The Oxford Handbook of Human Motivation

OXFORD LIBRARY OF PSYCHOLOGY

OXFORD LIBRARY OF PSYCHOLOGY

Editor in Chief PETER E. NATHAN

The Oxford Handbook of Human Motivation

Edited by

Richard M. Ryan

OXFORD
UNIVERSITY PRESS

Oxford University Press is a department of the University of Oxford.
It furthers the University's objective of excellence in research, scholarship,
and education by publishing worldwide.

Oxford   New York
Auckland   Cape Town   Dar es Salaam   Hong Kong   Karachi
Kuala Lumpur   Madrid   Melbourne   Mexico City   Nairobi
New Delhi   Shanghai   Taipei   Toronto

With offices in
Argentina   Austria   Brazil   Chile   Czech Republic   France   Greece
Guatemala   Hungary   Italy   Japan   Poland   Portugal   Singapore
South Korea   Switzerland   Thailand   Turkey   Ukraine   Vietnam

Oxford is a registered trade mark of Oxford University Press
in the UK and certain other countries.

Published in the United States of America by
Oxford University Press
198 Madison Avenue, New York, NY 10016

Library of Congress Cataloging-in-Publication Data
The Oxford handbook of human motivation / edited by Richard M. Ryan.
    p. cm. — (Oxford library of psychology)
ISBN 978-0-19-539982-0 (hardcover); 978-0-19-936623-1 (paperback)
    1. Motivation (Psychology)   I. Ryan, Richard M.
BF503.O94 2012
153.8—dc23
2011018564

9 8 7 6 5 4 3 2 1

Printed in the United States of America
on acid-free paper

SHORT CONTENTS

Oxford Library of Psychology vii

About the Editor ix

Contributors xi

Contents xv

Chapters 1–564

Index 565

OXFORD LIBRARY OF PSYCHOLOGY

The *Oxford Library of Psychology,* a landmark series of handbooks, is published by Oxford University Press, one of the world's oldest and most highly respected publishers, with a tradition of publishing significant books in psychology. The ambitious goal of the *Oxford Library of Psychology* is nothing less than to span a vibrant, wide-ranging field and, in so doing, to fill a clear market need.

Encompassing a comprehensive set of handbooks, organized hierarchically, the *Library* incorporates volumes at different levels, each designed to meet a distinct need. At one level are a set of handbooks designed broadly to survey the major subfields of psychology; at another are numerous handbooks that cover important current focal research and scholarly areas of psychology in depth and detail. Planned as a reflection of the dynamism of psychology, the *Library* will grow and expand as psychology itself develops, thereby highlighting significant new research that will impact on the field. Adding to its accessibility and ease of use, the *Library* will be published in print and, later on, electronically.

The *Library* surveys psychology's principal subfields with a set of handbooks that capture the current status and future prospects of those major subdisciplines. This initial set includes handbooks of social and personality psychology, clinical psychology, counseling psychology, school psychology, educational psychology, industrial and organizational psychology, cognitive psychology, cognitive neuroscience, methods and measurements, history, neuropsychology, personality assessment, developmental psychology, and more. Each handbook undertakes to review one of psychology's major subdisciplines with breadth, comprehensiveness, and exemplary scholarship. In addition to these broadly conceived volumes, the *Library* also includes a large number of handbooks designed to explore in depth more specialized areas of scholarship and research, such as stress, health and coping, anxiety and related disorders, cognitive development, or child and adolescent assessment. In contrast to the broad coverage of the subfield handbooks, each of these latter volumes focuses on an especially productive, more highly focused line of scholarship and research. Whether at the broadest or most specific level, however, all of the *Library* handbooks offer synthetic coverage that reviews and evaluates the relevant past and present research and anticipates research in the future. Each handbook in the *Library* includes introductory and concluding chapters written by its editor to provide a roadmap to the handbook's table of contents and to offer informed anticipations of significant future developments in that field.

An undertaking of this scope calls for handbook editors and chapter authors who are established scholars in the areas about which they write. Many of the nation's and world's most productive and best-respected psychologists have agreed to edit *Library* handbooks or write authoritative chapters in their areas of expertise.

For whom has the *Oxford Library of Psychology* been written? Because of its breadth, depth, and accessibility, the *Library* serves a diverse audience, including graduate students in psychology and their faculty mentors, scholars, researchers, and practitioners in psychology and related fields. Each will find in the *Library* the information they seek on the subfield or focal area of psychology in which they work or are interested.

Befitting its commitment to accessibility, each handbook includes a comprehensive index, as well as extensive references to help guide research. And because the *Library* was designed from its inception as an online as well as a print resource, its structure and contents will be readily and rationally searchable online. Further, once the *Library* is released online, the handbooks will be regularly and thoroughly updated.

In summary, the *Oxford Library of Psychology* will grow organically to provide a thoroughly informed perspective on the field of psychology, one that reflects both psychology's dynamism and its increasing interdisciplinarity. Once published electronically, the *Library* is also destined to become a uniquely valuable interactive tool, with extended search and browsing capabilities. As you begin to consult this handbook, we sincerely hope you will share our enthusiasm for the more than 500-year tradition of Oxford University Press for excellence, innovation, and quality, as exemplified by the *Oxford Library of Psychology*.

Peter E. Nathan
Editor-in-Chief
Oxford Library of Psychology

Richard M. Ryan

Richard M. Ryan, Ph.D., is a widely published researcher and theorist in the areas of human motivation, development, and well-being, with over 250 articles, chapters, and books. He is codeveloper (with Edward L. Deci) of Self-Determination Theory, an internationally researched theory that has been applied in hundreds of studies within areas such as development, education, work, relationships, medicine, psychical activity, and cross-cultural psychology. Ryan is also an award-winning teacher and researcher who has given addresses in over 60 universities worldwide. He is a Fellow of several professional organizations, including the American Psychological Association and the American Educational Research Association, and is an Honorary Member of the German Psychological Society. He has been a visiting scientist at the Max Planck Institute, a James McKeen Cattell Fellow, a Leverhulme Fellow, and recipient of other grants and awards. Recent research interests include the effects of intrinsic and extrinsic life goals on well-being; mindfulness and self-regulation; vitality; motivation in health care, education, and virtual environments.

CONTRIBUTORS

Henk Aarts
Department of Psychology
Utrecht University
Utrecht, The Netherlands

Mark D. Alicke
Department of Psychology
Ohio University
Athens, OH

Anthony J. Amorose
School of Kinesiology and Recreation
Illinois State University
Normal, IL

Larry C. Bernard
Psychology Department
Loyola Marymount University
Los Angeles, CA

Jenna Cambria
Department of Human Development
University of Maryland
College Park, MD

Charles S. Carver
Department of Psychology
University of Miami
Coral Gables, FL

Cecilia Sin-Sze Cheung
Department of Psychology
University of Illinois at
    Urbana–Champaign
Champaign, IL

Ruud Custers
Department of Psychology
Utrecht University
Utrecht, The Netherlands

Edward L. Deci
Department of Psychology
University of Rochester
Rochester, NY

Jacquelynne S. Eccles
Department of Psychology
University of Michigan
Ann Arbor, MI

Andrew J. Elliot
Department of Clinical & Social Sciences
    in Psychology
University of Rochester
Rochester, NY

Alexandra M. Freund
Department of Psychology
University of Zurich
Zurich, Switzerland

Ron Friedman
Department of Clinical & Social Sciences
    in Psychology
University of Rochester
Rochester, NY

Shelly L. Gable
Department of Psychological and Brain
    Sciences
University of California, Santa Barbara
Santa Barbara, CA

Guido H. E. Gendolla
Geneva Motivation Lab
FPSE, Department of Psychology
University of Geneva
Geneva, Switzerland

Peter M. Gollwitzer
Psychology Department
New York University/University of Konstanz
New York, NY/Konstanz, Germany

Adam M. Grant
The Wharton School
University of Pennsylvania
Philadelphia, PA

Martin S. Hagger
School of Psychology and
    Speech Pathology
Curtin University
Perth, Australia

Marie Hennecke
Department of Psychology
University of Zurich
Zurich, Switzerland

E. Tory Higgins
Department of Psychology
Columbia University
New York, NY

Martin Grosse Holtforth
Department of Psychology
University of Zurich
Zurich, Switzerland

Susan A. Jackson
Adjunct Senior Lecturer
School of Human Movement Studies
The University of Queensland
Brisbane, Australia
Flow Consultant and Writer
www.bodyandmindflow.com

Pelin Kesebir
Psychology Department
University of Colorado at Colorado Springs
Colorado Springs, CO

Lindsay E. Kipp
School of Kinesiology
University of Minnesota, Twin Cities
Minneapolis, MN

Woogul Lee
Division of Psychological and
    Quantitative Foundations
University of Iowa
Iowa City, IA

Nicole Legate
Department of Psychology
University of Rochester
Rochester, NY

Chris C. Martin
Department of Psychology
College of William and Mary
Williamsburg, VA

Laura A. Maruskin
Graduate School of Business
Stanford University
Stanford, CA

Johannes Michalak
Department of Psychology
University of Hildesheim
Hildesheim, Germany

Mark Muraven
Department of Psychology
University at Albany
Albany, NY

Kou Murayama
Department of Psychology
University of Munich
Munich, Germany

Maida Mustafić
Department of Psychology
University of Zurich
Zurich, Switzerland

Gabriele Oettingen
Psychology Department
New York University/University of Hamburg
New York, NY/Hamburg, Germany

Erika A. Patall
Department of Educational Psychology
The University of Texas at Austin
Austin, TX

Eva M. Pomerantz
Department of Psychology
University of Illinois at
    Urbana-Champaign
Champaign, IL

Thery Prok
Department of Psychological and Brain
    Sciences
University of California, Santa Barbara
Santa Barbara, CA

Tom Pyszczynski
Psychology Department
University of Colorado at Colorado Springs
Colorado Springs, CO

Lili Qin
Department of Psychology
University of Illinois at
    Urbana–Champaign
Champaign, IL

Johnmarshall Reeve
Department of Education
Korea University
Seoul, South Korea

K. Ann Renninger
Department of Educational Studies
Swarthmore College
Swarthmore, PA

Michael Richter
Geneva Motivation Lab
FPSE, Department of Psychology
University of Geneva
Geneva, Switzerland

Tomi-Ann Roberts
Department of Psychology
Colorado College
Colorado Springs, CO

Richard M. Ryan
Department of Psychology
University of Rochester
Rochester, NY

Michael F. Scheier
Department of Psychology
Carnegie Mellon University
Pittsburgh, PA

Abigail A. Scholer
Department of Psychology
University of Waterloo
Waterloo, ON, Canada

Dale H. Schunk
School of Education
University of North Carolina at Greensboro
Greensboro, NC

Constantine Sedikides
Center for Research on Self and Identity
School of Psychology
University of Southampton
Southampton, UK

Jihae Shin
The Wharton School
University of Pennsylvania
Philadelphia, PA

Paul J. Silvia
Department of Psychology
University of North Carolina at Greensboro
Greensboro, NC

Stephanie Su
Swarthmore College
Swarthmore, PA

Robert E. Thayer
Department of Psychology
California State University,
    Long Beach
Long Beach, CA

Todd M. Thrash
Department of Psychology
College of William and Mary
Williamsburg, VA

Ellen L. Usher
Department of Educational, School, and
    Counseling Psychology
University of Kentucky
Lexington, KY

Patricia L. Waters
Department of Psychology
Colorado College
Colorado Springs, CO

Maureen R. Weiss
School of Kinesiology
University of Minnesota, Twin Cities
Minneapolis, MN

Allan Wigfield
Department of Human Development
University of Maryland
College Park, MD

Rex A. Wright
Department of Psychology
University of North Texas
Denton, TX

CONTENTS

Part One • Introduction

1. Motivation and the Organization of Human Behavior:
   Three Reasons for the Reemergence of a Field 3
   Richard M. Ryan

Part Two • General Theories of Human Motivation

2. Social Cognitive Theory and Motivation 13
   Dale H. Schunk and *Ellen L. Usher*
3. Cybernetic Control Processes and the Self-Regulation of Behavior 28
   Charles S. Carver and *Michael F. Scheier*
4. The Role of Death in Life: Existential Aspects of Human Motivation 43
   Pelin Kesebir and *Tom Pyszczynski*
5. Too Much of a Good Thing? Trade-offs in Promotion and
   Prevention Focus 65
   Abigail A. Scholer and *E. Tory Higgins*
6. Motivation, Personality, and Development Within Embedded
   Social Contexts: An Overview of Self-Determination Theory 85
   Edward L. Deci and *Richard M. Ryan*

Part Three • Motivational Processes

7. Ego Depletion: Theory and Evidence 111
   Mark Muraven
8. Flow 127
   Susan A. Jackson
9. Implicit–Explicit Motive Congruence 141
   Todd M. Thrash, Laura A. Maruskin, and *Chris C. Martin*
10. Curiosity and Motivation 157
    Paul J. Silvia
11. Interest and Its Development 167
    K. Ann Renninger and *Stephanie Su*

Part Four • Goals and Motivation

12. Achievement Goals 191
    Kou Murayama, Andrew J. Elliot, and *Ron Friedman*
13. Goal Pursuit 208
    Peter M. Gollwitzer and *Gabriele Oettingen*

14. Unconscious Goal Pursuit: Nonconscious Goal Regulation
    and Motivation   232
    Henk Aarts and *Ruud Custers*
15. The Motivational Complexity of Choosing: A Review
    of Theory and Research   248
    Erika A. Patall
16. On Gains and Losses, Means and Ends: Goal Orientation
    and Goal Focus Across Adulthood   280
    Alexandra M. Freund, Marie Hennecke, and *Maida Mustafić*

Part Five • Motivation in Relationships
17. Self-Enhancement and Self-Protection Motives   303
    Constantine Sedikides and *Mark D. Alicke*
18. The Gendered Body Project: Motivational Components
    of Objectification Theory   323
    Tomi-Ann Roberts and *Patricia L. Waters*
19. Relatedness Between Children and Parents: Implications
    for Motivation   335
    Eva M. Pomerantz, Cecilia Sin-Sze Cheung, and *Lili Qin*
20. Avoiding the Pitfalls and Approaching the Promises
    of Close Relationships   350
    Shelly L. Gable and *Thery Prok*

Part Six • Evolutionary and Biological Perspectives
21. Neuroscience and Human Motivation   365
    Johnmarshall Reeve and *Woogul Lee*
22. Evolved Individual Differences in Human Motivation   381
    Larry C. Bernard
23. Moods of Energy and Tension That Motivate   408
    Robert E. Thayer
24. Effort Intensity: Some Insights From the Cardiovascular System   420
    Guido H. E. Gendolla, Rex A. Wright, and *Michael Richter*

Part Seven • Motivation in Application
25. Motivation in Psychotherapy   441
    Martin Grosse Holtforth and *Johannes Michalak*
26. Motivation in Education   463
    Allan Wigfield, Jenna Cambria, and *Jacquelynne S. Eccles*
27. Advances in Motivation in Exercise and Physical Activity   479
    Martin S. Hagger
28. Work Motivation: Directing, Energizing, and Maintaining
    Effort (and Research)   505
    Adam M. Grant and *Jihae Shin*

29. Youth Motivation and Participation in Sport and
    Physical Activity   520
    Maureen R. Weiss, Anthony J. Amorose, and *Lindsay E. Kipp*
30. Through a Fly's Eye: Multiple Yet Overlapping Perspectives
    on Future Directions for Human Motivation Research   554
    Richard M. Ryan and *Nicole Legate*

Index   *565*

PART 1

Introduction

Motivation and the Organization of Human Behavior: Three Reasons for the Reemergence of a Field

CHAPTER

1

Richard M. Ryan

Abstract

The fact that behavior is typically active, organized, and goal oriented represents one of the wonders of animate nature. Nonetheless, the organization and integrity of behavior can be disrupted by social contexts, implicit primes and motives, or by biological factors. There has been a strong resurgence in empirical research on these topics, as well as recognition of the potency of psychological factors. Three reasons for this resurgence of interest in the psychology of human motivation are reviewed in detail: (I) the theoretical depth and interdisciplinary nature of the field; (2) methodological innovations that have opened up new avenues of inquiry, and (3) the practical importance of motivation research as a translational science and for improving individual and community wellness through empirically supported interventions. Contributions within this volume are illustrative of all these factors, manifesting interdisciplinary depth, sophisticated methods, and practical applicability.

Key Words: motivation, organization, goals, regnant causes, implicit motives

The most salient and noteworthy feature of the behavior of animate entities is that it is *organized*. The actions of living things reflect a directed coordination of functions and processes toward specific ends. That behavior sequences are typically coherent and internally regulated, and thus demonstrate equifinality and adaptability is one of the great wonders of our science. It is also the central focus of the field of motivation.

This *Oxford Handbook of Motivation* is concerned in particular with human motivation, with all the complications that topic entails. Like that of other organisms, human behavior betrays an internal organization, actively operating within its environment, and employing layered, interacting functions and processes. Humans are clearly motivated, goal-directed, creatures. They seek out specific ends, ranging from concrete goals such as obtaining food and shelter to abstract ones such as developing a sense of meaning or attaining aesthetic ideals. Sometimes

people's motivation is explicit and conscious; at other times behavior is clearly energized and directed by nonconscious, implicit aims and attitudes. Finally, whether motives are implicit or explicit, the behavior organized by them will be variously successful. Effective motivation requires not only arousal or energy but also guidance by an affective and cognitive system that, at least for most of us, is susceptible to distraction or depletion. The authors represented in this handbook collectively address all of these facets and dynamics of human motivation, grappling with the multiple ways in which the integral organization of motivated action is maintained, as well as how *akrasia*, or motivational breakdowns, occur.

This timing of this *Handbook* is particularly apt, given that human motivation is being more intensively studied today than ever before. Broad, empirically based theories of motivation (many of the major ones represented within this volume) are again on the ascendance, influencing thinking across disciplines, domains, and applications of the behavioral sciences. I say "again" because the field of motivation has seen some rises and falls in its brief history.

In the early 20th century, motivational theories were the major organizing forces within both experimental and applied psychologies. Theorists of motivation such as Tolman (1932) and Hull (1943) on the behavioral side, and the formulations concerning motivation within psychodynamic camps (e.g., Freud, 1962/1923; Hartmann, 1939) spawned considerable empirical research that was integrated and interpreted through these paradigms. Yet following White's (1959) seminal review of the inadequacies of both behavioral and psychodynamic drive theories to explain active exploration, curiosity, and other phenomena associated with motivation, learning, and development, some major shifts happened within the discipline, and for many experimentalists, motivation faded as a focus of inquiry.

On the behavioral side, even before drive theories were stumbling, the cognitive revolution was beginning to supplant them. Indeed, Hilgard (1987) argued that cognitive approaches had presented a worldview in which questions of motivation as posed within drive theories were effectively "dead." In the cognitive tradition issues of motivation could be addressed in terms of acquired valences or preferences, attributions, and expectancies, all used to predict the direction and persistence of behavior. Indeed, I believe if Tolman were alive today he would feel vindicated in seeing the reliance of behavioral theorists on those "hypothetical" intervening variables that stand between the environment and manifest behavior.

Without tracing the history of this movement, it is no accident that this volume contains a very significant set of contributions that derive from the cognitive traditions within psychology, in particular the chapters on the topic of goals. As discussed by Murayama, Elliot, and Friedman (Chapter 12, this volume), *goals* can be defined as a form of regulation that guides behavior in the service of specific aims. Goals, they argue, help the individual to focus attention and to protect responses compatible with one's motives. This definition suggests how closely goals and motivation can be tied, insofar as goals are in many ways the servants of motives. For example, in Chapter 13, Gollwitzer and Oettingen demonstrate how explicitly set goals, especially when accompanied by specific implementation plans, enhance the likelihood that one's intentions reach fruition. In contrast, Aarts and Custers (Chapter 14) marvel at the power of motivated but nonconscious goals to entrain and direct behavior. Freund, Hennecke, and Mustafić (Chapter 16) distinguish between process and outcome-focused goals and the differential dynamics and influence of these goals across the life span. In all these cases motivation and goals are distinguished but interactive.

Alongside these cognitive/goal theories, frameworks concerned with fundamental motivations have also rearisen in the past two decades to be among the most actively researched topics in psychological science. These motivational theories replace, in a certain sense, the old drive theory accounts of Hull and Freud with a different set of "drivers." Rather than tracing motives to drive reduction these theories look to the evolved and acquired psychological needs and motives of individuals. Thus, within terror management theory (TMT; see Kesebir & Pyszczynski, Chapter 4, this volume) the dynamic driver of most behavior is *anxiety reduction*. People are motivated to pursue cultural goals and projects that help them feel esteemed and avoid awareness of vulnerability and mortality. Self-determination theory, on the other hand, focuses on intrinsic motivations and the basic psychological needs that support them as being fundamental to active behavior (see Deci & Ryan, Chapter 6). Sedikides and Alicke (Chapter 17) argue for self-esteem as a central motivational force, driving behaviors across cultures. These and other broad theories within this book thus look to psychological needs as giving rise to cognitive goals and the actions they guide.

As the examples illustrate, there is clearly a renewed energy surrounding the study of goals and motivation. There are many reasons for this, but three are especially worth elaboration: *(1)* the theoretical and multidisciplinary depth of motivational questions; *(2)* the methodological innovations in both quantitative and experimental tools that have facilitated exploration of motivational phenomena; and *(3)* the obvious practical and social importance of motivation research, with its utility as a translational, applicable science. Each shall be considered in turn.

Reason 1: The Theoretical Depth and Interdisciplinary Nature of Motivation Studies

The study of motivation drills at core foundational issues in the science. As stated earlier, what is most amazing about the behavior of organisms is the fact that it is spontaneously organized: It is both energized and directed. This is evident in what

Tolman (1932) understood to be the purposive nature of organisms, as they evidence effort, equifinality, and adaptive intelligence toward specific ends. The principles and mechanisms through which this occurs, as well as the conditions that support or thwart these spontaneous capabilities, are critical problems for scientists at all levels of behavior analysis, from physiological to cultural. Motivation is a problem unique to life scientists. Indeed it is the organized nature of actions that separates the life sciences from the physical sciences, where organized, purposive, behavior does not occur, and where entropy is the dominant force (Mayer, 1997). Instead, in the life sciences, and in the understanding of human behavior, the core interest is in discovering the bases of the negentropic, coherent, and integrated efforts of individuals as they pursue specific goals and outcomes.

Within this *Handbook* we see the problem of motivated, organized behavior viewed through multiple perspectives, including evolutionary (see Bernard, Chapter 22), physiological (e.g., Gendolla, Wright, & Richter, Chapter 24), neurological (Reeve & Lee, Chapter 21), cognitive (e.g., Carver & Scheier, Chapter 3), phenomenological/experiential (e.g., Jackson, Chapter 8), and cultural (e.g., Sedikedies & Alicke, Chapter 17), among others. At each level of analysis there are basic scientific questions concerning the processes that instigate and support versus disrupt or deplete motivational processes. In fact, the volume illustrates that motivation can be meaningfully studied through multiple levels of description and causal models.

Speaking of multiple levels or types of causality might give some scientists pause, particularly if they view the issue of causation reductively or narrowly. But it is clear that when it comes to motivation there is rarely if ever a singular cause at work. Rather, actions can be depicted best as outcomes of a set of determinative processes that can be described through various levels of analysis and theoretical models. One level of inquiry does not supplant or have epistemological priority over the others, but each has a different type of explanatory power and relevance to specific concerns and questions. Moreover, motivation is itself a phenomenon that resists simple reductionism, because an inventory of components and their functions does not by itself explain their emergent orchestration and directedness.

What shifts in scientific and practical discourse is not the plausibility, but the relevance, of different levels of analysis as explanations, making some causal analyses more regnant than others (Ryan & Deci, 2006). Regnant causes are those deemed most significant or functionally relevant to a problem, thus providing the most satisfying explanation of events. Many causally relevant analyses can be "correct" without being pertinent, or regnant in this sense. Indeed, rather than competing, each type of explanation and analysis must coordinate, even as some rightfully predominate because of their pragmatic utility or value.

The Unique Place of Psychological Theory

Causal explanations can operate at the level of physical/material causes, as well as at the level of cognitive, emotional, and social constructs as theorized and measured with the tools of psychology. Although some scientists early in the 20th century eschewed abstract or formal variables like those so frequently used in psychology, most all contemporary philosophers of science embrace them and acknowledge their necessity (Curd & Cover, 1998).

Psychological models of motivation, which make up the bulk of the current volume, operate on the level of inferred constructs, intended to capture the forces at work in energizing and directing action. Causal models at this level of analysis can be a particularly important point of entry into describing and predicting motivated behaviors. If one wants to intervene in intentional behaviors (e.g., dietary habits, work practices, physical activity and exercise), knowing the types of feedback, significant cognitions, meanings, and perceived social contexts that support or thwart these behaviors provides considerable leverage. Because the sources of variance accounting for molar behavior are so readily captured by the constructs and "causes" studied by psychologists, they represent among the most regnant levels of analysis for many human behaviors.

James (1892) clearly recognized this special power and utility of psychological theory, describing it as a science of "practical prediction and control" which when realized would represent "an achievement compared with which the control of the rest of physical nature would appear comparatively insignificant" (p. 148). Ok, perhaps astrophysicists would not agree! Nonetheless, the extent to which psychological interventions can impact important behaviors, from health maintenance to learning, is impressive. It is perhaps for this reason that psychological variables such as needs, goals, attributions, and perceptions even supply the target or criterion variables upon which other levels of analysis are often focused.

In addition to considerations of prediction and control, the psychological analysis of actions is also semantically meaningful in a way mere physical descriptions could never be. As Kauffman (2000) underscored, "compared to a hypothetical 'complete' physical description, the action-and-doing description picks out the relevant features with respect to the goals of the autonomous agent" (p. 126). Kauffmann further maintained that, once we are at the level of creatures that can have internal models of, and plans for, the future, we "seem to have arrived at a level of organization in which action and goal talk becomes essential" (p. 126). This is just to say again that reductionism is often a misplaced language game, in which the most important features of a situation are obscured rather than highlighted. In this regard, psychological explanations are not only often the most causally regnant, they also often make the most sense among explanations.

The fact that in this field we can plumb multiple levels of analysis from the molecular to the social and seek to coordinate them with psychological phenomena reflects the dynamic nature and complexity of motivation. The field thus befits the scientific ideal of *consilience* (Wilson, 1999) in which multiple levels of analysis mutually inform and constrain the problems in focus. Because science is inherently systematic, and totalizing, coordination between levels of analysis, or consilience, is logically demanded. Furthermore, in this reciprocal coordination the constraints, contours, and limits of prediction within any given level of analysis become apparent.

Theoretical depth leads to a richness and diversity of frameworks. The volume opens with chapters summarizing what are among the most vibrantly researched and integrative theories of human motivation on the current stage. They collectively attest to the multiple deep psychological accounts of human motivation that are supported by empirical research. Each of these theories was in fact selected for this volume because it represents a framework that is organizing significant scientific and scholarly inquiries around the globe, and often in multiple disciplines.

For example *social cognitive theory*, as developed by Bandura (1986) and described in this volume by Schunk and Usher (Chapter 2) emphasizes the idea that human learning and behavior are largely shaped by social environments, including the reactions and approval of others. As they observe and interact within social-cultural contexts, individuals learn about their own efficacy as well as the contingent consequences of specific behaviors. They then act in accordance with their beliefs about their capabilities and the expected outcomes of actions. Social cognitive theory is thus a broad and widely applied

view, which depicts human nature as relatively open to social and cultural conditioning and learning. It also emphasizes the importance of feelings of efficacy and competence, and how any factors that diminish that psychological experience undermine the subsequent probability of motivated action.

Control theory is presented in Chapter 3 by Carver and Scheier. They would likely not, when speaking technically, call their framework a theory of motivation, but rather a cybernetic model of behavior regulation. Yet in the editor's view, it needed to be included here anyway. Their influential perspective has generated more than three decades of careful research on goals and their successful, and unsuccessful, enactment. In terms of motivation, control theory interprets goal-directed action as reflecting a hierarchy of feedback processes that regulate behavior. In this model, affect and emotions are understood as both generated and intensified or dampened as an aspect of regulation, providing another set of feedback processes. This model leads to both expected and surprising predictions—among them that when we are feeling particularly good we are more likely to reduce effort on a task and "coast."

In Chapter 5 Scholer and Higgins discuss *regulatory focus theory*, first introduced by Higgins (1997), and consider two fundamental motivational systems: the promotion system and the prevention system. The theory is introduced largely in terms of individual differences—of the benefits and trade-offs faced by people who are *prevention oriented* (i.e., vigilant and security focused) versus *promotion oriented* (i.e., eager and accomplishment seeking). The former are highly sensitive to change and more oriented to "oughts" and "shoulds"; the latter are more interested in change and growth, and are oriented toward pursuing ideals. These distinct orientations have different adaptive value as a function of context, as Scholer and Higgins review, and each can mobilize approach or avoidance behaviors. The theory also assumes an underlying motivation for people to experience *regulatory fit*—that is, behavior that is consistent with their prevention or promotion orientation. Regulatory focus theory thus presents intersecting principles that afford a specificity of predictions concerning people's emotions and motivation in different situations.

Terror management theory, presented here by Kasebir and Pyszczynski, is a broad theory of human meaning and values derived from both existentialist reflections on death anxiety and the work of Ernst Becker, who once argued that the task of a unified science should be "the incessant implementation of human well-being" (Becker, 1968, p. xiii). TMT argues that our personal goals and cultural activities are mainly focused on self-esteem maintenance, which in turn serves as a buffer from awareness of mortality. Defense against the anxiety associated with death is thus in the TMT view a principal driving force of symbolic and cultural activities, and the generation of meanings and purposes. TMT has harnessed experimental techniques to assess attitudes and motivations following mortality salience events, with results that suggest that people are indeed often acting out of nonconscious defensive attempts to stave off existential threat. TMT challenges the view of humans as conscious and rational beings, showing instead that underlying ultimate concerns can in some individuals automatically activate complex, and sometimes defensive, behaviors and attitudes.

This *Handbook* also contains a chapter on *self-determination theory (SDT)*. Although presented here by Ed Deci and myself, the theory represents the efforts of a diverse yet cohesive community of scholars from around the world with interest in this perspective. SDT envisions an active, assimilative, and dynamic human nature, supported or thwarted in its basic psychological needs. In fact, SDT posits a specific human nature, one that thrives under conditions of support for competence, autonomy, and relatedness, and yet becomes defensive, reactive, and compliant under conditions of need deprivations or thwarts. The assumption of universal basic needs has been both descriptively and experimentally generative, addressing phenomena such as the undermining effect of controlling rewards, the characteristics that make an activity intrinsically motivated, the processes that facilitate greater internalization and integrated regulation of extrinsic motivation, and the reasons materialism leads to unhappiness. SDT has thus been broadly applied in domains from work, education, psychotherapy, and medicine to sport, play, and entertainment.

Outside of broad-based theories this volume also contains reviews of theory and research on specific motivational processes and phenomena that have big implications. For example, Chapter 7 by Muraven addresses a phenomenon that has captured the interests of dozens of experimental social psychologists for over a decade—namely *ego depletion*. Muraven, who is an originator of the ego-depletion concept and model, examines the myriad factors associated with the self-control of behaviors that require effort and drain human energies. Ego-depletion effects bear on the multiple ways that the human intentions and goal pursuits are vulnerable to akrasia, and

thus his chapter has broad relevance to both theories and practical models of motivation.

In Chapter 10, Silvia tackles that most important of motivational forces for development and learning, namely *curiosity*. He discusses curiosity as both an evolved feature of human nature, and as a motivational process that is strongly affected by social contexts and supports. Similarly, Renninger and Su take on the topic of personal *interests*—reviewing both the development of those abiding passions and investments that define us as individuals, and the factors that sustain them. Patall, in Chapter 15, reviews and integrates the vast literature on choice as it relates to motivation. She looks at the evidence that choice facilitates sustained motivation over time through enhancing commitment to actions; and how choice can entail costs, from cognitive load to cultural conflicts. Finally, in a quite unique chapter (Chapter 18) Roberts and Waters consider the issue of gender as it relates to motivation and interpersonal relationships. They specifically are concerned with objectification as an influence on women, and its costs for both their motivated performance and well-being. These topical reviews integrate an array of empirical findings on motivational processes and raise critical questions for continued research.

In short, the theoretical chapters in this volume represent some of the most important organizing frameworks in the science of motivation today. Each of these explanatory frameworks shifts out a distinct yield of predications, laws, and applications that are broadly influencing the scientific and applied communities. Looking across this collection, I am reminded here of the words of pioneer psychologist Robert S. Woodworth, who once stated about psychological schools of thought that: "Every school is good, though no one is good enough" (Woodworth, 1948, p. 255).

Reason 2: Methodological Innovations and the Resurgence in Motivation Studies

Although the romantic view of the development of new knowledge is that it is the product of individual insight and genius, many of the recent insights in the field of motivation were made possible less by individual genius and more by new and better tools for exploration. Explorers in a dark cave get farther when someone provides a better headlamp.

Among these new tools, several deserve to be highlighted as playing particularly strong roles in advancing the science of human motivation: Statistical advances in structural equation modeling, multilevel modeling, and growth-curve analysis;

experimental advances in the measurement and priming of implicit motivational processes; and new interfaces linking biology and neuropsychology to psychological models of behavior.

Changes in Statistical Methods

One of the characteristic features of behavioral science is its frequent use of statistical inference in the development of laws and principles. Although there are clearly limits to inductive-statistical explanations of events (see classic work by Hempel, 1965), the probabilistic and multidetermined nature of human behavior makes such methods essential tools of behavioral science. Yet these statistical tools themselves have traditionally had limitations in what they could describe, and what covariances and patterns could be detected. For example, the classical ANOVA approach to data restricts our imagination to what accounts for mean changes in a given variable, rather than trajectories, patterns, or intraindividual variability in change.

Recent methodological advances in quantitative analysis have thus lent new excitement to the field. In particular, *multilevel modeling* methods (e.g., Raudenbush & Bryk, 2002) have allowed investigators to look not only at how individuals differ from one another in motives and goal, but also at how and why an individual waxes and wanes in various motives and behavioral regulations across time or situations. Most every classical question in the field was originally posited as a "between persons" issue; yet for most of us personally and practically the core concern is at a "within-person" level of analysis, or what leads to rises and falls in motivation within individuals over time, settings, or events. Describing change over time, and what components of motivation remain stable or vary intra-individually becomes increasingly critical as we examine trajectories during or following critical events or planned interventions. These new tools have thus allowed us to at least begin to overcome the limitations of a cross-sectional psychology (see Lazarus, 2003) that hampered the study of motivation for so long.

New Experimental Methods and the Study of Implicit Motivation

Current experimental methods are allowing researchers to investigate previously underexplored phenomena, including the ubiquitous influence of nonconscious motivations. Clearly a great deal of human behavior is not consciously driven. We have many habitual and overlearned behaviors that can be performed without intention or conscious control.

But beyond habits, research suggests that much of the time our actions are being selected or sustained based on motivational dynamics of which we are unaware. Our attitudes and motives can be, to different degrees, *implicit*. Of course, as Westin (1998) points out, this is something long clear within psychodynamic circles, but there is a new vigor in experimental studies regarding this topic.

Many of the methods underlying recent research on nonconscious motivational processes build off of the idea of accessibility, in which reaction times are used to estimate how activated a motive or attitude is for a person. Related to the issue of activation are priming methods, in which motives or attitudes are potentiated by exposure to, or "priming" of, strongly associated constructs, thereby enhancing the accessibility of, and thus the likelihood of enacting, specific motives or goals (e.g., see Aarts, Custers, & Holland, 2007). Activating or priming a motive or goal can set in motion a rich network of cognitive, affective, and behavioral processes that provide both energy and direction (i.e., motivation) outside of conscious awareness. In fact, people's behavior can frequently be prompted by goals primed by situational elements of which they are not aware but that nonetheless make certain motives more accessible than others. Chapter 14 by Aarts and Custers in this volume provides an excellent review of some of these methods, along with considerable evidence that well-organized behaviors not only can be, but frequently are, under "unconscious control."

This strong renewed interest in nonconscious motivation has also opened up a dynamic new area of investigation where we can look not just beyond self-report, but at the interface of conscious (and reportable) and nonconscious motives, as Chapter 9 by Thrash, Maruskin, and Martin in this volume reviews. As they point out, as methodological refinements have occurred, correlations between implicit and explicit measures of motives and attitudes have increased, and these refinements have helped clarify more systematic individual and situational variations in implicit/explicit discrepancies. Such discrepancies, in turn, appear to be related to both developmental and proximal factors, and to predict well-being and motivational outcomes.

At the same time as studies impress us with the potential of nonconscious processes to organize intentional behaviors, the same methods allow researchers to demonstrate how individuals can exert tremendous regulatory control over their own actions. Thus, research has shown, for example, how people high in mindfulness and autonomy (see Deci & Ryan, Chapter 6, this volume), or in an implemental rather than deliberative phase of action (see Gollwitzer & Ottengen, Chapter 13) are more resilient in the face of depletion effects, threats, and challenges as they pursue goals. This is true even with respect to regulating implicit processes, which some can manage through volitional processes (e.g. Legault, Green-Demers, Grant, & Chung, 2007; Niemiec et al., 2010). Ironically, it seems, the very focus on the influence of nonconscious motivations over behavior has made salient the specific strengths and resources that allow some individuals to override such influences and more effectively pursue consciously endorsed goals.

Toward a Life Science: Beyond Reductionism to Coordinated Analyses

Robust advancements in methods have also been evident in a new synergism between biological and psychological inquiry. Methods such as functional magnetic resonance imaging (fMRI) allow us to link brain processes with specifically activated motives and inhibitions, clarifying the mechanics behind behavioral dynamics (see Chapter 21 by Reeve and Lee). More accurate physiological models of cardiovascular functioning allow better gauging of effort, and thus the study of its dynamics and determinants (e.g., Gendolla, Wright, & Richter, Chapter 24). In the area of coping, assays of cortisone and other biologic indicators also allow us to better gauge human reactivity, stress resources, and estimate the likelihood of goal success as a function of different sources of motivation. Finally, studies of how the physiological effects of diet and activity impact mood and motivation (see Chapter 23 by Thayer) show the import of biological factors on vitality and functioning.

As with statistical enhancements, these observational advances in the biological sphere, especially as they are linked with constructs of psychological interest, have tremendous promise for refining theory. The fact of the matter is that psychological processes are themselves *embodied*. The different constructs studied within social sciences must therefore map to distinct patterns of activation (Ryan, Kuhl, & Deci, 1997). Such mapping is not an acceptance of physicalism, but rather reflects integrative science rather than reductionism, and helps pave the "two-way street" that Reeve and Lee depict between neurosciences and psychology. More important, it facilitates tests of theory, harnessing biology to advance regnant psychological models, providing new avenues for examining covariations with external, social, and genetic influences. This is again congruent with the idea of consilience and the principle that all levels of analysis must be capable of coordination.

Reason 3: Practical Importance of Motivational Science as a Core *Translational and Applied Discipline*

Perhaps just as crucial to the resurgence of the field of motivation as these scientific advances is a renewed appreciation of its practical importance. As any good dialectical materialist might have predicted, it is probably more because motivation matters on the bottom line—for productivity at work, learning in schools, and adherence within clinics— than because it is of inherent intellectual or scientific interest that it is at the forefront of our thinking. Given that the most important societal goals require human energy and commitment to be actualized, motivation may in fact be the most critical applied topic of our field. Indeed, even for discoveries in other sciences to be applied, motivation represents a core *translational science*, because it addresses what must occur for new knowledge, products, or inventions to be adopted and actively used.

Chapters in this *Handbook* speak to myriad important applications of motivation theory. Indeed, reviewed in this volume are chapters on topics where motivation is clearly a central concern, including work (Grant & Shin, Chapter 28), education (Wigfield, Cambria, & Eccles, Chapter 26), psychotherapy (Holtforth & Michalak, Chapter 25), and exercise and sport (Hagger, Chapter 27; Weis, Ambrose, & Kipp, Chapter 29). Moreover, because motivation is so richly an interpersonal matter, also included is a section on motivation in relationships, which contains work on parenting (Pomerantz, Cheung, and Qin, Chapter 19), close relationships (Gable & Prok, Chapter 20), gender and objectification (Roberts & Waters, Chapter 18), and self-protection in the context of social comparisons (Sedikides & Alicke, Chapter 17). What one sees in each of these review chapters is a generative framework that not only is advancing the basic science but is also helping to translate that science into practices that yield better human outcomes from the workplace to the playground. These chapters, applied to everyday concerns and settings, make clear the extent to which motivation theories and research are organizing and informing significant practical activities and interventions in multiple fields of human endeavor.

The word *motivated* is not a complex term. It simply means "to be moved." Although human bodies can be physically moved by many forces, it is those animating energies that organize purposive action that are illuminated by the authors in this volume. And they are shedding light on phenomena that are not only of great practical concern to most of us but also represent one of the central scientific mysteries in our universe.

References

Aarts, H., Custers, R., & Holland, R. W. (2007). The non-conscious cessation of goal pursuit: When goals and negative affect are coactivated. *Journal of Personality and Social Psychology, 92,* 165–178.

Bandura, A. (1986). *Social foundations of thought and action: A social cognitive theory.* Englewood Cliffs, NJ: Prentice-Hall.

Becker, E. (1968). *The structure of evil.* New York: Braziller.

Curd, M., & Cover, J. A. (1998). *Philosophy of science: The central issues.* New York: Norton.

Freud, S. (1962). *The ego and the id.* New York: Norton. (Original work published 1923).

Hartmann, H. (1939). *Ego psychology and the problem of adaptation.* New York: International Universities Press.

Hempel, C. G. (1965). *Aspects of scientific explanation.* New York: Free Press.

Higgins, E. T. (1997). Beyond pleasure and pain. *American Psychologist, 52,* 1280–1300.

Hilgard, E. R. (1987). Psychology in America: A historical survey. New York: Harcourt, Brace.

Hull, C. L. (1943). *Principles of behavior: An introduction to behavior theory.* New York: Appleton-Century-Crofts.

James, W. (1892). A plea for psychology as a 'natural science.' *The Philosophical Review, 1,* 146–153.

Kauffman, S. (2000). *Investigations.* Oxford, England: Oxford University Press.

Lazarus, R. S. (2003). Does positive psychology have legs? *Psychological Inquiry, 14,* 93–109.

Legault, L., Green-Demers, I., Grant, P., & Chung, J. (2007). On the self-regulation of implicit and explicit prejudice: A self-determination theory perspective. *Personality and Social Psychology Bulletin, 33,* 732–749.

Mayer, E. (1997). *This is biology: The science of the living world.* Cambridge, MA: Harvard University Press.

Niemiec, C. P., Brown, K. W., Kashdan, T. B., Cozzolino, P. J., Breen, W. E., Levesque-Bristol, C., & Ryan, R. M. (2010). Being present in the face of existential threat: The role of trait mindfulness in reducing defensive responses to mortality salience. *Journal of Personality and Social Psychology, 99,* 344–365.

Raudenbush, S. W., & Bryk, A. S. (2002). *Hierarchical linear models: Applications and data analysis methods.* Newbury Park, CA: Sage

Ryan, R. M., & Deci, E. L. (2006). Self-regulation and the problem of human autonomy: Does psychology need choice, self-determination, and will? *Journal of Personality, 74,* 1557–1585.

Ryan, R. M., Kuhl, J., & Deci, E. L. (1997). Nature and autonomy: Organizational view of social and neurobiological aspects of self-regulation in behavior and development. *Development and Psychopathology, 9,* 701–728.

Tolman, E. C. (1932). *Purposive behavior in animals and men.* New York: Century.

Westin, D. (1998). The scientific legacy of Sigmund Freud: Toward a psychodynamically informed psychological science. *Psychological Bulletin, 124,* 333–371.

White, R. W. (1959). Motivation reconsidered: The concept of competence. *Psychological Review, 66,* 297–333.

Wilson, E. O. (1999) *Consilience: The unity of human knowledge.* New York: Vintage.

Woodworth, R. S. (1948). *Contemporary schools of psychology-revised edition.* New York: The Ronald Press.

General Theories of Human Motivation

Social Cognitive Theory and Motivation

Dale H. Schunk *and* Ellen L. Usher

Abstract

Social cognitive theory is a theory of psychological functioning that emphasizes learning from the social environment. This chapter focuses on Bandura's social cognitive theory, which postulates reciprocal interactions among personal, behavioral, and social/environmental factors. Persons use various vicarious, symbolic, and self-regulatory processes as they strive to develop a sense of agency in their lives. Key motivational processes are goals and self-evaluations of progress, outcome expectations, values, social comparisons, and self-efficacy. People set goals and evaluate their goal progress. The perception of progress sustains self-efficacy and motivation. Individuals act in accordance with their values and strive for outcomes they desire. Social comparisons with others provide further information on their learning and goal attainment. Self-efficacy is an especially critical influence on motivation and affects task choices, effort, persistence, and achievement. Suggestions are given for future research directions.

Key Words: social cognitive theory, vicarious processes, symbolic processes, self-regulatory processes, goals, self-evaluations of progress, outcome expectations, values, social comparisons, self-efficacy

Introduction

Motivation refers to the process whereby goal-directed activities are energized, directed, and sustained (Schunk, Pintrich, & Meece, 2008). Contemporary cognitive theories of motivation postulate that individuals' thoughts, beliefs, and emotions are central processes that underlie motivation. These cognitive perspectives stand in contrast both to early views that linked motivation with individual differences in instincts and traits and to behavioral theories that viewed motivation as an increased or continued level of responding to stimuli caused by reinforcements or rewards.

In this chapter we provide an account of motivation from the perspective of social cognitive theory. *Social cognitive theory* emphasizes the idea that much human learning and behavior occur in social environments.

By interacting with others, people learn knowledge, skills, strategies, beliefs, rules, and attitudes. Through their observations and interactions with others, individuals also learn about the appropriateness, usefulness, and consequences of behaviors. People act in accordance with their beliefs about their capabilities and the expected outcomes of actions.

Although there are different social cognitive perspectives on motivation, this chapter focuses on Bandura's (1977b, 1986, 1997, 2001) social cognitive theory of psychological functioning. Bandura's theory underscores the key roles of vicarious, symbolic, and self-regulatory processes in human learning and behavior. This social cognitive framework often is employed by researchers to explore the operation and outcomes of cognitive and affective processes hypothesized to underlie motivation.

The next section describes the conceptual framework of social cognitive theory to include the key roles played by vicarious, symbolic, and self-regulatory processes. Some key social cognitive motivational processes are discussed, including goals and self-evaluations of progress, outcome expectations, values, social comparisons, and self-efficacy. A separate section is devoted to discussing *self-efficacy*, or one's perceived capabilities for learning or performing actions at designated levels (Bandura, 1977a, 1997), given its centrality to learning and motivation. We conclude the chapter with suggestions for future research.

Conceptual Framework

This section discusses the conceptual framework of social cognitive theory. Of particular importance are the following: reciprocal interactions among personal, behavioral, and social/environmental factors; the differences between enactive and vicarious learning; the distinction between learning and performance; and the roles of vicarious, symbolic, and self-regulatory processes in psychological functioning.

Reciprocal Interactions

A central tenet of Bandura's (1977b, 1986, 1997, 2001) social cognitive theory is that human behavior operates within a framework of *triadic reciprocality* involving reciprocal interactions among three sets of influences: personal (e.g., cognitions, beliefs, skills, affect); behavioral; and social/environmental factors. This reciprocal network is illustrated in Figure 2.1.

These reciprocally interacting influences can be demonstrated using self-efficacy as the personal factor. With respect to the interaction of self-efficacy and behavior, much research shows that self-efficacy influences achievement behaviors such as task choice, effort, persistence, and use of effective learning strategies (person → behavior; Schunk & Pajares, 2009). These behaviors also affect self-efficacy. As students work on tasks and observe their learning progress, their self-efficacy for continued learning is enhanced (behavior → person).

The link between personal and environmental factors can be illustrated with students with learning disabilities, many of whom hold low self-efficacy for performing well (Licht & Kistner, 1986). Instructors in such environments may base their reactions to these students on perceived attributes about the students (e.g., low skills) rather than on students' actual capabilities (person → social/environment). In turn, environmental feedback can affect students' self-efficacy, such as when a teacher tells a student, "I know you can do this" (social/environment → person).

The link between behaviors and environmental factors is seen in many instructional sequences. Environmental factors can direct behaviors, such as when a teacher points to a display and says, "Look here," which students do without much conscious effort (social/environment → behavior). Students' behaviors can alter their instructional environments. When teachers ask questions and students give incorrect answers, teachers are apt to reteach the material rather than continue with the lesson (behavior → social/environment).

Social cognitive theory reflects a view of human *agency* in which individuals are proactively engaged in their own success and development (Schunk &

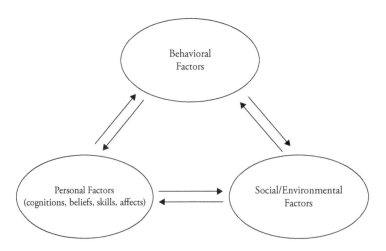

Fig. 2.1. Reciprocal interactions in social cognitive theory.

Pajares, 2005). These beliefs allow individuals to exert a large degree of control over their thoughts, feelings, and actions. In reciprocal fashion, people affect and are influenced by their actions and environments. But the scope of this reciprocal influence is broader than individuals because they live in social environments. *Collective agency* refers to people's shared perceived capabilities of accomplishing tasks as a group. As is true with individuals, groups also affect and are influenced by their actions and environments.

Enactive and Vicarious Learning

In social cognitive theory, learning occurs *enactively* through actual doing and *vicariously* through observing modeled performances (e.g., live, filmed, symbolic; Bandura, 1977b). Enactive learning involves learning from the consequences of one's actions, which can inform and motivate. Actions convey information about the accuracy or appropriateness of one's behaviors. People rewarded for their actions typically understand that they are performing well, whereas punishments signal behavioral inappropriateness. Individuals tend to be motivated to learn and perform behaviors that they believe will have desirable consequences and to avoid learning behaviors that they believe will be punished.

Much human learning occurs vicariously and therefore does not require actual performance by learners. Vicarious learning offers an efficient alternative to learning via direct experience. Humans would be hopelessly inefficient if their involvement were required for all learning. Vicarious learning also saves people from undesirable consequences. Observing or reading about safety techniques saves individuals from acting in potentially dangerous ways. As with enactive learning, observers are motivated to learn actions that lead to successes. People attend to successful models who demonstrate actions that they believe will benefit them (Schunk, 1987).

Learning of complex skills typically occurs both enactively and vicariously. By observing teacher models, students may learn some aspects of a complex skill. As students practice the skills, teachers provide feedback and corrective instruction as needed. Through observation, practice, and feedback, students learn skills and enjoy greater success.

Learning and Performance

Unlike older behavioral theories, social cognitive theory distinguishes new learning from performance of previously learned actions (Bandura, 1977b). The distinction is not apparent with enactive learning because persons demonstrate what they have learned. But vicarious learning may not be demonstrated until sometime after the modeled behavior occurs. Whether learning results in changed performances depends on factors such as learners' motivation, interests, incentives to perform, perceived needs, physical conditions, social pressures, and competing activities.

Students learn many new skills, strategies, and behaviors, only some of which they may demonstrate at the time of learning. Because teachers are responsible for ensuring that students learn, they assess student learning in various ways (e.g., tests, quizzes, assignments, homework). The assumption is that students will demonstrate what they have learned; however, this may not always happen. Able students who are motivated to be socially accepted by their peers may not demonstrate the full range of their learning so that they appear more in line with their classmates' competencies. Authentic assessments that take various forms can help teachers accurately gauge students' learning.

Vicarious, Symbolic, and Self-Regulatory Processes

Bandura's (1986) social cognitive theory stresses the idea that people possess capabilities that distinguish them as humans and motivate them to strive for a sense of agency. Among the most prominent of these are vicarious, symbolic, and self-regulatory processes.

Vicarious Processes

The capability for learning vicariously allows individuals to acquire beliefs, cognitions, affects, skills, strategies, and behaviors, from observations of others in their social environments. As noted earlier, this capability saves people time over what would be required if all learning had to be demonstrated at the time of learning. This capability also allows people to regularly shape their lives, because they select environmental features (e.g., individuals, materials) to which they want to attend. Thus, students who want to become teachers enroll in education programs and put themselves in situations where they can learn vicariously, such as by attending classes, observing and working with classroom teachers, and reading books and other materials. The models in individuals' environments serve as important sources of information and motivation. This section discusses the relevance of vicarious processes for learning and motivation.

TYPES OF VICARIOUS PROCESSES

Bandura (1986) distinguished three types of vicarious processes: response facilitation, inhibition and disinhibition, and observational learning (Table 2.1). *Response facilitation* refers to modeled actions that serve as social motivators for observers to act in the same fashion. Response facilitation effects are common in everyday life. An individual walking down a street who encounters a group of people looking in a store window may be motivated to stop and look in the window.

Response facilitation effects do not represent learning because people already know how to perform the actions. The behaviors of others motivate observers' actions. There is evidence that response facilitation effects can occur without conscious awareness (Chartrand & Bargh, 1999).

Inhibition and disinhibition effects result from models strengthening or weakening observers' tendencies to act in given ways. Inhibition can happen when models are punished for their actions, whereas disinhibition can result when models perform threatening or prohibited actions without negative consequences. Classroom misbehavior may be disinhibited when students observe other students misbehaving without being reprimanded by the teacher; a sudden reprimand may inhibit further misbehavior.

Like response facilitation, inhibition and disinhibition represent motivational effects on behavior, not new learning. A difference between these two categories is that, whereas response facilitation involves behaviors that are socially acceptable, inhibition and disinhibition typically involve actions that have moral or legal implications (e.g., breaking rules) or involve strong emotions (e.g., fears).

Observational learning through modeling occurs when observers perform behaviors that they had not learned prior to exposure to the models (Bandura, 1969). Observational learning has four component processes: attention, retention, production, and motivation.

Observational learning requires that observers attend to relevant features so that they can be perceived. Certain features of models and situations

Table 2.1. Types of Vicarious Processes

• Response facilitation
• Inhibition/disinhibition
• Observational learning

command better attention. Observers are more motivated to attend to models who have status and credibility, such as teachers. Task features can affect attention, such as when teachers use bright colors, oversized features, and interactive materials. Attention also is affected by observers' beliefs about the functional value of the modeled behaviors. Modeled activities that observers believe are important and likely to lead to desirable outcomes motivate them to pay attention. Students' attention should be raised when teachers provide verbal markers, such as when they announce that the material they are about to cover will be on a test.

Retention involves cognitively organizing, rehearsing, coding, and transforming information for storage in memory. Relative to the other processes of observational learning, social cognitive theory devotes less attention to this process. Theorists and researchers in the information processing tradition have addressed this aspect in depth (Matlin, 2009).

The third process—production—involves translating cognitive conceptions of modeled actions into behaviors. Especially with complex behaviors, it often is the case that observers will learn only some features. Learners refine their skills through practice and feedback that may include additional modeling.

Motivation is a key process in observational learning because onlookers are more apt to attend to, retain, and produce those modeled actions that they believe are important. People are selective; they do not learn or perform everything that they observe. Rather, they attempt to learn those actions that they believe will lead to desirable outcomes and help them attain their goals, and they avoid those actions that they believe will result in dissatisfying outcomes. As they observe the actions of others, people form expectations about different outcomes, which are based on their observations of models and their own experiences. Their learning and performances are based in part on these expectations.

MODEL CHARACTERISTICS

Researchers have investigated the characteristics of effective models. For example, perceived similarity between models and observers can affect modeling (Schunk, 1987). Similarity in important ways serves as a source of information for determining behavioral appropriateness, forming outcome expectations, and assessing one's self-efficacy. Age similarity between model and observer is important for gauging behavioral appropriateness but less so for actual learning, which is enhanced more by models whom observers believe are competent. When competence and age similarity do not match (e.g., younger model is more competent than a same-age model), children are swayed more by the competent model. Peers can be effective models when children hold self-doubts about their learning or performance capabilities. Viewing a similar peer successfully perform a task may raise observers' self-efficacy and motivate them to learn because they are apt to believe that if the model could learn, they can as well (Schunk, 1987).

Model gender can influence modeling by conveying information about task appropriateness. In general, observing a same-gender peer model perform a behavior without negative consequences conveys that the action is appropriate. Model gender is less important in learning academic skills and strategies (Schunk, 1987).

Researchers have also explored the effects of exposing students to mastery and coping models (Schunk, 1987). Mastery models demonstrate faultless performance from the outset. Coping models initially have difficulty learning skills but through effort gradually improve their skills and eventually perform as well as mastery models. Research shows that children who have experienced previous learning difficulties may benefit more from observing coping models (Schunk & Hanson, 1985). Such children may perceive themselves as more similar in competence to coping models, which can raise their self-efficacy and motivation for learning.

Viewing one's own performances, or *self-modeling*, can facilitate learning and motivation. In a study by Carroll and Bandura (1982), adults viewed models performing a motor skill, then attempted to reproduce it. Performances of some learners were taped and learners were allowed to watch this concurrent visual feedback while performing. Visual feedback given before learners had formed a mental model of the skill had no effect on performance; however, once learners had formed such a mental model, the visual feedback enhanced their production of the skill. The self-modeled feedback presumably helped to reduce discrepancies between learners' mental models and actual performances.

Observational learning is enhanced when modeled displays contain explanations and demonstrations (*cognitive modeling*). Schunk (1981) compared the effects of cognitive modeling with those of didactic instruction on children's long-division self-efficacy and achievement. Children who lacked division skills received instruction and practice over

sessions. Cognitive-modeling children observed an adult model explain and demonstrate division solution strategies while applying them to problems. Didactic-instruction children received written instructional material that explained and demonstrated the operations. Compared with didactic instruction, cognitive modeling promoted division achievement and accuracy of perceived division capabilities (i.e., self-efficacy was better aligned with actual skills).

Symbolic Processes

In addition to their capability for vicarious learning, individuals possess the capacity for symbolic representations, which involve language, mathematical and scientific notation, iconography, and cognition, and which help people adapt to and alter their environments (Bandura, 1986). They use symbolic processes to interpret actions and outcomes in their lives and to guide their future actions. Because of the human capacity to symbolize, people do not simply react to events in their lives but rather generate new courses of actions for solving problems. Symbolic processes also foster communications with others (e.g., in person, on the phone, electronically, in writing), which lead to further learning.

Self-Regulatory Processes

Social cognitive theory assigns a prominent role to self-regulatory processes (Bandura, 1986; Zimmerman, 2000). *Self-regulation* refers to the processes that individuals use to personally activate and sustain behaviors, cognitions, and affects, which are systematically oriented toward the attainment of goals (Zimmerman, 2000). Prior to embarking on a task, people set goals and determine which strategies to use. They then regulate their behaviors to conform to their internal standards and goals. As they work on tasks, they assess their progress toward their goals and decide whether to continue or alter their strategies. During breaks and when tasks are complete, they reflect on their experiences, seeking to make sense of them and to determine what their next steps should be. As they reflect on what they have done, their beliefs that they have learned and made progress strengthen their self-efficacy and motivate them to continue learning. We elaborate on these motivational processes next.

Motivational Processes

The preceding sections show how observational, symbolic, and self-regulatory processes can have motivational effects on individuals. Among the most

Table 2.2. Key Social Cognitive Motivational Processes

- Goals and self-evaluations of progress

- Outcome expectations

- Values

- Social comparisons

- Self-efficacy

critical are goals and self-evaluations of progress, outcome expectations, values, social comparisons, and self-efficacy (Table 2.2). These processes are covered in the following sections.

Goals and Self-Evaluations of Progress

Goals, or what people are consciously trying to attain, involve important symbolic and self-regulatory processes that people use to instigate and sustain actions. Initially, people must make a commitment to attempt to attain goals because goals do not affect behavior without commitment (Locke & Latham, 2002). As persons work on a task, they compare their current performance with their goals. Positive self-evaluations of progress strengthen self-efficacy and sustain motivation. A perceived discrepancy between present performance and the goal may create dissatisfaction, which can raise effort. Goals motivate people to expend effort necessary and persist at the task (Locke & Latham, 2002). Greater effort and persistence typically lead to better performance. Goals also help to direct people's attention to relevant task features, behaviors to be performed, and possible outcomes, and they can affect how people process information.

Although goals are important motivational processes, their effects depend on their properties: specificity, proximity, and difficulty. Goals that include specific performance standards are more likely to activate self-evaluations of progress and enhance motivation and learning than are general goals (e.g., "Do your best;" Bandura, 1986). Specific goals indicate the amount of effort needed to succeed, and evaluating progress toward specific goals is straightforward. Goals also are distinguished by how far they project into the future. Proximal, short-term goals enhance motivation and learning better than do distant, long-term goals, because it is easier to determine progress toward goals that are closer at hand (Bandura & Schunk, 1981).

Goal difficulty, which refers to the level of task proficiency required as assessed against a standard,

influences the amount of effort that people expend. In general, people work harder to attain goals perceived to be difficult than goals thought to be easier; however, perceived difficulty and motivation do not bear an unlimited positive relation to one another. Goals that people believe are overly difficult do not motivate because people hold low self-efficacy for attaining them. The opposite may also be true. Although people may feel efficacious for attaining goals perceived as very easy, these goals may not motivate because people often procrastinate in attempting them.

Another distinction can be made between learning and performance goals. A *learning goal* refers to what knowledge, behavior, skill, or strategy students are to acquire; a *performance goal* refers to what task students are to complete. These goals can have differential effects on achievement behaviors (Anderman & Wolters, 2006). Learning goals focus students' attention on processes and strategies that help them acquire competence and improve their skills. Focusing on knowledge and skill acquisition motivates behavior and sustains attention to important features. Students in pursuit of a learning goal are apt to feel self-efficacious for attaining it and be motivated to expend effort, persist, and use effective learning strategies. Self-efficacy is substantiated as they work toward their goal and assess their progress (Schunk, 1996).

In contrast, performance goals focus attention on completing tasks. They may not highlight the importance of the processes and strategies underlying task completion or raise self-efficacy for learning. As students engage in a task, they may be less likely to determine their progress by comparing their present and past performances. Performance goals can lead to social comparisons with the work of others to determine progress. These comparisons can lower self-efficacy among students who experience learning difficulties, which adversely affects motivation and learning.

Research supports these hypothesized effects of learning and performance goals (Anderman & Wolters, 2006). For example, Schunk (1996) conducted two studies in which elementary children with low fraction skills received instruction and practice on fractions over sessions. Children worked under conditions involving either a goal of learning how to solve problems or a performance goal of merely solving them. In the first study, half of the students in each goal condition completed a self-evaluation at the end of each instructional session in which they evaluated their progress in learning to solve the types of problems covered during that session. The learning goal with or without self-evaluation and the performance goal with self-evaluation led to higher motivation, self-efficacy, and achievement. In the second study, all students evaluated their learning progress at the end of the last instructional session. The learning goal led to higher motivation and achievement outcomes than did the performance goal.

Schunk and Ertmer (1999) conducted two studies with college undergraduates as they worked on computer projects over sessions. Students received a goal of learning computer applications or a goal of performing them. In the first study, half of the students in each goal condition evaluated their learning progress midway through the instructional program. The learning goal led to higher self-efficacy, self-judged progress, and self-regulatory competence and strategy use. The opportunity to self-evaluate progress promoted self-efficacy. In the second study, students in the self-evaluation condition assessed their progress after each instructional session. Frequent self-evaluation produced comparable results when linked with a learning or performance goal. These results suggest that infrequent self-evaluation of one's progress complements learning goals, but multiple self-evaluations can outweigh the benefits of learning goals and raise motivation and achievement outcomes.

Outcome Expectations

Outcome expectations are beliefs about the expected outcomes of actions. They can refer to external outcomes, such as "If I study hard, I should do well on the test." They also can refer to internal outcomes (e.g., "If I study hard, I will feel good about myself"), and to progress in learning (e.g., "If I study hard, I will learn more"). People form outcome expectations about the likely consequences of given actions based on personal experiences and observations of models (Bandura, 1986; Schunk & Zimmerman, 2006). Outcome expectations are a source of motivation. Individuals act in ways they believe they will be successful and attend to models whom they believe will teach them valued skills.

Outcome expectations can sustain behaviors over long periods when people believe their actions will eventually produce desired outcomes. Students who hold a sense of self-efficacy for succeeding and believe that their actions will result in positive outcomes are motivated to continue working even when progress occurs slowly. Conversely, those whose self-efficacy is weaker may, when they encounter difficulties,

work lackadaisically or give up readily. This situation can be demotivating; students may believe that positive outcomes will result but that they personally lack the self-efficacy to motivate themselves to continue. For example, they may believe that if they studied hard they would do well on the test, but they may doubt their self-efficacy to study hard.

Shell, Murphy, and Bruning (1989) obtained evidence of the influential role of outcome expectations. College students completed measures of self-efficacy and outcome expectations for reading and writing, as well as reading and writing achievement tests. For the self-efficacy assessment, students judged their competencies for performing various reading and writing tasks. For the outcome expectation measure, students judged the importance of reading and writing skills for achieving life goals, such as getting a job, being financially secure, and being happy.

Self-efficacy and outcome expectations related positively to achievement in both domains, although the relations were stronger for reading than for writing. In both domains, self-efficacy related more strongly to achievement than did outcome expectations, although the latter results were significant and added to the prediction of achievement. This study also found that self-efficacy and outcome expectations in each domain related significantly to achievement in the other domain, which suggests that improvements in students' self-efficacy and outcome expectations in one literacy area may generalize to other areas.

Values

Values are individuals' perceptions of the importance and utility of learning and acting in given ways. The role of values in motivation has been explored extensively by achievement motivation researchers (Eccles, 2005; Wigfield & Eccles, 2002; Wigfield, Tonks, & Eccles, 2004). Values enter prominently in a social cognitive account of motivation (Bandura, 1997). People who value attaining a sense of agency believe that they can exert a significant degree of control over important elements in their lives and are motivated to do so.

Individuals act in ways to bring about the outcomes they value and avoid actions leading to outcomes that are inconsistent with their values. They are motivated to learn when they deem that learning in a given area is important. Students who value mathematics may do so for various reasons, such as because they want to become mathematics teachers or because they believe that mathematics has many uses in everyday life. Valuing mathematics may lead them to take more mathematics courses and expend greater effort to succeed.

Investigations by achievement motivation researchers have shown that values and expectancy beliefs such as self-efficacy relate positively to students' achievement. When both expectancy beliefs and values are used to predict achievement, expectancy beliefs are significant predictors, whereas values are not. In contrast, values are better predictors of students' intentions to take future courses and actual enrollment in those courses than are expectancy beliefs (Wigfield & Eccles, 2002). Thus, values seem most important as contributors to individuals' choices, which are key motivational outcomes.

Social Comparisons

Given its emphasis on learning from the social environment and reciprocal interactions among personal, behavioral, and social/environmental variables, social cognitive theory underscores the importance of *social comparisons*, which refer to the process of comparing ourselves with others (Wheeler & Suls, 2005). Although people often compare their performances with objective standards, they also socially evaluate their capabilities, especially when objective standards are unclear or unavailable. Comparisons indicating that one is improving or more competent than others can raise self-efficacy and motivation; comparisons that result in negative self-evaluations can diminish these outcomes.

The most accurate self-evaluations arise from comparisons with others whom people believe are similar to themselves in the particular ability or characteristic being evaluated. The more alike observers are to models, the greater the probability that similar actions by observers will produce comparable results (Schunk, 1987). Model-observer perceived similarity in competence can improve learning (Braaksma, Rijlaarsdam, & van den Bergh, 2002). Observing similar others succeed can raise observers' self-efficacy and motivate them to try the task. Similarity may be especially influential with persons who have experienced difficulties and possess self-doubts about performing well.

Although social comparisons can motivate individuals, their effects are not automatic. Among elementary school children, Schunk (1983a) found that providing children with social comparative information about how their performances compared with those of others promoted their motivation but that pursuing goals enhanced their self-efficacy. Giving children both goals and comparative information led

to the best learning. Schunk (1983b) showed that difficult goals raised children's academic motivation more than easier goals, that persuasive self-efficacy feedback (e.g., "You can work 25 problems") raised self-efficacy more than feedback indicating how children's performances compared to those of peers, and that difficult goals plus persuasive feedback led to the highest achievement.

The effects of social comparisons on self-efficacy and motivation depend on the abilities of the comparison peers. Guay, Boivin, and Hodges (1999) found that the relation between children's perceived competence (analogous to self-efficacy) and achievement was stronger when best friends' achievement was low than when it was high. Students' social comparisons with close friends' achievement may make students' own performances look worse than they really are. In contrast, children may assess their capabilities more accurately when they have low-achieving friends because they rely less on social comparison and more on objective assessments of their progress and performances.

Thus, it seems that social comparisons can enhance motivation but not necessarily self-efficacy or learning. Social comparisons that focus students on the accomplishments of similar and average peers imply that they, too, are average and therefore have no reason to feel highly self-efficacious. Self-efficacy may decline when students socially compare themselves to high-achieving peers. Self-efficacy and motivation may benefit more from providing students with objective information indicating that they are making learning progress without referring to peers' accomplishments.

Self-Efficacy

Self-efficacy is a critical variable affecting learning and motivation (Bandura, 1997). This section discusses how individuals develop and alter their self-efficacy, the consequences of self-efficacy, research on self-efficacy in achievement situations, and collective self-efficacy.

Sources of Self-Efficacy Information

People acquire information to assess their self-efficacy from four primary sources: their mastery experiences (interpretations of actual performances), vicarious (modeled) experiences, forms of social persuasion, and physiological indexes (Bandura, 1997; Table 2.3). One's actual performances constitute the most reliable information because they typically are interpreted as tangible indicators of one's capabilities (Schunk & Pajares, 2009; Usher & Pajares, 2008b).

Table 2.3. Informational Sources of Self-Efficacy

- Mastery experiences (interpretations of actual performances)

- Vicarious (modeled) experiences

- Forms of social persuasion

- Physiological indexes

Successful performances raise self-efficacy, whereas failures may lower it, although an occasional failure or success after many successes or failures should not have much impact.

The influence of actual performances on self-efficacy depends on numerous circumstantial factors such as task difficulty, effort expended, aid received, and preconceptions of one's capabilities (Bandura, 1997). Consequently, the cognitive interpretations of the results of one's actions, not the actions themselves, determine the influence of past performances on efficacy judgments. For example, meeting the minimum requirements for passing geometry may not boost the mathematics self-efficacy of a student who holds extraordinarily high personal standards and who longs to be an engineer. For another student, whose values and interests lie elsewhere, an average performance in geometry may boost self-efficacy and lead to continued motivation in mathematics classes. Failures can also serve an important function when they lead to better strategies that make self-efficacy more robust.

Individuals acquire much information about their capabilities through social comparisons with others (Bandura, 1997). Similarity to others is a cue for gauging one's self-efficacy (Schunk, 1987). Observing similar others succeed can raise observers' self-efficacy and motivation when they believe that if others can perform well, they can too. But a vicarious increase in self-efficacy can be negated by subsequent failure. Persons who observe similar peers fail may believe they lack the competence to succeed, which can negatively affect motivation.

In their daily school environments, students likely compare themselves to particular classmates who are engaged in similar learning activities. Surpassing one's peers builds self-efficacy, whereas inferior performances lower it. Despite these tendencies, the influence of peer models on one's self-efficacy cannot be reliably predetermined. A high-achieving, competitive student might get a self-efficacy boost from being outperformed by a classmate (Usher, 2009). On the other hand, a student who stands out

for superior performance among classmates might make external attributions (e.g., "I did well because the test was easy") that leave self-efficacy relatively unchanged. Whether a vicarious experience raises or lowers self-efficacy depends on the models one selects for comparison, how similar the models are perceived to be, the models' attitudes, and disparities between the observers' and models' achievement and progress.

Teaching practices can also increase the frequency with which students compare their performances to those of others. Schools create comparative structures when they group students according to academic ability levels as measured by achievement test scores or similar criteria. Such practices can send students a public message of their (in)efficacy. And because exposure to multiple skilled models sustains learning self-efficacy, students who find themselves among highly talented peers may reap long-term self-efficacy benefits, whereas those surrounded by less-skilled peers may harbor similar self-doubts. Students who internalize personal standards may be less prone to making unfavorable comparisons (Pajares, 2006).

Because of the human capacity for symbolism and forethought, people are capable of cognitively generating events that can serve as guides for action. Students are, therefore, partial creators of their modeled experiences. Through cognitive self-modeling, people are able to visualize themselves confronting and overcoming challenges (Bandura, 1997). Envisioning one's academic success can raise self-efficacy, whereas imagining oneself failing lowers self-efficacy and can ensure the feared failure. The fact that this mode of cognitive influence has not been extensively examined need not suggest its impotence in changing self-efficacy. As William James remarked over a century ago, "The reaction due to things of thought is notoriously in many cases as strong as that due to sensible presences. It may be even stronger" (James, 1905, p. 53).

The third source of self-efficacy information on which individuals rely comes from the persuasive messages of others (e.g., "I know you can do this"; Bandura, 1997). But social persuasions must be credible for people to believe that success is attainable. Although positive feedback can raise individuals' self-efficacy, the increase will not endure if they subsequently perform poorly (Schunk & Pajares, 2009). Factors that influence the persuasory punch of a message include source credibility, valence of the message, and frequency. A youngster's self-efficacy is likely to suffer more from disparaging remarks than from positive ones (Bandura, 1997). Students who hear frequent messages from multiple sources that they are incapable may come to believe that to be the case.

People are more likely to attend to social messages about their capabilities when they lack adequate knowledge of what is required to succeed in a particular domain. To be most effective and motivating, persuasive messages from others must be matched to the individuals' current skill level. Students are quick to dismiss lofty praise or empty inspirational mantras. Those who are most skilled at building students' self-efficacy couple positive feedback about students' capabilities with scaffolded tasks that build mastery (Evans, 1989).

Individuals also can acquire self-efficacy information from physiological and emotional reactions such as anxiety and stress (Bandura, 1997). Strong emotional reactions provide cues about anticipated success or failure. For example, a student who feels a crippling fear when heading to advanced chemistry may interpret that fear as a sign of personal inefficacy. When people experience negative thoughts and fears about their capabilities (e.g., feeling nervous when thinking about taking a test), those affective reactions can lower self-efficacy. On the other hand, positive affect or excitement in learning can motivate. A student who feels energized by challenging academic work likely enjoys a sense of self-efficacy for succeeding. When people notice their stress abating (e.g., feeling less anxious while taking a test), they may experience higher self-efficacy for performing well.

As we noted earlier, informational sources related to one's abilities do not affect self-efficacy automatically (Bandura, 1997). Individuals interpret the results of events, and these interpretations provide the impetus for upward or downward shifts in one's self-efficacy (Schunk & Pajares, 2009). People weigh and combine information from the various sources to form self-efficacy judgments. Many factors influence the ways in which students interpret and integrate this information when forming their self-efficacy and motivation-related beliefs. For some individuals, the accumulation of informational sources enhances self-efficacy. Other people tend to rely on information from one source more than from others. For example, in a study of the sources of academic self-efficacy among middle school students, girls and African American students seemed more attuned to social persuasions when forming their self-efficacy than did boys and White students (Usher & Pajares, 2006).

The influence of these sources of self-efficacy might also be multiplicative, in that two sources combine interactively. Students who have had few mastery experiences in a given domain may be more likely to rely on what others tell them than would students who have had ample opportunities for mastery (Usher, 2009). Beliefs in one's personal efficacy for learning might also follow a transformational experience. A meaningful individual encounter with a caring teacher might have a more profound influence on one's self-efficacy than a year's worth of school. A disparaging remark can also leave a lasting bruise on one's sense of efficacy and undermine subsequent motivation. We now turn to the many outcomes that are influenced by these important self-beliefs.

Effects of Self-Efficacy

Within a social cognitive system of triadic reciprocality, self-efficacy is hypothesized to influence behaviors and environments and in turn be affected by them (Bandura, 1986, 1997). Self-efficacy exerts its influence through cognitive, motivational, affective, and selection processes. Students who feel efficacious about learning should engage in thoughts and actions that improve their learning, such as setting goals, using effective learning strategies, monitoring their comprehension, evaluating their goal progress, and creating effective environments for learning. In turn, self-efficacy is influenced by the outcomes of one's behaviors (e.g., goal progress, achievement) and by input from one's environment (e.g., feedback from teachers, social comparisons with peers; Schunk & Pajares, 2009).

Despite its benefits, self-efficacy is not the only influence on behavior. No amount of self-efficacy will produce a competent performance when individuals lack the needed skills to succeed (Schunk & Pajares, 2009). Discussed earlier was the importance of other motivating factors such as outcome expectations and values (Bandura, 1997; Wigfield et al., 2004). Even learners who feel highly efficacious about their mathematical skills will not become mathematics majors in college if they do not value a career as a mathematician, and they typically engage in activities that they believe will result in positive outcomes and avoid actions that they believe may lead to negative outcomes. Nonetheless, given requisite skills, positive values, and outcome expectations, self-efficacy is a key determinant of individuals' motivation, learning, self-regulation, and achievement (Schunk & Pajares, 2009).

Self-efficacy can have diverse effects in achievement contexts (Bandura, 1997; Pajares, 1996; Schunk & Pajares, 2009; Table 2.4). It can influence various motivational outcomes, including choice of tasks, effort, and persistence. Individuals are apt to select tasks and activities at which they feel competent and avoid those at which they do not. Self-efficacy can affect how much effort people expend on an activity, how long they persist when they encounter difficulties, and their levels of learning and achievement. People with high self-efficacy tend to set challenging goals, work diligently, persist in the face of failure, and recover their sense of efficacy after setbacks. As a consequence, they develop competence. On the other hand, those with low self-efficacy may set easier goals, expend little effort to succeed, give up readily when they experience difficulties, and feel dejected after they encounter failure, all of which negatively affect skill acquisition.

Self-efficacy also influences one's level of self-regulation (Schunk & Pajares, 2009; Zimmerman & Cleary, 2009). Those with higher self-efficacy for learning set challenging goals, employ what they believe are effective strategies, self-monitor their learning goal progress, make strategy adjustments and seek help as needed, and create an effective work environment. As formal and informal learning environments become increasingly technological, one's capabilities to minimize distractions and find reliable information are at a premium. In turn, these activities result in better performance and higher self-efficacy for continued improvement. We next highlight some specific research findings on the effects and sources of self-efficacy.

Research Evidence

Researchers have explored the operation of self-efficacy in various domains (e.g., education, health, business) and among individuals differing in age, developmental level, and cultural background. This research has shown that self-efficacy is a strong predictor of individuals' motivation, achievement,

Table 2.4. Effects of Self-Efficacy

- Motivational outcomes (task choices, effort, persistence)

- Learning

- Achievement

- Self-regulation

self-regulation, and life decisions in diverse contexts (Bandura, 1997; Klassen & Usher, 2010; Multon, Brown, & Lent, 1991; Pajares, 1997; Schunk & Pajares, 2009; Stajkovic & Luthans, 1998).

For example, much research shows that self-efficacy correlates with motivation, learning, and achievement (Schunk & Pajares, 2009). Using meta-analysis, Multon et al. (1991) found that self-efficacy was related to academic performance and accounted for 14% of the variance. Stajkovic and Luthans (1998) found that self-efficacy resulted in a 28% gain in work performance. Using path analysis, Schunk (1981) found that self-efficacy exerted a direct effect on children's mathematics achievement and persistence. Pajares and Kranzler (1995) found that mathematics self-efficacy had a direct effect on mathematics performance and mediated the influence of mental ability. Self-efficacy for self-regulated learning also predicts academic motivation, achievement, and continuation in school (Caprara et al., 2008; Usher & Pajares, 2008a).

Self-efficacy relates not only to task choice but also to career choice (Betz & Hackett, 1983). Social cognitive career theorists have demonstrated that basic social cognitive variables, including self-efficacy, outcome expectations, and goals, help explain career decision making and development (Brown & Lent, 2006). As learners grow and are given more choices over their decisions and activities, they are apt to select activities that involve capabilities they believe they can develop and turn away from areas in which they have doubts. The influence of self-efficacy on career development is partly mediated by perceived effort and persistence (Schunk & Pajares, 2009).

The relation of self-efficacy to effort and persistence is not always linear. In novel learning situations, students initially do not possess skills and must expend effort and persist to succeed. As skills develop, however, students should be able to attain the same level of performance with less effort in a shorter time. When this does not happen, self-efficacy may decline. Thus, if an advanced student believes she is capable in science but suddenly must exert a herculean effort to pass physics, she might begin to rethink her pursuit of a science-related career.

In addition to documenting the effects of self-efficacy, researchers have examined the influence of the four hypothesized sources on self-efficacy development. Mastery experiences have been shown to be the most powerful and consistent predictor of self-efficacy across academic domains and age levels

(Usher & Pajares, 2008b). Scaffolding instruction to provide for frequent successes offers learners many opportunities to build a sense of self-efficacy in their capabilities. The relative predictive power of the other three sources has been variable across studies. For example, in their study of the sources of academic and self-regulatory efficacy beliefs of sixth-grade students, Usher and Pajares (2006) found that girls and African American students relied on the social persuasions of others when forming their confidence, whereas this source was not a significant predictor of boys' or White students' self-efficacy. Klassen (2004) also found that Indo-Canadian students reported greater reliance on vicarious experiences and social persuasions than did Anglo-Canadian students. Investigating the importance of social messages, whether transmitted through vicarious enactment or verbal persuasion, for various groups of learners remains an important area of inquiry for understanding how efficacy beliefs take root.

Experimental research has shown that instructional and social processes that convey information to students that they are making learning progress and becoming more competent raise self-efficacy, motivation, and achievement (Schunk & Pajares, 2009). Other instructional strategies for building students' self-efficacy include having students pursue proximal and specific goals, using social models in instruction, providing social comparative information indicating competence, and having students self-monitor and evaluate their learning progress (Schunk & Ertmer, 2000). A noncompetitive classroom climate can lower students' anxiety, which can lead to a more favorable evaluation of their own capabilities (Bandura, 1997).

Collective Efficacy

Researchers have explored the operation of *collective efficacy* beliefs, or individuals' beliefs about their collective capabilities to learn or produce desired actions (Bandura, 1997). Collective efficacy perceptions are not simply the sum or average of the self-efficacy of individual group members; rather, they reflect individuals' perceptions of the capabilities of the group as a whole. In educational settings, collective teacher efficacy denotes the perceptions of the faculty as a whole to influence student outcomes (Goddard, Hoy, & Woolfolk Hoy, 2000; Henson, 2002).

The role of collective efficacy beliefs on group motivation may depend on the level of organizational coupling (Henson, 2002). In units that are loosely knit, collective efficacy beliefs may not predict outcomes well; rather, individual self-efficacy may be a better predictor. Conversely, in more tightly knit units—such as many elementary schools—the collective efficacy beliefs of teachers may be a better predictor of the efforts of the faculty as a whole to affect student learning (Henson, 2002).

The same four sources are important for the development of collective self-efficacy: performance attainments, vicarious experiences, social persuasion, and physiological indicators. Group members rely on what they know about the capabilities of each group member, as well as the group's collective capacity, when evaluating what they can do together (Bandura, 1997). When members work together successfully to implement changes, learn from one another and from other successful groups, receive encouragement for change from supervisors and others, and work together to cope with difficulties and alleviate stress, their beliefs about what they can do will be raised (Goddard, Hoy, & Woolfolk Hoy, 2004). Individuals who believe in their group's collective capabilities will be more motivated to work on the group's behalf, implement innovative ideas, and enact systemic change.

Educational research shows that collective self-efficacy is important for teachers' job satisfaction and motivation to remain in teaching. Researchers have found that teachers' collective self-efficacy bears a significant and positive relation to their job satisfaction in various contexts (Caprara, Barbaranelli, Borgogni, & Steca; 2003; Klassen, Usher, & Bong, 2010). Relatively less research attention has been given to the collective efficacy beliefs of students. Klassen and Krawchuk (2009) showed that the collective efficacy beliefs of early adolescents working in small groups became more strongly related to the group's success on an interdependent task over time. Perceived collective efficacy also depends on group members believing that others are working on their behalf. Consistent with Bandura's (1997) contention, however, even high self-efficacy will not lead to performance changes unless the environment in which groups function provides appropriate avenues for success.

Future Directions

Social cognitive theory offers a viable account of motivation, and researchers continue to test its predictions. But there remain several questions that should be addressed by investigators. In particular, research is recommended on the benefits of modeled observations, developmental appropriateness, and cross-cultural relevance.

Benefits of Modeled Observations

Individuals learn new skills and strategies by observing models. Modeled observations also motivate observers to improve their skills. In educational settings, use of models is apt to save instructional time as teachers or others can explain and demonstrate skills and strategies to be acquired. This also prevents students from learning inaccurately, as might happen if there were less structure.

Although models are important, their effects on students' self-efficacy and motivation are weaker than are those resulting from actual performance accomplishments. Researchers might explore how best to combine modeled demonstrations with learner practice to optimize motivational effects. In some situations, relatively little practice may be needed, but more is likely when skills to be learned are complex. Such research would contribute to clarifying how learners weigh and combine sources of self-efficacy information to arrive at self-efficacy judgments. For example, how is self-efficacy affected if models perform successfully but students then have difficulty when they practice? This type of research also would have instructional implications because it would suggest ways to effectively use instructional time to promote self-efficacy and motivation.

Technological innovations might facilitate this line of research. Computers and handheld devices make it possible for modeled experiences to be at students' fingertips. For example, researchers could use video recordings of models at varying skills levels to examine their influence on a diverse group of learners. An experimental design would enable varying of model characteristics such as similarity, proficiency, and degree of shared coping. Video playback of one's own performances could enhance students' ability for cognitive self-modeling as well. The changing nature and availability of technology make possible new and diverse modeling opportunities. If such videos of modeled skills prove to be effective, teachers could benefit from developing their own library of vicarious experiences for their students.

Developmental Appropriateness

Social cognitive theory emphasizes complex interactions among personal, social/environmental, and behavioral factors. This complexity leads to questions about the applicability of the theory to learners of all ages and developmental levels. For example, when assessing self-efficacy, individuals must weigh and combine information from the environment, their prior experiences, and their perceptions of the present situation. Such complex cognitive processing may be beyond the capabilities of young children, which can diminish the predictive utility of self-efficacy. Furthermore, mentally processing information conveyed by models can be complex, as when models demonstrate problem-solving strategies.

Children can learn from observing models and make reasonably valid self-efficacy judgments (Bandura, 1986). Models for children are effective when their explanations and demonstrations are brief and restricted to specific skills. Self-efficacy assessments typically contain a restricted range of choices, and children are given practice to ensure that they understand the nature of the judgment process. Thus, although social cognitive principles are assumed to apply to learners at different developmental levels, researchers might explore what constraints developmental factors place on applying these principles.

Longitudinal designs that track changes in learners' self-efficacy and motivation over time would help researchers understand the influence of developmental stages on efficacy appraisals. Such designs could also target changes in the efficacy-related information that students perceive. Multilevel modeling techniques could help document how self-efficacy levels fluctuate among groups of students (e.g., between grades 3 and 5) and could examine predictors of individual students' self-efficacy growth trajectories. Despite the costs of conducting longitudinal research, such designs will be able to clarify important questions related to developmental shifts in the sources and effects of self-efficacy that have not been clearly answered by cross-sectional designs.

Cross-Cultural Relevance

Pajares (2007) called for a careful consideration of cultural context in the investigation of academic motivation in general and self-efficacy in particular. Because the relation between self-efficacy, other motivation variables, and achievement varies in important ways across cultural groups, researchers should use caution when generalizing research results to other contexts. As Pajares (2007) noted, "Research findings must be carefully understood as being bounded by a host of situated factors" (p. 30), which limit what is known about a given variable.

Most social cognitive research relevant to motivation has been conducted with individuals in Western societies (Klassen & Usher, 2010). Fortunately this situation is changing as researchers are testing social cognitive ideas in settings globally.

As a research topic, self-efficacy has much international appeal, with the resulting increase in research in different cultures. While cross-cultural research has yielded differences (McInerney, 2008), overall the principles espoused by social cognitive theory have shown themselves to be cross-culturally relevant. Additional investigations will determine whether the motivational processes postulated by social cognitive theory operate consistently in diverse societies.

Conclusion

Social cognitive theory stresses learning from the social environment. The conceptual focus of Bandura's (1986) social cognitive theory postulates reciprocal interactions among personal, behavioral, and social/environmental factors. Social cognitive researchers have investigated the operation of vicarious, symbolic, and self-regulatory processes, in the various ways that individuals interact with their environments and one another.

A key point underlying social cognitive theory is that persons are motivated to develop a sense of agency for being able to exert a large degree of control over important events in their lives. Among the influential variables affecting motivation are goals and self-evaluations of progress, outcome expectations, values, social comparisons, and self-efficacy. Important questions remain to be addressed by researchers, which will further refine social cognitive theory and expand its applicability to motivation.

References

Anderman, E. M., & Wolters, C. A. (2006). Goals, values, and affects: Influences on student motivation. In P. A. Alexander & P. H. Winne (Eds.), *Handbook of educational psychology* (2nd ed., pp. 369–389). Mahwah, NJ: Erlbaum.

Bandura, A. (1969). *Principles of behavior modification.* New York: Holt, Rinehart & Winston.

Bandura, A. (1977a). Self-efficacy: Toward a unifying theory of behavioral change. *Psychological Review, 84,* 191–215.

Bandura, A. (1977b). *Social learning theory.* Englewood Cliffs, NJ: Prentice Hall.

Bandura, A. (1986). *Social foundations of thought and action: A social cognitive theory.* Englewood Cliffs, NJ: Prentice Hall.

Bandura, A. (1997). *Self-efficacy: The exercise of control.* New York: Freeman.

Bandura, A. (2001). Social cognitive theory: An agentic perspective. *Annual Review of Psychology, 52,* 1–26.

Bandura, A., & Schunk, D. H. (1981). Cultivating competence, self-efficacy, and intrinsic interest through proximal self-motivation. *Journal of Personality and Social Psychology, 41,* 586–598.

Betz, N. E., & Hackett, G. (1983). The relationship of mathematics self-efficacy expectations to the selection of science-based college majors. *Journal of Vocational Behavior, 23,* 329–345.

Braaksma, M. A. H., Rijlaarsdam, G., & van den Bergh, H. (2002). Observational learning and the effects of model-observer similarity. *Journal of Educational Psychology, 94,* 405–415.

Brown, S. D., & Lent, R. W. (2006). Preparing adolescents to make career decisions: A social cognitive perspective. In F. Pajares & T. Urdan (Eds.), *Adolescence and education, Vol. 5: Self-efficacy beliefs of adolescents* (pp. 201–223). Greenwich, CT: Information Age Publishing.

Caprara, G. V., Barbaranelli, C., Borgogni, L., & Steca, P. (2003). Efficacy beliefs as determinants of teachers' job satisfaction. *Journal of Educational Psychology, 95,* 821–832.

Caprara, G. V., Fida, R., Vecchione, M., Del Bove, G., Vecchio, G. M., Barbaranelli, C., & Bandura, A. (2008). Longitudinal analysis of the role of perceived efficacy for self-regulated learning in academic continuance and achievement. *Journal of Educational Psychology, 100,* 525–534.

Carroll, W. R., & Bandura, A. (1982). The role of visual monitoring in observational learning of action patterns: Making the unobservable observable. *Journal of Motor Behavior, 14,* 153–167.

Chartrand, T. L., & Bargh, J. A. (1999). The Chameleon Effect: The perception-behavior link and social interaction. *Journal of Personality and Social Psychology, 76,* 893–910.

Eccles, J. S. (2005). Subjective task value and the Eccles et al. model of achievement-related choices. In A. J. Elliot & C. S. Dweck (Eds.), *Handbook of competence and motivation* (pp. 105–121). New York: Guilford Press.

Evans, R. I. (1989). *Albert Bandura: The man and his ideas—a dialogue.* New York: Praeger.

Goddard, R. D., Hoy, W. K., & Woolfolk Hoy, A. (2000). Collective teacher efficacy: Its meaning, measure, and impact on student achievement. *American Educational Research Journal, 37,* 479–507.

Goddard, R. D., Hoy, W. K., & Woolfolk Hoy, A. (2004). Collective efficacy beliefs: Theoretical developments, empirical evidence, and future directions. *Educational Researcher, 33*(3), 3–13.

Guay, F., Boivin, M., & Hodges, E. V. E. (1999). Social comparison processes and academic achievement: The dependence of the development of self-evaluations on friends' performance. *Journal of Educational Psychology, 91,* 564–568.

Henson, R. K. (2002). From adolescent angst to adulthood: Substantive implications and measurement dilemmas in the development of teacher efficacy research. *Educational Psychologist, 37,* 137–150.

James, W. (1905). *Varieties of religious experience.* New York: Longmans, Green, and Co.

Klassen, R. M. (2004). A cross-cultural investigation of the efficacy beliefs of South Asian immigrant and Anglo non-immigrant early adolescents. *Journal of Educational Psychology, 96,* 731–742.

Klassen, R. M., & Krawchuk, L. L. (2009). Collective motivation beliefs of early adolescents working in small groups. *Journal of School Psychology, 47,* 101–120.

Klassen, R. M., & Usher, E. L. (2010). Self-efficacy in educational settings: Recent research and emerging directions. In T. C. Urdan & S. A. Karabenick (Eds.), *Advances in motivation and achievement: Vol. 16A. The decade ahead: Theoretical perspectives on motivation and achievement* (pp. 1–33). Bingley, UK: Emerald Publishing Group.

Klassen, R. M., Usher, E. L., & Bong, M. (2010). Teachers' collective efficacy, job satisfaction, and job stress in cross-cultural context. *Journal of Experimental Education, 78,* 464–486.

Licht, B. G., & Kistner, J. A. (1986). Motivational problems of learning-disabled children: Individual differences and their implications for treatment. In J. K. Torgesen & B. W. L. Wong (Eds.), *Psychological and educational perspectives on learning disabilities* (pp. 225–255). Orlando: Academic Press.

Locke, E. A., & Latham, G. P. (2002). Building a practically useful theory of goal setting and task motivation: A 35-year odyssey. *American Psychologist, 57,* 705–717.

Matlin, M. W. (2009). *Cognition* (7th ed.). Hoboken, NJ: Wiley.

McInerney, D. M. (2008). The motivational roles of cultural differences and cultural identity in self-regulated learning. In D. H. Schunk & B. J. Zimmerman (Eds.), *Motivation and self-regulated learning: Theory, research, and applications* (pp. 369–400). New York: Taylor & Francis.

Multon, K. D., Brown, S. D., & Lent, R. W. (1991). Relation of self-efficacy beliefs to academic outcomes: A meta-analytic investigation. *Journal of Counseling Psychology, 38,* 30–38.

Pajares, F. (1996). Self-efficacy beliefs in achievement settings. *Review of Educational Research, 66,* 543–578.

Pajares, F. (1997). Current directions in self-efficacy research. In M. Maehr & P. R. Pintrich (Eds.), *Advances in motivation and achievement* (Vol. 10, pp. 1–49). Greenwich, CT: JAI Press.

Pajares, F. (2006). Self-efficacy beliefs during adolescence: Implications for teachers and parents. In F. Pajares & T. Urdan (Eds.), *Adolescence and education, Vol. 5: Self-efficacy beliefs of adolescents* (pp. 339–367). Greenwich, CT: Information Age Publishing.

Pajares, F. (2007). Culturalizing educational psychology. In F. Salili & R. Hoosain (Eds.), *Culture, motivation, and learning* (pp. 19–42). Charlotte, NC: Information Age.

Pajares, F., & Kranzler, J. (1995). Self-efficacy beliefs and general mental ability in mathematical problem-solving. *Contemporary Educational Psychology, 20,* 426–443.

Schunk, D. H. (1981). Modeling and attributional effects on children's achievement: A self-efficacy analysis. *Journal of Educational Psychology, 73,* 93–105.

Schunk, D. H. (1983a). Developing children's self-efficacy and skills: The roles of social comparative information and goal setting. *Contemporary Educational Psychology, 8,* 76–86.

Schunk, D. H. (1983b). Goal difficulty and attainment information: Effects on children's achievement behaviors. *Human Learning, 2,* 107–117.

Schunk, D. H. (1987). Peer models and children's behavioral change. *Review of Educational Research, 57,* 149–174.

Schunk, D. H. (1996). Goal and self-evaluative influences during children's cognitive skill learning. *American Educational Research Journal, 33,* 359–382

Schunk, D. H., & Ertmer, P. A. (1999). Self-regulatory processes during computer skill acquisition: Goal and self-evaluative influences. *Journal of Educational Psychology, 91,* 251–260.

Schunk, D. H., & Ertmer, P. A. (2000). Self-regulation and academic learning: Self-efficacy enhancing interventions. In M. Boekaerts, P. R. Pintrich, & M. Zeidner (Eds.), *Handbook of self-regulation* (pp. 631–649). San Diego, CA: Academic Press.

Schunk, D. H., & Hanson, A. R. (1985). Peer models: Influence on children's self-efficacy and achievement. *Journal of Educational Psychology, 77,* 313–322.

Schunk, D. H., & Pajares, F. (2005). Competence perceptions and academic functioning. In J. Elliot & C. S. Dweck (Eds.), *Handbook of competence and motivation* (pp. 85–104). New York: Guilford Press.

Schunk, D. H., & Pajares, F. (2009). Self-efficacy theory. In K. R. Wentzel & A. Wigfield (Eds.), *Handbook of motivation at school* (pp. 35–53). New York: Routledge.

Schunk, D. H., Pintrich, P. R., & Meece, J. L. (2008). *Motivation in education: Theory, research, and applications* (3rd ed.). Upper Saddle River, NJ: Pearson Education.

Schunk, D. H., & Zimmerman, B. J. (2006). Competence and control beliefs: Distinguishing the means and ends. In P. A. Alexander & P. H. Winne (Eds.), *Handbook of educational psychology* (2nd ed., pp. 349–367). Mahwah, NJ: Erlbaum.

Shell, D. F., Murphy, C. C., & Bruning, R. H. (1989). Self-efficacy and outcome expectancy mechanisms in reading and writing achievement. *Journal of Educational Psychology, 81,* 91–100.

Stajkovic, A. D., & Luthans, F. (1998). Self-efficacy and work-related performances: A meta-analysis. *Psychological Bulletin, 124,* 240–261.

Usher, E. L. (2009). Sources of middle school students' self-efficacy in mathematics: A qualitative investigation of student, teacher, and parent perspectives. *American Educational Research Journal, 46,* 275–314.

Usher, E. L., & Pajares, F. (2006). Sources of academic and self-regulatory efficacy beliefs of entering middle school students. *Contemporary Educational Psychology, 31,* 125–141.

Usher, E. L., & Pajares, F. (2008a). Self-efficacy for self-regulated learning: A validation study. *Educational and Psychological Measurement, 68,* 443–463.

Usher, E. L., & Pajares, F. (2008b). Sources of self-efficacy in school: Critical review of the literature and future directions. *Review of Educational Research, 78,* 751–796.

Wheeler, L., & Suls, J. (2005). Social comparison and self-evaluations of competence. In A. J. Elliot & C. S. Dweck (Eds.), *Handbook of competence and motivation* (pp. 566–578). New York: Guilford Press.

Wigfield, A., & Eccles, J. S. (2002). The development of competence beliefs, expectancies for success, and achievement values from childhood through adolescence. In A. Wigfield & J. S. Eccles (Eds.), *Development of achievement motivation* (pp. 91–120). San Diego, CA: Academic Press.

Wigfield, A., Tonks, S., & Eccles, J. S. (2004). Expectancy value theory in cross-cultural perspective. In D. M. McInerney & S. Van Etten (Eds.), *Big theories revisited* (pp. 165–198). Greenwich, CT: Information Age Publishing.

Zimmerman, B. J. (2000). Attaining self-regulation: A social cognitive perspective. In M. Boekaerts, P. R. Pintrich, & M. Zeidner (Eds.), *Handbook of self-regulation* (pp. 13–39). San Diego, CA: Academic Press.

Zimmerman, B. J., & Cleary, T. J. (2009). Motives to self-regulate learning: A social cognitive account. In K. R. Wentzel & A. Wigfield (Eds.), *Handbook of motivation at school* (pp. 247–264). New York: Routledge.

Cybernetic Control Processes and the Self-Regulation of Behavior

Charles S. Carver *and* Michael F. Scheier

Abstract

This chapter describes a set of ideas bearing on the self-regulation of action and emotion that has been given labels such as cybernetic and feedback control processes. The ideas have roots in many sources, including the concept of homeostasis and attempts to create mechanical devices to serve as governors for engines. With respect to motivation, these ideas yield a viewpoint in which goal-directed action is seen as reflecting a hierarchy of feedback control processes and the creation and reduction of affect are seen as reflecting another set of feedback processes. The portion of the model devoted to affect is of particular interest in that it generates two predictions that differ substantially from those deriving from other theories. The first is that both approach and avoidance can give rise to both positive and negative feelings; the second is that positive affect leads to coasting, reduction in effort regarding the goal under pursuit. The latter suggests a way in which positive affect is involved in priority management when many goals are in existence at the same time. Recent interest in dual-process models, which distinguish between top-down goal pursuit and reflexive responses to cues of the moment, has caused us to reexamine some of our previous assumptions and to consider the possibility that behavior is triggered in two distinct ways. The chapter closes with a brief consideration of how these ideas might be compatible with other viewpoints on motivation.

Key Words: cybernetic, feedback loop, control theory, affect

This chapter describes several aspects of a viewpoint on the guidance of behavior that we have used throughout our careers in psychology. This viewpoint has roots in several places. One of them is the broad conception of homeostatic mechanisms, mechanisms that regulate diverse aspects of the body's physiological functioning (Cannon, 1932). Another source is ideas about mechanical governors and computing machines (e.g., Ashby, 1940; Rosenblueth, Wiener, & Bigelow, 1943; Wiener, 1948). In the middle of the 20th century, Wiener (1948) coined the term *cybernetic* (from the Greek word meaning "steersman") to characterize the overall functioning of this type of system. Cybernetic systems (whether mechanical, electronic, or living

systems) regulate some current condition so as to stay "on course." The idea that such systems underlie overt, intentional behavior as well as homeostatic self-regulation is the theme of this chapter. We amplify on this idea shortly, but first we'll provide a little more background.

Cybernetic ideas had a brief heyday in motivational psychology (broadly defined) in the 1950s through 1970s. Probably the best known example of this viewpoint was an engaging book by Miller, Galanter, and Pribram (1960). This book introduced into the psychological lexicon the acronym TOTE, which stands for test-operate-test-exit, a sequence of events that take place in a cybernetic control system. Miller et al. were not the only people to use cybernetic concepts during this period (ideas with a similar character were proposed, for example, by MacKay, 1956, 1966; for review see Miller et al., 1960), but Miller et al. received the most attention from psychologists. To some extent this may be attributable to the fact that the operation of a TOTE unit paralleled the operation of the basic element of a computer. Computers (which were fairly new at the time) were starting to influence people's thinking about the nature of cognition. Thus, Miller et al.'s book was very much in the spirit of its time.

Today when people use the word *cybernetic*, they generally are referring either to robotics or to the World Wide Web. It is also fairly common to associate the viewpoint we describe here with the discipline of engineering, partly because of its heritage in devices that govern engines and partly because of the usefulness of control theory in engineering applications. It's important, though, to keep in mind that these ideas have ties that extend well beyond engineering. As noted earlier, they pertain additionally to the homeostatic controllers of the body. They also pertain to diverse other complex systems in nature.

Thirteen years after Miller et al.'s (1960) intriguing volume came another book that had a particularly strong impact on our thinking. This book, written by William Powers (1973), was an extremely ambitious undertaking. Powers set out to portray how human behavior might reflect a hierarchy of cybernetic control processes. That is, he tried to account for how the nervous system creates the physical movements by which intentions and even abstract values are expressed in action. At center stage in his account was the feedback loop, the basic unit of cybernetic control. Powers set out to map several layers of postulated feedback processes to aspects of the nervous system. Perhaps even more than Miller et al. (1960), Powers made a compelling case for the idea that the feedback construct was up to the challenge of accounting for the complexity of behavior. He focused not on one single loop, but on an interwoven network of loops, dealing with regulation of diverse properties simultaneously.

We adopted the Powers (1973) model as a conceptual heuristic (Carver & Scheier, 1981). It helped us interpret a literature in personality and social psychology in which we were immersed at the time (see Carver & Scheier, 2112). And it provided a reference point for us for the next 30 years. Indeed, in some ways it serves as the conceptual backbone of this chapter.

Feedback Control

What are the elements of a cybernetic feedback control system? The term *feedback control* can seem quite forbidding. An easy point of entry into the logic behind it, however, is the goal concept, which is more intuitive. People have many goals, at varying levels of abstraction and importance. Goals energize and guide activities. Most goals can be reached in many ways, leading to the potential for vast complexity in the organization of action. This is a view that is easy and familiar for most people, and it is part of the conceptual landscape of contemporary psychology. From this view, the transition to thinking about cybernetic control is relatively straightforward.

Feedback Processes

The basic unit of cybernetic control is the feedback loop. A feedback loop has four elements (MacKay, 1966; Miller et al., 1960; Powers, 1973; Wiener, 1948): an input function, a reference value, a comparison process, and an output. Think of the input function as perception. The input function brings in information of some sort about present circumstances. Think of the reference value as a goal. The perceived input is compared to this value, to determine whether a difference exists. A discrepancy that is detected by this comparison creates what is called an "error signal." The output function is a response to any detected error (we treat the output here as equivalent to behavior, but sometimes the behavior is an internal signal rather than a physical movement).

If the comparison detects no discrepancy, the output remains as it was. If the comparison detects a discrepancy, the effect on output depends on what kind of loop it is. There are two kinds. In a discrepancy-reducing loop (also called negative, for negating), the output acts to reduce (or eliminate) the discrepancy. Homeostatic systems are examples of discrepancy-reducing systems. For example, if a person's internal temperature sensors detect that his body temperature is elevated above "normal," processes are engaged that serve to reduce body temperature so that it returns to that reference value. Specifically, sweat would be released, which cools the body as it evaporates. If the sensors detect a deviation below normal, rather than above, the output would be shivering, which generates heat via muscle contractions.

Discrepancy-enlarging feedback loops also exist, in which the output serves not to counter a discrepancy but to enlarge it (these are also called positive feedback loops). One might think of the reference value in this kind of loop as an "anti-goal." Discrepancy-enlarging loops are generally believed to be less common in living systems than discrepancy-reducing loops, because they are unstable. Unless overridden, they can enlarge discrepancies without end.

Some people believe that this kind of loop is always problematic and dysfunctional (Powers, 1973). Others believe that positive loops are an important part of complex systems (DeAngelis, Post, & Travis, 1986; Maruyama, 1963; McFarland, 1971), but that in living systems (and other cases in which positive feedback is adaptive), the effect of this loop is limited in some way or other. There may be a natural endpoint (e.g., sexual arousal prompts further increase in arousal to the point of orgasm, which ends the increase). Alternatively, the discrepancy-enlarging function may be constrained by a discrepancy-reducing function. To put it differently, avoidance of one reference point can give way to approach of another reference point.

Feedback Processes in Overt Behavior

A cybernetic approach to motivation generalizes these principles to behavioral goals, in which discrepancies are reduced by overt actions (Miller et al., 1960; Powers, 1973; Toates, 2006). Negative feedback processes, as applied to overt behavior, represent the engagement of effort to reach a valued goal, maintain a desired condition, or conform to some salient standard. Goal-directed behavior entails knowing (at some level) the desired end one wants to reach, knowing what the present condition is with respect to that desired end, and being able to decide whether the present condition does or does not match the desired end. It is also necessary, of course, to be able to create actions that will cause the present condition to change in appropriate ways. However, that ability would be of little help in itself if the other functions were not also operating.

In a way, this is the essence of what a cybernetic view brings to the motivational table: It forces the realization that all of those functions are necessary for successful goal pursuit, not just the capacity to act. It forces the realization that the action occurs in service to changing the input (Powers, 1973).

The principle of positive feedback can also be applied to overt behavior. What might be called "anti-goals" for behavior are conditions that one wants to avoid. An example would be a feared or disliked possible self (Carver, Lawrence, & Scheier, 1999; Markus & Nurius, 1986; Ogilvie, 1987), which one tries hard to not-be. Another example would be a scene of public humiliation, which most people will try to avoid.

As noted earlier, discrepancy-reducing and discrepancy-enlarging loops may work in concert, and it is fairly easy to point to such compound structures in behavior. An avoidance loop tries to distance from an anti-goal. But there may exist an approach goal that happens to be incompatible with the anti-goal. If the person adopts that approach goal, the tendency to avoid the anti-goal is joined by the tendency to move toward the approach goal. The approach loop pulls the behavior into its orbit. This pattern of dual influence describes what behavioral psychologists call active avoidance. In active avoidance an organism confronting a feared stimulus picks a relatively safe location to escape to and actively approaches that location.

Social and personality psychology also have good examples of discrepancy-enlarging loops being constrained by discrepancy-reducing loops. This pattern seems represented in Higgins's (1996) concept of the ought self (Carver et al., 1999) and in Ryan and Deci's (2000) concept of introjected values. In both of these constructs, the initial impetus to behavior is the desire to avoid social sanction of some sort. Thus, the starting point is an effort to create distance from an anti-goal. However, a good way to avoid social sanction is to locate a socially approved value that is different from (or even opposite to) the disapproved value, and move toward it. By homing in on the positive value, one simultaneously escapes the feared or disliked value. Thus, both ought selves and introjects represent positive values to conform to, but the motivational dynamic underlying them is more complex than the dynamic underlying other positive values.

Further Issues

At least a couple more issues should be noted before we move on. One of them concerns a common misconception about the nature of feedback processes. The other concerns a somewhat disconcerting reality about the nature of feedback processes.

As was described earlier, homeostasis is a common illustration of the feedback principle, because it is so easily understood. Another common illustration is the room thermostat, which senses deviations from a set point and engages devices that counter the deviations. Because of the common use of these illustrations, some people incorrectly infer that feedback loops can act only to create and maintain steady states. Some reference values (and goals) *are* indeed static end states or stable preferred conditions (e.g., to own one's home, to arrive at the end of the month with a balance above zero in one's checking account). But other reference values are dynamic and evolving (e.g., experiencing the pleasures of a month's vacation, raising children to become good citizens). In such cases, the goal for action regulation is the process of traversing the changing trajectory of the activity, not just the arrival at the endpoint. Feedback processes apply perfectly well to such moving targets (Beer, 1995).

Although the feedback loop is an abstract concept, it is not too hard to portray its elements conceptually. In some specific instances of feedback control (e.g., in artificial electronic systems), it is also easy to point to the physical existence of each element. In other instances, however, doing this is harder. In particular, some feedback loops have no explicit representation of a reference value. The system regulates around a value, but the value is not represented anywhere as a goal (Berridge, 2004; Carver & Scheier, 1999b, 2002).

Levels of Abstraction

Let us return, though, to cases with explicit reference points or goals, inasmuch as these cases are the focus of most of what we have to say. Goals vary quite considerably in how concrete or abstract they are. You can have the goal of being a good citizen, but you can also have the goal of recycling—a narrower goal that contributes to being a good citizen. To recycle entails other, more-concrete goals: placing newspapers or bottles and cans into containers and moving them to a pickup location. The fact that goals have subgoals leads to the idea that goals form a hierarchy (Powers, 1973; Toates, 2006; Vallacher & Wegner, 1987). Abstract goals are attained by the very process of attaining concrete goals that help define the abstract ones (Carver & Scheier, 1998, 1999a, 1999b, 2003).

Goals at different levels of abstraction have different kinds of characterizations. Some kinds of relatively low-level goals are defined by brief sequences of action: for example, picking up a pen or walking across the room. Such *sequences* (Powers, 1973) are fairly simple (though each can also be broken down further into subcomponents of motor control (e.g., Rosenbaum, Meulenbroek, Vaughan, & Jansen, 2001). Sequences have something of a self-contained quality about them, and they require little monitoring once they are triggered.

Such sequences can be organized into more elaborate strings of actions, which Powers (1973) called *programs*. These strings of action are more planful. They often require choices to be made at various points along the way, which depend on conditions that are encountered at those points. Programs are the level of the Powers hierarchy that most closely resembles Miller et al.'s TOTE construct, because of the sequencing of steps and subroutines that programs contain. There is some blurring between levels, however. Programs can become quite familiar, as a result of repetition. If they become familiar enough that they are executed all at a piece without much monitoring, they probably are no longer programs but instead have become sequences.

Programs are sometimes enacted in the service of broader guiding *principles*. Principles are more abstract qualities. They can provide a basis for making decisions at choice points within programs, and they can suggest that particular programs be undertaken or be refrained from. The term *principle* refers to the sorts of qualities that social psychologists often call values (Schwartz & Bilsky, 1990; Schwartz & Rubel, 2005). What defines a principle as such is its abstractness and broad applicability to diverse behaviors. Being a principle does not in itself imply anything about what behavior results. For example, one principle leads people to support affirmative action, whereas a different principle leads people to oppose it (Reyna, Henry, Korfmacher, & Tucker, 2006).

Even individual values are not the end of potential complexity and abstraction, though. Patterns of values coalesce to form the essence of a person's sense of desired (and undesired) self or a person's sense of desired (and undesired) community. These properties are very broad points of reference (goals).

Hierarchy of Processes in Action

Powers (1973) argued that, in a hierarchical organization, high-level control loops "behave" by setting and changing reference values for loops at the next lower level of control. Those loops, in turn act by setting reference values for lower levels, and so on (Fig. 3.1). At the very lowest level, the output is changes in muscle tensions. Thus, for a person to act in a way that is intended to exemplify a particular principle also requires the simultaneous involvement of all layers of control lower than the principle level.

In his statement about hierarchical organization of feedback processes, Powers (1973) devoted most of his attention to levels of abstraction that are even more basic than sequences. As personality-social psychologists, we have not found those lower levels of much direct interest. On the other hand, the argument that control of behavior relies on a single principle instantiated at multiple levels of

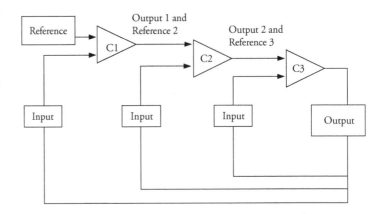

Fig. 3.1. Three-level hierarchy of feedback loops. The output from the comparison in a given loop is the reference value for the next lower level, and so on. The final (motoric) output creates a change in input that is (at varying levels of abstraction) relevant to all levels involved.

abstraction is a very interesting one, because it has a high degree of parsimony.

Knowledge of the nervous system has progressed enormously since 1973, of course, and parts of the picture that Powers created are doubtlessly contradicted by later evidence. However, the viability of the core idea that action reflects feedback processes engaged simultaneously at multiple levels of abstraction need not depend entirely on specific details.

From the point of view of personality-social psychology, goals from the ideal self down through sequences can be thought of as common starting points for self-regulation. All of them serve as classes of values to try to approximate or to deviate from. Any of them might be taken as the focal point for a given behavior (that is, the person could try to self-regulate at any of these levels). Once that value is adopted, lower levels are engaged automatically by the engagement of that one. Thus, it is easy to imagine cases in which a person is behaving according to a principle (e.g., a moral or ethical value), and it is easy to imagine cases in which the person is behaving according to a plan or program. It is also easy, however, to imagine cases in which the person is acting impulsively and spontaneously, without regard to either principle or plan. In all of these cases, the physical movements involved are being managed by systems automatically engaged by whichever level of control is in charge. Later in the chapter we reexamine this idea and consider some potentially important differences among these various levels of abstraction.

Approach and Avoidance

In some ways, the dual concepts of discrepancy-reducing and discrepancy-enlarging loops map nicely onto the general form of approach and avoidance processes. Incentives are approached by systems that close discrepancies between present conditions and

the incentives. Threats are avoided by systems that enlarge discrepancies between present conditions and the threats. The logic of feedback processes thus provides a way to think about this fundamental dichotomy among motivations, a dichotomy that plays a key role in many other ideas about motivation.

Feedback Processes and Affect

Motivation is partly about how people move from one place to another. However, it is also partly about the degree of urgency behind the action. A sense of urgency or intensity implies the involvement of affect, feelings that occur in the course of experience.

What is affect? Where does it come from? Affect is positive or negative feelings. Affect is the core of the experience of emotion, though the term *emotion* often incorporates connotations of physiological changes that frequently accompany hedonic experiences. A truism is that affect pertains to whether one's desires are being met (Clore, 1994; Frijda, 1986, 1988; Ortony, Clore, & Collins, 1988). But what is the internal mechanism by which feelings arise?

Mechanism

Many different kinds of answers to this question have been offered, ranging from neurobiological (e.g., Davidson, 1992) to cognitive (Ortony et al., 1988). We have proposed an answer that focused on what appear to be some of the functional properties of affect (Carver & Scheier, 1990, 1998, 1999a, 1999b). In suggesting this answer, we used feedback control as an organizing principle. Now, however, the control bears on a different quality.

We suggested that feelings arise as a consequence of a feedback loop that operates simultaneously with the behavior-guiding loop and in parallel to it. We regard its operation as automatic. The easiest characterization of what this second process is doing is that it is checking on how well the first process (the behavior loop) is doing. The input for this second loop thus is the *rate of discrepancy reduction in the action system over time*. (We focus first on discrepancy-reducing loops, then consider enlarging loops.)

Consider a physical analogy. Action implies change between states. Difference between states is distance. The action loop thus controls the psychological analog of distance. If the affect loop assesses the action loop's progress, then the affect loop is dealing with the psychological analog of velocity, the first derivative of distance over time. To the degree that this analogy is meaningful, the input to the affect loop should be the first derivative over time of the input used by the action loop.

Input (how well you are doing) does not by itself create affect; a given rate of progress has different affective consequences in different contexts. We argued that this input is compared to a reference value (cf. Frijda, 1986, 1988), just as in other feedback loops. In this case, the value is an acceptable or expected rate of behavioral discrepancy reduction. As in other feedback loops, the comparison checks for deviation from the standard. If there is a discrepancy, the error signal causes a change in the output function.

We think the error signal in this loop is manifest subjectively as affect, a sense of positive or negative valence. A rate of progress below the criterion yields negative affect. A rate high enough to exceed the criterion yields positive affect. If the rate is not distinguishable from the criterion, there is no valence. In essence, the argument is that feelings with positive valence mean you are doing better at something than you need to, and feelings with negative valence mean you are doing worse than you need to (for detail see Carver & Scheier, 1998, Chapters 8 and 9). The absence of affect means being neither ahead nor behind.

A couple of clarifications about what we do *not* mean to say here: We are not arguing for a deliberative thinking through of whether rate conforms to the criterion rate. We assume that the testing is continuous and automatic. Nor are we arguing for a deliberative thinking about what the affective valence means. We assume that the meaning (i.e., being ahead versus behind) is intrinsic to the affect's valence, which itself arises automatically.

One implication of this line of argument is that the affects that might potentially exist regarding any given action should fall on a bipolar dimension. That is, it should be the case that affect can be positive, neutral, or negative for any given goal-directed action, depending on how well or poorly the action seems to be attaining the goal.

Reference Criterion

What determines the criterion? There doubtlessly are many influences. Furthermore, the orientation that a person takes to an action can induce a different framing that may change the criterion (Brendl & Higgins, 1996). What is used as a criterion is probably quite flexible when the activity is unfamiliar. If the activity is very familiar, the criterion is likely to reflect the person's accumulated experience, in the form of an expected rate (the more experience you have, the more you know what is reasonable to expect). Whether "desired," "expected," or "needed" is most accurate as a depiction of the criterion rate may depend greatly on the context.

The criterion can also change, sometimes readily, sometimes less so. The less experience the person has in a domain, the easier it is to substitute one criterion for another. We believe, however, that change in rate criterion in a relatively familiar domain occurs relatively slowly. Continuing overshoots result automatically in an upward drift of the criterion; continuing undershoots result in a downward drift (see Carver & Scheier, 2000). Thus, the system recalibrates over repeated events. A (somewhat ironic) consequence of such recalibration would be to keep the balance of a person's affective experiences (positive to negative, across a span of time) relatively similar, even if the rate criterion changes considerably.

Two Kinds of Action Loops, Two Dimensions of Affect

So far we have addressed only approach loops. The view just outlined was that positive feeling exists when a behavioral system is making more than adequate progress *doing what it is organized to do*. The systems addressed so far are organized to reduce discrepancies. Yet there seems no obvious reason why the principle should not apply to systems that enlarge discrepancies. If such a system is making rapid enough progress attaining its ends, there should be positive affect. If it is doing poorly, there should be negative affect.

That affects of both valences are possible seems applicable to both approach and avoidance. That is, both approach and avoidance have the potential to induce positive feelings (by doing well), and both have the potential to induce negative feelings (by doing poorly). But doing well at *approaching an incentive* is not quite the same experience as doing well at *moving away from a threat*. Thus, there may be differences between the two positives, and between the two negatives.

Drawing on the work of Higgins (e.g., 1987, 1996), we have argued for two bipolar dimensions of affect, one bearing on approach, the other on avoidance (Carver, 2001; Carver & Scheier, 1998). Approach-related affect includes such positive affects as elation, eagerness, and excitement, and also such negative affects as frustration, anger, and sadness (Carver, 2004; Carver & Harmon-Jones, 2009). Avoidance-related affect includes such positive affects as relief, serenity, and contentment (Carver, 2009) and such negative affects as fear, guilt, and anxiety.

Affect and Action: Two Facets of One Event in Time

This two-layered viewpoint implies a natural connection between affect and action. That is, if the input function of the affect loop is a sensed rate of progress in action, the output function of the affect loop must be a change in the rate of progress in that action. Thus, the affect loop has a direct influence on what occurs in the action loop.

Some changes in rate output are straightforward. If you are lagging behind, you try harder. Some changes are less straightforward. The rates of many "behaviors" are defined not by pace of physical action but in terms of choices among potential actions, or entire programs of action. For example, increasing your rate of progress on a project at work may mean choosing to spend a weekend working rather than playing with family and friends. Increasing your rate of being kind means choosing to do an act that reflects kindness, when an opportunity arises. Thus, change in rate must often be translated into other terms, such as concentration or allocation of time and effort.

The idea of two feedback systems functioning jointly is something we stumbled into. It turns out, however, that this idea is quite common in control engineering (e.g., Clark, 1996). Engineers have long recognized that having two systems functioning together—one controlling position, one controlling velocity—permits the device they control to respond in a way that is both quick and stable, without overshoots and oscillations.

The combination of quickness and stability in responding is desirable in many of the devices engineers deal with. It is also desirable in human beings. A person with very reactive emotions is prone to overreact and oscillate behaviorally. A person who is emotionally unreactive is slow to respond even to urgent events. A person whose reactions are between those extremes responds quickly but without behavioral overreaction and oscillation.

For biological entities, being able to respond quickly yet accurately confers a clear adaptive advantage. We believe this combination of quick and stable responding is a consequence of having both behavior-managing and affect-managing control systems. Affect causes people's responses to be quicker (because this system is time sensitive); as long as the affective system is not overresponsive, the responses are also stable.

Our focus here is on how affects influence behavior, emphasizing the extent to which they are interwoven. However, note that the behavioral responses that are linked to the affects also lead to *reduction of the intensity of the affects*, returning them to the set point. We thus would suggest that the affect system is, in a very basic sense, self-regulating (cf. Campos, Frankel, & Camras, 2004). It is undeniable that people also engage in voluntary efforts to regulate their emotions (e.g., Gross, 2007; Ochsner & Gross, 2008), but the affect system does a good deal of that self-regulation on its own.

Affect Issues

This view of affect differs from most other theories bearing on emotion in at least two ways. One difference concerns the idea of dimensional structure underlying affect (Carver, 2001).

Two Underlying Bipolar Dimensions

In some theories (though not all) affects are seen as having underlying dimensionality (e.g., Watson, Wiese, Vaidya, & Tellegen, 1999). Our view has this character. It holds that affect generated through approach has the potential to range from positive (joy) through neutral to negative (anger, sadness); affect generated through avoidance also has the potential to range from positive (relief) through neutral to negative (fear, anxiety). Most dimensional models, however, are quite different from this one. They are unipolar. They ascribe affects with positive valence to an approach system and ascribe affects with negative valence to an avoidance system (e.g., Cacioppo, Gardner, & Berntson, 1999; Lang, Bradley, & Cuthbert, 1990; Watson et al., 1999).

There is at least some support for our view. There is evidence, albeit limited, that positive feelings of calmness and relief (as situationally relevant) relate to avoidance motivation (Carver, 2009; Higgins, Shah, & Friedman, 1997). There is far more evidence linking sadness to failure of approach (for reviews, see Carver, 2004; Higgins, 1996). There is also a good deal of evidence linking the approach system to the negative affect of anger (Carver & Harmon-Jones, 2009). Although it is clear that diverse negative feeling qualities coalesce with one another in mood states (Watson, 2009), the evidence does not make that case with regard to situation-specific affective responses.

This issue is important, because it has implications for any attempt to identify a conceptual mechanism underlying creation of affect. Theories positing two unipolar dimensions assume that greater activation of a system translates to more affect of that valence (or more potential for affect of that valence). If the approach system relates both to positive and to negative feelings, however, this direct transformation of system activation to affect is not tenable. A conceptual mechanism is needed that naturally addresses both valences within the approach function (and, separately, the avoidance function). The mechanism described here does so.

Counterintuitive Effect of Positive Affect

A second issue also differentiates this model from most other views (Carver, 2003; Carver & Scheier, 2009). Recall our argument that affect reflects the error signal from a comparison in a feedback loop. If this is so, affect is a signal to adjust rate of progress. This would be true whether the rate is above the mark or below it—that is, whether affect is positive or negative. For negative feelings, this is fairly intuitive. The first response to negative feelings about something is usually to try harder. If the person tries harder—and if more effort (or better effort) increases progress—the negative affect diminishes or ceases.

For positive feelings, prediction is counterintuitive. In this model, positive feelings arise when things are going better than they need to. But the feelings still reflect a discrepancy (albeit a positive one), and the function of a negative feedback loop is to keep discrepancies small. Such a system is organized in such a way that it "wants" to see neither negative nor positive affect. Either quality (deviation from the standard in either direction) would represent an "error" and lead to change in output that would eventually reduce it. This view argues that people who exceed the criterion rate of progress (and who thus have positive feelings) will automatically tend to reduce subsequent effort in this domain. They will "coast" a little—ease back. This prediction derives from a consideration of feedback principles, but a similar argument has been made

on other grounds by Izard (1977, p. 257; Izard & Ackerman, 2000, p. 258).

Expending greater effort to catch up when behind, and coasting when ahead, are both presumed to be specific to the goal domain to which the affect is attached, usually the goal from which the affect arises in the first place. We do not argue that positive affect creates a tendency to coast *in general*, but with respect to the activity producing the positive feelings. We should also be clear that we are talking about the current, ongoing episode of action. We are *not* arguing that positive affect makes people less likely to do the behavior later on.

Does positive affect lead to coasting? There is not a great deal of evidence on this question, but there is some. To test the idea requires generating positive affect (or creating the perception of being ahead of one's reference point) with respect to one behavioral domain and then measuring behavior in the same domain. Many studies have created positive affect in one context and assessed its influence on another task or in another context (e.g., Isen, 1987, 2000; Schwarz & Bohner, 1996). However, that does not test this question.

We know of three sources of evidence. One study found that professional basketball teams were more likely to lose after a playoff victory than after a defeat (Mizruchi, 1991). Although this is consistent with coasting after winning, it is also highly ambiguous. It is impossible to tell whether the pattern reflects coasting after success or renewed effort after failure or both. Less ambiguously, a series of three studies by Louro, Pieters, and Zeelenberg (2007) found consistent evidence that positive affect induces coasting, but only when goal attainment was imminent.

A more recent experience-sampling study had participants make a set of ratings pertaining to each of three goals, three times a day, for 21 days (Fulford, Johnson, Llabre, & Carver, 2010). The ratings included reports of effort toward the goal during the previous time block, perceived progress toward it during the previous time block, and expected progress in the forthcoming time block. Multilevel modeling revealed that instances of progress exceeding expectation were followed by reduction in effort toward that goal in the next time period.

Skepticism about the idea that positive affect (or getting ahead) leads to coasting stems in part from the fact that it is hard to see why a process would be built into the organism that limits positive feelings—indeed, dampens them. We see at least two bases for such an arrangement. The first lies in a basic biological principle: It is adaptive not to spend energy needlessly. Coasting prevents this. Indeed, Brehm built a motivational theory around the argument that people engage only as much effort as is needed to accomplish a given task—and no more (e.g., Brehm & Self, 1989; Wright & Kirby, 2001).

A second basis for such an arrangement stems from the fact that people have multiple simultaneous concerns. Given multiple concerns, people do not optimize their outcome on any one of them but "satisfice" (Simon, 1953)—that is, they do a good enough job on each concern to deal with it satisfactorily. This permits them to handle the many concerns adequately, rather than just any one of them. Coasting facilitates satisficing. A tendency to coast with respect to some goal virtually defines satisficing regarding that particular goal. A tendency to coast also fosters satisficing for a broader set of goals, by allowing easy shift to other domains at little or no cost (see Carver, 2003, for detail).

Affects and Priority Management

This line of argument brings up a broad function that deserves further attention: the shifting from one goal to another as focal in behavior (Dreisbach & Goschke, 2004; Shallice, 1978). This basic and very important phenomenon is often overlooked. People typically have many goals under pursuit simultaneously, but only one has top priority at a given moment. People need to shield and maintain intentions that are being pursued (cf. Shah, Friedman, & Kruglanski, 2002), but they also need to be able to shift flexibly among goals (Shin & Rosenbaum, 2002).

The issue of priority management was addressed very creatively many years ago by Simon (1967). He proposed that emotions are calls for reprioritization. He suggested that emotion arising with respect to a goal that is out of awareness eventually induces people to interrupt their behavior and give that goal a higher priority than it had. The stronger the emotion, the stronger is the claim that the unattended goal should have higher priority than the goal that is presently focal.

Simon's discussion focused on cases in which a nonfocal goal demands a higher priority and *intrudes* on awareness. By strong implication, his discussion dealt only with negative affect. However, there is another way for priority ordering to shift: The focal goal can *relinquish its place*. Perhaps positive feelings also pertain to reprioritization, but rather than a call for higher priority, they reflect *reduction* in priority. Positive affect regarding avoidance (relief or tranquility) indicates that a threat has dissipated, no longer requires so much attention, and can assume a lower priority. Positive feelings regarding approach (happiness, joy) indicate that an incentive is being attained and could temporarily be put on hold because you are doing so well; thus, this goal can assume a lower priority (see Carver, 2003).

Priority Management and Feelings of Depression

One more aspect of priority management must be addressed, concerning the idea that some goals are best abandoned. We have long held that sufficient doubt about goal attainment yields a tendency to disengage from effort, and even to disengage from the goal itself. This is certainly a kind of priority shift, in that the abandoned goal now has an even lower priority than it had before. But how does this case fit the ideas described thus far?

This case seems at first to contradict Simon's (1967) view that negative affect is a call for higher priority. But there is an important difference between two classes of negative affect related to approach (Carver, 2003, 2004; in this discussion we disregard avoidance). Some of these affects coalesce around frustration and anger. Others coalesce around sadness, depression, and dejection. The former relate to an increase in priority, the latter to a decrease.

Earlier in this section we characterized our view as implying that approach-related affects fall on a bipolar dimension. However, the dimension is not a simple straight line. Progress below the criterion creates negative affect, as the incentive slips away. Inadequate movement gives rise to frustration, irritation, and anger, prompting more effort to overcome obstacles and reverse the inadequate current progress. But efforts sometimes do not change the situation. Indeed, a loss precludes movement forward. In this case, the feelings are sadness, depression, despondency, and hopelessness. Behaviors also differ in this case. The person tends to disengage from—give up on—further effort.

In the first case, feelings of frustration and anger are a call for an upgrade in priority, an increase in effort, a struggle to gain the incentive despite setbacks. In the second case, feelings of sadness and depression accompany *reduction* of effort and a downgrade in priority. As described earlier, both the upgrade and the downgrade have adaptive functions in the appropriate situations.

Shifts in the Theoretical Landscape: Two Modes of Functioning

We now turn to an entirely different issue. During the last two decades, changes have occurred in how people view cognition and action. The implicit assumption that behavior is generally managed in a top-down, directive way has been challenged. Questions have been raised about the role of consciousness in many kinds of action. Interest has arisen in the idea that the mind has both explicit and implicit representations. These various issues have also influenced how we think about ideas we have been using.

Two-Mode Models

Several literatures have developed around the idea that there are two somewhat distinct modes of functioning (Carver, Johnson, & Joormann, 2008). In personality, Epstein (e.g., 1973, 1994) has long advocated such a view. He argues that people experience reality through two systems. What he calls a *rational* system operates mostly consciously, uses logical rules, is verbal and deliberative, and thus is fairly slow. In contrast, the *experiential* system is intuitive and associative in nature. It provides a quick and dirty way of assessing and reacting to reality. It relies on salient information and uses shortcuts and heuristics. It functions automatically and quickly. It is considered to be emotional (or at least very responsive to emotions) and nonverbal.

The experiential system is presumably older and more primitive neurobiologically. It dominates when speed is needed (as when the situation is emotionally charged). The rational system evolved later, providing a more cautious, analytic, planful way of proceeding. Operating in that way has important advantages, provided there is sufficient time and freedom from pressure to think things through. Both systems are presumed to be always at work, jointly determining behavior, though the extent of each one's influence can vary by situation and disposition.

A model in many ways similar to this was proposed by Metcalfe and Mischel (1999). Drawing on decades of work on delay of gratification, Metcalfe and Mischel (1999) proposed that two systems influence self-restraint. One they called a "hot" system: emotional, impulsive, and reflexive. The other they called a "cool" system: strategic, flexible, slower, and unemotional. How people respond to difficult situations depends on which system is in charge.

There are also several two-mode theories in social psychology (Chaiken & Trope, 1999). The essence of such a view has existed for a long time in the literature of persuasion. Strack and Deutsch (2004) have recently extended this reasoning more broadly into the range of behavioral phenomena of interest to social psychologists. They proposed a model in which overt social behavior is a joint output of two simultaneously operating systems that they termed *reflective* and *impulsive*. Again, differences in the systems' operating characteristics lead to differences in behavior. The reflective system anticipates the future, makes decisions on the basis of those anticipations, and forms intentions. It is planful and wide ranging in its search for relevant information. It is restrained and deliberative. The impulsive system acts spontaneously when its schemas or production systems are sufficiently activated. It acts without consideration for the future or for broader implications or consequences of the action. This depiction is very similar in some ways to the ideas of Epstein (1973, 1994) and Metcalfe and Mischel (1999).

Two-mode thinking has also been very influential in developmental psychology. Rothbart and her colleagues have argued for the existence of three temperament systems: two for reactive approach and reactive avoidance, and a third termed *effortful control* (e.g., Derryberry & Rothbart, 1997; Rothbart, Ahadi, & Evans, 2000; Rothbart & Posner, 1985; see also Nigg, 2000). Effortful control concerns (in part) the ability to suppress approach when it is situationally inappropriate. Effortful control is superordinate to approach and avoidance temperaments. The label *effortful* conveys the sense that this is an executive, planful activity, entailing the use of cognitive resources beyond those needed to react impulsively. This view of effortful control has substantial resemblance to depictions of the deliberative mode of the other two-mode models outlined earlier.

Hierarchicality Reexamined

Thus, several sources of theory suggest that the mind functions in two modes (indeed, the ones described earlier are far from an exhaustive list). All promote the view that a deliberative mode of functioning uses symbolic and sequential processing and thus is relatively slow; all suggest that a more impulsive or reactive mode of functioning uses associationist processing and is relatively fast. Many of the theories suggest that the two modes are semiautonomous in their functioning, competing with each other to influence actions. Indeed, many point to situational variables that influence which mode dominates at a given time.

These kinds of ideas have influenced how we think about the hierarchy of control that was proposed by Powers (1973). We said earlier that programs of action entail decisions. They seem to be managed top-down, using effortful processing. Planfulness, an element of programs, is also a common characterization of behavior managed by the reflective system. It seems reasonable to map program-level control onto the deliberative, reflective mode of functioning.

In contrast to this deliberative quality, well-learned *sequences* occur in a relatively automatic stream once they are triggered. Sequences (along with lower levels of control) are necessarily called up during the execution of programs. However, perhaps sequences can also be triggered more autonomously, without being specified by efforts toward a higher goal. Sequences may be triggered by the activation of strong associations in memory. In such cases, the operating characteristics would seem akin to those of the reactive mode of functioning.

In the past we have often noted that the level of control that is functionally superordinate can vary by situations and persons (e.g., Carver & Scheier, 1998, 1999a). As we said earlier, it is easy to imagine cases in which a person is behaving according to a principle (e.g., a moral or ethical value), and it is easy to imagine cases in which the person is behaving according to a plan or program. It is also easy, however, to imagine cases in which the person is acting impulsively and spontaneously, without regard to either principle or plan.

In making this case in the past, our emphasis generally focused simply on how sequences and programs differed. Now we are inclined to wonder if this particular differentiation is not perhaps more important than we had realized. Perhaps we have underappreciated the extent to which lower levels of self-regulatory structures can be triggered autonomously and their outputs enter the stream of ongoing action, without oversight from higher levels, and potentially even in conflict with values at higher levels. This seems an important question for further exploration.

Self-Control: Impulse and Restraint

The idea that conflicts exist between longer term and shorter term goals is also part of a literature on self-control and self-control failure (e.g., Baumeister, Heatherton, & Tice, 1994). This literature focuses on cases in which a person is both motivated to act and motivated to restrain that action. This is essentially the same case as examined by work on children's effortful control, and it is also the same logical structure as is in the delay of gratification paradigm. A difference is that in the self-control literature the intent often is to delay indefinitely rather than temporarily.

Although the self-control situation is often portrayed as pitting longer and shorter term goals against each other, a somewhat different view also seems plausible. The self-control situation may pit the two modes of processing against each other. This would be consistent with the literature on self-control failure, which tends to portray such failures as involving a relatively automatic tendency to act in one way, being opposed by a planful effort to restrain that act. The action being inhibited is often characterized as an impulse, a desire that is automatically translated into action unless it is controlled (often because the action is habitual). The restraint is presumed to be effortful and to depend on limited resources. If the planful part of the mind is able to attend adequately to the conflict, the person can resist the impulse. If not, the impulse is more likely to be expressed. This portrayal seems quite consonant with the two-mode models of functioning.

The How Versus the What of Motivation

The cybernetic approach to motivational issues is primarily about the structure and dynamics of behavior rather than the content of behavior. It is a depiction of relations among processes that occur as people negotiate the psychological and behavioral space of their lives. We think these principles are informative both about adaptive functioning and about problems in functioning. We also believe the ideas described in this chapter represent a viewpoint that is compatible with many other theories that are described in this book, standing alongside them rather than in place of them. In that sense, these ideas may be less a "theory" than a "meta-theory," a very general way of conceptualizing interwoven functions, a declaration of belief about how complex systems work.

However, this is a viewpoint that is primarily about the *how* of motivated behavior rather than the *what*. It bears on control of actions that are selfish as well as control of actions that are well socialized. Those actions differ not in their structure but in the content of the principles and programs (and perhaps the self) that exist in the persons who engage in the actions. This view thus is very different from views of motivation that address (for example) what specific core motives may underlie human growth and optimal functioning (e.g., Ryan & Deci, 2000, 2001). It was never the explicit goal of the feedback approach to speak to those issues.

On the other hand, it is also possible to stretch these ideas a bit more, to speak to at least some of those issues. It is inherent in a hierarchical organization of values that the values have some degree of compatibility. If there is too much inconsistency among goals, effort toward one of them enlarges discrepancies with respect to another. This is bad enough when the goals are simply in competition for devotion of time and resources to their attainment (for example, when taking extra time to work on a project at the office takes time away from engagement with one's family). It is even more problematic if the goals are intrinsically in conflict (for example, when taking a new job for oneself in a new town requires one's spouse to accept an inferior new job).

To the extent that the biological blueprint of a human being incorporates species-wide imperatives, goals at various lower levels of abstraction must be brought into at least some degree of compatibility with those imperatives. Precisely what species-wide imperatives are contained in that blueprint is a question on which there is a good deal of debate. Clearly the establishment of dominance hierarchies is one of them; relatedness to at least some other humans is another.

The upshot of this set of issues is that a model of hierarchical organization of the self and its goals appears to entail continuing pressure toward compatibility among the values that define the self and one's view of community. The attainment of lower order goals is the process by which higher order goals are realized, all the way to the highest values the person has.

Where Do New Goals Come From?

The principle that lower order goals have links to higher order ones also has implications for how new goals arise and are adopted as reference values (for broader treatment, see Carver & Scheier, 1999b).

A person's repertoire of goals changes in many ways over time. Some changes are very simple and restricted; other cases involve the adoption of goals that are very new.

Sometimes the change is limited to shifting one's level of aspiration. Goals that aren't being attained are scaled back to be less demanding. Goals that are attained too easily are raised to be more demanding. Such changes allow the person to continue in the same general domain of activity at a level that is both challenging and attainable. When such a change has been made, however, the goal is not quite the same as it was before.

Another small step in the direction of new goals would be cases in which a person engages in an activity for one purpose (e.g., going to a gym to work out, with the goal of staying healthy), and inadvertently finds that the activity also satisfies a second purpose (making new friends). The activity thereby acquires a second kind of usefulness and becomes connected to a different higher level goal than it was connected to before. This behavior has evolved a new link upward in the goal hierarchy (Fig. 3.2). The activity itself (going to the gym and exercising) already was in place as a goal, and thus it is not new itself. But its broader implications are now different—perhaps quite different—than they were. This change in a goal's connectedness to other aspects of the self structure also implies newness.

In many cases, new activities are undertaken precisely because they have been pre-identified as potentially relevant to a higher order goal in the person's life. For example, a person who is high in openness, who likes to explore diversity in life, may decide to take a vacation tour of Asia, try scuba diving, or experiment with bicycle racing. In such cases, the new activity is

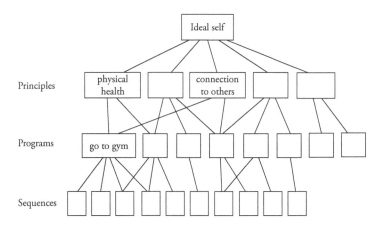

Fig. 3.2 Attainment of a goal at a relatively lower level of abstraction often can contribute to more than one goal at the next higher level. An example, also discussed in the text, is that going to the gym can contribute to the maintenance of physical health, and it can also be a way of making friends, thus enhancing connection to others.

Principles

Programs

Sequences

approached because it is identified as a possible means to satisfy the desire (the goal) of exploration.

Exploration provides an easy illustration, but it certainly is not the only higher level desire that can lead to new activities. Any time someone says, "You ought to try this—I think you might enjoy it," an inference is being made that the activity will satisfy a broader desire the person has. Anytime people contemplate undertaking new activities, they are considering how the activities might fit into their current patterns of preferences.

In these examples a link is prespecified between the "new" goal and an existing one. Sometimes, though, an activity seems to come together without much forethought or planning, and (when it occurs) is found to be enjoyable. In such cases, the person may actively seek to identify the activity's essence, so as to make the positive experience repeatable by intention. Thus, it becomes a new goal. That is, in order to make the experience repeatable, the person encodes its nature in memory in a manner that renders it accessible to top-down use later on. In this sort of case, a bottom-up self-assembly (component elements coming together without an explicit higher level reference value) leads to synthesis of a new reference value at the higher level.

What makes an experience unexpectedly enjoyable? Finding an experience enjoyable, we suggest, means that engaging in the experience serves to move the person toward another goal that already is in place as part of the self. The person may have had no idea beforehand that the new activity was going to connect to that already incorporated value. But because it does connect, the experience of the new activity creates positive affect. Thus, a new action, as well as an old one, can fairly quickly acquire an upward link to a higher order goal. A given principle (for example) can be fulfilled in myriad activities, even activities that might at first not have seemed relevant to the principle.

Closing Comment

We have chosen a rather unusual construct to be interested in for such a long time. We are, after all, personality psychologists, and these ideas are not exactly mainstream personality. We could have focused on goals and left it at that. But, no, we keep dragging in the idea that goal-directed action involves feedback processes. Why?

The answer is fairly simple. Scientists in diverse disciplines see feedback processes as among the basic building blocks of nature. Not of motivation, but of nature. It was suggested many years ago that

feedback loops are embedded in many different kinds of systems, at many levels of abstraction (e.g., Ford, 1987; von Bertalanffy, 1968). The principle of feedback control has been found useful in understanding phenomena as diverse as weather systems, the stability of ecological systems, and homeostasis. The argument that the same fundamental principle underlies even the regulation of overt action asserts a rather astonishing link between human experience and other aspects of nature, parts of nature that could hardly be more different from human life. The possibility that such a link is real is at least part of the fascination.

Acknowledgments

Preparation of this chapter was supported by grants from the National Cancer Institute (CA64710), the National Science Foundation (BCS0544617), and the National Heart, Lung, and Blood Institute (HL65111, HL65112, HL076852, and HL076858).

References

Ashby, W. R. (1940). Adaptiveness and equilibrium. *Journal of Mental Science, 86*, 478–483.

Baumeister, R. F., Heatherton, T. F., & Tice, D. M. (1994). *Losing control: Why people fail at self-regulation*. San Diego, CA: Academic Press.

Beer, R. D. (1995). A dynamical systems perspective on agent-environment interaction. *Artificial Intelligence, 72*, 173–215.

Berridge, K. C. (2004). Motivation concepts in behavioral neuroscience. *Physiology and Behavior. 81*, 179–209.

Brehm, J. W., & Self, E. A. (1989). The intensity of motivation. *Annual Review of Psychology, 40*, 109–131.

Brendl, C. M., & Higgins, E. T. (1996). Principles of judging valence: What makes events positive or negative? *Advances in experimental social psychology, 28*, 95–160.

Cacioppo, J. T., Gardner, W. L., & Berntson, G. G. (1999). The affect system has parallel and integrative processing components: Form follows function. *Journal of Personality and Social Psychology, 76*, 839–855.

Campos, J. J., Frankel, C. B., & Camras, L. (2004). On the nature of emotion regulation. *Child Development, 75*, 377–394.

Cannon, W. B. (1932). *The wisdom of the body*. New York: Norton.

Carver, C. S. (2001). Affect and the functional bases of behavior: On the dimensional structure of affective experience. *Personality and Social Psychology Review, 5*, 345–356.

Carver, C. S. (2003). Pleasure as a sign you can attend to something else: Placing positive feelings within a general model of affect. *Cognition and Emotion, 17*, 241–261.

Carver, C. S. (2004). Negative affects deriving from the behavioral approach system. *Emotion, 4*, 3–22.

Carver, C. S. (2009). Threat sensitivity, incentive sensitivity, and the experience of relief. *Journal of Personality, 77*, 125–138.

Carver, C. S., & Harmon-Jones, E. (2009). Anger is an approach-related affect: Evidence and implications. *Psychological Bulletin, 135*, 183–204.

Carver, C. S., Johnson, S. L., & Joormann, J. (2008). Serotonergic function, two-mode models of self-regulation, and vulnerability to depression: What depression has in common with impulsive aggression. *Psychological Bulletin, 134*, 912–943.

Carver, C. S., Lawrence, J. W., & Scheier, M. F. (1999). Self-discrepancies and affect: Incorporating the role of feared selves. *Personality and Social Psychology Bulletin, 25*, 783–792.

Carver, C. S., & Scheier, M. F. (1981). *Attention and self-regulation: A control-theory approach to human behavior.* New York: Springer Verlag.

Carver, C. S., & Scheier, M. F. (1990). Origins and functions of positive and negative affect: A control-process view. *Psychological Review, 97*, 19–35.

Carver, C. S., & Scheier, M. F. (1998). *On the self-regulation of behavior.* New York: Cambridge University Press.

Carver, C. S., & Scheier, M. F. (1999a). Themes and issues in the self-regulation of behavior. In R. S. Wyer, Jr. (Ed.), *Advances in social cognition* (Vol. 12, pp. 1–105). Mahwah, NJ: Erlbaum.

Carver, C. S., & Scheier, M. F. (1999b). Several more themes, a lot more issues: Commentary on the commentaries. In R. S. Wyer, Jr. (Ed.), *Advances in social cognition* (Vol. 12, pp. 261–302). Mahwah, NJ: Erlbaum.

Carver, C. S., & Scheier, M. F. (2000). Scaling back goals and recalibration of the affect system are processes in normal adaptive self-regulation: Understanding "response shift" phenomena. *Social Science and Medicine, 50*, 1715–1722.

Carver, C. S., & Scheier, M. F. (2002). Control processes and self-organization as complementary principles underlying behavior. *Personality and Social Psychology Review, 6*, 304–315.

Carver, C. S., & Scheier, M. F. (2003). Three human strengths. In L. G. Aspinwall & U. M. Staudinger (Eds.), *A psychology of human strengths: Fundamental questions and future directions for a positive psychology* (pp. 87–102). Washington, DC: American Psychological Association.

Carver, C. S., & Scheier, M. F. (2009). Action, affect, and two-mode models of functioning. In E. Morsella, J. A. Bargh, & P. M. Gollwitzer (Eds.), *Oxford handbook of human action* (pp. 298–327). New York: Oxford University Press.

Carver, C. S., & Scheier, M. F. (2112). A model of behavioral self-regulation. In P. A. M. Van Lange, A. W. Kruglanski, & E. T. Higgins (Eds.), *Handbook of theories of social psychology* (Vol. 1, pp. 505–525). Thousand Oaks, CA: Sage.

Chaiken, S. L., & Trope, Y. (Eds.). (1999). *Dual-process theories in social psychology.* New York: Guilford.

Clark, R. N. (1996). *Control system dynamics.* New York: Cambridge University Press.

Clore, G. C. (1994). Why emotions are felt. In P. Ekman & R. J. Davidson (Eds.), *The nature of emotion: Fundamental questions* (pp. 103–111). New York: Oxford University Press.

Davidson, R. J. (1992). Anterior cerebral asymmetry and the nature of emotion. *Brain and Cognition, 20*, 125–151.

DeAngelis, D. L., Post, W. M., & Travis, C. C. (1986). *Positive feedback in natural systems (Biomathematics, Vol. 15).* Berlin and New York: Springer-Verlag.

Derryberry, D., & Rothbart, M. K. (1997). Reactive and effortful processes in the organization of temperament. *Development and Psychopathology, 9*, 633–652.

Dreisbach, G., & Goschke, T. (2004). How positive affect modulates cognitive control: Reduced perseveration at the cost of increased distractibility. *Journal of Experimental Psychology: Learning, Memory, and Cognition, 30*, 343–353.

Epstein, S. (1973). The self-concept revisited: Or a theory of a theory. *American Psychologist, 28*, 404–416.

Epstein, S. (1994). Integration of the cognitive and the psychodynamic unconscious. *American Psychologist, 49*, 709–724.

Ford, D. H. (1987). *Humans as self-constructing living systems: A developmental perspective on behavior and personality.* Hillsdale, NJ: Erlbaum.

Frijda, N. H. (1986). *The emotions.* Cambridge, England: Cambridge University Press.

Frijda, N. H. (1988). The laws of emotion. *American Psychologist, 43*, 349–358.

Fulford, D., Johnson, S. L., Llabre, M. M., & Carver, C. S. (2010). Pushing and coasting in dynamic goal pursuit: Coasting is attenuated in bipolar disorder. *Psychological Science, 21*, 1021–1027.

Gross, J. J. (Ed.). (2007). *Handbook of emotion regulation.* New York: Guilford Press.

Higgins, E. T. (1987). Self-discrepancy: A theory relating self and affect. *Psychological Review, 94*, 319–340.

Higgins, E. T. (1996). Ideals, oughts, and regulatory focus: Affect and motivation from distinct pains and pleasures. In P. M. Gollwitzer & J. A. Bargh (Eds.), *The psychology of action: Linking cognition and motivation to behavior* (pp. 91–114). New York: Guilford.

Higgins, E. T., Shah, J., & Friedman, R. (1997). Emotional responses to goal attainment: Strength of regulatory focus as moderator. *Journal of Personality and Social Psychology, 72*, 515–525.

Isen, A. M. (1987). Positive affect, cognitive processes, and social behavior. In L. Berkowitz (Ed.), *Advances in experimental social psychology* (Vol. 20, pp. 203–252). San Diego, CA: Academic Press.

Isen, A. M. (2000). Positive affect and decision making. In M. Lewis & J. M. Haviland-Jones (Eds.), *Handbook of emotions* (2nd ed., pp. 417–435). New York: Guilford.

Izard, C. E. (1977). *Human emotions.* New York: Plenum.

Izard, C. E., & Ackerman, B. P. (2000). Motivational, organizational, and regulatory functions of discrete emotions. In M. Lewis & J. M. Haviland-Jones (Eds.), *Handbook of emotions* (2nd ed., pp. 253–264). New York: Guilford Press.

Lang, P. J., Bradley, M. M., & Cuthbert, B. N. (1990). Emotion, attention, and the startle reflex. *Psychological Review, 97*, 377–395.

Louro, M. J., Pieters, R., & Zeelenberg, M. (2007). Dynamics of multiple-goal pursuit. *Journal of Personality and Social Psychology, 93*, 174–193.

MacKay, D. M. (1956). Toward an information-flow model of human behavior. *British Journal of Psychology, 47*, 30–43.

MacKay, D. M. (1966). Cerebral organization and the conscious control of action. In J. C. Eccles (Ed.), *Brain and conscious experience* (pp. 422–445). Berlin: Springer-Verlag.

Markus, H., & Nurius, P. (1986). Possible selves. *American Psychologist, 41*, 954–969.

Maruyama, M. (1963). The second cybernetics: Deviation-amplifying mutual causal processes. *American Scientist, 51*, 164–179.

McFarland, D. J. (1971). *Feedback mechanisms in animal behavior.* New York: Academic Press.

Metcalfe, J., & Mischel, W. (1999). A hot/cool-system analysis of delay of gratification: Dynamics of willpower. *Psychological Review, 106*, 3–19.

Miller, G. A., Galanter, E., & Pribram, K. H. (1960). *Plans and the structure of behavior*. New York: Holt, Rinehart, & Winston.

Mizruchi, M. S. (1991). Urgency, motivation, and group performance: The effect of prior success on current success among professional basketball teams. *Social Psychology Quarterly, 54*, 181–189.

Nigg, J. T. (2000). On inhibition/disinhibition in developmental psychopathology: Views from cognitive and personality psychology as a working inhibition taxonomy. *Psychological Bulletin, 126*, 220–246.

Ochsner, K. N., & Gross, J. J. (2008). Cognitive emotion regulation: Insights from social cognitive and affective neuroscience. *Current Directions in Psychological Science, 17*, 153–158.

Ogilvie, D. M. (1987). The undesired self: A neglected variable in personality research. *Journal of Personality and Social Psychology, 52*, 379–385.

Ortony, A., Clore, G. L., & Collins, A. (1988). *The cognitive structure of emotions*. New York: Cambridge University Press.

Powers, W. T. (1973). *Behavior: The control of perception*. Chicago, IL: Aldine.

Reyna, C., Henry, P. J., Korfmacher, W., & Tucker, A. (2006). Examining the principles in principled conservatism: The role of responsibility stereotypes as cues for deservingness in racial policy decisions. *Journal of Personality and Social Psychology, 90*, 109–128.

Rosenbaum, D. A., Meulenbroek, R. G. J., Vaughan, J., & Jansen, C. (2001). Posture-based motion planning: Applications to grasping. *Psychological Review, 108*, 709–734.

Rosenblueth, A., Wiener, N., & Bigelow, J. (1943). Behavior, purpose, and teleology. *Philosophy of Science, 10*, 18–24.

Rothbart, M. K., Ahadi, S. A., & Evans, D. E. (2000). Temperament and personality: Origins and outcomes. *Journal of Personality and Social Psychology, 78*, 122–135.

Rothbart, M. K., & Posner, M. (1985). Temperament and the development of self-regulation. In L. C. Hartlage & C. F. Telzrow (Eds.), *The neuropsychology of individual differences: A developmental perspective* (pp. 93–123). New York: Plenum.

Ryan, R. M., & Deci, E. L. (2000). Self-determination theory and the facilitation of intrinsic motivation, social development, and well-being. *American Psychologist, 55*, 68–78.

Ryan, R. M., & Deci, E. L. (2001). On happiness and human potentials: A review of research on hedonic and eudaimonic well-being. *Annual Review of Psychology, 52*, 141–166.

Schwartz, S. H., & Bilsky, W. (1990). Toward a theory of the universal content and structure of values: Extensions and cross-cultural replications. *Journal of Personality and Social Psychology, 58*, 878–891.

Schwartz, S. H., & Rubel, T. (2005). Sex differences in value priorities: Cross-cultural and multimethod studies. *Journal of Personality and Social Psychology, 89*, 1010–1028.

Schwarz, N., & Bohner, G. (1996). Feelings and their motivational implications: Moods and the action sequence. In P. M. Gollwitzer & J. A. Bargh (Eds.), *The psychology of action: Linking cognition and motivation to behavior* (pp. 119–145). New York: Guilford.

Shah, J. Y., Friedman, R., & Kruglanski, A. W. (2002). Forgetting all else: On the antecedents and consequences of goal shielding. *Journal of Personality and Social Psychology, 83*, 1261–1280.

Shallice, T. (1978). The dominant action system: An information-processing approach to consciousness. In K. S. Pope & J. L. Singer (Eds.), *The stream of consciousness: Scientific investigations into the flow of human experience* (pp. 117–157). New York: Wiley.

Shin, J. C., & Rosenbaum, D. A. (2002). Reaching while calculating: Scheduling of cognitive and perceptual-motor processes. *Journal of Experimental Psychology: General, 131*, 206–219.

Simon, H. A. (1953). *Models of man*. New York: Wiley.

Simon, H. A. (1967). Motivational and emotional controls of cognition. *Psychology Review, 74*, 29–39.

Strack, F., & Deutsch, R. (2004). Reflective and impulsive determinants of social behavior. *Personality and Social Psychology Review, 8*, 220–247.

Toates, F. (2006). A model of the hierarchy of behaviour, cognition, and consciousness. *Consciousness and Cognition: An International Journal, 15*, 75–118.

Vallacher, R. R., & Wegner, D. M. (1987). What do people think they're doing? Action identification and human behavior. *Psychological Review, 94*, 3–15.

Von Bertalanffy, L. (1968). *General systems theory*. New York: Braziller.

Watson, D. (2009). Locating anger in the hierarchical structure of affect: Comment on Carver and Harmon-Jones. *Psychological Bulletin, 135*, 205–208.

Watson, D., Wiese, D., Vaidya, J., & Tellegen, A. (1999). The two general activation systems of affect: Structural findings, evolutionary considerations, and psychobiological evidence. *Journal of Personality and Social Psychology, 76*, 820–838.

Wiener, N. (1948). *Cybernetics: Control and communication in the animal and the machine*. Cambridge, MA: MIT Press.

Wright, R. A., & Kirby, L. D. (2001). Effort determination of cardiovascular response: An integrative analysis with applications in social psychology. In M. P. Zanna (Ed.), *Advances in experimental social psychology* (Vol. 33, pp. 255–307). New York: Academic Press.

The Role of Death in Life: Existential Aspects of Human Motivation

Pelin Kesebir *and* Tom Pyszczynski

Abstract

The capacity for self-reflection, which plays an important role in human self-regulation, also leads people to become aware of the limitations of their existence. Awareness of the conflict between one's desires (e.g., to live) and the limitations of existence (e.g., the inevitability of death) creates the potential for existential anxiety. In this chapter, we review how this anxiety affects human motivation and behavior in a variety of life domains. Terror management theory and research suggest that transcending death and protecting oneself against existential anxiety are potent needs. This protection is provided by an anxiety-buffering system, which imbues people with a sense of meaning and value that function to shield them against these concerns. We review evidence of how the buffering system protects against existential anxiety in four dimensions of existence: the physical, personal, social, and spiritual domains. Because self-awareness is a prerequisite for existential anxiety, escaping self-awareness can also be an effective way to obviate the problem of existence. After elaborating on how existential anxiety can motivate escape from self-awareness, we conclude the chapter with a discussion of remaining issues and directions for future research and theory development.

Key Words: terror management theory, experimental existential psychology, death anxiety, existential anxiety, motivation

Unlike any other animal, we humans live our lives starkly aware that, despite our most fervent desires, death will sooner or later come to us. This knowledge, combined with other uniquely human sophisticated mental abilities, inevitably leads people to ask questions about the meaning, value, and purpose of existence. Although writers and philosophers throughout the ages have pointed to the vital impact of existential concerns on the human psyche, systematic empirical investigation of how existential concerns affect human motivation began only relatively recently. The purpose of terror management theory (TMT; Greenberg, Pyszczynski, & Solomon, 1986) is to explain the role that awareness of the inevitability of death plays in diverse aspects of human life. In this chapter, we review what terror management

theory and research have revealed about existential anxiety and its effects on human behavior and experience. The main tenet of TMT is that the desire to transcend the fragility of human existence by construing oneself as a valuable contributor to a meaningful universe lies at the root of a diverse array of otherwise distinct human motives.

The research we will review in this chapter focuses on a uniquely human source of motivation. Although other animals react with fear to clear and present dangers that threaten their existence, only humans have the self-awareness that leads them to realize that death is inevitable. Like other evolutionary advances, this awareness led to changes in the way motivational systems operated by building on previous evolved adaptations. Thus, existential motivation operates on other more basic motive systems—co-opting them to meet new needs and changing the way other needs are pursued. We start by considering how the emergence of self-awareness changed the human condition.

Self-Awareness: A Blessing and a Curse

Awareness of self is a tremendously adaptive cognitive capacity that exponentially increases the flexibility of the system through which humans regulate their behavior (Becker, 1971; Duval & Wicklund, 1972; Leary, 2004; Pyszczynski & Greenberg, 1993). Self-awareness is a distinct type of consciousness that enables the human self to become an object to itself. Although some other species are capable of a rudimentary form of self-recognition, they lack the linguistic abilities to conceive of an abstract self and use it to structure their experiences and behavior (Mitchell, 2003). Self-awareness enables humans to step back, reflect on their circumstances, weigh multiple options for how to meet their needs and the chances of each one succeeding, and then select the option they believe will be most successful for achieving their goal. It greatly expands one's options for how to behave and gives greater executive control to the self over one's actions. Accompanied by other uniquely human capacities, such as language and symbolic thought, causal thinking, and imagination, reflexive self-awareness has been critical to the formation of complex human society and culture as we know it today. As Leary argues, "Science, philosophy, government, education, and health care would all be impossible if people could not consciously self-reflect" (2004, p. 12).

Contemporary thinking about the role of self-awareness in human behavior was stimulated by Duval and Wicklund's (1972) objective self-awareness theory. They pointed out that conscious attention can be directed either externally, toward the environment, or internally, toward the self. Objective self-awareness theory posits that directing attention toward the self instigates a self-evaluative process, in which one's current state on whatever dimension is currently salient is compared with salient standards for that dimension. The detection of discrepancies between current state and standards produces affect that motivates the person to either reduce any discrepancies or escape the self-focused state. Research has been highly supportive of these basic propositions (for reviews, see Carver & Scheier, 2002; Duval & Silvia, 2001; Pyszczynski & Greenberg, 1993). Carver and Scheier (1981; Carver, 1979) integrated these ideas with a very general cybernetic model of self-regulation in which this process

of comparing the self's current state to standards and the increased effort to reduce any discrepancies are viewed as the most basic process through which the self regulates its own actions. Self-awareness thus adds multiple layers of sophistication and flexibility to the simple system of comparing and matching to standards through which all self-regulating systems operate.

One of the most important innovations that Carver and Scheier (1981) brought to their synthesis of self-awareness and self-regulation was their conceptualization of a hierarchy of standards that integrated concrete physical actions and the even more concrete biological, chemical, and electrical changes through which these actions are accomplished, with the more abstract goals, identities, and sense of self-worth that these actions (and their lower level components) are oriented toward achieving. From this perspective, all behavior functions to simultaneously meet multiple hierarchically organized goals, and this organization gives coherence and flexibility to human action. The standard at any given level of abstraction is simultaneously a behavior through which the standard at a higher level of abstraction is met. For example, writing a paper for a college class is a behavior through which the standard of getting a good grade in the class is met; getting a good grade in the class is the behavior through which the more abstract standard of getting a college degree is met; getting a college degree is the behavior through which the more abstract standard of getting a good job is met; getting a good job is the behavior through which the more abstract standard of having a successful career is met; and having a successful career is the behavior through which the even more abstract goal of being a valuable person is met. One could also move down the hierarchy to consider the component behaviors through which writing a paper, gathering information, reading articles to provide that information, moving the focus of one's eyes across the words on the page are accomplished, and so on down to the biological and chemical reactions that underlie these actions.

Flexibility in behavior is provided by the fact that there are usually multiple behaviors through which any given standard can be met. For example, self-esteem can be achieved by means of success in one's career, relationships, community activities, or family. And there are many ways to succeed in any of these more specific endeavors, just as there are many particular routes through which any particular success could be attained. Self-awareness sets in motion a variety of executive processes through which choices among these multiple routes to goals at these various levels of abstraction are met. Of course this is a very complex system and we are able to provide only a brief overview here. For a more thorough presentation, see Carver and Scheier (1981; 2002). For present purposes, our goal is to make clear the central role and adaptive utility that self-awareness and hierarchical organization of standards and behavior play in human motivation and behavior. Put simply, self-awareness increases the human capacity for freedom and willful self-determined behavior.

Although self-awareness opened the door to many new opportunities for humans, it also set the stage for some uniquely human challenges. Perhaps the most basic problem born from self-awareness was the recognition of one's limits, one's perpetual vulnerability, and one's ultimate mortality. Human beings, compelled by their sophisticated mental abilities to be aware of their own existence, had to face the basic conditions of life and their limitations against them. The juxtaposition of what humans were born into and what they naturally desired created certain existential dilemmas with which they had to contend. Irvin Yalom (1980) delineated four ultimate concerns and proposed that the individual's confrontation with each of these "givens of existence" constituted a major existential conflict. These four concerns are *death*, *freedom*, *isolation*, and *meaninglessness*. Human beings wish to continue being, yet they are inevitably finite (*death*). They wish for ground and structure, yet there is no universal design or plan for human life other than that which humans create, leaving people responsible for creating themselves and their world (*freedom*). They wish for communion with others and to be part of something larger than themselves, yet they are born alone and ultimately die alone (*isolation*). They desperately seek meaning, yet there is no preordained, inherent meaning to the universe (*meaninglessness*). According to Yalom, each of these clashes between the structure of existence and the wishes of the self-reflective human being spawns conscious and unconscious fears and motives. Existential psychology is the branch of psychology that investigates how these fears and motives affect humankind, and how they interact with the other needs and desires that are essential to human existence

For most of the still brief history of psychology, the existential subdiscipline was synonymous with existential psychotherapy; its concepts and theories were scattered in a piecemeal fashion within the existing literature; and it had little interaction with empirically oriented psychological science (Jacobsen, 2007). The methodology of existential psychological research was qualitative and descriptive, with a particular emphasis on phenomenology. Notwithstanding the rich insights these methods are capable of yielding, causal inferences regarding the effect of existential realities on human motivation can be made only through rigorous experimental research. This is why terror management theory's application of experimental methods to existential psychological questions has been an invigorating contribution to existential psychology, resulting in the prolific subfield of social psychology known as experimental existential psychology (see Greenberg, Koole, & Pyszczynski, 2004; Pyszczynski, Greenberg, Solomon, & Koole, 2010).

Terror Management Theory

Terror management theory was inspired by cultural anthropologist Ernest Becker's (1971, 1973, 1975) attempts to integrate and synthesize what he viewed as the most important insights into the human condition provided by the social and natural sciences, as well as humanities. Building on the work of thinkers as diverse as Freud, Rank, Mead, Fromm, Kierkegaard, Heidegger, and Sartre, Becker built on the premise that the idea of death is unbearable to a self-aware animal: "To have emerged from nothing, to have a name, consciousness of self, deep inner feelings, an excruciating inner yearning for life and self-expression—and with all this yet to die" (1973, p. 87). To Becker, the terror inherent in this knowledge haunted humans like nothing else and was a mainspring of human activity: "Of all things that move man, one of the principal ones is his terror of death" (1973, p. 11). In his view, a major function of individual character and societal institutions was to deny one's mortality and avert this terror. He viewed human striving for a sense of value and unshakable meaning as the primary defense against the terror-inducing awareness of mortality, and he conceptualized this striving as taking place within the context of the cultural worldviews to which people subscribe. To Becker, participating in and contributing to a cultural system that imbues existence with order, purpose, and permanence provided the individual with a feeling of outliving or outshining death and the psychological equanimity that this produces.

TMT was initially developed to answer three fundamental questions about human nature: Why do people need self-esteem? Why do people need to believe that out of the multitude of ways that people construe reality, theirs happens to be the one that is ultimately correct? And why are interpersonal and intercultural relations so frequently ridden with conflict and violence? Becker's ideas offered potential answers to these and many other questions. TMT was an attempt to simplify Becker's ideas and integrate them with existing knowledge within the fields of social, personality, developmental, cognitive, and motivational psychology in a way that would generate testable hypotheses about the functions of self-esteem and culture. TMT posited that knowledge of inevitable mortality, when combined with the biologically rooted craving for life, creates a potential for paralyzing terror. To function effectively in the world, people must keep this terror at bay. Protection from this terror is provided by self-esteem and faith in one's cultural worldview (Solomon, Greenberg, & Pyszczynski, 1991). These two psychological entities function to buffer death-related anxiety. Later research revealed close interpersonal relations as an additional component of the anxiety-buffering mechanism (Mikulincer, Florian, & Hirschberger, 2003).

TMT posits that awareness of the inevitability of death is a powerful motivating force that influences the human needs for meaning, self-esteem, and close relationships. The precursors of these motives probably initially evolved because they solved practical problems of living that increased our ancestors' chances of passing on their genes by staying alive, mating, and caring for their offspring. However, once human intelligence had evolved to the point that awareness of death emerged, the need for protection from the fear that this awareness created led people to develop systems of meaning and value that provided protection from this fear. From this point on, people no longer simply needed meaning systems that helped them procure the necessities of life—now, their meaning systems also needed to help manage their potential for existential anxiety. The value of accuracy and practical utility of the meaning systems was usurped by the value of death transcendence, and from this point on the pursuit of truth and protection were often in conflict with each other.

Well over 400 separate studies conducted in over 20 countries have tested and supported hypotheses derived from TMT. These studies helped expand the theory beyond its initial focus and applied it to topics as varied as religion and spirituality, legal decision making, nostalgia, human sexuality, fascination with fame, creativity, materialism, and psychopathology. The fact that existential concerns have been shown to affect human behavior across so many domains suggests that existential anxiety is a central motivating force for the human psyche. In the next sections, we provide an overview of TMT findings that support this claim; however, we first describe the logic of the methods commonly employed in TMT studies.

The TMT Research Strategy

TMT research has been focused on three general hypotheses that have been combined in various ways to assess the basic propositions of the theory and applied to a diverse array of behaviors and social problems to document the generality and generativity of the theory. The earliest TMT studies (Greenberg et al., 1990; Rosenblatt, Greenberg, Solomon, Pyszczynski, & Lyon, 1989) used the mortality salience hypothesis to assess the theory's propositions, which has remained the most common approach to testing TMT. Indeed, according to a recent meta-analysis of 238 empirical TMT journal articles reporting 277 experiments, 83% directly tested this hypothesis (Burke, Martens, & Faucher, 2010). The mortality salience (MS) hypothesis states that to the extent a psychological structure (e.g., self-esteem, faith in one's cultural worldview) provides protection against death anxiety, reminders of death should intensify the need for this structure, and therefore lead to more positive reactions to people and ideas that support that structure and more negative reactions to people and ideas that threaten it. In a typical MS study, the experimental group is exposed to a reminder of death (mortality salience) and then compared to a control group that has not been reminded of death on the variable hypothesized to buffer against existential anxiety.

The most common mortality salience induction technique entails asking participants two open-ended questions about their own mortality, as first utilized by Rosenblatt et al. (1989). Specifically, participants are asked to "Please briefly describe the emotions that the thought of your own death arouses in you" and "Please jot down as specifically as you can what you think will happen to you as you physically die and once you are physically dead." In the control condition, participants respond to similarly worded questions regarding a neutral (e.g., watching TV) or negative topic not related to death (e.g., dental pain). Other techniques to manipulate MS include having participants complete fear of death scales, watch car crash or Holocaust videos, read an essay about cancer or the 9/11 attacks, exposing them to subliminal death primes, and interviewing them in front of a funeral home or cemetery. Findings have been highly consistent across these different mortality salience inductions.

In their meta-analysis, Burke and colleagues (2010) found that MS manipulations yielded moderate-to-large effects ($r = .35$, $d = .75$) on a wide range of attitudinal, behavioral, and cognitive dependent variables. This effect size reaches the top quartile of effects for psychology in general and the 80th percentile for theories in social psychology (Lipsey & Wilson, 1993; Richard, Bond, & Stokes-Zoota, 2003). The same meta-analysis revealed that a longer delay between MS manipulation and the dependent variable assessment yields larger effect sizes. This finding highlights an important finding regarding how people react to reminders of death—death-related thoughts elicit strongest defensive reactions when they are no longer in current focal attention, yet are still accessible. This led to a distinction between the types of defenses that people use to cope with conscious and nonconscious death-related thoughts (Pyszczynski, Greenberg, & Solomon, 1999). People deal with conscious thoughts of mortality using *proximal defenses* that operate in a relatively direct and rational fashion—for example, by reminding themselves of their excellent health or the "longevity gene" running in their family, by resolving to eat better, to exercise more, to have more regular checkups, and so on. Nonconscious thoughts of death, that is, thoughts that are highly accessible but not in current focal attention, lead to *distal defenses* that cope with the problem in a more indirect, symbolic manner. These distal defenses emerge only when thoughts of mortality have faded to the fringes of consciousness. Research showing that the removal of delay and distraction tasks eliminates effects of MS on worldview defense and self-esteem striving supports this dual process model of defense (Greenberg, Arndt, Simon, Pyszczynski, & Solomon, 2000). Hence, delay/distraction tasks (e.g., scales of positive and negative affect, word puzzles, anagram tasks) between the MS induction and measures of the dependent variable are essential for testing the MS hypothesis.

A second early approach to assessing TMT was the anxiety-buffer hypothesis. According to this hypothesis, to the extent that a psychological structure buffers anxiety, then strengthening that structure should lead to less anxiety in threatening situations and weakening it should lead to more anxiety. In the initial test of the anxiety-buffer hypothesis (Greenberg, Solomon et al., 1992), participants were given bogus positive or neutral personality profiles designed to either increase their self-esteem or have no effect on it. They then watched a graphic video of death-related scenes or a neutral film, after which their state anxiety was assessed. Although the death-related video led to significantly elevated

levels of anxiety in the neutral self-esteem condition, it had no effect on anxiety in the self-esteem boost condition. Follow-up studies by Greenberg et al. (1993) replicated this finding with different manipulations of self-esteem and threat and physiological measures of anxiety. These studies showed that both experimentally elevated and dispositionally high levels of self-esteem led to lower levels of death-denying defensive distortions, which presumably were decreased because of the anxiety-buffering effect of high self-esteem. Still other studies combined the anxiety-buffer and mortality salience hypotheses to show that bolstering self-esteem, faith in one's worldview, or close personal relationships eliminates the increase in defensiveness that reminders of death otherwise produce (e.g., Florian, Mikulincer, & Hirschberger, 2002; Harmon-Jones et al., 1997).

A third, increasingly common approach to assessing TMT is the death-thought accessibility (DTA) hypothesis. The hypothesis states that to the extent a psychological structure serves to protect against death anxiety, weakening this structure would increase, and strengthening it would decrease, the accessibility of death-related thoughts. According to a recent review (Hayes, Schimel, Arndt, & Faucher, 2010), there are over 80 published studies that have made use of the DTA concept in the context of TMT. The vast majority of these studies assessed DTA through the word-fragment completion task. This task, originally used by Greenberg et al. (1994), consists of word fragments, some of which can be completed in either death-related or death-unrelated ways (e.g., SK _ _ L can be completed as skull or skill). DTA is operationalized as the number of words completed in death-related ways. The successful use of this measure in languages other than English, including Hebrew, Chinese, French, and Dutch, attests to the construct validity and generality of the method. DTA studies were essential to the development of TMT, because they revealed that the anxiety buffer does not operate only when death thoughts are activated by external events (as studies testing the MS hypothesis show), but that they are continuously functioning to keep death-related thoughts beneath consciousness.

In our view, the most convincing aspect of the evidence for TMT is the high degree of consistency and convergence in findings across different methods. Although in some cases it may be possible to offer alternative explanations for specific findings, we have yet to encounter an attempt to provide an alternative account of the converging evidence provided by these diverse methods. We now discuss evidence obtained with these and other methods that reveal the role of existential anxiety in energizing and directing human behavior.

Evidence for the Motivational Role of Existential Anxiety

In presenting the findings on the diverse ways that the fear of death affects human behavior, we use a taxonomy widely used by existential psychologists (van Deurzen-Smith, 1984). According to this framework, humans experience the world on four basic dimensions, commonly referred to with their German names: physical dimension (*Umwelt*), personal dimension (*Eigenwelt*), social dimension (*Mitwelt*), and spiritual dimension (*Überwelt*). The first three dimensions are drawn from the work of Swiss psychiatrist Ludwig Binswanger (1946). Based on the writings of authors such as Buber (1923), Jaspers (1951), and Tillich (1952), existential psychotherapist van Deurzen-Smith (1984) proposed a fourth, spiritual dimension. According to van Deurzen-Smith (1997), all these dimensions have their own paradoxes and tensions, their own human objectives and aspirations, as well as their own ideals and evils. They create a complex four-dimensional field of forces that encompass the major aspects of the human experience. The four dimensions are obviously interrelated, with the self standing at the center of the person's entire network of physical, social, personal and spiritual relations. Indeed, these four dimensions overlap substantially with William James's four constituents of the self—the material self, social self, spiritual self, and the pure ego (1950). For organizational purposes, nonetheless, we will treat them separately and discuss how the human experience on each of these dimensions is affected by existential concerns.

The Physical Dimension

The physical dimension is concerned with how people relate to nature and the material world around them. Their relationship to their bodies, physical environment, concrete surroundings, and material possessions makes up this dimension (van Deurzen, 2002). How do existential motives shape human behavior and experience on the physical dimension?

THE PROBLEM OF THE BODY

Human beings are condemned to a dual existence: They are half animal and half symbolic—to use Becker's colorful metaphor, they are "gods with anuses" (1973, p. 51). The capacity for self-reflection that distinguishes the human race so sharply from

the rest of the animal kingdom ironically also leads to the realization that humankind is ultimately *part of nature* and subject to the same ultimate fate of death and decay. The knowledge that one is "up in the stars and yet housed in a heart-pumping, breath-gasping body" (Becker, 1973, p. 26), the awareness of one's common fate with all creatures, explains why people are often ill at ease with their own corporeality. Indeed, research has shown that reminders of death intensify the desire to distance oneself from other animals and from one's own body.

For example, Goldenberg and colleagues (2001) demonstrated that mortality salience leads to increased preference for an essay that describes humans as distinct from animals over one that emphasizes human-animal similarities. These researchers also found that mortality reminders increase disgust reactions to situations involving bodily products (e.g., "seeing a bowel movement left unflushed in a public toilet") and animals (e.g., "seeing maggots on a piece of meat in an outdoor garbage pail"). In a similar vein, viewing pictures of bodily wastes has been found to increase the accessibility of death-related thoughts (Cox, Goldenberg, Pyszczynski, & Weise, 2007). Other research has shown that intimations of the frailty of the human body, as in the case of elderly people (Martens, Greenberg, Schimel, & Landau, 2004) or persons with physical disabilities (Hirschberger, Florian, & Mikulincer, 2005), spontaneously increase the accessibility of death thoughts.

The urge to distance oneself from one's body in the face of death thoughts acquires great practical significance in the context of health behaviors. Ironically, the salience of mortality thoughts often poses a barrier to health-promoting behaviors that could actually forestall death (Goldenberg & Arndt, 2008). Research has shown, for example, that when mortality is salient, reminders of creatureliness decrease women's willingness to conduct breast self-examinations (Goldenberg, Arndt, Hart, & Routledge, 2008).

Interestingly, thoughts of death increase health-promoting behavior when they are in current focal attention, but they decrease such behavior when they are on the fringes of consciousness. This is consistent with the TMT distinction between proximal defenses, which deal with the problem of death in a rational way and emerge when one is consciously thinking about death, and distal defenses, which deal with the problem of death symbolically by boosting one's sense of meaning and value that emerge when such thoughts are accessible but not in focal attention. For example, Routledge, Arndt, and Goldenberg (2004) found that immediately after reminders of death people were more interested in using a sunscreen that provided a high level of protection (to reduce their chances of skin cancer), but after a delay and distraction, they were more interested in sunscreen with a lower level of protection (to get a better tan).

According to TMT, the great efforts individuals and societies put in denying and disguising the body's physicality are motivated, to a large extent, by a need to escape the creaturely aspects of existence. This need is perhaps nowhere more apparent than in the domain of human sexuality, which is a potent reminder of the fundamentally animal side of human nature. After all, as Cole Porter put it, "birds do it, bees do it, even educated fleas do it." Supporting the argument that sex is threatening when it is closely associated with creatureliness, research found that when similarities between humans and animals were salient, reminders of death resulted in decreased attraction to the physical, but not romantic (and hence uniquely human), aspects of sex (Goldenberg, Cox, Pyszczynski, Greenberg, & Solomon, 2002). These researchers also found that when participants were primed with human-animal similarities, thinking about physical, but not romantic, aspects of sex increased the accessibility of death-related thoughts. These findings suggest that construing human sex as indistinguishable from animal copulation can be uncomfortable due to the mortality concerns it arouses.

Confrontations with the natural world at its wildest can induce a similar sense of discomfort. Studies reveal that people have more death thoughts in wilderness settings compared to cultivated nature or urban settings, and that death reminders reduce the perceived beauty of wild landscapes and increase the perceived beauty of cultivated landscapes (Koole & Van den Berg, 2005). This helps explain the appeal of carefully mowed lawns and manicured gardens and the many hours that people devote to imposing unnatural order on their natural environment.

Finally, it has also been found that mortality thoughts increase people's desire to fly, whereas engaging in flight fantasies mitigates defensive reactions to mortality thoughts. These findings suggest that fantasies of flight can serve a terror management function by helping people to transcend physical confines, albeit in imagination only (Solomon, Greenberg, Pyszczynski, Cohen, & Ogilvie, 2009). All in all, our review indicates that existential concerns play a distinct role in humankind's relationships with their bodies and nature. Now we examine how existential concerns affect our relationship with material possessions.

MATERIALISM

Materialism, or the importance a person attaches to worldly possessions (Belk, 1985), has frequently been recognized by scholars as a way to secure meaning and transcend death. Irvin Yalom, for example, wrote that accumulating material wealth can become "a way of life which effectively conceals the mortal questions churning below" (1980, p. 121). Others contended that underlying the American ideology of affluence is the pursuit of secular personal immortality through material means (Hirschman, 1990). It has also been suggested that achieving immortality is a significant motivating force for collectors (e.g., Pearce, 1992).

Research inspired by TMT provides empirical support for this general line of thinking. Kasser and Sheldon (2000), for instance, demonstrated that participants primed with mortality thoughts not only reported higher financial expectations for themselves 15 years in the future but also became greedier and less environmentally sensitive in a forest-management simulation. Another study (Mandel & Heine, 1999) revealed that subtle reminders of mortality increase preference for high-status products such as Lexus automobiles or Rolex watches. Rindfleisch, Burroughs, and Wong (2009) similarly showed that the strong connections materialistic individuals form with their brands serve to buffer against existential insecurity. These and other parallel findings suggest that people often seek protection from existential anxiety in the sense of value and self-esteem provided by material objects.

The Personal Dimension

The personal dimension refers to how individuals relate to themselves (van Deurzen, 2002). It includes views about their identity, character, past experience, and future possibilities. In this section we examine how existential concerns affect human behavior and experience on the personal dimension, particularly in the context of self-esteem and psychopathology.

SELF-ESTEEM

Self-esteem refers to people's evaluations of themselves, and it is almost axiomatic in social psychology that people strive for positive self-esteem. The question of why people need self-esteem was, in fact, one of the original questions that begot TMT. The theory posits that self-esteem functions to keep death anxiety at bay (for a review, see Pyszczynski, Greenberg, Solomon, Arndt, & Schimel, 2004). According to TMT, self-esteem is attained by meeting or exceeding the standards of value that are part of one's cultural worldview; it is the sense that one is a valuable contributor to a meaningful universe. Although the standards upon which self-esteem is contingent vary across cultures and individuals, the underlying need for self-esteem is universal.

A large body of research supports the notion that self-esteem provides a buffer against existential anxiety. In the first test of this hypothesis, as we have seen, Greenberg, Solomon and colleagues (1992) showed that boosting participants' self-esteem through bogus positive feedback leads to lower levels of self-reported anxiety in response to graphic depictions of death, and lower physiological arousal when anticipating painful electric shocks. Other research revealed that both artificially enhanced and dispositionally high self-esteem are associated with lower levels of worldview defense and lower death-thought accessibility in response to mortality reminders (Harmon-Jones et al., 1997), as well as lower levels of defensive distortions aimed at denying vulnerability to early death (Greenberg et al. 1993). Studies also demonstrate that death-thought accessibility increases when participants think about their "undesired self" (Ogilvie, Cohen, & Solomon, 2008) or when their self-esteem is directly threatened, such as when they are informed that their personality is ill suited for their career aspirations (Hayes, Schimel, Faucher, & Williams, 2008). Conversely, having participants affirm their most important values reverses the effect of self-esteem threat on death-thought accessibility (Hayes et al., 2008).

In addition to evidence that self-esteem buffers death anxiety, research also shows that death reminders increase people's striving for self-esteem. In one dramatic illustration of this point, Israeli soldiers engaged in more risky driving behavior after mortality reminders, but only to the extent they derived self-esteem from their driving ability (Taubman Ben-Ari, Florian, & Mikulincer, 1999). Further support for the notion that existential anxiety increases striving for self-esteem in domains one is invested in is provided by studies showing that mortality salience improved strength performance among individuals invested in strength training, but it had no impact on those not invested in strength training (Peters, Greenberg, & Williams, 2005). Similarly, mortality salience increased identification with one's body and interest in sex among people high in body self-esteem, but not among those with low body self-esteem (Goldenberg, McCoy, Pyszczynski, Greenberg, & Solomon, 2000).

Existential anxiety also amplifies self-serving biases, which are perhaps the most commonly researched manifestation of the need for self-esteem.

Research shows, for example, that in achievement-related tasks, participants reminded of their mortality are more likely to attribute positive outcomes to internal, stable, and global causes and negative outcomes to external, unstable, and specific causes compared to participants in a control condition (Mikulincer & Florian, 2002). Furthermore, the accessibility of death-related thoughts induced by mortality reminders is mitigated when participants are given the opportunity to provide causal attributions excusing their failure.

The body of research reviewed here highlights the role of self-esteem in buffering existential anxiety. Humans struggle for a sense of identity and significance in the world, partly as a way to shield themselves from death and its attendant anxieties. This search for validation and value oftentimes takes the form of expanding oneself and merging with something larger than oneself. The family, nation, religion, science, or art can all serve as avenues for a person to find meaning and value in a vast arena that will not be shattered by one's death. These avenues for self-expansion provide the person with symbolic immortality—the sense that one is a valuable part of something larger, more significant, and longer lasting than one's individual existence. In the words of John Steinbeck, "After the bare requisites of living and reproducing, man wants most to leave some record of himself, a proof, perhaps, that he has really existed. He leaves his proof on wood, on stone, or on the lives of other people. This deep desire exists in everyone, from the boy who scribbles on a wall to the Buddha who etches his image in the race mind" (1995, p. 49). Lifton (1979) has elaborated on the various ways in which humans strive for symbolic immortality, the most common of which seem to be living on through one's progeny and through one's works.

In line with the idea that symbolic immortality can help to manage the threat of death, research has found an inverse correlation between self-reports of symbolic immortality and fear of personal death (Florian & Mikulincer, 1998). In the same study, a high sense of symbolic immortality also reduced participants' tendency to respond to mortality reminders with increased worldview defense, suggesting a protective, anxiety-buffering role for symbolic immortality. Interestingly, the desire for symbolic immortality may at times even trump the desire for life. In a study reported in *The Economist*, more than half of 198 Olympic-level American athletes said that they would take a banned drug if they knew that by taking it they would win every competition for the next 5 years but then die from the substance's side effects ("Superhuman Heroes," 1998). The case of suicide bombers is another illustration of how the quest for symbolic immortality can paradoxically lead to suicide (Kruglanski, Chen, Dechesne, Fishman, & Orehek, 2009).

In this section, we have reviewed evidence showing that a personal sense of worth and significance can effectively buffer anxiety. In the next section, we discuss findings from the emerging literature on the role of death anxiety in psychological disorders.

PSYCHOPATHOLOGY

TMT argues that successful management of existential anxiety is required for effective functioning and psychological well-being. If that is the case, then problems in managing this anxiety would be associated with psychological disturbances. Existentially oriented scholars have often argued that psychological disorders reflect extreme, graceless, or inefficient ways of dealing with existential anxiety (Becker, 1971, 1973; Lifton, 1979; Yalom, 1980). Becker (1973), for example, posited that mental illness results when people fail in their death-transcendence goals. Psychiatrist Irvin Yalom similarly noted: "Either because of extraordinary stress or because of an inadequacy of available defensive strategies, the individual who enters the realm called 'patienthood' has found insufficient the universal modes of dealing with death fear and has been driven to extreme modes of defense. These defensive maneuvers, often clumsy modes of dealing with terror, constitute the presenting clinical picture" (1980, p. 111).

Recent TMT studies provide empirical support for the proposition that psychological disorders are associated with mismanaged death anxiety (for a review, see Arndt, Routledge, Cox, & Goldenberg, 2005). Mortality reminders have been found to exacerbate anxiety symptoms in those who suffer from anxiety disorders such as phobia and obsessive-compulsive disorder (Strachan et al., 2007). In one study, clinically diagnosed spider phobics spent less time looking at pictures of spiders presented on a computer screen after mortality reminders, and they also rated the spiders in the pictures as more threatening. No such effect of mortality reminders was observed among nonphobic participants. In a similar vein, following mortality salience, college students who scored high on a measure of contamination obsession and compulsive hand-washing used more water to wash their hands after they had been soiled with gooey electrode gel. Other studies have shown that neuroticism, which refers to an enduring tendency to experience negative emotional states and which is robustly associated with a broad array of psychological disorders (Malouff, Thorsteinsson, & Schutte, 2005), makes it more difficult for individuals to manage death anxiety (e.g., Arndt & Solomon, 2003; Goldenberg, Pyszczynski, McCoy, Greenberg, & Solomon, 1999; Goldenberg, Routledge, & Arndt, 2009).

TMT has also recently been applied to the understanding of posttraumatic stress disorder (PTSD) in the form of anxiety-buffer disruption theory (Pyszczynski & Kesebir, 2011). Anxiety-buffer disruption theory posits that PTSD results from a breakdown in one's anxiety-buffering system, which normally provides protection from anxiety in general and death anxiety in particular. When the anxiety buffer stops functioning effectively due to a traumatic encounter, the individual becomes defenseless in the face of incapacitating fears and anxieties. As a consequence, he or she is flooded with overwhelming anxiety, leading to hyperarousability, intrusive thoughts, and avoidance behavior, the primary clusters of PTSD symptoms. Recent research has supported the hypothesis that if PTSD involves a disrupted anxiety buffer, PTSD-inflicted individuals would not respond to death reminders in the way that psychologically healthier individuals with functional anxiety buffers do. A study conducted in the aftermath of the 2005 Zarand earthquake in Iran, for example, showed that individuals with high PTSD symptom severity 2 years after the earthquake did not respond to mortality reminders with typical cultural worldview defenses (Abdollahi, Pyszczynski, Maxfield, & Luszczynska, in press). Another study conducted with survivors of the Ivory Coast civil war (Chatard et al., 2011) revealed that participants with high levels of PTSD symptoms did not respond to mortality reminders with the typical immediate suppression of death-related thoughts, while those with low PTSD symptom levels in the study did. These and similar studies (e.g., Edmondson, 2009; Kesebir, Luszczynska, Pyszczynski, & Benight, in press) provide encouraging initial support for anxiety-buffer disruption theory, though more research is of course needed. Although the well-functioning individuals who have been studied in the vast majority of TMT studies have shown little signs of the abject terror of death posited by the theory, presumably because their anxiety-buffer systems are intact, this terror is easy to see in those whose anxiety buffers are malfunctioning. Expanded use of TMT to understand psychological disorders seems a promising line of inquiry for the future.

The Social Dimension

The social dimension refers to our relationships with other people, the culture we live in, and the groups that make the social fabric of daily life. The need to belong to and affiliate is a powerful, fundamental, and extremely potent human motive (Baumeister & Leary, 1995). Although this need may have initially evolved because of the distinct evolutionary advantages that group living provides, TMT argues that with the evolution of sophisticated intelligence, it took on the existential function of helping people manage death-related anxiety. Here we present this literature in two major sections; first we review how existential motivation affects humans as they relate to the groups to which they belong (and do not belong) and then we review the role of existential motivation in close personal relationships.

GROUP BELONGING AND WORLDVIEW VALIDATION

According to TMT, faith in one's cultural worldview is a potent buffer against existential anxiety. The term *worldview* comes from the German word *Weltanschauung*, meaning a view or perspective on the world that encompasses one's total outlook on life, society, and its institutions (Koltko-Rivera, 2004). TMT defines cultural worldviews as personally and culturally held assumptions and beliefs about the nature of existence. Individuals construct their own individualized worldviews as they go through life by combining the beliefs and values of the individuals with whom they interact, the groups to which they belong, and the broader society that surrounds them. Cultural norms, moral values, and religious beliefs are among the most central cultural worldviews. They are "theories of reality" that explain what life is and how it should be lived. As such, they imbue existence with meaning, purpose, structure, and permanence, thereby helping to control anxiety.

Individuals are heavily invested in their worldviews and rely on them for navigating through life. Yet there is a problem with worldviews: It is impossible to definitively prove the accuracy or superiority of one's own worldview. As shared human constructions, cultural worldviews depend on social consensus for sustenance (Hardin & Higgins, 1996). The wide diversity of extant worldviews exacerbates people's motivation to validate their own worldviews as a protection against existential anxiety. This, from a TMT perspective, is the central reason people are attracted to those who share their cherished beliefs and values, and conversely, why they are generally uncomfortable around, and at times hostile toward, those who do not.

If cultural worldviews protect against the potential for terror inherent in the knowledge of one's mortality, then mortality reminders would intensify the need to hold on to one's ingroup and worldview and defend them against the outgroup and rival worldviews. In addition, threats to one's ingroup and cultural worldview should increase death-related thoughts and anxieties. Since the earliest days of TMT research, an avalanche of studies has supported these prepositions and demonstrated the role of these tendencies in ingroup bias and outgroup hostility. The first evidence of the role of death concerns in intergroup conflict came from a study by Greenberg and colleagues (1990) which showed that after mortality reminders, American Christians evaluated a fellow Christian student more positively and a Jewish student more negatively. Other studies found that mortality salience increases preference for an author with pro-American views over an author with anti-American views among American students (Greenberg et al., 1994), and it increases criticism of an anti-Japan essay writer among Japanese students (Heine, Harihara, Niiya, & 2002). Conversely, when participants heavily invested in their Canadian identity were exposed to material that derogates Canadian culture, they exhibited increased accessibility of death-related thoughts (Schimel, Hayes, Williams, & Jahrig, 2007).

Further corroborating the existential function served by the ingroup, a study conducted in Italy revealed that reminders of mortality increase peoples' identification with their ethnic identities as Italians, their belief in the entitativity of this identity, and their ingroup bias (Castano, Yzerbyt, Paladino, & Sacchi, 2002). These participants rated Italians as a significantly more stable, coherent, and distinct ethnic group after mortality reminders, while another study found mortality reminders to lead participants to view their ingroup as more human (Vaes, Heflick, & Goldenberg, 2010). Mortality reminders have been reported to intensify ingroup favoritism (e.g., Castano et al. 2002; Tam, Chiu, & Lau, 2007), and this bias seems to occur even when the group allocation is based on minimally meaningful criteria such as aesthetic preferences (Harmon-Jones, Greenberg, Solomon, & Simon, 1996).

It is important to note, however, that according to TMT, ingroups provide existential protection only to the extent that they are a source of value and meaning. The desire to affiliate with groups thus depends on the broader connotations and value of this affiliation for the individual. In support of this idea, Harmon-Jones and colleagues (1996) found that mortality primes did not increase ingroup bias when group assignment was entirely random. Similarly, participants reminded of their own death exhibited reduced identification with their college football team after the team's loss (Dechesne, Greenberg, Arndt, & Schimel, 2000); and Mexican American participants primed with mortality showed decreased affiliation with their ethnicity when they were exposed to a negative example of their ingroup by reading about a "Mexican drug cartel chief" (Arndt, Greenberg, Schimel, Pyszczynski, & Solomon, 2002).

A perceived threat to one's cherished beliefs can undermine the much-needed sense of meaning, value, and existential security, propelling people to defend their worldview and even resort to violence. This is why existential anxiety is not only associated with an intensified need to validate one's worldview and cling to one's ingroup but also with a host of unsavory behaviors such as outgroup derogation, stereotyping, prejudice, and discrimination. Reminders of death have been shown to increase stereotypic thinking about an outgroup and preference for those who confirm one's stereotypes (Schimel et al., 1999), as well as punitive reactions toward those who violate one's moral/cultural values (Rosenblatt et al., 1989).

The outrage felt at worldview-threatening others can also lead people to resort to violence, as exemplified by a study in which participants in a mortality salience condition administered a larger amount of hot sauce to a person who disliked hot sauce and disparaged their political ideology (McGregor et al., 1998). Furthermore, there is evidence that the annihilation of worldview-threatening others can mollify death anxiety. Hayes, Schimel, and Williams (2008) found that while Christian participants responded with increased death-thought accessibility to a news article reporting the Muslimization of Nazareth, informing them that many Muslims had died in a plane crash on their way to Nazareth eliminated this effect of worldview threat. Other studies revealed that existential fears can heighten the support for violence committed against worldview-threatening others. Pyszczynski et al. (2006) documented that mortality reminders increased Iranian college students' support for martyrdom attacks against the United States. A follow-up study by these authors found that reminders of death or 9/11 made politically conservative American college students more accepting of extreme military action in the War on Terror, such as the use of nuclear and chemical weapons, or the killing of thousands of civilians as collateral damage. Research has also shown that reminders of death lead conservative Israelis to view violence against Palestinians as more justified (Hirschberger & Ein-Dor, 2006).

These findings imply that the psychological protection that cultural worldviews provide against the reality of death often comes at the price of increased intergroup conflict and violence. Fortunately, the link between existential anxiety and intergroup conflict is neither automatic nor inevitable. An early study showed that a chronically high or temporarily heightened level of tolerance can eliminate negative reactions toward dissimilar others induced by mortality primes (Greenberg, Simon et al., 1992). Since then, research has revealed that the effect of mortality reminders on reactions to threatening others depends on the particular norms that are salient to the person. Jonas and colleagues (2008) demonstrated, for instance, that whereas a mortality prime led people to become harsher toward a moral transgressor when conservative values were made salient, a benevolence prime counteracted this effect. Others found that the violence-promoting effects of death anxiety can be attenuated or reversed when values such as compassion or shared humanity are salient (Motyl, Hart, & Pyszczynski, 2010; Rothschild, Abdollahi, & Pyszczynski, 2009). This line of research may suggest a promising direction for those who wish to promote peace in the face of ongoing intractable war and violence.

CLOSE PERSONAL RELATIONSHIPS

As Bowlby (1969) has pointed out, all infants are born with an attachment system oriented toward maintaining proximity to significant others in times of stress. To survive, children need caregivers who will provide protection and ensure that their needs are met. The attachment relationship to the caregiver helps children manage distress and feel secure, even before they possess the cognitive complexity to develop a sense of self or a concept of death. In the last decade, TMT research has demonstrated that the anxiety-buffering role of interpersonal attachments continues well into adulthood (Hart, Shaver, & Goldenberg, 2005; Mikulincer et al., 2003). Parents continue to function as a safe haven in the face of death thoughts, as revealed by studies showing that activating thoughts of one's parent in response to mortality reminders reduces death-thought accessibility and worldview defense (Cox et al., 2008). Close personal relationships—be they with family members, romantic partners, or friends—work in concert with faith in one's worldview and self-esteem in a dynamic, interrelated system to provide protection against existential anxiety.

In support of the anxiety-buffering function of personal relationships, mortality reminders have been found to increase people's willingness to initiate social interactions and decrease their sensitivity to rejection (Taubman Ben-Ari, Findler, & Mikulincer, 2002). Research has also shown that mortality thoughts lead to reports of increased commitment to one's romantic partner (Florian, Mikulincer, & Hirschberger, 2002). Conversely, inducing participants to think about their relationship problems (Florian et al., 2002) or about fear of intimacy (Taubman Ben-Ari, 2004) increases the accessibility of death-related thoughts. Consistent with the idea that close personal attachments serve to buffer death anxiety, writing about one's romantic commitment has been demonstrated to eliminate the need to resort to worldview defense after mortality reminders (Florian et al., 2002).

Research also shows that individual differences in attachment style predict differences in how people respond to existential threats. While correlational studies document that securely attached individuals report less fear of death than insecurely attached individuals (Mikulincer, Florian, & Tolmacz, 1990), experiments show that chronic attachment styles moderate terror management defenses. Mikulincer and Florian (2000), for example, found that mortality reminders led to harsher judgments about moral transgressions among insecurely attached, but not securely attached, individuals. In contrast, death thoughts led to an increase in one's sense of symbolic immortality and in the desire for intimacy among securely attached persons but not insecurely attached persons. From this body of research, close personal relationships emerge as an integral part of the existential anxiety-buffer system—intimately related to self-esteem and worldview validation needs, but distinct from them. It is possible that the reliance on interpersonal attachments as an existential defense involves more automatic and biologically based mechanisms, while worldview defense is mediated by cultural-symbolic processes (Wisman & Koole, 2003).

The social dimension constitutes an extraordinarily important aspect of the human experience—heaven, as well as hell, is indeed other people. In this section, we have reviewed the role that existential concerns play on this dimension. As we have seen, the groups to which we belong and the people with whom we relate can provide meaning, value,

a sense of security, and the hope of transcending death, thereby acting as a powerful balm against existential fear.

The Spiritual Dimension

The spiritual dimension entails the human proclivity to connect with something greater than oneself, typically involving abstract, supernatural, magical, or divine beings or entities. It encompasses our beliefs, values, and ideals pertaining to these entities as well as the experiences and altered states of consciousness that are often part of these relationships. From an existential perspective, the spiritual dimension functions to help people transcend the limitations of human existence in general and mortality in particular. In this section, we will review research on how concerns about mortality affect behavior on the spiritual dimension, particularly when it comes to the questions of meaning, religion, and spirituality.

Human beings require meaning, both to navigate through the mundane tasks of daily life and to imbue their lives with purpose and transcendent value (Frankl, 1963). To live without meaning, values, or ideals is distressing (Yalom, 1980), and many people are willing to live and die for their ideals and values. TMT posits that believing that things are as they are supposed to be—that the mundane ways of life make sense, and that human existence fits into some overall meaningful pattern—provides the coherence, structure, and security that protect people against death anxiety. Indeed, cultural worldviews and personal relationships can succeed as existential anxiety buffers only to the extent they provide the individual with this sense of meaning.

Supporting the notion that maintaining a meaningful view of reality is essential for protection against existential anxiety, research finds, for example, that reminders of mortality increase distaste for apparently meaningless art, particularly among those who dispositionally prefer unambiguous knowledge (Landau, Greenberg, Solomon, Pyszczynski, & Martens, 2006). Similarly, Vess, Routledge, Landau, and Arndt (2009) documented that death reminders bolster perceptions of life's meaning among participants with a high personal need for structure—those who are inclined to prefer simple and unambiguous interpretations of reality. Furthermore, death thoughts are found to lead people to imbue everyday actions with more meaning and to judge their current actions to be more meaningfully connected to their long-term goals (Landau, Kosloff, & Schmeichel, 2010). The desire to see the world as a just and orderly place (Lerner, 1980) can also be considered a manifestation of the fundamental need for meaning, structure, and comprehensibility. In line with this, Landau and colleagues (2004) found that for participants high in need for structure, reminders of mortality increased preference for narratives that suggest a just world and a benevolent causal order of events in the social world (see also Hirschberger, 2006).

This body of research, taken together, suggests that thoughts of death intensify the desire to see the world as a meaningful, structured, and ordered place, particularly for people who are predisposed to simpler interpretations of reality. Mortality thoughts also seem to intensify the need to find meaning on a larger scale, a so-called cosmic meaning—the sense that "life in general or at least human life fits into some overall coherent pattern" (Yalom, 1980, p. 423). In Becker's words, "man cannot endure his own littleness unless he can translate it into meaningfulness on the largest possible level" (1973, p. 196). The belief that there is some superordinate design to life and that each individual has some particular role to play in this design can thus be an extraordinary source of existential comfort.

Historically, religions have been the major sources of cosmic meaning, and despite the increase in popularity of atheistic worldviews (e.g., Dawkins, 2006; Harris, 2004; Hitchens, 2007), this is true for the vast majority of people today as well. Religions, typically, offer a comprehensive meaning schema, according to which the world and human life are part of a divinely ordained plan. This plan includes stories about the origin of the universe, clear moral guidelines, and theodicies that help people explain and endure suffering—all of which make the inevitability of death easier to handle. American historian and philosopher Will Durant talked about the "eternal hunger of mankind for supernatural consolations" (1932, p. 36), and TMT argues that this hunger stems largely from existential anxieties, and particularly the need to deal with the overwhelming reality of death (for a comprehensive review of the terror management function of religion, see Vail et al., 2010).

Religions, unlike any other institutions, are capable of promising literal immortality to their believers—in the form of heaven, reincarnation, or some other form of afterlife—which can be a powerful tool in mollifying death anxiety. Research shows, for example, that among those who believe in an afterlife, reminders of death increase this belief (Osarchuk & Tatz, 1973). Further support for the anxiety-buffering effects of belief in afterlife is provided by Dechesne and colleagues (2003), who found that exposure to scientific-looking evidence about the existence of life after death eliminates the typical increased worldview defense and striving for self-esteem that is produced by death primes. Mortality reminders have also been demonstrated to intensify faith in supernatural agents. Norenzayan and Hansen (2006) found that after the activation of death thoughts, North Americans, particularly those who were religiously affiliated, displayed stronger belief in God and divine intervention, even showing greater belief in spiritual entities associated with religious faiths other than their own.

Research also suggests that different orientations to religious faith have different psychological consequences. Whereas a fundamentalist orientation has been shown to be associated with a variety of socially undesirable tendencies, an intrinsic orientation appears to be especially effective in managing death-related fears. Religious fundamentalism refers to the belief that there is one absolute truth and that all other belief systems are wrong and evil. A large body of research has found religious fundamentalism to be positively associated with racial prejudice (e.g., Altemeyer, 2003; Altemeyer & Hunsberger, 1992; Laythe, Finkel, & Kirkpatrick, 2001), religious ethnocentrism (Altemeyer, 2003), and support for militarism (e.g., Henderson-King, Henderson-King, Bolea, Koches, & Kauffman, 2004; Nelson & Milburn, 1999). These attitudes are mediated by the absolutist authoritarian structure of the fundamentalist's belief system (Laythe et al., 2001). A rigid black-and-white orientation to truth is likely to make beliefs that deviate from one's own especially threatening and thus encourage more vigorous attempts to assert the correctness of those beliefs—derogation of and violence toward those with different beliefs are ways of bolstering confidence in the veracity of one's own beliefs.

Intrinsic religious orientation, on the other hand, seems to have more benefits and few costs. Batson, Schoenrade, and Ventis (1993) report that intrinsic religious beliefs are associated with lessened death anxiety and heightened existential well-being. Research also shows that people high in intrinsic religiousness do not engage in some forms of worldview defense after reminders of mortality, and experience lessened death-thought accessibility following mortality salience if they are given a chance to affirm their religious beliefs (Jonas & Fischer, 2006).

Becker (1973) notes the distinctive human need "to spiritualize human life, to lift it onto a special immortal plane, beyond the cycles of life and death that characterize all other organisms" (p. 231). While religions can effectively address this need for some people, others prefer less clearly structured forms of spirituality. Spirituality can be defined as a "personal quest for understanding answers to ultimate questions about life, about meaning, and about relationship to the sacred or transcendent" (Koenig, McCullough, & Larson, 2001, p. 18). The idea of the sacred is considered to be the distinctive core of spirituality (e.g., Pargament, 1999), and it has been frequently proposed that people fervently desire to live in a "sacralized cosmos" (Eliade, 1959). By providing a sense of transcendence, boundlessness, ultimate value and purpose, the sacred can alleviate the pain accompanying one's awareness of creatureliness, powerlessness, and ultimate finitude. Supporting this notion, studies show that construing different aspects of the world (e.g., nature, children, music) in sacred terms can protect the individual against death anxiety and its possibly destructive effects such as outgroup hostility and materialism (Kesebir, Chiu, & Pyszczynski, unpublished data).

The human predilection for a sacred, magical, divinely inspired view of reality can also manifest itself in the affection for charismatic leaders, for hero worshipping, and the fascination with celebrities. The word *charisma*, for example, originates from a Greek word meaning "divine gift," or "talent from God," and studies find that reminders of death intensify preference and support for charismatic leaders who proclaim the superiority of one's ingroup (Cohen, Solomon, Maxfield, Pyszczynski, & Greenberg, 2004). Cultural heroes, as well as famous people who represent individually and collectively held values, tend to be perceived as symbolically and literally immortal, which might help their admirers to transcend death and insignificance by proxy. In support of the existential function of famous people, Kesebir, Chiu, and Kim (unpublished data) demonstrated that after mortality reminders, participants expect famous people to be remembered for a longer time in the future, and this effect is qualified by how much the famous people represent cultural values. Similarly, the more a famous person was perceived to represent her culture's values, the less likely people thought that a plane she boarded would crash. These findings suggest that charismatic, heroic, or famous people might occupy a demigod status in the eyes of their fans, and in so doing provide them with meaning and existential stamina.

In this section, we have argued that humans harbor a potent need for an all-encompassing sense of meaning, an underlying reality that transcends everyday life, and a sacralized, magical cosmos—a need that is, at least partially, driven by existential concerns. This concludes our discussion of how existential motivation influences the human experience on the four dimensions of living. Our review suggests that on all the four dimensions—the physical, social, psychological, and spiritual—knowledge of one's mortality and accompanying existential concerns intensify people's striving for special meaning, value, and security. An inevitable fate of nonexistence, a realization that "our existence is but a brief crack of light between two eternities of darkness" (Nabokov, 1999, p. 9), is extremely difficult to accept, which renders the quest for assurances of invulnerability a primary human motive. As we have seen, a broad array of human behaviors—from self-esteem striving to outgroup derogation, from materialism to spirituality—serve to provide protection against existential dread. The breadth and depth of phenomena that have been subjected to research by TMT and shown to be affected by existential concerns testifies to the prominent role that existential motivation plays in human life. There remains, however, one last behavioral tendency that can be induced by existential motivation we have not yet explored.

Transcending Death by Escaping Self-Awareness

As discussed earlier in this chapter, self-awareness is a prerequisite for experiencing existential anxiety. In support of this claim, research shows that simple self-awareness manipulations, such as viewing oneself in a mirror, increase the accessibility of thoughts about both life and death (Silvia, 2001). This suggests that escaping self-awareness would be one way to obviate the problem of thoughts of death. Indeed, research has shown that participants induced to write about death spend less time on the task when they are made to feel self-aware (Arndt, Greenberg, Simon, Pyszczynski, & Solomon, 1998). This indicates that self-awareness makes mortality thoughts either more accessible or more threatening.

According to self-awareness theory (Duval & Wicklund, 1972), self-focused attention triggers evaluative processes in which people compare themselves to whatever standards and values are currently salient. If they perceive themselves as falling short of these standards, they either change their behavior in the direction of the standards or attempt to resolve the distress this produces by trying to lose self-awareness (Carver & Scheier, 1981; Duval & Wicklund, 1972).

TMT suggests that self-awareness leads to comparison with standards, and to behavior aimed at reducing any discrepancies that are detected, because self-awareness can cause a leakage of existential terror. As a way to buffer this terror, people strive to meet their standards of value and acquire the self-esteem this brings (Pyszczynski, Greenberg, Solomon, & Hamilton, 1990), which both require comparisons with standards to effectively accomplish. Consistent with this analysis, self-awareness has been shown to lead to a host of behaviors that are also induced by mortality reminders—behaviors more in tune with both personal and social standards of value (Diener & Wallbom, 1976; Scheier & Carver, 1988; Wicklund, 1975) or behaviors aimed at maintaining self-esteem such as the self-serving attributional bias (Duval & Silvia, 2002; Federoff & Harvey, 1976).

The human eagerness to lose self-awareness, escape consciousness, or enter a state of forgetfulness of existence can thus be a response to existential anxiety. The TMT analysis suggests that underlying the desire to escape self-awareness is something even deeper than the wish to escape thoughts of one's shortcomings or the modern culture's emphasis on and fascination with selfhood (Baumeister, 1991)—it is the need to evade confrontation with the existential reality of death and the potential for terror this invokes. A variety of behaviors have been shown to reduce levels of self-awareness, including alcohol consumption (Hull, 1981), binge eating (Heatherton & Baumeister, 1991), television viewing (Moskalenko, & Heine, 2003), and sexual masochism (Baumeister, 1988). Spiritual exercises such as meditation are also considered to lead to lower levels of self-awareness (Baumeister, 1991). A myriad of religious doctrines converge on the importance of shedding the self and emphasize mystical practices that help one lose self-consciousness—such as reaching Nirvana in Buddhism or fanaa in Sufism. In principle, any absorbing activity can provide an effective means of escape. Csikszentmihalyi's concept of flow, which he characterizes as a process that produces optimal human experience, similarly entails a loss of self-consciousness, a merging of action and awareness, and a transformation of one's perception of time (Csikszentmihalyi, 1975). It appears that avenues for escaping self-awareness can cover a broad range from the most sadly self-destructive to the most spiritually exalted, and according to TMT, they all help shield the individual from the existentially problematic implications of self-awareness.

Research testing the effects of mortality reminders on the desire to engage in activities that promote loss of self-awareness is still at a preliminary stage. Yet there are data showing that death-related stimuli increase consumers' desire to purchase higher quantities of food products and lead them to actually eat higher quantities, particularly among those who have low self-esteem (Mandel & Smeesters, 2008). Similarly, Hirschberger and Ein-Dor (2005) found that eating a tasty snack eliminated the effects of MS on defensive responses. There is also a plethora of anecdotal evidence suggesting that after the 9/11 attacks, Americans resorted to drinking, gambling, renting videos, watching television, and shopping as a way to deal with the shock (Pyszczynski, Solomon, & Greenberg, 2003). *The New York Times*, for example, reports three months after the event that according to liquor distributors, "the dramatic rise in consumption of alcoholic beverages immediately after September 11 was a nationwide phenomenon" (Burros, 2001). This could be interpreted as an attempt on the Americans' part to flee the massive existential insecurity produced by the 9/11 attacks. There is also indirect evidence for the idea that existential anxiety can generate the urge to escape self-awareness: Studies show that among restrained eaters, self-esteem threats increase the amount of eating (Heatherton, Herman, & Polivy, 1991; Polivy, Herman, & McFarlane, 1994), suggesting that a threat to one's existential anxiety buffer might intensify the desire to lose self-awareness.

Under what conditions would existential anxiety drive people to shut off self-awareness, and under what conditions would it lead to a more active striving for meaning, value, and security? This question is critical, considering that people's attempts to escape self-awareness sometimes occur through extremely self-destructive means. Previous research suggests that avoidance of self-awareness occurs primarily when people perceive the discrepancy between their current state and ideal state to be so high that it is unlikely to be reduced (Duval, Duval, & Mulilis, 1992). Drawing a parallel, we might predict that existential anxiety is most likely to lead to self-escapist behaviors when people perceive the gap between their actual self and ideal self as hardly bridgeable, when they are having extreme difficulties finding meaning in their lives or reconciling their worldviews with their life experiences. In other words, people would resort to escapism in the face of existential anxiety, when their anxiety buffers are— temporarily or chronically—not strong enough to provide protection. The most extreme, irreversible form of flight from the self is suicide (Baumeister, 1990), and in our analysis, people would be more likely to commit suicide when their anxiety buffers have stopped functioning entirely and the ensuing terror is overwhelming. An existence devoid of any meaning, value, or hope would turn self-awareness into an unbearable state and might make suicide an appealing escape. After all, ironically, dying seems to be the one certain way to rid oneself from existential anxiety for good (Greenberg, Solomon, & Arndt, 2008).

Escape from self-awareness might also be likely when people's self-regulatory energies are depleted and they lack the stamina needed for actively pursuing death transcendence. Gailliot, Schmeichel, and Baumeister (2006) reported an inverse relationship between strength of self-control and the accessibility of death thoughts—people who are good at self-control seem to have lower levels of chronic death-thought accessibility, while reminders of mortality are shown to lead to poorer self-regulation. When we consider that lack of self-control would be associated with behaviors aimed at escaping the self, the moderating role of self-control in the relationship between death thoughts and the demand for losing self-awareness becomes apparent: If death thoughts reduce the capacity for self-control, they would be even more likely to lead to self-escapist behaviors. Discovering ways to prevent the depletion of self-regulatory resources in the face of existential anxiety, or to replenish them, seems thus a worthy goal for future research.

In sum, the capacity for existential anxiety is a consequence of self-awareness and the existential burden is felt most deeply when we are self-aware. In some instances, particularly when the anxiety buffer is doing a poor job in counteracting existential anxiety, people might choose to avoid the self-focused state as a way to make the problem of existence disappear. We have initial evidence on the role of existential anxiety in prompting the desire to escape self-awareness; however, we believe that the topic needs to be explored further, given the serious costs associated with destructive escape strategies.

Remaining Issues and Future Directions

In the preceding sections, we have presented a myriad of studies demonstrating how existential concerns—and particularly death anxiety—can affect human behavior in diverse life domains. While we believe that the preponderance of evidence puts the role of existential anxiety as a motivational force for the human psyche beyond dispute, questions and unexplored areas, naturally, remain. We have touched upon some of these issues earlier in our discussion, and before concluding, we wish to briefly comment on a few others.

Over the years, TMT studies underwent a number of refinements and improvements in methodology. This allowed us to obtain converging support for the predictions of the theory through a variety of operationalizations and to broaden our understanding of the mechanisms involved in terror management. Open-ended items about mortality, death anxiety scales, proximity to funeral homes, and subliminal death primes, for example, have all been shown to instigate terror management responses—a testament to the validity of the role death concerns play in human motivation. When it comes to the topic of methodology, however, we should remember that a whopping majority of TMT studies test the mortality salience hypothesis; that is, they make mortality thoughts salient to assess their effects on the dependent variable (Burke et al., 2010). While this is a powerful and indispensable tool to test hypotheses derived from TMT, the theory would benefit from new and creative methods to explore the workings of terror management. In that sense, the increasingly common use of the death-thought accessibility methodology in the literature (Hayes et al., 2010) is encouraging, though not sufficient. We encourage researchers to venture beyond the tried-and-true methods.

Perhaps the most common criticism leveled against TMT has been that the effects obtained in response to mortality salience may not be unique to thoughts of death per se, but are due to some other aversive state elicited by death thoughts (e.g., negative affect, arousal) or some other threat inherent in the knowledge of mortality (e.g., meaninglessness, uncertainty, lack of control). Although some studies have found that threats to one's meaning system or sense of certainty produce the same effects as those produced by mortality reminders (e.g., Proulx & Heine, 2008; van den Bos, Poortvliet, Maas, Miedema, & van den Ham, 2005), the bulk of empirical evidence suggests that priming alternative topics (e.g., meaninglessness, uncertainty, cultural values, failure, giving a speech in public, worries about life after college, social exclusion, general anxiety, dental pain, general pain, paralysis) typically fails to produce the same defensive responses as priming mortality thoughts (Greenberg et al., 2008). Additionally, a recent meta-analysis finds that the effects produced by mortality salience follow the unique, signature time course—death thoughts have more influence on distal or symbolic TMT defenses after a delay—consistent with the dual process model described by Pyszczynski and colleagues (1999). Furthermore, a growing number of studies, as we reviewed earlier, reveal that threats to one's anxiety buffer make thoughts of death, but not thoughts of other threats, more accessible. We believe these findings constitute convincing evidence affirming the specific role of death concerns.

Although we attribute a unique quality to awareness of death for the human motivational system, by no means do we wish to intimate that threats to meaning or uncertainty are without consequence. On the contrary, as we repeatedly noted, meaning and certainty are essential components of the anxiety buffer. Indeed, TMT posits that elements of the anxiety-buffering system are effective only to the extent they are held with certainty or faith and provide the person with a sense of meaning and value. We view existential anxiety as a complex force that is born from the clash of human desires with the realities of existence. TMT construes the conflict between the biologically rooted desire for immortality and the inevitability of death as leading people to need certainty regarding whatever system of meaning they use to feel safe and secure.

One way of resolving this issue is to view threats to meaning, structure, and certainty as threatening for both epistemic and existential reasons. Epistemically, people need certainty about a structured and meaningful world because this provides a basis for confident action. This generally motivates people to seek accurate understandings that will help them attain their goals that ultimately relate to evolved proclivities for survival and reproductive success. These motives, at least in rudimentary form, probably exist in all animals (except perhaps the simplest ones). Although there may be rare instances in which an inaccurate understanding of reality facilitates the attainment of concrete goals, accuracy is the general rule. Existentially, people need certainty regarding well-structured meanings that help them cope with the fears that result from their awareness of the reality that existence is finite. This often, though not always, leads to a preference for fanciful wish-fulfilling beliefs that bear little relation to objective reality and to avoidance of and disdain for anything that might challenge these beliefs. It may be, then, that the biases and defenses instigated by epistemic and existential threats often take different *forms*, and this might help reconcile TMT with other theories that emphasize the needs for meaning and certainty (Heine, Proulx, & Vohs, 2006; Lind & van den Bos, 2002). That said, we believe that these accounts have more in common than not, and despite their differences, they all shed light on how existential anxiety motivates human behavior

(for a detailed discussion of how these accounts interrelate, see Pyszczynski, Greenberg, Solomon, & Maxfield, 2006).

Conclusion

"Death is immense/We all are his/with laughing mouths/When we are in/the midst of life/he dares to weep/right in our midst" goes the *End Poem* by celebrated Bohemian-Austrian poet Rainer Maria Rilke. These lines constitute a literary tribute to the role that knowledge of death plays in our lives, of which we are perhaps not sufficiently aware. In this chapter, we have tried to elucidate this role, based on TMT research that emerged over the last 25 years. We have argued that the desire to transcend death is a powerful motive in human life. A broad array of human behaviors seems to ultimately serve to render death anxiety and accompanying existential anxieties less accessible or less threatening.

Despite the problems that result from human awareness of the inevitability of death, many thinkers have argued that what gives life its depth and intensity is its limited duration. We echo these sentiments in suggesting that, though agonizing, heightened awareness of death—rather than a forgetfulness or denial of it—might ultimately lead us to happier, wiser, more authentic lives. The picture that emerged from terror management theory research regarding the role of death in human life to date has mostly been a dark, unappealing one. It is possible, however, that people can turn the reality of death into a constructive, empowering force for their lives. Research with people who had near encounters with death or those who experienced posttraumatic growth attests to the tremendously positive, transformative impact that death can have on some people. The next frontier of terror management theory might thus be a positive existential psychology—a research area that investigates how death thoughts can become a source of strength and virtue rather than a source of dread and destruction.

References

Abdollahi, A., Pyszczynski, T., Maxfield, M., & Luszczynska, A. (in press). Posttraumatic stress reactions as a disruption in anxiety-buffer functioning: Dissociation and responses to mortality salience as predictors of severity of post-traumatic symptoms. *Psychological Trauma: Theory, Research, Practice, and Policy*.

Altemeyer, B. (2003). Why do religious fundamentalists tend to be prejudiced? *The International Journal for the Psychology of Religion, 13*, 17–28.

Altemeyer, B., & Hunsberger, B. (1992). Authoritarianism, religious fundamentalism, quest, and prejudice. *The International Journal for the Psychology of Religion, 2*, 113–133.

Arndt, J., Greenberg, J., Schimel, J., Pyszczynski, T., & Solomon, S. (2002). To belong or not to belong, that is the question: Terror management and identification with gender and ethnicity. *Journal of Personality and Social Psychology, 83,* 26–43.

Arndt, J., Greenberg, J., Simon, L., Pyszczynski, T., & Solomon, S. (1998). Terror management and self-awareness: Evidence that mortality salience provokes avoidance of the self-focused state. *Personality and Social Psychological Bulletin, 24,* 1216–1227.

Arndt, J., Routledge, C., Cox, C. R., & Goldenberg, J. L. (2005). The worm at the core: A terror management perspective on the roots of psychological dysfunction. *Applied and Preventative Psychology, 11,* 191–213.

Arndt, J., & Solomon, S. (2003). The control of death and the death of control: The effects of mortality salience, neuroticism, and worldview threat on the desire for control. *Journal of Research in Personality, 37,* 1–22.

Batson, C. D., Schoenrade, P., & Ventis, W. L. (1993). *Religion and the individual: A social-psychological perspective.* New York: Oxford University Press.

Baumeister, R. F. (1988). Masochism as escape from self. *Journal of Sex Research, 25,* 28–59.

Baumeister, R. F. (1990). Suicide as escape from self. *Psychological Review, 97,* 90–113.

Baumeister, R. F. (1991). *Escaping the self: Alcoholism, spirituality, masochism, and other flights from the burden of selfhood.* New York: Basic Books.

Baumeister, R. F., & Leary, M. R. (1995). The need to belong: Desire for interpersonal attachments as a fundamental human motivation. *Psychological Bulletin, 117,* 497–529.

Becker, E. (1971). The *birth and death of meaning.* New York: Free Press.

Becker, E. (1973) *The denial of death.* New York: Free Press.

Becker, E. (1975). *Escape from evil.* New York: Free Press.

Belk, R. W. (1985). Materialism: Trait aspects of living in the material world. *Journal of Consumer Research, 12,* 265–280.

Binswanger, L. (1946). The existential analysis school of thought. In R. May, E. Angel, & H. F. Ellenberger (Eds.), *Existence* (pp. 191–213). New York: Basic Books.

Bowlby, J. (1969). *Attachment and loss: Attachment.* New York: Basic Books.

Buber, M. (1923). *I and thou* (Trans. W. Kaufmann). Edinburgh, Scotland: T&T Clark.

Burke, B. L., Martens, A., & Faucher, E. H. (2010). Two decades of terror management theory: A meta-analysis of mortality salience research. *Personality and Social Psychology Review, 14,* 155–195.

Burros, M. (2001, December 5). In a stressed city, no room at the bar. *The New York Times.* Retrieved from http://www.nytimes.com/2001/12/05/dining/in-a-stressed-city-no-room-at-the-bar.html

Carver, C.S. (1979). A cybernetic model of self-attention processes. *Journal of Personality and Social Psychology, 37,* 1251–1281.

Carver, C. S., & Scheier, M. F. (1981). *Attention and self-regulation: A control-theory approach to human behavior.* New York: Springer.

Carver, C. S., & Scheier, M. F. (2002). Control processes and self-organization as complementary principles underlying behavior. *Personality and Social Psychology Review, 6,* 304–315.

Castano, E., Yzerbyt, V., Paladino, M-P., & Sacchi, S. (2002). I belong, therefore, I exist: Ingroup identification, ingroup entitativity, and ingroup bias. *Personality and Social Psychology Bulletin, 28,* 135–143.

Chatard, A., Pyszczynski, T., Arndt, J., Selimbegović, L., Konan, P., & Van der Linden, M. (2011). Extent of trauma exposure and PTSD symptom severity as predictors of anxiety-buffer functioning. *Trauma Psychology: Theory, Research, Practice, and Policy,* doi: 10.1037/a0021085.

Cohen, F., Solomon, S., Maxfield, M., Pyszczynski, T., & Greenberg J. (2004). Fatal attraction: The effects of mortality salience on evaluations of charismatic, task-oriented, and relationship-oriented leaders. *Psychological Science, 15,* 846–851.

Cox, C. R., Arndt, J., Pyszczynski, T., Greenberg, J., Abdollahi, A., & Solomon, S. (2008). Terror management and adults' attachment to their parents: The safe haven remains. *Journal of Personality and Social Psychology, 94,* 696–717.

Cox, C. R., Goldenberg, J. L., Pyszczynski, T., & Weise, D. (2007). Disgust, creatureliness, and the accessibility of death related thoughts. *European Journal of Social Psychology, 37,* 494–507.

Csikszentmihalyi, M. (1975). *Beyond boredom and anxiety.* San Francisco, CA: Jossey-Bass, Inc.

Dawkins, R. (2006). *The God delusion.* London: Bantam.

Dechesne, M., Greenberg, J., Arndt, J., & Schimel, J. (2000). Terror management and the vicissitudes of sports fan affiliation: The effects of mortality salience on optimism and fan identification. *European Journal of Social Psychology, 30,* 813–835.

Dechesne, M., Pyszczynski, T., Arndt, J., Ransom, S., Sheldon, K. M., van Knippenberg, A., & Janssen, J. (2003). Literal and symbolic immortality: The effect of evidence of literal immortality on self-esteem striving in response to mortality salience. *Journal of Personality and Social Psychology, 84,* 722–737.

Diener, E., & Wallbom, M. (1976). Effects of self-awareness on antinormative behavior. *Journal of Research in Personality, 10,* 107–111.

Durant, W. (1932). *On the meaning of life.* New York: Ray Long & Richard R. Smith.

Duval, T., Duval, V., & Mulilis, J. (1992). Effects of self-focus, discrepancy between self and standard, and outcome expectancy favorability on the tendency to match self to standard and withdraw. *Journal of Personality and Social Psychology, 62,* 340–348.

Duval, T. S., & Silvia, P. J. (2001). *Self-awareness and causal attribution: A dual-systems theory.* Boston, MA: Kluwer Academic Publishers.

Duval, T. S., & Silvia, P. J. (2002). Self-awareness, probability of improvement, and the self-serving bias. *Journal of Personality and Social Psychology, 82,* 49–61.

Duval, S., & Wicklund, R. A. (1972) *A theory of objective self-awareness.* New York: Academic Press.

Edmondson, D. (2009). *From shattered assumptions to weakened worldviews: Evidence of anxiety buffer disruption in individuals with trauma symptoms.* Unpublished Ph.D. dissertation, University of Connecticut, Storrs.

Eliade, M. (1959). *The sacred and the profane.* (Trans. W. R. Trask). San Diego, CA: Harcourt.

Federoff, N. A., & Harvey, J. H. (1976). Focus of attention, self-esteem, and the attribution of causality. *Journal of Research in Personality, 10,* 336–345.

Florian, V., & Mikulincer, M. (1998). Symbolic immortality and the management of the terror of death: The moderating role of attachment style. *Journal of Personality and Social Psychology, 74*, 725–734.

Florian, V., Mikulincer, M., & Hirschberger, G. (2002). The anxiety-buffering function of close relationships: Evidence that relationship commitment acts as a terror management mechanism. *Journal of Personality and Social Psychology, 82*, 527–542.

Frankl, V. E. (1963). *Man's search for meaning.* New York: Simon & Schuster.

Gailliot, M. T., Schmeichel, B. J., & Baumeister, R. F. (2006). Self-regulatory processes defend against the threat of death: Effects of self-control depletion and trait self-control on thoughts and fears of dying. *Journal of Personality and Social Psychology, 91*, 49–62.

Goldenberg, J. L., & Arndt, J. (2008). The implications of death for health: A terror management model of behavioral health promotion. *Psychological Review, 15*, 1032–1053.

Goldenberg, J. L., Arndt, J., Hart, J., & Routledge, C. (2008). Uncovering an existential barrier to breast self-exam behavior. *Journal of Experimental Social Psychology, 44*, 260–274.

Goldenberg, J. L., Cox, C. R., Pyszczynski, T., Greenberg, J., & Solomon, S. (2002). Understanding human ambivalence about sex: The effects of stripping sex of meaning. *Journal of Sex Research, 39*, 310–320.

Goldenberg, J. L., McCoy, S. K., Pyszczynski, T., Greenberg, J., & Solomon, S. (2000). The body as a source of self-esteem: The effect of mortality salience on identification with one's body, interest in sex, and appearance monitoring. *Journal of Personality and Social Psychology, 79*, 118–130.

Goldenberg, J. L., Pyszczynski, T., McCoy, S. K., Greenberg, J., & Solomon, S. (1999). Death, sex, love, and neuroticism: Why is sex such a problem? *Journal of Personality and Social Psychology, 77*, 1173–1187.

Goldenberg, J. L., Pyszczynski, T., Greenberg, J., Solomon, S., Kluck, B., & Cornwell, R. (2001). I am not an animal: Mortality salience, disgust, and the denial of human creatureliness. *Journal of Experimental Psychology, 130*, 427–435.

Goldenberg, J. L., Routledge, C., & Arndt, J. (2009). Mammograms and the management of existential discomfort: Threats associated with the physicality of the body and neuroticism. *Psychology and Health, 24*, 563–581.

Greenberg, J., Arndt, J., Simon, L., Pyszczynski, T., & Solomon, S. (2000). Proximal and distal defenses in response to reminders of one's mortality: Evidence of a temporal sequence. *Personality and Social Psychology Bulletin, 26*, 91–99.

Greenberg, J., Koole, S., & Pyszczynski, T. (2004). *Handbook of experimental existential psychology.* New York: The Guilford Press.

Greenberg, J., Pyszczynski, T., & Solomon, S. (1986). The causes and consequences of a need for self-esteem: A terror management theory. In R. F. Baumeister (Ed.), *Public self and private self* (pp. 189–212). New York, NY: Springer-Verlag.

Greenberg, J., Pyszczynski, T., Solomon, S., Pinel, E., Simon, L., & Jordan, K. (1993). Effects of self-esteem on vulnerability-denying defensive distortions: Further evidence of an anxiety-buffering function of self-esteem. Journal of Experimental Social Psychology, 29, 229–251.

Greenberg, J., Pyszczynski, T., Solomon, S., Rosenblatt, A., Veeder, M., Kirkland, S., & Lyon, D. (1990). Evidence for terror management II: The effects of mortality salience on reactions to those who threaten or bolster the cultural worldview. *Journal of Personality and Social Psychology, 58*, 308–318.

Greenberg, J., Pyszczynski, T., Solomon, S., Simon, L., & Breus, M. (1994). Role of consciousness and accessibility of death-related thoughts in mortality salience effects. *Journal of Personality and Social Psychology, 67*, 627–637.

Greenberg, J., Simon, L., Pyszczynski, T., Solomon, S., & Chatel, D. (1992). Terror management and tolerance: Does mortality salience always intensify negative reactions to others who threaten one's worldview? *Journal of Personality and Social Psychology, 63*, 212–220.

Greenberg, J., Solomon, S., & Arndt, J. (2008). A basic but uniquely human motivation: Terror management. In J. Y. Shah & W. L. Gardner (Eds.), *Handbook of motivation science* (pp. 114–134). New York: The Guilford Press.

Greenberg, J., Solomon, S., Pyszczynski, T., Rosenblatt, A., Burling, J., Lyon, D.,...Pinel, E. (1992). Why do people need self-esteem? Converging evidence that self-esteem serves as an anxiety-buffering function. *Journal of Personality and Social Psychology, 63*, 913–922.

Hardin, C. D., & Higgins, E. T. (1996). Shared reality: How social verification makes the subjective objective. In R. M. Sorrentino & E. T. Higgins (Eds.), *Handbook of motivation and cognition. Vol. 3: The interpersonal context* (pp. 28–84). New York: The Guilford Press.

Harmon-Jones, E., Greenberg, J., Solomon, S., & Simon, L. (1996). The effects of mortality salience on intergroup bias between minimal groups. *European Journal of Social Psychology, 26*, 677–681.

Harmon-Jones, E., Simon, L., Greenberg, J., Pyszczynski, T., Solomon, S., & McGregor, H. (1997). Terror management theory and self-esteem: Evidence that increased self-esteem reduces MS effects. *Journal of Personality and Social Psychology, 72*, 24–36.

Harris, S. (2004). *The end of faith: Religion, terror, and the future of reason.* New York: W.W. Norton.

Hart, J., Shaver, P. R., & Goldenberg, J. L. (2005). Attachment, self-esteem, worldviews, and terror management: Evidence for a tripartite security system. *Journal of Personality and Social Psychology, 88*, 999–1013.

Hayes, J., Schimel, J., Arndt, J., & Faucher, E. H. (2010). A theoretical and empirical review of the death-thought accessibility concept in terror management research. *Psychological Bulletin, 136*, 699–739.

Hayes, J., Schimel, J., Faucher, E. H., & Williams, T. J. (2008). Evidence for the DTA hypothesis II: Threatening self-esteem increases death-thought accessibility. *Journal of Experimental Social Psychology, 44*, 600–613.

Hayes, J., Schimel, J., & Williams, T. J. (2008). Fighting death with death: The buffering effects of learning that worldview violators have died. *Psychological Science, 19*, 501–507.

Heatherton, T. F., & Baumeister, R. F. (1991). Binge eating as escape from self-awareness. *Psychological Bulletin, 110*, 86–108.

Heatherton, T. F., Herman, C. P., & Polivy, J. (1991). The effects of physical threat and ego threat on eating. *Journal of Personality and Social Psychology, 60*, 138–143.

Heine, S. J., Harihara, M., & Niiya, Y. (2002). Terror management in Japan. *Asian Journal of Social Psychology, 5*, 187–196.

Heine, S., Proulx, T., & Vohs, K. (2006). The meaning maintenance model: On the coherence of social motivations. *Personality and Social Psychology Review, 10*, 88–110.

Henderson-King, D., Henderson-King, E., Bolea, B., Koches, K., & Kauffman, A. (2004). Seeking understanding or sending bombs: Beliefs as predictors of responses to terrorism. *Peace and Conflict: Journal of Peace Psychology, 10,* 67–84.

Hirschberger, G. (2006). Terror management and attributions of blame to innocent victims: Reconciling compassionate and defensive responses. *Journal of Personality and Social Psychology, 91,* 832–844.

Hirschberger, G., & Ein-Dor, T. (2005). Does a candy a day keep the death thoughts away? The terror management function of eating. *Basic and Applied Social Psychology, 27,* 179–186.

Hirschberger, G., & Ein-Dor, T. (2006). Defenders of a lost cause: Terror management and violent resistance to the disengagement plan. *Personality and Social Psychology Bulletin, 32,* 761–769.

Hirschberger, G., Florian, V., & Mikulincer, M. (2005). Fear and compassion: A terror management analysis of emotional reactions to persons with disabilities. *Rehabilitation Psychology, 50,* 246–257.

Hirschman, E. C. (1990). Secular immortality and the American ideology of affluence. *Journal of Consumer Research, 17,* 31–42.

Hitchens, C. (2007). *God is not great: How religion poisons everything.* New York: Twelve Books.

Hull, J. G. (1981). A self-awareness model of the causes and effects of alcohol consumption. *Journal of Abnormal Psychology, 90,* 586–600.

Jacobsen, B. (2007). *Invitation to existential psychology: A psychology for the unique human being and its applications in therapy.* London: Wiley.

James, W. (1950). *The principles of psychology* (Vol. 1). New York: Dover Publications.

Jaspers, K. (1951). *Way to wisdom* (Trans. R. Manheim). New Haven and London: Yale University Press.

Jonas, E., & Fischer, P. (2006). Terror management and religion: Evidence that intrinsic religiousness mitigates worldview defense following mortality salience. *Journal of Personality and Social Psychology, 91,* 553–567.

Jonas, E., Martens, A., Niesta, D., Fritsche, I., Sullivan, D., & Greenberg, J. (2008). Focus theory of normative conduct and terror management theory: The interactive impact of mortality salience and norm salience on social judgment. *Journal of Personality and Social Psychology, 95,* 1239–1251.

Kasser, T., & Sheldon, K. M. (2000). Of wealth and death: Materialism, mortality salience, and consumption behavior. *Psychological Science, 11,* 348–351.

Kesebir, P., Luszczynska, A., Pyszczynski, T., & Benight, C. C. (in press). Posttraumatic stress disorder involves disrupted anxiety-buffer mechanisms. *Journal of Social and Clinical Psychology.*

Koenig, H. G., McCullough, M. E., & Larson, D. B. (2001). *Handbook of religion and health.* London: Oxford University Press.

Koltko-Rivera, M. E. (2004). The psychology of worldviews. *Review of General Psychology, 8,* 3–58.

Koole, S. L., & Van den Berg, A. E. (2005). Lost in the wilderness: Terror management, action orientation, and nature evaluation. *Journal of Personality and Social Psychology, 88,* 1014–1028.

Kruglanski, A. W., Chen, X., Dechesne, M., Fishman, S., & Orehek, E. (2009). Fully committed: Suicide bombers' motivation and the quest for personal significance. *Political Psychology, 30,* 331–357.

Landau, M. J., Greenberg, J., Solomon, S., Pyszczynski, T., & Martens, A. (2006). Windows into nothingness: Terror management, meaninglessness, and negative reactions to modern art. *Journal of Personality and Social Psychology, 90,* 879–892.

Landau, M. J., Johns, M., Greenberg, J., Pyszczynski, T., Solomon, S., & Martens, A. (2004). A Function of form: Terror management and structuring of the social world. *Journal of Personality and Social Psychology, 87,* 190–210.

Landau, M. J., Kosloff, S., & Schmeichel, B. (2010). Imbuing everyday actions with meaning in response to existential threat. *Self and Identity, 10,* 64–76.

Laythe, B., Finkel, D., & Kirkpatrick, L. A. (2001). Predicting prejudice from religious fundamentalism and right-wing authoritarianism: A multiple-regression approach. *Journal for the Scientific Study of Religion, 40,* 1–10.

Leary, M. R. (2004). *The curse of the self: Self-awareness, egotism, and the quality of human life.* New York: Oxford University Press.

Lerner, M. J. (1980). *The belief in a just world: A fundamental delusion.* New York: Plenum Press.

Lifton, R. J. (1979). *The broken connection: On death and the continuity of life.* New York: Simon & Schuster.

Lind, E. A., & van den Bos, K. (2002). When fairness works: Toward a general theory of uncertainty management. In B. M. Staw & R. M. Kramer (Eds.), *Research in organizational behavior* (Vol. 24, pp. 181–223). Greenwich, CT: JAI Press.

Lipsey, M. W., & Wilson, D. B. (1993). The efficacy of psychological, educational, and behavioral treatment: Confirmation from meta-analysis. *American Psychologist, 48,* 1181–1209.

Mandel, N., & Heine, S. J. (1999). Terror management and marketing: He who dies with the most toys wins. *Advances in Consumer Research, 26,* 527–532.

Mandel, N., & Smeesters, D. (2008). The sweet escape: The effects of mortality salience on consumption quantities for low and high self-esteem consumers. *Journal of Consumer Research, 35,* 309–323.

Malouff, J. M., Thorsteinsson, E. B., & Schutte, N. S. (2005). The relationship between the five-factor model of personality and symptoms of clinical disorders: A meta-analysis. *Journal of Psychopathology and Behavioral Assessment, 27,* 101–114.

Martens, A., Greenberg, J., Schimel, J., & Landau, M. J. (2004). Ageism and death: Effects of mortality salience and perceived similarity to elders on reactions to elderly people. *Personality and Social Psychology Bulletin, 30,* 1524–1536.

McGregor, H., A., Lieberman, J.D., Greenberg, J., Solomon, S. Arndt, J., Simon, L. & Pyszczynzki, T. (1998). Terror management and aggression: Evidence that mortality salience motivates aggression against worldview-threatening others. *Journal of Personality and Social Psychology, 74,* 590–605.

Mikulincer, M., & Florian, V. (2000). Exploring individual differences in reactions to mortality salience: Does attachment style regulate terror management mechanisms? *Journal of Personality and Social Psychology, 79,* 260–273.

Mikulincer, M., & Florian, V. (2002). The effect of mortality salience on self-serving attributions—Evidence for the function of self-esteem as a terror management mechanism. *Basic and Applied Social Psychology, 24,* 261–271.

Mikulincer, M., Florian, V., & Hirschberger, G. (2003). The existential function of close relationships: Introducing death into the science of love. *Personality and Social Psychology Review, 7,* 20–40.

Mikulincer, M., Florian, V., & Tolmacz, R. (1990). Attachment styles and fear of personal death: A case study of affect regulation. *Journal of Personality and Social Psychology*, *58*, 273–280.

Mitchell, R. W. (2003). Subjectivity and self-recognition in animals. In M. R. Leary & J. P. Tangney (Eds.), *Handbook of self and identity* (pp. 567–593). New York: The Guilford Press.

Moskalenko, S., & Heine, S. J. (2003). Watching your troubles away: Television viewing as a stimulus for subjective self-awareness. *Personality and Social Psychology Bulletin*, *29*, 76–85.

Motyl, M., Hart, J., & Pyszczynski, T. (2010). When animals attack: The effects of mortality salience, infrahumanization of violence, and authoritarianism on support for war. *Journal of Experimental Social Psychology*, *46*, 200–203.

Nabokov, V. (1999). *Speak, memory*. New York: Everyman's Library. (Original work published 1951).

Nelson, L. L., & Milburn, T. W. (1999). Relationships between problem-solving competencies and militaristic attitudes: Implications for peace education. *Peace and Conflict: Journal of Peace Psychology*, *5*, 149–168.

Norenzayan, A., & Hansen, I. G. (2006). Belief in supernatural agents in the face of death. *Personality and Social Psychology Bulletin*, *32*, 174–187.

Ogilvie, D. M., Cohen, F., & Solomon, S. (2008). The undesired self: Deadly connotations. *Journal of Research in Personality*, *42*, 564–576.

Osarchuk, M., & Tatz, S. J. (1973). Effect of induced fear of death on belief in afterlife. *Journal of Personality and Social Psychology*, *27*, 256–260.

Pargament, K. I. (1999). The psychology of religion and spirituality? Yes and no. *International Journal for the Psychology of Religion*, *9*, 3–16.

Pearce, S. M. (1992). *Museums, objects, and collections: A cultural study*. Leicester, England: Leicester University Press.

Peters, H. J., Greenberg, J., & Williams, J. M. (2005). Applying terror management theory to performance: Can reminding individuals of their mortality increase strength output? *Journal of Sport and Exercise Psychology*, *27*, 111–116.

Polivy, J., Herman, C. P., & McFarlane, T. (1994). Effects of anxiety on eating: Does palatability moderate distress-induced overeating in dieters? *Journal of Abnormal Psychology*, *103*, 505–510.

Proulx, T., & Heine, S. J. (2008). The case of the transmogrifying experimenter: Affirmation of a moral schema following implicit change detection. *Psychological Science*, *19*, 1294–1300.

Pyszczynski, T., Abdollahi, A., Solomon, S., Greenberg, J., Cohen, F., & Weise, D. (2006). Mortality salience, martyrdom, and military might: The Great Satan versus the Axis of Evil. *Personality and Social Psychology Bulletin*, *32*, 525–538.

Pyszczynski, T., & Greenberg, J. (1993). *Hanging on and letting go: Understanding the onset, maintenance, and remission of depression*. New York: Springer-Verlag.

Pyszczynski, T., Greenberg, J., & Solomon, S. (1999). A dual-process model of defense against conscious and unconscious death-related thoughts: An extension of terror management theory. *Psychological Review*, *106*, 835–845.

Pyszczynski, T., Greenberg, J., Solomon, S., Arndt, J., & Schimel, J. (2004). Why do people need self-esteem? A theoretical and empirical review. *Psychological Bulletin*, *130*, 435–468.

Pyszczynski, T., Greenberg, J., Solomon, S., & Hamilton, J. (1990). A terror management analysis of self-awareness and anxiety: The hierarchy of terror. *Anxiety Research*, *2*, 177–195.

Pyszczynski, T., Greenberg, J., Solomon, S., & Koole, S. L. (2010). Experimental existential psychology: Coping with the facts of life. In S. T. Fiske, D. T. Gilbert, & G. Lindzey (Eds.), *Handbook of social psychology* (5th ed., pp. 724–757). Hoboken, NJ: Wiley.

Pyszczynski, T., Greenberg, J., Solomon, S., & Maxfield, M. (2006). On the unique psychological import of the human awareness of mortality: Theme and variations. *Psychological Inquiry*, *17*, 328–356.

Pyszczynski, T., & Kesebir, P. (2011). Anxiety buffer disruption theory: A terror management account of posttraumatic stress disorder. *Anxiety, Stress, and Coping*, *24*, 3–26.

Pyszczynski, T., Solomon, S., & Greenberg, J. (2003). *In the wake of 9/11: The psychology of terror*. Washington, DC: American Psychological Association.

Richard, F. D., Bond, C. F., & Stokes-Zoota, J. J. (2003). One hundred years of social psychology quantitatively described. *Review of General Psychology*, *7*, 331–363.

Rindfleisch, A., Burroughs, J. E., & Wong, N. (2009). The safety of objects: Materialism, existential insecurity, and brand connection. *Journal of Consumer Research*, *36*, 1–16.

Rosenblatt, A., Greenberg, J., Solomon, S., Pyszczynski, T., & Lyon, D. (1989). Evidence for terror management theory I: The effects of mortality salience on reactions to those who violate or uphold cultural values. *Journal of Personality and Social Psychology*, *57*, 681–690.

Rothschild, Z., Abdollahi, A., & Pyszczynski, T. (2009). Does peace have a prayer? The effect of mortality salience, compassionate values and religious fundamentalism on hostility toward out-groups. *Journal of Experimental Social Psychology*, *45*, 816–827.

Routledge, C., Arndt, J., & Goldenberg, J. L. (2004). A time to tan: Proximal and distal effects of mortality salience on sun exposure intentions. *Personality and Social Psychology Bulletin*, *30*, 1347–1358.

Scheier, M. F., & Carver, C. S. (1988). A model of behavioral self-regulation: Translating intention into action. In L. Berkowitz (Ed.), *Advances in experimental social psychology* (Vol. 21, pp. 303–346). New York: Academic Press.

Schimel, J., Hayes, J., Williams, T., & Jahrig, J. (2007). Is death really the worm at the core? Converging evidence that worldview threat increases death-thought accessibility. *Journal of Personality and Social Psychology*, *92*, 789–803.

Schimel, J., Simon, L., Greenberg, J., Pyszczynski, T., Solomon, S., Wazmonsky, J., & Arndt, J. (1999). Stereotypes and terror management: Evidence that mortality salience enhances stereotypic thinking and preferences. *Journal of Personality and Social Psychology*, *77*, 905–926.

Silvia, P. J. (2001). Nothing or the opposite: Intersecting terror management and objective self-awareness. *European Journal of Personality*, *15*, 73–82.

Solomon, S., Greenberg, J., & Pyszczynski, T. (1991). A terror management theory of social behavior: On the psychological functions of self-esteem and cultural worldviews. In M. P. Zanna (Ed.), *Advances in experimental social psychology* (Vol. 24, pp. 93–159). San Diego, CA: Academic Press.

Solomon, S., Greenberg, J., Pyszczynski, T., Cohen, F., & Ogilvie, D. (2009). Teach these souls to fly: Supernatural as human adaptation. In M. Schaller, A. Norenzayan, S.

Heine, T. Yamagishi, & T. Kameda (Eds.), *Evolution, culture, and the human mind* (pp. 99–119) Mahwah, NJ: Lawrence Erlbaum.

Steinbeck, J. (1995). *Pastures of heaven.* New York: Penguin Classic.

Strachan, E., Schimel, J., Arndt, J., Williams, T., Solomon, S., Pyszczynski, T., & Greenberg, J. (2007). Terror mismanagement: Evidence that mortality salience exacerbates phobic and compulsive behaviors. *Personality and Social Psychology Bulletin, 33,* 1137–1151.

Superhuman heroes. (1998, June 6). *The Economist,* pp. 10–12.

Tam, K. P., Chiu, C. Y., & Lau, I. Y. (2007). Terror management among Chinese: Worldview defence and intergroup bias in resource allocation. *Asian Journal of Social Psychology, 10,* 93–102.

Taubman-Ben-Ari, O. (2004). Intimacy and risky sexual behavior—What does it have to do with death? *Death Studies, 28,* 865–887.

Taubman Ben-Ari, O., Findler, L., & Mikulincer, M. (2002) The effects of mortality salience on relationship strivings and beliefs: The moderating role of attachment style. *British Journal of Social Psychology, 41,* 419–441.

Taubman Ben-Ari, O., Florian, V., & Mikulincer, M. (1999). The impact of mortality salience on reckless driving: A test of terror management mechanisms. *Journal of Personality and Social Psychology, 76,* 35–45.

Tillich, P. (1952). *The courage to be.* Glasgow, Scotland: Collins/Fontana.

Vaes, J., Heflick, N., & Goldenberg, J. (2010)."We are people": Ingroup humanization as an existential defense. *Journal of Personality and Social Psychology, 98(5),* 750–760.

Vail, K., III, Rothchild, Z., Weise, D., Solomon, S., Pyszczynski, T., & Greenberg, J. (2010). A terror management analysis of the psychological functions of religion. *Personality and Social Psychology Review, 14,* 84–94.

van den Bos, K., Poortvliet, M., Maas, M., Miedema, J., & van den Ham, E. (2005). An enquiry concerning the principles of cultural norms and values: The impact of uncertainty and mortality salience on reactions to violations and bolstering of cultural worldviews. *Journal of Experimental Social Psychology, 41,* 91–113.

van Deurzen-Smith, E. (1984). Existential therapy. In W. Dryden (Ed.), *Individual therapy in Britain.* London: Harper and Row.

van Deurzen-Smith, E. (1997). *Everyday mysteries.* London: Routledge.

van Deurzen, E. (2002). *Existential counselling and psychotherapy in practice* (2nd ed.). London: Sage.

Vess, M., Routledge, C., Landau, M., & Arndt, J. (2009). The dynamics of death and meaning: The effects of death-relevant cognitions and personal need for structure on perceptions of meaning in life. *Journal of Personality and Social Psychology, 97,* 728–744.

Wicklund, R. A. (1975). Objective self awareness. In L. Berkowitz (Ed.), *Advances in experimental social psychology* (Vol. 8, pp. 233–275). San Diego, CA: Academic Press.

Wisman, A., & Koole, S. (2003). Hiding in the crowd: Can mortality salience promote affiliation with others who oppose one's worldviews? *Journal of Personality and Social Psychology, 84,* 511–526.

Yalom, I. (1980). *Existential psychotherapy.* New York: Basic Books.

Too Much of a Good Thing? Trade-offs in Promotion and Prevention Focus

Abigail A. Scholer *and* E. Tory Higgins

Abstract

Different kinds of motivational orientations provide distinctive ways of perceiving the world, dealing with life's inevitable slings and arrows, regulating challenges and opportunities, and creating success. In this chapter, we explore these differences in the two motivational systems outlined in regulatory focus theory: the promotion and prevention systems (Higgins, 1997). In particular, we discuss these systems in terms of the trade-offs in each; what are the benefits and costs of a strong promotion focus? What are the advantages and drawbacks of a strong prevention focus? We explore the trade-offs of each system with regard to three significant aspects of self-regulation and motivation: emotional experiences, the balance between commitment versus exploration, and performance. We conclude by discussing the importance of constraints on these systems for effective self-regulation and by suggesting avenues for future research.

Key Words: regulatory focus, motivation, self-regulation, emotion, commitment, performance

Air travel can provide not only logistical but also intellectual challenges. When you tell your seatmate that you study motivation, inevitably the question arises: "I'm having trouble motivating (substitute wife, son, employee). How can I get them *more* motivated?" Such is the typical conception of motivation. More is better. The problem is always that people are lacking in amount. If the maximum level of motivation can be achieved, all will be right with the world. And you can never have enough.

This chapter is dedicated to our fellow traveler. Is more motivation always better? The answer to this question, we believe, is consistent with what we face (sometimes resignedly) in most aspects of life: There are always *trade-offs*. Having a lot of a good thing means having at least some of a bad thing, too. Strength is intimately connected to weakness. Benefits come at some cost. This chapter is an exploration of such trade-offs within the two

fundamental motivational systems outlined in regulatory focus theory (Higgins, 1997): the promotion system and the prevention system. This chapter is a response to our seatmate (i.e., "It is not always about increasing motivation"), albeit with perhaps more nuance and complexity that one dares get into in Row 22.

We begin by introducing the promotion and prevention systems. We then explore what kind of life an individual would have if each system were totally unconstrained. In other words, what kind of life would a purely promotion-focused individual face? What kinds of opportunities and challenges would a purely prevention-focused individual confront? We explore the trade-offs of the pure forms of each system generally and the trade-offs in relation to specific situations. For instance, more promotion may be useful when brainstorming a new ad campaign (Friedman & Förster, 2001), but not so useful if overseeing the safety of one's employees (Wallace,

Little, & Shull, 2008). We organize our discussion of trade-offs around three significant issues in motivation and self-regulation: emotional life, commitment versus exploration, and performance. Lastly, we discuss the importance of constraints on these systems in order to achieve optimal self-regulation. We describe the ways in which the prevention and promotion systems may constrain each other, as well as how other motivational orientations (e.g., regulatory mode; Higgins, Kruglanski, & Pierro, 2003) may also provide constraints on these systems.

Overview of Regulatory Focus Theory

Building on earlier distinctions (Bowlby, 1969; 1973; Higgins, 1987; Mowrer, 1960), regulatory focus theory distinguishes between two coexisting motivational systems (promotion, prevention) that serve critically important but different survival needs (Higgins, 1997). The systems differ in what fundamentally motivates (nurturance versus security) and in what regulatory strategies are preferred (eagerness versus vigilance). Given that each system addresses a significant survival need, it is not surprising that people need both systems to be maximally effective in the world. However, in any given moment, one system is likely to predominate over the other, due to either chronic or situational differences in accessibility. In this chapter, we imagine what life would be like if an individual were purely promotion or prevention focused by exploring the benefits and costs of the extreme forms of each system.

The world of a promotion-focused individual is a world filled with possibility for advancement. An individual who is chronically promotion focused has been socialized to see that what matters in life is making good things happen—seeking the presence versus absence of positive outcomes. Caretaker–child interactions that support the development of a promotion focus direct attention to nurturance needs and emphasize desired end states as ideals (Higgins, 1987, 1997; Keller, 2008; Manian, Papadakis, Strauman, & Essex, 2006; Manian, Strauman, & Denney, 1998). Consequently, promotion-focused individuals are concerned with growth, advancement, and accomplishment that are served by using eager approach strategies in goal pursuit—approaching matches to desired end states and approaching mismatches to undesired end states (Crowe & Higgins, 1997; Higgins, Roney, Crowe, & Hymes, 1994; Liberman, Molden, Idson, & Higgins, 2001; Molden & Higgins, 2005; Wang & Lee, 2006). Advancements that count are those that result in positive deviations from the status quo or neutral state—the difference between "0" and "+1." Promotion-focused individuals are less sensitive to negative deviations from the status quo or neutral state, that is, the difference between "0" and "−1" (Brendl & Higgins, 1996; Higgins, 1997; Higgins & Tykocinski, 1992). In other words, promotion-focused individuals are maximally sensitive to gains versus nongains. Important gains are those related to their ideals, wishes, and aspirations.

In contrast, the world of a prevention-focused individual is a world filled with duty. An individual who is chronically prevention focused has been socialized to see that what matters in life is maintaining satisfactory states by preventing bad things from happening—ensuring the absence versus presence of negative outcomes. Caretaker–child interactions that encourage the development of a prevention focus direct attention to security needs and emphasize desired end states as oughts, duties, and obligations (Higgins, 1987, 1997; Keller, 2008; Manian et al., 1998; Manian et al., 2006). Consequently, prevention-focused individuals are concerned with safety and responsibility and focus on the necessity of maintaining the absence of negative outcomes. This orientation is best served by using vigilant avoidance strategies in goal pursuit—avoiding mismatches to desired end states and avoiding matches to undesired end states (Crowe & Higgins, 1997; Higgins et al., 1994; Liberman et al., 2001; Molden & Higgins, 2005; Wang & Lee, 2006). This sensitivity to the absence and presence of negative outcomes (nonlosses/losses) is reflected in greater assigned significance to the difference between "0" and "−1" than to the difference between "0" and "+1" (Brendl & Higgins, 1996; Higgins, 1997; Higgins & Tykocinski, 1992). Important nonlosses are those related to duties, oughts, and responsibilities.

Importantly, although the promotion and prevention systems are concerned with the regulation of different needs, promotion and prevention orientations *each* involve the approach and avoidance systems of self-regulation—each involve *both* approaching desired end states (e.g., approaching nurturance or safety, respectively) and avoiding undesired end states (e.g., avoiding nonfulfillment or danger, respectively). In other words, although at the strategic level promotion and prevention relate differentially to eager approach and vigilant avoidance strategies, at the system level each system is involved in both approach and avoidance (Scholer & Higgins, 2008). These differences mean that some desired end states will be more valuable or relevant in one system versus the other (Higgins, 2002). For instance, prevention-focused individuals may value the desired end state of an accident-free production line more than promotion-focused individuals (Henning, Stufft, Payne, Bergman, Mannan, & Keren, 2009). Additionally, the same desired end state can be presented in different ways by prevention- versus promotion-focused individuals. For example, the same desired end state, such as having a good marriage, may be represented as a duty or responsibility for prevention-focused individuals but as an ideal or aspiration for promotion-focused individuals. Furthermore, the fit (e.g., promotion eager) or nonfit (e.g., promotion vigilant) between an individual's underlying goal orientation and use of strategic means affects strength of engagement in the goal pursuit activity beyond any direct implications of either the system or the strategy itself (regulatory fit theory; Higgins, 2000). In other words, the effectiveness of a given strategy depends not only on the inherent properties of the strategy and task demands but also on whether the strategy sustains or fits an individual's underlying orientation. When individuals experience regulatory fit by using strategic means that sustain their underlying orientation, they "feel right" about and engage more strongly in what they are doing (Higgins, 2000, 2006).

As noted earlier, promotion and prevention orientations can arise either from chronic accessibility (personality differences) or from temporary accessibility (situational factors). Consequently, regulatory focus has been studied both as a personality variable with chronic strength or predominance of prevention or promotion orientations (e.g., Cunningham, Raye, & Johnson, 2005; Higgins et al., 2001; Higgins, Shah, & Friedman, 1997; Lockwood, Jordan, & Kunda, 2002; Ouschan, Boldero, Kashima, Wakimoto, & Kashima, 2007) and as a situational variable involving priming ideals or oughts or framing goal pursuits as potential gains or nonlosses (e.g., Friedman & Förster, 2001; Higgins et al., 1994; Liberman et al., 2001; Shah & Higgins, 1997; Shah, Higgins, & Friedman, 1998). Because we believe that what ultimately matters in terms of predicting behavior is the regulatory *state* that one is in, whether that arises from chronic or temporary accessibility (cf. Higgins, 1999), we review research that examines regulatory focus as both a measured and manipulated variable.

Trade-offs in Emotional Life

Few would argue with the claim that success feels better than failure. Yet what counts as a success or a failure and exactly how those triumphs and tragedies feel—both the precise quality and the intensity—depends at least in part on whether they are experienced within the promotion versus prevention systems. Additionally, the preferred strategic preferences of each system are sustained or disrupted by different affective states. In this section, we explore the trade-offs in the emotional life of a purely prevention-focused individual versus a purely promotion-focused individual.

The Price of Happiness, The Cost of Calm

Success and failure are defined differently within the promotion and prevention systems, have differential significance, and have distinct emotional signatures (Higgins, 1997, 2001). Success in a promotion focus reflects the presence of a gain: the positive outcome of an advancement, an improvement. In contrast, success in a prevention focus reflects just a nonnegative state: the establishment or maintenance of a satisfactory state. Thus, while promotion success requires progress or advancement from "0" to "+1," prevention success requires only maintenance of "0" such that a nonnegative, satisfactory state persists. Fundamentally, "success" in promotion requires positive *change* (gain), whereas "success" in prevention simply requires a state or condition that is satisfactory. This difference between requiring change (progress) versus requiring just a satisfactory state or condition constitutes a basic asymmetry between promotion and prevention.

Failure, too, is defined differently for promotion and prevention. For promotion-focused individuals, both "0" and "−1" are nongain, failure states. They both represent a failure to make progress, a failure to advance forward from "0." For prevention-focused individuals, however, only "−1" is experienced as failure (Brendl & Higgins, 1996; Higgins, 1997). Not making progress is not a failure.

This means that if both a promotion-focused individual and a prevention-focused individual are in a current state of loss ("−1"), acceptable movement for a prevention-focused individual requires reaching the satisfactory state of "0," whereas "0" holds no special meaning for a promotion-focused individual. Instead, acceptable movement for a promotion-focused individual means making progress beyond "0" towards "+1." Similarly, if both a promotion-focused individual and a prevention-focused individual have moved from "0" to a current state of "+1," the promotion-focused person would experience failure with a setback to "0" because it would represent a nongain, a removal of the previous progress, whereas the satisfactory state of "0" would still count as a success for a prevention-focused person.

Molden, Lucas, Gardner, Dean, and Knowles (2009) provide intriguing evidence for how different kinds of social losses "count" as promotion versus prevention failures. When asked to describe a time that they "did not belong," prevention-focused individuals were more likely to describe a time in which they were actively rejected ("−1" or an unsatisfactory state), whereas promotion-focused individuals were more likely to describe a time in which they had been more passively ignored (no opportunity to advance from "0" or a nongain). Similarly, Sassenberg and Hansen (2007) have shown that social discrimination based on "−1" unsatisfactory states increases distress for prevention-focused, but not promotion-focused, participants.

In addition to differences in what *counts* as success or failure, the *intensity* of the experience also differs for promotion and prevention individuals. For a prevention-focused individual who is sensitive to negative unsatisfactory states, "−1" failure is unacceptable in a way that it is not for a promotion-focused individual, and it is experienced more intensely by prevention-focused than promotion-focused individuals (Idson, Liberman, & Higgins, 2000). In contrast, "+1" success is more meaningful and experienced more intensely for promotion-focused than prevention-focused individuals (Idson, Liberman, & Higgins, 2000). This means that the potential for positive emotional intensity would be greater in the promotion system than the prevention system, that is, a promotion gain of "+1" is more intense than a prevention nonloss of "+1," whereas the potential for negative emotional intensity would be greater in the prevention system than the promotion system, that is, a prevention unsatisfactory state of "−1" is more intense than a promotion nongain of "−1."

It should be emphasized, however, that emotional intensity is not the same as level of pleasure or pain. The feeling of peace and calm from prevention success is not as intense as the feeling of joy and elation from promotion success, but this does not mean that the former is necessarily less pleasant than the latter. Similarly, the feeling of sadness and discouragement from promotion failure is not as intense as the feeling of anxiety and worry from prevention failure, but this does not mean that the former is necessarily less painful than the latter. Indeed, the feeling of depression from severe promotion failure is an extremely painful state precisely because its low motivational intensity reflects having no interest in engaging with life, a very painful psychological condition.

The distinct quality of prevention failure impacts how individuals anticipate and respond to failure. For example, prevention-focused individuals appear to be more susceptible to self-handicapping than promotion-focused individuals (Hendrix & Hirt, 2009), presumably because self-handicapping is a tactic for maintaining a current satisfactory state (e.g., the belief that you have high ability). In addition, after experiencing an unfavorable outcome that is represented as an unsatisfactory state, prevention-focused individuals are more upset if the process yielding that outcome was fair than unfair (Cropanzano, Paddock, Rupp, Bagger, & Baldwin, 2008). Cropanzano et al. (2008) suggest that because the fair process does not allow one to easily attribute failure to external causes, it is particularly threatening for prevention-focused individuals (see also Brockner, 2010). As we'll explore in more depth later, however, prevention failure, while painful, can also energize the system. Promotion failure generally provides no such benefit.

As described earlier when discussing the pleasures and pains of promotion and prevention, the *quality* of emotional response to success and failure also differs within the promotion and prevention systems. Success in the promotion system reflects the presence of a positive outcome (a gain or advancement) and results in cheerfulness-related emotions like happiness and joy. In contrast, success in the prevention system reflects the absence of a negative outcome (maintaining a satisfactory state) and results in quiescence-related emotions like peacefulness and calm. Failure in a promotion focus reflects the absence of a positive outcome (nongain or nonadvancement) and results in dejection-related emotions like sadness and disappointment. Because failure in a prevention focus reflects the presence of a negative outcome (an unsatisfactory or dangerous state), it results in agitation-related emotions like anxiety and worry (Higgins, 1997; Shah & Higgins, 2001). Consistent with these distinct emotional sensitivities, individuals in a promotion focus are faster at appraising how cheerful or dejected a given object makes them feel, whereas individuals in a prevention focus are faster at appraising how quiescent or agitated an object makes them feel (Shah & Higgins, 2001). Furthermore, these distinct emotional responses to failure mean that promotion and prevention individuals are differentially motivated by anticipating failure-related dejection versus agitation. Whereas promotion-focused individuals are more motivated to perform well when imagining potential dejection, prevention-focused individuals are more motivated to perform well when imagining potential agitation (Leone, Perugini, & Bagozzi, 2005).

A particularly significant type of failure that people experience occurs when their actual selves are discrepant from their desired selves—whether these desired selves are represented in the prevention system (ought selves) or the promotion system (ideal selves). In support of distinctive patterns of emotional response to this type of failure, several studies have found that priming ideal (promotion) discrepancies leads to increases in dejection, whereas priming ought (prevention) discrepancies leads to increases in agitation (Boldero, Moretti, Bell, & Francis, 2005; Higgins, Bond, Klein, & Strauman, 1986; Strauman, 1989; Strauman & Higgins, 1987). Not surprisingly, the magnitude of an emotional response to a discrepancy is related to that discrepancy's magnitude, accessibility, relevance to a particular context, and importance (Higgins, 1999). Simply encountering an individual who resembles a parent can activate self-discrepancies associated with that parent's ideals or oughts for the individual, producing dejected affect for parent-related ideal self-discrepancies and agitated affect for parent-related ought self-discrepancies (see Reznik & Andersen, 2007; Shah, 2003). Additionally, being socially rejected (a prevention negative state) leads to increased anxiety and withdrawal, but being socially ignored (a promotion nongain) leads to sadness and attempts to reengage (Molden et al., 2009).

These differences in the emotional dimensions associated with each system result in characteristic possibilities and vulnerabilities within each system (Brockner & Higgins, 2001; Higgins, 1987, 1997, 2001; Shah & Higgins, 2001). Both prevention- and promotion-focused individuals experience a sense of well-being when they successfully attain a goal. Both prevention- and promotion-focused individuals experience displeasure when they fail. However, the emotional trade-offs within each system are distinct, as we explore in more detail later. Only promotion goals provide the possibility of happiness (in the sense of joyful and ebullient). Only prevention goals provide the possibility of calm (in the sense of peace and serenity). However, within the promotion system, the *price of happiness* is vulnerability to depression. Within the prevention system, the *cost of calm* is vulnerability to anxiety.

Evidence of distinct patterns of intergoal inhibition supports the unique dynamics of emotional vulnerabilities within each system. Shah, Friedman, and Kruglanski (2002) found that individuals selectively showed greater intergoal inhibition for goals that could alleviate emotional distress. Shah et al. found that when participants were depressed, they showed greater intergoal inhibition for one type of focal goal—*ideal* goals—the goals that would result in happiness and satisfaction if obtained. Similarly, when participants were anxious, they selectively showed greater intergoal inhibition when the focal goal was an *ought* goal. In other words, participants were more likely to shield and protect a goal from competing goal alternatives when that goal could alleviate their emotional stress if it were attained.

One significant implication of the relation between regulatory focus concerns and emotional responses to success and failure is that it creates the possibility that individuals may be thwarted by misaligned emotional expectancies. To the extent that individuals experience successful self-regulation as being about *both* achieving the desired end state (e.g., going to the gym three times a week) *and* achieving the desired affective state (e.g., happiness), the impact of successes may be undermined if individuals expect promotion-related emotions from prevention successes (and vice versa). Individuals often have beliefs or hopes about how achieving a particular goal will make them feel (e.g., if I can go to the gym three times this week, I'll feel really happy). Someone who sets prevention goals and expects to be happy will be sorely disappointed.

In addition, setting promotion goals does not guarantee happiness either. The risk of aiming for happiness is that individuals become vulnerable to depression (Strauman, 2002; Strauman et al., 2006; Vieth et al., 2003). Indeed, it is when the motivational system is particularly strong (when promotion really matters to you) that individuals are most vulnerable to failures within the system (Higgins et al., 1997). Strauman (2002), in his self-regulation theory of depression, proposed that the chronic failure of promotion-focused individuals to meet promotion goals is a causal factor in the onset of depression. While the potential highs in promotion may be very high indeed (Idson et al., 2000, 2004), the lows embody the very depths of desolation. Several studies now support the link between failures in the promotion system and depression (Eddington et al., 2009; Jones, Papadakis, Hogan, & Strauman, 2009; Miller & Markman, 2007; Papadakis, Prince, Jones, & Strauman, 2006; Strauman et al., 2006;

Vieth et al., 2003) and suicidal ideation (Cornette, Strauman, Abramson, & Busch, 2009).

While promotion-focused individuals may be particularly susceptible to depression, coping styles and implicit beliefs about the nature of the failure may moderate the vulnerability (Cornette et al., 2009; Jones et al., 2009; Papadakis et al, 2006). In two studies, individuals who engaged in rumination and who had failures in the promotion system were more likely to show depressive symptoms. Individuals who had a more reflective coping style appeared to be buffered from the link between promotion failure and depression (Jones et al., 2009; Papadakis et al, 2006). Additionally, individuals who believed that their promotion failures (actual-ideal discrepancies) were stable and unchanging were most likely to show a relation between promotion failure and suicidal ideation (Cornette et al., 2009). Like reflective coping, belief in transitory failure appeared to provide a buffer against depression (Cornette et al., 2009). Together, these studies suggest that it is the "chronic and catastrophic" promotion failures that are likely to push individuals toward depression (Vieth et al., 2003, p. 249).

Self-system theory (SST) is a recently developed structured psychotherapy to treat the depression that is associated with individuals who have chronic promotion goals and are failing (Vieth et al., 2003). SST incorporates many principles from other forms of therapy such as cognitive therapy, interpersonal psychotherapy, and behavioral activation therapy. However, SST uses these principles in service of helping patients to identify their promotion and prevention goals, their strategies for attaining them, the obstacles they have encountered in goal pursuit, and how they can do things differently and/or more effectively. In a randomized trial comparing SST with cognitive therapy (Beck, Rush, Shaw, & Emery, 1979), SST, for individuals with a poor promotion effectiveness, was found to lead to reduced symptoms for depression and decreased dysphoric responses to promotion goals compared to cognitive therapy (Strauman et al., 2006). The effectiveness of SST speaks to the importance of understanding the trade-offs and vulnerabilities within a given motivational system.

The success of SST also supports the idea that some awareness of the trade-offs within systems may also be beneficial. As part of the educational and goal-setting aspects of the theory, therapist and client discuss the implications of the different concerns of the promotion and prevention systems. Interestingly, Vieth et al. (2003) describe a case study in which the client was under the mistaken impression that attaining prevention goals would lead to the happiness and satisfaction that she dearly wanted. Part of the usefulness of the therapy for her (and for other clients) appears to be learning that succeeding or failing at promotion versus prevention goals has distinct emotional consequences.

Less work has been done to examine the link between the prevention system and anxiety disorders (for a recent review, see Klenk, Strauman, & Higgins, 2011). However, some empirical evidence does suggest that chronic actual-ought discrepancies do predict certain patterns of anxiety (Scott & O'Hara, 1993; Strauman, 1989; Strauman et al., 2001). For instance, Strauman (1989) reported that social phobics had higher actual-ought discrepancy scores relative to depressed or control participants. Furthermore, social phobics exhibited increased agitation in response to actual-ought discrepancy priming relative to depressed or control participants. Scott and O'Hara (1993) extended this work to show that university students diagnosed with any one of a number of anxiety disorders (generalized anxiety disorder, panic attacks, agoraphobia, social phobia, or obsessive-compulsive disorder) also had higher actual-ought discrepancy scores than nonanxious or depressed students.

There is no doubt that failure in both the prevention and promotion systems is painful, albeit in different ways. However, as noted earlier, failure within the prevention system is not only painful but also unacceptable in a way that promotion failure is not, in the sense that prevention-focused individuals experience returning to a satisfactory "0" state as being a *motivational necessity*. This has significant implications for the actions that prevention-focused individuals are willing and motivated to take when in an unsatisfactory negative state. For prevention-focused individuals, a state of "–1" is intolerable; they should be willing to do *whatever is necessary* to get back to "0" or the status quo. "0" does not hold the same significance for promotion-focused individuals. While ultimately they are motivated to get to "+1," any progress away from "–1" is in service of that end; the status quo ("0") holds no special meaning as the state they want to reach. Consequently, when individuals are in an unsatisfactory state of "-1," it is prevention-focused individuals, rather than promotion-focused individuals, who have been found to be especially motivated to take risks that have the possibility of returning them to the status quo (Scholer, Zou, Fujita, Stroessner, & Higgins, 2010). For prevention-focused individuals at "–1," failure carries with it an increased likelihood of engaging in actions that are perceived as necessary to restore "0," even if they are risky.

Keeping the Engine Revved: Strategic Preferences and Life Experiences

Success and failure not only result in different emotional responses in the promotion versus prevention systems, but they also have distinct implications for the strategic inclinations that sustain each system and the motivational experiences that are associated with these strategic inclinations (i.e., eager and vigilant experiences). For promotion-focused individuals, failure is not only negative affectively, but it also reduces the strategic eagerness that sustains or fits the promotion system. In contrast, success is both affectively positive and sustains eagerness within the promotion system.

For prevention-focused individuals, on the other hand, failure poses no threat to the system's preferred strategic orientation. While failure in the prevention system is very emotionally negative, it increases the strategic vigilance that fits prevention (Idson et al., 2004). Success, however, while emotionally positive within the prevention system, has the potential to disrupt strategic vigilance that sustains the system's optimal effectiveness. Vigilance is hard to maintain in a state of calm and quiescence. Thus, while the pure promotion-focused individual would be wise to seek a life of half-full glasses in order to maintain eagerness, the pure prevention-focused individual would be better off seeing life's glasses as half-empty in order to maintain vigilance. The trade-offs, of course, are that the promotion-focused individual runs the risk of seeing good where there is none while the prevention-focused individual runs the risk of seeing no good when it's there.

To the extent that the strategic vigilance of prevention-focused individuals can become energized through failure, prevention-focused individuals should generally show better performance after failure feedback or when anticipating failure. In contrast, given that the strategic eagerness of promotion-focused individuals can become deflated after failure, promotion-focused individuals should show worse performance after failure feedback. Indeed, Idson and Higgins (2000) found that promotion-focused individuals showed a decline in performance after failure feedback relative to success feedback, whereas prevention-focused individuals showed the opposite pattern—better performance after failure feedback than after success feedback (see also Idson et al., 2000, 2004; Van-Dijk &

Kluger, 2004). But there is also a trade-off of failure for prevention-focused individuals. Because their increased vigilance after failure reduces the numbers of possible causes they consider for their failure, they are more likely than promotion-focused individuals to engage in self-serving attributions after failure (Molden & Higgins, 2008).

Notably, it is not the case that promotion-focused individuals simply give up after initial failure; rather, they are likely to respond to failure in ways that protect their eagerness for future performances. For example, after failure feedback in an ongoing performance situation, promotion-focused individuals show only slight decreases in expectancies for future performance (Förster, Grant, Idson, & Higgins, 2001). In addition, after failure they use tactics to maintain a positive self-evaluation, which supports the eagerness that serves their promotion (Scholer, Ozaki, & Higgins, 2011). Promotion-focused individuals are also more likely to generate additive (eager) counterfactuals when reflecting on past failures (Roese, Hur, & Pennington, 1999), and, indeed, when they engage in upward counterfactuals that sustain eagerness they perform better on subsequent tasks (Markman, McMullen, Elizaga, & Mizoguchi, 2006). Promotion-focused individuals also protect themselves against negative feedback by being generally optimistic (Grant & Higgins, 2003) and having high self-esteem (Higgins, 2008). Moreover, there is some evidence that promotion-focused individuals can be less distracted by negative feelings after making an error, such as action-oriented promotion-focused individuals being buffered from the negative impact of speed-related errors on subsequent trials (de Lange & van Knippenberg, 2009).

In contrast to promotion-focused individuals, prevention-focused individuals, in order to maintain their vigilance, respond to failure by lowering expectancies *even more* (Förster et al., 2001), and by maintaining relatively less positive self-evaluations in ongoing performance situations (Scholer, Ozaki, et al., 2011). Prevention-focused individuals are also more likely to generate subtractive (vigilant) counterfactuals when reflecting on past failures (Roese et al., 1999), and they perform better on subsequent tasks when they employ counterfactuals that sustain vigilance (Markman et al., 2006). Unlike promotion pride, prevention pride is uncorrelated with self-esteem (Higgins, 2008).

As noted earlier, these different strategic preferences in promotion and prevention create unique vulnerabilities within each system. The stronger the system, the more likely the individual is to embrace the preferred strategy, leaving the individual even more vulnerable to the potential downsides. Promotion-focused individuals may, at times, be overly optimistic and overeager (even manic), when a dose of realism would serve them well. Promotion-focused individuals may be less attentive to failure and areas that need improvement, which has the potential to reduce the effectiveness of learning. Promotion-focused individuals, for instance, are more likely to develop illusions of control regarding uncontrollable outcomes (Langens, 2007). While these illusions of control can help buffer them against the harsh realities of the world (Taylor, Lerner, Sherman, Sage, & McDowell, 2003), such illusions can, at times, be problematic. Eagerness carried too far simply leaves them untethered to reality.

Promotion-focused individuals are also vulnerable to the strategic nonfit of failure to their system. Accumulated failures deliver such a punch of nonfitness to the system from reduced eagerness that it can begin to break down, producing the anhedonia of depression (no interest in anything) discussed earlier (Strauman, 2002; Strauman et al., 2006). Prevention-focused individuals, on the other hand, may be overly attentive to negative signals, when a dose of optimism would serve them well. They may not give themselves or others enough credit for success and may be less likely to adopt those positive illusions that can buffer against a number of negative health outcomes (Taylor et al., 2003). Furthermore, while strategic vigilance generally serves them well, taken too far it may be problematic, even to the extent of producing pathological generalized anxiety disorder (Higgins, 2006; Klenk et al., 2011). Thus, while strong promotion and prevention systems both provide many benefits, the strengths do not come without the possibility of downsides in life experiences as well.

Trade-offs in Commitment Versus Exploration

Effective self-regulation requires both an ability to stay the course (even when sometimes difficult) as well as an openness to change course when necessary. Staying the course involves commitment, whether that is commitment to a goal, individual, or group. Openness to changing courses involves exploration, whether that is exploring other goals, other products, or other relationships. The prevention system, all else being equal, excels at commitment. The promotion system, all else being equal, excels at exploration. In this section, we explore the trade-offs of each system in turn; what

are the benefits and costs of a system that pushes for commitment versus a system that embraces exploration?

If It's Not Broke, Don't Fix It

A number of aspects of the prevention system converge to make prevention-focused individuals more likely to stay committed to a current course of action and less open to change in general. Increased prevention focus is associated with increased valuation of security and decreased valuation of openness to change (Higgins, 2008; Leikas, Lönnqvist, Verkasalo, & Lindeman, 2009; Vaughn, Baumann, & Klemann, 2008). Prevention-focused individuals, concerned with duties and obligations, are particularly likely to construe goals and actions as necessities (Shah & Higgins, 1997). To the extent that existing goals and loyalties are perceived as duties that *must* be upheld, prevention-focused individuals should cling more tightly to what they have (cf. Brickman, 1987). Furthermore, duties and obligations often involve responsibility to *others*. A number of studies have found support for an association between prevention focus and interdependent self-construals, such that prevention-focused individuals are more likely to view themselves within the context of a broader social network (Aaker & Lee, 2001; Lee, Aaker, & Gardner, 2000) and are more motivated by leadership styles that emphasize a sense of organizational duty and self-sacrifice (Choi & Mai-Dalton, 1999). Additionally, the prevention individual's acute sensitivity to loss and preference for vigilant strategies creates reluctance to take leaps that might expose him or her to potentially greater losses (Crowe & Higgins, 1997; Idson & Higgins, 2000).

Several studies support the idea that prevention focus is associated with commitment to the status quo (Chernev, 2004; Crowe & Higgins, 1997; Jain, Lindsey, Agrawal, & Maheswaran, 2007; Liberman, Idson, Camacho, & Higgins, 1999). For instance, prevention-focused participants are more likely to want to continue working on an interrupted task rather than begin a new one (Liberman et al., 1999). The endowment effect, in which people value an object more simply because they possess it, is uniquely associated with the prevention, but not promotion, system (Liberman et al., 1999). When prevention-focused individuals' initial preference in a consumer choice paradigm is framed as the status quo, they are particularly likely to stick with their initial choice (Chernev, 2004). Prevention-focused people's commitment to "the way things are" is also reflected in their relative reluctance to adopt new technology relative to promotion-focused people (Herzenstein, Posavac, & Brakus, 2007). This preference for the status quo appears to be due both to enhanced sensitivity to potential losses (Liberman et al., 1999) and increased motivation to minimize possible regret if things do not go well (Chernev, 2004).

To justify commitment to a chosen course of action (status quo or otherwise), prevention-focused people may sometimes see the world as a zero-sum game (i.e., if Product A is good, then Product B is bad). Disparaging alternatives and enhancing a chosen path is one way to increase commitment to that choice (cf. Gollwitzer, Heckhausen, & Steller, 1990). A study comparing the effect of different comparative frames in advertising on prevention-versus promotion-focused participants illustrates this well (Jain et al., 2007). Jain et al. (2007) compared the effectiveness of two possible comparative frames—positive versus negative. Positive comparative frames suggest that the advertised (target) brand is better than its comparison, whereas negative comparative frames suggest that the comparison brand is worse than the advertised (target) brand. The negative frame effectively marks the comparison brand as unacceptable, suggesting that the target brand is the safe, right one to choose.

Not only did prevention-focused participants evaluate the target brand more positively in the negative frame condition, but their ratings of the target and comparison products were also negatively correlated. In other words, as prevention-focused participants endorsed the target brand, they were more likely to disparage the comparison brand. Furthermore, the way in which prevention-focused participants approached the task suggested underlying vigilance against the perceived "other" (cf. Shah, Brazy, & Higgins, 2004); prevention-focused participants were more likely to evaluate the comparison brand first and remembered more advertised information about the comparison brand relative to the advertised brand (Jain et al., 2007). Consistent with this logic, prevention-focused individuals are also more likely to give more negative product evaluations, relative to promotion-focused individuals, when presented with two-sided product endorsements (e.g., the juice is natural but expensive) than with one-sided product endorsements (e.g., the juice is natural) (Florack, Ineichen, & Bieri, 2009).

When making decisions or comparing options, prevention-focused individuals are also likely to consider relatively few alternatives (Crowe & Higgins,

1997; Liberman et al., 2001; Molden & Higgins, 2004), consistent with a worldview that is less open to change (Higgins, 2008; Vaughn et al., 2008). By considering fewer possibilities, prevention-focused individuals are less likely to choose a wrong path or be tempted by alternate paths rather than doing just what is necessary. For instance, when sorting objects prevention-focused participants organize the objects into fewer categories than promotion-focused participants (Crowe & Higgins, 1997). Prevention-focused individuals generate fewer hypotheses when trying to explain someone else's behavior and are more likely to endorse only one (Liberman et al., 2001). Prevention-focused people in relationships pay less attention to romantic alternatives than promotion-focused participants (Finkel, Molden, Johnson, & Eastwick, 2009). Thus, by limiting the paths that they consider, prevention-focused individuals have a better chance of *protecting commitments* they have already made.

Prevention-focused individuals also consider fewer explanations for their successes and failures than promotion-focused individuals (Molden & Higgins, 2008). Although prevention-focused individuals may be motivated to consider fewer alternatives in order to minimize the possibility of mistakes, a restricted option set can sometimes increase error or bias. While prevention-focused individuals considered fewer explanations for successes and failures, these tended to be more self-serving (Molden & Higgins, 2008).

Part of the reason that prevention-focused individuals may be less open to considering a number of alternatives is that prevention-focused individuals are relatively more content with "safe" options that promise neither extreme highs nor lows (Zhang & Mittal, 2007). When given a choice between an enriched option (option with extreme values on its attribute—e.g., movie with great art direction but mind-numbing plot) versus an impoverished option (option with average values on its attributes—e.g., movie with average cinematography and average plot), prevention-focused individuals prefer the impoverished option (Zhang & Mittal, 2007). Because prevention-focused individuals weight the negative aspects more heavily, an option with average values wins out (Zhang & Mittal, 2007). This is also consistent with work that has shown that prevention-focused individuals, unlike promotion-focused individuals, are not trying to maximize outcomes in the world. In other words, the classic expectancy x value effect on goal commitment is not observed for prevention-focused individuals (Shah

& Higgins, 1997). When the world is construed in terms of duty and obligations, a relatively low expectancy does not necessarily diminish commitment for an important goal. If a goal is really valuable, such as maintaining a certain GPA being experienced as a *necessity*, then expectancy becomes irrelevant. And, again, there is a trade-off. While this prevention-focused orientation can support greater commitment to significant goals, the potential downside is that preferences and choices might not be optimized.

Nonetheless, greater commitment to important goals does have a number of benefits. Prevention-focused individuals who are chronically or temporarily concerned about health issues are more likely to engage in health care–taking behaviors, such as monitoring their health or signing up for cancer screenings (Uskul, Keller, & Oyserman, 2008). Fuglestad et al. (2008) also found that prevention-focused individuals were more successful at *maintaining* changes after successful initiation (weight loss and smoking cessation) than were promotion-focused individuals. Because successful behavior maintenance for changes like weight loss and smoking cessation requires being vigilant against backslides (Rothman, 2000), prevention-focused individuals may be particularly equipped for these kinds of challenges. Indeed, prevention-focused individuals outperform promotion-focused individuals under conditions in which they must resist distraction in order to stay focused on a focal task (Freitas, Liberman, & Higgins, 2002).

It is important to note that commitment to duties and obligations sometimes means that prevention-focused individuals will actually initiate action or change *more* quickly than promotion-focused individuals. If the current state is deemed to be an unacceptable, unsatisfactory state or if change itself is represented as a duty or responsibility, prevention-focused individuals may be especially likely to take action. Necessities and duties cannot be put away for another day. Individuals who are told that a product can prevent something negative (versus achieve something positive) remember more about the product and are more likely to sign up to test the product, as long as goal relevance is high (Poels & Dewitte, 2008). Prevention-focused participants initiate work on important goals (e.g., applying for a fellowship) earlier than promotion-focused participants (Freitas, Liberman, Salovey, & Higgins, 2002). Furthermore, because prevention-focused individuals are sensitive to loss, they will be motivated to do whatever it takes to get out of a current unacceptable state. For instance, when individuals have fallen below the status quo, as in a stock investment paradigm, prevention-focus strength, but not promotion-focus strength, predicts a willingness to take risks that have the possibility of returning participants to the status quo (Scholer et al., 2010). Thus, when change allows an individual to avoid losses, prevention-focused individuals should be especially motivated to take action.

The dynamics discussed in the previous paragraph highlight an important issue. Prevention-focused individuals are not arbitrarily committed to embracing the status quo and eschewing risk and change. It is not a love affair with the status quo itself, but with what the status quo represents. These preferences serve their underlying motivation to achieve security and act in accordance with duties and obligations. When things are going well and the world appears relatively safe, conservative biases in action (i.e., avoiding errors of commission) support the prevention system (Crowe & Higgins, 1997; Friedman & Förster, 2001). However, when things are not going well, the tactics that support the system may shift (Scholer & Higgins, 2008). For instance, while erring on the side of misses in a signal detection paradigm supports prevention motivation when the targets are neutral or positive, this tactical approach is folly when the targets are negative. Under these circumstances, prevention focus is associated with a risky bias (i.e., avoiding errors of omission); missing a negative signal (e.g., the potential mugger across the street) would be a serious threat to safety (Scholer, Stroessner, & Higgins, 2008).

The concern with missing negative signals and a desire to "play it safe" has a number of upsides for prevention-focused individuals. Prevention-focused individuals are more likely to fiercely defend that to which they are committed, whether that is a favorite product, their goals, or their close relationships. Prevention-focused individuals are likely to vigilantly monitor against potential health threats and to maintain health changes because of their vigilance against potential slippage. Because prevention-focused individuals are less likely to even consider how green the grass is on another hill, they are more likely to be content with the hill on which they stand, which is a definite plus for their marital partners.

However, putting aside the issue of marriage for a moment, sometimes other hills do offer better grass or better vistas. Prevention-focused individuals may miss opportunities to improve their situation because they are content with "good enough"—they are content with "0" being satisfactory and "+1" not being necessary. Furthermore, perceptions of current states can be amiss, and prevention-focused individuals may be more likely to stay in suboptimal states that they've categorized as "0" even though, in fact, they are negative. For instance, returning to marriage, prevention-focused individuals may be more likely to stay in bad or even abusive relationships, both out of a sense of duty and a belief that the relationship is "good enough." In sum, the significant benefits of high commitment within the prevention system do not come without a price.

Always on the Make

The promotion system pushes for exploration in the service of advancement. The promotion individual, especially sensitive to gains, is aware of the possible greener grass that might be just over the next hill. Furthermore, the preferred eager strategies of promotion-focused individuals suggest a world of better possibilities and opportunities. Motivated by the difference between "0" and "+1," promotion-focused individuals seek out many options in their aim for the ultimate experience. Consistent with this view, openness to experience (cf. John & Srivastava, 1999) has been shown to positively correlate with the promotion system (Higgins, 2008; Vaughn et al., 2008). Increased promotion focus is also negatively associated with values related to stability and tradition (Leikas et al., 2009).

The promotion individual's eagerness to pursue all possible paths means that promotion-focused individuals are less likely to stay committed to the status quo. Relative to prevention-focused individuals, promotion-focused individuals are more willing to give up an activity they are working on or a prize they currently possess for a new activity or prize (Chernev, 2004; Crowe & Higgins, 1997; Liberman et al., 1999). Promotion-focused individuals also value the desired end state of having all the latest and greatest technology more than prevention-focused individuals (cf. Herzenstein et al., 2007; Higgins, 2002) and are more likely to accept information technology changes at work (Stam & Stanton, 2010). Promotion-focused individuals own more new high-tech products than prevention-focused individuals and are more likely to buy cutting-edge, but not conventional, products (Herzenstein et al., 2007). Promotion-focused individuals' tendency to adopt new technology appears to be driven by their likelihood of seeing possibilities and opportunities, rather than lurking dangers and risks,

when given minimal or ambiguous information. When the risks of a new product were made salient, promotion-focused individuals were no more likely than prevention-focused individuals to buy the product (Herzenstein et al., 2007).

In search of the ultimate experience, promotion-focused individuals prefer extreme highs, even at the risk of some extreme lows, rather than a middling experience. When given a choice between enriched versus impoverished options, promotion-focused participants chose options with extreme attribute values (both positive and negative) rather than impoverished options with average attribute values (Zhang & Mittal, 2007). The greater attractiveness of enriched options appears to be due to the promotion system's greater weighting of positive versus negative attributes. When positive attributes are weighted more heavily, the enriched option trumps the impoverished one (Zhang & Mittal, 2007). Consistent with this, promotion-focused individuals are the epitome of the classic maximizer (Shah & Higgins, 1997); that is, promotion-focus individuals make decisions and evaluate commitment to goals using a value x expectancy calculation.

This desire for maximization is also observed in the promotion-focused individual's consideration of multiple alternatives and options when making decisions. Promotion-focused participants employ a greater number of categories when sorting objects relative to prevention-focused participants (Crowe & Higgins, 1997; Liberman et al., 2001; Molden & Higgins, 2004). When considering multiple options, promotion-focused individuals can embrace one option without derogating others; in other words, finding positives in Object A does not mean that Object B is negative or even needs to be discounted (Liberman et al., 2001). Unlike prevention-focused individuals, promotion-focused individuals are more persuaded by positive comparative frames (frames that suggest the advertised (target) brand is better than the comparison brand). Furthermore, their ratings of the target brand are uncorrelated with their ratings of the comparison brand. In other words, they can prefer one product while still acknowledging benefits in the other (Jain et al., 2007).

Being able to see the good in multiple paths, however, can bring challenges to relationships. As maximizers, promotion-focused individuals are more likely to ask themselves whether current relationships make the cut. Promotion-focused individuals report paying more attention to romantic alternatives and being more proactive about pursuing them relative to prevention-focused individuals. Even when in a long-term relationship, promotion-focused individuals show more positive evaluations of romantic alternatives than prevention-focused individuals. Although it is generally the case that individuals evaluate romantic alternatives less positively when they are committed to their current relationship, this effect is attenuated for promotion-focused individuals (Finkel et al., 2009). While the promotion-focused individual might be more likely to initially see the good in someone, he or she is also more likely to turn away and see the better in someone else.

Because promotion-focused individuals are more likely to make decisions in accordance with potential gains, they may open themselves up to unintended losses. Again, there is a trade-off. At times, an ignorance or inattention to losses can be beneficial. For instance, promotion-focused individuals are more successful at initiating certain health changes such as weight loss and smoking cessation, and Fuglestad et al. (2008) suggest that this is because successful initiation of such behaviors is often motivated by the perception of substantial gains (Foster, Wadden, Vogt, & Brewer, 1997). Thus, promotion-focused individuals may rise to the initiation challenge more eagerly than prevention-focused individuals.

Yet seeing the world through gains-colored glasses can also get promotion-focused individuals in trouble. When one is focused on possible gains (e.g., getting to enjoy this divine torte), it can be easy to miss the possible losses (e.g., not fitting into one's favorite jeans tomorrow). For example, promotion-focused individuals who tend to be chronic thrill-seekers are more likely to engage in health-detrimental behaviors, such as using stimulants to "push through" an illness (Uskul et al., 2008). If good health is seen as just another positive outcome (and not a necessity), it may be more likely to be overridden by other, conflicting goals. Promotion-focused individuals may not as easily resist tempting distractions (Freitas et al., 2002). Sengupta and Zhou (2007) have also shown that impulsive eaters, relative to nonimpulsive eaters, are more likely to show promotion system activation upon exposure to a tempting food; this activation mediates the effect of impulsivity on choice of the tempting food.

Promotion-focused individuals hold the world on a string. It can be a beautiful world, full of hope, possibility, and promise. Any peak experience may be topped tomorrow and the promotion-focused individual believes that you should never stop looking. Because of this worldview, promotion-focused

individuals are less likely to miss opportunities and more likely to extract all that they can from what the world has to offer (Galinsky, Leonardelli, Okhuysen, & Mussweiler, 2005). Yet promotion-focused individuals run the risk of always being on the make and never being satisfied with what they have. At times, promotion-focused individuals may have trouble committing to relationships, goals, or objects because of the nagging possibility that still more could be gained. Promotion-focused individuals may also run into trouble because they have not paid enough attention to negative signals. For instance, promotion-focused individuals may minimize accrued losses by focusing on the gains. Furthermore, because they are less concerned with the difference between "–1" and "0," promotion-focused individuals may be less likely to take action when things, in fact, are not satisfactory.

Trade-offs in Performance

Both promotion and prevention-focused individuals are motivated to perform well. As we've discussed previously, the systems are differentially sensitive to a number of factors that have the potential to influence performance—different kinds of desired end states (nurturance versus safety), outcomes (success versus failure), and strategies (eagerness versus vigilance). In this section, we discuss additional differences between the systems that impact productivity and performance. While the promotion system values speed, the prevention system values accuracy (Förster, Higgins, & Bianco, 2003). A promotion-focused individual is more likely to see the big picture, whereas a prevention-focused individual is more likely to see the dots of paint (Förster & Higgins, 2005; Semin, Higgins, de Montes, Estourget, & Valencia, 2005). Promotion focus facilitates creativity, while a prevention focus facilitates performance on analytical tasks (Friedman & Förster, 2001; Seibt & Förster, 2004). As we develop later, these differences have distinct advantages and disadvantages within each system. Furthermore, unlike some of the trade-offs that we've discussed in earlier sections, these trade-offs are often more closely tied to specific situations; for example, whether enhanced creativity will be a boon or a bust typically depends on the demands of a given task.

The promotion system is associated with greater creativity (Crowe & Higgins, 1997; Friedman & Förster, 2001) and a tendency to engage in more global processing (Förster & Higgins, 2005), including the use of more abstract language

(Semin et al., 2005). Eager strategies coupled with openness to novel and diverse ideas facilitate creative performance on many kinds of tasks. For instance, promotion-focused participants perform better than prevention-focused participants on creative insight problems and on tasks that require creative generation (e.g., generating creative uses for a brick).

The enhanced creativity of promotion-focused participants appears to be due, at least in part, to the fact that promotion-focused participants are less likely to be blocked by recently activated information that can interfere with novel production (Friedman & Förster, 2001). In addition, a promotion-focused individual is more likely to see the forest beyond the trees; global processing facilitates moving beyond concrete details in order to see new possibilities (Förster & Higgins, 2005). Consistent with this, promotion-focused individuals do better on tasks that require relational elaboration (Zhu & Meyers-Levy, 2007) and are better at "expanding the pie" in integrative negotiations (Galinsky et al., 2005). But what happens when there are obstacles to carrying out the creative task successfully and persistence is needed despite the likelihood of success being low? Once again there is a trade-off. The trade-off is that promotion-focused individuals generate more ideas than prevention-focused individuals, but prevention-focused individuals persevere in the creative project more than promotion-focused individuals in the face of obstacles (Lam & Chiu, 2002).

And there is another trade-off from a promotion focus as well. When tasks demand creativity, being in a chronically or temporarily promotion-focused state will serve one well. However, there are times when seeing the world more abstractly and globally can be problematic. Important details and errors can be missed. Sometimes the insight comes precisely from attention to concrete, logical connections. Weighting the abstract more heavily can even lead promotion-focused individuals to focus less on the concrete, pragmatic functions of products they are considering (Hassenzahl, Schöbel, & Trautmann, 2008).

Prevention-focused individuals, on the other hand, focus on the concrete more than the abstract, see the local rather than global features, and tend to perform worse on creative tasks and better on tasks that require analytical processing (Förster & Higgins, 2005; Friedman & Förster, 2001; Seibt & Förster, 2004; Semin et al., 2005). The vigilance of the prevention system against making mistakes works against taking some of the risks, opening up, and seeing the big picture that can support creative thought. For instance, prevention focus has been associated with increased perseverance on initially activated information, blocking the subsequent production of more novel responses (Friedman & Förster, 2001). But relative to promotion-focused individuals, prevention-focused individuals do better on tasks that require item-specific elaboration (Zhu & Meyers-Levy, 2007). Prevention-focused individuals focus on the concrete components of a visual scene; they are faster at identifying the smaller letters that make up a larger letter, whereas promotion-focused individuals show the opposite pattern (Förster & Higgins, 2005). A local processing approach supports a prevention-focused individual's concern with vigilantly maintaining security. To guard against possible danger and loss, it is necessary to be thoroughly aware of one's surroundings (e.g., Has someone moved that vase to the left?) and be prepared for action (e.g., There might be an intruder in the house). Additionally, local processing facilitates analytical thinking (Friedman, Fishbach, Förster, & Werth, 2003) and that may be one of the reasons that prevention-focused individuals tend to perform better on those kinds of tasks (Friedman & Förster, 2001; Seibt & Förster, 2004). Additionally, prevention-focused individuals are good at maintaining, that is, committing to, the necessary constraints involved in analytical reasoning.

The prevention system's focus on the concrete is also related to the prevention system's emphasis on accuracy in performance (Förster et al., 2003). Most tasks require some combination of speed (there is some deadline at some point) and accuracy (work riddled with errors is generally unacceptable). Prevention-focused individuals weight accuracy more heavily; a job well done is a job done without error (or at least minimized error). Across multiple studies, Förster et al. (2003) found that prevention focus was associated with greater accuracy and slower performance. Furthermore, the closer participants got to the goal, the more these effects were intensified. Prevention-focused participants are also more likely, relative to promotion-focused participants, to use a rereading strategy when they encounter confusing text (Miele, Molden, & Gardner, 2009). When rereading provides the possibility of clarification, this strategy relates to better performance. When rereading cannot clarify, however, this strategy is unrelated to performance, suggesting that prevention-focused individuals will sometimes be more likely to invest resources in thoroughness that is not rewarded.

This motivational concern with accuracy is also reflected in the prevention system's greater concern with safety (Henning et al., 2009; Van Noort, Kerkhof, & Fennis, 2008; Wallace & Chen, 2006; Wallace et al., 2008). Whether or not this focus on accuracy and safety is beneficial for performance depends on the demands of the situation. In many situations, accuracy and thoroughness in performance is valued. At times, however, in order to manage multiple demands, it is better to simply get a task done adequately, rather than complete only part of it well. Additionally, while high production and safe production can often coexist, there are times when one must be sacrificed for the other. Wallace et al. (2008) found that under normal conditions, prevention focus was related to good safety performance and was unrelated to productivity performance. Under high task complexity, however, the trade-offs between these concerns became hard to avoid, with prevention also becoming related to decreased productivity performance (the classic quality vs. quantity trade-off).

In contrast to the prevention system, the promotion system values speed in performance (Förster et al., 2003). The more quickly a task can be completed, the more quickly an individual can move on to the next potential gain. A job well done is a job done quickly and efficiently. Promotion-focused individuals generally perform faster and with less accuracy than prevention-focused individuals, with these effects intensifying the closer participants get to a goal (Förster et al., 2003). Similarly, promotion focus is associated with increased productivity performance (Wallace & Chen, 2006; Wallace et al., 2008).

The promotion system is also associated with increased reliance on affective information when making decisions and forming evaluations, which may be due, at least in part, to the fact that affect-based heuristics tend to less effortful and faster (Pham & Avnet, 2009). Under the right conditions, this emphasis on speed can serve the promotion-focused individual very well, sometimes not even at the cost of accuracy. For instance, Förster et al. (2003) found that, as predicted, promotion-focused individuals were faster at finishing a proofreading task compared to prevention-focused individuals. This speed, however, was actually associated with better performance for finding "easy" mistakes; while promotion-focused individuals were less likely to spot tricky or difficult errors, they were *more* likely to catch the obvious problems. At other times, however, the trade-offs are more evident. Sometimes what matters most is that a task is done right, even if that requires more time. When task complexity is high, promotion focus is associated with increased productivity performance and decreased safety performance (Wallace et al., 2008). Being less concerned about safety can have potentially devastating impacts on overall production if a serious mistake is made or a significant accident occurs.

Constraining the Systems

Being "more" motivated, in terms of increased promotion or prevention system activation, is not unequivocally a good thing. While increased strength of either the promotion system or the prevention system can have beneficial effects for well-being and self-regulation, one system is not better than the other, nor does increased motivation within a system come without costs. Rather, as we've explored in this chapter, with the increased benefits of more motivation come distinctive vulnerabilities. Some weaknesses/costs exist regardless of an individual's situation. For instance, in general, increased promotion focus is related to increased risk of depression (Strauman, 2002). Some costs emerge only under specific conditions. For example, the prevention system's concern with accuracy will be particularly problematic in situations that value speed or output quantity, not thoroughness or output quality. Additionally, some vulnerabilities may emerge when individuals are out of step with the dominant motivational orientation in their culture, as when well-being is reduced for individuals high in promotion focus who live in a culture such as Japan that is low in promotion as an aggregate (Fulmer et al., 2010) or for individuals high in prevention focus who live in a culture such as Italy that is low in prevention. These individuals can "feel wrong" in and disengage from the situations within their culture that are a nonfit for them (cf. Higgins, 2008). In many different ways, then, it is clear that the pure, unconstrained forms of each system present challenges.

Because of these challenges, constraints on the systems are important, both for effective self-regulation and optimal well-being (Higgins, 2011). Constraints allow for the systems to be kept in check. Constraints allow for flexible responding, such that promotion or prevention moments can shine brighter, less tarnished by potential downsides. Idealism can be reigned in by reminders of duties or possible dangers. Performance can be optimized when one balances the need for speed with a concern for accuracy. Constraints can come in a number of different forms. Constraints can come from within regulatory focus (e.g., prevention system constraining the promotion system) and from other motivational systems (e.g., regulatory mode; Kruglanski et al., 2000). Constraints can come from within an individual (e.g., their own prevention and promotion orientations interacting) or in dynamics that emerge in dyads or groups (cf. Bohns et al., 2011; Levine, Higgins, & Choi, 2000). Constraints can emerge from interactions between different chronic tendencies or between chronic tendencies and situational presses.

Within dyads and groups, the promotion and prevention systems can exert valuable constraining forces on each other. For instance, imagine a team that needs to create a new product idea and present it to a client. Team members who are promotion focused will tend to be better at generating innovative and creative ideas, but they may be likely to overlook potential problems or to miss errors in their presentation. Their creative contributions will result in a better output if they are balanced by prevention-focused members who are more likely to thoroughly analyze proposals for possible challenges and errors. Thus, teams made up of members with complementary regulatory focus may get the benefits of each system with fewer of the costs (cf. Bohns et al., 2011). Having a partner or team member with a complementary regulatory focus may also allow individuals to engage strategically in an activity in ways that fit both their orientation and the orientation of their partner, such as cooking a meal together and having the prevention partner take on the vigilant tasks and the promotion partner take on the eager tasks (Bohns et al., 2011). Given that regulatory focus orientations can be manipulated within groups (e.g., Levine et al., 2000), it is possible to create work environments that optimize the benefits of each system (for a locomotion plus assessment case of this, see Mauro, Pierro, Mannetti, Higgins, & Kruglanski, 2009). Exploring the most effective ways to do this is an exciting avenue for future research.

Even *within* individuals, the promotion and prevention systems, because they are orthogonal, can exert constraining influences on one another. In other words, individuals can be chronically strong in both the promotion *and* prevention systems. However, less is known about what factors make such high-promotion/high-prevention individuals more or less effective self-regulators. Simply being chronically strong in both systems may not be enough; it may also be important to have the skills to identify

which system best serves particular task demands and to be able to *flexibly* switch between systems. Exploring what factors—both within an individual and within environments—make it more or less likely that the dual strength of the systems can be utilized is an important question that remains to be explored.

Additionally, it is an open question how chronic and situationally induced temporary accessibility of the systems may work together dynamically in terms of constraining forces. For instance, how is a chronic promotion-focused individual served by a leadership style that induces prevention focus? On the one hand, such a situation can be problematic if the individual is in a consistent state of regulatory nonfit (Higgins, 2000). On the other hand, if the organization's primary objectives revolve around security, creating a prevention-focused environment at work may place important constraints on promotion-focused employees who would otherwise be less naturally inclined to attend to such issues. As another example, adding a coworker's prevention concern with reducing errors of commission to a personal promotion concern with reducing errors of omission could enhance someone's decision-making discriminability.

Though the promotion and prevention systems may place important constraints on each other, constraints can also come from other motivational systems. For example, individuals also differ in the extent to which they are motivated by two different aspects of self-regulation—initiating and maintaining smooth movement from state to state (locomotion) and comparing and critically evaluating options (assessment), a distinction highlighted in regulatory mode theory (Higgins et al., 2003; Kruglanski et al., 2000). Locomotors prefer action over inaction, such that they would rather do almost anything rather than nothing (Higgins et al., 2003). The locomotion system's preference for action can potentially provide a useful constraint on the prevention system's desire for thorough and careful analysis. Individuals who are chronically high in both prevention and locomotion may be better off than individuals who are chronically high in prevention and assessment, for instance. This latter combination may be particularly problematic in creating individuals who will carefully assess without end—going over and over a decision without being able to take action (e.g., being "lost in thought").

Though constraints on the systems are important, it is also important to recognize that sometimes what matters in terms of effective performance or well-being is not whether individuals are in a prevention- versus promotion-focused state, but whether individuals are in a state of regulatory fit, that is, pursuing goals using means that fit their underlying motivational orientation (Higgins, 2000). For instance, while in some situations prevention-focused individuals may be better at exhibiting self-control (e.g., resisting temptations) relative to promotion-focused individuals (Freitas et al., 2002), there are other situations in which both prevention- and promotion-focused individuals can be successful in exhibiting self-control when they use strategic means that fit their underlying orientation (Hong & Lee, 2008). Similarly, while in some situations promotion-focused individuals may be more open to change relative to prevention-focused individuals (Higgins, 2008), being in a state of regulatory fit may make *both* promotion- and prevention-focused individuals more flexible and open to alternatives. For instance, Maddox, Filoteo, Glass, and Markman (2010) found that individuals in regulatory fit showed better set shifting (abandoning a current rule for a new applicable rule) on a Wisconsin Card Sorting task relative to individuals in nonfit.

Concluding Comments

On the one hand, both promotion- and prevention-focused individuals can be successful in life pursuits; on the other hand, both promotion and prevention-focused individuals can experience difficulties. Having a lot of either promotion or prevention motivation does not guarantee a smooth ride; rather, there are trade-offs to being strongly motivated in either system. Having *more* motivation, then, is not always better. Having more motivation simply means that one is likely to experience both the upsides and the downsides of a particular motivational system. What those upsides and downsides are depends on whether an individual is in a promotion or prevention state. And how beneficial the upsides are or how detrimental the downsides are depends on the particular demands of the situation or task. What may matter most for effective self-regulation is having the *right* motivation that fits the demands of a particular situation, and understanding that even then, there can be trade-offs. Exploring how to negotiate these trade-offs in order to maximize the benefits and minimize the costs will continue to be an interesting and significant question going forward. As we hinted at earlier, we believe that the answer to effective self-regulation will need to go beyond promotion and prevention and add locomotion and assessment to the picture (Higgins,

2011). Future research will need to investigate how promotion, prevention, locomotion and assessment motivations function together effectively. It is this full organization of motivations, *working together*, that is critical.

References

Aaker, J. L., & Lee, A. Y. (2001). 'I' seek pleasures and 'we' avoid pains: The role of self-regulatory goals in information processing and persuasion. *Journal of Consumer Research, 28*, 33–49. doi:10.1086/321946

Beck, A. T., Rush, J., Shaw, B., & Emery, G. (1979). *Cognitive therapy of depression*. New York: The Guilford Press.

Bohns, V. K., Lucas, G. M., Molden, D. C., Finkel, E. J., Coolsen, M. K., Kumashiro, M.,...Higgins, E.T. (2011). When opposites fit: Increased relationship well-being from partner complementarity in regulatory focus. *Manuscript in preparation.*

Boldero, J. M., Moretti, M. M., Bell, R. C., & Francis, J. J. (2005). Self-discrepancies and negative affect: A primer on when to look for specificity, and how to find it. *Australian Journal of Psychology, 57*, 139–147. doi:10.1080/00049530500048730

Bowlby, J. (1969). *Attachment and loss. Vol. 1: Attachment..* New York: Basic Books.

Bowlby, J. (1973). *Attachment and loss. Vol. 2: Separation: Anxiety and anger*. New York: Basic Books.

Brendl, C. M., & Higgins, E. T. (1996). Principles of judging valence: What makes events positive or negative? *Advances in Experimental Social Psychology, 28*, 95–160. doi:10.1016/S0065–2601(08)60237–3.

Brickman, P. (1987). *Commitment, conflict, and caring*. Englewood Cliffs, NJ: Prentice-Hall.

Brockner, J. (2010). *A contemporary look at organizational justice: Multiplying insult times injury*. New York: Routledge.

Brockner, J., & Higgins, E. T. (2001). Regulatory focus theory: Implications for the study of emotions at work. *Organizational Behavior and Human Decision Processes, 86*, 35–66. doi:10.1006/obhd.2001.2972.

Chernev, A. (2004). Goal orientation and consumer preference for the status quo. *Journal of Consumer Research, 31*, 557–565. doi:10.1086/425090.

Choi, Y., & Mai-Dalton, R. R. (1999). The model of followers' responses to self-sacrificial leadership: An empirical test. *The Leadership Quarterly, 10*, 397–421. doi:10.1016/S1048–9843(99)00025–9.

Cornette, M. M., Strauman, T. J., Abramson, L. Y., & Busch, A. M. (2009). Self-discrepancy and suicidal ideation. *Cognition and Emotion, 23*, 504–527. doi:10.1080/02699930802012005.

Cropanzano, R., Paddock, L., Rupp, D. E., Bagger, J., & Baldwin, A. (2008). How regulatory focus impacts the process-by-outcome interaction for perceived fairness and emotions. *Organizational Behavior and Human Decision Processes, 105*, 36–51.

Crowe, E., & Higgins, E. T. (1997). Regulatory focus and strategic inclinations: Promotion and prevention in decision-making. *Organizational Behavior and Human Decision Processes, 69*, 117–132. doi:10.1006/obhd.1996.2675.

Cunningham, W. A., Raye, C. L., & Johnson, M. K. (2005). Neural correlates of evaluation associated with promotion and prevention regulatory focus. *Cognitive, Affective and Behavioral Neuroscience, 5*, 202–211. doi:10.3758/CABN.5.2.202.

Eddington, K. M., Dolcos, F., McLean, A. N., Krishnan, K. R., Cabeza, R., & Strauman, T. J. (2009). Neural correlates of idiographic goal priming in depression: Goal-specific dysfunctions in the orbitofrontal cortex. *Social Cognitive and Affective Neuroscience, 4,* 238–246. doi:10.1093/scan/nsp016.

Finkel, E. J., Molden, D. C., Johnson, S. E., & Eastwick, P. W. (2009). Regulatory focus and romantic alternatives. In J. P. Forgas, R. F. Baumeister, & D. M. Tice (Eds.), *Psychology of self-regulation: Cognitive, affective, and motivational processes. The Sydney symposium of social psychology* (pp. 319–335). New York: Psychology Press.

Florack, A., Ineichen, S., & Bieri, R. (2009). The impact of regulatory focus on the effects of two-sided advertising. *Social Cognition, 27,* 37–56. doi:10.1521/soco.2009.27.1.37.

Foster, G. D., Wadden, T. A., Vogt, R. A., & Brewer, G. (1997). What is a reasonable weight loss? Patients' expectations and evaluations of obesity treatment outcomes. *Journal of Consulting and Clinical Psychology, 65,* 79–85. doi:10.1037/0022–006X.65.1.79.

Förster, J., Grant, H., Idson, L. C., & Higgins, E. T. (2001). Success/failure feedback, expectancies, and approach/avoidance motivation: How regulatory focus moderates classic relations. *Journal of Experimental Social Psychology, 37,* 253–260. doi:10.1006/jesp.2000.1455.

Förster, J., & Higgins, E. T. (2005). How global versus local perception fits regulatory focus. *Psychological Science, 16,* 631–636. doi:10.1111/j.1467–9280.2005.01586.x.

Förster, J., Higgins, E. T., & Bianco, A. T. (2003). Speed/accuracy decisions in task performance: Built-in trade-off or separate strategic concerns? *Organizational Behavior and Human Decision Processes, 90,* 148–164. doi:10.1016/S0749–5978(02)00509–5.

Freitas, A., Liberman, N., & Higgins, E. (2002). Regulatory fit and resisting temptation during goal pursuit. *Journal of Experimental Social Psychology, 38,* 291–298.

Freitas, A., Liberman, N., Salovey, P., & Higgins, E. (2002). When to begin? Regulatory focus and initiating goal pursuit. *Personality and Social Psychology Bulletin, 28,* 121–130.

Friedman, R. S., Fishbach, A., Förster, J., & Werth, L. (2003). Attentional priming effects on creativity. *Creativity Research Journal, 15,* 277–286. doi:10.1207/S15326934CRJ152&3_18.

Friedman, R. S., & Förster, J. (2001). The effects of promotion and prevention cues on creativity. *Journal of Personality and Social Psychology, 81,* 1001–1013. doi:10.1037/0022–3514.81.6.1001.

Fuglestad, P. T., Rothman, A. J., & Jeffery, R. W. (2008). Getting there and hanging on: The effect of regulatory focus on performance in smoking and weight loss interventions. *Health Psychology, 27,* S260-S270. doi:10.1037/0278–6133.27.3.

Fulmer, C., Gelfand, M., Kruglanski, A., Kim-Prieto, C., Diener, E., Pierro, A., & Higgins, E.T. (2010). On "feeling right" in cultural contexts: How person-culture match affects self-esteem and subjective well-being. *Psychological Science, 21*(11), 1563–1569.

Galinsky, A. D., Leonardelli, G. J., Okhuysen, G. A., & Mussweiler, T. (2005). Regulatory focus at the bargaining table: Promoting distributive and integrative success. *Personality and Social Psychology Bulletin, 31,* 1087–1098. doi:10.1177/0146167205276429.

Gollwitzer, P. M., Heckhausen, H., & Steller, B. (1990). Deliberative and implemental mind-sets: Cognitive tuning toward congruous thoughts and information. *Journal of Personality and Social Psychology, 59,* 1119–1127.

Grant, H., & Higgins, E. T. (2003). Optimism, promotion pride, and prevention pride as predictors of quality of life. *Personality and Social Psychology Bulletin, 29,* 1521–1532. doi:10.1177/0146167203256919.

Hassenzahl, M., Schöbel, M., & Trautmann, T. (2008). How motivational orientation influences the evaluation and choice of hedonic and pragmatic interactive products: The role of regulatory focus. *Interacting with Computers, 20,* 473–479. doi:10.1016/j.intcom.2008.05.001.

Hendrix, K. S., & Hirt, E. R. (2009). Stressed out over possible failure: The role of regulatory fit on claimed self-handicapping. *Journal of Experimental Social Psychology, 45,* 51–59. doi:10.1016/j.jesp.2008.08.016.

Henning, J. B., Stufft, C. J., Payne, S. C., Bergman, M. E., Mannan, M. S., & Keren, N. (2009). The influence of individual differences on organizational safety attitudes. *Safety Science, 47,* 337–345. doi:10.1016/j.ssci.2008.05.003.

Herzenstein, M., Posavac, S. S., & Brakus, J. J. (2007). Adoption of new and really new products: The effects of self-regulation systems and risk salience. *Journal of Marketing Research, 44,* 251–260. doi:10.1509/jmkr.44.2.251.

Higgins, E. T. (1987). Self-Discrepancy: A theory relating self and affect. *Psychological Review, 94,* 319–340.

Higgins, E. T. (1997). Beyond pleasure and pain. *American Psychologist, 52,* 1280–1300. doi:10.1037/0003–066-X.52.12.1280.

Higgins, E. T. (1999). Persons or situations: Unique explanatory principles or variability in general principles? In D. Cervone & Y. Shoda (Eds.), *The coherence of personality: Social-cognitive bases of consistency, variability, and organization* (pp. 61–93). New York: Guilford Press.

Higgins, E. T. (2000). Making a good decision: Value from fit. *American Psychologist, 55,* 1217–1230.

Higgins, E. T. (2001). Promotion and prevention experiences: Relating emotions to nonemotional motivational states. In J. P. Forgas (Ed.), *Handbook of affect and social cognition* (pp. 186–211). London: Psychology Press.

Higgins, E. T. (2002). How self-regulation creates distinct values: The case of promotion and prevention decision making. *Journal of Consumer Psychology, 12,* 177–191. doi:10.1207/S15327663JCP1203_01.

Higgins, E. T. (2006). Value from hedonic experience and engagement. *Psychological Review, 113,* 439–460.

Higgins, E. T. (2008). Culture and personality: Variability across universal motives as the missing link. *Social and Personality Psychology Compass, 2,* 608–634. doi:10.1111/j.1751–9004.2007.00075.x.

Higgins, E. T. (2011). *Beyond pleasure and pain: How motivation works.* New York: Oxford University Press.

Higgins, E. T., Bond, R., Klein, R., & Strauman, T. (1986). Self-discrepancies and emotional vulnerability. How magnitude, accessibility, and type of discrepancy influence affect. *Journal of Personality and Social Psychology, 51,* 5–15.

Higgins, E. T., Friedman, R. S., Harlow, R. E., Idson, L. C., Ayduk, O. N., & Taylor, A. (2001). Achievement orientations from subjective histories of success: Promotion pride versus prevention pride. *European Journal of Social Psychology, 31,* 3–23. doi:10.1002/ejsp.27.

Higgins, E. T., Kruglanski, A. W., & Pierro, A. (2003). Regulatory mode: Locomotion and assessment as distinct orientations. *Advances in Experimental Social Psychology, 35,* 293–344. doi:10.1016/S0065–2601(03)01005–0.

Higgins, E. T., Roney, C., Crowe, E., & Hymes, C. (1994). Ideal versus ought predilections for approach and avoidance: Distinct self-regulatory systems. *Journal of Personality and Social Psychology, 66,* 276–286.

Higgins, E. T., Shah, J., & Friedman, R. (1997). Emotional responses to goal attainment: Strength of regulatory focus as moderator. *Journal of Personality and Social Psychology, 72,* 515–525. doi:10.1037/0022–3514.72.3.515.

Higgins, E. T., & Tykocinski, O. (1992). Self-discrepancies and biographical memory: Personality and cognition at the level of psychological situation. *Personality and Social Psychology Bulletin, 18,* 527–535. doi:10.1177/0146167292185002.

Hong, J., & Lee, A. Y. (2008). Be fit and be strong: Mastering self-regulation through regulatory fit. *Journal of Consumer Research, 34,* 682–695. doi:10.1086/521902.

Idson, L.C., & Higgins, E.T. (2000). How current feedback and chronic effectiveness influence motivation: Everything to gain versus everything to lose. *European Journal of Social Psychology, 30,* 583–592.

Idson, L. C., Liberman, N., & Higgins, E. T. (2000). Distinguishing gains from nonlosses and losses from nongains: A regulatory focus perspective on hedonic intensity. *Journal of Experimental Social Psychology, 36,* 252–274. doi:10.1006/jesp.1999.1402.

Idson, L., Liberman, N., & Higgins, E.T. (2004). Imagining how you'd feel: The role of motivational experiences from regulatory fit. *Personality and Social Psychology Bulletin, 30,* 926–937.

Jain, S. P., Lindsey, C., Agrawal, N., & Maheswaran, D. (2007). For better of for worse? Valenced comparative frames and regulatory focus. *Journal of Consumer Research, 34,* 57–65. doi:10.1086/513046.

John, O. P., & Srivastava, S. (1999). The Big Five Trait taxonomy: History, measurement, and theoretical perspectives. In L. A. Pervin & O. P. John (Eds.), *Handbook of personality: Theory and research* (2nd ed., pp. 102–138). New York: Guilford Press.

Jones, N. P., Papadakis, A. A., Hogan, C. M., & Strauman, T. J. (2009). Over and over again: Rumination, reflection, and promotion goal failure and their interactive effects on depressive symptoms. *Behaviour Research and Therapy, 47,* 254–259. doi:10.1016/j.brat.2008.12.007.

Keller, J. (2008). On the development of regulatory focus: The role of parenting styles. *European Journal of Social Psychology, 38,* 354–364. doi:10.1002/ejsp.460.

Klenk, M., Strauman, T., & Higgins, E. T. (2011). Regulatory focus and anxiety: A self-regulatory model of GAD-Depression comorbidity. *Personality and Individual Differences, 50,* 935–943.

Kruglanski, A., Higgins, E.T., Pierro, A., Thompson, E., Atash, M., Shah, J., & Spiegel, S. (2000). To "do the right thing" or to "just do it": Locomotion and assessment as distinct self-regulatory imperatives. *Journal of Personality and Social Psychology, 79,* 793–815.

Lam, T. W., & Chiu, C. (2002). The motivational function of regulatory focus in creativity. *Journal of Creative Behavior, 36,* 138–150.

de Lange, M. A., & van Knippenberg, A. (2009). To err is human: How regulatory focus and action orientation predict performance following errors. *Journal of Experimental Social Psychology, 45,* 1192–1199. doi:10.1016/j.jesp.2009.07.009.

Langens, T. A. (2007). Regulatory focus and illusions of control. *Personality and Social Psychology Bulletin, 33,* 226–237. doi:10.1177/0146167206293494.

Lee, A. Y., Aaker, J. L., & Gardner, W. L. (2000). The pleasures and pains of distinct self-construals: The role of interdependence in regulatory focus. *Journal of Personality and Social Psychology, 78,* 1122–1134. doi:10.1037/0022–3514.78.6.1122.

Leikas, S., Lönnqvist, J., Verkasalo, M., & Lindeman, M. (2009). Regulatory focus systems and personal values. *European Journal of Social Psychology, 39,* 415–429. doi:10.1002/ejsp.547.

Leone, L., Perugini, M., & Bagozzi, R. P. (2005). Emotions and decision making: Regulatory focus moderates the influence of anticipated emotions on action evaluations. *Cognition and Emotion, 19,* 1175–1198. doi:10.1080/02699930500203203.

Levine, J. M., Higgins, E. T., & Choi, H. (2000). Development of strategic norms in groups. *Organizational Behavior and Human Decision Processes, 82,* 88–101. doi:10.1006/obhd.2000.2889.

Liberman, N., Idson, L. C., Camacho, C. J., & Higgins, E. T. (1999). Promotion and prevention choices between stability and change. *Journal of Personality and Social Psychology, 77,* 1135–1145. doi:10.1037/0022–3514.77.6.1135.

Liberman, N., Molden, D. C., Idson, L. C., & Higgins, E. T. (2001). Promotion and prevention focus on alternative hypotheses: Implications for attributional functions. *Journal of Personality and Social Psychology, 80,* 5–18. doi:10.1037/0022–3514.80.1.5.

Lockwood, P., Jordan, C. H., & Kunda, Z. (2002). Motivation by positive or negative role models: Regulatory focus determines who will best inspire us. *Journal of Personality and Social Psychology, 83,* 854–864. doi:10.1037/0022–3514.83.4.854.

Maddox, W. T., Filoteo, J. V., Glass, B. D., & Markman, A. B. (2010). Regulatory match effects on a Modified Wisconsin Card Sort Task. *Journal of the International Neuropsychological Society, 16,* 352–359. doi:10.1017/S1355617709991408.

Manian, N., Papadakis, A. A., Strauman, T. J., & Essex, M. J. (2006). The development of children's ideal and ought self-guides: Parenting, temperament, and individual differences in guide strength. *Journal of Personality, 74,* 1619–1645. doi:10.1111/j.1467–6494.2006.00422.x.

Manian, N., Strauman, T. J., & Denney, N. (1998). Temperament, recalled parenting styles, and self-regulation: Testing the developmental postulates of self-discrepancy theory. *Journal of Personality and Social Psychology, 75,* 1321–1332.

Markman, K. D., McMullen, M. N., Elizaga, R. A., & Mizoguchi, N. (2006). Counterfactual thinking and regulatory fit. *Judgment and Decision Making, 1,* 98–107.

Mauro, R., Pierro, A., Mannetti, L., Higgins, E. T., & Kruglanski, A. W. (2009). The perfect mix: Regulatory complementarity and the speed-accuracy balance in group performance. *Psychological Science, 20,* 681–685. doi:10.1111/j.1467–9280.2009.02363.x.

Miele, D. B., Molden, D. C., & Gardner, W. L. (2009). Motivated comprehension regulation: Vigilant versus eager metacognitive control. *Memory and Cognition, 37,* 779–795. doi:10.3758/MC.37.6.779.

Miller, A. K., & Markman, K. D. (2007). Depression, regulatory focus, and motivation. *Personality and Individual Differences, 43*, 427–436. doi:10.1016/j.paid.2006.12.006.

Molden, D., & Higgins, E. (2004). Categorization under uncertainty: Resolving vagueness and ambiguity with eager versus vigilant strategies. *Social Cognition, 22*, 248–277.

Molden, D., & Higgins, E. (2008). How preferences for eager versus vigilant judgment strategies affect self-serving conclusions. *Journal of Experimental Social Psychology, 44*, 1219–1228.

Molden, D. C., & Higgins, E. T. (2005). Motivated thinking. In K. Holyoak and B. Morrison (Eds.), *Handbook of thinking and reasoning* (pp. 295–320). New York: Cambridge University Press.

Molden, D. C., Lucas, G. M., Gardner, W. L., Dean, K., & Knowles, M. L. (2009). Motivations for prevention or promotion following social exclusion: Being rejected versus being ignored. *Journal of Personality and Social Psychology, 96*, 415–431. doi:10.1037/a0012958.

Mowrer, O. (1960). *Learning theory and behavior.* New York: Wiley.

Ouschan, L., Boldero, J. M., Kashima, Y., Wakimoto, R., & Kashima, E. S. (2007). Regulatory Focus Strategies Scale: A measure of individual differences in the endorsement of regulatory strategies. *Asian Journal of Social Psychology, 10*, 243–457. doi:10.1111/j.1467–839X.2007.00233.x.

Papadakis, A. A., Prince, R. P., Jones, N. P., & Strauman, T. J. (2006). Self-regulation, rumination, and vulnerability to depression in adolescent girls. *Development and Psychopathology, 18*, 815–829. doi:10.1017/S0954579406060408.

Pham, M. T., & Avnet, T. (2009). Contingent reliance on the affect heuristic as a function of regulatory focus. *Organizational Behavior and Human Decision Processes, 108*, 267–278. doi:10.1016/j.obhdp.2008.10.001.

Poels, K., & Dewitte, S. (2008). Hope and self-regulatory goals applied to an advertising context: Promoting prevention stimulates goal-directed behavior. *Journal of Business Research, 61*, 1030–1040. doi:10.1016/j.jbusres.2007.09.019.

Reznik, I., & Andersen, S. M. (2007). Agitation and despair in relation to parents: Activating emotional suffering in transference. *European Journal of Personality, 21*, 281–301. doi:10.1002/per.628.

Roese, N. J., Hur, T., & Pennington, G. L. (1999). Counterfactual thinking and regulatory focus: Implications for action versus inaction and sufficiency versus necessity. *Journal of Personality and Social Psychology, 77*, 1109–1120. doi:10.1037/0022–3514.77.6.1109.

Rothman, A. J. (2000). Toward a theory-based analysis of behavioral maintenance. *Health Psychology, 19*, 64–69.

Sassenberg, K., & Hansen, N. (2007). The impact of regulatory focus on affective responses to social discrimination. *European Journal of Social Psychology, 37*, 421–444. doi:10.1002/ejsp.358.

Scholer, A. A., & Higgins, E. T. (2008). Distinguishing levels of approach and avoidance: An analysis using regulatory focus theory. In A. J. Elliot (Ed.), *Handbook of approach and avoidance motivation* (pp. 489–503). New York: Psychology Press.

Scholer, A. A., Ozaki, Y., & Higgins, E. T. (2011). Inflating and deflating the self: Sustaining motivational concerns through self-evaluation. *Under review.*

Scholer, A. A., Stroessner, S. J., & Higgins, E. T. (2008). Responding to negativity: How a risky tactic can serve a vigilant strategy. *Journal of Experimental Social Psychology, 44*, 767–774.

Scholer, A. A., Zou, X., Fujita, K., Stroessner, S. J., & Higgins, E. T. (2010). When risk-seeking becomes a motivational necessity. *Journal of Personality and Social Psychology, 99*, 215–231.

Scott, L., & O'Hara, M. W. (1993). Self-discrepancies in clinically anxious and depressed university students. *Journal of Abnormal Psychology, 102*, 282–287. doi:10.1037/0021–843X.102.2.282.

Seibt, B., & Förster, J. (2004). Stereotype threat and performance: How self-stereotypes influence processing by inducing regulatory foci. *Journal of Personality and Social Psychology, 87*, 38–56. doi:10.1037/0022–3514.87.1.38.

Semin, G. R., Higgins, E. T., de Montes, L. G., Estourget, Y., & Valencia, J. F. (2005). Linguistic signatures of regulatory focus: How abstraction fits promotion more than prevention. *Journal of Personality and Social Psychology, 89*, 36–45. doi:10.1037/0022–3514.89.1.36.

Sengupta, J., & Zhou, R. (2007). Understanding impulsive eaters' choice behaviors: The motivational influences of regulatory focus. *Journal of Marketing Research, 44*, 297–308. doi:10.1509/jmkr.44.2.297.

Shah, J., Brazy, P., & Higgins, E. T. (2004). Promoting us or preventing them: Regulatory focus and manifestations of intergroup bias. *Personality and Social Psychology Bulletin, 30*, 433–446.

Shah, J. (2003). The motivational looking glass: How significant others implicitly affect goal appraisals. *Journal of Personality and Social Psychology, 85*, 424–439. doi:10.1037/0022–3514.85.3.424.

Shah, J., & Higgins, E. T. (1997). Expectancy × value effects: Regulatory focus as determinant of magnitude and direction. *Journal of Personality and Social Psychology, 73*, 447–458. doi:10.1037/0022–3514.73.3.447.

Shah, J., & Higgins, E. T. (2001). Regulatory concerns and appraisal efficiency: The general impact of promotion and prevention. *Journal of Personality and Social Psychology, 80*, 693–705. doi:10.1037/0022–3514.80.5.693.

Shah, J., Higgins, E. T., & Friedman, R. S. (1998). Performance incentives and means: How regulatory focus influences goal attainment. *Journal of Personality and Social Psychology, 74*, 285–293. doi:10.1037/0022–3514.74.2.285.

Shah, J. Y., Friedman, R., & Kruglanski, A. W. (2002). Forgetting all else: On the antecedents and consequences of goal shielding. *Journal of Personality and Social Psychology, 83*, 1261–1280. doi:10.1037/0022–3514.83.6.1261.

Stam, K. R., & Stanton, J. M. (2010). Events, emotions, and technology: Examining acceptance of workplace technology changes. *Information Technology & People, 23*, 23–53. doi:10.1108/09593841011022537.

Strauman, T. J. (1989). Self-discrepancies in clinical depression and social phobia: Cognitive structures that underlie emotional disorders? *Journal of Abnormal Psychology, 98*, 14–22. doi:10.1037/0021–843X.98.1.14.

Strauman, T. J. (2002). Self-regulation and depression. *Self and Identity, 1*, 151–157. doi:10.1080/152988602317319339.

Strauman, T. J., & Higgins, E. T. (1987). Automatic activation of self-discrepancies and emotional syndromes: When cognitive structures influence affect. *Journal of Personality and Social Psychology, 53*, 1004–1014.

Strauman, T. J., Kolden, G. G., Stromquist, V., Davis, N., Kwapil, L., Heerey, E., & Schneider, K. (2001). The effects of treatments for depression on perceived failure in self-regulation. *Cognitive Therapy and Research, 25,* 693–712. doi:10.1023/A:1012915205800.

Strauman, T. J., Vieth, A. Z., Merrill, K. A., Kolden, G. G., Woods, T. E., Klein, M. H., ... Kwapil, L. (2006). Self-system therapy as an intervention for self-regulatory dysfunction in depression: A randomized comparison with cognitive therapy. *Journal of Consulting and Clinical Psychology, 74,* 367–376. doi:10.1037/0022–006X.74.2.367.

Taylor, S. E., Lerner, J. S., Sherman, D. K., Sage, R. M., & McDowell, N. K. (2003). Are self-enhancing cognitions associated with healthy or unhealthy biological profiles? *Journal of Personality and Social Psychology, 85,* 605–615. doi:10.1037/0022–3514.85.4.605.

Uskul, A. K., Keller, J., & Oyserman, D. (2008). Regulatory fit and health behavior. *Psychology and Health, 23,* 327–346. doi:10.1080/14768320701360385.

Van-Dijk, D., & Kluger, A. N. (2004). Feedback sign effect on motivation: Is it moderated by regulatory focus? *Applied Psychology: An International Review, 53,* 113–135. doi:10.1111/j.1464–0597.2004.00163.x.

Van Noort, G., Kerkhof, P., & Fennis, B. M. (2008). The persuasiveness of online safety cues: The impact of prevention focus compatibility of web content on consumers' risk perceptions, attitudes, and intentions. *Journal of Interactive Marketing, 22,* 58–72. doi:10.1002/dir.20121.

Vaughn, L. A., Baumann, J., & Klemann, C. (2008). Openness to experience and regulatory focus: Evidence of motivation from fit. *Journal of Research in Personality, 42,* 886–894. doi:10.1016/j.jrp.2007.11.008.

Vieth, A. Z., Strauman, T. J., Kolden, G. G., Woods, T. E., Michels, J. L., & Klein, M. H. (2003). Self-System Therapy (SST): A theory-based psychotherapy for depression. *Clinical Psychology: Science and Practice, 10,* 245–268. doi:10.1093/clipsy/bpg023.

Wallace, C., & Chen, G. (2006). A multilevel integration of personality, climate, self-regulation, and performance. *Personnel Psychology, 59,* 529–557. doi:10.1111/j.1744–6570.2006.00046.x.

Wallace, J. C., Little, L. M., & Shull, A. (2008). The moderating effects of task complexity on the relationship between regulatory foci and safety and production performance. *Journal of Occupational Health Psychology, 13,* 95–104. doi:10.1037/1076–8998.13.2.95.

Wang, J., & Lee, A. Y. (2006). The role of regulatory focus in preference construction. *Journal of Marketing Research, 43,* 28–38. doi:10.1509/jmkr.43.1.28.

Zhang, Y., & Mittal, V. (2007). The attractiveness of enriched and impoverished options: Culture, self-construal, and regulatory focus. *Personality and Social Psychology Bulletin, 33,* 588–598. doi:10.1177/0146167206296954.

Zhu, R., & Meyers-Levy, J. (2007). Exploring the cognitive mechanism that underlies regulatory focus effects. *Journal of Consumer Research, 34,* 89–96. doi:10.1086/513049.

Motivation, Personality, and Development Within Embedded Social Contexts: An Overview of Self-Determination Theory

Edward L. Deci *and* Richard M. Ryan

Abstract

Self-determination theory maintains and has provided empirical support for the proposition that all human beings have fundamental psychological needs to be competent, autonomous, and related to others. Satisfaction of these basic needs facilitates people's autonomous motivation (i.e., acting with a sense of full endorsement and volition), whereas thwarting the needs promotes controlled motivation (i.e., feeling pressured to behave in particular ways) or being amotivated (i.e., lacking intentionality). Satisfying these basic needs and acting autonomously have been consistently shown to be associated with psychological health and effective performance. Social contexts within which people operate, however proximal (e.g., a family or workgroup) or distal (e.g., a cultural value or economic system), affect their need satisfaction and type of motivation, thus affecting their wellness and effectiveness. Social contexts also affect whether people's life goals or aspirations tend to be more intrinsic or more extrinsic, and that in turn affects important life outcomes.

Key Words: self-determination, autonomy, motivation, control, autonomy support, social contexts, intrinsic motivation, life goals, autonomous motivation, embedded social contexts

To be autonomous means to behave with a sense of volition, willingness, and congruence; it means to fully endorse and concur with the behavior one is engaged in. Autonomy—this capacity for and desire to experience self-regulation and integrity—is a central force within both the life span development of individuals and in the movement of history toward greater freedom and voice for citizens within cultures and governments.

In healthy individual development, people move in the direction of greater autonomy. This entails internalizing and integrating external regulations over behavior, and learning to effectively manage drives and emotions. Additionally, it means maintaining intrinsic motivation and interest, which are vital to assimilating new ideas and experiences. When people are more autonomous, they exhibit greater engagement, vitality, and creativity in their life activities, relationships, and life projects.

Yet autonomy is not just an individual affair. Across history, groups of people have struggled to protect or gain autonomy, and to be free of coercive forces from their own dictatorial governments or from invasions by other collectives. They have fought, and often died, to be free of oppression, as well as to express and actualize their valued aims and ideals. These struggles continue today, with respect to both totalitarian regimes and the controlling forces of wealth and power wherever they subjugate or disenfranchise individuals or cultural subgroups.

Although autonomy is clearly a central issue in both individual and collective development and wellness, it is nonetheless a complex construct, manifest in different ways. Within self-determination theory (SDT), the concept of autonomy is, at different times, used to refer to a motivational state, to an enduring motivational orientation, and to a fundamental psychological need, depending on what problem is being addressed. Each of these more specific concepts relates to the formulations of autonomy and autonomy support within SDT, and the purpose of this chapter is to discuss these multiple aspects of the construct and their meanings within theory and practice.

A central function served by the concept of autonomy within SDT is to differentiate types of motivation with their corresponding qualities of functioning. Many historical and contemporary theories of motivation have treated motivation as a unitary concept, either by not specifying types of motivation or by specifying types but then adding them together to form total motivation (e.g., Bandura, 1996; Hull, 1943). Such theories have sometimes been able to effectively predict amount of behavior, but they have been much less effective in predicting qualities of behaviors. SDT maintains that knowing whether people's motivation is more *autonomous* or more *controlled* is far more important for making predictions about the quality of people's engagement, performance, and well-being than is the overall amount or intensity of motivation. And even more refined predictions can be made from the subtypes of either autonomous or controlled motivation, as we will explain in the pages ahead.

Motivation Within Embedded Contexts

Motivated individuals exist within social contexts, and research indicates that contexts vary in the degree to which they support the individuals' autonomy versus control their behaviors, thoughts, and feelings. Furthermore, at any given time people are under the influence of numerous embedded contexts (Bronfenbrenner, 1979; Connell & Wellborn, 1991). Both proximal interpersonal contexts (e.g., the behavior of people's parents or managers) and distal contexts (e.g., the cultural norms and economic structures of their society) can variously support or undermine intrinsic motivation and the integrative tendency, which together are the bases of autonomous behavior. Thus, SDT uses the quality of the social contexts within which people exist, as well as the individuals' own motivational states, orientations, and experiences of need satisfaction, to make predictions about such outcomes as the quality of behaviors, emotional experiences, cognitive structures, and psychological and physical health.

The majority of research within SDT has focused on people's proximal social contexts and the salient people within them: parents, teachers, coaches, managers, friends, physicians, and partners, for example (e.g., Deci & Ryan, 2008). Yet it is not just these immediate social connections that affect people's development and functioning, because each proximal interpersonal context is embedded in various other more distal ones. For example, classroom teachers create the interpersonal climate that affects the motivation of students on a daily basis, yet the classrooms are embedded within schools where key administrators also create broader climates, affecting the teachers' motivation, goals, and behaviors (Deci, Spiegel, Ryan, Koestner, & Kauffman, 1982; Pelletier, Séguin-Lévesque, & Legault, 2002). Schools in turn are embedded within school districts, and the key administrators of the districts affect the behaviors, motivations, and experiences of principals, and then onward down to teachers and students. District administrators, in turn, are impacted by local, state, and national government policies, which themselves will tend to be either autonomy supportive or controlling.

Ryan and Weinstein (2009) discussed an example of embedded effects, detailing how government policies concerning high-stakes testing have had a coercive influence on educational administrators' objectives and in turn on classroom practices. This has resulted in more teaching to tests, and less teacher and student autonomy, engagement, and satisfaction at the bottom of this chain of embedded contexts. In short, increasingly distal contexts such as government policies can affect individuals (in this example, the students), primarily via mediation by the important intervening contexts (viz., state governments, district administrators, principals, and teachers). This is true not only in relation to education; one sees similar embedded context affects in relation to work organizations, sport teams, health care practices, and in many other domains.

At the most distal levels of analysis, considerable research has examined how cultural contexts and values (e.g., individualism and collectivism) affect and characterize individual motivation and behaviors (e.g. Chirkov, Ryan, Kim, & Kaplan, 2003). Typically, the research focuses only on how various cultural dimensions describe individuals within a culture, but presumably much of the effect of the culture ripples through different embedded contexts at both distal and proximal levels. Parents and schools, for example, serve to transmit their cultures' values to the young people within those cultures. Cultures and countries differ not only in their ambient values, they also have economic systems (e.g., capitalism, socialism) and political systems (e.g., democracy, totalitarianism), which impact individuals—from the everyday motivations of workers, to the value systems and lifestyles embraced by their citizens (e.g., Kasser, Cohn, Kanner, & Ryan, 2007; Vansteenkiste, Ryan, & Deci, 2008). Furthermore, countries typically create laws that tend to be congruent with the economic and/or political systems and that either constrain or support the growth of competencies, the abilities of citizens to affiliate and connect, and the exercise of people's autonomy, and in so doing the laws affect the wellness and effectiveness of the citizens.

The social contexts at each of these levels of analysis can be examined with SDT concepts to investigate their effects on the behaviors, thoughts, feelings, and well-being of the people within those contexts. Throughout this chapter we will review research examining the effects of different levels of social contexts on individuals' motivation, integrity, and psychological health.

Contexts and Basic Psychological Needs

According to SDT, social contexts, whatever their level, have their impact on individuals by facilitating versus impairing satisfaction of *basic psychological needs*. We define *needs* as organismic necessities for health. Psychological needs are a subset of these necessities that are essential for psychological growth, integrity, and wellness. We have posited that people require three specific psychological nutriments for healthy functioning: They need to feel *competent* in negotiating their external and internal environments; they need to experience *relatedness* to other people and groups; and they need to feel *autonomy* or self-determination with respect to their own behaviors and lives. To the extent that these needs are satisfied, people will develop healthily and thrive, but to the extent that the needs are not satisfied, people will experience various psychological detriments. Social contexts at each level of proximity vary considerably in the degree to which they facilitate versus impair satisfaction of the basic psychological needs, and SDT is concerned in part with an examination of the factors within contexts that impact the degree to which basic psychological need satisfactions are afforded or frustrated.

It is worth noting that these three needs—for competence, relatedness, and autonomy—were not simply assumed or formulated based on casual theorizing

but were instead derived empirically. In other words, we found it necessary to posit these needs as human universals in order to provide meaningful interpretations of various phenomena that had emerged from research projects—phenomena such as the undermining of intrinsic motivation by tangible rewards (Deci, Koestner, & Ryan, 1999), contextual factors promoting the internalization of extrinsic motivation (Ryan & Connell, 1989), and goal contents and lifestyles affecting well-being (Vansteenkiste et al., 2008). Subsequent research was designed to test the existence and operation of these needs, and numerous studies have shown, for example, that across cultures (e.g., Chirkov et al., 2003), ages (e.g., Kasser & Ryan, 1999), and socioeconomic levels (Williams, McGregor, Sharp, Levesque, et al., 2006) people who experience greater satisfaction of the basic psychological needs also display greater psychological health.

In what follows, we first discuss the nature of autonomous and controlled motivation, focusing on differences in processes and outcomes that follow from the different kinds of motivation, reviewing studies that have confirmed these differences across many life domains—including home, school, work, leisure, and health care—in multiple developmental periods and cultural contexts. We begin with a focus on the more state-like or domain-specific experiences of autonomy and control, and we move on to the more enduring individual differences in autonomy and control that are termed *causality orientations* (Deci & Ryan, 1985). We then turn to different types of life goals or aspirations that have distinct motivational and well-being consequences. We also discuss social-contextual conditions at various levels as they affect the development and functioning of autonomous and controlled motivations and of intrinsic and extrinsic life goals. Finally, we review studies that have assessed satisfaction of the basic psychological needs as mediators between social contextual conditions and various outcomes such as performance and wellness, and we consider the relations of need satisfaction to motivations and goals.

Autonomous and Controlled Motivation

SDT has two important meta-theoretical assumptions concerning the nature of people that have played an important role in the theory's development. First, people are assumed to be inherently active and thus to proactively initiate engagement with their environments. *Intrinsic motivation* is the energizing basis for this activity. Second, people are assumed to have an evolved developmental tendency toward integration and organization of psychic material. This process includes taking in or *internalizing* various types of information from the external world (e.g., values, attitudes, contingencies, and knowledge), as well as integrating the regulation of internal forces (e.g., drives and emotions). These two fundamental assumptions are extremely important for our discussion of autonomous motivation, because autonomous motivation comprises two broad categories of motivation: intrinsic motivation, which is a manifestation of our active nature and is the prototype of autonomous motivation; and well-internalized extrinsic motivation, which develops because of the natural integrative tendency that is the basis of healthy development. Thus, nonintrinsic, socially transmitted motivations and regulations can become fully internalized and form the basis for autonomous or self-determined extrinsically motivated behavior (e.g., Ryan & Deci, 2003).

Intrinsic motivation involves doing an activity because it is interesting and enjoyable. It is often said that when people are intrinsically motivated, doing the activity is its own reward. However, although it may be heuristically useful to think about it that way, a more precise way of defining intrinsic motivation is in terms of the inherently satisfying internal conditions that occur when doing an intrinsically motivated behavior, thus helping to sustain it. These inherent satisfactions (experienced directly as interest and enjoyment) derive primarily from experiences of competence and autonomy as well as, in some cases, from relatedness.

One typically delightful example of intrinsically motivated behavior is children playing. In play, children are often wholly absorbed in activities, experiencing a sense of interest and joy as they manipulate objects and explore their environments. As this occurs, their basic psychological needs for competence and autonomy are likely being met, as they self-organize their actions and experience effectance. And through play, the children are learning. With adults as well, learning can be intrinsically motivated; people sometimes learn simply because they find the material or activity interesting. This is especially important because studies have shown that, when children (Grolnick & Ryan, 1987) or college students (Benware & Deci, 1984) are intrinsically motivated to learn, their learning tends to be deeper and more conceptual, and they tend to remember it longer, than when the learning is extrinsically motivated by grades or rewards. Similarly, accomplishment can be intrinsically motivated; that is,

people will often be eagerly engaged in activities because they enjoy the process of accomplishing some task or goal. At work or in sport, for example, people may be very immersed in doing a task well and experience deep satisfaction of competence and autonomy needs as they do.

In contrast to intrinsic motivation, *extrinsic motivation* involves doing an activity because it leads to a separable consequence—the goal is separate from the activity itself. Carrots (rewards or accolades) and sticks (punishments or threats) are the classic extrinsic motivators. Extrinsic motivation, when driven by such classic contingencies, is often experienced as controlled—that is, people often feel pressured, through the seduction of rewards or the coercion of threats, to do a task. Their behavior tends to become dependent on the contingencies, so they do not do the behaviors if the contingencies are not operative. To the extent that people do feel controlled by extrinsic motivators, their need for autonomy will be thwarted and some negative motivational, performance, and well-being consequences are likely to follow. Extrinsic motivation is not invariantly controlled, however, and to account for this phenomenon, SDT has differentiated extrinsic motivation using the concept of internalization.

Differentiation of Extrinsic Motivation

As noted, the classic example of being extrinsically motivated is acting in the pursuit of rewards or the avoidance of punishments. Within SDT we refer to this as *external regulation*, which is the type of regulation emphasized in operant psychology (Skinner, 1953). External regulation is a highly controlling form of motivation. Here the focus is on contingencies that are controlled by external agents, along with the resulting outcomes. However, Ryan, Connell, and Deci (1985) argued that people have an inclination, as part of the inherent integrative process, to internalize the regulation of behaviors that are valued by important others in their environments. Parents may convey to their children that they value an activity by doing it themselves, and the children may thus internalize the value of the behavior. Ryan and colleagues further argued that although internalization is typically treated as a dichotomous concept—that is, as being either external to the person or internal (Sears, Maccoby, & Levin, 1957)—it is useful to recognize that values or behavioral regulations can be internalized to differing degrees.

Specifically, Ryan et al. described three different types of internalization that differ in the degree to which they represent *full* internalization and thus the degree of autonomy of the resulting behaviors. The authors used the term *introjection* (e.g., Perls, 1973) to refer to the least autonomous form of internal regulation. Here, people have taken in a behavioral regulation, but it has retained more or less the same form it was in when it was still external. For example, parents may convey to their children that they will give them more rewards if the children do well in school and will reward them less, or punish them if they do not do well (Grolnick, 2003). Introjection of these contingencies would involve the children esteeming themselves to the degree that they do well in school. In short, their self-esteem would be contingent on doing their schoolwork well (Assor, Roth & Deci, 2004; Deci & Ryan, 1995). If they did not do well, they would feel unworthy and would have a general sense of being disapproved of by others (Roth, Assor, Niemiec, Ryan, & Deci, 2009). Although introjected regulations are "internal" or intrapersonal, they are nonetheless controlling in nature, as the individuals are being controlled by these contingencies of self-worth, which results in negative well-being consequences (Kernis & Paradise, 2002). Moreover, because the values enforced by these contingencies are only partially internalized, people typically do not feel fully volitional when enacting them so the behaviors are motivationally unstable and usually are either weakly related or unrelated to long-term commitment or performance (Deci & Ryan, 2000). Accordingly, external and introjected regulations are considered to be the two subtypes of controlled extrinsic motivation.

The regulation of extrinsically motivated behaviors is more autonomous when the individuals understand and accept the real importance of the activity for themselves. We refer to this type of regulation as *identified regulation* because the individuals have identified with the value of the behavior for themselves. The experience of identified regulation is thus distinct from the experience of introjected regulation, and the two have different correlates. For example, research has shown when the regulation of religious behaviors is introjected, such behaviors are negatively associated with well-being, whereas when the regulation is identified, religious behaviors are positively associated with well-being (Ryan, Rigby, & King, 1993). Finally, when an identification has become congruent with other identifications, needs, and experiences, the resulting regulation is referred to as *integrated regulation*, which represents the most highly autonomous form of extrinsic motivation.

We have now specified three subtypes of autonomous motivation: identified and integrated forms of extrinsic motivation, along with intrinsic motivation. Typically, behaviors that are initially extrinsically motivated are not transformed into intrinsically motivated behaviors, because they retain their instrumental focus; however, some behaviors are motivated by both intrinsic and extrinsic elements. These extrinsic motivations may begin as external or introjected regulations and be transformed into the more autonomous types of extrinsic motivation—namely, identified and integrated regulation—although they may be retained in a quite controlling form. Intrinsic motivation and integrated extrinsic motivation share various characteristics, such as flexibility and volitional engagement, but they are different because intrinsic motivation refers to doing the behavior because it is interesting and enjoyable in its own right, whereas integrated regulation refers to doing the behavior because it is personally, though instrumentally, important, valued, and meaningful for the person. Furthermore, studies have shown that, whereas intrinsic motivation tends to be the better predictor of being engrossed in an activity, identified and integrated regulations tend to be better predictors of doing more effortful tasks that require discipline (e.g., Burton, Lydon, D'Alessandro, & Koestner, 2006; Koestner, Losier, Vallerand, & Carducci, 1996).

Having specified different types of motivation, it is important to highlight that any given behavior can be energized by more than one of these motivations. For example, one might be both identified with the value of an action and also introjected concerning one's performance at it. One might pursue an activity that one identifies with and also feel intrinsic motivation while enacting at least parts of it. In other words, types of regulation can co-occur, and thus within SDT we often look at the overall *relative autonomy* of a person's actions, using procedures that aggregate these multiple motives (see Ryan & Connell, 1989).

Outcomes Associated With Autonomous Motivation

Ryan, Connell, and Plant (1990) found that students' intrinsic motivation for a learning task positively predicted their learning and recall both immediately following the reading and a week later. Wang (2008) found similar results among Chinese college students in that those who were more intrinsically motivated performed better on the final exam in the course, thus confirming the relation of intrinsic motivation to learning in an Eastern culture. Boiché, Sarrazin, Grouzet, and Pelletier (2008) assessed autonomous motivation (both intrinsic and identified) of high school physical education students and found that students who were more autonomously motivated performed better in the course activities than those who were lower on autonomous motivation. Lévesque, Zuehlke, Stanek, and Ryan (2004) found that autonomous motivation (as well as perceived competence) in both German and American college students positively predicted their well-being. Pelletiere, Fortier, Vallerand, and Brière (2001) found that elite swimmers who were more autonomously motivated persisted at their sport longer than those who were more controlled in their motivation.

Studies have also shown that when people are more autonomously motivated for changing their health-compromising behaviors—for example, stopping smoking, eating a healthier diet, or exercising more regularly—they are more successful in changing such behaviors and maintaining the changes over time. Such findings have been verified in multiple ways, including through physiological indicators such as decreases in glycosylated hemoglobin and LDL cholesterol (e.g., Williams, Freedman, & Deci, 1998; Williams, McGregor, Sharp, Kouides, et al., 2006). In a similar vein, studies have shown that when clients are more autonomous in their motivation for participating in psychotherapy, they experience more successful outcomes, such as decreased depression (Pelletier, Tuson, & Haddad, 1997; Zuroff et al., 2007). Other research has shown that people who are more autonomously motivated behave in healthier ways, such as consuming alcohol responsibly (Pavey & Sparks, 2009).

Research has further shown that autonomous motivation promotes not only behaviors that are personally healthy, but it also leads to behaviors that promote well-being of the collective. For example, Séguin, Pelletier, and Hunsley (1999) found that people who were more autonomously motivated to engage in pro-environmental behaviors sought out more information about environmental health risks and acted more pro-environmentally.

Furthermore, across these and other domains, research suggests that people who are more autonomously motivated display greater psychological wellness (e.g., Ryan et al., 1993; Sheldon, Ryan, Deci, & Kasser, 2004). This is important because SDT assumes that when afforded autonomy people are more apt to behave in ways that further their own capabilities and thriving (Vansteenkiste et al.,

2008). Stated differently, autonomy facilitates integrated action, need fulfillment, and wellness.

To summarize, we have reviewed just a few of the hundreds of studies, done in multiple domains and cultures and with participants of varied ages, that have shown that more autonomous motivations are more effective than controlled motivations with respect to learning, performing effectively, behaving in healthier ways, and other important outcomes.

Causality Orientations

The autonomous and controlled motivations being addressed thus far have been either (1) state-level motivations that people experience at a particular time and that might be prompted by a particular situation, or (2) domain-specific motivations—motivations in school, at home, or at work, for example—that are somewhat more stable than state motivations but apply just to specific areas of life. Yet autonomous functioning can also be studied at a more global, or individual difference, level, as specified within Vallerand's (1997) hierarchical model of motivation. Individual differences (i.e., between-person differences) in personality can have influences across domains and over time. We refer to this level of analysis of motivational types as causality orientations, and SDT specifies three such orientations—autonomous, controlled, and impersonal orientations—and maintains that all people have each orientation to some degree.

The autonomy orientation is defined as the degree to which people tend to be generally autonomous and also to interpret the environment as both being supportive of their autonomy and providing information relevant to choices they are making. When autonomy oriented, people regulate behavior on the basis of interests and abiding values. The controlled orientation indexes the level to which people are controlled across domains of their lives and interpret environments as being pressuring and coercive. When control oriented, people are focused on rewards or punishments, both tangible and social, in the regulation of behavior. The impersonal orientation refers to a general sense of not being intentional or motivated and of seeing the environment as providing obstacles to getting desired outcomes. When impersonally oriented, people feel little agency, and often fail to regulate their behavior effectively.

Considerable research has shown that the autonomy orientation is positively associated with self-actualization, self-esteem, ego development, and the tendency to support autonomy in others; it is also negatively associated with many indicators of ill-being. The controlled orientation is associated with such characteristics as public self-consciousness and the Type-A coronary-prone behavior pattern. The impersonal orientation is correlated with variables such as self-derogation, social anxiety, external locus of control, and depressive symptoms.

Williams, Grow, Freedman, Ryan, and Deci (1996) found that morbidly obese patients who were in a medically supervised dietary program were more likely to lose weight and keep it off for 2 years if they were high rather than low on the autonomy orientation. Baard, Deci, and Ryan (2004) found that employees of a banking firm who were high rather than low on the autonomy orientation experienced greater need satisfaction at work and received better performance evaluations from their managers. Knee, Patrick, Vietor, Nanayakkara, and Neighbors (2002) found in a laboratory study of romantic partners that individuals who were high on the autonomy orientation displayed fewer negative emotions, more positive behaviors, and more relationship-maintaining coping strategies; whereas those high on the controlled orientation were more negative and wanted their partners to be more like themselves.

Weinstein, Deci, and Ryan (2011) found that people high in the autonomy orientation integrated both positive and negative past identities into their current sense of self, whereas those high on the controlled orientation accepted their past positive, but rejected their past negative, identities. These findings were mediated by defensiveness, with people high in the controlled orientation also being higher in defense. The results followed up on a study by Hodgins, Koestner, and Duncan (1996), which found that college students who were high in autonomy were less defensive (i.e., more honest and disclosing) with their parents, reported more pleasant affect, and felt better about themselves in those interactions than were students high in the controlled orientation. Other studies by Hodgins and colleagues (Hodgins & Liebeskind, 2003; Hodgins, Liebeskind, & Schwartz, 1996) revealed that people higher in autonomy, relative to the other orientations, used fewer lies in explaining wrongdoings and provided more apologies when they had caused harm to others.

As noted, the SDT perspective maintains that all people have some level of all three causality orientations. One orientation may be much stronger than the others and thus, on average, be the dominant personality-level influence on a person's functioning; however, other orientations may be dominant at particular times. This happens in part because factors in the environment prime (i.e., nonconsciously prompt) specific orientations regardless of the ongoing levels in the strengths of the three orientations (e.g., Friedman, Deci, Elliot, Moller, & Aarts, 2010; Hodgins, Yacko, & Gottlieb, 2006). In the Weinstein et al. (2011) research mentioned earlier, some of the studies assessed causality orientations with the self-report measure, but others primed the autonomous and controlled orientations in people randomly assigned to conditions, thus making the primed orientations more salient. The researchers found that those primed to be autonomous integrated both positive and negative past identities, whereas those primed to be controlled integrated positive past identities but not negative ones, thus paralleling exactly the findings by these authors in which individual differences in causality orientations (assessed with a questionnaire) were used as predictors of integrating past identities. Similarly, Hodgins et al. (2006) primed causality orientations in college students and found that autonomy-primed individuals displayed lower use of the defenses such as self-serving bias and self-handicapping, whereas control-primed individuals were higher in self-serving responding and self-handicapping, results that paralleled those found in studies by Knee and Zuckerman (1996, 1998) who had used causality orientations assessed as individual differences.

To summarize, research on causality orientations has indicated that being more autonomy oriented has far more positive outcomes for effective performance and psychological health than being high on the other two orientations. Furthermore, studies have shown that subliminal prompts can prime causality orientations and produce effects that parallel those that are predicted by self-reported individual differences in causality orientations.

Intrinsic and Extrinsic Life Goals

Although SDT focuses primarily on the "why" of people's goals and behaviors (i.e., on autonomous versus controlled motivations), we have also studied the *contents* of people's goals, or the "what" of behavior. A central notion is that, because the effects of any behavior on wellness is mediated by basic psychological need satisfactions, "not all goals are created equal" (Ryan, Sheldon, Kasser, & Deci, 1996), because some goals are more directly satisfying of basic needs and some are less satisfying or even thwarting of basic need satisfaction, and thus have different effects on psychological wellness.

Pursuing Intrinsic and Extrinsic Aspirations

Especially studied in this regard are aspirations or life goals that people value, pursue, and sometimes attain. Kasser and Ryan (1996) found that, when participants reported how much importance they placed on a variety of life goals, the goals separated into two factors that the investigators referred to as *extrinsic* and *intrinsic aspirations* or *life goals*. The extrinsic aspirations that have been studied most are accumulating wealth, becoming famous, or having an attractive image. The intrinsic ones that have gotten considerable empirical attention are personal growth, developing meaningful relationships, contributing to the community, and being physically fit and healthy.

Much of the research has examined the association between the relative strength of the extrinsic versus intrinsic life goal pursuits and their relations to various indicators of psychological health and well-being. Consistently, the studies have shown that when people's aspirations for pursuing extrinsic outcomes are relatively stronger than their aspirations for pursuing intrinsic outcomes, individuals tend to have lower self-esteem and self-actualization, as well as higher depression, anxiety, narcissism, and Machiavellianism, among other outcomes (e.g., Kasser & Ryan, 1993; McHoskey, 1999). They also engage more in high risk behaviors (Williams, Cox, Hedberg, & Deci, 2000).

Some commentators (e.g., Carver & Baird, 1998) have suggested that the reason pursuing extrinsic goals is related to poorer psychological health than is pursuing intrinsic goals is that extrinsic goals are likely to be pursued for controlled motives, whereas intrinsic goals are likely to be pursued for autonomous motives. In other words, they argued that the problem is not in "what" was being pursued (the extrinsic goal) but in "why" it was being pursued (the controlled motive). Sheldon et al. (2004) tested this reasoning in three studies. They found that there was indeed a correlation between the "what" and the "why" of behavior— people more oriented toward extrinsic goals did tend to be more controlled and those oriented toward the intrinsic goals did tend to be more autonomous. However, when both the goals and the motives were entered simultaneously into regression analyses to predict well-being, results showed that both the what and the why accounted for independent variance. That is, what people pursue and why they pursue it both make a significant difference in their psychological well-being. In short, being controlled in one's motivation and pursuing extrinsic aspirations are both negative predictors of well-being.

The SDT interpretation of the results for aspirations is that the intrinsic goals are quite directly related to satisfaction of the basic psychological needs. Personal growth, for example, is closely related to becoming more integrated and autonomous, as well as somewhat more competent and, most likely, more related to others because personal growth tends to make satisfying relationships easier. Furthermore, both meaningful relationships and community involvement are strongly tied to satisfaction of the relatedness need and they are likely to relate to people feeling more autonomous and competent to the extent that the goals are pursued volitionally (e.g., see Weinstein & Ryan, 2010). In contrast, the extrinsic aspirations are typically at best only indirectly related to basic need satisfaction, and they may in many cases be antagonistic to satisfaction of the basic needs. For example, the pursuit of wealth is likely to leave people feeling less autonomous, as acting in the service of monetary rewards has been shown to undermine autonomy, and, furthermore, the time devoted to the pursuit of wealth is likely to interfere with relatedness satisfaction. Similar kinds of arguments can be made for fame and image when they are highly valued as life goals.

Attaining Intrinsic and Extrinsic Aspirations

Recently, Niemiec, Ryan, and Deci (2009) examined how the *attainment* (rather than the pursuit) of intrinsic versus extrinsic aspirations contributes to wellness versus distress in early adulthood. The study followed young adults beginning 1 year after they had graduated from college (Time 1) and ending 1 year after that (Time 2). At the beginning and end of that year four important concepts were assessed: *(1)* the personal importance of intrinsic and extrinsic goals, *(2)* the level of attainment of intrinsic and extrinsic goals, *(3)* the degree of satisfaction of the basic psychological needs, and *(4)* indicators of both well-being and ill-being. Results showed first that the importance people place on goals at Time 1 strongly predicted attainment of those goals at Time 2, and this was true for both intrinsic and extrinsic goals. People tended to attain that which they considered important. Second, increases in the attainment of intrinsic goals over the year related to increases in well-being and to decreases in ill-being over that period. In contrast, increases in attainment of extrinsic goals did *not* predict increases in well-being but did predict symptoms of ill-being. Finally, the research showed that the relations between changes in intrinsic goal attainment and changes in well-being were mediated by corresponding changes in satisfaction of the basic psychological needs (Niemiec et al., 2009). This study seems to be a warning: "Be careful what you wish for" because people tend to attain the goals they value, but the consequences of doing so may be negative for some of the goals.

Manipulating Goal Orientations

Thus far we have treated aspirations as individual differences that are learned as a function of satisfaction versus thwarting of the basic psychological needs during development, and the primary outcomes in the research have generally been well-being indicators. In another important strand of this research the salience of people's goals has been experimentally manipulated. Vansteenkiste, Simons, Lens, Sheldon, and Deci (2004) did two studies of college students and one of younger, physical education students in which all the students were engaged in learning activities and the introduction they received to the task oriented them toward viewing the task as leading to either an intrinsic goal or an extrinsic goal. For example, business students were given material to learn about communication processes; half were told the learning would help them understand themselves better (i.e., an intrinsic goal of personal growth) and the other half were told that the learning would help them earn more money in their business careers (i.e., an extrinsic goal of wealth). Results indicated that those who had been oriented toward the intrinsic goal learned the material better than those who had been oriented toward the extrinsic goal. Furthermore, 5 days later, when making a presentation about the material, the students who had learned with the intrinsic goal set were rated as having given better presentations. Additionally, those who had been given the intrinsic goal orientation spent more subsequent time exploring the topic by engaging in voluntary activities related to the learning.

Summary of Life Goals Research

Research shows that many life goals can be grouped into two categories: intrinsic aspirations such as growth, relationships, and community, and extrinsic aspirations such as wealth, fame, and image. Numerous studies further indicate that pursuit and attainment of the intrinsic aspirations is associated with greater well-being and less ill-being, whereas the pursuit and attainment of extrinsic aspirations is

associated with less well-being and greater ill-being. These relations tend to be mediated by satisfaction versus thwarting of the basic psychological needs, such that intrinsic goals tend to have a direct relation to satisfaction of the basic psychological needs, whereas extrinsic goals tend to be either indirectly related to or antagonistic to satisfaction of the basic needs. Finally, these intrinsic and extrinsic aspirations can also be manipulated by or primed within social contexts, such that, when extrinsic goals are made salient, performance and well-being tend to be worse, whereas when intrinsic goals are made salient performance and well-being tend to be better. We turn now to a consideration of how social contexts facilitate autonomous versus controlled motivations and intrinsic versus extrinsic aspirations.

Effects of Social Contexts on Motivation, Life Goals, Behavior, and Well-Being

Autonomous motivation, intrinsic aspirations, effective functioning, and well-being are theorized to be facilitated both developmentally and situationally by social contexts. As we noted earlier, facilitators of (and obstacles to) optimal functioning, of which autonomous motivation and intrinsic aspirations are a central components, are conceptualized within SDT in terms of supports (or thwarts) for satisfaction of the basic psychological needs for competence, autonomy, and relatedness.

Specific Contextual Factors and Autonomous Motivation

Some of the studies of social-contextual effects on motivation-related outcomes have been experiments examining specific factors such as the offer of rewards, provision of choice, imposition of deadlines, or introduction of competition as they affect autonomous motivation, and many of these have used intrinsic motivation as the dependent variable. For example, nearly 100 experiments have investigated whether tangible-reward contingencies tend to promote versus diminish intrinsic motivation, and the results confirmed that the use of the most common reward contingencies tend to decrease the experience of autonomy and promote controlled motivation (Deci et al., 1999). These authors interpreted this as indicating that, on average, the rewards thwart satisfaction of the need for autonomy while prompting a shift in the perceived locus of causality from internal to external (de Charms, 1968). Rewards have frequently been used to control people's behavior, so the rewards have tended to take on a controlling functional significance and to end up thwarting autonomy and undermining intrinsic motivation.

Other research revealed that threats of punishment, deadlines, evaluations, surveillance, and pressured competition also decreased intrinsic motivation because they too are often experienced as thwarting the autonomy need (see Ryan & Deci, 2000a for a review). Like rewards, these other specific aspects of social environments tend to be experienced as pressuring rather than supportive. In contrast, offering choice and acknowledging people's feelings enhanced intrinsic motivation and facilitated fuller internalization because they prompted an internal perceived locus of causality and satisfied people's need for autonomy (e.g., Deci, Eghrari, Patrick, & Leone, 1994; Koestner, Ryan, Bernieri, & Holt, 1984; Oliver, Markland, Hardy, & Petherick, 2008; Patall, Cooper, & Robinson, 2008).

Experiments have also examined the effects of feedback on autonomous motivation. In general, these studies indicate that positive feedback tends to enhance intrinsic motivation and facilitate internalization, because such feedback provides satisfaction of the competence need and may also support autonomy. That is, when people get positive feedback that is authentic, they are likely to infer that they are responsible for their good performance, thus experiencing autonomy as well as competence satisfactions. Situations that provide positive feedback and are accompanied by some support for autonomy are referred to as *informational*, and they have consistently been shown to enhance autonomous motivation (see Deci & Ryan, 2000). Yet when positive feedback is given in a controlling way—for example, in a form such as, "Good, you did just as you should"—it tends to be detrimental to autonomous motivation and to shift the perceived locus of causality toward external (Ryan, 1982). When feedback is negative, the message tends to convey "incompetence" and decreases autonomous motivation. If the negative feedback is persistent, and especially if it is demeaning, it will tend to result in amotivation.

Autonomy-Supportive and Controlling Climates

Other studies have examined autonomy-supportive versus controlling social environments as concepts that capture the quality of an interpersonal climate or the ambience of a situation—be it, say, a home, classroom, workgroup, or clinic. Autonomy-supportive environments are ones in which the perspectives of individuals in that environment are acknowledged (typically by an authority figure); the individuals are encouraged to experiment and are provided some choice; and the use of controlling language and contingencies is minimized. In contrast, controlling contexts are ones that pressure people to think, feel, or behave in specific ways (Deci & Ryan, 2000) through the use of coercive or seductive pressures and demands. The concept of an autonomy-supportive versus controlling climate has been assessed with several methods, including self-reports from the authority figures in the situations (e.g., teachers, managers, parents, coaches, physicians, or therapists); reported perceptions of the authorities' autonomy supportiveness from people for whom the authority is responsible; interviews with the authorities that are rated or coded for autonomy support; and direct observations that are, similarly, rated or coded.

As mentioned earlier, autonomy-supportive contexts of course support satisfaction of the autonomy need. It turns out, furthermore, that these contexts also tend, to some degree, to support the other basic psychological needs—the needs for relatedness and competence. First, when an authority takes another's perspective, the other typically feels like he or she has been related to in a genuine way, thus providing support for relatedness (e.g., La Guardia, Ryan, Couchman, & Deci, 2000). In addition, because autonomy support includes perspective taking, autonomy-supportive authorities will be more mindful of obstacles to satisfaction of the people's other needs—that is, of frustrations to competence and relatedness needs. Finally, when people are in situations where their autonomy is supported, they are likely to feel freer to do what is necessary to get their other needs satisfied.

RELATIONAL SUPPORTS AND STRUCTURE

It is important to note that there are factors other than autonomy support that specifically facilitate satisfaction of the basic needs for relatedness and competence. For example, direct expressions of caring, time spent together mutually sharing feelings, and involvement of one person in the life of another are examples of factors likely to promote satisfaction of the relatedness need (e.g., Grolnick, Benjet, Kurowski, & Apostoleris, 1997). Furthermore, providing noncontrolling *structure* and informational feedback are factors likely to promote satisfaction of the competence need (e.g., Jang, Reeve, & Deci, 2010; Ryan, 1982). In other words, research in SDT suggests specific nutriments that can enhance each of the basic need satisfactions, beyond the general facilitating impact of autonomy support.

STUDIES OF SOCIAL CONTEXTS IN VARIOUS DOMAINS

Many studies conducted over the past 30 years have examined the relations of autonomy-supportive contexts to motivation and other outcomes, beginning with Deci, Schwartz, Sheinman, and Ryan (1981). These investigators had elementary school teachers report on the degree of their own autonomy-supportive versus controlling classroom styles, and these teacher self-reports were then related to the students' experiences of intrinsic motivation, perceived competence for school, and self-esteem. It was found that when teachers were more autonomy supportive, their students became more intrinsically motivated and perceived themselves more positively by the end of the first 2 months of the school year. Ryan and Connell (1989) found that when elementary school teachers were perceived as more autonomy supportive, their students showed greater internalization of achievement-related values. Black and Deci (2000) found that college students taking organic chemistry from instructors who were more autonomy supportive became more autonomous and got higher grades in the course, after controlling for SAT scores and grade point averages.

Grolnick and Ryan (1989) in an interview study of the parents of elementary school students found that parents who were rated by interviewers as more autonomy supportive had children who were more autonomously motivated to do schoolwork, were rated by their teachers as more competent and better behaved, and got better grades. Landry et al. (2008) found that when mothers trusted in the natural developmental process, they were more autonomy supportive, and both the mothers and children evidenced more positive adaptation. Gagné, Ryan, and Bargmann (2003) found that when coaches were more autonomy supportive, gymnasts evidenced greater vitality, autonomous motivation, and well-being. These and many other similar studies have shown the pervasive effects of support for autonomy across youth development.

Similar evidence is found in the workplace (see Gagné & Deci, 2005). For example, managers of a Fortune 500 company who were more autonomy supportive had employees who were more satisfied with their jobs and more trusting of the company's top management (Deci, Connell, & Ryan, 1989). Baard et al. (2004) found that banking industry employees who perceived their managers as more autonomy supportive displayed better psychological well-being and received higher performance evaluations than employees who perceived their managers as more controlling.

In health care settings numerous studies have shown that patients who perceive their practitioners as more autonomy supportive tended to make greater improvements in health behaviors and outcomes. For example, when practitioners (e.g., physicians, nurses, health counselors, dental professionals) were perceived as more autonomy supportive, their patients were more likely to quit smoking (e.g., Williams, McGregor, Sharp, Levesque, et al., 2006); to more effectively regulate their glucose levels (e.g., Williams, McGregor, Zeldman, Freedman, & Deci, 2004); to achieve and maintain more weight loss (Williams et al., 1996); and to attend dental clinics more regularly (Münster Halvari, Halvari, Bjørnebekk, & Deci, 2010). Philippe and Vallerand (2008) found that when nursing home staff were more autonomy supportive, residents both reported more autonomy and displayed greater well-being.

Mutual Autonomy Support in Peer Relationships

In friendships and romantic relationships autonomy support also matters. Here, however, the situation is a bit different. In each of the relationships discussed earlier there was an authority differential between the two people in the relationship— teachers-students, managers-employees, and coaches-athletes, for example. With friends, relationships are typically more mutual. A study of friends by Deci, La Guardia, Moller, Scheiner, and Ryan (2006) found that the mutuality of autonomy support was indeed advantageous. Each relational partner benefited in terms of well-being not only when receiving autonomy support from his or her partner but also when giving autonomy support to the partner. Other studies of intimate relationships (Knee et al., 2002; La Guardia & Patrick, 2008) similarly attest to the impact of need-related supports in close relationships for enhancing versus debilitating people's healthy functioning and wellness.

Other research has shown positive effects on well-being of both giving and receiving help even to a stranger, assuming that the helping was autonomously done rather than being controlled. Weinstein and Ryan (2010) found in a series of diary studies and experiments that the more autonomously motivated an individual was to provide help to another, the more the helping predicted well-being outcomes not only in the helper but also in the recipients of that help. In short, it seems that giving to and caring for others can be very positive for both the giver and the receiver so long as the giver is autonomous in his or her actions.

Contextual Effect on Intrinsic and Extrinsic Aspirations

Studies have examined the effects of social contexts not only on autonomous and controlled motivation but also on the development of intrinsic and extrinsic life goals or aspirations. We saw earlier that having a strong extrinsic life-goal orientation tends to thwart basic psychological need satisfaction, resulting in more negative outcomes, such as increased ill-being. The SDT perspective suggests that it is also the case that the *development* of a strong extrinsic life-goal orientation tends to result from thwarting of basic psychological need satisfaction over time. This thwarting creates a sense of anxiety and inadequacy that leads to the pursuit of external indicators of worth in order to make up for the lack of inner feelings of worth. For example, Kasser, Ryan, Zax, and Sameroff (1995) studied the importance late teenagers' placed on the extrinsic aspiration for wealth, relative to intrinsic aspirations for growth, relatedness, and community. They found that teenagers who placed the strongest importance on wealth had mothers, according to reports from both the adolescents and their mothers, who were more authoritarian, controlling, and cold. This early thwarting of children's basic need satisfaction is assumed to have created an inner insecurity in the children for which they developed strong extrinsic aspirations in an attempt to compensate.

Similarly, Williams, Cox, Hedberg, and Deci (1999) found that adolescents who rated their parents as low in autonomy support placed stronger importance on the extrinsic relative to intrinsic aspirations, and this in turn was associated with the adolescents engaging in more risky behaviors such as early engagement in tobacco use, alcohol consumption, and sexual intercourse. Sheldon and Kasser (2008) found that when college students experienced psychological threats (including existential, financial, and interpersonal threats), they tended to become more strongly focused on extrinsic life goals. It seems from these various studies that when young people experience thwarting of their basic psychological needs they tend to become more oriented toward the extrinsic goals in order to compensate for the inner feelings of anxiety. Unfortunately, as we saw earlier, becoming more strongly oriented toward extrinsic aspirations in turn causes greater need thwarting and poorer outcomes, thus perpetuating a cyclical negative dynamic of need thwarting, causing a stronger extrinsic orientation and that in turn causing greater need thwarting.

More Distal and Pervasive Influences

Certainly proximal social contexts—our immediate interpersonal worlds—typically provide the most phenomenally salient experiences of autonomy support or control both situationally and developmentally. But from an SDT perspective the cultural, economic, and political contexts within which people live have overarching and pervasive, yet often hidden, roles in supporting or thwarting the fulfillment of their basic needs. These distal contexts both set horizons on people's possibilities and also introduce norms, constraints, and policies that either facilitate or diminish need fulfillments.

Cultural Values

AUTONOMOUS MOTIVATION AND WELLNESS

Chirkov et al. (2003) examined the relations of cultural values to the well-being of individuals in those cultures. The researchers focused on whether the cultures of South Korea, Russia, Turkey, and the United States tended to emphasize individualism or collectivism and whether the societies were more horizontal or vertical in their structures. The researchers found first that although the cultures differed in terms of the values placed on individualism versus collectivism, it was not the values themselves that predicted well-being; it was instead the degree to which people had internalized the values that predicted their well-being. In other words, autonomy (resulting from full internalization) was important for individuals' well-being in all these cultures, regardless of whether the cultures were oriented more toward the collective or more toward the individual.

The study further found that vertical structures were, on average, more difficult to internalize than were horizontal structures. We understand this as indicating that a vertical or hierarchical system is likely (though not invariantly) to be experienced as more controlling than a horizontal one and would thus tend to thwart people's need for autonomy, making it more difficult to accept the hierarchical structure as their own. This of course is merely an "on average" finding, and it remains for the issue of hierarchy to be disentangled from the experience of autonomy versus control at the cultural level. In principle, according to SDT, one could congruently assent to some hierarchical arrangements without losing a sense of autonomy in following that arrangement. This kind of integrated identification with a hierarchical structure would be facilitated by authorities who behave in a need-supporting way toward the individual or group, making acceptance and assimilation more possible.

CULTURE, ASPIRATIONS, AND WELL-BEING

The issue of broader contextual effects and well-being can also be addressed with respect to aspirations or life goal. The goals of wealth, fame, and image are very central to what we think of as the "American Dream"—that is, the set of values our culture and its economic system tend to promote. Indeed, having people within the culture be oriented toward the pursuit of wealth, fame, and attractiveness is necessary for the culture to grow (Kasser et al., 2007), so the advertising industry within America has become enormous, and its primary purpose is to get people to buy more goods and services that represent external indicators of worth—namely, appearing attractive, wealthy, and popular. Of course, doing that requires actually pursuing more wealth to pay for the goods and services, thus contributing to economic growth.

Our cultural context, emphasizing the American Dream, supplies the backdrop in which schools and parents are embedded as they influence children's motivation. Simply stated, the culture with its capitalist economic system strongly promotes extrinsic aspirations, through direct means such as advertising and through indirect means such as prompting stress within families and thus creating conditions of insecurity that conduce toward extrinsic valuing. While these psychological conditions may facilitate consumption and spending, they are unlikely to be conducive to wellness and high quality of life.

Twenge, Gentile, DeWall, Ma, Lacefield, and Schurtz (2010) recently examined cultural trends in the mental health of U.S. college students over the past seven decades. They first found a rather disconcerting pattern: Over this time U.S. college students evidenced increases in symptoms of depression, anxiety, and antisocial tendencies as detected with equated assessments. Examining numerous factors that might account for this negative trend toward greater distress and psychopathology, they ruled out numerous issues from prosperity to family structure. What they concluded was that the increasing shift toward poorer mental health and psychopathology may be "due to an increased focus on money, appearance, and status rather than on community and close relationships" (p. 153). That is, the slide toward more extrinsic life goals appears to have led

at least this U.S. cultural subgroup toward more distress and lower wellness.

CULTURAL VALUES AND NEED SATISFACTION

Together, these findings about cultures and values are important because they suggest that cultures play a role in whether the people can experience satisfaction of their basic needs. The results further suggest that having the need for autonomy satisfied in any culture, regardless of the culture's values, would contribute to psychological wellness. Conversely, studies show that people feel more estranged from and less accepting of their cultures to the degree that they are not experiencing basic need satisfaction (e.g., Chirkov, Ryan, & Willness, 2005). Thus, one basis for alienation and instability within any culture may be the extent to which the culture's ambient values and behavioral regulations fail to support or facilitate opportunities for basic need satisfaction among its constituents.

EVALUATING CULTURAL VALUES AND PRACTICES

It is of course treacherous for social scientists to evaluate cultural value systems or practices. Many scholars today in fact ascribe to a *cultural relativism* view, which maintains that it is not appropriate to evaluate any cultural milieu from the "outside." In this regard, SDT is in a particularly interesting position. In our view, need support means supporting the self-regulation of individuals so they can have the freedom to experience and pursue *their own* preferred values and life projects. In taking this *internal frame of reference*, SDT is therefore not imposing particular contents, but rather is specifying a criterion for evaluating any cultural value or practice. To the extent that the value or practice supports (rather than thwarts) satisfaction of the basic human needs underlying growth, effective functioning, and wellness, the evaluation would be positive.

Economic Systems

Just as cultural systems set affordances, constraints, and boundaries that affect people's pursuit and attainment of basic psychological need satisfactions, so too do economic systems. From the way in which work behavior is managed and regulated, to the macro-arrangements responsible for distributing wealth and caring for citizens, SDT takes interest in how various economic structures support or thwart people's basic psychological needs. We have already discussed how proximal management styles impact work motivation. Variations in macro-structures—from the direct deprivations of autonomy and competence often witnessed in central planning economies, to the economic and social oppression that can be experienced within market capitalisms also differentially support or diminish human wellness. SDT uses the construct of basic psychological needs as mediating factors to link these distal structures to the experiences and outcomes of particular individuals and communities. Although we have interest in varied economic systems (e.g., Deci et al., 2001), in what follows, we focus primarily on features found in modern corporate capitalism to illustrate how the standard market economy can affect individuals' motivation and well-being (e.g., Frey, 1997).

Corporate capitalism is most notable in part because of its increasing global reach and its capacity to transform the other cultures it reaches (Kasser et al., 2007). Still, the capitalist system has variations, in part because cultures have varied in the degree to which they have also embraced social-welfare policies. It is clear, for example, that these additions and variations to an unbridled or laissez-faire economic approach modify and constrain some of capitalism's influences on need satisfactions.

Briefly, capitalism is characterized by private ownership of capital and sale of goods and services at the highest price attainable. The basic idea is that people are acting in terms of their "self-interests" in a competitive system, so they are "free to choose" (Friedman & Friedman, 1990) how to act in an assumed attempt to maximize their earnings and wealth, whether they own capital or merely work for others who do. One's own labor, ideas, time, and products of effort are thus all commodities that can be exchanged or sold to others. From the perspective of SDT, capitalist systems are complex and have elements that both support and thwart autonomy.

First, modern corporate capitalism, relative to other styles of economic organization, provides a multitude of choices, and, when coupled with democracies, it also manifests as a relative absence of *direct* external control over lifestyles and vocations. Of course, choices may be *highly* constrained for some individuals or groups within capitalist societies, especially those without access to education or resources and who thus have few options to develop competencies or the autonomy to pursue valued ends. Yet the array of opportunities for many and the relative freedom to pursue preferred vocations and projects are in large part responsible for the high levels of entrepreneurial activity, productivity, and creativity evidenced within sectors of the capitalist system. Perhaps no other economic system in history has prompted so much productivity, both constructive and wasteful.

SDT research makes a compelling case for the significant role played by autonomy in fostering both creative development and amplifying "human capital" within an economic system. Within the workplace we know, for example, that autonomy maximizes creativity and flexible problem solving (Gagné & Deci, 2005). Similarly, at a systems level provision of choice and opportunities to develop competence (e.g., education, training) allow individuals to cultivate and apply more preferred talents and passions, which overall makes the system more effective and generative (e.g., Sen, 1999). Autonomy too is evident in the freedom to pursue innovation and expression, and it is enriched by shared ideas and flow of information. Autonomy, that is, is an engine of growth in its own right.

Accompanying these advantages, however, SDT highlights a number of less positive motivational implications associated with capitalism. Perhaps most salient is capitalism's capacity to externally regulate people's behavior. The outcomes of pay and other tangible rewards are viewed as the primary motivators of behavior and are offered with contingencies that are either directly (e.g., commissions, piece-rate payments, stock-option bonuses) or indirectly (salaries) related to people's performance on the job. As outlined by Deci et al. (1999), the contingencies widely used within the capitalist system are nearly always either engagement-contingent (pay depends on doing the job) or performance-contingent (pay depends on the quality of the work produced) with most of the people whose pay is performance-contingent not receiving the maximum amount possible. These contingencies are considered the key motivators of the principal-agent theory of the modern market economy (Petersen, 1993), and yet they are the ones that have been found to be most detrimental to human autonomy.

Specifically, research has shown that these reward contingencies have the negative consequences of undermining autonomy and intrinsic motivation (Deci et al., 1999) and can lead to poorer quality performance as reflected in more superficial learning, less flexible problem solving and heuristic processing, and less creativity (e.g., Ariely, Gneezy, Loewenstein, & Mazar, 2009; McGraw & McCullers, 1979). Thus, the controlling use of rewards, which is common within capitalism, can interfere with effort and quality of engagement, and, as we shall see later, can even lead people to distort or ignore organizational goals. Thus, as explained by Frey (1997), the external intervention of financial incentives can have the positive price effect emphasized by economics but at the same time have the negative undermining effect emphasized in SDT.

Furthermore, competition, which is a central aspect of capitalism, has also been found on average within the American culture to be controlling and undermining of autonomous motivation, especially when there is interpersonal pressure to beat the opponents (Reeve & Deci, 1996). Additionally, performance evaluations, which are a feature of most corporate organizations, have similarly been found to be detrimental to autonomy (e.g., Harackiewicz, Manderlink, & Sansone, 1984). In short, research has linked the controlling use of rewards, competition, and evaluations to decreases in basic psychological need satisfaction and autonomous motivation. Because these are all commonly used motivational elements in a capitalist system, the economic system can be expected to yield negative effects on the autonomous motivation and heuristic information processing of individuals. Furthermore, because the capitalist system, by its very nature, holds people directly accountable for results, it is likely that the system will make the managers who work within it more controlling (e.g., Deci et al., 1982), which is likely to represent yet another blow to the autonomy of employees.

Another feature of capitalism is its explicit support for lifestyles focused on achievement, competitiveness, consumerism, and material accumulation. Each of these orientations is fostered through embedded contexts, from parental and school ideologies to national values, that vary both in how controllingly they instill values and in the contents of those values. We maintain that capitalism as a system both directly and indirectly promotes extrinsic aspirations or life goals that focus on accumulation, personal gains, and recognition. As such, it is inherently in opposition to goals for community and thus global welfare (e.g., Kasser & Ryan, 1996). Kasser et al. (2007) discuss at length the antipodal nature of intrinsic and extrinsic values and their relation to capitalist social climates.

In sum, capitalism, like every complex economic system, has structures and features that can either support or thwart the autonomy, competence, and relatedness needs of the people within the system. The vitality and quality of the system's functioning reflects its supports for people's basic needs, including the three psychological needs. For example, where features enhance autonomy, more thriving is evidenced, and where autonomy is undermined, alienation, passivity, and gaming the system typically result.

High-Stakes Rewards and Sanctions

An example of traditional "rewards gone wrong" within capitalism is the current use of high-stakes bonuses, rewards, and sanctions to pressure people or organizations to attain specific outcomes. From the gargantuan financial bonuses and stock options doled out to executives for hitting stock-price targets, to sanctions on schools for not raising test scores, "accountability" enforced by high-stakes contingencies is in fashion. SDT has a particular take on such rewards that, sadly, is showing its validity across these multiple settings.

Notably, for example, around the globe various nations have applied *high-stakes tests* to drive higher achievement in students, with the ultimate aim of fostering greater economic productivity. The strategy of placing high-stakes contingencies behind test scores is based on an undifferentiated view of motivation that considers external incentives to be the effective way to foster motivation for all behaviors, from widget making to intellectual creativity. Policies such as the Bush-era *No Child Left Behind* and the Obama-era *Race to the Top* have threatened to close schools that did not perform sufficiently well on specific tests and to reward schools that excelled. Analogous strategies of rewarding states for holding their schools accountable, of paying teachers for their students' performance on achievement test, and even of paying students for attending school or doing well on tests have been increasingly advocated and, in some places, implemented despite well-known evidence of the negative effects of such reward structures on motivation, learning, and persistence.

Accordingly, as SDT predicts, accompanying the increased emphasis on high stakes has been research showing an increase in a variety of negative consequences that follow from it (see Nichols & Berliner, 2007, Ryan & Brown, 2005; Ryan & Weinstein, 2009, for reviews). These include increases in student dropout, failing to categorize all students who have left school as dropouts, excluding some students from taking the high-stakes tests so they wouldn't lower the school's scores, more teaching to the tests, more teaching of test-taking strategies, and less teaching of content. Additionally, there is evidence that "improvements" on high-stakes test scores often do not generalize to independent indices of achievement (e.g., the National Assessment of Educational Progress exams) that do not have teacher- or school-level stakes associated with them. This simply highlights that a "teach to the test" culture has been realized and appears not to be improving achievement.

Erroneously, backers of high stakes in education and elsewhere often suggest that their strategies are supported by behaviorist (i.e., operant) principles (Skinner, 1953). But in fact operant theory advocates rewarding *behaviors* and not *outcomes* (see Ryan & Brown, 2005; Ryan & Weinstein, 2009). In contrast, SDT predicts that making rewards contingent on outcomes typically has the functional effect of *reinforcing any route to the rewarded end* (e.g., Shapira, 1976). In addition, because the approach is controlling in nature, such rewards inspire a shortest-route mentality. This *contamination effect* is manifest in counterproductive activities intended to increase reward attainment, including "gaming" outcome data, sacrificing long-term organizational goals to reach short-term targets, and even outright cheating. SDT attributes such contamination effects to the controlling nature of outcome-focused rewards, and thus has anticipated many of the unintended negative results of high-stakes approaches, including how they undermine intrinsic motivation and internalization of values in students and teachers alike, and drive out best practices.

As we noted, high-stakes reward structures are not limited to schools. High-stakes bonus structures have been widely implemented to "drive results" on Wall Street, Tokyo, and other stock markets or to reap short-term profits. Where implemented, they have also driven myriad "bad behaviors" by executives, from excessive risk taking to outright "cooking the books." Indeed, the aforementioned contamination effect (Ryan & Brown, 2005) in which all routes to stock inflations or profits are reinforced has recently been the source of much economic stress and human misery across the globe, as well as selfish profit taking by the players at the top of many corporations, including failing ones. Here we see the direct relation between a distal structure involving controlling rewards that ultimately thwarts human need satisfaction and wellness on a broad scale. As high-stakes contingencies are imported into other spheres of life from health care to the coaching of sports, SDT suggests that there are strong, evidence-based reasons for concern.

It is precisely because economists, policy makers, politicians, and pundits often ignore the negative consequences associated with the controlling use of rewards, and the interplay of extrinsic and intrinsic values, that they support interventions that are likely to fail or backfire. Beyond obvious calculations of incentive or loss, external contingencies impact outcomes in part by thwarting versus satisfying people's basic psychological needs. To make effective predictions outside of formal exchange situations requires a focus on human psychological needs and on the conditions that support versus undermine them. That focus provides SDT with a critical lens through which to view both micro- and macro-economic factors.

Political Systems

In addition to an economic system, each country has a political system that tends toward either totalitarianism or democracy. Totalitarian systems are centered on individual dictators who hold absolute power over the lives of their citizens. Through the use of propaganda via state-controlled media and the support from the military, most aspects of citizens' lives are subjugated to the dictates of government. Typically, totalitarianism is accompanied by central planning economies, although modified totalitarian systems may have some degree of capitalism. Totalitarianism is straightforwardly antagonistic to satisfaction of the basic psychological needs. There is little opportunity for autonomy, except perhaps if one is working under the political umbrella of the dictator, but even then there is always the implicit or explicit threat of serious consequences if one offends someone higher in the hierarchy. As noted earlier, more vertical or hierarchical systems have been found to be more difficult to internalize, and this may be because the more hierarchical systems tend to be associated with at least some degree of totalitarianism.

Democracies, in contrast, are inherently oriented toward giving individuals some say in the processes that govern their lives. Through direct voting and by having representatives in all levels of government, individuals can, ideally, have the opportunity to contribute to the political process and to experience freedom from constraints other than those necessary to keep the system functioning effectively. There can be little doubt that, in general, the democratic system has great advantages relative to the totalitarian system in terms of human autonomy and satisfaction of the needs for competence and relatedness, which also tend to be diminished within a totalitarian system.

Nonetheless, democracies are vulnerable to distortion by forces within the countries. For example, in democratic systems individuals or groups can attain power by amassing huge wealth. Thus, through financial support of activities such as advertising and lobbying, the influence of wealth-based power can, through subtle or overt coercion or seduction, overrun the voices of the average citizens. Power through force can similarly yield undue influence within a democratic system and thus diminish the autonomy of individuals within the system. In such cases, it is the role both of the legislative system to create laws and regulatory agencies to limit the undue influence of the few and of the judicial system to prevent individuals and groups from acting outside the laws. Different cultures have been differentially effective in these regards.

Summary of Distal Social-Contextual Influences

Theory and research on social contexts, across levels of analysis from dyads to cultures, indicates that, to the degree that environmental factors are experienced as need supportive, they will foster greater autonomous motivation, more intrinsic aspirations, more effective performance, and higher well-being. Our analysis points to the embedded nature of contexts and suggests that the varied levels of analysis that support versus thwart human needs must be considered. In this section we have seen how the broadest level, cultural, economic, and political systems have substantial influences on individuals both directly and as mediated by various embedded contexts contained within the culture.

Basic Psychological Needs

As a motivational theory, SDT must account for the energization of behavior. The basic psychological needs for competence, autonomy, and relatedness represent one very important energizer of behavior. In support of the assertion that there are three universal psychological needs, we have reviewed evidence indicating that when social contexts in multiple cultures supported people's basic psychological needs, the people tended to thrive relative to people for whom the social contexts were thwarting of need satisfaction. In line with this, various studies have examined need satisfaction as a mediator both between autonomy-supportive contexts and positive outcomes such as well-being and between the pursuit and attainment of intrinsic versus extrinsic aspirations and positive outcomes.

For example, Adie, Duda, and Ntoumanis (2008) found that when coaches were more autonomy supportive, their adult athletes playing various team sports experienced greater satisfaction of the needs

for autonomy, competence, and relatedness, which in turn led to greater subjective vitality, with the autonomy and competence needs each being partial mediators of the relations. Deci et al. (2001) found support for a cross-cultural structural model in Bulgarian and American work organizations in which autonomy support led to greater need satisfaction, which in turn led to higher work engagement and greater well-being.

Studies of within-person need satisfaction over time (e.g., Reis, Sheldon, Gable, Roscoe, & Ryan, 2000; Sheldon, Ryan, & Reis, 1996), using multilevel modeling have further found that in addition to between-person relations of need satisfaction to well-being, daily fluctuations in satisfaction of each of the three needs predict unique variance in daily well-being. On days when people experience satisfaction of their basic psychological needs, they also feel happier and even physically healthier. For example, Ryan, Bernstein, and Brown (2010) recently demonstrated that the "weekend effect," in which U.S. workers experienced greater vitality and positive mood on weekends, is primarily a function of the low autonomy and relatedness satisfactions most workers experience in their Monday through Friday jobs. This brings us back to our earlier point that although capitalism offers its constituents choices and options, many of the vocations that are available and that people "have to" adopt involve jobs that thwart psychological needs.

Need satisfaction also turns up in odd places. For example, having identified that exposure to natural elements engenders greater vitality (Ryan et al., 2010), Weinstein, Przybylski, and Ryan (2009) showed that these positive effects were at least partially due to the increased autonomy and connectedness people feel when nature is salient to them. Przybylski, Ryan, and Rigby (2009) found that psychological need satisfaction could derive from certain elements in video games, but not from their violent content. Weinstein and Ryan (2010) studied the benefits of helping others, finding that autonomous helping fulfilled all three basic psychological needs, but controlled helping did not. These examples show how SDT research is always in search of sources, moderators, and obstacles to basic need satisfactions across the varied activities of life.

Earlier in the chapter we reviewed research by Niemiec et al. (2009) showing that people who attained intrinsic aspirations such as personal growth and community tended to display greater well-being and less ill-being but that those who attained extrinsic aspirations such as wealth and fame did not display enhanced well-being although they did display greater ill-being. The important point for the present discussion is that these effects on well-being and ill-being were mediated by satisfaction of the basic psychological needs for autonomy, competence, and relatedness.

Although need satisfaction supplies the essential nutriments for growth, integrity, and wellness, active thwarting of needs produces a range of negative outcomes, from defensiveness and aggression to psychopathology (Bartholomew, Ntoumanis, Ryan, & Thøgersen-Ntoumani, 2011; Ryan, Deci, Grolnick, & LaGuardia, 2006). Indeed, from an SDT view, behaviors such as aggression and violence are not themselves inherently motivated (Przybylski et al., 2009) but are instead consequences of need thwarting. That is, people are prone to aggression whenever basic functioning concerned with autonomy, competence, or relatedness is frustrated or threatened, rather than because it is an inherent drive or interest. More generally, the "dark sides" of human behavior can typically be traced to persistent or severe need thwarting and the substitute needs or compensatory activities related to it (Ryan & Deci, 2000b).

Awareness As an Important Part of Autonomy and Well-Being

Reviewing the powerful effects of proximal and distal contexts on human motivation, effective performance, and wellness, as mediated by basic psychological need satisfaction, might suggest to many a very deterministic and even passive view of human nature. But that is not the SDT viewpoint. It bears repeating that SDT assumes that people have an active, growth-oriented, challenge-seeking nature unless they experience pervasive conditions of threat and need thwarting, in which case defensive behaviors, need substitutes, and controlled and impersonal orientations can be catalyzed. When needs are satisfied, the inherent, active, and growth-oriented processes flourish. Part of the active nature that is supported by need satisfaction involves the development of integrative awareness (Hodgins & Knee, 2002).

According to SDT, autonomy is facilitated by awareness, which entails the authentic attempt to experience and become conscious of what is occurring within and around oneself. It is a relaxed and interested attention to what is happening within and without. One concept closely aligned with awareness is mindfulness, which refers to an open, receptive stance regarding what is occurring in any given moment (Brown & Ryan, 2003). Research has shown that mindfulness is associated with enhanced autonomous functioning—that is, people are more likely to act in accord with abiding values and interests when they are mindful (e.g., Niemiec et al., 2010). Moreover, mindfulness is associated with less focus on extrinsic values, more effective coping, and greater wellness, again in part because of its enhancement of autonomous functioning and fulfillment of the basic psychological needs (Weinstein, Brown, & Ryan, 2009). As such, awareness or mindfulness represents a very important means to take greater responsibility for oneself and thus to be less vulnerable to the controlling and amotivating forces that are all too prevalent in our social environments.

In this chapter, we have devoted considerable attention to social-environmental influences for two primary reasons. First, knowledge about the effects of social environments on the motivation, performance, and well-being of individuals provides a basis for creating systems—ranging, for example, from families, to corporations, to political policies—that conduce toward satisfaction of the basic psychological needs of individuals within those systems. Second, when people understand how social environments affect individuals, those people are more able to avoid or resist having the potentially negative effects impact them. Although we have emphasized social-contextual effects, we are equally as interested in people expanding their own awareness, for example, though mindfulness training, psychotherapy, and other such methods, in order to be more autonomous in managing their own lives and to be more autonomy supportive with others.

Summary and Conclusions

Herein, we have provided an overview of self-determination theory, arguing that the distinction between autonomous and controlled forms of motivation are crucial for making predictions about the quality of performance, well-being, and other important outcomes. We discussed the intrinsic, integrated, and identified forms of autonomous motivation, as well as the external and introjected forms of controlled motivation. Autonomous and controlled motivations were discussed in terms of the state level, the domain level, and the personality level, the last being referred to as causality orientations. Considerable research has verified that more autonomous motivation, both situationally and dispositionally considered, generally leads to more positive consequences than controlled motivation.

We then discussed research on people's life goals or aspirations, pointing out that these goals tend to fall into two categories, referred to as extrinsic aspirations (e.g., wealth, fame, and image) and intrinsic aspirations (e.g., growth, relationships, and community). The pursuit and attainment of extrinsic, relative to intrinsic, aspirations has been shown to be associated with poorer psychological health and inferior performance, because the intrinsic aspirations more directly lead to satisfaction of the basic psychological needs, whereas extrinsic aspirations are less closely instrumental to basic need satisfaction and may be hostile to it.

People's autonomous and controlled motivations, as well as their intrinsic and extrinsic life goals are influenced to a significant degree, in both the immediate situation and developmentally over time, by the degree to which their social contexts support versus thwart their basic psychological needs for competence, relatedness, and autonomy. We reviewed research and theory indicating that social contexts may be relatively proximal or increasingly more distal, with the more proximal being embedded within various levels of more distal contexts. An example of a proximal context is a child's home environment, and examples of more distal contexts are the neighborhood and, even more broadly, the culture, with its values, economics, and politics.

Today's increasingly global economic trends portend increased concentrations of wealth and power in the hands of a few, and at this global level raise concerns about increased top-down control and deprivations of autonomy, which is a threat to both national (Downie, Koestner, & Chua, 2007) and personal wellness (Twenge et al., 2010). Yet there are potentially offsetting trends as well. We live in a "wiki" world of fast Internet connections and instant communications that allow for much personal expression as well as bottom-up organization (e.g., Tapscott & Williams, 2006). In the context of these complex forces, understanding the basic needs of persons that are essential to wellness is crucial for interventions from levels of global policy (see, for example, work by the New Economics Foundation; http://www.neweconomics.org/) to individual psychotherapy (Ryan & Deci, 2008). The hope is that SDT research informs these policies and interventions and in doing so promotes more optimal functioning and wellness of both persons and the communities within which they are embedded.

References

Adie, J., Duda, J. L., & Ntoumanis, N. (2008). Autonomy support, basic need satisfaction and the optimal functioning of adult male and female sport participants: A test of basic needs theory. *Motivation and Emotion, 32,* 189–199.

Ariely, D., Gneezy, U., Loewenstein, G., & Mazar, N. (2009). Large stakes and big mistakes. *Review of Economic Studies, 75,* 1–19.

Assor, A., Roth, G., & Deci, E. L. (2004). The emotional costs of parents' conditional regard: A self-determination theory analysis. *Journal of Personality, 72,* 47–89.

Baard, P. P., Deci, E. L., & Ryan, R. M. (2004). Intrinsic need satisfaction: A motivational basis of performance and well-being in two work settings. *Journal of Applied Social Psychology, 34,* 2045–2068.

Bandura, A. (1996). *Self-efficacy: The exercise of control.* New York: Freeman.

Bartholomew, K. J., Ntoumanis, N., Ryan, R. M., & Thøgersen-Ntoumani, C. (2011). Psychological need thwarting in the sport context: Assessing the darker side of athletic experience. *Journal of Sport and Exercise Psychology, 33,* 75–102.

Benware, C., & Deci, E. L. (1984). Quality of learning with an active versus passive motivational set. *American Educational Research Journal, 21,* 755–765.

Black, A. E., & Deci, E. L. (2000). The effects of student self-regulation and instructor autonomy support on learning in a college-level natural science course: A self-determination theory perspective. *Science Education, 84,* 740–756.

Boiché, J. C., Sarrazin, P. G., Grouzet, F. M., & Pelletier, L. G. (2008). Students' motivational profiles in physical education and achievement outcomes: A self-determination theory perspective. *Journal of Educational Psychology, 100,* 688–701.

Bronfenbrenner, U. (1979). *The ecology of human development.* Cambridge, MA: Harvard University Press.

Brown, K. W., & Ryan, R. M. (2003). The benefits of being present: Mindfulness and its role in psychological well-being. *Journal of Personality and Social Psychology, 84,* 822–848.

Burton, K. D., Lydon, J. E., D'Alessandro, D. U., & Koestner, R. (2006). The differential effects of intrinsic and identified motivation on well-being and performance: Prospective, experimental and implicit approaches to self-determination theory. *Journal of Personality and Social Psychology, 91,* 750–762.

Carver, C. S., & Baird, E. (1998). The American dream revisited: Is it what you want or why you want it that matters? *Psychological Science, 9,* 289–292.

Chirkov, V. Ryan, R. M., Kim, Y., & Kaplan, U. (2003). Differentiating autonomy from individualism and independence: A self-determination theory perspective on internalization of cultural orientations and well-being. *Journal of Personality and Social Psychology. 84,* 97–110.

Chirkov, V. I., Ryan, R. M., & Willness, C. (2005). Cultural context and psychological needs in Canada and Brazil: Testing a self-determination approach to the internalization of cultural practices, identity, and well-being. *Journal of Cross-Cultural Psychology, 36,* 423–443.

Connell, J. P., & Wellborn, J. G. (1991). Competence, autonomy and relatedness: A motivational analysis of self-system processes. In M. R. Gunnar & L. A. Sroufe (Eds.), *The Minnesota symposium on child psychology: Self-processes in development* (Vol. 22, pp. 43–77). Hillsdale, NJ: Erlbaum.

de Charms, R. (1968). *Personal causation: The internal affective determinants of behavior*. New York: Academic Press.

Deci, E. L., Connell, J. P., & Ryan, R. M. (1989). Self-determination in a work organization. *Journal of Applied Psychology*, 74, 580–590.

Deci, E. L., Eghrari, H., Patrick, B. C., & Leone, D. R. (1994). Facilitating internalization: The self-determination theory perspective. *Journal of Personality*, 62, 119–142.

Deci, E. L., Koestner, R., & Ryan, R. M. (1999). A meta-analytic review of experiments examining the effects of extrinsic rewards on intrinsic motivation. *Psychological Bulletin*, 125, 627–668.

Deci, E. L., La Guardia, J. G., Moller, A. C., Scheiner, M. J., & Ryan, R. M. (2006). On the benefits of giving as well as receiving autonomy support: Mutuality in close friendships. *Personality and Social Psychology Bulletin*, 32, 313–327.

Deci, E. L., & Ryan, R. M. (1985). The General Causality Orientations Scale: Self-determination in personality. *Journal of Research in Personality*, 19, 109–134.

Deci, E. L., & Ryan, R. M. (1995). Human autonomy: The basis for true self-esteem. In M. Kernis (Ed.), *Agency, efficacy, and self-esteem* (pp. 31–49). New York: Plenum.

Deci, E. L., & Ryan, R. M. (2000). The "what" and "why" of goal pursuits: Human needs and the self-determination of behavior. *Psychological Inquiry*, 11, 227–268.

Deci, E. L., & Ryan, R. M. (2008). Facilitating optimal motivation and psychological well-being across life's domains, *Canadian Psychology*, 49, 14–23.

Deci, E. L., Ryan, R. M., Gagné, M., Leone, D. R., Usunov, J., & Kornazheva, B. P. (2001). Need satisfaction, motivation, and well-being in the work organizations of a former Eastern Bloc country. *Personality and Social Psychology Bulletin*, 27, 930–942.

Deci, E. L., Schwartz, A. J., Sheinman, L., & Ryan, R. M. (1981). An instrument to assess adults' orientations toward control versus autonomy with children: Reflections on intrinsic motivation and perceived competence. *Journal of Educational Psychology*, 73, 642–650.

Deci, E. L., Spiegel, N. H., Ryan, R. M., Koestner, R., & Kauffman, M. (1982). Effects of performance standards on teaching styles: Behavior of controlling teachers. *Journal of Educational Psychology*, 74, 852–859.

Downie, M., Koestner, R., & Chua, S. N. (2007). Political support for self-determination, wealth, and national subjective well-being. *Motivation and Emotion*, 31, 188–194.

Frey, B. S. (1997). *Not just for the money: An economic theory of personal motivation*. Northampton, MA: Edward Elgar.

Friedman, M., & Friedman, R. (1990). *Free to choose*. New York: Harcourt Brace Jovanovich.

Friedman, R., Deci, E. L., Elliot, A. J., Moller, A. C., & Aarts, H. (2010). Motivational synchronicity: Priming motivational orientations with observations of others' behaviors. *Motivation and Emotion*, 34, 34–38.

Gagné, M., & Deci, E. L. (2005). Self-determination theory and work motivation. *Journal of Organizational Behavior*, 26, 331–362.

Gagné, M., Ryan, R. M., & Bargmann, K. (2003). Autonomy support and need satisfaction in the motivation and well-being of gymnasts. *Journal of Applied Sport Psychology*, 15, 372–390.

Grolnick, W. S. (2003). *The psychology of parental control: How well-meant parenting backfires*. Mahwah, NJ: Erlbaum.

Grolnick, W. S., Benjet, C., Kurowski, C. O., & Apostoleris, N. H. (1997). Predictors of parent involvement in children's schooling. *Journal of Educational Psychology*, 89, 538–548.

Grolnick, W. S., & Ryan, R. M. (1987). Autonomy in children's learning: An experimental and individual difference investigation. *Journal of Personality and Social Psychology*, 52, 890–898.

Grolnick, W. S., & Ryan, R. M. (1989). Parent styles associated with children's self-regulation and competence in school. *Journal of Educational Psychology*, 81, 143–154.

Harackiewicz, J. M., Manderlink, G., & Sansone, C. (1984). Rewarding pinball wizardry: The effects of evaluation on intrinsic interest. *Journal of Personality and Social Psychology*, 47, 287–300.

Hodgins, H. S., & Knee, C. R. (2002). The integrating self and conscious experience. In E. L. Deci & R. M. Ryan (Eds.), *Handbook of self-determination research* (pp. 87–100). Rochester, NY: University of Rochester Press.

Hodgins, H. S., Koestner, R., & Duncan, N. (1996). On the compatibility of autonomy and relatedness. *Personality and Social Psychology Bulletin*, 22, 227–237.

Hodgins, H. S., & Liebeskind, E. (2003). Apology versus defense: Antecedents and consequences. *Journal of Experimental Social Psychology*, 39, 297–236.

Hodgins, H. S., Liebeskind, E., & Schwartz, W. (1996). Getting out of hot water: Facework in social predicaments. *Journal of Personality and Social Psychology*, 71, 300–314.

Hodgins, H. S., Yacko, H. A., & Gottlieb, E. (2006). Autonomy and nondefensiveness. *Motivation and Emotion*, 30, 283–293.

Hull, C. L. (1943). *Principles of behavior: An introduction to behavior theory*. New York: Appleton-Century-Crofts.

Jang, H., Reeve, J., & Deci, E. L. (2010). Engaging students in learning activities: It's not autonomy support or structure, but autonomy support and structure. *Journal of Educational Psychology*, 102, 588–600.

Kasser, T., Cohn, S., Kanner, A. D., & Ryan, R. M. (2007). Some costs of American corporate capitalism: A psychological exploration of value and goal conflicts. *Psychological Inquiry*, 18, 1–22.

Kasser, T., & Ryan, R. M. (1993). A dark side of the American dream: Correlates of financial success as a central life aspiration. *Journal of Personality and Social Psychology*, 65, 410–422.

Kasser, T., & Ryan, R. M. (1996). Further examining the American dream: Differential correlates of intrinsic and extrinsic goals. *Personality and Social Psychology Bulletin*, 22, 80–87.

Kasser, T., Ryan, R. M., Zax, M., & Sameroff, A. J. (1995). The relations of maternal and social environments to late adolescents' materialistic and prosocial values. *Developmental Psychology*, 31, 907–914.

Kasser, V. G., & Ryan, R. M. (1999). The relation of psychological needs for autonomy and relatedness to vitality, well-being, and mortality in a nursing home. *Journal of Applied Social Psychology*, 29, 935–954.

Kernis, M. H., & Paradise, A. W. (2002). Distinguishing between secure and fragile forms of high self-esteem. In E. L. Deci & R. M. Ryan (Eds.), *Handbook of *self-determination research* (pp. 339–360). Rochester, NY: University Of Rochester Press.

Knee, C. R., Patrick, H., Vietor, N. A., Nanayakkara, A., & Neighbors, C. (2002). Self-determination as growth motivation in romantic relationships. *Personality and Social Psychology Bulletin, 28,* 609–619.

Knee, C. R., & Zuckerman, M. (1996). Causality orientations and the disappearance of the self-serving bias. *Journal of Research in Personality, 30,* 76–87.

Knee, C. R., & Zuckerman, M. (1998). A nondefensive personality: Autonomy and control as moderators of defensive coping and self-handicapping. *Journal of Research in Personality, 32,* 115–130.

Koestner, R., Losier, G. F., Vallerand, R. J., & Carducci, D. (1996). Identified and introjected forms of political internalization: Extending self-determination theory. *Journal of Personality and Social Psychology, 70,* 1025–1036.

Koestner, R., Ryan, R. M., Bernieri, F., & Holt, K. (1984). Setting limits on children's behavior: The differential effects of controlling versus informational styles on intrinsic motivation and creativity. *Journal of Personality, 52,* 233–248.

La Guardia, J. G., & Patrick, H. (2008) Self-determination theory as a fundamental theory of close relationships. *Canadian Psychology, 49,* 201–209.

La Guardia, J. G., Ryan, R. M., Couchman, C. E., & Deci, E. L. (2000). Within-person variation in security of attachment: A self-determination theory perspective on attachment, need fulfillment, and well-being. *Journal of Personality and Social Psychology, 79,* 367–384.

Landry, R., Whipple, N., Mageau, G., Joussemet, M., Koestner, R., DiDio, L.,... Haga, S. M. (2008). Trust in organismic development, autonomy support, and adaptation among mothers and their children. *Motivation and Emotion, 32,* 173–188.

McGraw, K. O., & McCullers, J. C. (1979). Evidence of a detrimental effect of extrinsic incentives on breaking a mental set. *Journal of Experimental Social Psychology, 15,* 285–294.

McHoskey, J. W. (1999). Machiavellianism, intrinsic versus extrinsic goals, and social interest: A self-determination theory analysis. *Motivation and Emotion, 23,* 267–283.

Münster Halvari, A. E. M., Halvari, H., Bjørnebekk, G., & Deci, E. L. (2010). Motivation and anxiety for dental treatment: Testing a self-determination theory model of oral self-care behavior and dental clinic attendance. *Motivation and Emotion, 34,* 15–33.

Niemiec, C. P., Brown, K. W., Kashdan, T. B., Cozzolino, P. J., Breen, W. E., Levesque-Bristol, C., & Ryan, R. M. (2010). Being present in the face of existential threat: The role of trait mindfulness in reducing defensive responses to mortality salience. *Journal of Personality and Social Psychology, 99,* 344–365.

Niemiec, C. P., Ryan, R. M., & Deci, E. L. (2009). The path taken: Consequences of attaining intrinsic and extrinsic aspirations in post-college life. *Journal of Research in Personality, 43,* 291–306.

Nichols, S. L., & Berliner, D. C. (2007). *Collateral damage: How high-stakes testing corrupts America's schools.* Cambridge, MA: Harvard Education Press.

Oliver, E. J., Markland, D., Hardy, J., & Petherick, C. M. (2008). The effects of autonomy-supportive versus controlling environments on self-talk. *Motivation and Emotion, 32,* 200–212.

Patall, E. A., Cooper, H., & Robinson, J. C. (2008). The effects of choice on intrinsic motivation and related outcomes: A meta-analysis of research findings. *Psychological Bulletin, 134,* 270–300.

Pavey, L., & Sparks, P. (2009). Reactance, autonomy, and paths to persuasion: Examining perceptions of threats to freedom and informational value. *Motivation and Emotion, 33,* 277–290.

Pelletier, L. G., Fortier, M. S., Vallerand, R. J., & Brière, N. M. (2001). Associations among perceived autonomy support, forms of self-regulation, and persistence: A prospective study. *Motivation and Emotion, 25,* 279–306.

Pelletier, L. G., Séguin-Lévesque, C., & Legault L. (2002). Pressure from above and pressure from below as determinants of teachers' motivation and teaching behavior. *Journal of Educational Psychology, 94,* 186–196.

Pelletier, L. G., Tuson, K. M., & Haddad, N. K. (1997). Client motivation for therapy scale: A measure of intrinsic motivation, extrinsic motivation, and amotivation for therapy. *Journal of Personality Assessment, 68,* 414–435.

Perls, F. S. (1973). *The Gestalt approach and eyewitness to therapy.* Ben Lomond, CA: Science and Behavior Books.

Petersen, T. (1993). The economics of organization: The principal-agent relationship. *Acta Sociologica, 36,* 277–293.

Philippe, F. L., & Vallerand, R. J. (2008). Actual environments do affect motivation and psychological adjustment: A test of self-determination theory in a natural setting. *Motivation and Emotion, 32,* 81–89.

Przybylski, A. K., Ryan, R. M., & Rigby, C. S. (2009). The motivating role of violence in video games. *Personality and Social Psychology Bulletin, 35,* 243–259.

Reeve, J., & Deci, E. L. (1996). Elements within the competitive situation that affect intrinsic motivation. *Personality and Social Psychology Bulletin, 22,* 24–33.

Reis, H. T., Sheldon, K. M., Gable, S. L., Roscoe, J., & Ryan, R. M. (2000). Daily well-being: The role of autonomy, competence, and relatedness. *Personality and Social Psychology Bulletin, 26,* 419–435.

Roth, G., Assor, A, Niemiec, C. P., Ryan, R. M., & Deci, E. L. (2009). The emotional and academic consequences of parental conditional regard: Comparing conditional positive regard, conditional negative regard, and autonomy support as parenting practices. *Developmental Psychology, 45,* 1119–1142.

Ryan, R. M. (1982). Control and information in the intrapersonal sphere: An extension of cognitive evaluation theory. *Journal of Personality and Social Psychology, 43,* 450–461.

Ryan, R. M., Bernstein, J. H., & Brown, K. W. (2010). Weekends, work, and well-being: Psychological need satisfactions and day of the week effects on mood, vitality, and physical symptoms. *Journal of Social and Clinical Psychology, 29,* 95–122.

Ryan, R. M., & Brown, K. W. (2005). Legislating competence: The motivational impact of high stakes testing as an educational reform. In A. J. Elliot & C. S. Dweck (Eds.) *Handbook of competence* (pp. 354–374). New York: Guilford Press.

Ryan, R. M., & Connell, J. P. (1989). Perceived locus of causality and internalization: Examining reasons for acting in two domains. *Journal of Personality and Social Psychology, 57,* 749–761.

Ryan, R. M., Connell, J. P., & Deci, E. L. (1985). A motivational analysis of self-determination and self-regulation in education. In C. Ames & R. E. Ames (Eds.), *Research on motivation in education: The classroom milieu* (pp. 13–51). New York: Academic Press.

Ryan, R. M., Connell, J. P., & Plant, R. W. (1990). Emotions in non-directed text learning. *Learning and Individual Differences, 2*, 1–17.

Ryan, R. M., & Deci, E. L. (2000a). Intrinsic and extrinsic motivations: Classic definitions and new directions. *Contemporary Educational Psychology, 25*, 54–67.

Ryan, R. M. & Deci, E. L. (2000b). The darker and brighter sides of human existence: Basic psychological needs as a unifying concept. *Psychological Inquiry, 11*, 319–338.

Ryan, R. M., & Deci, E. L. (2003). On assimilating identities to the self: A self-determination theory perspective on internalization and integrity within cultures. In M. R. Leary & J. P. Tangney (Eds.), *Handbook of self and identity* (pp. 255–273). New York: Guilford.

Ryan, R. M., & Deci, E. L. (2008). A self-determination approach to psychotherapy: The motivational basis for effective change. *Canadian Psychology, 49*, 186–193.

Ryan, R. M., Deci, E. L., Grolnick, W. S., & LaGuardia, J. G. (2006) The significance of autonomy and autonomy support in psychological development and psychopathology. In D. Cicchetti & D. Cohen (Eds.), *Developmental psychopathology. Vol. 1: Theory and methods* (2nd ed., pp. 295–849). New York: John Wiley & Sons.

Ryan, R. M., Rigby, S., & King, K. (1993). Two types of religious internalization and their relations to religious orientations and mental health. *Journal of Personality and Social Psychology, 65*, 586–596.

Ryan, R. M., Sheldon, K. M., Kasser, T., & Deci, E. L. (1996). All goals are not created equal: An organismic perspective on the nature of goals and their regulation. In P. M. Gollwitzer & J. A. Bargh (Eds.), *The psychology of action: Linking cognition and motivation to behavior* (pp. 7–26). New York: Guilford.

Ryan, R. M., & Weinstein, N. (2009). Undermining quality teaching and learning: A self-determination theory perspective on high-stakes testing. *Theory and Research in Education, 7*, 224–233.

Ryan, R. M., Weinstein, N., Bernstein, J., Brown, K. W., Mistretta, L. & Gagne, M. (2010). Vitalizing effects of being outdoors and in nature. *Journal of Environmental Psychology, 30*, 159–168.

Sears, R. R., Maccoby, E., & Levin, H. (1957). *Patterns of child rearing.* Evanston, IL: Row, Peterson.

Séguin, C., Pelletier, L. G., & Hunsley, J. (1999). Predicting environmental behaviors: The influence of self-determination and information about environmental health risks. *Journal of Applied Social Psychology, 29*, 1582–160.

Sen, A. (1999). *Development as freedom.* New York: Alfred A. Knopf.

Shapira, Z. (1976). Expectancy determinants of intrinsically motivated behavior. *Journal of Personality and Social Psychology, 34*, 1235–1244.

Sheldon, K. M., & Kasser, T. (2008). Psychological threat and extrinsic goal striving. *Motivation and Emotion, 32*, 37–45.

Sheldon, K. M., Ryan, R. M., Deci, E. L., & Kasser, T. (2004). The independent effects of goal contents and motives on well-being: It's both what you pursue and why you pursue it. *Personality and Social Psychology Bulletin, 30*, 475–486.

Sheldon, K. M., Ryan, R. M., & Reis, H. T. (1996). What makes for a good day? Competence and autonomy in the day and in the person. *Personality and Social Psychology Bulletin, 22*, 1270–1279.

Skinner, B. F. (1953). *Science and human behavior.* New York: Macmillan.

Tapscott, D., & Williams, A. D. (2006). *Wikinomics: How mass collaboration changes everything.* New York: Penguin.

Twenge, J., Gentile, B., DeWall, C. N., Ma, D., Lacefield, K., & Schurtz, D. R. (2010). Birth cohort increases in psychopathology among young Americans, 1938–2007: A cross-temporal meta-analysis of the MMPI. *Clinical Psychology Review, 30*, 145–154.

Vallerand, R. J. (1997). Toward a hierarchical model of intrinsic and extrinsic motivation. In M. P. Zanna (Ed.), *Advances in experimental social psychology* (Vol. 29, pp. 271–360). San Diego, CA: Academic Press.

Vansteenkiste, M., Ryan, R. M., & Deci, E. L. (2008). Self-determination theory and the explanatory role of psychological needs in human well-being. In L. Bruni, F. Comim, & M. Pugno (Eds.), *Capabilities and happiness* (pp. 181–223). Oxford, England: Oxford University Press.

Vansteenkiste, M., Simons, J., Lens, W., Sheldon, K. M., & Deci, E. L. (2004). Motivating learning, performance, and persistence: The synergistic effects of intrinsic goal contents and autonomy-supportive contexts. *Journal of Personality and Social Psychology, 87*, 246–260.

Wang, F. (2008). Motivation and English achievement: An exploratory and confirmatory factor analysis of a new measure for Chinese students of English learning. *North American Journal of Psychology, 10*, 633–646.

Weinstein, N., Brown, K. W., & Ryan, R. M. (2009). A multimethod examination of the effects of mindfulness on stress attribution, coping, and emotional well-being. *Journal of Research in Personality, 43*, 374–385.

Weinstein, N., Deci, E. L., & Ryan, R. M. (2011). Motivational determinants of integrating positive and negative past identities. *Journal of Personality and Social Psychology, 100*, 527–544.

Weinstein, N., Przybylski, A. K., & Ryan, R. M. (2009). Can nature make us more caring? Effects of immersion in nature on intrinsic aspirations and generosity. *Personality and Social Psychology Bulletin, 35*, 1315–1329.

Weinstein, N., & Ryan, R. M. (2010). When helping helps: Autonomous motivation for prosocial behavior and its influence on well-being for the helper and recipient. *Journal of Personality and Social Psychology, 98*, 222–244.

Williams, G. C., Cox, E. M., Hedberg, V., & Deci, E. L. (2000). Extrinsic life goals and health risk behaviors in adolescents. *Journal of Applied Social Psychology, 30*, 1756–1771.

Williams, G. C., Freedman, Z. R., & Deci, E. L. (1998). Supporting autonomy to motivate glucose control in patients with diabetes. *Diabetes Care, 21*, 1644–1651.

Williams, G. C., Grow, V. M., Freedman, Z., Ryan, R. M., & Deci, E. L. (1996). Motivational predictors of weight loss and weight-loss maintenance. *Journal of Personality and Social Psychology, 70*, 115–126.

Williams, G. C., McGregor, H. A., Sharp, D., Kouides, R. W., Levesque, C., Ryan, R. M., & Deci, E. L. (2006). A self-determination multiple risk intervention trial to improve smokers' health. *Journal of General Internal Medicine, 21*, 1288–1294.

Williams, G. C., McGregor, H. A., Sharp, D., Levesque, C., Kouides, R. W., Ryan, R. M., & Deci, E. L. (2006). Testing a self-determination theory intervention for motivating tobacco cessation: Supporting autonomy and competence in a clinical trial. *Health Psychology, 25*, 91–101.

Williams, G. C., McGregor, H. A., Zeldman, A., Freedman, Z. R., & Deci, E. L. (2004). Testing a self-determination theory process model for promoting glycemic control through diabetes self-management. *Health Psychology, 23*, 58–66.

Zuroff, D. C., Koestner, R., Moskowitz, D. S., McBride, C., Marshall, M., & Bagby, M. (2007). Autonomous motivation for therapy: A new common factor in brief treatments for depression. *Psychotherapy Research, 17*, 137–147.

PART 3

Motivational Processes

Ego Depletion: Theory and Evidence

Mark Muraven

Abstract

Self-control all too often fails. Despite people's best intentions and considerable negative outcomes, people often find themselves at the losing end of resisting temptation, combating urges, and changing their behavior. One reason for these failures may be that exerting self-control depletes a limited resource (ego depletion) that is necessary for the success of self-control. Hence, after exerting self-control individuals are less able to resist temptations, fight urges, or stop a behavior, which results in a loss of self-control. This chapter reviews the evidence for this theory in a wide variety of domains and examines what behaviors appear to deplete ego strength and how depletion affects behavior. A comprehensive theory that examines how depletion operates is put forth and this theory is used to examine some factors that might moderate the depletion effect.

Key Words: self-control, ego depletion, willpower, motivation

Introduction

As most people can attest, dieting, quitting smoking, controlling one's temper, and working instead of playing are not easy. In fact, it often feels quite difficult to avoid immediate, pressing, or easy behaviors in order to follow rules, get along with others, or reach long-range goals. Moreover, such self-control efforts fail all too often. The point of the strength model of self-control (Muraven & Baumeister, 2000) is to better understand how people resist such temptations, understand why it fails (and why it succeeds) and what can be done to improve self-control.

Self-control is the process that enables organisms to override, inhibit, or stop urges, emotions and moods, thoughts, or behaviors in order to reach a long-term goal. These long-term goals can be personally set, such as losing weight or succeeding in school, or can be moral, interpersonal, or societal rules like not having premarital sex or not gossiping. Regardless of the type of goal, it typically requires the individual to forgo an immediate pleasure or

desire in order to reach a more desired state in the future. That is, the organism is seeking to gain a larger but delayed reward over a smaller but more immediate reward. To do so, the organism must resist the temptation to take the immediate reward. Self-control is the process that allows this to happen (Kanfer & Karoly, 1972; Mischel, Shoda, & Rodriguez, 1989).

There are significant and important differences between self-control and self-regulation worthy of mention. Although these terms are sometimes used interchangeably, self-control is an important subset of self-regulation. Self-regulation is the process by which individuals pursue all goals, both short and long term. The process of self-regulation incorporates both conscious and unconscious process, such as breathing, eating, or driving to work every day. On the other hand, self-control is a deliberative, conscious, effortful, and resource-intensive process of restraining an impulse in order to reach a long-term goal or follow a rule. To the extent that a situation requires inhibition, it demands self-control. This distinction is important, because tasks that may seem effortful, like memorizing a list of words or solving simple arithmetic problems only require self-control to the extent that the individual has to override an impulse.

The ability to exert self-control is one of the critical features that differentiate humans from other organisms (Baumeister, 1998, 2005). Although other animals can exert self-control (for instance, squirrels burying nuts for the winter), it is clear that the self-control demands on humans is much greater than the self-control demands on these other animals. Indeed, it has been argued (Sedikides & Skowronski, 1997) that the growth in the ability to exert self-control drove the development of human cognition, society, and the development of the self. Hence, understanding how self-control operates can give us insight into many critical features of the human experience.

Moreover, of course, understanding self-control has immense practical benefits as well. Self-control is critical to both preventing the initiation as well as the cessation of addictive behaviors (e.g., Brown, 1998; Wills, Sandy, & Yaeger, 2002). Other research has illustrated the importance of self-control in dieting (Heatherton, Striepe, & Wittenberg, 1998), overspending (Faber, 1992), relationship problems (Finkel & Campbell, 2001), violence (Stucke & Baumeister, 2006), and crime (Gottfredson & Hirschi, 1990). Given that many health problems can be linked to a lack of exercise, smoking, and poor eating habits, it is apparent that a lack of self-control is a major contributor to morbidity and mortality. Likewise, because many economic problems at both the personal and societal level follow from overspending, lack of consideration of future demands, and educational underachievement, a better understanding of how self-control operates is critical to our prosperity as well.

Ego Strength

An examination of past research on self-control (Muraven & Baumeister, 2000) suggested that self-control worsens over time. That is, after exerting self-control, subsequent attempts at self-control suffer. For instance, research on the effects of environmental stress (Glass, Singer, & Friedman, 1969) found that individuals who were exposed to uncontrollable or unpredictable noise subsequently performed more poorly on a test of persistence and frustration tolerance, after being moved to a quiet location, as compared to individuals who had been exposed to a controllable or predictable noise. These researchers argued that it was not the noise per se that affected performance, but rather the process of adapting and coping with the noise that depleted the individual so that he or she was less able to deal with future demands.

Such a depletion model can be contrasted with a constant resource or skill model. These models would predict that self-control should not be affected by previous demands, or it may even get better as the individual warms up and gains knowledge of the tasks. The depletion model specifically predicts an aftereffect of exerting self-control. That is, even after the initial self-control demand has been removed and a new situation introduced, there should be a carryover effect that leads to poorer self-control. Moreover, in order to be a unique prediction, this decline in performance should not arise from changes in mood, arousal, frustration, self-efficacy, or other well-established psychological processes.

Extensive research has strongly suggested that the depletion model is the best fit for the observed data on self-control. In experimental studies, individuals who exert self-control perform more poorly on subsequent tests of self-control as compared to individuals who initially worked on a task that did not require self-control. For example, Muraven, Collins, and Nienhaus (2002) had social drinkers either suppress the thought of a white bear (a difficult thought inhibition exercise; Wegner, Schneider, Carter, & White, 1987) or solve addition problems. These tasks did not differ in perceived unpleasantness, effort, or difficulty; the only reported difference was the amount of self-control required. Subsequently, participants were given the chance to drink alcohol, with the caveat that afterward they would take a driving simulator test and those who did well would win a prize. As compared to those who solved addition problems, individuals who had to suppress their thoughts drank more and become more intoxicated. This suggests that the exercise of suppressing thoughts leads to poorer control over alcohol intake subsequently. Indeed, participants' reports of the amount of self-control they exerted on the first task were related to the amount of alcohol they consumed. On the other hand, reports of mood, arousal, frustration, and displeasure were not related to the amount consumed. This strongly suggests that the loss of control over alcohol intake is being driven by the amount of self-control exerted in the first part of the experiment.

The initial exertion of self-control only affects tasks that require self-control, further giving evidence to the specificity of the depletion model. For instance, people who strongly desire to drink alcohol must exert greater self-control not to drink than people who desire alcohol less. Hence, in the alcohol study (Muraven et al., 2002), individuals who were not very tempted to drink were less affected by the initial exertion of self-control and drank less as compared to individuals who were higher in temptation. That is, the initial act of self-control reduced subsequent self-control performance, but it did not lead to a general increase in alcohol intake (see also Muraven, Collins, Shiffman, & Paty, 2005). Additional research has further illustrated that difficult tasks that do not require self-control are unaffected by initial acts of self-control (Muraven, Shmueli, & Burkley, 2006).

Given these results, it has been suggested (e.g., Muraven & Baumeister, 2000) that exerting self-control may deplete a conceptual resource called *ego strength* (alternatively called *self-control strength*). In particular, this resource is critical to any and all attempts at self-control. It is not needed for any activities except self-control. This ego strength is limited and the amount of strength is critical to the success of self-control, so that more is better. The exertion of self-control depletes some of this resource, so that after engaging in self-control, the individual has less ego strength. People in this state are said to be *ego depleted* (or just depleted).

If indeed the level of strength is critical to the success of self-control and that the exertion of self-control depletes some of this resource, it follows that after exerting self-control, subsequent attempts at self-control may be more likely to fail. A good amount of research, from around the world, using a variety of methods, has found this pattern of results.

As noted earlier, the observed effects do not appear to be a product of mood or arousal. In most studies, mood and arousal have not been found to differ between participants who exerted self-control and those who did not (e.g., Baumeister, Bratslavsky, Muraven, & Tice, 1998; Muraven, Tice, & Baumeister, 1998). Likewise, mood and arousal were not related to final self-control performance. The same is true for more specific mood items, such as frustration, irritation, annoyance, boredom, or interest as well. Likewise, Wallace and Baumeister (2002) directly manipulated feedback about success and failure of the self-control efforts and also found no effect. In short, the decline in self-control performance after exerting self-control appears to be directly related to the amount of self-control exerted and cannot be easily explained by other, well-established psychological processes.

What Causes Depletion

Overall, and consistent with the definition of self-control given earlier, researchers have found that anytime an individual overrides, inhibits, stops, or changes a mood, urge, thought, or behavior, it can lead to depletion and hence poorer self-control. For example, at the most basic level, Baumeister et al. (1998) showed that after resisting the temptation of eating chocolate chip cookies, participants quit working on a frustrating puzzle sooner than participants who had to resist eating radishes, which were not seen as tempting as the cookies. This suggests that overriding basic urges is depleting. Indeed, Muraven and Shmueli (2006) found a similar effect for alcohol and social drinkers, with the magnitude of the depletion effect being proportional to participants' self-reported desire to drink. Likewise, resisting the urge to eat cookies was more depleting to dieters than nondieters, further suggesting that the strength of the impulse being inhibited may partially determine how depleting an activity is (Vohs & Heatherton, 2000).

Interpersonal

However, research has shown that many other behaviors are also depleting. One particular area of interest is the depleting nature of interpersonal interactions. For instance, Vohs, Baumeister, and Ciarocco (2005) found that people who had to present themselves as competent and likeable to an audience motivated to believe otherwise were less able to regulate their emotions subsequently as compared to individuals who were asked to act naturally. Similarly, engaging in an interaction with a difficult, high-maintenance confederate led to greater depletion than interacting with a more receptive person (Finkel et al., 2006).

The difficulty of high-maintenance interactions seems to carry over to interracial interactions as well. Research has found that interracial interactions lead to poorer performance subsequently on the Stroop interference task as compared to same-race interactions (Richeson & Shelton, 2003; Richeson & Trawalter, 2005). This effect seems to exist for Black as well as White individuals (Richeson, Trawalter, & Shelton, 2005). Being the target of prejudice and stigma also appears to be depleting, as individuals try to cope with the negative feelings and behaviors of being the target of stigma (Inzlicht, McKay, & Aronson, 2007). Even more powerfully, people who were asked to ostracize someone by not talking to the person quit working on an unsolvable anagram task sooner than people who did not have to ostracize someone (Ciarocco,

Sommer, & Baumeister, 2001). These studies suggest that self-presentation and maintaining (or ending) relationships are tasks that often require self-control.

Changing the Self

Other activities that require the individual to change his or her behavior have also been found to be depleting. For instance, as would be expected, individuals who had to suppress their emotional reaction to a film designed to evoke sadness exhibited greater depletion than individuals who did not have to control their emotions (Muraven et al., 1998). However, individuals who had to control their emotions and increase their sadness in response to a video clip of animals dying in an environmental disaster also exhibited greater depletion, as evidenced by less persistence on a frustrating task subsequently. This indicates that the direction of control is far less important than the exercise of control. Subsequent research replicated this effect with disgust (Schmeichel, Demaree, Robinson, & Pu, 2006), while indicating that these effects were not due to arousal. Hence, behavior change in all its forms appears to be depleting.

The act of making choices also seems to be depleting. In one study, participants were told that they were going to have to give a speech on an issue that ran counter to their existing opinions. As compared to those who had no choice, those who were given a choice whether to make the speech persisted for less time on a difficult task afterward compared to those who were not given a choice (Baumeister et al., 1998). In later research, participants who made a series of consumer decisions subsequently drank less of a bad tasting drink than those who rated the products but did not make a choice (Vohs et al., 2008; see also Bruyneel, Dewitte, Vohs, & Warlop, 2006). This effect was even observed when making choices about pleasant outcomes and appears to be separate from implementing the choice.

Perhaps most intriguing is recent research that suggests that mentally simulating the self-control actions of others may also be depleting (Ackerman, Goldstein, Shapiro, & Bargh, 2009). Participants read a story about a waiter or waitress who was hungry but unable to eat the food that he or she served. Half the participants were told to simply read the story, whereas the other half were asked to imagine themselves as this waiter or waitress. The people who imagined themselves as the hungry but self-denying server reported being more willing to overpay for consumer products as compared to those who merely read the story. Although the exact mechanism for this effect remains unclear

(see later for a further discussion of the nature of self-control depletion), the researchers argued that imagining oneself exerting self-control may both activate expectancies about depletion as well as actually require self-control. This further illustrates that although tasks that require self-control appear to deplete self-control resources, we must look beyond simple inhibition if we wish to understand how individuals exert executive control and guide themselves to long-term goals.

Consequences of Depletion

Understanding how a state of ego depletion affects subsequent performance may also help to illuminate the processes involved in self-control. First, consistent with definitions outlined earlier, the most clear-cut consequence of depletion is a loss of self-control. This has been demonstrated in many different domains, some of which have already been described. For instance, after controlling their thoughts and not thinking about a white bear, participants had a harder time not smiling, laughing, or showing amusement at a humorous film as compared to individuals who did not control their thoughts (Muraven et al., 1998). This effect has carried over to many different domains. For instance, depleted individuals (especially dieters) tend to eat more (Kahan, Polivy, & Herman, 2003; Vohs & Heatherton, 2000). Perhaps most artfully, Hofmann, Rauch, and Gawronski (2007; see also Friese, Hofmann, & Wanke, 2008) found that the amount of candy individuals ate when not depleted was related to their self-report views toward food. However, when depleted, their implicit attitudes were a much better predictor of their consumption, which suggest that depletion reduced their ability to intentionally regulate their food intake (a similar study by Ostafin, Marlatt, and Greenwald, 2008, found the same pattern with implicit and explicit measures of attitudes toward drinking and actual alcohol consumption). Consistent with that perspective, depletion has been found to affect the controlled components of stereotype-based responses, but not the automatic component (Govorun & Payne, 2006).

Research on depletion has found similar patterns that depletion leads to poorer control over other behaviors of consequence as well. For instance, Muraven, Collins, and Nienhaus (2002) found that after controlling their thoughts, social drinkers consumed more alcohol despite incentives not to as compared to social drinkers who solved difficult and frustrating math problems that nonetheless did not require self-control. In a follow-up, a field study of underage social drinkers who carried palm top computers for 3 weeks to report their self-control demands and drinking behavior found that on days that their self-control demands were higher than their average, these drinkers were more likely to drink to excess (Muraven et al., 2005). The increased drinking was not apparently related to increased urges, greater negative affect, or a lack of desire to control drinking; instead it appeared to be related to an inability to regulate alcohol intake. Depletion of ego strength has also been found to affect smoking behavior (Leeman, O'Malley, White, & McKee, 2010), regulation of sexual urges (Gailliot & Baumeister, 2007), and impulse spending (Vohs & Faber, 2007).

Although the predominant model is that depletion reduces individuals' ability to inhibit urges (Govorun & Payne, 2006; Muraven & Shmueli, 2006; Ostafin et al., 2008), there is also some evidence that depletion can also lead to stronger emotions and urges. For instance, Schmeichel, Harmon-Jones, and Harmon-Jones, (2010) found that depletion increased individuals' approach motivation, so that they focused more on a reward-relevant stimulus than a reward-irrelevant stimulus. Ego depletion could therefore lead to poorer self-control by strengthening impulses, rather than undermining inhibition.

Broader Perspective

Less well investigated but important to understanding how depletion affects performance are studies on perception of time and passivity in depleted individuals. In particular, depletion apparently affects people's sense of the passage of time. Depleted individuals estimated that more time had passed while exerting self-control than nondepleted individuals (Vohs & Schmeichel, 2003). This might contribute to the poorer self-control among depleted individuals, especially on persistence-based tasks, as they may misjudge how long they have been acting on controlling themselves. More research is needed to better integrate these results into a more general theory of how self-control operates.

Similarly, Baumeister et al. (1998) found that depleted individuals were more passive than nondepleted individuals. When quitting a boring task (watching an unchanging video of a blank wall) required participants to initiate a button push, depleted participants watched longer than nondepleted participants. On the other hand, when quitting was the passive option and continuing required a response, depleted participants quit sooner. The extent to which many of the effects associated with depletion may spring from passivity and a general unwillingness to initiate an action is an unanswered question.

Interpersonal Effects

There are clear interpersonal consequences to depletion as well. As expected from the decline in self-control performance, depleted people appear to be less likely to follow basic social norms, both prescriptive and descriptive (DeBono, Shmueli, & Muraven, 2011). For instance, depleted individuals are more likely to cheat (Muraven, Pogarsky, & Shmueli, 2006), lie, and steal (DeBono et al., 2011). People whose self-control was depleted also engaged in more inappropriate social interactions, by talking too much, making too intimate interpersonal disclosures, or being arrogant (Vohs et al., 2005). Clearly, being socially appropriate and following norms requires self-control and is affected by depletion.

However, the effects of depletion extend beyond simple impulsive control. For example, depleted individuals are also more easily persuaded. Burkley (2008) found that resisting a persuasive attempt leads to a pattern of self-control outcomes consistent with depletion. In later studies, he found that depleted individuals were more easily persuaded, especially by strong arguments. Wheeler, Brinol, and Hermann (2007) found a similar pattern of results and persuasively argued that depleted individuals were more likely to agree with counterattitudinal statements. Interestingly, they found that depleted and nondepleted individuals thought equally hard about the message, but only depleted individuals were less likely to come up with counterarguments to the message. These results suggest that depletion leads to passivity and agreement among people.

This passivity and general lack of ability to engage in counterarguments may affect interpersonal perception as well. For example, individuals who were depleted rated African American targets more negatively than European American targets (Muraven, 2008b; Park, Glaser, & Knowles, 2008). Depleted people may be less willing to override their stereotypes and less likely to think of reasons to do so (Devine, 1989). Research has also found that depletion makes people less helpful (DeWall, Baumeister, Gailliot, & Maner, 2008; Fennis, Janssen, & Vohs, 2009). Consistent with that reduced helpfulness, depleted people are less forgiving in their relationships: Individuals who were depleted were less likely to engage in accommodation (Yovetich & Rusbult, 1994) and therefore responded less constructively to the negative behavior of their partner (Finkel & Campbell, 2001). Depleted individuals lie more as compared to nondepleted people as well (Mead, Baumeister, Gino, Schweitzer, & Ariely, 2009), which can also damage relationships.

The effects of depletion further extend into aggressive behavior. It is likely that individuals have to learn to restrain aggressive urges in order to maintain harmonious relationships and therefore depletion of self-control resources may lead to a breakdown in this restraint. Indeed, depleted individuals have been found to react to provocations with greater aggression than nondepleted individuals (DeWall, Baumeister, Stillman, & Gailliot, 2007; Stucke & Baumeister, 2006). As compared to participants who were asked to not eat radishes, participants who were asked to not eat a donut placed in front of them slipped more hot sauce into the foods that were to be given to a participant who gave them negative feedback on an essay. When participants received neutral feedback on their essay, there were no differences between depleted and nondepleted conditions. This suggests that depletion was simply potentiating the aggressive responses and was not a direct cause of it.

Cognition

Depletion also appears to affects cognition. For instance, Schmeichel (2007) found that individuals who were depleted by regulating their emotions, controlling their attention, writing in a nonnatural way, or taking a working memory test performed more poorly on subsequent tests of working memory span, reverse digit span, and response inhibition. Basic cognitive processes appear to be affected by depletion; the affected tests are considered to require substantial executive control and response inhibition. This decrease in mental efficiency apparently carries over to higher order functioning as well, as depleted individuals do worse on tests of logic and reasoning, reading comprehension, and a general test of fluid cognitive functioning than nondepleted individuals (Schmeichel, Vohs, & Baumeister, 2003; see also Shamosh & Gray, 2007). Depletion did not affect performance on a test of general knowledge or memorization and recall—tests that are presumed to require less higher order cognitive functioning.

As would be expected from the observed changes in cognition, depletion appears to affect decision making as well. In general, it appears that depleted individuals take greater risks, make poorer decisions, and fail to consider all alternatives as well as nondepleted individuals. For instance, Freeman and Muraven (2010) found that people who had to control their attention by ignoring information presented at the bottom of a video screen subsequently made more pumps on the Balloon Analogue Risk Task (Lejuez et al., 2003), a measure of risk taking. The link between negative

affect and risk taking was also found to be partially mediated by depletion—people's attempt to regulate their negative moods is depleting and this depletion leads to greater risk taking (Bruyneel, Dewitte, Franses, & Dekimpe, 2009). Depleted individuals also rely to a greater extent than nondepleted individuals on heuristics and fail to consider all options carefully in a consumer decision-making task, which leads to a suboptimal decision (Masicampo & Baumeister, 2008; Pocheptsova, Amir, Dhar, & Baumeister, 2009). In addition, it appears that depleted individuals are more likely to seek confirmatory information that is consistent with their existing viewpoints (Fischer, Greitemeyer, & Frey, 2008). Exerting self-control appears to reduce the motivation to search for and process new information. This research is particularly notable for showing that the effects of depletion on decision making and information processing appear to be different from the effects observed from cognitive load, ego threat, and mood.

This change in decision making and risk taking goes hand in hand with changes in self-perception. Depleted individuals are less optimistic about their abilities, have a lower sense of control, and are less optimistic about the future (Fischer, Greitemeyer, & Frey, 2007). Indeed, depleted individuals set lower standards for themselves and had less confidence in their ability to reach a goal than nondepleted individuals (DeBono & Muraven, in press). Optimistic perspectives and positive illusions are apparently not automatic but instead require the individual to override doubts and negativity. These findings need to be better integrated into the idea of "automatic egotism" (Paulhus, Graf, & Van Selst, 1989), as well as the findings that depletion leads to greater heuristic processing. They suggest that processes that consider egotism and self-enhancement automatic either need to be revised or that depletion contributes to a decline in positive illusions in a novel way. In short, the underlying mechanism of maintaining illusions and why it is vulnerable to depletion requires attention.

Physiological Markers of Depletion

Finally, research on biological markers of effort and motivation similarly point to decreased cognitive control among depleted individuals. For example, Bray et al. (2008) measured electromyographic (EMG) activation in depleted and nondepleted individuals as they isometrically squeezed a handgrip. Consistent with previous research (e.g., Muraven et al., 1998), depleted individuals were not able to hold the handgrip as long as nondepleted individuals. Moreover, depleted individuals had greater neuromuscular activation than nondepleted individuals, despite no differences in maximum strength. This indicates that the depletion is not the same as reduced motivation (which presumably would lead to reduced maximal output) and also represents increased effort as if the person needs to overcome a motivational deficit.

A similar conclusion can be drawn from Segerstrom and Nes (2007), who found that resisting eating cookies led to greater heart rate variability than resisting eating carrots and this heart rate variability correlated with persistence on a subsequent anagram task. This suggests that exerting self-control requires the mobilization of effort. The inability to maintain that effort over time may help explain how depletion arises. Indeed, that is the argument raised by Wright and colleagues (Wright et al., 2007; Wright, Martin, & Bland, 2003; Wright, Stewart, & Barnett, 2008): High levels of fatigue require increased mobilization of effort (as indexed by cardiovascular output), but when the effort required is perceived to be too great, then all efforts cease (Stewart, Wright, Azor Hui, & Simmons, 2009).

Intriguingly, research using electroencephalographic (EEG) methodology suggests that depletion can also be measured by changes in the event-related potential of error-related negativity (Inzlicht & Gutsell, 2007). Error-related negatively has been linked to preconscious error monitoring and correction and thus may be related to cognitive control over behavior. Individuals who had to control their emotions exhibited weaker error-related negativity signal while working on a Stroop task as compared to individuals in a control condition. Moreover, performance on the Stroop was related to magnitude of the error-related negativity signal, so that this neural signal mediated the link between initial self-control exertion and subsequent self-control performance. In short, depletion may affect neurological functioning and may be tied to specific changes in the neural system used for conflict monitoring.

How Depletion Operates

These biological markers of depletion provide some insight into how and why prior acts of self-control lead to subsequent self-control failure. As noted earlier, most research has been founded on the idea that depletion reduces individuals' ability to inhibit behaviors. The exact process underlying that effect is still an area of active investigation, with two main theoretical lines. The first focuses on a motivation or expectancy account, which suggests that

self-control fails because individuals hold certain beliefs about how self-control should operate. The biological account, on the other hand, suggests that ego depletion is more than a metaphor and actually represents the loss of crucial biological resources needed for the success of self-control. Ultimately, as with many dichotomies, the truth may lie in the integration of these accounts.

Expectancies

Arguments for the expectancy account for the depletion effect suggest that individuals hold beliefs that self-control is limited and therefore after exerting self-control, they expect to fail in subsequent attempts at self-control. For instance, individuals who felt that self-control was limited and depletes a limited resource were more affected by the initial self-control demand than individuals who did not subscribe to such a belief (e.g., Job, Dweck, & Walton, 2010; Martijn, Tenbuelt, Merckelbach, Dreezens, & de Vries, 2002). The researchers argued that this suggests that the depletion effect springs from expectancies about the nature of self-control. Indeed, in subsequent research, they found that individuals who were not paying attention to their self-control efforts exhibited less of a decline in self-control than individuals who were not distracted (Alberts, Martijn, Nievelstein, Jansen, & de Vries, 2008). This leads credence to the idea that some of the effects of exerting self-control on subsequent self-control performance are psychologically mediated and based on expectations of self-control demands.

Similarly, Clarkson et al. (2010) found that people's perceived levels of depletion predicted their performance on tasks that required self-control. Depleted (or not depleted) individuals were given (false) feedback about this depleting task that led them to attribute their resources to external or internal sources. For instance, participants crossed off the letter "e" that is next to or one away from another vowel (those in the control condition simply crossed off all e's). Crossed with this, participants were told that the color of the paper could either "*exhaust and deplete* their ability to attend to information" or "*energize and replenish* one's ability to attend to information" (p. 33, italics in original). In the low-depletion condition, the replenishment feedback led to greater persistence on a subsequent task than the depletion feedback. This pattern was reversed in the high-depletion condition. In short, people's perception of their level of self-control resource was a predictor of their subsequent self-control performance regardless of their actual level of resource.

In summary, the expectancy account of depletion suggests that people fail at self-control because they believe it should fail. Most people apparently subscribe to the belief that self-control is a limited resource and after exerting self-control this belief is typically activated, which leads to poorer self-control subsequently. This may explain many of the outcomes described earlier, although it may have greater difficulty in explaining situations in which the exertion or need for self-control is not apparent (e.g., cognitive performance) nor does it explain why seemingly difficult tasks (Muraven et al., 1998), like solving math problems, does not lead to a decline in self-control performance. This model suggests that people have a finely attuned sense of what requires self-control and what does not.

Biology

There are also some persuasive arguments that the effects of depletion may be biologically mediated. In particular, there is evidence that levels of glucose, particularly in the brain, may also explain the decline in self-control performance after exerting self-control. Glucose is the primary source of energy for all brain activity and therefore a decline in glucose may negatively affect executive functioning (Siesjö, 1978). For instance, low levels of glucose are related to poorer cognitive functioning in both rats (McNay, McCarty, & Gold, 2001) and humans (Benton, 1990; Martin & Benton, 1999). More recent research has directly linked glucose to self-control, as individuals with lower levels of blood glucose have been found to engage in greater discounting of the future. Consistent with this argument, the ingestion of sugar negates this drop in self-control (Wang & Dvorak, 2010).

Like the hypothesized ego strength, glucose can be consumed faster than it can be replenished under heavy cognitive demands. Hence, exerting self-control may deplete glucose, a vital fuel for cognitive efforts. Indeed, recent research found that dogs which were required to follow rules and resist a temptation had lower levels of glucose than dogs which were not required to be obedient (Miller, Pattison, DeWall, Rayburn-Reeves, & Zentall, 2010). A similar effect has been found in humans after engaging in tasks that likely require self-control (Fairclough & Houston, 2004; Gailliot, Baumeister, et al., 2007). For example, Gailliot, Baumeister, DeWall et al. (2007) reported that individuals who were instructed to deliberately ignore words at the bottom of a video clip suffered a greater drop in blood glucose levels from baseline than individuals who

saw the same clip but did not have to ignore the words. This change in glucose correlated with subsequent self-control performance. Later experiments showed that this decline in self-control performance after exerting self-control could be negated, however, by the ingestion of glucose (in the form of orange juice). Given that these patterns closely mirror the predictions of the ego strength model, it seems likely that some of the observed effects are being driven by the depletion of glucose in the brain. Sugar only improves the performance of depleted individuals and has no effect on nondepleted individuals, which suggests that depletion may be related to reduced levels of sugar (Masicampo & Baumeister, 2008; also found in dogs by Miller et al., 2010). This study also showed that the ingestion of a non-nutritive sugar substitute (Splenda) had no effect on depletion, which further indicates that the effects are not simply due to expectations or merely drinking a pleasant drink. Denson et al. (2010) replicated these findings in a study that looked at the effects of ego depletion on aggression.

In short, there are persuasive arguments that exerting self-control may require and deplete glucose and this drop in glucose may drive the decline in self-control performance. This helps to explain the specificity of the depletion on self-control and executive control and may fit well with the physiological effects associated with depletion. However, changes in glucose cannot be easily integrated with the fact that changes in expectancy for self-control apparently also lead to changes in self-control performance. The biological account also leaves little room for motivation in depletion.

Integration: Effects of Motivation and Conservation

Even if the depletion of glucose in the brain is a contributor to poorer self-control outcomes, the final result must be psychologically mediated. It is very unlikely that exerting self-control depletes all available glucose so that self-control becomes impossible. Indeed, except in very rare and unusual circumstances, most individuals who fail at self-control do not lose control over all actions and become completely animalistic. Individuals who exert self-control on a laboratory task and hence exhibit poorer self-control subsequently do not urinate on themselves but instead ask to be excused to go to the bathroom. Thus, a complete model of depletion needs to explain both the specificity of depletion to self-control and how it can be moderated by motivation.

Motivation

For instance, Muraven, Pogarsky, and Shmueli (2006) found that depleted individuals were more likely to lie and cheat on a laboratory task than non-depleted individuals. However, this was only true when the perceived probability of getting caught was low. When the odds of the experimenter discovering the deviance were high, depleted individuals were no more likely to cheat than nondepleted individuals. Likewise, Wan and Sternthal (2008) found that depleted individuals who were encouraged to engage in self-monitoring by being given a clock while working on a persistence task worked as long as nondepleted individuals. As self-monitoring has been found to increase motivation and goal adherence (Carver & Scheier, 1998), it is likely that this self-monitoring feedback led to increased motivation that negated the effects of depletion.

Even more directly, depleted individuals who were given an incentive to exert self-control, in the form of either money, social acceptance, or moral expectations, performed just as well on a subsequent self-control task as participants who were not depleted (Muraven & Slessareva, 2003). For instance, when paid a cent per cup, individual who had to suppress their emotional reaction to a humorous video clip drank less of a vinegar-flavored drink as compared to individuals who simply watched the video with no instructions to control their emotional reaction. On the other hand, when the incentive for drinking was high (25 cents per cup), individuals who had to suppress their emotional reaction drank just as much of the sour drink as individuals who did not suppress their reaction.

The motivation can apparently be unconsciously activated as well. For instance, Alberts et al. (2007) found that depleted individuals who were given primes related to persistence (either by unscrambling sentences with persistence words in them or seeing a screensaver with motivational images) performed better than depleted individuals not given these primes. Likewise, thinking of good self-control exemplars led to better self-control among depleted individuals than thinking of a neutral example (Martijn et al., 2007). Even the mere symbolic presence of family members appears to lead to better self-control in depleted individuals (Stillman, Tice, Fincham, & Lambert, 2009).

The results indicate that people can overcome depletion if sufficiently motivated. Thus, a reduction in glucose levels may increase the likelihood of self-control failure, but only when the individual is insufficiently motivated. Given that motivation plays a critical role in contributing to self-control failures, the question then arises why past self-control efforts matter at all. Further research, based on the idea of the conservation of limited resources, suggests they do.

Conservation

In particular, if self-control requires glucose or other limited resources, it makes sense to use this resource as wisely as possible. People should be judicious in how and when they exert self-control, so they can have resources for future demands or emergencies. This self-control resource can be compared to other limited resources, such as money. The sensible person keeps a cushion of money in his or her checking account, to pay for unexpected events. Moreover, consistent with prospect theory (Tversky & Kahneman, 1981), the less money one has, the more the remaining money should be valued.

Analogously, individuals should be concerned with conserving ego strength to the extent that it is perceived to be a limited resource. Depletion of this resource, through the exercise of self-control, should heighten this desire to conserve the remaining resource. It then follows that individuals who are motivated to conserve ego strength may be less likely to exert self-control, which therefore leads to poorer self-control performance. This may explain why depleted individuals typically perform more poorly on tasks that matter less to them, but perform just as well as nondepleted people on important, self-relevant, or externally motivated tasks.

Muraven, Shmueli, and Burkley (2006; see replication by Tyler & Burns, 2009) tested this idea by manipulating participants' expectations for the future. If people expect to exert self-control in the future, their motivation to conserve should be increased; this should be especially likely if their ego strength was already depleted. In one experiment, participants first had to control a well-learned pattern by typing a paragraph without hitting the "e" key (participants in the control condition just typed the paragraph as they saw it). They were then told that they would take two more tests. The first was a Stroop test, where they would have to state the font color of word. After that, they would have to solve anagrams that were either described as requiring them to "think hard" (low self-control) or "override impulses" (high self-control). Participants who had to exert self-control in the first part of the experiment and who expected to exert self-control in the future exhibited poorer self-control on the Stroop task as compared to those who did not exert self-control in the past or those who did not expect to exert self-control in the future.

Further evidence for conservation came from participants' actual performance on the final task. In particular, how long they persisted on difficult and frustrating anagrams before quitting. There was a negative correlation between Stroop performance and time spent on the anagrams, suggesting a trade-off in resource use. That is, worse performance on the Stroop (which would suggest conserving) was associated with greater self-control on the anagram. Janssen, Fennis, and Pruyn (2010) found a similar effect: Depleted individuals who were warned about an upcoming persuasive attempt conserved strength and hence generated better counterarguments and resisted the compliance more than depleted individual who were not forewarned.

In short, people appear to manage their self-control resources based on their past efforts and future demands. The desire to conserve strength can help both explain the specificity of the depletion effect to self-control and how motivation and expectancies can moderate this effect. The desire to conserve should not be necessarily interpreted as a conscious process, however. There is very limited evidence that people are aware of their self-control states; instead, there appears to be a complex process of unconscious weighing of alternatives. Further work is necessary to understand how these motivational processes work together to lead to self-control failures.

Moderators of Depletion

This conservation model of self-control failure points the way toward understanding when self-control is more likely to fail and when it is less likely. Hence, there may be processes that moderate the link between depletion and self-control failure. That is, there are some situations in which the link between depletion of ego strength and final self-control performance is weakened (or strengthened). These moderators may give some further insight into how depletion works and some limitation to our self-control.

Automatization

Intuitively, anything that reduces the self-control demand on a behavior should reduce how depleting it is. Indeed, as noted earlier, there is a relationship between how much self-control a task required and the subsequent decline in self-control performance (e.g., Muraven et al., 2002). Hence, it was suggested that implementation intentions

(Gollwitzer & Brandstätter, 1997) should help in the elimination of ego depletion. Implementation intentions help automatize behaviors by creating a clear link between when, where, and how an individual will strive for a goal. This helps reduce the self-control demand of a situation, as it forges an association between a cue and a response, thereby reducing the need for conscious control.

In an examination of the effects of implementation intentions on depletion, participants who created implementation intentions for the Stroop task (e.g., "As soon as I see the word I will ignore its meaning") subsequently persisted longer on a frustrating task than individuals who did the same Stroop task without the benefit of creating an implementation intention (Webb & Sheeran, 2003). In a second study, the opposite of this effect was found: Depleted individuals who created implementation intentions for a Stroop task read the list of words faster than depleted individuals who did not create a plan. Making a plan apparently reduced the resources required for self-control, so that tasks were less depleting and less affected by depletion.

Rest and Replenishment

There clearly must be some way to recover lost resources. However, to date, this topic has not received extensive attention. It is likely that rest from exerting self-control is one way in which resources are recovered. For instance, Shiffman et al. (1996) reported that although the urge to smoke is strongest in the morning, most lapses occur in the evening. This is consistent with the idea that in the morning people are rested and therefore have the strength to deal with their urges. Later in the day, however, more strength has been depleted and therefore their ability to resist the temptation to smoke has been diminished. Research that focused more directly on depletion on a smaller scale found a similar pattern (Tyler & Burns, 2008). Participants who had a 10-minute break between the first self-control task and the subsequence measure performed better than participants who did not have the break and equal to nondepleted individuals. A similar effect was found for participants who were induced into relaxing between tasks.

It may be possible to accelerate this recovery process through positive affect (Tice, Baumeister, Shmueli, & Muraven, 2007). Participants who were depleted by resisting the temptation of cookies and candy failed to persist as long on a frustrating task as compared to those who had to resist the temptation of eating radishes. However, if they watched a comedy between resisting the food and persisting, those who could not eat the cookies persisted just as long as those who could not eat the radishes. The general conclusion is that positive experiences negate the effects of ego depletion and the effects are not driven by arousal and distraction but are specific to tasks that require self-control. The researchers argued that positive affect may help to replenish lost ego strength. It may do this directly, by serving as a resource, or it may just increase motivation or willingness to exert self-control. That is, it might be like giving coffee to a tired person—it gets him or her going for a while, but a crash is inevitable, or it might be like getting a good night's sleep. Further empirical research is required to differentiate between these accounts.

Finally, affirming the self (Steele, 1988) appears to help negate the effects of depletion (Schmeichel & Vohs, 2009). Individuals who were depleted by having to write a story without using any words containing the letter "a" or "n" removed their hand from ice water sooner than participants who wrote a story without such restrictions. However, if the depleted individuals were given the chance to rank 11 values and personal characteristics in order of personal importance, this effect disappeared: Depleted individual held their hand in the water as long as nondepleted individuals. The effects were not related to changes in mood. Instead, the researchers argued that the self-affirmation led individuals to consider abstract, long-range outcomes, which improved their self-control performance.

Autonomy

Perhaps related to these replenishment findings is research on the effects of autonomy support on depletion. The idea of autonomy support is that some situations encourage and are more supportive of behaviors that are intrinsic and self-driven, whereas others take that feeling away (Ryan & Deci, 2000). Time pressures, external rewards, and authority figures cause individuals to feel compelled to act, which in turn diminishes the extent to which the behavior feels intrinsic, genuine, and self-motivated.

Several studies have clearly shown self-control that feels compelled by the situation is much more depleting than self-control that feels more autonomously driven. For instance, Moller, Deci, and Ryan (2006) gave some participants a choice between several different activities and then measured their self-control performance. They found that people given such a choice without any constraints exhibited

better self-control subsequently as compared to people who were told that although they were free to choose, the experimenter really needed them to select a particular activity. This effect was found to be mediated by feelings of self-determination, but not mood.

People's own reasons for exerting self-control can have a similar effect. A plate of cookies was placed in front of participants, with the instructions to please not eat them unless absolutely necessary (Muraven, 2008a). They were then asked why they did not eat the cookies, to measure their feelings of self-determination. People who did not eat the cookies for more self-determined reasons (e.g., because it matters to me) exhibited better self-control by squeezing a handgrip longer, as compared to those who did not eat the cookies for more extrinsic reasons (e.g., the experimenter would get mad at me).

These results suggest that autonomously driven self-control is less depleting than self-control that is compelled by others or the situation. Further research suggested that this outcome may be driven by the replenishment effect described earlier. Participants instructed to avoid thinking about a white bear by a warm, open, and friendly experimenter who tried to engage participants as a vital contributor to the research project subsequently exhibited better self-control on a dependent measure of self-control than participants who were instructed by a more distant and cold experimenter who treated participants like a "cog in the machine" (Muraven, Gagné, & Rosman, 2008; see also Muraven, Rosman, & Gagné, 2007). The participants in the autonomy supportive condition had greater feelings of subjective vitality (Nix, Ryan, Manly, & Deci, 1999; Ryan & Frederick, 1997), a positive state of aliveness and energy that arises from acting in self-actualizing ways. These feelings of vitality mediated the link between experimental condition and self-control outcomes, so that the reason why people in the autonomy supportive condition exhibited less depletion was because they felt more vital. This is consistent with the replenishment idea, and it further suggests that self-control behaviors that are associated with positive states should lead to less depletion of strength.

Building Strength

The research described earlier focuses primarily on the short-term effects of exerting self-control. A quick summary would suggest that people act as if self-control is a muscle, which gets fatigued with use. This fatigue effect is moderated by several different processes, and it may be related to glucose levels in the brain, as well as beliefs that self-control is limited.

Muscles do get fatigue through work, much like the effects observed with self-control. However, muscles also get stronger, providing they are worked hard and frequently and rest is taken. Is the same true with self-control? That is, can people strengthen their self-control muscle by exercising their self-control? The evidence suggests that they can.

In the first study on this process, Muraven, Baumeister, and Tice, (1999) asked participants to practice self-control by either maintaining a diary of food intake, keeping good posture, or regulating their moods to avoid negative emotions as much as possible. The control group had no special instructions and went about their daily life. Participants' handgrip squeezing time (relative to their baseline) after engaging self-control was assessed at the start of the study and again after they had practiced their assigned task for 2 weeks. Those who practiced self-control were less affected by the depleting task as compared to those who did not practice self-control and the effects were stronger for participants who practiced more. This is evidence that practicing self-control can increase self-control endurance, so that people are less affected by depletion. Put another way, practicing self-control increased their stamina, so that they were able to exert self-control even when already fatigued.

Comparably, research by Oaten and colleagues (Oaten & Cheng, 2006a, 2006b, 2007), as well as Gailliot and colleagues (Gailliot, Plant, Butz, & Baumeister, 2007) found that practicing self-control can also increase self-control power. That is, even in nondepleted states, participants who practiced self-control exhibited better self-control outcomes. This is the equivalent of strength, so that after practicing self-control individuals could overcome more powerful impulses. For instance, in Hui et al. (2009), participants either engaged in a strong training program (work on the Stroop task for 5 minutes twice daily for 2 weeks and rinse with a mouthwash that produces a powerful burning sensation) or a weak training program (no conflict between ink color and word; diluted mouthwash). At the end of this training, participants returned to the laboratory and engaged in several tasks that required self-control. As compared to those who had no training or those who had the weak training, those who underwent the strong training held their hand in ice water significantly longer. They also performed better on a visual search task that requires regulating attention and concentration, had better dental care (based on

amount of dental floss and toothpaste used), and reported better health-related behaviors.

Recent research by Muraven (2010a, 2010b) has further extended these findings to make it clear that the effects of practicing self-control are above and beyond any effects expected from expectation or self-efficacy. Smokers who were interested in quitting were assigned one of four tasks to practice for 2 weeks before beginning a cessation attempt. Two of these conditions required self-control (avoid eating sweets and squeeze a handgrip exercise for as long as possible twice a day) and two did not (maintain a diary of any time they exerted self-control and work on difficult math problems). Consistent with previous research, smokers who practiced tasks that required self-control remained abstinent longer than smokers who practiced tasks that did not require self-control. Moreover, the control tasks evoked awareness of self-control, increased self-monitoring, increased self-efficacy, and participants expected these tasks to be helpful in their cessation attempt. This means that the effects of practicing self-control on subsequent improvements in self-control are above and separate from the smokers' expectation that it should help them quit smoking, improvements in self-efficacy, or greater self-monitoring. Put another way, practicing self-control has a direct effect on subsequent self-control performance.

Conclusion

The depletion model of self-control suggests that self-control is bounded by a limited resource that gets depleted with use. A growing body of research, in a variety of domains, suggests that after exerting self-control, individuals have greater difficulty resisting subsequent self-control demands as this resource is taxed. Although this resource may be biologically mediated (possibly glucose), the process of self-control failure is also psychologically driven, as individuals use social cues in motivating themselves to exert self-control. It appears that the process of depletion can be moderated by individuals' mood, feelings toward the self-control activity, and ability to recover lost resources.

The model suggests that managing this resource is vital to the success of self-control. Given the wide range of behaviors that have been shown to be affected by depletion and depleting in themselves, including high-order cognition, controlling aggression, getting along with others, regulating moods, and resisting the temptations of sex, food, and drugs, clearly a better idea of how self-control operates is critical at the personal and societal level.

Future Directions

Indeed, the findings on building strength and how self-control is moderated by motivation may point the way for further research. A better understanding of how processes underlying the improvements observed after practicing self-control is critical to both advancing theory and crafting the best interventions. In particular, the process of building strength should probably be tied in the conservation model that links the biological and motivation accounts of strength. Such a complete theory should help in predicting which tasks will lead to the most improvement in self-control, how long they should be practiced, and how often.

The conservation model also would benefit from additional research to refine its predictions. For instance, it is not clear how people judge their future and past self-control demands, as well as introspect their levels of resource. This is an area ripe for investigation, as it may illuminate how people process information critical to self-control, which would lead to more powerful theories of self-control. Such a model of conservation might also better explain the processes underlying the replenishment effect of positive affect, as well as the findings that autonomously driven self-control is less depleting than self-control that feels compelled.

The findings that depletion leads to greater passivity and changes in time estimation likely need to be better integrated into the literature as well. These results may help to explain a wide variety of outcomes and may present an opportunity for creating a more unified theory of depletion. Ultimately, it may be possible to link these findings to changes in brain operation, for example, whether glucose is connected to passivity and a lack of motivation.

In the end, a comprehensive theory of self-control may be of profound practical and theoretical importance. Many of the problems facing people and society arise from or could be addressed from improvements in self-control. Moreover, because self-control is so critical to what makes us human and enables us to reach our full potential, a theory of self-control may help in explaining other important aspects of the human condition.

References

Ackerman, J. M., Goldstein, N. J., Shapiro, J. R., & Bargh, J. A. (2009). You wear me out: The vicarious depletion of self-control. *Psychological Science, 20*, 326–332.

Alberts, H. J. E. M., Martijn, C., Greb, J., Merckelbach, H., & de Vries, N. K. (2007). Carrying on or giving in: The role of automatic processes in overcoming ego depletion. *British Journal of Social Psychology, 46*, 383–399.

Alberts, H. J. E. M., Martijn, C., Nievelstein, F., Jansen, A., & de Vries, N. K. (2008). Distracting the self: Shifting attention prevents ego depletion. *Self and Identity, 7*, 322–334.

Baumeister, R. F. (1998). The self. In D. Gilbert, S. T. Fiske, & G. Lindzey (Eds.), *Handbook of social psychology* (4 ed., pp. 680–740). Boston, MA: McGraw-Hill.

Baumeister, R. F. (2005). *The cultural animal: Human nature, meaning, and social life.* New York: Oxford University Press.

Baumeister, R. F., Bratslavsky, E., Muraven, M., & Tice, D. M. (1998). Ego-depletion: Is the active self a limited resource? *Journal of Personality and Social Psychology, 74*, 1252–1265.

Benton, D. (1990). The impact of increasing blood glucose on psychological functioning. *Biological Psychology, 30*, 13–19.

Bray, S. R., Ginis, K. A., Hicks, A. L., & Woodgate, J. (2008). Effects of self-regulatory strength depletion on muscular performance and emg activation. *Psychophysiology, 45*, 337–343.

Brown, J. M. (1998). Self-regulation and the addictive behaviors. In W. R. Miller & N. Heather (Eds.), *Treating addictive behaviors* (2nd ed., pp. 61–73). New York: Plenum.

Bruyneel, S. D., Dewitte, S., Franses, P. H., & Dekimpe, M. G. (2009). I felt low and my purse feels light: Depleting mood regulation attempts affect risk decision making. *Journal of Behavioral Decision Making, 22*, 153–170.

Bruyneel, S. D., Dewitte, S., Vohs, K. D., & Warlop, L. (2006). Repeated choosing increases susceptibility to affective product features. *International Journal of Research in Marketing, 23*, 215–225.

Burkley, E. (2008). The role of self-control in resistance to persuasion. *Personality and Social Psychology Bulletin, 34*, 419–431.

Carver, C. S., & Scheier, M. F. (1998). *On the self-regulation of behavior.* New York: Cambridge University Press.

Ciarocco, N. J., Sommer, K. L., & Baumeister, R. F. (2001). Ostracism and ego depletion: The strains of silence. *Personality and Social Psychology Bulletin, 27*, 1156–1163.

Clarkson, J. J., Hirt, E. R., Jia, L., & Alexander, M. B. (2010). When perception is more than reality: The effects of perceived versus actual resource depletion on self-regulatory behavior. *Journal of Personality and Social Psychology, 98*, 29–46.

DeBono, A., & Muraven, M. (in press). Keeping it real: Self-control depletion increases accuracy but decreases confidence for performance. *Journal of Applied Social Psychology.*

DeBono, A., Shmueli, D., & Muraven, M. (2011). Rude and inappropriate: The role of self-control in following social norms. *Personality and Social Psychology Bulletin, 37*, 136–146.

Denson, T. F., von Hippel, W., Kemp, R. I., & Teo, L. S. (2010). Glucose consumption decreases impulsive aggression in response to provocation in aggressive individuals. *Journal of Experimental Social Psychology, 46*, 1023–1028.

Devine, P. G. (1989). Stereotypes and prejudice: Their automatic and controlled components. *Journal of Personality and Social Psychology, 56*, 5–18.

DeWall, C. N., Baumeister, R. F., Gailliot, M. T., & Maner, J. K. (2008). Depletion makes the heart grow less helpful: Helping as a function of self-regulatory energy and genetic relatedness. *Personality and Social Psychology Bulletin, 34*, 1653–1662.

DeWall, C. N., Baumeister, R. F., Stillman, T. F., & Gailliot, M. T. (2007). Violence restrained: Effects of self-regulation and its depletion on aggression. *Journal of Experimental Social Psychology, 43*, 62–76.

Faber, R. J. (1992). Money changes everything: Compulsive buying from a biopsychosocial perspective. *American Behavioral Scientist, 35*, 809–819.

Fairclough, S. H., & Houston, K. (2004). A metabolic measure of mental effort. *Biological Psychology, 66*, 177–190.

Fennis, M., Janssen, L., & Vohs, K. D. (2009). Acts of benevolence: A limited resource account of compliance with charitable requests. *Journal of Consumer Research, 35*, 906–924.

Finkel, E. J., & Campbell, W. K. (2001). Self-control and accommodation in close relationships: An interdependence analysis. *Journal of Personality and Social Psychology, 81*, 263–277.

Finkel, E. J., Campbell, W. K., Brunell, A. B., Dalton, A. N., Scarbeck, S. J., & Chartrand, T. L. (2006). High-maintenance interaction: Inefficient social coordination impairs self-regulation. *Journal of Personality and Social Psychology, 91*, 263–277.

Fischer, P., Greitemeyer, T., & Frey, D. (2007). Ego depletion and positive illusions: Does the construction of positivity require regulatory resources? *Personality and Social Psychology Bulletin, 33*, 1306–1321.

Fischer, P., Greitemeyer, T., & Frey, D. (2008). Self-regulation and selective exposure: The impact of depleted self-regulation resources on confirmatory information processing. *Journal of Personality and Social Psychology, 94*, 382–395.

Freeman, N., & Muraven, M. (2010). Self-control depletion leads to increased risk taking. *Social Psychological and Personality Science, 1*, 175–181.

Friese, M., Hofmann, W., & Wanke, M. (2008). When impulses take over: Moderated predictive validity of explicit and implicit attitude measures in predicting food choice and consumption behaviour. *British Journal of Social Psychology, 47*, 397–419.

Gailliot, M. T., & Baumeister, R. F. (2007). Self-regulation and sexual restraint: Dispositionally and temporarily poor self-regulatory abilities contribute to failures at restraining sexual behavior. *Personality and Social Psychology Bulletin, 33*, 173–186.

Gailliot, M. T., Baumeister, R. F., DeWall, C. N., Maner, J. K., Plant, E. A., Tice, D. M.,...Schmeichel, B. J. (2007). Self-control relies on glucose as a limited energy source: Willpower is more than a metaphor. *Journal of Personality and Social Psychology, 92*, 325–336.

Gailliot, M. T., Plant, E. A., Butz, D. A., & Baumeister, R. F. (2007). Increasing self-regulatory strength can reduce the depleting effect of suppressing stereotypes. *Personality and Social Psychology Bulletin, 33*, 281–294.

Glass, D. C., Singer, J. E., & Friedman, L. N. (1969). Psychic cost of adaptation to an environmental stressor. *Journal of Personality and Social Psychology, 12*, 200–210.

Gollwitzer, P. M., & Brandstätter, V. (1997). Implementation intentions and effective goal pursuit. *Journal of Personality and Social Psychology, 73*, 186–199.

Gottfredson, M. R., & Hirschi, T. (1990). *A general theory of crime.* Stanford, CA: Stanford University Press.

Govorun, O., & Payne, B. K. (2006). Ego-depletion and prejudice: Separating automatic and controlled components. *Social Cognition, 24*, 111–136.

Heatherton, T. F., Striepe, M., & Wittenberg, L. (1998). Emotional distress and disinhibited eating: The role of the self. *Personality and Social Psychology Bulletin, 24*, 301–313.

Hofmann, W., Rauch, W., & Gawronski, B. (2007). And deplete us not into temptation: Automatic attitudes, dietary restraint, and self-regulatory resources as determinants of eating behavior. *Journal of Experimental Social Psychology, 43*, 497–504.

Hui, S-K., Wright, R., Stewart, C., Simmons, A., Eaton, B., & Nolte, R. (2009). Performance, cardiovascular, and health behavior effects of an inhibitory strength training intervention. *Motivation and Emotion, 33*, 419–434.

Inzlicht, M., & Gutsell, J. N. (2007). Running on empty: Neural signals for self-control failure. *Psychological Science, 18*, 933–937.

Inzlicht, M., McKay, L., & Aronson, J. (2007). Stigma as ego depletion: How being the target of prejudice affects self-control. *Psychological Science, 18*, 262–269.

Janssen, L., Fennis, B. M., & Pruyn, A. T. H. (2010). Forewarned is forearmed: Conserving self-control strength to resist social influence. *Journal of Experimental Social Psychology, 46*, 911–921.

Job, V., Dweck, C. S., & Walton, G. M. (2010). Ego depletion: Is it all in your head? *Psychological Science, 21*, 1686–1693.

Kahan, D., Polivy, J., & Herman, C. P. (2003). Conformity and dietary disinhibition: A test of the ego-strength model of self-regulation. *International Journal of Eating Disorders, 33*, 165–171.

Kanfer, F. H., & Karoly, P. (1972). Self-control: A behavioristic excursion into the lion's den. *Behavior Therapy, 3*, 398–416.

Leeman, R. F., O'Malley, S. S., White, M. A., & McKee, S. A. (2010). Nicotine and food deprivation decrease the ability to resist smoking. *Psychopharmacology, 212*, 25–32.

Lejuez, C. W., Aklin, W. M., Jones, H. A., Richards, J. B., Strong, D. R., Kahler, C. W., & Read, J. P. (2003). The balloon analogue risk task (BART) differentiates smokers and nonsmokers. *Experimental and Clinical Psychopharmacology, 11*, 26–33.

Martijn, C., Alberts, H. J. E. M., Merckelbach, H., Havermans, R., Huijts, A., & de Vries, N. K. (2007). Overcoming ego depletion: The influence of exemplar priming on self-control performance. *European Journal of Social Psychology, 37*, 231–238.

Martijn, C., Tenbuelt, P., Merckelbach, H., Dreezens, E., & de Vries, N. K. (2002). Getting a grip on ourselves: Challenging expectancies about loss of energy after self-control. *Social Cognition, 20*, 441–460.

Martin, P. Y., & Benton, D. (1999). The influence of a glucose drink on a demanding working memory task. *Physiology and Behavior, 67*, 69–74.

Masicampo, E. J., & Baumeister, R. F. (2008). Toward a physiology of dual-process reasoning and judgment: Lemonade, willpower, and expensive rule-based analysis. *Psychological Science, 19*, 255–260.

McNay, E. C., McCarty, R. C., & Gold, P. E. (2001). Fluctuations in brain glucose concentration during behavioral testing: Dissociations between brain areas and between brain and blood. *Neurobiology of Learning and Memory, 75*, 325–337.

Mead, N. L., Baumeister, R. F., Gino, F., Schweitzer, M. E., & Ariely, D. (2009). Too tired to tell the truth: Self-control resource depletion and dishonesty. *Journal of Experimental Social Psychology, 45*, 594–597.

Miller, H. C., Pattison, K. F., DeWall, C. N., Rayburn-Reeves, R., & Zentall, T. R. (2010). Self-control without a "self"? *Psychological Science, 21*, 534–538.

Mischel, W., Shoda, Y., & Rodriguez, M. L. (1989). Delay of gratification in children. *Science, 244*, 933–938.

Moller, A. C., Deci, E. L., & Ryan, R. M. (2006). Choice and ego-depletion: The moderating role of autonomy. *Personality and Social Psychology Bulletin, 32*, 1024–1036.

Muraven, M. (2008a). Autonomous self-control is less depleting. *Journal of Research in Personality, 42*, 763–770.

Muraven, M. (2008b). Prejudice as self-control failure. *Journal of Applied Social Psychology, 38*, 314–333.

Muraven, M. (2010a). Building self-control strength: Practicing self-control leads to improved self-control performance. *Journal of Experimental Social Psychology, 46*, 465–468.

Muraven, M. (2010b). Practicing self-control lowers the risk of smoking lapse. *Psychology of Addictive Behaviors, 24*, 446–452.

Muraven, M., & Baumeister, R. F. (2000). Self-regulation and depletion of limited resources: Does self-control resemble a muscle? *Psychological Bulletin, 126*, 247–259.

Muraven, M., Baumeister, R. F., & Tice, D. M. (1999). Longitudinal improvement of self-regulation through practice: Building self-control strength through repeated exercise. *Journal of Social Psychology, 139*, 446–457.

Muraven, M., Collins, R. L., & Nienhaus, K. (2002). Self-control and alcohol restraint: An initial application of the self-control strength model. *Psychology of Addictive Behaviors, 16*, 113–120.

Muraven, M., Collins, R. L., Shiffman, S., & Paty, J. A. (2005). Daily fluctuations in self-control demands and alcohol intake. *Psychology of Addictive Behaviors, 19*, 140–147.

Muraven, M., Gagné, M., & Rosman, H. (2008). Helpful self-control: Autonomy support, vitality, and depletion. *Journal of Experimental Social Psychology, 44*, 573–585.

Muraven, M., Pogarsky, G., & Shmueli, D. (2006). Self-control depletion and the general theory of crime. *Journal of Quantitative Criminology, 22*, 263–277.

Muraven, M., Rosman, H., & Gagné, M. (2007). Lack of autonomy and self-control: Performance contingent rewards lead to greater depletion. *Motivation and Emotion, 31*, 322–330.

Muraven, M., & Shmueli, D. (2006). The self-control costs of fighting the temptation to drink. *Psychology of Addictive Behaviors, 20*, 154–160.

Muraven, M., Shmueli, D., & Burkley, E. (2006). Conserving self-control strength. *Journal of Personality and Social Psychology, 91*, 524–537.

Muraven, M., & Slessareva, E. (2003). Mechanisms of self-control failure: Motivation and limited resources. *Personality and Social Psychology Bulletin, 29*, 894–906.

Muraven, M., Tice, D. M., & Baumeister, R. F. (1998). Self-control as a limited resource: Regulatory depletion patterns. *Journal of Personality and Social Psychology, 74*, 774–789.

Nix, G., Ryan, R. M., Manly, J. B., & Deci, E. L. (1999). Revitalization through self-regulation: The effects of autonomous and controlled motivation on happiness and vitality. *Journal of Experimental Social Psychology, 35*, 266–284.

Oaten, M., & Cheng, K. (2006a). Improved self-control: The benefits of a regular program of academic study. *Basic and Applied Social Psychology, 28*, 1–16.

Oaten, M., & Cheng, K. (2006b). Longitudinal gains in self-regulation from regular physical exercise. *British Journal of Health Psychology, 11*, 717–733.

Oaten, M., & Cheng, K. (2007). Improvements in self-control from financial monitoring. *Journal of Economic Psychology, 28*, 487–501.

Ostafin, B. D., Marlatt, G. A., & Greenwald, A. G. (2008). Drinking without thinking: An implicit measure of alcohol motivation predicts failure to control alcohol use. *Behaviour Research and Therapy, 46*, 1210–1219.

Park, S. H., Glaser, J., & Knowles, E. D. (2008). Implicit motivation to control prejudice moderates the effect of cognitive depletion on unintended discrimination. *Social Cognition, 26*, 401–419.

Paulhus, D. L., Graf, P., & Van Selst, M. (1989). Attentional load increases the positivity of self-presentation. *Social Cognition, 7*, 389–400.

Pocheptsova, A., Amir, O., Dhar, R., & Baumeister, R. (2009). Deciding without resources: Resource depletion and choice in context. *Journal of Marketing Research, 46*, 344–355.

Richeson, J. A., & Shelton, J. (2003). When prejudice does not pay: Effects of interracial contact on executive function. *Psychological Science, 14*, 287–290.

Richeson, J. A., & Trawalter, S. (2005). Why do interracial interactions impair executive function? A resource depletion account. *Journal of Personality and Social Psychology, 88*, 934–947.

Richeson, J. A., Trawalter, S., & Shelton, J. N. (2005). African americans' implicit racial attitudes and the depletion of executive function after interracial interactions. *Social Cognition, 23*, 336–352.

Ryan, R. M., & Deci, E. L. (2000). Self-determination theory and the facilitation of intrinsic motivation, social development, and well-being. *American Psychologist, 55*, 68–78.

Ryan, R. M., & Frederick, C. (1997). On energy, personality, and health: Subjective vitality as a dynamic reflection of well-being. *Journal of Personality, 65*, 529–565.

Schmeichel, B. J. (2007). Attention control, memory updating, and emotion regulation temporarily reduce the capacity for executive control. *Journal of Experimental Psychology: General, 136*, 241–255.

Schmeichel, B. J., Demaree, H. A., Robinson, J. L., & Pu, J. (2006). Ego depletion by response exaggeration. *Journal of Experimental Social Psychology, 42*, 95–102.

Schmeichel, B. J., Harmon-Jones, C., & Harmon-Jones, E. (2010). Exercising self-control increases approach motivation. *Journal of Personality and Social Psychology, 99*, 162–173.

Schmeichel, B. J., & Vohs, K. (2009). Self-affirmation and self-control: Affirming core values counteracts ego depletion. *Journal of Personality and Social Psychology, 96*, 770–782.

Schmeichel, B. J., Vohs, K. D., & Baumeister, R. F. (2003). Intellectual performance and ego depletion: Role of the self in logical reasoning and other information processing. *Journal of Personality and Social Psychology, 85*, 33–46.

Sedikides, C., & Skowronski, J. J. (1997). The symbolic self in evolutionary context. *Personality and Social Psychology Review, 1*, 80–102.

Segerstrom, S. C., & Nes, L. S. (2007). Heart rate variability reflects self-regulatory strength, effort, and fatigue. *Psychological Science, 18*, 275–281.

Shamosh, N. A., & Gray, J. R. (2007). The relation between fluid intelligence and self-regulatory depletion. *Cognition and Emotion, 21*, 1833–1843.

Shiffman, S., Paty, J. A., Gnys, M., Kassel, J. A., & Hickcox, M. (1996). First lapses to smoking: Within-subjects analysis of real-time reports. *Journal of Consulting and Clinical Psychology, 64*, 366–379.

Siesjö, B. K. (1978). *Brain energy metabolism*. Chichester, England and New York: Wiley.

Steele, C. M. (1988). The psychology of self-affirmation: Sustaining the integrity of the self. In L. Berkowitz (Ed.), *Advances in experimental social psychology* (Vol. 21, pp. 261–302). New York, NY: Academic Press.

.Stewart, C. C., Wright, R. A., Azor Hui, S. K., & Simmons, A. (2009). Outcome expectancy as a moderator of mental fatigue influence on cardiovascular response. *Psychophysiology, 46,* 1141–1149.

Stillman, T., Tice, D., Fincham, F., & Lambert, N. (2009). The psychological presence of family improves self-control. *Journal of Social and Clinical Psychology, 28,* 498–529.

Stucke, T. S., & Baumeister, R. F. (2006). Ego depletion and aggressive behavior: Is the inhibition of aggression a limited resource? *European Journal of Social Psychology, 36,* 1–13.

Tice, D. M., Baumeister, R. F., Shmueli, D., & Muraven, M. (2007). Restoring the self: Positive affect helps improve self-regulation following ego depletion. *Journal of Experimental Social Psychology, 43,* 379–384.

Tversky, A., & Kahneman, D. (1981). The framing of decisions and the psychology of choice. *Science, 211,* 453–458.

Tyler, J. M., & Burns, K. C. (2008). After depletion: The replenishment of the self's regulatory resources. *Self and Identity, 7,* 305–321.

Tyler, J. M., & Burns, K. C. (2009). Triggering conservation of the self's regulatory resources. *Basic and Applied Social Psychology, 31,* 255–266.

Vohs, K. D., Baumeister, R. F., & Ciarocco, N. J. (2005). Self-regulation and self-presentation: Regulatory resource depletion impairs impression management and effortful self-presentation depletes regulatory resources. *Journal of Personality and Social Psychology, 88,* 632–657.

Vohs, K. D., Baumeister, R. F., Schmeichel, B. J., Twenge, J. M., Nelson, N. M., & Tice, D. M. (2008). Making choices impairs subsequent self-control: A limited-resource account of decision making, self-regulation, and active initiative. *Journal of Personality and Social Psychology, 94,* 883–898.

Vohs, K. D., & Faber, R. (2007). Spent resources: Self-regulatory resource availability affects impulse buying. *Journal of Consumer Research, 33,* 537–547.

Vohs, K. D., & Heatherton, T. F. (2000). Self-regulatory failure: A resource-depletion approach. *Psychological Science, 11,* 243–254.

Vohs, K. D., & Schmeichel, B. J. (2003). Self-regulation and extended now: Controlling the self alters the subjective experience of time. *Journal of Personality and Social Psychology, 85,* 217–230.

Wallace, H. W., & Baumeister, R. F. (2002). The effects of success versus failure feedback on further self-control. *Self and Identity, 1,* 35–42.

Wan, E., & Sternthal, B. (2008). Regulating the effects of depletion through monitoring. *Personality and Social Psychology Bulletin, 34,* 32.

Wang, X. T., & Dvorak, R. D. (2010). Sweet future. *Psychological Science, 21,* 183–188.

Webb, T. L., & Sheeran, P. (2003). Can implementation intentions help to overcome ego-depletion? *Journal of Experimental Social Psychology, 39,* 279–286.

Wegner, D. M., Schneider, D., Carter, S. R., & White, T. L. (1987). Paradoxical effects of thought suppression. *Journal of Personality and Social Psychology, 53,* 5–13.

Wheeler, S. C., Brinol, P., & Hermann, A. D. (2007). Resistance to persuasion as self-regulation: Ego-depletion and its effects on attitude change processes. *Journal of Experimental Social Psychology, 43,* 150–156.

Wills, T. A., Sandy, J. M., & Yaeger, A. M. (2002). Moderators of the relation between substance use level and problems: Test of a self-regulation model in middle adolescence. *Journal of Abnormal Psychology, 111,* 3–21.

Wright, R. A., Junious, T. R., Neal, C., Avello, A., Graham, C., Herrmann, L., Junious, S., & Walton, N. (2007). Mental fatigue influence on effort-related cardiovascular response: Difficulty effects and extension across cognitive performance domains. *Motivation and Emotion, 31,* 219–231.

Wright, R. A., Martin, R. E., & Bland, J. L. (2003). Energy resource depletion, task difficulty, and cardiovascular response to a mental arithmetic challenge. *Psychophysiology, 40,* 98–105.

Wright, R. A., Stewart, C. C., & Barnett, B. R. (2008). Mental fatigue influence on effort-related cardiovascular response: Extension across the regulatory (inhibitory)/non-regulatory performance dimension. *International journal of psychophysiology: official journal of the International Organization of Psychophysiology, 69,* 127–133.

Yovetich, N. A., & Rusbult, C. E. (1994). Accommodative behavior in close relationships: Exploring transformation of motivation. *Journal of Experimental Social Psychology, 30,* 138–164.

Flow

Susan A. Jackson

Abstract

The concept of flow is one that is central to understanding human motivation and the capacity of humans to function optimally in the psychological realm. In this chapter, the concept of flow is defined and described from its dimensional perspective. An overview of some of the research that has been conducted on flow is provided, measurement options are explored, and the critical question of how to facilitate this optimal psychological state is addressed.

Key Words: flow, optimal experience, flow measurement, facilitating flow

Introduction

Ten years after Seligman and Csikszentmihalyi (2000) presented a rationale for the advancement of positive psychology in the millennial issue of *American Psychologist*, the rebirth of a positive focus in psychology has grown from strength to strength. In 2007, The International Association for Positive Psychology (IPPA) was formed, and in 3 years, it has grown to a membership of 3,000, representing 70 countries. Seligman and Csikszentmihalyi (2000) outlined three areas central to the science of positive psychology: positive subjective experience, positive individual traits, and positive institutions. Seligman characterized the aim of positive psychology as "to catalyze a change in psychology from a preoccupation only with repairing the worst things in life to also building the best qualities in life" (Seligman, 2002, p. 3). The IPPA website defines positive psychology as "the scientific study of what enables individuals and communities to thrive."

Flow was identified by Seligman and Csikszentmihalyi (2000) as a key construct in the area of positive subjective experience, one of the three core areas of study identified for the field of positive psychology. Thus, flow has found a home in positive psychology.

This chapter will overview flow, providing definition and description of this positive psychology construct. Examples of the research that has been conducted on flow will be overviewed, centering on the themes of understanding flow, assessing flow, and factors found to be associated with flow. Future research directions for this exciting motivational concept will be explored.

Defining Flow

Flow represents those moments when everything comes together to create a special state of absorption and enjoyment in what one is doing (Csikszentmihalyi, 1975, 1990). Flow occurs when one is totally involved in the task at hand. Characteristics that identify a flow experience include the better-than-average nature of the experience, with heightened focus and high levels of enjoyment being key factors. Csikszentmihalyi (1990) considered flow to be an optimal experience, and he has used the terms "flow" and "optimal experience" interchangeably.

Through the 35 years of insightful writings on flow by Csikszentmihalyi, this construct has come to be universally regarded as a special psychological state, one that is intimately associated with motivation and enjoyment. Complete involvement in a task at hand—for the sake of the absorbing experience itself—defines flow. This "immersion for the sake of doing it" links flow with intrinsic motivation, and the initial name given by Csikszentmihalyi for flow (i.e., autotelic experience) translates as doing something for its own sake, and hence the links with intrinsic motivation are strong.

Flow can occur at different levels of complexity but, by definition, flow is intrinsically rewarding, regardless of whether it involves a simple game of throw and catch or a complicated and dangerous gymnastics routine. Csikszentmihalyi (1975) referred to the different levels of flow experience as micro and macro flow. Micro flow experiences are those that occur in everyday life, whereas macro flow are those experiences associated with higher levels of complexity and demand on the participant.

Macro flow experiences are similar to the concept of peak experience, first described by Abraham Maslow in the 1960s. Maslow (1968, 1970, 1973) asked groups of people such questions as what was "the single most joyous, happiest, most blissful moment of your life" (1973, p. 182). Maslow detailed the peak experience into 14 characteristics that reflected a variety of emotional and cognitive changes. These changes included a feeling of being detached from concerns, strong concentration, an egoless and unselfish perception, disorientation in time and space, and a feeling of life being meaningful, beautiful, and desirable.

Research has suggested that flow and peak experience are overlapping constructs and can co-occur (Jackson, 1996, 2000; McInman & Grove, 1991; Privette & Bundrick, 1997). Notwithstanding, the notion of peak experience is conceptually distinct from the optimal experience model of flow. For example, the flow model consists of not only an affective component but also several important cognitive components, as described in the following section. Furthermore, the flow construct is grounded in a multidimensional theory of optimal experience with a substantive empirical base drawn from a variety of life domains, such as work, school, leisure, and sports (Kowal & Fortier, 1999).

Flow is an internal, conscious process that lifts experience from the ordinary to the optimal. It is the simultaneous experiencing of several positive aspects that makes the flow experience so special (Jackson & Csikszentmihalyi, 1999). Some of these aspects, or dimensions of flow as they have come to be known, include total focus, involvement, and absorption in what one is doing, to the exclusion of all other thoughts and emotions. Mind and body work together effortlessly, so that there is an intrinsic experience of harmonious enjoyment (Jackson & Csikszentmihalyi, 1999). This leads to a feeling of being so involved in the activity that nothing else seems to matter and we continue in it "…even at great cost, for the sheer sake of doing it" (Csikszentmihalyi, 1990, p. 4).

Dimensions of Flow

Csikszentmihalyi (e.g., 1990) has conceptualized the flow construct in terms of a number of dimensions. Nine dimensions have been articulated, with more recent descriptions (e.g., Nakamura & Csikszentmihalyi, 2002) separating three of these dimensions into what have been described as preconditions for flow. The nine dimensions are, with the three preconditions listed first: challenge–skill balance, clear goals, unambiguous feedback, action-awareness merging, concentration on task, sense of control, loss of self-consciousness, time transformation, and autotelic experience. Together, they represent the optimal psychological state of flow; singly they signify conceptual elements of the flow experience.

Challenge–Skill Balance

During the experience of flow, a dynamic balance exists between challenges in the situation and a person's skills. Challenges can be thought of as opportunities for actions, or goals, while skills are the capacities the individual has to produce desired outcomes (Csikszentmihalyi, 1990). Both the challenge of the situation and our skills to meet the challenge need to be at personally high levels in order for us to be in a position to experience flow: "…it is not enough for challenges to equal skills; both factors need to be extending the person, stretching them to new levels" (Jackson & Csikszentmihalyi, 1999, p. 16). Critical to finding this balance is "what you *believe* you can do" (p. 17) and how you perceive the situation, rather than the actual demands or an objective level of abilities per se. It is the perception of the defined challenge that is critical to the occurrence of flow.

Action-Awareness Merging

This dimension involves a feeling of being "at one" with the activity being performed. It is through total absorption in what one is doing (see later for total concentration dimension of flow) that perception of oneness with the activity results, bringing harmony and peace to an active engagement with a task. When people are asked to describe what it feels like to be in flow, commentary on the merging of action and awareness is often central to their descriptions, exemplified in statements such as a sense of ceasing to be aware of themselves as separate from their actions and experiences. This is often accompanied by a sense of effortless ease and fluency in movement.

Clear Goals

Individuals describe the flow state as involving a clear sense of knowing what it is they are supposed to do. When in flow, this clarity of purpose occurs on a moment-by-moment basis, keeping the performer fully connected to the task and responsive to appropriate cues. In flow, it is clear, moment by moment, how one is doing. Goals provide a blueprint for what we need to do; then, while engaged in the activity, there is an ongoing awareness about what to do next as actions and goals become seamlessly intertwined (Jackson & Csikszentmihalyi, 1999).

Unambiguous Feedback

Hand in hand with clear goals comes the processing of information on how performance is progressing relative to these goals. When in flow, feedback information is unambiguous and effortlessly processed in producing actions consistent with the actor's desires.

Unambiguous feedback while undertaking an activity can be internal, such as kinaesthetic awareness, or it can come from external sources. Both types of feedback tell us how we are going and allow us to appraise the successfulness of our actions in an ongoing manner during the performance process. The unambiguous feedback provides a clear idea of the next action and enables us to know we are on track and headed toward achieving our goals.

Concentration on Task at Hand

Being totally connected to the task at hand epitomizes the flow state, and it is one of its most frequently mentioned characteristics. When in flow, one is totally focused in the present moment. There are no extraneous thoughts, and the distractibility that often accompanies involvement on any task is wonderfully absent. "In flow, there is no room for any thoughts other than what you are doing and feeling right at the moment, the 'now'" (Jackson & Csikszentmihalyi, 1999, p. 25). Full and sustained concentration, including the ability to exclude irrelevant or unhelpful thoughts from consciousness, and tune into the task at hand, characterizes this dimension.

Sense of Control

Another frequently mentioned flow characteristic is a feeling of being in control. Sometimes described as a sense of infallibility, this empowering feeling frees one from the all-too-frequent fear of failure that can so easily creep into performance. Failure thoughts are nowhere to be found during flow, enabling the individual to positively approach the challenges at hand.

Control, like the challenge–skills relationship, is a delicately balanced component of flow. Although the perception of control is inherent to the experience, it is actually a finely balanced equation where perceived skills are at a high level, but one commensurate with the challenge. One must experience challenge to experience flow; it is the possibility of being in control that can keep flow alive. If the feeling of being in control keeps going indefinitely, then the scales have tipped in favor of skills over challenge, and flow is lost.

Loss of Self-Consciousness

We can think of flow as non-self-conscious action. In flow, one is so totally absorbed in the activity that there is no room for worry about self or about the evaluations of others. It is liberating to be free of the voice within our head that questions whether we are living up to the standards that we perceive are important to be met. The losing of self-consciousness is thus one of the "hidden" benefits of flow, emanating from being fully present.

Time Transformation

Deep moments of flow seem to transform our perception of time. For some, the experience is that time stops. For others, time seems to slow. Or it may be that time seems to pass more quickly than expected. Because nothing else is entering our awareness during flow, we can be surprised to find that significant time has passed while in this state. The intensity of focus may also contribute to perceptions of time slowing, with a feeling of having all the time in the world to execute a move that is, in reality, very much time limited. It is through the total absorption that occurs in flow that the passage of time can become perceptually transformed in some way.

Autotelic Experience

Csikszentmihalyi (1990) coined the term "autotelic experience" to describe the intrinsically rewarding encounter that flow is for the individual. As described by Csikszentmihalyi, the word is derived from two

Greek words that describe doing something for its own sake: "auto" = self, and "telos" = goal. Flow is such an enjoyable experience that one is motivated to return to this state. Once experienced, flow becomes much sought after. Csikszentmihalyi described this dimension as the end result of the other eight flow dimensions. For many, flow is the defining motivation to keep pushing toward higher limits. It is generally upon reflection that the autotelic aspect of flow is realized and provides high motivation toward further involvement.

Considered together, these nine dimensions of flow provide an optimal experience. Considerable consistency of flow experience has been found across many different domains (see Csikszentmihalyi, 1990, 1997; Csikszentmihalyi & Csikszentmihalyi, 1988a). The dimensions of flow provide a conceptually coherent framework for understanding optimal experience.

The Critical Balance of Challenges and Skills

A central consideration to facilitating an environment conducive to flow is the existence of a challenging situation. Flow is defined by the appropriate mix of challenges and skills in a situation, as described earlier in the dimension of challenge–skill balance. When the challenges of an activity are balanced with the skills of the participant, flow can occur. It is a delicate balance, as other relative levels of challenge and skill can bring about quite different experiential states. These relationships between challenge and skill, and experience, are depicted in Figure 8.1.

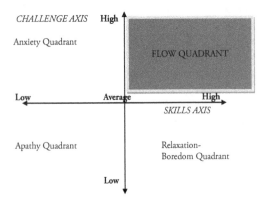

Fig. 8.1. Model of the flow state. (Adapted with permission from S.A. Jackson & M. Csikszentmihalyi, 1999, *Flow in sports*, Champaign, IL: Human Kinetics, p. 37. Adapted from M. Csikszentmihalyi & I. Csikszentmihalyi, 1988, *Optimal experience: Psychological studies of flow in consciousness*, with permission of Cambridge University Press.)

According to this model of flow, first developed by Csikszentmihalyi (1975) when he initially began investigating flow, it is the relative balance of challenges and skills that defines whether an individual experiences flow, anxiety, apathy, relaxation, or another psychological state. When the individual perceives that he or she has the skills to match a challenge, flow can occur. It is the person's *perception* of the level of challenge and degree of skill—and the balance between them—that is essential to flow (Csikszentmihalyi, 1990). When our perceived challenge of the activity is in balance with our perceived skill, we are setting ourselves up for an experience of flow.

Growing the Knowledge Base on Flow: Research Examples from 1975 to 2010

From enquiries into subjective experience, at times when everything "came together" during performance of one's chosen activity, Csikszentmihalyi (1975) developed the concept of flow. He coined the term *flow* to describe these experiences because of the use of this word in the descriptions of absorbing encounters by research participants. From artists to rock climbers, surgeons to musicians, a sense of actions flowing from one moment to the next prompted Csikszentmihalyi to adopt the term *flow* for what he initially described as autotelic experiences. Despite considerable diversity in settings where people were interviewed about being in flow, there was considerable consistency of responses regarding what was felt during these moments that stood out as being special, above-average experiences.

After the release of *Beyond Boredom and Anxiety* in 1975, Csikszentmihalyi and colleagues began exploring the flow concept at theoretical and empirical levels. There was interest in flow from a variety of domains, and the research of these formative early years is presented in Csikszentmihalyi and Csikszentmihalyi (1988a). One of the critical developments during this period of research was the development of the Experience Sampling Method, a tool to sample everyday experience, which is described in the section on "Measurement of Flow" in this chapter.

Drawn to the flow concept after reading Csikszentmihalyi's (1975) portrayal of his early investigations into this experience, and relating these experiences to her best moments as an athlete, Jackson's early research into flow was also primarily interview based, but focused on athletes, to assess the relevance of flow to sport experiences. Elite athletes were the initial focus, because of their expected familiarity with optimal performance and flow experiences

(Jackson, 1996). More generally, sport has been recognised as an excellent setting in which to examine flow (Csikszentmihalyi, 1990; Jackson & Csikszentmihalyi, 1999).

Sport offers the opportunity to do something better than it has been done before (Csikszentmihalyi, 1990), and so, once having made a choice to engage in a sport activity, a focused mindset generally results. Furthermore, the experience of sport is generally one of enjoyment—people engage in sport for the quality of experience it provides, as explained by Jackson and Csikszentmihalyi (1999, p. 4), "Contrary to what happens in most of life, sport can offer a state of being that is so rewarding one does it for no other reason than to be a part of it." Thus, sport can be considered an autotelic activity, and this also makes it an environment conducive to flow. A third advantage to studying flow in sport is that challenges and skills are in-built to the domain, are easily observable, and can be modified. Thus, in this chapter, the research that has investigated flow in sport, and other performance-based settings, will be a focus, to demonstrate what has been learned about flow in these settings.

Jackson and Roberts (1992) examined the association between peak performance and flow with 200 elite athletes from a wide-ranging sample of sports that included gymnastics, swimming, golf, track and field, cross-country running, tennis, and diving. Flow was related to athletes' peak performances. Furthermore, athletes high in orientation toward mastery of the task experienced flow more frequently than athletes low in mastery orientation. An opportunity to interview a subsample of this group of competitive athletes demonstrated clearly that the flow state was not only relevant to athletes; it was a treasured experience. This led Jackson to investigate flow experiences in athletes in greater depth.

Jackson (1992) interviewed U.S. national champion figure skaters to learn how performers in this graceful sport experience flow. A close agreement between the skaters' perceptions of flow and the theoretical descriptions of the flow construct (Csikszentmihalyi, 1990) was found. Jackson identified factors perceived as important for attaining flow and those perceived to prevent flow from occurring. In an extension of this qualitative research of flow, Jackson (1995, 1996) interviewed elite athletes from seven sports, to assess whether their descriptive accounts of their optimal sport experiences would also match Csikszentmihalyi's (1990) dimensional model of flow. Results showed a strong consistency in flow experience descriptions with Csikszentmihalyi's model and with the figure skating sample from the 1992 study. Antecedent and preventative flow factors were consistent with the skaters' experiences. These factors influencing flow are described in a later section of this chapter.

Grove and Lewis (1996) studied a noncompetitive sport sample of circuit training participants and found an association between hypnotic susceptibility and "flow-like" states. Highly hypnotic susceptible participants showed greater changes in their flow-like states than those with low susceptibility.

Catley and Duda (1997) tested psychological states both before and during a golf round and found consistency with Jackson's (1995) qualitative findings of factors influencing flow. Catley and Duda found confident readiness, positive focus, and pessimism had the strongest relationships with flow.

In a confirmation of the findings of Jackson and Roberts (1992) with regard to flow and task orientation, Kowal and Fortier (1999) found athletes motivated by intrinsic, self-determined reasons experienced flow more readily than those not intrinsically motivated. Their sample of 203 masters-level swimmers were described as either being motivated in a self-determined way, by engaging in swimming for their own pleasure, satisfaction, or benefit; versus those motivated for more external reasons. They also found that the situational determinants of perceived competence, autonomy, and relatedness were positively related to flow experiences.

Jackson and colleagues (Jackson, Kimiecik, Ford, & Marsh, 1998) examined the flow experience in nonelite, older athletic participants in World Masters Games participants in swimming, triathlon, cycling, and track and field. Using an early version of the Flow Scale (Jackson & Marsh, 1996; Marsh & Jackson, 1999), their findings gave support to Csikszentmihalyi's (1990) concept of an autotelic personality—where participants choose to undertake an activity for its own sake and where the activity provides its own reward. Factors found to be predictive of flow were perceived ability, intrinsic motivation, and anxiety.

Interest in flow as a research concept has continued to grow and flourish in the 21st century. Concurrent with this growing interest has been an interest in development and application of research tools to investigate what is by nature a somewhat elusive concept. One approach to the assessment of flow for research purposes has been the development of self-report instruments. These developments are described in a subsequent section of this chapter.

One approach to assessing flow that has been developed has been the Flow Scales (state and dispositional) by Jackson and colleagues (e.g., Jackson & Eklund, 2002; Jackson & Marsh, 1996). Using the original versions of the flow scales, Jackson et al. (2001) found that four of the flow dimensions assessed by the Flow Scales—challenge–skill balance, concentration on the task at hand, sense of control, and clear goals—were found to be most strongly associated with psychological skill proficiency and self-concept in a study of 236 competitive orienteers, surf life savers, and road cyclists Moreover, athletes with greater psychological skill proficiency and more positive self-perceptions were more likely to experience flow.

Karageorghis et al. (2000) investigated relationships between subjective feelings of enjoyment and flow in exercise. Using Jackson's flow scale, they found in their sample of 1,231 aerobic dance exercise participants a positive and significant association between levels of flow and the postexercise feelings of revitalization, tranquility, and positive engagement. This suggested that the experience of flow might play also a role in encouraging adherence to physical activity regimes through the experience of positive postexercise feelings.

A group of Italian researchers investigated the flow experience across a variety of sport settings, and an edited book (Muzio, 2004) summarizes findings from an array of research into aspects of flow. Included are reports on differences on an Italian version of the Flow State Scale (FSS; Jackson & Marsh, 1996) between fencers, skiers, swimmers, cyclists, and track and field athletes. The fencers were the most different from the other groups, which the researchers explained in terms of the high importance assigned to immediate feedback cues in fencing bouts. There was close similarity between the swimming, cycling, and track and field groups.

Vea and Pensgaard (2004) examined the relationship between perfectionism and flow in young elite Norwegian athletes. Perfectionism has been shown to have some negative repercussions, and the authors were interested in understanding the performance and well-being implications of perfectionism. Flow was selected as an indicator of potential to perform at optimal levels, as well as an indicator of subjective well-being. As expected, most of the perfectionism dimensions correlated negatively with flow dimensions, although there were a couple of unexpected positive associations.

Koehn (2007) investigated the frequency and intensity of flow in tennis competition in a sample of 271 junior athletes. The results showed that trait confidence, imagery use, and action control were significantly related to dispositional and state flow, whereas no significant links emerged between absorption and flow. In studying U.S. Division I college athletes, Wiggins and Freeman (2000) observed higher flow scores (i.e., global, unambiguous feedback, concentration, loss of self-consciousness) among athletes perceiving their anxiety as facilitative compared with those who perceived it as debilitative.

As has been discussed, sport, and more generally, performance-based domains, provide ideal contexts in which to research flow. Csikszentmihalyi (1975) initially began investigating flow through interviewing performers in varied domains—and was struck by the consistency of the flow experience across domains. Research continues to unfold in different contexts, including various domains of the performing arts (e.g., Jackson & Eklund, 2004; Martin & Cutler, 2002; Wrigley, 2005). For example, Wrigley (2005) using the FSS-2 and his music performance rating scale derived from live evaluations of over 30 teaching staff, measured the effect of the flow state on the performances of more than 200 tertiary music students from five instrument families—strings, piano, brass, woodwind, and voice—during their live performance examinations. Most of the students experienced flow infrequently during their performance and with a very similar pattern of subscale scores across instrument families. Those that did experience flow achieved significantly higher global and specific performance ratings from their examiners.

Perry (1999) studied creative writers, another activity conducive to flow. Perry's descriptions of the writers' experience of flow provide an in-depth analysis of the experience of writing in flow, as well as suggestions about how to make flow happen while writing.

Computer-mediated environments have also been a setting in which flow has been examined, especially Web instruction and design (e.g., Chen, Wigand, & Nilan, 1999; Novak, Hoffman, & Yung, 2000). Given the growing importance of computer technology, this is a timely direction in which the study of flow can move. Novak and colleagues (Novak, Hoffman, & Yung, 2000; Novak, Hoffman, & Duhachek, 2003) found support for their proposition that compelling online experiences are dependent on facilitating flow state. The experience of flow for Web users (Chen, Wigand, & Nilan, 1999) has been found to be similar to flow experiences in other settings.

Measurement of Flow

Flow is a subjective, experiential phenomenon and approaches to its measurement face the challenge that go with assessing a subjective state of consciousness. Csikszentmihalyi has presented a convincing argument that any measure of flow is only a "partial reflection" of the human experience (Csikszentmihalyi, 1992, p. 183). A multimodal approach that incorporates both qualitative and quantitative methods of measurement is likely to yield the greatest gains. A diversity of methodologies will offer the greatest potential to explain the "what" and "how" questions posed by the unique phenomenon of the flow experience. The measurement approaches that are described next are tools to tap into the flow experience, and they are presented with the understanding that no one empirical tool can fully capture flow.

Qualitative Methods

Csikszentmihalyi's (1975) early research, which brought to light the flow concept, involved qualitative interviews with people from a variety of life domains. Simarly, initial research of flow in sport (Jackson, 1992, 1995, 1996) used qualitative methods to assess the flow experience. Jackson developed in-depth interviews with elite athletes and inductive content analysis of their descriptions led to identification of factors inherent in their experiences. A qualitative approach was adopted in this early research because it was felt that this would facilitate the understanding of athletes' flow experiences, particularly as little prior research had been conducted in the area. By interviewing athletes about their flow experiences, it was possible to explore the understanding and meaning of flow from the perspective of the elite athlete.

The Development of Quantitative Methods

Csikszentmihalyi (1975) developed his model of flow through the use of experience sampling (Csikszentmihalyi & Larson, 1987). A concomitant quantitative approach has been developed in sport by Jackson (e.g., Jackson & Marsh, 1996; Jackson & Eklund, 2002), through the development of both the dispositional and flow state scales. These self-report scales were developed to facilitate the examination of the flow experience among sport and exercise participants and to assist with teasing out those factors that may be associated with its occurrence. Both the Experience Sampling Method (ESM) and Jackson's Flow Scales are described in the following sections.

THE EXPERIENCE SAMPLING METHOD

The Experience Sampling Method (ESM) involves the systematic measurement of individuals' experiences as they are interacting in their daily environment (Csikszentmihalyi & Larson, 1987; Hormuth, 1986). Participants carry some sort of paging system, which provides them with a randomly occurring signal several times during their day. Each time they receive the signal, they complete a questionnaire about their momentary experiences in the situation at the time. These measures are generally taken over a period of 1 week.

Analysis of the ESM data provides a description of the patterns of respondents' daily experiences. Compilation of many individuals' responses in particular situations can lead to development of patterns of commonality in experience in sampled settings (Csikszentmihalyi & Larson, 1987). Csikszentmihalyi and Larson (1987) stated, "ESM data allow examination of the magnitude, duration, and sequences of states, as well as an investigation of correlations between the occurrences of different experiences" (p. 533).

The ESM is a reliable and valid tool for assessing flow (Csikszentmihalyi & Larson, 1987), which has been used in many varied life settings (see Csikszentmihalyi & Csikszentmihalyi, 1988b). The ESM offers several advantages that are particularly useful in the study of flow. Measures of momentary thoughts and feelings and their effects can be taken in the person's naturalistic environment, without too much disruption. It is ecologically valid and offers a fine-grained assessment of temporal relationships between affects and changeable antecedents (Cerin, Szabo, & Williams, 2001).

There are obvious difficulties with implementing the ESM approach in sport settings and in other settings where performance is of a continuous nature and evaluated. Creative ways of applying the ESM approach will enable the benefits of this type of assessment to be realized in sport and other performance settings. A study by Cerin et al. (2001) demonstrated that the ESM can be used in performance-based settings. These authors randomly assigned 62 male competitive tae-kwon-do practitioners into three different measurement groups to ascertain their emotional states. While this study did not measure the flow experience, it provided strong evidence that the ESM can be used to assess dynamic psychological states during competitive sport. Continuing to develop creative and effective ways to adapt and apply the ESM approach to performance-based settings has the potential to open up greater understanding of flow through this dynamic measurement approach.

THE FLOW SCALES

Jackson and colleagues (Jackson & Eklund, 2002; Jackson & Marsh, 1996; Jackson, Martin, & Eklund, 2008; Martin & Jackson, 2008) have, over a number of years, developed a suite of scales—the LONG, SHORT, and CORE Flow Scales—providing a range of self-report instruments to suit a diversity of research and applied purposes. One general characteristic of this approach to assessing flow has been to do so at two levels: *(a)* the *dispositional level*, or frequency of flow experience across time in particular domains (e.g., sport, work, school), and *(b)* the *state level*, or extent of flow experienced in a particular event or activity (e.g., a race, a work project, or a test). The dispositional and state flow scales are parallel forms, with wording differences reflecting whether the disposition to experience flow, or a specific flow experience, is being assessed. By designing two versions of the scales, it is possible to assess both a general tendency to experience flow, as well as particular incidence (or nonincidence) of flow characteristics during a particular event.

There are three main flow instruments (each of which has a dispositional and a state version):

1. LONG Flow Scales: These are 36-item instruments, designed to assess the nine dimensions of flow (Csikszentmihalyi, 1990). The Long Flow Scales (i.e., Dispositional & State) are particularly useful when a detailed picture of flow experience is important for research or applied purposes. The Long Scales provide a multidimensional approach to assessing flow. These scales are the instruments of choice for targeted interventions, and/or when a detailed understanding of the flow dimensions is important.

2. SHORT Flow Scales: These are 9-item (Dispositional and State) scales, which are abbreviated versions of Long Flow. One item is used to represent each of the nine flow dimensions. The Short Flow Scales provide a brief assessment useful when research or practical constraints prevent use of a longer scale.

3. CORE Flow Scales: These are 10-item (Dispositional and State) scales, designed to assess the global phenomenology of flow. The Core Flow Scales provide an assessment of the central subjective experience and complement the dimensional assessments afforded by the Long and Short Flow Scales.

All versions of the scales have been validated through confirmatory factor analyses, and the scales have demonstrated good psychometric properties. Each of the scales is briefly described next.

The LONG Flow Scales
Flow State Scale-2 (FSS-2). The FSS-2 is a 36-item self-report questionnaire designed to measure the state of flow when participating in a specific activity. The FSS-2 was a revision of the original Long Flow scale developed by Jackson and Marsh (1996). It is designed to be given immediately or soon after a participant has completed an activity. The questionnaire has nine subscales each with four items, to assess the nine flow dimensions. Respondents indicate the extent to which they agree with each statement on a 5-point Likert scale, ranging from 1 (*Strongly disagree*) to 5 (*Strongly agree*).

Dispositional Flow Scale-2 (DFS-2). A dispositional version of the flow scale was developed to measure the frequency with which one typically experiences flow in a specific activity or setting (Jackson et al., 1998). The dispositional flow scale was developed to help understand the autotelic personality (see, e.g., Csikszentmihalyi, 1990), or individual differences in propensity to experience flow (Jackson et al., 1998). Jackson and Eklund (2002) developed the DFS-2, a revision of the original Long Flow scale developed by Jackson and Marsh (1996). The DFS-2 is essentially a parallel version of the FSS-2. It has 36 items, which are designed to assess to what degree an individual *generally* experiences the flow state while participating in a specified activity. It is therefore designed to be answered away from an immediate involvement in one's activity. The questionnaire has nine subscales with four items each, corresponding to the nine flow dimensions. Respondents indicate the frequency of each statement on a 5-point Likert scale, ranging from 1 (*Never*) to 5 (*Always*).

Psychometric Characteristics of the Long Flow Scales. A comprehensive construct validation approach has been undertaken for the purpose of evaluating the psychometric characteristics of the FSS-2 and DFS-2. Using confirmatory factor analyses (CFA), Jackson and Marsh (1996) demonstrated acceptable fit values for the FSS, as did Marsh and Jackson (1999) for the FSS and DFS. In both studies, a nine-factor, first-order model and a hierarchical model with one global flow factor were evaluated. The first-order model received stronger support due to the slightly weaker fit of the hierarchical model.

Across two large psychometric studies (i.e., Jackson & Eklund, 2002; Jackson, Martin, & Eklund, 2008), the FSS-2 and DFS-2 have demonstrated good reliability, with FSS-2 alphas ranging between .76 to .92, and the DFS-2 range being .78 to .90.

The DFS-2 and/or FSS-2 have been translated into several languages, including Greek (Stavrou & Zervas, 2004), French (Fournier et al., 2007), Japanese (Kawabata, Mallett, & Jackson, 2007), Finnish (Pekka Hämäläinen & Veli-Pekka Räty, personal communication, 2008), Spanish (Martínez-Zaragoza, Benavides, Solanes, Pastor, & Martin del Rio, personal communication, 2008), Hungarian (Bimbo, personal communication, 2009), and Hindi (Singh, personal communication, 2009) versions, with more translations presently underway.

Research has been conducted with the Long flow scales in a range of activities in settings including sport (e.g., Jackson et al., 1998), exercise (e.g., Karageorghis et al., 2000), yoga (Penman, Cohen, Stephens, & Jackson, 2006), music performance (Wrigley, 2005), and Web-based instructional activity (Chan & Repman, 1999). The author has communicated with researchers from diverse areas (such as gifted education, work addiction, yoga, and business) regarding application of the flow scales to their research setting. Moreover, there is considerable interest in examining flow in relationship to other psychological constructs across diverse settings. Relationships with concepts such as hope, cohesion, personality type, intrinsic motivation, burnout, self-efficacy, self-esteem, and anxiety have all captured the interest of flow researchers. There is considerable interest in examining flow across a range of settings and in relation to a diverse set of psychological constructs. With the recent introduction of two new brief measures of flow, researchers have several options for including flow as a focal, ancillary, or outcome measure.

The SHORT Flow Scales

Despite the psychometric advantages to longer, multidimensional instruments, practical considerations may dictate the need for shorter versions. For example, during a sports event, athletes and coaches may be willing to complete a 10-item scale, but not one four times that length. In large-scale projects involving many measures, short forms may be preferable to keep a questionnaire package to a reasonable size for participants, or because a particular construct is not the central focus and can be reasonably estimated with a short measure. It was for practical reasons such as these that Jackson and colleagues (Jackson et al., 2008; Martin & Jackson, 2008) developed two short scales to assess flow: the Short Flow Scales and the Core Flow Scales.

The Short flow scales are abbreviated versions of their predecessors, the FSS-2 and DFS-2. Both the Short Flow State Scale and the Short Dispositional Flow Scale contain nine items, one for each of the nine flow dimensions. The rating scales of the abbreviated instruments are the same as those used in their parent scales. They provide succinct measures of the higher order dimensional flow model described in CFA research with the 36-item scales. Initial psychometric support for the Short Flow Scales is promising. Being new scales, there is a need for research to assess their validity and utility across domains. Both dispositional and state forms have demonstrated good reliability in initial validation studies (Jackson, Martin, & Ekluund, 2008; Martin & Jackson, 2008).

The CORE Flow Scales

The rationale behind the Core flow scales was to devise a somewhat different approach to assessing flow to the Long and Short Flow Scales. The Core flow scales contain 10 items that are descriptions of what it feels like to be in flow during a target activity. The items were derived from qualitative research, specifically, elite athlete descriptions of the experience of being in flow (Jackson, 1992, 1995, 1996). Expressions used by athletes to describe what it is like to be in flow were adapted into short statements that are rated on similar rating scales to the other flow scales. Model fit and reliability for these scales have been strong in initial validation studies (Martin & Jackson, 2008).

THE POTENTIAL USES OF THE FLOW SCALES

The triad of flow scales developed by Jackson and colleagues (e.g., Jackson & Eklund, 2002; Jackson et al., 2008; Martin & Jackson, 2008) provides researchers and practitioners with a choice of measurement instruments to assess flow. The 36-item, or Long flow, scales have solid research evidence indicating they are robust instruments that can provide a detailed assessment of the dimensional flow model. When a fine-grained description of flow characteristics according to the dimensional flow model of Csikszentmihalyi (1990) is desired, then the Long flow scales are the best option. The Long scales are also ideally suited to intervention-based research, providing assessment of modifiable flow characteristics in the nine-dimensional approach.

The Short flow scales provide a practical tool for a brief assessment of flow from the nine-dimensional conceptualization. Grounded in a solid psychometric base, the nine-item Short Flow Scales provide an aggregate measure of the nine flow dimensions. The equally short (10-item) Core Flow Scales provide a valid and reliable assessment of the central, or core, subjective experience of being in flow. These two brief flow instruments offer different but complementary ways of assessing flow and open up possibilities for including flow as a focal construct across a range of settings. The items in Short and Core Flow Scales are applicable across domains, and the initial CFA research conducted with these scales has demonstrated good fit indices in sport, work, academic school work, and extracurricular activities.

In summary, Jackson and colleagues have developed a suite of self-report scales that provide multiple ways of tapping into flow. All of the current versions of the scales, and a manual detailing their use, are described in Jackson, Eklund, and Martin (2010).

Facilitating Flow

Understanding factors that facilitate flow has been a focus of Jackson's research (e.g., 1992, 1995, 1998, 2001), with the goal of developing the knowledge base of what can increase the likelihood of achieving this rewarding optimal experience.

In a qualitative study with U.S. national champion figure skaters, Jackson (1992) found that there were certain factors that helped or hindered the achievement of this state. Skaters were more likely to achieve flow when they held a positive mental attitude, experienced positive precompetitive and competitive affect, maintained appropriate focus, felt physically ready, and experienced a unity with their dance partner. Skaters' experience of flow was more likely to be prevented or disrupted if they experienced physical problems and made mistakes, had an inability to maintain focus, held a negative attitude, or experienced a lack of audience response.

In an extension of her 1992 study, Jackson (1995) considered the factors that facilitated, disrupted, and prevented the experience of flow—together with the perceived controllability of flow—with a larger and more diverse range of elite athletes across seven sports. Results showed considerable consistency with results from the earlier study with figure skaters (Jackson, 1992). Ten factors (see Box 8.1) were described by the athletes to influence their development of flow and included physical, psychological, nutritional, and situational variables. Support for the multidimensional nature of antecedent and preventive flow factors was provided by these findings. In relation to the question on perceived controllability of flow, athletes reported a range of responses, from perceiving little control to perceiving considerable control. A large percentage of the factors seen to facilitate or prevent flow were seen as controllable, whereas the factors seen as disrupting flow were largely perceived as being uncontrollable.

Karageorghis et al. (2000) made some suggestions to facilitate the flow experience among school students, which are equally applicable to other individuals interested in attaining flow. They suggested that students "set personal goals that are attainable, challenging and well-defined"; "give pupils a choice from time to time in the activities they engage in" to increase their autotelic experience; and

---

Box 8.1 Factors Influencing Flow

1. Being motivated to perform well.
2. Achieving an optimal arousal level before performing.
3. Having precompetitive and competitive plans so that the performer felt totally prepared and knew clearly what to do.
4. Knowing they had done the training and felt physically ready.
5. Optimal environmental and situational conditions and influences.
6. Feeling good during a performance.
7. Holding strong focus and concentration.
8. Feeling confident and having a positive mental attitude.
9. Having positive team play and interaction.
10. Feeling experienced as a competitor and in having experienced flow in the past.

Source: Jackson, 1995.

"use skill-learning techniques" to encourage persistence in mastering the tasks to increase their sense of control (p. 243).

Jackson and colleagues (Jackson, 1995; Jackson et al., 1998, 2001; Jackson & Roberts, 1992) have found that a high perception of their sporting ability was a crucial factor facilitating flow. This led Jackson (Jackson et al., 2001) to suggest that the perceived skills component of the challenge–skill balance that defines flow is a critical aspect in the acquisition of the flow state in sport or other performance-based domains.

Perceptions of skill and challenge in a situation, as described in the flow model (see Fig. 8.1) also help to explain when the experience of anxiety, rather than flow, is likely to occur. When the challenges are greater than perceived skills, anxiety is the predicted outcome, according to the flow model. There has been considerable research support for anxiety as a factor preventing flow (Jackson, 1995; Jackson & Roberts, 1992; Jackson et al., 1998; Stein, Kimiecik, Daniels, & Jackson, 1995; Taylor, 2001) and, furthermore, that the cognitive, rather than the physiological, components of anxiety are seemingly more detrimental to the flow experience.

As would be expected, self-determined, intrinsic motivation is the best type of motivation to facilitate flow. A study by Jackson et al. (1998), using a multidimensional measure of intrinsic motivation, showed that only an intrinsic motivation factor demonstrated substantive relationships with flow; the extrinsic factors were unrelated to flow. Further research in this area will increase understanding of how different forms of motivation are related to flow.

There has been some research suggesting that flow may be enhanced by hypnotic capacity and training in psychological skills. The results of a study by Grove and Lewis (1996) showed that the flow state can be enhanced by the capacity for hypnotic susceptibility. They found that high-susceptibility exercisers had greater increases in flow than low-susceptibility participants. Case studies by Pates and Maynard (2000) and Pates, Cummings, and Maynard (2002) found that hypnotic interventions using imagery, relaxation, hypnotic induction, regression, and triggers enhanced their experience of, and personal control over, flow. Using an imagery-based intervention in combination with relaxation techniques, Koehn, Morris, and Watt (2006) and Koehn (2007) used an imagery script that aimed to increase athletes' confidence and action control in order to facilitate flow state and performance in tennis competition.

The small sample size of four increased their service and groundstroke performance, and three participants attained higher flow levels following the intervention phase (Koehn, 2007).

Understanding the factors that facilitate flow has obvious important applied implications. While it is not possible to engineer a flow experience, it is possible to increase its occurrence, as Jackson and Csikszentmihalyi (1999, p.138) argued: "It is not possible to make flow happen at will . . . and attempting to do so will only make the state more elusive. However, removing obstacles and providing facilitating conditions will increase its occurrence . . ." (Jackson & Csikszentmihalyi, 1999, p. 138).

Future Directions

The pioneering efforts of Csikszentmihalyi (e.g., 1975, 1990, 1997, 2003) has opened a new level of understanding of what is involved when people become totally absorbed in what they are doing. Csikszentmihalyi has examined flow across settings ranging from daily living (e.g., Csikszentmihalyi, 1997) to research endeavor leading to major scientific discoveries (e.g., Csikszentmihalyi, 1996). As was observed in Csikszentmihalyi's (1975) initial investigations, remarkable consistency has continued to be encountered across the broadening array of activities and settings examined.

The way forward for research into the optimal experience of flow is promising and exciting. The measurement tools thus far developed to help assess flow provide much scope for researchers interested in furthering understanding of flow. The ESM, as had been discussed, has been the central method used by Csikszentmihalyi and colleagues for over 20 years (e.g., Csikszentmihalyi & Csikszentmihalyi, 1988a; Csikszentmihalyi & Nakamura, 1989) to assess flow, and it continues to provide an innovative way to tap into experiential states as they are occurring.

The Flow Scales developed by Jackson and colleagues (e.g., Jackson & Marsh, 1996; Jackson & Eklund, 2002; Jackson, Martin, & Eklund, 2008) provide valid and reliable tools for assessing specific experiences, as well as assessing general tendency to experience flow, respectively. The dispositional versions of the flow scales facilitate investigation of correlates of flow, while the state versions provide assessment of experience of flow characteristics within an event. The brief flow measures discussed in this chapter provide opportunity to assess flow during, or immediately after, performance, without imposing a time demand on participants. Both Short and Core flow can be completed in less than 2 minutes and could be used to gain multiple assessments of experience across time. Other advantages of the brief flow measures have already been highlighted, such as the inclusion of flow in multimeasure studies investigating a large number of constructs, gaining self-other ratings, and their generic item format that makes them easily applicable to many domains.

Knowing what is occurring at a neuro- or psychophysiological level during flow has long been regarded as a critical area for furthering understanding of this concept. Csikszentmihalyi (Csikszentmihalyi & Csikszentmihalyi, 1988a) referred to early neurological studies conducted by Hamilton (e.g., Hamilton, 1976, 1981), where attentional patterns associated with flow were first described. Mental effort, as measured by cortical activation, was shown to decrease in individuals with good ability to concentrate deeply on a task. The challenges of assessing internal, physiological states during flow have meant this area of research has moved ahead slowly. A promising study by de Manzano, Theorell, Harmat, and Ullen (2010) examined several psychophysiological parameters and flow state. With piano players as the participants, they found significant associations between flow and heart rate, blood pressure, zygomaticus muscle activity, and respiratory depth. With continuing technological advances, new levels of understanding of what happens when people are in flow will be possible.

Standard psychological measures, such as self-report, also hold promise for advancing understanding of factors influencing flow. Although there has been considerable research already conducted, future research could continue to explore dispositional characteristics that may make it more or less likely that flow will be experienced. Some individual difference factors that researchers could explore include such areas as general level of capacity to experience enjoyment and fun; emotional and personality characteristics, such as the autotelic personality trait; motivational orientations; cognitive styles and processes, including the capacity to concentrate and immerse oneself in an activity; and experience with, and use of, psychological skills.

In addition to individual difference factors, there are a host of situational factors that can help to extend understanding of flow. For example, do competitive or noncompetitive environments facilitate flow better? How does flow operate in group or team settings? Social factors, such as the impact of teaching and coaching styles, are likely to influence flow. Can we design programs that help to facilitate flow in learning environments? In organizational contexts, do organizational cultures or administration style impact on flow?

One of the most important research pursuits for the future will be the unravelling of the complex interplay between person and situational variables such as these. How do certain dispositional characteristics of an individual interact with situational variables to affect the experience of flow? Furthermore, do different individuals, or different settings, influence the relative endorsement of the nine flow dimensions that have been described in this chapter? Future research is required to tease out the interplay between the nine dimensions to flow and the pattern of relationships between these dimensions within different contexts and individuals (Jackson et al., 1998, 2001). For example, the loss of self-consciousness and time transformation dimensions have been found to receive lower endorsement and lower factor loadings in sport research (Jackson, 1996; Jackson & Marsh, 1996; Kowal & Fortier, 1999; Vlachopoulos et al., 2000). One future research direction would be to investigate how these two dimensions are experienced in different settings, and across different levels of performers. An exploratory study of the dimensions of flow using Rasch analyses (Tenenbaum, Fogarty, & Jackson, 1999) suggested that the loss of self-consciousness and time transformation dimensions might only be experienced in deeper levels of flow.

Another interesting direction for future research is to continue to examine the challenge–skill balance model of flow, how person and/or situational variables might influence the balance of challenges and skills, and whether there is individual variation in relative levels of challenge and skill for flow to occur. Although the operational definition of flow describes flow as occuring when challenges and skills are balanced, and extending the individual, there may be specific situations where the relative levels of challenges and skills vary from this standard definition. This potential variability has been discussed by Csikszentmihalyi (e.g., Moneta & Csikszentmihalyi, 1996), and a recent empirical study by Engeser and Rheinberg (2008) demonstrated that the challenge–skill relationship was moderated by perceived importance of the activity and by achievement motivation. As measurement tools are refined, and creative ways of tapping into flow developed, understanding of the concept of flow will continue to evolve.

Conclusion

Flow is a critical area to continue to research in order to help with finding out more about fostering the positive side of people's lived experience. In the end, our experience of life is what matters most, as Csikszentmihalyi so eloquently expressed when he wrote, "Subjective experience is the bottom line of existence" (Csikszentmihalyi, 1982). Or, as an elite athlete interviewed about his flow experience described, "I strive to get to that state of perfection" (Jackson, 1996). The concept of flow provides researchers and practitioners with the lofty goal of understanding those moments in time that make life worth living.

References

Catley, D., & Duda, J. L. (1997). Psychological antecedents of flow in golfers. *International Journal of Sport Psychology, 28,* 309–322.

Cerin, E., Szabo, A., & Williams, C. (2001). Is the Experience Sampling Method (ESM) appropriate for studying pre-competitive emotions? *Psychology of Sport and Exercise, 2,* 27–45.

Chan, T. S., & Repman, J. (1999). Flow in web based instructional activity: An exploratory research project. *International Journal of Educational Telecommunications, 5,* 225–237.

Chen, H., Wigand, R. T., & Nilan, M. S. (1999). Optimal experience of web activities. *Computers in Human Behavior, 15,* 585–608.

Csikszentmihalyi, M. (1975). *Beyond boredom and anxiety.* San Francisco, CA: Jossey-Bass.

Csikszentmihalyi, M. (1982). Towards a psychology of optimal experience. In L. Wheeler (Ed.), *Review of personality and social psychology* (Vol. 3, pp. 13–36). Beverly Hills, CA: Sage.

Csikszentmihalyi, M. (1990). *Flow: The psychology of optimal experience.* New York: Harper & Row.

Csikszentmihalyi, M. (1992). A response to the Kimiecik & Stein and Jackson papers. *Journal of Applied Sport Psychology, 4,* 181–183.

Csikszentmihalyi, M. (1996). *Creativity: Flow and the psychology of discovery and invention.* New York: Harper Collins.

Csikszentmihalyi, M. (1997). *Finding flow: The psychology of engagement with everyday life.* New York: Harper Collins.

Csikszentmihalyi, M. (2003). *Good business: Leadership, flow, and the making of meaning.* London: Hodder & Stoughton.

Csikszentmihalyi, M., & Csikszentmihalyi, I. (Eds.). (1988a). *Optimal experience: Psychological studies of flow in consciousness.* New York: Cambridge University Press.

Csikszentmihalyi, M., & Csikszentmihalyi, I. (1988b). Measurement of flow in everyday life: Introduction to part IV. In M. Csikszentmihalyi & I. Csikszentmihalyi. (Eds.), *Optimal experience: Psychological studies of flow in consciousness* (pp. 251–265). New York: Cambridge University Press.

Csikszentmihalyi, M., & Larson, R. (1987). Validity and reliability of the experience-sampling method. *The Journal of Nervous and Mental Disease, 175,* 526–536.

Csikszentmihalyi, M., & Nakamura, J. (1989). The dynamics of intrinsic motivation: A study of adolescents. In C. Ames & R. Ames (Eds.), *Research on motivation in education. Vol. 3: Goals and cognitions* (pp. 45–71). New York: Academic Press.

De Manzano, O., Theorell, T., Harmat, L., & Ullen, F. (2010). The psychophysiology of flow during piano playing. *Emotion, 10,* 301–311.

Engeser, S., & Rheinberg, F. (2008). Flow, performance, and moderators of challenge-skill balance. *Motivation and Emotion, 32,* 158–172.

Fournier, J., Gaudreau, P., Demontrond-Behr, P., Visioli, J., Forrest, J., & Jackson, S. A. (2007). French translation of the Flow State Scale-2: Factor structure, cross-cultural invariance, and associations with goal attainment. *Psychology of Sport and Exercise, 8,* 897–916.

Grove, J. R., & Lewis, M. A. (1996). Hypnotic susceptibility and the attainment of flow like states during exercise. *Journal of Sport and Exercise Psychology, 18,* 380–391.

Hamilton, J. A. (1976). Attention and intrinsic rewards in the control of psychophysiological states. *Psychotherapy and Psychosomatics, 27,* 54–61.

Hamilton, J. A. (1981). Attention, personality, and self-regulation of mood: Absorbing interest and boredom. In B.A. Maehr (Ed.), *Progress in experimental personality research, 10,* 282–315.

Hormuth, S. E. (1986). The sampling of experiences in situ. *Journal of Personality, 54,* 262–293.

Jackson, S. A. (1992). Athletes in flow: A qualitative investigation of flow states in elite figure skaters. *Journal of Applied Sport Psychology, 4,* 161–180.

Jackson, S. A. (1995). Factors influencing the occurrence of flow states in elite athletes. *Journal of Applied Sport Psychology, 7,* 135–163.

Jackson, S. A. (1996). Toward a conceptual understanding of the flow experience in elite athletes. *Research Quarterly for Exercise and Sport, 67,* 76–90.

Jackson, S. A. (2000). Joy, fun, and flow state in sport. In Y. Hanin (Ed.), *Emotions in sport* (pp. 135–156). Champaign, IL: Human Kinetics.

Jackson, S. A., & Csikszentmihalyi, M. (1999). *Flow in sports: The keys to optimal experiences and performances.* Champaign, IL: Human Kinetics.

Jackson, S. A., & Eklund, R. C. (2002). Assessing flow in physical activity: The FSS-2 and DFS-2. *Journal of Sport and Exercise Psychology, 24,* 133–150.

Jackson, S. A., & Eklund, R. C. (2004, September). *Relationships between quality of experience and participation in diverse performance settings.* Paper presented at the 39th Annual Conference of the Australian Psychological Society, Sydney, Australia. [*Australian Journal of Psychology, 56,* (Supplement), p. 193].

Jackson, S. A., Eklund, R. C., & Martin A. J. (2010). *The FLOW Manual.* Mind Garden Inc. Retrieved from, www.mindgarden.com/products/flow.htm

Jackson, S. A., Kimiecik, J., Ford, S., & Marsh, H.W. (1998). Psychological correlates of flow in sport. *Journal of Sport and Exercise Psychology, 20,* 358–378.

Jackson, S. A., & Marsh, H. W. (1996). Development and validation of a scale to measure optimal experience: The flow state scale. *Journal of Sport and Exercise Psychology, 18,* 17–35.

Jackson, S. A., Martin, A. J., & Eklund, R. C. (2008). Long and short measures of flow: Examining construct validity of the FSS-2, DFS-2, and new brief counterparts. *Journal of Sport and Exercise Psychology, 30,* 561–587.

Jackson, S. A., & Roberts, G. C. (1992). Positive performance states of athletes: Toward a conceptual understanding of peak performance. *The Sport Psychologist, 6,* 156–171.

Jackson, S. A., Thomas, P. R., Marsh, H. W., & Smethurst, C. J. (2001). Relationships between flow, self-concept, psychological skills, and performance. *Journal of Applied Sport Psychology, 13,* 154–178.

Karageorghis, C. I., Vlachopoulos, S. P., & Terry, P. C. (2000). Latent variable modelling of the relationship between flow and exercise-induced feelings: An intuitive appraisal perspective. *European Physical Education, 6*(3), 230–248.

Kawabata, M., Mallett, C., & Jackson, S. A. (2007). The Flow State Scale-2 and Dispositional Flow Scale-2: Examination of factorial validity and reliability for Japanese adults. *Psychology of Sport and Exercise, 9,* 465–485.

Koehn, S., (2007). *Propensity and attainment of flow state.* Unpublished Ph.D. dissertation, Victoria University, Melbourne, Australia.

Koehn, S., Morris, T., & Watt, A. P. (2006). Efficacy of an imagery intervention on flow and performance in tennis competitions *Society for Tennis Medicine and Science, 11,* 12–14.

Kowal, J., & Fortier, M. (1999). Motivational determinants of flow: Contributions from self-determination theory. *Journal of Social Psychology, 139*(3), 355–368.

Marsh, H. W., & Jackson, S. A. (1999). Flow experience in sport: Construct validation of multidimensional, hierarchical state and trait responses. *Structural Equation Modelling, 6,* 343–371.

Martin, J. J., & Cutler, K. (2002). An exploratory study of flow and motivation in theater actors. *Journal of Applied Sport Psychology, 14,* 344–352.

Martin, A. J., & Jackson, S. A. (2008). Brief approaches to assessing task absorption and enhanced subjective experience: Examining 'short' and 'core' flow in diverse performance domains. *Motivation and Emotion, 32,* 141–157.

Maslow, A. H. (1968). *Toward a psychology of being* (2nd ed.). New York: D. Van Nostrand.

Maslow, A. H. (1970). *Religions, values and peak-experiences.* New York: The Viking Press.

Maslow, A. H. (1973). *The farther reaches of human knowledge.* Pelican Books.

McInman, A. D., & Grove, J. R. (1991). Peak moments in sport: A literature review. *Quest, 43,* 333–351.

Moneta, G. B., & Csikszentmihalyi, M. (1996). The effect of perceived challenges and skills on the quality of subjective experience. *Journal of Personality, 64,* 274–310.

Muzio, M. (Ed.). (2004). *Sport: Flow e prestazione eccellente.* Milano, Italy: FrancoAngeli.

Nakamura, J., & Csikszentmihalyi, M. (2002). The concept of flow. In C. R. Snyder & S. J. Lopez (Eds.), *Handbook of positive psychology* (pp. 89–105). Oxford University Press.

Novak, T. P., Hoffman, D., & Duhachek, A. (2003). The influence of goal-directed and experiential activities on online flow experiences. *Journal of Consumer Psychology, 13,* 3–16.

Novak, T. P., Hoffman, D. L., & Yung, Y. F. (2000). Measuring the customer experience in online environments: A structural modeling approach. *Marketing Science, 19,* 22–44.

Pates, J., & Maynard, I. (2000). Effects of hypnosis on flow states and golf performance. *Perceptual and Motor Skills, 91,* 1057–1075.

Pates, J., Cummings, A., & Maynard, I. (2002). Effects of hypnosis on flow states and three-point shooting performance in basketball players. *The Sport Psychologist, 16,* 34–47.

Penman, S., Cohen, M., Stephens, P., & Jackson, S. A. (2006, April). *Results of the 'Yoga in Australia' survey.* International Aruyveda and Yoga Conference, Sydney, Australia. Retrieved from http://www.yogainaustralia.com/downloads/YogaInAustralia.pdf, November 27, 2011.

Perry, S. K. (1999). *Writing in flow.* Cincinnati, OH: Writer's Digest.

Privette, G., & Bundrick, C. M. (1997). Psychological processes of peak, average, and failing performance in sport. *International Journal of Sport Psychology, 28,* 323–334.

Seligman, M. E. P. (2002). Positive psychology, positive prevention, and positive therapy. In C. R. Snyder & S. J. Lopez (Eds.), *Handbook on positive psychology* (pp. 3–9). Oxford, England: Oxford University Press.

Seligman, M. E., & Csikszentmihalyi, M. (2000). Positive psychology: An introduction. *American Psychologist, 55*(1), 5–14.

Stavrou, N. A., & Zervas, Y. (2004). Confirmatory factor analysis of Flow State Scale in sports. *International Journal of Sport and Exercise Psychology, 2,* 161–181.

Stein, G., Kimiecik, J., Daniels, J., & Jackson, S. A. (1995). Psychological antecedents of flow in recreational sport. *Personality and Social Psychology Bulletin, 21,* 125–135.

Taylor, M. K. (2001*). The relationships of anxiety intensity and direction of flow in collegiate athletes.* Unpublished Master's thesis, University of North Carolina at Greensboro, North Carolina.

Tenenbaum, G., Fogarty, G. J., & Jackson, S. A. (1999). The flow experience: A Rasch analysis of Jackson's Flow State Scale. *Journal of Outcome Measurement, 3,* 278–294.

Vea, S., & Pensgaard, A.M. (2004, September). *The relationship between perfectionism and flow among young elite athletes.* Paper presented at the Advancement of Applied Sport Psychology Annual Conference, Minneapolis, MN.

Vlachopoulos, S. P., Karageorghis, C. I., & Terry, P. C. (2000). Hierarchical confirmatory factor analysis of the Flow State Scale in exercise. *Journal of Sport Sciences, 18,* 815–823.

Wiggins, M. S., & Freeman, P. (2000). Anxiety and flow: An examination of anxiety direction and the flow experience. *International Sports Journal, 4,* 78–87.

Wrigley, W. J. (2005). *An examination of ecological factors in music performance assessment.* Unpublished Ph.D. dissertation, Griffith University, Brisbane, Australia.

CHAPTER
9

Implicit–Explicit Motive Congruence

Todd M. Thrash, Laura A. Maruskin, *and* Chris C. Martin

Abstract

This chapter reviews the literature on congruence (consistency) between implicit (unconscious) and explicit (conscious) motives. The prevailing wisdom that implicit and explicit motives are uncorrelated is shown to be incorrect. When methodological shortcomings of past research (e.g., unreliability of measurement) are overcome, implicit and explicit motives are positively correlated. Nevertheless, the relation is weak enough that the discrepancy between implicit and explicit motives carries important information about personality congruence. The relation between implicit and explicit motives has been found to vary systematically and meaningfully as a function of substantive moderator variables, such as self-determination and self-monitoring. Motive congruence is predicted distally by satisfaction of basic needs during childhood and proximally by stress among individuals who have difficulty regulating affect. Motive congruence predicts important outcomes, including volitional strength, flow, and well-being. The chapter closes with a discussion of future research directions, such as the distinction between congruence and integration constructs.

Key Words: motive congruence, incongruence, implicit motives, explicit motives, moderators, self-determination, self-monitoring, well-being, personality, motivation

Introduction

A *motive* is a predisposition to approach a particular class of incentives, such as achievement, affiliation, or power, or to avoid a particular class of threats, such as failure, rejection, or domination by others. The study of motives began with the work of Henry Murray (1938), who, along with his colleagues at the Harvard Psychological Clinic, pioneered a sophisticated, multimethod approach to the assessment of human motives. Of the methods that Murray developed, two were particularly influential—self-report motive questionnaires and the Thematic Apperception Test (TAT). Motive questionnaires consist of a series of statements regarding motivation in a particular content domain, such as achievement, affiliation, or power. The participant reports the level of his

or her motivation using a set of numerical response options. In the TAT, the participant is shown a series of pictures and is asked to tell a story about each. The researcher interprets the stories in terms of their motivational content. David McClelland and other researchers later developed refined versions of the TAT, now called Picture-Story Exercises (PSEs), in which subjective interpretation of participants' stories is replaced by application of experimentally derived coding systems (e.g., McClelland, Atkinson, Clark, & Lowell, 1953). After 60 years of research in the McClelland tradition, the prevailing wisdom is that scores on questionnaire and PSE measures of motives tend to be uncorrelated, even when they concern the same content domain. For instance, within the achievement domain, the extent to which individuals report valuing achievement on a questionnaire is often unrelated to the level of concern with achievement that they reveal indirectly through the stories that they tell.

Most contemporary researchers interpret the lack of correlation between questionnaire and PSE measures as a substantive fact about underlying constructs. PSEs and questionnaires are thought to assess different kinds of motive constructs that are conceptually and statistically independent. Questionnaires assess *explicit motives*—verbally encoded values that are consciously accessible. PSEs assess *implicit motives*—spontaneously expressed concerns or preferences that are not verbally encoded or directly accessible to consciousness.

An important implication of the substantive interpretation of statistical independence is that individuals differ markedly in *motive congruence*—the extent to which an individual's levels of implicit and explicit motives are aligned. For the sake of illustration, we have depicted a correlation of $r = .00$ between implicit and explicit need for achievement (nAch) in Figure 9.1, based on hypothetical data. Each data point represents the implicit nAch and explicit nAch scores for a particular individual. Some individuals—those whose scores fall near the line $y = x$ (which runs from the lower left corner to the upper right corner)—have similar levels of implicit and explicit achievement motives; that is, the extent to which they value achievement is comparable to the level of concern with achievement that they reveal spontaneously through the stories that they tell. These individuals display a high level of motive congruence. Other individuals—those whose scores fall far from the line $y = x$ (those near the upper left corner or lower right corner)—have dissimilar levels of implicit and explicit achievement motives; that is, the extent to which they value achieve-

ment is much higher or lower than the level of concern with achievement that they reveal through their stories. These individuals display a low level of motive congruence (or, equivalently, a high level of incongruence). Motive congruence in important life domains, such as achievement, affiliation, and power, is regarded as a fundamental indicator of personality coherence and has been posited to have important implications for well-being (McClelland, Koestner, & Weinberger, 1989; Weinberger & McClelland, 1990).

This interpretation of the lack of correlation between PSE and questionnaire measures provides a rather unflattering portrait of the human condition—it suggests that the conscious sense of self is fundamentally divorced from underlying unconscious motivations. However, an alternative possibility is that PSEs and questionnaires are uncorrelated due to methodological shortcomings of one or both assessment methods. Thus, it may be the assessment methodology, rather than the human psyche, that is in disarray. Of course, these two possibilities are not mutually exclusive. Our objective in this chapter is to review the literature on the substantive and methodological factors that influence the relation between PSE and questionnaire motive measures, as well as the literatures on the antecedents of motive congruence and the consequences of congruence for well-being and other outcomes. In the following, we begin by providing a more detailed historical overview of traditional and contemporary perspectives on the relation between PSE and questionnaire motive measures.

The Relation Between PSE and Questionnaire Measures of Motives

In their classic book *The Achievement Motive*, McClelland et al. (1953) described a study in which their PSE measure of nAch was found to be uncorrelated with a three-item questionnaire concerning effort to achieve. Although significant positive correlations emerged in some subsequent studies (e.g., deCharms, Morrison, Reitman, & McClelland, 1955), most studies failed to document a significant relation between PSE and questionnaire measures of nAch (Spangler, 1992). Findings were similar for PSE and questionnaire measures of need for affiliation (nAff) and need for power (nPow). Accordingly, McClelland (1987) and others concluded that these two kinds of measures are statistically independent. McClelland et al. (1989) described the lack of relation between PSE and questionnaire measures as

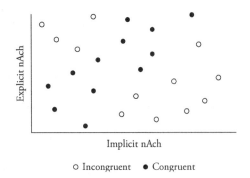

Fig. 9.1. Hypothetical data in which the correlation between implicit and explicit nAch is $r = .00$. Individuals who are more congruent have data points that fall closer to the line $y = x$.

being among the most well-established findings in psychology.

Statistical Independence as a Problem of Measurement

McClelland et al. (1989) observed that most researchers up to that point had interpreted the lack of correlation between PSEs and questionnaires as evidence that one method or the other is invalid (see also Weinberger & McClelland, 1990). The assumption underlying these interpretations is that PSEs and questionnaires represent alternative potential methods of assessing the same construct and therefore ought to converge if both are valid. This assumption has been most explicit among researchers employing the multitrait–multimethod (MTMM) matrix framework (Burwen & Campbell, 1957; Campbell & Fiske, 1959). In this approach, convergent validity depends upon robust relations between measures that concern the same content (here, motive domains) but that involve different assessment methods. Campbell and colleagues have reported that PSEs tend to show poor convergence with other methods, including self-reports. Campbell and Fiske (1959) concluded—at least as interpreted by McClelland et al. (1989)—that PSEs are therefore invalid. In contrast, Raven (1988) cited questionnaires as the cause of poor convergence, which he attributed to improper design. McClelland, similarly, has questioned the validity of questionnaires for the assessment of motives, particularly in his earlier writings (e.g., deCharms et al., 1955; McClelland, 1980).

Statistical Independence as a Substantive Fact of Personality Structure

Although McClelland has questioned the validity of questionnaires for the assessment of motives, his more central and long-standing explanation of the lack of correlation was that PSEs and questionnaires assess distinct and independent constructs. That is, he challenged the alternative-methods assumption. McClelland's early position was that PSEs assess motives, whereas so-called motive questionnaires assess schemata (McClelland, 1951) or values (McClelland, 1980). Later, McClelland concluded that the schemata or values assessed by questionnaires satisfy his criteria for the definition of a motive—they energize, direct, and select behavior—but he argued that PSEs and questionnaires assess different kinds of motives, which he called implicit motives and self-attributed (i.e., explicit) motives, respectively (McClelland et al., 1989).

McClelland's case for interpreting the lack of correlation between PSEs and questionnaires as evidence of independent constructs rests on data showing that they have distinct nomological networks. DeCharms et al. (1955) provided early evidence of distinct behavioral correlates, and McClelland et al.'s (1989) literature review made a particularly compelling case for distinct nomological networks more generally (see also Biernat, 1989; McClelland & Pilon, 1983; Schultheiss, 2001a). Implicit motives, according to McClelland and other theorists, appear to develop in early childhood through preverbal, affect-based associative learning, respond to task-based or experiential incentives, predict spontaneous behavior trends, and are introspectively inaccessible; explicit motives, in contrast, are thought to develop later in childhood through verbally mediated learning, are responsive to social-extrinsic or verbal-symbolic incentives, predict deliberate choices, and are accessible in the form of consciously articulated values. These findings provide evidence that PSEs and questionnaires are indicators of different constructs; therefore, the lack of correlation between PSEs and questionnaires was attributed to the independence of these underlying constructs.

Our reading of McClelland's various writings suggests that his position was stronger than one of attempting to explain post hoc why PSEs and questionnaires are unrelated; he argued that, in theory, they ought to be unrelated (e.g., McClelland, 1987). McClelland's theoretical grounds for predicting statistical independence appear to consist of two complementary arguments (see also Thrash, Elliot, & Schultheiss, 2007): *(a)* implicit and explicit motives have different developmental antecedents (e.g., they are acquired through nonverbal and verbal forms of socialization, respectively), and *(b)* implicit motives, which develop first, do not influence the development of explicit motives, because implicit motives are not accessible to consciousness. In short, if implicit and explicit motives develop independently, then there should be no correlation between them across individuals—developmental independence implies statistical independence.

Critique of McClelland's Substantive Interpretation of Independence

It is difficult to overstate the importance of McClelland's contribution. Virtually all motive researchers today acknowledge the discriminant validity of implicit and explicit motives and regard the implicit–explicit distinction as fundamentally important. Nevertheless, being a pioneer meant getting a few things wrong. We turn our attention now to two problems with McClelland's perspective and then propose a model that addresses these and other problems.

One problem is that McClelland's justifications for expecting statistical independence do not withstand scrutiny. We emphasize that we are not questioning the discriminant validity of implicit and explicit motives; we accept that implicit and explicit motives are distinct in the sense that the correlation between them is substantially less than $r = 1.00$ and that they have distinct nomological networks. Rather, we are questioning the justification for the stronger claim that these distinct constructs are statistically independent (i.e., correlated at $r = .00$).[1]

Consider the argument that distinct developmental antecedents (e.g., nonverbal and verbal socialization practices) lead to statistical independence. This argument rests on the unstated assumption that these antecedents are themselves uncorrelated. After all, if the parents who promote achievement through nonverbal behavior are more likely than other parents to also promote achievement through verbally mediated training, then implicit and explicit nAch would be positively correlated across children; distinct but related developmental processes would produce distinct but related motives. Thus, the expectation of independence derives from an assumption of independence and amounts to tautology. Moreover, the identification of particular developmental antecedents that distinctively promote implicit motives and of others that distinctively promote explicit motives does not imply that there exist no antecedents that promote the development of both, thereby producing a correlation between the implicit and explicit motives (Thrash, Cassidy, Maruskin, & Elliot, 2010).

Consider next the argument that implicit motives do not influence explicit motives because the former are not consciously accessible. We are aware of no affirmative evidence (not based on null effects) that individuals have no awareness of their levels of implicit motives, and there is some evidence to the contrary (e.g., Sherwood, 1966). Even if implicit motives are not directly accessible to consciousness, individuals may learn about their implicit motives indirectly, such as through feedback from others (Murray, 1938). Moreover, implicit and explicit motives could come into alignment through processes that do not require conscious awareness of implicit motives, such as those based on the reinforcing emotional consequences of motive congruence (Thrash et al., 2010).

Theoretical issues aside, the available empirical evidence suggests that implicit and explicit motives are positively related rather than uncorrelated. Spangler (1992) conducted a meta-analysis of 105 studies and found that, on average, implicit and explicit nAch were significantly positively correlated, albeit very weakly ($r = .09$). Although McClelland himself documented a significant positive correlation in some studies (e.g., deCharms et al., 1955),[2] he tended to downplay the meaningfulness of such findings. For instance, in his textbook on human motivation, McClelland (1987) stated: "The most reasonable interpretation of such findings is that these two types of measures are essentially independent, as they ought to be on theoretical grounds, and that when occasional correlations appear between them, they are the product of a peculiar set of circumstances related to the particular group being tested" (p. 521). McClelland's strong stance on independence is understandable in its historical context; an emphasis on independence may have been necessary to convince skeptics that PSEs and questionnaires assess different constructs. However, now that the discriminant validity of implicit and explicit motives is no longer in question, there is no reason to downplay evidence of a positive relation between them.

The other problem with McClelland's perspective is that, while challenging the assumption that a single construct underlies PSE and questionnaire measures, McClelland introduced a problematic assumption of his own—that PSEs and questionnaires are perfectly valid as measures of implicit and explicit motives, respectively. To be precise, McClelland certainly recognized that neither kind of measure is perfectly valid; nevertheless, he neglected this fact when he attributed the lack of correlation between PSEs and questionnaires to the independence of implicit and explicit motive constructs *instead of* (rather than *in addition to*) the imperfect relation between constructs and measures. The following quotation (in which *n* refers to implicit need and *v* refers to explicit value) illustrates his treatment of methodological and substantive explanations as mutually exclusive alternatives:

> This lack of correlation bothers a lot of people and they have used it as an argument that therefore, since the *v* Achievement measures are more reliable, this proves that the *n* Achievement is not valid. To me, it demonstrated that these measures get at different aspects of personality—*n* Achievement at operant trends I called motives and *v* Achievement at values I called schemas.
> (*McClelland*, 1980, p. 13)

Although Spangler's analysis suggests that the implicit–explicit correlation is very weak (*r* = .09), one could discover that the true correlation is considerably larger if the assumption of perfect validity is relaxed and threats to validity and reliability are actively identified and overcome. Indeed, the history of other literatures (e.g., attitude–behavior consistency, trait–behavior consistency, and implicit–explicit attitude consistency) indicates that as measurement and methods improve, effect sizes tend to increase.

An Integrative, General Model

We present the models in Figure 9.2 as a framework for understanding researchers' explanations of the lack of correlation between questionnaires and PSEs, as well as the assumptions that have led to these interpretations. Models representing researchers' explanations of the lack of correlation are illustrated in the right panel of Figure 9.2; models depicting the tacit assumptions that have led to these interpretations are shown in the middle panel; and a general model, in which these assumptions are relaxed, is shown in the lower left (Fig. 9.2b). After discussing

the implications stemming from this general model, we briefly discuss the model in the upper left, which is even more general (Fig. 9.2a).

The general model in Figure 9.2b includes two underlying constructs (in ovals): an implicit motive (e.g., implicit nAch) and the corresponding explicit motive within the same content domain (e.g., explicit nAch). The curved arrow represents the correlation between them. The underlying implicit and explicit motive constructs are posited to influence scores on PSE and questionnaire measures, respectively (rectangles). Because the measures are posited not to be perfectly reliable or valid, each is also posited to be influenced by an error term (circles). These error terms represent all influences on the measure other than the underlying construct, including extraneous constructs, method variance, and random error.

If one begins with the general model in Figure 9.2b and imposes the assumption that implicit and explicit motive constructs are correlated at *r* = 1.00, then one arrives at the alternative-methods model shown in Figure 9.2c, in which there is no distinction between implicit and explicit motive

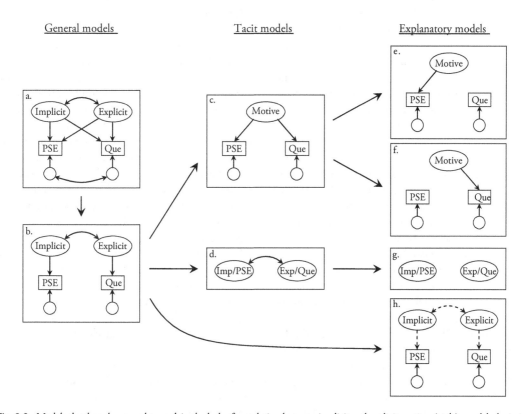

Fig. 9.2. Models that have been used to explain the lack of correlation between implicit and explicit motives (*right*); models depicting the tacit assumptions that underlie the explanatory models (*center*); and general models that are relatively free of assumptions (*left*).

constructs. It is understandable that researchers who relied on this tacit model attributed the lack of correlation between measures to inadequate validity of questionnaires (Fig. 9.2e) or PSEs (Fig. 9.2f). The reasoning is sound but the premise (assumption) is not, thus leading these researchers to the incorrect conclusion that one measure or the other is invalid.

If one begins with the general model and instead imposes the assumption that each measure is correlated at $r = 1.00$ with its underlying construct (i.e., each measure is perfectly valid), then one arrives at the model in Figure 9.2d, in which there is no distinction between constructs and measures. Relying on this tacit model, McClelland attributed the lack of correlation between measures to the independence of the underlying constructs (Fig. 9.2g). Again, the reasoning is sound but the premise (assumption) is not, leading McClelland to conclude, incorrectly it seems, that the implicit and explicit motive constructs are statistically independent.

We propose that the best route forward is to make neither assumption and to allow the general model itself (Fig. 9.2b) to guide theory and research. This model implies that the correlation between PSEs and questionnaires is a multiplicative function (for details, see Bollen, 1989) of (a) the true correlation between underlying implicit and explicit motive constructs, (b) the degree of relation between the implicit motive construct and the PSE measure, and (c) the degree of relation between the explicit motive construct and the questionnaire measure. Because assumptions have been relaxed, this model is underdetermined in the sense that a weak correlation between measures is of uncertain origin; it may result from a weak relation between underlying constructs, from poor validity of one or both measures, or from some combination of these. We presume that each of these factors contributes to the weak relation between PSE and questionnaire measures (Fig. 9.2h), but this is an empirical question. Our general model therefore calls for research on two kinds of influences on the relation between PSE and questionnaire measures: methodological factors concerning the relation between constructs and measures, and substantive factors concerning the relation between underlying constructs. This dual emphasis parallels similar historical developments in the attitude-behavior consistency and trait-behavior consistency literatures (Kraus, 1995). Next, we review the emerging literatures on methodological and substantive factors that influence the relation between PSE and questionnaire measures.

Before moving on to those literatures, we pause to specify some of the assumptions that underlie our own general model. In particular, the general model in Figure 9.2b rests on the assumptions that (a) implicit motives do not influence scores on questionnaires; (b) explicit motives do not influence scores on PSEs; and (c) PSEs and questionnaires do not share method variance. A model in which these assumptions are relaxed is shown in Figure 9.2a. We note that the assumptions underlying the model in Figure 9.2b are consistent with most existing theory; therefore, this model has greater parsimony and heuristic value than the model in Figure 9.2a for representing the diversity of assumptions and interpretations to date. However, we acknowledge that there may be grounds for challenging each of the assumptions that underlie the model in Figure 9.2b. Whereas we have used this model as a framework for depicting problematic assumptions in past research, a future reviewer may profit from using the model in Figure 9.2a for the same purpose.

Methodological Factors That Influence Estimates of the Implicit–Explicit Motive Correlation
Omnibus Effect of Multiple Methodological Factors

Sherwood (1966) noted that a variety of factors, such as lack of clarity about the task of introspection, defensiveness, and social desirability, may compromise the validity of questionnaire measures, at least as they are typically administered. Sherwood administered questionnaire measures of nAch and nAff under special conditions designed to minimize these problems. Specifically, he taught participants in detail about the implicit nAch and nAff constructs about which they were asked to report explicitly; he sought to maximize motivation to be accurate by framing the study as an opportunity to develop self-insight; and he conducted the study in the context of a trusting and nonevaluative relationship with the experimenter. Implicit nAch and nAff were assessed under standard conditions at the beginning of the study. Also noteworthy is a methodological refinement to which Sherwood himself drew little attention: His questionnaires were designed to correspond closely in content to the implicit motive coding systems. His findings were striking. Across two studies, the relationships between implicit and explicit measures were positive and significant for both nAch ($rs =.35, .42$) and nAff ($rs =.40, .34$). These correlations are among the strongest reported to date, suggesting that implicit and explicit motives are robustly related when care is taken to avoid problems that may compromise the validity of explicit measures. Unfortunately, it is impossible to know to what extent each of Sherwood's various methodological refinements was responsible for his findings. Next we turn to studies that have isolated particular methodological factors.

Correspondence of Content

Ajzen and Fishbein (1977) showed that attitude-behavior consistency is attenuated when attitudes and behaviors do not correspond closely in content or specificity. Thrash et al. (2007) suggested that a similar issue may apply to congruence between implicit and explicit motives. These authors argued that the relationship between implicit and explicit motives may have been underestimated in past research, because questionnaires and PSEs generally have not been designed to correspond directly in content. For example, many measures of explicit nAch are based on Murray's (1938) early conceptualization of nAch (e.g., Edwards, 1959), whereas McClelland's coding system for implicit nAch was derived empirically (McClelland et al., 1953) and deviates from Murray's conceptualization (Koestner & McClelland, 1990).

To examine the impact of correspondence of content, Thrash et al. (2007) administered a PSE measure of implicit nAch and four questionnaire measures of explicit nAch. Implicit nAch was assessed using Schultheiss's (2001b) translation of Heckhausen's (1963) coding system for hope for success. Three of the measures of explicit nAch were traditional measures that had not been designed to correspond in content to Heckhausen's coding system. The fourth measure was a new questionnaire (Schultheiss & Murray, 2002) that consisted of five pairs of items that corresponded directly to categories of Heckhausen's coding system (need for success, instrumental activity, expectation of success, praise, and positive affect). Results indicated that the traditional measures of explicit nAch were uncorrelated with implicit nAch (rs = .00 to .02), whereas the matched-content measure of explicit nAch was significantly related to implicit nAch (r = .17). The latter effect with matched-content measures was significantly stronger than two of the three null effects that were obtained using nonmatched measures. This study shows that correspondence of content influences estimates of the implicit–explicit correlation; implicit and explicit motives are positively related rather than unrelated when the measures are designed to cover the same content universe.

Schultheiss, Yankova, Dirlikov, and Schad (2009) sought to address the same issue but came to a different conclusion. These researchers assessed implicit nAch, nAff, and nPow using Winter's (1994) coding system and assessed explicit nAch, nAff, and nPow with a new measure that corresponded closely in content to the implicit measure. The implicit and explicit measures were also made to correspond in a second respect. The explicit motive questionnaire items were assessed with respect to the picture cues used in the PSE; participants were asked to look at the picture and respond to the questions as if they were a character in the picture. Schultheiss et al. reported that there was no relation between scores on these two sets of measures. They concluded, "Statistical independence between both construct types can also be observed when the explicit measure of motivation is made as similar as possible to the method of implicit motive assessment" (p. 78).

The contradiction between the conclusions of Thrash et al. (2007) and Schultheiss et al. (2009) may be reconciled if one distinguishes issues of statistical independence (i.e., whether the implicit–explicit correlation equals zero) and effect size (i.e., whether a nonzero correlation is small or large). Consider first the issue of statistical independence. Schultheiss et al. reported the following correlations between measures of implicit motives and matched-content measures of explicit motives: nPow, r = .18, p < .05; nAch, r = .11, ns; nAff, r = .12, ns. Interpretation of these findings depends on whether one accepts the logic of null hypothesis testing. If so, then one rejects the null hypothesis of independence in the case of nPow and draws no conclusion in the cases of nAch and nAff. If not, then the correlations may be interpreted as the midpoints of the following 95% confidence intervals: nPow, r = .18 ± .14; nAch, r = .11 ± .14; nAff, r = .12 ± .14. In this case, there is no more reason to interpret any of these effects as equaling r = .00 (which is near the bottom of the confidence intervals and therefore improbable as an estimate of the population effects) than there is to interpret them as equaling, say, r = .27 (which is near the top of the confidence intervals and therefore also improbable). The best point estimates of the population effects are the correlations themselves, which are uniformly weak, positive, and similar to the correlation of r = .17 reported by Thrash et al. (2007). Regardless, both interpretations provide at least qualified support for a proposal that, when the problem of correspondence of content is addressed, implicit and explicit motives are positively related. On the other hand, these effects are certainly small—this is the take-home message of the Schultheiss et al. findings in our view. We conclude that when the problem of poor correspondence is addressed, across studies the correlation between implicit and explicit motives is consistently positive but weak.[3]

These effects are not so weak that they should be disregarded, however. One reason is that, as suggested by Sherwood's (1966) findings, particular methodological factors are likely to have individually small but cumulatively robust effects. To further explore this possibility, we now consider a second specific methodological factor.

Reliability of Measurement

All measures demonstrate some degree of random measurement error, which attenuates effect sizes. If the correlation between implicit and explicit measures is not corrected for the unreliability of the measures—and generally it is not—then the correlation between underlying constructs is likely to be underestimated. The proper means of correction depends on the theorized measurement model—that is, the relation between the measured variables and the construct of interest. Unfortunately, measurement models are rarely explicitly specified or tested in PSE research, and the measurement models that have been proposed are often unconventional (e.g., Atkinson & Birch, 1970; for other possible models, see McClelland, 1987; Thrash et al., 2010). Because the issue of measurement models remains unresolved, we present the two most widely employed approaches to disattenuation. We illustrate the first approach using data from Thrash et al. (2007) and the second using data from Schultheiss et al. (2009).

One method of disattenuation is to use confirmatory factor analysis to remove the unique error variance from particular indicators of a construct, resulting in latent variables that correspond more closely to the construct of interest. Thrash et al. (2010) used this approach to reanalyze data from Thrash et al. (2007). An implicit nAch latent variable was modeled using separate nAch scores for each of five stories as indicators. A nonmatched-content explicit nAch latent variable was modeled using the three nonmatched measures as indicators. Finally, a matched-content explicit nAch latent variable was modeled using the 10 items from the matched-content questionnaire as indicators.

In theory, disattenuation should have less impact for nonmatched-content measures than for matched-content measures, because the true (disattenuated) correlation would be expected to be robust only in the latter case. As expected, disattenuation was found to modestly increase the effect size for nonmatched measures. As noted earlier, the implicit–explicit correlations for nonmatched measures ranged from $r = .00$ to $.02$ (ns). Use of latent variables increased the implicit–explicit correlation for nonmatched measures to $r = .07$ (ns). More important, disattenuation had a pronounced effect for matched measures. As noted earlier, the implicit–explicit correlation for matched measures reported by Thrash et al. (2007) was $r = .17$. Use of latent variables increased the implicit–explicit correlation to $r = .38$ ($p < .01$). Although the impact of disattenuation was itself substantial, particularly striking are the combined effects of addressing the correspondence and measurement error problems simultaneously. With nonmatching measures and without correcting for measurement error, the implicit-explicit correlations ranged from $r = .00$ to $.02$; with matching measures and with correction for measurement error, the implicit–explicit correlation was $r = .38$. The latter correlation is in the range reported by Sherwood (1966) who, as noted, also addressed multiple methodological problems simultaneously.

A second approach to disattenuation is to correct an observed correlation based on the reliabilities of the two variables. A standard approach based on traditional psychometric theory is to divide a correlation by the square root of the product of the internal consistencies of the two measures (Guilford & Fruchter, 1978). We used results reported by Schultheiss et al. (2009) to implement this technique. Schultheiss et al. (2009) did not report internal consistency values for the PSE variables, as is customary in PSE research. Internal consistency is underestimated for PSE measures, researchers have argued, because traditional psychometric models are not appropriate for the PSE. We therefore used the internal consistencies of Schultheiss et al.'s measures of explicit nPow (Cronbach's $\alpha = .64$), nAff (Cronbach's $\alpha = .74$), and nAch (Cronbach's $\alpha = .84$) as estimates of the internal consistencies of the corresponding PSE measures. This approach is reasonable in that the measures were designed to be as similar as possible. Correcting the implicit–explicit correlations for unreliability using the equation described earlier increases the implicit–explicit correlations as follows: for nPow, the correlation increases from $r = .18$ ($p < .05$) to $.28$ ($p < .0001$); for nAff, the correlation increases from $r = .12$ (ns) to $.16$ ($p < .05$); and for nAch, the correlation increases from $r = .11$ (*ns*) to $.13$ ($p = .07$). Thus, after disattenuation, two of the effects are significant and one is marginally significant. These analyses provide further evidence that unreliability may lead the implicit–explicit correlation to be underestimated. Moreover, although the effects remained modest in size in this data set, these findings nevertheless provide additional unambiguous support for the conclusion that the independence hypothesis does not hold when problems of correspondence of content and measurement error are addressed.

MTMM Analysis

As noted earlier, Campbell and colleagues concluded, based on inspection of MTMM matrices, that PSEs and questionnaires failed tests of convergence. However, now that the discriminant validity of implicit and explicit motives is well established, the relevant question is not whether they converge strongly enough to be considered alternative indicators of the same construct (i.e., whether the correlation approaches $r = 1.00$), but rather whether they converge at all (i.e., whether the correlation is greater than $r = .00$). We also note that Campbell and Fiske's (1959) approach is outdated in an important respect. Among their criteria for validity was the requirement that measures have more trait variance than method variance. With contemporary modeling techniques (e.g., CFA, multidimensional scaling [MDS]), this issue is relatively unimportant, because trait variance and method variance may be unconfounded through analysis of underlying latent variables or dimensions.

Recently, Bilsky and Schwartz (2008) used MDS to conduct a MTMM analysis of three previously published data sets in which both PSEs and questionnaires were used to measure motivations in the achievement, affiliation, and power domains. The aim of the MDS analysis was to derive a spatial representation (i.e., in two or three dimensions) of motive domain and method facets, such that more highly correlated measures are located closer together in physical space. The MDS approach is well suited for the question at hand, because it is based on the relative strengths of the correlations among measures and does not require that any of the correlations be strong in an absolute sense. In all three data sets, Bilsky and Schwartz found that motive domains formed pie-piece-like wedges in a two-dimensional space, whereas methods were represented by concentric circles, which varied from more implicit to more explicit or vice versa as the radius increased. This structure indicates that, as may be shown with

geometry, implicit and explicit measures are more strongly related when they concern the same domain than different domains. This finding is at odds with the independent-constructs perspective.

In sum, empirical evidence indicates that implicit and explicit motives are positively related, rather than unrelated, when methods are refined by improving correspondence of content, correcting for unreliability, or using contemporary modeling techniques. The effects of methodological factors tend to be individually modest but cumulatively robust. A large variety of other methodological factors remains to be investigated. We encourage researchers to look to other literatures, such as the attitude–behavior consistency, trait–behavior consistency, and implicit–explicit attitude consistency literatures, for precedents. Epstein's (1979) research, for instance, suggests that implicit–explicit correlations will increase if test–retest reliability is enhanced by aggregating motive scores from multiple occasions.

Substantive Variables That Moderate Implicit–Explicit Motive Congruence

The argument that implicit and explicit motive constructs are positively correlated rather than uncorrelated is more than an academic quibble; these two scenarios have very different implications for theory and application. A correlation of $r = .00$ between underlying constructs suggests (but does not guarantee) that no integrative mechanisms are operative. In contrast, a positive correlation suggests (but does not guarantee) that an integrative process is operative and calls for research focused on identifying such processes.

Moreover, a weak correlation is not necessarily evidence that integrative mechanisms tend to be ineffectual and therefore neglible. Another possibility is that integrative mechanisms are effectual but operative among some rather than all members of the population. Imagine that the true correlation between implicit and explicit nAch is $r = .35$. This correlation could be the net result of combining two subgroups of individuals: one in which integrative processes are operative (resulting in a correlation of, say, $r = .74$ within this subgroup), and another in which integrative processes are not operative (resulting in a correlation of, say, $r = .00$ within this subgroup). The effect of combining these two subgroups into one group is illustrated with hypothetical data in Figure 9.3. Within the past 10 years, researchers have begun to investigate substantive moderating variables that specify the groups of individuals (e.g., individuals with high or low levels of particular

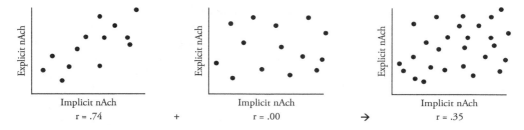

Fig. 9.3. Hypothetical data showing how a relatively weak correlation may be the net result of combining two subgroups, one in which the correlation is strong and one in which the correlation equals zero.

traits) among whom the implicit–explicit relation is weaker or stronger. We focus our review on studies of implicit and explicit motives per se. For recent reviews of studies of congruence between motives and goals, some of which preceded the motive congruence studies reviewed here (e.g., Schultheiss & Brunstein, 1999), see Brunstein (2010) and Thrash et al. (2010).

Self-Determination

The topic of personality congruence has been of interest not only in the motive literature but also in humanistic theories, including traditional theories, such as that of Rogers (1959), and contemporary theories, such as Deci and Ryan's self-determination theory (Deci & Ryan, 1991). Thrash and Elliot (2002) sought to integrate motive and humanistic approaches by showing that individuals who are more self-determined display greater motive congruence.

Self-determination refers to self-regulation in accord with one's authentic or true self. Individuals differ in self-determination, such that some individuals live according to their core interests and values, whereas others live according to others' expectations or controlling influences in the environment. Thrash and Elliot (2002) argued that the experience of self-determination may reflect (at least in part) the integration of explicit values with one's preexisting and deep-seated implicit motivational tendencies, as opposed to the internalization of explicit values arbitrarily from the environment regardless of their fit to one's implicit motives. As expected, self-determination was found to moderate the relation between implicit and explicit nAch. Among individuals high in self-determination, implicit nAch robustly predicted explicit nAch, $r = .40$, $p < .01$; in other words, self-determined individuals tended to be congruent. Among individuals low in self-determination, implicit and explicit nAch were largely unrelated, $r = -.07$, *ns*; in other words, individuals low in self-determination tended to be either congruent or incongruent, as would be expected by

chance if these individuals internalize values regardless of their fit with implicit motives.

More recently, Hofer, Busch, Bond, Kärtner, Kiessling, and Law (2010) tested the generalizability of the self-determination finding across cultures, using data from Cameroon, Germany, and Hong Kong. Consistent with the finding reported by Thrash and Elliot (2002), Hofer et al. reported that self-determination moderated the relation between implicit nAch and explicit achievement goals, such that implicit nAch and explicit achievement goals were positively related among individuals high, but not low, in self-determination. This moderation effect was found to be invariant across cultures.

Private Body Consciousness, Self-Monitoring, and Preference for Consistency

Thrash et al. (2007) argued that at least three distinct processes contribute to motive congruence: access to one's implicit motives, integration of one's explicit motives with one's implicit motives, and resistance to competing sources of values. Regarding access to implicit motives, Thrash et al. argued that motive congruence may be greater among individuals higher in private body consciousness; these individuals are sensitive to bodily states and therefore may perceive the effects of implicit motive arousal. Regarding integration, Thrash et al. argued that congruence may be greater among individuals higher in preference for consistency; these individuals would be particularly motivated to reconcile their explicit motives with any rudimentary knowledge of their implicit motives. Regarding resistance to competing sources of values, Thrash et al. argued that congruence may be greater among individuals lower in self-monitoring; these individuals are less likely to monitor others' expectations and to internalize others' values arbitrarily. As predicted, implicit nAch was found to predict explicit nAch among individuals high but not low in private body consciousness, high but not low in preference for consistency, and low but not high in self-monitoring.

Among individuals with the most advantageous profile of traits (i.e., high in private body consciousness, high in preference for consistency, and low in self-monitoring), the correlation between implicit and explicit nAch was $r = .46$ ($p < .05$); among individuals with the opposite profile of traits, the correlation was $r = -.30$ (*ns*). All three moderators were found to account for unique variance in motive congruence. Building on this multiple-process perspective, Thrash et al. (2010) recently developed a general meta-theoretical framework that may be useful in identifying additional processes through which motive congruence may emerge.

Antecedents of Motive Congruence

Next we review studies that address essentially the same issue as those in the last section, except that congruence is modeled differently. The studies in the prior section concerned independent variables that moderate the *relation* between implicit and explicit motives. For instance, self-determination was found to moderate the relation between implicit and explicit nAch. The studies in this section concern variables that predict the *discrepancy* between implicit and explicit motives; that is, the implicit and explicit motive variables are reduced to a single incongruence variable, which is treated as the dependent variable. For instance, if one were to test the self-determination hypothesis in this way, one would expect to find that individuals higher in self-determination have less of a discrepancy between implicit and explicit nAch. Consistent with the difference in modeling strategies, we refer to the predictor variables in this section as antecedents rather than moderators.

Need Satisfaction

Schattke, Koestner, and Kehr (2011) examined the childhood antecedents of incongruence in adults, with hypotheses grounded in self-determination theory. These authors predicted that childhood experiences that interfere with the development of self-determination—specifically, those that thwart satisfaction of the basic needs for relatedness and autonomy—would predict incongruence later in life. Based on new analyses of an archival data set (McClelland & Pilon, 1983; Sears, Maccoby, & Levin, 1957), Schattke et al. reported that experiences involving deprivation of the need for autonomy (e.g., maternal inhibition of sexuality) or of the need for relatedness (e.g., separation from the mother during the second year of life) predicted levels of incongruence 26 years later. Consistent with the

self-determination findings reported earlier, these findings suggest that explicit motives become integrated with implicit motives to the extent that the socialization environment supports satisfaction of the basic needs theorized to underlie self-determination.

Stress and Affect Regulation

Whereas Schattke et al. (2011) examined distal, developmental antecedents of congruence, Baumann, Kaschel, and Kuhl (2005) examined a proximal antecedent: stress. Working from the perspective of personality interactions theory, these authors argued that stress leads to motive incongruence among state-oriented (as opposed to action-oriented) individuals. State-oriented individuals have difficulty generating positive affect in response to demand-related stressors and/or difficulty overcoming negative affect in response to threat-related stressors. In two correlational studies and an experiment in which stress was manipulated, Baumann et al. reported that state orientation interacted with stress, such that greater stress predicted a greater discrepancy between implicit and explicit nAch among state-oriented individuals but not among action-oriented individuals. The relation between stress and motive incongruence among state-oriented individuals was theorized to reflect a disruption of communication between the memory systems associated with implicit and explicit motives (extension and intention memory, respectively).

The studies in the prior section (regarding moderators) and this section (regarding antecedents) provide additional evidence that implicit and explicit motives are not statistically independent. The positive correlation between implicit and explicit motives may be viewed as the overall or average relation. The studies in the moderator section showed that the correlation varies systematically as a function of third variables. The studies in this section, similarly, indicate that one's standing as congruent or incongruent varies systematically as a function of predictor variables. We caution, however, that stress was the only variable that was manipulated in these studies. Stress appears to play a role in causing incongruence, but the other moderators and antecedents of congruence may or may not be causes of congruence.

Consequences of Motive Congruence

Although, as we have shown, implicit and explicit motives are positively related when methodological shortcomings of past research are overcome, the correlation remains weak enough that the discrepancy between them carries important information about congruence of personality. This conclusion is suggested by the aforementioned moderator and antecedent findings and would be further supported by evidence that individuals' levels of congruence have theoretically meaningful consequences. Researchers are in agreement that congruence is beneficial relative to incongruence. In this section, we review the literature on variables that have been posited to be consequences of motive congruence.

Identity Status

Marcia's (1966) theory of identity recognizes four identity statuses: moratorium, achievement, diffusion, and foreclosure. Individuals who have actively searched for an identity have the status of *moratorium* if they have not yet committed themselves to an identity, or the status of identity *achievement* if they have. Individuals who have not actively searched for an identity have the status of *diffusion* if they have not yet committed to an identity, or the status of *foreclosure* if they have internalized an identity from the social environment despite lack of exploration.

Regarding individuals who have committed themselves to an identity, Hofer, Busch, Chasiotis, and Kiessling (2006) argued that identity achievement stems from discovering one's implicit motives and adopting explicit motives that are consistent with them, whereas foreclosure stems from adopting others' explicit values regardless of their compatibility with one's implicit motives. As predicted, Hofer et al. found that implicit and explicit nAff interacted in the prediction of identity achievement, such that explicit nAff was a more positive predictor of identity achievement among individuals higher in implicit nAff. Also as predicted, implicit and explicit nAff interacted in the prediction of foreclosure, such that explicit nAff was a more positive predictor of foreclosure among individuals lower in implicit nAff. No effects emerged for the statuses that do not involve commitment to an identity (i.e., moratorium, diffusion). These findings suggest that attaining a sense of identity requires discovery of one's implicit motives and embracing them as the foundation of one's values.

Volitional Strength

Kehr (2004) examined the relationship between implicit–explicit motive congruence and volitional regulation within a sample of managers. Kehr posited that discrepancies between implicit and explicit motives lead to psychological conflict and that resolution of this conflict requires volitional regulation.

Consistent with past findings (Muraven & Baumeister, 2000), such regulation was posited to deplete limited volitional resources. In Kehr's study, implicit motives were assessed using the Multi-Motive Grid (MMG; Sokolowski, Schmalt, Langens, & Puca, 2000), an instrument that we classify as implicit for present purposes but that also has some properties of explicit measures. As predicted, Kehr found that discrepancies between managers' implicit and explicit motives, averaged across content domains (achievement, affiliation, power), predicted lower levels of volitional strength 5 months later.

Flow

Flow refers to an optimal state in which one is completely involved in an activity, to the point of becoming unaware of anything else (Csikszentmihalyi, 1990). Rheinberg (2008) argued that the volitional regulation necessitated by motive incongruence hinders flow experiences. Consistent with this argument, Clavadetscher (2003) found that the discrepancy between implicit and explicit motives predicted less flow among workers. Schüler (2010) argued that such effects are likely to be manifest only when the situation involves achievement cues; in the presence of achievement cues, motive conflicts that are otherwise dormant are aroused and interfere with task engagement. Schüler confirmed this hypothesis in a series of three studies, including a longitudinal study in which the dependent variable represented change in flow and an experiment in which the presence of achievement incentives was experimentally manipulated.

Well-Being

Well-being is the outcome variable that has received the most attention to date. Kehr (2004) found that implicit–explicit motive discrepancies predicted lower levels of affective well-being longitudinally. Lower levels of volitional strength mediated (explained) this effect. Baumann et al. (2005) found that incongruence between implicit and explicit nAch predicted lower levels of subjective well-being and more psychosomatic complaints. Baumann et al. also showed that incongruence mediated the effect of the stress × state orientation interaction on these outcomes. Hofer, Chasiotis, and Campos (2006) found that congruence in the power domain, but not in the affiliation domain, predicted greater life satisfaction in three cultures. Kazén and Kuhl (2011) found that a directional nPow discrepancy, in which explicit nPow was strong and implicit nPow was weak, predicted lower levels of well-being and higher levels of stress among managers.

Null effects of motive congruence on well-being have also been reported (McAuley, Bond, & Ng, 2004). For this empirical reason, and based on theory about the conditions under which incongruence is more or less likely to be problematic, researchers have begun to document factors that moderate the effect of motive congruence on well-being. Motive incongruence has been found to be less problematic when the incongruent motives are not aroused through motive-relevant activity (Schüler, Job, Fröhlich, & Brandstätter, 2008), when motive expression is inhibited by a dispositional trait called activity inhibition (Langens, 2007), when the individual uses emotional disclosure as a coping strategy (Langan-Fox, Sankey, & Canty, 2009; Schüler, Job, Fröhlich, & Brandstätter, 2009), and among individuals high in self-directedness or internal locus of control (Langan-Fox et al., 2009).

In sum, motive congruence appears to have a variety of important consequences. Individuals who are more congruent have greater volitional strength, are more prone to flow experiences, and experience higher levels of well-being. These variables are generally posited to be effects of motive congruence. However, whether motive congruence is the cause of these outcomes has not been shown definitively; indeed, demonstrating effects of motive congruence is difficult, because motives (as aspects of personality) and the discrepancy between them are not readily amenable to experimental control. Thrash et al. (2010) identified several strategies for documenting causality that may be useful in future research on motive congruence.

Conclusion

In this chapter, we have shown to be incorrect the prevailing wisdom that implicit and explicit motives are uncorrelated. When care is taken to address methodological problems of past research, implicit and explicit motives are positively correlated across individuals. Nevertheless, the correlation is weak enough that the discrepancy between implicit and explicit motives carries important information. We have reviewed evidence showing that the relation between implicit and explicit motives varies systematically as a function of moderator variables. Motive congruence also has meaningful antecedents and important consequences. We are excited about the rapid development of the motive congruence literature and, in the following, identify several important questions to be addressed in future research.

Future Directions
How Should Motive Congruence Be Modeled?

Analytic strategies for modeling congruence have varied across studies. These strategies include the following: *(a)* testing moderation of the implicit-explicit relation (e.g., Thrash & Elliot, 2002); *(b)* computing difference scores based on standardized implicit and explicit motive variables (e.g., Kehr, 2004); *(c)* testing whether one motive moderates the effect of the other (i.e., implicit motive × explicit motive interactions; e.g., Hofer, Chasiotis et al., 2006); and, most recently, *(d)* using polynomial regression with response surface analysis (Kazén & Kuhl, 2011), a sophisticated variant of the implicit × explicit motive interaction approach (Edwards, 2002). In most cases, implicit and explicit motives are modeled as separate variables, but in some cases they are combined into a single discrepancy index. Most studies have examined nondirectional incongruence, which results from either motive being higher than the other, but some studies have examined incongruence in a particular direction. These various operationalizations of congruence, which imply subtly different conceptualizations of congruence and vary in statistical rigor, have not yet received detailed discussion. We encourage researchers to articulate the rationale for their operationalization and its suitability to the substantive issue that is being addressed. The robustness of findings across operationalizations of congruence is also in need of greater scrutiny.

What Can Motive Researchers Learn From Freud?

It is striking how similar the issues surrounding the topic of motive congruence are to the issues that interested Sigmund Freud and subsequent psychoanalysts. Nevertheless, motive researchers, like empirical researchers more generally, tend not to cite Freud's work (see Weinberger & McClelland, 1990, for a notable exception). It is not clear whether this inattention to Freud is based on the belief that Freud's writings have nothing to offer, or a fear that citing Freud will undermine the appearance of scientific credibility, or some other reason. Whatever the reason, we have found that Freud's writings contain many important insights (as well as claims that warrant skepticism) and believe that inattention to these insights undermines rather than serves scientific credibility and progress. We therefore encourage researchers to explore more fully the theoretical and historical underpinnings of their subject matter. This recommendation brings us to our next question for future research.

May Incongruence Be Integrated?

Freud (1909/1989) argued that an individual has three healthy options after bringing unconscious material into awareness: accept it, reject it, or sublimate it. In contrast, the prevailing assumption in the motive literature seems to be that there is one healthy option: accept it—that is, embrace one's implicit motives as the basis of explicit motive adoption. We encourage researchers to entertain the possibility that rejecting or rechanneling ("sublimating") one's implicit motives may sometimes be the healthier option, particularly in the case of implicit motives (e.g., implicit nPow or implicit avoidance motives) that do not promote, or that thwart, satisfaction of fundamental human needs. Thrash et al. (2010) proposed that a self-determined, mindful decision to reject an implicit motive represents a form of integrated incongruence that may be healthier than incongruence arising through other processes (e.g., chance). Integration, which refers to unity of structure and coordination of function, may ultimately be more important than the simpler mathematical notion of congruence or discrepancy.

May Congruence Be Unintegrated?

Regarding the literature on moderators of congruence, we have argued that integrative processes may be operative for individuals at one pole of a moderating variable and not operative for individuals at the other pole. A potentially important implication is that congruent individuals are found at both poles of the moderator, but they are congruent for different reasons. For instance, one would expect most individuals high in self-determination to be congruent as a result of an integrative process, and one would expect roughly half of the individuals low in self-determination to be congruent as a result of chance. In the literatures on antecedents and consequences of congruence, there has been no distinction between these two sets of congruent individuals. We speculate that unintegrated congruence—congruence that arises by chance (for a broader definition of unintegrated congruence, see Thrash et al., 2010)—may be less stable and beneficial than congruence that arises through an integrative process.

Does Congruence Vary at Other Levels of Analysis?

Researchers to date have focused on congruence at the between-person level of analysis. However, congruence between implicit and explicit motives (or between the levels of implicit and explicit motivational states) is likely to vary not only across individuals but also across time (for a particular individual), across content domains (for a particular individual), across countries (for the average individual), and so on. We believe that generalizing and extending conceptualizations of congruence to new levels of analysis will be among the most fruitful avenues for future research.

Notes

1. McClelland and others who have argued that implicit and explicit motives are statistically independent have sometimes qualified this claim by stating that implicit and explicit motives are "generally," "essentially," or "largely" independent. We acknowledge this fact but emphasize McClelland's focus on independence for the following reasons: (a) McClelland appeared to use these qualifications in order for his language to be consistent with the empirical facts, but these empirical facts appear not to have influenced his theorizing; (b) quite often, McClelland did not qualify the claim of statistical independence; (c) McClelland (1987) explicitly denied the meaningfulness of implicit–explicit correlations when they emerged; and (d) for theory to progress, it is necessary to sharpen distinctions (e.g., between "independent" and "essentially independent") that have been obscured in the past.

2. McClelland et al. (1989), and many others since, mistakenly stated that implicit and explicit nAch were uncorrelated in this study.

3. Part of Schultheiss et al.'s basis for concluding that implicit and explicit motives were statistically independent was that an omnibus test of a full correlation matrix was nonsignificant. This matrix included all nine pairwise correlations between implicit and explicit measures of nAch, nPow, and nAff. The three on-diagonal correlations in this matrix (i.e., the correlations between implicit and explicit nPow, between implicit and explicit nAch, and between implicit and explicit nAff) are the congruence coefficients that we have discussed. The six off-diagonal correlations involve mismatches of content domain (e.g., the correlation between implicit nPow and explicit nAff). We have disregarded this omnibus test, because it confounds our hypothesis (i.e., that implicit and explicit measures within the same content domain are correlated if their content is carefully matched) with a hypothesis that is at odds with our hypothesis (i.e., that implicit and explicit measures from entirely different content domains are correlated). Campbell and Fiske (1959) observed that the meaningfulness of the on-diagonal correlations is enhanced when the off-diagonal correlations are weak rather than strong.

References

Ajzen, I., & Fishbein, M. (1977). Attitude-behavior relations: A theoretical analysis and review of empirical research. *Psychological Bulletin, 84,* 888–918.

Atkinson, J. W., & Birch, D. (1970). *The dynamics of action.* New York: Wiley.

Baumann, N., Kaschel, R., & Kuhl, J. (2005). Striving for unwanted goals: Stress-dependent discrepancies between explicit and implicit achievement motives reduce subjective well-being and increase psychosomatic symptoms. *Journal of Personality and Social Psychology, 89,* 781–799.

Biernat, M. (1989). Motives and values to achieve: Different constructs with different effects. *Journal of Personality, 57,* 69–95.

Bilsky, W., & Schwartz, S. H. (2008). Measuring motivations: Integrating content and method. *Personality and Individual Differences, 44,* 1738–1751.

Bollen, K. A. (1989). *Structural equations with latent variables.* New York: Wiley.

Brunstein, J. C. (2010). Implicit motives and explicit goals: The role of motivational congruence in emotional well-being. In O. C. Schultheiss & J. C. Brunstein (Eds.), *Implicit motives* (pp. 347–374). New York: Oxford University Press.

Burwen, L. S., & Campbell, D. T. (1957). The generality of attitudes toward authority and nonauthority figures. *Journal of Abnormal and Social Psychology, 54,* 24–31.

Campbell, D. T., & Fiske, D. (1959). Convergent and discriminant validation by the multitrait–multimethod matrix. *Psychological Bulletin, 56,* 81–105.

Clavadetscher, C. (2003). *Motivation ehrenamtlicher Arbeit im Verein Mahogany Hall, Bern [Motivation for voluntary work in the association Mahogany Hall, Bern].* Bern, Switzerland: Abschlussarbeit NDS BWL/UF, Hochschule für Technik und Architektur.

Csikszentmihalyi, M. (1990). *Flow: The psychology of optimal experience.* New York: Harper & Row.

deCharms, R., Morrison, H. W., Reitman, W., & McClelland, D. C. (1955). Behavioral correlates of directly and indirectly measured achievement motivation. In D. C. McClelland (Ed.), *Studies in motivation* (pp. 414–423). New York: Appleton-Century-Crofts.

Deci, E. L., & Ryan, R. M. (1991). A motivational approach to self: Integration in personality. In R. Dienstbier (Ed.), *Nebraska symposium on motivation: Perspectives on motivation* (Vol. 38, pp. 237–288). Lincoln: University of Nebraska Press.

Edwards, A. L. (1959). *Edwards Personality Preference Schedule manual—revised.* Cleveland, OH: Psychological Corporation.

Edwards, J. R. (2002). Alternatives to difference scores: Polynomial regression analysis and response surface methodology. In F. Drasgow & N. W. Schmitt (Eds.), *Advances in measurement and data analysis* (pp. 350–400). San Francisco, CA: Jossey-Bass.

Epstein, S. (1979). The stability of behavior: I. On predicting most of the people much of the time. *Journal of Personality and Social Psychology, 37,* 1097–1126.

Freud, S. (1909/1989). *Five lectures on psycho-analysis: The standard edition.* New York: Norton & Co.

Guilford, J. P., & Fruchter, B. (1978). *Fundamental statistics in psychology and education* (6th ed.). New York: McGraw-Hill.

Heckhausen, H. (1963). *Hoffnung und Furcht in der Leistungsmotivation [Hope and fear components of achievement motivation].* Meisenheim am Glan, Germany: Anton Hain.

Hofer, J., Busch, H., Bond, M. H., Kärtner, J., Kiessling, F., & Law, R. (2010). Is self-determined functioning a universal prerequisite for motive-goal congruence? Examining the domain of achievement in three cultures. *Journal of Personality, 78,* 747–779.

Hofer, J., Busch, H., Chasiotis, A., & Kiessling, F. (2006). Motive congruence and interpersonal identity status. *Journal of Personality, 74,* 511–541.

Hofer, J., Chasiotis, A., & Campos, D. (2006). Congruence between social values and implicit motives: Effects on life satisfaction across three cultures. *European Journal of Personality, 20,* 305–324.

Kazén, M., & Kuhl, J. (2011). Discrepancies between explicit and implicit power motive decreases managers' well-being. *Motivation and Emotion.* doi: 10.1007/s11031–011-9219–8

Kehr, H. M. (2004). Implicit/explicit motive discrepancies and volitional depletion among managers. *Personality and Social Psychology Bulletin, 30,* 315–327.

Koestner, R., & McClelland, D. C. (1990). Perspectives on competence motivation. In L. A. Pervin (Ed.), *Handbook of personality: Theory and research* (pp. 527–548). New York: Guilford.

Kraus, S. J. (1995). Attitudes and the prediction of behavior: A metaanalysis of the empirical literature. *Personality and Social Psychology Bulletin, 21,* 58–75.

Langan-Fox, J., Sankey, M. J., & Canty, J. M. (2009). Incongruence between implicit and self-attributed achievement motives and psychological well-being: The moderating role of self-directedness, self-disclosure and locus of control. *Personality and Individual Differences, 47,* 99–104.

Langens, T. A. (2007). Congruence between implicit and explicit motives and emotional well-being: The moderating role of activity inhibition. *Motivation and Emotion, 31,* 49–59.

Marcia, J. E. (1966). Development and validation of ego identity status. *Journal of Personality and Social Psychology, 3,* 551–558.

McAuley, P. C., Bond, M. H., & Ng, I. W. (2004). Antecedents of subjective well-being in working Hong Kong adults. *Journal of Psychology in Chinese Societies, 5,* 25–49.

McClelland, D. C. (1951). *Personality.* New York: Sloane.

McClelland, D. C. (1980). Motive dispositions. The merits of operant and respondent measures. In L. Wheeler (Ed.), *Review of personality and social psychology* (Vol. 1, pp. 10–41). Beverly Hills, CA: Sage.

McClelland, D. C. (1987). *Human motivation.* New York: Cambridge University Press.

McClelland, D. C., Atkinson, J. W., Clark, R. A., & Lowell, E. L. (1953). *The achievement motive.* New York: Appleton-Century-Crofts.

McClelland, D. C., Koestner, R., & Weinberger, J. (1989). How do self-attributed and implicit motives differ? *Psychological Review, 96,* 690–702.

McClelland, D. C., & Pilon, D. A. (1983). Sources of adult motives in patterns of parent behavior in early childhood. *Journal of Personality and Social Psychology, 44,* 564–574.

Muraven, M., & Baumeister, R. F. (2000). Self-regulation and depletion of limited resources: Does self-control resemble a muscle? *Psychological Bulletin, 126,* 247–259.

Murray, H. A. (1938). *Explorations in personality.* New York: Oxford.

Raven, J. (1988). Toward measures of high-level competencies: A re-examination of McClelland's distinction between needs and values. *Human Relations, 41,* 281–294.

Rheinberg, F. (2008). Intrinsic motivation and flow experience. In H. Heckhausen & J. Heckhausen (Eds.), *Motivation and action* (pp. 323–348). Cambridge, England: Cambridge University Press.

Rogers, C. R. (1959). A theory of therapy, personality, and interpersonal relationships, as developed in the client-centered framework. In S. Koch (Ed.), *Psychology: A study of a science: Vol. 3. Formulations of the person and the social context* (pp. 184–215). New York: McGraw-Hill.

Schattke, K., Koestner, R., & Kehr, H. M. (2011). Childhood correlates of adult levels of incongruence between implicit and explicit motives. *Motivation and Emotion.* doi, *35*, 306–316.

Schüler, J. (2010). Achievement incentives determine the effects of achievement-motive incongruence on flow experience. *Motivation and Emotion, 34*, 2–14.

Schüler, J., Job, V., Fröhlich, S. M., & Brandstätter, V. (2008). A high implicit affiliation motive does not always make you happy: A corresponding explicit motive and corresponding behavior are further needed. *Motivation and Emotion, 32*, 231–242.

Schüler, J., Job, V., Fröhlich, S. M., & Brandstätter, V. (2009). Dealing with a 'hidden stressor': Emotional disclosure as a coping strategy to overcome the negative effects of motive incongruence on health. *Stress and Health, 25*, 221–233.

Schultheiss, O. C. (2001a). An information processing account of implicit motive arousal. In M. L. Maehr & P. Pintrich (Eds.), *Advances in motivation and achievement* (Vol. 12, pp. 1–41). Greenwich, CT: JAI.

Schultheiss, O. C. (2001b). *Manual for the assessment of hope of success and fear of failure* (English translation of Heckhausen's need for achievement measure). Department of Psychology, University of Michigan, Ann Arbor: Unpublished manuscript.

Schultheiss, O. C., & Brunstein, J. C. (1999). Goal imagery: Bridging the gap between implicit motives and explicit goals. *Journal of Personality, 67*, 1–38.

Schultheiss, O. C., & Murray, T. (2002). *Hope of success/fear of failure questionnaire.* Ann Arbor: University of Michigan, Department of Psychology.

Schultheiss, O. C., Yankova, D., Dirlikov, B., & Schad, D. J. (2009). Are implicit and explicit motive measures statistically independent? A fair and balanced test using the Picture Story Exercise and a cue- and response-matched questionnaire measure. *Journal of Personality Assessment, 91*, 72–81.

Sears, R. R., Maccoby, E. E., & Levin, H. (1957). *Patterns of child rearing.* Evanston, IL: Row Peterson.

Sherwood, J. J. (1966). Self-report and projective measures of achievement and affiliation. *Journal of Consulting Psychology, 30*, 329–337.

Sokolowski, K., Schmalt, H-D., Langens, T. A., & Puca, R. M. (2000). Assessing achievement, affiliation, and power motives all at once: The Multi-Motive Grid (MMG). *Journal of Personality Assessment, 74*, 126–145.

Spangler, W. D. (1992). Validity of questionnaire and TAT measures of need for achievement: Two meta-analyses. *Psychological Bulletin, 112*, 140–154.

Thrash, T. M., Cassidy, S. E., Maruskin, L. A., & Elliot, A. J. (2010). Factors that influence the relation between implicit and explicit motives: A general implicit-explicit congruence framework. In O. C. Schultheiss & J. C. Brunstein (Eds.), *Implicit motives* (pp. 308–346). New York: Oxford University Press.

Thrash, T. M., & Elliot, A. J. (2002). Implicit and self-attributed achievement motives: Concordance and predictive validity. *Journal of Personality, 70*, 729–755.

Thrash, T. M., Elliot, A. J., & Schultheiss, O. C. (2007). Methodological and dispositional predictors of congruence between implicit and explicit need for achievement. *Personality and Social Psychology Bulletin, 33*, 961–974.

Weinberger, J., & McClelland, D. C. (1990). Cognitive versus traditional motivational models: Irreconcilable or complementary? In E. T. Higgins & R. M. Sorrentino (Eds.), *Handbook of motivation and cognition* (Vol. 2, pp. 562–597). New York: Guilford.

Winter, D. G. (1994). *Manual for scoring motive imagery in running text* (4th ed.). Unpublished manuscript, Department of Psychology, University of Michigan, Ann Arbor.

Curiosity and Motivation

Paul J. Silvia

Abstract

Curiosity is an old, intriguing, and vexing construct in the psychology of motivation. This chapter reviews the major strands of thought on curiosity and motivation: *(1)* curiosity as a motive to reduce negative states, such as uncertainty, novelty, arousal, drive, or information gaps; *(2)* curiosity as a source of intrinsic motivation that fosters learning and exploring for their own sakes; and *(3)* curiosity as a stable motivational difference between people that leads to differences in knowledge, goals, achievement, and experience. The scope of psychological thought on curiosity defies a simple integration, but it offers inspiration for researchers curious about why people learn and explore in the absence of obvious external rewards.

Key Words: curiosity, interest, intrinsic motivation, personality

The joys of history are many. Some are guilty joys, like snickering at the weird use of semicolons and em-dashes in old scholarly books, but some are more noble, like recognizing that most of the major problems in psychology were identified prior to the invention of air conditioning, paperback books, or hierarchical linear modeling. Curiosity is an old concept in the study of human motivation, and like many of psychology's venerable problems, the problem of curiosity seems tractable enough to be intriguing but too complicated to ever solve. The history of psychology thus offers modern researchers a lot of interesting takes on curiosity: Most of the major schools of thought in motivation science have had something to say about what curiosity is, how it works, and what it does, if anything.

In this chapter, we'll consider some of the major themes that have emerged in the history of thought on curiosity and motivation. Our goal isn't to develop a unified model of curiosity by reinterpreting past work in terms of a modern theory. History provides many such models, and the fact that there are so many suggests that some history-induced

modesty is called for. Instead, we'll aim to cultivate a sense of perspective—some of psychology's problems should be appreciated rather than solved—and a sense of interest in the diverse, wide-ranging, and occasionally weird body of thought on curiosity.

This chapter extracts and explores the three major strands of thought on curiosity's motivational nature. The first strand proposes that curiosity is a kind of deficit motivation: It motivates people to fill gaps in knowledge, reduce unpleasant uncertainty, and minimize aversive states of drive. The second strand proposes that curiosity is a kind of intrinsic motivation: It motivates people to explore and learn for their own sakes. The third strand proposes individual differences in curiosity: Variation in curiosity translates into big differences in behavior and life outcomes, although the models disagree about the motivational nature of between-person variation.

Curiosity Is Motivation to Reduce Novelty and Uncertainty

Our first major strand of thought on curiosity's motivational nature proposes that curiosity and exploratory behavior represent attempts to reduce novelty and uncertainty. In such models, gaining knowledge and exploring the world are instrumental acts, not ultimate goals in themselves. Instead, learning and exploring allow people to reduce something unpleasant, such as feelings of uncertainty, ignorance, information deprivation, arousal, or drive. Curiosity is thus akin to scratching a mental itch or filling a mental hole.

Motivation psychology's grandest drive-reduction model comes from Clark Hull's body of work, which had a tremendous influence in its time. Hull certainly wasn't the first psychologist to propose a hydraulic approach to motivation, but his model of drive and reinforcement was probably the first major scientific theory of motivation to inspire extensive empirical research. We can't cover the complexity and development of Hull's model here—for the details, curious and motivated readers can consult Hull's (1943, 1952) own books or reviews by his contemporaries (Atkinson, 1964; Bolles, 1967).

In broad strokes, Hull formalized several ideas that had been proposed during the early writings on psychological drives. First, organisms experience a state of drive due to internal deficits or strong stimulation from the environment. Second, reducing the state of drive is rewarding, so behaviors that result in drive reduction are reinforced and hence more likely to happen during later periods of drive. This model thus accommodated both the intensity and direction aspects of motivation, and it integrated problems of motivation with problems of learning. But from the outset curiosity and exploratory behavior seemed hard to explain. Seeking stimulation and approaching unfamiliar stimuli increase drive; within Hull's model, it's not obvious why an organism at rest would cease resting and start exploring.

Unfortunately, the accumulation of facts interfered with Hull's elegant theory, a common occupational hazard in science. One peculiar phenomenon, and one predating Hull's work, was spontaneous alternation. Rats in T-mazes will often alternate between arms of the maze, presumably for no real reason apart from the variety afforded by the arm less traveled (Montgomery, 1951, 1952). Harlow showed similar findings with primates. When given puzzles to work with, the primates often worked on them vigorously in the absence of food rewards; if anything, food rewards and prior food deprivation seemed to interfere with learning these complex tasks (Harlow, 1953). Most fatal, however, was

research that showed that drive-increasing stimuli—such as novelty and intense stimulation—could reinforce learning. For example, the opportunity to view a novel maze compartment or complex display or to manipulate puzzles can reinforce other behaviors (e.g., Butler, 1953; Harlow & McClearn, 1954; Myers & Miller, 1954).

Eventually, it became clear that the classical drive-reduction model simply couldn't accommodate the many demonstrations of curiosity and exploration. Motivation psychologists thus searched for extensions and modifications of Hull's approach. The earliest models simply proposed a new drive, such as a curiosity drive, an exploration drive, or a boredom drive (see Fowler, 1965). These new drives didn't stick, but they were an ironic development—the behavior theorists had often mocked instinct theories of motivation for proposing new instincts to deal with challenging findings.

Berlyne (1960) proposed a particularly clever revision of drive theory in his first major model of curiosity. He suggested that organisms do indeed prefer a low level of arousal, but arousal is non–linearly related to the novelty, complexity, uncertainty, and conflict of stimuli in the environment. He suggested a U-shaped relationship between actual arousal and novelty: Arousal is high when stimuli are very low and very high in novelty. Understimulation and overstimulation thus both increase arousal, which then motivates arousal reduction. Understimulation promoted *diversive exploration*, in which bored organisms search for anything that would boost arousal potential; overstimulation promoted *specific exploration*, in which activated organisms examine the arousal-producing stimulus to reduce its novelty and arousingness. The nonlinear function relating arousal and arousal potential was clever, but it didn't catch on (Berlyne, 1967).

Another modification of Hull's approach was the *optimal arousal* approach, a family of models that proposed that the ideal level of arousal was moderate instead of low (Fiske & Maddi, 1961; Hebb, 1955; Hunt, 1965; Leuba, 1955; Zuckerman, 1969). As a result, many classic Hullian findings could be retained—organisms will act to reduce drive when arousal exceeds the optimal level—while accommodating curiosity. This is a neat idea, but optimal arousal models never inspired much research despite the broad interest in them in their time. As Hull's model ebbed and alternative models of motivation emerged, researchers moved away from the notion that reinforcement depends on arousal (Atkinson, 1964). Once this notion was dropped, optimal arousal models became a compromise for a conflict that no longer existed.

Modern work continues to develop the notion that curiosity is motivated by drive reduction. After reviewing past work on curiosity, Loewenstein (1994) proposed an information gap model of curiosity, which has its roots in information theory. His model proposes that someone becomes curious "when attention becomes focused on a gap in one's knowledge. Such information gaps produce the feeling of deprivation labeled *curiosity*. The curious individual is motivated to obtain the missing information to reduce or eliminate the feeling of deprivation" (p. 87). Information gaps are represented using information theory's uncertainty formula. This model thus has all the hallmarks of a Hullian-inspired curiosity model: Increases in information gaps create an aversive feeling of deprivation, which then motivates exploratory behavior.

The cardinal problem with the information gaps model is that it is a subset of Berlyne's (1960) model. To someone who has read Berlyne's work, Loewenstein's article seems odd. Berlyne first made his name by applying information theory to curiosity—this idea was developed in a *Psychological Review* article (Berlyne, 1957) and in Berlyne's (1960, 1965, 1971) books. Berlyne's concept of *specific curiosity* covers the dynamics of information gaps—uncertainty motivates exploration aimed at reducing it. And as a subset of Berlyne's work, Loewenstein's work is encumbered by the same problems that drive-reduction models of curiosity face, such as the classic studies of exploratory behavior from the 1950s that we reviewed earlier. Berlyne's concept of *diversive curiosity* at least attempted to explain such findings, but the information gaps model has little to say about them. It is in this sense that the information gaps model is a subset of Berlyne's model: They both concern specific curiosity, but only Berlyne's model grappled with the problems of diversive curiosity and novelty seeking. We can thus agree that research supports Loewenstein's predictions, but it is perhaps embarrassing that the predictions come from the 1960s.

With the perspective of history and the benefit of modern research, what can we conclude about the novelty-reduction tradition? People do seek information for many reasons, and some of those reasons resemble scratching mental itches. In the parlance of the lay epistemics model (Kruglanski & Fishman, 2009), people sometimes seek information because of a need for cognitive closure. At the same time, it seems obvious that a model of curiosity founded on reducing unpleasant states will struggle to explain a large literature on exploratory behavior, which suggests that novelty, variety, and uncertainty can themselves be valued and rewarding. As a result, most research on curiosity since the 1970s has shifted from drive models to intrinsic motivation models, the research tradition that we consider next.

Curiosity Is "For Its Own Sake" Motivation

Our second strand of thought views curiosity as a source of "for its own sake" motivation, as a source of inquiring, learning, and exploring in the absence of external sources of reward and punishment. In this tradition, curiosity is motivating in its own right, not because it allows people to reduce an unpleasant state. This tradition is the mainstream modern view of curiosity, so naturally it goes way back. J. Clark Murray (1904), author of an early textbook of psychology, considered curiosity one of the intellectual feelings: "The exertion of intellect, when not overstrained, is itself an agreeable activity.... It is not, therefore, difficult to explain the love of knowledge,—the feeling commonly treated by psychologists under the name of *curiosity*" (p. 470). Typical of his time (cf. McDougall, 1908/1960; Smith & Hall, 1907), there was a tacit snobbery to Murray's view of curiosity:

> During the earlier years of life, until the familiar facts of the world are mastered, curiosity forms a strong and useful impulse. In later life it is only among men of some education that it forms a useful and refining power. In vulgar minds it allies itself with the more petty instincts, and even with the malicious passions of human nature, degenerating into a prurient craving after the knowledge of facts too trivial or too pernicious to be worth knowing.
> (pp. 470, 471)

Although trivial and pernicious are in the eye of the beholder, one wonders what Murray would have thought of social networking Web pages and reality TV shows.

The intrinsic love of knowledge received a deeper treatment by Felix Arnold (1910) and John Dewey (1913), both of whom considered how interest aided education. Arnold viewed interest as having motor aspects and ideational aspects. The motor aspect of interest was essentially motivational— "interest is dynamic, it points ahead, it is a form of striving, of motor impulsion, and it is felt as a conation or motor attitude" (p. 186)—a view that prefigures later models of interest as a source of motivated action. The ideational aspect was essentially cognitive—interest evoked mental images related to the object of interest and the actions and goals it entailed.

John Dewey (1913), the better known of the pair, set forth a model of interest in *Interest and Effort in Education*, a small book that was overshadowed by his many later landmark works. Dewey contended that educators typically used one of two methods to motivate students, neither of which worked well. In the effort method, instructors use self-discipline and willpower as the main mechanisms of learning—if the material is tedious, students must simply slog through it. In the interest method, instructors use diverting, novel, and flashy elements to attract students' attention to basically boring material—"when things have to be *made* interesting, it is because interest itself is wanting," he quipped (p. 11).

As an alternative, Dewey proposed connecting material to students' own interests. Children already had important interests, and new activities could become interesting in their own right if they furthered or connected to an existing interest. Dewey argued that interest was a developmental process rather than a momentary state—it motivated people to immerse themselves in the activity, and it made the process valuable and self-relevant. Dewey's conception of interested action probably represents psychology's first fleshed-out treatment of interest and intrinsic motivation: Interested actions are internalized and autonomous, and over time they cultivate competence and successful development.

In the modern era, the notion of curiosity as a source of intrinsic, for-its-own-sake motivation emerged in many areas of psychology. Within social and personality psychology, the rise of models of intrinsic motivation in the 1970s (Deci, 1975)—particularly the line of work that developed into self-determination theory (Deci & Ryan, 1985, 2000)—is probably the best known example of a model of curiosity as a source of intrinsic motivation. Deci and Ryan (2000, p. 233) have argued that "intrinsically motivated behaviors are those that are freely engaged out of interest without the necessity of separable consequences," and research in this area commonly measures engagement, exploration, and interest (Deci, 1992, 1998; Krapp, 2002). This area of work is reviewed in Chapter 6 of this volume, so here we'll only express awe at the enormous amount of research that self-determination theory has inspired.

Within behavior theory, Berlyne (1971, 1973) proposed a new model of curiosity that shifted from the position that reinforcement and exploration depended on arousal reduction. As an alternative, he proposed that several brain systems interacted to promote exploratory behavior or avoidance. Figure 10.1 depicts how two of these systems relate to positive and negative affect. The first system, the primary reward system, generates positive affect as stimuli become more novel, complex, and uncertain. The positive affect motivates and rewards engagement with new things, so this model qualifies as a for-its-own-sake model of curiosity and motivation. A second system, the primary aversion system, generates negative affect as stimuli become more novel, complex, and uncertain. The aversion system, however, has a temporal offset—it takes higher levels of stimulation for it to kick in—so the combined effect of the two systems is to create positive approach and engagement and then eventual aversive withdrawal as stimuli increase in intensity.

Berlyne's (1971) reward–aversion model is important for historical reasons. Berlyne developed the model as part of a shift into the psychology of aesthetics (e.g., Berlyne, 1972, 1974), and his research team profoundly affected how the small but valiant community of aesthetics researchers thought about aesthetic preference and experience (Silvia, in press). The model itself, however, never stuck, perhaps because behavior theory was obviously waning in the 1970s and emerging approaches to curiosity and to the neuroscience of reward seemed more fresh and exciting.

Within emotion psychology, research on curiosity and interest got its start with the work of Silvan Tomkins (1962), who gave much of early emotion science its start. Tomkins argued that emotions were the organism's primary motivational system. First, at the level of action dynamics, emotions made some events significant and thus gave them priority. Tomkins proposed a central assembly that

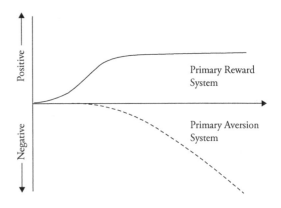

Fig. 10.1. Berlyne's model of reward and aversion systems.

organized the components of behavior into effective action. People can't do many behaviors at once, so they need a mechanism that elevates some tasks and situations over others. Tomkins's theory thus falls into the category of prioritization models of motivation, which tackle the problems of why people are doing a particular thing instead of something else and how action is stopped and redirected (cf. Atkinson & Birch, 1970).

Second, at the level of life span development, Tomkins proposed that emotions have broad adaptational functions. Darwin's (1872/1998) work on facial expressions heavily influenced Tomkins, whose theory of emotion was one of the first modern emotion theories colored by adaptational concepts. He gave particular attention to the communicative functions of emotion, such as expressions in the face, voice, and body; how the emotions developed in early childhood; and how emotions over the life span shaped a person's personality and worldview (Tomkins, 1965, 1979).

Curiosity appeared in Tomkins's (1962) work as the basic emotion of *interest–excitement*, which he felt was the "affect which has been most seriously neglected" (p. 337). Interest makes new things appealing and thus provides an innate incentive for engaging with new, unfamiliar things. Events that are novel enough to evoke interest—but not novel enough to evoke fear—thus gained priority in the central assembly over mundane events that evoked no affect. For example, people do forego food and sleep to pursue interesting things, which fits a priority view of motivation—interest make those actions more significant—but poses yet another problem for drive models of motivation. In the long run, the broad adaptational function served by interest is to motivate learning and development. In early childhood, interest is an engine of perceptual and cognitive development; in adulthood, it is the source of intrinsically motivated learning and intellectual creativity.

Since Tomkins's work, interest has been a controversial emotion: Some emotion theories retained it (e.g., Ellsworth & Smith, 1988; Izard, 1977) and others omitted it (e.g., Ekman, 1992; Lazarus, 1991). Nevertheless, a lot of work has accumulated on interest's emotional qualities (Silvia, 2006, 2008). For example, researchers have examined the production and recognition of facial and vocal expressions of interest (Banse & Scherer, 1996; Reeve, 1993; Sauter & Scott, 2007), the cognitive appraisals that predict interest and distinguish it from other states (Silvia, 2005, 2010; Turner & Silvia, 2006),

and how interest develops and operates in infancy and early childhood (Izard, 1978; Langsdorf, Izard, Rayias, & Hembree, 1983).

Most relevant to motivation, however, is the body of work on interest's influence on behavior. A lot of research supports Tomkins's view of interest as a source of intrinsic motivation. One line of work considers the action tendencies associated with being interested. Interest predicts many behavioral markers of exploration and knowledge seeking, such as how long people look at or listen to interesting things and how long they spend exploring objects or working on tasks (Berlyne, 1971; Sansone & Smith, 2000; Sansone & Thoman, 2005). Oddly enough, interest predicts behavioral exploration much more strongly than enjoyment does (Silvia, 2006). Another line of work considers learning outcomes, particularly text comprehension and educational achievement. Educational research has found that people get better grades in interesting classes, use deeper level reading and studying strategies for interesting texts and domains, and retain interesting material better (Hidi, 1990, 2001; Krapp, 1999, 2002; Sadoski & Paivio, 2001; Silvia, 2006).

For the most part, the intrinsic motivation approach to curiosity is more vibrant than the drive-reduction approach—it's the backdrop for the majority of contemporary work. The three domains we have covered—social and personality psychology, behavior theory, and emotion psychology—capture most of modern research. Social and personality psychology contains much of the experimental research on situational and dispositional influences on curiosity and interest; behavior theory has evolved into mature psychobiological models of novelty seeking and reward, such as Panksepp's (1998) SEEKING system; and emotion psychology continues to explore what makes things interesting, how interest operates across domains, and how interest develops.

Some People Are More Curious Than Others

Our third strand of thought concerns individual differences in curiosity. William McDougall (1908/1960), the notorious and maligned instinct theorist, was one of the first psychologists to speculate about stable between-person variability in curiosity. In modern terms, his instincts are modular and automated motivational systems that are evoked by stimuli and opportunities in the environment. Instinctive action has a cognitive aspect (an apprehension of an object), a behavioral tendency (a motivational urge to act), and an affective aspect (an emotional feeling).

McDougall proposed an instinct of curiosity, which was the instinct associated with exploratory behavior—the impulse "to approach and examine more closely the object that excites it" (p. 49)—and with the emotional state of wonder. He argued that "the native excitant of the instinct would seem to be any object similar to, yet perceptibly different from, familiar objects habitually noticed" (p. 47), while recognizing that higher levels of novelty and uncertainty evoked fear. It is tempting to make fun of poor McDougall and his many instincts, but for many decades the notion of a curiosity instinct was the prevailing model of the motivational basis of curiosity, and it had a big influence (e.g., Cameron, 1922).

McDougall (1908/1960) thought that the curiosity instinct was less important to humans, so he believed that it was more variable as a result:

> This instinct, being one whose exercise is not of prime importance to the individual, exhibits great individual differences as regards its innate strength; and these differences are apt to be increased during the course of life, the impulse growing weaker for lack of use in those in whom it is innately weak, stronger through exercise in those in whom it is innately strong. In men of the latter type it may become the main source of intellectual energy and effort; to its impulse we certainly owe most of the disinterested labors of the highest types of intellect.
> (p. 50)

This passage is doubly intriguing: It proposes individual differences in curiosity, a topic that has since been widely studied, and it suggests that these differences become exaggerated across the life span, a topic that hasn't.

Modern individual differences research got started a long time after McDougall's work, and models of trait-like curiosity represent both themes we have considered so far. It's hard to organize the hurly-burly world of self-report curiosity scales—there are a lot of scales and a lot of constructs. Some models have their roots in Berlyne's models of curiosity. Researchers have developed scales to measure individual differences in epistemic, sensory, specific, and diversive forms of curiosity (e.g., Collins, Litman, & Spielberger, 2004; Litman & Spielberger, 2003), and Spielberger and Starr (1994) proposed that trait curiosity corresponds to Berlyne's (1971) primary reward system and that trait anxiety corresponds to the primary aversion system. People high in trait curiosity can

thus tolerate more uncertainty and novelty before withdrawing.

For the most part, recent research has focused on global curiosity as a source of intrinsic motivation. Kashdan (2004, 2009), for example, approaches individual differences in curiosity from the perspective of positive psychology. In Kashdan's work, curiosity is a tendency to notice, seek, value, and embrace novelty, uncertainty, and challenge. The Curiosity and Exploration Inventory, a brief self-report scale, was developed to capture this model of curiosity (Kashdan et al., 2009; Kashdan, Rose, & Fincham, 2004). The model is explicitly motivational, in that curious people respond to novelty with an appetitive, approach-oriented response. As a consequence of exploring new and challenging things across the life span, curious people are expected to have a wide range of positive outcomes (Kashdan & Silvia, 2009; Silvia & Kashdan, 2009). For example, curious people typically have better academic achievement (Kashdan & Yuen, 2007), higher subjective well-being (Gallagher & Lopez, 2007), and a stronger sense that their daily lives and goals are meaningful (Kashdan & Steger, 2007).

Another model of trait curiosity, Litman's (2005) I-D model, combines the drive reduction and intrinsic motivation traditions of curiosity research. Litman proposes that curiosity consists of two major facets: curiosity as a feeling of interest (I-curiosity) and curiosity as a feeling of deprivation (D-curiosity). Interest is curiosity motivated by a desire to seek information for its own sake, whereas deprivation is curiosity motivated by a desire to reduce the uncertainty and frustration caused by knowledge gaps. The I-D model is thus a compromise between the two competing traditions. Most of the work testing Litman's model has used measures of individual differences (Litman & Jimerson, 2004). Curiosity scales seem to sort into these two I and D factors (Litman & Silvia, 2006), which are highly correlated, and the I and D traits predict different kinds of knowledge seeking in response to knowledge gaps (Litman, Hutchins, & Russon, 2005).

Most research on individual differences in curiosity has been conducted as part of research on *openness to experience*, a higher order trait that encompasses curiosity and related constructs. McCrae and Sutin (2009) describe open people as "imaginative, sensitive to art and beauty, emotionally differentiated, behaviorally flexible, intellectually curious, and liberal in values" (p. 258). Closed people, in contrast, are "down-to-earth, uninterested in art, shallow in affect, set in their ways, lacking curiosity, and traditional in values" (p. 258). Curiosity is thus one of several facets of openness.

Of the five factors, openness to experience has been the most controversial. It is the least well captured by trait terms, so the lexical tradition in personality research has yielded inconsistent pictures of how openness to experience is represented in natural languages (De Raad, 1994; Goldberg, 1994; McCrae, 1994). As a result, models of openness to experience define the construct somewhat differently. Some models cast openness to experience as an intellectual trait (Goldberg, 1990) or propose that openness and intellect are primary facets of the higher order trait of openness to experience (DeYoung, Quilty, & Peterson, 2007).

Differences between models aside, openness to experience is an important source of variability in curiosity. The literature on openness is massive, so we'll focus on two domains: aesthetic experience and creativity. Research on aesthetics finds wide differences in how interesting and pleasing people find works of art. People high in openness to experience generally find art more interesting than people low in openness (e.g., Feist & Brady, 2004), possess more expertise and knowledge related to the arts (Silvia, 2007; Silvia & Berg, 2011), listen to more complicated kinds of music in everyday life (Chamorro-Premuzic & Furnham, 2007; Rentfrow & Gosling, 2003), experience aesthetic chills—a feeling of goose bumps and chills down the spine (Grewe, Kopiez, & Altenmüller, 2009)—more often in response to art (McCrae, 2007), and find abstract, disturbing, and bizarre art intriguing and appealing (Rawlings, 2003; Rawlings, Twomey, Burns, & Morris, 2002).

In addition to their interest in the arts, people high in openness to experience are more creative, in several senses of the word. Openness to experience consistently appears as a major predictor of creativity across many domains (Feist, 1998, 2006), and it seems to foster creativity in part for motivational reasons. To do creative work, people must value novelty: They should see merit in doing something differently and in challenging established ideas. People who like things the way they are and who prefer the traditional over the novel lack the basic mindset needed for innovative behavior (Joy, 2004).

A large literature shows that people high in openness to experience are more creative. First, openness predicts divergent thinking, a creative cognitive trait (McCrae, 1987; Silvia et al., 2008, 2009). Second, cross-sectional studies show that people high in openness behave more creatively, ranging from everyday creativity (e.g., having creative hobbies) to significant creative accomplishment (Carson, Peterson, & Higgins, 2005; Silvia et al., 2009). Third, life span research shows that openness to experience predicts the accumulation of creative accomplishment and the likelihood of becoming creatively eminent. Feist and Barron (2003), for example, found that indicators of openness to experience measured at age 27 predicted creative achievements at age 72.

McDougall seems to have been on to something with his notion of individual differences in curiosity: Curious people and incurious people are pretty different. Modern researchers would disagree with McDougall that curiosity is both more variable and less important than other motivational traits, but they would agree that curiosity is important to achievements across the life span.

Conclusion

Curiosity touches on some of motivational psychology's most vexing problems: Why do people do something instead of nothing? Why do people persist on seemingly trivial activities in the absence of obvious external rewards and in the presence of more important goals? Why do apparently trivial things capture attention and action? The wellsprings of action proposed by motivation theories are usually abstract and vaunted, but the kinds of actions motivated by curiosity are usually mundane and capricious. Nevertheless, curiosity does seem to be an important mechanism in the development of knowledge and competence, so it's reassuring that something is coming out of the hours people spend scrambling around playgrounds, reading low-brow books, and street tuning old Honda Civics.

Future Directions

1. How can the different strands of thought on curiosity be connected? The urge to weave beats strong in the hearts of motivation psychologists. Within each strand, there could be interesting bridges. In the intrinsic motivation strand, there could be fertile connections between self-determination theory and emotion psychology, two areas that haven't had much to do with each other. In the drive-reduction strand, researchers could explore the value of a single broad model—something akin to Kruglanski's (2004) lay epistemics model or Litman's (2005) I-D model—for unifying curious and incurious motives for seeking knowledge. Between each strand, researchers could consider bridges between

intrinsic motivation and drive reduction. Such bridges would shift what the field means by curiosity, but they could illuminate the broader workings of cognitive motives.

2. How do curious traits influence curious states? Many models of individual differences invoke motivational mechanisms, largely along the lines of drive reduction, intrinsic motivation, or both. Despite this conceptual overlap, there isn't much integration between the state and the trait approaches to curiosity—with many interesting exceptions, naturally—perhaps because self-report assessment and cross-sectional designs dominate individual differences research. Future work on curious people ought to tackle the paradigms used in state research, particularly the measures of experience, cognition, and behavior used to illuminate knowledge seeking and exploration.

3. What does the midrange level of curious motivation look like? Most work on curiosity has explored situational aspects or stable individual differences. The midrange—the level of idiosyncratic personal goals—remains obscure. In everyday curiosity, people are probably exploring activities and domains that they have engaged with before and know a lot about (Prenzel, 1992)—their hobbies and interests are important to understanding how curiosity influences their behavior. So far, most of the work on hobbies and interests has been done in educational research, which emphasizes a distinction between situational interest and individual interest (Chapter 11, this volume; Schiefele, 2009). Future work should examine how interests relate to situational states and enduring traits (e.g., Durik & Harackiewicz, 2007) and how idiosyncratic interests develop (Hidi & Renninger, 2006; Silvia, 2006).

References

Arnold, F. (1910). *Attention and interest: A study in psychology and education.* New York: Macmillan.

Atkinson, J. W. (1964). *An introduction to motivation.* New York: Van Nostrand.

Atkinson, J. W., & Birch, D. (1970). *The dynamics of action.* New York: Wiley.

Banse, R., & Scherer, K. R. (1996). Acoustic profiles in vocal emotion expressions. *Journal of Personality and Social Psychology, 70*, 614–636.

Berlyne, D. E. (1957). Uncertainty and conflict: A point of contact between information-theory and behavior-theory concepts. *Psychological Review, 64*, 329–339.

Berlyne, D. E. (1960). *Conflict, arousal, and curiosity.* New York: McGraw–Hill.

Berlyne, D. E. (1965). *Structure and direction in thinking.* New York: Wiley.

Berlyne, D. E. (1967). Arousal and reinforcement. *Nebraska Symposium on Motivation, 15*, 1–110.

Berlyne, D. E. (1971). *Aesthetics and psychobiology.* New York: Appleton-Century-Crofts.

Berlyne, D. E. (1972). Ends and means of experimental aesthetics. *Canadian Journal of Psychology, 26*, 303–325.

Berlyne, D. E. (1973). The vicissitudes of aplopathematic and thelematoscopic pneumatology (or the hydrography of hedonism). In D. E. Berlyne & K. B. Madsen (Eds.), *Pleasure, reward, preference* (pp. 1–33). New York: Academic Press.

Berlyne, D. E. (Ed.). (1974). *Studies in the new experimental aesthetics: Steps toward an objective psychology of aesthetic appreciation.* Washington, DC: Hemisphere.

Bolles, R. C. (1967). *Theory of motivation.* New York: Harper & Row.

Butler, R. A. (1953). Discrimination learning by rhesus monkeys to visual-exploration motivation. *Journal of Comparative and Physiological Psychology, 46*, 95–98.

Cameron, E. H. (1922). *Psychology and the school.* New York: Century.

Carson, S. H., Peterson, J. B., & Higgins, D. M. (2005). Reliability, validity, and factor structure of the Creative Achievement Questionnaire. *Creativity Research Journal, 17*, 37–50.

Chamorro-Premuzic, T., & Furnham, A. (2007). Personality and music: Can traits explain how people use music in everyday life? *British Journal of Psychology, 98*, 175–185.

Collins, R. P., Litman, J. A., & Spielberger, C. D. (2004). The measurement of perceptual curiosity. *Personality and Individual Differences, 36*, 1127–1141.

Darwin, C. (1872/1998). *The expression of the emotions in man and animals* (3rd ed.). New York: Oxford University Press.

Deci, E. L. (1975). *Intrinsic motivation.* New York: Plenum.

Deci, E. L. (1992). The relation of interest to the motivation of behavior: A self-determination theory perspective. In K. A. Renninger, S. Hidi, & A. Krapp (Eds.), *The role of interest in learning and development* (pp. 43–70). Hillsdale, NJ: Lawrence Erlbaum Associates.

Deci, E. L. (1998). The relation of interest to motivation and human needs—The self-determination theory viewpoint. In L. Hoffman, A. Krapp, K. A. Renninger, & J. Baumert (Eds.), *Interest and learning* (pp. 146–162). Kiel, Germany: IPN.

Deci, E. L., & Ryan, R. M. (1985). *Intrinsic motivation and self-determination in human behavior.* New York: Plenum.

Deci, E. L., & Ryan, R. M. (2000). The "what" and "why" of goal pursuits: Human needs and the self-determination of behavior. *Psychological Inquiry, 11*, 227–268.

De Raad, B. (1994). An expedition in search of a fifth universal factor: Key issues in the lexical approach. *European Journal of Personality, 8*, 229–250.

Dewey, J. (1913). *Interest and effort in education.* Boston, MA: Riverside.

DeYoung, C. G., Quilty, L. C., & Peterson, J. B. (2007). Between facets and domains: 10 aspects of the Big Five. *Journal of Personality and Social Psychology, 93*, 880–896.

Durik, A. M., & Harackiewicz, J. M. (2007). Different strokes for different folks: Individual interest as a moderator of the effects of situational factors on task interest. *Journal of Educational Psychology, 99*, 597–610.

Ekman, P. (1992). An argument for basic emotions. *Cognition and Emotion, 6*, 169–200.

Ellsworth, P. C., & Smith, C. A. (1988). Shades of joy: Patterns of appraisal differentiating positive emotions. *Cognition and Emotion, 2*, 301–331.

Feist, G. J. (1998). A meta-analysis of personality in scientific and artistic creativity. *Personality and Social Psychology Review, 2*, 290–309.

Feist, G. J. (2006). *The psychology of science and the origins of the scientific mind*. New Haven, CT: Yale University Press.

Feist, G. J., & Barron, F. X. (2003). Predicting creativity from early to late adulthood: Intellect, potential, and personality. *Journal of Research in Personality, 37*, 62–88.

Feist, G. J., & Brady, T. R. (2004). Openness to experience, nonconformity, and the preference for abstract art. *Empirical Studies of the Arts, 22*, 77–89.

Fiske, D. W., & Maddi, S. R. (1961). A conceptual framework. In D. W. Fiske & S. R. Maddi (Eds.), *Functions of varied experience* (pp. 11–56). Homewood, IL: Dorsey.

Fowler, H. (1965). *Curiosity and exploratory behavior*. New York: Macmillan.

Gallagher, M. W., & Lopez, S. J. (2007). Curiosity and well-being. *Journal of Positive Psychology, 2*, 236–248.

Goldberg, L. R. (1990). An alternative "description of personality": The Big Five factor structure. *Journal of Personality and Social Psychology, 59*, 1216–1229.

Goldberg, L. R. (1994). Resolving a scientific embarrassment: A comment on the articles in this special issue. *European Journal of Personality, 8*, 351–356.

Grewe, O., Kopiez, R., & Altenmüller, E. (2009). The chill parameter: Goose bumps and shivers as promising measures in emotion research. *Music Perception, 27*, 61–74.

Harlow, H. F. (1953). Mice, monkeys, men, and motives. *Psychological Review, 60*, 23–32.

Harlow, H. F., & McClearn, G. E. (1954). Object discrimination learned by monkeys on the basis of manipulation motives. *Journal of Comparative and Physiological Psychology, 47*, 73–76.

Hebb, D. O. (1955). Drives and the C.N.S. (conceptual nervous system). *Psychological Review, 62*, 243–254.

Hidi, S. (1990). Interest and its contribution as a mental resource for learning. *Review of Educational Research, 60*, 549–571.

Hidi, S. (2001). Interest, reading, and learning: Theoretical and practical considerations. *Educational Psychology Review, 13*, 191–209.

Hidi, S., & Renninger, K. A. (2006). The four-phase model of interest development. *Educational Psychologist, 41*, 111–127.

Hull, C. L. (1943). *Principles of behavior*. New York: Appleton–Century–Crofts.

Hull, C. L. (1952). *A behavior system*. New Haven, CT: Yale University Press.

Hunt, J. M. (1965). Intrinsic motivation and its role in psychological development. *Nebraska Symposium on Motivation, 13*, 189–282.

Izard, C. E. (1977). *Human emotions*. New York: Plenum.

Izard, C. E. (1978). On the development of emotions and emotion–cognition relationships in infancy. In M. Lewis & L. A. Rosenblum (Eds.), *The development of affect* (pp. 389–413). New York: Plenum.

Joy, S. (2004). Innovation motivation: The need to be different. *Creativity Research Journal, 16*, 313–330.

Kashdan, T. B. (2004). Curiosity. In C. Peterson & M. E. P. Seligman (Eds.), *Character strengths and virtues: A handbook and classification* (pp. 125–141). New York: Oxford University Press.

Kashdan, T. B. (2009). *Curious? Discover the missing ingredient to a fulfilling life*. New York: William Morrow.

Kashdan, T. B., Gallagher, M. W., Silvia, P. J., Winterstein, B. P., Breen, W. E., Terhar, D., & Steger, M. F. (2009). The curiosity and exploration inventory–II: Development, factor structure, and psychometrics. *Journal of Research in Personality, 43*, 987–998.

Kashdan, T. B., Rose, P., & Fincham, F. D. (2004). Curiosity and exploration: Facilitating positive subjective experiences and personal growth opportunities. *Journal of Personality Assessment, 82*, 291–305.

Kashdan, T. B., & Silvia, P. J. (2009). Curiosity and interest: The benefits of thriving on novelty and challenge. In C. R. Snyder & S. J. Lopez (Ed.), *Handbook of positive psychology* (2nd ed., pp. 367–374). New York: Oxford University Press.

Kashdan, T. B., & Steger, M. F. (2007). Curiosity and pathways to well-being and meaning in life: Traits, states, and everyday behaviors. *Motivation and Emotion, 31*, 159–173.

Kashdan, T. B., & Yuen, M. (2007). Whether highly curious students thrive academically depends on the learning environment of their school: A study of Hong Kong adolescents. *Motivation and Emotion, 31*, 260–270.

Krapp, A. (1999). Interest, motivation and learning: An educational-psychological perspective. *European Journal of Psychology of Education, 14*, 23–40.

Krapp, A. (2002). An educational-psychological theory of interest and its relation to self-determination theory. In E. L. Deci & R. M. Ryan (Eds.), *Handbook of self-determination research* (pp. 405–427). Rochester, NY: University of Rochester Press.

Kruglanski, A. W. (2004). *The psychology of closed-mindedness*. New York: Psychology Press.

Kruglanski, A. W., & Fishman, S. (2009). The need for cognitive closure. In M. R. Leary & R. H. Hoyle (Eds.), *Handbook of individual differences in social behavior* (pp. 343–353). New York: Guilford.

Langsdorf, P., Izard, C. E., Rayias, M., & Hembree, E. A. (1983). Interest expression, visual fixation, and heart rate changes in 2- to 8-month old infants. *Developmental Psychology, 19*, 375–386.

Lazarus, R. S. (1991). *Emotion and adaptation*. New York: Oxford University Press.

Leuba, C. (1955). Toward some integration of learning theories: The concept of optimal stimulation. *Psychological Reports, 1*, 27–33.

Litman, J. A. (2005). Curiosity and the pleasures of learning: Wanting and liking new information. *Cognition and Emotion, 19*, 793–814.

Litman, J. A., Hutchins, T. L., & Russon, R. K. (2005). Epistemic curiosity, feeling-of-knowing, and exploratory behavior. *Cognition and Emotion, 19*, 559–582.

Litman, J. A., & Jimerson, T. L. (2004). The measurement of curiosity as a feeling of deprivation. *Journal of Personality Assessment, 82*, 147–157.

Litman, J. A., & Silvia, P. J. (2006). The latent structure of trait curiosity: Evidence for interest and deprivation curiosity dimensions. *Journal of Personality Assessment, 86*, 318–328.

Litman, J. A., & Spielberger, C. D. (2003). Measuring epistemic curiosity and its diversive and specific components. *Journal of Personality Assessment, 80*, 75–86.

Loewenstein, G. (1994). The psychology of curiosity: A review and reinterpretation. *Psychological Bulletin, 116*, 75–98.

McCrae, R. R. (1987). Creativity, divergent thinking, and openness to experience. *Journal of Personality and Social Psychology, 52*, 1258–1265.

McCrae, R. R. (1994). Openness to experience: Expanding the boundaries of Factor V. *European Journal of Personality, 8*, 251–272.

McCrae, R. R. (2007). Aesthetic chills as a universal marker of openness to experience. *Motivation and Emotion, 31*, 5–11.

McCrae, R. R., & Sutin, A. R. (2009). Openness to experience. In M. R. Leary & R. H. Hoyle (Eds.), *Handbook of individual differences in social behavior* (pp. 257–273). New York: Guilford.

McDougall, W. (1908/1960). *An introduction to social psychology.* London: Methuen.

Montgomery, K. C. (1951). The relationship between exploratory behavior and spontaneous alternation in the white rat. *Journal of Comparative and Physiological Psychology, 44*, 582–589.

Montgomery, K. C. (1952). A test of two explanations of spontaneous alternation. *Journal of Comparative and Physiological Psychology, 45*, 287–293.

Murray, J. C. (1904). *An introduction to psychology based on the author's handbook of psychology.* Boston, MA: Little, Brown, & Company.

Myers, A. K., & Miller, N. E. (1954). Failure to find a learned drive based on hunger; Evidence for learning motivated by "exploration." *Journal of Comparative and Physiological Psychology, 47*, 428–436.

Panksepp, J. (1998). *Affective neuroscience: The foundations of human and animal emotions.* New York: Oxford University Press.

Prenzel, M. (1992). The selective persistence of interest. In K. A. Renninger, S. Hidi, & A. Krapp (Eds.), *The role of interest in learning and development* (pp. 71–98). Hillsdale, NJ: Lawrence Erlbaum Associates.

Rawlings, D. (2003). Personality correlates of liking for "unpleasant" paintings and photographs. *Personality and Individual Differences, 23*, 395–410.

Rawlings, D., Twomey, F., Burns, E., & Morris, S. (2002). Personality, creativity, and aesthetic preference: Comparing psychoticism, sensation seeking, schizotypy, and openness to experience. *Empirical Studies of the Arts, 16*, 153–178.

Reeve, J. (1993). The face of interest. *Motivation and Emotion, 17*, 353–375.

Rentfrow, P. J., & Gosling, S. D. (2003). The do re mi's of everyday life: The structure and personality correlates of music preferences. *Journal of Personality and Social Psychology, 84*, 1236–1256.

Sadoski, M., & Paivio, A. (2001). *Imagery and text: A dual coding theory of reading and writing.* Mahwah, NJ.: Lawrence Erlbaum Associates.

Sansone, C., & Smith, J. L. (2000). Interest and self-regulation: The relation between having to and wanting to. In C. Sansone & J. M. Harackiewicz (Eds.), *Intrinsic and extrinsic motivation* (pp. 341–372). San Diego, CA: Academic.

Sansone, C., & Thoman, D. B. (2005). Interest as the missing motivator in self-regulation. *European Psychologist, 10*, 175–186.

Sauter, D. A., & Scott, S. K. (2007). More than one kind of happiness: Can we recognize vocal expressions of different positive states? *Motivation and Emotion, 31*, 192–199.

Schiefele, U. (2009). Situational and individual interest. In K. R. Wenzel & A. Wigfield (Eds.), *Handbook of motivation at school* (pp. 197–222). New York: Routledge.

Silvia, P. J. (2005). What is interesting? Exploring the appraisal structure of interest. *Emotion, 5*, 89–102.

Silvia, P. J. (2006). *Exploring the psychology of interest.* New York: Oxford University Press.

Silvia, P. J. (2007). Knowledge-based assessment of expertise in the arts: Exploring aesthetic fluency. *Psychology of Aesthetics, Creativity, and the Arts, 1*, 247–249.

Silvia, P. J. (2008). Interest—The curious emotion. *Current Directions in Psychological Science, 17*, 57–60.

Silvia, P. J. (2010). Confusion and interest: The role of knowledge emotions in aesthetic experience. *Psychology of Aesthetics, Creativity, and the Arts, 4*, 75–80.

Silvia, P. J. (in press). Human emotions and aesthetic experience: An overview of empirical aesthetics. In A. Shimamura (Ed.), *Aesthetic science: Connecting minds, brains, and experience.* New York: Oxford University Press.

Silvia, P. J., & Berg, C. (2011). Finding movies interesting: How expertise and appraisals influence the aesthetic experience of film. *Empirical Studies of the Arts, 29*, 73–88.

Silvia, P. J., & Kashdan, T. B. (2009). Interesting things and curious people: Exploration and engagement as transient states and enduring strengths. *Social and Personality Psychology Compass, 3*, 785–797.

Silvia, P. J., Nusbaum, E. C., Berg, C., Martin, C., & O'Connor, A. (2009). Openness to experience, plasticity, and creativity: Exploring lower-order, higher-order, and interactive effects. *Journal of Research in Personality, 43*, 1087–1090.

Silvia, P. J., Winterstein, B. P., Willse, J. T., Barona, C. M., Cram, J. T., Hess, K. I., ...Richard, C. A. (2008). Assessing creativity with divergent thinking tasks: Exploring the reliability and validity of new subjective scoring methods. *Psychology of Aesthetics, Creativity, and the Arts, 2*, 68–85.

Smith, T. L., & Hall, G. S. (1907). Curiosity and interest. In T. L. Smith (Ed.), *Aspects of child life and education* (pp. 84–141). Boston, MA: Ginn & Company.

Spielberger, C. D., & Starr, L. M. (1994). Curiosity and exploratory behavior. In H. F. O'Neil, Jr. & M. Drillings (Eds.), *Motivation: Theory and research* (pp. 221–243). Hillsdale, NJ: Lawrence Erlbaum Associates.

Tomkins, S. S. (1962). *Affect, imagery, consciousness. Vol. 1: The positive affects.* New York: Springer.

Tomkins, S. S. (1965). Affect and the psychology of knowledge. In S. S. Tomkins & C. E. Izard (Eds.), *Affect, cognition, and personality* (pp. 72–97). New York: Springer.

Tomkins, S. S. (1979). Script theory: Differential magnification of affects. *Nebraska Symposium on Motivation, 26*, 201–236.

Turner, S. A., Jr., & Silvia, P. J. (2006). Must interesting things be pleasant? A test of competing appraisal structures. *Emotion, 6*, 670–674.

Zuckerman, M. (1969). Theoretical formulations. In J. P. Zubeck (Ed.), *Sensory deprivation* (pp. 407–432). New York: Appleton–Century.

Interest and Its Development

K. Ann Renninger *and* Stephanie Su

Abstract

This chapter focuses on interest as a cognitive and affective motivational variable that develops and can be supported to develop. Interest and interest development as described by Hidi and Renninger's (2006) Four-Phase Model of Interest Development are *(a)* defined and then *(b)* contextualized in light of other conceptualizations that focus on specific aspects of interest (such as emotion, experience, task features, value, and vocational interest) and issues pertaining to the operationalization and measurement of interest. Following this, research addressing the development of interest is overviewed, with particular attention to *(a)* the triggering of interest in both earlier and later phases of interest, *(b)* maintaining interest once it has been triggered, *(c)* fluctuations in interest, and *(d)* shifts between phases in the development of interest. Finally, a Punnett square is employed to suggest next steps and open questions in the study of interest development.

Key Words: achievement, affect, interest, interest development, knowledge, metacognition, value

Introduction

This chapter overviews research that contributes to understanding interest as a cognitive and affective motivational variable that both develops and can be supported to develop. It includes studies that have been conducted in varying domains using different methods. The chapter centers on aspects of development that are not yet well understood. It begins with the case of Helen Keller and an analysis of a part of her autobiography, *The Story of My Life* (Keller, 1903).

Helen Keller was the first blind person to receive a bachelor's degree. She became a world-famous activist, wrote books about her experience and beliefs, and is now widely considered one of the most inspirational people of the 20th century. Through the support of her tutor Anne Sullivan, Helen "discovered" language, communication, and society. Helen's case, particularly as it is presented in her

autobiography, is used to illustrate critical aspects in the development of interest, the conditions that support interest to develop and deepen, with which researchers and practitioners continue to wrestle. These are elaborated on later in this chapter, starting with the initial triggering of interest through to the point where she asks questions, reflects on these, and independently follows through to seek answers and feedback. Helen's case of interest development is paraphrased briefly below:

> Rendered both deaf and blind at a young age, Helen stumbled around like a feral animal for many years. The adults around her were unable to reach or tame her, pitying her and letting her do anything she wanted. When Anne Sullivan, a young and financially strapped tutor, was hired to help Helen, she found a bright but horribly spoiled 7-year-old girl who was unable to see the implications of her own behavior

and its effect on other people. Anne did not approve of the way that Helen grabbed food from various people's dinner plates and broke things during temper tantrums. Anne disciplined, and Helen fought back both physically and with pranks.

Anne recognized that Helen was bright and decided to teach her how to finger spell, thinking that this might help her to communicate with others. Anne would put an object in one of Helen's hands, and in the other quickly spell the name for the object. Even though Helen could imitate well, she did not understand what Anne was trying to teach her. Her patience ran out quickly, and the lessons would end in tears and yelling.

Everything changed one day when Anne pumped water into Helen's hands and spelled "water." The event appeared to trigger Helen to make a connection between the fluttering movement in her hand and the cold liquid spilling over her skin. All of a sudden, Helen realized what Anne had been trying to show her as she had doggedly spelled word after word into her hand all those weeks. From then on, Anne could hardly keep up with Helen, who dragged her around demanding a word for everything she encountered, everything that had been there before.

Anne's efforts to help Helen make connections between signs and what they represent could be described as potential triggers for interest, and the incident with the water was a trigger that worked because with it she discovered the connection between the sign and water. We do not know why or how the trigger of the water served as a catalyst. In fact, Helen thought at first that this was some kind of game. It seems likely that many factors contributed to her revelation.

We know, however, that a few elements of Helen's story are particularly important to the description and understanding of interest development. First, the development of her interest involved extended, seemingly ineffective, external support before she made a connection between the finger spelling and the water and then engaged the challenge of revisiting the prior lessons that had been so very frustrating to her. She did not make a decision to be interested in communication. Rather, it seems that she needed to encounter the connection in order to communicate, and it was the connection that triggered her eventual interest in communication more generally.

Second, Helen was not aware that she was developing an interest as her tutor worked with her. The potential triggers of finger spelling did not "take"

until the incident with the water. Even at that point, it is not clear that she would have described finger spelling, or communication more generally, as something in which she was personally invested and that would hold her interest.

Third, Helen's interest developed in a context where her strengths and needs were accounted for and she was not being graded or assessed: Anne worked with her so that she would understand and be able to think and explore. She was extremely successful by any number of measures, once her interest began to develop.

Fourth, Helen's interest continued to develop because, once she made the connection between finger spelling and communicating, she then had curiosity questions for which she wanted answers—curiosity questions are questions that are novel to the learner but may not be novel to others (Renninger, 2000). Finding answers to these questions led her to continue to stretch her own understanding.

Fifth, once she began asking curiosity questions, Helen also began to self-regulate and to explore and seize opportunities to learn—opportunities that were ostensibly present before but that she was not in a position to see.

It is not until Helen makes the connection between finger spelling and communication that she begins to pose her own curiosity questions, seek answers, and reflect on them—a point when her interest is clearly developing. However, as Helen's case reveals, the development of interest has phases that precede what to the outside observer would be identified as "interest." Her interest also continues to develop beyond the phase that is detailed here. The present chapter focuses on the development of interest, from the point of potential triggering that "takes" to the point when the learner begins to ask his or her own curiosity questions, and then follows through to reflect on these and seek answers.

Misunderstood Aspects of Research on Interest Development

We next call attention to two often misunderstood aspects of research on the development of interest: awareness of interest (the learner's ability to cognitively evaluate engagement), and the essential role of knowledge, in addition to feelings and value, as an indicator of interest, especially in later phases of interest development.

Awareness of Interest

As Helen's case illustrates, the development of interest does not necessarily involve metacognitive, or reflective, awareness. This point has three implications for researchers, educators, and the learners themselves. First, learners are not necessarily dependent on their will to develop interest or be interested (Lipstein & Renninger, 2007). They may be dependent largely on supports to find ways to connect with the content that they are to learn, and while they need to make their own connections, they are also likely to need support to perceive them (Renninger, 2010). Second, while learners may make a cognitive evaluation about some content, like Helen they also may not be aware that their interest has been triggered until much later in the process of its development. In later phases of interest development too, they can be so engrossed in engagement that they are not reflecting on it.

A third implication is that having and developing an interest is not the same as being metacognitively aware of the role of interest in one's learning. The presence of metacognition impacts a learner's ability to take stock of his or her own goals and to act on them (see Flavell, 1976). In this sense, the learner's goals refer to what the learner wants to understand or do, not whether his or her goals would be considered mastery or performance goals, since a learner may possess both types of goals. Thus, while a person may or may not be aware of the process of engaging with an identified interest, the extent to which he or she is metacognitively aware of his or her interest and its role in learning is likely to impact *how*, not whether, he or she organizes as a learner and follows through to engage.

Knowledge and Interest

In its earliest phases, interest may be considered an emotion, or measured based on affect, or emotional response, and have minimal knowledge requirements (Ainley, 2007; Hidi, 2006; Reeve, Jang, Hardre, & Omura, 2002). As interest develops, knowledge and value, in addition to affect, need to be present (Renninger, 1990, 2000). More specifically, Hidi and Renninger (2006) argue that as interest develops and deepens, the desire for knowledge and value develop concurrently, while affect continues to be an important aspect of interest.

In distinguishing among the phases of interest development, content knowledge is also an important indicator. Without knowledge, a learner is not in a position to develop the types of curiosity questions that lead to reengagement, as well as the value that comes from asking these questions. Helen, for example, had no knowledge that finger spelling

allowed communication. It was only when she made this connection and began to build her knowledge that she then also had questions that she wanted to answer. This led to her continued reengagement to understand.

Defining Interest and Interest Development

In the present chapter, which focuses on interest and its potential to develop, interest is conceptualized as:

(a) referring to both a learner's state as well as his or her predisposition to return to engagement with a particular class of ideas (disciplinary content), events, or objects, and

(b) developing through four phases: triggered situational, maintained situational, emerging individual, and well-developed individual interest (see Table 11.1; Hidi & Renninger, 2006).

In this section of this chapter, the Four-Phase Model of Interest Development is described. This is followed by an overview of other approaches to the study of interest in order to provide a context for understanding a developmental approach. In later sections, research specific to interest development is reviewed and issues central to next steps in understanding its development are considered.

The Four-Phase Model of Interest Development

Hidi and Renninger's (2006) model identifies four phases in the development of interest based on existing empirical literature and extended previous discussions suggesting that there were two types of interest: situational and individual interest (e.g., Hidi, 1990; Krapp, Hidi, & Renninger, 1992; Renninger, 1990). Briefly, situational interest refers to the likelihood that particular content, activities, or events will trigger a response in the moment that may hold over time (Hidi & Baird, 1986; Mitchell, 1993). Individual interest, in contrast, refers to an ongoing and possible deepening of a person's relation to particular content. It includes a more enriched kind of value than situational interest, as well as an increasingly consolidated base of discourse knowledge (Renninger, 1990, 2000).

In the Four-Phase Model, Hidi and Renninger (2006) suggested that findings from studies of situational and individual interest were complementary and could be used to map the development of interest, beginning with forms of initial triggering that might be sustained to the relatively enduring predisposition to return to particular classes of content

Table 11.1. The four phases of interest development (Hidi & Renninger, 2006): Definitions and learner characteristics.

Phases of Interest Development			
Phase 1: Triggered Situational	Phase 2: Maintained Situational	Phase 3: Emerging Individual	Phase 4: Well-Developed Individual
Definition • Psychological state resulting from short-term changes in cognitive and affective processing	• Psychological state that involves focused attention and persistence over extended period, and/or reoccurs and persists	• Psychological state *and* the beginning of relatively enduring predisposition to seek reengagement with particular classes of content	• Psychological state *and* a relatively enduring predisposition to reengage particular classes of content
Learner Characteristics • Attends to content, if only fleetingly • Needs support to engage from others and through instructional design • May experience either positive or negative feelings • May or may not be reflectively aware of the experience	• Reengages content that previously triggered attention • Is supported by others to find connections among their skills, knowledge, and prior experience • Has positive feelings • Is developing knowledge of the content • Is developing a sense of the content's value	• Is likely to independently re-engage content • Has curiosity questions that leads and seeks answers • Has positive feelings • Has stored knowledge and stored value • Is very focused on his or her own questions	• Independently reengages content • Has curiosity questions • Self-regulates easily to reframe questions and seek answers • Has positive feelings • Can persevere through frustration and challenge in order to meet goals • Recognizes others' contributions to the discipline • Actively seeks feedback

over time. It was suggested that situational interest could develop into individual interest, but it was also suggested that situational interest could occur simultaneously with individual interest.

As described in Table 11.1, the four phases of interest are considered to be sequential and discrete, but as Hidi and Renninger (2006) also noted, they are phases rather than stages because the length and character of a given phase may vary among individuals based on, among other factors, experience and temperament. The first phase in the development of interest is conceptualized as being initiated by a triggered situational interest. If sustained, this first phase evolves into the second phase, maintained situational interest. The third phase of interest, emerging individual interest, may develop out of the second phase and may then lead to the fourth phase, a well-developed individual interest.

Helen's experience with finger signing provides an illustration of triggered and eventually maintained situational interest that evolved almost immediately into an emerging interest. Helen's interest was triggered it seems by the juxtaposition of the water and the finger signing: It represented the presence of a new concept, communication. Her interest for communicating using finger spelling was maintained following the triggering provided by the water, and although she first engaged communication as a game, it began to take on meaning for her. It also led her to ask questions because she wanted to understand, marking a shift in her phase of interest. Based on what Helen tells us in her autobiography, she appears to have transitioned through the phase of maintained situational interest almost immediately, possibly because she had Anne to respond and work with her to find answers to the curiosity questions she posed, as they emerged. As her autobiography also indicates, Helen continued to want to ask questions that allowed her to develop her knowledge. Her emerging individual interest rapidly developed into a well-developed individual interest.

The example of Helen demonstrates that once interest is triggered, it can be maintained and then progress as an individual interest. Her interactions with others were critical, a characteristic of interest development that is now well established (e.g., Barron, 2006; Nolen, 2007; Pasupathi & Rich, 2005). At first these interactions could be characterized as supporting the generation of her interest (e.g., Mitchell, 1993; Palmer, 2004, 2009). Later they involved the provision of information that led her to continue to stretch, engage, and explore the content of her interest (see Renninger, 2010) or to self-generate interest (Sansone, Weir, Harpster, & Morgan, 1992).

The match between the strengths and needs of the learner and available support, described by Eccles and Midgley (1989) as the stage-fit of the environment, was critical to Helen, and more generally to the development of interest. Available supports can include interactions with others, such as teachers, peers, parents, or museum personnel, and the tools that they have created (e.g., books, tasks, software, exhibits). However, the presence of supports and intended triggers does not necessarily guarantee triggering. Instead, interest appears to be both triggered and supported to develop when a task such as an assignment to set a goal for a class at the beginning of the term leads learners to find meaning for themselves (Hulleman, Durik, Schweigert, & Harackiewicz, 2008; Hulleman & Harackiewicz, 2009), or when learners are allowed or take charge of shaping class activity (Cobb & Hodge, 2004; Meyer & Turner, 2002).

When support from the learning environment is lacking (or perceived to be lacking), however, interest can fall off, go dormant, or disappear altogether (Bergin, 1999). Renninger (2000), for example, described the case of a talented chess player who ceased to continue to play chess because there was no one else to challenge him. Renninger and Lipstein (2006) also reported declines in interest when students did not perceive opportunities to connect to the work they are doing and/or for their ideas to be respected and heard. Their findings appear to be consistent with those of Kunter, Baumert, and Köller (2007) who found that within the same classroom there were students whose interest would develop and students whose interest would decrease. They observe that the development of interest is likely to be more related to students' personal experience of the classroom—for example, whether they feel they understand what is expected of them and have a teacher who is responsive and provides support for autonomy (see related discussions in Frenzel, Goetz, Pekrun, & Watt, 2010; Tsai, Kunter, Lüdtke, Trautwein, & Ryan, 2008). The stage-fit of the person to the environment has been described as supporting

feelings about the worth (the value, task interest, utility, cost) of continued engagement (e.g., Wigfield, Eccles, Schiefele, Roeser, & Davis-Kean, 2006). Whether a person is in a position to make an independent decision to reengage has also been found to impact the relation between the affective and cognitive components of interest, a relation that affects the experience of interest (Ainley, 2007; Sansone & Thoman, 2005a, b) as well as the likelihood that interest will develop and deepen (Renninger, 2000).

Although learners at all ages with varying experiences can develop new interests at any time, age also affects how and whether interest is likely to develop. Undergraduates, for example, may be able to self-generate ways in which to sustain interest in view of a task that they find boring by finding some reason that the task could be beneficial to them (e.g., Sansone, et al., 1992). This capacity is related to their metacognitive awareness of the situation (a boring task that needs to be completed) and their ability to generate strategies to address it. Conversely, younger children are more likely to generate means to continue to engage only when tasks are already of interest, although they also may be more open than older learners to trying to learn new topics or participate in new activities (Renninger, Sansone, & Smith, 2004). At about 8 to 10 years of age, they begin comparing their own capacities to those of others and then need a different form of support to persevere on tasks that they have not yet tried, or that they are aware others already do at a much more advanced level then they (Renninger, 2009).

Conceptualizations of Interest Not Specifically Focused on Development

Understanding how interest can be supported to develop is of particular concern to those who support others to learn, whether in or outside the school context. However, the conceptualization of interest as a cognitive and affective motivational variable that develops is only one of the ways in which interest is defined and studied. Krapp (2002, 2007), for example, describes interest development as a process of developing one's identity. Other conceptualizations of interest reflect a range of research questions and as a result address different aspects of the way in which a person engages (or does not engage) content to be learned. These perspectives contribute to understanding interest and its relation to learning but may not address the development of interest per se. However, each is a conceptualization on which the understanding of interest development builds.

Detailed considerations of interest can be described as focusing on emotion (e.g., Ainley, 2007; Silvia, 2006), task features and environment (e.g., Mayer, 2005; Sansone & Thoman, 2005 a, b), value (e.g., Schiefele, 2009; Wigfield et al., 2006), and vocational interest (e.g., Alexander, Johnson, Leibham, & Kelley, 2008; Holland, 1985/1997; Lent, Brown, & Hackett, 1994; see Renninger & Hidi, 2011). Briefly, conceptualizations of interest that focus on emotion are often concerned with the state of interest, rather than with interest as both a state and a predisposition to reengage particular content over time. They have determined, for example, that mood, disposition, and situation combine to influence students' affective reactions to tasks (Ainley & Patrick, 2006), and that interest may be either pleasant or unpleasant (Turner & Silvia, 2006), but little is known about whether and how the intensity and valence of affect changes with the development of interest.

Conceptualizations that have focused on interest in terms of task features or the environment have also pointed to the importance of the experience of interest to engagement. They find that interest is essential to the feelings of competence that accompany this experience and self-regulation (Sansone & Thoman, 2005 a, b), and they have indicated that interest can be distracting (e.g., Mayer, Griffith, Jurkowitz, & Rothman, 2008). However, because these approaches to interest address the state of interest in earlier phases of interest development, it is not clear whether and how the experience of interest then varies with development.

Conceptualizations that have focused on interest as value have further indicated that interest that is operationalized in terms of how much the respondent says he or she *likes* particular content will differentiate first in the expectancy value framework (Wigfield et al., 2006) and is linked to intrinsic motivation (Schiefele, 2009). In cross-sectional work with middle and high school students, Denissen, Zarrett, and Eccles (2007) reported that self-concept of ability and interest are coupled, but they also point out that when achievement is introduced, there is a higher degree of coupling between self-concept of ability and achievement than between interest and achievement. Because, however, the focus of studies of interest conceptualized in terms of value has been on an assessment of value at one point in time, little is understood about possible change in the development of interest in terms of expectancy value (see Wigfield & Cambria, 2010).

Conceptualizations that have focused on interest in terms of vocational or conceptual interest address the relation between a person's present abilities and possible occupations (e.g., Holland 1985/1997; see also Armstrong, Allison, & Rounds, 2008) or categories of children's interest engagement such as science or art (e.g., Alexander et al., 2008) and school readiness. One line of work within this framework draws on counseling psychology to suggest that environmental support can be provided to encourage those who presently lack interest to develop it (e.g., women who lack interest for engineering; Brown & Lent, 1996). Lent, Brown, and Hackett's (1994, 2000) Social Cognitive Career Theory describes interest development as determined by the individual's perceptions of his or her own competence, or ability to succeed.

Each of the conceptualizations overviewed indicates that interest can beneficially influence learning (although it can also be distracting) and that it is always linked to a particular disciplinary content, object, event, or idea. The conceptualizations also all acknowledge the role of affect, or feelings, as a component of interest, but they tend to vary in the extent to which affect, knowledge, and value are the focus of inquiry and measurement.

Some of the conceptualizations describe knowledge and value as components of interest (Ainley, 2007; Hidi & Renninger, 2006; Mayer, 2005; Sansone & Thoman, 2005 a, b; Silvia, 2006), whereas others focused on affect and value as established through cognitive evaluation (Krapp, 2005, 2007; Schiefele, 2009; Wigfield et al., 2006). Differences among the conceptualizations with respect to the role of knowledge reflect differences among research aims. The research questions being addressed do not necessarily assess change over time but instead focus on one or another aspect of interest that may be present and/or a factor in each phase of interest.

Operationalization and Measurement Considerations

There presently is no single correct measure or indicator of interest or interest development, and as Renninger and Hidi (2011) have noted, such a specification may not be possible because of differences in the structure of disciplinary domains, with some being more hierarchical than others (Lawless & Kulikowich, 2006), and/or differences in researchers' questions.

To date, interest development has been measured using both surveys (e.g., Chen, Darst, & Pangrazi, 1999; Häussler & Hoffmann, 2002;

Linnenbrink-Garcia et al., 2010; Schiefele, Krapp, Wild, & Winteler, 1993; Schraw, Bruning, & Svoboda, 1995) and behavioral measures, such as online experience sampling (Ainley, Hidi, & Berndorff, 2002), functional magnetic resonance imaging (fMRI; Kim, Lee, & Bong, 2009), or participant observation (Pressick-Kilborn & Walker, 2002; Nolen, 2007; Renninger & Wozniak, 1985). In its most well-developed form, interest has also been assessed based on participation (Azevedo, 2006; Barron, 2006; Fink, 1998) or membership (e.g., recreational figure skaters, see Green-Demers, Pelletier, Stewart, & Gushue, 1998; mathematicians, Gisbert 1998). However, Renninger, Cai, Lewis, Adams, and Ernst (2011) report that interest that is not well developed is not accurately predicted by participation alone.

While surveys capture respondent perceptions, behavioral measures capture respondent behaviors. Triangulating assessments is likely to be necessary in order to accurately capture differences among phases of interest. For example, while triggered interest may be assessed through behavioral measures, it is not likely to be easily assessed in the earlier phases of its development using self-reports alone given that respondents in this phase are often not aware that interest has been triggered. On the other hand, a respondent is in a position to report whether he or she works on more math problems than those that are assigned, suggesting that survey items that specify more developed forms of interest may be expected to provide a way to partition a sample.

Hidi and Renninger (2006) have suggested that while the earliest phases and the state of interest may be characterized and assessed by affective response, the identification of developed interest needs to account for the relation between feelings, value, and knowledge, and that change in this relation might be expected with development. Presently, efforts to distinguish phases of interest have focused on dichotomies such as situational and individual interest, earlier and later phases of interest, less developed and more developed interest, or low interest and high interest. Methods for identifying interest specific to each of the four phases of interest are presently being explored.

Two quasi-experimental studies of interest are described that suggest potential indicators of interest in each phase of development. These consider the relation among the phase of interest and other variables that describe learning and motivation, such as understanding of the discipline, goals, strategies, effort, self-efficacy, and feedback preferences. Both were mixed-method studies of middle school-age students; taken together, they suggest the need to further consider the role of the learning environment as another potential indicator of interest.

In each study, assessment of interest was based on an assessment of the feelings, value, and knowledge of participants relative to the other content, or subject matter, with which they were engaged. In the first, Lipstein and Renninger (2007) used survey items (Likert ratings and open-ended questions) and in-depth interviews to assess students' phase of interest for writing, and then developed portraits of students in each phase of interest. In the second, Renninger and Riley (in press) used participant observation notes and interviews collected at three time points during each of the 5 years to assess phase of interest. Their assessment procedures were informed by Renninger and Wozniak's (1985, see also Renninger, 1990) use of ethnographic methods to identify developed interest as including all of the following in relation to a particular class of objects, events, or ideas:

a. more engagement relative to other engagements,
b. voluntary return to engagement over time,
c. the ability to engage independently, and
d. engagement that is not simply exploratory.

Lipstein and Renninger (2007) undertook their study of student writers in order to explore potential indicators of each of the four phases of interest development. They developed portraits of middle school students' interest for writing by coupling information from surveys of 172 students and follow-up in-depth interviews. Each portrait provided an exemplar or generalized characterization of a writer in a given phase of interest and described the student's wants and needs as a learner.

As depicted in the description of the closed environment of Table 11.2, Lipstein and Renninger (2007) found that students with only a triggered situational interest were those with little knowledge of and value for writing but whose interest for writing could be triggered by the assignment of the "right" topic and/or feedback that appreciated their ideas and provided concrete suggestions for revision. Students with a maintained situational interest thought of writing in terms of rules, and they could be assisted to begin thinking like writers if they were provided with topics that were of interest to them and given supportive feedback. Students with an emerging individual interest for writing had

Table 11.2. Learner characteristics and needs in interest development generally, and by learning environment. Reprinted from Renninger, K. A. & Riley, K. R. (in press). Interest, cognition, and the case of L__ and science. In Kreitler, S. (Ed). *Cognition and motivation: Forging an interdisciplinary perspective.* **New York: Cambridge University Press.**

Phases of Interest Development			
Phase I: Triggered Situational	Phase 2: Maintained Situational	Phase 3: Emerging Individual	Phase 4: Well-Developed Individual

Learner Characteristics
• Attends to content, if only fleetingly
• Needs support to engage
  o From others
  o Through instructional design
• May experience either positive or negative feelings
• May or may not be reflectively aware of triggered interest
	• Reengages content that previously triggered attention
	• Is supported by others to find connections between skills, knowledge, and prior experience
	• Has positive feelings
	• Is developing knowledge of the content
	• Is developing a sense of the content's value
		• Is likely to independently re-engage content
		• Has curiosity questions that lead to seeking answers
		• Has positive feelings
		• Has stored knowledge and stored value
		• Is very focused on his/her own questions
			• Independently reengages content
			• Has curiosity questions
			• Self-regulates easily to reframe questions and seek answers
			• Has positive feelings
			• Can persevere through frustration and challenge in order to meet goals
			• Recognizes others' contributions to the discipline
			• Actively seeks feedback

Needs/More Closed Learning Environmen • To have his/her ideas respected • To feel genuinely appreciated for his/her efforts • To have others understand how hard work with this content is • A limited number of concrete suggestions	• To have his/her ideas respected • To feel genuinely appreciated for efforts • Support to explore his/her own ideas	• To have his/her ideas respected • To feel genuinely appreciated for his/her efforts • To feel that his/her ideas and goals are understood • Feedback that enables him/her to see how goals can be more effectively met	• To have his/her ideas respected • Information and feedback • To balance his/her personal standards with more widely accepted standards in the discipline • To feel that his/her ideas have been heard and understood • Constructive feedback • Challenge
Needs/More Open Learning Environment • To have his/her ideas respected • To feel genuinely appreciated for efforts made • To know that he/she understands the content	• To have his/her ideas respected • To feel genuinely appreciated for the efforts he/she has made • To know what he/she has learned and what he/she still wants to learn	• To have his/her ideas respected • To express his/her ideas • Not to be told to revise present efforts • To feel that this/her ideas and goals are understood • To feel genuinely appreciated for his/her efforts • Feedback that enables him/her to see how his/her goals were met	• To have his/her ideas respected • Information and feedback • To balance his/her personal standards with more widely accepted standards in the discipline • To feel that his/her ideas have been heard and understood • Constructive feedback • Challenge

begun to think of themselves as writers and were not interested in receiving feedback about either the organization or development of their writing. Students with a well-developed individual interest for writing also thought of themselves as writers, but, unlike those with an emerging individual interest, sought feedback and recognized that through feedback they could strengthen their abilities to communicate their ideas to others.

The characteristics of the learners in each of the four phases of interest suggest a preliminary set of indicators for each phase that includes information about what and how content is engaged and the forms of support that might be needed in order to enable it to develop (additional information is provided in both Lipstein & Renninger, 2007 and Renninger & Lipstein, 2006). However, Renninger and Riley's (in press) 5-year in-depth case study of inner-city participants in an out-of-school summer science workshop reveals a slightly different trajectory that they attribute to the workshops' out-of-school, nongraded context (see the description of the open environment in Table 11.2). The participants in the science workshops were in an environment that provided a lot of possible triggers for interest, and once their interest was maintained, it quickly shifted to being an emerging individual interest, where they sought input, readily asking and answering questions. This differed from the resistance to feedback that characterized the middle school writers identified as having an emerging individual interest, suggesting the possibility of the effects of environmental differences in constraint and opportunities for learning on the learners' interest trajectories.

Like findings reported by Frenzel et al. (2010), who studied the decline in students' interest for mathematics in three academic achievement tracks, it appears that trajectory of interest development may be impacted by how open the environment is to inquiry, or the press of the learning environment on achievement. Such findings suggest the need to consider not only the learners' feelings, value, and knowledge as a predictor of interest development but also the role of the environment.

Research on Interest Development

Studies that track the behaviors of individuals over time and studies of learners in earlier and/or later phases of interest (also described as situational and individual, less developed and more developed, or low interest and high interest) provide our present understanding of interest development. Findings from these two types of studies are described separately because they offer different insights. Studies that track the behaviors of individuals over time provide rich descriptive information that provides a basis for developing inductive models. Studies that have examined earlier and/or later phases of interest focus on studying one or more aspects of findings identified in more descriptive data with samples and methods that generalize.

A parsimonious selection of these studies is overviewed with particular attention to four questions central to supporting interest development: (a) the triggering of interest in both earlier and later phases of interest, (b) how and why interest is maintained once it has been triggered, (c) fluctuations in interest, and (d) shifts between phases in the development of interest. Following this, the generative potential of thinking across studies is suggested, using articles by Frenzel et al. (2010) and Pugh et al. (2010).

Studies That Track Interest Over Time

Interest development as described in studies that have tracked individuals over time is collected through interviews with the participant and/or significant others in the participant's life, surveys and interviews, the development of portraits based on interviews or surveys and interviews, experience sampling, course enrollments, and/or observation. Analysis of these studies together describes the development of interest as primarily a sequential process that evolves through interactions with the environment.

TRIGGERS FOR INTEREST DEVELOPMENT

Findings from studies that track the development of interest over time generally describe a changing relation between affect and knowledge as interest develops. They also describe triggers for interest (in this case, triggers that actually result in interest development) as supporting the making of connections to content in earlier phases of interest and opportunities to continue to develop understanding of content in later phases. Some examples include the following: girls in earlier phases of interest who wanted to pursue hard science were triggered by their desire to get their father's approval and also by opportunities to pursue mathematics (Gisbert, 1998), children's desires to express themselves as members of a "literate community" in their classroom acted as a trigger for their interest in reading and writing (Nolen, 2007), and instructional methods in Latin that students personalized themselves were successful triggers (Renninger et al., 2004).

Changes in the relation between affect and knowledge are also referenced in later phases of development, when the interest being studied already exists. Some examples include the following: descriptions of self-initiated work with technology in which adolescents seek additional resources, create new activities, pursue structured learning, and develop mentoring/knowledge-sharing relationships (Barron, 2006); the dyslexic adolescent who uses his or her more well-developed interest as a context within which to work on reading skills needed to develop further understanding (Fink, 1998); and business students whose interests were refined with the introduction of new opportunities (Krapp & Lewalter, 2001). Once interest is triggered and a connection to content occurs, it appears to continue to be triggered as interest develops, either by other people or the environment, challenging reading materials, or the development of nuanced understanding.

SUSTAINING INTEREST, FLUCTUATIONS, AND SHIFTS BETWEEN PHASES

Studies that have examined the development of interest over time suggest that, once triggered, interest is sustained based on the availability of opportunities to continue to learn and of support to be autonomous—meaning that there is ready scaffolding available for the learner who needs it. Such opportunities (or constraints on opportunities) can take the form of finances, timing, or access (Barron, 2006, Barron, Kennedy-Martin, Takeuchi, & Fithian, 2009), although the types of support or feedback required may depend on the phase of the interest. Mismatches between the learner's phase of interest and available supports have been found to result in marginalization and lack of identification (Nolen, 2007), a decrease in feelings of competence (Azevedo, 2006), and the falling off of interest (Renninger & Lipstein, 2006). Shifts between phases of interest and the development of interest, on the other hand, have been characterized as including developing feelings of competence, the acquisition of skills and knowledge (Nolen, 2007; Lipstein & Renninger, 2007), and/or identification with the domain of interest (see Krapp, 2003, 2005).

Assessed in terms of the individual learner and his or her development over time, studies that have mapped trajectories of interest development point to the critical role of environmental supports in triggering and sustaining interest. As interest develops, the supports need to shift from helping learners to make connections to particular content to

encouraging learners to fully engage, explore, and work with the content of the interest (Renninger, 2010). The studies allow identification of recurrent patterns within the ecology of the larger learning environment (Barron, 2006) and point to indicators that warrant further study and consideration. Such patterns are descriptive and specific to a particular context. Next steps to examine the issues that are uncovered include the kind of replication and validation undertaken in studies that have targeted earlier and/or later phases of interest.

Studies of Earlier and/or Later Phases of Interest

Studies contributing to the understanding of earlier and/or later phases of interest have typically not been undertaken to address interest development, but rather to understand and/or demonstrate the impact of interest as a motivational variable. In these studies, researchers usually partition the sample of participants whom they are studying into earlier or later phases of interest based on responses to survey items, rather than studying one or more individuals over time. Some of these studies have focused on participants in a particular phase of interest, while others have compared the responses of participants in two phases. The relation between affect and cognition in these studies is not central unless connections between the findings and a model of interest development is specified, in which case the shifting, or change, from one to another phase of interest is addressed (e.g., Harackiewicz, Durik, K. Barron, Linnenbrink, & Tauer, 2008). Most often, this type of study focuses on earlier phases of interest and has measured interest in terms of affect and value, rather than knowledge. Taken together, the studies confirm the importance of the relation among achievement, feelings of competence, and the development of interest. They also suggest a potentially critical role for metacognitive awareness.

TRIGGERS FOR INTEREST DEVELOPMENT

Findings from studies addressing earlier and/or later phases of interest development have focused on (a) the impact of triggers for situational or individual interest on learning and (b) the experience of the learning environment as a contributor to interest. Both situational interest and individual interest have been found to trigger interest. Situational interest has been found to promote reading comprehension and motivation among third graders (Guthrie et al., 2006), help high school students develop positive attitudes toward science (Palmer, 2009), and promote undergraduates' reading engagement and essay production (Flowerday, Schraw, & Stevens, 2004). Similarly, individual interest has been found to trigger learners to persevere in working with content that is complex and challenging. For example, middle school students were found to be more likely to persevere in working on math problems into which an individual interest had been inserted as a context (e.g., basketball) than problems into which content of less developed interest (e.g., football) were inserted (Renninger, Ewen, & Lasher, 2002; see also Hoffmann, 2002).

Having interest has also been described as a buffering factor that helps students to cope with unfavorable learning conditions (Katz, Assor, Kanat-Maymon, & Bereby-Meyer, 2006). For example, Tsai et al. (2008) reported that the climate of the classroom (e.g., the levels of autonomy support, controlling behaviors) influenced those with less developed interest more than those with well-developed interest. Similarly, Durik and Harackiewicz (2007) found that level of interest for math influenced the impact of catch (collative factors) and hold (situational factors that sustain interest) in an experimental manipulation of triggers for interest in solving math problems. Those with less interest for mathematics showed more interest in the collative-rich environment that provided triggers for novelty, and less interest in triggers for challenge, while those with more developed interest for mathematics were negatively affected by triggers for novelty and positively influenced by triggers for challenge.

Findings such as these suggest both that potential triggers for interest differ for learners with more and less developed interest, and the potential triggers of the learning environment may be particularly critical for those in earlier phases of interest development. They also suggest that the association between interest and experience that is independent of achievement, as is reported by Schiefele and Csikszentmihalyi (1994), is further indication that changed experience can impact interest (see also Pugh et al., 2010). However, Schiefele and Csikszentmihalyi (1995) also reported a correlation between grades and interest that, like Jacobs, Lanza, Osgood, Eccles, and Wigfield's (2002) findings, points to links between grades and valuing and contributes to the experience of interest.

Sansone and her colleagues' work suggest that interest experience reliably predicts task choice and persistence and is essential to self-regulation (e.g., Sansone & Thoman, 2005a, b). With interest the learner has a clear goal and is able to self-generate or trigger interest for himself or herself. Thus, while present perception and values may inform present interest, the experience of interest can change through the process of triggering that is provided either by other people or situations (e.g., Hulleman et al., 2008; Mitchell, 1993; Palmer, 2009) or by individuals who are in a position to self-generate interest (e.g., by finding a reason to persevere; Sansone et al., 1992).

SUSTAINING, FLUCTUATIONS, AND SHIFTS IN INTEREST DEVELOPMENT

Studies of both earlier and later phases of interest development suggest that situational factors, challenge, and personal investment are potential triggers for sustaining interest, and they provide a basis for shifts that occur in interest development. For example, experiences in which students are led to explore and work with the everyday meaning of science concepts in new ways are designed to promote meaningfulness and sustain engagement (e.g., Mitchell, 1993; Palmer, 2004, 2009; Pugh et al., 2010). They also support learners to set goals for themselves that involve them in asking curiosity questions, reflecting on these, and seeking resources to answer them (Renninger, 2000; Renninger, Bachrach, & Posey, 2008).

Like the process of triggering interest, whether interest is sustained and continues to develop appears to be linked to learners' perceptions of their experiences, as well as their abilities to set goals for themselves and self-regulate (see Sansone & Thoman, 2005b). Harackiewicz et al.'s (2008) findings indicate, for example, that the process of triggering interest and goal adoption differs for those who come to class with an already developed interest and those who do not. They found that undergraduates with low initial interest who reported having their interest triggered were also those who experienced shifts in the development of interest, suggesting that the triggering of interest can promote mastery goals and that mastery goals can promote interest development.

Harackiewicz et al. (2008) also found, however, that the simple presence of a trigger did not predict continued interest. Rather, the triggering of interest in addition to students' final grades in the course predicted their continued interest. These findings suggest the importance of both mastery and performance goals to the development of interest (see Harackiewicz, Barron, Tauer, & Elliot, 2002; Harackiewicz, Barron, Pintrich, Elliot, & Thrash, 2002). Moreover, analyses to examine the relation between interest (measured in terms of feelings and value) and background knowledge in the Harackiewicz et al. (2008) study revealed that initial interest was a particularly strong predictor of continued interest when paired with a high level of background knowledge, indicating the importance of content knowledge for interest development.

Interest that has been triggered has also been found to fluctuate, however. Consistent with the Harackiewicz et al. (Harackiewicz, Barron, Tauer, & Elliot, 2002; Harackiewicz, et al., 2008) findings, Denissen et al. (2007) found that students between 6 and 17 years of age felt competent and interested in the subjects in which they achieved and in which they perceived themselves to have ability. They also found an increase with age in the coordination of achievement, self-concept of ability, and/or interest, suggesting an increasingly influential role of student perceptions when the content with which they are working in school also reflects increases in difficulty (see Hidi & Ainley, 2008).

Repeated but not specifically examined in studies of earlier and/or later phases of interest development is the role of the learner's metacognitive awareness. Discussion has centered instead on perceptions of the environment and whether the learner responds to potential triggers or opportunities in the environment. The evidence suggests that when learner interest is triggered, it can be sustained, but if interest fluctuates this is linked to the learner's perceptions or experience of the environment.

The Harackiewicz et al. (2008) findings suggest that when undergraduates reported having a triggered situational interest, their interest developed. Harackiewicz et al. (2008) did not go on to suggest that if participants report having their interest triggered on a survey, then it also is the case that they have at least some level of metacognitive awareness and are positioned to set goals for themselves and self-regulate. This is an emergent finding of this review. One of the critiques of using surveys to assess earlier phases of interest has been that learners are not likely to know that their interest has been triggered. What the Harackiewicz et al. findings do suggest, however, is that when learners are able to report having a triggered interest, their interest then develops. This is not to say that interest cannot develop without this reflective awareness, but rather that interest can be expected to develop if this reflective awareness is present. Without metacognitive awareness, it may be that the learner can be supported to engage with content but may lack self-direction and need additional support to reflect on and continue to explore it.

Two Studies of Interest Development

Reviewing articles and chapters for this chapter called attention to the range of studies that contribute to our present understanding of interest development. It also pointed to the importance of their complementarities as sources of validation and emergent insight. In this section of this chapter, the questions, methods, and findings from two solid and seemingly different studies by Frenzel et al. (2010) and Pugh et al. (2010) are reviewed, and their joint contributions to interest development are considered. Two other studies could as easily have been selected for consideration; our choice was informed by the differences of their methods and the similarity of the age group that each addressed.

Frenzel et al.'s study is a quantitative longitudinal study of early adolescents' mathematics interest; Pugh et al.'s is a short-term qualitative study of high school students' transformative experiences with biology. Both studies assess the trajectory of interest development. Whereas Frenzel et al.'s study implies that the students' environment (e.g., teachers, parents, school) may influence and account for differences in their achievements and interest trajectories, Pugh et al.'s study suggests that individual learner characteristics contribute significantly to interest development. Together, these studies can be understood to suggest that interest development involves both internal and external factors and point to potential indicators and questions that the research on interest development still needs to address.

FRENZEL, GOETZ, PEKRUN, AND WATT (2010)

Frenzel et al. (2010) reported on a longitudinal study of the mathematical interests of 3,193 students (51% female) in grades 5 to 9 in the German school system based on surveys administered to the students and their parents. Using Likert scales assessing feelings, value, and knowledge to measure interest, four issues were addressed: (a) the characteristics of trajectories of interest development in mathematics, (b) the role of gender in the development of interest in mathematics, (c) the role of ability grouping in the development of interest in mathematics, and (d) the role of the values of significant others' in the development of interest in mathematics.

Frenzel et al. predicted that students would experience a generalized loss of interest across time. In particular, they hypothesized that students' intrinsic motivations for learning were likely to be in increasing conflict with school-ordained restrictions such as required courses, increased task complexity, and demands for academic effort and achievement.

Frenzel et al. focused on mathematics, noting that mathematics has long been considered a field preferred by males, and predicted that gender would influence the level of mathematics interest, in that females would have less interest than males, but that the level of female and male interest would not impact the expected decline in the trajectory of interest development given findings suggesting gender differences in the level of interest but not in the trajectory of its development (Fredricks & Eccles, 2002; Jacobs et al., 2002; Watt, 2004).

Frenzel et al. also predicted that ability grouping would impact interest development based on Marsh's (1987) findings from a study of the "Big Fish Little Pond Effect," which suggests negative effects for students placed into high-achievement groups and positive effects of placement into low-achievement groups. Taking advantage of the organization of the German school system, which tests and places students into one of three academic tracks based on academic achievement by the fourth grade, Frenzel et al. posited that students in Hauptschule (the lowest track) would report higher interest levels than students in either Realschule (the middle track) or Gymnasium (the highest track), due to the pressure in Realschule and Gymnasium to focus on achievement instead of personal development.

Finally, based on the findings of social cognitive theorists (e.g., Eccles, Wigfield, Harold, & Blumenfeld, 1993; Pekrun, 2000), Frenzel et al. predicted that significant others such as family, classmates/peers, and teachers would influence the formation of students' values and interest for mathematics. Family members, especially parents, have been found to be role models for their children's eventual interests and educational values (Jacobs, Davis-Kean, Bleeker, Eccles, & Malanchuk, 2005) and students can be expected to develop interests and values similar to those of their parents (Jacobs & Eccles, 2000).

Findings from Frenzel et al's study revealed an overall decline in mathematical interest over time, regardless of variables such as gender. In terms of gender, Frenzel et al. reported that girls had a lower initial level of interest, but as expected: There were no differences between the shapes of the trajectories of girls boys, suggesting that the areas of decline and stabilization on the growth trajectories may be the result of an intensification at earlier ages. In addition, differences were identified in the level of interest of students in each of the different ability groups. General/universal longitudinal interest declines aside, students in Hauptschule in grade 5 had slightly lower initial levels of interest but by grade 9 had managed to sustain interest, whereas students in both Realschule and Gymnasium evinced steeper declines in interest levels, leveling out at a lower level than Hauptschule students by grade 9. Finally, while family, peer, and teacher influences affected the formation of students' interest, it appears that, based on an assessment of interest trajectories, they did not influence the development of interest.

PUGH, LINNENBRINK-GARCIA, KOSKEY, STEWART, AND MANZY (2010)

Pugh et al. (2010) reported on a short-term study of transformative experience among 166 (66% female) 9th- and 10th-grade biology students, where transformative experience is characterized by "motivated use, expansion of perception, and experiential value" (p. 7), and interest and task value are described as supporting conceptual change (Dole & Sinatra, 1998). Prestudy, poststudy, and follow-up assessments of students' science knowledge, identity, and goals were undertaken using survey data. Interest was not assessed independently but as part of the construct of experiential value; Likert-items were used to assess student opinion about the value and utility of information about natural selection.

Pugh et al.'s research questions focused on three issues: *(a)* the prevalence of transformative experiences among high school biology students learning about natural selection; *(b)* the relation among transformative experience, science identity, and mastery goal orientation; and *(c)* the relation between transformative experience and both initial and enduring conceptual change and transfer. Based on findings from his earlier work, Pugh (2004) had described transformative experiences as occurring when students are motivated to apply what they have learned in the classroom outside of the classroom, experiences that led to expanded perception and value. These findings suggested that transformation is best measured by observing changes in students' conceptual understandings of science and whether they *transfer* their learning to other aspects of their lives, see aspects of the world in new ways, and find value in doing so (Pugh, 2004). Like findings from Girod, Twyman, and Wojcikiewicz's (2010) work with fifth graders, Pugh (2002) showed that biology students who had transformative experiences had more gains in conceptual understanding than those who did not. In the study examined here, he and his colleagues sought to explore transformative experiences in an expanded sample and sought to explore science identity and achievement goal orientation as predictors of transformative experience. They chose to focus on natural selection in the biology classroom because this is a topic about which students often have misconceptions.

Based on both Girod and Wong (2002) and Pugh (2004), it was expected that students who identified as having had transformative experiences were also those who saw the relevance of the science being taught. They conceptualized interest in this context in terms of value, and science identity as comprised of one's prior knowledge and one's identification with science as a strength or weakness. When students believed that they had a strong science identity, it was expected that they would thus see the relevance of the science unit being taught and were more likely to undergo transformative experiences (Girod & Wong, 2002; Pugh, 2004). Similarly, it was expected that a student's achievement goal orientation would affect the likelihood of transformative experiences.

Thus, Pugh et al. predicted that students with a mastery goal orientation would be more likely to report transformative experiences, given the focus of mastery goal orientation on learning. Pugh et al. also expected that students who either strongly identify with science or have a mastery approach toward learning would be more likely to experience transformative experiences than those with a less defined science identity and a performance approach (i.e., displaying competence but not necessarily comprehension).

Pugh and his colleagues found that both science identity and mastery goal orientations were positively associated with transformative experience. Students who both identified with science and had a mastery approach to learning were more likely to experience transformative experiences; they retained information and were able to independently apply it outside of the classroom. However, students with initially higher levels of knowledge about the information taught in the unit also reported having more transformative experiences, suggesting that the acquisition and development of knowledge and interest (defined as value and utility) may be mutually reinforcing.

Their results further suggested that students with a mastery goal orientation were more likely to report experiencing transformative experiences, and that mastery goal orientation mediated the relationship between science identity and transformative experience when prior science knowledge related to the unit taught was controlled. In other words, a strong science identity predicted a stronger endorsement of goal orientation, which in turn predicted the occurrence of transformative experiences. It appears that mastery orientation increased the likelihood of transformative experiences. On the strength of these findings, Pugh et al. pointed to the role of individual characteristics in the development of interest.

COMPLEMENTARY ASPECTS OF THE FRENZEL ET AL. AND PUGH ET AL. STUDIES

The findings of the Frenzel et al. and Pugh et al. studies mirror and extend present discussions of interest development. Together, their findings suggest that, at least for adolescents, interest develops in relation to both academic and personal satisfaction, and the keys to these lie in the balance and personalizing of external and internal, environmental and individual, factors.

Frenzel et al.'s findings confirm the existence of a general decline of interest over time spent within the academic system, and the influence of ability groups on students' interest development. Students in Hauptschule (the lower track) showed less steep declines in interest over time, compared to students in Realschule and Gymnasium. Frenzel et al. suggested that this might be a result of the less competitive atmosphere with fewer achievement-oriented demands in Hauptschule as compared to Realschule and Gymnasium. These findings also underscore the role of the learning environment as a support for (or constraint on) academic development, interest, and performance.

Similarly, Pugh et al.'s findings point to the importance of the learning environment as a support for comprehension and transfer, suggesting the further need to attend to the role of learner characteristics in the development of interest. When prior knowledge was controlled, students with a mastery approach to learning were found to have more comprehension and a greater ability to retain and transfer what they had learned to other aspects of their lives. These findings further suggest that a mastery goal orientation may compensate for less than ideal situational factors such as unsupportive environments, limited opportunities, and grade-oriented pressure. It also appears that whether interest develops depends on the learner: It may be the individual's approach to learning that most influences both comprehension and transfer.

Frenzel et al.'s and Pugh et al.'s studies also indicated that both situational and individual factors can result in a falling off of interest. According to the Frenzel et al. study, placement into a high-achievement ability group negatively influenced interest development, whereas placement in a low-achievement ability group had a positive effect. The interest levels of Hauptschule students declined at a slower rate than Realschule or Gymnasium students and eventually stabilized toward the later grades of high school. As this difference in decline in interest occurred regardless of the student's initial interest level, it suggests that the right combination of environmental factors and amount of external pressure can cause someone's interest to change, whether positively or negatively. Similarly, Pugh et al. found that intrinsic motivation, such as a mastery goal orientation, increased the likelihood of transformative experiences, more advanced conceptual understanding, and the transfer of learning.

KNOWLEDGE, A COMPONENT OF DEVELOPING INTEREST

Pugh et al.'s decision to assess interest using items addressing feelings and value (e.g., "During science class, I think the stuff we are learning about adaptation and/or natural selection is interesting." [p. 22]) and to control for prior knowledge influences what they can say about interest development. If interest develops through phases, and if transitions between phases of interest are dependent on developing understanding, then knowledge needs to be included in measures intended to distinguish between earlier and later phases of interest development. Pugh et al.'s findings provide information about the roles of knowledge and value in the process of making connections to content to be learned. However, their findings do not for sure address differences between those in earlier and later phases of interest, and their abilities to pose questions, seek answers, and so forth. While some participants may well have been in later phases of interest, distinguishing among students in terms of the possibility that some were in later phases of interest was not undertaken. Frenzel et al., on the other hand, used items to assess interest that tapped feelings and value, as well as the participants' relation to knowledge: "I would like to find out more about some of the things we deal with in our mathematics class." And, "I like to read books and solve brainteasers related to mathematics." (p. 532)

While both Pugh et al. and Frenzel et al. described their studies of interest in terms of low and high interest, the relation between their outcomes and interest theory suggest that what they are each describing differs. Pugh et al. appear to be describing either earlier and later phases of situational interest (triggered situational and maintained situational), or an earlier phase, consisting of triggered situational and maintained situational interest, and a later phase of emerging individual interest (see Table 11.1). Whereas, because they have included knowledge in their assessment of interest, Frenzel et al. appear to be distinguishing between earlier and later phases of interest for mathematics.

Consistent with descriptions of students in earlier phases of interest as mapped by Lipstein and Renninger (2007; see also Renninger & Riley, in press), the Pugh et al. and the Frenzel et al. studies suggest that it is the student who ultimately makes use of available supports, and whether students make this choice depends on whether they are enabled to make personalized, individualized connections to content that is a function of both their learning characteristics and the learning environment. This is an important point. While personalized content has for some time been recognized as important in generating interest (e.g., Mitchell, 1993), the findings from the Pugh et al. and Frenzel et al. studies point to the fact that it is the learner, not the teacher or the researcher, who decides what is meaningful—and also that this is the case whether intrest is in earlier or later phases of development. In other words, whether the student is positioned to take advantage of available resources may have to do with how and whether he or she understands the situation or the goal and his or her ability to recognize the utility of the particular resources or practices that would allow the goal to be realized. These findings further suggest that the degree to which the learner is metacognitively aware of his or her interest may be a critical indicator of interest development. Having an interest is not the same as being metacognitively aware of the role of interest in one's learning. Metacognition should allow for the possibility of change by enabling goal setting and self-regulation.

Conclusions

The studies by Frenzel et al. and Pugh et al. point to some potentially critical aspects and indicators of interest development, in particular the roles of situational influences such as the achievement demands of the learning environment and experiential valuing. Like the other studies of earlier and/or later phases of interest development, they note the role of the learner's metacognitive awareness as an indicator of what types of supports might be needed in order for interest to develop.

These aspects of interest development together form the basis of an inductive model for understanding the relation among the learner's phase of interest, achievement demands of the learning environment, and metacognitive awareness. Depicted in Figure 11.1 as a Punnett square, phase of interest forms one dimension and the achievement demands of the learning environment the other. The level of the learner's metacognition, or reflective ability to think about interest and learning, is also included in each quadrant. Framed in this way, it appears that metacognitive awareness, both in terms of the learner's reflection on content and abilities to self-regulate, is beneficial to the learner and supports interest to develop. Development of content knowledge can also support the learner's capacity to develop meaningful connections to the content, regardless of his or her initial phase of interest. However, the achievement demands of the learning environment may positively or negatively affect the learner's ability to make connections to the content and ask curiosity questions about it. If the learner is negatively affected, his or her content knowledge may develop but interest may not, thereby compromising his or her possibilities for learning.

To date, research on interest development has tended to focus on one or another aspect of interest and/or its development, using different measures and methods, and resulting in seemingly contradictory findings and conclusions between studies. It appears that for research on interest development it is important to look for complementarities among findings—a consideration that also requires attention to the way in which interest and its development is conceptualized and measured, how it is studied, with which populations (age and experience), and in what type of context (domain of study, achievement expectations, etc.).

The proposed Punnett square anchors the repeated evidence that interest develops through the interaction of the learner's individual learning characteristics and his or her environment. It includes information about a particular aspect of the learning environment: its achievement demands. It also calls attention to the emergent finding from the literature review in this chapter, which suggests that metacognitive awareness contributes to whether a learner responds to potential triggers. The Punnett square can also be used to describe the focus of support needed to enable shifts in interest development. Vertical movement along the Punnett square

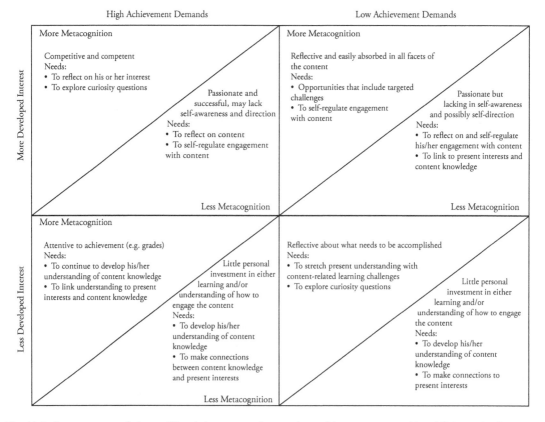

Fig. 11.1. Punnett square of the possible relations among learner phase of interest, metacognitive abilities, and achievement demands of the learning environment.

indicate shifts between earlier and later phases of interest, whereas horizontal movement refers to altering the learning environment, or achievement context.

Used for the purpose of revisiting findings from both studies of interest development over time and the studies of earlier and/or later phases in interest development, the Punnett square facilitates the discerning of patterns among individuals sharing trajectories of interest development. Patterns such as these are useful for researchers studying interest development, and for educators or anyone working with and hoping to support the interest development of others.

Mapping what we know of Helen's experience to the Punnett square, for example, suggests that her achievement demands were low. She was in an earlier phase of interest development at the beginning of her anecdote: She was less metacognitively aware and was unresponsive to potential triggers for interest. She then shifted from being less metacognitively aware and less developed in her interest to being more metacognitively aware and more developed in her interest.

Helen's interest developed outside of the school environment; it could be said to have been a context with low achievement demands, and that Anne, her tutor, provided appropriate types of support in order to allow her interest to develop. Based on Helen's account, she appears to have almost skipped through the phase of maintained situational interest once she made the connection between finger signing and the water, suggesting that maybe the maintaining of interest is an artifact of school-based learning, an interpretation that is suggested by the Renninger and Riley (in press) study as well. Reflecting on Helen's case, and the overviews of the literature provided, it is also noted that Helen is significantly younger than the adolescent learners of the Pugh et al. and Frenzel et al. studies, which suggests that for her, the development of this interest was possibly easier than it might have been for an older, more self-conscious student (see Renninger, 2009).

Further questions to be considered on the basis of the quadrants of the Punnett square in Figure 11.1 include the following: whether Helen's age changes the trajectory of interest development in some way; what difference a high achievement demand context would contribute to what is understood presently; and the particulars of her engagement with both less and more metacognitive awareness (her response to potential triggers, how and why she reacted to them,

and the focus and quality of supports that enabled shifts in her interest development).

Future Directions

Research on interest has demonstrated that it is a variable that develops over time and can be supported to develop at any age. Its presence has been repeatedly found to positively impact learners' attention, goal setting, and learning. Research on interest development, however, is in its infancy. This chapter has examined research on interest and its development, paying particular attention to little understood aspects of the development of interest: the triggering of interest in both earlier and later phases of interest, how interest is maintained once it is triggered, fluctuations in the development of interest, and shifts from one to another phase of interest development.

It is provocative, for example, that interest should be able to be sustained once a respondent can indicate that his or her interest is triggered. This finding also raises other questions, however. For example: Why and when is a potential trigger likely to come to the attention of a learner and work? Are potential triggers for interest the same in all disciplinary contexts, in naturally occurring and experimental contexts? Do potential triggers (e.g., novelty) hold the same meaning for learners in one versus another phase of interest and at different ages?

Similarly, findings suggesting that fluctuations in interest are likely to be due to the learners' perceptions or experience of the environment are critical and raise questions for further study. For example: Are there particular learner characteristics, or configurations of learner characteristics, that contribute to how the environment is perceived, experienced, and whether interest can be expected to develop? What types of environmental supports are needed for learners in different phases of interest? What is the role of metacognition in the development of interest and how might it be fostered?

In the present chapter we worked with aspects and dimensions of interest development that emerged in reviewing the research literature. Any number of Punnett squares could have been developed, drawing on already existing studies. Little research has yet been done on how findings from different studies interact with one another and/or contribute to interest development. The Punnett square proposed in this chapter is an example of a framework that could support the continued examination of complementarities among interest research. In selecting studies to examine, we strove to find complementarities, recognizing that differences of measures, methods, and disciplines provide insight and also present particular challenges. We suggest that forward progress in the understanding of interest and its development involves revisiting the differences and challenges of what has already been found.

Acknowledgments

We are appreciative of the thoughtful comments we received from Jessica E. Bachrach at different phases in this project, Nadine Kolowrat's editorial support, and Allison L. Gannett's help with figures. We also gratefully acknowledge funding for work on this chapter from a Joel Dean Summer Research Grant and the Swarthmore College Faculty Research Fund.

References

Ainley, M. (2007). Being and feeling interested: Transient state, mood, and disposition. In P. Schutz (Ed.), *Emotion in education* (pp. 141- 157). New York: Academic Press.

Ainley, M., & Patrick, L. (2006). Measuring self-regulated learning processes through tracking patterns of student interaction with achievement activities. *Educational Psychology Review*, 18, 267–286.

Ainley, M., Hidi, S., & Berndorff, D. (2002). Interest, learning, and the psychological processes that mediate their relationship. *Journal of Educational Psychology*, 94(3), 545–561.

Alexander, J. M., Johnson, K. E., Leibham, M. E., & Kelley, K. (2008). The development of conceptual interests in young children. *Cognitive Development*, 23, 324–334.

Armstrong, P. I., Allison, P., & Rounds, J. (2008). Development and initial validation of brief public domain RIASEC marker scales. *Journal of Vocational Behavior*, 73, 287–299.

Azevedo, F. S. (2006). Personal excursions: investigating the dynamics of student engagement. *International Journal of Computers for Mathematical Learning*, 11, 57–98.

Barron, B. (2006). Interest and self-sustained learning as catalysts of development: A learning ecology perspective. *Human Development*, 49, 193–224.

Barron, B., Kennedy-Martin, C., Takeuchi, L., & Fithian, R. (2009). Parents as learning partners in the development of technological fluency. *International Journal of Learning and Media*, 1(2), 55–77

Bergin, D. (1999). Influences on classroom interest. *Educational Psychologist*, 34(2), 87–98.

Brown, S., & Lent, R. (1996). A social cognitive framework for career choice counseling. *The Career Development Quarterly*, 44, 355–367.

Chen, A., Darst, P. W., & Pangrazi, R. P. (1999). What constitutes situational interest? Validating a construct in physical education. *Measurement in Physical Education and Exercise Science*, 3, 157–180.

Cobb, P., & Hodge, L. (2004, June). An initial contribution to the development of a design theory of mathematical interests: The case of statistical data analysis. Paper presented as part of the symposium, *Design Theories of Interest, Motivation, and Engagement for the Learning Sciences*. Sixth International Conference of the Learning Sciences, Santa Monica, CA.

Denissen, J. H., Zarrett, N. R., & Eccles, J. S. (2007). "I like to do it, I'm able, and I know I am": Longitudinal couplings between domain-specific achievement, self-concept, and interest. *Child Development*, 78, 430–447.

Dole, J. A., & Sinatra, G. M. (1998). Reconceptualizing change in the cognitive construction of knowledge. *Educational Psychologist*, 33, 109–128.

Durik, A., & Harackiewicz, J. M., (2007). Different strokes for different folks: How individual interest moderates the effects of situational factors on task interest. *Journal of Educational Psychology*, 99(3), 597–610.

Eccles, J. P., & Midgley, C. (1989). State/environment fit: Developmentally appropriate classrooms for early adolescents. In R. Ames & C. Ames (Eds.), *Research on motivation in education* (Vol. 3, pp. 139–181). New York: Guilford Press.

Eccles, J., Wigfield, A., Harold, R. D., & Blumenfeld, P. (1993). Age and gender differences in children's self- and task perceptions during elementary school. *Child Development*, 64(3), 830–847.

Fink, R. (1998). Interest, gender, and literacy development in successful dyslexics. In L. Hoffmann, A. Krapp, K. A. Renninger, & J. Baumert (Eds.), *Interest and learning: Proceedings of the Seeon Conference on Interest and Gender* (pp. 402–408). Kiel, Germany: IPN.

Flavell, J. H. (1976). Metacognitive aspects of problem solving. In L. B. Resnick (Ed.), *The nature of intelligence* (pp. 231–236). Hillsdale, NJ: Erlbaum.

Flowerday, T., Schraw, G., & Stevens, J. (2004). The role of choice and interest in reader engagement. *The Journal of Experimental Education*, 72(2), 93–114.

Fredricks, J. A., & Eccles, J. (2002). Children's competence and value beliefs from childhood through adolescence: Growth trajectories in two male-sex-typed domains. *Developmental Psychology*, 38, 519–533.

Frenzel, A. C., Goetz, T., Pekrun, R., & Watt, H. M. G. (2010). Development of mathematics interest in adolescence: Influences of gender, family, and school context. *Journal of Research on Adolescence*, 20(2), 507–537.

Girod, M., Twyman, T., & Wojcikiewicz, S. (2010). Teaching and learning science for transformative, aesthetic experience. *Journal of Science Teacher Education, 21*, 801–824.

Girod, M., & Wong, D. (2002). An aesthetic (Deweyan) perspective on science learning: Case studies of three fourth graders. *The Elementary School Journal*, 87, 574–587.

Gisbert, K. (1998). Individual interest in mathematics and female gender identity: Biographical case studies. In L. Hoffmann, A. Krapp, K. A. Renninger, & J. Baumert (Eds.), *Interest and learning: Proceedings of the Seeon Conference on Interest and Gender* (pp. 387–401). Kiel, Germany: IPN.

Green-Demers, I., Pelletier, L. G., Stewart, D. G., & Gushue, N. R. (1998). Coping with the less interesting aspects of training: Toward a model of interest and motivation enhancement in individual sports. *Basic and Applied Social Psychology*, 20(4), 251–261.

Guthrie, J. T., Wigfield, A., Humenick, N. H., Perencevich, K. C., Taboada, A., & Barbosa, P. (2006). Influences of stimulating tasks on reading motivation and comprehension. *Journal of Educational Research*, 99, 232–247.

Harackiewicz, J. M., Barron, K. E., Pintrich, P. R., Elliot, A. J., & Thrash, T. M. (2002). Revision of achievement goal theory: Necessary and illuminating. *Journal of Educational Psychology*, 94, 638–645.

Harackiewicz, J. M., Barron, K. E., Tauer, J. M., & Elliot, A. J. (2002). Predicting success in college: A longitudinal study of achievement goals and ability measures as predictors of interest and performance from freshman year through graduation. *Journal of Educational Psychology, 94,* 562–575.

Harackiewicz, J. M., Durik, A. M., Barron, K. E., Linnenbrink, L. & Tauer, J. M. (2008). The role of achievement goals in the development of interest: Reciprocal relations between achievement goals, interest, and performance. *Journal of Educational Psychology, 100*(1), 105–122.

Häussler, P., & Hoffmann, L. (2002). An intervention study to enhance girls' interest, self-concept, and achievement in physics classes. *Journal of Research in Science Teaching, 39*(9), 870–888.

Hidi, S. (1990). Interest and its contribution as a mental resource for learning. *Review of Educational Research, 60*(4), 549–571.

Hidi, S. (2006). Interest: A motivational variable with a difference. *Educational Research Review, 7,* 323–350.

Hidi, S., & Ainley, M. (2008). Interest and self-regulation: Relationships between two variables that influence learning. In D. H. Schunk & B. J. Zimmerman (Eds.), *Motivation and self-regulated learning: Theory, research, and application* (pp. 77–109). Mahwah, NJ: Erlbaum.

Hidi, S., & Baird, W. (1986). Interestingness—A neglected variable in discourse processing. *Cognitive Science, 10,* 179–194.

Hidi, S., & Renninger, K. A. (2006). The Four-Phase Model of Interest Development. *Educational Psychologist, 41*(2), 111–127.

Hoffmann, L. (2002). Promoting girls' learning and achievement in physics classes for beginners. *Learning and Instruction, 12,* 447–465.

Holland, J. L. (1985/1997). *Making vocational choices: A theory of vocational personalities and work environments.* Englewood Cliffs, NJ: Prentice Hall.

Hulleman, C. S., Durik, A. M., Schweigert, S. A., & Harackiewicz, J. M. (2008). Task values, achievement goals, and interest: An integrative analysis. *Journal of Educational Psychology, 100*(2), 398–416.

Hulleman, C., & Harackiewicz, J. (2009). Promoting interest and performance in high school science classes. *Science, 326*(5698), 1410–1412.

Jacobs, J. E., Davis-Kean, P., Bleeker, M. M., Eccles, J. S., & Malanchuk, O. (2005). 'I can, but I don't want to': The impact of parents, interests, and activities on gender differences in math. In A. M. Gallagher & J. C. Kaufman (Eds.), *Gender differences in mathematics: An integrative psychological approach* (pp. 246–263). New York: Cambridge University Press.

Jacobs, J. E., & Eccles, J. S. (2000). Parents, task values, and real-life achievement-related choices. In C. Sansone & J.M. Harackiewicz (Eds.), *Intrinsic and extrinsic motivation: The search for optimal motivation and performance* (pp. 405–439). San Diego, CA: Academic Press.

Jacobs, J., Lanza, S., Osgood, D. W., Eccles, J. S., & Wigfield, A. (2002). Ontogeny of children's self-beliefs: Gender and domain differences across grades one through 12. *Child Development, 73,* 509–527.

Katz, I., Assor, A., Kanat-Maymon, Y., & Bereby-Meyer, Y. (2006). Interest as a motivational resource: Feedback and gender matter, but interest makes the difference. *Social Psychology of Education, 9,* 27–42.

Keller, H. (with A. Sullivan & J. A. Macy). (1903). *The story of my life.* New York: Doubleday, Page & Co.

Kim, S., Lee, M. J., & Bong, M. (2009, April). *fMRI study on the effects of task interest and perceived competence during negative feedback processing.* Paper presented at the Meetings of the American Educational Research Association, San Diego, CA.

Krapp, A. (2002). An educational-psychological theory of interest and its relation to SDT. In E. L. Deci & R. M. Ryan (Eds.), *Handbook of self-determination research* (pp. 405–427). New York: University of Rochester Press.

Krapp, A. (2005). Basic needs and the development of interest and intrinsic motivational orientations. *Learning and Instruction, 12,* 383–409.

Krapp, A. (2007). An educational—psychological conceptualization of interest. *International Journal of Educational and Vocational Guidance, 7,* 5–21.

Krapp, A. (2003). Interest and human development: An educational-psychological perspective. In L. Smtih, C. Rogers, & P. Tomlinson (Eds.), *Development and motivation: Joint perspectives* (pp. 57–84). *British Journal of Educational Psychology Monograph Series, Development and Motivation, 2* (series II).

Krapp, A., Hidi, S., & Renninger, K. A. (1992). Interest, learning, and development. In K. A. Renninger, S. Hidi, & A. Krapp (Eds.), *The role of interest in learning and development* (pp. 3–25). Hillsdale, NJ: Erlbaum.

Krapp, A., & Lewalter, D. (2001). Development of interests and interest-based motivational orientations: A longitudinal study in vocational school and work settings. In S. Volet & S. Järvela (Eds.), *Motivation in learning contexts: Theoretical advances and methodological implications* (pp. 209–232). New York: Elsevier.

Kunter, M., Baumert, J., & Köller, O. (2007). Effective classroom management and the development of subject-related interest. *Learning and Instruction, 17*(5), 494–509.

Lawless, K. A., & Kulikowich, J. M. (2006). Domain knowledge and individual interest: The effects of academic level and specialization in statistics and psychology. *Contemporary Educational Psychology, 31,* 30–43.

Lent, R. W., Brown, S. D., & Hackett, G. (1994). Toward a unifying social cognitive theory of career and academic interest, choice, and performance. *Journal of Vocational Behavior, 45,* 79–122.

Lent, R. W., Brown, S. D., & Hackett, G. (2000). Contextual supports and barriers to career choice: A social cognitive analysis. *Journal of Counseling Psychology, 47,* 36–49.

Linnenbrink-Garcia, L., Durik, A. M., Conley, A. M., Barron, K. E., Tauer, J. M., Karabenick, S. A., & Harackiewicz, J. M. (2010). Measuring situational interest in academic domains. *Educational and Psychological Measurement, 70*(4), 647–671.

Lipstein, R., & Renninger, K. A. (2007). "Putting things into words": 12–15-year-old students' interest for writing. In P. Boscolo & S. Hidi (Eds.), *Motivation and writing: Research and school practice* (pp. 113–140). New York: Kluwer Academic/Plenum Press.

Marsh, H. W. (1987). The big-fish-little-pond effect on academic self-concept. *American Psychologist, 79,* 280–295.

Mayer, R. E. (2005). Cognitive theory of multimedia learning. In R. E. Mayer (Ed.), *The Cambridge handbook of multimedia learning* (pp. 31–48). New York: Cambridge University Press.

Mayer, R. E., Griffith, E., Jurkowitz, I. T. N., & Rothman, D. (2008). Increased interestingness of extraneous details in a multimedia science presentation leads to decreased learning. *Journal of Experimental Psychology: Applied, 14*(4), 329–339.

Meyer, D. K., & Turner, J. C. (2002). Discovering emotion in classroom motivation research. *Educational Psychologist, 37,* 107–114.

Mitchell, M. (1993). Situational interest: Its multifaceted structure in the secondary school mathematics classroom. *Journal of Educational Psychology, 85,* 424–436.

Nolen, S. B. (2007). Young children's motivation to read and write: Development in social contexts. *Cognition and Instruction, 25,* 219–270.

Palmer, D. H. (2004). Situational interest and the attitudes towards science of primary teacher education students. *International Journal of Science Education, 26*(7), 895–908.

Palmer, D. H. (2009). Student interest generated during an inquiry skills lesson. *Journal of Research in Science Teaching, 46*(2), 147–165.

Pekrun, R. (2000). A social-cognitive, control-value theory of achievement emotions. In J. Heckhausen (Ed.), *Motivational psychology of human development* (pp 143–163). Oxford, England: Elsevier.

Pugh, K. J. (2002). Teaching for idea-based, transformative experiences in science: An investigation of the effectiveness of two instructional elements. *Teachers College Record, 104,* 1101–1137.

Pugh, K. J. (2004). Newton's laws beyond the classroom walls. *Science Education, 88,* 182–196.

Pugh, K. J., Linnenbrink-Garcia, L., Koskey, K. L., Stewart, V. C., & Manzey, C. (2010). Motivation, learning, and transformative experience: A study of deep engagement in science. *Science Education, 94,* 1–28.

Pressick-Kilborn, K., & Walker, R. (2002). The social construction of interest in a learning community. In D. M. McInerney & S. Van Etten (Eds.), *Research on sociocultural influences on motivation and learning: An historical perspective* (Vol. 2, pp.153–182). Greenwich, CT: Information Age.

Reeve, J., Jang, H., Hardre, P., & Omura, M. (2002). Providing a rationale in an autonomy-supportive way as a strategy to motivate others during an uninteresting activity. *Motivation and Emotion, 26,* 183–207.

Renninger, K. A. (1990). Children's play interests, representation, and activity. In R. Fivush & J. Hudson (Eds.), *Emory cognition series. Vol. III: Knowing and remembering in young children* (pp. 127–165). New York: Cambridge University Press.

Renninger, K. A. (2000). Individual interest and its implications for understanding intrinsic motivation. In C. Sansone & J. M. Harackiewicz (Eds.), *Intrinsic motivation: Controversies and new directions* (pp. 373–404). San Diego, CA: Academic Press.

Renninger, K. A. (2009). Interest and identity development in instruction: An inductive model. *Educational Psychologist, 44*(2), 1–14.

Renninger, K. A. (2010). Working with and cultivating interest, self-efficacy, and self-regulation. In D. Preiss & R. Sternberg (Eds.), *Innovations in educational psychology: Perspectives on learning, teaching and human development* (pp. 107–138). New York: Springer.

Renninger, K. A., Bachrach, J. E., & Posey, S. K. E. (2008). Learner interest and achievement motivation. In M. L. Maehr, S. Karabenick, & T. Urdan (Eds.), *Social psychological perspectives. Vol. 15: Advances in motivation and achievement.* (pp.461–491) Bingley, England: Emerald Group.

Renninger, K. A., Cai, M., Lewis, M., Adams, M., & Ernst, K. (2011). Motivation and learning in an online, unmoderated, mathematics workshop for teachers. R. Small (Ed.), *Educational Technology, Research and Development* [Special Issue: Motivation and New Media], *59* (2), 229–247.

Renninger, K. A., Ewen, E., & Lasher, A. K. (2002). Individual interest as context in expository text and mathematical word problems. *Learning and Instruction, 12,* 467–491.

Renninger, K. A., & Hidi, S. (2011). Revisiting the conceptualization, measurement, and generation of interest. *Educational Psychologist, 46*(3), 168–184.

Renninger, K. A., & Lipstein, R. (2006). Come si sviluppa l'interesse per la scrittura; Cosa volgliono gli studenti e di cosa hannobisogno? [Developing interest for writing: What do students want and what do students need?] *Età Evolutiva,* 84, pp. 65–83.

Renninger, K. A., Ewen, E., & Lasher, A. K. (2002). Individual interest as context in expository text and mathematical word problems. *Learning and Instruction, 12,* 467–491.

Renninger, K. A., & Riley, K., (in press). Interest, cognition, and the case of L- and science. In S. Kreitler (Ed.). *Cognition and motivation: Forging an interdisciplinary perspective.* New York: Cambridge University Press.

Renninger, K. A., Sansone, C., & Smith, J. L. (2004). Love of learning. In C. Peterson & M.E.P. Seligman (Eds.), *Character strengths and virtues: A handbook and classification* (pp. 161–179). New York: Oxford University Press.

Renninger, K. A., & Wozniak, R. (1985). Effect of interest on attentional shift, recognition, and recall in young children. *Developmental Psychology, 21,* 624–632.

Sansone, C., & Thoman, D. B. (2005a). Does how we feel affect what we learn? Some answers and new questions. *Learning and Instruction, 15,* 507–515.

Sansone, C., & Thoman, D.B. (2005b). Interest as the missing motivator in self-regulation. *European Psychologist, 10*(3), 175–186.

Sansone, C., Weir, C., Harpster, L., & Morgan, C. (1992). Once a boring task always a boring task? Interest as a self-regulatory mechanism. *Journal of Personality and Social Psychology, 63,* 379–390.

Schiefele, U. (2009). Situational and individual interest. In K. Wentzel & A. Wigfield (Eds.), *Handbook of Motivation at School* (pp. 197–222). New York: Routledge.

Schiefele, U., & Csikszentmihalyi, M. (1994). Interest and the quality of experience in classrooms. *European Journal of Psychology of Education, 9*(3), 251–270.

Schiefele, U., & Csikszentmihalyi, M. (1995). Motivation and ability factors in mathematics experience and achievement. *Journal of Research in Mathematics Education, 26*(2), 163–181.

Schiefele, U., Krapp, A., Wild, K-P., & Winteler, A. (1993). Eine neue Version des Fragebogens zum Studieninteresse (FSI). Untersuchungen zur Reliabilität und Validität [A new version of the Study Interest Questionnaire (SIQ)]. *Diagnostica, 39,* 335–351.

Schraw, G., Bruning, R., & Svoboda, C. (1995). Sources of situational interest. *Journal of Reading Behavior, 27,* 1–17.

Silvia, P. J. (2006). *Exploring the psychology of interest.* New York: Oxford University Press.

Tsai, Y. M., Kunter, M., Lüdtke, O., Trautwein, U., & Ryan, R. M. (2008). What makes lessons interesting? The role of situational and individual factors in three school subjects. *Journal of Educational Psychology, 100*(2), 460–472.

Turner, S. A., Jr., & Silvia, P. J. (2006). Must things be pleasant? A test of competing appraisal structures. *Emotion, 6*(4), 670–674.

Watt, H. M. G. (2004). Development of adolescents' self-perceptions, values, and task perceptions according to gender and domain in 7th-through 11th-grade Australian students. *Child Development, 75*(5), 1556–1574.

Wigfield, A., & Cambria, J. (2010). Students' achievement values, goal orientations, and interest: Definitions, develop-ment, and relations to achievement outcomes. *Developmental Review, 30*, 1–35.

Wigfield, A., Eccles, J., Schiefele, U., Roeser, R., & Davis-Kean, P. (2006). Development of achievement motivation. In In R. Lerner & W. Damon (Series Eds.), N. Eisenberg (Vol. Ed.), *Handbook of child psychology. Vol. 3: Social, emotional, and personality development* (6th ed., pp. 933–1002). New York: Wiley.

PART 4

Goals and Motivation

Achievement Goals

Kou Murayama, Andrew J. Elliot, *and* Ron Friedman

Abstract

In this chapter, we describe the achievement goal construct's origin and highlight noteworthy developments in the literature. We then use this historical overview to provide the context for several key theoretical and empirical issues surrounding the current achievement goal approach, including the precise definition of achievement goals, the possible inclusion of additional goals into the achievement goal approach, the measurement of achievement goals, the debates surrounding performance-approach and performance-avoidance goals, contextual effects on achievement goals, and the consideration of methodological expansion.

Key Words: achievement motivation, achievement goals, approach-avoidance

Introduction

Central to the study of human motivation is the concept of goals, which can be defined as a form of self-regulation that guides people toward future-directed aims (Austin & Vancouver, 1996; Elliot & Fryer, 2008). Goals focus people's attention and facilitate responses that are compatible with their objectives, thereby promoting the achievement of desired outcomes or the avoidance of undesired outcomes. The content of people's goals varies widely, and researchers studying the antecedent and consequences of goals have categorized goals by specific features or common themes, in order to compare goals across different domains. One goal category that has received considerable attention within the field of psychology is that of achievement goals (Duda, 2005; Elliot, 2005; Kaplan & Maehr, 2007; Meece, Anderman, & Anderman, 2006; Senko, Durik, & Harackiewicz, 2008).

The achievement goal construct was originally developed in the late 1970s and has evolved considerably from its original form over 30 years ago. In this chapter, we start by presenting a history of the achievement goal construct, charting its development from initial conceptualization to its present-day form. We then use this historical overview to provide the context for several key theoretical and empirical issues surrounding the current achievement goal literature.

Historical Overview

The establishment of the achievement goal construct has occurred through the combined efforts of several theorists working both independently and collaboratively over a number of decades. Unlike most theoretical approaches in psychology, the achievement goal approach did not arise through the refinement of a single theoretical framework but emerged through the fusion of several distinct lines of thinking. In this sense, the research tradition on achievement goals does not constitute "achievement goal theory;" rather, it is best construed in terms of "theories of achievement goals" or "the achievement goal approach."

Dichotomous Model

The achievement goal construct originally emerged from the work of psychologists Carole Ames, Carol Dweck, Marty Maehr, and John Nicholls, each of whom led an independent research program at the

University of Illinois. In the fall of 1977, they began meeting regularly in a series of seminars on motivation at the Institute for Child Behavior and Development in the Children's Research Center (Elliot, 2005; Roberts, 2001). Shortly thereafter, a series of papers emerged (Maehr & Nicholls, 1980; Nicholls & Dweck, 1979) articulating the foundational ideas of the achievement goal approach.

It should be noted that research on achievement motivation in the 1970s was heavily influenced by the causal attribution tradition (Weiner, 1985; Weiner, Heckhausen, & Meyer, 1972; Weiner & Kukla, 1970) and the achievement motive tradition (Atkinson & Raynor, 1978; McClelland, Atkinson, Clark, & Lowell, 1976). The combined efforts of Ames, Dweck, Maehr, and Nicholls can be viewed, in part, as an attempt to overcome the weaknesses and limitations of the causal attribution and achievement motive traditions. The achievement goal construct was, therefore, not created ex nihilo.

A common feature of early work on the achievement goal construct is the usage of a *dichotomous model*, which distinguishes between two types of achievement goals. These distinctions typically center on the different foci an individual might bring to a given achievement activity (Dweck & Elliott, 1983; Nicholls, 1984). Two dichotomous models that were highly influential in the development of the achievement goal construct are Dweck's framework, grounded in the *learning-performance* distinction, and Nicholls's model, grounded in the *task-ego* distinction. The following section reviews these models and outlines the influence of each approach on later work.

DWECK'S CONCEPTUALIZATION

Dweck's achievement goal conceptualization emerged from her research with late grade-school-age children (Diener & Dweck, 1978, 1980; Dweck, 1975; Dweck & Reppucci, 1973). Dweck found that after experiencing failure on a task, some children exhibited "helpless" responses (characterized by decrements in persistence and performance, the onset of negative affect and expectancies, the attribution of failure to insufficient ability, and the avoidance of subsequent challenge), while others exhibited "mastery" responses (characterized by sustained or enhanced persistence and performance, continued positive affect and expectancies, the attribution of failure to insufficient effort, and the pursuit of subsequent challenge). Dweck was interested in identifying the underlying root of these distinct response patterns. The causal attribution tradition

suggests that children experience helplessness when they attribute failure to insufficient ability, but it does not explain what factors cause this maladaptive attribution pattern. The achievement motive tradition, on the other hand, overemphasized dispositions without sufficiently addressing the role of cognitions in predicting achievement behavior (Dweck & Wortman, 1982). In her work, Dweck sought to address these limitations and proposed that children's responses to failure were related to the *goals* they held for completing the task (Dweck, 1986, 1999; Dweck & Leggett, 1988).

According to Dweck's theorizing, children who adopt *learning goals* view achievement pursuits as opportunities to learn and increase their competence. Children with learning goals also view failure as important feedback on their progress, rather than an indictment of their ability. Consequently, the experience of failure leads children with learning goals to redouble their efforts, which is consistent with a mastery response pattern. In contrast, children who hold *performance goals* view achievement pursuits not as opportunities to learn but as opportunities to demonstrate their competence (Elliott & Dweck, 1988; Smiley & Dweck, 1994). To these children, failure is a signal that they do not possess the ability to succeed. After experiencing failure, children with performance goals reduce their efforts, which is consistent with a helpless response pattern.

Dweck further posited that the adoption of different achievement goals is influenced by one's implicit theories of ability. Implicit theories represent a person's beliefs about the relative stability or malleability of objective forms of competence. A belief that ability is a stable entity and not amenable to change (called *entity theory*) was posited to lead to performance goal adoption, while a belief that ability is malleable and highly amenable to change (called *incremental theory*) was posited to lead to learning goal adoption (Bempechat, London, & Dweck, 1991). Taken together, Dweck's work characterizes achievement goals as proximal predictors of failure responses that are influenced by a person's implicit theories of competence.

NICHOLL'S CONCEPTUALIZATION

Nicholls's work on achievement goals emerged from his research on the way children conceptualize ability. Nicholls argued that both the achievement motive and causal attribution traditions had failed to recognize that ability may be construed in different ways (Nicholls, 1983). According to Nicholls

(Jagacinski & Nicholls, 1984, 1987; Nicholls, 1976, 1978, 1980), children hold an *undifferentiated* view of ability through most of their early development; that is, they do not distinguish between ability and effort. Success is essentially equated with effort, and those who expend more effort are generally regarded as having greater ability. By roughly the age of 12, however, children acquire a more *differentiated* view of ability; that is, they gain the capacity to distinguish between ability and effort. Within this differentiated view, high ability is only inferred when one outperforms others while expending equal effort, or when one performs the same as others while expending less effort.

Nicholls argued that adolescents and adults can construe achievement situations in either an undifferentiated or a differentiated fashion, and these distinct views of ability form the basis for the two major achievement goals (Nicholls, 1984, 1989). People who pursue competence in an undifferentiated sense—meaning that they simultaneously focus on effort and learning—are said to be in a state of *task involvement*. People who pursue competence in a differentiated sense—meaning that they focus on outperforming others with limited effort—are said to be in a state of *ego involvement*. Importantly, task and ego involvement were posited by Nicholls to interact with perceived ability in predicting processes and outcomes. For example, ego involvement was said to lead to the selection of moderately challenging tasks when accompanied by high perceived ability (an adaptive response), but it was said to lead to the selection of very easy or very difficult tasks when accompanied by low perceived ability (a maladaptive response).

AMES'S INTEGRATION

While there are clear differences in the achievement goal conceptualizations proffered by Dweck and Nicholls, the similarities are far more striking. First, within each theory, one goal (learning/task) is characterized in terms of developing ability and seeking task mastery, while the other (performance/ego) is characterized in terms of demonstrating ability (often through normative competence). Second, both distinctions identify goals that ultimately yield fairly comparable outcomes. And third, in both conceptualizations, individuals' perceptions of their own ability are predicted to moderate the effect of achievement goal adoption. That is, performance/ego goals were posited to exert the most negative impact when accompanied by low perceptions of competence, whereas learning/ego goals were posited to exert the same positive impact across competence perceptions.

This convergence was not limited to the work of Dweck and Nicholls. Similar dichotomies were proposed by other achievement goal theorists, such as Maehr (Maehr, 1983), Ames (Ames, 1984), and Covington (Covington & Omelich, 1984). By the late 1980s, a wealth of empirical work had emerged supporting the idea that different achievement goals predict distinct achievement-related outcomes, yet researchers were using different (albeit overlapping) terminologies to describe these effects.

Noting the conceptual similarities, Ames and Archer (1987, 1988) argued that the achievement goal literature could be unified into a single framework that distinguishes between two types of goals: *mastery* and *performance*. This was a milestone event—the introduction of an integrative framework that brought cohesion to the field. Consequently, researchers have largely adopted Ames and Archer's (1987, 1988) terminological recommendation of *mastery* and *performance* goals, and research on achievement goals proliferated widely thereafter.

Early empirical work revealed a relatively clear and consistent picture of the consequences of mastery goal adoption. Mastery goals were shown to lead to positive processes and outcomes, such as task value and self-efficacy (Pintrich & DeGroot, 1990; Pintrich & Garcia, 1991), deep-processing learning strategies (Kaplan & Midgley, 1997; Nolen, 1988; Nolen & Haladyna, 1990a), self-regulated learning strategies (Bouffard, Boisvert, Vezeau, & Larouche, 1995; Middleton & Midgley, 1997; Miller, Greene, Montalvo, Ravindran, & Nicholls, 1996; Wolters, 1998), persistence (Elliott & Dweck, 1988), and adaptive help seeking (Butler & Neuman, 1995; Newman, 1998; Ryan & Pintrich, 1997). In sum, mastery goals were shown to lead to a host of adaptive outcomes.

The consequences of performance goal adoption were less clear. A number of theorists argued that performance goal adoption is associated with negative, maladaptive outcomes, due to its inherent focus on outperforming others (e.g., Ames, 1992; Urdan, 1997). Empirical findings, however, did not provide clear support for this assumption. For example, performance goals were shown to have a null or positive influence on adaptive outcomes in certain types of achievement contexts (Koestner, Zuckerman, & Koestner, 1987; Miller & Hom, 1990; Sansone, Sachau, & Weir, 1989). In addition, among those with certain types of personality dispositions, performance goals were associated with positive outcomes (Harackiewicz & Elliot, 1993; Harackiewicz & Sansone, 1991).

Approach-Avoidance Distinction: Trichotomous and 2 x 2 Models

To help resolve ambiguities surrounding the consequences of performance goals, and further refine the mastery-performance distinction, Elliot and colleagues (Elliot & Church, 1997; Elliot & Harackiewicz, 1996) introduced the approach-avoidance distinction to the achievement goal literature. The approach-avoidance distinction centers on whether an individual is focused on approaching a positive possibility (e.g., success) or on avoiding a negative possibility (e.g., failure). Although the approach-avoidance distinction had been largely ignored within the achievement goal literature, it had been readily acknowledged by a long line of researchers and theorists early in the study of achievement behavior. For example, Lewin and colleagues' (Lewin, Dembo, Festinger, & Sears, 1944) theory of resultant valence (the first formal model of achievement motivation) incorporated the *desire for success* and the *desire to avoid failure* as the two primary independent motivational orientations. Similarly, McClelland posited that the approach-avoidance distinction constitutes two different types of achievement motivation (McClelland, 1951). Atkinson introduced his classic need achievement theory, a mathematical framework that designated the *desire to approach success* and the *desire to avoid failure* as the primary determinants of achievement behavior (Atkinson, 1957).

The approach-avoidance distinction has also been incorporated well beyond the achievement motivation literature, ranging from traditional behavioral theories (e.g., Hull, 1943; Skinner, 1953), to developmental theories (e.g., Bowlby, 1969), to personality theories (e.g., Eysenck, 1967; Gray, 1987), to cognitive theories (e.g., Kahneman & Tversky, 1979), to neuroscience theories (e.g., Davidson, 2000; Rolls, 2005). Given the prevalence of the approach-avoidance distinction throughout psychology, it is not surprising that its application to the achievement goal literature has proven highly generative.

TRICHOTOMOUS MODEL OF ACHIEVEMENT GOALS

Initially, the approach-avoidance distinction was applied to performance goals to help explain inconsistent findings related to the consequences of performance goal adoption. Elliot and Harackiewicz (1996) separated the conventional performance goal construct into conceptually independent approach and avoidance goals, introducing three distinct achievement goals comprised of mastery, performance-approach, and performance-avoidance goals. When pursuing performance-approach goals, individuals aim to attain positive outcomes relative to others (e.g., "My goal is to perform better than others"), whereas individuals pursuing performance-avoidance goals aim to avoid negative outcomes compared to others (e.g., "My goal is to avoid doing poorly comparing to others"). The mastery goal construct was virtually the same in the dichotomous and trichotomous models.

Importantly, distinguishing between performance-approach goals and performance-avoidance goals helped elucidate when performance-based goals were most likely to have adaptive or maladaptive consequences. Reanalyses of extant data (Elliot & Moller, 2003; Harackiewicz, Barron, Pintrich, Elliot, & Thrash, 2002; Rawsthorne & Elliot, 1999), as well as newly emerging data, revealed similar findings (Elliot & Church, 1997; Elliot, McGregor, & Gable, 1999; Middleton & Midgley, 1997; Skaalvik, 1997; Vandewalle, 1997). Performance-avoidance goals were clearly linked to maladaptive learning behaviors and outcomes (e.g., disorganized study strategies, lower grades, lower intrinsic motivation), while performance-approach goals were linked to several positive behaviors and outcomes (e.g., effort, persistence, higher grades). This pattern of findings was observed in both experimental and correlational studies.

2 X 2 MODEL OF ACHIEVEMENT GOALS

Elliot and colleagues (Elliot, 1999; Elliot & McGregor, 2001; see also Pintrich, 2000a) then extended the approach-avoidance distinction to mastery goals, resulting in a 2 x 2 achievement goal model comprised of mastery-approach, mastery-avoidance, performance-approach, and performance-avoidance goals (Fig. 12.1). A key feature of the 2 x 2 model was the addition of *mastery-avoidance goals*, which focused on not doing worse than before or not failing to master a task (e.g., "My goal is not to do worse than before" or "My goal is to avoid not mastering a task"). Extant empirical work on mastery goals at that time focused exclusively on positive possibilities (i.e., approaching success), which were termed *mastery-approach goals* (e.g., "My goal is to do better than before" or "My goal is to master a task" within the 2 x 2 framework).

Although mastery-avoidance goals were presumed to be less prevalent than other achievement goals (mastery approach, performance approach, and performance avoidance), they were also thought to be common in certain instances. For example, mastery-avoidance goals were thought to become more salient as individuals enter later adulthood. As a person's physical and mental skills begin to decline, the person may shift his or her focus to "not losing important abilities." Similarly, athletes may also be prime candidates for mastery-avoidance goal adoption. When athletes reach their peak performance, they may begin to focus on not performing worse than they have performed to date. Factor analytic studies confirmed the validity of the 2 x 2 structure of achievement goals (Elliot & McGregor, 2001; Elliot & Murayama, 2008; Finney, Pieper, & Barron, 2004), and a cross-cultural replication was also largely supportive (Murayama, Zhou, & Nesbit, 2009). Mastery-avoidance goals have been linked to fewer adaptive processes and outcomes than mastery-approach goals but also fewer maladaptive processes and outcomes than performance-avoidance goals (Bong, 2009; Conroy, Elliot, & Hofer, 2003; Cury, Elliot, Fonseca, & Moller, 2006; Elliot & McGregor, 2001; Elliot & Murayama, 2008; Elliot & Reis, 2003; Sideridis, 2008). Research on mastery-avoidance goals, however, remains at a very early stage, and a full understanding of their antecedents and consequences is still developing.

Current Theoretical and Empirical Issues

Over the past few decades, the achievement goal construct has emerged as a central variable in the study of motivation. However, there remain a number of outstanding theoretical and empirical issues yet to be explored. In this section, using the historical context that we have discussed, we overview these issues, providing a broader perspective for the evolution of the achievement goal construct.

Definition of Achievement Goal Constructs

Motivational theorists often assume that a consensual definition of "achievement goal" has been established. However, a careful reading of the literature reveals a somewhat inconsistent picture (Elliot & Thrash, 2001; Kaplan & Maehr, 2007). Those offering definitions of the achievement goal construct have typically adopted one of three basic approaches.

ACHIEVEMENT GOALS AS AN OMNIBUS CONSTRUCT

The first approach, introduced by early researchers, describes achievement goals in terms of the *purpose for which a person engages in achievement behavior* (Dweck, 1986; Maehr, 1989; Nicholls, 1989). This approach is appealing because it intuitively captures what achievement motivation theorists, lay and trained alike, want to know: "For what purpose is the person engaging in behavior in this achievement situation?" However, it should be noted that the operative word in this definition, "purpose," can take on several different meanings. According to the *Random House Dictionary of the English Language* (1993), the word *purpose* can be defined in two primary ways: as "the reason for which something exists or is done, made, used, etc." and "an intended or desired result; end; aim; goal." Researchers who adopt this approach have implicitly employed a combination of both of these meanings simultaneously. That is, the term *achievement goal* has been used as both the reason for behavior in an achievement situation (e.g., the development or demonstration of ability) *and* as the aim or outcome that is sought in an achievement situation (e.g., normative ability or self-referential ability). Accordingly, this approach can be problematic because it defines the achievement goal construct in two different ways. For example, performance-approach goals can be conceptualized in terms of both the reason of impressing others *and* the aim of doing better than other people.

The second approach, which emerged through the conceptual integration of Ames and Archer (1987, 1988), characterizes achievement goals as *a network or integrated pattern of beliefs and feelings about success, effort, ability, errors, feedback, and standards of evaluation that together provide a wide-ranging framework or schema toward achievement tasks* (Ames, 1992; Kaplan & Maehr, 2007; Pintrich, 2000a). This comprehensive account—often labeled *achievement goal orientation*—is initially appealing in that it unifies many achievement-relevant variables into a single organizational system. However, upon careful consideration, this strength can also be viewed as a limitation. Because this definition includes a collection of variables, it is difficult to identify exactly which aspect of the achievement goal construct is responsible for any hypothesized or observed effects. The inability to differentiate antecedents and consequences from achievement goals per se may present significant impediments to researchers utilizing this approach.

ACHIEVEMENT GOALS AS SPECIFIC AIMS

A third approach, which was developed to address the limitations of previous definitions, is simply to describe achievement goals as an *aim with competence at its conceptual core* (Elliot & Murayama, 2008; Elliot & Thrash, 2001). Within this account, competence is integral with regard to both the definition and valence of a goal. That is, definition and valence are construed as necessary features of achievement goals because it is not possible to fully specify an achievement goal construct without identifying how competence is defined and valenced. The performance-mastery distinction maps onto the *definition* of competence, whereas approach-avoidance distinction maps on the *valence* of competence.

Competence is *defined* by the standard or referent that is used in evaluating it. Three different standards may be used: an absolute standard (the requirements of the task itself), an intrapersonal standard (one's own past attainment or maximum potential attainment), and a normative standard (the performance of others). That is, competence may be evaluated and therefore defined, in absolute terms according to one's mastery of a task, in *intra*personal terms according to one's personal trajectory, and in *inter*personal terms according to one's attainment relative to others. Absolute and intrapersonal competence share many conceptual and empirical similarities and, at present, may be considered jointly rather than separately. As such, competence may be defined in absolute/intrapersonal terms or in interpersonal terms, and two types of achievement goals may be delineated according to the type of competence that an individual commits to in an achievement situation. Mastery goals are posited to map onto an absolute/intrapersonal standard, while performance goals are posited to map onto an intrapersonal standard.

Competence is also *valenced* in that it can be construed in positive terms (i.e., competence or success) or in negative terms (i.e., incompetence or failure). Two types of achievement goals may be delineated according whether the competence-relevant focus is on approaching the positive possibility of competence, or on avoiding the negative possibility of incompetence. Approach goals represent positive concerns for competence, while avoidance goals represent negative concerns for incompetence. These two aspects of competence are combined to form the four different types of goals represented in the aforementioned 2 x 2 framework, which consists of mastery-approach, mastery-avoidance, performance-approach, and performance-avoidance goals (Fig. 12.1).

In sum, we have described three approaches to defining and conceptualizing achievement goal constructs. Our preferred perspective is that achievement goals are best defined by the third approach, which provides conceptual clarity—a critical requirement for scientific investigation. This approach also distinguishes achievement goals from the many different dispositions, tendencies, processes, and outcomes to which they are associated, allowing researchers to study the relationship between these constructs.

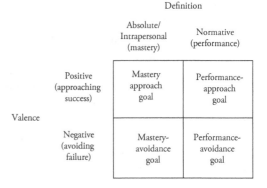

Fig. 12.1. The 2 x 2 achievement goal model. Definition and valence represent the two dimensions of competence. Absolute/intrapersonal and normative represent the two ways that competence may be defined; positive and negative represent the two ways that competence may be valenced.

There is, however, room for debate as to how achievement goals should be conceptualized, and continued discussion on this issue should result in theoretical and empirical progress in the field.

Other Achievement Goals

A number of theorists have introduced additional goal constructs to the established mastery-performance and approach-avoidance dichotomies (for early examples, see Maehr & Braskamp, 1986; Maehr & Nicholls, 1980). Several candidates for inclusion began to receive consideration and scrutiny in the early to mid 1990s, most notably, work-avoidance goals, extrinsic goals, and social goals (see Urdan, 1997, for a review).

Work-avoidance goals (also labeled "academic alienation") were defined in terms of trying to get away with putting as little work or effort as possible into achievement tasks (Meece, Blumenfeld, & Hoyle, 1988; Nicholls, Patashnick, & Nolen, 1985; Nolen, 1988). Work-avoidance goals were thought to differ from traditional avoidance goals in that it is the avoidance of work—and not failure—that is the main focus. Research findings have consistently shown a negative pattern of cognition, affect, and behavior for individuals pursuing work-avoidance goals (Archer, 1994; Meece et al., 1988; Nicholls et al., 1985; Nolen, 1988; Skaalvik, 1997).

Extrinsic goals were defined in terms of striving to succeed in order to earn a reward or avoid a punishment (Maehr, 1983; Midgley & Urdan, 1995; Pintrich & Garcia, 1991). Extrinsic goals were initially considered a form of performance goal (e.g., Pintrich, Smith, Garcia, & Mckeachie, 1993); however, recent studies have shown that while extrinsic goals may overlap with performance goals, the two constructs are not identical (Malka & Covington, 2005; Midgley et al., 1998). Several studies also found that in general, this orientation is associated with a maladaptive attitude toward achievement that includes placing a lower value on the task, reporting higher achievement anxiety, admitting to relatively more cheating, and using self-handicapping strategies (Anderman, Griesinger, & Westerfield, 1998; Ryan & Pintrich, 1997; Wolters, Yu, & Pintrich, 1996).

Social goals were defined as strivings that focus on interpersonal relationships (Maehr & Nicholls, 1980; Wentzel, 1989), and a number of different variants were introduced, including social approval goals, social responsibility goals, social status goals, prosocial goals, and affiliation goals (Urdan & Maehr, 1995). Among these iterations, social responsibility goals were posited to have the most positive impact on student learning (Wentzel, 1989, 1991, 1998).

While each of these classifications offers a unique and potentially valuable way of classifying people's strivings, the achievement goal literature has yet to develop an explicit criterion for determining inclusion. Our perspective is that establishing competence as the conceptual core of the achievement goal construct (the third definitional approach that we discussed earlier) provides clear guidelines for evaluating additional achievement goal candidates. According to this approach, achievement goals are considered cognitive aims that one adopts when striving for competence, and distinct achievement goals are characterized in terms of the definition and valence of competence (Elliot & Thrash, 2001). Using these guidelines, we can better assess the value of incorporating these additional classifications.

Work-avoidance goals differ from striving for competence, because work-avoidant individuals are trying to get away from commitment to a task and are therefore not focused on achieving competence or avoiding incompetence. Similarly, extrinsic goals do not focus on a competence-based striving per se, but on external factors such as monetary rewards. Some extrinsic goals may qualify as achievement goals; however, not all extrinsic goals are achievement goals. Social goals involve a focus on interpersonal considerations, rather than a focus on competence considerations (Wentzel, 1991). Therefore, social goals, as traditionally defined, are not achievement goals (although see Ryan and Shim, 2006, 2008; for goals that focus on social competence and are, therefore, a form of achievement goal).

The competence-based conceptualization of achievement goals also suggests a systematic guideline for consideration of additional achievement goals. As noted earlier, within the definition of mastery goal in the competence-based framework, competence is defined in terms of success relative to either an absolute (task-based) *or* intrapersonal standard. Accordingly, a straightforward theoretical extension would entail separating these absolute and intrapersonal standards, resulting in a 3 x 2 framework comprising six types of achievement goal: task-approach goals ("do a task well"), task-avoidance goals ("avoid doing poorly on a task"), self-approach goals ("do better than before"), self-avoidance goals ("avoid doing worse than before"), other-approach goals ("do better than others"), and other-avoidance goals ("avoid doing worse than others"). Empirical investigation of a 3 x 2 framework has just started (see Elliot, Murayama, & Pekrun, 2011) and is an intriguing topic that merits future inquiry.

Measurement of Achievement Goals

Another current issue in the achievement goal literature that warrants consideration is the usage of different measurement tools. Over the past two decades, a host of achievement goal measures have appeared in the educational psychology, industrial/organizational psychology, social-personality psychology, and sport and exercise psychology literatures. Some have focused on the mastery-performance distinction alone, while others have focused on both the mastery-performance and approach-avoidance distinctions (for reviews, see Elliot & Murayama, 2008; Fulmer & Frijters, 2009; Kaplan & Maehr, 2007). The use of different measurement tools is important because not all achievement goal measures are created equal; different measures tend to reflect distinct theoretical backgrounds. We therefore encourage researchers to consider measurement tools carefully when comparing results across studies.

As noted earlier, some research construes the achievement goal construct as an omnibus combination of variables reflecting an integrated pattern of beliefs and feelings. Accordingly, those who subscribe to this view utilize assessments that combine several distinct components of achievement goals into a single measure. For example, performance-approach goal measures commonly include items that combine a focus on *demonstrating competence* with a focus on *outperforming a normative standard* (e.g., "I'd like to show my teacher that I'm smarter than the other students"; Button, Mathieu, & Zajac, 1996; Elliot & Church, 1997; Greene & Miller, 1996; Harackiewicz, Barron, Elliot, Carter, & Lehto, 1997; Meece et al.,

1988; Midgley et al., 2000; Roberts & Treasure, 1995; Skaalvik, 1997; Stipek & Gralinski, 1996). Alternatively, some performance-based goal scales focus only on demonstrating competence, excluding a normative standard (Middleton & Midgley, 1997; Vandewalle, 1997; Zweig & Webster, 2004). Moreover, some measures include items that do not really focus on goals at all but attend to other aspects of achievement, including intrapersonal definitions of success (e.g. "I feel most successful when...", Button et al., 1996; Duda, Chi, Newton, Walling, & Catley, 1995; Duda & Nicholls, 1992; Roberts & Treasure, 1995; Skaalvik, 1997), the value of certain outcomes or experiences (e.g., "It is important for me to...", Bouffard et al., 1995; Conroy et al., 2003; Elliot & Church, 1997; Elliot & McGregor, 2001; Middleton & Midgley, 1997; Stipek & Gralinski, 1996; Vandewalle, 1997; Zweig & Webster, 2004), affective components (e.g., "I feel really pleased when...", Bouffard et al., 1995; Button et al., 1996; Elliot & Church, 1997; Harackiewicz et al., 1997; Middleton & Midgley, 1997; Skaalvik, 1997; Stipek & Gralinski, 1996; Vandewalle, 1997), and the consequences of failure (e.g., "My fear of performing poorly in this class is often what motivates me," Elliot & Church, 1997; Elliot & McGregor, 2001; Meece et al., 1988; Skaalvik, 1997; Vandewalle, 1997).

Elliot and Murayama (2008) recently developed a new 2 x 2 measure labeled the Achievement Goal Questionnaire Revised (AGQ-R), which eliminates goal-irrelevant features, such as motives and affect, common to previous measures. This measure specifically focuses on tapping cognitive aims and therefore makes it possible to assess achievement goals based on the competence-based framework discussed earlier.

Due in part to the wide variety of achievement goal measures, researchers in the field have yet to converge on a single scale that best captures the achievement goal construct. From our perspective, the choice of achievement goal measure depends on one's theoretical background. Ultimately, researchers must be attentive to the correspondence between how goals are conceptualized and how they are operationalized within a given assessment device. For example, when interested in assessing the influence of achievement goals on emotional states, we would recommend choosing an achievement goal measure that *does not* contain affective components in the items, so that the obtained relationship cannot be attributed to the overlap between items.

Similarly, when manipulating achievement goals in an experimental setting, researchers must take care to craft manipulations that correspond to elements of achievement goals of focal theoretical interest. As is the case with achievement goal measures, achievement goal manipulations are not uniform and researchers have used many different procedures in the past (Rawsthorne & Elliot, 1999; Utman, 1997). Here again, we recommend first settling on a theoretical position regarding the achievement goal construct, and then choosing (or designing) a manipulation that corresponds to that position.

Debates on Performance-Approach and Performance-Avoidance Goals

As noted earlier, motivation researchers have long debated whether performance-based goal adoption ultimately facilitates or impedes achievement (Brophy, 2005; Midgley, Kaplan, & Middleton, 2001; Urdan & Mestas, 2006). In 2001, Midgley, Kaplan, and Middleton attempted to resolve this dispute by suggesting that performance-approach goals are adaptive, but only when mastery-approach goal adoption is also present (see also Kaplan & Middleton, 2002). Later research has not supported this hypothesis, in that performance-approach goals alone are related to several types of positive outcomes (Elliot & Moller, 2003; Harackiewicz et al., 2002); however, Midgley et al.'s suggestion raises the interesting possibility that certain *interactions* of achievement goals (e.g., high mastery-approach goals and high performance-approach goals) may produce a pattern of results that differs from a simple combination of main effects. This perspective is known as the *multiple goals model* (Pintrich, 2000b; for other definitions of multiple goals model, see Barron & Harackiewicz, 2001; Senko, Hulleman, & Harackiewicz, 2011) and has been investigated using interaction effect analyses (e.g., Ames & Archer, 1988; Harackiewicz et al., 1997; Pintrich, 2000b; Wolters, 2004) and profile analyses (e.g., Daniels et al., 2008; Levy-Tossman, Kaplan, & Assor, 2007; Meece & Holt, 1993). Unfortunately, empirical investigations of multiple goal models have failed to yield consistent results to date. These inconsistencies, however, may be due to statistical difficulties in detecting interaction effects in field research (McClelland & Judd, 1993). We therefore believe that further research is needed to investigate the interactive influence of multiple achievement goals. Of particular interest is the combination of approach-based *and* avoidance-based goals. This issue has failed to receive attention from researchers, despite considerable interest from a number of pioneering achievement motivation theorists (see Atkinson, 1957; Lewin et al., 1944; Miller & Dollard, 1941).

Another intriguing possibility is that the reasons or motives *underlying* goal pursuits may strongly influence the consequences of specific goal adoption. According to this view, individuals may adopt the same goal for fundamentally different reasons, and their experiences and outcomes may differ as a function of their underlying motivation. For example, individuals may strive to outperform others because this goal represents an enjoyable challenge, provides meaningful competence information, or provides an opportunity to exercise their skills and capabilities. On the other hand, individuals may pursue performance-approach goals because they feel compelled to demonstrate their abilities, perhaps because they see doing so as a means of obtaining positive regard from others. When pursued for this reason, performance-approach goals are likely to be experienced as stressful and anxiety inducing, and they may lead to less adaptive outcomes. In short, some reasons for pursuing goals may lead to highly positive experiences and adaptive outcomes, whereas others may lead to less positive experiences and less adaptive outcomes. This combinatorial construct, which represents both the goal and the underlying reason that it is pursued, is known as a *goal complex* (Elliot, 2006; Elliot & Thrash, 2001). Goal complex research is now in the very early stages (see Dompnier, Darnon, & Butera, 2009), and it would greatly benefit from additional work that directly and systematically tests the consequences of distinct goal-based combinations.

Another issue that has been debated to some degree within the achievement goal literature concerns whether performance-avoidance goals warrant their own category. A number of psychologists have challenged the performance-approach and performance-avoidance distinction based on the finding that respondents rarely mention performance-avoidance goals in open-ended goal measures (Brophy, 2005; Lemos, 1996; Roeser, 2004; Roeser, Peck, Nasir, Alexander, & Winne, 2006; Urdan & Mestas, 2006; but see Senko, Hulleman, & Harackiewicz, 2011).

In our view, this criticism is unconvincing for several reasons. First, when it comes to assessing the value of psychological constructs, what matters most is not the mean level of occurrence but the construct's relations with other psychological outcomes. Many studies have clearly demonstrated the predictive utility of performance-avoidance goals (e.g., Bong, 2009; Elliot & Church, 1997; Elliot & Murayama, 2008; Middleton & Midgley, 1997; Pekrun, Elliot, & Maier, 2009), and to the extent that performance-avoidance goal adoption predicts unique outcomes,

there is value in attending to this construct. Second, there is considerable evidence showing that social comparison (normative competence) is automatically, nonconsciously processed (Mussweiler, 2003; Mussweiler & Epstude, 2009; Stapel & Koomen, 2001). The fact that performance-avoidance goals are not frequently mentioned in open-ended measures does not, therefore, necessarily indicate that these goals are not guiding people's behaviors in achievement situations.

A final criticism of the performance-approach/ performance avoidance-distinction highlights the high correlation between the two goals, suggesting that these goals are functionally indistinguishable (Duda, 2005; Roeser, 2004; Roeser et al., 2006; Urdan & Mestas, 2006). In fact, some have indicated that students cannot readily distinguish between performance-approach and performance-avoidance goals (Urdan & Mestas, 2006). However, a number of studies using factor analytic techniques have supported differentiating between performance-approach and performance-avoidance goals in both the trichotomous (Elliot & Church, 1997; Midgley et al., 1998; Vandewalle, 1997) and 2 x 2 models (Baranik, Barron, & Finney, 2007; Campbell, Barry, Joe, & Finney, 2008; Elliot & McGregor, 2001; Murayama et al., 2009), indicating that repondents do indeed distinguish between these two constructs (see Murayama, Elliot, & Yamagata, 2011, for a broader analysis on this issue). The high correlation between them may reflect the fact that the two goals share a normative standard for evaluating competence. Furthermore, there may be additional factors at work, and we believe that future research is needed to explore moderators of this relationship.

Contextual Effects on Achievement Goals

Within the achievement goal literature, the term *achievement goal orientation* is often used to refer to a broad network of beliefs and feelings, as well as a dispositional tendency to adopt a certain goal. Indeed many researchers in this area utilize the achievement goal construct in a dispositional manner in empirical work. This strong dispositional focus is surprising, because the achievement goal approach originated, in part, as a critique of dispositional constructs (especially the need for achievement), reflecting a desire to move toward a more specific, context-based level of analysis (see Dweck & Wortman, 1982; Maehr & Nicholls, 1980). When construed as a disposition, it is difficult to see how the achievement goal construct differs from the self-attributed achievement motive construct that has been articulated within the classic achievement motive tradition (see, for example, Spence and Helmreich's [1983] distinction between work-mastery and competitiveness in the self-attributed need for achievement). Furthermore, if achievement goal orientations are portrayed as general tendencies to adopt particular achievement goals in specific situations, and achievement goals in specific situations are viewed as direct regulators of achievement behavior, then it seems that achievement goal orientations merely serve a *descriptive* rather than an *explanatory* function. Thus, although the achievement goal construct has been utilized at both the dispositional and situation-specific levels, we believe it is best suited to the situation-specific level.

A good deal of research has been done to investigate the joint influence of contextual factors and achievement goals (Elliot, 2006; Elliot & Church, 1997). Classroom achievement goal structure, for example, which refers to *competence-relevant environmental emphases made through teachers' communications and general classroom practices*, has received a good deal of theoretical and empirical attention (Ames, 1992; Covington & Omelich, 1984; Epstein, 1988; Maehr & Midgley, 1996). The concept of classroom goal structure originated from early work by Ames, who was particularly interested in the contextual determinants of achievement goals (Ames, 1981; Ames & Ames, 1981, 1984). Research on classroom goal structures initially centered on two distinct types of structures: A *mastery goal structure*, in which an emphasis is placed on mastery, personal improvement, and understanding in the classroom, and a *performance goal structure*, in which an emphasis is placed on relative ability and competition in the classroom. Midgley and her colleagues (Midgley et al., 2000) subsequently applied the trichotomous model of personal achievement goals to the classroom context, differentiating the performance-based goal structure in terms of approach and avoidance. This resulted in three separate classroom goal structures: a *mastery goal structure*, in which the classroom environment focuses on engaging in academic work in order to develop competence, especially task-based and intrapersonally based competence; a *performance-approach goal structure*, in which the classroom environment focuses on engaging in academic work in order to demonstrate competence, often normative competence; and a *performance-avoidance goal structure*, in which the classroom environment focuses on engaging in academic work in order to avoid demonstrating incompetence, often normative incompetence. These goal structures were assessed either by student self-report (thus constituting "perceived"

classroom goal structure), teacher self-report, or classroom observation.

Research on classroom goal structures has revealed a relationship between achievement goals, classroom goal structures, and achievement-relevant outcomes (for reviews, see Linnenbrink, 2004; Meece et al., 2006; Murayama & Elliot, 2009; Urdan & Turner, 2005). For example, a number of studies have documented that classroom goal structures *indirectly* influence achievement-relevant outcomes through their impact on personal achievement goal adoption (Bong, 2005; Church, Elliot, & Gable, 2001; Greene, Miller, Crowson, Duke, & Akey, 2004; Kaplan & Maehr, 1999; Midgley, Anderman, & Hicks, 1995; Nolen & Haladyna, 1990b; Roeser, Midgley, & Urdan, 1996; Urdan, 2004). Within these studies, classroom goal structures prompt the adoption of corresponding achievement goals (e.g., mastery-approach goal structure facilitates the adoption of mastery-approach goals). Another set of studies showed a *direct* effect of classroom goal structure on achievement goals; that is, they demonstrated that classroom goal structures have an effect on outcomes over and above the effect of (personal) achievement goals (Kaplan, Gheen, & Midgley, 2002; Karabenick, 2004; Lau & Nie, 2008; Midgley & Urdan, 1995, 2001; Wolters, 2004; for a statistical formulization of contextual effects, see Enders & Tofighi, 2007; Hoffman & Stawski, 2009). These studies show that mastery goal structures positively influence achievement outcomes, while performance-approach goal structures have null or negative effects. The effects of performance-avoidance goal structures are not well established; however, Karabenick (2004) has shown that they can be associated with the avoidance of help-seeking behavior.

Taken together, these results highlight the contextual factors that play an important role in the functioning of achievement goals. These studies also underscore the need for future research in this domain. To date, only a few studies have investigated interaction effects, in which classroom goal structures moderate the influence of achievement goals on achievement-relevant outcomes (e.g., Lau & Nie, 2008; Linnenbrink, 2005; Murayama & Elliot, 2009). Given the extensive literature documenting the importance of person by situation interactions (Bretz & Judge, 1994; Cronbach & Snow, 1977; Higgins, 2000; Hunt, 1975; Mischel & Shoda, 1995; Oishi, Diener, Suh, & Lucas, 1999), there is considerable need for additional insight in this domain. Among the few studies that reveal an interaction, for example, Murayama and Elliot (2009) showed that the influence of performance-approach goals on intrinsic motivation varies between classrooms, and that the effect is positive in classrooms with high performance-approach goal structures.

In addition, empirical work on classroom goal structures has yet to incorporate the mastery-avoidance distinction. There is good reason to believe that investigating the influence of mastery-avoidance goal structures would be valuable, because instructional practices that convey mastery-avoidance goals (i.e., a mastery-avoidance goal structure) are relatively common in classroom setting (e.g., "Be careful not to make mistakes"). This mastery-avoidance goal structure could therefore have a substantial impact on the learning process.

While research on contextual factors has primarily focused on classroom goal structures, the notion of context can be thought of more broadly. For example, a number of researchers have raised the possibility that achievement goals are pursued differently in different cultures (Maehr & Nicholls, 1980; Urdan, 2004; Zusho & Njoku, 2007). To date, few empirical studies have tested cultural difference in achievement goals (e.g., Murayama et al., 2009; see Elliot, Chirkov, Kim, & Sheldon, 2001 for an analogous point regarding approach and avoidance goals more generally). From our perspective, competence strivings (i.e., achievement goals) are common to all individuals, across cultural boundaries (Li, 2003; Sheldon, Elliot, Kim, & Kasser, 2001; Van de Vliert & Janssen, 2002). Indeed, it is impossible to imagine a culture in which individuals do not have any achievement goals. However, the form that these strivings take may differ for people with distinct cultural backgrounds (Heine, Lehman, Markus, & Kitayama, 1999). Research has shown that relative to Western cultures (e.g., Canada, the United States, Western Europe), Eastern cultures (e.g., China, Japan, South Korea) appear to be more group and socially oriented (Chang, Wong, & Teo, 2000), more grounded in obligation and responsibility (Fuligni, Tseng, & Lam, 1999), more avoidance oriented (Eaton & Dembo, 1997; Elliot et al., 2001), and more focused on improvement (Heine et al., 2001). Furthermore, empirical studies show that competence-relevant words such as "success," "failure," and "learn" have different connotations in different countries (Li, 2003; Maehr & Nicholls, 1980). In sum, cross-cultural differences in achievement goal strivings may emerge as a function of distinct worldviews promoted within each culture.

Methodological Expansion

As this chapter demonstrates, the achievement goal literature has yielded a wealth of interesting findings over the past few decades. That said, we believe there remains substantial room for growth in the methodology approaches used by achievement goal researchers.

To date, nearly all achievement goal research has focused on between-person covariation, using persons as the unit of analysis (Borsboom, Mellenbergh, & van Heerden, 2003). This focus on between-person comparisons is limiting, particularly when the rest of personality/social psychology is moving in the direction of focusing on both between- and within-person covariation (Cervone & Shoda, 1999; Hamaker, Dolan, & Molenaar, 2005; Molenaar & Campbell, 2009). Within-person analyses, which involve collecting repeated measurements of items across time-points or situations and computing the covariance of the scores using the time-points or situations as the unit of analysis, allow researchers to directly investigate how psychological elements vary within individuals and interact with each other. Goal pursuit across time and situations, and regulatory shifts therein, can be monitored using within-person analyses, potentially shedding much needed light on an area about which little is presently known (see Murayama, Elliot, & Yamagata, 2011; Schantz & Conroy, 2009). Furthermore, the use of within-person methodologies, such as diary studies, can be used to test whether the psychological mechanisms identified through between-person research can be extended to the within-person level.

Another limitation of the methodologies commonly used in achievement goal research is the informal assumption that achievement goals are consciously accessible. While few present-day achievement goal researchers would argue that all goals are consciously accessible, the reality is that within the achievement goal literature, goals are operationalized as if they must be conscious. That is, in the vast majority of studies, achievement goals are assessed by self-report questionnaire or experimentally manipulated through verbal instruction (for an exception, see Niiya, Crocker, & Bartmess, 2004). However, recent research on social cognition has repeatedly shown that goals can be activated and operate in a thoroughly automatic, nonconscious fashion (Bargh, Gollwitzer, Lee-Chai, Barndollar, & Trotschel, 2001; Custers & Aarts, 2005). There is therefore a strong need for the introduction of experimental priming techniques and implicit assessments into the achievement goal literature. This work could advance existing research by disentangling conscious and nonconscious elements of achievement goal striving, thereby bringing a richer understanding to the field as a whole.

On a related note, the vast majority of current studies on achievement goals have relied on self-reported questionnaire studies. Although a number of studies have utilized experimental manipulations, interventions, and observational methods, these studies are relatively rare. In our view, these methodologies offer important findings that cannot be obtained by depending solely on questionnaire studies, including causal relationships. They also minimize bias inherent in subjective self-reports. We therefore encourage future studies to incorporate these methodologies.

Conclusion

In sum, the achievement goal construct has provided considerable conceptual and empirical utility over the past three decades. What began with the work of four independent researchers has quickly developed into a robust literature examining the thoughts, attitudes, and behaviors that characterize people's competence-based pursuits. Today, the achievement goal construct is utilized within a diverse range of psychological literatures, including developmental psychology, educational psychology, industrial-organizational psychology, social-personality psychology, cross-cultural psychology, and sport/exercise psychology. For the achievement goal literature to continue to grow, however, it must address the next generation research questions that we have highlighted herein, delivering more insight into the processes underlying goal pursuit. In this chapter, we have identified a number of exciting opportunities for building on existing research, leading us to believe that the future of the achievement goal literature is bright, with a number of unanswered empirical questions awaiting inquiry.

Future Directions

• Consider the possible extension of the achievement goal framework to a 3x2 model.

• Conduct additional research on the consequences of mastery-avoidance goal adoption.

• Integrate broader methodologies such as priming methodologies, diary methodologies, and continue work on interventions.

• Investigate the interrelationship between achievement goals, including the interaction between different achievement goals, contextual moderation effects, and cultural difference in the predictors and outcomes of achievement goals.

• Examine the many different achievement goal complexes that energize and direct individuals' behavior in real-world achievement settings.

References

Ames, C. (1981). Competitive versus cooperative reward structures: The influence of individual and group performance factors on achievement attributions and affect. *American Educational Research Journal, 18*, 273–287.

Ames, C. (1984). Achievement attributions and self-instructions under competitive and individualistic goal structures. *Journal of Educational Psychology, 76*, 478–487.

Ames, C. (1992). Classrooms: Goals, structures, and student motivation. *Journal of Educational Psychology, 84*, 261–271.

Ames, C., & Ames, R. (1981). Competitive versus individualistic goal structures: The salience of past performance information for causal attributions and affect. *Journal of Educational Psychology, 73*, 411–418.

Ames, C., & Ames, R. (1984). System of student and teacher motivation: Toward a qualitative definition. *Journal of Educational Psychology, 76*, 535–566.

Ames, C., & Archer, J. (1988). Achievement goals in the classroom: Students' learning strategies and motivation processes. *Journal of Educational Psychology, 80*, 260–267.

Ames, C., & Archer, R. (1987). Mother's beliefs about the role of ability and effort in school learning. *Journal of Educational Psychology, 79*, 409–414.

Anderman, E. M., Griesinger, T., & Westerfield, G. (1998). Motivation and cheating during early adolescence. *Journal of Educational Psychology, 90*, 84–93.

Archer, J. (1994). Achievement goals as a measure of motivation in university students. *Contemporary Educational Psychology, 19*, 430–446.

Atkinson, J. W. (1957). Motivational determinants of risk-taking behavior. *Psychological Review, 64*, 359–372.

Atkinson, J. W., & Raynor, J. O. (1978). *Personality, motivation, and achievement*: Oxford, England: Hemisphere.

Austin, J. T., & Vancouver, J. B. (1996). Goal constructs in psychology: Structure, process, and content. *Psychological Bulletin, 120*, 338–375.

Baranik, L. E., Barron, K. E., & Finney, S. J. (2007). Measuring goal orientation in a work domain: Construct validity evidence for the 2 x 2 framework. *Educational and Psychological Measurement, 67*, 697–718.

Bargh, J. A., Gollwitzer, P. M., Lee-Chai, A., Barndollar, K., & Trotschel, R. (2001). The automated will: Nonconscious activation and pursuit of behavioral goals. *Journal of Personality and Social Psychology, 81*, 1014–1027.

Barron, K. E., & Harackiewicz, J. M. (2001). Achievement goals and optimal motivation: Testing multiple goal models. *Journal of Personality and Social Psychology, 80*, 706–722.

Bempechat, J., London, P., & Dweck, C. S. (1991). Children's conceptions of ability in major domains: An interview and experimental study. *Child Study Journal, 21*, 11–36.

Bong, M. (2005). Within-grade changes in Korean girls' motivation and perceptions of the learning environment across domains and achievement levels. *Journal of Educational Psychology, 97*, 656–672.

Bong, M. (2009). Age-related differences in achievement goal differentiation. *Journal of Educational Psychology, 101*, 879–896.

Borsboom, D., Mellenbergh, G. J., & van Heerden, J. (2003). The theoretical status of latent variables. *Psychological Review, 110*, 203–219.

Bouffard, T., Boisvert, J., Vezeau, C., & Larouche, C. (1995). The impact of goal orientation on self-regulation and performance among college students. *British Journal of Educational Psychology, 65*, 317–329.

Bowlby, J. (1969). *Attachment*. New York: Basic Books.

Bretz, R. D., & Judge, T. A. (1994). The role of human-resource systems in job applicant decision-processes. *Journal of Management, 20*, 531–551.

Brophy, J. (2005). Goal theorists should move on from performance goals. *Educational Psychologist, 40*, 167–176.

Butler, R., & Neuman, O. (1995). Effects of task and ego achievement goals on help-seeking behaviors and attitudes. *Journal of Educational Psychology, 87*, 261–271.

Button, S. B., Mathieu, J. E., & Zajac, D. M. (1996). Goal orientation in organizational research: A conceptual and empirical foundation. *Organizational Behavior and Human Decision Processes, 67*, 26–48.

Campbell, H. L., Barry, C. L., Joe, J. N., & Finney, S. J. (2008). Configural, metric, and scalar invariance of the modified achievement goal questionnaire across African American and white university students. *Educational and Psychological Measurement, 68*, 988–1007.

Cervone, D., & Shoda, Y. (1999). Beyond traits in the study of personality coherence. *Current Directions in Psychological Science, 8*(1), 27–32.

Chang, W., Wong, W., & Teo, G. (2000). The socially oriented and individually oriented achievement motivation of Singaporean and Chinese students. *Journal of Psychology in Chinese Societies, 1*, 39–63.

Church, M. A., Elliot, A. J., & Gable, S. L. (2001). Perceptions of classroom environment, achievement goals, and achievement outcomes. *Journal of Educational Psychology, 93*, 43–54.

Conroy, D. E., Elliot, A. J., & Hofer, S. M. (2003). A 2 x 2 achievement goals questionnaire for sport: Evidence for factorial invariance, temporal stability, and external validity. *Journal of Sport & Exercise Psychology, 25*, 456–476.

Covington, M. V., & Omelich, C. L. (1984). Task-oriented versus competitive learning structures: Motivational and performance consequences. *Journal of Educational Psychology, 76*, 1038–1050.

Cronbach, L. J., & Snow, R. E. (1977). *Aptitudes and instructional methods: A handbook for research on interactions*. Oxford, England: Irvington.

Cury, F., Elliot, A. J., Fonseca, D. D., & Moller, A. C. (2006). The social-cognitive model of achievement motivation and the 2 X 2 achievement goal framework. *Journal of Personality and Social Psychology, 90*, 666–679.

Custers, R., & Aarts, H. (2005). Positive affect as implicit motivator: On the nonconscious operation of behavioral goals. *Journal of Personality and Social Psychology, 89*, 129–142.

Daniels, L. M., Haynes, T. L., Stupnisky, R. H., Perry, R. P., Newall, N. E., & Pekrun, R. (2008). Individual differences in achievement goals: A longitudinal study of cognitive, emotional, and achievement outcomes. *Contemporary Educational Psychology, 33*, 584–608.

Davidson, R. J. (2000). The functional neuroanatomy of affective style. In R. Lane, L. Nadel, J. Allen, A. Kaszniak, S. Rapcsak & G. Schwartz (Eds.), *Cognitive neuroscience of emotion* (pp. 371–388). New York: Oxford University Press.

Diener, C. I., & Dweck, C. S. (1978). An analysis of learned helplessness: Continuous changes in performance, strategy, and achievement cognitions following failure. *Journal of Personality and Social Psychology, 36*, 451–462.

Diener, C. I., & Dweck, C. S. (1980). An analysis of learned helplessness. The processing of success. *Journal of Personality and Social Psychology, 39*, 940–952.

Dompnier, B., Darnon, C., & Butera, F. (2009). Faking the desire to learn: A clarification of the link between mastery goals and academic achievement. *Psychological Science, 20*, 939–943.

Duda, J. L. (2005). Motivation in sport: The relevance of competence and achievement goals. In A. J. Elliot & C. S. Dweck (Eds.), *Handbook of competence and motivation* (pp. 318–335). New York: Guilford Press.

Duda, J. L., Chi, L., Newton, M. L., Walling, M. D., & Catley, D. (1995). Task and ego orientation and intrinsic motivation in sport. *International Journal of Sport Psychology, 26*, 40–63.

Duda, J. L., & Nicholls, J. G. (1992). Dimensions of achievement motivation in schoolwork and sport. *Journal of Educational Psychology, 84*, 290–299.

Dweck, C. S. (1975). The role of expectations and attributions in the alleviation of learned helplessness. *Journal of Personality and Social Psychology, 31*, 674–685.

Dweck, C. S. (1986). Motivational process affects learning. *American Psychologist, 41*, 1010–1018.

Dweck, C. S. (1999). *Self-theories: Their role in motivation, personality, and development*. New York: Psychology Press.

Dweck, C. S., & Elliott, E. (1983). Achievement motivation. In E. M. Hetherington (Ed.), *Handbook of child psychology* (4th ed., Vol. 4, pp. 643–691). New York: Wiley.

Dweck, C. S., & Leggett, E. L. (1988). A social-cognitive approach to motivation and personality. *Psychological Review, 95*, 256–273.

Dweck, C. S., & Reppucci, N. D. (1973). Learned helplessness and reinforcement responsibility in children. *Journal of Personality and Social Psychology, 25*, 109–116.

Dweck, C. S., & Wortman, C. (1982). Learned helplessness, anxiety, and achievement motivation: Neglected parallels in cognitive, affective, and coping responses. In H. Krohne & L. Laux (Eds.), *Achievement, stress, and anxiety* (pp. 92–126). Washington, DC: Hemisphere.

Eaton, M. J., & Dembo, M. H. (1997). Differences in the motivational beliefs of Asian American and non-Asian students. *Journal of Educational Psychology, 89*, 433–440.

Elliot, A. J. (1999). Approach and avoidance motivation and achievement goals. *Educational Psychologist, 34*, 169–189.

Elliot, A. J. (2005). A conceptual history of the achievement goal construct. In A. J. Elliot & C. S. Dweck (Eds.), *Handbook of competence and motivation* (pp. 52–72). New York: Guilford Press.

Elliot, A. J. (2006). The hierarchical model of approach-avoidance motivation. *Motivation and Emotion, 30*(2), 111–116.

Elliot, A. J., Chirkov, V. I., Kim, Y., & Sheldon, K. M. (2001). A cross-cultural analysis of avoidance (relative to approach) personal goals. *Psychological Science, 12*, 505–510.

Elliot, A. J., & Church, M. A. (1997). A hierarchical model of approach and avoidance achievement motivation. *Journal of Personality and Social Psychology, 72*, 218–232.

Elliot, A. J., & Fryer, J. W. (2008). The goal construct in psychology. In J. Shah & W. Gardner (Eds.), *Handbook of motivation science* (pp. 235–250). New York: Guilford Press.

Elliot, A. J., & Harackiewicz, J. M. (1996). Approach and avoidance achievement goals and intrinsic motivation: A mediational analysis. *Journal of Personality and Social Psychology, 70*, 461–475.

Elliot, A. J., & McGregor, H. A. (2001). A 2×2 achievement goal framework. *Journal of Personality and Social Psychology, 80*, 501–519.

Elliot, A. J., McGregor, H. A., & Gable, S. (1999). Achievement goals, study strategies, and exam performace: A mediational analysis. *Journal of Educational Psychology, 91*, 549–563.

Elliot, A. J., & Moller, A. C. (2003). Performance-approach goals: Good or bad forms of regualtion? *International Journal of Educational Research, 39*, 339–356.

Elliot, A. J., & Murayama, K. (2008). On the measurement of achievement goals: Critique, illustration, and application. *Journal of Educational Psychology, 100*, 613–628.

Elliot, A. J., Murayama, K., & Pekrun, R. (2011). A 3 x 2 achievement goal model. *Journal of Educational Psychology, 103*, 632–648.

Elliot, A. J., & Reis, H. T. (2003). Attachment and exploration in adulthood. *Journal of Personality and Social Psychology, 85*, 317–331.

Elliot, A. J., & Thrash, T. M. (2001). Achievement goals and the hierarchical model of achievement motivation. *Educational Psychology Review, 13*, 139–156.

Elliott, E. S., & Dweck, C. S. (1988). Goals: An approach to motivation and achievement. *Journal of Personality and Social Psychology, 54*, 5–12.

Enders, C. K., & Tofighi, D. (2007). Centering predictor variables in cross-sectional multilevel models: A new look at an old issue. *Psychological Methods, 12*, 121–138.

Epstein, J. L. (1988). Effective schools or effective students: Dealing with diversity. In R. Haskins & D. Macrae (Eds.), *Policies for America's public schools: Teachers, equity, and indicators* (pp. 89–126). Norwood, NJ: Ablex.

Eysenck, H. J. (1967). *The biological basis of personality*: Springfield, IL: Thomas.

Finney, S. J., Pieper, S. L., & Barron, K. E. (2004). Examining the psychometric properties of the achievement goal questionnaire in a general academic context. *Educational and Psychological Measurement, 64*, 365–382.

Fuligni, A. J., Tseng, V., & Lam, M. (1999). Attitudes toward family obligations among American adolescents with Asian, Latin American, and European backgrounds. *Child Development, 70*(4), 1030–1044.

Fulmer, S. M., & Frijters, J. C. (2009). A review of self-report and alternative approaches in the measurement of student motivation. *Educational Psychology Review, 21*, 219–246.

Gray, J. A. (1987). *The psychology of fear and stress* (2nd ed.). Cambridge, England: Cambridge University Press.

Greene, B. A., & Miller, R. B. (1996). Influences on achievement: Goals, perceived ability, and cognitive engagement. *Contemporary Educational Psychology, 21*, 181–192.

Greene, B. A., Miller, R. B., Crowson, H. M., Duke, B. L., & Akey, K. L. (2004). Predicting high school students' cognitive engagement and achievement: Contributions of classroom perceptions and motivation. *Contemporary Educational Psychology, 29*, 462–482.

Hamaker, E. L., Dolan, C. V., & Molenaar, P. C. M. (2005). Statistical modeling of the individual: Rationale and application of multivariate stationary time series analysis. *Multivariate Behavioral Research, 40*, 207–233.

Harackiewicz, J. M., Barron, K. E., Elliot, A. J., Carter, S. M., & Lehto, A. T. (1997). Predictors and consequences of achievement goals in the college classroom: Maintaining interest and making the grade. *Journal of Personality and Social Psychology, 73*, 1284–1295.

Harackiewicz, J. M., Barron, K. E., Pintrich, P. R., Elliot, A. J., & Thrash, T. M. (2002). Revision of achievement goal theory: Necessary and illuminating. *Journal of Educational Psychology, 94*, 638–645.

Harackiewicz, J. M., & Elliot, A. J. (1993). Achievement goals and intrinsic motivation. *Journal of Personality and Social Psychology, 65*, 904–915.

Harackiewicz, J. M., & Sansone, C. (1991). Goals and intrinsic motivation: You can get there from here. In M. L. Maehr & P. R. Pintrich (Eds.), *Advances in motivation and achievement* (Vol. 7, pp. 21–49). Greenwich, CT: JAI Press.

Heine, S. J., Kitayama, S., Lehman, D. R., Takata, T., Ide, E., Leung, C., & Matsumoto, H. (2001). Divergent consequences of success and failure in Japan and North America: An investigation of self-improving motivations and malleable selves. *Journal of Personality and Social Psychology, 81*, 599–615.

Heine, S. J., Lehman, D. R., Markus, H. R., & Kitayama, S. (1999). Is there a universal need for positive self-regard? *Psychological Review, 106*, 766–794.

Higgins, E. T. (2000). Making a good decision: Value from fit. *American Psychologist, 55*, 1217–1230.

Hoffman, L., & Stawski, R. S. (2009). Persons as contexts: Evaluating between-person and within-person effects in longitudinal analysis. *Research in Human Development, 6*, 97–120.

Hull, C. L. (1943). *Principles of behavior: an introduction to behavior theory*: Oxford, England: Appleton-Century.

Hunt, D. E. (1975). Person-environment interaction: A challenge found wanting before it was tried. *Review of Educational Research, 45*, 209–230.

Jagacinski, C. M., & Nicholls, J. G. (1984). Conceptions of ability and related affects in task involvement and ego involvement. *Journal of Educational Psychology, 76*, 909–919.

Jagacinski, C. M., & Nicholls, J. G. (1987). Competence and affect in task involvement and ego involvement: The impact of social comparison information. *Journal of Educational Psychology, 79*, 107–114.

Kahneman, D., & Tversky, A. (1979). Prospect theory: An analysis of decision under risk. *Econometrica, 47*, 263–291.

Kaplan, A., Gheen, M., & Midgley, C. (2002). Classroom goal structure and student disruptive behaviour. *British Journal of Educational Psychology, 72*, 191–212.

Kaplan, A., & Maehr, M. L. (1999). Achievement goals and student well-being. *Contemporary Educational Psychology, 24*, 330–358.

Kaplan, A., & Maehr, M. L. (2007). The contributions and prospects of goal orientation theory. *Educational Psychology Review, 19*, 141–184.

Kaplan, A., & Middleton, M. J. (2002). Should childhood be a journey or a race? Response to Harackiewicz et al.(2002). *Journal of Educational Psychology, 94*, 646–648.

Kaplan, A., & Midgley, C. (1997). The effects of achievement goals: Does level of perceived academic competence make a difference? *Contemporary Educational Psychology, 22*, 415–435.

Karabenick, S. A. (2004). Perceived achievement goal structure and college student help seeking. *Journal of Educational Psychology, 96*, 569–581.

Koestner, R., Zuckerman, M., & Koestner, J. (1987). Praise, involvement, and intrinsic motivation. *Journal of Personality and Social Psychology, 53,* 383–390.

Lau, S., & Nie, Y. (2008). Interplay between personal goals and classroom goal structures in predicting student outcomes: A multilevel analysis of person-context interactions. *Journal of Educational Psychology, 100,* 15–29.

Lemos, M. S. (1996). Students' and teachers' goals in the classroom. *Learning and Instruction, 6,* 151–172.

Levy-Tossman, I., Kaplan, A., & Assor, A. (2007). Academic goal orientations, multiple goal profiles, and friendship intimacy among early adolescents. *Contemporary Educational Psychology, 32,* 231–252.

Lewin, K., Dembo, T., Festinger, L., & Sears, P. S. (1944). Level of aspiration. In *Personality and the behavior disorders* (pp. 333–378). Oxford, England: Ronald Press.

Li, J. (2003). U.S. and Chinese cultural beliefs about learning. *Journal of Educational Psychology, 95,* 258–267.

Linnenbrink, E. A. (2004). Person and context: Theoretical and practical concerns in achievement goal theory. In P. R. Pintrich & M. L. Maehr (Eds.), *Advances in motivation and achievement: Motivating students, improving schools: The legacy of Carol Midgley* (Vol. 13, pp. 159–184). Greewich, CT: JAI.

Linnenbrink, E. A. (2005). The dilemma of performance-approach goals: The use of multiple goal contexts to promote students' motivation and learning. *Journal of Educational Psychology, 97,* 197–213.

Maehr, M. L. (1983). On doing well in science: Why Johnny no longer excels, why Sarah never did. In S. Paris, G. Olson, & H. Stevenson (Eds.), *Learning and motivation in the classroom* (pp. 179–210). Hillsdale, NJ: Erlbaum.

Maehr, M. L. (1989). Thoughts about motivation. In C. Ames & R. Ames (Eds.), *Research on motivation in education: Goals and cognitions* (Vol. 3, pp. 299–315). San Diego, CA: Academic Press.

Maehr, M. L., & Braskamp, L. A. (1986). *The motivation factor: A theory of personal investment.* Lexington, MA: Lexington Books.

Maehr, M. L., & Midgley, C. (1996). *Transforming school cultures.* Boulder, CO: Westview Press.

Maehr, M. L., & Nicholls, J. G. (1980). Culture and achievement motivation: A second look. In N. Warren (Ed.), *Studies in cross cultural psychology* (Vol. 3, pp. 221–267). New York: Academic Press.

Malka, A., & Covington, M. V. (2005). Perceiving school performance as instrumental to future goal attainment: Effects on graded performance. *Contemporary Educational Psychology, 30,* 60–80.

McClelland, D. C. (1951). *Personality.* New York: William Sloane Assoc.

McClelland, D. C., Atkinson, J. W., Clark, R. A., & Lowell, E. L. (1976). *The achievement motive*: Oxford, England: Irvington.

McClelland, G. H., & Judd, C. M. (1993). Statistical difficulties of detecting interactions and moderator effects. *Psychological Bulletin, 114,* 376–390.

Meece, J. L., Anderman, E. M., & Anderman, L. H. (2006). Classroom goal structure, student motivation, and academic achievement. *Annual Review of Psychology, 57,* 487–503.

Meece, J. L., Blumenfeld, P. C., & Hoyle, R. H. (1988). Student's goal orientations and cognitive engagement in classroom activities. *Journal of Educational Psychology, 80,* 514–523.

Meece, J. L., & Holt, K. (1993). A pattern analysis of students' achievement goals. *Journal of Educational Psychology, 85,* 582–590.

Middleton, M. J., & Midgley, C. (1997). Avoiding the demonstration of lack of ability: An underexplored aspect of goal theory. *Journal of Educational Psychology, 89,* 710–718.

Midgley, C., Anderman, E., & Hicks, L. (1995). Differences between elementary and middle school teachers and students: A goal theory approach. *Journal of Early Adolescence, 15,* 90–113.

Midgley, C., Kaplan, A., & Middleton, M. (2001). Performance approach goals: Good for what, for whom, under what circumstances, and at what cost? *Journal of Educational Psychology, 93,* 77–86.

Midgley, C., Kaplan, A., Middleton, M., Maehr, M. L., Urdan, T., Anderman, L. H., . . . Roeser, R. (1998). The developmental and validation of scales assessing students' achievement goal orientations. *Contemporary Educational Psychology, 23,* 113–131.

Midgley, C., Maehr, M. L., Hruda, L. Z., Anderman, E., Anderman, L., Freeman, K. E., . . . Urdan, T. (2000). *Manual for the Patterns of Adaptive Learning Scales (PALS).* Ann Arbor: University of Michigan Press.

Midgley, C., & Urdan, T. (1995). Predictors of middle school students' use of self-handicapping strategies. *The Journal of Early Adolescence, 15,* 389–411.

Midgley, C., & Urdan, T. (2001). Academic self-handicapping and achievement goals: A further examination. *Contemporary Educational Psychology, 26,* 61–75.

Miller, A., & Hom, H. L. (1990). Influence of extrinsic and ego incentive value on persistence after failure and continuing motivation. *Journal of Educational Psychology, 82,* 539–545.

Miller, N. E., & Dollard, J. (1941). *Social learning and imitation.* New Haven, CT: Yale University Press.

Miller, R. B., Greene, A., Montalvo, G. P., Ravindran, B., & Nicholls, J. D. (1996). Engaging in academic work: The role of learning goals, future consequences, pleasing others, and perceived ability. *Contemporary Educational Psychology, 21,* 388–422.

Mischel, W., & Shoda, Y. (1995). A cognitive-affective system theory of personality: Reconceptualizing situations, dispositions, dynamics, and invariance in personality structure. *Psychological Review, 102,* 246–268.

Molenaar, P. C. M., & Campbell, C., G. (2009). The new person-specific paradigm in psychology. *Current Directions in Psychological Science, 18,* 112–116.

Murayama, K., & Elliot, A. J. (2009). The joint influence of personal achievement goals and classroom goal structures on achievement-relevant outcomes. *Journal of Educational Psychology, 101,* 432–447.

Murayama, K., Elliot, A. J., & Yamagata, S. (2011). Separation of performance-approach and performance-avoidance achievement goals: A broader analysis. *Journal of Educational Psychology, 103,* 238–256.

Murayama, K., Zhou, M., & Nesbit, J. C. (2009). A cross-cultural examination of the psychometric properties of responses to the Achievement Goal Questionnaire. *Educational and Psychological Measurement, 69,* 432–447.

Mussweiler, T. (2003). Comparison processes in social judgment: Mechanisms and consequences. *Psychological Review, 110,* 472–489.

Mussweiler, T., & Epstude, K. (2009). Relatively fast! Efficiency advantages of comparative thinking. *Journal of Experimental Psychology: General, 138,* 1–21.

Newman, R. S. (1998). Students' help seeking during problem solving: Influences of personal and contextual achievement goals. *Journal of Educational Psychology, 90,* 644–658.

Nicholls, J. G. (1976). Effort is virtuous, but it's better to have ability: Evaluative responses to perceptions of effort and ability. *Journal of Research in Personality, 10,* 306–315.

Nicholls, J. G. (1978). The development of the concepts of effort and ability, perception of academic attainment, and the understanding that difficult tasks require more ability. *Child Development, 49,* 800–814.

Nicholls, J. G. (1980). The development of the concept of difficulty. *Merrill-Palmer Quarterly: Journal of Developmental Psychology, 26,* 271–281.

Nicholls, J. G. (1983). Conceptions of ability and achievement motivation. In R. Ames & C. Ames (Eds.), *Research on motivation in education* (Vol. 3, pp. 185–218). New York: Academic Press.

Nicholls, J. G. (1984). Achievement motivation: Conceptions of ability, subjective experience, task choice, and performance. *Psychological Review, 91,* 328–346.

Nicholls, J. G. (1989). *The competitive ethos and democratic education*: Cambridge, MA: Harvard University Press.

Nicholls, J. G., & Dweck, C. S. (1979). A definition of achievement motivation. Unpublished manuscript. University of Illinois at Champaign-Urbana.

Nicholls, J. G., Patashnick, M., & Nolen, S. B. (1985). Adolescents' theories of education. *Journal of Educational Psychology, 77,* 683–692.

Niiya, Y., Crocker, J., & Bartmess, E. N. (2004). From vulnerability to resilience: Learning orientations buffer contingent self-esteem from failure. *Psychological Science, 15,* 801–805.

Nolen, S. B. (1988). Reasons for studying: Motivational orientations and study strategies. *Cognition and Instruction, 5,* 269–287.

Nolen, S. B., & Haladyna, T. M. (1990a). Personal and environment influences on students' beliefs about effective study strategies. *Contemporary Educational Psychology, 15,* 116–130.

Nolen, S. B., & Haladyna, T. M. (1990b). Personal and environmental influences on students' beliefs about effective study strategies. *Contemporary Educational Psychology, 15,* 116–130.

Oishi, S., Diener, E., Suh, E., & Lucas, R. E. (1999). Value as a moderator in subjective well-being. *Journal of Personality, 67,* 157–184.

Pekrun, R., Elliot, A. J., & Maier, M. A. (2009). Achievement goals and achievement emotions: Testing a model of their joint relations with academic performance. *Journal of Educational Psychology, 101,* 115–135.

Pintrich, P. R. (2000a). An achievement goal theory perspective on issues in motivation terminology, theory, and research. *Contemporary Educational Psychology, 25,* 92–104.

Pintrich, P. R. (2000b). Multiple goals, multiple pathways: The role of goal orientation in learning and achievement. *Journal of Educational Psychology, 92,* 544–555.

Pintrich, P. R., & DeGroot, E. V. (1990). Motivational and self-regulated learning components of classroom academic performance. *Journal of Educational Psychology, 82,* 33–40.

Pintrich, P. R., & Garcia, T. (1991). Student goal orientation and self-regulation in the college classroom. In M. L. Maehr & P. R. Pintrich (Eds.), *Advances in motivation and achievement* (Vol. 7, pp. 371–402). Greenwich, CT: JAI Press.

Pintrich, P. R., Smith, D. A. F., Garcia, T., & Mckeachie, W. (1993). Reliability and predictive validity of the motivated strategies for learning questionaire(MSLQ). *Educational and Psychological Measurement, 53,* 801–813.

Rawsthorne, L. J., & Elliot, A. J. (1999). Achievement goals and intrinsic motivation: A meta-analytic review. *Personality and Social Psychology Review, 3,* 326–344.

Roberts, G. C. (2001). Understanding the dynamics of motivation in physical activity: The influence of achievement goals on motivational processes. In G. C. Roberts (Ed.), *Advances in motivation in sport and exercise* (pp. 1–50). Champaign, IL: Human Kinetics.

Roberts, G. C., & Treasure, D. C. (1995). Achievement goals, motivational climate and achievement strategies and behaviors in sport. *International Journal of Sport Psychology, 26,* 64–80.

Roeser, R. W. (2004). Competing schools of thought in achievement goal theory? In P. R. Pintrich & M. L. Maehr (Eds.), *Advances in motivation and achievement. Vol. 13: Motivating students, improving schools: The legacy of Carol Midgley* (pp. 265–299). Oxford, England: Elsevier.

Roeser, R. W., Midgley, C., & Urdan, T. C. (1996). Perceptions of the school psychological environment and early adolescents' psychological and behavioral functioning in school: The mediating role of goals and belonging. *Journal of Educational Psychology, 88,* 408–422.

Roeser, R. W., Peck, S. C., Nasir, N. S., Alexander, P. A., & Winne, P. H. (2006). Self and identity processes in school motivation, learning, and achievement. In P. Alexander & P. H. Winne (Eds.), *Handbook of educational psychology* (pp. 391–424). Mahwah, NJ: Erlbaum.

Rolls, E. T. (2005). *Emotion explained*. Oxford, England: Oxford University Press.

Ryan, A. M., & Pintrich, P. R. (1997). Should I ask for help? The role of motivation and attitudes in adolescents' help seeking in math class. *Journal of Educational Psychology, 89,* 329–341.

Ryan, A. M., & Shim, S. O. (2006). Social achievement goals: The nature and consequences of different orientations toward social competence. *Personality and Social Psychology Bulletin, 32,* 1246–1263.

Ryan, A. M., & Shim, S. S. (2008). An exploration of young adolescents' social achievement goals and social adjustment in middle school. *Journal of Educational Psychology, 100,* 672–687.

Sansone, C., Sachau, D. A., & Weir, C. (1989). Effects of instruction on intrinsic interest: The importance of context. *Journal of Personality and Social Psychology, 57,* 819–829.

Schantz, L. H., & Conroy, D. E. (2009). Achievement motivation and intraindividual affective variability during competence pursuits: A round of golf as a multilevel data structure. *Journal of Research in Personality, 43,* 472–481.

Senko, C., Durik, A. M., & Harackiewicz, J. M. (2008). Historical perspectives and new directions in achievement goal theory: Understanding the effects of mastery and performance-approach goals. In J. Shah & W. Gardner (Eds.), *Handbook of motivation science* (pp. 100–113). New York: Guilford Press.

Senko, C., Hulleman, C. S., & Harackiewicz, J. M. (2011). Achievement goal theory at the crossroads: Old controversies, current challenges, and new directions. *Educational Psychologist, 46,* 26–47.

Sheldon, K. M., Elliot, A. J., Kim, Y., & Kasser, T. (2001). What is satisfying about satisfying events? Testing 10 candidate psychological needs. *Journal of Personality and Social Psychology, 80,* 325–339.

Sideridis, G. D. (2008). The regulation of affect, anxiety, and stressful arousal from adopting mastery-avoidance goal orientations. *Stress and Health: Journal of the International Society for the Investigation of Stress, 24,* 55–69.

Skaalvik, E. M. (1997). Self-enhancing and self-defeating ego orientation: Relations with task and avoidance orientation, achievement, self-perceptions, and anxiety. *Journal of Educational Psychology, 89,* 74–81.

Skinner, B. F. (1953). *Science and human behavior.* Oxford, England: Macmillan.

Smiley, P. A., & Dweck, C. S. (1994). Individual differences in achievement goals among young children. *Child Development, 65,* 1723–1743.

Spence, J. T., & Helmreich, R. L. (1983). Achievement-related motives and behavior. In J. T. Spence (Ed.), *Achievement and achievement motives: Psychological and sociological approaches* (pp. 10–74). San Francisco, CA: Freeman.

Stapel, D. A., & Koomen, W. (2001). The impact of interpretation versus comparison mindsets on knowledge accessibility effects. *Journal of Experimental Social Psychology, 37,* 134–149.

Stipek, D., & Gralinski, J. H. (1996). Children's beliefs about intelligence and school performance. *Journal of Educational Psychology, 88,* 397–407.

Urdan, T. C. (1997). Achievement goal theory: Past results, future directions. In M. L. Maehr & A. L. Pincus (Eds.), *Advances in motivation and achievement* (Vol. 10, pp. 99–141). Greenwich, CT: JAI Press.

Urdan, T. C. (2004). Predictors of academic self-handicapping and achievement: Examining achievement goals, classroom goal structures, and culture. *Journal of Educational Psychology, 96,* 251–264.

Urdan, T. C., & Maehr, M. L. (1995). Beyond a two-goal theory of motivation and achievement: A case for social goals. *Review of Educational Research, 65,* 213–243.

Urdan, T. C., & Mestas, M. (2006). The goals behind performance goals. *Journal of Educational Psychology, 98,* 354–365.

Urdan, T. C., & Turner, J. C. (2005). Competence motivation in the classroom. In A. J. Elliot & C. S Dweck (Eds.), *Handbook of competence and motivation* (pp. 297–317). New York: Guilford Press.

Utman, C. H. (1997). Performance effects of motivational state: A meta-analysis. *Personality and Social Psychology Review, 1,* 170–182.

Van de Vliert, E., & Janssen, O. (2002). Competitive societies are happy if the women are less competitive than the men. *Cross-Cultural Research: The Journal of Comparative Social Science, 36*(4), 321–337.

Vandewalle, D. (1997). Development and validation of a work domain goal orientation instrument. *Educational and Psychological Measurement, 57,* 995–1015.

Weiner, B. (1985). Spontaneous causal thinking. *Psychological Bulletin, 97,* 74–84.

Weiner, B., Heckhausen, H., & Meyer, W-U. (1972). Causal ascriptions and achievement behavior: A conceptual analysis of effort and reanalysis of locus of control. *Journal of Personality and Social Psychology, 21,* 239–248.

Weiner, B., & Kukla, A. (1970). An attributional analysis of achievement motivation. *Journal of Personality and Social Psychology, 15,* 1–20.

Wentzel, K. R. (1989). Adolescent classroom goals, standards for performance, and academic achievement: An interactionist perspective. *Journal of Educational Psychology, 81*(2), 131–142.

Wentzel, K. R. (1991). Social competence at school: Relation between social responsibility and academic achievement. *Review of Educational Research, 61*(1), 1–24.

Wentzel, K. R. (1998). Social relationships and motivation in middle school: The role of parents, teachers, and peers. *Journal of Educational Psychology, 90,* 202–209.

Wolters, C. A. (1998). Self-regulated learning and college students' regulation of motivation. *Journal of Educational Psychology, 90,* 224–235.

Wolters, C. A. (2004). Advancing achievement goal theory: Using goal structures and goal orientations to predict students' motivation, cognition, and achievement. *Journal of Educational Psychology, 96,* 236–250.

Wolters, C. A., Yu, S. L., & Pintrich, P. R. (1996). The relation between goal orientation and students' motivational beliefs and self-regulated learning. *Learning and Individual Differences, 8,* 211–238.

Zusho, A., & Njoku, H. (2007). Culture and motivation to learn: Exploring the generalizability of achievement goal theory. In F. Salili & R. Hoosain (Eds.), *Culture, motivation, and learning: A multicultural perspective* (pp. 91–113). Charlotte, NC: Information Age Publishing.

Zweig, D., & Webster, J. (2004). Validation of a Multidimensional Measure of Goal Orientation. *Canadian Journal of Behavioural Science/Revue canadienne des sciences du comportement, 36,* 232–248.

Goal Pursuit

Peter M. Gollwitzer *and* Gabriele Oettingen

Abstract

We start out with describing how the goal concept emerged in the history of the psychology of motivation to better understand the important role it plays in current research on motivation. We then suggest a differentiation between studies targeting the setting of goals versus the implementation of goals to get a grip on the host of empirical work the goal concept has triggered. With respect to goal setting, we first discuss studies that explore determinants affecting the content and structure of set goals (e.g., entity vs. incremental theories of intelligence influence the setting of performance vs. learning goals). We then turn to studies on the self-regulation of goal setting and discuss in detail how a self-regulation strategy called mental contrasting of future and reality facilitates strong commitment to feasible goals but dissolves commitment to unfeasible ones. With respect to goal implementation we first refer to studies on the determinants of effective goal striving (e.g., the framing of the set goal in terms of approach vs. avoidance) and then turn to analyzing the effective self-regulation of goal implementation. Here we focus on the strategy of forming implementation intentions (i.e., if-then plans) and explicate in detail how such planning helps in overcoming classic hurdles to goal attainment (e.g., distractions). We will end the chapter by reporting the results of recent intervention studies that successfully enhanced goal attainment in the health, academic, and interpersonal domains by combining the self-regulation strategy of mental contrasting with that of forming implementation intentions.

Key Words: goal setting, goal implementation, goal commitment, obstacles, mental contrasting, implementation intentions, self-regulation, self-control, willpower, behavior change interventions

It is Friday afternoon. On Monday, there is an important presentation you have to give. Even though you are highly motivated to give a great talk (i.e., desirability and feasibility are high), you did not find the time to prepare the talk during the week. So you set yourself the goal to use the weekend to prepare a nice presentation. But how do you arrive at a strong commitment to attain this goal? And how do you ensure that you will indeed implement your goal? In the present chapter we will discuss research on self-regulation strategies that benefit *(a)* committing to goals and *(b)* implementing goals that one wants to attain (i.e., one feels committed to).

Goals Versus Motivation

The term *motivation* is commonly used to explain *why a person in a given situation selects one response over another or makes a given response with great energization or frequency.* Imagine a person looking for someone else in a crowd. She gets excited when she finds that person, and then she runs toward him. Each of these responses involves motivation, which can manifest itself cognitively (e.g., looking), affectively (e.g., excitement), and behaviorally (e.g., running). To the question of what drives motivation, the history of the psychology of motivation has offered ever more sophisticated answers.

Based on learning theory advanced by early animal psychologists (Hull, 1943; Spence, 1956), the strength of the tendency to make a response was at first considered to be a function of an organism's skills (or habit strength), its needs, and the incentive value of the desired outcome. For example, how fast an animal runs toward a box containing food depends on its habit strength, its hunger, and the quality and quantity of food. However, with the advance of the cognitive revolution in psychology, these determinants of motivation as well as the concept of motivation itself became more elaborated. Tolman (1932) postulated various mental processes "which intermediate in the causal equation between environmental stimuli and…overt behavior" (Tolman, 1932, p. 2). These intermediate processes entailed concepts of purpose (ends and means) as well as expectations (e.g., means-expectations, end-expectations, and means-end-expectations). A few years later, Festinger (1942) and Atkinson (1957) drew on that work in their research on what motivates humans to select and perform tasks of varying difficulty. They suggested that people weight the incentive value of the desired outcome with the expectancy that it would actually occur.

Social cognitive learning theorists (e.g., Bandura, 1977) went a step further, factoring in whether one could successfully perform the necessary behavior required to arrive at a desired outcome (so-called efficacy or control beliefs). These theorists also alluded to further relevant expectancies, such as whether the situation by itself would produce the desired outcome (Heckhausen, 1977; Mischel, 1973), whether performing a given behavior would lead to the desired outcome (Bandura, 1977), whether achieving the desired outcome would be instrumental to accruing further positive consequences (Vroom, 1964), whether the desired outcome could be brought about somehow by one's actions (Oettingen, 1996), and whether the future in general would be bright (Abramson, Seligman, & Teasdale, 1978; Scheier & Carver, 1987).

Adding these expectancy-related variables helped to explicate in more detail the *can*-aspect (or feasibility aspect) of the motivation to make a certain response: *Can* the desired outcome be brought about? But the cognitive revolution also helped to explain the *want*-aspect (or desirability aspect) of the motivation to make a certain response: Do I really want the desired outcome? This desirability issue was originally captured by Hull (1943) and

Spence (1956) as the concept of need and the concept of incentive. With respect to need, the cognitively inspired psychology of motivation ventured into the concept of motives (for a summary, see McClelland, 1985a), defined as the class of incentives that a person finds attractive (e.g., achievement, power, affiliation, intimacy). More important, McClelland (1985b) discovered that depending on whether this preference for certain classes of incentives was measured implicitly (as assessed by the Thematic Apperception Test; TAT) or explicitly (as assessed by attitude questionnaires), it predicts the execution of different types of motive-related responses: actions people spontaneously engage in versus actions people decide to engage in after thoughtful deliberation.

It was also found that whether an incentive is hoped for versus feared matters. For instance, a person with a strong achievement motive, longing for the pride associated with success, will choose a task of medium difficulty to pursue; this level of difficulty provides the most information about achievement level. However, a person who abhors the shame associated with failure (Atkinson, 1958) will choose either a very easy or a very difficult task, which is an effective strategy to avoid shame (as very easy tasks are likely to be solved, and failure on too-difficult tasks can easily be explained). Finally, researchers have differentiated among types of incentives as well (Heckhausen, 1977). For instance, in the realm of achievement, anticipation of positive self-evaluations (e.g., "I did really well!"), positive evaluations by others (e.g., praise by the teacher), higher order positive consequences (e.g., successful professional career), and consequences that go beyond achievement (e.g., having a good time with coworkers) can all motivate people to do well on given tasks.

Given this increasing differentiation in thinking about the determinants of motivation (i.e., needs, incentives, and expectancies), one may wonder whether the concept of goals is at all needed. In our opinion, the concept of goals helps the cognitive explication of the readiness to make a certain response. Importantly in this regard, Ajzen and Fishbein (1969) suggested that this readiness should be assessed in terms of a person's intention to make the response. Mischel (1973) went a step further and argued that such intentions can be conceived as self-imposed or assigned goals that imply standards that the person intends to meet (with respect to quality and quantity criteria). Doing so allows asking new questions such as how people arrive at their goals and how they strive to achieve them. Noticing the unique nature of both of these problems, Kurt Lewin (Lewin, Dembo, Festinger, & Sears, 1944) suggested adopting a distinct theoretical perspective for goal setting versus goal striving. Present-day researchers have rediscovered Kurt Lewin's approach (see, e.g., the action phases model; Gollwitzer, 1990; Heckhausen & Gollwitzer, 1987). Today, research on goals explicitly targets either the determinants and processes of goal setting or the determinants and processes of goal striving and successful goal attainment. In the subsequent discussion of current research on goals, we will therefore group the presented research into *goal setting* versus *goal striving* (goal implementation).

Goal Setting
Determinants of Goal Content and Structure

Most theories addressing the issue of goal setting focus on the question of what goals people are setting themselves: What types of contents and what type of framing is preferred? With respect to content, the perceived desirability and feasibility of the goal matters. Perceived desirability is high when the goal is in line with the person's needs (e.g., *needs* for autonomy, competence, and social integration; Hagger, Chatzisarantis, & Harris, 2006; Ryan, Sheldon, Kasser, & Deci, 1996), wishes (e.g., possible selves; Oyserman, Bybee, & Terry, 2006), higher order goals (e.g., identity goals; Gollwitzer & Kichhof, 1998), and attitudes (i.e., the expected value of achieving the goal at hand; Ajzen & Fishbein, 1980). But perceived feasibility also matters. As suggested by Bandura (1997), feasibility concerns play an important role in setting goals of certain contents as well. It matters whether people feel that they can make the responses that produce the desired goal. Self-efficacy beliefs need to be high (or control beliefs as referred to by Ajzen, 1991, in his theory of planned behavior) for strong intentions (goal commitments) to emerge.

Recent research has turned its focus on the question of what makes people reflect on the desirability or feasibility (or both) of a given goal choice. For instance, Epstude and Roese (2008; McCrea, 2008) observed that failing to reach a set goal (e.g., not doing well in a midterm exam where one set out to receive an A) triggers thoughts such as: "If only I had studied harder, I would have done better on the midterm exam!" Such counterfactual thought in turn triggers reflections on the desirability and feasibility of studying harder for the class, potentially leading to the goal to study harder for this class in the future.

It is important to recognize that goals of the same content can be framed in different ways. Accordingly, goal research has analyzed what makes people favor a certain framing over another. For instance, a person who wants to be a good student may frame the goal of doing well in class as either approaching good grades (earning A's and B's) or avoiding bad grades (no C's and D's). Whether approach or avoidance framing is chosen depends on various attributes of the person (e.g., the trait disposition of extraversion vs. neuroticism, Larsen & Augustine, 2008; reward sensitivity vs. punishment sensitivity, Gray, 1994; their motive dispositions of hope for success versus fear of failure, Elliot, 1997, Gable, 2006).

A further framing variation pertains to promotion strategy goals versus prevention strategy goals (Higgins, 1997; Scholer & Higgins, 2008) as one may want to approach a desired end state either by promotion strategies (i.e., with eagerness) or prevention strategies (i.e., with vigilance). Equally, when one moves away from an undesired end state, one can also use either promotion strategies (eagerness) or prevention strategies (vigilance). The framing of strategy goals in terms of promotion versus prevention has been found to be a consequence of whether people construe their self either as an *ideal* self that they desire to be or as an *ought* self that they feel compelled to be: Ideal-self individuals prefer a promotion framing, whereas ought-self individuals favor a prevention framing.

Dweck (1996) has suggested a framing distinction between *performance goals* and *learning goals*. Goals in the achievement domain, for example, may either focus on finding out how capable one is (performance goals) or on learning from the task (learning goals). Molden and Dweck (2006) argue that implicit theories on the nature of ability determine the preference for performance versus learning goals. If people believe that ability is fixed and cannot be easily changed (i.e., hold an entity theory of ability), they prefer setting performance goals. However, if people believe that ability can be improved by learning (i.e., hold an incremental theory of ability), they prefer setting learning goals.

Another structural feature of goals is their level of *abstractness*. People generally prefer to set themselves abstract goals. They adopt concrete goals predominantly when they run into problems attaining an abstract goal (see action identification theory; Vallacher & Wegner, 1987). Finally, goals of any content (e.g., solving a math problem, writing a book, getting to know a stranger) can be specified at different levels of *difficulty*. Which level is preferred depends on whether a person's achievement motive is dominated by hope for success or fear of failure (Atkinson, 1957), whether the goal is made public (Hollenbeck, Williams, & Klein, 1989), and whether one has successfully achieved an earlier goal (Bandura, 1997).

Knowing the determinants of the content and structure of the goals people set themselves still does not answer the question of what people can do to promote strong goal commitments. Perceiving a goal as desirable and feasible does not guarantee that one actually commits strongly and then sets out to strive for this goal. For instance, one may wish to learn to play the violin because one loves to make music and feels capable of doing so (after all one knows how to sing well), yet actually committing oneself to realize this wish takes a further step, and there are certain self-regulatory strategies that facilitate making this step.

Self-Regulation of Goal Setting

Various mental strategies advance the transition from one's wishes and fantasies to goal commitments. The *theory of fantasy realization* specifies three respective self-regulation strategies (Oettingen, 2000): mental contrasting, indulging, and dwelling. In mental contrasting, people first imagine the fulfillment of a wish or fantasy (e.g., giving a good presentation at a conference) and then reflect on the present reality that stands in the way of attaining the desired future (e.g., evaluation anxiety). Mental contrasting is a problem-solving strategy that makes people recognize that they have not yet fulfilled their wish and that they need to take action in order to achieve the desired future. As a consequence, expectations of attaining the desired future become activated and determine a person's goal commitment and subsequent striving to attain the desired future. When perceived expectations of success are high, people will actively commit to realizing the desired future; when expectations of success are low, people will refrain from doing so, and thus they will venture on alternative wishes and desired futures. In this way, mental contrasting helps people discriminate between feasible and unfeasible goals.

The theory of fantasy realization specifies two further routes to goal setting. People may engage either in indulging (envisioning only the attainment of the wished-for future) or in dwelling (reflecting only on the present negative reality). Neither of these mental strategies produces any discrepancy between future and reality, and thus the individual fails to recognize that actions (making responses) are necessary to achieve the desired future. Therefore, expectations of success do not become activated, and goal setting does not reflect the perceived likelihood of reaching the desired future. Individuals who indulge and dwell show a medium level of goal commitment, even though the resource-efficient strategy to follow would be for no engagement in the case of low expectations of success, and full engagement in the case of high expectations of success. For example, when it comes to the goal of giving a good presentation at a conference, both an indulging and a dwelling person will show moderate preparation, regardless of whether a successful performance is perceived as within one's reach or as hardly possible.

Various experiments support these claims (e.g., Oettingen, 2000; summary by Oettingen & Stephens, 2009). In one study (Oettingen, Pak, & Schnetter, 2001, Study 4), first-year students enrolled in a vocational school for computer programming indicated their expectations of excelling in mathematics. Next, they named positive aspects that they associated with excelling in mathematics (e.g., feelings of pride, increasing job prospects) and negative aspects of reality, that is, potential obstacles (e.g., being distracted by peers or feeling lazy). In the mental contrasting condition, participants had to elaborate in writing two aspects of the desired future and two aspects of present reality, in alternating order beginning with the aspect of the desired future. Participants in the indulging condition were asked to elaborate four aspects of the desired future only; in the dwelling condition they instead elaborated four aspects of the present reality only. As a dependent variable, participants indicated how energized they felt with respect to excelling in math (e.g., how active, eventful, energetic).

Two weeks after the experiment, the participants' teachers reported how much effort each student had invested over the interim and provided each student with a grade for that time period. As predicted, only in the mental contrasting condition did the students feel energized, exerted effort, and earned grades based upon their expectations of success. Those with high expectations of success felt the most energized, invested the most effort, and received the highest course grades; those with low expectations of success felt the least energized, invested the least effort, and received the lowest course grades. To the contrary, participants in both the indulging and dwelling conditions felt moderately energized, exerted medium effort, and received medium grades independent of their expectations of success.

A variety of studies pertaining to different life domains replicated this pattern of results, for example, experiments on studying abroad, acquiring a second language, getting to know an attractive stranger, finding a balance between work and family life, self-improvement, and fulfilling idiosyncratic interpersonal wishes of great importance (Oettingen, 2000; Oettingen, Hönig, & Gollwitzer, 2000; Oettingen et al., 2001; Oettingen, Mayer, Thorpe, Janetzke, & Lorenz, 2005). Furthermore, strength of goal commitment was assessed by cognitive (e.g., making plans), affective (e.g., feelings of frustration), motivational (e.g., feelings of energization), and behavioral (e.g., amount of invested effort) indicators. These indicators were measured via self-report or observations, either directly after the experiment or weeks later. All of these studies evidenced the same patterns of results: Given high expectations of success, participants in the mental-contrasting group showed the strongest goal commitment; given low expectations, mental-contrasting participants showed least goal commitment. Participants who indulged in positive images about the future or dwelled on negative images of reality showed medium commitment no matter whether expectations of success were high or low. It is important to note that the outcomes of mental contrasting do not occur as a result of changes in the level of expectations (feasibility) or incentive valence (desirability) but rather as a result of the mode of self-regulatory thought (i.e., mental contrasting, indulging, dwelling), with mental contrasting aligning strength of goal commitment to expectations. Furthermore, the effects of mental contrasting depend on the person perceiving the present reality as an obstacle, that is, as standing in the way of realizing the desired future (Oettingen et al., 2001, Study 3). Thus, when mentally contrasting, people need to first elaborate the desired future and only then reflect the present reality; the reverse order (reverse contrasting) fails to connect future and reality in the sense of the reality standing in the way of realizing the desired future outcome (Oettingen et al., 2001; A. Kappes & Oettingen, 2011).

The pattern of results, seen as a whole, shows that mental contrasting is a mode of thought that people can use to wisely regulate their goal pursuit. First, it helps people to build strong commitments to feasible desired future outcomes (i.e., high expectations of success); however, equally important, mental contrasting also fosters disengagement from unfeasible desired future outcomes (i.e., low expectations of success). Thereby mental contrasting allows people to orient themselves toward alternative, more promising endeavors and to actively search for new venues.

Recent research suggests that mental contrasting not only regulates goal setting and goal disengagement but also promotes the choice of suitable means for effective goal striving. Oettingen, Stephens, Mayer, and Brinkmann (2010) examined the mental-contrasting effects on seeking and giving help as means to an end. For college students, mental contrasting about attaining academic help (more than indulging and dwelling) led to expectancy-dependent commitment to seek help (Study 1), while for critical care nurses mental contrasting about helping patients' relatives led to expectancy-dependent commitment to give help (Study 2). Thus, next to regulating commitment to goals, mental contrasting also regulates the selection of appropriate means to achieve goals.

Goal commitment instilled by mental contrasting equips people to successfully master negative feedback. A series of three studies (A. Kappes, Oettingen, & Pak, 2011; Oettingen & A. Kappes, 2009) shows that mental contrasting regulates the mastery of negative feedback in three different ways. When expectations of success were high, mental contrasting promoted the processing of relevant negative feedback, protected participants' self-view of competence against negative feedback, and led to optimistic as well as effort-related (rather than ability-related) attributions in response to negative feedback. Thus, mental contrasting can be used as an effective strategy to strengthen goal commitment in the sense that it prepares people to master upcoming negative feedback.

So far, we reported findings about mental contrasting of a positive desired future with a negative present reality. However, mental contrasting does not have to pertain to the attainment of a positive future; people can also fantasize about a negative future and contrast fantasies about a negative feared future with reflection on the positive present reality. Oettingen, Mayer, Thorpe, Janetzke, and Lorenz (2005) observed in a group of xenophobic high school students that when negative fantasies (i.e., fears that social conflicts would arise from foreign youth moving into their neighborhood) are contrasted with reflections on a positive reality standing in the way of the feared future (i.e., youth having wonderful and exciting soccer matches with foreigners), mental contrasting produced expectancy-dependent goal commitments as well (i.e., more tolerance and the goal of approaching the foreigners by investing time and effort in welcoming them into one's neighborhood). Thus, mental contrasting can be used to create *approach* goals that make people successfully conquer a feared future. In addition, Oettingen, Mayer, and Thorpe (2010) found that mental contrasting can also be used to create *avoidance* goals that make people successfully evade a feared future. In a study with chronic cigarette smokers, they found that setting oneself the goal of avoiding the feared consequences of smoking can be facilitated by mentally contrasting the feared future of negative health consequences with the current positive reality of still having a healthy body.

The mediating processes of mental contrasting pertain to both cognitive and motivational processes. As for cognitive processes, mental contrasting modulates the strength of the association between future and reality and between reality and instrumental means. In a series of four studies employing a primed lexical decision task to measure strength of association between future and reality, A. Kappes and Oettingen (2011) observed that when expectations of successfully reaching a desired future were high, mental contrasting strengthened the association between the desired future and the reality; when expectations were low, mental contrasting weakened future-reality associations. These results were obtained no matter whether expectations were measured or manipulated. Importantly, the future-reality associations in turn mediated mental-contrasting effects on self-reported (e.g., feelings of responsibility) and other-rated goal commitment (e.g., raters scored quality of performance on giving a talk and solving a creativity test). Finally, mental-contrasting effects on future-reality associations vanished when participants were informed that the goal was achieved, implying that future-reality associations wax and wane with the upholding versus accomplishment of the goal that was generated by mental contrasting.

Mental contrasting not only links future and reality but also connects present reality to relevant instrumental means (i.e., means instrumental to overcome or circumvent the present reality to attain the desired future). In two studies, A. Kappes, Singman, and Oettingen (2011) showed that mental contrasting paired with high expectations established strong associations between present reality and instrumental behavior, whereas paired with low expectations of success, it weakened reality-behavior associations. Importantly, the strength of the reality-behavior associations mediated goal commitment as indicated by actual performance (e.g., performance of taking the stairs instead of the elevator to achieve the goal of getting physically fit).

Mediating processes of mental contrasting on goal commitment pertain also to motivational processes. Oettingen et al. (2009) investigated energization as a primary indicator of motivational processes. Specifically, they found that mentally contrasting a desired future with present reality leads to energization, which in turn creates goal commitments strong enough to lead to effective goal striving and successful goal attainment. Mediating effects of energization on goal commitment are shown on physiological indicators of energization (i.e., systolic blood pressure) as well as on experiential indicators (self-report of feeling energized). Mental contrasting also spurs various forms of planning, a known cognitive mediator between expectations of success and goal attainment (Oettingen et al., 2001, 2005; Oettingen & Stephens, 2009).

Finally, mental contrasting, as it is a problem-solving strategy, necessitates heightened cognitive activity. A recent experiment attesting to this idea used continuous magnetoencephalography (MEG), a brain imaging technique measuring magnetic fields produced by electrical activity in the brain (Achtziger, Fehr, Oettingen, Gollwitzer, & Rockstroh, 2009). Mental contrasting as compared to indulging or simply resting produced heightened brain activity in areas associated with working memory, episodic memory, intention maintenance, action preparation, and vivid visualization. That is, mental contrasting implies vividly imagining a desired future, anticipating hindrances to realizing this future, and making plans on how to overcome these barriers. The brain activity associated with indulging, on the other hand, did not differ from resting.

Given this latter finding, one might think that indulging in the future could potentially lead to strong goal commitments as well—if only individuals managed to intensely engage in highly positive fantasies about the future. But research on engaging in positive versus negative fantasies about the future speaks against this argument. Early on, Oettingen and Wadden (1991) observed that obese women who spontaneously indulge in positive fantasies about their weight loss were less successful in achieving a lower body mass index (after 4 months and 2 years) than obese women whose spontaneously produced fantasies were more negative. Moreover, Oettingen and Mayer (2002) observed that people who indulge in positive fantasies (valence and frequency) show comparatively weaker goal commitments (as assessed by their efforts to strive for the goal) in the areas of academic achievement (i.e., achieving a good grade in a psychology class), professional achievement (i.e., finding a job after graduation), interpersonal relations (i.e., finding a romantic partner), and health (i.e., recovering from hip surgery). Importantly, it did not matter whether the spontaneously produced positive fantasies pertained to the desired outcome or to the ways of getting there. Additionally, goal commitment in these studies was assessed 2 weeks or even 2 years after the assessment of the spontaneously produced positive future fantasies. More recently, H. B. Kappes and Oettingen (2011) investigated the effects of experimentally induced positive fantasies on energization, hypothesizing that low energy is a mechanism by which positive fantasies translate into poor achievement. Indeed, induced positive fantasies resulted in less energy (as measured by physiological and behavioral indicators) than fantasies that questioned the desired future, negative fantasies, or neutral fantasies. Additionally, energy measured right after the induction of the positive fantasies mediated accomplishment in everyday life a week later. Finally, positive fantasies yielded a larger decrease in energy when they pertained to a more rather than less pressing need (e.g., need achievement), further suggesting that it is the positivity of fantasies that quells energization. Altogether the results indicate that one reason positive fantasies predict poor achievement is because they sap energy required to pursue the desired future.

At first sight, the reported findings seem to be in contrast to research observing facilitating effects of positive affect on performance in executive function tasks (Dreisbach & Goschke, 2004; Gable & Harmon-Jones, 2008; Kazen & Kuhl, 2005). However, these facilitating effects evince for individuals who perform tasks while being in a positive affective state. Note that in the studies reported earlier, it is not positive affect per se that is measured or manipulated, but the positivity of fantasies that depict the person already having attained the specified desired future. The mental experience of having already reached the desired outcome and of savoring the wished-for consequences reduces the energy required to reach the outcome in actuality. Only when such positive fantasies pertain to feasible futures and are mentally contrasted with the impeding reality will people muster the energy to excel in actuality (Oettingen et al., 2009).

Goal Striving

Once people have set themselves goals, it cannot be assumed that attaining the goal is inevitable; rather, only the first step has been taken. People need then to move on and to engage in *goal striving*. Whether a goal is ultimately attained depends on how well this goal striving is executed. Successful goal striving depends first of all on what kind of goals people have set for themselves; again, the relevant variables are goal content and how this content is structured or framed. However, successful goal striving also depends on coping effectively with a few typical problems: getting started with the initiation of goal-directed actions, persisting in the face of difficulties, shielding the goal from distractions, disengaging from ineffective means, and not overextending oneself. This self-regulatory issue of what people can do to make their goal striving more effective in the face of these problems (i.e., the effective self-regulation of goal striving) has recently received much attention.

Determinants of Goal Striving

Goal content strongly affects the chances of implementing a goal successfully. For instance, Ryan et al. (1996) have argued that goals of autonomy, competence, and social integration favor creativity, cognitive flexibility, deep processing of information, and effective coping with failure. These effects are assumed to be mediated by an intrinsic self-regulation (see the self-concordance model by Sheldon & Elliot, 1999), as the needs of autonomy, competence, and social integration are associated with intrinsic goal striving in line with a person's interests or core values, rather than with extrinsic goal striving in line with environmental pressures or internal sanctions. Intrinsic goal striving is preferred by individuals with positive self-regard (Judge, Bono, Erez, & Locke, 2005), and it can be facilitated from outside by teachers who provide autonomy support (e.g., when law school faculty provide autonomy support, grade point average improves; Sheldon & Krieger, 2007).

In addition to goal content, structural features of set goals also affect whether goal striving is successful. For example, goal striving is said to depend on the strength of the goal ("I really want to reach goal x!"; Ajzen, 1991; Ajzen & Fishbein, 1980). But most tests of this goal-behavior relation involve only correlational studies that preclude causal inferences. A recent meta-analysis by Webb and Sheeran (2006) took a closer look at this assumption by selecting studies where the strength of the goal was manipulated relative to a control group, and differences in subsequent goal-directed behavior were observed. They found 47 experimental tests of the intention (goal)–behavior relation that actually used an experimental manipulation of the strength of the goal (intention). The meta-analysis showed that the medium-to-large change in strength of intention (d = 0.66) led to a small-to-medium change in respective behavior (d = 0.36).

But success in goal striving does not only depend on the strength of the goal; it also depends on what kind of aspiration or standard is specified in the goal (i.e., whether the person wants to achieve a lot or only a little). Locke and Latham (2002, 2006) report that participants are more likely to attain challenging goals that are spelled out in specific terms than moderately specific goals or challenging but vague goals (i.e., "do your best"). This effect has a number of prerequisites: frequent performance feedback, strong goal commitment, low goal complexity, and that the necessary skills and means are available to the individual. What does not seem to matter is whether goal setting is determined from outside (assigned goals), freely chosen by individuals (self-set goals), or chosen in interaction with others (participative goals). As potential mediators of the goal-specificity effect, Locke and Latham point to heightened persistence, attention to the execution of goal-directed behaviors, a greater readiness to plan the goal pursuit, and to feedback and self-monitoring advantages.

Goal implementation is also affected by the structural features of time frame and goal orientation (i.e., approach vs. avoidance orientation, promotion vs. prevention, learning versus performance orientation, low versus high psychological distance, and low versus high identity-relation). Note that the earlier discussion of goal setting pertained to what determines that a person sets goals with various structural features. Here we asked the question of what kind of consequences choosing one or the other structural framing has for successful goal attainment.

Framing of the orientation of social goals in terms of *approach versus avoidance* clearly affects their attainment. For instance, striving for the goal of making new friends versus striving for the goal of not being lonely produces quite different outcomes. With respect to the outcome variable of satisfaction with one's social bonds versus loneliness, the latter leads to less favorable results than the former (Elliot, Gable, & Mapes, 2006; Strachman & Gable, 2006). Recent research suggests that these differences are mediated by differential attention and memory processes, differential interpretation and weighting of available information, and differential evaluation of the progress made toward goal attainment.

Higgins (2000; Förster, Higgins, & Idson, 1998; Shah, Higgins, & Friedman, 1998) reports that

approach goals benefit more from goal striving that makes use of eagerness-related approach strategies (such as pulling things toward oneself) than from vigilance-related avoidance strategies (such as pushing things away from oneself), whereas the reverse is true for avoidance goals. The assumed reason for this is *value from fit*. Higgins (2006) argues that people engage more in goal striving when the strategies used match the goal orientation (i.e., eagerness strategies/positive outcome focus; vigilance strategies/negative outcome focus) than when there is a mismatch (i.e., vigilance strategies/positive outcome focus; eagerness strategies/negative outcome focus). This heightened engagement in turn leads to higher perceived value and strength of attraction to this outcome.

Framing goals in terms of *learning versus performance* has been found to have different effects on achievement (Dweck, 1996). Learning goals lead to better achievement than performance goals because the former allow for a more effective coping with negative feedback than the latter. For people with performance goals, negative feedback signals failure and lack of ability and thus causes them to give up prematurely. People with learning goals, on the other hand, view negative feedback as setbacks and as valuable cues on how to focus on new strategies, ultimately furthering goal attainment. Elliot and Church (1997) observed that performance goals are less detrimental when they are framed as approach goals (e.g., I want to get good grades) rather than avoidance goals (e.g., I do not want to get bad grades). Recent studies by Darnon, Harackiewicz, Butera, Mugny, and Quiamzade (2007), however, show that this is only true when the achievement context does not allow for the emergence of fear of failure (i.e., the task is easy; the feedback on one's achievement is unambiguously positive). Recent research on the framing of achievement goals in terms of learning versus performance has also investigated its influence on interactions in social achievement situations (Poortvliet, Janssen, Van Yperen, & Van de Vliert, 2007). People with learning goals are oriented reciprocally. They give information openly, and they process received information with a focus on those pieces of information that fit well and add value to their own chosen task strategy. On the other hand, people with performance goals are oriented exploitatively. They provide information to others reluctantly, and they process received information with a suspicious attitude that leads them to focus on detecting and disregarding low-quality information that might hurt their own task performance.

Another relevant structural feature is *psychological distance*. Liberman, Trope, McCrea, and Sherman (2007) had research participants indicate either *why* or *how* another person would perform an activity (e.g., open a bank account) and then ask them to guess when this person would enact the activity. As it turned out, why-construals of the activity revealed longer time estimates than how-construals. McCrea, Liberman, Trope, and Sherman (2008) recently assessed actual enactment times of intended activity (i.e., returning a filled-out questionnaire to the experimenter on time) that was framed in terms of high versus low psychological distance. Even though psychological distance was manipulated by a variety of different methods, low psychological distance led to earlier enactment of the intended activity than high psychological distance. It appears, then, that framing a goal in terms of high versus low psychological distance engenders the risk of procrastinating about the goal pursuit.

Finally, it matters whether a person frames a given task goal in terms of its *identity-relatedness*. For instance, the task of solving a certain arithmetic problem can be approached with the goal of solving it effectively or the goal of identifying oneself as a mathematician. The latter goal has been referred to as a self-defining goal or *identity* goal, as it specifies an identity as a desired end state. Self-completion theory (Wicklund & Gollwitzer, 1982) proposes that people who are committed to identity goals can undertake a variety of activities to claim identity-goal attainment, because many different behaviors indicate the possession of such identities. For a scientist, for example, such self-symbolizing activities might include engaging in professional duties (e.g., giving lectures), making positive self-descriptions (e.g., "I discovered a new principle!"), exerting identity-relevant social influence (e.g., advising students), or acquiring respective skills, tools, and material symbols (e.g., programming skills, fast computers, large office).

Failing to perform an identity-relevant activity or lacking an identity symbol produces a state of incompleteness; to restore completeness, people engage in self-symbolizing efforts (summary by Gollwitzer & Kirchhoff, 1998). People then emphasize the possession of alternative symbols or set out to acquire new identity symbols (e.g., engaging in identity-relevant activities, Brunstein & Gollwitzer, 1996; describing oneself as having the required personality attributes, Gollwitzer & Wicklund, 1985; showing off relevant status symbols, Harmon-Jones, Schmeichel, & Harmon-Jones, 2009). Importantly,

affirming one's general self-integrity or bolstering one's self-esteem are not sufficient to offset incompleteness regarding an identity goal; rather, one must acquire specific identity symbols (Ledgerwood, Liviatan, & Carnevale, 2007).

Research on self-completion theory has discovered that a higher level of completeness is reached when a social audience notices the individual's self-symbolizing activities (Gollwitzer, 1986). In addition, incomplete individuals are more concerned with finding an audience for their identity strivings than are completed individuals (Brunstein & Gollwitzer, 1996). This self-symbolizing, however, has its costs. Self-symbolizing individuals see others only in terms of the potential to notice their compensatory efforts; thus, they lack social sensitivity (Gollwitzer & Wicklund, 1985). Most interestingly, when people make public their intention to acquire a certain self-definitional indicator (e.g., when a person who wants to become a great student publicly utters the behavioral intention to enroll in an inspiring course), it turns out that actual efforts toward completion are reduced (Gollwitzer, Sheeran, Michalski, & Seifert, 2009). Apparently, when others take notice of a stated identity-relevant behavioral intention, the superordinate goal of claiming the identity is already reached, and thus performing the intended behavior becomes less necessary. This finding is in line with results of earlier self-completion studies; public, positive self-descriptions claiming the possession of an identity symbol produced the same sense of self-definitional completeness as actual identity-relevant achievements (Brunstein & Gollwitzer, 1996; Gollwitzer, Wicklund, & Hilton, 1982).

Striving for a given goal does not only depend on the content of the goal and its structural features. It also depends on the *context* in which the person is situated. Recent research on context variables in goal striving differentiates various context variables that relate to the person's affective state, the array of competing action tendencies, and the power position of the goal striver.

For instance, Tice, Bratislavsky, and Baumeister (2001) focused on negative *affect* and observed that feeling emotionally distraught (i.e., having been asked to imagine that one has caused a traffic accident that killed a child) makes it difficult to follow through with goals of not eating unhealthy food or delaying gratification to attain better long-term rewards. Moreover, this emotionally negative state also intensifies procrastination; for example, people did not use the time provided to study for an upcoming test. In all of these studies it appeared that the reason people did not act on their goals was simple; they felt that inaction would alleviate their negative emotional states.

Positive affect, on the other hand, has been observed to facilitate goal striving. Kazen and Kuhl (2005; Kuhl & Kazen, 1999) argue that even though decreases in positive affect make it easier to maintain an intention in working memory, it takes an increase in positive affect to facilitate the successful behavioral implementation of difficult intentions (e.g., to do well on the Stroop task). Tamir and Robinson (2007) report data suggesting that positive moods (measured or induced) are associated with selective attention to reward stimuli. Gable and Harmon-Jones (2008) observed that positive affect induced by imagining rewards (such as tasty desserts) reduced the breadth of attentional focus, which facilitates focusing on specific action tendencies and thus tenacious goal striving. Apparently, positive affect makes people focus on rewarding stimuli that in turn produce a narrowing of attentional focus that makes it easy to strive for the goal at hand.

Given that positive affect seems to foster goal striving on well-structured tasks (e.g., Stroop and task-switching paradigms), this does not imply that positive affect is beneficial to striving for all kinds of tasks. Complex and ill-defined tasks require that people anticipate potential obstacles and hindrances. This is easier when people experience negative affect. Not surprisingly then, for complex and ill-defined tasks positive affect was found to be a hindrance rather than a facilitator of goal attainment (Markman, Lindberg, Kray, & Galinsky, 2007; Oettingen & Mayer, 2002; Taylor, Pham, Rivkin, & Armor, 1998). And people are found to prefer to be in negative emotional states if those states better facilitate goal striving; for instance, soldiers entering battle or football players during a game prefer an angry, aggressive (negative) mood rather than a relaxed, positive mood (Tamir, 2009).

The success of goal striving in situational contexts that are filled with *powerful distractions* depends on whether the individual is capable of shielding goal striving from these distractions. Accordingly, the analysis of the determinants of effective goal shielding has received much research attention recently. For instance, Shah, Friedman, and Kruglanski (2002) observed that high commitment to the focal goal facilitates goal shielding (measured in terms of reduced accessibility of a competing goal), whereas feeling anxious and sad hinders it. Moreover, when people consider the progress they have made toward the goal there is less goal shielding,

as people open up to competing goals; this effect occurs even when people are told merely to intend to make progress in the future (Fishbach & Dhar, 2005). However, this negative effect of goal progress on goal shielding should only be expected if the goal-directed actions taken (or intended) are interpreted by the individual as completing the goal; if the action is instead interpreted as indicating a strong commitment to the focal goal, then improved goal shielding would be expected (Fishbach, Dhar, & Zhang, 2006; Koo & Fishbach, 2008). In line with this reasoning, Louro, Pieters, and Zeelenberg (2007) report on the basis of diary and experimental studies that the effects of perceived proximity to the goal are moderated by the experience of positive or negative goal-related emotions. That is, when the attainment of the focal goal is remote, positive emotions promote goal shielding, whereas negative emotions hinder it; in this case, positive emotions apparently indicate a feeling of high goal commitment. When closer to the goal, positive emotions decrease shielding of the focal goal, whereas negative emotions prompt increased goal shielding; here, positive emotions apparently indicate a feeling of high goal attainment.

Recently, researchers have focused on the contextual variable of being in a position of *power* versus being powerless. Power has been manipulated experimentally in several ways: Participants remember an incident in which they had power over someone or someone had power over them, they imagine or actually act in a powerful (manager, evaluator) or a powerless role (subordinate, worker), or power is primed outside of awareness (e.g., by having participants perform a scrambled sentences task using words related to having power—e.g., authority, dominate—or to lacking power—e.g., subordinate, obey). These studies have shown that not only do powerful (as compared to powerless) participants relate differently to people by treating them as a means to the attainment of their goals (i.e., objectivation; Gruenfeld, Inesi, Magee, & Galinsky, 2008); they also differ in the ways in which they strive for personal goals.

Guinote (2007) observed that people in power procrastinate less in pursuing their goals, they persist longer in the face of difficulties, they show more willingness to try out different strategies to attain the goal, and they more readily seize good opportunities to make goal-directed responses. In addition, they more readily recognize whether a given situation can be used to serve their goals and then allow suitable situations to guide their behavior

(Guinote, 2008). All of this appears to be facilitated by a change in executive functioning. Smith, Jostmann, Galinsky, and van Dijk (2008) report that powerful individuals are better than powerless ones at updating goal-relevant information (i.e., new information is monitored for goal relevance, and relevant information replaces old, irrelevant information in working memory). They are also better at inhibiting responses that may interfere with the present goal, and at planning by continuously switching between the main goal and respective subgoals. Finally, these "powerful" participants show less goal neglect (i.e., forgetting to strive for the goal; Kane & Engle, 2003) by actively maintaining the goal in working memory. Future research could profitably explore the extent to which these effects are mediated by heightened efficacy beliefs or control beliefs that may be stimulated by the power manipulations.

Self-Regulation of Goal Striving

The earlier discussion considered goal content and structure, as well as contextual variables (e.g., relative power) as determinants of successful goal striving and goal attainment. The self-regulation approach to goal striving, on the other hand, focuses on what the individual can do to master the problems inherent in goal striving. One very powerful strategy is planning out goal striving in advance. Gollwitzer (1993, 1999) has proposed a distinction between goal intentions and implementation intentions. Goal intentions (goals) have the structure of "I intend to reach Z!" whereby Z may relate to a certain outcome or behavior to which the individual feels committed. Implementation intentions (plans) have the structure of "If situation X is encountered, then I will perform the goal-directed response Y!" Both goal and implementation intentions are set in an act of will: The former specifies the intention to meet a goal or standard; the latter refers to the intention to perform a plan. For instance, a possible implementation intention for the goal intention to eat healthy food could link a suitable situational context (e.g., one's order is taken at a restaurant) to an appropriate behavior (e.g., asking for a low-fat meal). Whereas goal intentions merely specify desired end states ("I want to achieve goal X!"), the if-component of an implementation intention specifies when and where one wants to act on this goal, and the then-component of the plan specifies how this will be done. Implementation intentions thus delegate control over the initiation of the intended goal-directed behavior to a specified opportunity by creating a strong link between a situational cue and a goal-directed response.

Implementation intentions have been found to help people close the gap between setting goals and actually realizing these goals. Evidence that forming if-then plans enhances rates of goal attainment and behavioral performance has now been obtained in many studies on a whole array of different goals. A recent meta-analysis (Gollwitzer & Sheeran, 2006) involving over 8,000 participants in 94 independent studies revealed a medium-to-large effect size ($d = .65$; Cohen, 1992) of implementation intentions on goal achievement in a variety of domains (e.g., interpersonal, environmental, health) on top of the effects of mere goal intentions. This size of the implementation intention effect is noteworthy, given that goal intentions by themselves already have a facilitating effect on behavior enactment (Webb & Sheeran, 2006).

Research on the underlying mechanisms of implementation intention effects has discovered that implementation intentions facilitate goal attainment on the basis of psychological mechanisms that relate to the anticipated situation (specified in the if-part of the plan), the intended behavior (specified in the then-part of the plan), and the mental link forged between the if-part and the then-part of the plan. Because forming an implementation intention implies the selection of a critical future situation, the mental representation of this situation becomes highly activated and hence more accessible (Gollwitzer, 1999). This heightened accessibility of the if-part of the plan has been observed in several studies testing this hypothesis by using different experimental paradigms: for example, lexical decision tasks, Webb and Sheeran (2004), Parks-Stamm, Gollwitzer, and Oettingen (2007); dichotic-listening paradigm, Achtziger, Bayer, and Gollwitzer (in press; Study 1); and cued recall (Achtziger et al., in press, Study 2). There are even some studies showing that the heightened accessibility of the mental representation of critical cues as specified in an implementation intention mediates the attainment of the respective goal intention (e.g., Aarts, Dijksterhuis, & Midden, 1999). More recent studies indicate that forming implementation intentions not only heightens the activation (and thus the accessibility) of the mental presentation of the situational cues specified in the if-component, it also forges a strong associative link between the mental representation of the specified opportunity and the mental representation of the specified response (Webb & Sheeran, 2007, 2008). These associative links seem to be quite stable over time (Papies, Aarts, & de Vries, 2009), and they allow for priming the mental representation of the specified response (the plan's then-component) by subliminal presentation of the specified critical situational cue (if-component) (Webb & Sheeran, 2007). Moreover, mediation analyses suggest that cue accessibility and the strength of the cue-response link together mediate the impact of implementation intention formation on goal attainment (Webb & Sheeran, 2007, 2008).

Gollwitzer (1999) suggests that the upshot of the strong associative (critical situation—goal-directed response) links created by forming implementation intentions is that—once the critical cue is encountered—the initiation of the goal-directed response specified in the then-component of the implementation intention exhibits features of automaticity, including immediacy, efficiency, uncontrollability, and redundancy of conscious intent. Evidence that if-then planners act quickly (Gollwitzer & Brandstätter, 1997, Experiment 3), deal effectively with cognitive demands (i.e., speed up effects still evidence under high cognitive load; Brandstätter, Lengfelder, & Gollwitzer, 2001), show uncontrolled attention to the specified cues (Wieber & Sassenberg, 2006), and do not need to consciously intend to act in the critical moment is consistent with this idea (i.e., implementation intention effects are observed even when the critical cue is presented subliminally; Bayer, Achtziger, Gollwitzer, & Moskowitz, 2009).

The postulated and observed component processes underlying implementation intention effects (enhanced cue accessibility, strong cue-response links, automation of responding) mean that if-then planning allows people to see and seize good opportunities to move toward their goals. Fashioning an if-then plan thus strategically automates goal striving; people intentionally make if-then plans that delegate control of goal-directed behavior to preselected situational cues with the explicit purpose of reaching their goals. This delegation hypothesis has recently been tested by in a functional magnetic resonance imaging (fMRI) study reported by Gilbert, Gollwitzer, Cohen, Oettingen, and Burgess (2009). In this study, participants had to perform a prospective memory task on the basis of either goal or implementation intention instructions. Acting on the basis of goal intentions was associated with brain activity in the lateral rostral prefrontal cortex, whereas acting on the basis of implementation intentions was associated with brain activity in the medial rostral prefrontal cortex. Brain activity in the latter area is known to be associated with

bottom-up (stimulus) control of action, whereas brain activity in the former area is known to be related to top-down (goal) control of action (Burgess, Simons, Dumontheil, & Gilbert, 2005).

Support for the delegation hypothesis also comes from studies using critical samples—that is, individuals with poor self-regulatory abilities such as people with schizophrenia and people with substance abuse disorders (Brandstätter et al., 2001, Studies 1 & 2), people with frontal lobe damage (Lengfelder & Gollwitzer, 2001), and children with attention-deficit/hyperactivity disorder (ADHD; Gawrilow & Gollwitzer, 2008, Paul et al., 2007). For instance, Brandstätter et al. (2001, Study 1) assigned hospitalized opiate addicts under withdrawal the goal to write a short CV before the end of the day; half of the participants formed relevant implementation intentions (they specified when and where they would start to write what), and the other half (control group) formed irrelevant implementation intentions (when and where they would eat what for lunch). Eighty percent of the relevant implementation intention participants had written a short CV at the end of the day, whereas none of the participants with the irrelevant implementation intention succeeded in doing so.

Implementation intentions have also been found to benefit children with ADHD who are known to have difficulties with tasks that require response inhibition (e.g., Go/NoGo tasks). For example, it was observed that the response inhibition performance in the presence of stop signals can be improved in children with ADHD by forming implementation intentions (Gawrilow & Gollwitzer, 2008, Studies 1 & 2). This improved response inhibition is reflected in electrocortical data as well (Paul et al., 2007). Typically, the P300 component evoked by NoGo stimuli has greater amplitude than the P300 evoked by Go stimuli. This difference is less pronounced in children with ADHD. Paul et al. (2007) found that if-then plans improved response inhibition and increased the P300 difference (NoGo—Go) in children with ADHD. Recently, Gawrilow, Gollwitzer, and Oettingen (2011a) observed that children with ADHD can use implementation intentions to support executive functions in addition to inhibition (i.e., set shifting and working memory).

Additional process mechanisms to the stimulus perception and response initiation processes documented in the findings described earlier have been explored. For instance, furnishing goals with implementation intentions might produce an increase in goal commitment or self-efficacy, which in turn cause heightened goal attainment. However, this hypothesis has not received any empirical support. A recent meta-analysis on 66 implementation intention studies that assessed goal commitment or self-efficacy after the formation of if-then plans revealed negligible effects on both of these variables (Webb & Sheeran, 2008); accordingly, neither an increase in goal commitment nor self-efficacy qualifies as a potential mediator of implementation intention effects. Additionally, having to furnish their goals with implementation intentions may suggest to research participants that the experimenter wants them to do well on the goal at hand. However, when experimenter demand was checked in studies assigning goals versus implementation intentions, participants who performed the task goals at hand under these different instructions did not in felt experimenter demand (e.g., Schweiger Gallo, Keil, McCulloch, Rockstroh, & Gollwitzer, 2009; Kirk, Gollwitzer, & Carnevale, 2011). Finally, one might argue that implementation intentions have positive effects on goal attainment because they provide extra strategy knowledge. In fact, several studies have critically tested this idea by adding to the design a further goal condition in which the critical strategy information was provided as well. However, this condition never showed the beneficial effects on goal attainment observed in the respective implementation intention condition (e.g., Oettingen et al., 2000; Palayiwa, Sheeran, & Thompson, 2010; Webb, Ononaiye, Sheeran, Reidy, & Lavda, 2010).

Research on the facilitating effects of forming implementation intentions on goal attainment has targeted all of the four major problems that are known to doom effective goal striving: getting started, staying on track, failing to call a halt to futile goal striving, and overextending oneself. Given that forming implementation intentions automates goal striving, people who form implementation intentions should actually have it easier when they are confronted with these four central problems of goal implementation. Indeed, numerous studies suggest that problems of getting started on one's goals can be solved effectively by forming implementation intentions. For instance, Gollwitzer and Brandstätter (1997, Study 2) analyzed a goal intention (i.e., writing a report about how the participants spent Christmas Eve) that had to be performed at a time when people are commonly busy with other things (i.e., during the subsequent 2 days which are family holidays in Europe). Still, research participants who had furnished their goal intention with an implementation intention that specified when, where,

and how one wanted to get started on this project were about three times as likely to actually write the report than mere goal intention participants. Other studies found that implementation intentions foster striving toward goals involving behaviors that are somewhat unpleasant to perform (e.g., to recycle, Holland, Aarts, & Langendam, 2006; and to engage in physical exercise, Milne, Orbell, & Sheeran, 2002), even though there is an initial reluctance to execute these behaviors. Moreover, implementation intentions were associated with goal attainment in domains where it is easy to forget to act (e.g., regular intake of vitamin pills, Sheeran & Orbell, 1999; attendance for cervical cancer screening, Sheeran & Orbell, 2000; the signing of work sheets by the elderly, Chasteen, Park, & Schwarz, 2001).

But many goals cannot be accomplished by a simple discrete one-shot action as they require that people keep striving over an extended period of time. Such staying on track may become very difficult when certain internal stimuli (e.g., being anxious, tired, overburdened) or external stimuli (e.g., temptations, distractions) interfere with ongoing goal pursuit. Implementation intentions can prevent the negative influence of interferences from outside the person (e.g., disruptions by attractive video shows; Gollwitzer & Schaal, 1998). For this purpose, implementation intentions may take very different forms. For instance, if a person wants to avoid being unfriendly to a friend who is known to make outrageous requests, she can form implementation intentions such as: "And if my friend approaches me with an outrageous request, then I will not respond in an unfriendly manner!" The then-component of suppression-oriented implementation intentions does not have to be worded in terms of not showing the critical behavior; it may also specify an alternative antagonistic behavior ("..., then I will respond in a friendly manner!") or focus on ignoring the critical cue ("..., then I'll ignore it!"). Recent research suggests that the negation implementation intention ("..., then I will not respond in an unfriendly manner") is the least effective as it is associated with an ironic activation of the mental representation of the unwanted behavior (Adriaanse, Van Oosten, De Ridder, De Wit, & Evers, 2011). Interestingly, implementation intentions can be used to curb the negative effects not only of interfering external events but also of interfering inner states. Achtziger, Gollwitzer, and Sheeran (2008), for instance, report two field experiments concerned with dieting (i.e., reduce snacking; Study 1) and athletic goals (i.e., win a competitive tennis match; Study 2) in which goals were shielded by implementation intentions geared toward controlling potentially interfering inner states (i.e., cravings for junk food in Study 1, and disruptive thoughts, feelings, and physiological states in Study 2).

An alternative way of using implementation intentions to protect ongoing goal striving from derailment is to form implementation intentions geared toward stabilizing the ongoing goal pursuit at hand (Bayer, Gollwitzer, & Achtziger, 2010). Using again the example of a person who is approached by her friend with an outrageous request, let us assume that the person who is the recipient of the request is tired or irritated and thus particularly likely to respond in an unfriendly manner. If this person has stipulated in advance in an implementation intention what she will converse about with her friend, the interaction may come off as planned, and being tired or irritated should fail to affect the person's behavior toward her friend. Bayer et al. (2009) tested this hypothesis in a series of experiments in which participants were asked to make plans (i.e., form implementation intentions) or not, regarding their performance on an assigned task. Prior to beginning the task, participants' self-states were manipulated, so that the task at hand became more difficult (e.g., a state of self-definitional incompleteness prior to a task that required perspective taking; Gollwitzer & Wicklund, 1985; a good mood prior to a task that required evaluation of others nonstereotypically; Bless & Fiedler, 1995; and a state of ego depletion prior to solving difficult anagrams; Baumeister, 2000; Muraven, Tice, & Baumeister, 1998). The results suggested that the induced critical self-states negatively affected task performance only for those participants who had not planned out work on the task at hand via implementation intentions (i.e., had only set themselves the goal to come up with a great performance). Apparently, task performance (i.e., taking the perspective of another person, judging people in a nonstereotypical manner, solving difficult anagrams) does not suffer any impairment because of the respective detrimental self-states (e.g., self-definitional incompleteness, mood, and ego depletion) if performing these tasks has been planned out in advance via implementation intentions.

The self-regulatory problem of calling a halt to a futile goal striving (i.e., disengaging from a chosen but noninstrumental means or from a chosen goal that has become unfeasible or undesirable) can also be ameliorated by forming implementation intentions. People often fail to readily disengage from chosen means and

goals that turn out to be faulty because of a strong self-justification motive (i.e., we tend to adhere to the irrational belief that decisions we have made deliberately must be good; Brockner, 1992). Such escalation effects of sticking with a chosen means or goal even if negative feedback on goal progress amounts and alternative means and goals are available are reduced effectively, however, by the use of implementation intentions. These implementation intentions only have to specify receiving negative feedback as the critical cue in the if-component and switching to available alternative means or goals as the appropriate response in the then-component (Henderson, Gollwitzer, & Oettingen, 2007).

Finally, the assumption that implementation intentions subject behavior to the direct control of situational cues (i.e., strategic automation of goal striving; Gollwitzer, 1999) implies that the person does not have to exert deliberate effort when behavior is controlled via implementation intentions. As a consequence, the self should not become depleted (Muraven & Baumeister, 2000) when task performance is regulated by implementation intentions, and thus for individuals using implementation intentions, not overextending themselves should become easier. Indeed, using different ego depletion paradigms, research participants who used implementation intentions to self-regulate in one task do not show reduced self-regulatory capacity in a subsequent task (e.g., Webb & Sheeran, 2003).

LACK OF WILLPOWER

A new line of research on implementation intentions has been stimulated by Aristotle's concept of akrasia (lack of willpower). It is argued that any willful strategy of goal striving (such as if-then planning) has to prove itself under conditions where people commonly fail to demonstrate willpower. Three such conditions have been analyzed so far: *(a)* situations in which a person's knowledge and skills constrain performance such as taking academic tests, *(b)* situations in which an opponent's behavior limits one's performance such as negotiation settings, and *(c)* situations in which the wanted behavior (e.g., no littering) runs into conflict with habits favoring an antagonistic response.

The litmus test for any strategy to improve willpower is enhanced performance in a *delay of gratification* task. Children with impulse control deficits (i.e., children with ADHD) are known to have particularly pronounced problems with delaying gratifications. Accordingly, Gawrilow, Gollwitzer, and Oettingen (2011b) analyzed whether delay of gratification can be facilitated by forming implementation intentions even in children with ADHD. A computer task was developed in line with the delay of gratification paradigms developed by Walter Mischel (1974) and Sonuga-Barke (2002)—waiting in the presence of a suboptimal cue to make money for a delayed optimal cue to make money led to a higher total amount of money earned. In two studies it was observed that the goal intention to do well on the task did not improve performance as compared to a control group that received mere task instructions specifying the reward contingencies. However, when the goal intention was furnished with an implementation intention that linked a waiting response to the suboptimal cue, a significantly higher amount of money was earned, indicating a heightened ability to delay gratification.

Willpower is also called for when working on *academic performance tests* (math tests, general intelligence tests) as a good performance is commonly not only determined by a person's knowledge, analytic capability, and cognitive skills but also by a person's motivation to do well as a consequence of perceived desirability and feasibility of successful test performance. To increase test scores on the spot by exerting willpower, a person may thus focus on holding up her motivation (e.g., by increasing her self-efficacy feelings). Accordingly, Bayer and Gollwitzer (2007, Study 2) tested whether it is possible to increase self-efficacy beliefs by forming implementation intentions. They asked college students to take the Raven Intelligence Test: One group of participants formed a mere goal intention to do well ("I will correctly solve as many test items as possible!"), whereas the implementation intention group added the following if-then plan: "And whenever I start a new test item, then I'll tell myself: I can solve it!" Participants in the implementation intention condition performed better than those in the mere goal intention to perform well condition; implementation intention participants also performed better than participants in a further condition where a self-efficacy strengthening goal intention had to be performed ("I will tell myself: I can do these test items!").

Often our goals are constrained by others who are competing with us for positive outcomes or have competing goals for the use of the situation at hand. In such *competitive situations* exerting willpower involves effectively protecting one's goal striving from the unwanted influences generated by the goals of others (e.g., Martin, Sheeran, Slade, Wright, & Dibble, 2009). In their negotiation research, Trötschel and Gollwitzer (2007) targeted the sharing of a common good and explored whether the self-regulation strategy of forming implementation intentions enables negotiators to find agreements even if they have to operate under the adverse conditions of a loss frame (i.e., participants see how many points they lose rather than win and thus they are reluctant to make concessions; e.g., Bottom & Studt, 1993). When looking at the agreements achieved (i.e., level of joint outcomes), it was observed that pairs of loss-frame negotiators with a prosocial goal intention managed to somewhat reduce the resistance to concession making arising from the loss-frame negotiation context, but that only negotiators who furnished their prosocial goal intentions with respective implementation intentions were successful in completely abolishing the negative impact of the loss-frame negotiation context (i.e., showed a negotiation performance that was not different from that of gain-frame negotiators). In addition, action control via implementation intentions was found to be very efficient (i.e., implementation intentions abolished the negative effects of loss framing by leaving the negotiators' cognitive capacity intact); negotiators who had formed implementation intentions were more likely to use the cognitively demanding integrative negotiation strategy of logrolling (i.e., making greater concessions on low rather than high priority issues). More recent negotiation research by Kirk, Gollwitzer, and Carnevale (2011) used a different negotiation task: the ultimatum game. The participants acted as receivers of a series of fair but also unfair offers. It is commonly found that impulsive anger in response to unfair offers leads to rejections—and in turn to a financial cost to the receiver. It was found that entering the ultimatum game with goals to make a personal profit only then curbed impulsive rejections by increasing the frequency of accepting unfair offers when these goals were furnished with respective implementation intentions.

The self-regulation of one's goal striving becomes particularly difficult when *habitual responses* conflict with initiating and executing the needed goal-directed responses instrumental to goal attainment (e.g., Wood & Neal, 2007). In such cases, showing willpower means asserting one's will to attain the chosen goal against unwanted habitual responses. But can the self-regulation strategy of forming if-then plans help people to let their goals win out over their habitual responses? By assuming that action control by implementation intentions is immediate and efficient, and adopting a simple horse race model of action control

(Gurney, Prescott, & Redgrave, 2001a, b), people might be in a position to break habitualized responses by forming implementation intentions (e.g., by forming if-then plans that spell out a response that is contrary to the habitualized response to the critical situation; Holland, Aarts, & Langendam, 2006).

Research on the control of automatic responses by implementation intentions has targeted cognitive, affective, and behavioral responses. With respect to *cognitive* responses it has been shown that automatic cognitive biases such as stereotyping can by successfully controlled by forming implementation intentions. Extending earlier work by Gollwitzer and Schaal (1998), Stewart and Payne (2008) examined whether implementation intentions designed to counter automatic stereotypes (e.g., "When I see a black face, I will then think 'safe'") could reduce stereotyping toward a category of individuals (versus a single exemplar). The authors used the Process Dissociation Procedure (PDP; Jacoby, 1991) to estimate whether the reduction in automatic stereotyping came about by reducing automatic stereotyping, increasing control, or a combination of these two processes. It was found that implementation intentions reduced stereotyping in a weapon identification task (Studies 1 and 2) and an IAT task (Study 3) by reducing automatic effects of the stereotype (without increasing conscious control). This reduction in automatic race bias held for even new members of the category (Study 2). These studies suggest that implementation intentions are an efficient way to overcome automatic stereotyping.

Schweiger Gallo, Keil, McCulloch, Rockstroh, and Gollwitzer (2009, Study 3) analyzed whether it is possible to curb habitual *affective* responses by forming implementation intentions. They found that implementation intentions specifying an ignore response in the then-component helped control fear in response to pictures of spiders in participants with spider phobia—to the low level that was experienced by participants who did not report any spider phobia. The obtained electrocortical correlates (the authors had used dense-array EEG) revealed that those participants who bolstered their goal intention to stay calm with an ignore-implementation intention showed significantly reduced early activity in the visual cortex in response to spider pictures, as reflected in a smaller P1 (assessed at 120 milliseconds [msec] after a spider picture was presented). This suggests that the ignore-implementation intention assigned to spider phobics lead to a strategic automation of the specified goal-directed response (in the present case, an ignore response) when the critical cue (in the present case, a spider picture) was encountered, so that—using the horse race metaphor—the planned response (i.e., ignore response) could outrun the habitual response (i.e., fear response).

Various studies have analyzed the control of habitual *behavioral* responses. For instance, Cohen, Bayer, Jaudas, and Gollwitzer (2008, Study 2; see also Miles & Proctor, 2008) explored the suppression of habitual responses by implementation intentions using the Simon task. In this task paradigm, participants are asked to respond to a nonspatial aspect of a stimulus (i.e., whether a presented tone is high or low) by pressing a left or right key, and to ignore the location of the stimulus (i.e., whether it is presented on one's left or right side). The difficulty of this task is in ignoring the spatial location (left or right) of the tone in one's classification response (i.e., pressing a left or right response key; Simon, 1990). The cost in reaction times is seen when the location of the tone (e.g., right) and required key press (e.g., left) are incongruent, as people habitually respond to stimuli presented at the right or left side with the corresponding hand. Cohen et al. (2008, Study 2) found that implementation intentions eliminated the Simon effect for the stimulus that was specified in the if-component of the implementation intention. Reaction times for this stimulus did not differ between the congruent and incongruent trials (i.e., they were fast throughout).

Further studies on the control of habitual behavioral responses by implementation intentions analyzed reducing the behavioral expression of stereotypical bias (using the shooter paradigm; Mendoza, Gollwitzer, & Amodio, 2010), abolishing concept and goal priming effects on behavior (using different concept and goal priming methods; Gollwitzer, Sheeran, Trötschel, & Webb, 2011), stopping overlearned responses to critical stimuli (using the stop signal task in children with ADHD, Gawrilow & Gollwitzer, 2008), and breaking bad eating habits (using a lexical decision task presenting the unwanted food item as the critical word; Adriaanse, Gollwitzer, De Ridder, De Wit, & Kroese, 2011).

Still, one wonders whether forming implementation intentions will always block habitual responses. Using a *horse race metaphor*, the answer has to be no. Whether the habitual response or the if-then guided response will win the race depends on the relative strength of the two behavioral orientations. If the habitual response is based on strong habits (Webb, Sheeran, & Luszczynska, 2009) and the if-then guided response is based on weak implementation intentions, then the habitual response should win over the if-then planned response; and the reverse should be true when weak habits are sent into a race with strong implementation intentions. This implies that controlling behavior that is based on strong habits requires the formation of strong implementation intentions. One effective strategy pertains to creating particularly strong links between situational cues (if-component) and goal-directed responses (then-component). Knäuper, Roseman, Johnson, and Krantz (2009; see also Papies, Aarts, & de Vries, 2009) asked participants to use mental imagery when linking situational cues to goal-directed responses in their if-then plans, and found that the rate of initiation of the planned response increased by almost 50%. Finally, using the if-then format for spelling out one's implementation intentions benefits their effectiveness. Chapman, Armitage, and Norman (2009) observed that for the goal to increase one's fruit and vegetable intake an if-then implementation intention had greater impact than an implementation intention that settled with simply listing the when, where, and how of acting toward the goal.

What else strengthens (or weakens) the effects of implementation intentions? For strong implementation intention effects to occur people need to be highly committed to the superordinate goal intention (e.g., Gollwitzer 1999; De Nooijer, De Vet, Brug, & De Vries, 2006; Orbell, Hodgkins, & Sheeran, 1997; Sheeran, Webb, & Gollwitzer, 2005, Study 1; Verplanken & Faes, 1999), which is facilitated when this goal is self-concordant (Koestner, Lekes, Powers, & Chicoine, 2002) and the self-efficacy to reach the goal is high (Koestner et al., 2006, Study 2; Wieber, Odenthal, & Gollwitzer, 2010); furthermore, the goal needs to be in a state of activation (Sheeran et al., 2005, Study 2). These prerequisites help flexible goal striving because they prevent rigid plan enactment even when people have reached the goal, disengaged from the goal, or are in a situation where striving for the goal is inappropriate; in other words, the automaticity achieved by implementation intentions is a goal-dependent automaticity (Bargh, 1989). There may, however, be a cost to this flexibility associated with goal dependency: Recent research by Wieber et al. (2011) finds that people who have formed implementation intentions for the goal of eating more healthy food, but subsequently are induced to reflect on the reasons for striving to reach this goal (such as, e.g., a better health, a more beautiful body) no longer benefit from their if-then plans. Apparently, any doubts about the reasons for striving for a goal can undermine the effectiveness of respective if-then plans. This is in line with findings that the induction of the distinct emotion of sadness leads to weaker implementation intention effects as compared to the induction of the distinct emotion of anger (Maglio, Gollwitzer, & Oettingen, in press).

Not surprisingly, it was found that the commitment to the formed implementation intention also needs to be strong to produce beneficial effects of if-then planning (e.g., Achtziger, Bayer, & Gollwitzer, 2010, Study 2). When participants doubted the appropriateness of forming implementation intentions, no implementation intention effects emerged. Additionally, people should find it easier to commit to if-then plans that specify feasible (i.e., high self-efficacy feelings) and desirable (i.e., high instrumentality beliefs; the intrinsic value or activity incentive is perceived as high, Koestner et al., 2006) responses in their then-part. In any case, the requirement of commitment to the if-then plan for implementation intentions to have an effect ensures that incidental if-then plans do not impair flexibility in striving for goal attainment (e.g., Gollwitzer, Parks-Stamm, Jaudas, & Sheeran, 2008).

Finally, personality attributes have been examined as moderators of implementation intention effects in two lines of research (Powers, Koestner, & Topciu, 2005; Webb, Christian, & Armitage, 2007). In the first set of studies (Powers et al., 2005), perfectionism was examined whereby self-oriented perfectionism was distinguished from socially prescribed perfectionism. Whereas the standards for self-oriented perfectionists are set by the people themselves, socially prescribed perfectionists try to conform to standards and expectations that are prescribed by others. Powers et al. assessed goal progress with respect to New Year's resolutions (i.e., three personal goals) in participants who formed implementation intentions as compared to participants who received control instructions only. Whereas for participants being high on self-oriented perfectionism, forming implementation intentions actually did improve goal progress, social perfectionists failed to benefit from implementation intentions. Perhaps social perfectionists find it difficult to commit to implementation intentions, as they may feel that the expectations and standards prescribed by others often change unexpectedly, and flexibly responding to such changes may be seen as impossible when one incurs a strong commitment to a given if-then plan.

In the second line of research on relevant personal attributes for implementation intention effects, conscientiousness was examined (Webb, Christian,

& Armitage, 2007). In an experimental study using undergraduate students, the goal of regularly attending class was studied as a function of conscientiousness and implementation intentions. Whereas class attendance of highly conscientious students was not changed by forming implementation intentions (as it was high to begin with and stayed high), low and moderately conscientious people significantly benefited from forming implementation intentions. If one assumes that being on time is easy for people with high conscientiousness but difficult for people who are low on this personal attribute, this finding is in line with the general observation that it is in particular the difficult goals that benefit from forming implementation intentions (Gollwitzer & Sheeran, 2006). Apparently, when goal striving is easy the help of the self-regulation strategy of forming implementation intentions is not needed; easy goals can be striven for effectively without having to prepare goal striving by forming implementation intentions (e.g., Wieber, Odenthal, & Gollwitzer, 2010; Wieber, von Suchodoletz, Heikamp, Trommsdorff, & Gollwitzer, 2011). Alternatively, it seems possible that highly conscientious people routinely form implementation intentions by themselves to live up to their high standards of self-control (Gollwitzer & Brandstätter, 1997, Study 1).

Future Goal Research: Interventions

How can the research on goal setting and goal striving reported earlier be used to help people wisely select their goals and then meet them? First, knowledge about the determinants about effective goal setting and goal striving allows one to establish these determinants, and this can be done by the individuals themselves or people (e.g., parents, teachers, instructors) who want to help others in their goal setting and goal striving. Second, knowledge about effective strategies of goal setting and goal striving allows one to construct interventions that teach people how to effectively set and implement goals by themselves. One such intervention (developed by Oettingen and her colleagues: Oettingen & Gollwitzer, 2010; Oettingen & Stephens, 2009; Adriaanse et al., 2010; Stadler, Oettingen, & Gollwitzer, 2009, 2010) combines mental contrasting with forming implementation intentions into one metacognitive strategy called MCII (i.e., Mental Contrasting with Implementation Intentions). To unfold their beneficial effects, implementation intentions require that strong goal commitments are in place (Sheeran, Webb, & Gollwitzer, 2005, Study 1), and mental contrasting creates such strong commitments (Oettingen et al., 2001). Implementation intentions are also found to show enhanced benefits when the specification of the if-component is personalized (Adriaanse, De Ridder, & De Wit, 2009), and mental contrasting guarantees the identification of personal critical obstacles that can then used as the critical situation in the if-component of an implementation intention.

Indeed, in a recent intervention study with middle-aged women (Stadler, Oettingen, & Gollwitzer, 2009), participants were taught the cognitive principles and individual steps of the MCII self-regulation strategy. This intervention allowed participants to apply MCII to their idiosyncratic everyday wishes and concerns. Specifically, participants were taught to apply MCII by themselves to the wish of exercising more whenever possible. Hence, MCII is referred to as a *metacognitive* self-regulation strategy. Participants were free to choose whatever form of exercising they wished, and they were encouraged to anticipate exactly those obstacles that were personally most relevant and to link them to exactly those goal-directed responses that personally appeared to be most instrumental. As dependent measures, participants maintained daily behavioral diaries to keep track of the amount of time they exercised every day. Overall, teaching the MCII technique enhanced exercise more than the information-only control intervention; this effect showed up immediately after the interventions and it stayed stable throughout the entire period of the study (16 weeks after the intervention). More specifically, participants in the MCII group exercised nearly twice as much: an average of 1 hour more per week than participants in the information-only control group.

Conducting the same MCII intervention to promote healthy eating in middle-aged women (i.e., eating more fruits and vegetables) also produced the desired behavior change effects, and these persisted even over the extensive time period of 2 years (Stadler, Oettingen, & Gollwitzer, 2010). In another study, Adriaanse, Oettingen, Gollwitzer, et al. (2010) targeted the negative eating habit of unhealthy snacking in college students. MCII worked for both students with weak and strong such habits, and notably, it was more effective than mental contrasting or formulating implementation intentions alone. Moreover, MCII was observed to benefit chronic back pain patients in increasing their health behaviors (Christiansen, Oettingen, Dahme, & Klinger, 2010). Over a period of both 3 weeks and 3 months patients increased their exercise as compared to a standard treatment control group. Exercise was measured by objective (i.e., bicycle ergometer test and number of lifts achieved in 2 minutes) and subjective indicators (reported physical functioning). Finally, MCII has shown beneficial effects outside the health area. For example, it benefited study efforts in adolescents preparing for standardized tests (Duckworth, Grant, Loew, Oettingen, & Gollwitzer, 2011). Together, these findings suggest that MCII is a cost- and time-effective self-regulation technique when it comes to the effective self-regulation of goal pursuit.

Conclusion and Outlook

The research on goals presented in this chapter paints a picture of an agentic individual who wisely sets goals and effectively acts upon them. She only needs to apply the self-regulatory strategies of goal setting and goal striving, that is, mental contrasting and implementation intentions. These strategies allow people to pursue realizing their idiosyncratic wishes and timber their own development according to principles of what is desirable and feasible. When applied in metacognitive form, mental contrasting and implementation intentions and especially their combined usage (MCII) will liberate people from being bound to erroneous engagement and bad habits. How these strategies can be applied to create goals of content and structure that best serve the realizing of people's individual wishes (e.g., learning goals if the future outcome is to accumulate knowledge and performance goals when outperforming others is at stake) will need to be explored in future research.

References

Aarts, H., Dijksterhuis, A., & Midden, C. (1999). To plan or not to plan? Goal achievement or interrupting the performance of mundane behaviors. *European Journal of Social Psychology*, 29, 971–979.

Abramson, L. Y., Seligman, M. E. P., & Teasdale, J. D. (1978). Learned helplessness in humans: Critique and reformulation. *Journal of Abnormal Psychology*, 87, 49–74.

Achtziger, A., Bayer, U. C., & Gollwitzer, P. M. (in press). Committing to implementation intentions: Attention and memory effects for selected situational cues. *Motivation and Emotion*.

Achtziger, A., Fehr, T., Oettingen, G., Gollwitzer, P. M., & Rockstroh, B. (2009). Strategies of intention formation are reflected in continuous MEG activity. *Social Neuroscience*, 4, 11–27.

Achtziger, A., Gollwitzer, P. M., & Sheeran, P. (2008). Implementation intentions and shielding goal striving from unwanted thoughts and feelings. *Personality and Social Psychology Bulletin*, 34, 381–393.

Adriaanse, M. A., de Ridder, D. T. D., & de Wit, J. B. F. (2009). Finding the critical cue: Implementation intentions

to change one's diet work best when tailored to personally relevant reasons for unhealthy eating. *Personality and Social Psychology Bulletin*, 35, 60–71.

Adriaanse, M. A., Gollwitzer, P. M., De Ridder, D. T. D., De Wit, J. B. F., & Kroese, F. M. (2011). Breaking habits with implementation intentions: A test of underlying processes. *Personality and Social Psychology Bulletin*, 37, 502–513.

Adriaanse, M. A., Oettingen, G., Gollwitzer, P. M., Hennes, E. P., De Ridder, D. T. D., & De Wit, J. B. F. (2010). When planning is not enough: Fighting unhealthy snacking habits by mental contrasting with implementation intentions (MCII). *European Journal of Social Psychology*, 40, 1277–1293.

Adriaanse, M. A., Van Oosten, J. M. F., De Ridder, D. T. D., De Wit, J. B. F., & Evers, C. (2011). Planning what not to eat: Ironic effects of implementation intentions negating unhealthy habits. *Personality and Social Psychology Bulletin*, 37, 69–81.

Ajzen, I. (1991). The theory of planned behavior. *Organizational Behavior and Human Decision Processes*, 50, 179–211.

Ajzen, I., & Fishbein, M. (1969). The prediction of behavioral intentions in a choice situation. *Journal of Experimental Social Psychology*, 5, 400–416.

Ajzen, I., & Fishbein, M. (1980). *Understanding attitudes and predicting social behavior*. Englewood Cliffs, NJ: Prentice-Hall.

Atkinson, J. W. (1957). Motivational determinants of risk-taking behavior. *Psychological Review*, 64, 359–372.

Atkinson, J. W. (1958). Towards experimental analysis of human motivation in terms of motives, expectancies and incentives. In J. W. Atkinson (Ed.), *Motives in fantasy, action, and society* (pp. 288–305). Princeton, NJ: Van Nostrand.

Bandura, A. (1977). Self-efficacy: Toward a unifying theory of behavioral change. *Psychological Review*, 84, 191–215.

Bandura, A. (1997). *Self-efficacy: The exercise of control*. New York: Freeman.

Bargh, J. A. (1989). Conditional automaticity: Varieties of automatic influence in social perception and cognition. In J. S. Uleman & J. A. Bargh (Eds.), *Unintended thought* (pp. 3–51). New York: Guilford Press.

Baumeister, R. E. (2000). Ego-depletion and the self's executive function. In A. Tesser, R. B. Felson, & J. M. Suls (Eds.), *Psychological perspectives on self and identity* (pp. 9–33). Washington, DC: American Psychological Association.

Bayer, U. C., Achtziger, A., Gollwitzer, P. M., & Moskowitz, G. (2009). Responding to subliminal cues: Do if-then plans facilitate action preparation and initiation without conscious intent? *Social Cognition*, 27, 183–201.

Bayer, U. C., & Gollwitzer, P. M. (2007). Boosting scholastic test scores by willpower: The role of implementation intentions. *Self and Identity*, 6, 1–19.

Bayer, U. C., Gollwitzer, P. M., & Achtziger, A. (2010). Staying on track: Planned goal striving is protected from disruptive internal states. *Journal of Experimental Social Psychology*, 46, 505–514.

Bless, H., & Fiedler, K. (1995). Affective states and the influence of activated general knowledge. *Personality and Social Psychology Bulletin*, 21, 766–778.

Bottom, W. P., & Studt, A. (1993). Framing effects and the distributive aspect of integrative bargaining. *Organizational Behavior and Human Decision Processes*, 56, 459–474.

Brandstätter, V., Lengfelder, A., & Gollwitzer, P. M. (2001). Implementation intentions and efficient action initiation. *Journal of Personality and Social Psychology*, 81, 946–960.

Brunstein, J. C., & Gollwitzer, P. M. (1996). Effects of failure on subsequent performance: The importance of self-defining goals. *Journal of Personality and Social Psychology, 70,* 395–407.

Brockner, J. (1992). The escalation of commitment to a failing course of action: Toward theoretical progress. *Academy of Management Review, 17,* 39–61.

Burgess, P. W., Simons, J. S., Dumontheil, I., & Gilbert, S. J. (2005). The gateway hypothesis of rostral PFC function. In J. Duncan, L. Phillips, & P. McLeod (Eds.), *Measuring the mind : Speed control and age* (pp. 215–246). New York: Oxford University Press.

Chapman, J., Armitage, C. J., & Norman, P. (2009). Comparing implementation intention interventions in relation to young adults' intake of fruit and vegetables. *Psychology and Health, 24,* 317–332.

Chasteen, A. L., Park, D. C., & Schwarz, N. (2001). Implementation intentions and facilitation of prospective memory. *Psychological Science, 12,* 457–461.

Cohen, J. (1992). A power primer. *Psychological Bulletin, 112,* 155–159.

Cohen, A-L., Bayer, U. C., Jaudas, A., & Gollwitzer, P. M. (2008). Self-regulatory strategy and executive control: Implementation intentions modulate task switching and Simon task performance. *Psychological Research, 72,* 12–26.

Christiansen, S., Oettingen, G., Dahme, B., & Klinger, R. (2010). A short goal-pursuit intervention to improve physical capacity: A randomized clinical trial in chronic back pain patients. *Pain, 149,* 444–452.

Darnon, C., Harackiewicz, J. M., Butera, F., Mugny, G., & Quiamzade, A. (2007). Performance-approach and performance-avoidance goals: When uncertainty makes a difference. *Personality and Social Psychology Bulletin, 33,* 813–827.

De Nooijer, J., De Vet, E., Brug, J., & De Vries, N. K. (2006). Do implementation intentions help to turn good intentions into higher fruit intakes? *Journal of Nutrition Education and Behavior, 38,* 25–29.

Dreisbach, G., & Goschke, T. (2004). How positive affect modulates cognitive control: Reduced perseveration at the cost of increased distractibility. *Journal of Experimental Psychology: Learning, Memory, and Cognition 30,* 343–353.

Duckworth, A. L., Grant, H., Loew, B., Oettingen, G., & Gollwitzer, P. M. (2011). Self-regulation strategies improve self-discipline in adolescents: Benefits of mental contrasting and implementation intentions. *Educational Psychology 31,* 17–26.

Dweck, C. S. (1996). Implicit theories as organizers of goals and behavior. In P. M. Gollwitzer & J. A. Bargh (Eds.), *The psychology of action: Linking cognition and motivation to behavior* (pp. 69–90). New York: Guilford Press.

Elliot, A. J. (1997). Integrating the "classic" and "contemporary"approaches to achievement motivation: A hierarchical model of approach and avoidance achievement motivation. In M. Maehr & P. Pintrich (Eds.), *Advances in motivation and achievement* (pp. 243–279). Greewich, CT: JAI Press.

Elliot, A. J., & Church, M. A. (1997). A hierarchical model of approach and avoidance achievement motivation. *Journal of Personality and Social Psychology, 72,* 218–232.

Elliot, A. J., Gable, S. L., & Mapes, R. R. (2006). Approach and avoidance motivation in the social domain. *Personality and Social Psychology Bulletin, 32,* 378–391.

Epstude, K., & Roese, N. J. (2008). The functional theory of counterfactual thinking. *Personality and Social Psychology Review, 12,* 168–192.

Festinger, L. (1942). A theoretical interpretation of shifts in level of aspiration. *Psychological Review, 49,* 235–250.

Fishbach, A., & Dhar, R. (2005). Goals as excuses or guides: The liberating effect of perceived goal progress on choice. *Journal of Consumer Research, 32,* 370–377.

Fishbach, A., Dhar, R., & Zhang, Y. (2006). Subgoals as substitutes or compliments: The role of goal accessibility. *Journal of Personality and Social Psychology, 91,* 232–242.

Förster, J., Higgins, E. T., & Idson, L. C. (1998). Approach and avoidance strength during goal attainment: Regulatory focus and the "goal looms larger"effect. *Journal of Personality and Social Psychology, 75,* 1115–1131.

Gable, P. A. (2006). Approach and avoidance social motives and goals. *Journal of Personality, 74,* 175–222.

Gable, P. A., & Harmon-Jones, E. (2008). Approach-motivated positive affect reduces breadth of attention. *Psychological Science, 19,* 476–482.

Gawrilow, C., & Gollwitzer, P. M. (2008). Implementation intentions facilitate response inhibition in ADHD children. *Cognitive Therapy and Research, 32,* 261–280.

Gawrilow, C., Gollwitzer, P. M., & Oettingen, G. (2011a). If-then plans benefit executive functions in children with ADHD. *Journal of Social and Clinical Psychology 30,* 616–646.

Gawrilow, C., Gollwitzer, P. M., & Oettingen, G. (2011b). If-then plans benefit delay of gratification performance in children with and without ADHD. *Cognitive Therapy and Research, 35,* 442–455.

Gilbert, S. J., Gollwitzer, P. M., Cohen, A-L., Oettingen, G., & Burgess, P. W. (2009). Separable brain systems supporting cues versus self-initiated realization of delayed intentions. *Journal of Experimental Psychology: Learning, Memory, and Cognition, 35,* 905–915.

Gollwitzer, P. M. (1986). Striving for specific identities: The social reality of self-symbolizing. In R. F. Baumeister (Ed.), *Public self and private self* (pp. 143–159). New York: Springer.

Gollwitzer, P. M. (1990). Action phases and mind-sets. In E. T. Higgins & R. M. Sorrentino (Eds.), *Handbook of motivation and cognition: Foundations of social behavior* (Vol. 2, pp. 53–92). New York: Guilford Press.

Gollwitzer, P. M. (1993). Goal achievement: The role of intentions. *European Review of Social Psychology, 4,* 141–185.

Gollwitzer, P. M. (1999). Implementation intentions: Strong effects of simple plans. *American Psychologist, 54,* 493–503.

Gollwitzer, P. M., & Brandstätter, V. (1997). Implementation intentions and effective goal pursuit. *Journal of Personality and Social Psychology, 73,* 186–199.

Gollwitzer, P. M., & Kirchhof, O. (1998). The willful pursuit of identity. In J. Heckhausen & C. S. Dweck (Eds.), *Motivation and self-regulation across the life span* (pp. 389–423). Cambridge, England: Cambridge University Press.

Gollwitzer, P. M., Parks-Stamm, E. J., Jaudas, A., & Sheeran, P. (2008). Flexible tenacity in goal pursuit. In J. Shah & W. Gardner (Eds.), *Handbook of motivation science* (pp. 325–341). New York: Guilford Press.

Gollwitzer, P. M., & Schaal, B. (1998). Metacognition in action: The importance of implementation intentions. *Personality and Social Psychology Review, 2,* 124–136.

Gollwitzer, P. M., & Sheeran, P. (2006). Implementation intentions and goal achievement: A meta-analysis of effects and processes. *Advances in Experimental Social Psychology, 38*, 69–119.

Gollwitzer, P. M., Sheeran, P., Michalski, V., & Seifert, A. E. (2009). When intentions go public: Does social reality widen the intention-behavior gap? *Psychological Science, 20*, 612–618.

Gollwitzer, P. M., Sheeran, P., Trötschel, R., & Webb, T. L. (2011). Self-regulation of primimg effects on behvaior. *Psychological Science, 22*, 901–911.

Gollwitzer, P. M., & Wicklund, R. A. (1985). Self-symbolizing and the neglect of others' perspectives. *Journal of Personality and Social Psychology, 48*, 702–715.

Gollwitzer, P. M., Wicklund, R. A., & Hilton, J. L. (1982). Admission of failure and symbolic self-completion: Extending Lewinian theory. *Journal of Personality and Social Psychology, 43*, 358–371.

Gray, J. A. (1994). Three fundamental emotion systems. In P. Ekman & R. J. Davidson (Eds.), *The nature of emotion* (pp. 243–247). New York: Oxford University Press.

Gruenfeld, D. H., Inesi, M. E., Magee, J. C., & Galinsky, A. D. (2008). Power and the objectification of social targets. *Journal of Personality and Social Psychology, 95*, 111–127.

Guinote, A. (2007). Power and goal pursuit. *Personality and Social Psychology Bulletin, 33*, 1076–1087.

Guinote, A. (2008). Power and affordances: When the situation has more power over powerful than powerless individuals. *Journal of Personality and Social Psychology, 95*, 237–252.

Gurney, K., Prescott, T. J., & Redgrave, P. (2001a). A computational model of action selection in the basal ganglia I: A new functional anatomy. *Biological Cybernetics, 84*, 401–410.

Gurney, K., Prescott, T. J., & Redgrave, P. (2001b). A computational model of action selection in the basal ganglia II: Analysis and simulation of behavior. *Biological Cybernetics, 84*, 411–423.

Hagger, M. S., Chatzisarantis, N. L. D., & Harris, J. (2006). From psychological need satisfaction to intentional behavior: Testing a motivational sequence in two behavioral contexts. *Personality and Social Psychology Bulletin, 32*, 131–148.

Harmon-Jones, C., Schmeichel, B. J., & Harmon-Jones, E. (2009). Symbolic self completion in academia: Evidence from department web pages and email signatures files. *European Journal of Experimental Social Psychology, 39*, 311–316.

Heckhausen, H. (1977). Achievement motivation and its constructs: A cognitive model. *Motivation and Emotion, 1*, 283–329.

Heckhausen, H., & Gollwitzer, P. M. (1987). Thought contents and cognitive functioning in motivational versus volitional states of mind. *Motivation and Emotion, 11*, 101–120.

Henderson, M., Gollwitzer, P. M., & Oettingen, G. (2007). Implementation intentions and disengagement from a failing course of action. *Journal of Behavioral Decision Making, 20*, 81–102.

Higgins, E. T. (1997). Beyond pleasure and pain. *American Psychologist, 52*, 1280–1300.

Higgins, E. T. (2000). Making a good decision: Value from fit. *American Psychologist, 55*, 1217–1230.

Higgins, E. T. (2006). Value from hedonic experience and engagement. *Psychological Review, 113*, 439–460.

Holland, R. W., Aarts, H. & Langendam, D. (2006). Breaking and creating habits on the working floor: A field-experiment on the power of implementation intentions. *Journal of Experimental Social Psychology, 42*, 776–783.

Hollenbeck, J. R., Williams, C. R., & Klein, H. J. (1989). An empirical examination of the antecedents of commitment to difficult goals. *Journal of Applied Psychology, 74*, 18–23.

Hull, C. L. (1943). *Principles of behavior*. New York: Appleton-Century-Crofts.

Jacoby, L. L. (1991). A process-dissociation framework: Separating automatic from intentional uses of memory. *Journal of Memory and Language 30*, 513–541.

Judge, T. A., Bono, J. E., Erez, A., & Locke, E. A. (2005). Core self-evaluations and job and life satisfaction: The role of self-concordance and goal attainment. *Journal of Applied Psychology, 90*, 257–268.

Kane, M. J., & Engle, R. W. (2003). Working-memory capacity and the control of attention: The contributions of goal neglect, response competition, and task set to Stroop interference. *Journal of Experimental Psychology: General, 132*, 47–70.

Kappes, A., & Oettingen, G. (2011). *The emergence of goals: Mental contrasting connects future and reality*. Manuscript under revision.

Kappes, A., Singman, H., & Oettingen, G. (2011). *Mental contrasting links reality to instrumental means*. Manuscript under review.

Kappes, A., Oettingen, G. & Pak, H. (2011). *Mental contrasting and the self-regulation of responding to negative feedback*. Manuscript under revision.

Kappes, H. B., & Oettingen, G. (2011). Positive fantasies about idealized futures sap energy. *Journal of Experimental Social Psychology 47*, 719–729.

Kazen, M., & Kuhl, J. (2005). Intention memory and achievement motivation: Volitional facilitation and inhibition as a function of affective contents of need related stimuli. *Journal of Personality and Social Psychology, 89*, 426–448.

Kirk, D., Gollwitzer, P. M., & Carnevale, P. J. (2011). Self-regulation in ultimatum bargaining: Goals and plans help accept unfair but profitable offers. *Social Cognition 29*, 528–546.

Knäuper, B., Roseman, M., Johnson, P., & Krantz, L. (2009). Using mental imagery to enhance the effectiveness of implementation intentions. *Current Psychology, 28*, 181–186.

Koestner, R., Horberg, E. J., Gaudreau, P., Powers, T. A., Di Dio, P., Bryan, C., & Salter, N. (2006). Bolstering implementation plans for the long haul: The benefits of simultaneously boosting self-concordance or self-efficacy. *Personality and Social Psychology Bulletin, 32*, 1547–1558.

Koestner, R., Lekes, N., Powers, T. A., & Chicoine, E. (2002). Attaining personal goals: Self-concordance plus implementation intention equals success: *Journal of Personality and Social Psychology, 83*, 231–244.

Koo, M., & Fishbach, A. (2008). Dynamics of self-regulation: How (un)accomplished goal actions affect motivation. *Journal of Personality and Social Psychology, 94*, 183–195.

Kuhl, J., & Kazen, M. (1999). Volitional facilitation of difficult intentions: Joint activation of intention memory and positive affect removes Stroop interference. *Journal of Experimental Psychology: General, 128*, 382–399.

Larsen, R. J., & Augustine, A. A. (2008). Basic personality dispositions related to approach and avoidance: Extraversion/neuroticism, BAS/BIS, and positive/negative affectivity. In A. J. Elliot (Ed.), *Handbook of approach and avoidance motivation* (pp. 151–164). Philadelphia, PA: Psychology Press.

Ledgerwood, A., Liviatan, I., & Carnevale, P. J. (2007). Group identity completion and the symbolic value of property. *Psychological Science, 18*, 873–878.

Lengfelder, A., & Gollwitzer, P. M. (2001). Reflective and reflexive action control in frontal lobe patients. *Neuropsychology*, *15*, 80–100.

Lewin, K., Dembo, T., Festinger, L., & Sears, P. S. (1944). Level of aspiration. In J. McHunt (Ed.), *Personality and the behaviour disorders* (Vol. 1, pp. 333–378). New York: Ronald.

Liberman, N., Trope, Y., McCrea, M. S., & Sherman, S. (2007). The effect of level of construal on the temporal distance of activity enactment. *Journal of Experimental Social Psychology*, *43*, 143–149.

Locke, E. A., & Latham, G. P. (2002). Building a practically useful theory of goal setting and task performance: A 35 year odyssey. *American Psychologist*, *57*, 705–717.

Locke, E. A., & Latham, G. P. (2006). New directions in goal-setting theory. *Current Directions in Psychological Science*, *15*, 265–268.

Louro, M. J., Pieters, R., & Zeelenberg, M. (2007). Dynamics of multiple-goal pursuit. *Journal of Personality and Social Psychology*, *93*, 174–193.

Maglio, S. J., Gollwitzer, P. M., & Oettingen, G. (in press). Action control by implementation intentions: The role of discrete emotions. In A. Clark, J. Kiverstein, & T. Vierkant (Eds.), *Decomposing the will*. New York: Oxford University Press.

Markman, K. D., Lindberg, M. J., Kray, L. J., & Galinsky, A. D. (2007). Implications of counterfactual structure for creativity and analytical problem solving. *Personality and Social Psychology Bulletin*, *33*, 312–324.

Martin, J., Sheeran, P., Slade, P., Wright, A., & Dibble, T. (2009). Implementation intention formation reduces consultations for emergency contraception and pregnancy testing among teenage women. *Health Psychology*, *28*, 762–769.

McClelland, D. C. (1985a). *Human motivation*. Glenview, IL: Scott, Foresman.

McClelland, D. C. (1985b). How motives, skills, and values determine what people do. *American Psychologist*, *41*, 812–825.

McCrea, S. M. (2008). Self-handicapping, excuse-making, and counterfactual thinking: Consequences for self-esteem and future motivation. *Journal of Personality and Social Psychology*, *95*, 274–292.

McCrea, S. M., Liberman, N., Trope, Y., & Sherman, S. J. (2008). Construal level and procrastination. *Psychological Science 19*, 1308–1314.

Mendoza, S. A., Gollwitzer, P. M., & Amodio, D. M. (2010). Reducing the expression of implicit stereotypes: Reflexive control through implementation intentions. *Personality and Social Psychology Bulletin*, *36*, 512–523.

Miles, J. D., & Proctor, R. W. (2008). Improving performance through implementation intentions: Are preexisting response biases replaced? *Psychonomic Bulletin and Review*, *15*, 1105–1110.

Milne, S. E., Orbell, S. & Sheeran, P. (2002). Combining motivational and volitional interventions to promote exercise participation: Protection motivation theory and implementation intentions. *British Journal of Health Psychology*, *7*, 163–184.

Mischel, W. (1973). Toward a cognitive social learning reconceptualization of personality. *Psychological Review*, *80*, 252–283.

Mischel, W. (1974). Processes in delay of gratification. In L. Berkowitz (Ed.), *Advances in experimental social psychology* (Vol. 7, pp. 249–292). New York: Academic Press.

Molden, D. C., & Dweck, C. S. (2006). Finding "meaning" in psychology. A lay theories approach to self-regulation, social perception, and social development. *American Psychologist*, *61*, 192–203.

Muraven, M., & Baumeister, R. F. (2000). Self-regulation and depletion of limited resources: Does self-control resemble a muscle? *Psychological Bulletin*, *126*, 247–259.

Muraven, M., Tice, D. M., & Baumeister, R. F. (1998). Self-control as a limited resource: Regulatory depletion patterns. *Journal of Personality and Social Psychology*, *74*, 774–789.

Oettingen, G. (1996). Positive fantasy and motivation. In P. M. Gollwitzer, & J. A. Bargh (Eds.), *The psychology of action: Linking cognition and motivation to behavior* (pp. 236–259). New York: Guilford.

Oettingen, G. (2000). Expectancy effects on behavior depend on self-regulatory thought. *Social Cognition 18*, 101–129.

Oettingen, G., & Gollwitzer, P. M. (2010). Strategies of setting and implementing goals: Mental contrasting and implementation intentions. In J. E. Maddux & J. P. Tangney (Eds.), *Social psychological foundations of clinical psychology* (pp. 114–135). New York: Guilford Press.

Oettingen, G., Hönig, G., & Gollwitzer, P. M. (2000). Effective self-regulation of goal attainment. *International Journal of Educational Research*, *33*, 705–732.

Oettingen, G., & Kappes, A. (2009). Mental contrasting of the future and reality to master negative feedback. In K. D. Markman, W. M. P. Klein, & J. A. Suhr (Eds.), *Handbook of imagination and mental simulation*. (pp. 395–412). New York: Psychology Press.

Oettingen, G., & Mayer, D. (2002). The motivating function of thinking about the future: Expectations versus fantasies. *Journal of Personality and Social Psychology*, *83*, 1198–1212.

Oettingen, G., Mayer, D., Sevincer, A. T., Stephens, E. J., Pak, H., & Hagenah, M. (2009). Mental contrasting and goal commitment: The mediating role of energization. *Personality and Social Psychology Bulletin*, *35*, 608–622.

Oettingen, G., Mayer, D., & Thorpe, J. S (2010). Promotion and prevention fantasies and the self-regulation of goal commitment to reduce cigarette consumption. *Psychology and Health*, *25*, 961–977.

Oettingen, G., Mayer, D., Thorpe, J. S., Janetzke, H., & Lorenz, S. (2005). Turning fantasies about positive and negative futures into self-improvement goals. *Motivation and Emotion*, *29*, 237–267.

Oettingen, G., Pak, H., & Schnetter, K. (2001). Self-regulation of goal-setting: Turning free fantasies about the future into binding goals. *Journal of Personality and Social Psychology*, *80*, 736–753.

Oettingen, G., & Stephens, E. J. (2009). Fantasies and motivationally intelligent goal setting. In G. B. Moskowitz & H. Grant (Eds.), *The psychology of goals* (pp. 153–178). New York: Guilford Press.

Oettingen, G., Stephens, E. J., Mayer, D., & Brinkmann, B. (2010). Mental contrasting and the self-regulation of helping relations. *Social Cognition*, *28*, 490–508.

Oettingen, G., & Wadden, T. A. (1991). Expectation, fantasy, and weight loss: Is the impact of positive thinking always positive? *Cognitive Therapy and Research*, *15*, 167–175.

Orbell, S., Hodgkins, S., & Sheeran, P. (1997) Implementation intentions and the theory of planned behavior. *Personality and Social Psychology Bulletin*, *23*, 953–962.

Oyserman, D., Bybee, D., & Terry, K. (2006). Possible selves and academic outcomes: How and when possible selves impel action. *Journal of Personality and Social Psychology*, *91*, 188–204.

Palayiwa, A., Sheeran, P., & Thompson, A. (2010). "Words will never hurt me!" Implementation intentions regulate attention to stigmatizing comments about appearance. *Journal of Social and Clinical Psychology, 29*, 575–598.

Papies, E., Aarts, H., & de Vries, N. K. (2009). Grounding your plans: Implementation intentions go beyond the mere creation of goal-directed associations. *Journal of Experimental Social Psychology, 45*, 1148–1151.

Parks-Stamm, E. J., Gollwitzer, P. M., & Oettingen, G. (2007). Action control by implementation intentions: Effective cue detection and efficient response initiation. *Social Cognition, 25*, 248–266.

Paul, I., Gawrilow, C., Zech, F., Gollwitzer, P. M., Rockstroh, B., Odenthal, G., Kratzer, W., & Wienbruch, C. (2007). If-then planning modulates the P300 in children with attention deficit hyperactivity disorder. *NeuroReport, 18*, 653–657.

Poortvliet, P. M., Janssen, O., Van Yperen, N. W., & Van de Vliert, E. (2007). Achievement goals and interpersonal behavior: How mastery and performance goals shape information exchange. *Personality and Social Psychology Bulletin, 33*, 1435–1447.

Powers, T. A., Koestner, R., & Topciu, R. A. (2005). Implementation intentions, perfectionism, and goal progress: Perhaps the road to hell is paved with good intentions. *Personality and Social Psychology Bulletin, 31*, 902–912.

Ryan, R. M., Sheldon, K. M., Kasser, T., & Deci, E. L. (1996). All goals are not created equal: An organismic perspective on the nature of goals and their regulation. In P. M. Gollwitzer & J. A. Bargh (Eds.), *The psychology of action: Linking cognition and motivation to behavior* (pp. 7–26). New York: Guilford Press.

Scheier, M. F., & Carver, C. S. (1987). Dispositional optimism and physical well-being: The influence of generalized outcome expectancies. *Journal of Personality, 55*, 169–210.

Scholer, A. A., & Higgins, E. T. (2008). Distinguishing levels of approach and avoidance: A analysis using regulatory focus theory. In A. J. Elliot (Ed.), *Handbook of approach and avoidance motivation* (pp. 489–503). New York: Psychology Press.

Schweiger Gallo, I., Keil, A., Mc Culloch, K. C., Rockstroh, B., & Gollwitzer, P. M. (2009). Strategic automation of emotion control. *Journal of Personality and Social Psychology, 96*, 11–31.

Shah, J. Y., Friedman, R., & Kruglanski, A. W. (2002). Forgetting all else: On the antecedents and consequences of goal shielding. *Journal of Personality and Social Psychology, 83*, 1261–1280.

Shah, J., Higgins, E. T., & Friedman, R. S. (1998). Performance incentives and means: How regulatory focus influences goal attainment. *Journal of Personality and Social Psychology, 74*, 285–293.

Sheeran, P., & Orbell, S. (1999). Implementation intentions and repeated behavior: augmenting the predictive vailidity of the theory of planned behaviour. *European Journal of Social Psychology 29*, 349–369.

Sheeran, P., & Orbell, S. (2000). Using implementation intentions to increase attendance for cervical cancer screening. *Health Psychology, 19*, 283–289.

Sheeran, P., Webb, T. L., & Gollwitzer, P. M. (2005). The interplay between goal intentions and implementation intentions. *Personality and Social Psychology Bulletin, 31*, 87–98.

Sheldon, K. M., & Elliot, A. J. (1999). Goal striving, need satisfaction, and longitudinal well-being: The self-concordance model. *Journal of Personality and Social Psychology, 76*, 482–497.

Sheldon, K. M., & Krieger, L. S. (2007). Understanding the negative effects of legal education on law students: A longitudinal test of self-determination theory. *Personality and Social Psychology Bulletin, 33*, 883–897.

Simon, J. R. (1990). The effects of an irrelevant directional cue on human information processing. In R. W. Proctor & T. G. Reeve (Eds.), *Stimulus-response compatibility: An integrative perspective* (pp. 31–86). Amsterdam: North-Holland.

Smith, P. K., Jostmann, N. B., Galinsky, A. D., & van Dijk, W. W. (2008). Lacking power impairs executive functions. *Psychological Science, 19*, 441–447.

Sonuga-Barke, E. J. S. (2002). Psychological heterogenity in ADHD—A dual pathway model of behavior and cognition. *Behavioral Brain Research, 130*, 29–36.

Spence, K. W. (1956). *Behavior theory and conditioning.* New Haven, CT: Yale University Press.

Stadler, G., Oettingen, G., & Gollwitzer, P. M. (2009). Physical activity in women. Effects of a self-regulation intervention. *American Journal of Preventive Medicine, 36*, 29–34.

Stadler, G., Oettingen, G., & Gollwitzer, P. M. (2010). Intervention effects of information and self-regulation on eating fruits and vegetables over two years. *Health Psychology, 29*, 274–283.

Stewart, B. D., & Payne, B. K. (2008). Bringing automatic stereotyping under control: Implementation intentions as efficient means of thought control. *Personality and Social Psychology Bulletin, 34*, 1332–1345.

Strachman, A., & Gable, S. L. (2006). What you want (and do not want) affects what you see (and do not see): Avoidance social goals and social events. *Personality and Social Psychology Bulletin, 32*, 1446–1458.

Tamir, M. (2009). What do people want to feel and why? Pleasure and utility in emotion regulation. *Current Directions in Psychological Science, 18*, 101–105.

Tamir, M., & Robinson, M. D. (2007). The happy spotlight: Positive mood and selective attention to rewarding information. *Personality and Social Psychology Bulletin, 33*, 1124–1136.

Taylor, S. E., Pham, L. B., Rivkin, I. D., & Armor, D. A. (1998). Harnessing the imagination: Mental simulation, self-regulation, and coping. *American Psychologist, 53*, 429–439.

Tice, D. M., Bratslavsky, E., & Baumeister, R. F. (2001). Emotional distress regulation takes precedence over impulse control: If you feel bad, do it! *Journal of Personality and Social, 80*, 53–67

Tolman, E. C. (1932). *Purposive behavior in animals and men.* New York: Appleton-Century.

Trötschel, R., & Gollwitzer, P. M. (2007). Implementation intentions and the willful pursuit of prosocial goals in negotiations. *Journal of Experimental Social Psychology, 43*, 579–589.

Vallacher, R. R., & Wegner, D. M. (1987). What do people think they're doing? Action identification and human behavior. *Psychological Review, 94*, 215–228.

Verplanken, B., & Faes, S. (1999). Good intentions, bad habits, and effects of forming implementation intentions on healthy eating. *European Journal of Social Psychology, 29*, 591–604.

Vroom, V. H. (1964). *Work and motivation.* New York: Wiley.

Webb, T. L., Christian, J., & Armitage C. J. (2007). Helping students turn up for class: Does personality moderate the effectiveness of an implementation intention intervention? *Learning and Individual Differences, 17*, 316–327.

Webb, T. L., Ononaiye, M. S. P., Sheeran, P., Reidy, J. G., & Lavda, A. (2010). Using implementation intentions to overcome the effects of social anxiety on attention and appraisals of performance. *Personality and Social Psychology Bulletin, 36,* 612–627.

Webb, T. L., & Sheeran, P. (2003). Can implementation intentions help to overcome ego-depletion. *Journal of Experimental Social Psychology, 39,* 279–286.

Webb, T. L., & Sheeran, P. (2004). Identifying good opportunities to act: Implementation intentions and cue discrimination. *European Journal of Social Psychology, 34,* 407–419.

Webb, T. L., & Sheeran, P. (2006). Does changing behavioral intentions engender behavior change? A meta-analysis of the experimental evidence. *Psychological Bulletin, 132,* 249–268.

Webb, T. L., & Sheeran, P. (2007). How do implementation intentions promote goal attainment? A test of component processes. *Journal of Experimental Social Psychology, 43,* 295–302.

Webb, T. L., & Sheeran, P. (2008). Mechanisms of implementation intention effects: The role of goal intentions, self-efficacy, and accessibility of plan components. *British Journal of Social Psychology, 47,* 373–395.

Webb, T. L., Sheeran, P., & Luszczynska, A. (2009). Planning to break unwanted habits: Habit strength moderates implementation intention effects on behavior change. *British Journal of Social Psychology, 48,* 507–523.

Wicklund, R. A., & Gollwitzer, P. M. (1982). *Symbolic self-completion.* Hillsdale, NJ: Erlbaum.

Wieber, F., Odenthal, G., & Gollwitzer, P. M. (2010). Self-efficacy feelings moderate implementation intention effects. *Self and Identity, 9,* 177–194.

Wieber, F., & Sassenberg, K. (2006). I can't take my eyes off of it—attention attraction of implementation intentions. *Social Cognition, 24,* 723–752.

Wieber, F., von Suchodoletz, A., Heikamp, T., Trommsdorff, G., & Gollwitzer, P. M. (2011). If-then planning helps school-aged children to ignore attractive distractions. *Social Psychology 42,* 39–47.

Wood, W., & Neal, D. T. (2007). A new look at habits and the habit–goal interface. *Psychological Review, 114,* 842–862.

Unconscious Goal Pursuit: Nonconscious Goal Regulation and Motivation

Henk Aarts *and* Ruud Custers

Abstract

Experimental research in psychology has discovered that human goal pursuit originates and unfolds in the unconscious. Our behavior is directed and motivated by goals outside of conscious awareness in the current situation or environment. In this chapter we review past and current research that examines these goal-priming effects. Our review is organized around two themes. The first theme deals with research that analyzes how people control their goal pursuit in the absence of conscious awareness, and it examines goal pursuit as automated behaviors resulting from habits as well as flexible behaviors that occur when habitual responding is not adequate to attain goals. The second theme concerns the quest to understand the unconscious source of human goal pursuit, and it explores recent work that considers the fundamental role of positive affect in reward processing and implicit motivation.

Key Words: priming, goal pursuit, unconscious processes, motivation, regulation

Observing other people's and one's own behavior sometimes may lead to the conclusion that the human behavioral system throws in responses to situations by trial and error. Our behavior can be fairly unpredictable and even chaotic. However, whereas human behavior occasionally appears to consist of a random selection of responses, often it is not. Our behavior is very sensitive to learning and strongly influenced by past experiences, and it tends to be highly organized and structured in the service of future action. Indeed, research in the tradition of behaviorism has shown that human behavior follows from rigid responses to environmental stimuli that are learned and reinforced by rewards (Skinner, 1953; Watson, 1925). When chained together—it is reasoned—such responses can even make up complicated patterns of action, setting each other off like toppling domino stones. According to this view, the environment organizes and determines human behavior.

Obviously, the environment plays a crucial role in directing behavior. However, acting on fixed stimulus-response rules—such as smashing a beeping alarm clock in the morning—is not the whole story. A substantial part of human behavior seems to be directed at desired outcomes that reliably control and motivate the behavioral system in a dynamic world. This flexibility to produce the same desired outcomes under varying circumstances comes from our capacity to mentally represent what we want and do: to build and store representations of goals. These goal representations function as beacons for behavior, motivating action and guiding its course.

The idea that our behavior is directed by goals is explicitly articulated in different models and theories of human behavior (e.g., Bandura, 1986; Deci & Ryan, 1985; Locke & Latham, 1990). Importantly, in most of these models and theories people's goal pursuit is assumed to be governed by a kind of inner agent such as "consciousness" or "the will." There is common agreement that goal setting is accompanied by conscious awareness, and that goal pursuit is associated with conscious intent. For Descartes, the role of consciousness in goal pursuit even provided proof of our very existence. It is we who consciously decide what we want and do; and it is up to us to consciously act upon it. It does not come as a surprise, then, that the scientific investigation of human behavior—heavily influenced by Descartes—has assigned a key role to consciousness.

However, whereas the causal status of consciousness in human behavior is often taken for granted, over the last 15 years or so several lines of experimentation have discovered that our goal-directed behaviors can be under "unconscious control" (Custers & Aarts, 2010). This large body of evidence for the occurrence of nonconscious social behavior resonates well with prevailing views on the limited role of consciousness in human functioning. According to these views, our thinking and doing is produced by mental processes that are not open to introspection, and hence, in essence *all* our behaviors start and unfold in the unconscious (Libet, 1985; Nørretranders, 1991). In other words, human behavior is not (always) governed by a social agent that motivates and directs behavior consciously and intentionally (Bargh, 1997; Wegner, 2002; Wilson, 2002). Instead, our behavior is directed and motivated by goals outside of conscious awareness in the current situation or environment, even though we share the experience and belief that we consciously set and pursue goals. This notion not only pertains to simple motor movements and skills such as flexing an index finger, pushing keys on a computer keyboard, or driving a car but also to social behavior resulting from higher cognitive processes such as our goal pursuit.

In the present chapter, we discuss social cognition research that examines the possibility that human goal pursuit emerges in the absence of conscious intent and without awareness of the cause of the goal pursuit. This chapter is organized around two themes. The first theme deals with research that analyzes how people are able to control and regulate their goal pursuit in the absence of conscious awareness. Therefore, we examine goal pursuit as automated behaviors resulting from habits as well as flexible behaviors that occur when habitual responding is not adequate to attain goals. The second theme concerns the question of what motivates goal pursuit unconsciously. Specifically, we discuss recent work that considers the fundamental role

of positive affect in reward processing and implicit motivation to offer insight into the unconscious sources of our goal pursuit. Before we discuss this work in more detail, we will briefly address some general issues pertaining to the conceptualization of unconscious goal pursuit.

The Concept of Unconscious Goal Pursuit

At first glance, the notion that goal pursuit occurs nonconsciously and is controlled by the environment brings us back to behaviorism. However, the modern conceptualization of unconscious goal pursuit is different in one important way (e.g., Aarts & Dijksterhuis, 2000; Bargh, 1990). It follows the modern view on human functioning that analyzes the involvement of mental processes and the role of knowledge acquisition and utilization in nonconscious learning and environmental control over behavior. For instance, several studies on the role of reinforcement in classical and instrumental conditioning have stressed the importance of incentives or goals in motivating and directing behavior of animals, humans included, in the absence of conscious awareness (Berridge, 2001). Furthermore, basic and applied work on preference learning suggests that humans implicitly form mental representations of rewarding goal-objects when these objects co-occur with affective (e.g., rewarding) stimuli (De Houwer, Thomas, & Baeyens, 2001; Hofmann, De Houwer, Perugini, Baeyens, & Crombez, 2010). In addition, people have been shown to learn rules that predict the occurrence of complex sequences of stimuli and responses without their ability to consciously verbalize these rules (Reber, 1993). Accordingly, research on unconscious goal pursuit goes beyond behaviorism (Bargh & Ferguson, 2000) by scrutinizing the mental processes that underlie the influence of the environment on the activation and operation of goal-directed behavior.

Analogous to research on conscious goal pursuit, the study on unconscious goal pursuit assumes that goals are mentally represented as desired behaviors or outcomes (e.g., Carver & Scheier, 1998; Gollwitzer & Moskowitz, 1996). These goal representations can differ in their level of abstractness. For instance, while socializing or earning money are representations of complex goals that usually require a series of actions to be achieved, using a phone or producing matching symbols on a slot machine are results which can be attained by a few button presses or a simple hand movement. Thus, human goal-directed behavior is commonly understood to evolve from more simple movement goals to more complex social goals. We first have to learn to orchestrate and coordinate our motor movements before we can operate a phone and to make a date to go out, so to speak.

In contrast to research on conscious goal pursuit, however, the study on unconscious goal pursuit explicitly assumes that goals and their pursuit can be controlled in the absence of conscious awareness. An important foundation for this assumption pertains to the empirical observation that humans represent their actions in terms of their observable effects or outcomes, and they establish associations between the outcomes and the motor programs that produce the outcome (Hommel, Müsseler, Aschersleben, & Prinz, 2001; Jeannerod, 1997; Prinz, 1997; Vallacher & Wegner, 1987). As a consequence, action can follow from an ideomotor principle (James, 1890): Merely thinking about or priming a certain outcome moves and programs the human body in the service of achieving that outcome without a conscious decision to act. In addition, representing actions in terms of their potentially desirable outcomes allows people to direct their behavior at the level of the specific outcome, in that they serve as reference points that guide and adjust ongoing actions toward producing the desired goal.

Furthermore, our personal goal pursuit is assumed to be part of knowledge structures including the context, the goal itself, and actions as well as opportunities that may aid goal pursuit, that are shaped by direct experience and other types of learning (Aarts & Dijksterhuis, 2000; Aarts & Dijksterhuis 2003; Bargh & Gollwitzer, 1994; Kruglanski et al., 2002). For example, the goal of consuming fruit may be related to eating a banana while having lunch in the university cafeteria. Or a visit to an exclusive restaurant or bar may be connected to interacting with good friends and the desire to socialize and go out. Thus, when activating or priming a goal (e.g., eating fruit, socializing), we do not access a single concept, but rather a rich structure containing, among others, cognitive, affective, behavioral information (Bargh, 2006). According to the concept of unconscious goal pursuit, then, the direction and motivation of people's thinking and doing can start and proceed outside of conscious awareness, because one can directly rely on accessible goal-relevant representations that are primed by contextual as well as behavioral information.

One of the first empirical demonstrations of this notion comes from Bargh and others' (2001) research program on goal-priming effects on achievement. In one of their studies, they unobtrusively exposed students to words such as "strive" and "succeed" to prime the goal of achievement, and then gave them the opportunity to perform well (finding as many words as possible in an anagram puzzle task). Results indicated that students primed with the achievement goal outperformed those who were not primed with the goal. Further experimentation demonstrated that such goal priming leads to qualities associated with motivational states or volition, such as persistence in solving puzzles and increased flexibility on the Wisconsin Card Sorting Task (Hassin, 2008), a standard measure of flexibility in cognitive processing (Miyake, Friedman, Emerson, Witzki, Howerter, & Wager, 2000). Extensive debriefing revealed that the students did not experience an influence of the first task (in which they were exposed to achievement-related words) on their responses to the second. These findings indicate that the mere activation of a goal representation suffices to motivate and direct people to work on the primed goal without conscious thought and intent.

The work alluded to earlier shows that goal pursuit can be automatically put in place if the representation of the goal is *directly* primed (for more evidence of direct achievement goal priming effects, e.g., Bongers, Dijksterhuis, & Spears, 2010; Custers, Aarts, Oikawa, & Elliot, 2009; Eitam, Hassin, & Schul, 2008; Engeser, Wendland, & Rheinberg, 2006; Hart & Albarracín, 2009; Oikawa, 2004; Shantz & Latham, 2009). Recently, researchers have started to identify the specific aspects in the social environment that may cause people to automatically set and pursue goals. Through their associations with particular goals, these aspects *indirectly* prime or activate goal representations. For instances, there is research to suggest that goal pursuit is automatically triggered when goals are inferred from the behavior of others, an effect termed *goal contagion* (Aarts, Gollwitzer, Hassin, 2004; Dik & Aarts, 2007; Friedman, Deci, Elliot, Moller, & Aarts, 2010; Loersch, Aarts, Payne, & Jefferis, 2008). Aarts et al. (2004) demonstrated that participants who observed another person's behavior that implied the goal of making money were more motivated to make money themselves by engaging in a task that gave access to a lottery.

Furthermore, goals and their pursuit seem to be activated in the presence of important others (Fitzsimons & Bargh, 2003; Kraus & Chen, 2009; Shah, 2003). In a study among undergraduate students (Fitzsimons & Bargh, 2003), subliminal priming of the name of one's parents was demonstrated to trigger the motivation to achieve, and exposure to names of good friends primed the goal and resultant behavior of helping. In a recent line of experimentation, these goal-priming effects have been replicated and extended in the realm of social stereotypes (Aarts et al., 2005; Custers, Maas, Wildenbeest, & Aarts, 2008; Moskowitz, Gollwitzer, Wasel, & Schaal, 1999). For instance, priming members of social groups that contain the representation of a goal that is believed to be held by that group has been shown to cause people to automatically pursue the goals, such as the goals of helping or making money that are stereotypical for nurses or stockbrokers, respectively.

While divergent, these findings have a common theme. They suggest that an appreciation of the goals motivating other people we interact with allows one to entertain similar goals and to try to attain them oneself. It promotes successful pursuit of one's own needs, desires, and goals. Furthermore, by pursuing the goals of others, people may become more similar in what they desire and strive for, and hence in their plans for the future (Aarts, Dijksterhuis, & Dik, 2008). Given this compelling and pervasive social influence on human pursuit, we will now discuss how goals are primed and control overt behavior without an act of conscious will.

The Control of Unconscious Goal Pursuit

In this section we address the question of how people control their goal pursuit unconsciously. That is, we will examine how the mere activation of a goal representation produces actions leading to the goal. Two issues are important here. First, unconscious goal pursuit is the result of well-established habits. Second, because habits may fail to produce actions directed at goals, human goal pursuit needs to be flexible and adaptive. Accordingly, researchers have started to examine whether people are capable of regulating their personal goals without being aware of the activation and operation of the goal. We will first address the habitual nature of unconscious goal pursuit, and then discuss research that aims to demonstrate that goal pursuit is flexible without an act of conscious will.

The Role of Habits in Unconscious Goal Pursuit

The nonconscious execution of goal-directed behavior has been initially understood and appreciated in terms of habits. That is, in line with contemporary social cognition research on the establishment of automatic and unconscious processes, goals prime

behavior as a result of practice and the automation of skills. In general, there are two different views to this issue that can be characterized as representing either low-level stimulus-response learning and performance or a higher cognitive level of goal-directed learning and performance.

UNCONSCIOUS GOAL PURSUIT AND STIMULUS-RESPONSE RULES

At the lowest level of analysis, habits can be regarded as stimulus-response links that are established and reinforced by rewards which follow certain responses to a stimulus. If, for example, one feels pleasantly satisfied after eating a crunchy chocolate bar, the sight of chocolate may later evoke the action of grabbing it in order to eat. Eventually, when a behavior has repeatedly been executed in response to a certain stimulus and the stimulus-response association has become well established, the perception of the stimulus may automatically trigger the execution of the associated behavior.

This view that, after sufficient practice, behavior becomes completely stimulus controlled and independently of the rewards (e.g., reducing hunger) that initially reinforced the behavior suggests that the behavior is no longer motivational and goal directed in nature (Dickinson, Balleine, Watt, Gonzales, & Boakes, 1995). However, there are two scientific discoveries that do not agree with this automatic stimulus-response habit perspective. First, theories on incentive learning propose that stimuli themselves may act as incentives for which the organism is willing to work. These theories grew out of several remarkable findings in different animal labs that shed new light on the role of reinforcement in learning processes following the stimulus-response habit paradigm (Skinner, 1953; Watson, 1925). For instance, operant stereotypes or misbehaviors were discovered during operant conditioning experiments (Breland & Breland, 1961). One such behavior is autoshaping (Brown & Jenkins, 1968; Williams & Williams, 1969). It has, for example, been shown that pigeons, for which free presentation of food is repeatedly paired with a light signal, start to vigorously pick at the light bulb, although this behavior is not explicitly reinforced. This phenomenon, in which an animal shapes itself, occurs because the positive affect or pleasure aroused by the food has now become linked to the light bulb, which therefore serves as an incentive for which the animal is motivated to work.

Biological grounding of this "transfer of positive affect to stimuli" effect comes from research suggesting that so-called pleasure centers in the brain (mainly targeting the nucleus accumbens) are involved in the mechanism that creates incentives (Shizgal, 1999). For example, rats that have learned to perform an arbitrary behavior such as pressing a lever in a cage that is followed by electrical stimulation of the mesolimbic brain area become highly motivated to perform that behavior (as the behavior activates the brain's pleasure center, and hence, triggers positive affect; Olds & Milner, 1954). It appears as if pushing the lever becomes a goal in itself. Illustrative of the motivational strength of this type of incentive learning, it has been established that animals run uphill and leap over hurdles (Edmonds & Gallistel, 1974) and cross electrified grids (Olds, 1958) in order to engage in the behavior. Importantly, such enhanced effort effects occur even in the absence of physiological deprivation states such as thirst or hunger (Shizgal, 1997). This research demonstrates that practice does not only lead to automatic stimulus-response rules, but it can also install a form of unconscious goal pursuit that is motivational and goal directed, in that the stimulus acquires goal properties that work as a reward signal and motivate behavior.

A second line of research that diverges from the automatic stimulus-response habit perspective comes from context learning. Specifically, several studies suggest that, even though habits may rely on nonmotivational well-practiced stimulus-response structures, these structures are not as rigid and automatic as one may think (Hommel, 2000). Most notably, some stimulus-response links appear to be conditional on a particular goal or context, and as such renders the activation and application of stimulus-response links more flexible. Upon hearing the sound of the alarm clock, someone may stumble to the shower on a workday when she has to get to the office, but she may without much thought stumble downstairs to pick up the Saturday paper on the weekend. Depending on the person's goal (work or leisure), the same stimulus may set off a different response that promotes the completion of the goal at hand. This flexibility in switching between different stimulus-response relations is reflected in work demonstrating that people are able to quite easily switch between different well-learned stimulus-response rules according to task instructions, such as has been shown for context effects on spatial mapping of stimulus-response relations (Hommel, 1993) or approach/avoidance movements toward valenced stimuli (Eder & Rothermund, 2008). In this way, some stimulus-response habits can be

regarded as goal dependent that are selected in the course of attaining a specific goal.

UNCONSCIOUS GOAL PURSUIT AND SKILLS DIRECTED BY GOALS

Considering habits as single responses to stimuli may work well for basic actions such as walking to the door when the bell rings. However, most actions in daily life—such as making coffee, driving to work, or even uttering words that make up sentences—are far more complicated. Nonetheless, these actions can be executed in a habitual manner without much conscious thought. How do these skills develop and what do their underlying structures look like?

One way to consider these skills is to regard them as a chain of responses instigated by a particular stimulus (e.g., Adams, 1984; Wickelgren, 1969). When one prepares coffee in the morning, for example, pouring the water may trigger getting a filter from the cupboard, putting the filter in the machine triggers getting the coffee powder, and so forth. Such action chains can be conceptualized as open-loop mechanisms that enable the efficient execution of behavior when the exact same sequence of actions is required every time the behavior is performed. In these types of habits, once the behavior is initiated, it runs to completion in a ballistic fashion and does not allow for adjustments of the ongoing process. Relying on such an open-loop mechanism, which does not take into account the result of the performed responses, may be the only way to execute complex behavioral patterns when there is no time to process such feedback information (e.g., when playing a fast sequence of notes on a piano). However, this mechanism only works when the exact same sequence of responses is required. Any small change in the environment or execution of previous actions will lead the mechanism astray and cause the chain to break.

As the execution of behavior often happens under such dynamic conditions, researchers have suggested that another type of habitual behavior operates via a feedback-control system, in which one's actions are directed by goals and can be adjusted in an ongoing manner. More specifically, in such closed-loop processes, the result of one action forms the input for the next one, thereby allowing for constant adjustments and efficient regulation of skillful actions in changing circumstances (e.g., Cooper & Shallice, 2006; Frith, Blakemore, & Wolpert, 2000; Powers, 1973). When driving one's car, for example, the required behavior is largely the same every time one takes the usual route to work. Still, slightly different actions are needed on different occasions, such as when the traffic light is red instead of green, there is a slow car in front, or a steady side wind requires adjusting one's steering wheel. Such adjustments of one's habitual behavior can be made in a nonconscious manner by monitoring the results of one's actions and using perceptual feedback to fine-tune the execution of the necessary skills and responses (Bargh & Ferguson, 2000; Custers & Aarts, 2010; Fourneret & Jeannerod, 1998). This way, the operation of a perceptual feedback-control system ensures that the same goals can be attained under different circumstances.

When pursuing a goal, however, how is the selection of a course of action made in the first place? Out of a variety of behaviors that could potentially lead to the attainment of a goal, how does the mental system supporting unconscious goal pursuit decide which path to follow? All else being equal, one is likely to do things as one did them before, and this is certainly true for nonconscious goal-directed behavior. Repeatedly pursuing a goal via a certain course of behavior forges a strong cognitive link between the goal representation and the representation of this behavior, so that activation of a goal can automatically lead to the activation of the habitual means for goal pursuit. This way, for example, we do not have to think deliberately how to get to work in the morning, as the goal of going to work automatically activates the idea of using one's bike or car; we do not have to consider all available supermarkets when having to do the groceries, since the goal of grocery shopping automatically activates the representation of the store we usually go to. Thus, habitual behavior involves not only the skilled execution but also the initial selection of a means for goal pursuit, which can be automatized based on earlier behavior and later executed in an efficient, nonconscious fashion.

The idea that habitual behavior comprises the automatic selection of a course of action upon the priming of a goal has received empirical support in a number studies, and it was first tested in the domain of travel behavior (e.g., Aarts & Dijksterhuis, 2000). Here, participants who had been primed with certain travel goals (e.g., going to follow classes) showed increased activation of certain means for traveling (e.g., biking). However, this effect occurred only among those students who habitually used the bicycle to reach their travel goals. These findings were replicated and extended in the domain of the habitual drinking of alcohol among students in the United Kingdom (Sheeran

et al., 2005), where it was shown that activating the goal of socializing increased the accessibility of the concept of drinking, but only among those student participants who were regular drinkers of alcohol in social situations. In addition, after a socializing prime, these students were more likely to drink alcohol as a reward for their participation in the experiment. These results indicate that the activation of a goal automatically activates its associated habitual means, making the repeated selection of this means for goal pursuit more likely.

The idea of habits as a form of automatic goal-directed behavior has been pushed even a bit further. Specifically, although most models on goal-directed behavior assume that the goals that we set eventually originate from a conscious reflection process and thus are the result of conscious intent, research on nonconscious goal pursuit suggest that our goals can be activated outside of conscious awareness themselves to then have their effect on behavior. Recurrent and consistent pursuit of a goal upon perception of a specific (social) situation is thought to strengthen the link between the representations of the situation and the goal. Consequently, the mere perception of the situation or environment causes the goal-directed behavior to be triggered directly. This notion has been corroborated by a host of studies that show that goal pursuit is launched when people are exposed to goal-related stimuli (Aarts et al., 2008).

To recap, practice and habits play an important role in the automation of goal pursuit. Actions instrumental in attaining goals that are repeatedly and consistently selected and performed in the same context become habitual and associated with the goal in the given context. Accordingly, goal-directed behavior no longer needs to be guided by conscious intentions to attain the goal, but, instead, it is activated and maintained by the representation of the goal without conscious intervention.

It is important to emphasize here that, in line with the behaviorists' perspective, habits have often been (and are still) conceptualized as rigid responses that are directly triggered by environmental cues, while goal-directed behaviors are exclusively seen as the result of conscious intentional processes (see, e.g., Wood & Neal, 2007). In other words, goals are treated as inherently equivalent to conscious intentions and, hence, the obvious cause of the instigation of behavior to attain specific goals always relies on consciousness. The research on habitually driven goal-directed behavior discussed here goes beyond this conventional approach. Specifically, the observation that our goal pursuits can emerge from nonconscious cognitive processes as a result of practice suggests that intentions and goals are distinct concepts that can operate independently from each other, served by different processes (see also Bargh, 1990). In line with this idea, neuroscientific research on motor skill control suggests that conscious intentions are recruited and handled by the medial prefrontal cortex, whereas the control of goals occurs in more posterior, parietal areas interconnected with motor and sensory areas in the cortex to enable action preparation and execution (e.g. Frith et al., 2000). Therefore, priming these goal representations causes the organism to recruit the associated means or skills directly, and thus goal-directed behavior is triggered and guided in the situation at hand without conscious intent and awareness.

When Habits Fail: Unconscious Goal Pursuit Is Flexible and Adaptive

Thus far, unconscious goal pursuit is mainly explored as a form of habit: Once the goal is activated by the situation, habitual behavior follows a well-practiced route to completion with some degrees of freedom by the operation of a perceptual feedback-control system. Sometimes, however, the situation does not allow for a direct execution of habitual means or skills, or it contains distractions and temptations that push our current goal out of the attentional system. In that case, we may need to postpone our goals, shield them from interfering or prepotent responses, and act on opportunities to attain these goals. For example, a person who frequently pursues the goal of being popular may need to wait for the right moment or adjust his behavior to the context at hand to successfully attain the goal (e.g., telling sexually explicit jokes when sitting in a pub with friends, but gossiping about the minister of education during lunch with colleagues). Furthermore, when having the goal to use healthy food at lunch, one may need to resist the temptation to eat the delicious snacks abundantly available in the cafeteria; or one needs to switch to alternatives when one discovers that the cafeteria is currently out of one's habitually selected bananas, in order to eat healthy food.

An important issue, then, is how unconscious goal pursuit proceeds when habits are inadequate and fail to produce goals. The traditional answer would be that we do not: Unconscious goal pursuit, like every other automatic process, is limited to circumstances in which habits can be applied successfully. If they cannot be applied successfully, then unconscious goal pursuit is bound to fail and conscious processes are called to the fore. It is this episode of awareness that is said to typify a shift from habitual to intentional control (e.g., James, 1890; Louis & Sutton, 1991; Norman & Shallice, 1986).

Although tempting, this suggestion is questionable. Given the acknowledged limitations of conscious attention on the one hand (Kahneman, 1973), and the dynamic nature of the world on the other (Powers, 1973), it seems that people should be able to go beyond routines to efficiently adapt to the environment, even during unconscious goal pursuit (see also Wilson, 2002). Indeed, previous work on goal priming indicates that people who are unconsciously primed with goals display behavior in novel settings, overcome obstacles, and invest effort to achieve the primed goal. In other words, unconscious goal pursuit is flexible and adaptive. This observation has led researchers to posit that nonconscious goals operate via cognitive processes that follow principles of self-regulation or executive control and working memory (Aarts, 2007; Hassin, Aarts, Custers, Eitam, & Kleinman, 2009). Whereas commonly conceived of as belonging to the realm of consciousness, executive processes supporting goal pursuit are proposed to operate in the absence of awareness of the activation and operation of the goal. While this may be a controversial proposition, there is accumulating evidence for it.

ACTIVE MAINTENANCE OF GOAL-RELEVANT REPRESENTATIONS

The activation of semantic items decays in short-term memory over very short periods of time, usually within a couple of seconds, unless some intervention or goal holds the items active (Baddeley & Logie, 1999; McKone, 1995). Exploiting this notion, research has demonstrated that goals that are activated unconsciously can keep relevant information active as well (Aarts, Custers, & Holland, 2007; Aarts, Custers, & Marien, 2009; Aarts, Custers, & Veltkamp, 2008). For instance, Aarts, Custers, and Holland (2007) examined how the mental accessibility of a goal after a short interval changes as a function of subliminally priming the goal. In one of their studies, participants were either primed with the goal to socialize or not, and 2.5 minutes later tested for accessibility of the goal in a lexical decision task by measuring the speed of recognizing words related to the goal as existing words. Results showed that the representation of the goal remained accessible when participants were primed to attain the goal. Similar persistent activation effects—even after 5 minutes of goal priming—have been obtained for behavioral measures (Aarts et al., 2004; Bargh et al., 2001), suggesting that some kind of updating or active maintenance process keeps goal-relevant information alive nonconsciously. From a functional point of view, this observation makes sense: When a goal operates as a desired state it should be kept actively in mind, thereby increasing the probability of acting on it when encountering goal-relevant opportunities (e.g., asking a colleague that enters one's office to meet up later on in the bar).

INHIBITION OF GOAL-INTERFERING REPRESENTATIONS

Furthermore, recent work has started to explore whether humans can keep their eyes on their ongoing goal pursuit in a nonconscious manner when competing information conflicts with these pursuits (Aarts et al., 2007; Papies, Stroebe, & Aarts, 2008; Shah, Friedman, & Kruglanski, 2002). People usually engage in this type of self-regulatory process when they have to deal with interference that stems from other goals or temptations that compete for attention and behavior; a process that is commonly conceived of as requiring conscious and intentional control (see, e.g., work on delay of gratification; Mischel, Shoda, & Rodriguez, 1989). However, there are studies that tell a somewhat different story. For instance, Shah and colleagues (2002) demonstrated that when participants are nonconsciously instigated to pursue a given goal (by subliminal exposure to words representing the goal, e.g., of studying), they inhibit competing accessible goals (e.g., going out), and moreover, this inhibition facilitated the achievement of the nonconsciously activated goal. These findings provide support for the existence of a nonconscious attention/inhibition mechanism that shields goals from distracting thoughts. Shah et al. speculated that these goal-shielding effects require extensive practice, thus arguing for a habitual and well-learned automated mechanism. Recent studies, however, indicate that the inhibitory effects in goal-directed behavior may kick in rather rapidly—that is, after a few practice trials (Danner, Aarts, & De Vries, 2007; McCulloch, Aarts, Fujita, & Bargh, 2008; Veling & Aarts, 2009).

GOAL MONITORING AND FEEDBACK PROCESSING

Finally, there are a few studies that tested whether situations that are discrepant with nonconsciously activated goals encourage people to exploit opportunities in novel settings without awareness of operation of the goal (Aarts et al., 2004; Custers & Aarts, 2005a; 2007a). For instance, Aarts et al. (2004) showed that priming the goal of earning money encouraged participants to engage in a lottery that gave access to money, but only when they were in need of money, that is, when the primed desired goal state was discrepant with the actual state. Participants claimed that they were not aware of the priming effects, thus showing that the detection and reduction of discrepancies may occur in the absence of conscious awareness. In another, more compelling study, Custers and Aarts (2007a) investigated the goal of looking well groomed, a goal which typically needs to be maintained over time and was highly desirable to participants. In their study, they subliminally primed the goal or not, just before participants were confronted with a situation that was discrepant with the goal (e.g., the shoes they put on were dirty). Then, they implicitly measured the accessibility of actions that are instrumental in reducing the discrepancy (e.g., polishing) in action-identification reaction time task. Their findings showed that subliminal priming facilitated the identification of instrumental actions. Additional studies showed that these priming effects do not emerge when the situation is not discrepant with the primed goal (Custers & Aarts, 2005a). Together, these data suggest that unconscious goal pursuit is supported by monitoring and feedback processing.

In sum, several lines of research suggest that nonconscious goals not only run off in a habitual, automatic way, but they may serve flexible functions that operate via cognitive processes following principles of executive control and working memory that rely on the mobilization of effort and the recruitment of resources (Baddeley & Hitch, 1974; Miyake & Shah, 1999). Contrary to most current views (e.g., Baars & Franklin, 2003; Baddeley, 1993), however, these processes (and the information on which they operate) seem to run below the threshold of consciousness (see also Dijksterhuis & Aarts, 2010).

The findings discussed earlier raise the interesting issue of how people mobilize effort and allocate resources to pursue a primed goal without an act of conscious will. That is, what is the nonconscious source that motivates people to initiate and regulate their goals in the first place? This is the issue to which we turn now.

Unconscious Motivation: Positive Affect and Reward Processing

When scrutinizing the scientific literature on the pressing question of what motivates people to set and pursue their goals, most answers boil down to the idea that humans are equipped with an internal agent that prioritizes and decides what we want and do. That is, the step from priming a cognitive representation of a goal to the process of motivating goal pursuit involves an act of conscious will (e.g., Gollwitzer, 1990; Locke & Latham, 1990; Monsell & Driver, 2000). Research on nonconscious goal pursuit suggests that this assumption may not be entirely right: The step from goal priming to motivated behavior can be taken nonconsciously. An important issue, though, concerns the question of how this works: How do people resolve whether to pursue and to invest effort or recruit resources to attain a given goal without involvement of conscious will?

Current social cognition research tends to answer this question by proposing that the process of forming an intention or decision to pursue a goal can take place outside awareness. Whereas this proposition led researchers to come up with original terms to conceptualize the source of human goal pursuit, such as automated will (Bargh et al., 2001), implicit intention (Wood, Quinn, & Kashy, 2002), or implicit volition (Moskowitz, Li, & Kirk, 2004), these terms merely stretch the applicability of inherently conscious concepts featured in existing models to the unconscious level. Obviously, this strategy has certainly helped to put the exciting notion of nonconscious goal pursuit on the scientific research agenda, but it does not tell us much about how the unconscious, rather than consciousness, determines whether to pursue a goal or not.

Another approach is to make an inventory of what people can do unconsciously and construct a hypothesis in line with that knowledge. According to almost all models of goal pursuit, whether a goal is pursued depends on the rewarding value of the goal state. The best candidate for a mechanism that could determine the value of a primed goal outside conscious awareness would therefore be one that relies on affective processes. It is known that affect plays a fundamental role in motivating human action and can be evoked quite quickly without reaching conscious awareness (e.g., Damasio, 1994; Dijksterhuis & Aarts, 2003; Fazio, 2001; LeDoux, 1996; Zajonc, 1980). For instance, in several experiments it has been shown that affective words (e.g., summer, shark) are classified in terms of their valence before participants know the meaning of the word. Furthermore, the affective tone associated with options in a decision problem (e.g., while inspecting the several occasions at the local car garage the

TOYOTA COROLLA evokes a better gut feeling than the NISSAN SUNNY) often determines what people decide to do without them being aware of the influence of the affective signal. Thus, if goal representations would contain an affective component that reflects the rewarding value of the goal, this information could be used to nonconsciously determine whether a primed goal is desired, which renders conscious deliberations redundant.

In line with this notion, neuroimaging research has discovered that reward cues are processed by limbic structures such as the nucleus accumbens and the ventral striatum. These subcortical areas play a central role in determining the rewarding value of outcomes and are connected to frontal areas in the cortex that facilitate goal pursuit (e.g., Aston-Jones & Cohen, 2005). These reward centers in the brain respond to evolutionarily relevant rewards such as food and sexual stimuli but also to learned rewards (e.g., money, status) or words (e.g., good, nice) that are associated with praise or rewards (Schultz, 2006). This demonstrates that regardless of their shape or form, such positive stimuli induce a reward signal that is readily picked up by the brain (Shizgal, 1997).

Other recent research has demonstrated that subliminal primes that are specifically related to rewards can motivate people to increase the effort they invest in behaviors. In one study (Pessiglione et al., 2007), participants could earn money by squeezing a handgrip. Before each squeeze, the money that could be earned was indicated by a one-pound or one-penny coin on the screen. Whereas on some trials the coin was clearly visible, on others it was presented subliminally. Thus, effects of conscious and unconscious reward cues could be compared within one experiment. It was found that people squeezed harder on high- than on low-reward trials, regardless of whether the reward was consciously visible. Moreover, this effect was accompanied by activation in the brain areas that play a role in reward processing and in the recruitment of effort for action. Similar effects of unconscious (and conscious) monetary rewards have been established in cognitive tasks that require flexibility and cognitive resources (Bijleveld, Custers, & Aarts, 2009, 2010; Zedelius, Veling, & Aarts, 2011). These findings indicate that conscious and unconscious reward cues have similar effects on effort and flexible cognitive processing, which suggests that conscious awareness of rewards is not needed for goal pursuit to occur.

The observation that a variety of reward cues are encoded by the same brain system to motivate cognition and action and can be processed unconsciously has led to the proposal that a positive reward signal associated with outcomes plays a crucial role in unconscious goal pursuit (Custers & Aarts, 2010). Specifically, when a desired outcome or goal is primed, activation of the mental representation of this outcome is immediately followed by the activation of an associated positive affective tag, which acts as a reward signal for pursuing the primed goal. The positive reward signal attached to a goal thus unconsciously facilitates the actual selection of the goal and the subsequent mobilization of effort and resources to maintain the goal, unless other (e.g., more rewarding) goals gain priority. This affective-motivational process relies on associations between the representations of outcomes and positive reward signals that are shaped by one's history (e.g., when a person was happy when making money or performing well). In this case, the goal is said to preexist as a desired state in the mind. Priming this goal representation not only prepares the appropriate instrumental actions but also motivates behavior, rendering it persistent and flexible, directed at attaining the desired outcome.

A recent set of studies tested investigated the role of this positive reward signal attached to a goal in the effects of subliminal goal priming in teenagers and young adults (Custers & Aarts, 2007b; Ferguson, 2007). For instance, Custers and Aarts (2007b) subliminally primed participants or not with the goal of going out socially. Next, they performed a mouse-click task that, if sufficient time was left, was followed by a lottery in which they could win tickets for a popular student party. Thus, working hard (or fast) on the task can be seen as a means to get to the goal of socializing. It was established that participants put more effort into the instrumental task to attain the goal state when the goal concept of "socializing" was primed, and that this effect was more pronounced when the goal concept was more positive (which was assessed in a separate implicit affective association task). These findings show that goal-priming effects on motivated behavior and action control are conditional on the positive valence attached to the primed goal. Similar effects of positive reward value attached to a goal have been documented for other, perhaps more consequential behaviors. Priming an egalitarian goal, for instance, changes people's voting behavior to the extent that this goal is represented as positive or rewarding (Ferguson, 2007).

The findings presented earlier indicate that unconscious goal pursuit may result when a preexisting desired goal is activated, which, because of its association with positive affect, sets off a positive reward signal. In theory, this process could be simulated by externally triggering the affective signal just after activation of a neutral goal concept (i.e., a goal concept that provides a reference point for action but does not designate a current desired state that people are motivated to pursue). This ability to respond to the mere coactivation of goal representations and positive affective cues is thought to play a fundamental role in social learning (Miller & Dollard, 1941) and considered as basic in motivational analyses of human behavior (Shizgal, 1997). Thus, when a child observes ones mother's smile upon munching homemade cookies, a student witnesses a hilarious joke upon entering the classroom, or a person strolling around in the mall hears people laugh while reading on a billboard "start your holiday here," this can cause the goal representations that are primed by those situations (eating candy, achieving at school, booking a vacation) to acquire an intrinsic reward value, which prepares and regulates goal-directed behavior.

This hypothesis that the mere coactivation of a neutral goal concept and positive affect produces unconscious goal pursuit has been tested as well (Aarts, Custers, & Veltkamp, 2008; Van den Bos & Stapel, 2009; Custers & Aarts, 2005b; Holland et al., 2009; Veltkamp, Aarts, & Custers, 2008, 2009). In these studies, goal concepts were paired with positively valenced information outside of conscious awareness by exploiting the evaluative conditioning paradigm (De Houwer et al., 2001). For instance, it has been shown that repeated pairing of the representation of a neutral goal concept (e.g., words such as drinking, cleaning up, doing puzzles) and positive affect (e.g., words such as summer or nice) motivates participants to work harder on an intervening task to secure engagement in the behavior (Custers & Aarts, 2005b). In another study, effects of linking the behavioral concept of drinking to positive affect were compared with the deprivation of water on the amount of water that was consumed in a tasting task. The results of this study showed that deprivation increased the amount of drinking, and that shaping drinking more positively caused participants to drink more water only when they were not deprived. These findings indicate that linking neutral goal concepts to positive affect simulates effects of actual needs (Veltkamp et al., 2009).

Furthermore, extending past research into the relation between motivation and functional perception (Bruner & Goodman, 1947; Bruner & Postman, 1948), other research demonstrated that the nonconscious goal-shaping treatment (e.g., of drinking) affected size perception of goal-related objects (e.g., a glass of water): participants saw them as being bigger in size (Veltkamp et al., 2008). Moreover, these motivated functional perception effects were manifested even after a period of 3 minutes, suggesting that some kind of rehearsal or active maintenance process kept the nonconsciously shaped goal alive in the mind (Aarts, Custers, & Veltkamp, 2008). Importantly, these effects could not be attributed to initial differences in activation of the goal concept as all participants were primed with the mental representation of the goal before the dependent variables were assessed. What mattered was the fact that the goal concept was activated in temporal proximity to the activation of positive affect, and as a consequence, evoked in people a state of readiness for goal pursuit that not only prepared but also regulated their behavior to attain the goal.

A recent study examined the effects of coactivating goal representations and positive reward signals on the preparation and motivation of behavior in more detail. In this study, healthy young adults had to squeeze a handgrip in response to a start sign while the timing and persistence of their behavior were measured (Aarts, Custers, & Marien, 2008). Prior to this task, words pertaining to the goal of physical exertion were subliminally presented (or not) together with positive words that signal rewards (e.g., good, nice) or not. In line with the ideomotor principle, research participants who were subliminally primed with the goal of exertion started to squeeze earlier. However, only participants for whom the goal was coactivated with a positive reward signal recruited more resources to execute this goal, as was evidenced by more forceful and persistent squeezing. It was found that consciously reported motivation did not show any relation with the subliminal goal-priming manipulation. Hence, activating a goal representation gives behavior a head start, whereas the accompanying reward signal motivates behavior outside awareness. Other studies have shown that this coactivation procedure yields effects that are similar to those of conscious goals (induced by conscious goal instructions or by making people aware of their current needs) on tasks that require flexibility and effort in novel situations (Custers & Aarts, 2005b; Veltkamp et al., 2009).

Conclusion and Future Directions

The present review indicates that unconscious goal pursuit relies on automated habitual behaviors as well as flexible behaviors that occur when habitual responding is not adequate to attain goals. Furthermore, this unconscious control of goal pursuit is initiated and maintained by the mere processing of reward signals that accompany the priming of the representation of a goal. This way, people can pursue and attain desired outcomes without being aware of the activation and operation of the goal leading to the outcome. Whereas the amount of scientific evidence for the occurrence of unconscious goal pursuit is still growing, there are several issues that require further scrutiny to offer a more comprehensive understanding and examination of the role of nonconscious processes in human goal pursuit. We will briefly address three of them here.

The first issue pertains to the question of whether people are truly unaware of the goal that produces their behavior. It is clear that the notion of unconscious goal pursuit is not readily appreciated and endorsed by all people. After all, we all share the experience that our behavior is accompanied by conscious awareness, and it feels odd to assume that these conscious experiences have no causal status in the process of goal pursuit. Accordingly, the idea that consciousness does not mediate goal-priming effects is still a matter of debate.

To offer compelling evidence that goal pursuit can be truly unconscious, researchers have tried to do their best to conceal the purpose of their study to participants (in the so-called unrelated studies setup) or took pains to prime goals unconsciously by subliminal presentation techniques. In addition, some studies asked participants in retrospect to indicate whether they were influenced by the primes or motivated to pursue the primed goal. The general finding of these checks is that although reported motivation sometimes correlates with behavior (people who worked harder report to be more motivated), these reports are not influenced by the primes. This suggests that subliminal priming of the goal does not affect goal pursuit because people become conscious of their motivation to pursue the goal after it is primed. Participants may become conscious of their motivation after the behavior is performed and when they are explicitly probed to reflect on it. We believe that such checks should be a default part of the experimental setup in the study on unconscious goal pursuit, and future research should even try to go further by designing new and more fine-grained ways to examine whether consciousness plays a causal role in the priming of goal pursuit (e.g., Seth, Dienes, Cleeremans, Overgaard, & Pessoa, 2008).

The second issue concerns the observation that the control of unconscious goals is flexible and effortful, suited to meet the dynamics of the environment. Such unconscious flexibility fits well with research that has discovered that human functioning (information encoding, memory use, evaluation, inferences, social perception and judgment) is largely rooted in cognitive processes and does not require conscious control. However, understanding exactly how unconscious goals flexibly control behavior remains a challenge for future research. It has been argued that goals direct attention and behavior, even in the absence of conscious awareness of the goal (Bargh & Ferguson, 2000; Dijksterhuis & Aarts, 2010). That is, the operation of cognitive processes supporting goal pursuit (also conceptualized as working memory or executive control) does not care much about the conscious state of the individual. This view concurs with recent insights that attention and consciousness are distinct (Dehaene et al., 2006; Koch & Tsuchiya, 2006; Lamme, 2003).

The research discussed here suggests that conscious goals (often induced by explicit task instructions) and unconscious goals (induced by priming) have similar effects on tasks that rely on executive control. However, it is too early to conclude that consciousness is redundant in the pursuit of goals, as we do not yet know whether there are special cases in which consciousness (apart from attention) facilitates performance. In fact, we only know that we can become consciously aware of the decisions that we make and the goals we pursue without having a proper empirical test telling us how consciousness itself exactly influences our behavior. Future research thus will have to explore when consciously and unconsciously activated goals direct the operation of cognitive functions and brain systems supporting goal pursuit in similar or distinct manners.

A third issue that may be worth examining is the idea that a potential role for consciousness may lie not in the starting and steering of behavior, but in stopping it. Whereas the brain is designed to realize desired outcomes, in today's society the well-being of the individual may for a large part be dependent on the ability to prevent oneself from engaging in rewarding behaviors that have undesired personal and social long-term consequences (e.g., eating junk food, derogating others). Whereas it is known that ongoing and impulsive behaviors can be inhibited directly by environmental stimuli or well-learned stop rules (Verbruggen & Logan, 2009), we do not yet know whether and how people can express an unconscious volitional veto, or whether

consciousness as a relatively new knack of human evolution is required to overrule the labor of the older reward system involved in unconscious goal pursuit.

Recently, researchers have started to explore the role of negative affect in this process, and it turns out that negative stimuli that are coactivated with the subliminal priming of goals can put unconscious goal pursuit on a hold (e.g., Aarts, Custers, & Holland, 2007; Veling, Aarts, & Stroebe, 2011). Importantly, this modulating effect of negative affect on the cessation of unconscious goal pursuit may not be so general, as other studies suggest that people can also be motivated by negative affect, such as when goals are associated with anger (Aarts, Ruys, Veling, Renes, de Groot, van Nunen, & Geertjes, 2010; Carver & Harmon-Jones, 2009). It remains to be seen, then, whether and how negative affect accompanying the activation of goals serves as an unconscious veto to not engage in goal pursuit itself.

Acknowledgment

The preparation of this chapter was supported by VICI-grant 453-06-002 from the Netherlands Organization for Scientific Research.

References

Aarts, H. (2007). Health behavior and the implicit motivation and regulation of goals. *Health Psychology Review*, *1*, 53–82.

Aarts, H., Chartrand, T. L., Custers, R., Danner, U., Dik, G., Jefferis, V., & Cheng, C. M. (2005). Social Stereotypes and automatic goal pursuit. *Social Cognition*, *23*, 464–489.

Aarts, H., Custers, R., & Holland, R. W. (2007). The nonconscious cessation of goal pursuit: When goals and negative affect are coactivated. *Journal of Personality and Social Psychology*, *92*, 165–178.

Aarts, H., Custers, R., & Marien, H. (2008). Preparing and motivating behavior outside of awareness. *Science*, *319*, 1639.

Aarts, H., Custers, R., & Marien, H. (2009). Priming and authorship ascription: When nonconscious goals turn into conscious experiences of self-agency. *Journal of Personality and Social Psychology*, *96*, 967–979.

Aarts, H., Custers, R., & Veltkamp, M. (2008). Goal priming and the affective-motivational route to nonconscious goal pursuit. *Social Cognition*, *26*, 497–519.

Aarts, H., & Dijksterhuis, A. (2000). Habits as knowledge structures: Automaticity in goal-directed behavior. *Journal of Personality and Social Psychology*, *78*, 53–63.

Aarts, H., & Dijksterhuis, A. (2003). The silence of the library: Environment, situational norm and Social behavior. *Journal of Personality and Social Psychology*, *84*, 18–28.

Aarts, H., Dijksterhuis, A., Dik, G. (2008). Goal contagion. In J. Y. Shah & W. Gardner (Eds.), *Handbook of motivation science* (pp. 265–280). New York: Guilford.

Aarts, H., Gollwitzer, P. M., & Hassin, R. R. (2004). Goal contagion: Perceiving is for pursuing. *Journal of Personality and Social Psychology*, *87*, 23–37.

Aarts, H., Ruys, K. I., Veling, H., Renes, R. A., de Groot, J. H. B., van Nunen, A. M., & Geertjes S. (2010). The art of anger: Reward context turns avoidance responses to anger-related objects into approach. *Psychological Science, 21,* 1406–1410.

Adams, J. A. (1984). Learning of motor movement. *Psychological Bulletin, 96,* 3–28.

Aston-Jones, G., & Cohen, J. D. (2005). An integrative theory of locus coeruleus-norepinephrine function: Adaptive gain and optimal performance. *Annual Review of Neuroscience, 28,* 403–450.

Baars, B. J., & Franklin, S. (2003). How conscious experience and working memory interact. *Trends in cognitive science, 7*(4), 166–172.

Baddeley, A. D. (1993). Working memory and conscious awareness. In A. Collins & S. Gathercole (Eds.), *Theories of memory* (pp. 11–28). Hillsdale, NJ: Lawrence Erlbaum Associates.

Baddeley, A. D., & Hitch, G. (1974). Working memory. In G. Bower (Ed.), *The psychology of learning and motivation: Advances in research and theory* (Vol. 8, pp. 47–89). New York: Academic Press.

Baddeley, A. D., & Logie, R. H. (1999). Working memory: The multiple-component model. In A. Miyake & P. Shah (Eds.), *Models of working memory: Mechanisms of active maintenance and executive control* (pp. 28–61). New York: Cambridge University Press.

Bandura, A. (1986). *Social foundations of thought and action: A social cognitive theory.* Englewood Cliffs, NJ: Prentice-Hall.

Bargh, J. A. (1990). Goal not-equal-to intent: Goal-directed thought and behavior are often unintentional. *Psychological Inquiry, 1,* 248–251.

Bargh, J. A. (1997). The automaticity of everyday life. In R. S. Wyer (Ed.), *The automaticity of everyday life: Advances in social cognition* (Vol. 10, pp. 1–61). Mahwah, NJ: Erlbaum.

Bargh, J. A. (2006). What have we been priming all these years? On the development, mechanisms, and ecology of nonconscious social behavior. *European Journal of Social Psychology, 36,* 147–168.

Bargh, J. A., & Ferguson, M. J. (2000). Beyond behaviorism: On the automaticity of higher mental processes. *Psychological Bulletin, 126,* 925–945.

Bargh, J. A., & Gollwitzer, P. M. (1994). Environmental control of goal-directed action: Automatic and strategic contingencies between situations and behavior. In W. D. Spaulding (Ed.), *Integrative views of motivation, cognition, and emotion. Nebraska symposium on motivation* (Vol. 41, pp. 71–124). Lincoln: University of Nebraska Press.

Bargh, J. A., Gollwitzer, P. M., Lee Chai, A., Barndollar, K., & Trötschel, R. (2001). The automated will: Nonconscious activation and pursuit of behavioral goals. *Journal of Personality and Social Psychology, 81,* 1014–1027.

Berridge, K. C. (2001). Reward learning: Reinforcement, incentives, and expectations. In D. L. Medin (Ed.), *The psychology of learning and motivation: Advances in research and theory* (Vol. 40, pp. 223–278). San Diego, CA: Academic Press.

Bijleveld, E., Custers, R., & Aarts, H. (2009). The unconscious eye opener: Pupil dilation reveals strategic recruitment of mental resources upon subliminal reward cues. *Psychological Science, 20,* 1313–1315.

Bijleveld, E., Custers, R., & Aarts, H. (2010). Unconscious reward cues increase invested effort, but do not change speed-accuracy tradeoffs. *Cognition, 115,* 330–335.

Bongers, K. C. A., Dijksterhuis, A., & Spears, R. (2010). On the role of consciousness in goal pursuit. *Social Cognition, 28,* 262–272.

Breland, K., & Breland, M. (1961). The misbehavior of organisms. *American Psychologist, 16,* 681–684.

Brown, P. L., & Jenkins, H. M. (1968). Auto-shaping of the pigeon's key-peck. *Journal of the Experimental Analysis of Behavior, 11,* 1–8.

Bruner, J. S., & Goodman, C. C. (1947). Value and need as organizing factors in perception. *Journal of Abnormal and Social Psychology, 42,* 33–44.

Bruner, J. S., & Postman, L. (1948). Symbolic value as an organizing factor in perception. *Journal of Social Psychology, 27,* 203–208.

Carver, C. S., & Harmon-Jones, E. (2009). Anger is approach-related affect: Evidence and implications. *Psychological Bulletin, 135,* 183–204.

Carver, C. S., & Scheier, M. F. (1998). *On the self-regulation of behavior.* New York: Cambridge University Press.

Cooper, R. P., & Shallice, T. (2006). Hierarchical schemas and goals in the control of sequential behavior. *Psychological Review, 113,* 887–916.

Custers, R., & Aarts, H. (2005a). Beyond accessibility: The role of affect and goal-discrepancies in implicit processes of motivation and goal-pursuit. *European Review of Social Psychology, 16,* 257–300.

Custers, R., & Aarts, H. (2005b). Positive affect as implicit motivator: On the nonconscious operation of behavioral goals. *Journal of Personality and Social Psychology, 89,* 129–142.

Custers, R., & Aarts, H. (2007a). Goal-discrepant situations prime goal-directed actions if goals are temporarily or chronically accessible. *Personality and Social Psychology Bulletin, 33,* 623–633.

Custers, R., & Aarts, H. (2007b). In search of the nonconscious sources of goal pursuit: Accessibility and positive affective valence of the goal state. *Journal of Experimental Social Psychology, 43,* 312–318.

Custers, R, & Aarts, H. (2010). The unconscious will: How the pursuit of goals operates outside of conscious awareness. *Science, 329,* 47–50.

Custers, R., Aarts, H., Oikawa, M., & Elliot, A. (2009). The nonconscious road to perceptions of performance: Achievement priming, success expectations and self-agency. *Journal of Experimental Social Psychology, 45,* 1200–1208.

Custers, R., Maas, M., Wildenbeest, M., & Aarts, H. (2008). Nonconscious goal pursuit and the surmounting of physical and social obstacles. *European Journal of Social Psychology, 38,* 1013–1022.

Damasio, A. R. (1994). *Descartes' error: Emotion reason, and the human brain.* New York: Putnam.

Danner, U. N., Aarts, H., & De Vries, N. K. (2007). Habit formation and multiple options to goal attainment: Repeated selection of targets means causes inhibited access to alternatives. *Personality and Social Psychology Bulletin, 33,* 1367–1379.

Deci, E. L., & Ryan, R. M. (1985). *Intrinsic motivation and self-determination in human behavior.* New York: Plenum Press.

Dehaene, S., Changeux, J. P., Naccache, L., Sackur, J., & Sergent, C. (2006). Conscious, preconscious, and subliminal processing: A testable taxonomy. *Trends in Cognitive Sciences, 10,* 204–211.

De Houwer, J., Thomas, S., & Baeyens, F. (2001). Association learning of likes and dislikes: A review of 25 years of research on human evaluative conditioning. *Psychological Bulletin, 127*, 853–869.

Dickinson, A., Balleine, B., Watt, A., Gonzales, F., & Boakes, R. A. (1995). Motivational control after extended instrumental training. *Animal Learning and Behavior, 23*, 197–206.

Dik, G., & Aarts, H. (2007). Behavioral cues to others' motivation and goal-pursuits: The perception of effort facilitates goal inference and contagion. *Journal of Experimental Social psychology, 43*, 727–737.

Dijksterhuis, A., & Aarts, H. (2003). On wildebeests and humans: The preferential detection of negative stimuli. *Psychological Science, 14*, 14–18.

Dijksterhuis, A., & Aarts, H. (2010). Goals, attention, and (un) consciousness. *Annual Review of Psychology, 61*, 467–490.

Eder, A., & Rothermund, K. (2008). When do motor behaviors (mis)match affective stimuli? An evaluative coding view of approach and avoidance reactions. *Journal of Experimental Psychology: General, 137, 262–281*.

Edmonds, D. E., & Gallistel, C. R. (1974). Parametric analysis of brain stimulation reward in the rat: III. Effect of performance variables on the reward summation function. *Journal of Comparative and Physiological Psychology, 87*, 876–883.

Eitam, B., Hassin, R. R., & Schul, Y. (2008). Nonconscious goal pursuit in novel environments: The case of implicit learning. *Psychological Science, 19*, 261–267.

Engeser, S., Wendland, M., & Rheinberg, F. (2006). Nonconscious activation of behavioral goals, a methodologically refined replication. *Psychological Reports, 99*, 963.

Fazio, R. H. (2001). On the automatic activation of associated evaluations: An overview. *Cognition and Emotion, 15*, 115–141.

Ferguson, M. J. (2007). On the automatic evaluation of end-states. *Journal of Personality and Social Psychology, 92*, 596–611.

Fitzsimons, G. M., & Bargh, J. A. (2003). Thinking of you: Nonconscious pursuit of interpersonal goals associated with relationship partners. *Journal of Personality and Social Psychology, 84*, 148–163.

Fourneret, P., & Jeannerod, M. (1998). Limited conscious monitoring of motor performance in normal subjects. *Neuropsychologia, 36*, 1133–1140.

Friedman, R., Deci, E.L., Elliot, A., Moller, A., & Aarts, H. (2010). Motivation synchronicity: Priming motivational orientations with observations of others' behavior. *Motivation and Emotion, 34*, 34–38.

Frith, C. D., Blakemore, S-J., & Wolpert, D. M. (2000). Abnormalities in the awareness and control of action. *Philosophical Transactions of the Royal Society of London, 355*, 1771–1788.

Gollwitzer, P. M. (1990). Action phases and mindsets. In R. M. Sorrentino & E. T. Higgins (Eds.), *Handbook of motivation and cognition* (pp. 53–92). New York: Guilford Press.

Gollwitzer, P. M., & Moskowitz, G. B. (1996). Goal effects on action and cognition. In E. Higgins & A. W. Kruglanski (Eds.), *Social psychology: Handbook of basic principles* (pp. 361–399). New York: Guilford Press.

Hart, W., & Albarracín, D. (2009). The effects of chronic achievement motivation and achievement primes on the activation of achievement and fun goals. *Journal of Personality and Social Psychology, 97*, 1129–1141.

Hassin, R. R., Aarts, H., Custers, R., Eitam, B., & Kleiman, T. (2009). Non-conscious goal pursuit, working memory, and the effortful control of behavior. In E. Morsella, J. A. Bargh, & P. M. Gollwitzer (Eds.), *Oxford handbook of human action* (pp. 549–566). New York: Oxford University Press.

Hassin, R. R. (2008). Being open minded without knowing why: Evidence from nonconscious goal pursuit. *Social Cognition, 26*, 578–592.

Hofmann, W., De Houwer, J., Perugini, M., Baeyens, F., & Crombez, G. (2010). Evaluative conditioning in humans: A meta-analysis. *Psychological Bulletin, 136*, 390–421.

Holland, R. W., Wennekers, A. M., Bijlstra, G., Jongenelen, M. M., & Van Knippenberg, A. (2009). Self-symbols as implicit motivators. *Social Cognition, 27*, 579–600.

Hommel, B. (1993). Inverting the Simon effect by intention: Determinants of direction and extent of effects of irrelevant spatial information. *Psychological Research, 55*, 270–279

Hommel, B. (2000). The prepared reflex: Automaticity and control in s-r translation. In S. Monsell & J. Driver (Eds.), *Control of cognitive processes: Attention and performance XVIII.* (pp. 247–273). Cambridge, MA: MIT Press.

Hommel, B., Müsseler, J., Aschersleben, G., & Prinz, W. (2001). The theory of event coding (tec): A framework for perception and action planning. *Behavioral and Brain Sciences, 24*, 849–937.

James, W. (1890). *The principles of psychology.* London: Macmillan.

Jeannerod, M. (1997). *The cognitive neuroscience of action.* Oxford, England: Blackwell Publishers.

Kahneman, D. (1973). *Attention and effort.* Englewoods Cliff, NJ: Prentice-Hall.

Koch, C., & Tsuchiya, N. (2006). Attention and consciousness: Two distinct brain processes. *Trends in Cognitive Sciences, 11*, 16–22.

Kraus, M. W., & Chen, S. (2009). Striving to be known by significant others: Automatic activation of self-verification goals in relationship contexts. *Journal of Personality and Social Psychology, 97*, 58.

Kruglanski, A. W., Shah, J. Y., Fishbach, A., Friedman, R., Chun, W. Y., & Sleeth-Keppler, D. (2002). A theory of goal-systems. In M. P. Zanna (Ed.), *Advances in experimental social psychology* (Vol. 34, pp. 331–378). New York: Academic Press.

Lamme, V. A. F. (2003). Why visual attention and awareness are different. *Trends in Cognitive Sciences, 7*, 12–18.

LeDoux, J. (1996). *The emotional brain.* New York: Simon & Schuster.

Libet, B. (1985). Unconscious cerebral initiative and the role of conscious will in voluntary action. *Behavioural and Brain Science, 8*, 529–566.

Locke, E. A., & Latham, G. P. (1990). *A theory of goal setting and task performance.* Englewood Cliffs, NJ: Prentice Hall.

Loersch, C., Aarts, H., Payne, B. K., & Jefferis, V. E. (2008) The influence of social groups on goal contagion. *Journal of Experimental Social Psychology, 44*, 1555–1558.

Louis, M. R., & Sutton, R. I. (1991). Switching cognitive gears: From habits of mind to active thinking. *Human Relations, 44*, 55–76.

McCulloch, K. C., Aarts, H., Fujita, J., & Bargh, J. A. (2008). Inhibition in goal systems: A retrieval-induced forgetting account. *Journal of Experimental Social Psychology, 44*, 857–865.

Mckone, E. (1995). Short-term implicit memory for words and nonwords. *Journal of Experimental Psychology: Learning, Memory and Cognition, 21*, 1108–1126.

Miller, N. E., & Dollard, J. (1941). *Social learning and imitation*. New Haven, CT: Yale University Press.

Mischel, W., Shoda,Y., & Rodriguez, M.I. (1989). Delay of gratification in children. *Science, 244*, 933–938.

Miyake, A., Friedman, N. P., Emerson, M. J., Witzki, A. H., Howerter, A., & Wager, T. D. (2000). The unity and diversity of executive functions and their contributions to complex "Frontal lobe" Tasks: A latent variable analysis. *Cognitive Psychology, 41*, 49–100.

Miyake, A., & Shah, P. (1999). *Models of working memory: Mechanisms of active maintenance and executive control*. New York: Cambridge University Press.

Monsell, S., & Driver, J. (2000). *Control of cognitive processes: Attention and performance XVIII*. Cambridge, MA: The MIT Press.

Moskowitz, G. B., Gollwitzer, P. M., Wasel, W., & Schaal, B. (1999). Preconscious control of stereotype activation through chronic egalitarian goals. *Journal of Personality and Social Psychology, 77*, 167–184.

Moskowitz, G. B., Li, P., & Kirk, E. R. (2004). The implicit volition model: On the preconscious regulation of temporarily adopted goals. In M. P. Zanna (Ed.), *Advances in experimental social psychology* (Vol. 36, pp. 317–404). New York: Academic Press.

Norman, D. A., & Shallice, T. (1986). Attention and action: Willed and automatic control of behavior. In R. J. Davidson, G. E. Schwartz, & D. Shapiro (Eds.), *Consciousness and self-regulation: Advances in research and theory* (Vol. 4, pp. 1–18). New York: Plenum.

Nørretranders, T. (1991). *The user illusion: Cutting consciousness down to size*. New York: Penguin.

Oikawa, M. (2004). Moderation of automatic achievement goals by conscious monitoring. *Psychological Reports, 95*, 975–980.

Olds, J. (1958). Self-stimulation of the brain. *Science, 127*, 315–324.

Olds, J., & Milner, P. (1954). Positive reinforcement produced by electrical stimulation of septal area and other regions of rat brain. *Journal of Comparative and Physiological Psychology, 47*, 419–427.

Papies, E. K., Stroebe, W., & Aarts, H. (2008). Healthy cognition: Processes of self-regulatory success in restrained eating. *Personality and Social Psychology Bulletin, 34*, 1290–1300.

Pessiglione, M., Schmidt, L., Draganski, B., Kalisch, R., Lau, H., Dolan, R. J., & Frith, C. D. (2007). How the brain translates money into force: A neuroimaging study of subliminal motivation. *Science, 316*, 904–906.

Powers, W. T. (1973). *Behavior: The control of perception*. Chicago, IL: Aldine.

Prinz, W. (1997). Perception and action planning. *European Journal of Cognitive Psychology, 9*, 129–154.

Reber, A. S. (1993). *Implicit learning and tacit knowledge: An essay on the cognitive unconscious*. New York: Oxford University Press.

Schultz, W. (2006). Behavioral theories and the neurophysiology of reward. *Annual Review of Psychology, 57*, 87.

Seth, A. K., Dienes, Z., Cleeremans, A., Overgaard, M., & Pessoa, L. (2008). Measuring consciousness: Relating behavioural and neurophysiological approaches. *Trends in Cognitive Sciences, 12*, 314–321.

Shah, J. Y. (2003). Automatic for the people: How representations of significant others implicitly affect goal pursuit. *Journal of Personality and Social Psychology, 84*, 661–681.

Shah, J. Y., Friedman, R., & Kruglanski, A. W. (2002). Forgetting all else: On the antecedents and consequences of goal shielding. *Journal of Personality and Social Psychology, 83*, 1261–1280.

Shantz, A., & Latham, G. P. (2009). An exploratory field experiment of the effect of subconscious and conscious goals on employee performance. *Organizational Behavior and Human Decision Processes, 109*, 9–17.

Sheeran, P., Aarts, H., Custers, R., Rivis, A., Webb, T. L., & Cooke, R. (2005). The goal-dependent automaticity of drinking habits. *British Journal of Social Psychology, 44*, 47–63.

Shizgal, P. (1997). Neural basis of utility estimation. *Current Opinion in Neurobiology, 7*, 198–208.

Shizgal, P. (1999). On the neural computation of utility: Implications from studies of brain stimulation reward. In D. Kahneman, E. Diener, & N. Schwarz (Eds.), *Well-being: The foundations of hedonic psychology* (pp. 500–524). New York: Russell Sage Foundation.

Skinner, B. F. (1953). *Science and human behavior*. Oxford, England: Macmillan.

Vallacher, R. R., & Wegner, D. M. (1987). What do people think they're doing? Action identification and human behavior. *Psychological Review, 94*, 3–15.

Van den Bos, A., & Stapel, D. A. (2009). Why people stereotype affects how they stereotype: The differential influence of comprehension goals and self-enhancement goals on stereotyping. *Personality and Social Psychology Bulletin, 35*, 101–113.

Veling, H., & Aarts, H. (2009). Putting behavior on hold decreases reward value of need-instrumental objects outside of awareness. *Journal of Experimental Social Psychology, 45*, 1020–1023.

Veling, H., Aarts, H., & Stroebe, W. (2011). Fear signals inhibit impulsive behavior toward rewarding food objects. *Appetite, 56*, 643–648.

Veltkamp, M., Aarts, H., & Custers, R. (2008). Perception in the service of goal pursuit: Motivation to attain goals enhances the perceived size of goal-instrumental object. *Social Cognition, 26*, 720–736.

Veltkamp, M., Aarts, H., & Custers, R. (2009). Unravelling the motivational yarn: A framework for understanding the instigation of implicitly motivated behaviour resulting from deprivation and positive affect. *European Review of Social Psychology, 20*, 345–381.

Verbruggen, F., & Logan, G. D. (2009). Automaticity of cognitive control: Goal priming in response-inhibition paradigms. *Journal of Experimental Psychology: Learning Memory and Cognition, 35*, 1381.

Watson, J. B. (1925). *Behaviorism*. New York: Norton and Company.

Wegner, D. M. (2002). *The illusion of conscious will*. Cambridge, MA: MIT Press.

Wickelgren, W. A. (1969). Auditory and articulatory coding in verbal short-term memory. *Psychological Review, 76*, 233–235.

Williams, D. R., & Williams, H. (1969). Auto-maintenance in the pigeon: Sustained pecking despite contingent non-reinforcement. *Journal of the Experimental Analysis of Behavior, 12*, 511–520.

Wilson, T. D. (2002). *Strangers to ourselves: Discovering the adaptive unconscious*. Cambridge, MA: Belknap Press of Harvard University Press.

Wood, W., & Neal, D. T. (2007). A new look at habits and the interface between habits and goals. *Psychological Review, 114,* 843–863.

Wood, W., Quinn, J. M., & Kashy, D. A. (2002). Habits in everyday life: Thought, emotion, and action. *Journal of Personality and Social Psychology, 83,* 1281–1297.

Zajonc, R. B. (1980). Feeling and thinking: Preferences need no inferences. *American Psychologist, 35,* 151–175.

Zedelius, C. M., Veling, H., & Aarts, H. (2011). Boosting or choking—How conscious and unconscious reward processing modulate the active maintenance of goal-relevant information. *Consciousness and Cognition, 20,* 355–362.

The Motivational Complexity of Choosing: A Review of Theory and Research

Erika A. Patall

Abstract

Years of research have implicated a complex set of motivational causes and consequences of choice. Psychological theory has often prescribed the benefits of choosing, though limitations to this view of choice as being ubiquitously positive are apparent. In this chapter, the relation between choice and motivation is examined. Conceptualizations of choice as both an outcome of motivation and a motivational experience are described. The benefits and determinants of receiving and perceiving choice for motivation are then discussed according to various psychological theories. Next, the complex and often contradictory findings regarding the relation between choice and motivation are discussed in light of various factors (e.g., characteristics of choices, persons, and situations) that may influence those effects. Issues that have yet to be adequately addressed in the research on choice effects and the directions that future research might take are briefly discussed.

Key Words: provision of choice, perceived choice, decision making, autonomy, motivation

Introduction

People make a multitude of choices every day. Considering any one of a number of personal choices you may have made today will reveal that choices vary in type and are influenced by numerous factors. Not only is the motivation that underlies choice making complex, but the consequences of choosing may be powerful. Most people believe that having the freedom to choose is an essential determinant of happiness and health, allowing them to control their fate and express individuality. Few other beliefs are more fundamental to Western culture than the belief that individuals have the right to freedom, liberty, and choice.

Given this colloquial understanding of the complexity and importance of choosing, it comes as no surprise that choice is implicated in numerous psychological theories, either as an outcome of some motivational process or as a predictor of

motivation. In this chapter, the relation between choice and motivation is examined. First, an array of important factors that influence choice making are briefly highlighted to illustrate how choice is often conceptualized as the outcome of a motivational process. I then turn to a more central focus of the chapter, to discuss how various psychological theories have conceptualized choice as an influential predictor of motivation. In this section, research emphasizing both the benefits of choosing and the detriments of choosing is presented. Next, in an attempt to understand the complex and often contradictory relations that have been revealed between choice and various motivation-related outcomes, factors that may influence choice effects are discussed. Finally, issues that have yet to be adequately addressed in the research on choice effects and the directions that future research might take are briefly discussed.

The Motivation to Choose

Over time, choice has been conceptualized and operationally defined in a variety of different ways in theories of human behavior. Consequently, the study of choice and its relation with motivation reflect this variability. In much theory and research, choice is an outcome that can be explained by some motivational process. That is, choice is the end result of a decision-making process in which an individual has some freedom regarding whether to engage in one behavior or not or one behavior over another. When looking at choice as a behavioral outcome, virtually any theory of human behavior might be conceived to have something to say regarding the relation between motivation and choice. Likewise, the research on what motivates people to choose as they do provides a long list of influential factors.

For example, from the standpoint of early drive theories (Maslow, 1954; Murray, 1938), people choose one object or activity over another to the extent that it satisfies one or more of many basic physiological and psychological needs (i.e., hunger, thirst, love, or achievement). According to Maslow (1954), needs exist in a hierarchical organization, such that lower level "deficit" needs (physiological and safety needs) are required to be satisfied before higher level "growth" needs (belongingness, esteem, and self-actualization needs). As such, when faced with a situation in which an individual has the choice of objects and activities that satisfy existing needs at varying levels in the hierarchy, the object or activity that satisfies lower level needs will be chosen.

A number of theories suggest that people simply choose the best or most rewarding option among the alternatives and avoid options that lead to undesirable outcomes. From a traditional behaviorist standpoint, a particular behavior will be chosen and initiated over another behavior to the extent that it has been frequently paired with a stimulus or followed by a reinforcing consequence in the past (Skinner, 1953; Thorndike, 1913). Similarly, according to rational choice theory, an influential theory in social sciences such as sociology, economics, and political science, individuals are motivated to choose the best option given their goals and information they have about the conditions under which they are acting (Scott, 2000). Rational individuals must anticipate the outcome of each alternative course of action and will choose the alternative that will lead to the greatest satisfaction (Carling, 1992; Coleman, 1973; Heath, 1976). Despite this hedonic assumption, the decisions people make do not always conform to conventional assumptions of rational choice. Rather, people are often engaging in satisficing, accepting a choice that is good enough, due to their cognitive limitations, limited information, and the complexity of environment that limits their ability to make a perfect choice (Simon, 1982, 1987). Likewise, irrational choices may be a function of a number of judgment heuristics and biases that influence the way people assess probabilities under uncertain conditions and, thus, influence the decisions they make (Kahneman & Tversky, 1979; Tversky & Kahneman, 1974, 1981).

A great deal of research and theory has highlighted the important role that expectancies about one's abilities or the outcomes of behaving, as well as one's values for a particular object or behavior, play in influencing the choices an individual makes (Ajzen, 1985; Atkinson, 1964; Bandura, 1977; Eccles & Wigfield, 2002; Edwards, 1954; Feather, 1988; Lewin, 1936; Rotter, 1954; Tolman, 1932; Vroom, 1964). Self-efficacy or expectations regarding one's ability to adequately execute a specific behavior or sequence of behaviors relative to a particular goal or criterion influence which behaviors one chooses to engage in (Bandura, 1977, 1986, 1997). For example, students with higher mathematical self-efficacy were found to be more likely to choose to engage in the math task compared to other types of tasks (Bandura & Schunk, 1981), and measures of self-efficacy have been found to correlate significantly with career choices and students' choice of majors in college (Betz & Hackett, 1981, 1983; Hackett & Betz, 1981, 1989). Going further, maladaptive choices may be made as a result of expectancies for failure and self-presentational concerns. For example, Berglas and Jones (1978) demonstrated in their research on self-handicapping that compared to undergraduate students that were led to believe they had performed well on a series of analogy problems due to their high aptitude, students who were led to believe they had performed well on the task due to lucky guessing (and thus would be unlikely to do well on future tasks) were more likely to choose to take a performance-inhibiting drug rather than a performance-enhancing drug for a second round of problems.

Expectancy-value theories of motivation suggest that the choices an individual makes are a function of the interaction between an individual's beliefs about his or her ability to produce a particular outcome and his or her value for the task or attaining a particular outcome (Ajzen, 1985; Atkinson, 1964; Edwards, 1954; Feather, 1988; Lewin, 1936;

Rotter, 1954; Vroom, 1964). For example, Vroom's expectancy theory (1964), Atkinson's theory of achievement motivation (1964), and Rotter's social learning theory (1954) all predict that an individual's choices are a function of the product of an individual's beliefs about his or her ability to produce a particular outcome or consequence and the desirability or his or her value for attaining that particular outcome. The greater the product of these elements, the more likely an individual will be to choose a particular option or course of action. Research has been consistent with these notions. For example, the combination of expectancies and values has been found to predict occupational choice (Mitchell, 1974; Van Eerne & Thierry, 1996) and students' academic choices (Feather, 1988) rather well. Feather (1988) found that college students who had a higher value and perceptions of their ability in math were more likely to enroll in science courses, whereas students who had higher value and perception of their ability in English were less likely to enroll in science courses and more likely to enroll in humanities.

Similar predictions are made according to the theory of planned behavior (Ajzen, 1985). Specifically, outcome expectancies and values lead to a favorable or unfavorable attitude toward a behavior and influence one's intentions to perform a particular behavior, along with perceptions of the social pressure to engage or not engage in a behavior and perceptions of one's ability to perform a given behavior. Consequently, one behavior will be chosen over alternatives to the extent that the intention to perform that behavior is stronger than the intention to perform alternative behaviors and when an individual has a sufficient degree of actual control over the behavior (Ajzen, 1988, 2002; Sheppard, Hartwick, & Warshaw, 1988). For example, people's voting intentions, assessed a short time prior to a presidential election, tend to correlate with actual voting choice in the range of .75 to .80 (see Fishbein & Ajzen, 1981). Mothers' choice of feeding method (breast versus bottle) for newborn babies has been found to have a strong correlation with intentions expressed several weeks prior to delivery (Manstead, Proffitt, & Smart, 1983).

Contemporary expectancy-value theories within the academic domain (Eccles, 1987; Eccles et al., 1983; Eccles & Wigfield, 2002; Wigfield & Eccles, 1992, 2001) also assert that the choices that individuals make when given some autonomy in their decision making are influenced by expectancy-related beliefs about how well they will do on a task either immediately or in the future and the extent to which an activity is valued. Although early expectancy-value theory and research (e.g., Atkinson, 1964; Vroom, 1964) suggested that expectancies were related to task choices, more recent research has suggested that value beliefs are a better predictor of students' academic choices than expectancies (Eccles, 1987; Eccles et al., 1983; Eccles et al., 1984; Feather, 1988; Meece, Wigfield, & Eccles, 1990; Wigfield & Eccles, 1992). For example, Eccles (1984) showed that fifth- through twelfth-grade students' valuing of math predicted their intentions to keep taking more math courses more strongly than their expectancies for success. Likewise, Eccles, Adler, and Meece (1984) showed that eighth- through tenth-grade students' valuing of math strongly predicted their decisions to enroll in advanced high school math courses. Whereas for younger students, interest may be the strongest predictor of academic choices, for older students, both interest and perceived usefulness may both be strong predictors (Wigfield & Eccles, 1989).

A number of theories emphasize how one's goals motivate choices in the context of self-regulation (Carver & Scheier, 2002; Markus & Nurius, 1986). For example, according to Carver and Scheier's (1982, 2002; also see Chapter 3, this volume) control theory, people monitor the discrepancy between their current state and a goal and will try to move toward a desirable goal (or away from a goal with an undesirable outcome) as a way to reduce the discrepancy (or enlarge it in the case of goals to avoid undesirable outcomes). Thus, a person's choice to engage in one behavior over another is the result of the ability of a behavior to reduce the discrepancy between one's current state and ideal state or goal. Similarly, individuals' positive and negative visions of themselves in the future or their possible selves (Markus & Nurius, 1986; Oyserman & James, 2008) may influence the choices an individual makes. Possible selves can act as a guidepost and orient an individual to make choices that bring them closer to desired possible selves and farther from undesirable possible selves (Hoyle & Sherrill, 2006; Oyserman & Fryberg, 2006; Oyserman & James, 2008).

Various personal orientations that people have will influence their choices. For example, in Atkinson's (1957, 1964) early expectancy-value theory, an individual's choice of tasks was hypothesized to be a function of relatively enduring motives to approach success and avoid failure, in addition to expectancies and value for success. People high in the motive to approach success were expected to choose tasks of intermediate difficulty because motivation was expected to be highest for intermediate tasks. In contrast, people who were high in the motive to avoid failure were expected to choose tasks that were very easy or very difficult. In one case, negative affect (the fear of failure) would be minimized because very easy tasks would ensure success. Likewise, negative affect could be minimized by choosing a very difficult task because success would not be expected on difficult tasks. Empirical findings have supported predictions of Atkinson's expectancy-value theory, showing that most people choose tasks of intermediate difficulty and that individuals high in the motive to approach success were more likely to choose tasks of intermediate difficulty compared to individuals high in the motive to avoid failure (Weiner, 1992). For example, Atkinson and Litwin (1960) showed that individuals high in the motive to approach success stood at a moderately challenging distance from pegs for a ring-toss game, whereas individuals high in the motive to avoid failure stood either very close or very far from the peg. In the context of an academic environment, the extent to which a student is focused on mastery versus performance goals (Ames, 1992; Dweck & Leggett, 1988; Maehr & Midgley, 1991) or holds an entity versus incremental theory of intelligence (Dweck, 1986, 1999; Dweck & Bempechat, 1983) may lead a student to choose options and activities that are reflective of his or her personal orientation. For instance, students with performance goals or entity theories of intelligence are likely to choose easier tasks, while students with mastery tasks or incremental theories of intelligence are likely to choose more personally challenging tasks (Ames, 1992; Anderman & Maehr, 1994; Bandura & Dweck, 1985 (unpublished data); Dweck, 1986; 1999; Elliott & Dweck, 1988, ; Nicholls, 1984). As another example, according to regulatory focus theory (Higgins, 1997, 2000; also see Chapter 5, this volume), people pursue goals in line with their regulatory focus orientation or their particular manner of approaching pleasure and avoiding pain. Individuals with a promotion focus are concerned with gains, advancements, and accomplishments, whereas individuals with a prevention focus are primarily concerned with safety, responsibilities, and avoiding losses. Regulatory focus will influence the choice of behavior an individual engages in to achieve a goal, as well as the value of various options. That is, people choose to engage in behaviors that allow them to achieve a goal in a way that is consistent with their regulatory focus orientation (e.g., Crowe & Higgins, 1997) and have greater value for and commitment to decisions in which there is a fit between their regulatory orientation and behavior (e.g., Förster, Higgins, & Idson, 1998; Förster, Higgins, & Strack, 2000; Idson, Liberman, & Higgins, 2000).

It is also important to note that the choice an individual makes is not only the end result of some motivational process, but it is an index of motivation. That is, when an individual has the freedom to choose among objects or activities, what he or she chooses indicates where the individual's motivation lies. Fairly common is the experimental design in which a factor is manipulated to observe its impact on the participant's motivation to engage in a task by observing his or her selection of a task under free-choice conditions (e.g., Lepper, Greene, & Nisbett, 1973; Zuckerman, Porac, Lathin, Smith, & Deci, 1978).

Finally, for some choices, motivation may not even be part of the equation. Theorists have noted that some choices may not require intentional analytical reasoning; rather, some choices are made quickly and spontaneously based on nonconscious processes, including affective feelings (Bargh, 1997; Bargh & Chartrand, 1999; Kahneman, 2003). According to automaticity scholars, conscious choice based on one's preferences, goals, and expectations may initially be needed to perform a desired behavior. However, to the extent the same option is chosen across similar situations, choice becomes an automatic process (Bargh & Chartrand, 1999).

As the earlier discussion illustrates, when choice is conceptualized inclusively as the selection between objects, the initiation of one behavior over another, or the initiation of behavior over doing nothing at all, the list of possible psychological and social theories that can illuminate our understanding of the impact of motivation on one's choices is virtually endless. However, more limited in scope is theory and research that has studied choice as an experience that has consequences for an individual's motivation to engage in subsequent behaviors. I turn my attention to this conceptualization of choice next.

Choice as an Experience
Choice as a Motivator

The presumption that feelings of having choice can be a powerful motivator is pervasive in motivation theory and research. Kurt Lewin (1952) provided one of the earliest proposals of the notion that having choice was a powerful motivator, demonstrating that people would be more likely to engage in an activity if they believed they had freely chosen it.

The motivating role of having choice is apparent in many foundational theories in social psychology.

Dissonance theory suggests that people dislike inconsistency between the beliefs they have about themselves and the behavior they engage in, and therefore, people will strive for their thoughts to be consistent with other thoughts and with their behavior (Aronson, 1969, 1992, 1999; Brehm, 1962; Festinger, 1957). When a person's thoughts are inconsistent with one another or inconsistent with one's behavior, an aversive motivational state of dissonance is aroused (Elliot & Devine, 1994) in which an individual will be motivated to resolve dissonance (Gerard, 1992; Harmon-Jones & Mills, 1999) by one of a number of strategies: *(1)* removing the dissonant belief, *(2)* reducing the importance of the dissonant belief, *(3)* adding new beliefs that are consonant with behavior, or *(4)* increasing the importance of the new consonant belief (Festinger, 1957; Harmon-Jones & Mills, 1999; Simon, Greenberg, & Brehm, 1995).

Choice making plays an important role in cognitive dissonance in several ways. First, the experience of making a difficult choice is one important source of dissonance and motivates strategies to reduce dissonance (Festinger, 1964). For example, in Brehm's (1956) classic study examining the role of choice making, after receiving a chosen household appliance among several options, participants who chose between appliances similar in desirability according to their own initial ratings were found to subsequently rate the chosen object as more desirable and the unchosen object as less desirable. However, participants who were assigned to receive a particular appliance or who were asked to choose between appliances that they initially viewed as highly discrepant in desirability, showed little change in their attitudes toward the appliances after receiving the one they were assigned or had chosen. Subsequent studies provided additional support for the notion that choice making itself can motivate an individual to shift his or her attitudes in an effort to reduce dissonance (Brehm & Cohen, 1959; Gerard & White, 1983; Lyubomirsky & Ross, 1999; Shultz, Léveillé, & Lepper, 1999).

Second, refinements of dissonance theory suggested that dissonance and corresponding dissonance-reducing strategies will only occur when people perceive that they have freely chosen to engage in a behavior and can therefore accept responsibility for an action (Cooper & Fazio, 1984; Goethals & Cooper, 1972; Harmon-Jones, Brehm, Greenberg, Simon, & Nelson, 1996; Helmreich & Collins, 1968; Linder, Cooper, & Jones, 1967; Scher & Cooper, 1989; Sherman, 1970). For example, Croyle and Cooper (1983) found that when participants were asked to write a counterattitudinal essay, participants who felt they had a great deal of choice compared to those who perceived having little choice regarding whether to write the essay demonstrated greater physiological arousal construed as a dissonant motivational state. Likewise, individuals who perceived having chosen to write an essay that was contrary to their personal beliefs subsequently changed their attitudes, while individuals who felt they were forced to write the counterattitudinal essay did not change their attitudes (Cooper & Fazio, 1984). Similarly, participants who were given a choice compared to no choice as to whether to write that they liked an unpleasant-tasting drink or that they thought a boring passage was interesting shifted their attitudes in the direction of what they wrote. Furthermore, the more choice participants felt they had over what they wrote, the more they shifted their attitudes (Harmon-Jones et al., 1996).

Choice is also at the core of attribution theory (Kelley, 1967, 1973) and self-perception theory (Bem, 1967). According to attribution theory, people will assign dispositional meaning to behavior after a careful assessment of the possible explanatory power of controlling influences in the environment. Thus, if a person feels that a behavior was freely chosen, he or she will be more likely to infer from that behavior information about the actor's traits and attitudes (Jones & Harris, 1967; Jones, Worchel, Goethals, & Grumet, 1971).

Self-perception theory makes a similar claim. Challenging the notion that people experience an aversive motivational state known as dissonance, self-perception theory suggested that rather "individuals come to know their own attitudes, emotions, and other internal states partially by inferring them from observations of their own overt behavior and/or the circumstances in which this behavior occurs" (Bem, 1972, p. 2). Like dissonance theory, self-perception theory maintained the notion that that in order for individuals to be motivated to form attitudes that reflect their overt behavior, they must believe that they freely chose to engage in the behavior self-observed (Bem, 1972; Bem & McConnell, 1971). That is, individuals who experienced a choice as to whether to engage in a particular behavior will observe that overt behavior and conclude that they must have an attitude in line with that behavior. In contrast, individuals who did not experience a choice will observe their behavior and evaluate the conditions in which they acted and conclude that their behavior was the result of not having a choice, rather than their internal beliefs. Subsequent research attempting to resolve the discrepancies between dissonance theory and self-perception theory demonstrated that both were correct under various circumstances. In particular, when initial attitudes are weak or unimportant individuals may form (or change) their beliefs upon observing their own behavior (Chaiken & Baldwin, 1981; Fazio, 1981; Fazio, Zanna, & Cooper, 1977). In contrast, when initial attitudes are strong or important, attitude change may be motivated by dissonance (Chaiken & Baldwin, 1981; Fazio, 1981; Fazio, Zanna, & Cooper, 1977). However, both situations require that a person believe that he or she freely chose to engage in the behavior in order to motivate the formation or shifting of an attitude in line with behavior.

Furthermore, the motivating effects of choice go beyond the formation or change of an attitude to affect other subsequent behaviors. For example, the basic finding of research examining the "foot-in-the-door" technique is that once a person freely chooses to comply with a small request, he or she will be more likely to comply with more substantial subsequent requests (Freedman & Fraser, 1966; Uranowitz, 1975). Similarly, people may remain committed to a course of action if they freely chose it in the first place. For example, even when presented with information suggesting that a chosen investment was not profitable, participants given a choice of investments subsequently allocated more money to their chosen investment compared to people who were not given a choice (Staw, 1976).

The role of choice is well defined in studies evaluating its effects on intrinsic motivation and outcomes related to intrinsic motivation from a self-determination perspective. According to self-determination theory, people are naturally inclined to interact with the environment in ways that promote learning and mastery (Deci & Ryan, 1985; Ryan & Deci, 2000). The theory posits that autonomy, competence, and relatedness are three fundamental needs that underlie people's intrinsic motivation or the propensity to engage in a behavior for its own sake (or out of enjoyment; Deci, 1971). Social contexts that satisfy these needs will enhance intrinsic motivation (Ryan & Deci, 2000). Therefore, intrinsic motivation is enhanced when an individual feels autonomous and in control of his or her outcomes and when information is provided about the individual's competence at navigating the social environment. When the environment is experienced as controlling, self-determination and intrinsic motivation are diminished (Deci, Connell, & Ryan, 1989).

Given the importance placed on one's need for autonomy in supporting intrinsic motivation, self-determination theory holds that having choice should result in enhanced intrinsic motivation, as well as other positive motivational and performance outcomes supported by intrinsic motivation (Deci, 1980; Deci & Ryan, 1985; Ryan & Deci, 2000). Much research has supported this postulate of self-determination theory, demonstrating that choice leads to enhanced intrinsic motivation (e.g., Cordova & Lepper, 1996; Iyengar & Lepper, 1999; Patall, Cooper, & Robinson, 2008; Swann & Pittman, 1977; Zuckerman, Porac, Lathin, Smith, & Deci, 1978), as well as enhanced effort, task performance, subsequent learning, perceived competence, preference for challenge, and creativity (e.g., Amabile, 1979, 1983; Amabile, Hennessey, & Grossman, 1986; Becker, 1997; Cordova & Lepper, 1996; Iyengar & Lepper, 1999; Kernan, Heimann, & Hanges, 1991; Patall, Cooper, & Robinson, 2008). For example, in one seminal study on the effect of choice on intrinsic motivation, Zuckerman, Porac, Lathin, Smith, and Deci (1978) found that participants who were asked to choose three puzzles to work on among six options spent more time engaged in the puzzle-solving task in a subsequent free-play period compared to participants who were assigned to work on three of the six puzzles. Iyengar and Lepper (1999) found that Caucasian American elementary school students were the most motivated and demonstrated the best performance when they made personal choices about which tasks to engage in rather than having the task chosen for them. Similarly, children provided with various choices during a computerized math activity, such as the opportunity to choose their game name or various icons in the math game, demonstrated greater intrinsic motivation and learning as measured by the number of problems answered correctly on a math test compared to children who were not provided with choices (Cordova & Lepper, 1996). Amabile and Gitomer (1984) found that children who were given choices of which task materials to use when creating a collage produced collages that were assessed to be more creative than those produced by children given no choice. Likewise, Greenberg (1992) found that participants who were given choice in selecting which problems to work on produced more creative outputs. Most recently, a meta-analysis of 41 studies examining the effect of choice on intrinsic motivation and related outcomes in a variety of settings indicated that overall, providing choice indeed enhanced intrinsic motivation, effort, task performance, and perceived competence, among other outcomes (Patall, Cooper, & Robinson, 2008).

In addition to being an important antecedent of feelings of autonomy, subsequent motivational and performance benefits of choice may lie in its ability to support the perception or experience of having control (Langer, 1975; Rotter, 1966; Taylor, 1989) and the need for competence (Cordova & Lepper, 1996; Henry, 1994; Henry & Sniezek, 1993; Katz & Assor, 2007; Monty & Perlmuter, 1987; Patall et al., 2008; Perlmuter & Monty, 1977; Perlmuter, Scharff, Karsh, & Monty, 1980; Tafarodi, Milne & Smith, 1999; Tafarodi, Mehranvar, Panton, & Milne, 2002). Based on a series of studies showing that choice of either stimulus or response words in a paired-associates memory task led to enhanced performance outcomes (Monty & Perlmuter, 1975; Monty, Rosenberger, & Perlmuter, 1973; Perlmuter & Monty, 1973; Perlmuter, Monty, & Kimble, 1971), Perlmuter and Monty (1977) argued that the performance benefits of choice are a result of increased motivation in the form of enhanced perceived control and subsequent increased arousal and cognitive engagement with the task (Monty & Perlmuter, 1987; Perlmuter et al., 1980). Similarly, Henry (1994; Henry & Sniezek, 1993) argued that the benefits of choice lie in its ability to increase perceived control and subsequent self-efficacy. Furthermore, the power of choice to enhance perceptions of control and perceived competence has been found to be independent of its effect on either actual performance or intrinsic motivation. For example, in two studies examining the effects of choice, college students were asked to read and understand a short story. Those who selected names to be used in the story reported enhanced perceived control and felt more confident about their performance than did those who were assigned names, although the groups in fact performed equally and did not differ in reports of interest for the task (Tafarodi et al., 1999).

In fact, so strong is the relationship between choice, perceived control, and feelings of competence, that choice may have a motivational quality even when the choices one makes have no relation with outcomes (Langer, 1975). Langer (1975) argued that as a result of people's cumulative experience in which having choice allows one to perform better on a task by picking options that are tailored to one's preferences and abilities, even providing choices that have no relation with the outcomes obtained can lead to heightened expectations of success. Furthermore, the cue that choice provides of an increased probability of success (Estes, 1976) may support motivation and increased resilience even in the wake of initial failure (Mikulincer, 1988). Consistent with these notions, Henry (1994) found that allowing male participants to choose between two sets of almanac questions produced enhanced perceptions of competence prior to engaging in the task, though the only information provided was uninformative labels for the questions (i.e., Set A or Set B). Similarly, Langer (1975) found that expectancies for success were greater when participants were given a choice of ticket in the lottery, even though outcomes in a lottery are determined by chance.

In line with self-determination theorists and others, the importance of providing choices has also been emphasized in theories of academic achievement motivation. For example, achievement goal orientation theorists have suggested that to the extent that it is a way to support students' feelings of autonomy and control and emphasizes the process of learning, the provision of choice may be one of a number of key instructional practices that differentiate mastery compared to performance classroom goal structure (Ames, 1992; Ames & Archer, 1988; Epstein, 1989; Maehr & Midgley, 1991; Meece, Anderman, & Anderman, 2006). In particular, providing students with options and opportunities to make choices regarding tasks, materials, learning methods, or pace of learning in the classroom has been theorized to be an important part of implementing a mastery goal structure (e.g., an emphasis on developing skills and learning), whereas restricting options and choices may be consistent with a performance goal structure (e.g., an emphasis on demonstrating competence and performing better than others). Though few empirical examples exist to support the supposition, the provision of choice in the classroom is expected to encourage students to adopt a personal mastery goal orientation when engaging in achievement behaviors (Ames, 1992; Epstein, 1989; Maehr & Midgley, 1991; Meece, Anderman, & Anderman, 2006) and, in turn, support a constellation of adaptive motivational and performance outcomes that mastery goal orientations have generally been found to be positively associated with (e.g., increases in effort, persistence, self-efficacy, intrinsic motivation, and self-regulation; see Ames, 1992; Harackiewicz, Barron, Pintrich, Elliot, & Thrash, 2002; Linnenbrink-Garcia, Tyson, & Patall, 2008; Meece et al., 2006; Midgley, Kaplan, & Middleton, 2001 for relevant reviews).

Also building on the notion that the provision and/or perception of having choices will support student feelings of autonomy and intrinsic motivation a la a self-determination perspective, interest theorists have suggested that choice may be an important antecedent to students' situational interest and the subsequent development of individual (personal) interest for a domain (Krapp, 2005; Schraw, Flowerday, & Lehman, 2001; Tsai et al., 2008; Zahorik, 1996).

Individual interest is relatively stable and resides within the individual (c.f., Hidi & Renninger, 2006; Krapp, 2005; Renninger, 2009; Renninger, Hidi, & Krapp, 1992; Schiefele, 1991, 2001). It includes a deep, personal connection, enjoyment, and valuing of a domain as well as a willingness to reengage in the domain over time. Renninger and her colleagues (Hidi & Renninger, 2006; Lipstein & Renninger, 2007; Renninger, 1992, 2009) further suggest that knowledge is a critical component of well-developed individual interest in that as interest develops, a person gains a more in-depth knowledge, value, and advanced epistemic understanding of the domain based on his or her experiences. In contrast, situational interest refers to interest that emerges from and is supported by the context (Hidi & Baird, 1986; Hidi & Renninger, 2006; Krapp, 2002), and it may support intrinsic motivation for learning and the development of individual interest (Hidi & Renninger, 2006; Krapp, 2002; Renninger, 2009; Schiefele, 2009).

In line with the notion that choice may be an important practice used to support situational interest, Schraw, Flowerday, and Reisetter (1998) reported that giving college students choices about what they read increased situational interest in the material. Linnenbrink-Garcia, Patall, and Messersmith (unpublished data) found that controlling for students' initial individual interest or perceived competence for science, the perception of having choices supported talented adolescents' situational interest for a science course during a 3-week summer program, as well as subsequent individual interest and perceived competence in science at the end of the program.

Likewise, academic expectancy-value theorists have made use of the notion that supporting the fundamental need for autonomy can have important motivating consequences. That is, supporting autonomy by providing students with the opportunity to make choices may be critical to creating contexts in which values for a task may develop and lead to enhanced self-perceptions and expectancies for success, as well as long-term engagement in that task (Jacobs & Eccles, 2000). During the transition to junior high school, students were more likely to feel competent and to value schoolwork if they felt they had some autonomy about choosing the activity (Midgley & Feldlaufer, 1987). Similarly, college students' perceptions that they were afforded greater opportunities for decision making in a college course predicted greater course self-efficacy and value for the course (Garcia & Pintrich, 1996).

In sum, a number of psychological theories, including dissonance theory, self-perception theory, attribution theory, self-determination theory, and related academic motivation theories have suggested that choice may be an influential motivator. According to these perspectives, choice is expected to motivate behavior and lead to a variety of benefits. Formation or change of attitudes, enhanced commitment, as well as greater feelings of autonomy, control, intrinsic motivation, and a number of adaptive learning-related outcomes (e.g., perceived competence, effort, engagement, task performance, learning, creativity, situational and individual interest, mastery goals, and task value) are among the many outcomes on which choice has been found to have a motivating effect.

The Effectiveness of Choice and Choice as a Demotivator

Despite a great deal of theory and research suggesting that choice is a powerful motivator of behavior, not all studies within the various motivational perspectives described previously have found choice to be a ubiquitous motivator. A number of studies find that choice may have no effect or even a negative effect on adaptive motivation and performance outcomes (Overskeid & Svartdal, 1996; Parker & Lepper, 1992; Reeve, Nix, & Hamm, 2003). Likewise, not all studies from dissonance and attribution theory perspectives have found that greater choice conditions produce greater dissonance and attitude change (Collins, Ashmore, Hornbeck, & Whitney, 1970; Melson, Calder, & Insko, 1969), greater internal attributions (Fitch, 1970), or dispositional attributions to actors by observers (Calder, Ross, & Insko, 1973).

For example, in a series of studies, Flowerday and colleagues (Flowerday & Schraw, 2003; Flowerday, Schraw, & Stevens, 2004) found choice had few positive effects. For example, giving students a choice between working on a crossword puzzle or essay task showed no effect on engagement and task performance (Flowerday & Schraw, 2003). Students in the choice condition demonstrated reduced effort compared to students not given a choice of tasks. In a second study, students allowed to choose the pacing of the task spent less time studying and performed more poorly on cognitive measures compared to students whose pace was dictated by the experimenter (Flowerday & Schraw, 2003). In two additional studies, no-choice participants were found to write higher quality essays compared to students who were given choice. Choice had no effect on a subsequent test to assess learning (Flowerday, Schraw, & Stevens, 2004). In models exploring the nature of perceived autonomy (or self-determination) and its relation to intrinsic motivation, Reeve, Nix, and Hamm (2003) found that internal locus of causality (e.g., an individual's perception that his or her actions are initiated and controlled by the individual rather than by external forces; deCharms, 1968) and volition (e.g., sense that individuals feel free rather than forced to engage in a behavior), but not perceived choice or the external event of provision of choice, constituted valid indicators of self-determination. Through structural equation models, the authors compared a series of models containing one, two, or all three qualities of perceived self-determination to find the best-fitting model. The inclusion of perceived choice or provision of choice was consistently found to reduce the fit of the model and reduced the strength of the relationship between perceived self-determination and intrinsic motivation. Similar findings were reported by Assor, Kaplan, and Roth (2002) when they distinguished between three forms of teacher practices meant to support the need for autonomy among students: fostering relevance by articulating the importance of a task for students' personal goals, allowing students to express dissatisfaction with learning tasks, and providing opportunities to make choices. They found that while allowing students to express their concerns if they do not like a task and fostering the relevance of a task promoted engagement, perceptions of provision of choice had little impact.

In line with null and negative findings, some psychologists have suggested that choice may have disadvantages. Schwartz (2000) argues that Americans now live in a world in which the ability to choose everything from breakfast cereal to the way one wants to live is greater than ever before, though depression and unhappiness are on the rise. That is, although some choice may have benefits, as the number of options and opportunities for making choices becomes excessive, motivation and well-being suffer due to the cost of giving up alternatives and regret with the choices made. Accordingly, Schwartz (2000, 2004) and colleagues (2002) argue that constraints on choosing may often be beneficial.

According to the self-regulatory perspective proposed by Baumeister, Muraven, and colleagues (Baumeister, Bratslavsky, Muraven, & Tice, 1998; Muraven & Baumeister, 2000; Muraven, Baumeister, & Tice, 1999), all acts of choice or self-control are effortful and draw on a limited resource that can be depleted, analogous to a source of energy or strength. Since all acts of volition or self-regulation draw on the same resource, any act of volition or self-regulation will have detrimental effects on subsequent acts that continue to require self-regulation. Consequently, engaging in a choice can result in a state of fatigue called ego depletion, in which the individual experiences a decrement in the capacity to initiate activity, make choices, or further self-regulate.

Baumeister and colleagues (1998) have proposed that making choices is one form of self-control that can result in ego depletion. In particular, the process of deliberation among the options and making a specific choice produces depletion (Vohs et al., 2008; Vohs, Finkenauer, & Baumeister, 2011). Several studies have demonstrated the depleting effect of choice. Baumeister and colleagues (1998) found that participants who were given a choice of which side to take in a debate persisted for less time and made fewer attempts at solving subsequent puzzles compared to participants who were not asked to make a debating choice. In other studies, participants who made choices among household products, among college courses, or about the content of courses demonstrated a reduced ability to exert self-control on a subsequent task (Vohs et al., 2008). Specifically, participants who made choices drank less of a bad-tasting beverage, showed reduced persistence on a cold water pressure task, procrastinated more on a math task, showed less persistence in the face of failure on an unsolvable tracing task or solvable math task, and performed worse on a math test. In yet another study, people who reported making more choices during a shopping trip performed more poorly on a subsequent math task (Vohs et al., 2008).

Burger (1989) proposed a variety of circumstances under which the provision of choice may lead to maladaptive outcomes due to the relationship between having choice and perceptions of control. In particular, having a choice can also increase self-presentational concerns or feelings of responsibility about making the correct choice or performing well. This concern over self-presentation may lead to various negative outcomes. For example, in a series of studies, participants were given a choice of three tasks to work on during a 20-min testing session, one of which they had been told they were likely to do well on based on earlier trials. All participants chose the task they expected to do well on. Other participants were given identical feedback, but they were assigned the task for the testing session. Participants given the choice of tasks scored lower on measures of self-esteem and higher on measures of anxiety and hostility than did subjects given no choice of tasks. However, when participants were led to believe that whether they had made a choice would not be known to the experimenter who was to administer the test, there was no increase in negative affect. Similarly, participants given a choice of words in a paired-associate memory study and told that both the experimenters and the professor supervising the project would return to discuss their performance performed worse on the memory task than those who anticipated the same discussion but did not choose the words (Burger, 1988, unpublished data).

In sum, not all research examining the effects of choice has found choosing to enhance motivation. In some instances choice has been found to have few beneficial effects on intrinsic motivation, perceived competence, engagement, learning and performance, among other adaptive outcomes. As we have seen, some theorists have suggested that in line with null or even negative choice effects that have been found, there may be limitations or drawbacks of choosing. In particular, choice is an effortful and sometimes ego-involved process that may deplete resources and motivation to engage in subsequent behavior.

Factors That Influence the Effects of Choice

There is little doubt that the relationship between choice and motivation is complex. It would seem that choice has the potential to promote motivation, to protect motivation, and to diminish motivation depending on a variety circumstances. Characteristics of the choice, the person, and the situation may all influence the effects of being provided or perceiving one has a choice.

Characteristics of the Choice
PERCEIVED VERSUS ACTUAL CHOICE

One factor that may be important to consider in determining when choice has versus does not have an effect (whether beneficial or detrimental) may be the extent to which it is real or illusory. The finding that choice can be totally illusory and need not have any real consequences in order for it to have an effect on motivation or performance has already been highlighted (e.g., Langer, 1975; Taforodi,

Milne, & Smith, 1999). That is, as long as the individual still perceives increased control over outcomes as a function of his or her choices, choice may yield motivational benefits. For example, Dember and colleagues (1992) found that participants who were given a choice between completing an "easy" or a "hard" version of a vigilance task performed better compared to participants not given a choice, though in reality, everyone was given the same task regardless of the choice made.

However, more surprising might be the notion that an individual need not have had the opportunity to make an actual choice (regardless of its relationship with outcomes) in order for the effects of choice to be experienced. It would be expected that the provision of choice would be an effective way to enhance perceived choice, and in fact, research has suggested that having the opportunity to make choices does increase the perception of choice (e.g., Patall, Cooper, & Wynn, 2010; Reeve et al., 2003). However, akin to the claim made by many control theorists that perceived control is a more powerful predictor than actual control (Averill, 1973; Burger, 1989; Langer, 1975, 1979), choice is unlikely to have an effect if its provision and significance is unrecognized by the individual. In this way, perceived choice may be a more powerful and essential predictor than the actual choice. One study explicitly tested the role of perceived compared to actual choice in motivation. Detweiler, Mendoza, and Lepper (1996) asked preschool children to draw a picture using a set of eight colored markers. Actual choice was manipulated by either allowing the children to choose the subject of their drawing from a list of eight possibilities or assigning the children subjects for the drawing. Perceptions of choice were manipulated by showing children in the high perceived-choice condition only eight markers and emphasizing to them that they could use any of the eight, while participants in the low perceived-choice condition were showed a set of 32 markers, though they too could use any makers of a set of eight. Participants in the perceived-choice condition demonstrated greater intrinsic motivation for the drawing activity in a later free-play period compared to students in the low perceived-choice condition. Moreover, the effect of low compared to high perceived choice was greater than that of low compared to high actual choice.

CHOICES THAT SUPPORT PERCEPTIONS OF CONTROL, COMPETENCE, AND AUTONOMY

There are a number of constructs, many previously mentioned, that are so intimately related to the provision or perception of choice (and each other) that they are sometimes viewed as synonymous with choice. Although increased perceptions or experiences of control, competence, autonomy, volition, or locus of causality may often result as a function of having or perceiving opportunities to choose, the provision or perception of having an opportunity to select an option among alternatives is separable from each of these related constructs. That said, a survey of the literature would suggest that when choice is divorced from some or all of these related constructs, it may lose its power to motivate.

Control may be conceptualized as the opportunity or perception that *(1)* an individual has the ability to perform a particular behavior, *(2)* the particular behavior will be likely to lead to a desirable end, and so ultimately, *(3)* the individual will obtain a particular outcome (Bandura, 1977, 1997; Burger, 1989; Skinner, 1996). As previously discussed, some research and theory suggests that the effects of choice may be owed at least partly to the power of choice to enhance perceptions of control (Burger, 1989; Henry, 1994; Langer, 1975; Monty & Perlmuter, 1977). Work on reactance theory (see Brehm, 1966; Wortman & Brehm, 1975) has suggested that when people expect to be able to control important outcomes, explicitly eliminating an option in the context of giving choice will cause a state of psychological reactance in which they will be highly motivated to regain and defend their personal freedom. This threat of restriction or elimination of the individual's ability to choose will cause the individual to evaluate more positively the alternatives he or she was not allowed to choose, while the remaining alternatives are evaluated more negatively. People will continue to experience a motivational state of reactance and engage in coping behaviors designed to regain their personal freedom as long as behaviors associated with this reactance are perceived to affect outcomes.

In fact, it would seem that when choice does not support the experience of control, it may have no or negative effects. For example, work on learned helplessness has demonstrated that motivation to engage in a behavior and learning are impaired when people experience outcomes as independent of their choice of actions and consequently feel they have no control over a situation (Seligman, 1975). Furthermore, mental health suffers under conditions of learned helplessness; in particular, depression and anxiety result when an individual experiences life choices as irrelevant (e.g., Abramson, Metalsky, & Alloy, 1989;

Abramson, Seligman, & Teasdale, 1978; Maier & Seligman, 1976; Peterson, Maier, & Seligman, 1993; Peterson & Seligman, 1984; Seligman, 1975). When choice does not support perceptions of control because the chooser feels insufficiently informed or overly rushed to make decisions, choice may be experienced as stressful and can diminish self-confidence (Paterson & Neufeld, 1995; Rodin, Rennert, & Solomon, 1980). Similarly, Tafarodi and colleagues (1999) showed that perceptions of competence in understanding a story and performing well on a subsequent test were heightened only when participants chose names used in the story relative to those who made no choices or those who chose names not used in the story. Similarly, choice may be less beneficial when divorced from the need for competence. For example, Burger (1987, 1989) showed that having choice was more beneficial when it provided an opportunity to demonstrate competence. Undergraduate students allowed to select the response word for a paired-associate memory task performed better when told that the experimenter would know about their choice and performance compared to participants who did not choose or chose but were not told the experimenter would know about their choice and performance (Burger, 1987).

According to self-determination theory, perceptions of choice are conceptualized as being an important condition to the experience of autonomy, and in turn, this experience of autonomy supports other adaptive outcomes (Deci & Ryan, 1987). However, perceived choice is just one of several aspects of autonomy. Specifically, autonomy is experienced when actions are perceived as *(a)* stemming from an internal locus of causality or individuals' perceptions that their actions are initiated and controlled by them rather than by external forces (deCharms, 1968) and *(b)* volitional, or the sense that individuals feel free rather than forced to engage in a behavior (Rogers, 1969). Choice is viewed as the condition needed to induce the experiential shift "from pawn to origin" and "from forced to free" (Deci & Ryan, 1985).

However, not all choices (or perceptions of choices) facilitate an internal locus of causality or volition. Reeve and colleagues (2003) suggested as much based on a review of existing literature and their own series of studies in which it was shown that when choice was designed in such a way that it enhanced perceptions of an internal locus of causality and volition (e.g., participants were given ongoing action choices in which the initiation and regulation of their behavior could be freely chosen), it effectively enhanced intrinsic motivation. However, when choice was designed to only enhance the perception of choice and not locus of causality or volition (e.g., participants were given choices of experimenter-determined task options), then it did not successfully enhance intrinsic motivation.

Moller and colleagues (Moller, Deci, & Ryan, 2006) also highlighted the importance of considering how the choices being given support feelings of autonomy in an attempt to integrate contradictory predictions from self-determination theory perspective compared to a self-regulatory strength depletion framework. Specifically, Moller et al. (2006) suggested that contradictory findings result from the lack of differentiation between choices that either promoted participants' sense of autonomy or provided them with a controlled form of choice. Moller and colleagues (2006) suggested that most often in studies of ego depletion, a controlled form of choice is implemented in which participants are led to pick a particular option. That is, while participants are told they have a choice among options, they are subtly pressured to pick a particular option. In contrast, studies coming out of the self-determination perspective generally provide an unrestricted choice with no indication provided as to which option should be chosen. In support of their hypothesis that differentiating between autonomous and controlled forms of choice would reconcile discrepancies, Moller and colleagues (2006) found that when an unrestricted autonomous form of choice was provided, it had a beneficial effect in terms of persistence and performance outcomes, whereas ego depletion resulted when a controlled choice was provided. In fact, the relatively little controversy over the role of choice in dissonance or self-perception motivated attitude change may be a function of the fact that the choice manipulation consistently used in these studies is intentionally designed to make the participant feel responsible for his or her action because he or she freely chose to engage in an attitude-discrepant behavior (Brehm & Cohen, 1962; Cooper & Fazio, 1984). That is, choice manipulations often used in dissonance research may inherently support feeling of autonomy because they usually involve giving the participant the choice to engage in an attitude-discrepant behavior or not.

A recent meta-analysis my colleagues and I conducted of the effect of choice on intrinsic motivation provided additional support for the notion that the effects of choice might in part depend on the extent to which feelings of autonomy are enhanced (Patall et al., 2008). First, this meta-analysis suggested that

study designs in which participants were subtly pressured to choose a particular option or provided options grossly dissimilar in attractiveness to increase the likelihood that all participants would choose a particular target option had the undesirable effect of reducing the sense of having a true choice, resulting in a smaller effect size for this group of studies compared to those with other study designs. Second, the meta-analysis found that the effect of choice was essentially zero when a reward external to the choice manipulation was provided compared to when the participants chose a reward they would receive or when no reward was involved, presumably because providing rewards in this fashion seems to communicate to the individual that he or she is being controlled by forces external to the self.

The importance of autonomy in choice provision goes beyond avoiding the overt pressure or control that may characterize some forms of choice. Katz and Assor (2007) adopted a useful differentiation in terminology to express when choice will be most likely to facilitate adaptive motivational outcomes by differentiating between "picking" and "choosing" (Ullmann-Margalit & Morgenbesser, 1997). That is, choosing allows for one's preferences to be expressed, while picking does not necessarily. Choices that allow for the expression of one's preferences are likely to better facilitate a sense of autonomy and subsequent motivation. In fact, there is evidence to suggest that the greater the extent to which choosing supports feelings of autonomy, the greater the benefits. For example, research has suggested that choices that allow for personalization may be particularly effective (e.g., Cordova & Lepper, 1996). Tafarodi Mehranvar, Panton, and Milne (2002) found in two studies that only choices reflecting personal preferences increased confidence in the task outcome and boosted performance-related self-esteem. Choice had few effects when participants were asked to select options based on what they thought the majority of people similar to them would most prefer. Similarly, variety (or the mere appearance of variety) may effectively enhance the benefits of choice by increasing feelings of autonomy from choosing. A series of studies found that when choosers are unfamiliar with the domain or options they are asked to choose among, being presented with a greater rather than fewer number of categories (holding constant the number of individual options) positively influenced their satisfaction (Mogilner, Rudnick, & Iyengar, 2008). Presumably, the presence of categories signals greater variety among the available options. This in turn may enhance the sense that one can truly express his or her personal preferences from choosing and thus increases feelings of autonomy. All in all, these examples serve to illustrate the point that more powerful choices are those that effectively enhance feelings of autonomy.

LEVEL OF EFFORT

In addition to the extent to which choices provided enhance perceptions of control, competence, or autonomy, the extent to which a choice is effortful may also play a role in determining when choice may lead to motivational benefits or decrements. That is, in line with a self-regulatory strength model, making a choice has a cost for expenditure of effort. The greater the extent to which making a choice is an effortful process, the less likely it will be to afford motivational benefits. Given that choosing may simultaneously support feelings of control, autonomy, and competence, while being an effortful process, it seems reasonable that positive and negative consequences can both occur under various conditions and can even occur together.

There is some research to support this assertion that there are limited benefits to choosing when greater effort is needed to make choices. For example, in one study designed to investigate the role of inner effort, Vohs and colleagues (2008) found that making choices about a computer and associated services, support options, and accessories required more effort and resulted in less persistence on a subsequent anagram task than the process of just thinking about and forming a preference regarding the options or implementing choices previously made by others. Similarly, Vohs, Finkenauer, and Baumeister (2011) had participants either execute preordained choices without thinking about them, deliberate between options without choosing, or both deliberate and choose. The last condition was the most depleting on subsequent tasks, whereas executing choices without deliberating produced little depletion. Deliberating without choosing still depleted some resources, but not as much as deliberating and choosing.

The extent to which options are similar or attractive may influence the effort needed to make a decision and the benefits of choosing. For example, choosers make suboptimal choices and delay making choices when confronted with equally attractive or highly risky options (Luce, 1998; Mischel & Ebbesen, 1970; Shafir, Simonson, & Tversky, 1993; Shafir & Tversky, 1992; Yates & Mischel, 1979). Higgins, Trope, and Kwon (1999) found that children demonstrated less intrinsic motivation when

given two equally preferred activities to choose from compared to when just one preferred activity was offered. Likewise, when required to choose among unwanted options (as opposed to choosing to do something undesirable or nothing at all, as is common in dissonance research), the effort needed to make a decision may be greater (Higgins, 1998; Janis & Mann, 1977; Lewin, 1951), diminishing the benefits of choosing. In one study (Botti & Iyengar, 2004), participants were asked to either choose or not choose among either appealing or unappealing yogurt flavors. Although all of the subjects preferred to choose for themselves, choosers reported greater satisfaction than nonchoosers only when the yogurt options were appealing. When the yogurt options were unappealing, choosers were less satisfied than nonchoosers. Furthermore, when the yogurt flavors were unappealing, choosers ate less yogurt than nonchoosers.

Wang and colleagues (Wang, Novemsky, Dhar, & Baumeister, in press) found that the structure of the options influenced whether making choices was depleting. In one condition, participants made a choice in which there was a fairly linear trade-off between cost and quality across options, so that each increase in price yielded a roughly proportional increase in quality. In another condition, however, the trade-offs were not linear, and one of the choices yielded the best value in the sense that it offered much higher quality for only a slight increase in price. Participants who made the latter choice were more likely to make more virtuous future decisions compared to participants who made the former choices, presumably because the nonlinear trade-off choices produced greater depletion by requiring greater effort to make a good decision.

On the flip side, it is often noted that studies in which seemingly trivial choices presumably requiring little effort in order to make decisions provide significant motivational, performance, and well-being benefits. A rather dramatic example is provided by Langer and Rodin (1976) who conducted a field study in a nursing home in which a group of patients were given choices to make relatively inconsequential decisions, such as choosing when to watch a movie or how to arrange their bedroom furniture, or had these same decisions made for them by the nursing home staff. The results showed an increase in choosers' happiness and activity levels relative to nonchoosers, as well as better health conditions and even lower death rates in the long run. Cordova and Lepper (1996) examined the effects of choices over "instructionally irrelevant aspects of the task" among elementary school children involved in an educational computer activity. Participants who were given the opportunity to choose features such as the icon representing them on the game board, the name of their spaceship, and the name of their opponent's spaceship demonstrated enhanced motivation and learning of the mathematical concepts involved in the game compared to participants who were not given a choice. Tafarodi and colleagues (1999) intentionally attempted to trivialize the choice manipulation by giving participants a choice among unusual names to be used in a story. The name options were made highly similar by transposing one pair of consonants within a root name to create each of the options (e.g., Ojebeta, Obejeta, Otebeja, Ojeteba, Otejeba, Obeteja). However, even this somewhat trivial choice led to enhanced perceptions of competence. In a meta-analysis of the effects of choice on intrinsic motivation, my colleagues and I (Patall et al., 2008) found evidence to support the notion that these trivial or instructionally irrelevant choices are the most effective in supporting intrinsic motivation compared to instructionally relevant choices, choices among task, versions of a task, or rewards. We hypothesized that this effect was the result of variation in self-regulatory effort that various kinds of choices requires. That is, instructionally relevant choices (e.g., choosing the method or strategy used to engage in the task, pacing, or who to work with) were hypothesized to be more effortful to the extent that they both provide an opportunity to personalize the task and have potentially influential consequences for learning and performance. Because people are likely aware of the potential for these types of choice to have important consequences, they are more difficult to make, particularly when the choices are equally desirable, because the consequences of that decision are likely to be important to the individual. In contrast, when a choice is of little instructional significance, such as choosing what color paper to write on or what pen to write with, it may be relatively "easier" to make a choice because the implications are minimal, no matter what option is chosen. Nevertheless, these forms of choice still provide the opportunity to personalize the task and gain a sense of autonomy without the cost of having expended a great deal of effort. Consequently, it may be these "easy" choices require the least effort and allow for more positive effects of being given a choice.

For similar reasons, the number of options provided or the total number of choices an individual makes within a limited time frame may also moderate the effects of providing choice. While a self-determination model might predict that too few options or choices may not be powerful enough to bolster the individual's sense of autonomy, a self-regulatory model would suggest that many options or choices requires exertion of more effort and energy. As the cognitive "workload" of deciding between options and making choices increases with the number of options and discrete choices available, choice may come to be experienced as overwhelming rather than motivating and decision making may become impaired as a consequence (Botti & Iyengar, 2006; Greenleaf & Lehmann, 1995; Huffman & Kahn, 1998; Malhotra, 1982; Payne, Bettman, & Johnson, 1993; Shugan, 1980).

In fact, research has supported the proposition that more choice does not necessarily lead to greater motivation. In a series of three studies, Iyengar and Lepper (2000) asked that participants choose between 6 or 24 options. They found that people were more likely to purchase gourmet jams or chocolates or undertake an optional class essay assignment when offered the small array of options to choose among. Other studies across a variety of contexts have found that offering too many options may have detrimental effects. For example, the presence of more rather than fewer options has been found to make decision makers more likely to decide against choosing, even when the choice of opting out has negative consequences for their future well-being (Iyengar, Jiang, & Kamenica, 2006, (unpublished data); see Botti & Iyengar, 2006). In one study (Chua & Iyengar, 2005), when participants were given an extensive choice of initial themes from which to generate ideas for a print advertisement and told their goal was to be creative, they demonstrated less creativity and more frustration compared to those who were given fewer themes. Furthermore, participants in the limited choice condition reported more interest in participating in similar future studies than those in the extensive choice condition. Similarly, job seekers who pursued more rather than fewer job opportunities were less satisfied with their accepted job offer and reported less commitment to their position (Iyengar, Elwork, & Schwartz, 2006). Likewise, as employers increase the number of investment options provided to employees in 401(k) plans, employees become less likely to participate in any, even though this often means forgoing an employer match of several thousand dollars per year (Iyengar, Jiang, & Huberman, 2004). However, when the cognitive effort needed to make choices is alleviated, the benefits of choosing may be apparent even when the set of options is extensive. For example, providing categories may allow choosers to clearly perceive the variety available in extensive choice sets and reduce the effort needed to differentiate among options and make a choice. Consequently, grouping options into categories appears to alleviate the detrimental effects of having an extensive set of options to choose among (Mogilner et al., 2008).

Furthermore, in addition to the number of options one has, the number of discrete choices one makes in a limited time frame may also have limited benefits. The meta-analysis by myself and colleagues (Patall et al., 2008) suggested that, indeed, there were an optimal number of choices to be made. Specifically, studies in which participants made between two and four choices produced the greatest effect on intrinsic motivation compared to when participants made more or fewer choices. Similarly, Vohs and colleagues (2008) found that as the amount of time engaging in a choice-making task (choosing items for a wedding registry) and therefore the number of choices made increased, the more depletion participants demonstrated. Specifically, participants asked to engage in the choice-making task for a longer compared to shorter duration waited more time to tell the researcher that there was a technical problem occurring on a subsequent task that prevented them from continuing. All in all, it would seem that making more choices requires more effort expenditure and there is likely a point at which the balance among motivational effects of choosing are tipped from beneficial to null or even deleterious.

FRAME OF REFERENCE

Clearly, there are a variety of factors that influence the motivational effects of choice. However, it also matters how one is treated when choices are intentionally restricted. The assumptions of theories previously mentioned have attested to this. According to self-determination theory, conditions that are experienced as controlling will diminish intrinsic motivation (Deci et al., 1989). Similarly, reactance theory (Brehm, 1966) suggests that when an option or alternative course of action is explicitly eliminated, people will evaluate whatever options are left more negatively, and those they were not allowed to choose more positively.

In line with both theories, the meta-analysis of empirical studies on the impact of choice on intrinsic motivation I conducted with colleagues (Patall et al., 2008) suggested that the effect of choice was stronger when participants given choice were compared to the most controlling forms of no-choice conditions. Specifically, the effect of choice was strongest in comparison to no-choice conditions in which participants' lack of choice was made salient by explicitly denying choice. Similarly, the effect of choice on intrinsic motivation was greatest in comparison to control conditions in which participants were aware that there were alternatives not open to them versus control conditions in which participants were not aware of alternatives. Under these conditions, participants likely experienced a decrement in intrinsic motivation. Consequently, the difference in intrinsic motivation between the choice conditions and these most controlling no-choice conditions was greater than the difference between the choice condition and less controlling no-choice conditions, such as when participants were randomly assigned an option, were assigned an option by an individual who was not significant to the participant in any way (e.g., the experimenter), or were unaware that options other than their assignment existed.

SUMMARY

Clearly, choices vary in form and type. Not all choices are equally motivating and in fact some choices may be depleting. A review of existing research suggests several underlying themes may explain when choice has positive, negative, or no effects. In particular, while choice need not be explicit, individuals need to perceive that they have the freedom to choose in order for effects (whether beneficial or detrimental) to be experienced. Choices that effectively enhance feelings of autonomy, control, and competence are likely to successfully motivate behavior and facilitate adaptive outcomes. Likewise, choices that lack the ability to support feelings of autonomy, control, or competence, or are experienced as controlling, are unlikely to lead to beneficial effects and may even diminish motivation or lead to detrimental outcomes. The previous review also highlights that choices may often come with a cost. That is, choice can be an effortful process. A look at the literature on various types and forms of choice suggests that when choice is made to be a more effortful process (e.g., choices require greater deliberation, more complex cognitive evaluation in order to determine the best option, reflect greater similarity between options, or the number of options and choices are extensive), the benefits of choosing become more unlikely and the detriments of choosing become more likely. Given that choice may vary both in the level of effort required as well as the extent to which feelings of autonomy, control, or competence is supported, choice may have simultaneously positive and negative effects that must be negotiated. On one side, choices that are highly effortful and lack support for important psychological needs are likely to lead to detrimental outcomes. Conversely, choices that minimize the cognitive effort needed to make a decision, while still enhance feelings of control, autonomy, or competence, may provide the greatest benefits. However, the complexity of choosing becomes clear upon considering that most choices will require both some level of effort and provide some level of support for important psychological needs. How the effects of these choices become negotiated in a cost–benefit-like analysis is less clear, but it would seem that trade-offs must occur in most choice situations. Finally, the previous review illustrated that not only does the type or form of choice given impact the effects observed, but it also matters how individuals are treated when not given a choice. In line with the notion that it is the sense of control, autonomy, and competence that underlies the powerful effects of choosing, when these needs are diminished in no-choice situations, the difference between choosing and not choosing may become even more apparent.

Characteristics of the Individual

Clearly, the type, number, and various other characteristics of the choice and options provided can influence the effects of receiving or perceiving choices. However, people bring with them an array of individual characteristics that are likely to influence how choice is interpreted. An individual's initial levels of interest, value, and perceived competence for the options or tasks, cultural or socioeconomic background, or developmental level may all influence the effect of choice.

INITIAL LEVELS OF INTEREST, PERCEIVED COMPETENCE, AND VALUE FOR TASKS AND OPTIONS

Individuals are expected to vary in their initial levels of interest and motivation for the tasks involved, as well as their preferences and values for the particular options available in any choice-making situation. As such, this individual variation may influence how choice is experienced by one person to the next. Some research has suggested that providing choices may be particularly beneficial for those individuals who lack existing motivation and personal interest for the task at hand (Flowerday & Schraw, 2000; Schraw, Flowerday, & Lehman, 2001). That is, for those who lack initial interest in

an activity, the ability to choose aspects of it may create interest and motivation where little previously existed. This is particularly relevant to the educational setting. In a phenomenological study of teachers' beliefs about instructional choice (Flowerday & Schraw, 2000), teachers reported that choice was perceived to be especially beneficial for students who had low interest and little motivation for the task at hand. In particular, many teachers reported that they believed choice increased the motivation of students with low initial interest because it gave them a sense of control. A similar pattern was found in one set of experiments that isolated the effects of choice and personal interest on situational interest and text comprehension. Personal interest ratings were made prior to reading a text. Some students then were given a choice of what to read, whereas others were assigned a text. Results suggested that only for students with low personal interest, having a choice of what to read significantly increased situational interest (see Schraw, Flowerday, & Lehman, 2001 for a description of this unpublished finding). In fact, this notion may be the very base on which a dissonance effect operates. That is, in the traditional dissonance study, it is inherent to the design that participants have little motivation to perform a behavior counter to their existing attitudes. However, freely choosing to engage in that counterattitudinal behavior motivates a shift in attitudes.

Likewise, an individual's perception of competence for the tasks involved may also influence the effects of choice. On one hand, when individuals feel that they may be somewhat inadequate in performing a task, having a choice may alleviate some of those concerns by allowing them to choose aspects of the task most preferred and tailor the task to their particular interests, values, and skills. That is, choosing may lead to motivational benefits for individuals with low perceptions of competence, in particular because choosing allows them to feel that the task is more manageable than would have been the case if they had not been given the opportunity to choose. Whereas for individuals with high perceptions of competence for a task, choosing may confer little additional advantage if they feel that the task is manageable regardless of their ability to tailor it to their particular preferences, interests, and skills. Alternatively, it seems reasonable to propose the opposite pattern. That is, individuals who perceive themselves to be highly competent on a task may benefit most from having choice, given their greater expertise and potentially enhanced ability to make effective decisions. Whereas individuals who perceive themselves to lack competence on a task may feel overwhelmed by having to make choices. Furthermore, when the number of options or choices to be made becomes excessive, individuals with low perceived competence for the task at hand may be particularly likely to feel overwhelmed, given their perception of having more limited expertise. There is some evidence to suggest possibilities. For example, exploratory analyses in one series of experimental studies repeatedly revealed a trend in which the effect of choice appeared to be more beneficial for individuals with low perceived competence and the effect of restricting choice appeared to be more detrimental to individuals with high perceived competence (Patall, 2009). Another study suggested that among college students who were given feedback to lead them to believe they would perform very well on an upcoming task, choice had a positive effect on motivation for the task. However, for college students who were led to believe that they would perform poorly on an upcoming task, choice had a negative effect on motivation (Patall, Dacy, & Han, unpublished data). Further, Chua and Iyengar (2005) found that an individual's level of self-efficacy may moderate when an extensive set of options becomes overwhelming and when it is motivating. That is, in one experiment, participants were assigned to either a high-choice condition, in which they were given six types of ribbon and four types of wrapping paper for a gift-wrapping task, or a low-choice condition in which they were given only two types of ribbon and two types of wrapping paper. For each of the choice conditions, half of the subjects were told that the goal was to come up with as creative a gift wrap as possible (creativity goal) while the other half of the subjects were simply told to do their "best" in the gift-wrapping task (performance goal). Results showed that there was no difference in divergent thinking (i.e., use of more unusual materials in gift wrapping) among subjects with high creative self-efficacy as a function of choice set provided. However, participants with low creative self-efficacy were more likely to think divergently when given fewer as opposed to greater options. More specifically, for subjects with high creative self-efficacy, a greater number of options led to more divergent thinking when the goal was to be as creative as possible.

Once in the choice-making situation, if an individual personally values the options and enjoys the process of making a choice, he or she may be more likely to experience the benefits and less likely to experience the costs of choice making due to an increased sense of autonomy from making choices reflective of the self and his or her personal autonomy

(Baumeister & Vohs, 2007; Deci & Ryan, 1985; Katz & Assor, 2007; Reeve, Nix, & Hamm, 2003; Ryan, 1993; Williams, 1998). Conversely, when an individual has little value for the options provided, choice making may be experienced ambivalently or even negatively. This assertion seems probable in light of the evidence previously reviewed suggesting that choices that are intentionally constructed to facilitate preference matching and that allow individuals to experience a greater sense of autonomy (i.e., through personalization, variety, or unconstrained options) often yield impressive benefits. However, even in situations in which choices are intentionally created to allow individuals to freely choose and express their preferences among options, individuals may still vary in their value for the options available or the choice-making process. There is some evidence to suggest that indeed, experiencing the choice-making process as enjoyable may protect individuals from experiencing costs associated with choice making, at least within limits. For example, in one study (Vohs et al., 2008), participants were asked to make a series of choices in the context of creating a bridal registry (i.e., selecting wedding presents to receive). Some participants enjoyed the choice-making task, whereas others found it aversive. Results suggested that individuals who liked the bridal registry task did not experience depletion on subsequent activities as long as the task was brief, that is, only a moderate number of choices were made. When the bridal registry task was long, that is, many decisions had to be made, participants experienced depletion on subsequent tasks, regardless of whether they liked the task or detested it.

While little direct evidence exists on the topic as of yet, an individual's personal choice-making strategy may be one factor likely to influence the motivational benefits and detriments of choosing. According to Simon (1955, 1956, 1957), choice-making strategies can be distinguished as either "maximizing" versus "satisficing." For the individual who engages in a maximizing choice-making strategy, the strategy is to seek out the best alternative by engaging in an exhaustive search of all possibilities (Schwartz et al., 2002). For the individual who engages in a satisficing choice-making strategy, the strategy is to determine an acceptable option or option that is "good enough." Thus, a satisficing strategy requires only that the individual search until an option is encountered that crosses the threshold of acceptability. Research has suggested that individuals who engage in maximizing choice-making strategies may make better decisions. For example, in one study, maximizers performed better in the job search process than satisficers, earning higher salaries in their resulting job (Iyengar, Wells, & Schwartz, 2006). However, despite being more likely to make successful decisions and obtain desirable outcomes in the long run, maximizers may also be less satisfied with the choice process and the outcomes of choosing. In this same study, maximizers reported feeling more "pessimistic," "stressed," "tired," "anxious," "worried," "overwhelmed," and "depressed" throughout the entire choice process and with their resulting jobs (Iyengar, Wells, & Schwartz, 2006). Given this relation, it seems likely that one's preferred choice-making strategy will impact the motivational benefits or detriments of choosing to the extent that the experience of choice will be less enjoyable, satisfying, or rewarding for maximizers compared to satisficers, particularly when an extensive set of options are provided. While choosing may lead to motivational benefits for satisficers, maximizers may be more likely to experience the costs associated with choosing.

An individual's regulatory focus might also be particularly important in determining how different individuals will perceive choice or will value various options (Higgins, 1998). According to the regulatory focus theory (Higgins, 1998) all goal-directed behaviors are regulated by two distinct motivational systems: promotion and prevention focus. Promotion-focused individuals are primarily concerned with accomplishment and advancement. They in turn, tend to use an "approach" strategy to gain accomplishments. In contrast, prevention-focused individuals are more concerned with safety and fulfillment of responsibilities. They, in turn, tend to use an "avoidance" strategy to avoid losses. Consequently, an individual's personal orientation to either approach may influence the value attributed to options provided in a choice-making context. Research has in fact suggested that when an object or course of action is consistent with one's regulatory focus, that option will be allocated more value (Forster et al., 1998, 2000; Idson, Liberman, & Higgins, 2000). Based on this relation between regulatory focus and value for a course of action, it seems reasonable to suggest that benefits of choosing will be more apparent if available options are consistent with an individual's regulatory focus. However, again, there is little evidence that addresses these predictions.

Going further, to the extent that one knows what he or she wants and can therefore make a choice based on his or her own values and preferences, having the ability to choose is likely to empower and motivate.

However, many times people do not know their own preferences before making a decision and construct them on the spot during the decision-making process (Feldman & Lynch, 1988; Payne, Bettman, & Johnson, 1993). In this case in which personal preferences are not well known, choice may have more limited benefits as the cognitive effort needed to make a decision can be great even in the context of a limited number of options or decisions to be made (Chernev, 2003; Dhar, 1997; Huffman & Kahn, 1998; Shafir, Simonson, & Tversky, 1993). Furthermore, the limited benefits and potential costs of making choices when one's preferences are unclear may only be exacerbated as the number of options increases (Chua & Iyengar, 2006).

In sum, individual differences in levels of initial interest and perceived competence for tasks, as well as variation in one's value for the options and the choice-making process, play a complex role in determining the effects of choice. Though the evidence is currently limited, findings suggest that choice may be especially beneficial for those who lack initial interest for the task at hand. It remains unclear as of yet whether choice is more or less beneficial for those who feel least competent for the task, though the benefits of providing an extensive amount of choice may be limited to those who are the most confident. Furthermore, once in a choice-making situation, it may be important that individuals value the options provided and enjoy the choice-making process in order for choice making to afford motivational advantages and avoid costs. One's regulatory orientation and preferred choice-making strategy may be important in determining which options are likely to be valued and when the choice-making process will be enjoyable for particular individuals. Furthermore, the extent to which preferences are clearly known to the individual may also determine when choosing is more or less effortful, enjoyable, and in turn, motivating or detrimental. Additional research is needed to investigate these possibilities.

CULTURAL AND SOCIOECONOMIC DIFFERENCES

An individual's cultural or socioeconomic background has also been found to influence the motivating effects of choice. Culture has been hypothesized to moderate the effects of choice or lack of personal choice in light of seminal work suggesting that in individualistic cultures (including the United States), personal agency and independence may be central to one's self-concept (Markus & Kitayama, 1991). However, in more collectivistic cultures (such as those in Asian countries) agency may have less importance. Instead, non-Westerners may have more interdependent self-concepts in which the goal of belongingness is achieved by acting in accordance with one's social obligations to others (Markus & Kitayama, 1991). Consequently, making personal choices without reference to significant others may not hold as much importance for individuals from interdependent cultures as it does for those from independent cultures. In fact, evidence suggests that individuals from more interdependent cultures construe fewer actions of themselves and others as choices, are more likely to construe actions as choices when it involved a response to another person, and are less likely to choose based on their own personal preferences (Savani, Markus, & Conner, 2008; Savani, Markus, Naidu, Kumar, & Berlia, 2010). Furthermore, under circumstances in which significant others are considered, not choosing may support important psychological needs, including autonomy, and enhance subsequent motivation for individuals from interdependent opposed to independent cultures.

In line with this reasoning, previous research has suggested that one's cultural background may influence the extent to which a motivational state of dissonance is experienced as a function of choosing. For example, Heine and Lehman (1997) found that after choosing among similarly desirable CDs, Canadians demonstrated the classic dissonance finding, expressing increased liking for chosen CDs and decreased liking for unchosen CDs. However, Japanese participants demonstrated no such spreading of alternatives. Similarly, Kitiyama, Snibbe, Markus, and Suzuki (2008) showed that the standard dissonance paradigm did not produce dissonance reduction among Japanese participants. However, when asked to estimate the preference of the average college student before making choices, Japanese participants demonstrated a spreading of alternatives, whereas American participants demonstrated a significant spread of alternatives regardless of whether they were primed to think of others or not. That is, for European American participants, choosing produces dissonance to the extent that one is worried about his or her own competence. However, for Japanese participants, choosing produces dissonance to the extent that one is worried about possible rejection by others.

Furthermore, the effect of choice on intrinsic motivation, learning, and performance-related outcomes may vary depending on the culture of the individual. For example, in a field study in which an extensive questionnaire was given to Citigroup employees in nine different countries ranging in levels of individualism (Iyengar, Lepper, Hernandez, DeVoe, & Alpert, 2001 (unpublished data); see Chua & Iyengar, 2006), results suggested that perceptions of choice predicted job satisfaction, intrinsic motivation, perceptions of fair treatment at work, and job performance (as reported by the employees managers) significantly better for employees in the United States as compared to employees in Asian countries. Furthermore, comparisons among various ethnic groups in the United States indicated that the perception of choice was a stronger predictor of these outcomes for European, African, and Hispanic Americans as compared to Asian Americans.

Experimental evidence has further teased apart cultural variation in the effects of choice on motivation. Iyengar and Lepper (1999) found that intrinsic motivation was enhanced for students of all cultural backgrounds when a personal choice was made compared to when an unfamiliar person (i.e., the experimenter) made a choice for the individual. However, among Asian American students, intrinsic motivation, performance, learning, and other related outcomes were enhanced most when trusted authority figures or peers made choices for them compared to when a personal choice was made. For Caucasian American students, motivation and performance were most enhanced when making a personal choice. Similarly, in another study (Katz & Assor, 2003), the provision of choice was found to undermine the intrinsic motivation of collectivistically oriented Bedouin children. Somewhat in contrast, Bao and Lam (2008) found that Chinese students reported greater motivation for a word task or a school course and greater task performance for a word task when they had made a personal choice compared to when their mothers or teachers had made the choice for them. However, this effect was moderated by the level of closeness Chinese students felt toward their mother or teacher. For Chinese students who were close to their mothers or teachers, having a choice made for them by their mother or teacher enhanced motivation for the target task just as well as making a personal choice. But for students who were not close to their mothers or teachers, making a personal choice enhanced motivation more than when mothers or teachers chose for the student. Finally, Bao and Lam (2008) showed in an additional study that unlike their findings regarding choosing, students' level of autonomous motivation positively related to self-reported behavioral engagement regardless of how close students felt to their teacher. Together these findings suggest a point made previously, namely, choosing is not synonymous with autonomy. To the extent that having another person make a choice for an individual is perceived to be an autonomous experience (as may be the case for individuals from more collectivistic cultures in which the needs or desires of personally significant others are internalized as part of one's own self-concept), a lack of choice may be equally or more motivating than making a personal choice.

Somewhat parallel to theoretical perspectives of cultural differences in the choice experience, individuals' socioeconomic background may influence their choice-making experience. Scholars have suggested that choice may be particularly relevant to higher socioeconomic status individuals (i.e., those with a college degree or higher) because agency for these individuals emphasizes the expression of uniqueness and control over the environment (Snibbe & Markus, 2005). To the extent that choice is a way to express one's unique preferences and exert control over the environment, choice may be particularly important to individuals of high socioeconomic status. In contrast, among lower socioeconomic status individuals (i.e., those without a college degree), notions of agency emphasize integrity, honesty, and the expression of self-control. For these individuals, personal choice may be less important or may reflect one's connection to others (Snibbe & Markus, 2005; Stephens, Markus, & Townsend, 2007).

In line with this reasoning that individuals from different classes differ in their models of agency, Stephens, Markus, and Townsend (2007) found that the choices of individuals from higher socioeconomic status backgrounds reflected attempts to differentiate themselves from others, whereas the choices of individuals from lower socioeconomic status backgrounds reflected attempts to be similar and connected to others. For example, participants from working class compared to middle class backgrounds more often chose pens that appeared similar to, rather than different from, other pens in the set of options, and they more often chose images they had previously been told were chosen by another participant. Participants from working class relative to middle class backgrounds also liked their chosen objects better when someone else had chosen similarly (either a confederate or a friend). Going further, Snibbe and Markus (2005) found that subjects who held college degrees demonstrated the classic dissonance effect of evaluating chosen objects more positively and rejected objects less positively. However, this effect was not found among those subjects who were high school graduates; for these subjects,

evaluations of chosen objects remained unchanged. In a second study, participants approached in a shopping center were assigned to one of two conditions. Participants in the free-choice condition were asked to choose a pen that they liked from among five types of pens, test out the pen, and complete a pen evaluation survey. Participants in the no-choice condition were denied the pen of their choice due to scarcity and offered a different pen that they subsequently tested and evaluated. The results indicated that college graduate subjects in the no-choice condition evaluated their pens less favorably than those in the free-choice condition. Conversely, high school graduate subjects evaluated their pens equally favorably irrespective of the experimental condition.

DEVELOPMENTAL LEVEL

Developmental level may also be an important characteristic of the individual that may influence how choice is experienced and the effect of choice on subsequent cognitive and motivational outcomes. In particular, developmental level may be important because individuals of different ages may vary in their cognitive capacity to process choices and may be afforded fewer opportunities for choosing (Bereby-Meyer, Assor, & Katz, 2004; Patall et al., 2008). Limited evidence exists to suggest that there are differences in the effects of choice depending on developmental level. In fact, there is no single study in which age has been varied in order to explore possible differences in the effects of choice among individuals of different developmental levels. However, in a recent meta-analysis (Patall et al., 2008) my colleagues and I found that choice had a greater effect on intrinsic motivation for children than for adults. We hypothesized that this effect might be a function of the possibility that children experience fewer opportunities to make choices and to enhance their sense of autonomy than do adults. Consequently, when a child encounters an opportunity to make choices and to experience a sense of autonomy, the effect is more powerful. Future research should systematically investigate how the experience and effects of choice may vary by developmental level.

SUMMARY

Not only does the form and type of the choice given influence the observed effects of choosing but individual differences among the people doing the choosing are likely to influence when choice is more or less beneficial. While the research is limited, there is some evidence to suggest that choice will confer greater motivational benefits and fewer costs when an individual has a clear conception of his or her preferences, values the options available, and enjoys the process of choosing and its outcomes. Likewise, one's initial level of interest and feelings of competence for the tasks involved may influence the extent to which choice is perceived to afford advantages or not and thus have a motivating effect. Due to its relation with one's construal of the self and the importance of personal choice to the self, an individual's cultural or socioeconomic background may influence the experience and effects of choice. In particular, agency may be less central and social connectedness more central to the self-concepts of individuals from more interdependent cultures or lower socioeconomic backgrounds. Consequently, the benefits and detriments of making personal choices or lacking personal choice may be different depending on one's cultural or socioeconomic background and the social conditions under which choices are provided or limited. Finally, given the cognitive complexity of choosing and the extent to which choosing is available to children compared to adults, the effects of choice may vary depending on one's developmental age. Limited evidence has suggested thus far that choosing may be particularly beneficial for children compared to adults, possibly due to children having fewer opportunities for choice. This review of existing research pointed to a number of potentially influential characteristics of the individual that may explain when choice is more or less motivating. However, additional research is needed.

Characteristics of the Situation

Finally, in addition to characteristics of the choices provided and characteristics of the individual doing the choosing, various characteristics of the situation may also influence the effects of choice. In particular, the extent to which the situation emphasizes self-presentational concerns and the level of realism within which choices are provided may be situational factors that influence when choice leads to motivational benefits or detriments. Although little evidence is available in order to examine their impact, several additional situational factors may also be important, including type of the tasks involved, the desirability of subsequent outcomes, and the correspondence between the choices made and the target for which motivation is measured.

SITUATIONS THAT ENHANCE
SELF-PRESENTATIONAL CONCERNS

Burger (1989) suggested that at moderate levels of self-presentational concern, providing choice may indeed lead to motivational and performance benefits through its impact on perceptions of control. For example, in one experiment (Burger, 1987), undergraduates either were or were not allowed to select the response words for a paired-associate memory task. In addition, half the subjects were led to believe that the experimenter who knew of their choice would also know of their performance on the task. The other half thought that the experimenter would not know of their choice or their performance. It was found that choice improved performance on the task only when subjects also believed the experimenter would know of their choice and performance. In a second experiment, participants given a choice of which cognitive aptitude test to take did better on the test than the no-choice participants, but only when they believed their choice and performance would be known by the experimenter and other participants.

However, while the intensification of self-presentational concerns at moderate levels may often facilitate the benefits of choice on motivation and performance, motivation may be hindered when choice is accompanied by factors that raise awareness of public evaluation to distracting or anxiety-provoking levels (Burger, 1989). For example, Burger (1988) found that participants who were given a choice of words in a paired-associates task and a told that both the experimenters and the professor supervising the project would return to discuss their performance did worse on the memory task than those who anticipated the same discussion but did not choose the words. That is, when self-presentational concerns were high, choice had few motivational and performance benefits. However, consistent with choice findings in which only a moderate level of self-presentational concern was created, participants who believed their performance would be known only to one undergraduate experimenter showed an increase in performance when allowed to select the words compared to those who were not given a choice.

LEVEL OF REALISM

The context in which choice is administered may also affect its impact on motivation. That is, choice may be particularly beneficial in settings in which it makes intuitive sense to have choices, seems most realistic, or is most meaningful. For example, choice may be expected to have a larger effect when it is administered in a classroom with students or in a workplace with workers as opposed to in a contrived laboratory setting in which choice may often be experienced as meaningless or inauthentic. In fact, in a recent meta-analysis (Patall et al., 2008), my colleagues and I found that the effect of choice varied as a function of setting. Specifically, choice had the greatest effect on intrinsic motivation when the choice manipulation was implemented in a well-controlled natural setting, for example, when students were taken to a separate room within the school they attend or employees were taken to a separate room within their workplace in order to examine the effects of giving them choices, compared to when choices were examined in a traditional laboratory setting. That is, when the choices given are experienced as more authentic, their impact may be greater.

TYPE OF TASKS

It has been suggested that choice may be particularly motivating when it involves a task that is not interesting to begin with (e.g., Tafarodi et al., 1999), although there is little evidence to examine this supposition. That is, the increase in motivation as a function of choosing will be more consequential for a task that is not especially motivating to begin with than for one that is already highly motivating. For highly engaging and naturally interesting activities, it is possible that the benefits of choosing may be more limited. In line with this notion, it is worth noting that many demonstrations of improved motivation and performance due to choice have involved neutral or lackluster activities, such as solving anagram puzzles and paired-associate word learning (e.g., Iyengar & Lepper, 1999; Monty, Rosenberger, & Perlmuter, 1973; Perlmuter & Monty, 1973). A recent demonstration of the classroom effects of choice with a traditionally boring task, homework, showed that when high school students were allowed to choose among homework options identical in the content covered, they reported greater interest and enjoyment for their homework, greater perceived competence for homework, enhanced homework completion, and improved test scores at the end of the instructional unit (Patall, Cooper, & Wynn, 2010).

DESIRABILITY OF OUTCOMES

Related to the notion that the benefits of choosing are limited to conditions in which the choice involves attractive rather than unappealing options (Botti & Iyengar, 2004), motivation and related benefits of choosing may also be restricted to situations in which the outcomes of choosing bring about desirable outcomes. That is, there may be

fewer benefits and greater costs of choosing under tragic circumstances in which undesirable outcomes will be experienced regardless of the choice made. For example, Beattie and colleagues (1994) found that when people were asked to make choices about very consequential decisions with undesirable outcomes regardless of the decision (e.g., a parent was confronted with having to choose which of two children would receive a bone marrow transplant when both children will die without the procedure), not only did parents experience guilt, regret, and psychological distress, but they also preferred that the decision be left to fate or another decision maker. Similarly, Botti, Orfali, and Iyengar (2009) found that when faced with the consequential decision of having to discontinue their infants' life support, people experienced greater negative feelings and less coping ability than when the same choices were made by a physician. Although participants faced with this kind of tragic decision were resistant to giving up the option to choose, they had a weaker desire for autonomy and disliked having to make a decision. Given such aversive affective and well-being responses to choosing, as well as the reduced desire to choose, it seems reasonable to suggest that the motivation to engage in behaviors related to such tragic choices would be limited to nonexistent.

CORRESPONDENCE BETWEEN CHOICE OPTIONS AND MOTIVATION TARGET

Finally, one potentially influential factor may be the correspondence between the choices made and the target for which motivation is being considered. According to a self-determination perspective, choice making is expected to enhance subsequent persistence and liking for those objects and activities which relate to the choices previously made. In contrast, a self-regulatory strength depletion model suggests that choice making will diminish persistence on subsequent activities. However, there is an important methodological difference between the self-regulatory depletion and self-determination perspectives. Namely, the effect of making choices within the context of the self-regulatory depletion framework has always been tested by examining subsequent persistence on a task separate from the choice-making activity. Within the self-determination theory perspective, the effects of choice are typically examined for the same tasks for which choices were originally made. Going further, even from a self-determination perspective, choice making would be expected to have few benefits when motivation was assessed for targets unrelated to the choice-making activity. It seems reasonable to suggest that choice making may provide motivational benefits for those activities and objects related to the choices previously made and simultaneously incur undesirable motivational and self-regulatory costs for activities and objects unrelated to the choice made. While the correspondence between choice content and motivational target has yet to be the focus of study in understanding the effects of choices, the preponderance of evidence supporting both self-determination and self-regulatory depletion perspectives (as previously reviewed) suggest that this is likely to be an important factor.

SUMMARY

In this section, the roles of various situational characteristics in choice effects were described. Though existing evidence is limited, several factors may help to explain variation in the effects of choice. First, choices may be less beneficial when self-presentational concerns are heightened to anxiety-producing levels or when outcomes are undesirable despite having been chosen. Second, settings which promote the perception that choosing is a meaningful and authentic experience are more likely to produce strong effects of choice. Benefits of choosing may also be particularly likely when the tasks involved are not interesting to begin with. That is, actors may be more likely to benefit from having choices for dull tasks because choosing allows them to make the task more personally interesting, relevant, or meaningful. Finally, it seems important to consider the methodological underpinnings of studies looking at the effects of choosing in order to explain variation in effects. In particular, there may be little reason to expect a motivating effect of choosing when there is little correspondence between the subject of the choice and the motivational target.

Lingering Issues in Determining the Motivational Effects of Providing Choices

As the previous review suggests, the experience and effects of choice are not uniform across outcomes, settings, and people. A look at the cumulative evidence suggests that in many cases, opportunities for choosing may motivate behavior in various ways and through a variety of mechanisms. However, there appear to be many limits to the benefits of choosing. That said, a number of lingering issues continue to obfuscate our understanding of the effects of choosing.

The Role of Preferences

One such issue is that of the role of preference matching in the effect of choice. That is, it remains in question as to whether there is any motivational effect of choosing beyond that of having one's preferences. This issue has recently emerged in the cognitive dissonance literature (Chen, 2008; Chen & Risen, 2009; Sagarin, & Skowronski, 2008). Specifically, Chen (2008) has argued that a methodology central to the cognitive dissonance literature (the free-choice paradigm in which participants' rank several options, choose or do not choose between two approximately equally attractive options, then rerank the items) has suffered from an inability to separately measure how much choices affect people's preferences and how much they simply reflect those preferences. The argument is that the traditional paradigm cannot properly test for dissonance because it fails to account for revealed preferences. That is, preranking only ensures that the choices are approximately equal in attractiveness, not exactly equal and that people simply choose the option that they prefer, even if the difference is minimal. Thus, even without the motivating effect of cognitive dissonance, a subject's choices among objects will change subsequent rankings. This is because if the initial ranking is an imperfect measure of preferences, then a subject's choice is new information about his or her preferences; choices reflect how subjects feel about the goods they are choosing between. The option chosen is not random, and comparisons which use that option must take this into account. In defense of the traditional paradigm, other scholars have argued that people do not always choose the option most preferred (Sagarin & Skowronski, 2008). Even so, it seems reasonable to suggest that when testing for choice effects, it is necessary to begin with an experimental design that explicitly controls for revealed preferences (Chen, 2008).

A similar issue exists in the literature looking at the effects of choosing on intrinsic motivation, effort, persistence, performance, learning, and related outcomes. In fact, few if any studies designs have successfully addressed the confounding between choosing and having one's preference. A common design among studies looking at the effects of choosing on intrinsic motivation and related outcomes is to use yoking or matching in order to control for the particular task or options that the individual receives. Specifically, in a yoked design, the experimenter matches a control participant with an experimental participant so that in both conditions there are an equal number of participants doing the same task or having the same task options (e.g., Iyengar & Lepper, 1999; Zuckerman et al., 1978). In this way, a yoked design will perfectly control for the confounding effect of the task or option the participant chose or is assigned. Matched designs also attempt to control for the confounding effect of task; however, this is accomplished by excluding participants who do not engage in a target activity or option. While these design strategies rule out the possibility that differences between the choice and no-choice conditions can be attributed to the fact that participants in the choice condition chose different options than those that were assigned to participants in the no-choice condition, they do not successfully control for the preference matching that is possible in the choice condition. That is, even though a no-choice participant was assigned the same option as his or her choice participant counterpart, this assigned option may not reflect the no-choice participant's preferences. As such, differences attributed to choice making may actually be attributable to the fact that participants in one group received options that they prefer, while participants in the other condition did not. It is possible that the act of personally choosing may confer no additional benefit beyond having received one's preferences.

There is little evidence that partitions the effect of choosing from the effect of having one's preference. One study suggested that choosing, even when preference matching is near impossible, may still confer motivational benefits (Henry, 1994). Henry (1994) attempted to separate the effect of choosing from preference by having participants choose or be assigned almanac questions based only on an uninformative label (Set A or Set B) with no information on characteristics that might differentiate the options given. She found that among males, having a choice produced enhanced perceptions of competence prior to engaging in the task, although having this type of choice produced no performance benefits. Other studies have found that choice may have few if any benefits when information about the options is unavailable, and therefore preference matching is impossible. In two studies, Flowerday and colleagues (Flowerday et al., 2004) had participants choose between two sealed packets of materials (Packet A and Packet B) without other information presented on which to base a decision. In this case, choice had no benefits for participants' attitudes (i.e., motivation, enjoyment, satisfaction) toward the reading task, their engagement in the task, or subsequent learning, controlling for prior interest in the reading topic or interest for the reading material reported after engaging in the task. In contrast, students' reports of the interest experienced while reading the text significantly predicted attitudes and engagement in the task.

With such limited information on the effects of choice when separated from the role of preferences it is difficult as of yet to tell whether the power of choice goes beyond the effect of having one's preferences. However, several points seem warranted based on the accumulated evidence and theory on choice effects. Given that much of the power of choice seems to be dependent on the extent to which choosing supports feelings of control, competence, and autonomy, choices that are made without information on which to base a decision are unlikely to have benefits. That is, undecipherable choices are unlikely to have benefits because, aside from not being able to preference match, these sorts of choices do not lead the actor to feel more in control of outcomes, more competent, or more autonomous. As such, these designs may not be the best way to separate the independent effect of choosing from having one's preference. In fact, based on the previous review, being asked to choose without information to base one's decision would be expected to yield no or even negative effects to the extent this type of situation may be perceived as highly controlling. A preferred research design strategy would be to assess preferences in advance of providing choices so that no-choice participants may be assigned their preferences. This suggestion would be relevant even in cases in which choice is illusory. For example, in a case in which the options participants choose have no bearing on the task they are asked to engage in, as we have seen, a powerful effect may still lie in the mere perception of having chosen one's preferences. It remains relevant to assess one's prior preferences even if in the end the choice or assignment is only between different labels for a single option. Furthermore, given the seeming importance of people's needs for control and autonomy under many circumstances, it seems reasonable to suggest that choosing is likely to yield small benefits above and beyond having one's preference. However, certainly the most pronounced effects of choosing are likely to emerge when comparing those who choose based on personal preferences to those who do not choose or receive their preferences.

Future Research on Factors That Enhance or Inhibit Choice Effects

This review has highlighted a number of potentially influential factors in determining when choosing is more or less motivating and when it may even be detrimental. However, as has been highlighted throughout, many of these factors have yet to be the systematic focus of study in single experimental designs. Rather, in this narrative review (as is often the case, even in quantitative reviews using meta-analysis), many important factors have been identified using patterns that emerge across studies rather than within studies. For example, much of the evidence drawn on to conclude that choice effects vary with the extent to which choosing is an effortful process makes assumptions about particular kinds of choices being more or less effortful and draw comparisons across studies. Research in which the effort exerted in making a choice is systematically varied in a single experimental design is needed to explicitly test these assertions. Similarly, though an initial look at the existing research suggests that factors such as the frame of reference, initial levels of value, interest, or perceived competence for options and tasks, developmental age, type of task, or correspondence between the choice options and motivational target are likely to be important factors, there is limited evidence on which such claims are made. Furthermore, influential factors are likely to interact in complex ways. The burden falls on future research to systematically investigate factors suggested here and elsewhere in well-controlled experimental designs. Additional research is needed to reveal which factors are truly influential moderators as well as examine the complex relationships that may exist among these moderators. Finally, as can be garnered by this review, choice has been linked to a variety of motivation-related outcomes. It seems reasonable to suggest that various outcomes may be differentially related to choice when various moderators are taken into consideration. As one example, some choices may more effectively enhance feelings of control, while other forms of choice may more effectively enhance feelings of autonomy. Various motivational consequences, such as intrinsic motivation or perceived competence, may be differentially impacted to the extent that choices are intentionally designed to satisfy each of these various needs. Likewise, the interaction of choice making with other important moderators may lead to different effects depending on what motivational outcome is considered. Future research is needed to tease apart the differential pathways by which choice may lead to various motivational outcomes.

Conclusions

A review of the relations between choice and motivation suggests that the relationship is far reaching, reciprocal, and complex. Choice making has been implicated in numerous psychological theories, as well as in social science theories more broadly. The motivational factors implicated to influence choice making are numerous—too numerous in fact to even adequately review here. However, perhaps equally complex is the influence of the experience of choice on motivation. The cumulative evidence suggests that under most circumstances, the presence of choice may have powerful motivating effects, helping to shape attitudes, enhance perceptions of control and competence, intrinsically motivate behavior, as well as enhance a variety of adaptive outcomes (e.g., learning, performance, effort, satisfaction, and creativity, among others). However, choosing is likely not equal across all types of choices, people, and circumstances, and the benefits of choosing are not had without cost. Whether for bad or good, choosing is a necessity in most people's lives. Furthermore, the potential benefits and limits of choice suggest that there are practical implications of understanding choice effects for classroom, workplace, and therapeutic settings. As such, it is important for both theory and practice that future research continue to provide a firm foundation on which to base conclusions about the circumstances under which choice is more or less beneficial. Although simplicity is always desirable, an accurate understanding of choice effects requires this more complex analysis of the phenomena.

Future Directions

1. Few of the choice-, person-, and situation-related characteristics proposed to moderate the effect of choice on motivation are well established based on existing literature. As such, what are the most important factors in determining when choosing will lead to motivational benefits or decrements, and stronger or weaker effects?

2. How do important choice-, person-, and situation-related factors moderating the role of choice interact to affect the relation between choice and motivation?

3. How do the effects of choice vary from one motivational outcome to the next (e.g., intrinsic motivation versus perceived competence versus task value) when considering the role of important choice-, person-, and situation-related moderating factors?

4. What is the effect of choice on motivation after accounting for the role of preference matching?

References

Ajzen, I. (1985). From intentions to actions: A theory of planned behavior. In J. Kuhl & J. Beckman (Eds.),

Action-control: From cognition to behavior (pp. 11–39). Heidelberg, Germany: Springer.

Ajzen, I. (1988). *Attitudes, personality, and behavior*. Chicago, IL: Dorsey Press.

Ajzen, I. (2002). Perceived behavioral control, self-efficacy, locus of control, and the theory of planned behavior. *Journal of Applied Social Psychology, 32*, 665–683.

Amabile, T. M. (1979). Effects of external evaluation on artistic creativity. *Journal of Personality and Social Psychology, 37*, 221–233.

Amabile, T. M. (1983). The social psychology of creativity: A componential conceptualization. *Journal of Personality and Social Psychology, 45*, 357–376.

Amabile, T. M., & Gitomer, J. (1984). Children's artistic creativity: Effect of choice in task materials. *Personality and Social Psychology Bulletin, 10*, 209–215.

Amabile, T. M., Hennessey, B. A., & Grossman, B. S. (1986). Social influence on creativity: The effects of contract-for rewards. *Journal of Personality and Social Psychology, 50*, 14–23.

Abramson, L. Y., Metalsky, F. I., & Alloy, L. B. (1989). Hopelessness depression: A theory based subtype of depression. *Psychological Review, 96*, 358–372.

Abramson, L. Y., Seligman, M. E. P., & Teasdale, J. (1978). Learned helplessness in humans. Critique and reformulation. *Journal of Abnormal Psychology, 87*, 49–74.

Ames, C. (1992). Classrooms: Goals, structures, and student motivation. *Journal of Educational Psychology, 84*, 261–271.

Ames, C., & Archer, J. (1988). Achievement goals in the classroom: Students' learning strategies and motivation processes. *Journal of Educational Psychology, 80*, 260–267.

Anderman, E. M., & Maehr, M. L. (1994). Motivation and schooling in the middle grades. *Review of Educational Research, 64*, 287–309.

Aronson, E. (1969). A theory of cognitive dissonance: A current perspective. In L. Berkowitz (Ed.), *Advances in experimental social psychology* (Vol. 4, pp. 1–34) New York: Academic Press.

Aronson, E. (1992). The return of the repressed: Dissonance theory makes a comeback. *Psychological Inquiry, 3*, 303–311.

Aronson, E. (1999). Dissonance, hypocrisy, and the self-concept. In E. Harmon-Jones & J. Mills (Eds.), *Cognitive dissonance: Progress on a pivotal theory in social psychology* (pp. 103–126). Washington, DC: American Psychological Association.

Assor, A., Kaplan, H., & Roth, G. (2002). Choice is good, but relevance is excellent: Autonomy-enhancing and suppressing teacher behaviors predicting students' engagement in school work. *British Journal of Educational Psychology, 72*, 261–278.

Atkinson, J. W (1957). Motivational determinants of risk-taking behavior. *Psychological Review, 64*, 359–372

Atkinson, J. W. (1964). *An introduction to motivation*. Princeton, NJ: Van Nostrand.

Atkinson, J. W., & Litwin, G. H. (1960). Achievement motive and test anxiety as motive to approach success and motive to avoid failure. *Journal of Abnormal and Social Psychology, 60*, 52–63.

Averill, J. R. (1973). Personal control over aversive stimuli and its relationship to stress. *Psychological Bulletin, 80*, 286–303.

Bandura, A. (1977). Self-efficacy: Toward a unifying theory of behavioral change. *Psychological Review, 84*, 191–215.

Bandura, A. (1986). *Social foundations of thought and action: A social cognitive theory*. Englewood Cliffs, NJ: Prentice-Hall.

Bandura, A. (1997). *Self-efficacy: The exercise of control*. New York: Freeman.

Bandura, A., & Schunk, D. H. (1981). Cultivating competence, self-efficacy, and intrinsic interest through proximal self-motivation. *Journal of Personality and Social Psychology, 41*, 586–598.

Bao, X., & Lam, S. (2008). Who makes the choice? Rethinking the role of autonomy and relatedness in Chinese children's motivation. *Child Development, 79*, 269–283.

Bargh, J. A. (1997). The automaticity of everyday life. In R. S. Wyer, Jr. (Ed.), *The automaticity of everyday life: Advances in social cognition* (Vol. 10, pp. 1–61). Mahwah, NJ: Erlbaum.

Bargh, J. A., & Chartrand, T. L. (1999). The unbearable automaticity of being. *American Psychologist, 54*, 462–479.

Baumeister, R. F., Bratslavsky, E., Muraven, M., & Tice, D. M. (1998). Ego-depletion: Is the active self a limited resource? *Journal of Personality and Social Psychology, 74*, 1252–1265.

Baumeister, R. F., & Vohs, K. D. (2007). Self-regulation, ego depletion, and motivation. *Social and Personality Psychology Compass, 1*, 1–14.

Beattie, J., Baron, J., Hershey, J. C., & Spranca, M. D. (1994). Psychological determinants of decision attitude. *Journal of Behavioral Decision Making, 7*, 129–144.

Becker, D. A. (1997). The effects of choice on auditors' intrinsic motivation and performance. *Behavioral Research in Accounting, 9*, 1–19.

Bem, D. J. (1967). Self-perception: An alternative interpretation of cognitive dissonance phenomena. *Psychological Review, 74*, 183–200.

Bem, D. J. (1972). Self-perception theory. In L. Berkowitz (Ed.), *Advances in Experimental Social Psychology* (Vol. 6, pp. 1–62). New York: Academic Press.

Bem, D. J., & McConnell, H. K. (1971). Testing the self-perception explanation of dissonance phenomena: On the salience of premanipulation attitudes. *Journal of Personality and Social Psychology, 14*, 23–31.

Bereby-Meyer, Y., Assor, A., & Katz, I. (2004). Children's choice strategies: The effects of age and task demands. *Cognitive Development, 19*, 127–146.

Berglas, S., & Jones, E. E. (1978). Drug choice as a self-handicapping strategy in response to noncontingent success. *Journal of Personality and Social Psychology, 36*(4), 405–417.

Betz, N. E., & Hackett, G. (1981). The relationship of career-related self-efficacy expectation to perceived career options in college women and men. *Journal of Counseling Psychology, 28*, 399–410.

Betz, N. E., & Hackett, G. (1983). The relationship of mathematics self-efficacy expectations to the selection of science-based college majors. *Journal of Vocational Behavior, 23*, 329–345.

Botti, S., & Iyengar, S. S. (2004). The psychological pleasure and pain of choosing: When people prefer choosing at the cost of subsequent outcome satisfaction. *Journal of Personality and Social Psychology, 87*, 312–326

Botti, S., & Iyengar, S. S. (2006). The dark side of choice: When choice impairs social welfare. *Journal of Public Policy and Marketing, 25*, 24–38.

Botti, S., Orfali, K., & Iyengar, S. S. (2009). Tragic choices: Autonomy and emotional response to medical decision. *Journal of Consumer Research, 36*, 337–352.

Brehm, J. (1956). Post-decision changes in desirability of alternatives. *Journal of Abnormal and Social Psychology, 52*, 384–389.

Brehm, J. W. (1962). *A dissonance analysis of attitude-discrepant behavior*. New York: Gaines Dog Research Center.

Brehm, J. W. (1966). *A theory of psychological reactance*. New York: Academic Press.

Brehm, J. W., & Cohen, A. R. (1959). Re-evaluation of choice alternatives as a function of their number and qualitative similarity. *Journal of Abnormal Social Psychology, 58*, 373–378.

Brehm, J. W., & Cohen, A. R. (1962). *Explorations in cognitive dissonance*. New York: Wiley.

Burger, J. M. (1987). Increased performance with increased personal control: A self-presentation interpretation. *Journal of Experimental Social Psychology, 23*, 350–360.

Burger, J. M. (1989). Negative reactions to increases in perceived personal control. *Journal of Personality and Social Psychology, 56*, 246–256.

Calder, B., Ross, M., & Insko, C. (1973). Attitude change and attitude attribution: Effects of incentive, choice, and consequence. *Journal of Personality and Social Psychology, 25*, 84–99.

Carver, C. S., & Scheier, M. F. (1982). Control theory: A useful conceptual framework for personality-social, clinical, and health psychology. *Psychological Bulletin, 92*, 111–135.

Carver, C. S., & Scheier, M. F. (2002). Control processes and self-organization as complementary principles underlying behavior. *Personality and Social Psychology Review, 6*, 304–315.

Carling, A. (1992). *Social divisions*. London: Verso.

Chaiken, S., & Baldwin, M. W. (1981). Affective–cognitive consistency and the effect of salient of behavioral information on the self-perception of attitudes. *Journal of Personality and Social Psychology, 41*, 1–12.

Chen, K. (2008). *Rationalization and cognitive dissonance: Do choices affect or reflect preferences?* [Discussion Paper No. 1669]. Cowles Foundation for Research in Economics, Yale University. Retrieved July 2011, from http://cowles.econ.yale.edu/P/cd/d16b/d1669.pdf

Chen, M. K., & Risen, J. L. (2009). Is choice a reliable predictor of choice? A comment on Sagarin and Skowronski. *Journal of Experimental Social Psychology, 45*, 425–427.

Chernev, A. (2003). When more is less and less is more: The role of ideal point availability and assortment in choice. *Journal of Consumer Research, 30*, 170–183

Chua, R. Y. J., & Iyengar, S. (2005). *The effects of choice, goal, and creative self-efficacy on divergent thinking and creative outcomes*. Academy of Management Conference. Hawaii.

Chua, R. Y.J., & Iyengar, S. (2006). Empowerment through choice? A critical analysis of the effects of choice in organizations. *Research in Organizational Behavior 27*, 41–79.

Coleman, J. (1973). *The mathematics of collective action*. London: Heinemann.

Collins, B. E., Ashmore, R. D., Hornbeck, F. W., & Whitney, R. E. (1970). Studies in forced compliance: XIII and XV in search of dissonance producing forced compliance paradigm. *Representative Research in Social Psychology, 1*, 11–23.

Cooper, J., & Fazio, R. H. (1984). A new look at dissonance theory. In L. Berkowitz (Ed.), *Advances in experimental social psychology* (Vol. 17, pp. 229–266). New York: Academic Press.

Cordova, D., & Lepper, M. (1996). Intrinsic motivation and the process of learning: Beneficial effects of contextualization, personalization, and choice. *Journal of Educational Psychology, 88*, 715–730.

Crowe, E., & Higgins, E. T. (1997). Regulatory focus and strategic inclinations: Promotion and prevention in decision-making. *Organizational Behavior and Human Decision Processes, 69*, 117–132.

Croyle, R. T., & Cooper, J. (1983). Dissonance arousal: Physiological evidence. *Journal of Personality and Social Psychology, 45*, 782–791.

DeCharms, R. (1968). *Personal causation*. New York: Academic Press.

Deci, E. L. (1971). Effects of externally mediated rewards on intrinsic motivation. *Journal of Personality & Social Psychology, 18*, 105–115.

Deci, E. L. (1980). *The psychology of self-determination*. Lexington, MA: Heath.

Deci, E. L., Connell, J. P., & Ryan, R. M. (1989). Self-determination in a work organization. *Journal of Applied Psychology, 74*, 580–590.

Deci, E. L., & Ryan, R. M. (1985). *Intrinsic motivation and self-determination in human behavior*. New York: Plenum.

Deci, E. L., & Ryan, R. M. (1987). The support of autonomy and the control of behavior. *Journal of Personality and Social Psychology, 53*, 1024–1037.

Dember, W. N., Galinsky, T. L., & Warm, J. S. (1992). The role of choice in vigilance performance. *Bulletin of the Psychonomic Society, 30*, 201–204.

Detweiler, J. B., Mendoza, R. J., & Lepper, M. R. (1996, June). *Perceived versus actual choice: High perceived choice enhances children's task engagement*. Paper presented to the 8th Annual Meeting of the American Psychological Society, San Francisco, CA.

Dhar, R. (1997). Consumer preference for a no-choice option. *Journal of Consumer Research, 24*, 215–231.

Dweck, C. S. (1986). Motivational processes affecting learning. *American Psychologist, 41*, 1040–1048.

Dweck, C. S. (1999). *Self-theories: Their role in motivation, personality, and development*. Philadelphia, PA: The Psychology Press.

Dweck, C., & Bempechat, J. (1983). Children's theories of intelligence. In S. Paris, G. Olsen, & H. Stevenson (Eds.), *Learning and motivation in the classroom* (pp. 239–256). Hillsdale, NJ: Erlbaum.

Dweck, C. S., & Leggett, E. L. (1988). A social-cognitive approach to motivation and personality. *Psychological Review, 95*, 256–273.

Eccles, J. S. (1984). Sex differences in achievement patterns. In T. Sonderegger (Ed.), *Nebraska symposium on motivation, 1983* (pp. 97–132). Lincoln: University of Nebraska Press.

Eccles, J. S. (1987). Gender roles and women's achievement related decisions. *Psychology of Women Quarterly, 11*, 135–172.

Eccles, J. S., Adler, T. F., Futterman, R., Goff, S. B., Kaczala, C. M., Meece, J., & Midgley, C. (1983). Expectancies, values and academic behaviors. In J. T. Spence (Ed.), *Achievement and achievement motives* (pp. 75–146). San Francisco, CA: W. H. Freeman.

Eccles, J. S., Adler, T., & Meece, J. L. (1984). Sex differences in achievement: A test of alternate theories. *Journal of Personality and Social Psychology, 46*, 26–43.

Eccles, J. S., & Wigfield, A. (2002). Motivational belief, values, and goals. *Annual Review of Psychology, 53*, 109–132.

Edwards, W. (1954). The theory of decision making. *Psychological Bulletin, 51*, 380–417.

Elliot, A. J., & Devine, P. G. (1994). On the motivational nature of cognitive dissonance: Dissonance as psychological discomfort. *Journal of Personality and Social Psychology, 67*, 382–394.

Elliott, E. S., & Dweck, C. S. (1988). Goals: An approach to motivation and achievement. *Journal of Personality and Social Psychology, 54,* 5–12.

Epstein, J. (1989). Family structure and student motivation: A developmental perspective. In C. Ames & R. Ames (Eds.), *Research on motivation in education* (Vol. 3, pp. 259–295). San Diego, CA: Academic Press.

Estes, W. K. (1976). The cognitive side of probability learning. *Psychological Review, 83,* 37–64.

Fazio, R. H. (1981). On the self-perception explanation of the overjustification effect: The role of salience of initial attitude. *Journal of Experimental Social Psychology, 17,* 417–426.

Fazio, R. H., Zanna, M. P., & Cooper, J. (1977). Dissonance and self-perception: An integrative view of each theory's proper domain of application. *Journal of Experimental Social Psychology, 13,* 464–479.

Feather, N. T. (1988). Values, valences, and course enrollment: testing the role of personal values within an expectancy-value framework. *Journal of Educational Psychology, 80,* 381–391.

Feldman, J. M., & Lynch, J. G., Jr. (1988). Self-generated validity and other effects of measurement on belief, attitude, intention and behavior. *Journal of Applied Psychology, 73,* 421–435.

Festinger, L. (1957). *A theory of cognitive dissonance.* Stanford, CA: Stanford University Press.

Festinger, L. (1964). *Conflict, decision, and dissonance.* Stanford, CA: Stanford University Press.

Fitch, G. (1970). Effects of self-esteem, perceived performance and choice on causal attributions. *Journal of Personality and Social Psychology, 16,* 311–315

Fishbein, M., & Ajzen, I. (1981). Attitudes and voting behaviour: An application of the theory of reasoned action. In G. M. Stephenson & J. M. Davis (Eds.), *Progress in applied social psychology* (Vol. 1, pp. 95–125). London: Wiley.

Flowerday, T., & Schraw, G. (2000). Teacher beliefs about instructional choice: A phenomenological study. *Journal of Educational Psychology, 92,* 634–645.

Flowerday, T., & Schraw, G. (2003). Effect of choice on cognitive and affective engagement. *Journal of Educational Research, 96,* 207–215.

Flowerday, T., Schraw, G., & Stevens, J. (2004). The role of choice and interest in reader engagement. *The Journal of Experimental Education, 72,* 93–114

Förster, J., Higgins, E. T., & Idson, L. C. (1998). Approach and avoidance strength during goal attainment: Regulatory focus and the "goal looms larger" effect. *Journal of Personality and Social Psychology, 75,* 1115–1131.

Förster, J., Higgins, E. T., & Strack, F. (2000). When stereotype disconfirmation is a personal threat: How prejudice and prevention focus moderate incongruency effects. *Social Cognition, 18,* 178–197.

Freedman, J. L., & Fraser, S. C. (1966). Compliance without pressure: The foot-in-the-door technique. *Journal of Personality and Social Psychology, 4,* 196–202

Garcia, T., & Pintrich, P. R. (1996). The effects of autonomy on motivation and performance in the college classroom. *Contemporary Educational Psychology, 21,* 477–486.

Gerard, H. (1992). Dissonance theory: A cognitive psychology with a engine. *Psychological Inquiry, 3,* 323–327

Gerard, H. B., & White, G. L. (1983). Post-decisional reevaluation of choice alternatives. *Personality and Social Psychology Bulletin, 9,* 365–369.

Goethals, G. R., & Cooper, J. (1972). Role of intention and postbehavioral consequence in the arousal of cognitive dissonance. *Journal of Personality and Social Psychology, 23,* 293–301

Greenberg, E. (1992). Creativity, autonomy, and evaluation of creative work: Artistic workers in organizations. *Journal of Creative Behavior, 26,* 75–80

Greenleaf, E. A., & Lehmann, D. R. (1995). Reasons for substantial delay in consumer decision making. *Journal of Consumer Research, 22,* 186–199.

Hackett, G., & Betz, N. E. (1981). A self-efficacy approach to the career development of women. *Journal of Vocational Behavior, 18,* 326–336.

Hackett, G., & Betz, N. E. (1989). An exploration of the mathematics self-efficacy/mathematics performance correspondence. *Journal for Research in Mathematics Education, 20,* 261–273.

Harackiewicz, J. M., Barron, K. E., Pintrich, P. R., Elliot, A. J., & Thrash, T. M. (2002). Revision of achievement goal theory: Necessary and illuminating. *Journal of Educational Psychology, 94,* 638–645.

Harmon-Jones, E., Brehm, J. W., Greenberg, J., Simon, L., & Nelson, D. E. (1996). Is the production of aversive consequences necessary to create cognitive dissonance? *Journal of Personality and Social Psychology, 70,* 5–16.

Harmon-Jones, E., & Mills, J. (1999). *Cognitive dissonance: Progress on a pivotal theory in social psychology.* Washington, DC: American Psychological Association.

Helmreich, R., & Collins, B. E. (1968). Studies in forced compliance: Commitment and magnitude of inducement to comply as determinants of opinion change. *Journal of Personality and Social Psychology, 10,* 75–81.

Heath, A. (1976). *Rational choice and social exchange.* Cambridge, England: Cambridge University Press.

Heine, S. J., & Lehman, D. R. (1997). Culture, dissonance, and self-affirmation. *Personality and Social Psychology Bulletin, 23,* 389–400.

Henry, R. A. (1994). The effects of choice and incentives on the overestimation of future performance. *Organizational Behavior and Human Decision Processes, 57,* 210–225.

Henry, R. A., & Sniezek, J. A. (1993). Situational factors affecting judgments of future performance. *Organizational Behavior and Human Decision Processes, 54,* 104–132.

Hidi, S., & Baird, W. (1986). Interestingness—A neglected variable in discourse processing. *Cognitive Science, 10,* 179–194.

Hidi, S., & Renninger, K. A. (2006). The four-phase model of interest development. *Educational Psychologist, 41,* 111–127.

Higgins, E. T. (1998). From expectancies to worldviews: Regulatory focus in socialization and cognition. In J. M. Darley & J. Cooper (Eds.), *Attribution and social interaction: The legacy of Edward E. Jones* (pp. 243–309). Washington, DC: American Psychological Association.

Higgins, E. T. (2000). Making a good decision: Value from fit. *American Psychologist, 55,* 1217–1230.

Higgins, E. T., Trope, Y., & Kwon, J. (1999). Augmentation and undermining from combining activities: The role of choice in activity engagement theory. *Journal of Experimental Social Psychology, 35,* 285–307.

Hoyle, R. H., & Sherrill, M. R. (2006). Future orientation in the self-system: Possible selves, self-regulation, and behavior. *Journal of Personality, 74,* 1673–1696.

Huffman, C., & Kahn, B. E. (1998). Variety for sale: Mass customization or mass confusion? *Journal of Retailing, 74,* 491–513.

Idson, L. C., Liberman, N., & Higgins, E. T. (2000). Distinguishing gains from nonlosses and losses from nongains: A regulatory focus perspective on hedonic intensity. *Journal of Experimental Social Psychology, 36*, 252–274.

Iyengar, S. S., Elwork, R. F., & Schwartz, R. (2006). Doing better but feeling worse: Looking for the 'best' job undermines satisfaction. *Psychological Science, 17*, 143–150.

Iyengar, S. S., Jiang, W., & Huberman, G. (2004). How much choice is too much: Determinants of individual contributions in 401K retirement plans. In O. S. Mitchell & S. Utkus (Eds.), *Pension design and structure: New Lessons from Behavioral Finance,* (pp. 83–97). Oxford, England: Oxford University Press.

Iyengar, S. S., & Lepper, M. R. (1999). Rethinking the value of choice: A cultural perspective on intrinsic motivation. *Journal of Personality and Social Psychology, 76*, 349–366.

Iyengar, S. S., & Lepper, M. R. (2000). When choice is demotivating: Can one desire too much of a good thing? *Journal of Personality and Social Psychology, 79*, 995–1006.

Iyengar, S. S., Wells, R., & Schwartz, B. (2006). Doing better but feeling worse: Looking for the "best" job undermines satisfaction. *Psychological Science, 17*, 143–150.

Janis, I. L., & Mann, L. (1977). *Decision making, a psychological analysis of conflict, choice and commitment.* New York: The Free Press.

Jacobs, J., & Eccles, J. S. (2000). Parents, task values, and real life achievement-related choices. In C. Sansone & J. M. Harackiewicz (Eds.), *Intrinsic and extrinsic motivation: The search for optimal motivation and performance* (pp. 405–439). San Diego, CA: Academic Press.

Jones, E. E., & Harris, V. A. (1967). The attribution of attitudes. *Journal of Experimental Social Psychology, 3*, 1–24.

Jones, E. E., Worchel, S., Goethals, G. R., & Grumet, J. F. (1971). Prior expectancy and behavioral extremity as determinants of attitude attribution. *Journal of Experimental Social Psychology, 7*, 59–80.

Kahneman, D. (2003). A perspective on judgment and choice. *American Psychologist, 58*, 697–720.

Kahneman, D., & Tversky, A. (1979). Prospect theory: An analysis of decisions under risk. *Econometrika, 47*, 263–291.

Katz, I., & Assor, A. (2003). *Is autonomy important for nonwestern students? Examining autonomy as a universal human propensity.* Paper presented at the 84th Annual Meeting of the American Educational Research Association, Chicago, IL.

Katz, I., & Assor, A. (2007). When choice motivates and when it does not. *Educational Psychology Review, 19*, 429–442.

Kelley, H. H. (1967). Attribution theory in social psychology. In D. Levine (Ed.), *Nebraska symposium on motivation.* Lincoln: University of Nebraska Press.

Kelley, H. H. (1973). The process of causal attribution. *American Psychologist, 28*, 107–128.

Kernan, M. C., Heimann, B., & Hanges, P. J. (1991). Effects of goal choice, strategy choice, and feedback source on goal acceptance, performance, and subsequent goals. *Journal of Applied Social Psychology, 21*, 713–733

Kitiyama, S., Snibbe, A. C., Markus, H. R., & Suzuki, T. (2008). Is there any "free" choice? Self and dissonance in two cultures. *Psychological Science, 15*, 527–533.

Krapp, A. (2002). An educational-psychological theory of interest and its relation to SDT. In E. L. Deci & R. M. Ryan (Eds.), *The handbook of self-determination research* (pp. 405–427). Rochester, NY: Rochester University.

Krapp, A. (2005). Basic needs and the development of interest and intrinsic motivational orientations. *Learning and Instruction, 15*, 381–395.

Langer, E. (1975). The illusion of control. *Journal of Personality and Social Psychology, 32*, 311–328.

Langer, E. (1979). The illusion of control. *Journal of Personality and Social Psychology, 32*, 311–328.

Langer, E. J., & Rodin, J. (1976). The effects of choice and enhanced personal responsibility for the aged: A field experiment in an institutional setting. *Journal of Personality and Social Psychology, 34*, 191–198.

Lepper, M. R., Greene, D., & Nisbett, R. E. (1973). Undermining children's intrinsic interest with extrinsic rewards: A test of the "overjustification" hypothesis. *Journal of Personality and Social Psychology, 28*, 129–137.

Lewin, K. (1936). *Principles of topological psychology.* New York: McGraw-Hill.

Lewin, K. (1951). *Field theory in social science; selected theoretical papers.* (D. Cartwright Ed.). New York: Harper & Row.

Lewin, K. (1952). Group decision and social change. In G. E. Swanson, T. M. Newcomb, & E. L. Hartley (Eds.), *Readings in social psychology* (pp. 459–473). New York: Henry Holt.

Linder, D. E., Cooper, J., & Jones, E. E. (1967). "Decision freedom as a determinant of the role of incentive magnitude in attitude change." *Journal of Personality and Social Psychology, 6*, 245–254.

Linnenbrink-Garcia, L., Tyson, D., & Patall, E. A. (2008). When are achievement goal orientations beneficial for academic achievement? A closer look at main effects and moderating factors. *International Review of Social Psychology, 21*, 19–70.

Lipstein, R., & Renninger, K. A. (2007). "Putting things into words": The development of 12–15-year-old students' interest for writing. In P. Boscolo & S. Hidi (Eds.), *Motivation and writing: Research and school practice* (pp. 113–140). New York: Elsevier.

Luce, M. (1998). Choosing to avoid: Coping with negatively emotion-laden consumer decisions. *The Journal of Consumer Research, 24*, 409–433.

Lyubomirsky, S., & Ross, L. (1999). Changes in attractiveness of elected, rejected, and precluded alternatives: A comparison of happy and unhappy individuals. *Journal of Personality and Social Psychology, 76*, 988–1007.

Maehr, M. L., & Midgley, C. (1991). Enhancing student motivation: A schoolwide approach. *Educational Psychologist, 26*, 399–427.

Maier, S. F., & Seligman, M. E. P. (1976). Learned helplessness: Theory and evidence. *Journal of Experimental Psychology: General, 105*, 3–46.

Malhotra, N. K. (1982). Information load and consumer decision making. *Journal of Consumer Research, 8*, 419–430.

Manstead, A. S. R., Proffitt, C., & Smart, J. L. (1983). Predicting and understanding mothers' infant feeding intentions and behavior: Testing the theory of reasoned action. *Journal of Personality and Social Psychology, 44*, 657–671.

Markus, H., & Kitayama, S. (1991). Culture and the self: Implications for cognition, emotion and motivation. *Psychological Review, 98*, 224–253.

Markus, H., & Nurius, P. (1986). Possible selves. *American Psychologist, 41*, 954–969.

Maslow, A. (1954). *Motivation and personality.* New York: Harper.

Meece, J. L., Wigfield, A., & Eccles, J. S. (1990). Predictors of math anxiety and its influence on young adolescents' course enrollment intentions and performance in mathematics. *Journal of Educational Psychology, 82,* 60–70.

Meece, J., Anderman E. M., & Anderman, L. H. (2006). Structures and goals of educational settings: Classroom goal structure, student motivation, and academic achievement. In S. T. Fiske, A. E. Kazdin, & D. L. Schacter (Eds.), *Annual review of psychology* (Vol. 57, pp. 487–504). Stanford, CA: Annual Reviews.

Melson, W. H., Calder, B. J., & Insko, C. A. (1969). The social psychological status of reward. *Psychonomic Science, 17,* 240–242.

Midgley, C., & Feldlaufer, H. (1987). Students' and teachers' decision-making fit before and after the transition to junior high school. *Journal of Early Adolescence, 7,* 225–241.

Midgley, C., Kaplan, A., & Middleton, M. J. (2001). Performance-approach goals: Good for what, for whom, under what circumstances, and at what cost? *Journal of Educational Psychology, 93,* 77–86.

Mikulincer, M. (1988). Freedom of choice, control, and learned helplessness. *Journal of Social and Clinical Psychology, 7,* 203–213.

Mischel, W., & Ebbesen, E. B. (1970). Attention in delay of gratification. *Journal of Personality and Social Psychology, 16,* 329–337

Mitchell, T. R. (1974). Expectancy models of job satisfaction, occupational preference and effort: A theoretical, methodological, and empirical appraisal. *Psychological Bulletin, 81,* 1053–1077

Mogilner, C., Rudnick, T., & Iyengar, S. S. (2008). The mere categorization effect: How the presence of categories increases choosers' perceptions of assortment variety and outcome satisfaction. *Journal of Consumer Research, 35,* 202–215.

Moller, A. C., Deci, E. L., & Ryan, R. M. (2006). Choice and ego-depletion: The moderating role of autonomy. *Personality and Social Psychology Bulletin, 32,* 1024–1036.

Monty, R. A., & Perlmuter, L. C. (1975). Persistence of the effects of choice on paired-associate learning. *Memory and Cognition, 3,* 183–187.

Monty, R. A., & Perlmuter, L. C. (1987). Choice, control, and motivation in the young and the aged. In M. L. Maehr & D. L. Kleiber (Eds.), *Advances in motivation and achievement. Vol. 5: Enhancing motivation* (pp. 99–122). Greenwich, CT: JAI.

Monty, R. A., Rosenberger, M. A., & Perlmuter, L. C. (1973). Amount and locus of choice as sources of motivation in paired-associate learning. *Journal of Experimental Psychology, 97,* 16–21.

Muraven, M., & Baumeister, R. F. (2000). Self-regulation and depletion of limited resources: Does self-control resemble a muscle? *Psychological Bulletin, 126,* 247–259.

Muraven, M., Baumeister, R. F., & Tice, D. M. (1999). Self-control as limited resource: Regulatory depletion patterns. *Journal of Personality and Social Psychology, 74,* 774–789.

Murray, H. A. (1938). Explorations in personality. New York: Oxford University Press.

Nicholls, J. G. (1984). Achievement motivation: Conceptions of ability, subjective experience, task choice, and performance. *Psychological Review, 91,* 328–346.

Oyserman, D., & Fryberg, S. (2006). The possible selves of diverse adolescents: Content and function across gender, race and national origin. In C. Dunkel & J. Kerpelman (Eds.),

Possible selves: Theory, research, and application (pp. 17–39). Huntington, NY: Nova.

Oyserman, D., & James, L. (2008). Possible selves: From content to process. In K. Markman, W. M. P. Klein, & J. A. Suhr (Eds.), *The handbook of imagination and mental stimulation* (pp. 373–394). New York: Psychology Press.

Overskeid, G., & Svartdal, F. (1996). Effects of reward on subjective autonomy and interest when initial interest is low. *The Psychological Record, 46,* 319–331.

Patall, E. A. (2009). *The motivational benefits and limits of choice.* (Unpublished doctoral dissertation). Duke University, Durham, NC.

Patall, E. A., Cooper, H., & Robinson, J. C. (2008). The effects of choice on intrinsic motivation and related outcomes: A meta-analysis of research findings. *Psychological Bulletin, 134,* 270–300.

Patall, E. A., Cooper, H., & Wynn, S. R. (2010). The effectiveness and relative importance of providing choices in the classroom. *Journal of Educational Psychology, 102,* 896–915.

Parker, L. E., & Lepper, M. R. (1992). Effects of fantasy contexts on children's learning and motivation: Making learning more fun. *Journal of Personality and Social Psychology, 62,* 625–633.

Paterson, R. J., & Neufeld, R. W. J. (1995). What are my options? Influences of choice availability on stress and the perception of control. *Journal of Research in Personality, 29,* 145–167.

Payne, J. J., Bettman, J. R., & Johnson, E. R. (1993). *The adaptive decision maker.* Cambridge, England: Cambridge University Press.

Perlmuter, L. C., & Monty, R. A. (1973). Effect of choice of stimulus on paired-associate learning. *Journal of Experimental Psychology, 99,* 120–123.

Perlmuter, L. C., & Monty, R. A. (1977). The importance of perceived control: Fact or fantasy? *American Scientist, 65,* 759–765.

Perlmuter, L. C., Monty, R. A., & Kimble, G. A. (1971). Effect of choice on paired-associate learning. *Journal of Experimental Psychology, 91,* 47–53.

Perlmuter, L. C., Scharff, K., Karsh, R. A., & Monty, R. A. (1980). Perceived control: A generalized state of motivation. *Motivation and Emotion, 4,* 35–45.

Peterson, C., Maier, S. F., & Seligman, M. E. P. (1993). *Learned helplessness.* Oxford, England: Oxford University Press.

Peterson, C., & Seligman, M. E. P. (1984). Causal explanations as a risk factor for depression: Theory and evidence. *Psychological Review, 91,* 347–374.

Reeve, J., Nix, G., & Hamm, D. (2003). Testing models of the experience of self-determination in intrinsic motivation and the conundrum of choice. *Journal of Educational Psychology, 95,* 375–392.

Renninger, K. A. (1992). Individual interest and development: Implications for theory and practice. In K. A. Renninger, S. Hidi, & A. Krapp (Eds.), *The role of interest in learning and development* (pp. 361–376). Hillsdale, NJ: Erlbaum.

Renninger, K. A. (2009). Interest and identity development in instruction: An inductive model. *Educational Psychologist, 44,* 1–14.

Renninger, K. A., Hidi, S., & Krapp, A. (1992). *The role of interest in learning and development.* Hillsdale, NJ: Erlbaum.

Rodin, J., Rennert, K., & Solomon, S. K. (1980). Intrinsic motivation for control: Fact or fiction? In A. Baum & J. E. Singer (Eds.), *Advances in environmental psychology.*

Vol 2: Applications of personal control (pp. 131–148). Hillsdale, NJ: Erlbaum.

Rogers, C. R. (1969). *Freedom to learn.* Columbus, OH: Merrill.

Rotter, J. B. (1954). *Social learning and clinical psychology.* New York: Prentice-Hall.

Rotter, J. B. (1966). Generalized expectancies for internal versus external control of reinforcement. *Psychological Monographs, 80,* 1–28.

Ryan, R. M. (1993). Agency and organization: Intrinsic motivation, autonomy, and the self in psychological development. In J. E. Jacobs (Ed.), *Nebraska Symposium on Motivation. Vol. 40: Developmental perspectives on motivation* (pp. 1–56). Lincoln: University of Nebraska Press.

Ryan, R. M., & Deci, E. L. (2000). Self-determination theory and the facilitation of intrinsic motivation, social development, and well-being. *American Psychologist, 55,* 68–78.

Sagarin, B. J., & Skowronski, J. J. (2008). The implications of imperfect measurement for free choice carry-over effects: Reply to M. Keith Chen (2008) Rationalization and cognitive dissonance: Do choices affect or reflect preferences? *Journal of Experimental Social Psychology, 45,* 421–423.

Savani, K., Markus, H. R., & Conner, A. L. (2008). Let your preference be your guide? Preferences and choices are more tightly linked for North Americans than for Indians. *Journal of Personality and Social Psychology, 95,* 861–876.

Savani, K., Markus, H. R., Naidu, N. V. R., Kumar, S., & Berlia, N. (2010). What counts as a choice? U.S. Americans are more likely than Indians to construe actions as choices. *Psychological Science, 21,* 391–398.

Scher, S., & Cooper, J. (1989). The motivational basis of dissonance: The singular role of behavioral consequences. *Journal of Personality and Social Psychology, 56,* 899–906.

Schiefele, U. (1991). Interest, learning, and motivation. *Educational Psychologist, 26,* 299–323.

Schiefele, U. (2001). The role of interest in motivation and learning. In J. Collis & S. Messick (Eds.), *Intelligence and personality: Bridging the gap in theory and measurement* (pp. 163–194). Mahwah, NJ: Erlbaum.

Schraw, G., Flowerday, T., & Lehman, S. (2001). Promoting situational interest in the classroom. *Educational Psychology Review, 13,* 211–224.

Schraw, G., Flowerday, T., & Reisetter, M. F. (1998). The role of choice in reader engagement. *Journal of Educational Psychology, 90,* 705–714.

Schwartz, B. (2000). Self-determination: The tyranny of freedom. *American Psychologist, 55,* 79–88.

Schwartz, B. (2004, April). The tyranny of choice. *Scientific American,* 71–75.

Schwartz, B., Ward, A. H., Monterosso, J., Lyubomirsky, S., White, K., & Lehman, D. (2002). Maximizing versus satisficing: Happiness is a matter of choice. *Journal of Personality and Social Psychology, 83,* 1178–1197.

Scott, J. (2000). Rational choice theory. In G. Browning, A. Haleli, & F. Webster (Eds.), *Understanding contemporary society: Theories of the present* (pp. 126–138). London: Sage.

Seligman, M. E. P. (1975). *Helplessness: On depression, development, and death.* San Francisco, CA: W. H. Freeman.

Shafir, E., Simonson, I., & Tversky, A. (1993). Reason-based choice. *Cognition, 49,* 11–36.

Shafir, E., & Tversky, A. 1992. Thinking through uncertainty: Nonconsequential reasoning and choice. *Cognitive Psychology, 24,* 449–474.

Sheppard, B. H., Hartwick, J., & Warshaw, P.R (1988). The theory of reasoned action: A meta-analysis of past research with recommendations for modifications and future research. *Journal of Consumer Research, 15,* 325–343.

Sherman, S. J. (1970). Attitudinal effects of unforeseen consequences. *Journal of Personality and Social Psychology, 16,* 510–520.

Shugan, S. M. (1980). The cost of thinking. *Journal of Consumer Research, 7,* 99–111.

Shultz, T. R., Leveille, E., & Lepper, M. R. (1999). Free-choice and cognitive dissonance revisited. *Personality and Social Psychology Bulletin, 25,* 40–48.

Simon, H. A. (1955). A behavioral model of rational choice. *Quarterly Journal of Economics, 59,* 99–118.

Simon, H. A. (1956). Rational choice and the structure of the environment. *Psychological Review, 63,* 129–138.

Simon, H. A. (1957). *Models of man, social and rational: Mathematical essays on rational human behavior.* New York: Wiley.

Simon, H. A. (1982). *Models of bounded rationality.* Cambridge, MA: MIT Press.

Simon, H. A. (1987). Rationality in psychology and economics. In R. M. Hogarth & M. W. Reder (Eds.), *Rational choice: The contrast between economics and psychology* (pp. 25–40). Chicago, IL: University of Chicago Press.

Simon, L., Greenberg, J., & Brehm, J. (1995). Trivialization: The forgotten mode of dissonance reduction. *Journal of Personality and Social Psychology, 68,* 247–260.

Skinner, B. F. (1953). *Science and human behavior.* New York: Macmillan.

Skinner, E. A. (1996). A guide to constructs of control. *Journal of Personality and Social Psychology, 71,* 549–570.

Snibbe, A., & Markus, H. R. (2005). You can't always get what you want: Educational attainment, agency, and choice. *Journal of Personality and Social Psychology, 88,* 703–720.

Staw, B. M. (1976). Knee-deep in the big muddy: A study of escalating commitment to a chosen course of action. *Organizational Behavior and Human Performance, 16,* 27–44.

Stephens, N., Markus, H. R., & Townsend, S. S. M. (2007). Choice as an act of meaning: The case of social class. *Journal of Personality and Social Psychology, 93.* 814–830.

Swann, W., & Pittman, T. (1977). Initiating play activity of children: The moderating influence of verbal cues on intrinsic motivation. *Child Development, 48,* 1128–1132.

Tafarodi, R. W., Mehranvar, S., Panton, R. L., & Milne, A. B. (2002). Putting oneself in the task: Choice, personalization, and confidence. *Personality and Social Psychology Bulletin, 28,* 648–658.

Tafarodi, R. W., Milne, A. B., & Smith, A. J. (1999). The confidence of choice: Evidence for an augmentation effect on self-perceived performance. *Personality and Social Psychology Bulletin, 25,* 1405–1416.

Taylor, S. (1989). *Positive illusions: Creative self-deception and the healthy mind.* New York: Basic Books.

Thorndike, E. (1913). *Educational psychology: The psychology of learning.* New York: Teachers College Press.

Tolman, E. C. (1932). *Purposive behavior in animals and men.* New York: Appleton-Century-Crofts.

Tsai, Y., Kunter, M., Ludtke, O., Trautwein, U., & Ryan, R. M. (2008). What makes lessons interesting? The role of situational and individual factors in three school subjects. *Journal of Educational Psychology, 100,* 460–472.

Tversky, A., & Kahneman, D. (1974). Judgment under uncertainty: Heuristics and biases. *Science, 185,* 1124–1131.

Tversky, A., & Kahneman, D. (1981). The framing of decisions and the psychology of choice. *Science, 211,* 453–458.

Ullmann-Margalit, E., & Morgenbesser, S. (1997). Picking and choosing. *Social Research, 44,* 757–785.

Uranowitz, S. W. (1975). Helping and self-attributions: A field experiment. *Journal of Personality and Social Psychology, 31,* 852–854.

Van Eerne, W., & Thierry, H. (1996). Vroom's expectancy models and work-related criteria: A meta-analysis. *Journal of Applied Psychology, 81,* 575–586.

Vohs, K. D., Baumeister, R. F., Schmeichel, B. J., Twenge, J. M., Nelson, N. M., & Tice, D. M. (2008). Making choices impairs subsequent self-control: A limited resource account of decision making, self-regulation, and active initiative. *Journal of Personality and Social Psychology, 94,* 883–898.

Vohs, K., Finkenauer, C., & Baumeister, R. F. (2011). The sum of friends' and lovers' self-control scores predicts relationship quality. *Social Psychological and Personality Science, 2,* 138–145.

Vroom, V. H. (1964). *Work and motivation.* New York: Wiley

Wang, J., Novemsky, N., Dhar, R. and Baumeister, R. (in press). Tradeoffs and depletion in choice. *Journal of Marketing Research.*

Weiner, B. (1992). *Human motivation: Metaphors, theories, and research.* Newbury Park, CA: Sage.

Wigfield, A., & Eccles, J. (1989). Test anxiety in elementary and secondary school students. *Educational Psychologist, 24,* 159–183.

Wigfield, A., & Eccles, J. (1992). The development of achievement task values: A theoretical analysis. *Developmental Review, 12,* 265–310.

Wigfield, A. L., & Eccles. J. S. (2001). Development of achievement motivation. San Diego, CA: Academic Press.

Williams, S. (1998). An organizational model of choice: A theoretical analysis differentiating choice, personal control, and self-determination. *Genetic, Social and General Psychology Monographs, 124,* 465–492.

Wortman, C. B., & Brehm, J. W. (1975). Response to uncontrollable outcomes: An integration of reactance theory and the learned helplessness model. In L. Berkowitz (Ed.), *Advances in Experimental Social Psychology* (Vol. 8, pp. 277–336). New York: Academic Press.

Yates, B. T., & Mischel, W. (1979). Young children's preferred attentional strategies for delaying gratification. *Journal of Personality and Social Psychology, 37,* 286–300.

Zahorik, J. A. (1996). Elementary and secondary teachers' reports of how they make learning interesting. *Elementary School Journal, 96,* 551–564.

Zuckerman, M., Porac, J., Lathin, D., Smith, R., & Deci, E., (1978). On the importance of self-determination for intrinsically-motivated behavior. *Personality and Social Psychology Bulletin, 4,* 443–446.

On Gains and Losses, Means and Ends: Goal Orientation and Goal Focus Across Adulthood

Alexandra M. Freund, Marie Hennecke, *and* Maida Mustafić

Abstract

Personal goals guide behavior toward a desired outcome, motivate behavior over time and across situations, provide direction and meaning, and contribute to the acquisition of skills and subjective well-being. The adaptiveness of goals, however, might vary with dimensions such as their orientation toward the achievement of gains, maintenance of functioning, or the avoidance of losses. We argue that goal orientation is most adaptive when it corresponds to the availability of resources and the ubiquity of losses. In line with this argument, younger adults show a predominant orientation toward the promotion of gains, whereas goal orientation shifts toward maintenance and avoidance of loss across adulthood. This shift in goal orientation seems adaptive both regarding subjective well-being as well as engagement in goal pursuit. A second goal dimension that has been largely overlooked in the literature is the cognitive representation of goal pursuit primarily in terms of its means (i.e., process focus) or its ends (i.e., outcome focus). This chapter investigates the antecedents and consequences of goal focus. In particular, it highlights the importance of factors related to chronological age (i.e., the availability of resources, future time perspective, goal orientation, motivational phase) for the preference for and adaptiveness of an outcome or process focus. Finally, we posit that a process focus leads to more adaptive behavioral and affective reactions when people encounter failure during goal pursuit.

Key Words: adult development, goal orientation, goal focus, means, ends, resources, time perspective, failure

Introduction

Imagine a young woman in her early 20s and her grandmother, an older woman in her early 70s. Now think about the personal goals they might pursue. Most likely, the younger woman will pursue goals related to finding a life partner, finishing her education, and establishing a professional career. The goals of the older woman are more likely to center around the domains of health, cognitive functioning, independence, and the well-being of her loved ones (Freund & Riediger, 2006). Beyond the differences in content, however, two other age-related differences in the goals of a younger and an older adult might

be evident. First, the orientation of goals is likely to shift from gains in young adulthood to maintenance in middle adulthood and the prevention of losses in older age (e.g., Freund & Ebner, 2005). For example, a young woman might aim at improving her fitness level, whereas her grandmother might be more likely to try to maintain her physical fitness in the face of age-related losses in health. Second, younger adults might focus more on the outcome of goal pursuit, whereas older adults might focus more on the process (Freund, Hennecke, & Riediger, 2010). For example, the young woman might focus on the desired outcome of exercising regularly such as her body shape and her overall fitness. In contrast, her grand-mother might think primarily about how she can exercise regularly in a manner that even makes her feel good while she is exercising. In this chapter we aim at integrating these two dimensions of personal goals and discuss their change across adulthood. First, however, we want to highlight the importance of personal goals throughout the life span.

The Importance of Goals for Adult Development

Laypeople as well as motivation researchers seem to agree that setting and pursuing goals has positive consequences. Goals give life meaning, direction, and contribute to happiness and subjective well-being (e.g., Emmons, 1996; Klinger, 1977; Little, 1989). Goals have been defined as cognitive representations of personally desired (or dreaded) states to be approached (or avoided) through action, such as becoming a nurse (or not becoming like one's parents). More specifically, they encompass *means* of goal pursuit and desired *outcomes* of it (e.g., Kruglanski, 1996). The activation of goals affects the encoding, storage, and retrieval of information and guides attention as well as behavior (e.g., Wyer & Srull, 1986). As goals are comprised of means and ends, goals might channel and organize information in terms of means and ends (e.g., Woike, Lavezzary, & Barsky, 2001). Each time a goal is activated, the associated means and ends (as well as their emotional correlates such as enjoyment or fear) are also activated. Consequently, the activation of goals enhances the likelihood of engaging in goal-relevant behaviors (i.e., means), which can occur even automatically (e.g., Bargh & Ferguson, 2000; Bargh & Gollwitzer, 1994). Goals, then, direct attention and information processing and motivate behavior. Thereby, goals organize behavior over time and across situations, and provide a sense of direction and purpose in life (Freund, 2007). Moreover, research suggests that goal pursuit enhances performance (e.g., Austin & Vancouver, 1996; Emmons, 1989, 1996; Freund, 2007). Therefore, it is not surprising that the goal concept seems particularly well suited for understanding how people develop successfully over time.

However, as Ryan and colleagues put it: Not all goals are created equal (Ryan, Sheldon, Kasser, & Deci, 1996). Goals differ in their content, concreteness, difficulty, time frame, and their orientation toward gains and losses (e.g., Austin & Vancouver, 1996; Freund & Ebner, 2005; Little, 1989; Locke & Latham, 2002; Wiese & Freund, 2005).

Such goal dimensions influence the adaptiveness of goals. Various goal dimensions have been distinguished, such as approach—avoidance (e.g., Elliott & Friedman, 2007), promotion—prevention (e.g., Higgins, 1997), intrinsic—extrinsic (e.g., Deci, Koestner, & Ryan, 1999), and mastery—performance (e.g., Dweck & Leggett, 1988). This chapter centers around two goal dimensions that we believe to change systematically across adulthood: *(1)* Goal orientation: the orientation of personal goals toward gains, maintenance, or the prevention of losses (e.g., Freund & Ebner, 2005), and *(2)* Goal focus: whether a person focuses on the *outcome* of goal pursuit (short-term and long-term consequences) or on the *process* of goal pursuit (means of goal attainment) (e.g., Freund et al., 2010; Sansone & Thoman, 2005; Zimmerman & Kitsantas, 1997).

The importance of personal goals for adult development has been acknowledged by different action-theoretical approaches (e.g., Brandtstädter & Renner, 1990; Freund & Baltes, 2000; Heckhausen & Schulz, 1995). In particular, the model of selection, optimization, and compensation (SOC model, Baltes & Baltes, 1990) has stressed the importance of setting, pursuing, and maintaining personal goals for successful development.

Successful Development Through Personal Goals

One of the central propositions of lifespan psychology is the *multidirectionality* of development. That is, development comprises not only trajectories of growth but also trajectories of decline (Baltes, 1987; Labouvie-Vief, 1981). Successful development has often been defined as the maximization of gains and the simultaneous minimization of losses (see Freund & Riediger, 2003, for a review of definitions of successful development). According to the SOC model (Baltes & Baltes, 1990), an optimal ratio of gains to losses can be achieved by the orchestrated use of three processes of developmental regulation, namely selection, optimization, and compensation. As elaborated in more detail elsewhere (e.g., Freund, 2006; Freund & Baltes, 2000; Freund, Li, & Baltes, 1999), the action-theoretical specification of the SOC model posits that developing and committing to a hierarchy of personal goals (i.e., *elective selection*) and engaging in goal-directed actions and means (i.e., *optimization*) are essential for achieving higher levels of functioning (i.e., maximizing gains). To maintain a given level of functioning in the face of inevitable losses in resources people encounter throughout their lives, people need to *compensate* for their losses (e.g., by substituting goal-relevant means that are no longer available). When the costs for optimization or compensation outweigh the expected gains, according to the SOC model it is more adaptive to reconstruct one's goal hierarchy by focusing on the most important goals, developing new goals, or adapting goal standards (i.e., *loss-based selection*). Thus, the SOC model conceptualizes processes promoting gains (elective selection, optimization) but also processes to counteract losses (compensation, loss-based selection).

Empirical evidence supports the adaptiveness of self-reported selection, optimization, and compensation throughout adolescence (Gestsdottir & Lerner, 2007), adulthood, and into very old age (e.g., Freund & Baltes, 1998; 2002; Wiese, Freund, & Baltes, 2000; 2001; Ziegelmann & Lippke, 2007). The use of SOC strategies seems to be particularly helpful for persons with fewer resources (Jopp & Smith, 2006; Lang, Rieckmann, & Baltes, 2002; Young, Baltes, & Pratt, 2007).

Goal Selection: Managing Multiple Goals

A series of studies by Riediger and colleagues (Riediger & Freund, 2004, 2006, 2008; Riediger, Freund, & Baltes, 2005) demonstrated the role of the *selection* of goals for successful goal pursuit. More specifically, results by Riediger and colleagues stress the importance of considering the interrelations of personal goals. Conflict between goals might occur because resources are insufficient to support both goals at the same time through incompatible strategies. For instance, wanting to enjoy food and trying to lose weight imply incompatible eating behaviors, leading to goal conflict. Goals can facilitate each other by sharing the same strategies. For example, the two goals to lose weight and to lead a healthy lifestyle are both served by the same strategy of working out regularly. Goal conflict and facilitation are two largely independent goal dimensions and show differential associations with affective experience and goal-relevant behavior. Goal conflict seems to impair affective well-being; facilitation is associated with goal pursuit in everyday life and subsequent goal attainment (Riediger et al., 2005). Interestingly, older adults appear to gain in motivational competence regarding the selection of goals. They report more goal facilitation and less conflict among their goals than younger adults (Riediger et al., 2005). Importantly, this result is not simply due to a reduction in the number of goals but to focusing on personally important, superordinate goals. Focusing one's goals on central and similar life domains contributes to higher facilitation among goals, which, in turn, leads to stronger goal engagement and achievement (Riediger & Freund, 2006). Age-related increases in motivational selectivity, then, are one way of managing the increasing limitation of resources in adulthood. Another way of dealing with conflicts due to goals competing for the same limited resources is prioritizing. Wiese and Freund (2001) showed that young adults who experience conflicts between work- and family-related goals report fewer strains and higher subjective well-being when they prioritize one goal (and temporally postpone the other). Taken together, this research supports the importance of selection as a key process for successfully managing multiple goals.

Optimization and Compensation: A Tale of the Shifting Goal Orientation Across Adulthood

As mentioned earlier, one of the central tenets of lifespan developmental psychology holds that development encompasses both gains and losses throughout the life span. Examples of ubiquitous losses in later adulthood are health-related and cognitive decline or the loss of social partners and social status through retirement (Baltes & Smith, 2003). In contrast, affective well-being (e.g., Röcke, Li, & Smith, 2009), motivational competence (e.g., Riediger & Freund, 2008), and self-regulation (Hennecke & Freund, 2010) appear to increase across adulthood and into old age. The ratio of gains to losses, however, changes across the life span, encompassing decreasing gains and increasing losses throughout adulthood and into old age (e.g., Baltes, 1997; Baltes, Lindenberger, & Staudinger, 1998; Heckhausen, Dixon, & Baltes, 1989). Addressing this changing ratio of gains to losses, the SOC model holds that goals directed at the optimization of gains might be more important at younger ages, whereas goals directed at the maintenance and avoidance of losses might gain in importance with increasing age.

Arguing from an evolutionary standpoint as well as from a developmental perspective, it is advantageous to possess as many resources as possible (see Freund & Riediger, 2001). Resources are essential for reproductive success and survival. They signal success, relative social standing, and good genetic material to potential mates. They enhance attractiveness and successful reproduction and provide for the upbringing of offspring (Buss, 1999). Gaining resources appears to be a primary motivation in young adulthood, a phase in life when most people have not yet had opportunities to accumulate many resources that are advantageous for their reproductive success. Moreover, social expectations and developmental tasks for young adults are geared toward gains (e.g., gaining education or professional skills, founding a family, building a home, establishing a career). Young adults have large potentials for functional gains and still need to realize these potentials. As Raynor (1982) puts it, younger adults are still in the process of "becoming." In other words, before younger adults can start protecting and conserving resources, they need to acquire skills and resources and build upon their status. In contrast, with increasing age, one is increasingly likely to have reached one's personal asymptote of performance in many areas of life, making the achievement of new gains less and less likely. Moreover, throughout their lives older adults have accumulated resources, including skills, material belongings, as well as social relations that need to be protected against losses. Given the ubiquity of losses in older adulthood and the corresponding social expectations (Heckhausen et al., 1989), older adults are likely to be chronically aware of threatening losses.

In late adulthood, then, preserving resources and counteracting losses may become the primary motivation outweighing tendencies to accumulate new resources (Freund & Ebner, 2005; Staudinger, Marsiske, & Baltes, 1995).

Consistent with this hypothesis, J. Heckhausen (1999) found that younger adults reported more goals in domains associated with striving for gains and fewer goals in domains reflecting the avoidance of losses than middle-aged or old adults. Similarly, Ebner, Freund, and Baltes (2006) showed that, compared to older adults, younger adults rated their personal goals as having a stronger focus on gains. Conversely, older adults reported a higher focus on maintenance and prevention of loss in their personal goals than younger adults. Moreover, in two further studies using a forced-choice paradigm for tasks pertaining to physical fitness and cognitive functioning, younger adults were more likely to adopt goals focusing on achieving new gains compared to older adults who preferred goals focusing on the maintenance of their level of functioning. Attesting to the role of resources for goal orientation, Ebner et al. (2006) showed that younger adults shifted to a preference for maintenance goals when resources were perceived as being limited.

The shift in goal orientation across adulthood seems adaptive. Whereas younger adults seem to suffer from a goal orientation toward maintenance and avoidance of loss, older adults' subjective well-being was positively related to a maintenance orientation. Using behavioral indicators of goal pursuit, Freund (2006) showed that younger adults pursue a given goal more persistently when it is oriented toward achieving gains (optimization goal), whereas older adults are more persistent when pursuing the goal to counteract losses (compensation goal). In addition, when confronted with a resource loss, compensatory activities are related to positive affect in older adults (Duke, Leventhal, Brownlee, & Leventhal, 2002).

In sum, then, goal orientation toward gains and losses appears to change with the shifting ratio of gains to losses across adulthood. Moreover, this shift in goal orientation seems adaptive both regarding subjective well-being as well as actual goal pursuit.

Goal Focus: Process or Outcome

The previous sections focused on *goal selection* and the shift in goal orientation toward gains and losses across adulthood. In the following, we want to address how the cognitive representation of *goal pursuit* primarily in terms of its means (process focus) or its outcome (outcome focus) might affect goal-relevant behavior as well as affect, and how it might change with age.

Let us open this section with an example of process and outcome focus. Two people pursuing the goal of completing a 20-km hike in the Alps within 5 hours may focus on very different aspects of this goal: One of them might focus primarily on the consequences of successfully reaching the destination within the allotted time, while the other might focus more on pacing herself by monitoring her pulse rate and breathing. What factors determine whether a person focuses more on the outcome or the process when pursuing goals? Are there differences in adaptiveness of a stronger focus on the outcome or the process of goal pursuit? We posit that factors related to chronological age, namely the availability of (physical and cognitive) resources, future time perspective, and a goal orientation toward achieving gains or maintenance of functioning contributes to a preference for and adaptiveness of either an outcome or a process focus during goal pursuit. In addition, taking a closer look at the dynamics of goal setting and pursuit, we posit that the motivational phase and the closeness to a deadline determine whether people focus on the process or the outcome of goal pursuit. Finally, we discuss the role of goal focus when goal pursuit is hampered by setbacks or failure.

The concept of outcome and process focus is related—but not identical—to the concepts of extrinsic and intrinsic motivation as well as performance and mastery orientation. In accordance with Sansone and Thoman (2005), we define *outcome focus* as the motivation to engage in an activity because it is a means to a certain *end*. We define *process focus* as the cognitive salience of aspects of the goal that are related to the *means*, whereas Sansone and Thoman define it as the (expected) experience of interest in an activity. It is likely that people only persist in a certain activity for longer periods of time, however, if they experience it as being somehow rewarding, be it due to their interest in it, their positive affect, or its instrumentality for achieving a desired outcome. Focusing on the outcome or the process of goal pursuit is like beaming a flashlight on either the means or the end of goal pursuit, thus highlighting aspects of goal pursuit either related to the process (e.g., Do I have the means necessary to achieve this goal?) or the outcome (e.g., When will I achieve the goal?).

Differentiating Goal Focus From Related Constructs

LINKING OUTCOME AND PROCESS FOCUS TO EXTRINSIC AND INTRINSIC MOTIVATION

Extrinsic motivation is characterized by a focus on the consequences of goal achievement (e.g., external rewards for achieving a certain goal), whereas intrinsic motivation is typically defined as a focus on the task at hand (e.g., enjoyment of or interest in the goal-relevant activity). Compared to extrinsic motivation, intrinsic motivation is associated with voluntary involvement, more interest, and higher persistence in a task (e.g., Deci, Koestner, & Ryan, 1999; Krapp, 2005; Lepper, 1981). Intrinsic motivation implies that a person focuses on the satisfaction derived from the activity rather than on the external consequences of goal achievement. For instance, when one's goal is to paint a picture, either the amount of money the picture will bring in at the next exhibition (i.e., extrinsic motivation) or the enjoyment of and interest in the activity of painting (i.e., intrinsic motivation) could be in the foreground. Engaging in goal pursuit for tangible, external rewards has been shown to undermine intrinsic motivation (Deci, Koestner, & Ryan, 1999).

At first glance, the definition of intrinsic and extrinsic motivation greatly resembles process and outcome focus. Intrinsic motivation entails a focus on the process, whereas extrinsic motivation entails a focus on the consequences of attaining a certain outcome. The opposite is not true, however, as the concept of goal focus is mute regarding the underlying reasons for engaging in goal pursuit. For instance, a person might focus on the outcome of goal pursuit (e.g., a beautiful painting) for a goal that was set autonomously and will bear no further consequences such as praise or tangible rewards. Extrinsic motivation implies a concern about the *consequences* of attaining an outcome (e.g., receiving a monetary reward from parents for achieving a good grade), not about the outcome itself. Regarding process focus, a person might focus on the process of goal pursuit (e.g., painting) because she is positively reinforced for doing so (e.g., through teachers' praise for her talent and perseverance). Process focus, then, is not necessarily associated with intrinsic motivation.

LINKING OUTCOME AND PROCESS FOCUS TO PERFORMANCE AND MASTERY GOAL ORIENTATION

Another goal dimension related to goal focus is performance and mastery goal orientation. Dweck (e.g., Dweck & Leggett, 1988) defines performance goal orientation as a focus on how well one is doing (particularly as compared to others), whereas mastery goal orientation represents a focus on learning and mastering a skill. Dweck traces these two types of goal orientation back to beliefs about skills as fixed (i.e., an entity) or malleable (i.e., incremental), respectively. In the first case (entity theory), performance is seen as an indicator of the underlying ability and provides feedback about an unchanging trait. In the latter case (incremental theory), feedback is a means of improving one's skill level. A number of studies in educational settings have shown that setting mastery goals promotes interest in and enjoyment of goal pursuit, but that performance goals are typically associated with a higher level of performance (e.g., Harackiewicz, Barron, Trauer, Carter, & Elliot, 2000; for a review, see Dweck & Molden, 2005). In the area of organizational behavior, however, mastery goals (in this context often labeled "learning" goals) have been shown to be positively linked to the successful acquisition of new skills, feedback seeking, and performance (e.g., VandeWalle, 2001; VandeWalle, Brown, Cron, & Slocum, 1999).

Seijts and Latham (2005) posit that the adaptiveness of goal focus depends on the goal at hand. If the means and strategies of goal pursuit are not (yet) known or mastered, learning goals should enhance performance because attention is focused on the means of goal pursuit, whereas focusing on performance might actually distract and hinder successful goal pursuit. In a similar vein, and using the terminology of process and outcome focus, Zimmerman and Kitsantas (1997, 1999) point out that, when learning to master a new task, people are more likely to adopt a process focus, defined by these authors as a focus on the acquisition of (strategic) skills (i.e., mastering the various elements and steps of a complex skill such as writing or dart throwing) or, in other words, on the means for achieving a given outcome. Outcome focus, in contrast, presupposes mastery of the different elements of which a complex skill is comprised and denotes a focus on the actual outcome (i.e., performance level). In line with Seijts and Latham (2005), Zimmerman and Kitsantas found that a focus on the acquisition of skills and means (i.e., adopting a process focus) is beneficial when learning a new skill, whereas adopting an outcome focus enhances performance when the means need to be implemented as an integrated whole in the service of goal attainment (Zimmerman & Kitsantas, 1997, 1999). This result can be taken as first evidence for the hypothesis that goal focus and its adaptiveness depend on skill level.

Before we elaborate on the role of age for goal focus, let us summarize the main differences between process and outcome focus.

MAIN DIFFERENCES BETWEEN PROCESS AND OUTCOME FOCUS

Table 16.1 summarizes the main differences between process and outcome goal focus, which will be elaborated below.

First, let us point out that the differences highlighted in Table 16.1 are relative, not absolute. Typically, however, actions and the means of goal pursuit are more concrete than outcomes (Carver & Scheier, 1998). Similarly, actions take place in specific situational contexts (e.g., studying for the SAT), whereas outcomes are more decontextualized

(e.g., achieving a certain SAT score). Another feature distinguishing outcome and process focus is the clarity of standards of comparison between actual and desired states. Outcome focus is more likely than process focus to provide a clear standard of comparison because outcomes typically entail criteria regarding when they are reached (e.g., arriving at a destination within 5 hours). By comparison, it is much more difficult to define the standards of comparison for the means of goal pursuit without referring to the outcome (e.g., enjoying a hike is less clearly defined than reaching the destination in a given amount of time). Finally, researchers agree that higher-order, abstract goal representations (i.e., outcome focus) provide direction and meaning in life, whereas lower-order, concrete goal representations (i.e., process focus) provide guidelines for action (e.g., Emmons, 1996; Klinger, 1977; Little, 1989). As Little (1989) pointed out, however, people do not want to know *why* they are doing something but also *what* they should be doing. It seems, then, that neither of the two is in and of itself more adaptive. Instead, as discussed in the next section, the effects of goal focus are hypothesized to depend on factors related to chronological age.

Age and Goal Focus

As for the development of skills during adulthood, one could argue that skill level is associated with age. In many domains of life, young adults are still in the process of acquiring the means and skills relevant for goal pursuit, such as skills needed in the professional/work domain or in the area of establishing a long-term partnership and family. This might force young adults to focus more closely on the acquisition of skills or the process of goal pursuit (see Zimmermann & Kitsantas, 1997, 1999). Middle-aged and older adults are more likely to have acquired most of the skills necessary to pursue their goals in both the work as well as the social domain and, thus, could be seen as being

Table 16.1. Differences Between Process and Outcome Goal Focus

Process Goal Focus	Outcome Goal Focus
action/means	end state
subordinate goals (concrete)	superordinate goals (abstract)
contextualized	decontextualized
provides vague or no standard of comparison	provides clear standard
provides guidelines for action	provides direction, meaning

more likely to focus on the outcome of goal pursuit. Moreover, as Kanfer and Ackerman (2004) point out, skills can also be defined in terms of the balance between investment of resources and payoff. In the context of work-related motivational development during adulthood, they argue that the payoff for resource investment decreases with age, leading younger adults to be more focused on resource investment and older adults on the outcome. Next, we will argue, however, that other factors related to chronological age—the availability of resources, future time perspective, goal orientation toward gains or maintenance/avoidance of loss—suggest that, overall, the primary goal focus is expected to shift from the outcome to the process of goal pursuit across adulthood.

Some goals might lend themselves more to a process focus than others. For instance, goals related to an enduring characteristic (e.g., to be a friendly person) or maintaining some state (e.g., to stay healthy) require working constantly on the goal and might therefore be more suitable for a process focus than goals specifying an endpoint (e.g., to pass an exam). Therefore, maintenance goals may be more likely to be associated with a process focus, whereas goals involving the achievement of new outcomes (i.e., growth) should be more likely to invoke an outcome focus. As has been shown by Ebner et al. (2006), availability of resources is one of the factors determining whether growth or maintenance goals are adopted. When resources are perceived as being limited, people might feel that achieving new outcomes (growth) is less likely and desirable than focusing on the task at hand, namely, the process of goal pursuit. Similarly, as suggested by construal level theory (Trope & Liberman, 2003), goals that are temporally distant are more likely to be represented in an abstract way and in terms of ends, whereas shorter temporal distance of goals

should lead to a more concrete representation of the means ("do" goals, according to Carver & Scheier, 1998). Taken together, preference for a certain goal focus might vary by variables such as time perspective (Carstensen, Isaacowitz, & Charles, 1999) and availability of resources (e.g., Freund & Ebner, 2005). Both time perspective and available resources have been shown to be negatively related to chronological age (e.g., Baltes & Smith, 2003; Lang & Carstensen, 2002). Therefore, one could expect an increase in process focus and a decrease in outcome focus during adulthood (see Fig. 16.1).

As pointed out earlier, the developmental tasks of young adults entail the achievement of growth goals, which have an inherent *outcome*-oriented aspect due to the tangible nature of task achievement consequences (viz., a diploma, a job, a mate, a child). Thus, young adults may develop a more outcome-oriented approach to task achievement, and *outcomes* are likely to become highly salient during young adulthood. Later on, however, adults'—especially older adults'—goal orientation shifts toward maintaining one's level of functioning and avoiding losses (Ebner et al., 2006; Freund, 2006). Orientation toward maintenance/avoidance of losses implies a constant monitoring of one's actual performance vis-à-vis a progressively declining level of functioning. Thus, orientation toward maintenance and loss avoidance has an inherent *process*-oriented aspect. Accordingly, older adults may develop a more process-oriented approach to goal achievement. In addition, achieving new outcomes typically takes time. However, when one's future becomes more and more limited, growth goals with their inherently more distant outcomes might be viewed as less applicable to one's own life than maintenance goals with their inherently more immediate nature (as necessitated by constant monitoring). Thus, given that future time perspective decreases with age (Lang & Carstensen,

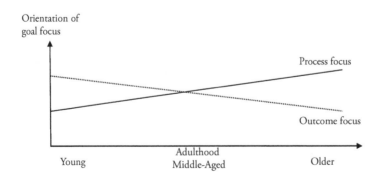

Fig. 16.1. Hypothesized relation of the development of goal focus across adulthood.

2002), one might expect older adults to be more process focused.

RESOURCES AND GOAL FOCUS

The importance of achieving gains and accumulating new resources in young adulthood (see earlier) is likely to result in a focus on achieving certain outcomes. Middle-aged adults might hold an equally strong process and outcome focus because, on the one hand, they are starting to experience a shift in resources toward decline and are, in many areas, at their peak in performance, making achievement of new outcomes less likely. This should lead to a stronger focus on the process of goal pursuit. At the same time, middle-aged adults typically still experience their resources such as (life-) time and vigor as plentiful, and they might therefore still aspire to reach certain outcomes because gains are still possible (Baltes et al., 1998; Freund & Ebner, 2005; Staudinger et al., 1995). This pattern clearly changes in old age, when resources decline (Baltes & Smith, 2003) and achieving new outcomes becomes less likely and goal orientation shifts toward maintenance and loss avoidance. As maintenance goals lend themselves more to process focus than do growth goals, older adults should also be more likely than younger or middle-aged adults to adopt a process focus.

This hypothesis is also consistent with Kanfer's resource model (e.g., Kanfer, 1987; Kanfer & Ackerman, 2004), which proposes that motivation (defined here as effort) depends on the perceived effort-performance function (i.e., the expected level of performance upon investing a certain amount of effort into a task at hand), the performance-utility function (i.e., the consequences of attaining a certain level of performance), and the effort-utility function (i.e., the payoff for investing effort into a task at hand). When resources decrease (e.g., as does fluid intelligence during adulthood), the expected payoff for investing effort declines, so older adults are expected to invest less effort into tasks involving resources on the decline. When resources are plentiful or even increasing (e.g., crystallized intelligence during adulthood), the expected payoff for investing effort increases, so effort will be invested into tasks involving resources that are increasing. Applied to the work domain, Kanfer and Ackerman (2004) propose that "among older workers, work motivation will be less determined by level of performance achievement and, rather, more determined by judgments of how much effort is required for requisite performance...and the utility of allocating that

effort" (p. 451). This proposition is consistent with the view that older adults' goal focus shifts from being primarily concerned with achieving a specific outcome (i.e., performance level) and more with the process of goal achievement (i.e., investment of effort).

TIME PERSPECTIVE AND GOAL FOCUS

Attempting to achieve certain outcomes requires adopting a future time perspective. Zimbardo and Boyd (1999) even view outcome focus and the ability to postpone immediate gratification in order to attain a goal at some later point in time as part of their concept of future time perspective. In contrast, present orientation is characterized by a more hedonic approach to life with a focus on more immediate gratification and less concern for consequences that lie in the farther future. Therefore, one could argue that an extended future time perspective is more likely to be associated with outcome focus, whereas shorter future time expansion might be associated with a focus on the process of goal pursuit that is taking place in the present. Investing into the future only makes sense when there is a future in which to reap the fruits of one's efforts. Consistent with this view, in their studies testing socioemotional selectivity theory (SST), Carstensen and her colleagues (e.g., Carstensen, Isaacowitz, & Charles, 1999) consistently show that a limited future time perspective is related to focusing on emotionally meaningful social goals. In contrast, a longer future time perspective is associated with information seeking, which can be seen as an investment in the future. As Fung and Carstensen (2004) put it, "When the future is perceived as open-ended, future-oriented goals weigh most heavily and individuals pursue goals that optimize long-range outcomes" (p. 68), and "when time is perceived as limited, emotionally meaningful goals (...) are pursued because such goals have more immediate payoffs" (p. 68).

In her studies, Carstensen shows that, different to younger adults, older people are more likely to restrict their social contacts to close social partners and emotionally meaningful social interactions. It is not old age per se, SST argues, but the shorter future time perspective of older people that is responsible for this shift in social goals. In fact, Lang and Carstensen (2002) show that age is negatively related to future time perspective. Moreover, when experimentally restricting younger adults' time perspective, they orient themselves more toward meaningful interactions with close social partners rather than investing into the future by selecting partners that might provide useful information (for a summary, see Carstensen, et al., 1999). Research on SST suggests that an extended future time perspective is likely to be associated with a focus on the outcomes of goal pursuit, whereas a limited time perspective brings about a focus on the present and, therefore, a more immediate payoff. With a limited future time perspective, people should be more concerned with the more immediate process of goal pursuit rather than the more distant outcome thereof.

Change Versus Stability Orientation and Goal Focus

In this section, we take a different perspective on gain and maintenance/avoidance of loss goal orientation by shifting the emphasis of this distinction away from gains and losses toward stability and change. From a developmental viewpoint, striving for the achievement of new gains implies an orientation toward *change* (e.g., "I want to become better in Spanish"), whereas striving for maintenance/avoidance of loss implies an orientation toward *stability* (e.g.., "I want to maintain my Spanish at the current level and not get worse"). Different to the distinction of gain versus maintenance/loss-avoidance orientation, change as well as stability goal orientation might be approach- as well as avoidance-motivated. In other words, change and stability goals can be either approach or avoidance oriented (see Table 16.2). When approaching a change goal, people are oriented toward a future state (e.g., "I want to *become* better"), whereas approaching a stability goal implies the wish to maintain an actual state (e.g., "I want to *stay* good"). Similarly, avoiding change is directed at an actual state (e.g., "I do not want to change"), whereas avoiding stability comprises a future state (e.g., "I do not want to *become* different").

Goal orientation toward stability or change is theoretically related to goal focus and thereby contributes to the hypothesized age-related differences in process and outcome focus. As we will elaborate

next, we posit that a change goal orientation might be associated with a stronger outcome focus and stability goal orientation might be related to a stronger process focus.

One of the main reasons why change and stability goal orientation might contribute to goal focus is that they imply a different discrepancy between the actual and the desired state. The very definition of a change goal is that it entails a significant discrepancy between the actual and the desired state. In contrast, there is no discrepancy between the actual and the desired state in a stability goal—the desired state is to maintain this lack of a discrepancy. Feedback-loop models of goals (Carver & Scheier, 1998; Miller, Galanter, & Pribram, 1960) suggest that, as long as a discrepancy reduction between the actual and desired state is intended and the outcome is not reached, a "tension state" toward the outcome exists; that is, the cognitive accessibility of outcome-related information might be higher *before* than after goal fulfillment (see Förster, Liberman, & Friedman, 2007). In a change goal orientation, a person attempts at reducing the discrepancy to the outcome ("negative feedback loop," Miller, Galanter, & Pribram, 1960). This should render the outcome cognitively more accessible than a stability goal orientation, where the desired outcome state has already been achieved.

Another line of argument for the association of change versus stability orientation and process versus outcome goal focus stems from the temporal value asymmetry assumptions (Caruso, Gilbert, & Wilson, 2008). Accordingly, people value future events more than equivalent events in the equidistant past. Future outcomes in change goal orientation should therefore have a higher value than outcomes already reached in stability goal orientation. Consequently, change goal orientation should lead to a stronger focus on the outcome than stability goal orientation. Taken together, then, the larger discrepancy of the actual and desired state in a change goal should lead to a stronger outcome focus when compared to a stability goal. Conversely,

Table 16.2. Difference Between Change and Stability Goal Orientation with Respect to Approach and Avoidance Motivation

Motivational system	Goal Orientation	
	change	stability
Approach	Future state	Actual state
Avoidance	Actual state	Future state

stability goals should be associated with a process focus because there is no discrepancy between the desired and the actual state.

Furthermore, change and stability goal orientation might lead to different goal foci due to *(1)* how resource demanding the pursuit of a goal is, and *(2)* the frequency of means usage for change and stability goals over time.

AD (1): RESOURCE DEMANDS

Means might vary in different regards, as making one of them more desirable, for example, for being less resource demanding than the other. Investing highly resource-demanding means might be acceptable if they help achieving a certain goal quickly and the investment of the means does not have to be repeated often. This is more likely to be the case in a change as compared to a stability goal that typically requires investment of resources as long as the goal itself exists (e.g., maintaining a certain diet in order to keep one's weight stable). Consequently, as means have to be selected more carefully when pursuing a stability goal, the focus should also be on means rather than the outcome of goal pursuit.

AD (2): FREQUENCY OF MEANS USAGE

Successful stabilization of achieved outcomes is often achieved by repeating already established goal-relevant behavior that helped attaining the now to-be-maintained state. Maintaining a certain state typically requires engaging in goal-relevant behaviors as long as people hold the respective goal. Stability goals (e.g., "I want to maintain my weight") are typically not achieved at one specific point in time and therefore do not render themselves to one-shot goal pursuit. Stability goals, then, are more likely to be pursued for longer periods of time than change goals that typically specify a certain end point when the goal is achieved (e.g., "I want to lose 5 pounds"). Therefore, as goal pursuit stretches over a longer period of time, people are also more likely to use the means for goal pursuit more often than when they pursue change goals that are more likely to specify certain end points. Frequency here refers to the absolute number of times means are applied (not to the interval between using the means during a fixed time period). According to semantic memory theories (Collins & Loftus, 1975) or spreading activation models (Bower, 1981), the more recently or frequently a concept (such as a goal orientation) has been used in the past, the more often it is activated, and the more cognitively accessible it is. Therefore, if people use means more often in a stability as

compared to a change goal orientation, means should also be more cognitively accessible.

ADAPTIVENESS OF GOAL FOCUS FOR CHANGE AND STABILITY GOAL ORIENTATION

There might be an adaptive correspondence between mental representations of either means or outcomes and change or stability goal orientation. As the pursuit of change and stability goals poses different challenges to goal pursuit, process and outcome focus might be differentially adaptive. In particular, we posit that the challenge of a change goal lies in successfully reducing the discrepancy between the actual and desired state within a certain time (e.g., Carver & Scheier, 1998), which should require more intense and immediate effort mobilization, whereas the challenge of pursuing a stability goal lies in maintaining it potentially endlessly, which should demand adaptive adjustment of means.

Let us first address the challenge of pursuing a change goal, namely to reduce efficiently the discrepancy between the actual and desired state. We maintain that an outcome focus might provide motivational resources helpful when people experience goal pursuit as effortful and demanding. As decision theories propose, outcomes are generally evaluated compared to the costs of attaining them, that is, the effort invested in the pursuit of a goal (e.g., Kahneman & Tversky, 1979). Given the same costs, the higher (i.e., the more abstract) an outcome is set, the more it is perceived to be worth investing energy in it. Furthermore, Fujita, Trope, Liberman, and Levin-Sagi (2006) demonstrated that focusing on higher-order goals (i.e., outcomes) increases people's motivation and mobilizes efforts for outcome attainment. A focus on outcomes leads to a preference for delayed outcomes compared to immediate ones, greater physical endurance, more self-control, and less positive evaluations of temptations that undermine self-control. Fujita and Han (2009) showed that changes in the evaluation of temptations depend on whether a goal is represented in more concrete or more abstract terms. This, in turn, might explain that an outcome focus can foster self-control when facing temptations. Additionally, Manderlink and Harackiewicz (1984) theorize that a focus on outcomes increases intrinsic motivation. Therefore, an outcome focus should be more likely than a process focus to mobilize motivational resources for optimal outcome attainment. Furthermore, the approach toward the desired outcome and the reduction of the actual-desired state discrepancy is evaluated and experienced as more positive the nearer one gets to the outcome (Carver & Scheier, 1982). In contrast, focusing on a discrepancy where none exists, as in the case of a stability goal, does not provide any further information regarding goal pursuit or potential for experiencing positive emotions.

Turning to stability goals, the main challenge is the length of goal pursuit. For instance, keeping one's weight is not reached at a certain point in time but instead requires constant adherence to a certain eating or exercising regimen. Because of the long-term aspect of stability goal orientation, the means must have the potential to be used for as long as the goal is held. This is not necessarily true for change goals where, once a goal is reached, it is either abandoned (e.g., I want to pass this exam) or translated into a stability goal (e.g., "I want to lose 10 pounds," once achieved, might turn into "I want to keep my weight down"). Because of the longer time frame of a stability goal, people have to pay more attention to how resource demanding their means are. Taken together, this suggests that, when pursuing a change goal, an outcome focus might be more adaptive, whereas the pursuit of a stability goal should profit more from a process focus.

As was elaborated earlier, older adults report a stronger orientation toward the maintenance of functioning, whereas younger adults are more oriented toward achieving new gains. Taking a stability versus change perspective, older adults should be more stability oriented, younger adults more change oriented. If, as we posit, stability orientation is related to a stronger process focus and change orientation to a stronger outcome focus, once again, we would predict that younger adults should focus more on the outcome of goal pursuit, whereas older adults should focus more on the process.

DOES PROCESS AND OUTCOME GOAL FOCUS CHANGE WITH AGE?

A short-term longitudinal study by Freund, Hennecke, and Riediger (2010) provides first evidence for an age-related shift in primary goal focus. In this study, younger and older exercise beginners' process and outcome focus were assessed using an exercise motivation scale. Outcome focus comprised such items as wanting to lose weight, becoming more physically attractive, or improving one's appearance in general. Process focus was operationalized as wanting to have fun, socializing with friends, or making new acquaintances. As expected, younger adults focused more on the outcome of their exercise goal, whereas older adults focused more on the process thereof. Moreover, outcome and process focus were differentially associated with goal-relevant exercise outcomes. Adults with a stronger process focus tended to experience a decrease in the distance to their goal over time and rated it as more attainable and important; they also reported higher goal involvement and satisfaction as compared to adults with an outcome focus. One of the shortcomings of this study is that outcome and process focus were assessed indirectly via the motivation to exercise.

Addressing this shortcoming, Freund and Hennecke (in press) demonstrated that a directly assessed process focus helped overweight women to successfully pursue the goal to lose weight over a period of six weeks. Moreover, in another study reported by Freund et al. (2010) presented four goals (e.g., to quit smoking) to younger and older adults. Each goal was described by five process-related statements (e.g., throw away cigarettes) and five outcome-related statements (e.g., improve health). Participants were asked to select five out of these ten statements per goal. As hypothesized, younger but not older adults showed a significant preference for outcome-related descriptors, indicating their stronger outcome orientation. A third study investigated age-related differences in and affective consequences of goal focus. Both younger and older adults were to choose between two "thinking exercises," one of them focusing on the desired outcomes of personal goals (i.e., outcome-related exercise), the other one focusing on means to pursue these personal goals (i.e., process-related exercise). Participants who selected the process-related exercise then had to list two successive means by which one could pursue the goal of having a good vacation. Participants who selected the outcome-related exercise had to list two successive desired outcomes of having a good vacation (see also Freitas, Gollwitzer, & Trope, 2004). Again, younger adults showed a preference for the outcome-focused exercise, whereas older adults showed no preference for either type. Affect measures were administered after conducting the exercises. A significant age by goal focus interaction indicated that older adults showed higher positive affect after the process-related exercise. Interestingly, younger adults showed more intense negative affect after conducting the outcome-focused exercise, which they had chosen more often. Even though younger adults appear to prefer an outcome focus, then, they experience more negative affect when adopting an outcome rather than a process focus.

Focus

model of action
'1991) and the
s accompanying
iollwitzer, 1996;
ler, 1990), we
es according to

iishes four con-
process[1]: In the
eliberate about
heir short- and
is their subjec-
s made, people
ifferent options
Steller, 1990).
on formulating
:tion plans that
ı the final *post-*
evaluated. Note
ases is idealized.
s, people might
, reentering the
:y employ (i.e.,
iaybe leading to
isen means. The
ausen proposes
dence) that the
r and prototypi-
ie hypothesized
s in the action
)89/1991), aug-
J. Heckhausen

If a goal is not externally set (e.g., by teachers, parents, boss), people have to come to a decision if they want to adopt a certain goal or not. During this phase, the *predecisional phase*, we propose that people are likely to adopt an outcome focus. This is because during this phase, they deliberate about the advantages and disadvantages of one or more temporally distant outcomes. Weighing consequences of different options is likely to direct attention to abstract, global features of the goal rather than the concrete goal process. At this stage, people think about whether they want or like to attain something in general before engaging in laying out a roadmap as to how to reach the goal. This is not to say that considerations about whether one believes to have, in principle, good chances of achieving the goal do not play a role. They clearly do, as research on goal setting shows (for an overview of this literature, see H. Heckhausen, 1989/1991). As the literature in the context of bounded rationality and the use of heuristics for making decisions suggests, however, people do not typically have elaborate lists in mind for integrating the various goal-relevant means, weighted by subjective likelihood of attaining each step (Gigerenzer, Todd, & the ABC research group, 1999; see also H. Heckhausen, 1989/1991). Even if all the necessary information were available, such an approach would overburden cognitive capacities and might not even lead to better decisions (Gigerenzer et al., 1999). Therefore, focusing on the outcome and the value attached to the consequences of a potential goal before making a decision seems more likely *and* more adaptive than taking a detailed stock of the necessary means attached to

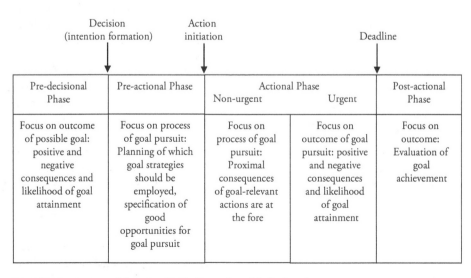

	Decision (intention formation)	Action initiation		Deadline
Pre-decisional Phase	Pre-actional Phase	Actional Phase Non-urgent	Urgent	Post-actional Phase
Focus on outcome of possible goal: positive and negative consequences and likelihood of goal attainment	Focus on process of goal pursuit: Planning of which goal strategies should be employed, specification of good opportunities for goal pursuit	Focus on process of goal pursuit: Proximal consequences of goal-relevant actions are at the fore	Focus on outcome of goal pursuit: positive and negative consequences and likelihood of goal attainment	Focus on outcome: Evaluation of goal achievement

Fig. 16.2. Integrating goal focus into H. Heckhausen's model of action phases.

the different outcomes also into account. In fact, H. Heckhausen and Gollwitzer (1987) showed that people focus more on the values of the outcome than on strategies of goal pursuit during the predecisional phase.

If a goal is not self-selected but instead externally imposed (and accepted as a goal by the individual), the predecisional phase is not relevant and people move directly to the *preactional phase*, which describes the phase after having committed to a goal and before actually engaging in goal-relevant actions. In the preactional phase, people plan the implementation of intentions as to how, when, and where to start goal-relevant actions and means. If the means of goal pursuit are well established and highly routinized, it is likely that people will immediately proceed to implementing goal-relevant actions, sometimes even in an automatic way, as Bargh and Gollwitzer (1994) posit in their automotive theory of goal pursuit. If, however, the means are not yet known and routinized, the focus is likely to lie on finding out the best way to pursue the goal (see also Zimmerman & Kitsantas, 1997, 1999). In line with this, H. Heckhausen and Gollwitzer (1987) demonstrated that the postdecisional phase is associated with the elaboration of plans and strategies of how to implement goal pursuit. Findings on the *implementational mindset* are highly compatible with the assumption of a predominant process focus during this motivational phase. Moreover, in a number of studies, Gollwitzer and his colleagues (for an overview, see Gollwitzer, 1996) showed repeatedly and consistently that clear and strong implementation intentions contribute to goal achievement. Implementation intentions specify goal-related means and actions, situations in which to apply those means, and also the right timing of acting on a given goal. Moreover, implementation intentions have important cognitive effects (i.e., implemental mindset): They focus attention on goal-relevant information and ward off distractions (including questioning the value of the selected goal), they heighten the accessibility of situational cues allowing goal-related actions (thereby enhancing the likelihood of seizing the right moment and opportunity), and lead to being particularly optimistic about achieving the goal. All of these characteristics of planning enhance the likelihood of actually initiating and completing intended goal-related actions or applying goal-related means (Gollwitzer & Brandstätter, 1997). Taken together, the literature suggests that during the preactional phase, people focus on the actual *process* of goal pursuit rather than the outcome.

In the *actional phase*, the primary task is to invest goal-relevant means and engage in goal-relevant actions in the interest of goal achievement. H. Heckhausen and colleagues claim that a focus on the outcome on a rather abstract level of cognitive representation might be predominant and adaptive during this phase. In contrast, we posit that focusing on the outcome might distract from good opportunities to implement goal-relevant plans and might thereby actually hinder goal achievement. Particularly when long-term goals are pursued that require maintenance of goal-relevant actions over an extended period of time, focusing on the activities related to goal pursuit (rather than the negative discrepancy to a desired outcome) should help maintaining motivation even in the face of hindrances or setbacks (see Kuhl & Beckmann, 1994). This should be the case because, if the very process of goal pursuit is in the foreground, the distance to the outcome becomes less salient. For instance, when the goal is to lose weight and the goal-relevant means is exercising regularly, a lack of weight loss over a certain period of time is less likely to discourage from exercising if the focus is on jogging every morning rather than on the weight one brings to the scale every morning. If an outcome orientation prevails, the person might give up exercising if no weight reduction is seen within a certain period of time. This might also be why many weight loss programs advise not to get on the scale too often.

In line with this idea, Houser-Marko and Sheldon (2006) found that formulating an existing goal in terms of "self as a doer" (e.g., "jogger" instead of "jogging regularly") leads to higher goal attainment in the domains of academic performance (Study 1) and exercising (Study 2). In contrast, research on positive fantasies, which can be defined as an extreme version of a positive outcome focus, has been shown to have detrimental effects for actual goal pursuit during the actional phase. Oettingen and colleagues have demonstrated repeatedly and in different goal domains (e.g., academic achievement, dieting) that indulging in positive fantasies about the desired outcome seems to undermine actual goal pursuit (see Oettingen & Hagenah, 2005). The authors speculate that the rewarding experience of anticipated goal attainment on an imaginary level might seduce people to fantasize rather than engage in the more laborsome process of the acquisition and investment of goal-relevant means.

The hypothesis of a predominant focus on goal pursuit during the actional phase is also in line with research on automatic goal pursuit. According to the automotive model by Bargh and Gollwitzer (1994), the repeated activation of a goal in a certain situation leads to an association of the respective goal and situational cues. Such situational features can then automatically trigger goal-relevant actions without being consciously aware of the respective goal (Bargh & Ferguson, 2000). This suggests that, during the actional phase, conscious awareness of the outcome is not necessary in order to pursue a goal. It might even happen that—temporarily or permanently—the process itself takes over as the goal and the outcome is either regarded as relatively unimportant or abandoned as irrelevant (e.g., jogging every morning for 45 minutes becomes a goal and techniques are acquired to improve running performance, whereas losing weight might be seen as a nice side effect of jogging but no longer as the goal). As these examples show, means and ends can change their status during the motivational process (see Kruglanski, 1996). Means sometimes become outcomes. Attention then shifts to the subordinate means to achieve the new goal (formerly known as means).

A different situation arises when a (self-set or imposed) deadline is approaching (J. Heckhausen, 1999). In this case the outcome will again become more salient. A deadline (e.g., losing 3 pounds until the night of the high school prom a week from now) revives the importance of the outcome and decreases the importance of the valence of the process. In such cases, the most effective (and not necessarily the most enjoyable) way of attaining one's goal needs to be identified and implemented so as to reach it in time. Closely monitoring the distance to an outcome becomes adaptive and adjusting means of goal pursuit accordingly is required (e.g., Schmitz & Wiese, 1999).

If the means for achieving a goal are not positively valued, even if the outcome is, people are tempted to procrastinate and not engage in goal-relevant activities. In this case, a deadline and the perceived negative consequences of missing it (i.e., not achieving the outcome) serve as incentives to get to work. The valence of the more abstract outcome representation (i.e., the positive valence of achieving the outcome, or the negative valence of failure) is helpful for overriding the negative valence of the concrete goal-relevant means. In fact, research suggests that deadlines increase performance and goal attainment and, moreover, that people even self-impose binding deadlines to counteract procrastination (e.g., Ariely & Wertenbroch, 2002). Thus, people might use deadlines to induce a shift from

process to outcome focus, thereby motivating themselves to strive for the positively valued goal instead of focusing on negative aspects of goal pursuit. Note that not only achievement-related goals can have such deadlines, but they can be applied to other life domains as well. An example of a (external) developmental deadline in the family domain is menopause for reproduction in women.

Adopting an outcome goal when a deadline is looming might, on the one hand, help to mobilize increased efforts of goal pursuit and attain a goal within a certain time frame. On the other hand, however, outcome focus might also hinder flexible adjustment of means and emphasize the importance of investing maximum effort over efficient use of goal pursuit strategies (Schmitz & Wiese, 1999). Hence, if a deadline is introduced too early in the motivational process, that is, when the most adaptive means or strategies of pursuing the goal are not yet established, goal attainment might come at a relatively high cost or people might not live up to their optimal performance level (see also Ariely & Wertenbroch, 2002). In cases where no deadline is set, people are expected not to undergo a shift from process to outcome focus during goal pursuit. The same holds true for goals consisting of a state to be reached and maintained (e.g., "I want to be happy.") rather than an endpoint (e.g., "I want to get married."). State goals do not have clear endpoints but instead stretch over an extended period of time. As continued engagement in goal pursuit is needed for such goals, they should be generally more conducive to process focus. This contrasts with goals that specify an outcome that can be reached at a certain point in time. Upon reaching such a goal—or after deciding to give it up (e.g., because a deadline has passed)—people enter the postactional phase, in which they evaluate the means and the degree to which they reached the outcome. If the goal will have to be reached again (e.g., taking an exam in school), it is likely that people are motivated to evaluate the quality of the means in order to be able to optimize goal pursuit in the next round (i.e., maintain a focus on processes for some time). With increasing temporal distance, however, people will focus primarily on the outcome (Trope & Liberman, 2003).

Taken together, goal focus is proposed to change relative salience depending on motivational phase. During the predecisional and, again, when urgency in attaining the goal is experienced, outcome focus should be predominant. During the preactional and nonurgent actional phase, process focus is expected to be more salient.

Consequences of Goal Focus After Failure

After having discussed antecedents of goal focus related to age, resources, time perspective, goal orientation, and motivational phase, we now turn to the *consequences* of goal focus when people have to cope with failure.

Previous research on the consequences of goal focus has shown that mentally simulating the process of goal pursuit (e.g., studying for an exam) is more beneficial than mentally simulating its attainment (e.g., receiving a good grade; Pham & Taylor, 1999; Taylor, Pham, Rivkin, & Armor, 1998). However, not much is known about the *underlying mechanisms* that render process or outcome focus more adaptive. We propose that one mechanism might be the reaction to failures and setbacks that might depend on the goal focus. More specifically, we put forth that a process focus is more beneficial because it fosters adaptive affective and behavioral reactions in the event of failure.

There are many typical situations in which goal pursuit is hampered by setbacks or failure: Dieters are frustrated when their weight goes up instead of down, students fail to pass their exams, and sportsmen do not win a competition. As setbacks and failures are a major threat to future persistence and subjective well-being (Carver & Scheier, 1990; Pomerantz, Saxon, & Oishi, 2000), psychological research has long been interested in how people cope with them: Under what conditions does a person remain persistent and substitutes his or her means of goal pursuit? When will someone give up his or her goal and decide to head for other desirable outcomes instead? One prominent determinant of affective and behavioral consequences of failure is attribution to internal or external, stable or instable, global or unspecific causes (Abramson, Seligman, & Taesdale, 1978). We argue that goal focus is another important determinant of affective and behavioral reactions to failure because it might influence whether the inappropriate implementation of means or the failed accomplishment of desired outcomes is in the foreground of failure identification.

FRAMING FAILURE AS MEANS- VERSUS OUTCOME-RELATED

Feedback is essential to evaluate progress toward a desired outcome (e.g., Carver & Scheier, 1981, 1982). Sometimes such feedback can refer explicitly to either the processes of goal pursuit (i.e., failure to implement the right means) or the outcome states (i.e., failure to achieve a desired result; Earley, Northcraft, Lee, & Lituchy, 1990). In the absence of explicit feedback, people can internally frame failure either as failure to implement the right means or as failure to achieve the desired outcome. Whether failure is framed as means- or as outcome-related should partly depend on goal focus. Thinking about means (process focus) should be associated with the cognitive accessibility of these means, whereas thinking about outcomes (outcome focus) should be associated with the cognitive accessibility of these outcomes. Conversely, as highly accessible goals or constructs influence information processing (e.g., Bargh, Gollwitzer, Lee-Chai, Barndollar, & Trötschel, 2001; Bargh & Pratto, 1986; Förster, Liberman, & Higgins, 2005; Higgins, Bargh, & Lombardi, 1985), a person who primarily focuses on means will be more likely to frame her setbacks as a failure to implement the necessary or appropriate means of goal pursuit (e.g., "I did not use the right dieting strategies to lose weight."), whereas a person who primarily focuses on the outcome will be more likely to frame her failure as failure to attain desired outcomes (e.g., "I did not achieve the weight loss I was hoping for."). In other words: Beaming a flashlight on the means of goal pursuit will more likely also highlight the blocked path, whereas beaming it on the desired outcomes will highlight the blocked outcome. Failure, then, should be framed as process-related in an outcome focus and as outcome-related in an outcome focus.

BEHAVIORAL CONSEQUENCES OF GOAL FOCUS AFTER FAILURE

Framing failure as process-related should have different effects on subsequent behavior than framing failure as outcome-related. After experiencing failure, people usually face different behavioral options: First, means that are thwarted or resulted in failure can be substituted by others (equifinality; Kruglanski, 1996; Kruglanski et al., 2002). Different outcomes can be attained via the same means (multifinality; Kruglanski & Jaffe, 1988; Kruglanski et al., 2002). A person trying to lose weight could, for example, try another diet if he realized that the one he has tried before does not bring about the desired results. In a process focus, when the means of goal pursuit are identified as problematic and inappropriate, means substitution (i.e., compensation; see Freund & Baltes, 2000, 2002) seems like the self-evident behavioral reaction.

Second, a person can decide to pursue another goal, if she perceives the desired outcome as blocked. Switching to another desirable outcome, that is, disengaging from the goal at hand and selecting a new one (outcome substitution or loss-based selection; Freund & Baltes, 2000, 2002), should be the more straightforward reaction in an outcome focus.

In line with this rationale, some researchers have also argued that "what the hell" cognitions result from identifying behaviors on higher, more abstract levels (Cochran & Tesser, 1996). "What the hell" cognitions typically occur in dieters. After having failed to resist a temptation (e.g., a piece of cake), they interrupt their dieting for a day or even completely disengage from their weight loss goal. As a consequence, they show disinhibited eating (e.g., more pieces of cake; Polivy & Herman, 1985). This breakdown of self-regulation might be caused by framing failure as failure to bring about desired outcomes ("I am not successful in reducing my weight"). Perceiving a goal as blocked might cause people to disengage from it and switch to the tangible goal of eating enjoyment (for a similar argumentation, see also Stroebe, Mensink, Aarts, Schut, & Kruglanski, 2008). In fact, we have shown that dieters who focus on a more abstract and outcome-related level of their goal (weight loss, improving their appearance, health, and well-being) show more disinhibited eating after failure than dieters who focus on a more concrete process-related level (the way they diet, persist, resist temptations, and change their eating behavior; Hennecke & Freund, in revision). In addition, a recent study by Burnette (2010) has shown that dieters who might tend to attribute failure to the outcome of dieting, as they believe body weight to be fixed (entity theorists) rather than malleable by the use of appropriate means (incremental theorists), report less persistence following setbacks. Moreover, findings of our own self-report study (Hennecke & Freund, in revision) also supported the predicted link between goal focus and a preference for means substitution versus loss-based selection after failure in other goal domains. Participants were asked to name two personal goals and indicate how much they think about the means of goal pursuit (process focus) and about the desired outcomes (outcome focus). As expected, process focus was strongly positively related to means substitution as opposed to loss-based selection. Outcome focus was slightly negatively related to means substitution; hence, it had a positive impact on the loss-based selection of new outcomes after failure.

AFFECTIVE CONSEQUENCES OF GOAL FOCUS AFTER FAILURE

What are the affective consequences of process and outcome focus when people encounter failure?

According to Carver and Scheier (e.g., 1981), feelings arise as a consequence of an automatic feedback process. The feedback process continually checks how well one's actions reduce the discrepancy between the actual and a desired state. If goal progress is below a criterion that refers to an acceptable rate of discrepancy reduction, negative affect arises. If goal progress exceeds the criterion, positive affect arises. If it is identical with the criterion, no affect arises (Carver, 2004). Failure of goal pursuit can be defined as a progress rate below this criterion or even stagnation. Accordingly, failure elicits negative affect (see also Hsee & Abelson, 1991). We propose that, especially when goals are difficult to attain and goal pursuit is hampered by setbacks, focusing on and valuing primarily the outcome has negative consequences because it makes the discrepancy between the actual and the desired state more salient.

A second explanation for the detrimental effects of outcome focus on affective well-being is based on the hierarchic organization of goals and goal-directed behavior (e.g., Carver & Scheier, 1982, 1990; Emmons, 1996; Vallacher & Wegner, 1985). Means are often referred to as subgoals that serve the attainment of more abstract, superordinate goals, the respective outcomes. As goals that are placed higher in a personal goal hierarchy are more important and central to the self (Austin & Vancouver, 1996; Boden, 1973), outcomes, by definition, should be more valuable than their respective subgoals or means; they might even be valuable only to the extent that they serve a desired outcome. Self-regulation is required when people engage in activities that are not intrinsically motivated or positively valued in and of themselves (e.g., eating low-caloric food instead of tasty but high-caloric food) but instead represent means in the service of pursuing higher-order goals (e.g., becoming more attractive). If means of goal achievement come to bear intrinsic value (e.g., if someone joins a gym to lose weight and experiences exercising as fun), the former means might change their status to a desired outcome (e.g., wanting to have the fun experience of exercising).

However, the opposite effect can come about when intrinsically rewarding activities become means of achieving extrinsic rewards. The vast literature on the detrimental effects of extrinsic rewards on intrinsic motivation demonstrates that activities can lose their intrinsic appeal if they are tied to extrinsic rewards (Deci et al., 1999; Lepper, Greene, & Nisbett, 1973). Moreover, Newman and Taylor (1992) have demonstrated the relatively lower value of means as compared to outcomes in a study with children who were given a snack as a reward for consuming another snack. Independent of prior ratings of how much children liked the snacks, they ended up liking the snack that was given as a reward for consuming another snack more than the "means-snacks," even though the position of the respective snack in the goal system was assigned arbitrarily.

Martin and Tesser (1989) also assume that the higher a goal in the hierarchy, the more likely it is that a threat to it will elicit rumination, the tendency to carry negative thoughts and feelings after being exposed to unpleasant events. Taken together, as a means is subordinate to its desired outcome, a threat to a means should be less severe than a threat to an outcome. Houser-Marko and Sheldon (2008) have supported this hypothesis when showing that failure feedback has stronger negative effects on mood when it is related to the process (in their terms: primary goal level) as compared to the outcome (in their terms: subgoal level). Moreover, Emmons (1992) demonstrated that people who focus on concrete goals show less severe depressive symptoms than people whose goals are rather abstract. Our own research supports our assumptions as well: We have found that framing failure experience during a low-calorie diet as failure to attain desired outcomes was related to significantly lower levels of affective well-being (Hennecke & Freund, in revision).

In addition to these direct effects of goal focus on affect, an indirect effect might result from the behavioral outcomes of each focus. When goals are higher in the goal hierarchy than their subordinate means, disengaging from a goal to switch to another (outcome substitution or loss-based selection) should impede affective well-being more strongly than disengaging from a means and switching to another (means substitution). In fact, we have found that means substitution (as opposed to loss-based selection) is positively related to affective well-being (Hennecke & Freund, in revision).

In sum, then, a process focus might be generally more adaptive after failure because it should lead to failure framing that refers to the means rather than to the desired outcomes of goal pursuit. This, in turn, should foster the substituting of means rather than the loss-based selection of a new outcome. Finally, focusing on means has positive effects on affective reactions to failure, whereas focusing on the outcome should make the discrepancy between the actual and the desired state even more salient.

Conclusion

Goals have wonderful qualities: They motivate behavior, help us organize behavior into action sequences over time and situations, and thus provide our lives with direction and meaning. Although we wholeheartedly agree with this assessment, we would like to distinguish at least two goal dimensions that modulate the adaptiveness of goals. Depending on the availability of resources, it might be better to orient one's goals toward gains, maintenance, or the avoidance of loss. Goal orientation, in turn, might affect goal focus on the process or the outcome of goal pursuit. We argued that a gain (change) orientation is likely to be related to an outcome focus, whereas maintenance (stability) orientation is likely to be related to a process focus. Moreover, we elaborated that the motivational phase might influence the goal focus (during the predecisional phase and close to a deadline, an outcome focus is more likely to occur, whereas during the actional phase a process focus should prevail). Importantly, regarding the consequences of goal focus, we argued that process focus might lead to higher persistence and higher affective well-being when people encounter difficulties during goal pursuit. Research on goal focus is just at the beginning of empirically testing these hypotheses. Initial results, however, are largely supportive of the ideas presented here. Future research will have to prove the incremental validity of goal focus over other constructs such as intrinsic and extrinsic motivation.

Acknowledgments

This chapter represents work that is currently pursued in a grant to the first author and financially supporting the second and third author. The grant ("Process and outcome focus—The role of age," ID: 100013–116528) is financed by the Swiss National Foundation.

Note

Unlike H. Heckhausen (1989), we use the term "motivational phase" to refer to all phases from setting to attaining (or abandoning) a goal.

References

Abramson, L. Y., Seligman, M. E. P., & Taesdale, J. P. (1978). Learned helplessness in humans: Critique and reformulation. *Journal of Abnormal Psychology, 87*, 49–74.

Ariely, D., & Wertenbroch, K. (2002). Procrastination, deadlines, and performance: Self-control by precommitment. *Psychological Science, 13*, 219–224.

Austin, J. T., & Vancouver, J. B. (1996). Goal constructs in psychology: Structure, process, and content. *Psychological Bulletin, 120*, 338–375.

Baltes, P. B. (1987). Theoretical propositions of life-span developmental psychology: On the dynamics between growth and decline. *Developmental Psychology, 23,* 611–626.

Baltes, P. B. (1997). On the incomplete architecture of human ontogeny: Selection, optimization, and compensation as foundation of developmental theory. *American Psychologist, 52,* 366–380.

Baltes, P. B., & Baltes, M. M. (1990). Psychological perspectives on successful aging: The model of selective optimization with compensation. In P. B. Baltes & M. M. Baltes (Eds.), *Successful aging: Perspectives from the behavioral sciences* (pp. 1–34). New York: Cambridge University Press.

Baltes, P. B., Lindenberger, U., & Staudinger, U. M. (1998). Life-span theory in developmental psychology. In R. M. Lerner (Ed.), *Handbook of child psychology. Vol. 1: Theoretical models of human development* (5th ed., pp. 1029–1143). New York: Wiley.

Baltes, P. B., & Smith, J. (2003). New frontiers in the future of aging: From successful aging of the young old to the dilemmas of the fourth age. *Gerontology, 49,* 123–135.

Bargh, J. A., & Ferguson, M. J. (2000). Beyond behaviorism: On the automaticity of higher mental processes. *Psychological Bulletin, 126,* 925–945.

Bargh, J. A., & Gollwitzer, P. M. (1994). Environmental control of goal-directed action: Automatic and strategic contingencies between situations and behavior. *Nebraska Symposium on Motivation, 41,* 71–124.

Bargh, J. A., Gollwitzer, P. M., Lee-Chai, A., Barndollar, K., & Trötschel, R. (2001). The automated will: Nonconscious activation and pursuit of behavioral goals. *Journal of Personality and Social Psychology, 81,* 1014–1027.

Bargh, J. A., & Pratto, F. (1986). Individual construct accessibility and perceptual selection. *Journal of Experimental Social Psychology, 22,* 293–311.

Boden, M. A. (1973). The structure of intentions. *Journal for the Theory of Social Behaviour, 3,* 23–46.

Bower, G. H. (1981). Mood and memory. *American Psychologist, 36,* 129–148.

Brandtstädter, J., & Renner, G. (1990). Tenacious goal pursuit and flexible goal adjustment: Explication and age-related analysis of assimilative and accommodative strategies of coping. *Psychology and Aging, 5,* 58–67.

Burnette, J. L. (2010). Implicit theories of body weight: Entity beliefs can weigh you down. *Personality and Social Psychology Bulletin, 36,* 410–422.

Buss, D. M. (1999). *Evolutionary psychology: The new science of the mind.* Needham Heights, MA: Allyn & Bacon.

Carstensen, L. L., Isaacowitz, D. M., & Charles, S. T. (1999). Taking time seriously: A theory of socio-emotional selectivity. *American Psychologist, 54,* 165–181.

Caruso, E. M., Gilbert, D. T., & Wilson, T. D. (2008). A wrinkle in time: Asymmetric valuation of past and future events. *Psychological Science, 19,* 796–801.

Carver, C. S. (2004). Self-regulation of action and affect. In R. F. Baumeister & K. D. Vohs (Eds.), *Handbook of self regulation: Research, theory, and applications* (pp. 13–39). New York: Guilford Press.

Carver, C. S., & Scheier, M. F. (1981). *Attention and self-regulation: A control-theory approach to human behavior.* New York: Springer.

Carver, C. S., & Scheier, M. F. (1982). Control theory: A useful conceptual framework for personality, social, clinical, and health psychology. *Psychological Bulletin, 92,* 111–135.

Carver, C. S., & Scheier, M. F. (1990). Origins and functions of positive and negative affect: A control-process view. *Psychological Review, 97,* 19–35.

Carver, C. S., & Scheier, M. F. (1998). *On the self-regulation of behavior.* New York: Cambridge University Press.

Cochran, W., & Tesser, A. (1996). The "what the hell" effect: Some effects of goal proximity and goal framing on performance. In L. L. Martin & A. Tesser (Eds.), *Striving and feeling: Interactions among goals, affect and self-regulation* (pp. 99–120). Mahwah, NJ: Erlbaum.

Collins, A. M., & Loftus, E. F. (1975). A spreading activation theory of semantic processing. *Psychological Review, 83,* 407–428.

Deci, E. L, Koestner, R., & Ryan, R. M. (1999). A meta-analytic review of experiments examining the effects of extrinsic rewards on intrinsic motivation. *Psychological Bulletin, 125,* 627–668.

Duke, J., Leventhal, H., Brownlee, S., & Leventhal, E. A. (2002). Giving up and replacing activities in response to illness. *Journal of Gerontology: Psychological Sciences, 57,* 367–376.

Dweck, C. S., & Leggett, E. (1988). A social-cognitive approach to motivation and personality. *Psychological Review, 95,* 256–273.

Dweck, C. S., & Molden, D. C. (2005). Self-theories: Their impact on competence motivation and acquisition. In A. J. Elliot & C. S. Dweck (Eds.), *Handbook of competence and motivation* (pp. 122–140). New York: Guilford Press.

Earley, P. C., Northcraft, G. B., Lee, C., & Lituchy, T. R. (1990). Impact of process and outcome feedback on the relation of goal setting to task performance. *Academy of Management Journal, 33,* 87–105.

Ebner, N. C., Freund, A. M., & Baltes, P. B. (2006). Developmental changes in personal goal orientation from young to late adulthood: From striving for gains to maintenance and prevention of losses. *Psychology and Aging, 21,* 664–678.

Elliott, A. J., & Friedman, R. (2007). Approach-avoidance: A central characteristic of personal goals. In B. R. Little, K. Salmela-Aro, J. E. Nurmi, & S. D. Phillips (Eds.), *Personal project pursuit: Goals, action and human flourishing* (pp. 97–118). Mahwah, NJ: Erlbaum.

Emmons, R. A. (1989). The personal striving approach to personality. In L. A. Pervin (Ed.), *Goal concepts in personality and social psychology* (pp. 87–126). Hillsdale, NJ: Erlbaum.

Emmons, R. A. (1992). Abstract versus concrete goals: Personal striving level, physical illness, and psychological well-being. *Journal of Personality and Social Psychology, 62,* 292–300.

Emmons, R. A. (1996). Striving and feeling: Personal goals and subjective well-being. In P. M. Gollwitzer & J. A. Bargh (Eds.), *The psychology of action: Linking cognition and motivation to behavior* (pp. 313–337). New York: Guilford Press.

Förster, J., Liberman, N., & Friedman, R. S. (2007). Seven principles of goal activation: A systematic approach to distinguishing goal priming from priming of non-goal constructs. *Personality and Social Psychology Review, 11,* 211–233.

Förster, J., Liberman, N., & Higgins, E. T. (2005). Accessibility from active and fulfilled goals. *Journal of Experimental Social Psychology, 41,* 220–239.

Freitas, A. L., Gollwitzer, P. M., & Trope, Y. (2004). The influence of abstract and concrete mindsets on anticipating and guiding others' self-regulatory efforts. *Journal of Experimental Social Psychology, 40,* 739–752.

Freund, A. M. (2006). Differential motivational consequences of goal focus in younger and older adults. *Psychology and Aging, 21,* 240–252.

Freund, A. M. (2007). Levels of goals: Understanding motivational processes across adulthood. In B. R. Little, K. Salmela-Aro, & S. D. Phillips (Eds.), *Personal project pursuit: Goals, action and human flourishing* (pp. 87–116). Mahwah, NJ: Erlbaum.

Freund, A. M., & Baltes, P. B. (1998). Selection, optimization, and compensation as strategies of life-management: Correlations with subjective indicators of successful aging. *Psychology and Aging, 13*, 531–543.

Freund, A. M., & Baltes, P. B. (2000). The orchestration of selection, optimization and compensation: An action-theoretical conceptualization of a theory of developmental regulation. In W. J. Perrig & A. Grob (Eds.), *Control of human behavior, mental processes, and consciousness: Essays in honor of the 60th birthday of August Flammer* (pp. 35–58). Mahwah, NJ: Erlbaum.

Freund, A. M., & Baltes, P. B. (2002). Life-management strategies of selection, optimization, and compensation: Measurement by self-report and construct validity. *Journal of Personality and Social Psychology, 82*, 642–662.

Freund, A. M., & Ebner, N. C. (2005). The aging self: Shifting from promoting gains to balancing losses. In W. Greve, K. Rothermund, & D. Wentura (Eds.), *The adaptive self: Personal continuity and intentional self-development* (pp. 185–202). Ashland, OH: Hogrefe & Huber.

Freund, A. M., & Hennecke, M. (in press). Changing eating behavior vs. losing weight: The role of goal focus for weight loss in overweight women. *Psychology and Health.*

Freund, A. M., Hennecke, M., & Riediger, M. (2010). Age-related differences in outcome and process goal focus. *European Journal of Developmental Psychology, 7*, 198–222.

Freund, A. M., Li, K. Z. H., & Baltes, P. B. (1999). Successful development and aging: The role of selection, optimization, and compensation. In J. Brandtstädter & R. M. Lerner (Eds.), *Action and self-development: Theory and research through the life span* (pp. 401–434). Thousand Oaks, CA: Sage.

Freund, A. M., & Riediger, M. (2001). What I have and what I do: The role of resource loss and gain throughout life. *Applied Psychology: An International Review, 50*, 370–380.

Freund, A. M., & Riediger, M. (2003). Successful aging. In R. M. Lerner, A. Easterbrooks, & J. Mistry (Eds.), *Comprehensive handbook of psychology. Volume 6: Developmental psychology* (pp. 601–628). New York: Wiley.

Freund, A. M., & Riediger, M. (2006). Goals as building blocks of personality and development in adulthood. In D. K. Mroczek & T. D. Little (Eds.), *Handbook of personality development* (pp. 353–372). Mahwah, NJ: Erlbaum.

Fujita, K., & Han, H. A. (2009). Moving beyond deliberative control of impulses: The effect of construal levels on evaluative associations in self-control conflicts. *Psychological Science, 20*, 799–804.

Fujita, K., Trope, Y., Liberman, N., & Levin-Sagi, M. (2006). Construal levels and self-control. *Journal of Personality and Social Psychology, 90*, 351–367.

Fung, H. H., & Carstensen, L. L. (2004). Motivational changes in response to blocked goals and foreshortened time: Testing alternatives to socioemotional selectivity theory. *Psychology and Aging, 19*, 68–78.

Gestsdottir, S., & Lerner, R. M (2007). Intentional self-regulation and positive youth development in early adolescence: Findings from the 4-H Study of Positive Youth Development. *Developmental Psychology, 43*, 508–521.

Gigerenzer, G., Todd, P. M., & The ABC Research Group. (1999). *Simple heuristics that make us smart: Evolution and cognition.* London, England: Oxford University Press.

Gollwitzer, P. M. (1996). The volitional benefits of planning. In P. M. Gollwitzer & J. A. Bargh (Eds.), *The psychology of action* (pp. 287–312). New York: Guilford Press.

Gollwitzer, P. M., & Brandstätter, V. (1997). Implementation intentions and effective goal pursuit. *Journal of Personality and Social Psychology, 73*, 186–199.

Gollwitzer, P. M., Heckhausen, H., & Steller, B. (1990). Deliberative and implemental mind-sets: Cognitive tuning toward congruous thoughts and information. *Journal of Personality and Social Psychology, 59*, 119–127.

Harackiewicz, J. M., Barron, K. E., Trauer, J. M., Carter, S. M., & Elliot, A. J. (2000). Short-term and long-term consequences of achievement goals: Predicting interest and performance over time. *Journal of Educational Psychology, 92*, 316–330.

Heckhausen, H. (1991). *Motivation and action* (P. K. Leppmann, Trans.). New York: Springer. (Original work published 1989).

Heckhausen, H., & Gollwitzer, P. M. (1987). Thought contents and cognitive functioning in motivational versus volitional states of mind. *Motivation and Emotion, 11*, 101–120.

Heckhausen, J. (1999). *Developmental regulation in adulthood: Age-normative and sociostructural constraints as adaptive challenges.* New York: Cambridge University Press.

Heckhausen, J., Dixon, R. A., & Baltes, P. B. (1989). Gains and losses in development throughout adulthood as perceived by different adult age groups. *Developmental Psychology, 25*, 109–121.

Heckhausen, J., & Schulz, R. (1995). A life-span theory of control. *Psychological Review, 102*, 284–304.

Hennecke, M., & Freund, A. M. (2010). Staying on and getting back on the wagon: Age-related improvement in self-regulation during a low-calorie diet. *Psychology and Aging, 25*, 876–885.

Hennecke, M., & Freund, A. M. (in revision). The path or the goal? Process versus outcome focus and the mastery of failure.

Higgins, E. T. (1997). Beyond pleasure and pain. *American Psychologist, 52*, 1280–1300.

Higgins, E. T., Bargh, J. A., & Lombardi, W. (1985). Nature of priming effects on categorization. *Journal of Experimental Psychology: Learning, Memory, and Cognition, 11*, 58–69.

Houser-Marko, L., & Sheldon, K. (2006). Motivating behavioral persistence: The self-as-doer construct eyes on the prize or nose to the grindstone: The effects of level of goal evaluation on mood and motivation. *Personality and Social Psychology Bulletin, 32*, 1037–1049.

Houser-Marko, L., & Sheldon, K. (2008). Eyes on the prize or nose to the grindstone: The effects of level of goal evaluation on mood and motivation. *Personality and Social Psychology Bulletin, 34*, 1556–1569.

Hsee, C. K., & Abelson, R. P. (1991). Velocity relation: Satisfaction as a function of the first derivative of outcome over time. *Journal of Personality and Social Psychology, 60*, 341–347.

Jopp, D., & Smith, J. (2006). Resources and life-management strategies as determinants of successful aging: On the protective effect of selection, optimization, and compensation. *Psychology and Aging, 21*, 253–265.

Kahneman, D., & Tversky, A. (1979). Prospect theory: An analysis of decision under risk. *Econometrica, 47*, 263–291.

Kanfer, R. (1987). Task-specific motivation: An integrative approach to issues of measurement, mechanisms, processes, and determinants. *Journal of Social and Clinical Psychology, 5*, 237–264.

Kanfer, R., & Ackerman, P. L. (2004). Aging, adult development, and work motivation. *Academy of Management Review, 3,* 440–458.

Klinger, E. (1977). *Meaning and void: Inner experience and the incentives in people's lives.* Minneapolis: University of Minnesota Press.

Krapp, A. (2005). Basic needs and the development of interest and intrinsic motivational orientations. *Learning and Instruction, 15,* 381–395.

Kruglanski, A. W. (1996). Goals as knowledge structures. In P. M. Gollwitzer & J. A. Bargh (Eds.), *The psychology of action: Linking cognition and motivation to behavior* (pp. 599–618). New York: Guilford Press.

Kruglanski, A. W., & Jaffe, Y. (1988). Curing by knowing: The epistemic approach to cognitive therapy. In L. Abramson (Ed.), *Social cognition and clinical psychology* (pp. 254–291). New York: Guilford Press.

Kruglanski, A. W., Shah, J. Y., Fishbach, A., Friedman, R., Chun, W. Y., & Sleeth-Keppler, D. (2002). A theory of goal systems. In M. P. Zanna (Ed.), *Advances in experimental social psychology* (Vol. 34, pp. 331–378). San Diego, CA: Academic Press.

Kuhl, J., & Beckmann, J. (1994). *Volition and personality: Action versus state orientation.* Seattle, WA: Hogrefe & Huber.

Lang, F. R., & Carstensen, L. L. (2002). Time counts: Future time perspective, goals, and social relationships. *Psychology and Aging, 17,* 125–139.

Lang, F. R., Rieckmann, N., & Baltes, M. M. (2002). Adapting to aging losses: Do resources facilitate strategies of selection, compensation, and optimization in everyday functioning? *The Journals of Gerontology Series B: Psychological Sciences and Social Sciences, 57,* 501–509.

Labouvie-Vief, G. (1981). Proactive and reactive aspects of constructivism: Growth and aging in life-span perspective. In R. M. Lerner & N. A. Busch-Rossnagel (Eds.), *Individuals as producers of their development* (pp. 197–230). New York: Academic Press.

Lepper, M. (1981). Intrinsic and extrinsic motivation in children: Detrimental effects of superfluous social controls. In W. W. Collins (Ed.), *Minnesota Symposium on Child Psychology* (Vol. 14, pp. 155–214). Hillsdale, NJ: Erlbaum.

Lepper, M. R., Greene, D., & Nisbett, R. E. (1973). Undermining children's intrinsic interest with extrinsic reward: A test of the "overjustification" hypothesis. *Journal of Personality and Social Psychology, 28,* 129–137.

Little, B. R. (1989). Personal projects analysis: Trivial pursuits, magnificent obsessions, and the search for coherence. In D. M. Buss & N. Cantor (Eds.), *Personality psychology: Recent trends and emerging directions* (pp. 15–31). New York: Springer.

Locke, E. A., & Latham, G. P. (2002). Building a practically useful theory of goal setting and task motivation: A 35-year odyssey. *American Psychologist, 57,* 705–717.

Manderlink, G., & Harackiewicz, J. M. (1984). Proximal versus distal goal setting and intrinsic motivation. *Journal of Personality and Social Psychology, 47,* 918–928.

Martin, L. L., & Tesser, A. (1989). Toward a motivational and structural theory of ruminative thought. In J. S. Uleman & J. A. Bargh (Eds.), *Unintended thought* (pp. 306–326). New York: Guilford Press.

Miller, G. A., Galanter, E., & Pribram, K. H. (1960). *Plans and the structure of behavior.* New York: Henry Holt.

Newman, J., & Taylor, A. (1992). Effect of a means-end contingency on young children's food preferences. *Journal of Experimental Psychology, 64,* 200–216.

Pham, L. B., & Taylor, S. E. (1999). From thought to action: Effects of process- versus outcome-based mental simulations on performance. *Personality and Social Psychology Bulletin, 25,* 250–260.

Oettingen, G., & Hagenah, M. (2005). Fantasies and the self-regulation of competence. In A. Elliot & C. Dweck (Eds.), *Handbook of competence and motivation* (pp. 647–665). New York: Guilford.

Polivy, J., & Herman, C. P. (1985). Dieting as a problem in behavioral medicine. In E. Katkin & S. Manuck (Eds.), *Advances in behavioral medicine* (pp. 1–37). New York: SAI.

Pomerantz, E. M., Saxon, J. L., & Oishi, S. (2000). The psychological trade-offs of goal investment. *Journal of Personality and Social Psychology, 79,* 617–630.

Raynor, J. O. (1982). A theory of personality functioning and change. In J. O. Raynor & E. E. Entin (Eds.), *Motivation, career striving and aging* (pp. 249–302). Washington, DC: Hemisphere Publishing Corporation.

Riediger, M., & Freund, A. M. (2004). Interference and facilitation among personal goals: Differential association with subjective well-being and persistent goal pursuit. *Personality and Social Psychology Bulletin, 30,* 1511–1523.

Riediger, M., & Freund, A. M. (2006). Focusing and restricting: Two aspects of motivational selectivity in adulthood. *Psychology and Aging, 21,* 173–185.

Riediger, M., & Freund, A. M. (2008). Me against myself: Motivational conflicts and emotional development in adulthood. *Psychology and Aging, 23,* 479–494.

Riediger, M., Freund, A. M., & Baltes, P. B. (2005). Managing life through personal goals: Intergoal facilitation and intensity of goal pursuit in younger and older adulthood. *Journals of Gerontology: Psychological Sciences, 60B,* 84–91.

Röcke, C., Li, S-C., & Smith, J. (2009). Intraindividual variability in positive and negative affect over 45 days: Do older adults fluctuate less than young adults? *Psychology and Aging, 24,* 863–878.

Ryan, R. M, Sheldon, K. M., Kasser, T., & Deci, E. L. (1996). All goals are not created equal: An organismic perspective on the nature of goals and their regulation. In P. M. Gollwitzer & J. A. Bargh (Eds.), *The psychology of action: Linking cognition and motivation to behavior* (pp. 7–26). New York: Guilford Press.

Sansone, C., & Thoman, D. B. (2005). Interest as the missing motivator in self-regulation. *European Psychologist, 10,* 175–186.

Schmitz, B., & Wiese, B. S. (1999). Eine Prozessstudie selbstregulierten Lernenverhaltens im Kontext aktueller affektiver und motivationaler Faktoren [A process study of self-regulated learning behavior in the context of motivational and emotional states]. *Zeitschrift für Entwicklungspsychologie und Pädagogische Psychologie, 31,* 157–170.

Seijts, G. H., & Latham, G. P. (2005). Learning versus performance goals: When should each be used? *Academy of Management Executive, 19,* 124–131.

Staudinger, U. M., Marsiske, M., & Baltes, P. B. (1995). Resilience and reserve capacity in later adulthood: Potentials and limits of development across the life span. In D. Cicchetti & D. Cohen (Eds.), *Developmental psychopathology* (Vol. 2, pp. 801–847). New York: Wiley.

Stroebe, W., Mensink, W., Aarts, H., Schut, H., & Kruglanski, A. (2008). Why dieters fail: Testing the goal conflict model of eating. *Journal of Experimental Social Psychology, 44*, 26–36.

Taylor, S. E., Pham, L. B., Rivkin, I. D., & Armor, D. A. (1998). Harnessing the imagination: Mental simulation, self-regulation, and coping. *American Psychologist, 53*, 429–439.

Trope, Y., & Liberman, N. (2003). Temporal construal. *Psychological Review, 110*, 403–421.

Vallacher, R. R., & Wegner, D. M. (1985). *A theory of action identification.* Hillsdale, NJ: Erlbaum.

VandeWalle, D. (2001). Goal orientation: Why wanting to look successful doesn't always lead to success. *Organizational Dynamics, 30*, 162–171.

VandeWalle, D., Brown, S. P., Cron, W. L., & Slocum, J. W., Jr. (1999). The influence of goal orientation and self-regulation tactics on sales performance: A longitudinal field test. *Journal of Applied Psychology, 84*, 249–259.

Wiese, B. S., & Freund, A. M. (2001). Zum Einfluss persönlicher Prioritätensetzungen auf Masse der Stimuluspräferenz [The impact of personal priorities on stimulus preference]. *Zeitschrift für Experimentelle Psychologie, 48*, 57–73.

Wiese, B. S., & Freund, A. M. (2005). Goal progress makes one happy, or does it? Longitudinal findings from the work domain. *Journal of Occupational and Organizational Psychology, 78*, 287–304.

Wiese, B. S., Freund, A. M., & Baltes, P. B. (2000). Selection, optimization, and compensation: An action-related approach to work and partnership. *Journal of Vocational Behavior, 57*, 273–300.

Wiese, B. S., Freund, A. M., & Baltes, P. B. (2001). Longitudinal predictions of selection, optimization, and compensation. *Journal of Vocational Behavior, 59*, 1–15.

Woike, B., Lavezzary, E., & Barsky, J. (2001). The influence of implicit motives on memory processes. *Journal of Personality and Social Psychology, 81*, 935–945.

Wyer, R. S., & Srull, T. K. (1986). Human cognition in its social context. *Psychological Review, 93*, 322–359.

Young, L. M., Baltes, B. B., & Pratt, A. K. (2007). Using selection, optimization, and compensation to reduce job/family stressors: Effective when it matters. *Journal of Business and Psychology, 21*, 511–539.

Ziegelmann, J. P., & Lippke, S. (2007). Use of selection, optimization, and compensation strategies in health self-regulation: Interplay with resources and successful development. *Journal of Aging and Health, 19*, 500–518.

Zimbardo, P. G., & Boyd, J. N. (1999). Putting time in perspective: A valid reliable individual-differences metric. *Journal of Personality and Social Psychology, 77*, 1271–1288.

Zimmerman, B. J., & Kitsantas, A. (1997). Developmental phases in self-regulation: Shifting from process to outcome goals. *Journal of Educational Psychology, 89*, 29–36.

Zimmerman, B. J., & Kitsantas, A. (1999). Acquiring writing revision skill: Shifting from process to outcome self-regulatory goals. *Journal of Educational Psychology, 91*, 241–250.

PART 5

Motivation in Relationships

Self-Enhancement and Self-Protection Motives

Constantine Sedikides *and* Mark D. Alicke

Abstract

People desire to maximize the positivity, and minimize the negativity, of their self-views. The tendency to exalt one's virtues and soften one's weaknesses, relative to objective criteria, manifests itself in many domains of human striving. We focus illustratively on three strivings: the self-serving bias (crediting the self for successes but blaming others or situations for failures), the better-than-average effect (considering the self superior to the average peer), and selective self-memory (disproportionately poor recall for negative self-relevant information). Nonmotivational factors (e.g., expectations, egocentrism, focalism, individuated-entity versus aggregate comparisons) are not necessary for the emergence of these strivings. Instead, the strivings are (at least partially) driven by the self-enhancement and self-protection motives, as research on self-threat and self-affirmation has established. The two motives serve vital functions: They confer benefits to psychological health and psychological interests (e.g., goal pursuit).

Key Words: self-enhancement, self-protection, self-serving bias, better-than-average effect, self-memory, psychological health

Introduction

Individuals routinely appraise their qualities, performance, behavior, and feedback they receive from others. They also choose activities in which to engage, allocate credit or blame for dyadic and group task outcomes, recollect events from their lives, use self-knowledge to understand other people, and judge the value of their relationships or the groups to which they belong. We suggest, in the current chapter, that these and similar domains of human functioning can be motivated, and we proceed to discuss the role of two pivotal motives: self-enhancement and self-protection.

Self-enhancement and self-protection are instances of self-evaluation motives (Sedikides & Strube, 1995), which themselves are a class of the hedonic or pleasure/pain drive (Alicke & Sedikides, 2011a). Self-evaluation motives guide processing and appraisal of

self-relevant information, broadly defined (Sedikides, 1993; Sedikides & Strube, 1997). Self-enhancement in particular refers to the desire and preference for maximizing the positivity of self-views, whereas self-protection refers to the desire and preference for minimizing the negativity of self-views. Self-enhancement and self-protection are reflected in individuals' tendency to exaggerate their strengths and to underrate their weaknesses more so than objective standards would warrant. The two motives are also reflected in individuals' tendency to construe or remember events in a manner that places their self-attributes in the most favorable light that is credible to themselves and to others (Sedikides & Gregg, 2003). Finally, the motives energize and guide attributions, task involvement, and behavior. In the long run, self-enhancement and self-protection foster psychological health (Sedikides, Gregg, & Hart, 2007) and assist in the advancement and protection of psychological interests (e.g., goals; Alicke & Sedikides, 2009).

We begin our excursion into self-enhancement and self-protection with a brief historical overview. We then provide key examples of motive instantiation, what we call self-enhancement and self-protection strivings (Alicke & Sedikides, 2011b; Sedikides & Gregg, 2008). These striving are the self-serving bias, the better-than-average effect, and selective self-memory. In discussing each of these strivings, we consider the perennial "cognition-motivation" debate. We acknowledge, of course, that cognition and motivation are closely intertwined (Kruglanski, 1989; Kunda, 1990; Pyszczynski & Greenberg, 1987). Yet we aim to provide evidence that the strivings are motivated and, in particular, that they cannot be exclusively accounted for by the vagaries of information processing (Sedikides, 2012). Next, we discuss the functional benefits of the two motives: promotion of psychological health and psychological interest. We conclude with a consideration of issues worthy of further empirical attention.

A Historical Overview

The seeds for modern theorizing on self-enhancement and self-protection motivation were sown in classical times. The Cyrenaics (founder: Aristippus; Tatarkiewicz, 1976) and Epicureans (founder: Epicurus; De Witt, 1973) thought that hedonism drives human action. They observed that people want to feel good, or avoid feeling bad, about themselves, and they further proposed that humans want and pursue pleasurable experiences, while detesting and eschewing unpleasant ones. Notably, Demosthenes, the orator of antiquity, remarked insightfully on self-deception: "Nothing is so easy as to deceive oneself; for what we wish, we readily believe."

The role of hedonism as the master motive receded while rationalism was in ascendance. This philosophical school, building on Plato's ideas (Bloom, 1991), depicted an objective reality that all individuals with correct understanding ("orthodoxy") could readily discern (Kenny, 1986; Loeb, 1981). Continental rationalists (Descartes, Leibniz, Spinoza), for example, opined that selfish, irresponsible, or malicious behavior was due to flawed knowledge. Erudition would cure personal and social ills such as immorality or the prioritization of personal over societal goals.

The pendulum swung back with Renaissance philosophers (Macfarlane, 1978) and the British empiricists. Mandeville (1705) argued that humans overvalue themselves and expect others to do the same. Hobbes (1651/1991) believed that behavior was driven by the unbridled pursuit of pleasure rather than by a failure to grasp a priori truths. "Men [are] vehemently in love with their own opinions" (p. 48), he proclaimed. The position that humans have an excessively positive view of themselves and of the objects (e.g., persons, possessions) associated with them was reflected in the utilitarianism of Bentham (1789/1982) and John Stuart Mill (1863/2004), the forewarning of Nietzsche (1886/1972) for the power of pride to rewrite memory (Maxim 68, p. 72), and the contemplations of La Rochefoucauld (1678/1827), Schopenhauer (1844/1996), and Freud (1905/1961a) on the curious human capacity for self-deception.

William James (1890) was the first psychologist to systematize various philosophical accounts and propose a unifying principle. He observed that thinking about one's self gives rise to the emotions of "*self-complacency* and *self-dissatisfaction*" (p. 305). He also remarked on "social self-seeking," people's persistent concern with the achievement of tangible successes and public acclaim. "Each of us," James stated, "is animated by a *direct feeling of regard for his [self]*" (p. 308). He proceeded to define the self (empirical "me") as a repository of ego-relevant matters. James' key animating principle, self-enhancement, found fertile ground in Gordon Allport's (1937) theorizing. He advocated that humans have a need for self-positivity, and he also regarded self-protection as "nature's eldest law." Heider (1958) similarly argued that subjective needs, desires, and preferences partially serve to maintain an individual's positive outlook. Rogers (1961) proposed the construct of positive self-regard, a form of self-appreciation achieved by satisfying one's own, rather than others', standards and expectations. In the meantime, Sigmund Freud (1915/1961b, 1923/1961c, 1926/1961d) and Anna Freud (1936/1946) were pioneering the analysis of defense mechanisms. The scientific study of self-enhancement and self-protection was born.

Instantiations of Self-Enhancement and Self-Protection

How have scientists approached self-enhancement and self-protection? They have done so through experimental and correlational investigations of over 60 instantiations (or implementations) of the motives. These marks of self-enhancement and self-protection have recently been summarized through factor-analytic techniques, with both Western (Hepper, Gramzow, & Sedikides, 2010) and East-Asian (Hepper, Sedikides, & Cai, in press) samples, into four factors: positivity embracement, defensiveness, favorable construals, and self-affirming reflections.

Positivity embracement reflects the acquisition of positive feedback (e.g., self-serving attributions for success), whereas defensiveness reflects the protection of self from threat (e.g., self-serving attributions for failure). A striving that exemplifies both factors is the *self-serving bias*, the tendency to credit the self for successes but to blame others (e.g., dyadic partners, ingroup, situations) for failures. Favorable construals reflects flattering portrayals of the self in the social world. An exemplary striving here is the *better-than-average effect*, the tendency to regard the self as superior to others in many domains of functioning. Finally, self-affirming reflections refers to securing favorable, or bypassing unfavorable, self-views and outcomes. A key mechanism through which this process is attained is *selective self-memory*, or disadvantageous recall for negative as opposed to positive feedback.

Next we review literature on the self-serving bias, the better-than-average effect, and selective self-memory. Although we fully endorse the close interweaving of cognition and motivation (Kruglanski, 1989; Kunda, 1990; Pyszczynski & Greenberg, 1987), we venture to make the case for motivation. That is, we attempt to document that this class of purposive goal strivings cannot be accounted for purely and exclusively by nonmotivational antecedents. Instead, each striving is, at least in part, an outcome of the self-enhancement and self-protection motives in action.

The Self-Serving Bias

"If more than one person is responsible for a miscalculation, none will be at fault," Murphy's law advocates. Weiner's (1972) attributional analysis of achievement motivation documented this pattern. Actors attribute their successful outcomes to internal factors (e.g., ability, effort, discipline) and their unsuccessful outcomes to external factors (e.g., bad luck, task difficulty, harsh course instructor). More generally, assuming the lion's share of responsibility for desirable events and denying responsibility or displacing it to external causes for undesirable events has come to be known as the self-serving bias (SSB; Miller & Ross, 1975).

The SSB is a robust and pervasive phenomenon. It is evident among university students (Zuckerman, 1979), athletes (De Michele, Gansneder, & Solomon, 1998), and drivers (Stewart, 2005). It occurs in the arena of interpersonal influence (Arkin, Cooper, & Kolditz, 1980), naturalistic sports (Mullen & Riordan, 1988), and organizations (Corr & Gray, 1996). It is manifested by children, adolescents, and adults (Mezulis, Abramson, Hyde, & Hankin, 2004). And it is found both in Western and non-Western cultures (Brown & Kobayashi, 2002; Mezulis et al., 2004).

Next, we will consider reasons why the self-serving bias is motivated or why it cannot be accounted for solely by nonmotivational factors. Specifically, we will discuss the role of self-threat, self-affirmation, expectancies, and impression management. We will offer representative examples in each case.

SELF-THREAT

From a self-protection perspective, when people feel threatened, they become defensive (Roese & Olson, 2007). Given an outlet, such as the opportunity to deflect attributions regarding task outcomes, they will grab it to footprint their defensiveness. Assuming that the self-protection motive underlies the SSB, the more threatened people feel, the stronger the magnitude of the SSB will be. A meta-analysis by Campbell and Sedikides (1999) tested whether the SSB waxes and wanes as function of self-threat, operationalized as negative feedback. This meta-analysis examined several moderators of the SSB, such as role, self-focused attention, and interpersonal orientation.

In particular, each moderator was classified as high or low in self-threat potential. For example, the moderator *role* was classified in terms of actor or observer. Actors presumably experience more self-threat than observers, given that actors' self-views are directly challenged by negative feedback. The moderator *self-focused attention* was classified as self-focused or other-focused attention. Self-focused attention presumably involves more threat, given that participants in this experiential state are more likely to become aware of the discrepancy between their actual and ideal/ought self. Hence, their focus on performance standards would intensify the psychological impact of negative feedback. Finally, the moderator *interpersonal orientation* was classified as competitive or cooperative. Some participants competed (actually or ostensibly) with another person, whereas others cooperated (actually or ostensibly) with another person, on a task. Failed competitive participants would presumably experience the highest level of self-threat because they would have the most at stake on the task outcome.

The meta-analysis proceeded to test the effectiveness of the SSB moderators. The proposition that self-threat magnifies the SSB was supported. For example, actors, self-focused, and competing participants displayed the SSB, but their respective counterparts (observers, other-focused, and cooperative participants) did not do so. In all, this meta-analysis illustrated that, the more threatened individuals feel, the more likely they are to resort to the SSB.

This conclusion is bolstered in research by Kernis, Cornell, Sun, Berry, and Harlow (1993) and by Crocker, Voelkl, Testa, and Major (1991). Undergraduate students are quick to find flaws in a test when they fail it but quick to stress its validity when they pass it (Wyer & Frey, 1983). This pattern is especially pronounced among individuals with unstable self-esteem, suggesting that these individuals use the SSB when threatened to shore up a fragile sense of personal worth (Kernis et al., 1993). Black American students experience a drop in self-esteem when the negative feedback is administered by a White evaluator believed to be unaware of their race; however, their self-esteem is unaffected when the evaluator is believed to be aware of their race. In the latter case, participants attribute their failure to racial prejudice, thus denying the validity of the test (Crocker et al., 1991). Here, the SSB is not only a mode to respond to self-threat but also a means to alleviate the consequences of threat (i.e., drop in self-esteem).

SELF-AFFIRMATION

As discussed earlier, self-threat intensifies the SSB. It follows that the SSB will be attenuated or cancelled when the self-threat is assuaged. One way of reducing self-threat is via self-affirmation (Sherman & Hartson, 2011). Here, individuals affirm a domain (e.g., values) irrelevant to self-threat. For example, they explain in writing, before or after they receive negative feedback, why some values are important to them. This self-affirmation procedure reduces defensiveness (and even buffers neuroendoctrine and psychological responses to stress; Creswell et al., 2005) by making individuals feel more secure in their self-worth. Self-affirmation, then, would reduce, if not eliminate, the SSB.

Sherman and Kim (2005) tested these ideas in field experiments with volleyball and basketball athletes. The experiments were conducted at the conclusion of a game, with positive feedback operationalized as a win and negative feedback as a loss. Immediately after the game, athletes were escorted into a conference room and undertook a self-affirmation manipulation. They rated and ranked five values (aesthetics, religion, social, political, theoretical) in terms of personal importance. Then, participants in the control condition received a 10-item scale corresponding to their least important value, whereas participants in the self-affirmation condition received a 10-item

scale corresponding to their most important value. Each item consisted of two statements, one describing a facet of the relevant value, the other being neutral (i.e., filler). Participants proceeded to rate their agreement with each statement. Participants in the control condition displayed the SSB. However, participants in the self-affirmation condition refrained from it. In all, self-affirmation eclipsed the proclivity to respond defensively to self-threat, a pattern tracked by the vanishing of the SSB.

NONMOTIVATIONAL EXPLANATIONS

We will now turn to the nonmotivational explanations of expectancies and impression management.

Expectancies

It has been argued that differential expectancies for success and failure account for the SSB (Miller & Ross, 1975). Based on prior experience (Kelley & Michela, 1980; Tetlock & Levin, 1982), individuals expect success more frequently than failure. As such, they make internal attributions for expected outcomes and external attributions for unexpected outcomes (i.e., SSB).

There is evidence that expectations can influence the SSB. For example, individuals with chronic expectations of superior task performance (e.g., high self-esteemers, normals) manifest strongly the SBB relative to individuals with chronic expectations of inferior task performance (low self-esteemers, depressed; Blaine & Crocker, 1993; Tennen & Herzberger, 1987). Similarly, participants who regard a task as important (and hence likely have chronic expectations of superior performance) demonstrate the SSB to a greater degree than participants who regard a task as unimportant (Miller, 1976).

Nevertheless, expectations are not a necessary component of the SSB (Weary, 1979; Weary Bradley, 1978; Zuckerman, 1979). Of the various moderators in the Campbell and Sedikides (1999) meta-analysis discussed earlier, expectations did not play a substantial role. Actors and observers approach the experimental situation with the same expectations, yet only actors display the SSB. Furthermore, it is not clear why a momentary state of self-focused versus other-focused attention, or a state of competitive versus cooperative interpersonal orientation, would influence task expectancies. Yet the SSB was manifested by some of these participants (i.e., actors, state-self-focused persons, competitive persons) but not others. Finally, the SSB is observed even when controlling for task importance (Sedikides, Campbell, Reeder, & Elliot, 1998).

Impression Management

Participants may display the SBB in a strategic maneuver to present themselves favorably to others (Miller, 1978; Weary, 1979). Impression management, of course, aims at the enhancement or protection of one's public image (Forsyth & Schlenker, 1985), although such aims are not always felicitous (Miller & Schlenker, 1985; Sedikides, Gregg, et al., 2007). Nevertheless, strategic enhancement/protection of one's public image does not necessitate the concurrent enhancement/protection of one's private self. Impression management may be superficial and short lived (i.e., driven by the moment or situation) rather than authentic. It may merely reflect putting on a persona or playing a role rather than expressing a cherished self-belief.

Impression management concerns can influence the SSB (Arkin, Appelmen, & Burger, 1980; House, 1980). Such concerns, however, are not necessary for its occurrence. Sedikides et al. (1998) tested undergraduate students at a large university. The participants worked together, as members of a dyad, on an interdependent-outcomes task. They were unacquainted and thus unlikely to anticipate future interactions. In addition, care was taken to ensure that participants expected not to meet each other after the experiment and not to discuss this experiment even if they happened to encounter each other on campus. Finally, all procedures were private, anonymous, and confidential, with each participant being unaware of the other's contribution to the interdependent-outcomes task. These procedures were intended to minimize impression management concerns. The experimental task ostensibly assessed creativity. Following bogus success or failure feedback at the dyadic level, participants did manifest the SSB.

Greenberg, Pyszczynski, and Solomon (1982) put the impression management explanation of the SSB directly to test. Participants took an alleged intelligence test ("Culture Fair Test of g"). Half of them learned that the experimenter was interested in their performance on the test and therefore would collect their named answer sheets and record their scores (public performance condition: presence of impression management concerns). The other half of participants learned that the experimenter was disinterested in their performance and had no way of knowing how well they had done on the test (private performance condition: absence of impression management concerns). Participants displayed the SSB in both conditions. Remarkably, the SSB was stronger in the private than public performance

condition. In all, impression management concerns cannot fully account for the SSB.

SUMMARY

Although nonmotivational factors play a role in the SSB, they cannot account singly for it. Expectations or strategic self-management is not necessary for the emergence of the SSB. In contrast, research on self-threat and self-affirmation makes a compelling case that the SSB is a valid signature of the self-enhancement and self-protection motives.

The Better-Than-Average Effect

Garrison Keillor's Lake Wobegon is a fictional location, where "all the women are strong, all the men are good looking, and all the children are above average." This characterization describes succinctly the human tendency for overestimation of one's merits and underestimation of one's liabilities, in comparison to other persons. Research has confirmed this tendency. Most people judge themselves as better than their average peer (Alicke & Govorun, 2005; Brown, 1998; Dunning, Heath, & Suls, 2004), and they truly believe they are so (Williams & Gilovich, 2008). The phenomenon of rating oneself above the average peer standing on positive characteristics, or rating oneself below the average peer standing on negative characteristics, has been labeled the better-than-average effect (BTAE).

The BTAE is robust and pervasive. It is found among undergraduate students rating their leadership skills, athletic prowess, ability to get along with others (Brown, 1986; College Board Exams, 1976), intentions (Kruger & Gilovich, 2004), resistance to socially undesirable media messages (Davison, 1983), complexity of personality (Sande, Goethals, & Radloff, 1988), possessions (Nesselroade, Beggan, & Allison, 1999), and, indeed, their very humanness (Haslam, Bain, Douge, Lee, & Bastian, 2005); drivers rating their driving skills, while in a hospital due to a car accident they had caused (Preston & Harris, 1965); college instructors rating their teaching ability (Cross, 1977); social psychologists rating the quality of their research (Van Lange, Taris, & Vonk, 1997); students assessing their dating popularity (Preuss & Alicke, 2009) or couples assessing the quality of their marriage (Rusbult, Van Lange, Wildschut, Yovetich, & Verette, 2000); and adults assessing their happiness (Freedman, 1978). In addition, individuals suffering from rheumatoid arthritis rate their symptoms as less severe than those of the average patient (DeVellis et al., 1990), and elderly persons judge that they are less at risk for age-related problems than their peers

(Schulz & Fritz, 1987). The BTAE has also been found among preschoolers (Weiner, 1964), elementary school children (Albery & Messer, 2005), high school students (Kurman, 2002), and representative community samples (Andrews & Whitey, 1976; Heady & Wearing, 1988). Ironically, people believe that they are less prone to the BTAE than the average person (Pronin, Lin, & Ross, 2002).

Next we will discuss five reasons why the BTAE is motivated. These pertain to attribute valence and controllability, attribute importance (in cross-cultural context), attribute verifiability, self-threat, and self-affirmation. We will also consider nonmotivational accounts of the effect.

ATTRIBUTE VALENCE AND CONTROLLABILITY

Self-enhancement and self-protection strivings are tactical (Sedikides & Strube, 1997; see also Sedikides & Gebauer, 2010). People do not self-enhance or self-protect across the board; instead, they are selective on the attributes that they will tout or undervalue. For example, they may be more likely to self-enhance on positive attributes over which they have high control (e.g., resourceful) than positive attributes of which they have low control (e.g., mature). Conversely, they may be more likely to self-protect on negative attributes over which they have high control (e.g., unappreciative) than negative attributes over which they have low control (e.g., humorless).

The results of a study by Alicke (1985) demonstrated that the BTAE effect indeed varies as a function of attribute valence and controllability. Undergraduates rated themselves more favorably on positive traits, and less favorably on negative traits, compared to their average peer. Thus, the BTAE increased as the valence of the self-attribute increased. In addition, participants rated themselves more favorably on positive controllable traits, and more unfavorably on negative controllable traits, compared to their average peer. Finally, they rated themselves more favorably on positive controllable than positive uncontrollable traits, and rated themselves less favorably on negative uncontrollable than negative controllable traits, compared to their average peer. This latter finding in essence illustrates that people self-aggrandize the most when they feel responsible for their positive traits, and self-aggrandize the least when they believe that fate is responsible for their negative traits.

ATTRIBUTE IMPORTANCE: ON THE PANCULTURALITY OF THE BTAE

Self-enhancement and self-protection strivings are also tactical in another way. People are more likely to assert their self-superiority on their important (e.g., trustworthy) than their unimportant (e.g., punctual) attributes (Sedikides & Strube, 1997). This principle is illustrated in recent work by Brown (2011, Studies 1–4), where participants indeed showed a stronger tendency to evaluate themselves more positively on important than unimportant traits (Study 1). This principle is also illustrated when placing the BTA effect in cultural context.

Important self-attributes are those that imply successful role fulfillment or enactment of culturally sanctioned roles. They imply that one is a valued member of a given culture, given that one excels on culturally (and personally) important characteristics, no matter if one falls behind on culturally (and personally) unimportant characteristics. Members of all cultures, then, will appraise themselves positively on important (but not necessarily on unimportant) attributes.

For Western culture important attributes are those conveying agency (e.g., personal effectiveness, competence), whereas for Eastern culture important attributes are those conveying communion (e.g., personal integration, other-orientation). Hence, Westerners will display the BTAE on agentic attributes, whereas Easterners will display the BTAE on communal attributes. Westerners, for example, will rate themselves as better than their average peer on originality or independence but not on loyalty or respectfulness, but Easterners will rate themselves as better than their average peer on loyalty or respectfulness but not on originality or independence. This hypothesis has been confirmed both by primary studies (Brown & Kobayashi, 2002; Gaertner, Sedikides, & Chang, 2008; Sedikides, Gaertner, & Toguchi, 2003) and meta-analytic investigations (Sedikides, Gaertner, & Vevea, 2005, 2007; for more general discussions, see Brown, 2003, 2010). The findings attest to the panculturality of the BTAE.

ATTRIBUTE VERIFIABILITY

There is another way in which self-enhancement and self-protection are tactically expressed. It involves attribute verifiability. Some attributes (e.g., those belonging to the moral or social domain) are more difficult to verify objectively than others (e.g., those belonging to the intellectual or physical domain; Reeder & Brewer, 1979; Rothbart & Park, 1986). Therefore, moral attributes leave more latitude for self-enhancement strivings than intellectual ones. The BTAE, then, will be stronger in the case of moral than intellectual attributes.

This pattern has been empirically supported. Participants firmly believe that they have enacted more moral behaviors than their average peer. However, they believe rather tentatively that they have enacted more intellectual behaviors than their peers (Allison, Messick, & Goethals, 1980; Van Lange & Sedikides, 1998). In addition, participants rate themselves as better than average on traits that are either preclassified as ambiguous or are manipulated to be ambiguous (Critcher, Helzer, & Dunning, 2011). These findings illustrate that self-enhancement and self-protection strivings, albeit "dying to come out," are susceptible to reality constraints (Gramzow, 2011; Sedikides & Gregg, 2008).

SELF-THREAT

A self-protection perspective would predict that, when individuals feel threatened, they will become defensive (Roese & Olson, 2007). We have discussed evidence that self-threat intensifies the SSB. Does self-threat also intensify the BTAE?

Research by Brown (2011, Study 4) showed that it does. All participants took the Remotes Associates Test (RAT; Mednick, 1962), ostensibly a test of the cognitive ability of integrative orientation (defined as creativity). The RAT consists of a series of three words; in each case, participants are asked to generate a fourth word that relates in some way to the other three. All RAT problems were difficult, and participants received either bogus negative feedback or no feedback. Subsequently, participants completed a BTAE task: They rated both themselves and most other people on important and unimportant traits. Participants who received negative feedback manifested a stronger BTAE effect (compared to those who did not receive feedback). In particular, they rated themselves as superior to others on important than unimportant traits, but they rated others as superior on unimportant than important traits. These results underscore the motivational relevance of the BTAE (see also: Brown, Collins, & Schmidt, 1988; Brown & Gallagher, 1992; Dunning, Leuenberger, & Sherman, 1995).

Self-Affirmation

Does self-affirmation reduce the BTAE? An experiment by Guenther (2011) addressed this question. Participants were assigned to either a self-affirmation or a control condition. The manipulation was a hybrid of two established procedures introduced by Blanton, Pelham, DeHart, and Carvallo (2001) and by Wiesenfeld, Brockner, Petzall, Wolf, and Bailey (2001). Specifically, self-affirmation participants described an accomplishment or achievement that made them feel good about themselves. Control participants, on the other hand, described the student union building on campus. Subsequently, all participants rated their standing, relative to that of their average academic peer, on a variety of traits (e.g., cooperative, truthful, athletic, attractive, imaginative, tolerant).

The results were revealing. The BTAE emerged, as expected, among participants in the control condition, but it was attenuated among participants in the self-affirmation condition. Self-affirmation reduced defensiveness or the need to assert one's superiority over others. These findings attest to the motivational underpinnings of the BTAE.

NONMOTIVATIONAL EXPLANATIONS

The three most prominent nonmotivational explanations for the BTAE effect are egocentrism, focalism, and individuated-entity versus aggregate comparisons. We consider them next along with a fourth possibility, that the BTAE reflects simple contrast of oneself from the average peer.

Egocentrism

According to egocentrism, when participants compare their attributes to those of the average peer, they think selectively about their own strengths or about their peer's weaknesses (Champers, Windschitl, & Suls, 2003; Moore, 2007; Moore & Kim, 2003; Weinstein, 1980). However, selective recruitment of one's assets or of peers' liabilities may themselves be expressions of self-enhancement and self-protection (Brunot & Sanitioso, 2004; Sanitioso & Niedenthal, 2006). In addition, egocentrism cannot explain why the BTAE is obtained not only with direct measures (where participants compare the self to the average peer on a single scale) but also with indirect measures (where participants rate the self and average peer on separate and scales that are counterbalanced) (Alicke & Govorun, 2005). Moreover, egocentrism has trouble accounting for why the BTAE is stronger on unverifiable than verifiable traits (Allison et al., 1989; Critcher et al., 2011) and for why self-affirmation reduces the BTAE (Guenther, 2011). Finally and importantly, the BTAE is observed even when behavioral evidence for attributes is equated for self and others. This pattern was demonstrated by Alicke, Vredenburg, Hiatt, and Govorun (2001). Participants first estimated the percentage of times they enacted various trait-relevant behaviors (e.g., percentage of times they were uncooperative or cooperative, when the opportunity arose). A month and a half later, participants received the very same estimates but were led to believe that the estimates were provided by their average peer. Still, participants rated themselves more favorably than "their average peer" on almost all traits. Participants claimed that they were superior to themselves.

Focalism

According to focalism, people put greater weight on whatever entity is currently the focus of their attention. By asking participants to compare their attributes to those of their average peer, research on the BTAE places the self in the focal position and the average peer in the referent position. Self-representations consist of a higher number of unique attributes than other-representations (Karylowski, 1990; Karylowski & Skarzynska, 1992). Hence, focusing on the self highlights those unique attributes and leads to perceiving the self as less similar than the average peer (Moore & Kim, 2003; Otten & van der Pligt, 1996; Pahl & Eiser, 2006, 2007; Windschitl, Kruger, & Sims, 2003). However, focalism cannot provide an adequate account of why the BTAE varies as a function of attribute valence, controllability, importance, and verifiability. In addition, focalism cannot explain why the BTAE is obtained with indirect measures (Alicke & Govorun, 2005), when behavioral base rates for relevant traits are the same for self and other (Alicke et al., 2001), and even when the referent is highly concretized (Alicke, Klotz, Breitenbecher, Yurak, & Vredenburg, 1995). Finally, focalism cannot explain why participants manifest a stronger BTAE on important than unimportant traits, even when the self constitutes the referent and "most other people" constitute the target (Brown, 2011, Study 3).

Individuated-Entity Versus Aggregate Comparisons

This nonmotivational account refers to a single entity (e.g., a person, an object) being compared with an aggregate (e.g., the average peer, the average object). Klar and his colleagues (Giladi & Klar, 2002; Klar, 2002; Klar & Giladi, 1997) showed that any member of a liked group (e.g., a randomly selected student at one's university, police officer, soap fragrance) is rated more positively than the group average (e.g., average student at one's university, average police officer, average fragrance), and that any member of a disliked group is rated more negatively than the group average. These findings raise the possibility that the BTAE is due to the self being an individuated entity and the average peer being an aggregate. However, the BTAE is still present when the individuated entity is the self; that is, the effect emerges even when the self is compared to any other individuated entity (Alicke et al., 1995). In addition, this nonmotivational alternative cannot explain why the effect ebbs and flows as a function of the motivational significance of the judgment (e.g., attribute valence, controllability, verifiability, importance). Moreover, the alternative cannot easily explain why self-affirmation weakens the effect and, importantly, why the effect emerges even under cognitive load (Alicke et al., 1995, Study 7)—a pattern indicative of automatic self-enhancement (Paulhus, 1993). Finally, the alternative cannot explain why participants manifest a stronger BTAE on important than unimportant traits, even when they compare themselves with a single person (Brown, 2011, Study 2).

Assimilation and Contrast

Although some researchers have conjectured that self versus average peer judgments are made by anchoring on the self and contrasting the average peer from that point (e.g., Kruger, 1999), until recently, no studies had been designed specifically to examine this facet of the BTAE. To address this question, Guenther and Alicke (2010) constructed an experimental design that was equipped to test whether self versus average peer judgments represent assimilation or contrast, and in what direction assimilation or contrast might occur. In the first study, participants first made either self or average peer ratings in a pretesting session. Later in the semester, their original ratings were returned and they were now asked to rate the other target (i.e., those who rated the self in the first phase now rated the average peer in relation to their self-ratings, and those who rated the average peer in the first phase now rated the self in relation to their average peer ratings). Comparisons with the ratings provided by a group that simply made simultaneous ratings of self and the average peer showed that self-ratings were unaltered as a result of whether self and average peer were rated simultaneously, self was rated in relation to the average peer, or the average peer was rated in relation to the self. This shows clearly that the self anchors these judgments. The findings also demonstrated that ratings of the average peer were higher when made in relation to self-ratings than when self and average peer were rated simultaneously. Contrary to the common assumption that judgments of an average peer are contrasted *from* the self, average peer ratings were assimilated *toward* the self.

The fact that people move evaluations of the average peer closer to the self seems to contradict self-enhancement assumptions. However, most modern self-enhancement perspectives (Alicke & Sedikides, 2009; Sedikides & Gregg, 2003, 2008) acknowledge that such tendencies occur in concert with many nonmotivational forces, including relatively automatic anchoring and adjustment processes. Guenther and Alicke (2010) next designed a study to assess whether self-enhancement motives could be discerned in light of these assimilative comparative judgments.

In this study (Guenther & Alicke, 2010, Study 2), participants made self-judgments on various trait dimensions during pretesting. The returned later in the semester and were provided with the self-ratings they had completed during pretesting. This time, they were asked to evaluate the average college student with reference to these self-ratings. Most important, half of the participants were led to think that the ratings they now received were those provided by a randomly selected student instead of by themselves. The critical comparison was between ratings of the average peer made with reference to scale points that participants believed were their own ratings, and those made with reference to identical points that were believed to belong to another student. Participants assimilated their ratings of average toward the scale points provided to a lesser degree when those scale points were described as self-ratings compared to when the identical points were attributed to another individual. Thus, although anchoring comparative judgments on the self induces average-peer assimilation because of the fact that self-ratings constitute high scale points, participants' desire to maintain favorable self-concepts restricts this assimilative process and thereby maximizes the distance between the self and the average peer.

SUMMARY

As with the SSB, nonmotivational explanations for the BTAE are rather unsatisfactory. Egocentrism, focalism, individuated-entity versus aggregate comparisons, and assimilation/contrast cannot account for the fluctuation of the BTAE as a function of assessment technique (i.e., indirect measures, equation of behavioral evidence for self and other, cognitive load), motivational relevance (attribute valence, controllability, importance, verifiability), and referent individuation. On the other hand, research on self-threat, self-affirmation, and the motivational relevance of the BTAE makes a compelling case

that this effect is a legitimate signature of self-enhancement and self-protection motivation.

Selective Self-Memory

"It's not only the most difficult thing to know one's self, but the most inconvenient," quipped Josh Billings. The empirical evidence has treated Billings kindly. People indeed remember poorly their weaknesses compared to their strengths, a memorial pattern that does not occur for other people's weaknesses and strengths (Sedikides & Green, 2009; Skowronski, 2011). We refer to this phenomenon as selective self-memory. Next we discuss it by reviewing research both from the autobiographical and experimental literatures.

Selective self-memory is robust and pervasive. It has been observed in the domain of feedback (Crary, 1966; Sedikides & Green, 2000), social act frequencies (Gosling, John, Craik, & Robins, 1998), possessions and places (Zauberman, Ratner, & Kim, 2009), relationship-relevant behaviors (Van Lange, Rusbult, Semin-Goossens, Goerts, & Stalpers, 1999), personality traits (Messick, Bloom, Boldizar, & Samuelson, 1985; Mischel, Ebbesen, & Zeiss, 1976), life events (Ross & Wilson, 2002; Skowronski, Betz, Thompson, & Shannon, 1991), and emotionally charged (i.e., pride-inducing and shame-inducing) events (D'Argembeau & Van der Linden, 2008). It has also been observed not only in Western but also in non-Western or East-Asian cultures (Kwon, Scheibe, Samanez-Larkin, Tsai, & Carstensen, 2009; Schrauf & Hoffman, 2007). Selective self-memory emerges early in life. Children, for example, ascribe more serious transgressions to their siblings than to themselves in their recollections of sibling conflict (Wilson, Smith, Ross, & Ross, 2004). Finally, selective self-memory is found both among younger and older adults (Field, 1981, 1997; Wagenaar & Groeneweg, 1990; Yarrow, Campbell, & Burton, 1970).

Selective self-memory may be due to an encoding bias. People avoid attending to unfavorable feedback (Baumeister & Cairns, 1992; Sedikides & Green, 2000, Experiment 3), thus impeding its registration. However, selective self-memory may also be due to a retrieval bias. Evidence for this processing mechanism is found in memory for behaviors that exemplify desirable traits (Sanitioso, Kunda, & Fong, 1990), satisfying interpersonal relationships (Murray & Holmes, 1993), and health-boosting habits (Ross, McFarland, & Fletcher, 1981). Finally, selective self-memory may be due to retention. The negative affect associated with autobiographical memories fades faster across time than the positive affect associated with such memories (Landau & Gunter, 2009; Ritchie, Skowronski, Hartnett, Wells, & Walker, 2009; Walker, Skowronski, & Thompson, 2003).

We will examine next why selective self-memory is motivated. In particular, we will zero in on the role of self-threat and self-affirmation in selective self-memory. We will also consider the nonmotivational accounts of differential expectancies and inconsistency between information valence and self-view valence.

Self-Threat

Sedikides and colleagues (Sedikides & Green, 2009; Sedikides, Green, & Pinter, 2004) tested experimentally the role of self-threat in selective self-memory. In the standard paradigm, participants first receive behavioral feedback. Some are then asked to imagine, or are led to believe, that they are likely to perform the behaviors contained in the feedback. Other participants are asked to imagine, or are led to believe, that another person (Chris) is likely to perform the very same behaviors. These behaviors are either negative or positive, and they exemplify either central (e.g., unkind vs. kind, untrustworthy vs. trustworthy) or peripheral (e.g., complaining vs. uncomplaining, unpredictable vs. predictable) traits. Next, participants engage in a surprise recall task. The typical finding is that participants recall poorly behaviors that are negative, exemplify central traits, and refer to the self (e.g., unkind or untrustworthy behaviors) compared to all other categories of behavior (e.g., those that are positive, exemplify central traits, and refer to the self; those that are negative exemplify central traits but refer to Chris). For example, participants recall poorly the behaviors "you would borrow other people's belongings without their knowledge" (untrustworthy) and "you would refuse to lend classnotes to a friend who was ill" (unkind). However, participants recall relatively well the behaviors "Chris would borrow other people's belongings without their knowledge" and "Chris would refuse to lend classnotes to a friend who was ill" (unkind). Additionally, they recall relatively well the behaviors "you would keep secrets when asked to" (trustworthy) and "you would offer to care for a neighbor's child when the babysitter couldn't come" (kind). This recall discrepancy has been labeled *mnemic neglect* and has been attributed to the self-threat potential of the feedback.

Research has consistently supported the idea that self-threat underlies mnemic neglect. In general, the more threatening the feedback is perceived, the more defensive participants become (i.e., more likely to exhibit mnemic neglect). For example, the effect is obtained when the behaviors are high on diagnosticity (e.g., "you would be unfaithful when in an intimate relationship"), but it is cancelled when the behaviors are low on diagnosticity (e.g., "would forget for a week to return a borrowed book to a friend") (Green & Sedikides, 2004). This is because high-diagnosticity behaviors can really reveal whether one is untrustworthy or unkind, and are thus threatening. In addition, the effect is obtained when participants are led to believe that their traits are unmodifiable, but it is cancelled when they are led to believe their traits are modifiable (Green, Pinter, & Sedikides, 2005). This is because learning that one was born untrustworthy or unkind and will be so for life makes untrustworthiness or unkindness feedback threatening. Relatedly, the effect is obtained when participants are deprived of the opportunity to improve on feedback-relevant dimensions (e.g., to become less untrustworthy or less unkind) and are thus threatened, but it is cancelled when participants are offered the opportunity to improve (Green, Sedikides, Pinter, & Van Tongeren, 2009). In all, this research shows that selective self-memory is motivated.

Self-Affirmation

Does self-affirmation reduce or negate selective self-memory? Green, Sedikides, and Gregg (2008, Experiment 2) addressed this question. All participants took a test ostensibly assessing their cognitive ability (i.e., creativity). In the self-threat condition, participants learned that they had performed poorly on the test. In the self-affirmation condition, however, participants learned that they had performed well on the test. Subsequently, all participants proceeded to an "impression" task, which was actually the standard mnemic neglect paradigm (i.e., behavioral feedback).

The results were, once again, telling. Self-threatened participants evinced mnemic neglect, whereas self-affirmed participants did not. Self-affirmation relaxed defensiveness, as tracked by the abolishment of mnemic neglect. These results are consistent with the idea that mnemic neglect is a motivated phenomenon.

Nonmotivational Explanations

We next turn to two nonmotivational explanations of selective self-memory: differential expectancies and inconsistency between information valence and self-view valence.

DIFFERENTIAL EXPECTANCIES

In a review of the literature, Walker et al. (2003) concluded that the base rate of negative versus positive life events is unequal. That is, negative events are half as frequent as positive events (25% vs. 50%). Differential base rates may also be involved in mnemic neglect. People may process shallowly and recall negative feedback poorly because they do not expect to receive it; based on prior experience, such feedback is implausible.

Can differential expectancies account for selective self-memory? We (Sedikides et al., 2004; Sedikides & Green, 2009) addressed this issue in the context of the mnemic neglect paradigm. As described earlier, this research was concerned with the on-line processing of a concrete and experimentally provided array of feedback as opposed to the reconstruction of pleasant or unpleasant life events, thus exerting tight control over the to-be-remembered material. The ratio of negative to positive information was equal. In addition, the relevance of self versus other memories was taken into consideration: The same information was self-referent in one condition and other-referent in another condition. More important, the research addressed the issue of whether mnemic neglect is due to expectancies (Sedikides & Green, 2004, Experiment 1).

All participants received hypothetical behavioral feedback. However, the referent of the feedback varied. A quarter of the participants received feedback about themselves, and another quarter about Chris. The third quarter of participants received feedback about a person described in glowing terms, such as extraordinarily trustworthy and kind (glowing Chris condition). The fourth quarter of participants received feedback about a close friend. Pretest had established that participants held the most positive expectancies for glowing Chris, considering him or her as most likely to enact positive behaviors and least likely to enact negative behaviors. Expectancies for close friend and self were virtually identical, and they were both more positive than expectancies for (mere) Chris. If expectancies constituted a sufficient explanation for mnemic neglect, then the effect would be more strongly evident in the glowing Chris than the self condition, and it would be equally strong in the close friend and self conditions. This was not the case. Participants evidenced the most neglect in the self condition, followed by the friend condition, and then by the glowing Chris and Chris conditions (which did not differ significantly).

These findings were conceptually replicated by Newman, Nibert, and Winer (2009). In a separate session after the usual exposure to and recall of behavioral feedback, participants provided expectancies for each behavior for either the self or Chris. That is, they estimated the extent to which they could imagine either themselves or Chris performing the behavior. Expectancies and recall were uncorrelated for most but a subset of participants. This subset was defensive pessimists, who as hypothesized, did not show the typical mnemic neglect pattern. In conclusion, differential expectancies, albeit relevant to recall of autobiographical information (Walker et al., 2003), cannot account solely for mnemic neglect and more generally selective self-memory.

INCONSISTENCY BETWEEN INFORMATION VALENCE AND SELF-VIEW VALENCE

Another alternative, though, is worth considering, specifically, inconsistency between the valence of one's self-views and the valence of feedback (Abelson et al., 1968). Mnemic neglect, in particular, may reflect processing of information whose valence is inconsistent with the valence of self-conceptions. Most participants have a positive self-concept (Ogilvie, 1987; Schwartz, 1986). Hence, they recall negative feedback poorly because it is inconsistent with their self-views. This alternative explanation leads to an interesting prediction. Inconsistency will also drive mnemic neglect among participants with a negative self-concept. These participants will recall positive feedback poorly, because it is inconsistent with their self-views.

An experiment (Sedikides & Green, 2004, Experiment 2) tested whether feedback inconsistency (behaviors that are inconsistent with the self-view) or feedback negativity (behaviors that are negative regardless of whether they are consistent or inconsistent with the self-view) drives mnemic neglect. A pretest identified two groups of participants: those with positive self-views (i.e., trustworthy, kind) and those with negative self-views (i.e., untrustworthy, unkind). These participants were then brought in the laboratory and exposed to the usual mnemic neglect paradigm. The inconsistency alternative would predict that participants with positive self-views would recall poorly untrustworthy and unkind behaviors, whereas participants with negative self-views would recall poorly trustworthy and kind behaviors. The results ran contrary to this alternative. All participants, regardless of the valence of their self-conception, manifested mnemic neglect. That is, even individuals who regarded themselves as untrustworthy or unkind recalled poorly untrustworthy or unkind behaviors. This is additional evidence that feedback negativity (i.e., self-threat) underlies mnemic neglect. In conclusion, inconsistency between the valence of one's self-views and the valence of feedback, albeit relevant to autobiographical recall (Gramzow & Willard, 2006), cannot account singly for mnemic neglect and more generally selective self-memory.

SUMMARY

As with the SSB and the BTAE, nonmotivational explanations for selective self-memory are not particularly persuasive. Differential expectancies and inconsistency between information valence and self-view valence cannot provide a satisfactory account for poor recall of negative, central, self-referent feedback. Instead, the threat potential of such feedback, including research on self-affirmation, can. The extant evidence points to mnemic neglect as a valid signature of the self-protection motive.

But is self-threatening feedback always recalled poorly? Research on trauma would seem to indicate that it is not: Traumatic events are well remembered (Berntsen, 2001; McNally, 2003). Such events, though, are extreme, and event extremity is associated with superior recall (Thompson, Skowronski, Larsen, & Betz, 1996). And yet event valence predicts recall independently of event extremity (Thompson et al., 1996, Chapter 4). Finally, in the mnemic neglect paradigm, behavioral feedback was moderate rather than extreme (Sedikides & Green, 2000, pilot studies). Selective self-memory, then, is applicable to the domain of mild, as opposed to extreme, feedback or events.

What Are Self-Enhancement and Self-Protection Good For?

Self-enhancement and self-protection strivings have functional advantages for the individual. Next we will consider two critical domains of functionality: psychological health and psychological interests.

Psychological Health

The SSB is linked to a variety of psychological health benefits. For example, the SSB is related to positive mood (McFarland & Ross, 1982) and high subjective well-being (Rizley, 1978), improved problem solving (Isen & Means, 1983), reduced depression (Abramson & Alloy, 1981), better immune functioning (Taylor et al., 2000), and lower mortality and morbidity longitudinally (Peterson & Seligman, 1987). On the other hand, a weak or absent SSB is related to depression (Sweeney, Anderson, & Bailey, 1986), deteriorating physical health (Peterson,

Seligman, & Vaillant, 1998), and poorer athletic, academic, and work performance (Peterson & Barrett, 1987; Seligman, Nolen-Hoeksema, Thornton, & Thornton, 1990). The positive association between the SSB and psychological health has been found not only in Western culture but also in East-Asian culture (China; Anderson, 1999).

The BTAE is also strongly linked to psychological health. For example, the BTAE is positively related to indices of thriving (e.g., subjective well-being, purpose in life, positive relations, self-acceptance), positively related to resources (optimism, extraversion, self-esteem, family support), and negatively related to indices of distress (e.g., loneliness, depression, anxiety) (Brown, 1991, 1998; Marshall & Brown, 2007; Taylor, Lerner, Sherman, Sage, & McDowell, 2003a). Similar patterns have been obtained in several East-Asian cultures such as China (Brown & Cai, 2009; Cai, Wu, & Brown, 2009; O'Mara, Gaertner, Sedikides, Zhou, & Liu, 2010), Japan (Kobayashi & Brown, 2003), Korea (Chang, Sanna, & Yang, 2003), Taiwan (Gaertner et al., 2008), and Singapore (Kurman & Sriram, 1997). In addition, longitudinal studies, in Western and non-Western culture, indicate that the BTAE promotes subsequent psychological health under adverse conditions (Bonanno, Field, Kovacevic, & Kaltman, 2002; Bonanno, Rennicke, & Dekel, 2005; Gupta & Bonanno, 2010; Zuckerman & O'Loughlin, 2006). Moreover, the BTAE serves a stress-buffering function: As a response to stress, the BTAE is related to lower cardiovascular response, more rapid cardiovascular recovery, and lower baseline cortisol level (Taylor, Lerner, Sherman, Sage, & McDowell, 2003b).

Finally, selective self-memory in autobiographical recall is also associated with psychological health. For example, selective self-memory is related to lack of dysphoria (Walker, Skowronski, Gibbons, Vogl, & Thompson, 2003), reduced depression (Williams et al., 2007), a future orientation (Brunson, Wheeler, & Walker, 2010), social connectedness or better interpersonal relations (Wildschut, Sedikides, Arndt, & Routledge, 2006), felt continuity between one's past and one's present (Sedikides, Wildschut, Gaertner, Routledge, & Arndt, 2008), perceptions of life as meaningful (Routledge et al., 2011), and reduced existential anxiety (Juhl, Routledge, Arndt, Sedikides, & Wildschut, 2010). Relatedly, selective self-memory is linked to fewer symptoms of psychopathology and better psychological health over time (Bonanno, Keltner, Holen, & Horowitz, 1995; Bonanno, Znoj, Siddique, & Horowitz, 1999; Newton & Contrada, 1992). In conclusion, self-enhancement and self-protection strivings are associated with, or promote, psychological health.

Psychological Interests

Psychological interests include love/security, social status, and popularity, as well as skills and abilities (e.g., musicality, athleticism, intelligence). Interests are hierarchically organized from the general (e.g., being a good student, being a good friend) to the specific (e.g., performing well on a task, providing support to a friend in need) ones. Furthermore, interests can entail private matters (e.g., meeting one's personal standards) or public matters (e.g., meeting organizational standards) and can extend to close relations or important groups. Finally, interests can be negative or positive. Negative interests include matters that individuals wish to circumvent or shun (e.g., relationship breakup, achievement failure), whereas positive interest include matters that individuals wish to possess or attain (e.g., two-story house, managerial position) (Alicke & Sedikides, 2009).

A vital function of self-enhancement and self-protection is the pursuit of psychological interests (Alicke & Sedikides, 2009). This pursuit is carried out through either primary or secondary means. (These constructs correspond to notions of primary and secondary control; Rothbaum, Weisz, & Snyder, 1982.) Primary means refer to changing an objective state of affairs by assuming instrumental action. In that capacity, self-enhancement entails effective action that promotes oneself and one's prospects. Secondary means refers to psychological mechanisms that regulate events by altering how one perceives or interprets them. In that capacity, self-protection entails effective intervention that obviates failing below one's standards. Self-enhancement and self-protection, then, contribute effectively to the successful pursuit of psychological interests of the effective avoidance of harm to those interests.

The three self-enhancement and self-protection strivings serve psychological interests. Let us first consider the SSB. Seligman et al. (1990) examined the role of the SSB in predicting athletic performance. They found that varsity swimmers prone to the SSB (assessed at the start of the season) performed better at sporting competitions than swimmers not prone to the SSB. Additionally, Peterson and Barrett (1987) reported that undergraduate students prone to the SSB (assessed at the beginning of their first year at university) received higher grades during their freshman year compared to students not prone to the SSB. This pattern held after controlling for initial ability (measured by the Scholastic Aptitude

Test) and initial depression. Students prone to SSB were more likely to have specific academic goals and to make use of academic advising.

The BTAE is similarly implicated in the facilitation of psychological interests. Taylor et al. (2003a) showed that the BTAE is positively related to active coping, positive reframing, planning, achievement, mastery, and personal growth. In addition, Wright (2000) demonstrated that undergraduate students who are more likely to manifest the BTAE (assessed in the beginning of the semester) achieved higher grades during the semester compared to students less likely to manifest the BTAE. Moreover, students who exaggerate reporting of their grade point average perform better than those who do not (Gramzow, 2011). In general, the BTAE is associated with working harder and longer on tasks (Taylor & Brown, 1988) and with performing better on tasks (Armor & Taylor, 2003).

Finally, selective self-memory in autobiographical recall is also involved in the promotion of psychological interests. Such memory has approach rather than avoidance consequences (Stephan et al., 2011; Walker & Skowronski, 2009) and, as such, it can motivate individuals to engage and persist in goal pursuit (Sedikides & Hepper, 2009; Walker & Skowronski, 2009). Indeed, forms of selective self-memory have been found to be associated with resilience (Coifman, Bonanno, Ray, & Gross, 2007), improved coping following traumatic life events (Janoff-Bulman, 1992), and, in general, the implementation of active coping strategies in times of stress (Langens & Moerth, 2003) and in attempting to master life challenges (Walker & Skowronski, 2009).

SUMMARY

A psychological health and psychological interests analysis addresses squarely the issue of why people self-enhance and self-protect. They do not do so for a whim, or just to feel good, or for short-lived impression management purposes. Rather, they do so, and they do so persistently, because self-enhancement and self-protection strivings confer both momentary and long-term benefits (i.e., ways in which psychological health and psychological interests are advanced) and deter both momentary and long-term harms (i.e., ways in which psychological health interests are regressed or thwarted).

Conclusions

In his *An Outline of Intellectual Rubbish* (1943), Bertrand Russell was duly impressed by the influence of motives on human judgment. "Man is a rational animal—so at least I have been told. [...] I have looked diligently for evidence in favor of this statement, but so far I have not had the good fortune to come across it [...]," he exclaimed in wonder (p. 73). We have focused in this chapter on two self-evaluation motives that might have confounded Russell, self-enhancement and self-protection.

We defined self-enhancement as the desire and preference for maximizing the positivity of one's self-views, and we defined self-protection as the desire and preference for minimizing the negativity of one's self-view. We argued that the tendency to exalt one's virtues and make light of one's weaknesses, relative to impartial criteria, manifests itself in a variety of strivings. Due to space limitations, we restricted our discussion to three key strivings: the SSB (crediting the self for successes but blaming others for failures), the BTAE (considering the self superior to others), and selective self-memory (disadvantageous recall for negative feedback).

Although we acknowledged that cognition and motivation are closely intertwined, we proceeded to make a case for the motivational underpinnings of these strivings. We aimed to provide evidence that self-enhancement and self-protection strivings cannot be exclusively accounted for by nonmotivational (i.e., information processing) factors. The nonmotivational explanations of expectations and impression management were not deemed necessary for the occurrence of the SSB. Likewise, egocentrism, focalism, and individuated-entity versus aggregate comparisons were not deemed necessary for the occurrence of the BTAE. And similarly, differential expectancies and inconsistency between self-view valence and feedback were not deemed necessary for the occurrence of selective self-memory. In contrast, evidence from research on self-threat and self-affirmation testifies to the motivational underpinnings of the strivings. The SSB, BTAE, and selective self-memory are driven, in part, by the self-enhancement and self-protection motives.

We drew to a conclusion by asking why individuals self-enhance and self-protect. A partial answer lies in the functionality of self-enhancement and self-protection strivings: They accrue benefits pertaining to psychological health and psychological interests. Self-enhancement and self-protection strivings are associated with, or confer, a host of psychological health advantages, and they advance a host of psychological interests. Mild self-enhancement and self-protection continue to be markers of psychological health.

Future Directions

There are several issues in need of further empirical attention. We will briefly touch upon four of them. First, what is the interplay between the two motives? Although self-enhancement and self-protection are occasionally treated as polar ends of a single dimension, the empirical evidence suggests that a lot will be gained if they are treated separately (Elliot & Mapes, 2005). Yet the relation between the two motives is complex. They can operate independently, one motive may facilitate the other, or one motive may impede the other. Second, and relatedly, what is the interplay between implicit and explicit self-enhancement and self-protection? In particular, what is the relation between implicit and explicit self-enhancement and self-protection strategies (Arndt & Goldenberg, 2011) or between implicit and explicit self-esteem (Gregg & Sedikides, 2010)? Third, what is the interplay between the self-enhancement and self-protection motives on the one hand and other self-evaluation motives on the other? These other motives are self-assessment (i.e., pursuit of accurate self-knowledge; Gregg, Sedikides, & Gebauer, 2011), self-improvement (i.e., pursuit of one's betterment; Sedikides & Hepper, 2009), and self-verification (i.e., pursuit of self-confirmation; Swann, Rentfrow, & Guinn, 2003). Finally, what are the boundary conditions—both situational demands and individual differences—that constrain self-enhancement or self-protection (Gramzow, 2011)? And what are the intrapersonal and interpersonal consequences of such constraints upon motive emergence or manifestation? These and other issues are worth exploring. As La Rouchefoucauld (1678/1827) prophetically noted, "Whatever discoveries have been made in the land of self-love, many territories remain to be discovered."

References

Abelson, R, Aronson, E., McGuire, W., Newcomb, T., Rosenberg, M., & Tannenbaum, P. (Eds.). (1968). *The cognitive consistency theories: A source book.* Chicago, IL: Rand McNally.

Abramson, L. Y., & Alloy, L. B. (1981). Depression, nondepression, and cognitive illusions: Reply to Schwartz. *Journal of Experimental Psychology, 110*, 436–447.

Albery, I. P., & Messer, D. (2005). Comparative optimism about health and nonhealth events in 8- and 9-year old children. *Health Psychology, 24*, 316–320.

Alicke, M. (1985). Global self-evaluation as determined by the desirability and controllability of trait adjectives. *Journal of Personality and Social Psychology, 49*, 1621–1630.

Alicke, M., & Govorun, O. (2005). The better-than-average effect. In M. D. Alicke, D. A. Dunning, & J. I. Krueger (Eds.), *The self in social judgment* (pp. 85–106). New York: Psychology Press.

Alicke, M. D., Klotz, M. L., Breitenbecher, D. L., Yurak, T. J., & Vredenburg, D. S. (1995). Personal contact, individuation, and the better-than-average effect. *Journal of Personality and Social Psychology, 68*, 804–825.

Alicke, M., & Sedikides, C. (2009). Self-enhancement and self-protection: What they are and what they do. *European Review of Social Psychology, 20*, 1–48.

Alicke, M. D., & Sedikides, C. (2011a). Self-enhancement and self-protection: Historical overview and conceptual framework. In M. D. Alicke & C. Sedikides (Eds.), *The handbook of self-enhancement and self-protection* (pp. 1–19). New York: Guilford Press.

Alicke, M. D., & Sedikides, C. (2011b). (Eds.). *The handbook of self-enhancement and self-protection*. New York: Guilford Press.

Alicke, M. D., Vredenburg, D. S., Hiatt, M., & Govorun, O. (2001). The "better than myself effect." *Motivation and Emotion, 25*, 7–22.

Allison, S. T., Messick, D. M., & Goethals, G. R. (1989). On being better but not smarter than others: The Muhammad Ali effect. *Social Cognition, 7*, 275–296.

Allport, G. W. (1937). *Personality: A psychological interpretation.* New York: Holt.

Anderson, C. A. (1999). Attributional style, depression, and loneliness: A cross-cultural comparison of American and Chinese students. *Personality and Social Psychology Bulletin, 25*, 482–499.

Andrews, F. M., & Whitey, S. B. (1976). *Social indicators of well-being*. New York: Plenum Press.

Arkin, R. M., Appelmen, A. J., & Burger, J. M. (1980). Social anxiety, self-presentation, and the self-serving bias in causal attribution. *Journal of Personality and Social Psychology, 38*, 23–25.

Arkin, R. M., Cooper, H. M., & Kolditz, T. A. (1980). A statistical review of the literature concerning the self-serving attribution bias in interpersonal influence situations. *Journal of Personality, 48*, 435–448.

Armor, D. A., & Taylor, S. E. (2003). The effects of mindset on behavior: Self-regulation in deliberative and implemental frames of mind. *Personality and Social Psychology Bulletin, 29*, 86–95.

Arndt, A., & Goldenberg, J. L. (2011). When self-enhancement drives health decisions: Insights from a terror management health model. In M. D. Alicke & C. Sedikides (Eds.), *The handbook of self-enhancement and self-protection* (pp. 380–398). New York: Guilford Press.

Baumeister, R. F., & Cairns, K. J. (1992). Repression and self-presentation: When audiences interfere with self-deceptive strategies. *Journal of Personality and Social Psychology, 62*, 851–862

Bentham, J. (1982). *An introduction to the principles of morals and legislation* (J. H. Burns & H. L. A. Harts, Eds.). London, England: Methuem. (Original work published 1789).

Berntsen, D. (2001). Involuntary memories of emotional events: Do memories of traumas and extremely happy events differ? *Applied Cognitive Psychology, 15*, 135–158.

Blaine, B., & Crocker, J. (1993). Self-esteem and self-serving bias in reactions to positive and negative events: An integrative review. In R. F. Baumeister (Ed.), *Self-esteem: The puzzle of low self-regard* (pp. 55–85). New York: Plenum.

Blanton, H., Pelham, B. W., DeHart, T., & Carvallo, M. (2001). Overconfidence as dissonance reduction. *Journal of Experimental Social Psychology, 37*, 373–385

Bloom, A. (Trans.). (1991). *The republic of Plato* (2nd ed.). New York: Basic Books.

Bonanno, G. A., Field, N. P., Kovacevic, A., & Kaltman, S. (2002). Self-enhancement as a buffer against extreme adversity: Civil War in Bosnia and traumatic loss in the United States. *Personality and Social Psychology Bulletin, 28*, 184–196.

Bonanno, G. A., Keltner, D., Holen, A., & Horowitz, M. J. (1995). When avoiding unpleasant emotions might not be such a bad thing: Verbal-autonomic response dissociation and midlife conjugal bereavement. *Journal of Personality and Social Psychology, 69*, 975–989.

Bonanno, G. A., Rennicke, C., & Dekel, S. (2005). Self-enhancement among high-exposure survivors of the September 11th terrorist attacks: Resilience or social maladjustment? *Journal of Personality and Social Psychology, 88*, 984–998.

Bonanno, G. A., Znoj, H., Siddique, H. I., & Horowitz, M. J. (1999). Verbal autonomic dissociation and adaptation to midlife conjugal loss: A follow-up at 25 months. *Cognitive Therapy and Research, 23*, 605–624.

Brown, J. D. (1986). Evaluations of self and others: Self-enhancement biases in social judgments. *Social Cognition, 4*, 353–376.

Brown, J. D. (1991). Accuracy and bias in self-knowledge. In C. R. Snyder & D. F. Forsyth (Eds.), *Handbook of social and clinical psychology: The health perspective* (pp. 158–178). New York: Pergamon Press.

Brown, J. D. (1998). *The self*. New York: McGraw-Hill.

Brown, J. D. (2003). The self-enhancement motive in collectivistic cultures: The rumors of my death have been greatly exaggerated. *Journal of Cross-Cultural Psychology, 34*, 603–605.

Brown, J. D. (2010). Across the (not so) great divide: Cultural similarities in self-evaluative processes. *Social and Personality Psychology Compass, 4*, 318–330.

Brown, J. D. (2011). *Understanding the better than average effect: Motives matter*. Unpublished manuscript, University of Washington.

Brown, J. D., & Cai, H. (2009). Self-esteem and trait importance moderate cultural differences in self-evaluations. *Journal of Cross-Cultural Psychology, 41*, 116–122.

Brown, J. D., Collins, R. L., & Schmidt, G. W. (1988). Self-esteem and direct versus indirect forms of self-enhancement. *Journal of Personality and Social Psychology, 55*, 445–453.

Brown, J. D., & Gallagher, F. M. (1992). Coming to terms with failure: Private self-enhancement and public self-effacement. *Journal of Experimental Social Psychology, 28*, 3–22.

Brown, J. D., & Kobayashi, C. (2002). Self-enhancement in Japan and America. *Asian Journal of Social Psychology, 5*, 145–168.

Brunot, S., & Sanitioso, R. B. (2004). Motivational influences on the quality of memories: Recall of general autobiographical memories related to desired attributes. *European Journal of Social Psychology, 34*, 627–635.

Brunson, C. A., Wheeler, D., & Walker, W. R. (2011). *Testing two alternative explanations for a fading affect bias in autobiographical memory*. Manuscript under review.

Cai, H., Wu, Q., & Brown, J. D. (2009). Is self-esteem a universal need? Evidence from the People's Republic of China. *Asian Journal of Social Psychology, 12*, 104–120.

Campbell, K. W., & Sedikides, C. (1999). Self-threat magnifies the self-serving bias: A meta-analytic integration. *Review of General Psychology, 3*, 23–43.

Champers, J. R., Windschitl, P. D., & Suls, J. (2003). Egocentrism, event frequency, and comparative optimism: When what happens frequently is "more likely to happen to me." *Personality and Social Psychology Bulletin, 29,* 1343–1356.

Chang, E. C., Sanna, L. J., & Yang, K. (2003). Optimism, pessimism, affectivity, and psychological adjustment in US and Korea: A test of mediation model. *Personality and Individual Differences, 34,* 1195–1208.

Coifman, K. G., Bonanno, G. A., Ray, R. D., & Gross, J. J. (2007). Does repressive coping promote resilience? Affective-autonomic response discrepancy during bereavement. *Journal of Personality and Social Psychology, 92,* 745–758.

College Board. (1976–1977). *Student descriptive questionnaire.* Princeton, NJ: Educational Testing Service.

Corr, P., & Gray, J. (1996). Attributional style as a personality factor in insurance sales performance in the UK. *Journal of Occupational and Organizational Psychology, 69,* 83–87.

Crary, W. G. (1966). Reactions to incongruent self-experiences. *Journal of Consulting Psychology, 30,* 246–252.

Creswell, J. D., Welch, W. T., Taylor, S. E., Sherman, D. K., Gruenewald, T. L., & Mann, T. (2005). Affirmation of personal values buffers neuroendocrine and psychological stress responses. *Psychological Science, 16,* 846–851.

Critcher, C. R., Helzer, E. G., & Dunning, D. (2011). Self-enhancement via redefinition: Defining social concepts to ensure positive views of self. In M. D. Alicke & C. Sedikides (Eds.), *The handbook of self-enhancement and self-protection* (pp. 69–91). New York: Guilford Press.

Crocker, J., Voelkl, K., Testa, M., & Major, B. (1991). Social stigma: The affective consequences of attributional ambiguity. *Journal of Personality and Social Psychology, 60,* 218–228.

Cross, P. (1977). Not can but will college teachers be improved? *New Directions for Higher Education, 17,* 1–15.

Davison, W. P. (1983). The third-person effect in communication. *Public Opinion Quarterly, 47,* 1–15.

D'Argembeau, A., & Van der Linden, M. (2008). Remembering pride and shame: Self-enhancement and the phenomenology of autobiographical memory. *Memory, 16,* 538–547.

De Michele, P. E., Gansneder, B., & Solomon, G. B. (1998). Success and failure attributions of wrestlers: Further evidence of the self-serving bias. *Journal of Sport Behavior, 21,* 242–255.

DeVellis, R. F., Holt, K., Renner, B. R., Blalock, S. J., Blanchard, L. W., Cook, H. L.,…Harring, K. (1990). The relationship of social comparison to rheumatoid arthritis symptoms and affect. *Basic and Applied Social Psychology, 11,* 1–18.

De Witt, N. W. (1973). *Epicurus and his philosophy.* Westport, CT: Greenwood Publishing Group.

Dunning, D., Heath, C., & Suls, J. M. (2004). Flawed self-assessment: Implications for health, education, and the workplace. *Psychological Science in the Public Interest, 5,* 69–106.

Dunning, D., Leuenberger, A., & Sherman, D. A. (1995). A new look at motivated inference: Are self-serving theories of success a product of motivational forces? *Journal of Personality and Social Psychology, 69,* 58–68.

Elliot, A. J., & Mapes, R. R. (2005). Approach-avoidance motivation and self-concept evaluation. In A. Tesser, J. V. Wood, & D. A. Stapel (Eds.), *On building, defending and regulating the self: A psychological perspective* (pp. 171–196). New York: Psychology Press.

Field, D. (1981). Retrospective reports by healthy intelligent elderly people of personal events of their adult lives. *International Journal of Behavioral Development, 4,* 77–97.

Field, D. (1997). "Looking back, what period of your life brought you the most satisfaction?" *International Journal of Aging and Human Development, 45,* 169–194.

Forsyth, D. R., & Schlenker, B. R. (1985). Attributing the causes of group performance: Effects of performance quality, task importance, and future testing. *Journal of Personality, 45,* 220–236.

Freedman, J. (1978). *Happy people: What happiness is, who has it, and why.* New York: Harcourt Brace Jovanovich.

Freud, A. (1946). *The ego and the mechanisms of defense.* New York: International Universities Press. (Originally work published in 1936).

Freud, S. (1961a). Three essays on the theory of sexuality. In J. Strachey (Ed. & Trans.), *The standard edition of the complete psychological works of Sigmund Freud* (Vol. 19, pp. 3–66). London, England: Hogarth Press. (Original work published 1905).

Freud, S. (1961b). Instincts and their vicissitudes. In J. Strachey (Ed. & Trans.), *The standard edition of the complete works of Sigmund Freud* (Vol. 14, pp. 111–142). London, England: Hogarth Press. (Original work published in 1915).

Freud, S. (1961c). The ego and the id. In J. Strachey (Ed. & Trans.), *The standard edition of the complete works of Sigmund Freud* (Vol. 19, pp. 12–66). London, England: Hogarth Press. (Original work published in 1923).

Freud, S. (1961d). Inhibitions, symptoms, and anxiety. In J. Strachey (Ed. & Trans.), *The standard edition of the complete works of Sigmund Freud* (Vol. 20, pp. 77–178). London, England: Hogarth Press. (Original work published in 1926).

Gaertner, L., Sedikides, C., & Chang, K. (2008). On pancultural self-enhancement: Well-adjusted Taiwanese self-enhance on personally-valued traits. *Journal of Cross-Cultural Psychology, 39,* 463–477.

Giladi, E. E., & Klar, Y. (2002). When standards are wide of the mark: Nonselective superiority and bias in comparative judgments of objects and concepts. *Journal of Experimental Psychology: General, 131,* 538–551.

Gosling, S. D., John, O. P., Craik, K. H., & Robins, R. W. (1998). Do people know how they behave? Self-reported act frequencies compared with on-line codings by observers. *Journal Personality and Social Psychology, 74,* 1337–1349.

Gramzow, R. H. (2011). Academic exaggeration: Pushing self-enhancement boundaries. In M. D. Alicke & C. Sedikides (Eds.), *The handbook of self-enhancement and self-protection* (pp. 455–471). New York: Guilford Press.

Gramzow, R. H., & Willard, G. (2006). Exaggerating current and past performance: Motivated self-enhancement versus reconstructive memory. *Personality and Social Psychology Bulletin, 32,* 1114–1125.

Green, J. D., Pinter, B., & Sedikides, C. (2005). Mnemic neglect and self-threat: Trait modifiability moderates self-protection. *European Journal of Social Psychology, 35,* 225–235.

Green, J. D., & Sedikides, C. (2004). Retrieval selectivity in the processing of self-referent information: Testing the boundaries of self-protection. *Self and Identity, 3,* 69–80.

Green, J. D., Sedikides, C., & Gregg, A. P. (2008). Forgotten but not gone: The recall and recognition of self-threatening memories. *Journal of Experimental Social Psychology, 44,* 547–561.

Green, J. D., Sedikides, C., Pinter, B., & Van Tongeren, D. R. (2009). Two sides to self-protection: Self-improvement strivings and feedback from close relationships eliminate mnemic neglect. *Self and Identity, 8,* 233–250.

Greenberg, J., Pyszczynski, T., & Solomon, S. (1982). The self-serving attributional bias: Beyond self-presentation. *Journal of Experimental Social Psychology, 18,* 56–67.

Gregg, A. P., & Sedikides, C. (2010). Narcissistic fragility: Rethinking its links to explicit and implicit self-esteem. *Self and Identity, 9,* 142–161.

Gregg, A. P., Sedikides, C., & Gebauer, J. E. (2011). Dynamics of identity: Between self-enhancement and self-assessment. In S. J. Schwartz, K. Luyckx, & V. L. Vignoles (Eds.), *Handbook of identity theory and research* (Vol. 1, pp. 305–327). New York: Springer.

Guenther, C. (2011). *Self-affirmation and the better-than-average effect.* Manuscript submitted for publication, Creighton University.

Guenther, C. L., & Alicke, M. D. (2010). Deconstructing the better-than-average effect. *Journal of Personality and Social Psychology, 99,* 755–770.

Gupta, S., & Bonanno, G. A. (2010). Trait self-enhancement as a buffer against potentially traumatic events: A prospective study. *Psychological Trauma: Theory, Research, Practice, and Policy, 2,* 83–92.

Haslam, N., Bain, P., Douge, L., Lee, M., & Bastian, B. (2005). More human than you: Attributing humanness to self and others. *Journal of Personality and Social Psychology, 98,* 937–950.

Heady, B., & Wearing, A. (1988). The sense of relative superiority—central to well-being. *Social Indicators Research, 20,* 497–516.

Heider, F. (1958). *The psychology of interpersonal relations.* New York: Wiley.

Hepper, E. G., Gramzow, R., & Sedikides, C. (2010). Individual differences in self-enhancement and self-protection strategies: An integrative analysis. *Journal of Personality, 78,* 781–814.

Hepper, E. G., Sedikides, C., & Cai, H. (in press). Self-enhancement and self-protection strategies in China: Cultural expressions of a fundamental human motive. *Journal of Cross-Cultural Psychology.*

Hobbes, T. (1991). *Leviathan.* Cambridge, England: Cambridge University Press. (Original work published 1651).

House, W. C. (1980). Effects of knowledge that attributions will be observed by others. *Journal of Personality and Social Psychology, 14,* 528–545.

Isen, A. M., & Means, B. (1983). The influence of positive affect on decision-making strategies. *Social Cognition, 2,* 18–31.

James, W. (1890). Principles of psychology (Vols. 1–2). New York: Holt.

Janoff-Bulman, R. (1992). *Shattered assumptions: Towards a new psychology of trauma.* New York: Free Press.

Juhl, J., Routledge, C., Arndt, J., Sedikides, C., & Wildschut, T. (2010). Fighting the future with the past: On the death-anxiety buffering function of nostalgia. *Journal of Research in Personality, 44,* 309–314.

Karylowski, J. (1990). Social reference points and accessibility of trait-related information in self-other comparisons. *Journal of Personality and Social Psychology, 58,* 975–983.

Karylowski, J., & Skarzynska, K. (1992). Asymmetric self-other similarity judgments depend on priming self-knowledge. *Social Cognition, 10,* 235–254.

Kelley, H. H., & Michela, J. L. (1980). Attribution theory and research. *Annual Review of Psychology, 31,* 457–501.

Kenny, A. (1986). *Rationalism, empiricism and idealism.* Oxford, England: Oxford University Press.

Kernis, H. H., Cornell, D. P., Sun, C-R., Berry, A., & Harlow, T. (1993). There's more to self-esteem than whether it's high or low: The importance of stability of self-esteem. *Journal of Personality and Social Psychology, 65,* 1190–1204.

Klar, Y. (2002). Way beyond compare: Nonselective superiority and inferiority biases in judging randomly assigned group members relative to their peers. *Journal of Experimental Social Psychology, 38,* 331–351.

Klar, Y., & Giladi, E. E. (1997). No one in my group can be below the group's average: A robust positivity bias in favor of anonymous peers. *Journal of Personality and Social Psychology, 73,* 885–901.

Kobayashi, C., & Brown, J. D. (2003). Self-esteem and self-enhancement in Japan and America. *Journal of Cross-Cultural Psychology, 34,* 567–580.

Kruger, J. (1999). Lake Wobegon be gone! The "below-average effect" and the egocentric nature of comparative ability judgments. *Journal of Personality and Social Psychology, 77,* 221–232.

Kruger, J., & Gilovich, T. (2004). Actions, intentions, and self-assessment: The road to self-enhancement is paved with good intentions. *Personality and Social Psychology Bulletin, 30,* 328–339.

Kruglanski, A. W. (1989). *Lay epistemics and human knowledge: Cognitive and motivational biases.* New York: Plenum Press.

Kunda, Z. (1990). The case for motivated reasoning. *Psychological Bulletin, 108,* 480–498.

Kurman, J. (2002). Measured cross-cultural differences in self-enhancement and the sensitivity of the self-enhancement measure to the modesty response. *Cross-Cultural Research, 36,* 73–95.

Kurman, J., & Sriram, N. (1997). Self-enhancement, generality of self-evaluation, and affectivity in Israel and Singapore. *Journal of Cross-Cultural Psychology, 28,* 421–441.

Kwon, Y., Scheibe, S., Samanez-Larkin, G. R., Tsai, J. L. & Carstensen, L. L. (2009). Replicating the positivity effect in picture memory in Koreans: Evidence for cross-cultural generalizability. *Psychology and Aging, 24,* 748–754.

La Rochefoucauld, F. (1827). *Reflections: Or sentences and moral maxims* (J. W. W. Bund & J. H. Friswell, Trans.). London, England: Simpson, Low, Son, & Marston. (Original work published 1678).

Landau, J. D, & Gunter, B. C. (2009). "Don't worry; you really will get over it": Methodological investigations of the fading affect bias. *American Journal of Psychology, 122,* 209–217.

Langens, T. A., & Moerth, S. (2003). Repressive coping and the use of passive and active coping strategies. *Personality and Individual Differences, 35,* 461–473.

Loeb, L. (1981). *From Descartes to Hume: Continental metaphysics and the development of modern philosophy.* Ithaca, NY: Cornell University Press.

Macfarlane, A. (1978). *The origins of English individualism: The family, property, and social transition.* New York: Cambridge University Press.

Mandeville, B. (1705). *The fable of the bees: or private vices, public benefits* (Vol. 1). Oxford, England: Clarendon Press.

Marshall, M. A., & Brown, J. D. (2007). On the psychological benefits of self-enhancement. In E. Chang (Ed.), *Self-enhancement and self-criticism: Theory, research, and clinical implications* (pp. 19–35). New York: American Psychological Association.

McFarland, C., & Ross, M. (1982). Impact of causal attributions on affective reactions to success and failure. *Journal of Personality and Social Psychology, 45,* 937–946.

McNally, R. J. (2003). *Remembering trauma.* Cambridge, MA: Belknap Press/Harvard University Press.

Mednick, S.A. (1962). The associative basis of the creative process. *Psychological Review, 69,* 220–232.

Messick, D. M., Bloom, S., Boldizar, J. P., & Samuelson, C. D. (1985). Why are we fairer than others? *Journal of Experimental Social Psychology, 21,* 480–500.

Mezulis, A. H., Abramson, L. Y., Hyde, J. S., & Hankin, B. L. (2004). Is there a universal positive bias in attributions? A meta-analytic review of individual, developmental, and cultural differences in the self-serving attributional bias. *Psychological Bulletin, 130,* 711–747.

Mill, J. S. (2004). *Utilitarianism.* Adelaide, Australia: ebooks@ Adelaide. Retrieved July 2011, from, http://etext.library. adelaide.edu.au/m/mill/john_stuart/m645u/ (Original work published 1863).

Miller, D. T. (1976). Ego involvement and attributions for success and failure. *Journal of Personality and Social Psychology, 34,* 901–906.

Miller, D. T. (1978). What constitutes a self-serving attributional bias? A reply to Bradley. *Journal of Personality and Social Psychology, 36,* 1221–1223.

Miller, D. T., & Ross, M. (1975). Self-serving bias in the attribution of causality: Fact or fiction? *Psychological Bulletin, 82,* 213–225.

Miller, R. S., & Schlenker, B. R. (1985). Egotism in group members: Public and private attributions of responsibility for group performance. *Social Psychology Quarterly, 48,* 85–89.

Mischel, W., Ebbesen, E. B., & Zeiss, A. R. (1976). Determinants of selective memory about the self. *Journal of Consulting and Clinical Psychology, 44,* 92–103.

Moore, D. A. (2007). Not so above average after all: When people believe they are worse than average and its implications for theories of bias in social comparison. *Organizational Behavior and Human Decision Processes, 102,* 42–58.

Moore, D. A., & Kim, T. G. (2003). Myopic social prediction and the solo comparison effect. *Journal of Personality and Social Psychology, 85,* 1121–1135.

Murray, S. L., & Holmes, J. G. (1993). Seeing virtues in faults: Negativity and the transformation of interpersonal narratives in close relationships. *Journal of Personality and Social Psychology, 65,* 707–722.

Mullen, B., & Riordan, C. A. (1988). Self-serving attributions for performance in naturalistic settings: A meta-analytic review. *Journal of Applied Social Psychology, 18,* 3–22.

Nesselroade, K. P., Beggan, J. K., & Allison, S. T. (1999). Possession enhancement in an interpersonal context: An extension of the mere ownership effect. *Psychology and Marketing, 16,* 21–34.

Newman, L. S., Nibert, J. A., & Winer, E. S. (2009). Mnemic neglect is not an artifact of expectancy: The moderating role of defensive pessimism. *European Journal of Social Psychology, 39,* 477–486.

Newton, T. L., & Contrada, R. L. (1992). Repressive coping and verbal-autonomic dissociation: The influence of social context. *Journal of Personality and Social Psychology, 62,* 159–167.

Nietzsche, F. (1972). *Beyond good and evil* (R. J. Hollongdale, Trans.). London, England: Penguin Books. (Original work published 1886).

Ogilvie, D. M. (1987). The undesired self: A neglected variable in personality research. *Journal of Personality and Social Psychology, 52,* 379–385.

O'Mara, E. M., Gaertner, L., Sedikides, C., Zhou, X., & Liu, Y. (2010). An experimental test of the panculturality of self-enhancement: Self-enhancement promotes psychological well-being both in the West and the East. Manuscript submitted for pulbication, University of Dayton.

Otten, W., & van der Pligt, J. (1996). Context effects in the measurement of comparative optimism in probability judgments. *Journal of Social and Clinical Psychology, 15,* 80–101.

Pahl, S., & Eiser, J. R. (2006). The focus effect and self-positivity in ratings of self-other similarity and difference. *British Journal of Social Psychology, 45,* 107–116.

Pahl, S., & Eiser, J. R. (2007). How malleable is comparative self-positivity? The effects of manipulating judgemental focus and accessibility. *European Journal of Social Psychology, 37,* 617–627.

Paulhus, D. L. (1993). Bypassing the will: The automatization of affirmations. In D. M. Wegner & J. M. Pennebaker (Eds.), *Handbook of mental control* (pp. 573–587). Englewood Cliffs, NJ: Prentice Hall.

Peterson, C., & Barrett, L. C. (1987). Explanatory style and academic performance among university freshmen. *Journal of Personality and Social Psychology, 53,* 603–607.

Peterson, C., & Seligman, M. E. (1987). Explanatory style and illness. *Journal of Personality, 55,* 237–265.

Peterson, C., Seligman, M. E., & Vaillant, G. E. (1998). Pessimistic explanatory style is a risk factor for physical illness: A thirty-five-year longitudinal study. *Journal of Personality, 55,* 23–27.

Preston, C. E., & Harris, S. (1965). Psychology of drivers in traffic accidents. *Journal of Applied Psychology, 49,* 284–288.

Preuss, G. S., & Alicke, M. D. (2009). Everybody loves me: Self-evaluations and metaperceptions of dating popularity. *Personality and Social Psychology Bulletin, 35,* 937–950.

Pronin, E., Lin, D. Y., & Ross, L. (2002). The bias blind spot: Perceptions of bias in self versus others. *Personality and Social Psychology Bulletin, 3,* 369–381.

Pyszczynski, T., & Greenberg, J. (1987). Toward an integration of cognitive and motivational perspectives on social inference: A biased hypothesis-testing model. *Advances in Experimental Social Psychology, 20,* 297–340.

Reeder, G. D., & Brewer, M. B. (1979). A schematic model of dispositional attribution in interpersonal perception. *Psychological Review, 86,* 61–79.

Ritchie, T., Skowronski, J. J., Hartnett, J. Wells, B., & Walker, W. R. (2009). The fading affect bias in the context of emotion activation level, mood, and personal theories of emotion change. *Memory, 17,* 428–444.

Rizley, R. (1978). Depression and distortion in the attribution of causality. *Journal of Abnormal Psychology, 87,* 32–48.

Roese, N. J., & Olson, J. M. (2007). Better, stronger, faster: Self-serving judgment, affect regulation, and the optimal vigilance hypothesis. *Perspectives on Psychological Science, 2,* 124–141.

Rogers, C. R. (1961). *On becoming a person.* Boston, MA: Houghton Mifflin.

Ross, M., & Wilson, A. E. (2002). It feels like yesterday: Self-esteem, valence of personal past experiences, and judgments of subjective distance. *Journal of Personality and Social Psychology, 82,* 792–803.

Ross, M., McFarland, C., & Fletcher, G. J. (1981). The effect of attitude on the recall of personal histories. *Journal of Personality and Social Psychology*, *40*, 627–634.

Rothbart, M., & Park, B. (1986). On the confirmability and disconfirmability of trait concepts. *Journal of Personality and Social Psychology*, *50*, 131–142.

Rothbaum, F., Weisz, J. R., & Snyder, S. S. (1982). Changing the world and changing the self: A two-process model of perceived control. *Journal of Personality and Social Psychology*, *42*, 5–37.

Routledge, C., Arndt, J., Wildschut, T., Sedikides, C., Hart, C. M., Juhl, J., & Vingerhoets, A., & Schlotz, W. (2011). The past makes the present meaningful: Nostalgia as an existential resource. *Journal of Personality and Social Psychology*, *101*, 638–652.

Rusbult, C. E., Van Lange, P. A. M., Wildschut, T., Yovetich, N. A., & Verette, J. (2000). Perceived superiority in close relationships: Why it exists and persists. *Journal of Personality and Social Psychology*, *79*, 521–545.

Russell, B. (1943). *An outline of intellectual rubbish*. Girard, KS: Haldeman-Julius.

Sande, G., Goethals, G., & Radloff, C. (1988). Perceiving one's own traits and others': The multifaceted self. *Journal of Personality and Social Psychology*, *54*, 13–20.

Sanitioso, R., Kunda, Z., & Fong, G. T. (1990). Motivated recruitment of autobiographical memories. *Journal of Personality and Social Psychology*, *59*, 229–241.

Sanitioso, B. R., & Niedenthal, P. M. (2006). Motivated self-perception and perceived ease in recall of autobiographical memories. *Self and Identity*, *5*, 73–84.

Schopenhauer, A. (1996). *The world as will and representation* (Vol. 2; E. F. J. Payne, Trans.) New York: Dover Publications. (Original work published 1844).

Schrauf, R. W., & Hoffman, L. (2007). The effects of revisionism on remembered emotion: The valence of older, voluntary immigrants' pre-migration autobiographical memories. *Applied Cognitive Psychology*, *21*, 895–913.

Schulz, R., & Fritz, S. (1987). Origins of stereotypes of the elderly: An experimental study of the self-other discrepancy. *Experimental Aging Research*, *13*, 189–195.

Schwartz, R. M. (1986). The internal dialogue: On the asymmetry between positive and negative coping thoughts. *Cognitive Therapy and Research*, *10*, 591–605.

Sedikides, C. (1993). Assessment, enhancement, and verification determinants of the self-evaluation process. *Journal of Personality and Social Psychology*, *65*, 317–338.

Sedikides, C. (2012). Self-protection. In M. R. Leary & J. P. Tangney (Eds.), *Handbook of self and identity* (2nd ed.) (pp. 327–353). New York: Guilford Press.

Sedikides, C., Campbell, W. K., Reeder, G., & Elliot, A. J. (1998). The self-serving bias in relational context. *Journal of Personality and Social Psychology*, *74*, 378–386.

Sedikides, C., Gaertner, L., & Toguchi, Y. (2003). Pancultural self-enhancement. *Journal of Personality and Social Psychology*, *84*, 60–70.

Sedikides, C., Gaertner, L., & Vevea, J. L. (2005). Pancultural self-enhancement reloaded: A meta-analytic reply to Heine (2005). *Journal of Personality and Social Psychology*, *89*, 539–551.

Sedikides, C., Gaertner, L., & Vevea, J. L. (2007). Inclusion of theory-relevant moderators yield the same conclusions as Sedikides, Gaertner, and Vevea (2005): A meta-analytic reply to Heine, Kitayama, and Hamamura (2007). *Asian Journal of Social Psychology*, *10*, 59–67.

Sedikides, C., & Gebauer, J. E. (2010). Religiosity as self-enhancement: A meta-analysis of the relation between socially desirable responding and religiosity. *Personality and Social Psychology Review*, *14*, 17–36.

Sedikides, C., & Green, J. D. (2000). On the self-protective nature of inconsistency/negativity management: Using the person memory paradigm to examine self-referent memory. *Journal of Personality and Social Psychology*, *79*, 906–922.

Sedikides, C., & Green, J. D. (2004). What I don't recall can't hurt me: Information negativity versus information inconsistency as determinants of memorial self-defense. *Social Cognition*, *22*, 4–29.

Sedikides, C., & Green, J. D. (2009). Memory as a self-protective mechanism. *Social and Personality Psychology Compass*, *3*, 1055–1068.

Sedikides, C., Green, J. D., & Pinter, B. (2004). Self-protective memory. In D. R. Beike, J. M. Lampinen, & D. A. Behrend (Eds.), *The self and memory* (pp. 161–179). Philadelphia, PA: Psychology Press.

Sedikides, C., & Gregg, A. P. (2003). Portraits of the self. In M. A. Hogg & J. Cooper (Eds.), *Sage handbook of social psychology* (pp. 110–138). London, England: Sage Publications.

Sedikides, C., & Gregg, A. P. (2008). Self-enhancement: Food for thought. *Perspectives on Psychological Science*, *3*, 102–116.

Sedikides, C., Gregg, A. P., & Hart, C. M. (2007). The importance of being modest. In C. Sedikides & S. Spencer (Eds.), *The self: Frontiers in social psychology* (pp. 163–184). New York: Psychology Press.

Sedikides, C., & Hepper, E. G. D. (2009). Self-improvement. *Social and Personality Psychology Compass*, *3*, 899–917.

Sedikides, C., & Strube, M. (1995). The multiply motivated self. *Personality and Social Psychology Bulletin*, *21*, 1330–1335.

Sedikides, C., & Strube, M. J. (1997). Self-evaluation: To thine own self be good, to thine own self be sure, to thine own self be true, and to thine own self be better. In M. P. Zanna (Ed.), *Advances in Experimental Social Psychology*, *29*, 209–269. New York: Academic Press.

Sedikides, C., Wildschut, T., Gaertner, L., Routledge, C., & Arndt, J. (2008). Nostalgia as enabler of self-continuity. In F. Sani (Ed.), *Self-continuity: Individual and collective perspectives* (pp. 227–239). New York: Psychology Press.

Seligman, M. E., Nolen-Hoeksema, S., Thornton, N., & Thornton, K. M. (1990). Explanatory style as a mechanism of disappointing athletic performance. *Psychological Science*, *1*, 143–146.

Sherman, D. K., & Hartson, K. A. (2011). Reconciling self-protection with self-criticism: Self-affirmation theory. In M. D. Alicke & C. Sedikides (Eds.), *The handbook of self-enhancement and self-protection* (pp. 128–151). New York: Guilford Press.

Sherman, D. K., & Kim, H. S. (2005). Is there an "I" in "Team"? The role of the self in group-serving judgments. *Journal of Personality and Social Psychology*, *88*, 108–120.

Skowronski, J. J. (2011). The positivity bias and the fading affect bias in autobiographical memory: A self-motives perspective. In M. D. Alicke & C. Sedikides (Eds.), *The handbook of self-enhancement and self-protection* (pp. 211–231). New York: Guilford Press.

Skowronski, J. J., Betz, A. L., Thompson, C. P., & Shannon, L. (1991). Social memory in everyday life: Recall of self-events and other-events. *Journal of Personality and Social Psychology*, *60*, 831–843.

Stephan, E., Sedikides, C., Wildschut, T., & Routledge, C., Zhou, X., Kuang, L., & Vingerhoets, J. J. M. (2011). *Nostalgia regulates avoidance and approach motivation*. Unpublished manuscript, University of Southampton.

Stewart, A. E. (2005). Attributions of responsibility for motor vehicle crashes. *Accident Analysis and Prevention, 37,* 681–688.

Swann, W. B., Jr., Rentfrow, P. J., & Guinn, J. (2003). S elf-verification: The search for coherence. In M. Leary & J. Tangney (Eds.), *Handbook of self and identity* (pp. 367–383). New York: Guilford.

Sweeney, P. D., Anderson, K., & Bailey, S. (1986). Attributional style in depression: A meta-analytic review. *Journal of Personality and Social Psychology, 50,* 974–991.

Tatarkiewicz, W. (1976). *Analysis of happiness*. Warsaw, Poland: Polish Scientific Publishers.

Taylor, S. E., & Brown, J. D. (1988). Illusion and well-being: A social psychological perspective on mental health. *Psychological Bulletin, 103,* 193–210.

Taylor, S. E., Klein, L. C., Lewis, B. P., Gruenewald, T. L., Gurung, R. A. R., & Updegraff, J. A. (2000). Biobehavioral responses to stress in females: Tend-and-befriend, not fight-or-flight. *Psychological Review, 107,* 411–429.

Taylor, S. E., Lerner, J. S., Sherman, D. K., Sage, R. M., & McDowell, N. K. (2003a). Portrait of the self-enhancer: Well-adjusted and well-liked or maladjusted and friendless? *Journal of Personality and Social Psychology, 84,* 165–176.

Taylor, S. E., Lerner, J. S., Sherman, D. K., Sage, R. M., & McDowell, N. K. (2003b). Are self-enhancing cognitions associated with healthy or unhealthy biological profiles? *Journal of Personality and Social Psychology, 85,* 605–615.

Tennen, H., & Herzberger, S. (1987). Depression, self-esteem, and the absence of self-protective attributional biases. *Journal of Personality and Social Psychology, 52,* 72–80.

Tetlock, P. E., & Levin, A. (1982). Attribution bias: On the inconclusiveness of the cognition-motivation debate. *Journal of Experimental Social Psychology, 18,* 68–88.

Thompson, C. P., Skowronski, J. J., Larsen, S. F., & Betz, A. (1996). *Autobiographical memory: Remembering what and remembering when*. New York: Erlbaum.

Van Lange, P. A. M., Rusbult, C. E., Semin-Goossens, A., Goerts, C. A, & Stalpers, M. (1999). Being better than others but otherwise perfectly normal: Perceptions of uniqueness and similarity in close relationships. *Personal Relationships, 6,* 269–289.

Van Lange, P. A. M., & Sedikides, C. (1998). Being more honest but not necessarily more intelligent than others: Generality and explanations for the Muhammad Ali effect. *European Journal of Social Psychology, 28,* 675–680.

Van Lange, P. A. M., Taris, T. W., & Vonk, R. (1997). The social psychology of social psychologists: Self-enhancing beliefs about own research. *European Journal of Social Psychology, 27,* 675–685.

Wagenaar, W. A., & Groeneweg, J. (1990). The memory of concentration camp survivors. *Applied Cognitive Psychology, 4,* 77–87.

Walker, W. R., & Skowronski, J. J. (2009). The Fading Affect Bias….But what the hell is it for? *Applied Cognitive Psychology, 23,* 1122–1136.

Walker, W. R., Skowronski, J. J., Gibbons, J. A., Vogl, R. J., & Thompson, C. P. (2003). On the emotions accompanying autobiographical memory: Dysphoria disrupts the fading affect bias. *Cognition and Emotion, 17,* 703–724.

Walker, W. R., Skowronski, J. J., & Thompson, C. P. (2003). Life is pleasant—and memory helps to keep it that way. *Review of General Psychology, 7,* 203–210.

Weary, G. (1979). Self-serving biases in attribution process: A re-examination of the fact or fiction question. *Journal of Personality and Social Psychology, 36,* 56–71.

Weary Bradley, G. (1978). Self-serving attributional biases: Perceptual or response distortions? *Journal of Personality and Social Psychology, 37,* 1418–1420.

Weiner, B. (1972). *Theories of motivation: From mechanism to cognition*. Chicago, IL: Rand McNally.

Weiner, P. S. (1964). Personality correlates of self-appraisal in four-year-old children. *Genetic Psychologic Monographs, 70,* 329–365.

Weinstein, N. D. (1980). Optimistic biases about personal risks. *Science, 246,* 1232–1233.

Wiesenfeld, B., Brockner, J., Petzall, B., Wolf, R., & Bailey, J. (2001). Stress and coping among layoff survivors: A self-affirmation analysis. *Anxiety, Stress and Coping, 1,* 15–34.

Wildschut, T., Sedikides, C., Arndt, J., & Routledge, C. D. (2006). Nostalgia: Content, triggers, functions. *Journal of Personality and Social Psychology, 91,* 975–993.

Williams, E. F., & Gilovich, T. (2008). Do people really believe they are above average? *Journal of Experimental Social Psychology, 44,* 1121–1128.

Williams, J. M. G., Barnhofer, T., Crane, C., Hermans, D., Raes, F., Watkins, E., & Dalgleish, T. (2007). Autobiographical memory specificity and emotional disorder. *Psychological Bulletin, 133,* 122–148.

Wilson, A. E., Smith, M. D., Ross, H. S., & Ross, M. (2004). Young children's personal accounts of their sibling disputes. *Merrill-Palmer Quarterly, 50,* 39–60.

Windschitl, P. D., Kruger, J., & Sims, E. N. (2003). The influence of egocentrism and focalism on people's optimism and competition: When what affects us equally affects me more. *Journal of Personality and Social Psychology, 85,* 389–408.

Wright, S. S. (2000). Looking at the self in a rose-colored mirror: Unrealistically positive self-views and academic performance. *Journal of Social and Clinical Psychology, 19,* 451–462.

Wyer, R. S., & Frey, D. (1983). The effects of feedback about self and others on the recall and judgments of feedback-relevant information. *Journal of Experimental Social Psychology, 19,* 540–559.

Yarrow, M. R., Campbell, J. D., & Burton, R. V. (1970). Recollections of childhood: A study of the retrospective method. *Monographs of the Society for Research in Child Development, 35,* 1–83.

Zauberman, G., Ratner, R. K., & Kim, K. (2009). Memories as assets: Strategic memory protection in choice over time. *Journal of Consumer Research, 35,* 715–728.

Zuckerman, M. (1979). Attribution of success and failure revisited, or: The motivational bias is alive and well in attributional theory. *Journal of Personality, 47,* 245–287.

Zuckerman, M., & O'Loughlin, R. E. (2006). Self-enhancement by social comparison: A prospective analysis. *Personality and Social Psychology Bulletin, 32,* 751–760.

The Gendered Body Project: Motivational Components of Objectification Theory

Tomi-Ann Roberts *and* Patricia L. Waters

Abstract

In this chapter, we attempt to explore the motivational questions that arise when we view the psychology of women through the lens of objectification theory, which highlights the centrality of appearance concerns, or "body projects," for girls and women today. We examine theoretical perspectives on what motivates the sexual objectification of women, considering the ways this treatment may reflect an adaptive evolutionary mating strategy, may serve as a tool for the maintenance of patriarchal power, or may lend existential "protection" against the creaturely, death reminders that women's bodies provide. We then investigate both developmental processes and situational/contextual features that motivate girls and women to internalize a sexually objectifying view on their physical selves. And, finally, we review evidence that self-objectification, though motivating in itself, carries significant consequences for their health and well-being.

Key Words: sexual objectification, self-objectification, body, gender, motivation

New Year's Resolution: I will try to make myself better in any way I possibly can, with the help of my budget and babysitting money. I will lose weight, get new lenses, a new haircut, good makeup, new clothes and accessories.
(adolescent girl's diary entry, Brumberg, 1997, p. xxi)

In a fascinating if disheartening historiography, Joan Brumberg (1997) examined the ways adolescent girls described their self-improvement goals in their diaries over the past 100 years. The change over time was clear. Whereas girls of yesteryear focused on improving their manners or their study habits, in the more recent years, girls' focus has become almost exclusively the enhancement of their physical appearance. It was not that 19th-century girls were not aware of beauty imperatives, but rather that these were not linked to self-worth or personhood in the ways they appear to be for 21st-century girls, whose motivational concern with the shape and appearance

of their bodies becomes the primary expression of their individual identity. Because of the centrality of appearance concerns to girls and women today, Brumberg called this their "body projects."

Objectification theory (Fredrickson & Roberts, 1997), published the same year as Brumburg's book, provided a theoretical framework from within psychology for understanding the gendered body project. This framework argues that the ubiquitous sexual objectification of the female body provides the cultural milieu in which girls develop into women. The theory proposes that girls and women are coaxed through both social and cultural experiences of sexual objectification to treat them*selves* as objects to be gazed at and evaluated based on physical appearance, an effect termed "self-objectification" (Fredrickson & Roberts, 1997).

In this chapter, we explore the motivational questions that arise when we view the psychology of women through the lens of objectification theory.

First, we ask: What motivates the sexual objectification of women, both culturally and interpersonally? When, where, and why does this perspective on the female body get adopted, and what function does it serve? Next we examine the question of what motivates *self*-objectification, or the internalization of a sexually objectifying perspective on the bodily self, among girls and women. How do cultural and interpersonal experiences of objectification translate into and take hold of girls' and women's own trait-level self-concepts? What developmental processes are involved? What situational or contextual features of girls' and women's environments motivate states of self-objectification? Finally we argue that, despite its motivating elements, the "body project" that girls and women appear to be engaged in carries a host of cognitive, emotional, behavioral and even health consequences.

Theoretical Frameworks on the Sexual Objectification of Women

Philosopher Martha Nussbaum (1995) defined sexual objectification as the treating of persons as sexual "things" or objects, separating them from their human attributes or characteristics. Nussbaum (1999) identified seven components of objectification: *instrumentality* and *ownership* involve treating a person as a tool or commodity; *denial of autonomy* and *inertness* involve seeing a person as lacking self-determination and agency; *fungibility* is characterized by viewing a person as interchangeable with others of his or her "type"; *violability* represents someone as lacking boundary integrity; and *denial of subjectivity* involves believing that a person's experiences and feelings can be neglected.

Sexual objectification has been discussed by feminist philosophers and social scientists for over a century, and it has typically been linked to cultural representations of women in pornography (e.g., LeMoncheck, 1985). Indeed, each of Nussbaum's (1999) components can be seen in such cultural representations, as well as interpersonal treatment of women and girls. In psychology, Fredrickson and Roberts (1997) argued that sexual objectification occurs along a continuum, extending beyond pornography to the wider cultural context, which normalizes the commodification of women's bodies just about everywhere, and that this cultural context induces girls and women to adopt a third-person perspective on their own bodies (i.e., to self-objectify).

But what motivates this cultural and interpersonal treatment of women's bodies? Here we will outline three theoretical views that have been brought to bear on this question. First, evolutionary psychologists argue that such treatment of women serves an adaptational function. Second, feminists argue that such treatment serves to uphold hegemonic masculine patriarchal structures of power. And finally, existential theorists point to the psychic distancing from the animal body that objectification serves.

Objectification as Evolutionary Adaptation

Evolutionary psychologists argue that the sexual objectification of women's bodies is part and parcel of the naturally selected mating strategy of human males. This perspective takes as a starting point that physical appearance in women provides a wealth of cues to fertility and reproductive value. Secondly, these theorists argue that standards of physical attractiveness in human females are not arbitrary or infinitely culturally variable (Buss, 2007). So this framework argues for an evolution of standards of female beauty: Visually observable cues to fertility and reproductive value will become essential to what humans find attractive in females. As David Buss (2007) has put it, "beauty is in the psychological adaptations of the beholder" (p. 506).

In a large cross-cultural study, Buss and his colleagues (Buss, 1989; Buss et al., 1990) found that men place a greater emphasis on physical attractiveness (or "good looks") in potential mates than do women and men want mates who are more youthful than they themselves are. Theorists have suggested that the visually observable cues to fertility and reproductive value that are considered "good looking" in women include a low waist-to-hip ratio, full lips, lustrous hair, long hair, clear skin, and facial femininity (Buss, 2007).

So the evolutionary perspective on sexual objectification argues that men's visual inspections of women's bodies, the emphasis placed on women's bodies as the most important feature of them, and even women's own attention to and enhancement of their attractiveness are all motivated by a drive for heterosexual mating. There are several problems with this explanation for sexual objectification, however. First, in Buss et al.'s (1990) cross-cultural study, physical attractiveness was ranked by males, on average, not first but *third* on a list of desirable characteristics of a potential female sex partner. Both kindness and intelligence ranked ahead of physical attractiveness on the list of what men want in a mate. Perhaps some men's treatment of women as sexual objects is motivated by desire to reproduce, but some men are not as motivated as others by heterosexual sex, and clearly some sexual objectification by men is not a reflection of wanting to mate.

Of the many features of women's bodies considered signals of reproductive value by evolutionary psychologists, only the waist-to-hip ratio has received much attention in research. Here, studies show that men do find a lower ratio more attractive than a higher (e.g., Singh, 1993). However, in a study of the eye movements male and female participants made while judging the attractiveness of photographs of female bodies, researchers found no evidence for fixations on the pelvic or hip area. That is, waist-to-hip ratio assessments had no impact on attractiveness judgments overall (Cornelissen, Hancock, Kiviniemi, George, & Tovée, 2009). We do not know the role the other hypothesized signals of female attractiveness play in actually attracting men to want to mate with them.

Finally, numerous critics have pointed out that, although heterosexual intercourse is necessary for species survival, it is not necessary for individual survival or even well-being (e.g., Hartlaub, 2007). Plenty of people have lived long prosperous lives without having heterosexual intercourse. Therefore, hinging the ubiquitous cultural and interpersonal sexual objectification of women on men's evolved strategy for mating falls seriously short. Clearly other motivations for this phenomenon must exist.

Objectification as Maintenance of Hegemonic Masculinity

Hegemonic masculinity is defined as "the maintenance of practices that institutionalize men's dominance over women" (Connell, 1987, p. 185). One of these practices is the sexual objectification of women. Dworkin (1987) argues that women are socialized into heterosexual womanhood, which is the same as being socialized into subordination. For Dworkin, heterosexuality is organized around male dominance, which is heterosexual maleness, and female subordination, which is heterosexual femaleness. Women are socialized to be heterosexual females, and hence sexualized to the liking of heterosexual men, which is to be subordinate, which is to be unable to meaningfully consent to what is actually their own subordination. To the extent that women are complicit in this arrangement, it is because they have formed a kind of slave mentality to escape punishment or curry favor. Dworkin's colleague Catherine MacKinnon wrote, "sexual objectification is the primary process of the subjection of women. It unites act with word, construction with expression, perception with enforcement, myth with reality. Man fucks woman; subject verb object" (1983, p. 635).

This framework links objectification with power. However, the literature reveals a somewhat complex psychological relationship between felt power and likelihood to objectify. Is it that feelings of power motivate objectification, or is objectification a defensive reaction against feelings of powerlessness? There is evidence for both.

In one study, when a female participant was cast as subordinate, males who possessed power over her and who endorsed survey items indicating a likelihood to sexually harass found her more attractive than those without power or the propensity toward sexual harassment (Bargh, Raymond, Pryor, & Strack, 1995). A more recent study examined the relationship between power and the instrumentality feature of objectification, and it showed that felt power fundamentally alters how targets are perceived. Gruenfeld, Inesee, Magee, and Galinsky (2008) demonstrated sexual objectification of a moderately competent female prospective work partner by men assigned to the role of boss. When participants had concurrent sex and performance goals, those in the high-power condition were more interested in working with a female target who was instrumental for sexual purposes than were those in the low-power condition.

So felt power appears to heighten approach toward instrumental ("useful") social targets. In other words, this feature of sexual objectification (treating others as sexual tools) appears to be motivated in part by power. Indeed, news stories of men in positions of power sexually exploiting others are so common as to be almost humdrum. From Italy's Sylvio Berlusconi to our own Eliot Spitzer, Clarence Thomas, Bill Clinton, or John Edwards, the list of powerful men treating women as sexual tools is long. Such men seem willing to risk a great deal—even the loss of their hard-earned power—to do so.

On the other hand, evidence also exists for quite the opposite relationship between power and objectification. For example, Krings and Facchin (2009) found that men's sexual harassment of women (which we would argue is an interpersonal form of sexual objectification) is motivated by the perception of low interactional justice in their workplace. That is, when men feel they themselves are not being treated fairly, this appears to fuel a desire to exert power, to "get even," by harassing or objectifying women.

A similar theme is found in the literature on the motives of rapists. Numerous studies have found that men who rape confess to underlying feelings of insecurity about their masculinity, and they report feeling a need to exert power over women. Studies show similar feelings in a wide range of men who engage in sexual violence, from those incarcerated for attacking strangers (e.g., Scully & Marolla, 1985), to college students who coerce unwanted sex from acquaintances (Lisak & Roth, 1988; Malamuth, 1986). As Lisak and Roth (1990) showed, such men feel threatened by women and compensate for their insecurity by seeking to dominate and control them.

Contrary to the evolutionary view, this perspective on objectification argues that it is not motivated by sex or mating goals alone. In the Gruenfeld et al. (2008) study, having sex on their mind was not sufficient motivation for males to prefer to work with an attractive female on a complex task. Men did not act on their sex goal unless they were also powerful. Whether sexual objectification is fueled by a feeling of being in power over others, who become attractive sexual instruments, or whether objectification of others is a way for the relatively disenfranchised to reinstate dominance, it is clear that power plays a role. Furthermore, one structural outcome of the sexual objectification of women is certainly the maintenance of the societal power inequity between the sexes.

Objectification as Existential Protection

The previous two explanations for what motivates the sexual objectification of women, while offering significant insights, fail in at least two important ways. First, they do not adequately account for the fact that objectification occurs along a continuum from dehumanizing (e.g., rape, trafficking) to seemingly benign or even benevolent (e.g., widespread cultural displays of idealized women's bodies). In other words, sexual objectification does not just "keep women down" it also sometimes "puts them up." Second, they do not provide satisfying explanations for why women themselves often take this perspective on their own bodies; they do not, in other words, provide a meaningful account of the phenomenon of self-objectification.

More psychodynamically oriented feminist thinkers, such as Dorothy Dinnerstein (1976) add anxiety to the question of what motivates this treatment of women and their bodies. In this view, women are regarded as dangerous because they are the ones who first introduce all of us to the mixed blessing of being human (Snitow, 1978). For Dinnerstein, men have subordinated women across culture and time because women, in giving life, also, by association, give death. The threat men feel toward women's life-and-death giving "powers" is the impetus behind their efforts to control women. For if men can control women's bodies they also, in effect, control nature and mortality itself.

Building on Dinnerstein's view, Goldenberg and Roberts (2004, 2011) further articulated an existential motivation for the sexual objectification of women's bodies and women's own self-objectification. They point out that there are two conflicting views historically on women's bodies. On the one hand, there is a long tradition of construing women as closer to animals and nature (Ortner, 1974), yet on the other hand there are also ample cultural examples of women being elevated above nature, idealized, even worshipped as goddesses. So stereotypes about women are paradoxical, because they contain both negative and seemingly positive judgments, as Glick and Fiske's (1996) revelation of "benevolent sexism" attests. With respect to women's bodies, research shows that women's reproductive and bodily functions (menstruation, pregnancy, breastfeeding) are often viewed with derision, but, on the other hand, other features of their bodies are revered as cultural symbols of beauty and male desire.

Goldenberg and Roberts (2004, 2011) argue that the objectification of women is motivated by a desire to strip women of their connection to nature, and it serves as a form of symbolic drapery that enables a transformation of "natural," creaturely woman (and thus a reminder of our animal nature, and hence also of death) into "object" of beauty and desire. What becomes clear when scrutinizing the ubiquitous cultural presentation of women's idealized bodies is that, regardless of the particular features deemed essential by a culture for feminine beauty, it is specifically when the more creaturely features and functions of women's bodies are actually or symbolically removed from the presentation that the female body is publicly acceptable and attractive.

Breasts provide an illustrative example. Iris Marion Young once wrote of women's breasts, "Cleavage is good; nipples are a no-no" (1992; p. 220). Breasts are multidimensional. They are not only a source of food for offspring but also the objects of sexual desire. Interestingly, we do not seem capable of sustaining both of these orientations toward breasts at once. Studies indeed show that the extent to which both men and women view breasts as objects to be enjoyed by men predicts negative attitudes toward breastfeeding. In one qualitative study, a mother negatively disposed toward breastfeeding her infant was quoted as saying, "Yuck, those are for your husband!" (Morse, 1989, p. 239). In a more recent quantitative investigation, Ward, Merriwether, and Caruthers (2006) found that the more men engaged with popular men's magazines, the more they construed women as sexual objects, and this attitude predicted more negative views toward breastfeeding and more concern that breastfeeding interferes with sexual relations.

Menstruation provides another example. Roberts, Goldenberg, Power, and Pyszczynski (2002) found that male and female participants exhibited negative reactions to a woman who made her menstrual status known by inadvertently dropping a wrapped tampon out of her backpack. Not only was the woman viewed as less competent and less likable than when she dropped a less "offensive" but equally feminine item—a hair barrette—from her bag, but the mere presence of the tampon also led participants to distance themselves physically from the woman by sitting farther away from her. Furthermore, not only were negative reactions exhibited in response to the individual woman who dropped the tampon, but when participants were asked to describe their attitudes toward women more generally, those who had seen the tampon rather than the hair barrette were particularly likely to sexually objectify women's bodies.

Construing women as objects also requires downplaying their explicit sexuality as well. Putting "beautiful" (good) women on an objectified pedestal may also serve the function of protecting men from the threat associated with their own animalistic urges toward them. Landau et al. (2006) found that inducing male participants to contemplate their mortality led to reduced sexual interest in a seductive woman, but this effect was eliminated when the woman appeared more wholesome.

This position fits with the findings of Glick and Fiske (e.g., 2001), who have observed that prejudice against women takes the form not only of overtly hostile sexism but also benevolent sexism (i.e., "characterizing women as pure creatures who ought to be protected, supported, and adored and whose love is necessary to make a man complete"; Glick & Fiske, 2001, p. 109). The primary theoretical explanation for benevolent sexism is that it enables interaction between the sexes, while simultaneously pacifying women. Seemingly benevolent sexual objectification, when viewed as motivated by existential concerns, appears not only to pacify women but also to *protect both men and women*. Men's physical, animal desires should be rendered less threatening if the target of these desires is construed as a pure and wholesome object of worship. And, to the extent that women themselves self-objectify, they are afforded the protection of psychically distancing from their own animal nature.

The Hows and Whys of Self-Objectification

We come now to the question of how and why girls and women adopt an observer's point of view on their bodily selves, how and why they undertake their own "body projects." As Brumberg's (1997) work on diaries illustrates, today's girls have come to focus almost exclusively on the enhancement of their physical appearance as their most important self-improvement goal. Empirical studies indeed show that girls as young as 12 years old self-objectify; they place significantly greater emphasis on their body's appearance than on its competence, health, or well-being (Slater & Tiggemann, 2002). Other evidence shows that even younger girls are already dissatisfied with their bodies, and especially their weight (Phares, Steinberg, & Thompson, 2004). And what starts young, sticks around. For example, one survey showed that more than 70% of normal-weight women aged 30–75 are dissatisfied with their body's appearance (Allaz, Bernstein, Rouget, Archinard, & Morabia, 1998). Feminists have argued that, over the course of women's development across the life span, their dissatisfaction with their weight and physical attractiveness is so widespread as to constitute a "normative discontent" (Rodin, Silberstein, & Striegel-Moore, 1984).

Objectification theory provided a comprehensive framework for understanding how the cultural milieu of the sexual objectification of female bodies delivers a kind of instructional backdrop for women's development across the life span (Fredrickson & Roberts, 1997). Girls and women encounter this treatment second hand, through media and marketers' representations (e.g., Kilbourne & Jhally, 2000), as well as in actual interpersonal encounters (e.g., Swim, Hyers, Cohen, & Ferguson, 2001). The theory argues that girls and women are coaxed through these social and cultural experiences of sexual objectification to treat them*selves* as objects to be gazed at and evaluated based on physical appearance, that is, to self-objectify (Fredrickson & Roberts, 1997).

Exactly how does this coaxing occur? What motivates self-objectification? Fredrickson and Roberts (1997) argued that this view of self can manifest on a trait level, but it also can be induced by situational and contextual cues. On the one hand, some people are more likely to define themselves stably in ways that emphasize a third-person, over a first-person, point of view on their bodies. Women consistently score higher than men in trait self-objectification (e.g., Fredrickson, Roberts, Noll, Quinn, & Twenge, 1998). Furthermore, similarities override differences among subgroups of women in self-objectification.

White and non-White women as well as heterosexual and sexual minority women report similar levels of self-objectification (Downs, James, & Cowan, 2006; Harrison & Fredrickson, 2003; Kozee & Tylka, 2006). The adoption of this perspective on the self is likely a developmental process in which a sexually objectified standard of femininity is cultivated.

On the other hand, certain situations appear to call greater attention to the body as observed, encouraging a state of self-objectification. Again, women appear to be more susceptible than men to the experimental inductions of a state of self-objectification (Moradi & Huang, 2008). Here we will attempt to organize our understanding of what motivates the gendered body project both in terms of the development of trait-level self-objectification in girls and women, as well as the more situation-specific, proximal contexts that induce this perspective on self.

Girls' Gender Development in the Culture of Sexual Objectification

Theories of gender development may help to make sense of how cultural messaging around sexual objectification, as well as interpersonal sexualized or sexually objectifying treatment, get translated and incorporated into the self system of girls as they develop within a sexually objectifying culture.

SOCIALIZATION THEORIES

Ample research suggests that from the moment children are born they are treated differently based on their sex (Maccoby, 1998). By as early as 2 years old, children consistently label themselves and those around them as either male or female, and they are busy about the business of modeling behaviors that are consistent with cultural gender norms (Campbell, Shirley, & Candy, 2004). Social learning theorists (e.g., Bussey & Bandura, 1999) posit that children learn gender-appropriate behaviors by observing the praise and recognition others receive for gender-consistent behavior, and by noting sanctions against gender-inconsistent behavior (Rust, Golombok, Hines, Johnston, & Golding, 2000). From a social learning theory perspective then, little girls emulate feminine models because they are praised for doing so ("My, how pretty you look!"), and because they see that others are positively reinforced for doing so.

COGNITIVE DEVELOPMENTAL THEORIES

Cognitive developmentalists emphasize the child's active participation in forming an identity and argue that children construct a schema or framework for organizing gender-relevant information. From this perspective, children mark and quarter their realities along gender lines, allowing stereotype-consistent behavior in and ruling stereotype-inconsistent behavior out (Martin, Ruble, & Szkrybalo, 2002). However, the extent to which cultural modeling about beauty is internalized by young girls and whether there is a critique of cultural ideals is influenced by cognitive development.

While gender is only one part of the identity equation, it is one of the earliest emerging facets of identity and, since it develops so early, it can appear quite rigid. Parents often remark on their daughters' desire to dress in highly feminine outfits even when the situation might not warrant it, and this has led researchers to conclude that children both observe and construct notions about gender-appropriate behavior based on their cognitive abilities (Maccoby, 1998). Researchers argue that rigidity about gender-appropriate behavior (and dress) reflect preschoolers' erroneous beliefs that it is not biology, but the clothes (and other trappings of gender) that make the man (or woman). While this confusion is cleared up by the advent of gender constancy around 4 to 5 years old (Kohlberg & Zigler, 1967; Ruble et al., 2007), the fact that girls as young as 3 years old are already policing the femininity of their outfits suggests that the roots of self-objectification are deep indeed.

The basic schema for gender continues to become elaborated and solidified as part of one's larger identity across childhood and adolescence. However, in these earliest years, information about gender is consumed relatively uncritically. In preschool and early childhood, it is clear that children are preoccupied with learning the rules of the game, not with dismantling them (Piaget, 1965). Acquiring rules for gender-appropriate appearance and behaviors comes in a variety of sources, including family members, peers, teachers, but one of these ways is through media and toy exposure. The average preschooler watches more than 21 hours of TV a week and yet they are the least able to critically evaluate media messaging (Kunkel et al., 2004; Robinson & Bianchi, 1997). This is especially problematic given that even among young women and adults, the more exposure to mainstream media content the more likely females are to uncritically endorse sex-role stereotypes (Ward, 2002; Ward & Rivadeneyra, 1999).

Across early and middle childhood advances in perspective-taking ability pave the way for increasingly sophisticated interpretations of the social realm

(Higgins, 1991; Selman, 1980). In school-aged children these comparisons center around concrete attributes such as appearance. Given this, how explicitly sexually objectifying material is incorporated into the self at different ages is likely to change with the type of gender role models children encounter. The subtle shift in toys from Barbie with the hypersexualized *body* to Bratz dolls with a girlish body juxtaposed with hypersexualized *clothes and facial features* makes room for ever younger girls to don the mantle of sexuality even if they don't have the body for it (Roberts, in press).

At adolescence, normative developmental processes may heighten girls' sensitivity to sexually objectifying cultural messages. At puberty, girls begin to acquire formal operational thought and the capacity to compare themselves against multiple standards. However, the capacity to understand the self in increasingly complex and differentiated terms develops gradually and inconsistently across adolescence and may be accompanied by cognitive errors. Elkind (1967) dubbed one of these the "imaginary audience," which he argued was a "failure of under differentiation" between the self and other that leads adolescents to believe that others are as preoccupied with them as they are with themselves. In terms of objectification theory, the heightened self-consciousness associated with this cognitive error leaves early adolescents ripe for the self-surveillance aspects associated with self-objectification.

During the same period at the neurological level, a gradual process of synaptic pruning and consolidation of neural architecture occurs in the prefrontal cortex—the seat of judgment, reasoning, and planning—and this is coupled with more pronounced development in the amygdala (emotion regulation) and changes in the availability of dopamine and GABA (Baird et al., 1999; Kalivas, Churchill, & Klitenick, 1993; Spear, 2000). Taken together, these changes are associated with a heightened sensitivity to emotionally evocative material (e.g., media/advertising) coupled with relatively few cognitive "breaks" on the system. Researchers have associated these shifts with adolescents' penchant for risk taking and decision making that favors immediate over long-term rewards (Reyna & Farley, 2006; Spear, 2000), but in the context of objectification theory, it is conceivable that they are also associated with difficulty in critically analyzing provocative cultural messaging around appearance.

Self-objectification may also play a role in the social comparisons associated with creating a coherent and integrated identity during adolescence. Research on the development of the self concept demonstrates that while early adolescents are able to generate multiple self-descriptors, they see no apparent contradiction in describing themselves as entirely opposite in one setting versus another (Harter, 1999). Harter argued that this is due to emergent formal operational development in which the individual is able to generate multiple perspectives on the self but is not yet able to hold contradictory descriptors as objects for purposes of comparison. It is plausible then that the 12-year-old girl could hold completely contradictory views, recognizing at once that the media images are "stupid and unrealistic" and yet unproblematically working mightily to attain the ideal body. Appreciating the inconsistencies between these two ideas is likely to cause increasing distress only at mid-adolescence when contradictory information about the self becomes highly salient but integration of inconsistencies is still beyond the cognitive reach of the mid-adolescent (Harter, 1999). In the context of objectification theory, it is conceivable that self-objectification contributes to increased body surveillance and body shame, as the mid-adolescent works to integrate what she knows (e.g., "These media images are unrealistic and stupid, nobody dresses like that!") with what she feels (e.g., "If I look hot for this party, people will like me").

This assertion, however, is largely speculative given the lack of research examining the relationship between cognitive development and self-objectification. Even among older samples, studies that explicitly examine developmental processes in the motive to self-objectify have been few and far between. One notable exception is McKinley's (2006a; 2006b) sequential study of mothers and daughters at two points in time, 10 years apart. McKinley (2006a) found that college women reported higher levels of body shame and body surveillance than did their middle-aged mothers or their male peers and the link between body shame and body surveillance was stronger in younger women than in middle-aged women. Ten years later, both groups of women continued to report higher levels of self-objectification than males. However, the younger cohort of women reported significantly less self-objectification at the second assessment, and they no longer differed significantly from their mothers (McKinley, 2006a). McKinley explained that during emerging adulthood, young women may be more motivated to self-objectify because they are engaged in life span tasks such as establishing intimate relationships (Erikson, 1959) and beginning careers (Arnett, 2000), both of which implicate appearance for women. Ten years later, as careers and intimate relationships are solidifying, the motivation to self-objectify may lessen.

To sum up, objectification theory's concept of self-objectification provides an intrapsychic contribution to our understanding of gender development in girls. During their early years of gender socialization, perhaps through reinforcements as social learning theorists would argue, or even through normative cognitive and neurological changes as constructivists would argue, girls learn to internalize a sexually objectified view of their bodies. Once they have done so, they set about the work of solidifying their identity as a physically attractive female. The media steps in to supply increasingly impossible standards of sexy attractiveness to which they can aspire and marketers sell them the products and procedures that promise to help them meet that standard (Lamb & Brown, 2006). Once in place at the trait level, self-objectification provides the motivational fuel for the body project in which girls and women appear to remain engaged for much of their lives.

The Situational Motivators of Self-Objectification

In addition to its cultivation within girls and women as a trait, a number of studies manipulating the level of exposure to sexually objectifying versus control situations lend support for the notion that self-objectification can be induced as a state by subtle cues in the environment (e.g., Calogero, 2004; Fredrickson et al., 1998; Quinn, Kallen, & Cathey, 2006; Roberts & Gettman, 2004). The classic study of heightening self-objectification by manipulating appearance pressure involved women performing tasks in a mirrored dressing room while wearing either a swimsuit or a sweater (Fredrickson et al., 1998). Those in the heightened self-objectification condition (wearing swimsuits) reported higher levels of body shame, reduced task performance, and restrained food intake compared to control groups dressed in sweaters. Restrained eating occurred even after delaying the food intake assessment until after participants redressed, suggesting that the effects of the prime remained even after the initial manipulation (Quinn et al., 2006).

In other experiments, priming women to anticipate an interaction with a male stranger increased state self-objectification phenomena, including body shame and appearance anxiety (Calogero, 2004). Still other inductions that have been demonstrated to lead to heightened state self-objectification include exposure to sexually objectifying words or images (Aubrey, 2006; Monro & Huon, 2005; Roberts & Gettman, 2004), overhearing other women speak disparagingly of their own bodies (Gapinski, Brownell, & LaFrance, 2003), and being filmed by a male with a focus on the body, not the face (Gay & Castano, 2010). The salience of these primes suggests that contextual factors contribute to self-objectification and lend support for the argument that self-objectification derives from cultural messaging around expected appearance norms.

However, not all girls and women read cultural messages about beauty with the same urgency, nor do all females interpret cultural beauty ideals as mandates for body projects. The extent to which individual differences in self-objectification are trait-like or are the product of the social milieu remains speculative. Several studies have demonstrated connections between self-reported self-objectification (the trait), body surveillance, body shame, and negative outcomes. Jones (2004), for example, found that the more 7th and 10th grade girls engaged in *appearance conversations with friends* and the more social comparison they made concerning appearance, the more body dissatisfaction they reported. In this study, *appearance conversations with friends* played as significant a role as internalizing media ideals in shaping body dissatisfaction. It could be that conversations with peers concerning body issues are analogous to co-rumination, a phenomenon that has been tied to depressive symptoms (Broderick & Korteland, 2002; Rose, 2002; Rose & Rudolph, 2006). Could these conversations amount to *co-objectification*? When a girl asks a question like "Do these pants make my butt look big?" is she enlisting peers' help in her own body surveillance? If co-objectification is one of the factors contributing to body dissatisfaction in the middle and high school years, interventions in the context of peer interactions may be especially important.

Summary

We have argued that one of the reasons girls and women are motivated to self-objectify is that bringing the self into compliance with sociocultural norms yields positive benefits. We have also suggested that how self-objectification motivates behavior will vary depending on age and normative developmental processes, including cognitive and neurological maturation. It seems likely that adolescent girls may be especially sensitized to cultural information about appearance as they work to create a coherent self-concept. Research also suggests that young women who are in the emerging adulthood phase of life will be particularly motivated to engage in self-objectification because it is during these times that the social benefits of conforming to appearance standards are particularly salient. It is also clear that just how self-objectification informs girls' and women's choices varies depending on contextual phenomena such as the extent to which girls co-objectify by talking to each other about appearance concerns, and whether and how they encounter objectifying treatment and media.

The Motivating But Consequential Body Project

Self-objectification can be thought of as a kind of external locus of control, for it frames girls' and women's lives around their physical attractiveness or sexual appeal to others. On the other hand, the "body project" has its internally motivated elements as well. Girls and women have every reason to value the positive feedback they receive from their own efforts at appearance enhancement. Studies have shown that women's appearance control beliefs have a paradoxical relationship to their well-being. That is, those who endorse a more internal locus of control with respect to their appearance ("buying," in other words, what advertisers for the myriad of body-enhancing products and procedures marketed to females in this culture are really selling) tend to have somewhat higher body esteem, but engage in more restricted eating and other body-altering practices that can be hazardous (McKinley & Hyde, 1996). Despite its motivating elements, a decade of research since the publication of "Objectification theory" has demonstrated that the body project in which girls and women appear to be engaged carries a host of cognitive, emotional, behavioral, and even health consequences.

The most well-documented consequences of self-objectification are in the arena of body esteem. Moradi and Huang (2008) reviewed this literature and concluded that experimental data strongly suggest that heightened self-objectification promotes body shame, appearance anxiety, and negative affect in both White and racially and ethnically diverse samples of women as well as girls as young as 12 years old. Why do girls and women experience body shame upon viewing the self as an object? The conceptual reasons for this rest on observations that a disparity between the real and the ideal self contributes to low self-esteem, dissatisfaction with one's body, and dysphoria (Harter, 1999; Horney, 1945; James, 1892; McKinley, 1998). The thinning down of the feminine body ideal over

the past 40 years has increased the disparity between women's real bodies and media ideals. This widening gap motivates the self-surveillance that results in feelings of failure (shame) at attaining the increasingly impossible ideal (McKinley, 1998; Stice, 1994).

Moradi and Huang (2008) also reviewed correlational studies that support links between self-objectification and body shame with negative outcomes for girls' and women's mental health, including low self-esteem and depressive symptoms. The body shame associated with self-objectification appears to motivate eating disordered behaviors and even smoking behaviors (e.g., Fiissel & Lafreniere, 2006; Harrell, Fredrickson, Pomerleau, & Nolen-Hoeksema, 2006; Tylka & Hill, 2004). Self-objectification and its attendant body shame have also been linked with poor outcomes related to women's sexual motivations, such as reduced interest in sex, nonassertive and risky sexual behaviors, greater appearance concern during sexual intimacy, and even lower reported sexual pleasure and arousability (e.g., Hirschman, Impett, & Schooler, 2006; Sanchez & Kiefer, 2007).

However, while mere exposure to thin media ideals increases self-objectification and thus motivates unhealthy behaviors like disordered eating, smoking, or poor sexual decision making, it is increasingly clear that self-objectification is associated not only with exposure, but with the extent to which women *internalize* the beauty ideal (Moradi, Dirks & Matteson, 2005; Morry & Staska, 2001). In Morry and Staska's study, college women's self-reported exposure to beauty (as compared to fitness) magazines was tied to self-objectification and to symptoms of disordered eating, but this effect was mediated by self-reported internalization. In other words, it is likely not exposure alone, but the degree to which girls and women take on ideals for beauty as self-relevant and motivating that predicts noxious outcomes.

To sum up, the internalization of sexual objectification means that many girls and women chronically monitor their body's appearance. Their body projects can be very motivating indeed, and advertisers promise the products, clothing, procedures, and diets that provide the tools for their undertaking. But the project is costly, not only in terms of time and money, but, studies have clearly shown, also in terms of girls' and women's well-being. It is also never finished. The comparisons girls and women make to the idealized feminine beauty proliferated by 24–7 media nearly invariably result in body shame, which, in turn, leads to a host of negative consequences for the quality of their lives.

Concluding Comments

We have suggested that objectification and self-objectification can be viewed as motivated processes. We have suggested alternative explanations for why objectification takes place in the culture, and we have developed a rationale for viewing self-objectification, and its attendant self-surveillance and body shame, as a motivational set. The empirical literature on self-objectification suggests that it is contingent upon a complex interaction between the person and the situation. In a decade of investigation, much has been illuminated about the activating role of self-objectification in motivating girls' and women's body projects. In this chapter, we have attempted to illustrate how these projects can be seen as the logical outcome of normative developmental processes within a framework on gender where femininity is narrowly construed as emphasizing sexually attractive physical appearance. Gender identity formation in childhood, self-concept in adolescence, and intimacy and career establishment in emerging adulthood are all inflected through this lens.

Just how these processes unfold and the extent to which individual differences impact the motivation to engage in body projects and produce maladapted outcomes have been the subjects of considerable investigation, some of which has been reviewed in this chapter. And it is clear from the evidence gathered to this point that the motivation to self-objectify varies in response to priming. It remains unclear, however, why some individuals are motivated to engage in self-objectification to the detriment of their health and psychological well-being and self-esteem and others remain resilient in the face of pressures to conform to appearance ideals. Unraveling these questions will be important for research if we are to imagine interventions to undermine the sexual objectification of girls and women, as well as to relieve so many of them of the maladaptive body projects in which they are engaged.

References

Allaz, A. F., Bernstein, M., Rouget, P., Archinard, M., & Morabia, A. (1998). Body weight preoccupation in middle age and ageing women: A general population survey. *International Journal of Eating Disorders, 23*, 287–294.

Arnett, J. (2000). Emerging adulthood: A theory of development from the late teens through the twenties, *American Psychologist, 55*(5), 469–480.

Aubrey, J. S. (2006). Effects of sexually objectifying media on self-objectification and body surveillance in undergraduates: Results of a 2-year panel study. *Journal of Communication, 56*, 366–386.

Baird, A. A., Gruber, S. A., Cohen, B. M., Renshaw, P. F., Steingard, R. J., & Yurgelun-Todd, D. A. (1999). fMRI of the amygdala in children and adolescents. *Journal of the American Academy of Child and Adolescent Psychiatry, 38*(2), 195–199.

Bargh, J. A., Raymond, P., Pryor, J. B., & Strack, F. (1995). Attractiveness of the underling: An automatic power—sex association and its consequences for sexual harassment and aggression. *Journal of Personality and Social Psychology, 68*, 768–781.

Broderick, P. C., & Korteland, C. (2002). Coping styles and depression in early adolescence: Relationships to gender, gender role, and implicit beliefs. *Sex Roles, 46*, 201–213.

Brumberg, J. J. (1997). *The body project: An intimate history of American girls.* New York: Vintage.

Buss, D. M. (1989). Sex differences in human mate preferences: Evolutionary hypotheses testing in 37 cultures. *Behavioral and Brain Sciences, 12*, 1–49.

Buss, D. M. (2007). The evolution of human mating. *Acta Psychologica Sinica, 39*, 502–512.

Buss, D. M., Abbott, M., Angleitner, A., Biaggio, A., Blanco-Villasenor, A., Bruchon-Schweitzer, M. . . . Yang, K-S. (1990). International preferences in selecting mates: A study of 37 societies. *Journal of Cross Cultural Psychology, 21*, 5–47.

Bussey, K., & Bandura, A. (1999). Social cognitive theory and gender development and differentiation. *Psychological Review, 106*, 676–713.

Calogero, R. M. (2004). A test of objectification theory: The effect of the male gaze on appearance concerns in college women. *Psychology of Women Quarterly, 28*, 16–21.

Campbell, A., Shirley, L., & Candy, J. (2004). A longitudinal study of gender-related cognition and behavior. *Developmental Science, 7*, 1–9.

Connell, R. W. (1987). *Gender and power: Society, the person and sexual politics.* Stanford, CA: Stanford University Press.

Cornelissen, P. L., Hancock, P. J. B., Kiviniemi, V., George, H. R., & Tovée, M. J. (2009). Patterns of eye movements when male and female observers judge female attractiveness, body fat and waist to hip ratio. *Evolution and Human Behavior, 30*, 417–428.

Dinnerstein, D. (1976). *The mermaid and the minotaur: Sexual arrangements and human malaise.* New York: Harper Collins.

Downs, D. M., James, S., & Cowan, G. (2006). Body objectification, self-esteem, and relationship satisfaction: A comparison of exotic dancers and college women. *Sex Roles, 54*, 745–752.

Dworkin, A. (1987). *Intercourse.* London: Arrow Books.

Elkind, D. (1967). Egocentrism in adolescence. *Child Development, 38*, 1025–1034.

Erikson, E. (1959). *Childhood and society.* New York: Norton.

Fiissel, D. L., & Lafreniere, K. D. (2006). Weight control motives for cigarette smoking: Further consequences of the sexual objectification of women? *Feminism and Psychology, 16*, 327–344.

Fredrickson, B. L., & Roberts, T-A. (1997). Objectification theory: Toward understanding women's lived experiences and mental health risks. *Psychology of Women Quarterly, 21*, 173–206.

Fredrickson, B. L., Roberts, T-A., Noll, S. M., Quinn, D. M., & Twenge, J. M. (1998). That swimsuit becomes you: Sex differences in self-objectification, restrained eating, and math performance. *Journal of Personality and Social Psychology, 75*, 269–285.

Gapinski, K. D., Brownell, K. D., & LaFrance, M. (2003). Body objectification and "Fat Talk": Effects on emotion, motivation, and cognitive performance. *Sex Roles, 48*, 377–388.

Gay, R. K., & Castano, E. (2010). My body or my mind: The impact of state and trait objectification on women's cognitive resources. *European Journal of Social Psychology*, *40*, 695–703.

Glick, P., & Fiske, S. T. (1996). The ambivalent sexism inventory: Differentiating hostile and benevolent sexism. *Journal of Personality and Social Psychology*, *70*, 491–512.

Glick, P., & Fiske, S. T. (2001). An ambivalent alliance: Hostile and benevolent sexism as complementary justifications for gender inequality. *American Psychologist*, *56*, 109–118.

Goldenberg, J. L., & Roberts, T-A. (2004). The beast within the beauty: An existential perspective on the objectification and condemnation of women. In J. Greenberg, S. L. Koole, & T. Pyszczynski (Eds.), *Handbook of experimental existential psychology* (pp. 71–85). New York: Guilford Press.

Goldenberg, J. L., & Roberts, T-A. (2011). The birthmark: An existential account of the objectification of women. In R. M. Calogero, S. Tantleff-Dunn, & J. K. Thompson (Eds.), *Self-objectification in women: Causes, consequences, and counteractions* (pp. 77–99). Washington, DC: American Psychological Association Press.

Gruenfeld, D. H., Inesi, M. E., Magee, J. C., & Galinsky, A. D. (2008). Power and the objectification of social targets. *Journal of Personality and Social Psychology*, *95*, 111–127.

Harrell, Z. A. T., Fredrickson, B. L., Pomerleau, C. S., & Nolen-Hoeksema, S. (2006). The role of trait self-objectification in smoking among college women. *Sex Roles*, *54*, 735–743.

Harrison, K., & Fredrickson, B. L. (2003). Women's sport media, self-objectification, and mental health in black and white adolescent females. *Journal of Communication*, *53*, 216–232.

Harter, S. (1999). *The construction of self: A developmental perspective*. New York: Guilford Press.

Hartlaub, M. G. (2007). Celebrating the natural. *Journal of Sex Research*, *44*, 220–222.

Higgins, E. T. (1991). Development of self-regulatory and self-evaluative processes: Costs, benefits, and tradeoffs. In M. R. Gunnar & A. Sroufe (Eds.), *Self-processes and development: The Minnesota Symposia on Child Development* (Vol. 23, pp. 135–166). Hillsdale, NJ: Erlbaum.

Hirschman, C., Impett, E. A., & Schooler, D. (2006). Dis/embodied voices: What late-adolescent girls can teach us about objectification and sexuality. *Sexuality Research and Social Policy: A Journal of the NSRC*, *3*, 8–20.

Horney, K. (1945). *Our inner conflicts*. New York: Basic Books.

James, W. (1892). *Psychology: The briefer course*. New York: Henry Holt.

Jones, D. (2004). Body image among adolescent girls and boys: A longitudinal study. *Develomental Psychology*, *40*(5) 823–835.

Kalivas, P. W., Churchill, L., & Klitenick, M. A. (1993). The circuitry mediating the translation of motivational stimuli into adaptive motor responses. In P. W. Kalivas & C. D. Barnes (Eds.), *Limbic motor circuits and neuropsychiatry* (pp. 237–287). Boca Raton, FL: CRC Press.

Kilbourne, J. (Producer), Jhally, S. (Director). (2000). Killing us softly 3: Advertising images of women [videorecording]. Available from Media Education Foundation. http://www.mediaed.org/cgi-bin/commerce.cgi?preadd=action&key=206

Kohlberg, L., & Zigler, E. (1967). The impact of cognitive maturity upon the development of sex-role attitudes in the years four to eight. *Genetic Psychology Monographs*, *75*, 91–165.

Kozee, H. B., & Tylka, T. L. (2006). A test of objectification theory with lesbian women. *Psychology of Women Quarterly*, *30*, 348–357.

Krings, F., & Facchin, S. (2009). Organizational justice and men's likelihood to sexually harass: The moderating role of sexism and personality. *Journal of Applied Psychology*, *94*, 501–510.

Kunkel, D., Wilcox, B. L., Cantor, J., Palmer, E., Linn, S. & Dowrick, P. (2004, February 20). *Report of the APA task force on advertising and children*. Washington, DC: American Psychological Association.

Lamb, S., & Brown, L. M. (2006). *Packaging girlhood: Rescuing our daughters from marketers' schemes*. New York: St. Martin's Press.

Landau, M. J., Goldenberg, J. L., Greenberg, J., Gillath, O., Solomon, S., Cox, C.,... & Pyszczynski, T. (2006). The siren's call: Terror management and the threat of sexual attraction. *Journal of Personality and Social Psychology*, *90*, 129–146.

LeMoncheck, L. (1985). *Dehumanizing women: Treating persons as sex objects*. Totowa, NJ: Rowman & Allanheld.

Lisak, D., & Roth, S. (1988). Motivational factors in nonincarcerated sexually aggressive men. *Journal of Personality and Social Psychology*, *55*, 795–802.

Lisak, D., & Roth, S. (1990). Motives and psychodynamics of self-reported, unincarcerated rapists. *American Journal of Orthopsychiatry*, *60*, 268–280.

Maccoby, E. E. (1998). *The two sexes: Growing up apart, coming together*. Cambridge, MA: Belknap Press.

MacKinnon, C. (1983). *Feminism, Marxism, method, and the state: Toward feminist jurisprudence. Signs: Journal of Women in Culture and Society*, *8*, 635–658.

Malamuth, N. M. (1986). Predictors of naturalistic sexual aggression. *Journal of Personality and Social Psychology*, *50*, 953–962.

Martin, C. L., Ruble, D. N., & Szkrybalo, J. (2002). Cognitive theories of early gender development. *Psychological Bulletin*, *128*, 903–933.

McKinley, N. M. (1998). Gender differences in undergraduates' body esteem: The mediating effect of objectified body consciousness and actual/ideal weight discrepancy. *Sex Roles*, *39*, 113–123.

McKinley, N. M. (2006a). Longitudinal gender differences in objectified body consciousness and weight-related attitudes and behaviors: Cultural and developmental contexts in the transition from college. *Sex Roles*, *54*, 159–173.

McKinley, N. M. (2006b). The development and cultural contexts of objectified body consciousness: A longitudinal analsyis of two cohorts of women. *Developmental Psychology*, *42*(4), 679–687.

McKinley, N. M., & Hyde, J. S. (1996). The objectified body consciousness scale: Development and validation. *Psychology of Women Quarterly*, *20*, 181–215.

Monro, F., & Huon, G. (2005). Media-portrayed idealized images, body shame, and appearance anxiety. *International Journal of Eating Disorders*, *38*, 85–90.

Moradi, B., Dirks, D., & Matteson, A. (2005). Roles of sexual objectification experiences and internalization of sociocultural standards of beauty in eating disorder symptomatology: An examination and extension of objectification theory. *Journal of Counseling Psychology*, *52*, 420–428.

Moradi, B., & Huang, Y. P. (2008). Objectification theory and psychology of women: A decade of advances and future directions. *Psychology of Women Quarterly*, *32*, 377–398.

Morry, M. M., & Staska, S. L. (2001). Magazine exposure: Internalization, self-objectification, eating attitudes, and body satisfaction in male and female university students. *Canadian Journal of Behavioral Sciences, 4,* 269–279.

Morse, J. M. (1989). "Euch, those are for your husband!" Examination of cultural values and assumptions about breast feeding. *Health Care for Women International, 11,* 223–232.

Nussbaum, M. C. (1995). Objectification. *Philosophy and Public Affairs, 24,* 249–291.

Nussbaum, M. C. (1999). *Sex and social justice.* Oxford, England: Oxford University Press.

Ortner, S. B. (1974). Is female to male as nature is to culture? In M. Z. Rosaldo & M. Lamphere (Eds.), *Women, culture and society* (pp. 173–253). Stanford, CA: Stanford University Press.

Phares, V., Steinberg, A. R., & Thompson, J. K. (2004). Gender differences in peer and parental influences: Body image disturbance, self-worth and psychological functioning in preadolescent children. *Journal of Youth and Adolescence, 33,* 421–429.

Piaget, J. (1965). *The moral judgment of the child.* New York: Free Press.

Quinn, D. M., Kallen, R. W., & Cathey, C. (2006). Body on my mind: The lingering effect of state self-objectification. *Sex Roles, 55,* 869–874.

Reyna, V. F., & Farley, F. (2006). Risk and rationality in adolescent decision-making: Implications for theory, practice and public policy. *Psychological Science in the Public Interest, 7*(1) 1–44.

Roberts, T-A. (in press). "She's so pretty, she looks just like a Bratz doll!" Theoretical foundations for understanding girls' and women's self-objectification. In E. Zurbriggen & T-A. Roberts (Eds.), *The sexualization of girls and girlhood* New York: Oxford University Press.

Roberts, T-A., & Gettman, J. Y. (2004). Mere exposure: Gender differences in the negative effects of priming a state of self-objectification. *Sex Roles, 51,* 17–27.

Roberts, T-A., Goldenberg, J. L., Power, C., & Pyszczynski, T. (2002). "Feminine protection:" The effects of menstruation on attitudes toward women. *Psychology of Women Quarterly, 26,* 131–139.

Robinson, A. P., & Bianchi, S. (1997). The children's hours. *American Demographics, 19,*, 20–23.

Rodin, J., Silberstein, L., & Striegel-Moore, R. (1984). Women and weight: A normative discontent. *Nebraska Symposium on Motivation, 32,* 267–307

Rose, A. J. (2002). Co-rumination in the friendships of girls and boys. *Child Development, 73,* 1830–1843.

Rose, A. J., & Rudolph, K. D. (2006). A review of sex differences in peer relationship processes: Potential tradeoffs for the emotional and behavioral development of girls and boys. *Psychological Bulletin, 132,* 98–131.

Ruble, D. N., Taylor, L. J., Cyphers, L., Greulich, F. K., Lurye, L. E., & Shrout, P. E. (2007). The role of gender constancy in early gender development. *Child Development, 78*(4), 1121–1136.

Rust, J., Golombok, S., Hines, M., Johnston, K., & Golding, J. (2000). The role of brothers and sisters in the gender development of preschool children. *Journal of Experimental Child Psychology, 77,* 292–303.

Sanchez, D. T., & Kiefer, A. K. (2007). Body concerns in and out of the bedroom: Implications for sexual pleasure and problems. *Archives of Sexual Behavior, 36,* 808–820.

Selman, R. L. (1980). *The growth of interpersonal understanding.* New York: Academic Press.

Scully, D., & Marolla, J. (1985). "Riding the bull at Gilley's:" Convicted rapists describe the rewards of rape. *Social Problems, 32,* 251–263.

Singh, D. (1993). Body shape and women's attractiveness— the critical role of waist-to-hip ratio. *Human Nature, 4,* 297–321.

Slater, A., & Tiggemann, M. (2002). A test of objectification theory in adolescent girls. *Sex Roles, 46,* 343–349.

Snitow, A. (1978). Thinking about the *Mermaid and the Minotaur. Feminist Studies, 4,* 190–198.

Spear, L. (2000). The adolescence brain and age-related behavioral manifestations. *Neuroscience and Biobehavioral Reviews, 24*(4) 417–463.

Stice, E. (1994). Review of the evidence for a sociocultural model of bulimia nervosa and an exploration of the mechanisms of action. *Clinical Psychology Review, 14*(7), 633–661.

Swim, J. K., Hyers, L. L., Cohen, L. L., & Ferguson, M. J. (2001). Everyday sexism: Evidence for its incidence, nature, and psychological impact from three daily diary studies. *Journal of Social Issues, 57,* 31–53.

Tylka, T. L., & Hill, M. S. (2004). Objectification theory as it relates to disordered eating among college women. *Sex Roles, 51,* 719–730.

Ward, L. M. (2002). Does television exposure affect emerging adults' attitudes and assumptions about sexual relationships? Correlational and experimental confirmation. *Journal of Youth and Adolescence, 31,* 1–15.

Ward, L. M., Merriwether, A., & Caruthers, A. (2006). Breasts are for men: Media use, masculinity ideology, and men's beliefs about women's bodies. *Sex Roles, 55,* 703–714.

Ward, L. M., & Rivadeneyra, R. (1999). Contributions of entertainment television to adoelscents' sexual attitudes and expectations: The role of viewing amount versus viewer involvement. *Journal of Sex Research, 36,* 237–249.

Young, I. M. (1992). Breasted experience: The look and the feeling. In D. Leder (Ed.), *The body in medical thought and practice* (pp. 215–230). Boston, MA: Kluwer.

Relatedness Between Children and Parents: Implications for Motivation

Eva M. Pomerantz, Cecilia Sin-Sze Cheung, *and* Lili Qin

Abstract

A significant goal in many countries around the world is promoting children's motivation so that ultimately they achieve at their full potential. There is much evidence supporting the idea that parents play a significant role in either facilitating or undermining children's motivation. The focus of this chapter is on how relatedness between children and their parents shapes the development of children's motivation as well as achievement. Three sets of ideas about how relatedness between children and their parents contributes to children's motivation are reviewed. An integration of the three is provided to highlight key themes as well as suggest key directions for future research.

Key Words: achievement, attachment, motivation, parent–child relations, parenting

Feeling related to others is fundamental to human functioning (Baumeister & Leary, 1995; Deci & Ryan, 2000). For most humans, their first experience with relatedness takes place in the context of their relationships with their parents. Such relationships are unique in that they are often the first in children's lives, with children depending on their parents to provide them with important physical and psychological resources (Clutton-Brock, 1991; Thompson et al., 2005). It is thus not surprising that even as children enter into relationships with others such as their peers, their relationships with their parents retain substantial significance throughout adolescence, if not into adulthood as well (Collins & Steinberg, 2006; Offer & Offer, 1975). Indeed, children's relationships with their parents have been identified as key contexts for virtually all aspects of their psychological development (for reviews, see Cassidy & Shaver, 2008; Thompson, 2006). Although much of the attention in this vein has been directed toward the development of children's functioning in the social arena, the

development of children's functioning in the academic arena has also been of interest.

The central goal of this chapter is to integrate several lines of theory and research in which children's relationships with their parents serve as a context for the development of their motivation, with implications for their achievement (for recent reviews of other ways in which parents contribute to children's motivation, see Eccles, 2007; Grolnick, Friendly, & Bellas, 2009; Pomerantz & Moorman, 2010; Pomerantz, Moorman, & Litwack, 2007). After briefly describing the major categories of motivation studied among children, we highlight the relevant postulates, as well as supportive research, of the two foremost theories linking relatedness between children and their parents to children's academic functioning: We review Bowlby's (1969, 1973, 1980) attachment theory and its extensions to the development of such functioning (e.g., Bretherton, 1985; van IJzendoorn, Dijksta, & Bus, 1995); we then discuss Deci and Ryan's (1985, 2000) self-determination theory, with a focus on its application to parents' socialization of children's motivation (e.g., Grolnick, Deci, & Ryan, 1997; Grolnick & Farkas, 2002). We next move beyond the focus of these theories on the quality of relationships between children and their parents to children's sense of responsibility to their parents. In the final section before concluding, we integrate the different ideas about the role of children's relatedness to their parents in their academic functioning, suggesting key questions to be answered in the future.

Major Categories of Children's Motivation

Theory and research concerned with children's academic functioning has generally focused on three major categories of motivation (Eccles & Wigfield, 2002; Eccles, Wigfield, & Schiefele, 1998). First, a key category is that of how *capable* children feel they are in regard to accomplishing the learning tasks they encounter. This includes children's perceptions of competence, expectations for future performance, feelings of efficacy, and sense of control. Second, children's *investment* and *engagement* in learning tasks is of import, including not simply the value children assign to such tasks and the amount of time they spend on them but also their use of effective learning strategies, such as the planning and monitoring of their learning. A third category is the *reasons* behind children's investment and engagement. One of the most studied set of reasons is children's internal or autonomous (e.g., enjoyment and personal importance) versus external or controlled (e.g., avoidance of shame and attainment of rewards) reasons—what is known as intrinsic (versus extrinsic) motivation. Also receiving substantive attention is the extent to which children are concerned with developing (i.e., mastery motivation) rather than demonstrating (i.e., performance motivation) their competence. All three categories appear to play a role in children's achievement (for a review, see Wigfield, Eccles, Schiefele, Roeser, & Davis-Kean, 2006). Thus, they have all received attention in the theory and research concerned with the role of parents in the development of children's academic functioning.

The Attachment Theory Perspective

The idea that children's relationships with their parents contribute to their motivation has received support in Bowlby's (1969, 1973, 1980) and Ainsworth's (Ainsworth, Blehar, Waters, & Wall, 1978; Caldwell & Ricituti, 1973) writings in the context of attachment theory (see also Bretherton, 1985). Focusing on the first 2 years of life, both Bowlby and Ainsworth make the case that the quality of children's attachment to their primary caregivers, who are often their parents, shapes children's exploration (i.e., examining their environment so that they are ultimately knowledgeable about it). Among children who are securely attached, parents serve as a reliable base from which children can explore their world: Children are able to trust that their parents will be there for them if they are needed; their parents serve as a safe haven, thereby permitting effective concentration among children, which may be of particular import in the face of challenge. For these children, their attachment and exploration systems are balanced, which is unfortunately not the case for children who are insecurely attached to their parents. Such children experience anxiety over the possibility of losing their parents' attention, which interferes with their exploration.

Several studies find that when children are securely attached to their parents in the early years of life, they are better able to explore their environment at this time, often demonstrating enhanced competence (e.g., Belsky, Garduque, & Hrncir, 1984; Frodi, Bridges, & Grolnick, 1985). For example, Matas, Arend, and Sroufe (1978) observed that children securely (versus insecurely) attached to their mothers at 18 months were more effective in their problem solving 6 months later in that they spent more time working on problem-solving tasks, with heightened enthusiasm and dampened frustration. Perhaps because of their enhanced exploration, securely attached children are more cognitively competent (e.g., their language is more developed) than are insecurely attached children; notably, this is not accounted for by children's early IQ (e.g., O'Connor & McCartney, 2007; van IJzendoorn et al., 1995). Children with an ambivalent insecure attachment to their parents (i.e., children alternate between resistance and passivity toward their parents) appear to be at greater risk for a lack of exploration than are their counterparts with an avoidant insecure attachment (i.e., children physically and affectively avoid their parents; e.g., Belsky et al., 1984; Frodi et al., 1985). Frodi and colleagues (1985) speculate that although both types of insecurely attached children feel anxious over obtaining their parents' attention, avoidant children are more likely to displace their anxiety by engaging in activities that give the appearance of greater exploration compared to their ambivalent counterparts.

A critical question is whether the early attachments children have to their parents make contributions to children's academic functioning over the longer term as children progress through school. A key mechanism by which such attachments may do so is through the internal working models children develop of themselves and others (Jacobsen, Wolfgang, & Hofman, 1994; van IJzendoorn et al., 1995). Bowlby (1969, 1973) maintains that when children have secure attachments to their parents, they develop internal working models in which the self is seen as worthy of love and others are seen as trustable. Such models may not only contribute to the effective exploration of securely attached children described earlier but also generate confidence among them. Seeing oneself as worthy of love may lead to perceptions that one is competent; such perceptions, in conjunction with seeing others as trustable and thus as able to provide a safe haven when needed, may lead children to feel in control. These views of the self as capable may set the foundation for children's effective investment and engagement. In contrast, when children are insecurely attached to their parents, they possess internal working models in which people, including themselves, are viewed in a negative light. This may ultimately lead them to feel incapable, thereby undermining effective investment and engagement among children.

Consistent with this perspective, the quality of children's attachment to their parents, often as manifest in their representations of it, is predictive of their motivation as well as achievement during not only the childhood and adolescence years (e.g., Granot & Mayseless, 2001; Stams, Juffer, & van IJzendoorn, 2002) but also the transition to adulthood (e.g., Elliot & Reis, 2003; Larose, Bernier, & Tarabulsky, 2005). For example, Moss and St-Laurent (2001) found that children who were securely attached to their mothers at 6 years of age were more effectively engaged while working with their mothers on a problem-solving task at this age than were insecurely attached children; moreover, 2 years later, securely attached children were more mastery motivated in the academic arena. This may be responsible for the effects of children's attachment—or at least their representations of it—on their subsequent achievement (Jacobsen & Hofman, 1997). Notably, Jacobsen and colleagues (1994) demonstrated that when children hold secure (versus insecure) representations of attachment at 7 years of age, they appear more confident at this age, which accounts for the effect of their attachment representations on their later cognitive competence, over and above their earlier IQ.

It is unclear whether these effects reflect the influence of the quality of children's *early* attachment to their parents. Some investigators have put forth what Fraley (2002) refers to as revisionist perspectives of attachment in which internal working models are constantly updated to incorporate ongoing attachment experiences so that such models may or may not map onto children's early attachment to their parents. However, Fraley's (2002) review indicates that the data are more in line with what Fraley refers to as prototype perspectives in which internal working models are updated but maintain core dimensions of children's early attachment to their parents. In line with the idea that the quality of children's attachment to their parents early in life matters for children's academic functioning later in life, studying children who were raised in their initial years on an Israeli kibbutz, Aviezer, Sagi, Resnik, and Gini (2002) observed that children's early (i.e., at 13 to15 months) attachment to their mothers, but not fathers, was predictive of children's motivation (e.g., persistence and attention) and skills (e.g., writing and oral abilities), but not grades, in the academic arena during early adolescence over and above children's early IQ. When Stams and colleagues (2002) examined the link between adopted children's attachment to their biologically unrelated parents at 12 months and a composite of children's motivation, skills, and grades in the academic arena at 7 years of age, they found that the children with the most insecure attachments to their parents (i.e., disorganized) experienced problems in the academic arena; however, this effect was evident only among children who also had a difficult temperament early in life.

Building on the original tenets of attachment theory, contemporary investigators have speculated that several other mechanisms may also contribute to the role of children's attachment to their parents in their academic functioning (for additional mechanisms not discussed here, see Bergin & Bergin, 2009; van IJzendoorn et al., 1995). Such speculation is of import because constructs reflecting children's exploration (e.g., mastery motivation) and internal working models (e.g., self-confidence) do not fully account for the link between children's attachment to their parents and their achievement (e.g., Aviezer et al., 2002; Jacobsen & Hofman, 1997). For one, when children are securely attached to their parents, they may be both more able and willing to meet the learning demands of their parents, often adopting them as their own. In this vein, in what they term the attachment-teaching hypothesis, van IJzendoorn and colleagues (1995) make the case that when children are securely attached to their parents, they may be better able than their insecurely attached counterparts to attend to their parents' learning practices (e.g., instruction) because they are not distracted by concerns about their relationships with their parents; instead they feel safe even when confronted with challenge—a common occurrence in the learning context. In addition, because they trust their parents, securely (versus insecurely) attached children may be more willing to take on the values conveyed by their parents' learning-related practices (Furrer & Skinner, 2003; Kochanska, Aksan, Knaack, & Rhines, 2004). Thus, children's secure attachment to their parents may lead parents' learning-related practices to be particularly effective in enhancing children's motivation and ultimately achievement. Suggestive of this idea, the more mothers characterize their relationships with their kindergarten children as warm, the more positive the effects of their involvement in their children's learning for children's achievement at this phase of development (Simpkins, Weiss, McCartney, Kreider, & Dearing, 2006).

Much of the theory and research generated by Bowlby's attachment theory has focused on the implications of the quality of children's attachments to their parents for children's relationships with others—particularly, their peers and teachers (for a review, see Schneider, Atkinson, & Tardiff, 2001). The key idea is that the internal working models children develop in the context of their relationships with their parents are applied by children to their relationships with others (Bretherton, 1985; Main, Kaplan, & Cassidy, 1985). These relationships, in turn, may promote children's motivational development in two key ways. First, children's relationships with their peers contribute to their academic functioning (for a review, see Ladd, 2003): The more positive children's relationships with their peers, the less they are at risk for motivational as well as achievement problems as they are not preoccupied with relational difficulties in the classroom. Van IJzendoorn and colleagues (1995) also make the case that children's relationships with their peers can be cognitively stimulating, but only if there is trust in the relationships which allows children to use their peers' resources optimally. Second, the quality of children's attachment to their parents may shape the quality of their relationships with their teachers; this may contribute to how children are treated by their teachers as well as children's responsiveness to their teachers' instruction, thereby influencing children's academic functioning (Bergin & Bergin, 2009; Pianta, Nimetz, & Bennett, 1997).

Consistent with this idea, the effect of children's attachment to their parents on their subsequent cognitive competence is due in part to the quality of children's relationships with their teachers (O'Connor & McCartney, 2007).

Given that the quality of children's attachment to their parents appears to contribute to their motivation as well as achievement in the academic arena, the issue of how to foster secure attachments between children and their parents is of import. Bowlby (1969) postulates that the quality of children's attachment to their parents is dependent to a large extent on parents' sensitivity to children's needs and desires (see also Ainsworth et al., 1978), with much evidence to support this idea (for a review, see Wolff & van IJzendoorn, 1997). Of particular import to fostering children's academic functioning, there is some evidence that when parents are sensitive early in children's lives, such functioning among children is enhanced (e.g., Frodi et al., 1985; Stams et al., 2002). For example, Tamis-LeMonda, Bornstein, and Baumwell (2001) observed that mothers' heightened sensitivity during the first year of children's lives is predictive over time of children's advanced language development. Moreover, as delineated in the next section, starting in the preschool years, parents' emotional support, which is considered a core component of their sensitivity (Wolff & van IJzendoorn, 1997), is predictive of children's subsequent motivation as well as achievement (e.g., Estrada, Arsenio, Hess, & Holloway, 1987; Grolnick, Kurowski, Dunlap, & Hevey, 2000; Pomerantz, Wang, & Ng, 2005). However, research is necessary to determine whether children's attachment to their parents—rather than other mechanisms (e.g., children's feelings of autonomy)—underlies the effects of parents' sensitivity or other related dimensions of parenting, such as emotional support, on children's academic functioning.

Summary

In sum, from an attachment theory perspective, children's relationships with their parents serve as an important context for the development of their motivation, thereby contributing to their achievement. Multiple mechanisms have been posited to account for the role of the quality of children's attachment to their parents in their academic functioning. Early on, investigators focused on the idea of securely attached children using their parents as a trusted base from which to explore, with positive internal working models also being influential. However, as more attention was directed to the issue, other mechanisms were posited—for example, the ensuing response of children to their parents' instruction as well as children's ensuing relationships with their peers and teachers. There is some evidence that the early attachments children have with their parents play a role in their later academic functioning, but it remains an area for further investigation.

The Self-Determination Theory Perspective

Investigators working from a self-determination theory perspective have also deemed children's relatedness to their parents of import in children's academic functioning. In the context of self-determination theory, Deci and Ryan (1985, 2000) posit that critical to motivation is the fulfillment of basic psychological needs, which they view as specifying "innate psychological nutrients" (p. 227, Deci & Ryan, 2000) without which psychological functioning suffers. Relatedness represents one of the three central needs, with the other two being autonomy and competence. The relatedness need is fulfilled when children have a sense of security in the context of their relationships with significant others as well as feel that such others consider them as worthy of affection and positive regard (Connell & Wellborn, 1990). Self-determination theory does not give the relationships children have with their primary caretakers in the early years the special status that such relationships are given in attachment theory. Thus, relationships with others at various points across the life span are viewed as able to fulfill relatedness needs, relatively independent of early relationships with primary caretakers.

Deci and Ryan (2000) make the case that although the early relationships between children and their parents contribute to feelings of relatedness later in life, critical to such feelings are the psychological resources provided in the *proximal* environment. In this vein, in her application of self-determination theory to parents' socialization of children, Grolnick and colleagues (e.g., Grolnick, Deci, et al., 1997; Grolnick & Farkas, 2002) highlight the import of parents' involvement in their children's lives in facilitating the satisfaction of children's need for relatedness. These investigators maintain that parents' involvement, which they define as parents' dedication of resources to children as manifest in such practices as spending time with children, efforts to learn about children's lives, and warmth toward children, fosters the development of feelings of relatedness among children. Similar to

the attachment theory perspective, the relatedness that ensues from parents' involvement is postulated to have a validating function in that it indicates that the central figures in children's lives care about them, allowing children to feel worthy. Ultimately, children may come to view themselves as capable, with such feelings leading to investment and engagement (Grolnick, Deci, et al., 1997; Grolnick & Farkas, 2002). In addition, children's relatedness to their parents is viewed as facilitating children's internalization of their parents' values (Grolnick & Slowiaczek, 1994). In a somewhat different vein, relatedness has been posited to have a direct energizing function that permits engagement with the world; when there is a lack of relatedness, disaffection occurs (Connell & Wellborn, 1990; Deci & Ryan, 2000; Furrer & Skinner, 2003).

In line with Grolnick and colleagues' application of self-determination theory to parents' socialization of children, parents' involvement in their children's lives is associated with enhanced feelings of capability among children (for recent reviews, see Grolnick et al., 2009; Pomerantz & Moorman, 2010). In both concurrent and longitudinal investigations focusing on the academic arena, the more parents are involved in their children's learning (e.g., attending school events or reading with children), the more positively children perceive their competence as well as feel in control in school (e.g., Dearing, McCartney, Weiss, Kreider, & Simpkins, 2004; Grolnick & Slowiaczek, 1994; Hong & Ho, 2005). Such involvement also foreshadows children's heightened investment and engagement in school (Cheung & Pomerantz, 2011). The motivation developed by parents' involvement appears to pay off as parents' involvement consistently predicts children's heightened achievement (for reviews, see Fan & Chen, 2001; Hill & Tyson, 2009), even when children's earlier achievement (e.g., Cheung & Pomerantz, 2011; Izzo, Weissberg, Kasprow, & Fendrich, 1999) as well as socioeconomic status (e.g., Deslandes, Bouchard, & St-Amant, 1998; Jeynes, 2005; Senechal & LeFevre, 2002) is taken into account. Notably, children's beliefs about their capability in the academic arena account in large part for the association between parents' involvement and children's achievement (Dearing et al., 2004; Grolnick & Slowiaczek, 1994; Hong & Ho, 2005). However, research has not examined whether the effect of parents' involvement on children's academic functioning is due to children's relatedness to their parents.

As research by Pomerantz, Wang, and Ng (2005) reveals, parents' involvement as reflected in their warmth is also of import: The more positive mothers' affect when interacting with their children on days children have homework, the less children's negative affect in this often frustrating context is detrimental to their subsequent perceptions of competence as well as intrinsic and mastery motivation (see also Hokoda & Fincham, 1995; Nolen-Hoeksema, Wolfson, Mumme, & Guskin, 1995). Although parents' warmth is clearly of import to the development of children's motivation, it needs to be unconditional in that it is not expressed only when children do as parents desire. When parents make their warmth conditional on children thinking, feeling, or acting as parents desire, they lead children to feel pressured by a fear of losing their parents' positive regard (Roth, Assor, Niemiec, Ryan, & Deci, 2009). Indeed, when parents' positive regard for their children is contingent on their children doing well in the academic arena, children are engaged for performance rather than mastery reasons (Roth et al., 2009).

Although relatedness is viewed as important for the development of motivation in self-determination theory, it is not viewed as the only influence on motivation—or even the most important. Indeed, Grolnick and colleagues (e.g., Grolnick, Deci, et al., 1997; Grolnick & Farkas, 2002) argue that once parents are involved in their children's lives, key to promoting children's intrinsic motivation is parents' autonomy support: When parents support children's autonomy instead of exerting control over them by allowing children to take initiative rather than dictating what children do, parents facilitate the development of children's feelings of autonomy, thereby allowing for the development of intrinsic motivation among children. This process appears to begin early in children's lives as evidenced by Frodi and colleagues' (1985) finding that when mothers are autonomy supportive during children's first 2 years, children display heightened persistence in problem solving during this phase of development. As children move into the school years, the more parents support children's autonomy rather than exert control over children, the more children are intrinsically motivated in the academic arena (e.g., d'Ailly, 2003; Grolnick & Ryan, 1989; Grolnick, Ryan, & Deci, 1991). Parents' autonomy support is also associated with children feeling more capable as well as being more invested and engaged, with heightened achievement (e.g., Grolnick & Ryan, 1989; Hess & McDevitt, 1984; Ng, Kenney-Benson, & Pomerantz, 2004; Steinberg, Elmen, & Mounts, 1989; Wang, Pomerantz, & Chen, 2007).

Although both parents' involvement and autonomy support appear to lead children to experience themselves as capable, Grolnick and colleagues (e.g., Grolnick, Deci, et al., 1997; Grolnick & Farkas, 2002) maintain that particularly critical in this vein is parents' structure. Structure involves parents' provision of clear and consistent guidelines, expectations, and rules for children. Structuring parents also communicate predictable consequences for children's actions (e.g., what will happen if rules are violated). In addition, structure includes providing children with instruction that takes into account children's capacity. Such parenting can promote feelings of capability in that it assists children in not only identifying societally valued standards but also developing the skills to achieve them. Although parents' structure is not associated with children's intrinsic motivation (Grolnick & Ryan, 1989), it is associated with heightened feelings of capability, both in terms of perceptions of competence and a sense of control, among children (e.g., Grolnick & Ryan, 1989; Skinner, Johnson, & Snyder, 2005). This is likely due in part to the effects of parents' structure on children's skills. Research conducted by Englund and colleagues (2004), for example, reveals that the more structured mothers' instruction when children are 3 years old, the higher children's cognitive competence at 5 years old, and the better their achievement in the first and third grades (see also Pianta et al., 1997).

Summary

Similar to the attachment theory perspective, the self-determination theory perspective regards children's relatedness to their parents as important in the development of children's motivation, thereby shaping their achievement. Also like the attachment theory perspective, the self-determination theory perspective posits that children's relatedness to their parents may serve a validating function that allows them to feel worthy, with implications for their feelings of capability. However, there is a focus not evident in attachment theory on the proximal forces that lead to children's relatedness; consequently, parents' involvement in their children's lives is seen as key to facilitating children's fulfillment of their relatedness needs, thereby playing a role in children's academic functioning. Moreover, according to self-determination theory, other needs and thus dimensions of parenting other than involvement are central in the development of children's motivation: Parents must not only be involved in their children's lives but also autonomy supportive and structuring so that in addition to feeling related, children feel autonomous and competent.

Beyond Relationship Quality: Children's Sense of Responsibility to Their Parents

At the heart of both the attachment theory and self-determination theory perspectives is children's relatedness to their parents as reflected in the *quality* of their relationships with their parents—that is, the extent to which children have secure (versus insecure) or positive (versus negative) relationships with their parents. Although the quality of children's relationships with their parents is clearly of significance to children's academic functioning, it is not the only form that children's relatedness to their parents takes (Hardway & Fuligni, 2006; Pomerantz, Qin, Wang, & Chen, 2009). In this section, we focus on another form that is of import to children's motivation with their parents: *Children's sense of responsibility to their parents*—that is, the belief among children that it is important that they provide psychological or material assistance to their parents (e.g., by meeting their parents' expectations for their performance or helping with chores around the house). Children's sense of responsibility to their parents has been studied by Fuligni and colleagues (e.g., Fuligni, Tseng, & Lam, 1999; Fuligni & Zhang, 2004) as manifest in their feelings of obligation to their family. Pomerantz, Qin, Wang, and Chen (2011) make the case that children's sense of responsibility to their parents is also manifest in their motivation to please their parents—that is, children's pursuit of goals to obtain their parents' approval.

These two manifestations of children's sense of responsibility to their parents may enhance children's academic functioning by leading children to use their parents' values as guides as they attempt to fulfill their responsibilities to them (Fuligni & Flook, 2005). Fuligni and colleagues (Fuligni & Flook, 2005; Telzer & Fuligni, 2009) contend that children's feelings of obligation to their family along with the activities motivated by such feelings are beneficial in that they provide children with a sense of purpose, often evident in feelings of role fulfillment. Although some parents do not see children's learning in the academic arena as a priority, many parents place at least some value on this arena. Thus, children's sense of responsibility to their parents may often lead children to place value on the academic arena. As a consequence, children harboring a sense of responsibility to their parents may be more invested and engaged, albeit not necessarily more confident in their capabilities or intrinsically motivated, in the academic arena, which may benefit their achievement.

Although this process may be driven by controlled motivation – for example, children's fear of losing their parents' positive regard, it may be effective in ensuring children are engaged in school, particularly during adolescence. Controlled motivation, which may be fostered by rewards or punishment, is useful when autonomous motivation does not already exist (for a review, see Deci, Koestner, & Ryan, 1999), as is often the case for children in the academic context during adolescence (for a review, see Wigfield & Wagner, 2005). Indeed, controlled motivation may promote engagement and achievement—at least when deep processing is not necessary (Vansteenkiste, Simons, Lens, Soenens, & Matos, 2005). It is also possible that children's sense of responsibility to their parents is in part a form of autonomous motivation because it grows out of a relationship of reciprocal give and take between children and their parents (Pomerantz, Qin, Wang, & Chen, 2011), so that children view their responsibilities to their parents as personally important. Indeed, children's sense of responsibility to their parents is associated not only with children's controlled, but also autonomous, motivation in the academic context (Pomerantz et al., 2011).

Growing evidence reveals that children's sense of responsibility to their parents contributes to their academic functioning. In both the United States and China, the more children feel obligated to their family during the high school years, the more they value school (Fuligni et al., 1999; Fuligni & Zhang, 2004; Pomerantz et al., 2011). Research conducted in the United States also indicates that children of European, Chinese, and Mexican heritage who feel obligated to their family during adolescence are particularly likely to devote time to their schoolwork (Fuligni, Yip, & Tseng, 2002; Hardway & Fuligni, 2006). However, children's feelings of obligation to their family are not associated with their enhanced achievement—perhaps because other obligations to the family (e.g., doing chores and taking care of siblings) interfere with the effectiveness of their academic efforts so that children are not optimally focused. Notably, children's sense of responsibility to their parents as manifest in their motivation in school to please them appears to foster their motivation as well as achievement. Studying children in the United States and China during early adolescence, Pomerantz and colleagues (2011) found that the more motivated children were to please their parents, the greater their investment and engagement as well as grades in school 2 years later, even after taking into account children's earlier academic functioning.

The greater children's sense of responsibility to their parents (i.e., the more they feel obligated to their parents and the more motivated they are to please their parents), the better the quality of their relationships with their parents (e.g., Fuligni et al., 1999; Fuligni & Zhang, 2004; Pomerantz et al., 2011). Although the associations are not strong enough to suggest that children's sense of responsibility to their parents is simply a reflection of the quality of their relationships with them, they beg the question of whether the effects of children's sense of responsibility to their parents remain once the quality of their relationships with their parents is taken into account. Notably, when Pomerantz and colleagues (2011) statistically controlled for the quality of children's relationships with their parents, children's sense of responsibility to their parents continued to exert an effect over time on children's academic functioning. A key issue that has unfortunately not received attention is the extent to which children's adoption of their parents' values accounts for the effects of children's sense of responsibility to their parents on children's motivation. It is possible that other mechanisms may also be at work—for example, children's sense of responsibility to their parents may facilitate their spontaneous disclosure about their daily lives to their parents which has been argued to provide an important context for parents to gain knowledge about their children's lives (e.g., Kerr & Stattin, 2000). This may allow parents to provide support to children in the academic arena.

Summary

Although the quality of children's relationships with their parents is of import to children's academic functioning as postulated in the attachment theory and self-determination theory perspectives, other forms of children's relatedness to their parents appear to be instrumental as well. Here, we have focused on children's sense of responsibility to their parents, which appears to facilitate children's academic functioning during the adolescent years. Children's sense of responsibility to their parents may be particularly functional during this phase of development given children's declining interest in school. Notably, the effects of children's sense of responsibility to their parents on children's motivation as well as achievement are distinct from the effects of the quality of their relationships with their parents. Future research is needed to identify the mechanisms by which children's sense of responsibility to their parents enhances their academic functioning.

Integrating the Different Ideas About Relatedness

The three sets of ideas we have reviewed share an emphasis on children's relatedness to their parents as a significant force in the development of their motivation, with implications for their achievement. Although there is convergence among the three along some lines (e.g., children's relatedness to their parents is viewed as leading children to take on their parents' values), there is also divergence (e.g., the form of relatedness deemed of import varies). In this section, we offer an integration of the three sets of ideas. Such integration is a fruitful step toward fully elucidating how children's relatedness to their parents contributes to their academic functioning across different phases of their development in different cultural contexts. We outline three key themes that evolve from considering the different perspectives together. In doing so, we highlight critical questions that may serve to guide future research and theory.

Theme 1: Early Relatedness Matters, But Is Not Deterministic

Consistent with the attachment theory perspective, children's early relatedness to their parents may set an important foundation for children's later academic functioning. Indeed, as reviewed earlier, there is much evidence that the security of children's attachment to their parents during the first few years of their life contributes to their motivation as well as achievement during these years. Moreover, it appears that such relatedness is of import for children as they enter the school system where they may be confronted with new challenges. The extent to which children's early attachment to their parents continues to exert an influence over their academic functioning in the later years of children's development, however, is unclear. Indeed, research on the longer term effects is sparse. Although the one study in this vein of which we are aware provides evidence for such effects into adolescence, the effects are quite small, evident among mothers but not fathers, and do not reach significance when it comes to children's grades (Aviezer et al., 2002).

These findings along with the ideas put forth by investigators working from the self-determination theory perspective suggest that as children develop, although their early relatedness to their parents plays a role in their motivation, children's later environments are influential as well. Ultimately, children's early attachment to their parents may not be deterministic as it may be overridden—at least in part—by the subsequent environment created by their parents or other significant figures in their lives such as their peers or teachers. Parents may undo the costs or benefits of their early attachment relationships with their children through their involvement in their children's lives, which is influenced in part by parents' physical and psychological resources (for a review, see Pomerantz, Moorman, & Cheung, 2011). Such resources may change over the course of children's development, thereby changing parents' involvement. For example, when a family's income increases over time, parents create better learning environments for their children along physical as well as psychological lines (e.g., Dearing & Taylor, 2007). Parents may also experience changes in their social support over time that may lead to changes in their involvement in children's lives (e.g., Gavidia-Payne & Stoneman, 1997; Grolnick, Benjet, Kurowski, & Apostoleris, 1997; Sheldon, 2002).

The proposal that the effects of children's early relatedness to their parents are superseded to some extent by children's later relatedness to their parents fostered in part by their parents' involvement begs empirical examination of two key questions. First, to what extent are the effects of children's early attachment to their parents and their parents' later involvement in their lives independent of one another? On the one hand, it is possible that the two are entirely overlapping. Parents' early involvement may contribute to an early secure attachment; over the course of children's development, parents' continued involvement may maintain such an attachment, thereby fostering children's motivation. On the other hand, it is possible that although parents' involvement may contribute to early attachment, parents' involvement changes over time as their physical and psychological resources change, thereby changing children's motivational trajectory stemming from their early attachment.

Second, if parents' later involvement has an independent effect, to what extent does it do so through its impact on children's relatedness to their parents? A key tenet of the self-determination theory perspective is that parents' involvement fosters relatedness, which in part is responsible for its role in children's academic functioning. As highlighted earlier,

however, this important issue has not received empirical attention. Such attention is needed given other viable alternatives: Parents' involvement—at least in children's learning—may directly enhance children's skills (Senechal & LeFevre, 2002) or indirectly do so by leading teachers to give children more attention in the classroom (Epstein & Becker, 1982), both of which may enhance children's motivation as well as achievement.

The security of children's early attachment to their parents may also work synergistically with parents' later involvement to shape children's academic functioning. On the one hand, children's attachment may serve an amplifying function such that a secure (versus insecure) attachment sets a foundation among children allowing them to reap greater benefits from their parents' later involvement in their learning (e.g., van IJzendoorn et al., 1995). On the other hand, children's attachment may serve a compensatory function: A secure (versus insecure) attachment early in children's lives may make up for dampened involvement among parents in their children's learning later in children's lives. That is, when parents do not have the desire or resources to be involved in their children's learning, children may still make motivational gains if their secure attachment to their parents provides them with a trustable base from which to explore as well as other resources such as positive internal working models.

Distinguishing between the amplifying and compensating functions of children's early attachment to their parents requires research examining whether such relatedness moderates the effect of parents' subsequent involvement in their children's learning on children's academic functioning. Simpkins and colleagues' (2006) research showing that children who have warm relationships with their mothers as well as highly involved mothers have higher achievement than other children is a step in this direction. However, the focus of this research, which is suggestive of the amplifying function, was not on children's early attachment to their parents; thus, it is unclear what kind of foundation such relatedness provides for the success of subsequent parenting in promoting children's academic functioning. Moreover, an endeavor of this sort should look at the mechanisms underlying the synergy of children's early attachment to their parents and their parents' later involvement. Also in need of attention is the possibility that children's early attachment changes how parents are involved, with secure attachment driving more positive, effective involvement on parents' part (van IJzendoorn et al., 1995).

Indeed, there is some evidence supportive of this possibility (O'Connor & McCartney, 2007).

Theme 2: There Are Contextual Variations in the Role of Relatedness

For quite some time the attachment theory and self-determination theory perspectives have served to guide research on how relatedness between children and their parents contributes to children's academic functioning; this has led to a focus on the quality of relationships between children and their parents. However, more recent theory and research on the adolescent years has highlighted the significance of another form of children's relatedness to their parents—children's sense of responsibility to them—that while related to the quality of children's relationships with their parents, is distinct from it with unique effects on children's academic functioning. Children's sense of responsibility to their parents may be of particular import in two key contexts: *(1)* during phases of children's development when their interest in learning declines and *(2)* in cultures, such as that characteristic of East Asian countries, in which children may not have particularly positive relationships with their parents, but learning may be particularly important.

Although it is likely that children's sense of responsibility to their parents develops prior to adolescence, playing a role in their academic functioning during these earlier years, its role may be of most significance during adolescence. It is well documented that as children move into adolescence their investment and engagement in school declines, with a parallel decline in their achievement (for a review, see Wigfield et al., 2006). Eccles and colleagues (1993) have argued that such decrements are due in part to a poor fit between children's concerns as they move into adolescence (e.g., with establishing independence and avoiding negative evaluation) and the environment provided by the middle schools that they transition into from elementary school (e.g., teachers' heightened control and evaluative feedback). During adolescence, the quality of children's relationships with their parents is predictive of their academic functioning (e.g., Furrer & Skinner, 2003; Ryan, Stiller, & Lynch, 1994), but alone it may not be enough to sustain children during this phase of development. Optimal motivation may require additional forces that are instrumental in moving children toward adopting the values of their parents, which are less likely to deviate from those endorsed by society than are the values of children's peers who often attain heightened

significance in children's lives during adolescence (e.g., Furman & Buhrmester, 1992; Larson, Richards, Moneta, Holmbeck, & Duckett, 1996).

Direct empirical examination of this developmental hypothesis is necessary. The contribution of children's sense of responsibility to their parents, along with the quality (e.g., security or positivity) of children's relationships with their parents, should be identified from the earliest to the latest school years. The effect of children's sense of responsibility to their parents on their motivation may become larger over time as children move into adolescence, whereas that of the quality of children's relationships with their parents may be maintained. In this context, attention needs to be given to the possibility that children's sense of responsibility to their parents grows out of a positive relationship with them, thereby acting as a mechanism through which the quality of children's relationships with their parents enhances their motivation.

Also worthy of consideration is that children's sense of responsibility to their parents may be most beneficial when parents remain involved in their children's academic lives during adolescence—a time when the norm is often for parents to become less involved in this arena of children's lives (e.g., Cheung & Pomerantz, 2011; Cooper, Lindsay, & Nye, 2000). By being involved in their children's learning, parents may convey to children that they value school, leading children to view doing well in school as their responsibility. Indeed, during early adolescence, the more parents are involved in children's learning, the more children are motivated in school to please their parents, which is predictive of children's subsequent engagement and ultimately achievement (Cheung & Pomerantz, 2009). Through their involvement in children's academic lives, parents may also support children as they attempt to fulfill their academic responsibilities. For example, by being involved parents may provide children with encouragement when children experience difficulty as may often be the case during adolescence. In addition, through their involvement, parents may provide instruction that allows children to develop the abilities necessary to meet their responsibilities in the academic arena.

Children's sense of responsibility to their parents may be of particular import not only during adolescence but also in cultures where much emphasis is placed on learning as well as filial piety, as is the case in East Asian countries, such as China. In fact, considering children's sense of responsibility to their parents may be key to understanding the apparent paradox that despite reporting poorer quality relationships with their parents during adolescence (e.g., Pomerantz et al., 2009), East Asian children are more motivated, with heightened achievement, compared to American children during this phase of development (e.g., Stevenson, Chen, & Lee, 1993; Wang & Pomerantz, 2009). This paradox is particularly intriguing given that the quality of children's relationships with their parents appears to make equal contributions to children's academic functioning in China and the United States (Cheung, Pomerantz, & Dong, 2010). Thus, a key question is what compensates for the poorer quality relationships among children and their parents in East Asia (versus the United States) in motivating children. Although there are a variety of possibilities (e.g., teaching and parenting practices), children's sense of responsibility to their parents is likely to be influential.

The focus on children's sense of responsibility to their parents emerged largely in the context of efforts to understand children from cultural backgrounds in which the family looms larger than it does in European American culture (e.g., Fuligni et al., 1999). For example, in East Asian countries where Confucian philosophy is central, children's sense of responsibility to their parents may grow out of the notion of filial piety, which involves, among other things, children repaying their family for their efforts in raising them, bringing honor to their family, making sacrifices for their family, and psychologically and materially supporting their family (Chao & Tseng, 2002; Ho, 1996). Doing well in school may be a central way for children to fulfill their responsibilities to their parents in East Asian countries given the import of learning in Confucian philosophy (Ho, 1994; Yu, 1996) as well as professional and financial success (Tang, Luk, & Chiu, 2000).

In line with such reasoning, soon after entering adolescence, children of Chinese heritage—both residing in China and the United States—feel more obligated to their parents and more motivated in school to please them than do children of European heritage residing in the United States (e.g., Fuligni et al., 1999; Hardway & Fuligni, 2006; Pomerantz et al., 2011). Chinese (versus American) children's greater sense of responsibility to their parents may compensate for the poorer quality relationships they have with their parents during adolescence. Indeed, focusing on ethnic differences in the United States in the value children place on school during adolescence, Fuligni (2001) reports that the heightened feelings of obligation to their families of children of Chinese

and Latin heritage accounts for the heightened value they place on school compared to their American counterparts of other ethnic heritage. Further examination of the issue between countries is needed to ensure that the effects are not due to immigrant or minority status. In this context, other dimensions of children's motivation besides value should be examined, as should children's achievement.

Theme 3: Relatedness Is Not All That Matters

Most reviews focusing on the role of parents in children's academic functioning highlight the *practices* that parents employ that facilitate or undermine such functioning (e.g., Eccles, 2007; Grolnick et al., 2009; Pomerantz & Moorman, 2010; Pomerantz et al., 2007). Indeed, there is a sizeable body of research indicating that multiple dimensions of parenting contribute to children's motivation as well as achievement. Our goal in this chapter was to go beyond these prior reviews to emphasize the import of relatedness between children and their parents—whether it be established in the earliest years of children's lives or the later years, and whether it be the quality of the relationships between children and their parents or children's sense of responsibility to their parents. However, as is emphasized in self-determination theory, although relatedness is of import to children's motivational development, it is certainly not the only force.

If parents create an environment, often through their involvement, in which children feel related to them, this on its own may not necessarily translate into motivation among children that optimizes their achievement. Although parents' involvement in children's lives is a critical first step toward promoting children's motivation, such involvement likely needs to be accompanied by autonomy support and structure (Grolnick et al., 2009; Pomerantz, Grolnick, & Price, 2005; Pomerantz et al., 2007). Autonomy-supportive and structuring practices may afford key resources to children that no degree of relatedness may afford. For example, even if children have established a positive relationship with their parents, if their parents do not employ structuring practices, the feelings of capability fostered by children's relatedness with their parents may be undermined as children do not develop necessary skills.

In the two earlier themes we delineated, we highlighted how children's relatedness to their parents may work synergistically with their parents' involvement in shaping their academic functioning. Children's relatedness to their parents, as well as the involvement assumed to foster it, may also work synergistically with parents' autonomy support and structure. On the one hand, children's relatedness may serve an amplifying function. For example, the reduced anxiety produced by children's secure attachment to their parents may allow them to capitalize on their parents' autonomy support in that they are able to take full advantage of autonomy opportunities, such as making choices or solving problems on their own. Children's sense of responsibility to their parents may also lead children to use autonomy opportunities to pursue societally valued goals held by their parents. On the other hand, children's relatedness to their parents may play a compensatory function by providing them with resources to buffer the undermining effects of parenting that is not autonomy supportive or structuring. For example, children residing in a home without structure may have a trustable base from which to find structure outside of their home, such as that supplied by teachers, coaches, and friends' parents.

Empirical tests of the ideas outlined here are needed. Perhaps most notably, investigation of the synergies is an important direction for future research. Suggestive of such interactions are findings yielded by research conducted by Kochanska and colleagues (2004): Consistent with the idea of an amplifying function, parents' responsiveness (which involves some autonomy support) and gentle discipline (which is an aspect of structure) during the early years of children's lives mattered most for children in terms of their subsequent conscience when children were securely (versus insecurely) attached to their parents during the early years. However, there is no evidence to date as to whether children's relatedness moderates the effects of parents' learning-related practices on their academic functioning in such a manner. Examination of the moderating role of children's relatedness to their parents as manifest both in the quality of their relationships with their parents as well as their sense of responsibility to them is of much import.

Conclusions

Children's relatedness to their parents appears to play a fundamental role in the development of their motivation, ultimately having implications for their achievement. Such relatedness, whether reflected in the quality of children's relationships with their parents or their sense of responsibility to their parents, is predictive of children's subsequent academic functioning across multiple phases of the life span, taking into account children's earlier functioning in the academic context. However, there are still key issues to be resolved in understanding the role of children's relatedness to their parents. We highlighted three themes that emerge from an integration of the three different sets of ideas we reviewed on the role of relatedness between children and their parents in children's academic functioning: *(1)* Both the early attachment between children and their parents and the later environment created by parents are of import to children's academic functioning; *(2)* there is contextual variation in the effects of children's relatedness to their parents, particularly in regard to children's sense of responsibility to their parents; and *(3)* although children's relatedness to their parents is instrumental in their academic functioning, it alone may not be sufficient in optimizing it. A comprehensive understanding of the role of relatedness between parents and children in children's motivation as well as achievement requires empirical tests of these themes.

References

Ainsworth, M. D. S., Blehar, M. C., Waters, E., & Wall, S. (1978). *Patterns of attachment: A psychological study of the strange situation.* Hillsdale, NJ: Erlbaum.

Aviezer, O., Sagi, A., Resnick, G., & Gini, M. (2002). School competence in young adolescence: Links to early attachment relationships beyond concurrent self-perceived competence and representations of relationships. *International Journal of Behavioral Development, 26*, 397–409.

Baumeister, R. F., & Leary, M. R. (1995). The need to belong: Desire for interpersonal attachments as a fundamental human motivation. *Psychological Bulletin, 117*, 497–529.

Belsky, J., Garduque, L., & Hrncir, E. (1984). Assessing performance, competence, and executive capacity in infant play: Relations to home environment and security of attachment. *Developmental Psychology, 20*, 406–417.

Bergin, C., & Bergin, D. (2009). Attachment in the classroom. *Educational Psychology Review, 21*, 141–170.

Bowlby, J. (1969). *Attachment and loss. Vol 1: Attachment.* New York: Basic Books.

Bowlby, J. (1973). *Attachment and loss. Vol 2: Separation: Anxiety and anger.* New York: Basic Books.

Bowlby, J. (1980). *Attachment and loss. Vol. 3: Loss.* New York: Basic Books.

Bretherton, I. (1985). Attachment theory: Retrospect and prospect. In I. Bretherton & E. Waters (Eds.), Growing points of attachment theory and research. *Monographs of the Society for Research in Child Development, 50*, Serial No. 209 (1–2), pp. 3–35.

Caldwell, B., & Ricituti, H. (Eds.). (1973). *The development of infant-mother attachment.* New York: Russell Sage.

Cassidy, J., & Shaver, P. R. (Eds.). (2008). *Handbook of attachment: Theory, research, and clinical application* (2nd ed.). New York: Guilford Press.

Chao, R. K., & Tseng, V. (2002). Parenting of Asians. In M. H. Bornstein (Ed.), *Handbook of parenting. Vol. 4: Social conditions and applied parenting* (2nd ed., pp. 59–93). Mahwah, NJ: Erlbaum.

Cheung, C. S., & Pomerantz, E. M. (2011). Parents' involvement in children's academic lives in the US and China: Implications for children's academic and emotional adjustment. *Child Development, 82*, 932–950.

Cheung, C. S., & Pomerantz, E. M. (April, 2009). *Social motivation mediates the effects of parents' involvement on children's school engagement in the US and China.* Paper presented at the Society for Research on Child Development, Denver, CO.

Cheung, C. S., Pomerantz, E. M., & Dong, W. (March, 2010). *Youth's disclosure of everyday activities to parents in the United States and China: Implications for youth's academic functioning.* Paper presented at the Society for Research on Adolescence, Philadelphia, PA.

Clutton-Brock, T. H. (1991). *The evolution of parental care.* Princeton, NJ: Princeton University Press.

Collins, W. A., & Steinberg, L. (2006). Adolescent development in interpersonal context. In N. Eisenberg (Ed.), *Handbook of child psychology. Vol. 3: Social, emotional, and personality development* (6th ed., pp. 1003–1067). Hoboken, NJ: Wiley.

Connell, J. P., & Wellborn, J. G. (1990). Competence, autonomy, and relatedness: A motivational analysis of self-system processes. In M. Gunnar & A. Sroufe (Eds.), *Minnesota Symposium on Child Psychology* (Vol. 23, pp. 43–77). Hillsdale, NJ: Erlbaum.

Cooper, H., Lindsay, J. J., & Nye, B. (2000). Homework in the home: How student, family, and parenting-style differences relate to the homework process. *Contemporary Educational Psychology, 25*, 464–487.

d'Ailly, H. (2003). Children's autonomy and perceived control in learning: A model of motivation and achievement in Taiwan. *Journal of Educational Psychology, 95*, 84–96.

Dearing, E., McCartney, K., Weiss, H. B., Kreider, H., & Simpkins, S. (2004). The promotive effects of family educational involvement for low-income children's literacy. *Journal of School Psychology, 42*, 445–460.

Dearing, E., & Taylor, B. A. (2007). Home improvements: Within-family associations between income and the quality of children's home environments. *Journal of Applied Developmental Psychology, 28*, 427–444.

Deci, E. L., Koestner, R., & Ryan, R. M. (1999). A meta-analytic review of experiments examining the effects of extrinsic rewards on intrinsic motivation. *Psychological Bulletin, 125*, 627–668.

Deci, E. L., & Ryan, R. M. (1985). *Intrinsic motivation and self-determination in human behavior.* New York: Plenum.

Deci, E. L., & Ryan, R. M. (2000). The "what" and "why" of goal pursuits: Human needs and the self-determination of behavior. *Psychological Inquiry, 11*, 227–268.

Deslandes, R., Bouchard, P., & St-Amant, J. (1998). Family variables as predictors of school achievement: Sex differences in Quebec adolescents. *Canadian Journal of Education, 23*, 390–404.

Eccles, J. S. (2007). Families, schools, and developing achievement-related motivation and engagement. In J. E. Grusec & P. D. Hastings (Eds.), *Handbook of socialization: Theory and research* (pp. 655–691). New York: Guilford Press.

Eccles, J. S., Midgley, C., Wigfield, A., Buchanan, C. M., Reuman, D., Flanagan, C., & Iver, D. M. (1993). Development during adolescence: The impact of stage-environment fit on young adolescents' experiences in schools and in families. *American Psychologist, 48*, 90–101.

Eccles, J. S., & Wigfield, A. (2002). Motivational beliefs, values, and goals. *Annual Review of Psychology, 53*, 109–132.

Eccles, J. S., Wigfield, A., & Schiefele, U. (1998). Motivation to succeed. In N. Eisenberg (Ed.), *Handbook of child psychology. Vol. 3: Social, emotional, and personality development* (5th ed., pp. 1017–1095). New York: Wiley.

Elliot, A. J., & Reis, H. T. (2003). Attachment and exploration in adulthood. *Journal of Personality and Social Psychology, 85*, 317–331.

Englund, M. M., Luckner, A. E., Whaley, G. J. L., & Egeland, B. (2004). Children's achievement in early elementary school: Longitudinal effects of parental involvement, expectations, and quality of assistance. *Journal of Educational Psychology, 96*, 723–730.

Epstein, J. L., & Becker, H. J. (1982). Teachers' reported practices of parent involvement: Problems and possibilities. *Elementary School Journal, 83*, 103–113.

Estrada, P., Arsenio, W. F., Hess, R. D., & Holloway, S. D. (1987). Affective quality of the mother-child relationship: Longitudinal consequences for children's school-relevant cognitive functioning. *Developmental Psychology, 23*, 210–215.

Fan, X., & Chen, M. (2001). Parental involvement and students' academic achievement: A meta-analysis. *Educational Psychology Review, 13*, 1–22.

Fraley, C. (2002). Attachment stability from infancy to adulthood: Meta-analysis and dynamic modeling of developmental mechanisms. *Personality and Social Psychology Bulletin, 2*, 123–151.

Frodi, A., Bridges, L., & Grolnick, W. S. (1985). Correlates of mastery-related behavior: A short-term longitudinal study of infants in their second year. *Child Development, 56*, 1291–1298.

Fuligni, A. J. (2001). Family obligation and the academic motivation of adolescents from Asian, Latin, and European American backgrounds. In A. J. Fuligni (Ed.), *Family obligation and assistance during adolescence: Contextual variations and developmental implications* (pp. 61–75). San Francisco, CA: Jossey-Bass.

Fuligni, A. J., & Flook, L. (2005). A social identity approach to ethnic differences in family relationships. In R. Kail (Ed.), *Advances in child development and behavior* (Vol. 33, pp. 61–75). New York: Academic Press.

Fuligni, A. J., Tseng, V., & Lam, M. (1999). Attitudes toward family obligation among American adolescents with Asian, Latin American, and European American backgrounds. *Child Development, 70*, 1030–1044.

Fuligni, A. J., Yip, T., & Tseng, V. (2002). The impact of family obligation on the daily activities and psychological well-being of Chinese American adolescents. *Child Development, 73*, 302–314.

Fuligni, A. J., & Zhang, W. (2004). Attitudes toward family obligation among adolescents in contemporary urban and rural China. *Child Development, 75*, 180–192.

Furman, W., & Buhrmester, D. (1992). Age and sex differences in perceptions of networks of personal relationships. *Child Development, 63*, 103–115.

Furrer, C., & Skinner, E. (2003). Sense of relatedness as a factor in children's academic engagement and performance. *Journal of Educational Psychology, 95*, 148–162.

Gavidia-Payne, S., & Stoneman, Z. (1997). Family predictors of maternal and paternal involvement in programs for young children with disabilities. *Child Development, 68*, 701–717.

Granot, D., & Mayseless, O. (2001). Attachment security and adjustment to school in middle childhood. *Internaltional Journal of Behavioral Development, 25*, 530–541.

Grolnick, W. S., Benjet, C., Kurowski, C. O., & Apostoleris, N. H. (1997). Predictors of parent involvement in children's schooling. *Journal of Educational Psychology, 89*, 538–548.

Grolnick, W. S., Deci, E. L., & Ryan, R. M. (1997). Internalization within the family: The self-determination theory perspective. In J. Grusec & L. Kuczynski (Eds.), *Parenting and children's internalization of values: A handbook of contemporary theory* (pp. 135–161). New York: Wiley.

Grolnick, W. S., & Farkas, M. (2002). Parenting and the development of children's self-regulation. In M. Bornstein (Ed.), *Handbook of parenting. Vol. 5: Practical issues in parenting* (2nd ed., pp. 89–110). Mahwah, NJ: Erlbaum.

Grolnick, W. S., Friendly, R. W., & Bellas, V. M. (2009). Parenting and children's motivation at school. In K. R. Wenzel & A. Wigfield (Eds.), *Handbook of motivation at school* (pp. 279–300). New York: Routledge/Taylor & Francis.

Grolnick, W. S., Kurowski, C. O., Dunlap, K. G., & Hevey, C. (2000). Parental resources and the transition to junior high. *Journal of Research on Adolescence, 10*, 465–488.

Grolnick, W. S., & Ryan, R. M. (1989). Parent styles associated with children's self-regulation and competence in school. *Journal of Educational Psychology, 81*, 143–154.

Grolnick, W. S., Ryan, R. M., & Deci, E. L. (1991). Inner resources for school achievement: Motivational mediators of children's perceptions of their parents. *Journal of Educational Psychology, 83*, 508–517.

Grolnick, W. S., & Slowiaczek, M. L. (1994). Parents' involvement in children's schooling: A multidimensional conceptualization and motivational model. *Child Development, 64*, 237–252.

Hardway, C., & Fuligni, A. J. (2006). Dimensions of family connectedness among adolescents with Mexican, Chinese, and European backgrounds. *Developmental Psychology, 42*, 1246–1258.

Hess, R. D., & McDevitt, T. M. (1984). Some cognitive consequences of maternal intervention: A longitudinal study. *Child Development, 55*, 2017–2030.

Hill, N. E., & Tyson, D. (2009). Parental involvement in middle school: A meta-analytic assessment of the strategies that promote achievement. *Developmental Psychology, 45*, 740–763.

Ho, D. Y. F. (1994). Cognitive socialization in Confucian heritage culture. In P. M. Greenfield & R. R. Cocking (Eds.), *Cross-cultural roots of minority child development* (pp. 285–313). Mahwah, NJ: Lawrence Erlbaum.

Ho, D. Y. F. (1996). Filial piety and its psychological consequences. In M. H. Bond (Ed.), *Handbook of Chinese psychology* (pp. 155–165). New York: Oxford University Press.

Hokoda, A., & Fincham, F. D. (1995). Origins of children's helpless and mastery achievement patterns in the family. *Journal of Educational Psychology, 87*, 375–385.

Hong, S., & Ho, H. (2005). Direct and indirect longitudinal effects of parental involvement on student achievement: Second-order latent growth modeling across ethnic groups. *Journal of Educational Psychology, 97*, 32–42.

Izzo, C. V., Weissberg, R. P., Kasprow, W. J., & Fendrich, M. (1999). A longitudinal assessment of teacher perceptions of parent involvement in children's education and school performance. *American Journal of Community Psychology, 27*, 817–839.

Jacobsen, T., & Hofman, V. (1997). Children's attachment representations: Longitudinal relations to school behavior and academic competency in middle childhood and adolescence. *Developmental Psychology, 33*, 703–710.

Jacobsen, T., Wolfgang, E., & Hofman, V. (1994). A longitudinal study of the relation between representations of attachment in childhood and cognitive functioning in childhood and adolescence. *Developmental Psychology, 30*, 112–124.

Jeynes, W. H. (2005). A meta-analysis of the relation of parental involvement to urban elementary school student academic achievement. *Urban Education, 40*, 237–269.

Kerr, M., & Stattin, H. (2000). What parents know, how they know it, and several forms of adolescent adjustment: Further support for a reinterpretation of monitoring. *Developmental Psychology, 36*, 366–380.

Kochanska, G., Aksan, N., Knaack, A., & Rhines, H. M. (2004). Maternal parenting and children's conscience: Early security as a moderator. *Child Development, 75*, 1229–1242.

Ladd, G. W. (2003). Probing the adaptive significance of children's behavior and relationships in the school context: A child by environment perspective. In R. Kail (Ed.), *Advances in child development and behavior* (Vol. 31, pp. 43–104). Sand Diego, CA: Academic Press.

Larose, S., Bernier, A., & Tarabulsky, G. M. (2005). Attachment state of mind, learning dispositions, and acadmic performance during the college transition. *Developmental Psychology, 41*, 281–289.

Larson, R. W., Richards, M. H., Moneta, G., Holmbeck, G., & Duckett, E. (1996). Changes in adolescents' daily interactions with their families from ages 10 to 18: Disengagement and transformation. *Developmental Psychology, 32*, 744–754.

Main, M., Kaplan, N., & Cassidy, J. (1985). Security in infancy, childhood, and adulthood: A move to the level of representation. In I. Bretherton & E. Waters (Eds.), Growing points of attachment theory and research. *Monographs of the Society for Research in Child Development, 50*, Serial No. 209 (1–2), pp. 66–104.

Matas, L., Arend, R., & Sroufe, A. (1978). Continuity and adaptation in the second year: The relationship between quality of attachment and later competence. *Child Development, 49*, 547–556.

Moss, E., & St-Laurent, D. (2001). Attachment at school age and academic performance. *Developmental Psychology, 37*, 863–874.

Ng, F. F., Kenney-Benson, G. A., & Pomerantz, E. M. (2004). Children's achievement moderates the effects of mothers' use of control and autonomy support. *Child Development, 75*, 764–780.

Nolen-Hoeksema, S., Wolfson, A., Mumme, D., & Guskin, K. (1995). Helplessness in children of depressed and nondepressed mothers. *Developmental Psychology, 31*, 377–387.

O'Connor, E., & McCartney, K. (2007). Attachment and cognitive skills: An investigation of mediating mechanisms. *Journal of Applied Developmental Psychology, 28*, 458–476.

Offer, D., & Offer, J. B. (1975). *Teenage to young manhood: A psychological study.* New York: Basic Books.

Pianta, R. C., Nimetz, S. L., & Bennett, E. (1997). Mother-child relationships, teacher-child relationships, and school outcomes in preschool and kindergarten. *Early Childhood Research Quarterly, 12*, 263–280.

Pomerantz, E. M., Grolnick, W. S., & Price, C. E. (2005). The role of parents in how children approach school: A dynamic process perspective. In A. J. Elliot & C. S. Dweck (Eds.), *The handbook of competence and motivation* (pp. 259–278). New York: Guilford Press.

Pomerantz, E. M., & Moorman, E. A. (2010). Parents' involvement in children's schooling: A context for children's development. In J. L. Meece & J. Eccles (Eds.), *Handbook of research on schools, schooling, and human development* (pp. 398–416). New York: Routledge.

Pomerantz, E. M., Moorman, E. A., & Cheung, C. S. (2011). Parents' involvement in children's learning. In K. R. Harris, S. Graham, & T. C. Urdan (Eds.), *APA educational psychology handbook* (pp. 417–440). Washington DC: APA.

Pomerantz, E. M., Moorman, E. A., & Litwack, S. D. (2007). The how, whom, and why of parents' involvement in children's schooling: More is not necessarily better. *Review of Educational Research, 77*, 373–410.

Pomerantz, E. M., Qin, L., Wang, Q., & Chen, H. (2009). American and Chinese early adolescents' inclusion of their relationships with their parents in their self-construals. *Child Development, 80*, 792–807.

Pomerantz, E. M., Qin, L., Wang, Q., & Chen, H. (2011). Changes in early adolescents' sense of responsibility to their parents in the United States and China: Implications for their academic functioning. *Child Development, 82*, 1136–1151.

Pomerantz, E. M., Wang, Q., & Ng, F. F. (2005). Mothers' affect in the homework context: The importance of staying positive. *Developmental Psychology, 42*, 414–427.

Roth, G., Assor, A., Niemiec, C. P., Ryan, R. M., & Deci, E. L. (2009). The emotional and academic consequences of parental conditional regard: Comparing conditional positive regard, conditional negative regard, and autonomy support as parenting practices. *Developmental Psychology, 45*, 1119–1142.

Ryan, R. M., Stiller, J. D., & Lynch, J. H. (1994). Representations of relationships to teachers, parents, and friends as predictors of academic motivation and self-esteem. *Journal of Early Adolescence, 14*, 226–249.

Schneider, B. H., Atkinson, L., & Tardiff, C. (2001). Child-parent attachment and children's peer relations: A quantitative review. *Developmental Psychology, 37*, 86–100.

Senechal, M., & LeFevre, J. (2002). Parental involvment in the development of children's reading skill: A five year longitudinal study. *Child Development, 73*, 445–460.

Sheldon, S. B. (2002). Parents' social networks and beliefs as predictors of parent involvement *The Elementary School Journal, 102*, 301–316.

Simpkins, S. D., Weiss, H. B., McCartney, K., Kreider, H. M., & Dearing, E. (2006). Mother-child relationship as a moderator of the relation between family educational involvement and child achievement. *Parenting: Science and Practice, 6*, 49–57.

Skinner, E., Johnson, S., & Snyder, T. (2005). Six dimensions of parenting: A motivational model. *Parenting: Science and Practice, 5*, 175–235.

Stams, G. J. M., Juffer, F., & van IJzendoorn, M. H. (2002). Maternal sensitivity, infant attachment, and temperament in early childhood predict adjustment in middle childhood: The case of adopted children and their biologically unrelated parents. *Developmental Psychology, 38*, 806–821.

Steinberg, L., Elmen, J. D., & Mounts, N. S. (1989). Authoritative parenting, psychosocial maturity, and academic success among adolescents. *Child Development, 60*, 1424–1436.

Stevenson, H. W., Chen, C., & Lee, S-Y. (1993). Mathematics achievement of Chinese, Japanese, and American children: Ten years later. *Science, 259*, 53–58.

Tamis-LeMonda, C. S., Bornstein, M. H., & Baumwell, L. (2001). Maternal responsiveness and children's acheivement of language milestones. *Child Development, 72*, 748–767.

Tang, T. L-P., Luk, V. W-M., & Chiu, R. K. (2000). Pay differentials in the people's Republic of China: An examination of internal equity and external competitiveness. *Compensation Benefits Review, 32*, 43–49.

Telzer, E. H., & Fuligni, A. J. (2009). Daily family assistance and the psychological well-being of adolescents from Latin American, Asian, and European backgrounds. *Developmental Psychology, 45*, 1177–1189.

Thompson, R. A. (2006). The development of the person: Social understanding, relationships, conscience, self. In N. Eisenberg (Ed.), *Handbook of child psychology. Vol. 3: Social, emotional, and personality development* (6th ed., pp. 24–98). Hoboken, NJ: Wiley.

Thompson, R. A., Braun, K., Grossmann, K. E., Gunnar, M. R., Heinrichs, M., Keller, H.,... Wang, S. (2005). Early social attachment and its consequences: The dynamics of a developing relationship. In C. S. Carter, L. Ahnert, K. E. Grossmann, M. Lamb, S. Porges, & N. Sachser (Eds.), *Attachment and bonding: A new synthesis (Dahlem Workshop report 92)* (pp. 349–383). Cambridge, MA: MIT Press.

van IJzendoorn, M. H., Dijksta, J., & Bus, A. G. (1995). Attachment, intelligence, and language: A meta-analysis. *Social Development, 4*, 115–128.

Vansteenkiste, M., Simons, J., Lens, W., Soenens, B., & Matos, L. (2005). Examining the motivational impact of intrinsic versus extrinsic goal framing and autonomy-supportive versus internally controlling communication style on early adolescents' academic achievement. *Child Development, 76*, 483–501.

Wang, Q., & Pomerantz, E. M. (2009). The motivational landscape of early adolescence in the US and China: A longitudinal investigation. *Child Development, 80*, 1280–1296.

Wang, Q., Pomerantz, E. M., & Chen, H. (2007). The role of parents' control in early adolescents' psychological functioning: A longitudinal investigation in the United States and China. *Child Development, 78*, 1592–1610.

Wigfield, A., Eccles, J. S., Schiefele, U., Roeser, R. W., & Davis-Kean, P. (2006). Development of achievement motivation. In N. Eisenberg (Ed.), *Handbook of child psychology. Vol. 3: Social, emotional, and personality development* (6th ed., pp. 933–1002). Hoboken, NJ: Wiley.

Wigfield, A., & Wagner, A. L. (2005). Competence, motivation and identity development during adolescence. In A. J. Elliot & C. S. Dweck (Eds.), *Handbook of competence and motivation* (pp. 222–239). New York: Guilford Press.

Wolff, D., & van IJzendoorn, M. H. (1997). Sensitivity and attachment: A meta-analysis on parental antecedents of infant attachment. *Child Development, 68*, 571–591.

Yu, A-B. (1996). Ultimate life concerns, self, and Chinese achievement motivation. In M. H. Bond (Ed.), *The handbook of Chinese psychology* (pp. 227–246). Hong Kong: Oxford University Press.

Avoiding the Pitfalls and Approaching the Promises of Close Relationships

Shelly L. Gable *and* Thery Prok

Abstract

People are powerfully motivated to form and maintain social relationships. Indeed, health and well-being are strongly tied to the course and quality of social bonds. However, while close relationships provide people with many advantages such as intimacy and social support, relationships can also be a detriment, such as when they are wrought with hostility and potential rejection. We present a framework of social and relationship motivation that simultaneously accounts for people's tendencies to both approach the incentives and avoid the threats in close relationships. Research examining the correlates of approach and avoidance motives and goals in relationships is reviewed and mediating mechanisms are explored. The implications and advantages of an approach and avoidance model of social motivation are highlighted and future research directions are discussed.

Key Words: close relationships, approach motivation, avoidance motivation, social isolation, loneliness

Introduction
Motivation for Social Bonds

Humans *need* social contact. Some of the most compelling evidence for this simple truth can be found in reports of what happens to us when we are not able to form or maintain interpersonal bonds. The empirical literature on the effects of social isolation clearly shows that social relationships are critical to health and well-being. For decades we have known that social isolation is associated with a substantial increase in all-cause mortality risk and psychological dysfunction (e.g., Berkman & Syme, 1979; Durkheim, 1897; House, Landis, & Umberson, 1988). More recent work has begun to unravel the complex mechanisms responsible for these links (e.g., Carter, 1996; Cohen, 2005; Kiecolt-Glaser, 1999; Uchino, Cacioppo, & Kiecolt-Glaser, 1996; Whisman, 2001). This research shows that extended loneliness and social isolation is associated with downstream alterations in multiple biological systems (e.g., cardiovascular, inflammatory;

Hawkley, Mesi, Berry, & Cacioppo, 2006; McDade, Hawkley, & Cacioppo, 2006), psychological processes and disorders (e.g., executive functioning, depression, anxiety; Cacioppo & Hawkley, 2009; Cacioppo et al., 2006; Joiner, 1997), which likely contribute to increased mortality and decreased well-being.

The negative impact that social isolation has on health and well-being likely reflects the rich social context of human evolutionary history. Social bonds increased fitness, which, over time, likely conferred cognitive, affective, and behavioral responses designed to regulate interpersonal relations (Reis, Collins & Berscheid, 2000). In short, the legacy of our evolutionary past is that modern human beings possess a powerful *motivation* to form and maintain strong and stable interpersonal relationships (e.g., Baumeister & Leary, 1995; Cantor & Malley, 1991; McAdams, 1982). These nontransient relationships have a robust influence on daily life and vary in terms of their function and structure, taking the form of attachment bonds, hierarchical relationships, mating relationships, coalitions, and communal bonds (Bugental, 2000; Fiske, 1992). The motivation to connect with others is powerful and ubiquitous. For example, compared to people whose social needs are being met, those who feel lonely are more likely to ascribe human characteristics to inanimate objects, presumably in an attempt to feel more socially connected (Epley, Waytz, Akalis, & Cacioppo, 2008).

Even though the motivation to form and maintain strong interpersonal bonds is rooted deep in our evolutionary psyche, people are keenly aware of their need for close relationships, as beautifully illustrated in poetry and song lyrics. When asked about their most important life goals, successful close relationships are often high on the list (e.g., Emmons, 1986. Moreover, people who do not make their social goals a high priority have poorer mental and physical health than those who do rank social goals high among their life goals (Kasser & Ryan, 1996). The popularly held belief that "people need people" is expounded in the psychological literature. Prominent models of well-being propose that satisfying ongoing relationships are a necessary component of psychological and physical health (e.g., Deci & Ryan, 1985; Diener & Biswas-Diener, 2008; Keyes, 1998; Ryff, 1995).

Recent research has also demonstrated that the impact of our basic motivation to form and maintain close relationships reaches far beyond our interaction with others. That is, interpersonal motives and goals influence cognition, emotion, and behavior in domains that once were thought to be independent of close relationships. Overall, this body of research clearly demonstrates that motives for close relationships influence how people think, feel, and act in novel social interactions and seemingly nonsocial contexts (e.g., Andersen, Reznik, & Manzella, 1996; Baldwin, Carrell, & Lopez, 1990; Mikulincer, 1998). For example, the motives and goals people have for their close relationships affect psychological processes in the seemingly unrelated domain of performance on achievement tasks, and this occurs without their awareness (Shah, 2003).

In short, there is compelling evidence that people are motivated to form and maintain stable interpersonal bonds. When people are unable to fulfill these needs, their health and well-being suffer. Moreover, social motivation influences cognition, affect, and behavior in social and nonsocial contexts. However, close relationships in themselves are not necessarily positive and beneficial. That is, while close relationships provide people with many benefits such as social support and connection, relationships can also be harmful, such as when they are wrought with hostility and potential rejection. In the following section, we briefly outline the evidence that the road to close relationships contains both promises and pitfalls.

Promises and Pitfalls of Close Relationships

Close relationships are the source of both pleasure and pain. Although people cite close relationships most often when asked what gives their life meaning (e.g., Klinger, 1977), they are also very likely to cite relationship problems when asked what is not going well in their lives (Veroff, Douvan, & Kulka, 1981). The potential rewards of close relationships are numerous and highly valued; these incentives include companionship, passion, and intimacy. The potential pitfalls are equally plentiful and impactful; these threats include betrayal, jealously, and criticism.

One potential benefit of close relationships is social support, or more accurately the perception that others will be there if needed during times of stress. In fact, social support has been widely linked to various mental and physical health processes (e.g., Cohen & Willis, 1985; Cutrona, Russell, & Rose, 1986; Dunkel-Schetter & Bennett, 1990; Lakey & Cassady, 1990). Another potential benefit of social bonds is that close others often facilitate one's ideal personal development and goal pursuit (e.g., Rusbult, Kumashiro, Kubacka, & Finkel, 2009). On the other hand, threats to relationship stability and problems within relationships also contribute to psychopathological symptoms such as depression, anxiety, and substance abuse (e.g., Davila, Bradbuy, Cohan, & Tochluk, 1997; Whisman, 2001; Whisman, Uebelacker, & Settles, 2010). Specifically, conflict, rejection, and abandonment are among the threats with well-documented detrimental links to psychological health (e.g., Baron et al., 2007; Downey, Feldman, & Ayduck, 2000; Mikulincer, 1998).

In addition to the psychological impact of social bonds, there are numerous physical benefits and risks of relationships (e.g., Kiecolt-Glaser, Gouin, & Hantsoo, 2010). For example, emotionally supportive relationships facilitate recovery from illness, whereas marital conflict increases the likelihood of cardiac death (Eaker et al., 2007; Wilcox, Kasl, & Berkman, 1994). The specific physiological processes that are responsible for seemingly direct effects that relationship incentives and threats have on physical health are also beginning to be unraveled (e.g., Cacioppo & Patrick, 2008; Carter, 1996). For example, fear of negative social evaluation is linked to a biological stress response (Dickerson & Kemeny, 2004).

Taken together this research shows that some aspects of social bonds and close relationships are positively associated with psychological and physical health, whereas other aspects of social bonds and close relationships pose significant risks to health and well-being. Perhaps in no other domain of life is the simultaneous potential for rewards and threats so clear as it is for interpersonal relationships. And, given the human need for social connection, one can not avoid the potential pitfalls of social bonds (and forego any possible promises) by simply not having them. Therefore, it is our thesis that people are motivated to approach the rewards and avoid the punishments inherent in social relationships. Models of social and relationship motivation need to account simultaneously for the regulation of incentives and threats. Fortunately, decades of research on approach and avoidance motivation laid the groundwork for the model described in the remainder of this chapter.

Approach and Avoidance Motivation

The history of distinguishing approach and avoidance dimensions is almost as long as the history of psychology itself (Gray, 1970; Pavlov, 1927; Schneirla, 1959). For example, Miller (1959, 1961) conducted his classic research on separate approach and withdrawal learning processes and made graphical representations of their interplay in the form of approach and avoidance conflict gradients that continue to inspire current research (e.g., Cacioppo, Gardner, & Berntson, 1997). Over time, theoretical and empirical work across diverse areas of psychology has either explicitly or implicitly adopted a view of separate incentive approach and threat avoidance systems (see Carver, 1996; Gable, Reis, & Elliot, 2003, for reviews).

Specifically in the areas of motivation and behavior regulation, several theories have featured the approach and avoidance distinction (see Elliot, 2008). For example, Carver and Scheier described a model of self-regulation (1990) that entails feedback processes such that the current environment is compared to some internal goal, the person acts, the situation is reevaluated and the comparison made again, and the process continues. More important, these feedback processes can either lead to behaviors that move the person closer to the object of his or her goal (approach), or they can lead to behaviors that move the person away from the object of his or her goal (avoidance). Similarly, Elliot (1997) made the distinction between approach- and avoidance-focused motives and goals in the achievement domain. He separated approach motives, those consisting of the need for achievement, from avoidance motives, those focused on a fear of failure.

What is clear from all of this work is that beyond the content of the motives or goals (e.g., achievement, power, social), the focus of those motives and goals is critical for understanding a variety of psychological processes. That is, the approach and avoidance motivational distinction has been shown to have important implications for perception, cognition, emotion, behavior, health, and well-being (e.g., Derryberry & Reed, 1994; Elliot & Sheldon, 1998; Higgins, Shah, & Friedman, 1997). For example, in terms of basic attention, individuals with strong approach motivation are biased toward cues indicating gain of an incentive and those with strong avoidance motivation are biased toward cues indicating threat or loss (Derryberry & Reed, 1994). In the area of emotion, Carver (2001) argues that the function of emotions lies in their utility to motivate the organism and regulate behavior regarding incentives (approach) and threats (avoidance). Thus, there are positive incentive-related emotions (e.g., joy) and negative incentive-related emotion (e.g., disappointment). Likewise, there are positive threat-related emotions (e.g., relief) and negative threat-related emotions (e.g., anxiety). In the area of well-being, Elliot and Sheldon (1998) examined the links between approach and avoidance personal goals and found that people with more avoidance goals for their lives had lower well-being. Goal direction (approach or avoid) was associated with current well-being as well as changes in well-being over time.

Several researchers have argued that the reason that the approach-avoidance distinction emerges frequently in motivation research is because they are based on distinct neurobiological systems or structures (e.g., Gray, 1987). For example, researchers who have used electroencephalographic (EEG) technology to examine relative prefrontal brain asymmetry and activity in these regions have found that strong dispositional approach motives or signals of possible reward correspond to greater left prefrontal activation and strong dispositional avoidance motives or signals of possible punishment correspond to greater right prefrontal activation (e.g., Harmon-Jones & Allen, 1997; Sobotka, Davidson, & Senulis, 1992). The separate biological systems research is consistent with work examining the underlying factor structure of different measures of individual differences in motivation, personality, and affect (e.g., Gable, Reis, & Elliot, 2003; Laurenceau, Troy, & Carver, 2005).

These studies have found that approach and avoidance dimensions, while correlated with one another, are independent. Also consistent with theoretical models and empirical data is the idea that each operates through different processes. For example, Gable, Reis, and Elliot (2000) showed that the relationship between approach motivation and positive emotion was accounted for differential exposure processes (higher approach motives predicted a greater number of pleasant daily events). The relationship between avoidance motivation and negative emotion was mediated by differential sensitivity processes (higher avoidance motives predicted stronger reactions to negative events when they occurred, but not a higher frequency of them).

Social and Relationship Motivation
EARLY SOCIAL MOTIVATION RESEARCH: AFFILIATION MOTIVES

Early work on social motivation hinted at the need for understanding both the regulation of incentives and the regulation of threats. For example, among Murray's (1938) several socially based needs (e.g., deference, nurturance) the one that subsequently received the most empirical and theoretical attention was the need for affiliation (nAff). Shipley and Veroff (1952) viewed the need for affiliation as stemming from interpersonal insecurity. They measured the strength of the need for affiliation in open-ended stories written to explain ambiguous pictures (Thematic Apperception Test; Morgan & Murray, 1935). Their research showed that themes of social separation were more common in the stories of recently rejected men, compared to controls.

Later work showed that those who had a strong need for affiliation were less popular in their social groups, had more confidence, but sought the approval of others more often than those with weaker need for affiliation (Atkinson, Heyns, & Veroff, 1954). Atkinson and his colleagues explained the seemingly mixed results of the work on nAff by suggesting that social situations aroused two needs: hope of affiliation and fear of rejection. The idea that social needs took the form of independent approach and avoidance motives was further explicated by DeCharms (1957), who attempted to separately measure approach affiliative motives and avoidance affiliative motives. Sticking with the prevailing paradigm of the time, he further refined and expanded a TAT coding scheme; coding responses concerned with positive relationships and attaining affiliation as approach affiliation (+Aff) and responses concerned with separation and rejection as avoidance affiliation (–Aff).

However, up to this point most of these studies were conducted in the context of laboratory-formed groups doing achievement-relevant tasks, not with existing or naturally formed close relationships.

Later, Boyatzis (1973) further delineated approach and avoidance social motivation by pointing that affiliation motivation can be expressed in two ways; one is approach oriented and the other is avoidance oriented. The approach affiliative motive is focused on a positive outcome, obtaining closeness and intimacy, whereas the avoidance affiliative motive seems focused on a negative outcome, avoiding rejection or loneliness. Boyatzis' conclusions mirrored those of Mehrabian and colleagues, even though their work grew out a different perspective, that of reward and expectancy theories (Mehrabian, 1976; Mehrabian & Ksionzky, 1974). Specifically, Mehrabian (1976) posited that expectancies of positive and negative reinforcers in interpersonal relationships shaped approach and avoidance social motivation, respectively, which he called affiliation tendency and sensitivity to rejection. Mehrabian found that approach motives targeted different outcomes than avoidance motives. People high on affiliative tendency were less anxious, elicited more positive affect from others, were more self-confident, and saw themselves as similar to others. People high in sensitivity to rejection were less confident, more anxious, and were judged less positively by others than people low on sensitivity to rejection.

BEYOND AFFILIATION MOTIVATION

Although most scholars of close relationships would agree that the need for close bonds is a fundamental human motive, the examination of relationship motivation seemed to take a hiatus for close to 25 years. There were, of course, important exceptions. For example, McAdams (1982) conducted research on intimacy motivation. The primary assessment of these motives was again the TAT; however, motivation for intimacy and motivation for affiliation were assessed separately. He found that those with stronger intimacy motivation had more spontaneous thoughts about relationships and relationship partners, experienced more positive emotions in interpersonal situations, disclosed and listened more to friends, spent more time communicating with others, and had greater concern for others' well-being than those with weaker intimacy motives (McAdams & Constantian, 1983; McAdams, Healy, & Krause, 1984).

McAdams and colleagues' work on intimacy motivation is important to the current thesis because it highlights the relevance of social goals to established, ongoing close relationships. This was a departure from much of the previous work that examined the role of social goals in more general social processes (e.g., popularity, self-confidence) or in the context of newly or laboratory-formed groups and dyads. Moreover, subsequent research on intimacy motivation found that intimacy motives were associated with a variety of important relationship processes, including relationship satisfaction in dating relationships, friendships, and marriages (Sanderson & Cantor, 1997, 2001; Sanderson, Rahm, & Beigbeder, 2005). Although this work expanded the social motivation research beyond the original focus on the need to affiliate with others, little attention has been paid, until recently, to the need to simultaneously regulate incentives and threats. In the following sections we describe such a model of approach and avoidance social motivation and the empirical evidence supporting it.

Approaching Incentives and Avoiding Threats in Relationships

Modeled on other hierarchical motivation and goal theories (e.g., Elliot, 2006) and rooted in the previous work that separated fear of rejection from hope for affiliation motives (e.g., Mehrabian, 1976), Gable (2006) proposed a model of approach and avoidance social goals. The model describes predicted associations between approach and avoidance motives and different interpersonal outcomes as well as the processes that mediate those associations. Specifically, the model proposes that people can have two distinct types of goals. Approach social goals are aimed at obtaining desired outcomes such as intimacy and pleasure in their close relationships, whereas avoidance social goals direct individuals away from potentially undesirable outcomes such as conflict and rejection. The model posits that individual differences in dispositional threat and incentive sensitivities (i.e., relatively stable traits) as well as aspects of a person's current social environment (i.e., recent events in a person's particular relationship) influence the type of short-term goals that people adopt.

We view goals as the short-term cognitive representations of wants and fears that are influenced by both dispositional motivational tendencies (e.g., need for affiliation and fear of rejection) and situational cues (e.g., current social incentives and threats in the environment; Elliot, Gable, & Mapes, 2006; Gable, 2006). For example, when out on a date with a new partner, a person who has strong approach goals may be concerned with making a good impression and having an interesting conversation, whereas someone with weak approach goals would be less concerned with these outcomes. Strong approach goals in this scenario might stem from high dispositional levels of hope for affiliation and/or prior cues of warmth and interest from his date. Someone with strong avoidance goals may be concerned with not making a fool of himself and avoiding controversial conversation topics, whereas someone with weak avoidance goals would be less concerned with these things. Strong avoidance goals in this scenario might stem from high dispositional fear of rejection and/or prior cues of aloofness or disinterest from his date. Although the content of the goals in both of these examples is very similar, the manner in which individuals frame their goals makes all the difference.

MOTIVES AND CURRENT ENVIRONMENT SHAPE GOALS

Empirical evidence supports the premise that individual differences in distal social motives and attachment dimensions predict more proximal social and relationship goals (e.g., Gable, 2006; Impett, Gordon, & Strachman, 2008). For example, several studies found that people with strong approach motives were more likely to adopt short-term approach social goals such as wanting to make new friends, and those with strong avoidance motives were more likely to adopt short-term avoidance social goals such as not wanting to be lonely (e.g., Gable, 2006). Similar associations between dispositional motives and short-term goals for specific interactions in a romantic relationship have also been demonstrated (e.g., Impett, Gable, & Peplau, 2005).

Although there is less work on the associations among current cues of incentives and threats in the social environment and the adoption of approach and avoidance goals in relationships, existing data are consistent with the prediction that the perception of current incentives is positively associated with approach goal strength and the perception of current threats is positively associated with avoidance goal strength (e.g., Elliot et al., 2006). However, interpretation of these findings is complicated because current goals are likely to bias the interpretation of social cues in the environment, such as whether neutral or ambiguous social information is interpreted as an incentive or threat (Strachman & Gable, 2006). These processes are discussed in more detail in the following section.

Approach and Avoidance Goals and Interpersonal Outcomes

Because approach goals are focused on potential incentives, and avoidance goals are focused on potential threats, they should be linked with different outcomes in relationships. Specifically, approach goals should be associated with outcomes defined by the presence or absence of positive outcomes, such as passion and intimacy. Avoidance goals should be associated with outcomes defined by the presence or absence of negative outcomes, such as security and conflict. Results from several studies are consistent with this idea. In one study, participants' self-generated social goals and romantic goals were later coded as either approach or avoidance. Whereas approach goals were associated with more satisfaction and with social life and less loneliness, avoidance goals were associated with increased anxiety and loneliness 8 weeks later (Gable, 2006). Loneliness has historically been defined as being both about lacking positive relationships or having problematic or insecure relationships (e.g., Perlman & Peplau, 1981); thus, it is theoretically consistent with the model that both types of goals would be associated with changes in loneliness.

Similarly Elliot, Gable, and Mapes (2006) developed and validated an eight-item measure of approach and avoidance social goals in a short-term longitudinal study. Consistent with the model, they found that approach social goals were associated with greater subjective well-being, whereas avoidance social goals were associated with more self-reports of physical health symptoms 3.5 months later. The aforementioned studies examined peoples' level of relationship goals at a global level, aggregating across friendships, family relationships, and intimate relationships. However, additional studies have focused on people's approach and avoidance goals in a specific relationship and have found parallel results that are consistent with the hierarchical model. For example, in a series of studies, Impett and colleagues found that people in relatively new romantic relationships with strong approach goals maintained high levels of sexual desire over time, whereas those with weak approach goals showed the typical decline in sexual desire that has been observed in other studies (Impett, Strachman, Finkel, & Gable, 2008). In addition, in a study of married couples, Gable (2000) found that those who had strong avoidance goals reported greater insecurity than those with weaker avoidance goals. On the other hand, the strength of approach goals positively predicted daily positive affect during marital interactions.

There are data showing that the goals people have for specific interactions are also important. For example, in one study, the type of goals people had for everyday sacrifices (i.e., enacting behaviors that are not preferred for the sake of their partners, such as accompanying a partner to a dull work function or not spending time on a hobby) influenced their relationship outcomes (Impett, Gable, & Peplau, 2005). Specifically when people engaged in these behaviors for approach motives (e.g., to promote intimacy), they reported greater positive affect and relationship satisfaction. However, when they did the same behaviors for avoidance motives (e.g., to prevent my partner from becoming upset), they reported greater negative affect, lower relationship satisfaction, and more conflict. The more often people sacrificed for avoidance motives over the course of the study, the less satisfied they were with their relationships at the follow-up assessment 6 weeks later and the more likely they were to have broken up. Finally, in a recent observational study of newlywed couples, Laurenceau, Kleinman, Kaczynski, and Carver (2010) examined how incentive and threat sensitivities were associated with outcomes regarding specific interactions. They found that relationship incentive sensitivity was positively associated with positive affect during a discussion of the loving aspects of the relationship, whereas relationship threat sensitivity predicted greater anxiety when discussing a significant marital problem.

To summarize, the previous section reviewed several studies that demonstrated the links between approach and avoidance relationship motivation and outcomes. These studies employed diverse methods (cross-sectional, daily experience, longitudinal data, observational), focused on different close relationships such as friendships, romantic relationships, and family bonds, and examined associations at the level of global social relationships, specific relationships, and particular interactions. The results all showed that approach and avoidance goals were associated with important relationship outcomes. In addition, these data suggest that approach goals are more strongly associated with outcomes defined by the presence of incentives (e.g., sexual desire), whereas avoidance goals are more strongly associated with outcomes defined by the absence of threats (e.g., security). Global outcomes that involve both incentives and threats, such as overall relationships satisfaction and loneliness, were correlated with both approach and avoidance goals. The next question centers on how goals influence outcomes—the cognitive, behavioral, and affective processes that mediate the links summarized in this section.

Processes Linking Goals to Outcomes

Our theoretical model suggests that the processes that mediate the links between approach goals and outcomes are not necessarily the same as those that mediate the links between avoidance goals and outcomes. An illustration of this point comes from a series of studies examining how threat and reward sensitivities were associated with daily affect (Gable, Reis, & Elliot, 2000). Specifically, threat sensitivity was assessed with Carver and White's (1994) measure of individual differences in the Behavioral Inhibition System (BIS), and incentive sensitivity was assessed with the corresponding scale assessing individual differences in the Behavioral Activity System (BAS); both scales are based on Gray's reinforcement sensitivity theory (e.g., Gray, 1987, 1990). The results showed that, as expected, high BIS sensitivity was associated with more daily negative affect (NA) and high BAS sensitivity was predictive of increased daily positive affect (PA).

Across three studies the occurrence and impact of daily positive and negative events were also assessed, and the results suggested that the relationship between BAS and PA was explained by a differential exposure process and the relationship between BIS and NA was explained by a differential sensitivity hypothesis. People with more sensitive BAS experienced more daily PA because they experienced more frequent positive events (differential exposure), and people with more sensitive BIS did not report experiencing more frequent negative events; however, they reacted more strongly to the occurrence of negative events (differential reactivity). In another series of studies focused on social motives and goals and social events, results were consistent with these findings (Gable, 2006).

Specifically, approach social motives and goals were associated with increased exposure to social positive events, such that strong approach relationship motives and goals predicted increased frequency of the occurrence of positive social events (Gable, 2006). The frequency of positive social events mediated the link between approach relationship motives and outcomes; and as expected approach relationship motives and goals did not predict the frequency of negative social events. The link between avoidance goals and outcomes was associated with a different process, reactivity to negative social events (Elliot et al., 2006; Gable, 2006). Specifically, when negative social events happened, those with strong avoidance

relationship motives and goals rated them as more important and showed more changes in their well-being than those with weak avoidance goals. Exposure to negative events was not consistently related to avoidance goals. In the subsequent section, studies examining other possible mediators of the links between social goals and outcomes are reviewed.

MEMORY AND INTERPRETATION OF AMBIGUOUS INFORMATION

Previous research has clearly shown that motives and goals influence basic cognitive processes (e.g., Kunda, 1990). Much of this work has examined how the content of goals (e.g., self-protection motives, accuracy goals) directs cognitive processes. For example, Maner and colleagues (2005) reported that when participants were motivated by a self-protection goal, they perceived greater anger in the faces of outgroup members and when they had goals related to finding a mate, male participants perceived more sexual arousal in attractive female targets. In addition to the content of goals influencing basic cognitive processes, research has also suggested that the focus of motives and goals influences cognitive processes. For example, Higgins and Tykocinski (1992) found that participants who had promotion-focused motives (concerned with aspirations and growth) had better recall of information from a previously presented story when it was related to positive outcomes. Those with prevention-focused motives (concerned with obligations and security) remembered more information related to negative outcomes in the story.

Strachman and Gable (2006) investigated how goals focused on social incentives and those focused on social threats influenced two basic processes: recall of social information and interpretation of ambiguous social information. In one study, individual differences in the strength of approach and avoidance goals for current friendships were assessed. After reading a story containing positive, negative, and neutral information regarding the interactions of two relationship partners, participants with strong avoidance social goals recalled more of the negative information in the story than those with weak avoidance goals (Strachman & Gable, 2006, Study 1). In another study, social goals for an upcoming interaction with a stranger were experimentally manipulated; half of the participants were provided with an approach goal for a conversation with a stranger and half were given avoidance goals (e.g., try to make a good impression, try not to make a bad impression). They then were given a self-description ostensibly written by their future interaction partner. Those in the avoidance goal condition remembered more negative information about and expressed more dislike for the other person than those in the approach goal condition.

A significant proportion of social information that people receive on a daily basis can be ambiguous in nature. A smile from a stranger can be a sign of good manners or genuine warmth and interest. The quiet demeanor of a spouse can be indicative of a bad day at work or lingering animosity about a marital disagreement the night before. Strachman and Gable (2006) also analyzed their participants' interpretation of the information they did recall from the story they read. That is, they examined how closely their recalled information matched the information presented in the story. The results showed that those with strong avoidance goals were more likely to interpret seemingly neutral and positive information from the story with a more negative spin than people with avoidance goals. For example, when describing an originally neutral aspect of the scenario such as "he picked her up at 10:00," those with high avoidance goals were likely to view that as being picked up late. Memory of social information and biases in interpretation are particularly important processes in close relationships because people have repeated interactions with the same people across multiple contexts. Thus, there are ample opportunities for pertinent memories to form and for ambiguous information to be interpreted in a manner consistent with goals. Moreover, as demonstrated by Neuberg (e.g., 1996), these cognitive processes lead to expectations, which in turn influence the information sought from social partners, how people behavior toward a social partner, and how the social partner behaves in return.

WEIGHT OF SOCIAL INFORMATION

Although the strength of approach goals is primarily associated with incentive-based outcomes such as passion, and threat-based outcomes such as security, in the end, people make more global evaluations in relationships and decisions to act or not act in certain ways (e.g., file for divorce or stay in a marriage). Thus, another process by which approach and avoidance goals influence outcomes is by influencing the weight of different types of information in global evaluations and decisions. Specifically, those with strong approach goals likely weigh the presence (or absence) of incentives in their relationships more heavily in global evaluations than those with weaker approach goals. And those with strong avoidance goals likely place more weight on the presence (or absence) of threats in their relationships when making global evaluations than those with weaker avoidance goals. Consistent with this idea, Updegraff, Gable, and Taylor (2004) found that global life-satisfaction ratings were more strongly tied to positive affect for people with strong approach motivation than for those with weaker approach motivation.

Examining this idea in close relationships, Gable and Poore (2008) conducted a signal-contingent daily experience study in which participants were beeped at several random intervals throughout the day and reported their feelings of passion for and security regarding their romantic partners at that very moment. Prior to the beginning of the study, they reported the strength of their approach and avoidance relationship goals. At the end of the day, they also reported their general feeling of satisfaction with their relationships. The authors found that participants with strong avoidance social goals put more weight on security in their end-of-day reports of satisfaction than those with weaker avoidance social goals; moreover, those with strong approach goals put more weight on their feelings of passion in their end-of-day reports of relationship satisfaction than those low in approach goals. Thus, when people had strong avoidance goals they reported less relationship satisfaction on days they felt more insecure than they typically felt, but if they had weak avoidance goals their satisfaction did not go down on days they felt more insecure than they typically felt. Similarly, when people had strong approach goals they reported greater satisfaction on days they felt more passion than they typically reported feeling, but if they had weak approach goals they did not report a boost in their relationship satisfaction on days they felt more passion than they typically felt. It seems that the very definition of satisfaction—the presence of incentives or the absence of threats—was tied to goals.

EMOTION IN SOCIAL INTERACTION AND CLOSE RELATIONSHIPS

Motivation and emotion are closely tied (Keltner & Lerner, 2009) and approach and avoidance motives have been tied to positive and negative affect, respectively (e.g., Larsen & Ketelaar, 1991). For example, studies have found that approach motives and goals were positively correlated with positive affect on a daily basis and avoidance motives and goals were correlated with negative affect on a daily basis (e.g. Gable et al., 2000). More important, there is little evidence that approach motivation is associated with negative affect and that avoidance motivation is associated with positive affect (Gable et al., 2000).

Recently, Impett and colleagues (2010) examined the experience of affect in close relationships. In terms of ongoing relationships, Impett and colleagues conducted two studies investigating the role of positive emotions in the link between relationship goals and satisfaction in dating couples. They found that people high in approach goals experienced more positive emotions on a daily basis, which mediated their greater feelings of satisfaction with their relationships. Moreover, participants with high approach goals also had *partners* who experienced more positive emotions, which also contributed to participants' higher feelings of satisfaction with the relationship. More research is needed to understand how avoidance goals and negative emotions might mediate the link between avoidance goals and relationship outcomes; however, Impett and colleagues' findings are consistent with Fredrickson's (1998) broaden-and-build theory of positive emotions. That is, one interpretation of these data is that positive emotions broaden people's attention and thinking and these broadened outlooks help people to discover and build consequential personal resources such as social support and enhanced feelings of satisfaction (Fredrickson, Cohn, Coffey, Pek, & Finkel, 2008).

Conclusions

People are strongly motivated to form and maintain strong and stable bonds and their health and well-being are closely tied to those relationships. However, research has also clearly demonstrated that interpersonal relationships present both incentives and threats. Thus, our view is that no model of social motivation is complete unless it simultaneously addresses the regulation of both rewards and punishments. However, although the approach and avoidance motivation distinction has a long and prolific history in several domains of human endeavors, it has not been applied to close relationships research consistently until recently. This is likely a lost opportunity because such a frame explicitly describes the regulation of the inherent incentives and threats in social relationships and may offer insights into understanding different patterns of functioning in relationships. For example, some unstable and unsatisfying close relationships are lacking incentives and other unstable and unsatisfying close relationships are ripe with threats. Approach and avoidance motives and goals are likely operating differently in these two types of relationships, and more importantly, any attempt to better these relationships needs to address both dimensions of the relationship.

Future Directions

Although there has been empirical progress on approach and avoidance social motivation, there are several directions in need of further study. First, the bulk of studies have focused on existing individual differences in social motives, but the situational influences on interpersonal goal pursuit have been largely unexamined. For example, the cues in the social environment that signal incentives or threats, and their impact on goal adoption in relationships and interpersonal interactions, are not well understood. Another future direction is examining whether people can change their motivation through effort. Given the benefits of approach goal pursuit in close relationships (e.g., Gable & Poore, 2008; Impett et al., 2008), examining whether it is possible for people with chronically low levels of approach goals or high levels of avoidance goals to learn to focus on incentives in relationships is important. In addition, part of the definition of close relationships is that they are nontransient, consisting of interactions that take place over some period of time. Thus, a future direction of research is to more carefully examine how motives and goals unfold over time in long-term relationships.

For example, the manner in which approach and avoidance goals operate in a new friendship may be different than the way they operate for two lifelong best friends. Similarly, it may be that the associations between relationship motivation and relationship quality may be different in married couples than in dating couples. Another benefit of studying motivation in relationships over time is an increased understanding of how progress on goals is evaluated over time, across repeated interactions with the same person. It is likely that definition of progress and rate of that progress are assessed differently for approach compared to avoidance goals (e.g., Carver & Scheier, 1990). For example, the man who has the goal of not saying anything embarrassing on a first date is only one faux pas away from failure the whole evening, regardless of how many funny, smart, and kind comments he makes. Finally, research on approach and avoidance goals in relationships has focused on explicit or consciously accessible goals, but work from several other researchers on the power that seemingly nonconscious goal pursuit has on behavior in close relationship is compelling (e.g., Anderson et al., 1996; Baldwin et al., 1990; Fitzsimons & Bargh, 2003; Scinta & Gable, 2007). Future studies need to examine nonconscious incentive- and threat-based motivation.

Note

1. For reviews of the approach and avoidance distinction in motivation, see Elliot (1999), Higgins (1998), and Schleirna (1959).

References

Anderson, S. M., Reznik, I., & Manzella, L. M. (1996). Eliciting facial affect, motivation, and expectancies in transference: Significant-other representations in social relations. *Journal of Personality and Social Psychology, 71*, 1108–1129.

Atkinson, J. W., Heyns, R. W., & Veroff, J. (1954). The effect of experimental arousal of the affiliation motive on thematic apperception. *Journal of Abnormal and Social Psychology, 49*(3), 405–410.

Baldwin, M. W., Carrell, S. E., & Lopez, D. F. (1990). Priming relationship schemas: My advisor and the pope are watching me from the back of my mind. *Journal of Experimental Social Psychology, 26*(5), 435–454.

Baron, K. G., Smith, T. W., Butner, J., Nealey-Moore, J., Hawkins, M. W., & Uchino, B. N. (2007). Hostility, anger, and marital adjustment: Concurrent and prospective associations with psychosocial vulnerability. *Journal of Behavioral Medicine, 30*(1), 1–10.

Baumeister, R. F., & Leary, M. R. (1995). The need to belong: Desire for interpersonal attachments as a fundamental human motivation. *Psychological Bulletin, 117*, 497–529.

Berkman, L. F., & Syme, S. L. (1979). Social networks, host-resistance, and mortality—9-year follow-up-study of alameda county residents. *American Journal of Epidemiology, 109*(2), 186–204.

Boyatzis, R. E. (1973). Affiliation motivation: A review and a new perspective. In D. C. McClelland & R. S. Steele (Eds.), *Human motivation: A book of readings.* Morristown, NJ: General Learning Press.

Bugental, D. B. (2000). Acquisition of the algorithms of social life: A domain-based approach. *Psychological Bulletin, 26*, 187–209.

Cacioppo, J. T., & Hawkley, L. C. (2009). Perceived social isolation and cognition. *Trends in Cognitive Sciences, 13*(10), 447–454.

Cacioppo, J. T., & Patrick, W. (2008). *Loneliness: Human nature and the need for social connection.* New York: W. W. Norton & Co.

Cacioppo, J. T., Hughes, M. E., Waite, L. J., Hawkley, L. C., & Thisted, R. A. (2006). Loneliness as a specific risk factor for depressive symptoms: Cross-sectional and longitudinal analyses. *Psychology and Aging, 21*(1), 140–151.

Cacioppo, J. T., Gardner, W. L., & Berntson, G. G. (1997). Beyond bipolar conceptualizations and measures: The case of attitudes and evaluative space. *Personality and Social Psychology Review, 1*(1), 3–25.

Cantor, N., & Malley, J. (1991). Life tasks, personal needs, and close relationships. In G. J. O. Fletcher & F. D. Fincham (Eds.), *Cognition in close relationships* (pp. 101–125). Hillsdale, NJ: Erlbaum.

Carver, C. S. (1996). Neuroendocrine perspectives on social attachment and love. *Psychoneuroendocrinology, 23*, 779–818.

Carver, C. S. (2001). Affect and the functional bases of behavior: On the dimensional structure of affective experience. *Personality and Social Psychology Review, 5*(4), 345–356.

Carver, C. S., & Scheier, M. F. (1990). Origins and functions of positive and negative affect: A control-process view. *Psychological Review, 97*(1), 19–35.

Carver, C. S., & White, T. L. (1994). Behavioral inhibitions, behavioral activation, and affective responses to impending reward and punishment: The BIS/BAS Scales. *Journal of Personality and Social Psychology, 67*(2), 319–333.

Cohen, S. (2005). The Pittsburgh Common Cold Studies: Psychosocial predictors of susceptibility to respiratory infectious illness. *International Journal of Behavioral Medicine, 12*, 123–131.

Cohen, S., & Willis, T. A. (1985). Stress, social support, and the buffering hypothesis. *Psychological Bulletin, 98*, 310–357.

Cutrona, C., Russell, D., & Rose, J. (1986). Social support and adaptation to stress by the elderly. *Psychology and Aging, 1*, 47–54.

Davila, J., Bradbury, T. N., Cohan, C. L., & Tochluk, S. (1997). Marital functioning and depressive symptoms: Evidence for a stress generation model. *Journal of Personality and Social Psychology, 73*(4), 849–861.

DeCharms, R. (1957). Affiliation motivation and productivity in small groups. *The Journal of Abnormal and Social Psychology, 55*(2), 222–226.

Deci, E. L., & Ryan, R. M. (1985). *Intrinsic motivation and self-determination in human behavior.* New York: Plenum.

Derryberry, D., & Reed, M. A. (1994). Temperament and attention: Orienting toward and away from positive and negative signals. *Journal of Personality and Social Psychology 66*(6), 1128–1139.

Dickerson, S. S., & Kemeny, M. E. (2004). Acute stressors and cortisol responses: A theoretical integration and synthesis of laboratory research. *Psychological Bulletin, 130*(30), 355–391.

Diener, E., & Biswas-Diener, R. (2008). *Happiness: Unlocking the mysteries of psychological wealth.* Malden, MA: Blackwell Publishing.

Downey, G., Feldman, S., & Ayduk, O. (2000). Rejection sensitivity and male violence in romantic relationships. *Personal Relationships, 7*, 45–61.

Dunkel-Schetter, C., & Bennett, T. L. (1990). Differentiating the cognitive and behavioral aspects of social support. In I. G. Sarason, B. R. Sarason, & G. R. Pierce (Eds.), *Social support: An interactional view* (pp. 267–296). New York: Wiley.

Durkheim, E. (1897/1951). *Suicide: A study in sociology.* (J. A. Spaulding & G. Simpson, Trans.). New York: The Free Press.

Eaker, E. D., Sullivan, L. M., Kelly-Hayes, M., D'Agostino, R. B., & Benjamin, E. J. (2007). Marital status, marital strain, and risk of coronary heart disease or total mortality: The Framingham offspring study. *Psychosomatic Medicine, 69*(6), 509–551.

Elliot, A. J. (1997). Integrating the "classic" and "contemporary" approaches to achievement motivation: A hierarchical model of approach and avoidance achievement motivation. In M. Maehr & P. Pintrich (Eds.), *Advances in motivation and achievement* (Vol. 10; pp. 243–279). Greenwich, CT: JAI Press.

Elliot, A. J. (1999). Approach and avoidance motivation and achievement goals. *Educational Psychologist, 34*, 149–169.

Elliot, A. J. (2006). A hierarchical model of approach and avoidance motivation. *Motivation and Emotion, 30*, 111–116.

Elliot, A. J. (2008). *Handbook of approach and avoidance motivation.* Mahwah, NJ: Lawrence Erlbaum Associates.

Elliot, A. J., Gable, S. L., & Mapes, R. R. (2006). Approach and avoidance motivation in the social domain. *Personality and Social Psychology Bulletin, 32*, 378–391

Elliot, A. J., & Sheldon, K. M. (1998). Avoidance personal goals and the personality-illness relationship. *Journal of Personality and Social Psychology, 75*(5), 1282–1299.

Emmons, R. A. (1986). Personal strivings: An approach to personality and subjective well-being. *Journal of Personality and Social Psychology, 51*, 1058–1068.

Epley, N., Akalis, S., Waytz, A., & Cacioppo, J. T. (2008). Creating social connection through inferential reproduction: Loneliness and perceived agency in gadgets, gods, and greyhounds. *Psychological Science, 19*(2), 114–120.

Epley, N., Waytz, A., Akalis, S., & Cacioppo, J. T. (2008). When we need a human: Motivational determinants of anthropomorphism. *Social Cognition, 26*(2), 143–155.

Fiske, A. P. (1992). The four elementary forms of sociality: Framework for a unified theory of social relations. *Psychological Review, 99*(4), 689–723.

Fitzsimons, G. M., & Bargh, J. A. (2003). Thinking of you: Nonconscious pursuit of interpersonal goals associated with relationship partners. *Journal of Personality and Social Psychology, 84*(1), 148–164.

Fredrickson, B. L. (1998). What good are positive emotions? *Review of General Psychology, 2*, 300–319.

Fredrickson, B. L., Cohn, M. A., Coffey, K. A., Pek, J., & Finkel, S. M. (2008). Open hearts build lives: Positive emotions, induced through loving-kindness mediation, build consequential personal resources. *Journal of Personality and Social Psychology, 95*, 1045–1062.

Gable, S. L. (2000). *Appetitive and aversive social motivation*. Unpublished Ph.D. dissertation, University of Rochester, Rochester, NY.

Gable, S. L. (2006). Approach and avoidance social motives and goals. *Journal of Personality, 71*, 175–222.

Gable, S. L., & Poore, J. (2008). Which thoughts count? Algorithms for evaluating satisfaction in relationships. *Psychological Science, 19*, 1030–1036

Gable, S. L., Reis, H. T., & Elliot, A. J. (2000). Behavioral activation and inhibition in everyday life. *Journal of Personality and Social Psychology, 78*, 1135–1149.

Gable, S. L., Reis, H. T., & Elliot, A. J. (2003). Evidence for bivariate systems: An empirical test of appetition and aversion across domains. *Journal of Research in Personality, 37*, 349–372.

Gray, J. A. (1970). The psychophysiological basis of introversion-extraversion. *Behaviour Research & Therapy, 8*(3), 249–266.

Gray, J. A. (1987). *The psychology of fear and stress* (2nd ed.). New York: Cambridge University Press.

Gray, J. A. (1990). Brain systems that mediate both emotion and cognition. *Cognition and Emotion, 4*, 269–288.

Harmon-Jones, E., & Allen, J. J. B. (1997). Behavioral activation sensitivity and resting frontal EEG asymmetry: Covariation of putative indicators related to risk for mood disorders. *Journal of Abnormal Psychology, 106*, 159–163.

Hawkley, L. C., Masi, C. M., Berry, J. D., & Cacioppo, J. T. (2006). Loneliness is a unique predictor of age-related differences in systolic blood pressure. *Psychology and Aging, 21*(1), 152–164.

Higgins, E. T. (1998). Promotion and prevention: Regulatory focus as a motivational principle. *Advances in Experimental Social Psychology, 30*, 1–46.

Higgins, E. T., Shah, J., & Friedman, R. (1997). Emotional responses to goal attainment: Strength of regulatory focus as moderator. *Journal of Personality and Social Psychology, 72*(3), 515–525.

Higgins, E. T., & Tykocinski, O. (1992). Self-discrepancies and biographical memory: Personality and cognition at the level of psychological situation. *Personality and Social Psychology Bulletin, 18*(5), 527–535.

House, J. S., Landis, K. R. & Umberson, D. (1988). Social relationships and health. *Science, 241*, 540–545.

Impett, E., Gable, S. L. Peplau, L. A. (2005). Giving up and giving in: The costs and benefits of daily sacrifice in intimate relationships. *Journal of Personality and Social Psychology, 89*, 327–344.

Impett, E. A., Gordon, A. M., Kogan, A., Oveis, C., Gable, S. L., & Keltner, D. (2010) Approaching happiness: Daily and long-term consequences of approach and avoidance goals in romantic relationships. *Journal of Personality and Social Psychology, 99*, 948–963.

Impett, E. A., Gordon, A. M., & Strachman, A. (2008). Attachment and daily sexual goals: A study of dating couples. *Personal Relationships, 15*(3), 375–390.

Impett, E., Strachman, A., Finkel, E. & Gable, S. L. (2008). Maintaining sexual desire in intimate relationships: The importance of approach goals. *Journal of Personality and Social Psychology, 94*, 808–823.

Joiner, T. E., Jr. (1997). Shyness and low social support as interactive diatheses, with loneliness as mediator: Testing an interpersonal-personality view of vulnerability to depressive symptoms. *Journal of Abnormal Psychology, 106*(3), 386–394.

Kasser, T., & Ryan, R. M. (1996). Further examining the American dream: Differential correlates of intrinsic and extrinsic goals. *Personality and Social Psychology Bulletin 22*, 80–87.

Keltner, D., & Lerner, J. S. (2009) Emotion. In D. Gilbert, S. Fiske, & G. Lindsey (Eds.), *The handbook of social psychology* (5th ed., pp 312–347). New York: McGraw Hill.

Keyes, C. L. M. (1998). Social well-being. *Social Psychology Quarterly, 61*, 121–140.

Kiecolt-Glaser, J. K. (1999). Stress, personal relationships, and immune function: Health implications. *Brain, Behavior and Immunity, 13*(1), 61–72.

Kiecolt-Glaser J. K., Gouin J. P., & Hantsoo L. (2010). Close relationships, inflammation, and health. *Neuroscience Biobehavioral Review, 35*(1), 33–38.

Klinger, E. (1977). *Meaning and void: Inner experience and the incentives in people's lives*. Minneapolis: University of Minnesota Press.

Kunda, Z. (1990). The case for motivated reasoning. *Psychological Bulletin, 108*, 480–498.

Lakey, B., & Cassady, R B. (1990). Cognitive processes in perceived social support. *Journal of Personality and Social Psychology, 59*, 331–343.

Larsen, R. J., & Ketelaar, T. (1991). Personality and susceptibility to positive and negative emotional states. *Journal of Personality and Social Psychology, 61*, 132–140.

Laurenceau, J., Kleinman, B. M., Kaczynski, K. J., & Carver, C. S. (2010). Assessment of relationship-specific incentive and threat sensitivities: Predicting satisfaction and affect in adult intimate relationships. *Psychological Assessment, 22*(2), 407–419.

Laurenceau, J., Troy, A. B., & Carver, C. S. (2005). Two distinct emotional experiences in romantic relationships: Effects of perceptions regarding approach of intimacy and avoidance of conflict. *Personality and Social Psychology Bulletin, 31*(8), 1123–1133.

Maner, J. K., Kenrick, D. T., Becker, D. V., Robertson, T., Hofer, B., Neuberg, S. L.,...Schaller, M. (2005). Functional projection: How fundamental social motives can bias interpersonal perception. *Journal of Personality and Social Psychology*, *88*, 63–78.

McAdams, D. P. (1982). Intimacy motivation. In A. J. Stewart (Ed.), *Motivation and society* (pp. 133–171). San Francisco, CA: Jossey-Bass Publishers.

McAdams, D. P., & Constantian, C. A. (1983). Intimacy and affiliation motives in daily living: An experience sampling analysis. *Journal of Personality and Social Psychology*, *45*, 851–861.

McAdams, D. P., Healy, S., & Krause, S. (1984). Social motives and patterns of friendship. *Journal of Personality and Social Psychology*, *47*, 828–838.

McDade, T. W., Hawkley, L. C., & Cacioppo, J. T. (2006). Psychosocial and behavioral predictors of inflammation in middle-aged and older adults: The Chicago health, aging, and social relations study. *Psychosomatic Medicine*, *68*(3), 376–381.

Mehrabian, A. (1976). Questionnaire measures of affiliative tendency and sensitivity to rejection. *Psychological Reports*, *38*, 199–209.

Mehrabian, A., & Ksionzky, S. (1974). *A theory of affiliation*. Lexington, MA: D.C. Heath.

Mikulincer, M. (1998). Attachment working models and the sense of trust: An exploration of interaction goals and affect regulation. *Journal of Personality and Social Psychology*, *74*, 1209–1224.

Miller, N. E. (1959). Liberalization of basic S-R concepts: Extensions to conflict behavior, motivation, and social learning. In S. Koch (Ed.). *Psychology: A study of science, Study 1* (pp. 198–292). New York: McGraw-Hill.

Miller, N. E. (1961). Learning and performance motivated by direct stimulation of the brain. In D. E. Sheer (Ed.), *Electrical stimulation of the brain* (pp. 387–396). Austin, TX: University of Texas Press.

Morgan, Ch. D., & Murray, H. A. (1935). A method for investigating fantasies: The Thematic Apperception Test. *Archives of Neurology and Psychiatry*, *34*, 289–306.

Murray, H. A. (1938). *Explorations in personality*. New York: Oxford University Press.

Neuberg, S. L. (1996). Expectancy influences in social interaction: The moderating role of social goals. In P. M. Gollwitzer & J. A. Bargh (Eds.), *The psychology of action: Linking cognition and motivation to behavior* (pp. 529–552). New York: Guilford Press.

Pavlov, I. (1927). *Conditioned reflexes: An investigation into the physiological activity of the cortex* (G. Anrep, Trans.). New York: Dover.

Perlman, D., & Peplau, L. A. (1981). Toward a social psychology of loneliness. In S. Duck & R. Gilmour (Eds.), *Personal relationships 3: Personal relationships in disorder* (pp. 31–55). London: Academic Press.

Reis, H. T., Collins, W. A., & Berscheid, E. (2000). The relationship context of human behavior and development. *Psychological Bulletin*, *126*(6), 844–872.

Ryff, C. D. (1995). Psychological well-being in adult life. *Current Directions in Psychological Science*, *4*, 99–103.

Rusbult, C. E., Kumashiro, M., Kubacka, K. E., & Finkel, E. J. (2009). "The part of me that you bring out": Ideal similarity and the Michelangelo phenomenon. *Journal of Personality and Social Psychology*, *96*(1), 61–82.

Sanderson, C. A., & Cantor, N. (1997). Creating satisfaction in steady dating relationships: The role of personal goals and situational affordances. *Journal of Personality and Social Psychology*, *73*(6), 1424–1433.

Sanderson, C. A., & Cantor, N. (2001). The association of intimacy goals and marital satisfaction: A test of four mediational hypotheses. *Personality and Social Psychology Bulletin*, *27*(12), 1567–1577.

Sanderson, C. A., Rahm, K. B., & Beigbeder, S. A. (2005). The link between the pursuit of intimacy goals and satisfaction in close same-sex friendships: An examination of the underlying processes. *Journal of Social and Personal Relationships*, *22*(1), 75–98.

Schneirla, T. C. (1959). An evolutionary and developmental theory of biphasic processes underlying approach and withdrawal. *Nebraska Symposium on Motivation* (Vol. 7, pp. 1–43). Lincoln, Nebraska: University of Nebraska Press.

Scinta, A., & Gable, S. L. (2007). Automatic and self-reported attitudes in romantic relationships. *Personality and Social Psychology Bulletin*, *33*(7), 1008–1022.

Shah, J. Y. (2003). The motivational looking glass: How significant others implicitly affect goal appraisals. *Journal of Personality and Social Psychology*, *85*, 424–439.

Shipley, T. E., & Veroff, J. (1952). A projective measure of need for affiliation. *Journal of Experimental Psychology*, *43*, 349–356.

Sobotka, S. S., Davidson, R. J., & Senulis, J. A. (1992). Anterior brain electrical asymmetries in response to reward and punishment. *Electroencephalography and Clinical Neurophysiology*, *83*, 236–247.

Strachman, A., & Gable, S. L. (2006). What you want (and don't want) affects what you see (and don't see): Avoidance social goals and social events. *Personality and Social Psychology Bulletin*, *32*, 1446–1458.

Uchino, B. N., Cacioppo, J. T., & Kiecolt-Glaser, J. K. (1996). The relationship between social support and physiological processes: A review with emphasis on underlying mechanisms and implications for health. *Psychological Bulletin*, *119*, 488–531

Updegraff, J. A., Gable, S. L., & Taylor, S. E. (2004). What makes experiences satisfying? The interaction of approach-avoidance motivations and emotions in well-being. *Journal of Personality and Social Psychology*, *86*, 496–504.

Veroff, J., Douvan, E., & Kulka, R. A. (1981). *Mental health in America: Patterns of help-seeking from 1957 to 1976*. New York: Basic Books.

Whisman, M. A. (2001). Marital adjustment and outcome following treatments for depression. *Journal of Consulting and Clinical Psychology*, *69*(1), 125–129.

Whisman, M. A., Uebelacker, L. A., & Settles, T. D. (2010). Martial distress and the metabolic syndrome: Linking social functioning with physical health. *Journal of Family Psychology*, *24*(3), 367–370.

Wilcox, V. L., Kasl, S. V., & Berkman, L. F. (1994). Social support and physical disability in older people after hospitalization: A prospective study. *Health Psychology*, *13*(2), 170–179.

Evolutionary and Biological Perspectives

Neuroscience and Human Motivation

Johnmarshall Reeve *and* Woogul Lee

Abstract

Recognizing the potential for interdisciplinary research in motivational neuroscience, the goal of the present chapter is to show the relevance of neuroscience research to human motivation researchers and to suggest ways to expand their programs of research, methodological options, and theoretical conceptualizations of the motivational constructs with which they work. To illustrate the neural bases of human motivation, we highlight 15 key motivation-relevant brain structures, identify the neural core of reward-based motivated action, and discuss a range of brain-generated motivational states that extend from those that are relatively automatic and stimulus dependent (e.g., pleasure from taste) to those that are relatively intentional and context sensitive (e.g., goals). We then examine the following 10 well-researched concepts from the human motivation literature to suggest how each might be enriched through neuroscientific investigation: agency, volition, value, intrinsic motivation, extrinsic motivation, flow, expectancy, self-efficacy, self-regulation, and goals. We conclude with suggestions for future research.

Key Words: motivation, neuroscience, striatum, reward, dopamine, prefrontal cortex

Introduction

The "and" in the chapter title is important, as it reflects the contemporary view that human motivation study and neuroscience are two different fields. That is, the people who study human motivation, the journals they publish in, and the empirical methods they rely on are not generally populated by a neuroscience focus, though these same researchers (and journals) recognize the potential contribution of neuroscience to human motivation study. Neuroscientists often study the same content—the same motivational constructs, though they routinely conceptualize these motivational constructs more narrowly. Neuroscientists also tend to study basic, stimulus-driven motivations, such as hunger, thirst, pleasure and reward, though more complex motivations (e.g., volition, self-regulation) are also investigated. Overall, equal measures of optimism and

skepticism are in the air when human motivation researchers sit down at the table with neuroscientists to discuss collaborations and points of integration.

A decade ago, Richard Mayer (1998) characterized the relationship between neuroscience and his field—educational psychology—through the imagery of dead-end, one-way, and two-way streets. He characterized (and lamented) the then-present relation between neuroscience and his field as an intellectual landscape characterized by dead-end streets in which the two fields of study had little in common and contributed little to the enrichment of the other. He also observed (and again lamented) an intellectual landscape of one-way streets in which neuroscience research was unidirectionally applied to educational psychology. For instance, neuroscientists identified the limits of hippocampal-based short-term memory (e.g., cognitive overload), and educational psychologists revised their theories of learning and their recommendations for the design of instruction accordingly (e.g., Paas, Tuovinen, Tabbers, & Van Gerven, 2003).

The metaphor Mayer offered to enrich interdisciplinary activity was that of a two-way street. In this scenario, neuroscience study influences motivation research, while motivation study influences neuroscience research. Such a two-way relationship is only possible with the emergence and contributions of interdisciplinary researchers. Interdisciplinary researchers are those who feel free and able to traverse not only the landscape of their home field of study but also the landscape of the allied field. Several examples of such successful interdisciplinary research have emerged, including cognitive neuroscience (Gazzaniga, Ivry, & Mangun, 2008), affective neuroscience (Davidson & Sutton, 1995), social neuroscience (Decety & Cacioppo, 2010), and neuroeconomics (Loewenstein, Rick, & Cohen, 2008).

The goal of the present chapter is to embrace this two-way street imagery and, in doing so, embrace the potential value in interdisciplinary motivational

neuroscience. If interdisciplinary motivational neuroscientists are to become a critical mass of scholars, researchers in both fields will need to consider the merits of reengineering these otherwise one-way and dead-end streets into two-way streets of information, methodology, and theory development. To facilitate such progress in the present chapter, we first overview the neuroscience research that is broadly relevant to probably all contemporary human motivation study as we illuminate the biological substrates of human motivation. We then address conceptual points of convergence and divergence between neuroscience and human motivation study across the following 10 frequently studied motivational constructs: agency, volition, value, intrinsic motivation, extrinsic motivation, flow, expectancy, self-efficacy, self-regulation, and goals.

Any new field of study (e.g., motivational neuroscience) necessarily begins with description and taxonomy. In that spirit, Figure 21.1 lists 15 key brain structures identified by neuroscience research as motivation relevant and illustrates the anatomic location for each. Five structures reside within the neocortex: prefrontal cortex, ventromedial prefrontal cortex, dorsolateral

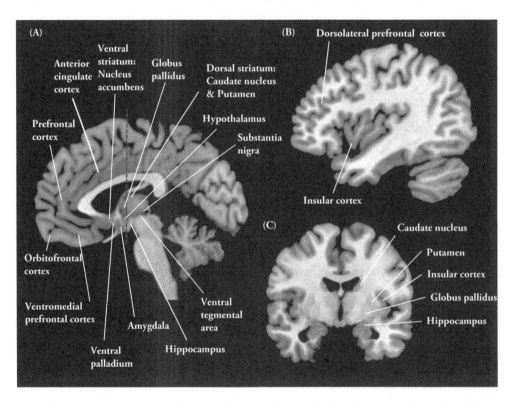

Fig. 21.1. Anatomic location of 15 key motivation-relevant brain structures. (*A*) A medial sagittal section of the brain. The dotted line represents the point that a coronal section of the brain (*C*) is acquired. (*B*) A lateral sagittal section of the brain.

prefrontal cortex, orbitofrontal cortex, and anterior cingulate cortex. Six structures reside with the basal ganglia: dorsal striatum—caudate nucleus and putamen, ventral striatum—nucleus accumbens, globus pallidus, ventral tegmental area, substantia nigra, and ventral palladium. And four structures reside within the limbic system: amygdala, hypothalamus, hippocampus, and insular cortex. It is with these 15 brain structures that we will illustrate the neural bases of human motivation.

When defined in the context of behavioral science, motivation concerns the study of all those processes that give behavior its energy and direction (Reeve, 2009). In neuroscience, motivation is generally conceptualized as energy for behaviors related to obtaining rewarding stimuli or situations (Mogenson, Jones, & Yim, 1980; Robbins & Everitt, 1996). That which energizes behavior is subscribed to a rather narrow set of neural processes, such as those in the mesolimbic dopamine system. While these basic neural processes energize behavior, the sources that activate these basic neural processes are many (e.g., natural rewards, social rewards; Berridge, 2004; Berridge & Robinson, 2003; Wise, 2004). In the next section, we summarize the basic subcortical neural core that energizes reward-related action. Once done, we overview the more specific types of motivation that activate these basic subcortical neural processes.

Neural Core of Reward-Based Motivated Action

From a biological perspective, the role of reward in motivation is fundamental. It is fundamental to survival, to learning, to well-being, and to the generation of goal-directed effort (Schultz, 2000). The energization or generation of goal-directed effort (motivated action) follows from and is dependent on first extracting reward-related information from environmental objects, events, and circumstances, and this reward-related information consists largely of the release of the neurotransmitter dopamine (Berridge & Kringelbach, 2008).[1] The reward-related information that people extract from their surroundings includes the presence and availability of reward, the value of the available reward, the predictability of the reward, and the costs associated with trying to obtain that reward.

In addition, repeated experiences with objects and events allow people to form mental representations in which these environmental stimuli come to signal reward information in a predictive fashion. In this way, past reward-related information helps establish an anticipatory motivational value of objects and events. Reward receipt and reward expectation both involve neural activations that typically give rise to pleasant feelings and a good mood and, hence, to the subjective experiences of pleasure and positive affect (at least in humans). This same reward-related information also serves as the basis of future goals, which are mental representations of sought-after (reward-related) environmental events. In addition, when the reward values of multiple environmental events are compared, people show preferences (in terms of choice and the amount of effort expended) for different objects and events. Hence, biologically experienced reward serves as the basis not only for reward but for the additional motivational constructs of value, expectancy, pleasure/affect, goal, and preference.

The neural substrates of this dopaminergic family of reward-based motivational states appear in Figure 21.2. The neural core of goal-directed motivated action is the pathway from the motivation-generating dopamine system to the movement-preparation and behavior-generating supplementary motor area and premotor cortex (see right side of Fig. 21.2). Within the phrase "motivated action," the *Dopamine system* box represents the fundamental core of "motivated" while the *Substantia nigra, globus pallidus* box represents the fundamental core of "action." Feeding into this basic reward processing core are a number of brain areas that process reward information by releasing dopamine, such as responsiveness to natural rewards (hypothalamus), the particular characteristics of any one particular reward in the limbic regions (e.g., amygdala), and the interoceptive information of rewards in the limbic-related regions (e.g., insular cortex) as well as responsiveness to the values (and relative values) of various rewards (orbitofrontal cortex), the mental representation of reward as a goal object (dorsolateral prefrontal cortex), and executive control over goal-directed action (anterior cingulate cortex). In addition, as depicted in the boldface double-sided arrow on the left-hand side of the figure, reciprocal relations connect the limbic regions with the prefrontal cortex as limbic regions generally feed-forward projections into the prefrontal cortex while prefrontal regions generally feed-back projections to the various limbic regions. Lastly, as depicted in the six double-sided arrows in the center of the figure, reciprocal relations connect the dopamine system with the limbic regions and prefrontal cortex.

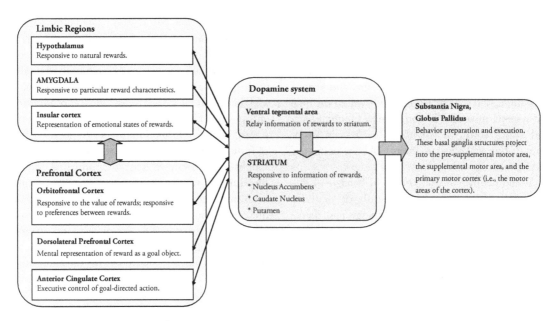

Fig. 21.2. Neural core of reward-based motivated action.

Sources of Reward-Based Motivation

It is important to understand the nature of various biological sources of motivation (depicted on the left-hand side of Fig. 21.2) because different sources of motivation lead to different types of motivation. For instance, some sources of motivation are implicit and objective (e.g., thirst, hunger), while other sources are more conscious and cognitive (e.g., ultimate goals). As we will see, the types of motivation induced by relatively implicit and objective sources tend to generate rather automatic motivational states, whereas the types of motivation induced by more conscious and cognitive sources tend to be rather rational motivational states. Accordingly, to classify and to understand the different types of biologically generated motivational states, we need to think carefully about *(1)* what the sources of the motivational state are, *(2)* how much the source of the motivational state is implicit and objective (versus explicit and cognitive), and *(3)* how much the various sources of motivation conflict when sources of motivation are divergent. Based on these considerations, we present four sections to illustrate a range of brain-generated motivational states that extend from those that are largely subcortical, relatively automatic, and stimulus dependent (e.g., pleasure from taste) to those that are largely cortical, intentional, and context sensitive (e.g., personal strivings).

Relatively Automatic Motivational States

Neuroscientific approaches to motivation do a particularly good job of explaining relatively automatic homeostatic motivational processes that are driven by ingestibles (or consumables), such as food and water. Ingested substances are natural rewards (e.g., food, water) that play a key role in energizing consumatory behaviors that then lead to changes in homeostatic and hedonic motivational states. These motivational states are closely monitored and regulated by subcortical limbic structures (Saper, Chou, & Elmquist, 2002), as the hypothalamus plays an important role in relatively automatic consumatory behavior while the dopamine-based mesolimbic system plays an important role in learned instrumental behaviors. Homeostatic motivational states such as hunger (appetite) and satiety arise rather automatically (and reliably) from cooperative networks distributed throughout the body, including those in the brain (hypothalamus, mesolimbic system) but also those in the endocrine/hormonal and autonomic systems (Powley, 2009).

Thirst is a brain-generated motivational state that arises when people physiologically need to ingest water to maintain adequate fluid balance throughout the body. Reduced water generates thirst—the urge to ingest water, and the body's remarkable constancy of intracellular and extracellular water is regulated by neural, hormonal/endocrine, and behavioral mechanisms (McKinley, 2009). Though hypothalamic-based thirst contributes to water intake (drinking) and to the involuntary regulation of water conservation (e.g., hormone release, kidney function), most human beverage consumption is determined by the reward aspects of the ingested fluid, including those related to taste, odor, temperature, alcohol, caffeine, and social consequences (Booth, 1991). Thus, brain structures such as the orbitofrontal cortex and amygdala respond to the rewarding properties of fluid intake (Rolls, 2000), and these brain structures then feed this reward-related information into the striatum that underlies the dopamine reward system that energizes fluid intake (Wise, 2002), as depicted in Figure 21.2. Recognizing the important motivational role of the rewarding properties of ingestibles (e.g., sweet taste) expands the neural bases of motivation from hypothalamic-centric homeostatic motivational states to include stimulus-driven, dopamine-centric motivational states (i.e., incentive motivation).

Motivational States Based on Associative Learning (Close to Automatic)

Environmental incentives are those we tend to approach and return to after experiencing their rewarding properties. Incentives have rewarding properties and promote approach-oriented behavior because they send information through the five senses that reach the mesolimbic dopamine-based reward circuitry to *(1)* activate those reward pathways (e.g., Fig. 21.2), *(2)* activate those reward pathways powerfully (above threshold), *(3)* activate those reward pathways with little delay in reinforcement (so to yield a high degree of reward effectiveness), and *(4)* produce rewarding effects that decay rapidly (half-second after onset) (Wise, 2002). Some incentive values are universal or objective, such as a sweet taste or a toxic smell. Other incentive values (e.g., color preference) are learned subjectively or circumstantially. The more an incentive value is universal or objective, the more it will be associated with motivational states that are automatic.

The learning (remembering, conditioning) of the incentive value of environmental events takes place in several brain areas. The amygdala evaluates a stimulus as associated with either reward or punishment, signals that it is potentially important (or not), and evaluates the stimulus as unpredicted or not (Whalen, 1999, 2007). In this way, amygdala activity builds associative knowledge about a stimulus's motivational and emotional significance (Baxter et al., 2000; Baxter & Murray, 2002; Schoenbaum, Chiba, & Gallagher, 1999). This information is mainly stored in the hippocampus and insular cortex, though it is also stored in cortical regions as well, including the orbitofrontal cortex. The more automatic or simple the incentive-based information is, the more likely it is that it will be stored subcortically in the limbic system or in the limbic-related regions (e.g., insular cortex); the more cognitive and less automated the incentive-based information is, the more likely it is that it will be stored cortically in the orbitofrontal cortex. When instrumental behaviors are needed, these various brain regions deliver their stored incentive value information to the mesolimbic dopamine system, which then energizes consumatory motivated action (when intense enough to exceed a threshold of response). In addition, the nucleus accumbens (within the ventral striatum) is active in the experience of rewarding and pleasurable feelings, as the presentation of pleasant images, pleasant tastes, and many addictive drugs (e.g., opiates, cocaine, amphetamine) are dopamine releasers in the nucleus accumbens (Sabatinelli et al., 2007; Wise, 2002).

To explain how associative learning processes occur, some researchers parse reward information into three psychological components—learning, affect (emotion), and motivation (Berridge, 2004; Berridge & Robinson, 2003). Learning has two forms—associative and cognitive. Associative learning refers to the relatively automatic forms of incentive learning, while cognitive refers to the relatively more complex and less automatic learning related to activities in the cortex (e.g., orbitofrontal cortex). Affect also has two forms: liking and conscious pleasure. Liking is one's implicit (nonconscious), hedonic reaction to an objective environmental stimulus (e.g., sweet taste) that arises from nondopamine mesolimbic activity (e.g., opioid neurotransmission). Conscious pleasure is a more general form of liking that involves awareness and arises from cortical activity. Motivation too has two forms—wanting which is implicit (nonconscious) and objective, and wanting that is cognitive, conscious, and goal directed.

The affective distinction between implicit liking and explicit pleasure and the motivational distinction between implicit desire and explicit goal striving is important for several reasons. First, affect and motivation can diverge. Liking and wanting typically converge in natural situations (i.e., we want and like the same thing), but they can diverge, as when a medicine smells or tastes disgusting (no liking) yet is wanted for health reasons (cognitive wanting) or when one craves an addictive drug (implicit wanting) that brings little or no pleasure (conscious liking). Second, these two forms of liking and these two forms of wanting mean that incentive values will sometimes be conflicting in naturally occurring behavior (e.g., should I watch the television show I like or should I go to a social event to meet potential new friends?). In these situations, people need to resolve these motivational conflicts using higher order cognitive, emotional, and motivational processes (Litman, 2005).

Implicit Motivational States Involved in Decision Making and Action

Subcortical (limbic system) processing of environmental events plays an important role in decision making and action. In daily life, few situations involve only a single stimulus, as decision making in the face of diverging and conflicting incentive values is the norm (two restaurants, two social events, 30 different chapters in this Handbook). When people make decisions, they rely on a great deal on both cognitive processes and emotional processes, even to the point that it is difficult to separate out cognitive activity from emotional activity, as the two are so neurally intertwined that it makes little sense to treat them as separate entities during decision making. In this section, we review how nonconscious processing creates feelings (e.g., affect, intuition) that bias what memory content emerges into conscious awareness that is then acted on in terms of decision making and action. Such affectively based decision making can be demonstrated through the dopamine hypothesis of positive affect, priming, and the somatic marker hypothesis.

DOPAMINE HYPOTHESIS OF POSITIVE AFFECT

Positive affect influences decision making and problem solving such that people who feel good, compared to people in a neutral mood, are more likely to recall positive material from memory, and this accessibility has been shown to promote flexibility in thinking, creative problem solving, efficiency and thoroughness in decision making, improved thinking on complex tasks, variety seeking, enhanced intrinsic motivation, and a greater willingness to help (Isen, 1987, 2003). The dopamine hypothesis of positive affect (Ashby, Isen, & Turken, 1999) proposes that the presence of mild positive feelings systemically affects cognitive processes and that it is increased dopamine in certain brain regions that produces the mild positive feelings and facilitating effects on cognition. For instance, the receipt of a small unexpected positive event (unexpected gift,

humor, task success) activates dopamine neurons in the ventral tegmental area, which sends dopamine projections into many cortical areas, including (a) the prefrontal cortex, which enriches working memory, openness to information, willingness to explore, creative problem solving, and the integration of ideas; and (b) the anterior cingulate cortex, which increases attention, flexible thinking, switching easily among alternative objects or action plans, and the sort of enhanced perspective taking that leads to prosocial behaviors such as cooperativeness, generosity, social responsibility, and improved negotiating skills (Ashby et al., 1999).

Crucially, the dopamine hypothesis of positive affect proposes that it is only mild, everyday positive feelings—the type of positive affect that remains outside of conscious attention—that produces these facilitating effects on decision making, problem solving, creativity, and prosocial behavior (Isen, 2003). If the dopamine increase is relatively large or if the person is made aware of the positive affect state (e.g., "My, aren't we in a good mood today?"), then research shows that the facilitating effect is lost (Isen, 1987). The dopamine hypothesis, however, seems to contradict the wanting versus liking distinction introduced in the previous section, as liking is not dopamine based. The difference between the two hypotheses might suggest that the positive affect (liking) is epiphenomenal and that it is only the dopamine increase (not the positive affect experience per se) that facilitates cognitive processes and prosocial behavior.

PRIMING

Priming is the procedure that evokes an implicit response from an individual upon exposure to a stimulus that is outside his or her conscious awareness. While priming occurs outside of the person's conscious awareness, the prime itself can be delivered unconsciously or consciously. An example of an unconsciously delivered prime might be a word that is flashed so briefly on a computer screen (e.g., 30 msec) that it is not recognized, though it still produces an implicit effect. An example of a consciously delivered prime might occur as the person is asked to judge if a dot appears above or below a word, a word whose content induces an implicit effect (e.g., the words "good" or "pleasant" might produce implicit positive feelings).

Primes that activate a mental representation of a behavior (outside the person's awareness) prepare people to enact behaviors consistent with that mental representation. For instance, the smell of a cleaning solution, the site of a briefcase, and viewing a library painting lead people to engage in cleaning behavior, competitive behavior, and hushed conversation, compared to the absence of these primes, though participants report being unaware of the aroma, briefcase, or painting (Aarts & Dijksterhuis, 2003; Holland, Hendriks, & Aarts, 2005; Kay, Wheeler, Bargh, & Ross, 2004). These findings show that nonconscious primes prepare (i.e., motivate) action.

Primes also influence a wide range of motivations. Primes have been shown to activate implicit motives such as power and affiliation (Schultheiss, 2008), outcome expectancies (Custers, Aarts, Oikawa, & Elliot, 2009), autonomous motivations (Hodgins, Yacko, & Gottlieb, 2006), and so forth. For instance, students who were asked to solve language puzzles populated by achievement-related words ("win") outperformed and outpersisted students who were asked to solve the same language puzzles populated by neutral words when both groups worked on a second task unrelated to the language-puzzle task (Bargh et al., 2001). This means that the nonconscious activation of the motivational state promotes behavioral activation if the motivational state itself is associated with positive valence (Aarts, Custers, & Marien, 2008; Custers & Aarts, 2005). That is, primes facilitate motivated action by activating mental representations of action (i.e., the subliminal presentation of the words "exert" and "vigorous"), implicit motivational states, and positive affect; furthermore, these effects occur even though participants are unaware of the presentation of the primes.

SOMATIC MARKER HYPOTHESIS

Another hypothesis about the role of feelings in decision making is the somatic marker hypothesis (Bechara & Damasio, 2005; Bechara, Damasio, & Damasio, 2000). In this hypothesis, the key brain structure is the insular cortex (Singer, Critchley, & Preuschoff, 2009). The insula (insular cortex) processes interoceptive (visceral, homeostatic) information about the state of one's body and allows the person to construct a consciously aware representation of how he or she feels (Craig, 2009; Wicker et al., 2003). Furthermore, insula activity seems to be involved in practically all subjective feelings (Craig, 2009). In the anterior insula, people consolidate this feeling-state information with social-contextual information about the task they are involved in and the people around them to form a basis of the conscious experience (subjective awareness) of emotion or affect (Craig, 2002, 2008). The insular also

processes and learns about risk and uncertainty. This is important because the role of the insula seems to be to integrate current feeling, a risk prediction forecast (that has a degree of uncertainty) that arises from the anticipation or consideration of the future outcomes of one's actions, and contextual information to produce a global feeling state that guides decision making (Singer et al., 2009).

The somatic marker hypothesis was originally based on observations that patients with ventromedial prefrontal cortex lesions commonly showed emotional impairments and made destructive social decisions, even though their cognitive capacities were unaffected. Based on these clinical observations, researchers proposed that emotional processes (bodily states and feelings in this case) played an important and constructive role in the decision-making process (Damasio, 1994, 1996). The body's primary inducer of bodily states is the amygdala, and the ventromedial prefrontal cortex works as a secondary inducer of bodily states (e.g., pain, heartbeat awareness, rhythm, affiliation) (Baxter & Murray, 2002; Baxter et al., 2000; Schoenbaum et al., 1999). As incentive-related events (those associated with motivational and emotional significance for the person) change the body, the insula integrates these changes into a conscious, subjective emotional experience (much in the spirit of the James-Lange theory of emotion; James, 1894).

Neural Bases of Rational Motivational States in Decision Making and Action

Several regions in the prefrontal cortex exert executive or cognitive control over decision making and action. For instance, the medial prefrontal cortex (both dorsal and ventral), inferior frontal cortex, dorsal section of the anterior cingulate cortex, and the dorsolateral prefrontal cortex all work for cognitive control of decision making and action (Davidson & Irwin, 1999; Ochsner & Gross, 2005; Ridderinkhof, van den Wildenberg, Segalowitz, & Carter, 2004). As a case in point, the dorsolateral prefrontal cortex activations occur when one pursues a long-term reward in favor of a shorter term, striatum-based reward (McClure, Laibson, Loewenstein, & Cohen, 2004).

In understanding the cognitive control over decision making and action, one needs to recognize the massive cortical feedback that occurs throughout the brain. For instance, the amygdala not only processes the emotional significance of sensory information and sends that information to the prefrontal cortex (feed-forward), but the amygdala also receives information from the prefrontal cortex (Freese & Amaral, 2005). Similar (and massive) feedback flows of information occur throughout cortical and subcortical brain regions (as depicted by the large double-sided arrow between them in Fig. 21.2). This prefrontal cortex flow of feedback information adds information about the environmental context and conscious intentions into the neural core depicted on the right-hand side of Figure 21.2. Furthermore, this prefrontal lobe information comes in cycles of continuous information and, according to some estimates, these top-down feedback projections likely exceed the number of bottom-up feed-forward projections, at least with adults (Salin & Bullier, 1995). The result is an integrated feed-forward and feedback system in which basic sensory information feeds-forward rather automatically and rapidly, while top-down deliberative information (intentions, goals), which is affected and biased by the aforementioned feed-forward information, contributes regulatory and intentional processing (Cunningham & Zelazo, 2007; Miller & Cohen, 2001).

Motivationally relevant brain structures are clearly reactive and responsive to environmental events. In this sense, motivation "happens" to the person as an adaptive reaction to these environmental events. It is also true, however, that brain activity is proactive in that people regularly anticipate the future (Bar, 2007). According to Bar, people are not so much passively waiting to be activated by environmental events as they are continuously busy generating predictions about the future. These predictions have motivational and emotional implications and therefore focus attention on the neural bases of proactive and purposive motivational states.

At one extreme, the brain is involved in proximal predictions, such as expecting to receive a shot upon walking in the doctor's office. But, at another extreme, the brain is involved in distal predictions, as the person anticipates experiences, plans far ahead, and uses memory-guided simulations to mentally travel into the future (Szpunar, Watson, & McDermott, 2007; Addis, Wong, & Schacter, 2007). The important point is that people plan, imagine, and project themselves into the future in a way that allows them to better prepare for that future, and these activities are subserved by brain processes specific for complex executive forecasts and predictions. Necessarily, these future-oriented forecasts, intentions, decisions, and plans take place under conditions of uncertainty (Cohen & Aston-Jones, 2005; Daw, O'Doherty, Dayan, Seymour, & Dolan,

2006). It is this set of complex executive predictions and forecasts that dominate current thinking about human motivation (e.g., goals, plans, expectations, future time perspective, possible selves), the topic to which we now turn.

Key Motivational Constructs in Human Motivation Study

To this point in the chapter, the conversation has been rather one sided, as we have presented and summarized the neuroscientific perspective on motivation. In the present section, we focus on several central motivational constructs that are richly studied in the human motivation research literature that occurs outside of a neuroscience focus. In doing so, we will compare and contrast the human motivation understanding of these complex motivational states with the neuroscientific understanding of these same phenomena. In particular, we discuss agency, volition, value, intrinsic motivation, extrinsic motivation, flow, expectancy, self-efficacy, self-regulation, and goals.

Agency

Agency is the sense that "I did that," and it lies at the center of intentional, voluntary, and purpose-driven action. Human motivation researchers tend to study agency broadly, defining it, for instance, as self-generated motivation to act on the environment—the proactive desire to create, manipulate, influence, and transform the environment that one is in so to improve it in some way (Bandura, 2006). Neuroscientists study agency more narrowly, as they contrast an experience of self-as-cause versus other-as-cause of an action (Engbert, Wohlschlager, & Haggard, 2008; Farrer & Frith, 2002; Spengler, von Cramon, & Brass, 2009). In these investigations, the person performs a simple action (e.g., move a joystick) that causes an event to happen (e.g., make an image appear on the screen), and the causal source of that action is manipulated experimentally such that what happens is directly linked to the person's own intentions and behaviors or is unrelated to them, because a computer program or the experimenter causes the action such that anything done by the participant is superfluous. Results show that an experience of agency is closely linked to and dependent on the activities of motor-related brain regions, such as the supplemental motor area and the presupplemental motor area, which plan and enact an efferent motor command—that is, agency arises from a tight relation between action and effect as the person must self-generate the motor instruction to perform an action to feel a true sense of personal agency. If the person enacts the same behavior without self-instruction to do so (e.g., an outside agent actually causes the person's behavior), little agency is experienced. Furthermore, the greater the length of time that elapses between one's action and the effect it produces, the less the resulting sense of agency will be, as the sense of "I did that" is put into doubt by the rival belief that "maybe something or someone else did it" (Spengler et al., 2009). Such agency is associated with activation in the insula, while such nonagency is associated with activation in the inferior parietal cortex (Farrer et al., 2003; Farrer & Frith, 2002). Pressing a button while lying in an fMRI machine is a long way from improving one's working conditions or changing one's career path, but the premise is the same—"unless people believe they can produce desired effects by their actions, they have little incentive to act" (Bandura, 2006, p. 170).

Volition

Some neuroscientists study mental control over action as volition, rather than as agency (Haggard, 2008). In this research, neuroscientists use experimental tasks that give participants freedom whether to perform actions, when to perform actions, or how many times to perform actions, and they then search for related neural activities (Haggard, 2008; Libet, Gleason, Wright, & Pearl, 1983; Nachev, 2006; Nachev, Rees, Praton, Kennard, & Husain, 2005). The results consistently indicate that *(1)* voluntary control activates motor-related brain regions, such as the supplementary motor area and the presupplementary motor area, and *(2)* conflict monitoring during this voluntary control activates the dorsal anterior cingulate cortex, as the individual attempts to cope with the cognitive conflicts that arise. In the human motivation research literature, Heinz Heckhausen distinguished what was termed agency in the preceding paragraph from volition by defining agency (motivation) as that which initiates action (e.g., need, goal), whereas volition involved the persistent striving of that motivated action over time and in the face of obstacles (Heckhausen, 1977). In other words, human motivation researchers view volition as the cognitive, emotional, and motivational control that occurs over time to carry out (not to initiate) goal-directed behavior (Gollwitzer, 1996). As such, volition encompasses diverse cognitive, emotional, and motivational processes (e.g., conflict monitoring). To expand the study of volition beyond that of agency, it would seem that interdisciplinary motivational neuroscience

researchers need to examine the neural circuits of various aspects of cognitive, emotional, and motivational control over action, and some neuroscientist have begun to do this (Haggard, 2008; Nachev, 2006; Nachev et al., 2005).

Value

Value is a central concept in contemporary motivation study, as it serves as the core construct underlying the expectancy X value family of motivation theories (Wigfield & Eccles, 2002). In expectancy X value theories, value is a multidimensional construct composed of four divergent sources: intrinsic interest, utility value, attainment value, and cost. High values on each of these components of value (cost needs to be reversed scored) generally correlate with choice behavior and persistence (Wigfield & Eccles, 2002). This conceptualization of value is noticeably different from the neuroscience conceptualization of value, which is the incentive-based, reward-related information of an object or event, and that reward value is sometimes natural (e.g., water, orange juice) but often learned or conditioned (Dickinson & Balleine, 2002). When the learned reward-based information is subjective or circumstantial (rather than universal or objective), orbitofrontal cortex information is active and, once the incentive value of various environmental objects and events is learned, activity in the orbitofrontal cortex helps people make choices between options, consider their options, remember the incentive value associated with each of those options, and make their selection among the differently valued objects to pursue (Arana et al., 2003; Rushworth, Behrens, Rudebeck, & Walton, 2007).

While expectancy X value theorists emphasize divergent sources of valuing, neuroscientists generally do the opposite and emphasize the converging sources of valuing. The orbitofrontal-striatal circuit is viewed as a valuation system in which this circuit continually computes valuation (how rewarding, how punishing) across a broad range of stimuli and environmental events (Montague & Berns, 2002). It does so by valuing all these potential stimuli and events on a common dopamine-based scale, which is sort of like the neural equivalent of monetary currency in a nation's economic system. Rewards vary on their type, magnitude, salience, and immediacy, and the orbitofrontal-striatal circuit (and the striatum in particular) convert and integrate these diverse sources of reward-based information into a common currency and, by doing so, value all rewards on a common scale. Once diverse environmental incentives can be compared and contrasted via a common currency, people can compare disparate stimuli (which would you rather do—drink a glass of orange juice, go for a walk in the park, or play a videogame?) so to assign their attention and plan their action. Perhaps some similar process allows people to integrate the various sources of value within expectancy X value theory (intrinsic value, utility value, and attainment value) on a common scale to compare the value of an interesting but not useful event (play) with an uninteresting but useful event (work).

A second perspective on value in the human motivation literature conceptualizes it as an internalization process in which socially recommended prescriptions ("do this, believe that") and proscriptions ("don't do this, don't believe that") are accepted as one's own (Ryan & Connell, 1989). The internalization process of valuing is not so much an emotionally associative process (as valuing is studied in neuroscience) as it is a process in which a particular way of thinking, feeling, or behaving is accepted as personally beneficial for self-functioning (similar to the "utility value" in expectancy X value theories). It is an active and intentional process that is based not on reward but in self-development and adjustment (Ryan, 1993). In both the expectancy X value literature and in the internalization literature, value (like volition in the previous section) is conceptualized more broadly than it is in the neuroscience literature.

Intrinsic Motivation and Extrinsic Motivation

Intrinsic motivation is the inherent propensity to engage one's interests and to exercise one's capacities and, in doing so, to seek out and master optimal challenges (Deci & Ryan, 1985). When people are intrinsically motivated, they act out of interest and because they find the task at hand to be inherently enjoyable—producing spontaneous satisfactions such as "It's fun" and "Its interesting" during activity engagement. This behavior occurs spontaneously and is not enacted for any instrumental (extrinsic) reasons. Intrinsic motivation is a concept that neuroscientists have not been able to explain (or understand). What is known, however, is that during greater insular cortical activity people become aware of how the task they are engaged in is affecting their subjective feelings and they consolidate this feeling-state information with social-contextual information about their task engagement (e.g., is there a deadline involved?) to form a global conscious experience of

"my feelings about that thing" (Craig, 2009, p. 65). As one example, people experience greater insular activity as they enjoy (experience spontaneous satisfactions from the experience) music (Koelsch, Fritz, Cramon, Muller, & Friederici, 2006).

In the neuroscience literature, extrinsic motivation is synonymous with incentive motivation, which we reviewed under the heading of "Motivational States Based on Associative Learning." In the human motivation literature, extrinsic motivation arises from environmental incentives and consequences (e.g., food, money, tokens, extra credit points) in which approach motivation is based not on the characteristics of the task itself but on the conditioned incentive value of the separate environmental event/consequence. As people experience extrinsic motivation toward a task, they show greater orbitofrontal cortex activity as they weigh the value of the incentive being offered and greater anterior cingulate cortex as they go through a decision-making process as to whether engagement in the activity will bring enough benefit to justify the effort expenditure (Plassmann, O'Doherty, & Rangel, 2007). In the human motivation literature, however, extrinsic motivation is a complex construct in which types of extrinsic motivation exist, including external regulation (the prototype of extrinsic motivation, which is incentive motivation), introjected regulation (the person—rather than the environment per se—self-administers rewards and punishments, as in feeling contingent pride or contingent shame), and identified regulation (discussed in the previous section as the internalized process of valuing). This differentiated view of extrinsic motivation has not been explored in the neuroscientific research literature. Furthermore, almost no research exists to date on the neuroscientific study of intrinsic motivation.

Intrinsic motivation and extrinsic motivation interact with one another, and the tendency of highly salient extrinsic rewards to decrease intrinsic motivation represents the "undermining effect" in the human motivation literature (Deci, Koestner, & Ryan, 1999). To investigate this social psychological process within a neuroscience perspective, one group of researchers asked participants to engage themselves in an interesting task either with the promise of a contingent extrinsic reward (money) or simply to experience the inherently interesting sense of challenge within the task itself (Murayama, Matsumoto, Izuma, & Matsumoto, 2010). By itself, the interesting, challenging task generated meaningful striatal and lateral prefrontal cortical activity, activations that confirmed that the challenging task was inherently rewarding and cognitively engaging. When the same task was paired with the promise of a contingent monetary reward, striatal and lateral prefrontal cortical activity increased significantly, suggesting that the extrinsic reward added to the task-inherent intrinsic motivation. In a second phase of the study, the extrinsic reward was removed. The researchers then examined how much striatal and lateral prefrontal cortical activity the task itself could generate. For participants in the no-reward condition, striatal and lateral prefrontal cortical activity were essentially the same on the second encounter with the activity—the task was just as rewarding and engaging as before. For participants in the reward condition, however, striatal and lateral prefrontal cortical activity practically disappeared—the capacity of the once interesting and challenging task to generate pleasure (striatum) and cognitive engagement (lateral prefrontal cortex) had been undermined by the previously contingent extrinsic reward. This program of research nicely shows how a complex human motivational concept (intrinsic motivation) can be better understood by a neuroscience emphasis, and it therefore provides an exemplary model for how future researchers might integrate neuroscientific methods and perspectives within human motivation study.

Flow

Flow is a state of concentration that involves a holistic absorption and deep involvement in an activity (Csikszentmihalyi, 1990). It is a highly pleasurable feeling that involves a sense of optimal challenge and perceived competence, and it is characterized by a loss of time perspective in which time passes relatively slowly. The anterior insular cortex integrates feelings generated by homeostatic, environmental, hedonic, motivational, social, and cognitive inputs to produce a "global emotional moment," which represents conscious awareness of one's feelings at one (present) moment in time (Craig, 2008, 2009). Under conditions of strong emotion (joy, or flow from achieving competent functioning during a challenging task), the anterior insular cortex produces a dilation of time in which many global emotional moments occur rapidly (Tse, Intriligator, Rivest, & Cavanagh, 2004). Hence, subjective time dilates, as the actor subjectively feels that little time has passed even when engagement has continued for an objectively long(er) period of time. Like the study of the undermining effect of rewards on intrinsic motivation, the human motivation and neuroscientific studies of flow represent

a second case of rather high convergence between these two literatures.

Expectancy

Expectancy is a central concept in the contemporary study of human motivation; it serves as the core explanatory construct underlying motivations such as personal control beliefs, mastery motivation, self-efficacy, and learned helplessness, among others (Skinner, 1995, 1996). These "expectancy-of-control" constructs involve the interrelations among person, behavior, and outcome such that people have expectancies of being able to generate effective coping behavior (e.g., efficacy expectations) and they have expectancies of whether their coping behavior, once enacted, will produce the outcome they seek (outcome expectations). In neuroscientific investigations of reward learning, however, expectancy is largely investigated as how expected a reward is.

This research, which takes place under the umbrella term of "reward prediction error" (Schultz, 1998), shows that dopamine neurons are responsive when a reward is received unexpectedly. When that same reward is expected, based on prior experience, the neurons respond not to reward receipt but to the informative nature of the predictive cue. Thus, dopamine neurons are responsive to reward-related novelty (Schott et al., 2004), the anticipation of cued reward (Schott et al., 2008), and the difference between expected reward and actual reward, which is the reward prediction error (Schultz, 1998). Overall, dopamine neurons throughout the basal ganglia—dorsal striatum, ventral striatum, ventral tegmental area, and substantia nigra—report ongoing reward prediction errors, and they do so by providing anticipatory, unexpected, and actual signals of motivational relevance (i.e., reward cues). This information is then passed on to target brain regions, including the prefrontal cortex and anterior cingulate cortex, to coordinate reward-based learning and the motivation to learn about goals. For instance, once this information is passed on to the anterior cingulate cortex, approach versus avoidance decisional conflicts can be resolved based on expected probabilities of reward, payoff, and costs, just as this same information can be passed on to the prefrontal cortex to guide goal setting and prioritizing.

The neuroscientific study of reward prediction errors is similar to the "outcome expectancy" concept in the human motivation literature. Reward prediction errors mostly serve the function of learning (not of motivation per se), as dopamine neurons activate with unexpected reward experiences to produce new learning. However, these same dopamine-based responses can be used to influence future choice behavior (Schultz, Dayan, & Montague, 1997). That is, as people navigate their surroundings, they evaluate various courses of action that have differential predictions of reward associated with them. These predictions of future rewards (outcomes) are influenced by past expected reward learning. Hence, dopamine responses provide information to enact the most basic expectancy-based motivational principle—namely, approach and engage in action correlated with increased dopamine activity and avoid action correlated with decreased dopamine activity.

Dopamine-based learning plays a key role in reward expectation and receipt, which are closely related to outcome expectancies. But it also facilitates episodic memory formation that is used for future adaptive behavior. That is, dopamine information during learning helps build and enable the forging of memory from one's past experience that then becomes the basis for future adaptive behavior (Shohamy & Adcock, 2010). It is this "adaptive memory" that then forms the basis of the second major type of expectancy motivation studied in the human motivation literature—namely, self-efficacy.

Self-Efficacy

Efficacy expectations are rooted in questions such as "Can I cope well with the task at hand?" and "If things start to go wrong during my performance, do I have the personal resources within me to cope well and turn things around for the better?" Self-efficacy is the generative capacity in which the individual (the "self" in self-efficacy) organizes and orchestrates his or her skills in the pursuit of goal-directed action to cope with the demands and circumstances he or she faces. Formally defined, self-efficacy is one's judgment of how well (or poorly) one will cope with a situation, given the skills one possesses and the circumstances one faces (Bandura, 1997). The precuneus (embedded within the parietal lobe) is involved in many of these processes, including self-related imagery, episodic memory retrieval, preparing future action, and the experience of agency (Cavanna & Trimble, 2006; den Ouden, Frith, Frith, & Blakemore, 2005).

The primary determinant of self-efficacy expectations is one's history of episodic memory-based mastery enactments, which might be conceptualized by neuroscientists as perceived skill in that domain. Studies of motor skill acquisition (Poldrack et al., 2005) and cognitive skill acquisition (Fincham & Anderson, 2006) show that trained individuals come to direct

their attention not to intermediate goal-directed steps but to the larger aim (as automation of skill occurs). Automation of procedural skills allows one to focus attention to environmental demands and challenges, retrieve relevant episodic memories, and predict and plan effective future courses of action, while it further lessens cognitive confusion and anxiety (Bandura, 1988). The hippocampus is important to automation of procedural knowledge, and the downregulation of competent self-representations has been shown to lessen negative affect, affect intensity, and cortisol reactivity during coping (Sapolsky, 1992).

Perhaps the most productive way that human motivation research on self-efficacy can contribute to interdisciplinary motivational neuroscience research is to stress the point that neural systems that focus attention, mentally represent value, detect the causal structure of the world, and integrate this information into effective decision making and action is only one part of the adaptive story (Bandura, 2001). The other part of the adaptive story is self-efficacy-fueled agency in which people proactively devise ways to adapt flexibly to a wide range of physical and social environments to redesign them to their liking and controllability. Such a perspective places lesser influence on environmentally responsive and adaptive brain processes and relatively greater influence on proactive and agentic brain processes in the exercise of personal control over environments to be encountered in the future.

Self-Regulation and Goals

Self-regulation is an ongoing, cyclical process that involves forethought, action, and reflection (Zimmerman, 2000). Forethought involves goal setting and strategic planning, while reflection involves assessment and making adjustments to produce more informed forethought prior to the next performance opportunity. What is regulated during self-regulation are the person's goals (and, to a lesser extent, the means to these goals, such as plans, strategies, emotions, and environments). In the human motivation literature, goals are future-focused cognitive representations that guide behavior to an end state that the individual is committed to either approach or avoid (Hulleman, Schrager, Bodmann, & Harackiewicz, 2010). It is the prefrontal cortex that houses a person's conscious goals (Miller & Cohen, 2001), and this information is used in goal-directed action in the top-down flow of information depicted in Figure 21.2.

From a neuroscience point of view, several brain structures exercise executive control and inhibition over action. The prefrontal cortex contributes top-down control that guides behavior by activating internal representations of action such as goals and intentions by sending information to other areas of the brain to promote goal-relevant actions. While the prefrontal cortex generates goals and intentions, executive control over action seems to be carried out in many additional prefrontal cortex regions, including the ventral medial prefrontal cortex, the anterior cingulate cortex, and the dorsolateral prefrontal cortex, as each is involved in a high-level regulation of action, including self-control and the self-regulation of action such as planning, organizing, and changing action (Damasio, 1994, 2003; Oschsner & Gross, 2005; Rueda et al., 2004). The anterior cingulate cortex, for example, plays a high-level role in the regulation of action, as it not only receives information about sensory events, monitors conflict, and integrates emotional information (Botvinick et al., 2004; Craig, 2008), it is active during any decision to change one's course of action (Devinsky, Morrell, & Vogt, 1995) and is involved in adjusting past learning about environmental contingencies when their reliability changes over time (Behrens, Woolrich, Walton, & Rushworth, 2007). These research findings suggest a possible convergence between human motivation researchers and neuroscientists, as neuroscientists have done an especially impressive job in explaining the neural bases of forethought, decision making, and reflective action.

Conclusion

The intellectual landscape that connects human motivation study and neuroscience is not currently populated by ever-present two-way information highways in which the methodologies, findings, and theoretical developments in one field flow into the other and return back in a more informed and sophisticated way. It is clear, however, that human motivation researchers have a lot to gain from such interconnectivity. To date, the most obvious benefit for human motivation research has been that neuroscientific investigations have brought to light the neural meditational processes that underlie the how and the why of the basic motivation mediation model: environment → motivation → adaptive action. That is, neuroscientific investigations have enriched the understanding of both the generation of motivational states (i.e., environment → neural activations → motivation) and their adaptive functions (motivation → neural activations → adaptive functioning).

It is equally clear that neuroscience researchers have gained from greater motivation-neuroscience interconnectivity. The most obvious benefit for neuroscience research has been to gain a greater

theoretical depth and complexity for the motivational constructs it studies. Motivational concepts such as volition, agency, value, intrinsic motivation, self-efficacy, and self-regulation can be understood more richly when neuroscientific analyses are supplemented and informed by behavioral and psychological findings, methodologies, and especially theories. Once understood in their theoretical richness, these motivational constructs can be studied in ways that increasingly map onto and reflect what is known about them from traditional human motivation study. Such integration, if it is to occur, will likely be carried out by a generation of interdisciplinary motivation neuroscience researchers— scholars whose interests, professional training, and intellectual home is as much in neuroscience as it is in human motivation study, and vice versa.

Future Directions

1. Will the relationship between neuroscience and human motivation become more reciprocal and bidirectional in the future, or will it remain largely a landscape of one-way—and even dead-end—streets? This trend will depend on human motivation researchers' openness to neuroscience and to their willingness to form collaborations and learn the methods and knowledge base of neuroscience.

2. Is neuroscience relevant to only some classes or facets of motivation—for example, homeostasis and reward—or is it more generally relevant to more complex motivations such as intrinsic motivation and self-efficacy? This is a question of whether the motivation-neuroscience collaboration will be a narrow or a broad one.

3. What are the benefits of maintaining the existing distinction between the two different levels of analyses (neurological versus behavioral and self-report) embraced by neuroscience on the one hand and human motivation study on the other? How well can the dependent measures used in neuroscience (e.g., reaction times, neural activations) align with the dependent measures used in human motivation study (e.g., effort, phenomenology)? This future direction will likely be determined by the extent to which neural-dependent measures align (correlate) with behavioral and self-report measures of motivation.

4. Can the brain generate motivation of its own? Or is brain-based motivation always an adaptive response to environmental events? Neuroscientific investigations of motivation have

revealed much about environmental sources of motivation and reward. It is still an open question, however, as to how much this paradigm might reveal about intrinsic sources of motivation.

5. Lastly, the past decade of motivational neuroscience has largely sought to identify the neural bases of various motivational states. This has been and continues to be a productive enterprise. As the neural bases of various motivational states become well understood, motivational neuroscience will need to ask new questions and take on a new sense of purpose. It is interesting to speculate what this future direction will be, but it will like be one that transcends description (e.g., the amygdala is involved in this, the anterior cingulate cortex is involved in that) to address explanation.

Acknowledgments

This research was supported by the WCU (World Class University) Program funded by the Korean Ministry of Education, Science and Technology, consigned to the Korea Science and Engineering Foundation (grant R32–2008–000-20023-0).

Note

1. While dopamine is the key neurotransmitter involved in the processing of reward, other neurotransmitters also contribute to the processing of reward, including choline, GABA, glutamate, opiod, and serotonin (Knapp & Kornetsky, 2009).

References

Aarts, H., Custers, R., & Marien, H. (2008). Preparing and motivating behavior outside of awareness. *Science, 319*, 1639.

Aarts, H., & Dijksterhuis, A. (2003). The silence of the library: Environment, situational norm, and social behavior. *Journal of Personality and Social Psychology, 84*, 18–28.

Addis, D. R., Wong, A. T., & Schacter, D. L. (2007). Remembering the past and imaging the future: Common and distinct neural substrates during event construction and elaboration. *Neuropsychologia, 45*, 1363–1377.

Arana, F. S., Parkinson, J. A., Hinton, E., Holland, A. J., Owen, A. M., & Roberts, A. C. (2003). Dissociable contributions of the human amygdala and orbitofrontal cortex to incentive motivation and goal selection. *Journal of Neuroscience, 23*, 9632–9638.

Ashby, F. G., Isen, A. M., & Turken, A. U. (1999). A neuropsychological theory of positive affect and its influence on cognition. *Psychological Review, 106*, 529–550.

Bandura, A. (1988). Self-efficacy conception of anxiety. *Anxiety Research, 1*, 77–98.

Bandura, A. (1997). *Self-efficacy: The exercise of control.* New York: W. H. Freeman.

Bandura, A. (2001). Social cognitive theory: An agentic perspective. *Annual Review of Psychology, 52*, 1–26.

Bandura, A. (2006). Toward a psychology of human agency. *Perspectives on Psychological Science, 1*, 164–180.

Bar, M. (2007). The proactive brain: Using analogies and associations to generate predictions. *Trends in Cognitive Sciences, 11*, 280–289.

Bargh, J. A., Gollwitzer, P. M., Lee-Chai, K., Barndollar, K., & Trotschel, R. (2001). The automated will: Nonconscious activation and pursuit of behavioral goals. *Journal of Personality and Social Psychology, 82*, 1014–1027.

Baxter, M. G., & Murray, E. A. (2002). The amygdala and reward. *Nature Reviews Neuroscience, 3*, 563–573.

Baxter, M. G., Parker, A., Lindner, C. C. C., Izquierdo, A. D., & Murray, E. A. (2000). Control of response selection by reinforcer value requires interaction of amygdala and orbital frontal cortex. *Journal of Neuroscience, 20*, 4311–4319.

Bechara, A., & Damasio, A. R. (2005). The somatic marker hypothesis: A neural theory of economic decision. *Games and Economic Behavior, 52*, 336–372.

Bechara, A., Damasio, H., & Damasio, A. R. (2000). Emotion, decision-making, and the orbitofrontal cortex. *Cerebral Cortex, 10*, 295–307.

Behrens, T. E. J., Woolrich, M. W., Walton, M. E., & Rushworth, M. F. (2007). Learning the value of information in an uncertain world. *Nature Neuroscience, 10*, 1214–1221.

Berridge, K. C. (2004). Motivation concepts in behavioral neuroscience. *Physiology and Behavior, 81*, 179–209.

Berridge, K. C., & Kringelbach, M. (2008). Affective neuroscience and pleasure: Reward in humans and animals. *Psychopharmacology, 191*, 391–431.

Berridge, K. C., & Robinson, T. E. (2003). Parsing reward. *Trends in Neurosciences, 26*, 507–513.

Booth, D. (1991). Influences on human fluid consumption. In D. J. Ramsay & D. A. Booth (Eds.), *Thirst: Physiological and psychological aspects* (pp. 53–73). London: Springer Verlag.

Botvinick, M., Cohen, J. D., & Carter, C. S. (2004). Conflict monitoring and anterior cingulate cortex: An update. *Trends in Cognitive Sciences, 8*, 539–546.

Cavanna, A. E., & Trimble, M. R. (2006). The precuneus: A review of its functional anatomy and behavioural correlates. *Brain, 129*, 564–583.

Cohen, J. D., & Aston-Jones, G. (2005). Cognitive neuroscience: Decision amid uncertainty. *Nature, 436*, 471–472.

Craig, A. D. (2002). How do you feel? Interoception: The sense of the physiological condition of the body. *Nature Reviews Neuroscience, 3*, 655–666.

Craig, A. D. (2008). Interoception and emotion: A neuroanatomical perspective. In M. Lewis, J. M. Haviland-Jones, & L. F. Barrett (Eds.), *Handbook of emotions* (3rd ed., pp. 272–288). New York: Guilford.

Craig, A. D. (2009). How do you feel—now? The anterior insula and human awareness. *Nature Review of Neuroscience, 10*, 59–70.

Csikszentmihalyi, M. (1990). *Flow: The psychology of optimal experience.* New York: Harper & Row.

Cunningham, W., & Zelazo, P. D. (2007). Attitudes and evaluation: A social cognitive neuroscience perspective. *Trends in Cognitive Sciences, 11*, 97–104.

Custers, R., & Aarts, H. (2005). Positive affect as implicit motivator: On the nonconscious operation of behavioral goals. *Journal of Personality and Social Psychology, 89*, 129–142.

Custers, R., Aarts, H., Oikawa, M., & Elliot, A. (2009). The nonconscious road to perceptions of performance: Achievement priming augments outcome expectancies and experienced self-agency. *Journal of Experimental Social Psychology, 45*, 1200–1208.

Damasio, A. R. (1994). *Descartes' error*. New York: Grosset/Putnam.

Damasio, A. R. (1996). The somatic marker hypothesis and the possible functions of the prefrontal cortex. *Philosophical Transactions of the Royal Society B: Biological Sciences, 35*, 1413–1420.

Damasio, A. R. (2003). *Looking for Spinoza: Joy, sorrow and the feeling brain*. New York: Harcourt.

Davidson, R. J., & Irwin, W. (1999). The functional neuroanatomy of emotion and affective style. *Trends in Cognitive Science, 3*, 11–21.

Davidson, R. J., & Sutton, S. K. (1995). Affective neuroscience: The emergence of a discipline. *Current Opinion in Neurobiology, 5*, 217–224.

Daw, N. D., O'Doherty, J. P., Dayan, P., Seymour, B., & Dolan, R. J. (2006). Cortical substrates for exploratory decisions in humans. *Nature, 441*, 876–879.

Decety, J., & Cacioppo, J. T. (2010). *Handbook of social neuroscience*. New York: Oxford University Press.

Deci, E. L., Koestner, R., & Ryan, R. M. (1999). A meta-analytic review of experiments examining the effects of extrinsic rewards on intrinsic motivation. *Psychological Bulletin, 125*, 627–668.

Deci, E. L., & Ryan, R. M. (1985). *Intrinsic motivation and self-determination in human behavior*. New York: Plenum.

den Ouden, H. E. M., Frith, U., Frith, C., & Blakemore, S-J. (2005). Thinking about intentions. *NeuroImage, 28*, 787–796.

Devinsky, O., Morrell, M. J., & Vogt, B. A. (1995). Contributions of anterior cingulate cortex to behaviour. *Brain, 118*, 279–306.

Dickinson, A., & Balleine, B. (2002). The role of learning in the operation of motivational systems. In C. R. Gallistel (Ed.), *Stevens' handbook of experimental psychology: Learning, motivation, and emotion* (Vol. 3, pp. 497–534). New York: Wiley.

Engbert, K., Wohlschlager, A., & Haggard, P. (2008). Who is causing what? The sense of agency is relational and efferent-triggered. *Cognition, 107*, 693–704.

Farrer, C., Franck, N., Georgieff, N., Frith, C. D., Decety, J., & Geannerod, M. (2003). Modulating the experience of agency: A positron emission tomography study. *NeuroImage, 18*, 324–333.

Farrer, C., & Frith, C. D. (2002). Experiencing oneself vs. another person as being the cause of an action: The neural correlates of the experience of agency. *NeuroImage, 15*, 596–603.

Fincham, J. M., & Anderson, J. R. (2006). Distinct roles of the anterior cingulate and prefrontal cortext in the acquisition and performance of a cognitive skill. *Proceedings of the National Academy of Sciences USA, 103*, 12941–12946.

Freese, J. L., & Amaral, D. G. (2005). Neuroanatomy of the primate amygdala. In R. J. Whalen & E. A. Phelps (Eds.), *The human amygdala* (pp. 3–42). New York: Guilford Press.

Gazzaniga, M. S., Ivry, R., & Mangun, G. R. (2008). *Cognitive neuroscience: The biology of the mind* (3rd ed.). New York: W. W. Norton.

Gollwitzer, P. M. (1996). The volitional benefits of planning. In P. M. Gollwitzer & J. A. Bargh (Eds.), *The psychology of action: Linking cognition and emotion to behavior* (pp. 287–312). New York: Guilford Press.

Haggard, P. (2008). Human volition: Towards a neuroscience of will. *Nature Reviews Neuroscience, 9*, 934–946.

Heckhausen, H. (1977). Achievement motivation and its constructs: A cognitive model. *Motivation and Emotion, 1*, 283–329.

Hodgins, H. S., Yacko, H. A., & Gottlieb, E. (2006). Autonomy and nondefensiveness. *Motivation and Emotion, 30*, 283–293.

Holland, R. W., Hendriks, M., & Aarts, H. (2005). Nonconscious effects of scent on cognition and behavior. *Psychological Science, 16*, 689–693.

Hulleman, C. S., Schrager, S. M., Bodmann, S. M., & Harackiewicz, J. M. (2010). A meta-analytic review of achievement goal measures: Different labels for the same constructs or different constructs with similar labels? *Psychological Bulletin, 136*, 422–449.

Isen, A. M. (1987). Positive affect, cognitive processes, and social behavior. In L. Berkowitz (Ed.), *Advances in experimental social psychology* (Vol. 20, pp. 203–253). New York: Academic press.

Isen, A. M. (2003). Positive affect as a source of human strength. In L. G. Aspinwall & U. Staudinger (Eds.), *A psychology of human strengths* (pp. 175–195). Washington, DC: American Psychological Association.

James, W. (1894). The physical basis of emotion. *Psychological Review, 1*, 516–529.

Kay, A. C., Wheeler, S. C., Bargh, J. A., & Ross, L. (2004). Material priming: The influence of mundane objects on situational construal and competitive behavioral choice. *Organizational Behavior and Human Decision Processes, 95*, 83–96.

Knapp, C. M., & Kornetsky, C. (2009). Neural basis of pleasure and reward. In G. G. Berntson & J. T. Cacioppo (Eds.), *Handbook of neuroscience for the behavioral sciences* (Vol. 2, pp. 781–806). Hoboken, NJ: Wiley.

Koelsch, S., Fritz, T., Cramon, D. Y. V., Muller, K., & Friederici, A. D. (2006). Investigating emotion with music: An fMRI study. *Human Brain Mapping, 27*, 239–250.

Libet, B., Gleason, C. A., Wright, E. W., & Pearl, D. K. (1983). Time of conscious intention to act in relation to onset of cerebral activity (readiness-potential). The unconscious initiation of a freely voluntary act. *Brain, 106*, 623–642.

Litman, J. (2005). Curiosity and the pleasures of learning: Wanting and liking new information. *Cognition and Emotion, 19*, 793–814.

Loewenstein, G., Rick, S., & Cohen, J. D. (2008). Neuroeconomics. *Annual Review of Psychology, 59*, 647–672.

Mayer, R. E. (1998). Does the brain have a place in educational psychology? *Educational Psychology Review, 10*, 389–396.

McClure, S. M., Laibson, D. I., Loewenstein, G., & Cohen, J. D. (2004). Separate neural systems value immediate and delayed monetary rewards. *Science, 306*, 503–507.

McKinley, M. J. (2009). Thirst. In G. G. Berntson & J. T. Cacioppo (Eds.), *Handbook of neuroscience for the behavioral sciences* (Vol. 2, pp. 680–709). Hoboken, NJ: Wiley.

Miller, E. K., & Cohen, J. D. (2001). An integrative theory of prefrontal cortex function. *Annual Review of Neuroscience, 24*, 167–202.

Mogenson, G. J., Jones, D. L., & Yim, C. Y. (1980). From motivation to action: Functional interface between the limbic system and the motor system. *Progress in Neurobiology, 14*, 69–97.

Montague, P. R., & Berns, G. S. (2002). Neural economics and the biological substrates of valuation. *Neuron, 36*, 265–284.

Murayama, K., Matsumoto, M., Izuma, K., & Matsumoto, K. (2010). Neural basis of the undermining effect of monetary reward on intrinsic motivation. *Proceedings of the National Academy of the Sciences USA, 107*, 20911–20916.

Nachev, P. (2006). Cognition and medial frontal cortex in health and disease. *Current Opinion in Neurology, 19*, 586–592.

Nachev, P., Rees, G., Praton, A., Kennard, C., & Husain, M. (2005). Volition and conflict in human medial frontal cortex. *Current Biology, 15*, 122–128

Oschsner, K. N., & Gross, J. J. (2005). The cognitive control of emotion. *Trends in Cognitive Sciences, 9*, 242–249.

Paas, F., Tuovinen, J. E., Tabbers, H., Van Gerven, P. W. M. (2003). Cognitive load measurement as a means to advance cognitive load theory. *Educational Psychologist, 38*, 63–71.

Plassmann, H., O'Doherty, J., & Rangel, A. (2007). Orbitofrontal cortex encodes willingness to pay in everyday economic transactions. *Journal of Neuroscience, 27*, 9984–9988.

Poldrack, R. A., Sabb, F. W., Foerde, K., Tom, S. M., Asarnow, R. F., Bookheimer, S. Y., & Knowlton, B. J. (2005). The neural correlates of motor skill automaticity. *Journal of Neuroscience, 25*, 5356–5364.

Powley, T. L. (2009). Hunger. In G. G. Berntson & J. T. Cacioppo (Eds.), *Handbook of neuroscience for the behavioral sciences* (Vol. 2, pp. 659–679). Hoboken, NJ: Wiley.

Reeve, J. (2009). *Understanding motivation and emotion* (5th ed.). Hoboken, NJ: Wiley.

Ridderinkhof, K. R., van den Wildenberg, W. P. M., Segalowitz, S. J., & Carter, C. S. (2004). Neurocognitive mechanisms of cognitive control: The role of prefrontal cortex in action selection, response inhibition, performance monitoring, and reward-based learning. *Brain and Cognition, 56*, 129–140.

Robbins, T. W., & Everitt, B. J. (1996). Neurobehavioral mechanisms of reward and motivation. *Current Opinion in Neurobiology, 6*, 228–236.

Rolls, E. T. (2000). The orbitofrontal cortex and reward. *Cerebral Cortex, 10*, 284–294.

Rueda, M. R., Posner, M. I., & Ruthbart, M. K. (2004). Attentional control and self-regulation. In R. F. Baumeister & K. D. Vohs (Eds.), *Handbook of self-regulation: Research, theory, and applications* (pp. 283–300). New York: Guilford Press.

Rushworth, M. F., Behrens, T. E., Rudebeck, P. H., & Walton, M. E. (2007). Contrasting roles for cingulate and orbitofrontal cortex in decisions and social behaviour. *Trends in Cognitive Sciences, 4*, 168–176.

Ryan, R. M. (1993). Agency and organization: Intrinsic motivation, autonomy, and the self in psychological development. In J. E. Jacobs (Ed.), *Nebraska Symposium on Motivation: Developmental perspectives on motivation* (Vol. 40, pp. 1–56). Lincoln: University of Nebraska Press.

Ryan, R. M., & Connell, J. P. (1989). Perceived locus of causality and internalization: Examining reasons for acting in two domains. *Journal of Personality and Social Psychology, 57*, 749–761.

Sabatinelli, D., Bradley, M. M., Lang, P. J., Costa, V. D., & Versace, F. (2007). Pleasure rather than salience activates human nucleus accumbens and medial prefrontal cortex. *Journal of Neurophysiology, 98*, 1374–1379.

Salin, P. A., & Bullier, J. (1995). Corticocortical connections in the visual system: Structure and function. *Physiological Review, 75*, 107–154.

Saper, C. B., Chou, T. C., & Elmquist, J. K. (2002). The need to feed: Homeostatic and hedonic control of eating. *Neuron, 36*, 199–211.

Sapolsky, R. (1992). *Stress, the aging brain and the mechanisms of neuron death*. Cambridge, MA: MIT Press.

Schoenbaum, G., Chiba, A. A., & Gallagher, M. (1999). Orbitofrontal cortex and basolateral amygdala encode expected outcomes during learning. *Nature: Neuroscience, 1*, 155–159.

Schott, B. H., Sellner, D. B., Lauer, C-J., Habib, R., Frey, J. U., Guderian, S.,…Duzel, E. (2004). Activation of midbrain structures by associative novelty and the formation of explicit memory in humans. *Learning and Memory, 11*, 383–387.

Schott, B. H., Minuzzi, L., Krebs, R. M., Elmenhorst, D., Lang, M., Winz, O. H.,…Bauer, A. (2008). Mesolimbic functional magnetic resonance imaging activations during reward anticipation correlate with reward-related ventral striatal dopamine release. *Journal of Neuroscience, 28*, 14311–14319.

Schultheiss, O. C. (2008). Implicit motives. In O. P. John, R. W. Robins, & L. A. Pervin (Eds.), *Handbook of personality: Theory and research* (3rd ed., pp. 603–633). New York: Guilford.

Schultz, W. (1998). Predictive reward signal of dopamine neurons. *Journal of Neurophysiology, 80*, 1–27.

Schultz, W. (2000). Multiple reward signals in the brain. *Nature Reviews: Neuroscience, 1*, 199–207.

Schultz, W., Dayan, P., & Montague, P. R. (1997). A neural substrate of prediction and reward. *Science, 275*, 1593–1599.

Shohamy, D., & Adcock, R. A. (2010). Dopamine and adaptive memory. *Trends in Cognitive Science, 14*, 464–472.

Singer, T., Critchley, H. D., & Preuschoff, K. (2009). A common role of insula in feelings, empathy, and uncertainty. *Trends in Cognitive Sciences, 13*, 334–340.

Skinner, E. A. (1995). *Perceived control, motivation, and coping*. Newbury Park, CA: Sage.

Skinner, E. A. (1996). A guide to constructs of control. *Journal of Personality and Social Psychology, 71*, 549–570.

Spengler, S., von Cramon, D. Y., & Brass, M. (2009). Was it me or was it you? How the sense of agency originates from ideomotor learning revealed by fMRI. *NeuroImage, 46*, 290–298.

Szpunar, K. K., Watson, J. M., & McDermott, K. B. (2007). Neural substrates of envisioning the future. *Proceedings of the National Academy of Sciences USA., 104*, 642–647.

Tse, P. U., Intriligator, J., Rivest, J., & Cavanagh, P. (2004). Attention and the subjective Expansion of time. *Perceptual Psychophysics, 66*, 1171–1189.

Whalen, P. J. (1999). Fear, vigilance, and ambiguity: Initial neuroimagining studies of the human amygdala. *Current Directions in Psychological Science, 7*, 177–187.

Whalen, P. J. (2007). The uncertainty of it all. *Trends in Cognitive Science, 11*, 499–500.

Wicker, B., Keysers, C., Plailly, J., Royet, J., Gallese, V., & Rizzolatti, G. (2003). Both of us disgusted in my insula: The common neural basis of seeing and feeling disgust. *Neuron, 40*, 655–664.

Wigfield, A., & Eccles, J. (2002). *The development of achievement motivation*. San Diego, CA: Academic Press.

Wise, R. A. (2002). Brain reward circuitry: Insights from unsensed incentives. *Neuron, 36*, 229–240.

Wise, R. A. (2004). Dopamine, learning and motivation. *Nature Reviews Neuroscience, 5*, 1–12.

Zimmerman, B. J. (2000). Attaining self-regulation: A social cognitive perspective. In M. Boekaerts, P. R. Pintrich, & M. Zeidner's (Eds.), *Handbook of self-regulation* (pp. 13–39). San Diego, CA: Academic Press.

Evolved Individual Differences in Human Motivation

Larry C. Bernard

Abstract

Three social science approaches—evolutionary psychology, behavioral ecology, and behavioral genetics—share the metatheory of evolution. They also suggest several mechanisms that may account for heritable individual differences in personality and motivation, including stabilizing selection, fluctuating selection, trade-offs, balancing selection, life history theory, and behavioral syndromes. These mechanisms are discussed as possible explanations for individual differences in the five-factor model of personality and in a new theory of human motivation. The theory postulates that 15 latent motive dimensions evolved in humans to facilitate behavior in five social domains. Trade-offs that, in combination with fluctuating and balancing selection, might have maintained individual differences in motive phenotypes are described. The reliability and validity of a method to assess individual differences in the strength of these motive dimensions is also discussed.

Key Words: individual differences, motivation, personality, evolutionary psychology, behavioral ecology, life history theory, behavioral genetics, trade-offs, balancing selection, behavioral syndromes

Introduction

Many evolutionary psychologists would consider the phrase "evolved individual differences" to be an oxymoron because it would appear to violate two important assumptions of evolutionary biology and evolutionary psychology: *(1)* that advantageous traits spread and become species typical while any heritable individual differences that arise in them are eliminated, and *(2)* that individual differences that do exist may be no more than noise in the operation of psychological adaptations (Buss, 2009). In contrast, the psychology of individual differences is a science of variation. Its primary research methods, such as factor analysis and multiple regression, are correlational and depend on variance (Revelle, 2007). The identification and confirmation of a dimension, latent trait, or construct in personality, require that people differ in it. If all people had the

same level of outgoing behavior, they would not describe each other as "introverted" or "extraverted" and psychologists would not be interested in the assessment of Extraversion.

Personality psychologists accept dimensions like Extraversion as important descriptors and predictors of behavior, and they are generally satisfied when a personality dimension can be demonstrated to be relatively stable, expressed across situations, and a valid predictor of behavior (Chamorro-Premuzic, 2007; McAdams & Pals, 2007). But evolutionary psychologists would not be satisfied until at least two additional questions were answered: *(1)* Is a personality dimension related to important outcomes such as fitness? and *(2)* If so, what mechanisms can account for its evolution?

These questions are rarely asked by individual differences psychologists and the dependence of personality psychology on variation has been a barrier to its acceptance by evolutionary psychologists (Buss, 2009). Selection pressures are thought to work in only one direction, variance reduction, to the point where a trait emerges universally, and nearly identically, in all members of a species (Tooby & Cosmides, 1990, 1992). The primary challenge for individual differences psychologists, then, is to conceptualize mechanisms by which selection can maintain variance in a functional dimension of behavior and put them to the test. Recent developments in behavioral ecology, behavioral genetics, evolutionary psychology, and comparative psychology have led to more willingness to explore the possibility of evolved individual differences in personality. These developments include life history theory (MacArthur & Wilson, 1967; Reznick, Bryant, & Bashey, 2002; Rushton, 2004; Stearns, 1992), balancing selection (Penke, Denissen, & Miller, 2007), fluctuating selection and trade-offs (Nettle, 2007), and behavioral syndrome theory (Roff, 2001; Sih, Bell, & Johnson, 2004a, 2004b) all of which suggest mechanisms by which heritable individual differences may evolve. Buss (1991) was one of the first evolutionary psychologists to recognize these developments and suggest the importance of their implications for personality, as well as evolutionary, psychology. These developments may one day turn "evolved individual differences" into a congruous term.

Evolutionary theory has played an important role in unifying the biological sciences, and it may play a similar role in the social sciences (de Waal, 2002). Evolutionary theory has great explanatory power, particularly when it addresses the interaction of brain *and* social (cultural) development, and may ultimately help in understanding the origin of individual differences in personality and motivation. Evolutionary psychology emphasizes the *function* of evolved solutions to adaptive problems, the recognition that *selective processes* are involved in the development of the brain, and the expectation that there should be a large number of *domain-specific* psychological mechanisms (Buss & Greiling, 1999; Ermer, Cosmides, & Tooby, 2007). (For a discussion of current issues in evolutionary psychology, see Confer et al., 2010.) This last emphasis is consistent with personality psychology's interest in multiple latent factors that may be responsible for individual differences in observed behavior. And personality psychologists are beginning to recognize the heuristic value of evolutionary psychology's adaptationist approach in their work (Penke et al., 2007).

This chapter presents a recent application of evolutionary theory to the study of individual differences in motivation. However, some of the first applications of evolutionary theory to individual differences involved personality constructs, specifically those in the five-factor model (FFM; Costa & McCrae, 1992; Digman, 1996; Goldberg, 1993). Therefore, this chapter will begin with the FFM, because it laid the groundwork for development of an evolutionary approach to individual differences in motivation.

The Five-Factor Model of Personality
Background
The FFM is one of the most widely studied personality models (e.g., Costa & McCrae, 1992; Digman, 1996; Goldberg, 1993). It is a taxonomic model of personality that emerged from factor analyses of the English lexicon of adjectives describing human behavior. It is based on the assumption that terms used to describe the most salient and socially relevant individual differences in behavior will become part of common language usage. Hundreds of such terms were factor analyzed until five meaningful dimensions emerged: Neuroticism, Extraversion, Openness, Conscientiousness, and Agreeableness. Although the FFM does have its limitations, it will probably continue to be the most popular model for personality assessment in the foreseeable future (Merenda, 1999, 2008). Meta-analyses of the FFM and both work performance (Barrick & Mount, 1991; Hough, Eaton, Dunnette, Kamp, & McCloy, 1990) and academic performance (Poropat, 2009) support its relationship with important behavioral outcomes. An emerging body of literature has proposed an evolutionary basis to, and the heritability of, the FFM (e.g., Jang, McCrae, Angleitner, Riemann, & Livesley, 1998; Reimann, Angleitner, & Strelau, 1997). Research has found that between 40% and 50% of variance in the FFM dimensions is due to genetic influences (Plomin, Happe, & Caspi, 2002; see Nettle, 2006, for a review of the heritability of the FFM). This has led to several proposed mechanisms that may be relevant to the evolution of individual differences dimensions in the FFM and a description of them follows.

Proposed Mechanisms for Evolution of the Five-Factor Model Dimensions
STABILIZING SELECTION
Wilson (1994) was one of the first evolutionary psychologists to propose that phenotypic differences between individuals could be the result of underlying genotypic polymorphisms, rather than primarily the result of proximal causes (i.e., phenotypic plasticity). MacDonald (1995, 1998) shared

this view and addressed the key assumption of evolutionary biology—that individual differences in adaptations should be eliminated by selection—by proposing that a personality dimension represents a continuous distribution of phenotypes. The phenotypes represent different behavioral strategies for negotiating a competitive social environment, and "stabilizing selection" is selection against extremes of the distribution (MacDonald, 2005). Stabilizing selection is based partly on Hogan's (1996) proposal that the environment of evolutionary adaptedness (EEA; see Hogan, 2005, for a discussion of this term) of *Homo sapiens* was comprised of hierarchical living groups wherein competition for social status could result in reproductive success or failure. Hogan contended that the FFM provided an indication of an individual's "reputation," of how well that individual "…is doing in the game of life…as it concerns reproductive success" (1996, p. 173).

Phenotypic behavioral strategies that fall in the tails of a normally distributed personality dimension might represent higher risk evolutionary strategies that could result in reduced fitness outcomes. In fact, extremes on FFM dimensions are associated with psychopathology (Costa & Widiger, 1994). In stabilizing selection, at different times in evolutionary history, phenotypes at different points on a personality dimension would be favored by selection, leading to niches for risk takers and risk avoiders alike. Over time, in the aggregate, selection against the extremes could provide a moderating influence, with the majority—but not all—individuals ending up in the middle of the distribution of phenotypes.

FLUCTUATING SELECTION AND TRADE-OFFS

There might be fitness disadvantages to phenotypes at the extremes of normal personality dimensions. However, any such disadvantages may not be stable, as proposed by stabilizing selection; rather, the effects of selection pressures themselves may fluctuate to sometimes increase a trait and sometimes decrease it. Therefore, stabilizing selection may not have made adequate use of the concept of trade-offs to explain variance, particularly in the middle range of a personality dimension, or to take into account possible disadvantages *and* advantages of phenotypes in the extremes of a distribution (Nettle, 2006).

When two levels along the continuum of a particular trait produce a relatively equal fitness outcome, if a different level of the trait increases a component of fitness, then it must also decrease other components of fitness. The benefit produced by increasing a trait must come at a cost, otherwise

there is no trade-off, and natural selection would be directional toward the higher value of the trait. If selection were directional, then it would decrease individual differences over time. The effect of trade-offs over time should be more variance in levels of a trait. This consideration of trade-offs has also been called the "optimality approach" (Kaplan & Gangestad, 2007). This approach takes into account that individuals live with finite resource "budgets," which must be allocated among various behavioral strategies. Because a finite budget necessitates trade-offs, there should be no optimal solutions to adaptive problems.

Fluctuating selection and trade-offs are not entirely incompatible with the key assumption of evolutionary psychology—that individual differences are mere noise in the operation of psychological adaptations (Tooby & Cosmides, 1990, 1992). However, they suggest a different conclusion about how variation can persist in the face of fitness-relevant selection processes (Nettle, 2006). First, genetic influences should be thought of as constraining, rather than determining, traits (Kagan, 2003). Second, mutation, by altering the constraining influence of a trait, is the starting point of variation. If a trait is the result of a single gene, selection pressures will keep variations close to zero because mutations occur infrequently and there is time for selection to operate. Single gene mutations account for rare serious disorders such as severe mental retardation and early-onset Alzheimer's disease (Plomin, DeFries, Craig, & McGuffin, 2003). However, because the probability of mutations rises with the number of genes involved in a trait, a polygenic trait has ample room for variance. Additionally, selection does not remove the mutations expediently, so there remains some variation in a trait even in the face of strong selection pressures (Houle, 1998). Polygentic traits—quantitative trait loci (QTL)—are more likely to result in quantitative distributions (such as those found in dimensions of personality) than they are to result in qualitative dichotomies such as those that underlie severe maladaptive or psychopathological disorders (Plomin et al., 2003).

The personality dimensions that may arise from QTLs would not simply increase or decrease fitness. Instead, overall fitness is a trade-off that balances the advantages and disadvantages of occupying a particular position in the distribution of a dimension. There should be fitness disadvantages associated with being in the tails of a personality dimension, but "The *retention* of a normal distribution is a consequence of the *inconsistency* of the direction of selection, not its stabilizing form" (Nettle, 2006, p. 628, italics added). Observations of the size to which male pygmy swordtail, *Xiphophorous nigrensis*, grow and its function in reproductive fitness demonstrate this point (Nettle, 2006). Large males are preferred by females, engage in elaborate courtship displays, and take 27 weeks to reach maturity at great cost in time and metabolic investment. In contrast, small males take only 14 weeks to mature and do not engage in the same courtship displays; therefore, more time and energy are available to "sneak" copulation with females (Zimmer & Kallman, 1989). Each variation in size has its fitness advantages and disadvantages and different sizes can be maintained through selection.

Trade-offs are also applicable to the FFM (Nettle, 2006). For example, people who score higher on Extraversion have more sexual partners and greater social support (Buchanan, Johnson, & Goldberg, 2005) but also engage in more risky behavior and are more likely to be hospitalized (Nettle, 2005) and arrested (Samuels et al., 2004). By implication, there should also be fitness trade-offs associated with low extraversion scores, for example, people who score lower may be exposed to less risk but would also have less opportunity to find mates of higher quality.

Both MacDonald's and Nettle's views of the evolutionary basis for personality dimensions have had to rely on post hoc analysis. Nettle (2006) acknowledged potential criticisms of trade-off theory as speculative and anticipated problems with the post hoc nature of his analysis of trade-offs in maintaining human personality variation. Many explanations of personality variation are open to such criticisms, and Nettle attempted to address them by making several specific testable predictions based on the theory.

BALANCING SELECTION

In balancing selection, selective forces are balanced for either extreme of a trait and both extremes could be favored by selection to the same extent but under different conditions (Penke et al., 2007). Several variations of balancing selection are likely candidates for maintaining personality variation (Penke et al., 2007). One is environmental heterogeneity, which relates more to the physical environment and occurs when a trait's fitness effect varies across space and time. When selection pressures vary spatially or temporally, a trait's fitness effect would be nearly neutral when averaged across them. Another variation is negative frequency-dependent selection, and it is a special case of environmental heterogeneity in which the spatial and temporal variations occur in the social environment. Different phenotypic personalities,

on a continuum, could result from social environmental variation across time and space.

Both of these variations are consistent with fluctuating selection/trade-offs, but balancing selection has led to a different emphasis in research with the FFM (Penke et al., 2007). In particular, personality dimensions have been conceptualized in terms of reaction range, which might help account for the dual role of the environment as a source of phenotypic plasticity and fluctuating selection pressures. Reaction range incorporates the idea of genes setting constraints that restrict outcomes along a personality dimension, rather than determining outcomes. Reaction range emphasizes the Person x Situation interaction in assessment. To illustrate this point, Penke et al. (2007) reasoned that "...some people may be socially confident at informal parties but not at public speaking, whereas for others, the opposite may apply. To class them both as 'extraverts' may conflate disparate genotypes that lead to distinct endophenotypes, behavioural strategies, reaction norms, and fitness payoffs" (p. 574). The applicability of this approach has been demonstrated with the FFM dimensions (Denissen & Penke, 2008). The dimensions were reconceptualized as motivational systems, and questionnaire items were developed to specifically tap reaction norms in the form of Person x Situation interactions. The results indicated that, while reaction norm-based items were different in content from those in other FFM measures, this did not negatively affect the factor structure or predictive validity of the FFM dimensions.

COMPARATIVE PSYCHOLOGY

Animal models have largely been missing from personality psychology, which could partially account for our poor understanding of the evolutionary basis of human personality (Figueredo et al., 2005). In contrast, animal models play a very important role in behavioral ecology, which focuses on the behavioral roles that enable a species to adapt to its environmental niche (Burkhardt, 2005; Krebs & Davies, 1997; Smith, 2000). Fairly compelling evidence has been developed for evolved personality differences in nonhuman species (Gosling, 2001; Gosling & Vazire, 2002), for example, shyness-boldness in wolves (MacDonald, 1983) and sunfish (Wilson, 1994). In particular, three FFM dimensions—Extraversion, Agreeableness, and Neuroticism—have been found in diverse species, such as primates, guppies, and octopuses (Gosling & John, 1999). Evolutionary biologists and ecologists have also found evidence of some non-FFM dimensions used to describe human personality in birds and fish (Coleman & Wilson, 1998; Groothuis & Carere, 2005; Wilson, Clark, Coleman, & Dearstyne, 1994).

As a result of such findings, Wolf, van Doorn, Leimar, and Weissing (2007) suggested that the "phenomenon of animal personalities is one of the most intriguing challenges to the adaptationist programme in behavioural research" (p. 581). This challenge goes directly to the key assumption of evolutionary psychology—that individual differences may be no more than noise in the operation of psychological adaptations—because the finding of some of the same individual differences dimensions in humans and other species suggests that the dimensions may have evolved and are not the result of proximal sources of variation alone.

To demonstrate that individual differences in animal personalities could have evolved, Wolf et al. (2007) conducted a simulation study based on the prediction that current and future reproduction trade-offs could result in polymorphic populations of individuals, some of whom would emphasize future fitness returns more than others. Those whose expectation is for future fitness should engage in less risk-taking behavior, operationalized in personality terms as less "aggressiveness" and "boldness." Wolf et al.'s mathematical simulation model showed that, over 1,000 generations, stable individual differences traits of aggressiveness and boldness could evolve under conditions in which predation risk and resource quality were varied. Their model was limited to these risk-taking dimensions of personality and was not intended to explain other dimensions such as "cooperativeness." However, it does suggest that selection pressures can give rise to stable individual differences.

LIFE HISTORY THEORY: K- AND R-SELECTED SPECIES

Life history theory originated with the work of MacArthur and Wilson (1967) to explain how selection pressures may operate to produce variation in the life histories of species. The original notion was that different strategies may ultimately produce the same fitness outcome depending on population density and resource availability. Two particular life history strategies came to be known as "K" and "r" (Pianka, 1970). K-selected species utilize a low-fecundity, high-survivorship strategy that is presumed to have evolved in a stable environment with a low risk of premature death. In contrast, r-selected species utilize a high-fecundity, low-survivorship strategy that is presumed to have evolved in an unstable environment with a high risk of mortality and varying availability of resources. Many species can be identified as K or r strategists. Populations of K-selected species, such as humans, tend to be near the density/resource capacity of their environments, while populations of r-selected species, such as rabbits, may exceed the density/resource capacity of their environments from time to time.

With subsequent modifications (e.g., Stearns, 1992), life history theory has received empirical support and become influential in behavioral ecology (Reznick et al., 2002; Rushton, 2004). Life history theory is relevant to the present discussion because it has been used to predict within-species variation among r- and K-selected species (Figueredo et al., 2005; Figueredo, Vásquez, Brumbach, & Schneider, 2007). Adaptive individual within-group differences in life history strategies have been found in several species in addition to humans (Rowe, 2000).

Figueredo et al. (2005) hypothesized that K-selection theory could lend itself to a latent variable, individual differences model comprised of a single factor (K) that underlies various life history variables such as sexual, reproductive, parental, and social behavior, reflective of a K-selected species. They provided empirical evidence of a single common factor, identified as "K," that was consistent with life history theory and weakly correlated with at least one FFM dimension, Neuroticism. Figueredo et al. (2007) also identified three common factors: *(1)* "K," which was related to life history theory and reflected personal, familial, and social functioning consistent with a K-selected species; *(2)* "Covitality," which reflected well-being, negative and positive affect, general health, and medical symptoms; and *(3)* "Personality," which reflected FFM dimensions. These factors were all moderately intercorrelated, suggesting relationships between K, health/well-being, and personality.

BEHAVIORAL SYNDROMES

The concept of behavioral syndromes developed in behavioral ecology and has not been applied specifically to the FFM. "Behavioral syndromes" refers to "suites" of correlated characteristics or behaviors that occur *across situations* (Roff, 2001). Cross-situational manifestation of behavior—its consistency—is an essential assumption for individual differences in human personality dimensions (Pervin & John, 1999) and may be observed in diverse animal species (Sih et al., 2004a, 2004b). Until recently, behavioral ecologists had been studying animal behavior individually, but behavioral syndrome theory suggests that behaviors should be studied "as a package," with a species exhibiting a "behavioral syndrome" and individuals manifesting different types (e.g., bold or shy) (Sih et al., 2004a, 2004b).

Behavioral syndromes are conceived as heritable styles of responding that are maintained by trade-offs. In some contexts, a behavioral syndrome could result in maladaptive behavior but be maintained because of fluctuating environmental selection. There may be environments in which no particular phenotype is optimum, for example, situations in which high and low Extraversion may be equally adaptive. Thus, variation could persist due to multiple optima in a single environment. This is in contrast to behavioral ecology's tendency to ignore variation and evolutionary psychology's concept of it as noise.

Behavioral syndrome theory has generated much research, most of it in nonhuman species. Intriguingly, again some of the behavioral syndromes that have been identified in nonhumans are similar to human personality traits. For example, evidence has been found for a boldness-aggression syndrome in zebrafish (*Danio rerio*) (Moretz, Martins, & Robison, 2007), an exploratory syndrome in the lizard (*Eulamprus heatwolei*) (Stapley & Keogh, 2005), and boldness, aggression, and risk-avoidance syndromes in farmed and wild fish (Huntingford & Adams, 2005). The identification of a bold syndrome in the fishing spider (*D. triton*) is particularly noteworthy, because an individual spider's boldness was consistent across situations and boldness in one context could be predicted from boldness in other contexts (Johnson & Sih, 2007).

SUMMARY

The widespread use of the FFM, and its relationships with important social outcomes, probably accounts for its central role in most of these proposed mechanisms to explain evolved individual differences. However, the task of providing an evolutionary rationale for personality dimensions may have been limited by the fact that the FFM was developed empirically and is atheoretical. In addition, at its inception, no claim was made, nor rationale provided, for an evolutionary basis to its dimensions; the heritability of its dimensions was investigated only after the fact.

Another problem with the use of the FFM dimensions is their relatively broad bandwidth. The five dimensions are general personality domains. In some measures of the FFM, such as the NEO PI-R (Costa & McCrae, 1992), the dimensions are comprised of facets or subscales. The facets are conceived as

first-order factors (i.e., with a narrower range or bandwidth of behavioral influence) and the FFM dimensions are conceived as second-order factors (i.e., with a broad range or bandwidth of behavioral influence). This can complicate interpretation because statistically significant relationships may be observed with the five broad dimensions that are due to differences within only one or two of the narrow facets that comprise them (Ones & Viswesvaran, 1996; Tett, Steele, & Beauregard, 2003). Bandwidth would be an issue when trying to understand which dimension or dimensions are heritable. Is it Extraversion or one or more of its facets—warmth, gregariousness, assertiveness, activity, excitement-seeking, and positive emotions—that is heritable? And it is conceivable that there are different selection pressures and trade-offs for each of these facets. Narrow bandwidth dimensions are probably best to control potentially confounding factors and also fit better with evolutionary psychology's emphasis on multiple, independent, domain-specific, rather than domain-general, evolved mental mechanisms (Cosmides & Tooby, 1992).

Evolved Individual Differences in Motivation
Background

Research with the FFM suggests that at least some heritable personality dimensions may be forms of strategic individual differences shaped by environmentally fluctuating, but ultimately balancing, selection forces and trade-offs. It may be possible to extend this reasoning to dimensions of motivation. From the beginnings of modern psychology—from James (1890), Freud (1955), McDougall (1933), to Murray (1938)—motivation has been an integral part of personality psychology (Fiske, 2008). However, there are some important distinctions between personality and motivational psychology. Personality psychology focuses more on *temperament, traits, and types*. Motivational psychology focuses more on the *dynamics of action*, on instincts, drives, needs, values, incentives, and goals (McAdams & Pals, 2007). Personality psychologists attempt to answer the question: "What is the structure of individuality?" Motivational psychologists attempt to answer the question: "What energizes and directs people's behavior?" Therefore, personality and motivational constructs are conceptually different. Traits are, by definition, enduring characteristics. Is it possible there can be enduring dynamics of action; can there be individual differences dimensions—traits—in motivation?

From a recent categorization of 75 years of measures used in motivation research it appears that many researchers would answer "yes;" dozens of instruments, many of them trait measures, have been used in hundreds of studies (Mayer, Faber, & Xu, 2007). While many of these instruments are unidimensional (e.g., The Need for Uncertainty; Sorrentino, Holmes, Hanna, & Sharp, 1995), many are multidimensional. One multidimensional instrument is R. B. Cattell and his colleagues' Motivation Analysis Test (MAT; Cattell, Horn, Sweney, & Radcliffe, 1964), which is comprised of scales to assess these dimensions: Career, Home-Parental, Fear, Narcism (sic), Superego, Self-sentiment, Mating, Pugnacity, Assertiveness, and Sweetheart-Spouse. The MAT incorporated innovations not widely used then or now. Unfortunately, one of these, ipsative scoring, is psychometrically problematic and the MAT has not been revised since it was introduced (Bernard, Walsh, & Mills, 2005).

Another multidimensional measure of individual differences in motivation is the Personality Research Form (PRF; Jackson, 1999), which is based on Murray's (1938) concept of needs. The PRF Form A/B is comprised of scales to assess these dimensions: Achievement, Affiliation, Aggression, Autonomy, Dominance, Endurance, Exhibition, Harmavoidance, Impulsivity, Nurturance, Order, Play, Social Recognition, and Understanding.

Both the MAT and PRF are comprised of relatively independent, narrow bandwidth scales assessing purported dimensions of motivation. However, while Cattell did propose a genetic basis to personality and motivational dimensions (e.g., Cattell & Dreger, 1977; Cattell, Radcliffe, & Sweney, 1963), neither MAT nor PRF scales were based on evolutionary theory. In 75 years of motivation research only two instruments were categorized as biologically based, and none were identified as evolutionary based (Mayer et al., 2007).

An Individual Differences Theory of Human Motivation

Buss (1991) proposed a rationale for joining evolutionary, motivational, and personality psychology. My colleagues and I were influenced by Buss's proposal, as well as Cattell's attempt to assess motivational traits multidimensionally, when we developed a new approach to the study of individual differences in human motivation based on evolution (Bernard, Mills, Swenson, & Walsh, 2005). We could have undertaken a post hoc analysis of the MAT or PRF dimensions from an evolutionary perspective, like what had been done with the FFM, but opted for a theory-based approach that would be compatible

with mainstream evolutionary psychology, behavioral ecology, and behavioral genetics—the three social science approaches that share the metatheory of evolution (Smith, 2000). Buss's (2009) rationale and the promising work of those who proposed evolutionary mechanisms for FFM dimensions both figured prominently in the development of this theory. The development of this theory is ongoing and has followed a logical, step-by-step procedure.

The first step was to describe the EEA in which human motivational dimensions may have evolved. Bugental (2000) and Kenrick, Li, and Butner (2003) had suggested that five or six overlapping social domains existed in the EEA of humans. Each of these domains is related to a different sized group. Evidence had suggested that the size of the human neocortex and the size of social groups in which humans interact had coevolved (Dunbar, 2007). Bernard et al. (2005) took this into account in organizing the domains hierarchically by size: Individual, Dyad, Small Group, Large Group, and Very Large Group.

The second step was to propose recurring fitness challenges that may have been present in each social domain in the EEA of humans. Kenrick et al.'s (2003) suggestions formed a basis for this. We identified seven fitness challenges. The social domains, their sizes, constituents, and fitness challenges are listed in Table 22.1. Three social groups, similar to the first three listed in Table 22.1, have also been identified in the social ecology of other primates: Solitary, Pairs, and Group-Living (Kappeler & van Schaik, 2002). The primate Group-Living domain was operationalized as at least three adults of both sexes and the upper limit size for gorillas in this domain is probably 20 members (Harcourt & Stewart, 2007), which places the primate Group-Living domain between the human Small Group and Large Group domains in terms of size. The larger social domains that humans negotiate probably necessitated the evolution of additional motive dimensions and larger and more complex brains.

The third step was to identify the behavioral syndromes that might have addressed each of the fitness challenges. A behavioral syndrome represents correlated strategies for overcoming a fitness challenge, and a brain that is prepared to facilitate certain strategies may have a fitness advantage (Sih et al., 2004a, 2004b). Each syndrome was hypothesized to be a dimension that varies in strength (i.e., the *amount* of resources in the form of time, effort, energy, money, etc.) an individual expends on it. Under some environmental conditions, maximum strength would

Table 22.1. Human Social Domains, Size, Constituents, and Recurring Fitness Challenges

Domain	Size	Constituents	Recurring Fitness Challenge
Individual	1	Single individual	(1) How to protect oneself (2) How to identify environmental and interpersonal resources and hazards
Dyadic	2	Pairs of intrasexual and inter-sexual individuals	(3) How to compete for mates (4) How to develop social status and mating desirability
Small Group	2–20	Mate and kin	(5) How to establish cooperative relationships for mating and support of kin
Large Group	20–150	Coalitions of mostly nonkin (neighborhoods, towns, social clubs)	(6) How to develop individual-to-individual reciprocation among nonkin
Very Large Group	1,000+	Coalitions of overwhelmingly nonkin (political parties, religions, ethnic groups, nations)	(7) How to develop group-to-individual reciprocation among nonkin ("institutionalized reciprocity")

Note: Once a successful adaptation to a fitness challenge in a domain has developed, it may be successful in meeting challenges in other domains as well.

produce better fitness, in others, minimal strength, and in most, a moderate level of strength. An individual's strength level in a dimension is phenotype, partly influenced by the genotype of a brain prepared to set a certain level (reaction range) for the latent trait that produces the behavioral syndrome and partly influenced by local environmental circumstances, including threats, resource availability, cultural expectations, roles, learning, and cues. The dimensions associated with each phenotypic behavioral syndrome are considered latent variables—called "motives" for short—and each was identified by a label for convenience.

Research has suggested that adapted mental mechanisms are not domain general, but rather evolved independently to accomplish domain-specific tasks (e.g., Cosmides & Tooby, 1992; Gigerenzer & Hug, 1992). Each motive was assumed to have developed independently and to be mediated by a relatively independent, domain-specific mental mechanism. The brain contains many such mental mechanisms, each one of which evolved to facilitate behavior that increased fitness in the EEA (Hagen & Symons, 2007; see Bernard et al., 2005, for a discussion of the neuropsychological structures that may underlie various motive mental mechanisms). The motives, operational definitions, and behavioral syndromes are listed in Table 22.2.

The fourth step was to propose a rationale for the development and heritability of these individual differences dimensions. Balancing/fluctuating selection (Penke et al., 2007) and trade-offs (Nettle, 2006) provide the basis for the theory. When environmental conditions fluctuate such that different levels of a trait are favored at different times, genetic variation in the trait can be maintained. An example of this is depicted in Figure 22.1 . As Figure 22.1 suggests, polygenic variations could result in structural and functional differences in brain development. Genotypic differences in brain development could result in different reaction ranges that restrict potential phenotypic outcomes along a motive dimension. Different phenotypes produce different levels of *strength* in a latent predisposition—a motive—to engage in a particular behavioral syndrome at a certain level of activity. Different levels of strength in a behavioral syndrome have different trade-offs. Higher strength generally requires more resources (e.g., time, effort, energy, wealth), while lower strength generally conserves resources. Any level of strength of a behavioral syndrome could increase fitness, depending on environmental conditions and the return on investment of resources (trade-offs) in terms of survival and reproductive/inclusive fitness.

Various levels of a motive's strength would be favored by selection to some extent but under

Table 22.2. Motives, Operational Definitions, and Behavioral Syndromes

Social Domain	Motive	Operational Definition	Behavioral Syndrome Examples
Individual	Environmental Inquisitiveness	Use resources to explore the physical environment; evaluate resource availability and hazards in new and different things, places, and situations	Investigating the physical environment and the unknown; investigating places; finding out how things work; trying out resources
	Illness Avoidance	Use resources to maintain bodily integrity and health	Avoiding unhealthy or toxic substances; maintaining physical integrity; maintaining cleanliness of one's person and surroundings; having health checkups; maintaining a healthy diet
	Threat Avoidance	Use resources to maintain the safety of one's person; avoid challenges to one's person and resources	Taking precautionary actions; avoiding potential conflicts and threats; securing one's person and property; pacifying others
Dyad	Aggression	Use resources to acquire and control additional resources; challenge and intimidate others for control of resources; approach challenges to one's person and resources with combative and intimidating displays and actions	Threatening or assaulting others; striving for leadership; engaging in challenging and dangerous activities that signal fearlessness and dominance
	Interpersonal Inquisitiveness	Use resources to explore the social environment; test limits, traditions, and how others act, react, and interact; compare oneself to others	Investigating the social environment; jesting, mocking, playful engagement with others; game playing; using humor and sarcasm; testing interpersonal limits
	Appearance[1]	Use resources to compete for status on the basis of physical appearance	Grooming and adornment; attempting to increases one's attractiveness comparatively and competitively (tanning, cosmetic surgery, makeup, fragrances, jewelry)
	Mental[1]	Use resources to compete for status on the basis of intellectual capacities and knowledge, as well as skills, abilities, and talents	Increasing knowledge; exploiting talent; developing creative or artistic abilities; participating in competitions that signal (gender-appropriate) intellectual ascendancy (spelling bees, chess and card tournaments, dance and music competitions)
	Physical[1]	Use resources to compete for status on the basis of physical strength, endurance, size, shape, and stature	Increasing bodily strength and endurance; participating in competitions that signal (gender-appropriate) physical ascendancy; altering and enhancing bodily shape to culturally appropriate norms
	Wealth[1]	Use resources to compete for status on the basis of acquiring material resources	Obtaining wealth and material possessions; signaling ascendancy on the basis of access to and control of resources
	Sex	Seek sexual activity	Pursuing sexual partners and sexual variety; engaging in frequent sexual activity

(*Continued*)

Table 22.2. Continued

Social Domain	Motive	Operational Definition	Behavioral Syndrome Examples
Small Group	Commitment[2]	Transfer of resources to mates and offspring; development of tender, intimate, supportive attachments with others	Giving mates and offspring resources and tangible signs of affection and emotional support; fidelity (e.g., refraining from sharing resources with others); signaling a desire for intimacy
Large Group	Altruism[2]	Transfer of resources to kin without expectation of immediate self-benefit (but at a cost to oneself that is generally lower than the benefits to others multiplied by their degree of genetic relatedness)	Using resources to protect kin and help kin succeed
	Social Exchange[2]	Enter into reciprocal, mutually beneficial exchanges of resources with nonkin; share resources fairly and without cheating; do what is legally and socially prescribed and avoid what is proscribed	Demonstrating reliability and trustworthiness; not taking advantage of others; not cheating others; living up to contracts and bargains; following social expectations, rules, regulations, and laws
Very Large Group	Legacy[2]	Transfer of resources to institutions that benefit nonkin as much as, or more than, kin without the expectation of direct reciprocity to oneself	Contributing resources to the commonweal and future generations; bequeathing resources to institutions (schools, hospitals, charities); self-sacrifice for nonkin
	Meaning	Use resources to identify with, construct, and maintain a philosophy, purpose, or rationalization for existence (and nonexistence); attempt to arrive at an understanding and peace with the presumed purpose of life	Using resources to investigate and support meaning-generating paradigms involving spirituality, religion, philosophy, science or any other system of knowledge; constructing a belief system; studying or engaging in the practice of philosophy, science, or religion

Note. Resources include time, energy, effort, wealth, and reputation. Since the theory was introduced, the motives have been renamed to better reflect their underlying dimensions and redefined and recategorized to conform more closely to evolutionary theory; this table reflects the theory in its current form.

[1] "S" or "status motive" the goal of which is to increase one's social standing through competitive behavior intended to increase personal resources within its behavioral domain.

[2] "C" or "cooperative motive" the goal of which is to increase one's reputation for reliability as a partner in relationships and coalitions through direct and indirect reciprocal transfers of resources.

different environmental conditions. There should also be trade-offs in the costs and benefits of different levels of a behavioral syndrome such that different levels of strength in a motive dimension could produce relatively equal fitness outcomes at different times and in different contexts in evolutionary history (MacArthur & Wilson, 1967; Reznick et al., 2002; Rushton, 2004; Stearns, 1992). Extreme environmental conditions have probably been less common over time, such that very high or very low strength in a motive dimension is less common than a moderate level. Therefore, aggregating

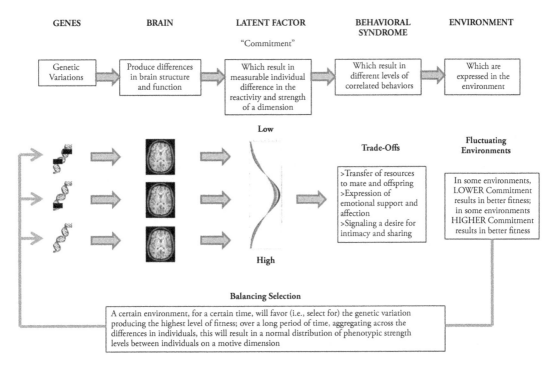

Fig. 22.1. The development of motive dimensions maintained by fluctuating/balancing selection: Example with the commitment motive.

motive strength across individuals should produce a relatively normal distribution of strength along a motive dimension.

To complete the fourth step, it is necessary to identify some of the possible trade-offs that may have allowed individual differences in the proposed motives to evolve. A preliminary rationale for motive trade-offs follows.

Hypothesized Motive Trade-Offs
INDIVIDUAL DOMAIN
Threat Avoidance

Threat Avoidance may be a better fitness strategy than Aggression in some cases where cost is high, and even "posturing," a mixture of aggression and threat avoidance, may be a better fitness strategy in other cases (Fournier, Moskowitz, & Zuroff, 2002). Panksepp (1998, 2000) identified several genetically-coded emotional operating systems, one of which he called "fear." This system mediates freezing, flight, or escape. Threat Avoidance combines a fear of harm to oneself and a desire to escape to safety (O'Connor, Berry, Weiss, Schuweiter, & Sevier, 2000). Social comparison helps humans determine when to submit (Buunk & Brenninkmeyer, 2000)—when the costs outweigh the benefits of standing ground—and humans have developed a variety of submission strategies (Fournier et al., 2002; Gil-

bert, 2000). Interestingly, one submission strategy is to signal cooperation, which could overlap with the cooperative motives described later. However, because submission to others results in aggressors gaining more access to available resources, submissive strategies should also involve costs that could maintain heritable individual differences.

Illness Avoidance

Illness Avoidance may also be related to Panksepp's (1998, 2000) fear system. In this sense, engaging in many healthy behaviors could represent a "flight into health" in order to escape fear of contamination and illness. In a study of 37 cultures, both women and men judged "good health" to be highly desirable in a mate (Buss, 1989). Individual differences in Illness Avoidance may be selectively maintained because it could increase fitness and the probability of selection as a mate. Avoiding illness may require more resources but result in better health and more access to mates. Illness avoidance should also vary with the presence and ease of transmission of pathogens in a particular environment, and this has been shown to affect sociosexuality and personality (Schaller & Murray, 2008).

Research on disgust offers another perspective on the Illness Avoidance motive. Disgust has been identified as a basic human facial expression in infants and has been part of many evolutionary and neural theories of emotion (Plutchik, 2003). Disgust has been defined as revulsion at the prospect of putting an offensive substance in one's mouth (Rozin & Fallon, 1987), but this seems overly narrow. People disgusted by something actually avoid proximity with it and do not want to touch or taste it (Rozin, Haidt, McCauley, Dunlop, & Ashmore, 1999; Rozin, Millman, & Nemeroff, 1986). Furthermore, even foods once preferred can become disgusting if a person has become nauseated and vomited after eating it once (Logue, 1985; Rozin & Kalat, 1971). Experimental stimuli that evoke such responses include rotting meat, feces, vomit, cockroaches, phlegm, and similar bodily fluids, and all of these could spread illness. In an evolutionary sense, individual differences in a motive to avoid contamination could be maintained because it may have resulted in trade-offs in survival and fitness benefits. Extreme illness avoidance could reduce exposure to toxins but could also restrict food intake and calories, while indiscriminate food intake could increase calories and nutrition but might lead to more frequent exposure to unwholesome or toxic substances. The fitness outcomes of high versus low Illness Avoidance would also depend on the fluctuating availability and quality of food.

Environmental Inquisitiveness

Panksepp (1998, 2000) called this the "seeking/expectancy" system, which controls general engagement with the environment, leading to exploration, investigation, and anticipation of rewards. He also noted its role in learning and memory and suggested that it allows an organism "to develop a sense of causality from the perception of correlated environmental events" (2000, p. 160). A strong motive to be inquisitive about the environment and explore it should involve trade-offs. Exploratory behavior requires resources in terms of time and effort. Knowledge gained may increase survival and fitness; however, exploration may involve exposure to unknown dangers that could reduce fitness.

DYADIC DOMAIN

Interpersonal Inquisitiveness

This is related to Panksepp's (1998, 2000) "play and dominance system," which recognizes the role play can have in establishing social dominance. Individual differences in play are observed in rats. For example, rats that exhibited the highest levels of juvenile play also became more dominant as adults. Human play is quite complex and numerous types

have been identified, such as relational, dramatic, constructive, sensorimotor, and rough-and-tumble (Scott & Panksepp, 2003; Slade & Wolf, 1994).

The Interpersonal Inquisitiveness motive was operationalized as rough-and-tumble play and simple fun rather than other types of play. Human rough-and-tumble play probably allows individuals to "size each other up" in mock situations that are not supposed to lead to outright aggression. For example, research suggests that children value sports achievements higher than any other (Eccles, Wigfield, Harold, & Blumenfeld, 1993), and men appear to have evolved mental mechanisms to allow them to assess each other's fighting ability and do so more than women (Fox, 1997). However, there are only modest differences in boys' and girls' rough-and-tumble play (Scott & Panksepp, 2003).

In addition, there is evidence that Environmental Inquisitiveness, in the form of play, improves cognitive functioning (Dansky & Silverman, 1973) and helps individuals learn to negotiate the social environment (Berkoff, 2001). A strong motive to be inquisitive about other people and the social environment could improve knowledge about other individuals' cooperation, fairness, and trustworthiness (Berkoff, 2001). On the other hand, rough-and-tumble play could lead to increased exposure to pathogens, and the risk of escalation of aggression could lead to physical injury.

Aggression

When attempting to survive, reproduce, and acquire resources, animals will threaten, attack, and kill each other (Mason & Mendoza, 1993). Another of Panksepp's (1998, 2000) four genetically coded emotional operating systems is "rage," which mediates aggressive behaviors such as attacking, biting, and fighting in non-humans. In humans, subtler forms of aggression, such as school yard bullying in order to gain resources (toys, designer clothes, or lunch money), are common in children (Campbell, 1993; Olweus, 1978). In a coalition-forming species such as humans, competition for friends can also result in "relational aggression" (Crick, Casas, & Mosher, 1997). Men sometimes kill other men who have cuckolded them, coopting their reproductive resource, and males commit more than 99% of intrasex homicides (Daly & Wilson, 1988). Aggression, as a strategy, can be used to acquire and secure resources of all kinds (mates, territory, food), but it can lead to counteraggression, and cycles of escalation can incur costs for the initial aggressor (Berkowitz, 1993). Therefore, aggressive behavior involves trade-offs in terms of costs such as physical injury. Aggression should be context dependent, and heritable individual differences could develop in it (Buss & Duntley, 2006). Innovative research with chimpanzees (*Pan troglodytes*) has found that dominance is heritable and correlated with subjective well-being (Weiss, King, & Enns, 2002), which may be a trade-off for the costs incurred by the risk of counteraggression and escalating violence.

Sex

Humans engage in pluralistic mating strategies (Gangestad & Simpson, 2000) and are prepared for short- and long-term relationships (Buss & Schmitt, 1993). Human females have "concealed ovulation" with a vague estrus cycle that is not evident through physical changes as in other primates. Therefore, human sexuality is not linked directly to reproduction. As Panksepp (1998) noted, "It was a remarkable feat of nature to weave powerful sexual feelings and desires in the fabric of the brain, without revealing the reproductive purposes of those feelings to the eager participants" (p. 228). In the absence of such knowledge, humans had to be motivated to engage in sex so that reproduction could occur. Sexual motivation is complex and mediated partly by neurohormonal activation and partly by the reward of physical contact and orgasm. The inherent level of neurohormonal activation should be correlated with the strength of the Sex motive, which is a testable hypothesis.

During orgasm, activity in the cerebral cortex decreases and activity in the hypothalamus and adjacent midline structures increases (Georgiadis et al., 2006; Holstege et al., 2003). These structures also respond more actively to heroin exposure and rely on dopamine, which is involved in pleasure and reward circuits (Panksepp, 1998). The benefits/rewards of sex are among the most intense pleasures experienced. However, that sex can have its costs is evident in some species, such as the wolf spider (*Hogna helluo*) where females eat males after mating presumably as nourishment for offspring.

The remaining four motives in the Dyadic Domain all involve different strategies to increase social status and desirability as a mate. It is likely that these motives arose through intrasexual and intersexual competition as well as sexual selection consistent with parental investment theory (Trivers, 1972). One strategy for maintaining friendships and coalitions may be to increase one's personal attributes, reputation, and irreplaceability, in short, one's status (Tooby & Cosmides, 1996). This is consistent with

the important role status and resources play in choosing a mate (Buss & Schmitt, 1993; Gangestad & Simpson, 2000). The four status/competitive motives could be maintained as individual differences dimensions because, although they can require considerable resources, their benefit is increased access to mates and reproductive fitness.

Appearance

Research has suggested that face and body symmetry—which can indicate genetic soundness and developmental stability—are the markers of "beauty" in mate selection (e.g., Gangestad, Thornhill, & Yeo, 1994; Shakelford & Larsen, 1997). Therefore, physical appearance is a proxy for good health. The nucleus accumbens of heterosexual males is differentially activated by female faces that range in attractiveness (Aharon et al., 2001). It becomes hyperactivated in response to images of attractive females but not to images of average females and attractive and average males. This region is the "pleasure center" of the brain and part of its reward circuitry. Cross-cultural research also supports a very strong desire for physical attractiveness in a long-term mate, although it is consistently stronger in males than females (Buss & Schmitt, 1993).

The Appearance motive is the strength of interest in increasing status through appearance-enhancing behaviors and can be measured by the amount of resources one puts into them. Examples of such behaviors include cosmetic surgery (which could correct asymmetries in body and face), dieting and fat reduction procedures (liposuction) where food is abundant and inexpensive, greater food intake where food is not abundant and costly, and body decoration and adornments that may serve to camouflage or distract from physical shortcomings. These can involve considerable costs in terms of resources, but a trade-off may be better quality mates.

Mental

Psychometric intelligence or "*g*" is related to socioeconomic status (SES) and the control of resources (e.g., Gottfredson, 1997, 2004; Jensen, 1998; Nyborg & Jensen, 2001; Scullin, Peters, Williams, & Ceci, 2000). Individuals with higher SES also have better physical health and a longer life span (Adler et al., 1994; Bradley & Corwyn, 2002), which suggests the evolutionary benefits of intelligence. Therefore, it is not surprising that intelligence is a highly valued quality in mate selection (Buss et al., 1990).

Bernard et al. (2005) posited that individuals might compete for status by attempting to increase and signal knowledge acquisition. For example, many cultures hold educators and the educated in high regard. Education costs time, wealth, and effort, but it can increase earning potential, reputation, and status. However, Bernard et al. adopted a broader definition of knowledge than academic achievement. They proposed that the Mental motive behavioral syndrome encompasses the development of nonintellectual talents and abilities such as in the creative arts (painting, sculpture) or performing arts (acting, dancing, singing, playing a musical instrument, composing). All of these might be avenues for increasing one's status, reputation, and irreplaceability (Tooby & Cosmides, 1996). This is consistent with the description of nonacademic talents and abilities as "multiple intelligences," which include musical intelligence and bodily/kinesthetic intelligence (Gardner, 1993). The time and effort to develop any of these talents and abilities is costly and must be diverted from other endeavors, but the benefit in better quality mates may offset this under certain environmental conditions.

Physical

Physical stature and status are important in mate selection. Women prefer potential partners to be tall, physically strong, and athletic (Buss & Schmitt, 1993) and men are intimidated by other men who are taller, have greater shoulder width, and more upper body musculature (Barber, 1995). Men prefer women whose waist-to-hip ratio (WHR) is between 0.67 and 0.80 (Singh, 1993, 2000; Singh & Young, 1995). WHR of men is in the range of 0.85 to 0.95, similar to what both men's and women's WHR is before puberty. The reduction in the ratio in women after puberty is an accurate indicator of women's better reproductive status. However, preferences in weight and body fat tend to be context dependent. In areas where food is more available, attractiveness is enhanced by a thinner appearance (Symons, 1979) and in areas where food is less available, attractiveness is enhanced by a heavier appearance (Rosenblatt, 1974).

Bernard et al. (2005) were aware of this and attempted to operationalize the Physical motive so that the behavioral syndrome would not be restricted to certain contexts and would reflect general attempts to improve one's physical stature and status. In contrast with the Appearance motive, which concerns body adornment, the Physical motive concerns actual attempts to alter one's physique, body type, and physical prowess. These may involve exercising and attempts to improve physical fitness, endurance, strength, and flexibility. Such activities can involve considerable costs in terms of effort, energy, and injury, yet they may result in higher status and better quality mates.

Wealth

A mate who has material resources may be valued as more irreplaceable or indispensable than a poorer rival (Tooby & Cosmides, 1996). Consistent with parental investment theory (Trivers, 1972), women place a premium on economic resources in a mate (e.g., Buss et al., 1990; Buss, Shackelford, Kirkpatrick, & Larsen, 2001; Kenrick, Sadalla, Groth, & Trost, 1990; Wiederman, 1993). Men do not discount the importance of economic resources, but women accord it more weight than men do in mate selection. Men should also value a mate who has her own resources more, because this could leave his resources intact. This could be the basis for some arranged marriages and would certainly be represented in the tradition of the dowry. People who are more acquisitive may accumulate more wealth and gain an advantage in competition for mates, but acquiring wealth may require a greater expense of other resources such as energy and time. The accumulation of material resources would, therefore, involve trade-offs that could permit individual differences to develop in the strength of resource acquisition behavior.

SMALL GROUP DOMAIN
Commitment

Commitment involves the transfer of resources to mate and offspring and provides the framework for family interrelationships. Comparative research suggests that a variety of neural circuits—for example, the dorsal preoptic area (Jirikowski, Caldwell, Stumpf, & Pedersen, 1988)—and hormones and neurotransmitters—vasopressin, oxytocin, prolactin, and progesterone (e.g., Carmichael, Warburton, Dixen, & Davidson, 1994; Insel, Winslow, Wang, & Young, 1998; Mann & Bridges, 2001; Panksepp, 1981; Rosenblatt, 2001)—are found in males *and* females and are involved in *sexual* as well as *affectionate* (caregiving or "maternal")behavior. The concept of "love" appears to be nearly universal in human cultures (Jankowiak, 1995; Jankowiak & Fischer, 1992), and it seems to be defined by men and women specifically in terms of commitment behaviors such as giving up other sexual and romantic partners, remaining faithful, marriage, and a desire to have children (Buss, 1988). The extent of commitment predicts satisfaction in relationships (Rusbult, 1983) and groups (Van Vugt & Hart, 2004) and commitment may be necessary in order for cooperative motives such as Altruism and Social Exchange (see later) to develop (Nesse, 2001; Rusbult & Van Lange, 2003; Van Vugt & Hart, 2004).

In addition, women prefer men who are more affectionate to children (La Cerra, 1994, as cited in Buss, 2004), supporting the evolutionary concept that men may have been selected by women not only for their ability to commit to a partner but also for their ability to commit to offspring. The formation of pair bonds increases inclusive fitness, because of the beneficial effects a partnership has on raising offspring (Geary, 2000). However, alternative strategies to increase fitness—such as promiscuity—also exist. As mammals, one of the most outstanding features of parental care is human males' involvement in parenting that is facultatively expressed based on contingent conditions and therefore could evolve (Geary, 2005). In terms of trade-offs, a cost of Commitment is reduced resources for the individual, while a benefit would be increased inclusive fitness.

LARGE GROUP DOMAIN

Bernard et al. (2005) proposed that the four remaining motives operated in Large and Very Large Group domains of mostly nonkin. Three of these—Altruism, Social Exchange, and Legacy—are considered "cooperative motives," due to their role in promoting coalition formation. Coalitions are typically defined as alliances of two or more individuals who take collective action to accomplish a goal. The cooperative motives help individuals balance the status/competitive motives that are involved in more individualistic and/or self-protective behavior. The benefit of coalitions is increased survivability of oneself and one's kin through the mutual protection and shared resources that a large group provides. For separately reproducing individuals, humans are exceptionally cooperative, and we cooperate in groups to compete with other groups (Alexander, 2005; Wrangham, 1999). This involves a fundamental trade-off in terms of the individual costs of being in a coalition versus perhaps the greater costs of *not* being in a coalition (Flinn & Coe, 2007). The increased social challenges and computations that group-living primates would have faced required greater social intelligence, which in turn bought increased brain size as well as developments in computational mechanisms to serve these additional adaptive motivations (Byrne & Corp, 2004; Byrne & Whiten, 1988; Dunbar, 2007; Kudo & Dunbar, 2001).

Multilevel selection theory (Wilson & Sober, 1998) probably also plays a role in the evolution of the cooperative motives. The mechanisms of balancing/fluctuating selection and trade-offs are usually understood to apply at the level of individual selection, but selection can operate at multiple levels. Groups can become higher-level "organisms" subject to the pressures of natural selection and this is probably necessary for adaptations such as altruism and morality to develop. Group selection had been rejected earlier but is now viewed as plausible in some circumstances (Wilson, 2007). Human evolution may represent a major transition in multilevel selection and this may be expressed in the cooperative motives (Wilson, Van Vugt, & O'Gorman, 2008).

Altruism

Bernard et al. (2005) noted Hamilton's (1964) "rule" that altruism could develop if the costs to oneself were outweighed by the benefit to the recipient, multiplied by the degree of genetic relatedness to the recipient. Indeed, research has found that altruistic behavior is more likely between relatives (Burnstein, Crandall, & Kitayama, 1994), and it is mediated by the degree of perceived emotional closeness (Korchmaros & Kenny, 2001; Neyer & Lang, 2003). Social species of insects engage in self-sacrificing behaviors but usually only within families of genetically related individuals when their interests overlap (Wilson, 1975).

Bernard et al. (2005) originally defined the Altruism motive in terms of "strong reciprocity," the predisposition to cooperate with nonkin. However, the theory now defines Altruism in terms of Hamilton's "rule." The Altruism motive applies to kin and facilitates sharing resources with a wider circle of kin than the Commitment motive does. It supports the development of larger family groups than Commitment. "Strong reciprocity" is now operationalized in the Social Exchange and Legacy motives, which involve exchange or transfer of resources to nonkin. In terms of trade-offs, as with Commitment, a cost of Altruism is reduced resources for the individual, while a benefit would be increased inclusive fitness through resource sharing with kin who share at least some of the individual's genes.

Social Exchange

Altruism involves an apparent unequal exchange—a *transfer* of resources to kin—whereas Social Exchange involves an equal—or reciprocal—*exchange* of resources with nonkin, either with immediate reciprocity or with the expectation of future reciprocity (Trivers, 1971). Altruism can increase inclusive fitness, but, as Hamilton's (1964) "rule" states, it would decline as the degree of genetic relatedness is reduced. Altruism would, therefore, not facilitate the formation of nonkin coalitions, but the Social Exchange motive would. Social Exchange can operate in large social groups whereby an individual transfers resources to another member of the group and receives reciprocation from the individual or a third party or institution (Alexander, 1987). For example, a soldier risks his or her life for a comrade in battle and receives veterans' benefits such as mortgage assistance or college tuition from the government in return.

The Social Exchange motive promotes individual sacrifice in the form of *not* taking advantage of others to gain resources, even when there is opportunity to gain an advantage that could increase an individual's fitness. Gradually, an individual's reputation for trustworthiness is enhanced through social exchanges and results in others being more willing to engage in exchanges to the mutual benefit of both parties. Those who enter into reciprocal exchanges of resources more frequently risk being taken advantage of, but they may benefit from enhancing their own reputation as a trusted partner. Research suggests that about 60% of people appear to be interested in maximizing mutual, rather than individual, gain (Van Lange & Kuhlman, 1994; Van Lange, Otten, De Bruin, & Joireman, 1997). Humans do engage in strong reciprocity—transfer of resources to nonkin—in large social groups (Fehr & Fischbacher, 2003) and this can be maintained by frequency-dependent selection (Mealey, 1995). In larger groups the detection of freeloaders can be more difficult, but larger groups provide better protection and access to resources as a trade-off.

Social Exchange requires the development of strong social institutions as well as cheater detection to reduce exploitation (Cosmides & Tooby, 1992). Therefore, Social Exchange should work best where reputations are known. However, some human groups are so large that it is impossible to be acquainted with more than a fraction of their members personally (Van Vugt, Snyder, Tyler, & Biel, 2000). Examples of such groups are nations, religions, linguistic, and ethnic groups. In large groups, membership is often formalized through requirements (e.g., place of birth or parentage), declarations of allegiance (e.g., loyalty oaths, catechism), initiation rituals (e.g., baptism, circumcision), and obligations (dues, taxes, military service). Formalization of membership is consistent with the idea that humans should exhibit "discriminate sociality"; they should seek the benefits of socializing in groups

while limiting costs such as increased potential for conflicts and exposure to pathogens (Kurzban & Leary, 2001). Formalizing membership may help identify in-group members from out-group members and insure that members participate at some minimal level, thereby reducing the costs of free-loading. Collateral institutions also develop that help members track each other's reputations for trustworthiness, for example, public trials, gossip, online social networking, and news media.

VERY LARGE GROUP DOMAIN

Very Large groups can command a strong sense of affiliation and can result in extreme sacrifices to the group, including death. Tooby and Cosmides (1988) have noted that war is a highly cooperative endeavor and, as such, it should involve the cooperative motives. Bernard et al. (2005) originally identified this very large social domain of nonkin as "memetic," because motives in this social domain are dependent on cultural transmission of memes of identity, meaning, and obligation (Dawkins, 1989). These memes can operate as cultural norms—as exemplars of culturally valued behavior—that increase cooperation and sacrifice in very large groups (de Waal, 1996). Motives in this domain are primarily cultural adaptations (Boyd, 2007) and learning plays an important role in their shaping and expression. This is because humans are a species that is not only subject to operant conditioning (Thorndike's law regarding learning from the consequences of one's actions) but also *aware* of its subjectivity to it. Group selection acting on culture may be partly responsible for the development of motives in the very large group domain and cultures may transmit valuable adaptive as well as maladaptive information (Boyd, 2007). Bernard et al. (2005) proposed two evolved individual differences dimensions in this very large social domain, the Legacy and Meaning motives.

Legacy

The third of the cooperative motives, Legacy, is not based on an equal exchange of resources. Legacy mediates the transfer of resources to nonkin without an expectation of reciprocity. Bernard et al. (2005) used the example of donating money to a university as an example of Legacy. Such a transfer of resources may provide no direct fitness benefit to the donor or his or her kin. The university is culturally valued and, presumably, perpetuates values consistent with the donor's, but a donation to the university probably tangibly benefits rivals' kin *more* than one's own. Another example of the Legacy motive is a soldier who gives his or her life in battle. This is the ultimate self-sacrifice to a perceived higher purpose (honor, duty, patriotism) that exists only as a meme. In the nonmemetic, material world, where resources are finite (nothing more so than mortality), such extreme self-sacrifice cannot benefit the individual's fitness. However, it may increase the self-sacrificing individual's inclusive fitness, because his or her kin may benefit from membership in a stronger, safer nation. Very large groups also develop institutionalized systems for third-party reciprocity through which, for example, individuals are "paid back" for dying (keeping their part of the bargain with society) by the government transferring resources (e.g., "survivor benefits") to a dead soldier's spouse and children.

This third-party reciprocal arrangement can work in evolutionary terms only if it increased the group's (society's or nation's) ability to prevail in competition with other groups or otherwise had the effect of increasing the commonweal, the resources generally available to the group. The reputation of the donor or dead soldier may also be enhanced and, in turn, increases the donor's attractiveness as a partner in social exchange or the soldier's offspring's status as a hero's progeny (Alexander, 1987; McAndrew, 2002). In this way, a good reputation is extended to kin, thereby increasing the donor's and the soldier's inclusive fitness. In terms of trade-offs, the costs in such cases are often large, while the benefits in terms of a return on investment beyond reputation are difficult to discern, which is why cultural memes must play an important role. There are, perhaps, some quantifiable returns to society and the strength of its institutions that benefit its members, but many of the benefits to the individual who engages in Legacy-motivated behaviors are perceptions and abstractions based on memes about generosity, patriotism, sacrifice, religious duty, and heroism.

Meaning

Access to resources in contemporary human existence involves living in smaller groups of kin, while simultaneously living in and depending on very large groups and institutions for resources (Tooby & Cosmides, 1996). And obtaining resources in such large groups requires the negotiation of numerous complex social exchanges. Bernard et al. (2005) suggested that meaning—the development of a personal ontology, a rationale or explanation for one's existence and place in the world—serves a survival function as an antidote to the despair that can arise in the social environment of very large groups.

Such a personal ontology would be essential in a species that is aware of its mortality.

As social animals, humans must accommodate or reconcile their nature in terms of balancing the trade-offs of individual self-interest versus communal group deference and cooperation. Bernard et al. (2005) believed that this situation can lead to alienation and despair. In fact, alienation and anonymity are associated with increased selfishness and antisocial behavior (Prentice-Dunn & Rogers, 1980; Zimbardo, 1970). Although behavior motivated by Meaning could increase an individual's level of cooperation with others, this would be a byproduct. Therefore, Meaning is not categorized as a cooperative motive.

Instead, Bernard et al. (2005) proposed that there are individual differences in the extent to which people are motivated to construct meaning out of existence. This is controversial, but in evolutionary terms, being motivated to seek, adopt, and/or construct meaning may result in benefits such as better psychological coping abilities—hardiness, resilience, fitness, even—when it comes to meeting existential challenges. Cultural myths, particularly of legendary heroes, which are a form of meme (Dawkins, 1989), exist because they function to provide ready models of meaning for members of a group (Campbell, 2008; Campbell & Moyers, 1991). Some people could find meaning by accepting a particular religious belief, and most religions come with an explanation of the individual's place in the world. In fact, an epidemiological analysis of mental representations suggested that motivation may even be driving the evolution of religious representations (Nichols, 2004). Others may find meaning in scientific pursuits or the enjoyment of nature. Some may even find meaning in amassing great fame and fortune and, with them, influence. In terms of trade-offs, even the pursuit of meaning has resource costs associated with it in terms of time, energy, effort, and wealth. There may be benefits, however, in terms of psychological fitness, which may increase one's attractiveness as a mate.

Summary

As noted in the introduction to this chapter, the primary challenge for individual differences psychologists is to conceptualize a means by which selection can maintain variance in a functional dimension of behavior. These proposed trade-offs that may have existed in the evolutionary history of the motive dimensions offer promise in addressing this challenge. However, the trade-offs proposed for the motive dimensions are only tentative first steps.

Furthermore, the proposal of an evolved individual differences theory of motivation is a highly speculative endeavor. First, in the long history of motivational psychology, except for the MAT and PRF, there are very few attempts to study motivation from a multidimensional, trait-based perspective. Second, the relevance of individual differences to evolutionary psychology is a source of much debate and is not widely accepted (see Gangestad & Simpson, 2007). The advantage of combining individual differences and evolutionary theory, particularly trade-offs, should be the ability to explain *why* certain motives are expressed today in human behavior and to put the development of these motives into historical context with respect to selection rather than to merely describe proximal processes in motivation (Buss, 1991, 1999). Due to their presumed heritability, evolved motives should be operating in, and should be able to be measured as, individual differences in contemporary behavior (Bernard et al., 2005). At this point, the theory and the motive constructs required empirical support, which necessitated development of a means of assessing them.

Development of a Motive Assessment Strategy

The development of new psychological constructs requires these steps: *(1)* base constructs on a theory, *(2)* operationally define the constructs, and *(3)* determine the relationships between the proposed constructs and behavior and other constructs (Cronbach & Meehl, 1955). The previous discussion has described how Steps 1 and 2 were accomplished. Step 3 required a programmatic series of studies designated the "Assessment of Individual Motives." The term "individual" was chosen to connote the presumed domain-specific (i.e., independent) nature of the motive dimensions. These studies resulted in several questionnaire versions of the 15 motive dimensions referred to together as the Assessment of Individual Motives-Questionnaire (AIM-Q; Bernard, Mills, Swenson, & Walsh, 2008). This section summarizes the psychometric properties of the AIM-Q. Our theory of motivation depends on whether the motive dimensions are able to be identified and assessed reliably and validly in contemporary samples.

RELIABILITY

The first challenge for the theory was to provide empirical evidence that the motive constructs could be reliably assessed, are unidimensional, and are relatively independent of one another and other

personality constructs. The AIM-Q consists of three versions of somewhat different questionnaire tasks (see Bernard et al., 2008, for descriptions of the versions). This permitted a multitrait-multimethod analysis of its psychometric properties. Overall, the AIM-Q scales assessing the 15 motive dimensions have good psychometric properties and the scales have good convergent and discriminant validities in a multitrait-multimethod matrix (Bernard et al., 2008). This suggests that the dimensions are not method-dependent artifacts and emerge across different assessment strategies. It also suggests that the dimensions, as represented in the AIM-Q, are relatively independent. The motive scales also have good internal consistency reliabilities and test-retest reliabilities across several different samples (Bernard et al., 2008).

Another method of establishing a new scales' reliability is consensual methodology. This approach compares self-reports to observer ratings on the same dimensions (Costa & McCrae, 1992). Mean correlations between self-friend and self-relative ratings of AIM-Q motive scores compared favorably to mean self-peer correlations for the five NEO PI-R domain scores (Costa & McCrae, 1992, Table 8). They also compared favorably to the mean of self-peer correlations reported by Cheek (1982) for a variety of aggregated personality measures (Bernard, 2009). This convergence of self-friend and self-relative ratings on the AIM-Q scales suggests that the motives represent dimensions on which there is agreement that people differ in meaningful ways (McCrae & Weiss, 2007).

VALIDITY

To better understand the meaning of scores on the AIM-Q motive scales, it is necessary to study their relationships to other important individual differences dimensions (Messick, 1995). Scores on the AIM-Q scales are correlated with scores on other reliable and valid measures of aggression, cognition, playfulness, and sexuality (Bernard, 2007a), providing evidence of the construct validity of some of the AIM-Q dimensions. It is also necessary to investigate relationships between the AIM-Q motive dimensions and personality dimensions, especially those represented in the FFM because of its proposed evolutionary basis. Recent research tested hypotheses predicting relationships between the motive dimensions and dimensions of the FFM (Bernard, 2010). Two general hypotheses predicting that the motive and personality dimensions would be related, but not strongly overlap, were supported. This suggests that motivational and personality constructs are conceptually different and that motivation, while related to personality, requires assessment by different psychological dimensions. In addition, 21 of 24 hypotheses of specific relationships between the motives and FFM dimensions based on Nettle's (2006, 2007) analysis of potential trade-offs in FFM dimensions were also supported.

AIM-Q items were written and edited to have face sex neutrality (Bernard et al., 2008). However, even with sex-neutral wording of the items, there should be mean sex differences in certain motive scale *scores* consistent with sexual selection and parental investment theory (Trivers, 1972). In fact, empirical evidence suggests that sex differences in scores on the Affection, Aggression, Appearance, Physical, and Sex motives are consistent with evolutionary theory (Bernard, 2007b).

One of the most important methods of establishing the validity of new dimensions is to use them to predict behaviors of some social importance. If a dimension can account for a meaningful amount of the variance in "real-world" behaviors, then it may be more than just an artifact of measurement on paper. Therefore, AIM-Q scale scores have also been used to predict the frequency of a variety of behaviors (Bernard, 2009). Although these behaviors were self-reported, their self-report was confirmed through observer ratings. Some of the more important relationships included the following: *(1)* Sex motive scores accounted for 11% of the variance in the frequency of sex; *(2)* Wealth motive scores accounted for 14% of the variance in money spent on clothing; *(3)* Illness Avoidance and Physical motive scores accounted for 15% of the variance in cigarette smoking and 42% of the variance in exercising; *(4)* Interpersonal Inquisitiveness motive scores accounted for 17% of the variance in illegal substance use; and *(5)* Aggression and Mental motive scores accounted for 29% of the variance in leadership among peers. These effect sizes are not trivial because behaviors such as these have multiple determinants. They suggest that the motive dimensions are related to socially important behaviors.

SUMMARY

These studies have relied on relatively large samples that now cumulatively total more than 3,500 adults. This research has been done only with English-language versions of the AIM-Q; however, there is ample evidence of the reliability and validity of the motive dimensions in these samples. The AIM-Q is being translated into other languages such as German and Spanish. These new versions may provide crucial additional information about the validity of the motive dimensions, because the theory requires that the motive dimensions be found independently of language and culture in all human societies.

Future Research Directions

Together, these results suggest that the AIM-Q motive dimensions predicted by the theory are reliable and, to some degree, valid. However, the demonstration of adequate psychometric properties is not evidence in support of the evolutionary theory or the proposed trade-offs on which the motives are based. Such evidence will require additional research as well as support from other avenues of investigation, including comparative psychology and behavioral genetics, and it may be some time before "evolved individual differences" is fully accepted as a congruent term by evolutionary biologists and psychologists. An example of other avenues of investigation that could facilitate this acceptance is Hogan's (2005) description of a number of behavior motivational systems in other species that includes parenting (Commitment?), aggression, sex, self-maintenance, fear (Threat Avoidance? Illness Avoidance?), and exploration (Environmental Inquisitiveness? Interpersonal Inquisitiveness?). Hogan suggested that these systems can interact to release and inhibit one another hydraulically to affect the direction of behavior. If there are links between the motives and these animal behavior systems, the links might be used to identify an evolved basis for the motives in other species.

Bernard et al. (2005) anticipated this notion of "hydraulic" interaction among motive dimensions, suggesting that multiple, even conflicting, motives may combine to shape behavior. The motives reflect complex decision rules that underlie the behavioral syndromes and even these rules may vary as a function of local trade-offs and the characteristics of other individuals in the local social network (Kenrick & Sundie, 2007). Our theory also incorporates roles for energy, emotion, and cognition, which help determine a direction for action when motives conflict. These roles are reflected in two additional individual differences dimensions that complete the theory: Vigor, which is an individual's level of raw behavioral activation/energy, and Deliberation, which is the extent to which an individual delays action/gratification in order to consider the consequences of conflicting motivated behaviors (Bernard, 2008). The deliberation process involves cognition and emotions that inform and expedite the process.

Another promising avenue of investigation is Kurzban and Aktipis' (2006) evolutionary psychology approach to social cognition. It suggests viewing social cognition from the perspective of "multiple minds, multiple motives," a brain architecture consisting of multiple discrete information processing systems. The motives were hypothesized to emerge from brain architecture and function (Bernard et al., 2005) and the AIM-Q scales could be used in studies of individual differences in social cognition and discrete informational processing systems. Hypothetically, different strengths in motive dimensions should shape the direction and content of social cognition.

One last promising avenue of investigation is experimental personality research (Revelle, 2007). In this approach, individual differences dimensions are assessed and then experimental conditions are manipulated. The effects of both are then jointly analyzed on states that mediate ongoing behavior. Such designs could be developed within one of the most active research paradigms in behavioral economics, "game theory" (for an overview see Camerer, 2003).

Game theory concerns people's interactive behavior. In the "games," people interact over obtaining, controlling, sharing, and using resources, which are behaviors of interest to evolutionary psychologists as well as economists. In some games, there are theoretically "optimal" strategies (equilibria), which, if followed, should result in the maximization of resources for each player. However, players sometimes adopt strategies that do not maximize their payoffs. Games can be used to investigate such phenomena as dominance, bargaining, social reputation, trust, and cooperativeness and, overall, there are substantial individual differences observed in games (Camerer, 2003). Typically, in a game theory experiment, individual differences are treated as nuisance variance and relegated to the error term. In the proposed experimental personality approach, the strength of certain motives and motive combinations would be used to predict who would be more dominant, trustworthy, or cooperative, for example. Thus, variations from game strategy equilibria due to individual differences would be "captured" and used to predict behavior. The accuracy of such predictions could provide further evidence for the validity of the motive dimensions.

Conclusion

Buss (1991) issued an early call for an evolutionary personality psychology: "Because personality psychology is dedicated to studying human nature in all of its individually different manifestations, this field is uniquely positioned to contribute to, and become informed by, evolutionary psychology" (p. 460). Almost two decades later, there is scant evidence that Buss's call has been answered by personality psychologists. For example, there is but a single brief reference to evolutionary theory in the 37 chapters of a recent volume that its editors call: "…a guide for researchers…that describes…*all* of the resources in the methodological toolkit of the personality psychologist" (Robins, Fraley, & Krueger, 2007, p. ix; italics added).

Despite this situation, there have been a few attempts to approach individual differences research from an evolutionary perspective. Stabilizing selection (MacDonald, 1998), fluctuating selection/ trade-offs (Nettle, 2006), and K-factor selection theory (Figueredo et al., 2005) all suggest that dimensions of personality, such as those that comprise the FFM, can be understood through the lens of evolution and may ultimately be explained as evolved adaptations. In addition, behavioral syndromes (Sih et al., 2004a, 2004b) and balancing selection (Penke et al., 2007) have much in common, even though the former is an outgrowth of behavioral ecology and the latter of behavioral genetics. Both use the concept of "reaction norms," which is also used in Person x Situation assessments in personality research. This suggests that the three social science approaches that share the basic metatheory of evolution may yet find common ground within personality psychology. Some behavioral geneticists have indeed been enthusiastic about the role the field may play in personality psychology (e.g., Ebstein, Benjamin, & Belmaker, 2003).

As with personality, there have been only a few attempts to apply evolutionary theory to motivation. Control theory (Heckhausen, 2000), behavior production theory (Aunger & Curtis, 2008), and the Zurich Model of Social Motivation (Bischof, 1975, 1993, 2001) have all suggested specific evolved motivational modules or behavior production systems in the human brain. All of these attempts are intriguing and may have potential for broadening our understanding of human motivation from an evolutionary perspective. However, none of these initially used an individual differences approach. Recently, a new questionnaire for the Zurich Model of Social Motivation has been developed to assess individual differences in the model's three dimensions: Security, Arousal, and Autonomy (Schönbrodt, Unkelbach, & Spinath, 2009).

Our theory combines individual differences and evolution and suggests that there may be multiple heritable individual differences dimensions of motivation that could be used to help understand and predict purposeful behavior. Some issues with the motive dimensions remain to be addressed empirically. For example, are they defined in too narrow a bandwidth, and are they too domain specific or not specific enough? Ultimately, the motives may provide a bridge between understanding human evolutionary past and understanding contemporary behavior. They should permit motivational psychologists to theorize about and predict behavior with some understanding of why it takes the forms and directions that it does, particularly when contemporary behavior is abnormal. The motive dimensions should also have applicability in basic research fields beyond motivation, such as behavioral genetics, behavioral economics, and neuroscience. With respect to the last of these, the original theory suggested some of the neuropsychological structures that may be involved with specific motives (Bernard et al., 2005). The availability of reliable and valid motive scales should permit these predictions to be tested with imaging techniques.

Despite early critics (e.g., Mischel, 1968), personality and individual differences psychology has demonstrated its usefulness in the clinic (e.g., Meyer et al., 2001) and as a valid predictor of important life outcomes (Roberts, Kuncel, Shiner, Caspi, & Goldberg, 2007). Therefore, one of the more practical outcomes of the study of evolved individual differences in motivation may be its potential utility in applied areas such as educational, industrial/organizational, health, and clinical psychology.

Years after his initial call for an evolutionary personality psychology, and noting the scant progress that had been made in the interim, Buss (1999) was still convinced that "Goal-directed tactics and strategies…are promising units for personality psychology…Discovery of the underlying species-typical goal structure and the corresponding evolved strategic solutions will constitute a major and lasting scientific contribution of personality psychologists *informed by evolutionary theory*" (p. 485).

Acknowledgments

The author is grateful to his many colleagues and students who have contributed to the development and study of this theory, in particular, to Michael Mills, Leland Swenson, and R. Patricia Walsh, who were part of the original research team that conceived the theory.

References

Adler, N. E., Boyce, T., Chesney, M. A., Cohen, S., Folkman, S., Kahn, R. L., & Syme, S. L. (1994). Socioeconomic status and health: The challenge of the gradient. *American Psychologist, 49*, 15–24.

Aharon, I., Etcoff, N., Ariely, D., Chabris, C. F., O'Connor, E., & Breiter, H. C. (2001). Beautiful faces have variable reward value: fMRI and behavioral evidence. *Neuron, 32*, 537–551.

Alexander, R. D. (1987). *The biology of moral systems.* Hawthorne, NY: De Gruyter.

Alexander, R. D. (2005). Evolutionary selection and the nature of humanity. In V. Hosle & C. Illies (Eds.), *Darwinism and philosophy* (pp. 301–348). South Bend, IN: University of Notre Dame Press.

Aunger, R., & Curtis, V. (2008). Kinds of behaviour. *Biology and Philosophy, 23*, 317–345.

Barber, N. (1995). The evolutionary psychology of physical attractiveness: Sexual selection and human morphology. *Ethology and Sociobiology, 16*, 395–424.

Barrick, M. R., & Mount, M. K. (1991). The Big Five personality dimensions and job performance: A meta-analysis. *Personality Psychology, 44*, 1–26.

Berkoff, M. (2001). Social play behavior: Cooperation, fairness, trust, and the evolution of morality. *Journal of Consciousness Studies, 8*, 81–90.

Berkowitz, L. (1993). *Aggression.* New York: McGraw-Hill.

Bernard, L. C. (2007a). Assessing individual differences in motivation: Convergent validity of the Assessment of Individual Motives-Questionnaire [AIM-Q] and measures of aggression, cognition, playfulness, and sexuality. *Individual Differences Research, 5*, 158–174.

Bernard, L. C. (2007b). Sex and motivation: Differences in evolutionary psychology-based motives. In P. W. O'Neal (Ed.), *Motivation of health behavior* (pp. 65–84). Hauppauge, NY: Nova Science Publishers.

Bernard, L. C. (2008). Individual differences in vigor and deliberation: Development of two new measures from an evolutionary psychology theory of human motivation. *Psychological Reports, 103*, 243–270.

Bernard, L. C. (2009). Consensual and Behavioral Validity of a Measure of Adaptive Individual Differences Dimensions in Human Motivation. *Motivation and Emotion, 33*, 303–319.

Bernard, L. C. (2010). Motivation and personality: Relationships between putative motive dimensions and the five factor model of personality. *Psychological Reports, 106*, 1–19.

Bernard, L. C., Mills, M., Swenson, L., & Walsh, R. P. (2005). An evolutionary theory of human motivation. *Genetic, Social, and General Psychology Monographs, 131*, 129–184.

Bernard, L. C., Mills, M., Swenson, L., & Walsh, R. P. (2008). Measuring motivation multidimensionally: Development of the assessment of individual motives-questionnaire [AIM-Q]. *Assessment, 15*, 16–35.

Bernard, L. C., Walsh, R. P., & Mills, M. (2005). The Motivation Analysis Test: An historical and contemporary evaluation. *Psychological Reports, 96*, 464–492.

Bischof, N. (1975). A systems approach toward the functional connections of attachment and fear. *Child Development, 46*, 801–817.

Bischof, N. (1993). Untersuchungen zur Systemanalyse der sozialen Motivation I: Die Regulation der sozialen Distanz—Von der Feldtheorie zur Systemtheorie [On the regulation of social distance—From field theory to systems theory]. *Zeitschrift für Psychologie, 201*, 5–43.

Bischof, N. (2001). *Das Rätsel Oedipus. Die biologischen Wurzeln des Urkonflikts von Intimität und Autonomie* [The riddle of Oedipus: The biological roots of the core conflict between intimacy and autonomy]. Munich, Germany: Piper.

Boyd, R. (2007). Cultural adaptation and maladaptation: Of kayaks and commissars. In S. W. Gangestad & J. A. Simpson (Eds.), *The evolution of mind: Fundamental questions and controversies* (pp. 327–331). New York: Guilford Press.

Bradley, R. H., & Corwyn, R. F. (2002). Socioeconomic status and child development. *Annual Review of Psychology, 53,* 371–399.

Buchanan, T., Johnson, J. A., & Goldberg, L. R. (2005). Implementing a five-factor personality inventory for use on the internet. *European Journal of Psychological Assessment, 21,* 115–127.

Bugental, D. B. (2000). Acquisition of the algorithms of social life: A domain-based approach. *Psychological Bulletin, 126,* 187–219.

Burkhardt, R. W., Jr. (2005). *Patterns of behavior: Konrad Lorenz, Niko Tinbergen, and the founding of ethology.* Chicago, IL: University of Chicago Press.

Burnstein, E., Crandall, C., & Kitayama, S. (1994). Some neo-Darwinian decision rules for altruism: Weighing cues for inclusive fitness as a function of the biological importance of the decision. *Journal of Personality and Social Psychology, 67,* 773–789.

Buss, D. M. (1988). Love acts: The evolutionary biology of love. In R. J. Sternberg & M. L. Barnes (Eds.), *The psychology of love* (pp. 100–118). New Haven, CT: Yale University Press.

Buss, D. M. (1989). Sex differences in human mate preferences: Evolutionary hypotheses testing in 37 cultures. *Brain and Behavioral Sciences, 12,* 1–49.

Buss, D. M. (1991). Evolutionary personality psychology. *Annual Review of Psychology, 42,* 459–491.

Buss, D. M. (1999). Evolutionary personality psychology. *Annual Review of Psychology, 42,* 459–491,

Buss, D. M. (2004). *Evolutionary psychology: The new science of the mind.* Boston, MA: Pearson.

Buss, D. M. (2009). How can evolutionary psychology successfully explain personality and individual differences? *Perspectives on Psychological Science, 4,* 359–366.

Buss, D. M., Abbott, M., Angleitner, A., Asherian, A., Biaggio, A., Blanco-Villasenor, A.... Yang, K. (1990). International preferences in selecting mates: A study of 37 cultures. *Journal of Cross-Cultural Psychology, 21,* 5–47.

Buss, D. M., & Duntley, J. D. (2006). The evolution of aggression. In M. Schaller, J. A. Simpson, & D. T. Kenrick, *Evolution and social psychology* (263–285). New York: Psychology Press.

Buss, D. M., & Greiling, H. (1999). Adaptive individual differences. *Journal of Personality, 67,* 209–243.

Buss, D. M., & Schmitt, D. P. (1993). Sexual strategies theory: An evolutionary perspective on human mating. *Psychological Review, 100,* 204–232.

Buss, D. M., Shackelford, T. K., Kirkpatrick, L. A., & Larsen, R. J. (2001). A half century of American mate preferences. *Journal of Marriage and the Family, 63,* 491–503.

Buunk, B. P., & Brenninkmeyer, V. (2000). Social comparison processes among depressed individuals: Evidence for the evolutionary perspective on involuntary subordinate strategies? In L. Sloman & P. Gilbert (Eds.), *Subordination and defeat: An evolutionary approach to mood disorders and their therapy* (pp. 147–164). Mahwah, NJ: Erlbaum.

Byrne, R. W., & Corp, N. (2004). Neocortex size predicts deception rate in primates. *Proceedings of the Royal Society of London B, 271,* 1693–1699.

Byrne, R. W., & Whiten, A. (Eds.). (1988). *Machiavellian intelligence: Social expertise and the evolution of intellect in monkeys, apes and humans.* Oxford, England: Oxford University Press.

Camerer, C. F. (2003). *Behavioral game theory: Experiments in strategic interaction.* New York: Princeton University Press.

Campbell, A. (1993). *Men, women, and aggression.* New York: Basic Books.

Campbell, J. (2008). *The hero with a thousand faces.* Novato, CA: New World Library.

Campbell, J., & Moyers, B. (1991). *The power of myth.* New York: Anchor Books.

Carmichael, M. S., Warburton, V. L., Dixen, J., & Davidson, J. M. (1994). Relationships among cardiovascular, muscular, and oxytocin responses during human sexual activity. *Archives of Sexual Behavior, 23,* 59–79.

Cattell, R. B., & Dreger, R. M. (Eds.). (1977). *Handbook of modern personality theory.* Washington, DC: Hemisphere Publishing.

Cattell, R. B., Horn, J. L., Sweney, A. B., & Radcliffe, J. A. (1964). *Handbook for the motivation analysis test.* Champaign, IL: Institute for Personality and Ability Testing.

Cattell, R. B., Radcliffe, J. A., & Sweney, A. B. (1963). The nature and measurement of components of motivation. *Genetic Psychology Monographs, 68,* 49–211.

Chamorro-Premuzic, T. (2007). *Personality and individual differences.* Malden, MA: Blackwell Publishing.

Cheek, J. M. (1982). Aggregation, moderator variables, and the validity of personality tests: A peer-rating study. *Journal of Personality and Social Psychology, 43,* 1254–1269.

Coleman, K., & Wilson, D. (1998). Shyness and boldness in pumpkinseed sunfish: Individual differences are context-specific. *Animal Behaviour, 56,* 927–936.

Confer, J. C., Easton, J. A., Fleischman, D. S., Goetz, C. D., Lewis, D. M. G., Perilloux, C., & Buss, D. M. (2010). Evolutionary psychology: Controversies, questions, prospects, and limitations. *American Psychologist, 65,* 110–126.

Cosmides, L., & Tooby, J. (1992). Cognitive adaptations for social exchange. In J. Barkow, L. Cosmides, & J. Tooby (Eds.), *The adapted mind* (pp. 163–228). New York: Oxford University Press.

Costa, P. T., Jr., & McCrae, R. R. (1992). *Revised NEO Personality Inventory (NEO PI-R) and NEO Five-Factor Inventory (NEO-FFI) professional manual.* Odessa, FL: Psychological Assessment Resources, Inc.

Costa, P. T., Jr., & Widiger, T. A. (1994). Summary and unresolved issues. In P. T. Costa, Jr. & T. A. Widiger (Eds.), *Personality and the five-factor model of personality* (pp. 1–20). Washington, DC: American Psychological Association.

Crick, N. R., Casas, J. F., & Mosher, M. (1997). Relational and overt aggression in preschool. *Developmental Psychology, 33,* 579–588.

Cronbach, L. J., & Meehl, P. E. (1955). Construct validity in psychological tests. *Psychological Bulletin, 52,* 281–302.

Daly, M., & Wilson, M. (1988). *Homicide.* New York: Aldine.

Dansky, J. L., & Silverman, I. W. (1973). Effects of play on associative fluency in preschool-aged children. *Developmental Psychology, 9,* 28–43.

Dawkins, R. (1989). *The selfish gene*. Oxford, England: Oxford University Press.

Denissen, J. A., & Penke, L. (2008). Motivational individual reaction norms underlying the Five-Factor model of personality: First steps towards a theory-based conceptual framework. *Journal of Research in Personality, 42*, 1285–1302.

de Waal, F. (1996). *Good natured: The origins of right and wrong in humans and other animals*. Cambridge, MA: Harvard University Press.

de Waal, F. B. M. (2002). Evolutionary psychology: The wheat and the chaff. *Current Directions in Psychological Science, 11*, 187–191.

Digman, J. M. (1996). The curious history of the f ive-factor model. In J. S. Wiggins (Ed.), *The five-factor model of personality: Theoretical perspectives* (pp. 1–20). New York: Guilford.

Dunbar, R. (2007). Evolution of the social brain. In S. W. Gangestad & J. A. Simpson (Eds.), *The evolution of mind: Fundamental questions and controversies* (pp. 280–286). New York: Guilford Press.

Ebstein, R. P., Benjamin, J., & Belmaker, R. H. (2003). Behavioral genetics, genomics, and personality. In R. Plomin, J. C. Defries, I. W. Craig, & P.McGuffin (Eds.), *Behavioral genetics in the postgenomic era* (pp. 365–388). Washington, DC: American Psychological Association.

Eccles, J., Wigfield, A., Harold, R. D., & Blumenfeld, P. (1993). Age and gender differences in children's self- and task perceptions during elementary school. *Child Development, 64*, 830–847.

Ermer, E., Cosmides, L., & Tooby, J. (2007). Functional specialization and the adaptationist program. In S. W. Gangestad & J. A. Simpson (Eds.), *The evolution of mind: Fundamental questions and controversies* (pp. 153–160). New York: Guilford Press.

Fehr, E., & Fischbacher, U. (2003). The nature of human altruism. *Nature, 425*, 785–791.

Figueredo, A. J., Vásquez, G., Brumbach, B. H., & Schneider, S. M. R. (2007). The K-factor, covitality, and personality. *Human Nature, 18*, 47–73.

Figueredo, A. J., Vásquez, G., Brumbach, B. H., Sefcek, J., Kirsner, B. R., & Jacobs, W. J. (2005). The K-factor: Individual differences in life history strategy. *Personality and Individual Differences, 39*, 1349–1360.

Fiske, S. T. (2008). Core social motivations: Views from the couch, consciousness, classroom, computers, and collectives. In J. Y. Shah & W. I. Gardner (Eds.), *Handbook of motivation science* (pp. 3–22). New York: Guilford Press.

Flinn, M., & Coe, K. (2007). The linked red queens of human cognition, coalitions, and culture. In S. W. Gangestad & J. A. Simpson (Eds.), *The evolution of mind: Fundamental questions and controversies* (pp. 339–347). New York: Guilford Press.

Fournier, M. A., Moskowitz, D. S., & Zuroff, D. C. (2002). Social rank strategies in hierarchical relationships. *Journal of Personality and Social Psychology, 83*, 425–433.

Fox, A. (1997, June). *The assessment of fighting ability in humans*. Paper presented at the Ninth Annual Meeting of the Human Behavior and Evolution Society, University of Arizona, Tucson, AZ.

Freud, S. (1955). Beyond the pleasure principle. In J. Strachey (Ed. & Trans.), *The standard edition of the complete psychological works of Sigmund Freud* (4th ed., Vol. 2, pp. 3–64). London: Hogarth Press.

Gangestad, S. W., & Simpson, J. A. (2000). The evolution of human mating: Trade-offs and strategic pluralism. *Behavioral and Brain Sciences, 23*, 573–587.

Gangestad, S. W., & Simpson, J. A. (Eds.). (2007). *The evolution of mind: Fundamental questions and controversies*. New York: Guilford Press.

Gangestad, S. W., Thornhill, R., & Yeo, R. A. (1994). Facial attractiveness, developmental stability, and fluctuating asymmetry. *Ethology and Sociobiology, 15*, 73–85.

Gardner, H. (1993). *Frames of mind* (2nd ed.). London: HarperCollins.

Geary, D. C. (2000). Evolution and proximate expression of human paternal investment. *Psychological Bulletin, 126*, 55–77.

Geary, D. C. (2005). Evolution of parental investment. In D. M. Buss (Ed.), *The handbook of evolutionary psychology* (pp. 483–505). Hoboken, NJ: John Wiley & Sons.

Georgiadis, J. R., Kortekaas, R., Kuipers, R., Nieuwenburg, A., Pruim, J., Reinders, A. A., Holstege, G. (2006). Regional cerebral blood flow changes associated with clitorally induced orgasm in healthy women. *European Journal of Neuroscience, 24*, 3305–3316.

Gigerenzer, G., & Hug, K. (1992). Domain-specific reasoning: Social contracts, cheating, and perspective change. *Cognition, 43*, 127–171.

Gilbert, P. (2000). Varieties of submissive behavior as forms of social defense: Their evolution and role in depression. In L. Sloman & P. Gilbert (Eds.), *Subordination and defeat: An evolutionary approach to mood disorders and their therapy* (pp. 3–46). Mahwah, NJ: Erlbaum.

Goldberg, L. R. (1993). The structure of phenotypic personality traits. *American Psychologist, 48*, 26–34.

Gosling, S. D. (2001). From mice to men: What can we learn about personality from animal research? *Psychological Bulletin, 127*, 45–86.

Gosling, S. D., & John, O. P. (1999). Personality dimensions in nonhuman animals: A cross-species review. *Current Directions in Psychological Science, 8*, 69–75.

Gosling, S. D., & Vazire, S. (2002). Are we barking up the right tree? Evaluating a comparative approach to personality. *Journal of Research in Personality, 36*, 607–614.

Gottfredson, L. (1997). Why g matters: The complexity of everyday life. *Intelligence, 24*, 79–132.

Gottfredson, L. (2004). Intelligence: Is it the epidemiologists' elusive "fundamental cause" of social class inequalities in health? *Journal of Personality and Social Psychology, 86*, 174–199.

Groothuis, T. G. G., & Carere, C. (2005) Avian personalities: Characterization and epigenesis. *Neuroscience and Biobehavioral Reviews, 29*, 137–150.

Hagen, E. E. (2005). Controversial issues in evolutionary psychology. In D. M. Buss (Ed.), *The handbook of evolutionary psychology* (pp. 145–174). New York: Wiley.

Hagen, E. H., & Symons, D. (2007). Natural psychology: The environment of evolutionary adaptedness and the structure of cognition. In S. W. Gangestad & J. A. Simpson (Eds.), *The evolution of mind: Fundamental questions and controversies* (pp. 38–52). New York: Guilford Press.

Hamilton, W. D. (1964). The genetical evolution of social behavior. *Journal of Theoretical Biology, 7*, 1–52.

Harcourt, A. H., & Stewart, K. J. (2007). Gorilla society: What we know and don't know. *Evolutionary Anthropology, 16*, 147–158.

Heckhausen, J. (2000). Evolutionary perspectives on human motivation. *The American Behavioral Scientist, 43*, 1015–1029.

Hogan, J. (2005). Motivation. In J. J. Bolhuis (Ed.), *The behavior of animals: Mechanisms, function, and evolution* (pp 41–70). Malden, MA: Blackwell Publishing.

Hogan, R. (1996). A socioanalytic perspective on the five-factor model. In J. S. Wiggins (Ed.), *The five-factor model of personality: Theoretical perspectives* (pp. 163–179). New York: Guilford.

Holstege, G., Georgiadis, J., R., Paans, A. M., Meiners, L. C., van der Graaf, F. H., & Reinders, A. A. (2003). Brain activation during human male ejaculation. *Journal of Neuroscience, 23*, 9185–9193.

Hough, L. M., Eaton, N. K., Dunnette, M. D., Kamp, J. D., & McCloy, R. A. (1990). Criterion-related validities of personality constructs and the effect of response distortion on those validities. *Journal of Applied Psychology, 75*, 581–595.

Houle, D. (1998). How should we explain variation in the genetic variance of traits? *Genetica, 102–103*, 241–253.

Huntingford, F., & Adams, C. (2005). Behavioural syndromes in farmed fish: Implications for production and welfare. *Behaviour, 142*, 1207–1221.

Insel, T. R, & Winslow, J. T. (1998). Serotonin and neuropeptides in affiliative behaviors. *Biological Psychiatry, 44*, 207–219.

Jackson, D. N. (1999). *Personality research form manual* (3rd ed.). Port Huron, MI: Sigma Assessment Systems, Inc.

James, W. (1890). *The principles of psychology* (2 vols.). New York: Holt.

Jang, K. L., McCrae, R. R., Angleitner, A., Riemann, R., & Livesley, W. J. (1998). Heritability of facet-level traits in a cross-cultural twin study: Support for a hierarchical model of personality. *Journal of Personality and Social Psychology, 74*, 1556–1565.

Jankowiak, W. (Ed.). (1995). *Romantic passion: A universal experience?* New York: Columbia University Press.

Jankowiak, W., & Fischer, R. (1992). A cross-cultural perspective on romantic love. *Ethnology, 31*, 149–155.

Jensen, A. R. (1998). *The g factor: The science of mental ability.* Westport, CT: Praeger.

Jirikowski, G. F., Caldwell, J. D., Stumpf, W. E., & Pedersen, C. A. (1988). Estradiol influences oxytocin immunoreactive brain systems. *Neuroscience, 25*, 237–248.

Johnson, J. C., & Sih, A. (2007). Fear, food, sex, and parental care: A syndrome of boldness in the fishing spider, Dolomedes triton. *Animal Behaviour, 74*, 1131–1138.

Kagan, J. (2003). A behavioral science perspective. In R. Plomin, J. C. DeFries, I. W. Craig, & P. McGuffin (Eds.), *Behavioral genetics in the postgenomic era* (pp. xvii–xx). Washington, DC: American Psychological Association.

Kaplan, H. S., & Gangestad, S. W. (2007). Optimality approaches and evolutionary psychology. Evolution of the social brain. In S. W. Gangestad & J. A. Simpson (Eds.), *The evolution of mind: Fundamental questions and controversies* (pp. 121–129). New York: Guilford Press.

Kappeler, P. M., & van Schaik, C. P. (2002). Evolution of primate social systems. *International Journal of Primatology, 23*, 707–740.

Kenrick, D. T., Li, N. P., & Butner, J. (2003). Dynamical evolutionary psychology: Individual decision rules and emergent social norms. *Psychological Review, 110*, 3–28.

Kenrick, D. T., Sadalla, E. K., Groth, G., & Trost, M. R. (1990). Evolution, traits, and the stages of human courtship: Qualifying the parental investment model. *Journal of Personality, 58*, 97–116.

Kenrick, D. T., & Sundie, J. M. (2007). Dynamical evolutionary psychology and mathematical modeling. In S. W. Gangestad & J. A. Simpson (Eds.), *The evolution of mind: Fundamental questions and controversies* (pp. 137–144). New York: Guilford Press.

Korchmaros, J. D., & Kenny, D. A. (2001). Emotional closeness as a mediator of the effect of genetic relatedness on altruism. *Psychological Science, 12*, 262–265.

Krebs, J. R., & Davies, N. B. (Eds.). (1997). *Behavioural ecology: An evolutionary approach* (4th ed.). Oxford, England: Blackwell.

Kudo, H., & Dunbar, R. I. M. (2001). Neocortex size and social network size in primates. *Animal Behaviour, 62*, 711–722.

Kurzban, R., & Aktipis, C. A. (2006). Modular minds, multiple motives. In M. Schaller, J. A. Simpson, & D. T. Kenrick (Eds.), *Evolution and social psychology* (pp. 39–53). Madison, CT: Psychosocial Press.

Kurzban, R., & Leary, M. R. (2001). Evolutionary origins of stigmatization: The functions of social exclusion. *Psychological Bulletin, 127*, 187–208.

Logue, A. W. (1985). Conditioned food aversion learning in humans. *Annals of the New York Academy of Sciences, 443*, 316–329.

MacArthur, R. H., & Wilson, E. O. (1967). *The theory of island biogeography.* Princeton, NJ: Princeton University Press.

MacDonald, K. B. (1983). Stability of individual differences in behavior in a litter of wolf cubs *(Canis Lupus). Journal of Comparative Psychology, 2*, 99–106.

MacDonald, K. (1995). Evolution, the 5-factor model, and levels of personality. *Journal of Personality, 63*, 525–567.

MacDonald, K. (1998). Evolution, cu lture, and the five-factor model. *Journal of Cross-Cultural Psychology, 29*, 119–149.

MacDonald, K. (2005). Personality, evolution, and development. In R. L. Burgess & K. MacDonald (Eds.), *Evolutionary perspectives on human development* (2nd ed., pp. 207–242). Thousand Oaks, CA: Sage.

Mann, P. E., & Bridges, R. S. (2001). Lactogenic hormone regulation of maternal behavior. *Progress in Brain Research, 133*, 251–262.

Mason, W. A., & Mendoza, S. P. (1993). *Primate social conflict.* Albany: State University of New York Press.

Mayer, J. D., Faber, M. A., & Xu, X. (2007). Seventy-five years of motivation measures (1930–2005): A descriptive analysis. *Motivation and Emotion, 31*, 83–103.

McAdams, D. P., & Pals, J. L. (2007). The role of theory in personality research. In R. W. Robins, R. C. Fraley, & R. F. Krueger (Eds.), *Handbook of research methods in personality psychology* (pp. 3–20). New York: Guilford Press.

McAndrew, F. T. (2002). New evolutionary perspectives on altruism: Multi-level selection and costly signaling theories. *Current Directions in Psychological Science, 11*, 79–82.

McCrae, R. R., & Weiss, A. (2007) Observer ratings of personality. In R. W. Robins, R. C. Fraley, & R. F. Krueger (Eds.), *Handbook of research methods in personality psychology.* New York: Guilford Press.

McDougall, W. (1933). *The energies of men.* New York: Scribner.

Mealey, L. (1995). The sociobiology of sociopathy: An integrated evolutionary model. *Behavioral and Brain Sciences, 18*, 523–599.

Merenda, P. F. (1999). Theories, models, and factor approaches to personality, temperament, and behavioral styles: Postulations and measurement in the second millennium A.D. *Psychological Reports, 85*, 905–932.

Merenda, P. F. (2008). Update on the debate about the existence and utility of the big five: A ten-year follow-up on Carroll's "The five factor personality model: How complete and satisfactory is it?" *Psychological Reports, 103*, 931–942.

Messick, S. (1995). Validity of psychological assessment: Validation of inferences from persons' responses and performances as scientific inquiry into score meaning. *American Psychologist, 50*, 741–749.

Meyer, G. J., Finn, S. E., Eyde, L. D., Kay, G. G., Moreland, K. L., Dies, R. R....Reed, G. M. (2001). Psychological testing and psychological assessment. *American Psychologist, 56*, 128–165.

Mischel, W. (1968). *Personality and assessment.* New York: Wiley.

Moretz, J. A., Martins, E. P., & Robison, B. D. (2007). Behavioral syndromes and the evolution of correlated behavior in zebrafish. *Behavioral Ecology, 18*, 556–562.

Murray, H. (1938). *Explorations in personality.* New York: Oxford University Press.

Nesse, R. M. (Ed.) (2001). *Evolution and the capacity for commitment.* New York: Russell Sage Fondation.

Nettle, D. (2005). An evolutionary approach to the extraversion continuum. *Evolution and Human Behavior, 26*, 363–373.

Nettle, D. (2006). The evolution of personality variation in humans and other animals. *American Psychologist, 61*, 622–631.

Nettle, D. (2007). Traits and trade-offs are an important tier. *American Psychologist, 62*, 1074–1075.

Neyer, F. J., & Lang, F. R. (2003). Blood is thicker than water: Kinship orientation across adulthood. *Journal of Personality and Social Psychology, 84*, 310–321.

Nichols, S. (2004). Is religion what we want? Motivation and the cultural transmission of religious representations. *Journal of Cognition and Culture,4*, 347–371.

Nyborg, H., & Jensen, A. R. (2001). Occupation and income related to psychometric *g. Intelligence, 29*, 45–55.

O'Connor, L. E., Berry, J. W., Weiss, J., Schweitzer, D., & Sevier, M. (2000). Survivor guilt, submissive behaviour and evolutionary theory: The down-side of winning social competition. *British Journal of Medical Psychology, 73*, 519–530.

Olweus, D. (1978). *Aggression in schools.* New York: Wiley.

Ones, D. S., & Viswesvaran, C. (1996). Bandwidth-fidelity dilemma in personality measurement for personnel selection. *Journal of Organizational Behavior, 17*, 609–626.

Panksepp, J. (1981). Brain opioids: A neurochemical substrate for narcotic and social dependence. In S. Cooper (Ed.), *Progress in theory in psychopharmacology* (pp. 149–175). London: Academic Press.

Panksepp, J. (1998). *Affective neuroscience: The foundations of human and animal emotions.* New York: Oxford University Press.

Panksepp, J. (2000). Emotions as natural kinds within the mammalian brain. In M. Lewis & J. M. Haviland-Jones (Eds.), *Handbook of emotions* (pp. 137–156). New York: Guilford Press.

Penke, L., Denissen, J. J. A., & Miller, G. F. (2007). The evolutionary genetics of personality. *European Journal of Personality, 21*, 549–587.

Pervin, L., & John, O. P. (Eds.). (1999). *Handbook of personality: Theory and research* (2nd ed.). New York: Guilford Press.

Pianka, E. R. (1970). On r- and K-selection. *American Naturalist, 104*, 592–596.

Plomin, R., DeFries, J. C., Craig, I. W., & McGuffin, P. (2003). Behavioral genetics. In R. Plomin, J. C. DeFries, I. W. Craig, & P. McGuffin (Eds.), *Behavioral genetics in the postgenomic era* (pp. 3–15). Washington, DC: American Psychological Association.

Plomin, R., Happe, F., & Caspi, A. (2002). Personality and cognitive abilities. In P. McGuffin, M. J. Owen, & I. I. Gottesman (Eds.), *Psychiatric genetics and genomics* (pp. 77–112). Oxford, England: Oxford University Press.

Plutchik, R. (2003). *Emotions and life: Perspectives from psychology, biology, and evolution.* Washington, DC: American Psychological Association.

Poropat, A. E. (2009). A meta-analysis of the Five Factor Model of personality and academic performance. *Psychological Bulletin, 135*, 322–338.

Prentice-Dunn, S., & Rogers, R. W. (1980). Effects of deindividuating situational cues and aggressive models on subjective deindividuation and aggression. *Journal of Personality and Social Psychology, 39*, 104–113.

Reimann, R., Angleitner, A., & Strelau, J. (1997). Genetic and environmental influences on personality: A study of twins reared together using the self- and peer report NEO-FFI scales. *Journal of Personality, 65*, 449–475.

Revelle, W. (2007). Experimental approaches to the study of personality. In R. W. Robins, R. C. Farley, & R. F. Krueger (Eds.), *Handbook of research methods in personality psychology* (pp. 37–61). New York: Guilford Press.

Reznick, B. M., Bryant, M. J., & Bashey, F. (2002). r- and K-selection revisited: The role of population regulation in life-history evolution. *Ecology, 83*, 1509–1520.

Roberts, B. W., Kuncel, N. R., Shiner, R., Caspi, A., & Goldberg, L. R. (2007). The power of personality: The comparative validity of personality traits, socioeconomic status, and cognitive ability for predicting important life outcomes. *Perspectives on Psychological Science, 2*, 313–345.

Robins, R. W., Fraley, R. C., & Krueger, R. F. (2007). Preface. In R. W. Robins, R. C. Fraley, & R. F. Krueger (Eds.), *Handbook of research methods in personality psychology* (pp. ix-x). New York: Guilford Press.

Roff, D. A. (2001). *The evolution of life histories: Theory and analysis.* New York: Chapman & Hall.

Rosenblatt, J. (2001). Hormone-behavior relationships in the regulation of parental behavior. In J. B. Becker, S. M. Breedlove, & D. Crews (Eds.), *Behavioral endocrinology* (pp. 219–260). Cambridge, MA: MIT Press.

Rosenblatt, P. C. (1974). Cross-cultural perspectives on attractiveness. In T. L. Huston (Ed.), *Foundations of interpersonal attraction* (pp. 79–95). New York: Academic Press.

Rowe, D. C. (2000). Environmental and genetic influences on pubertal development: Evolutionary life history traits? In J. L. Rodgers, D.C. Rowe, & W. B. Miller (Eds.), *Genetic influences on human fertility and sexuality: Recent empirical and theoretical findings* (pp. 147–168). Boston, MA: Kluwer.

Rozin, P., & Fallon, A. (1987). A perspective on disgust. *Psychological Review, 94*, 23–41.

Rozin, P., Haidt, J., McCauley, C., Dunlop, L., & Ashmore, M. (1999). Individual differences in disgust sensitivity: Comparisons and evaluations of paper-and-pencil versus behavioral measures. *Journal of Research in Personality, 33*, 330–351.

Rozin, P., & Kalat, J. W. (1971). Specific hungers and poison avoidance as adaptive specializations of learning. *Psychological Review, 78*, 459–486.

Rozin, P., Millman, L., & Nemeroff, C. (1986). Operation of the laws of sympathetic magic in disgust and other domains. *Journal of Personality and Social Psychology, 50,* 703–712.

Rusbult, C. E. (1983). A longitudinal test of the investment model: The development (and deterioration) of satisfaction and commitment in heterosexual involvements. *Journal of Personality and Social Psychology, 45,* 101–117.

Rusbult, C. E., & Van Lange, P. A. M. (2003). Interdependence, interaction, and relationships. *Annual Review of Psychology, 54,* 351–375.

Rushton, J. P. (2004). Placing intelligence into an evolutionary framework, or how *g* fits into the r-K matrix of life history traits, including longevity. *Intelligence, 32,* 321–328.

Samuels, J., Bienvenu, O. J., Cullen, B., Costa, P. T., Eaton, W. W., & Nestadt, G. (2004). Personality dimensions and criminal arrest. *Comprehensive Psychiatry, 45,* 275–280.

Schaller, M., & Murray, D. R. (2008). Pathogens, personality, and culture: Disease prevalence predicts worldwide variability in sociosexuality, extraversion, and openness to experience. *Journal of Personality and Social Psychology, 95,* 212–221.

Schönbrodt, F. D., Unkelbach, S. R., & Spinath, F. M. (2009). Broad motives in short scales: A questionnaire for the Zurich model of social motivation. *European Journal of Psychological Assessment, 25,* 141–149. doi: 10.1027/1015-5759.25.3.141.

Scott, E., & Panksepp, J. (2003). Rough-and-tumble play in human children. *Aggressive Behavior, 29,* 539–551.

Scullin, M. H., Peters, E., Williams, W. M., & Ceci, S. J. (2000). The role of IQ and education in predicting later labor market outcomes: Implications for affirmative action. *Psychology, Policy, and Law, 6,* 63–89.

Shakelford, T. K., & Larsen, R. J. (1997). Facial asymmetry as indicator of psychological, emotional, and physiological distress. *Journal of Personality and Social Psychology, 72,* 456–466.

Sih, A., Bell, A., & Johnson, J. C. (2004a). Behavioral syndromes: An ecological and evolutionary overview. *Trends in Ecology and Evolution, 19,* 372–378.

Sih, A., Bell, A., Johnson, J. C., & Ziemba, R. E. (2004b). Behavioral syndromes: An integrative overview. *The Quarterly Review of Biology, 79,* 241–277.

Singh, D. (1993). Body shape and women's attractiveness: The critical role of waist-to-hip ratio. *Human Nature, 4,* 297–321.

Singh, D. (2000). Waist-to-hip ratio: An indicator of female mate value. *International Research Center for Japanese Studies, International Symposium 16,* pp. 79–99.

Singh, D., & Young, R. K. (1995). Body weight, waist-to-hip ratio, breasts, and hips: Role in judgments of female attractiveness and desirability for relationships. *Ethology and Sociobiology, 16,* 483–507.

Slade, A., & Wolf, D. P. (Eds.). (1994).*Children at play.* New York: Oxford University Press.

Smith, E. A. (2000). Three styles in the evolutionary analysis of human behavior. In L. Cronk, N. Chagnon, & W. Irons (Eds.), *Adaptation and human behavior: An anthropological perspective* (pp. 27–46). New York: Aldine De Grutyer.

Sorrentino, R. M., Holmes, J. G., Hanna, S. E., & Sharp, A. (1995). Uncertainty orientation and trust in close relationships: Individual differences in cognitive styles. *Journal of Personality and Social Psychology, 68,* 314–327.

Stapley, J., & Keogh, J. S. (2005). Behavioral syndromes influence mating systems: Floater pairs of a lizard have heavier offspring. *Behavioral Ecology, 16,* 514–520.

Stearns, S. C. (1992). *The evolution of life histories.* Oxford, England: Oxford University Press.

Symons, D. (1979). *The evolution of human sexuality.* New York: Oxford.

Tett, R. P., Steele, J. R., & Beauregard, R. S. (2003). Broad and narrow measures on both sides of the personality-job performance relationship. *Journal of Organizational Behavior, 24,* 335–356.

Tooby, J., & Cosmides, L. (1988, April). *The evolution of war and its cognitive foundations.* Institute for Evolutionary Studies, Technical Report #88–1. Paper presented at the Evolution and Human Behavior Meetings, Ann Arbor, Michigan, retrieved from: http://www.psych.ucsb.edu/research/cep/papers/Evolofwar.pdf

Tooby, J., & Cosmides, L. (1990). On the universality of human nature and the uniqueness of the individual: The role of genetics and adaptation. *Journal of Personality, 58,* 17–68.

Tooby, J., & Cosmides, L. (1992). The psychological foundation of culture. In J. H. Barkow, L. Cosmides, & J. Tooby (Eds.), *The adapted mind* (pp. 19–136). New York: Oxford University Press.

Tooby, J., & Cosmides, L. (1996). Friendship and the banker's paradox: Other pathways to the evolution of adaptations for altruism. *Proceedings of the British Academy, 88,* 119–143.

Trivers, R. L. (1971). The evolution of reciprocal altruism. *Quarterly Review of Biology, 46,* 35–57.

Trivers, R. L. (1972). Parental investment and sexual selection. In B. Campbell (Ed.), *Sexual selection and the descent of man, 1871–1971* (pp. 136–179). Chicago, IL: Aldine.

Van Lange, P. A. M., & Kuhlman, D. M. (1994). Social value orientations and impressions of partner's honesty and intelligence: A test of the might versus morality effect. *Journal of Personality and Social Psychology, 67,* 126–141.

Van Lange, P. A. M., Otten, W., De Bruin, E. M. N., & Joireman, J. A. (1997). Development of prosocial, individualistic, and competitive orientations: Theory and preliminary evidence. *Journal of Personality and Social Psychology, 73,* 733–746.

Van Vugt, M., & Hart, C. M. (2004). Social identity as social glue: The origins of group loyalty. *Personality and Social Psychology Bulletin, 25,* 731–745.

Van Vugt, M., Snyder, M., Tyler, T., & Biel, A. (2000). *Cooperation in modern society: Promoting the welfare of communities, states, and organizations.* London: Routledge.

Weiss, A., King, J. E., & Enns, R. M. (2002). Subjective well-being is heritable and genetically correlated with dominance in chimpanzees (*Pan troglodytes*). *Journal of Personality and Social Psychology, 83,* 1141–1149.

Wiederman, M. W. (1993). Evolved gender differences in mate preferences: Evidence from personal advertisements. *Ethology and Sociobiology, 14,* 331–352.

Wilson, D. S. (1994). Adaptive genetic variation and human evolutionary psychology. *Ethology and Sociobiology, 15,* 219–235.

Wilson, D. S. (2007). The role of group selection in human psychological evolution. In S. W. Gangestad & J. A. Simpson (Eds.), *The evolution of mind: Fundamental questions and controversies* (pp. 213–220). New York: Guilford Press.

Wilson, D. S. Clark, A. B., Coleman, K., & Dearstyne, T. (1994). Shyness and boldness in humans and other animals. *Trends in Ecology and Evolution, 9,* 442–446.

Wilson, D. S. & Sober, E. (1998). Multilevel selection and the return of group-level functionalism. *Brain and Behavioral Sciences, 21,* 305–306.

Wilson, D. S., Van Vugt, M., & O'Gorman, R. (2008). Multilevel selection theory and major evolutionary transitions: Implications for psychological science. *Current Directions in Psychological Science, 17,* 6–9.

Wilson, E. O. (1975). *Sociobiology: The new synthesis.* Cambridge, MA: Harvard University.

Wolf, M., van Doorn, G. S., Leimar, O., & Weissing, F. J. (2007). Life-history trade-offs favour the evolution of animal personalities. *Nature, 447,* 581–585.

Wrangham, R. W. (1999). Evolution of coalitionary killing. *Yearbook of Physical Anthropology, 42,* 1–30.

Zimbardo, P. G. (1970). The human choice: Individuation, reason, and order versus deindividuation, impulse, and chaos. In W. J. Arnold & D. Levine (Eds.), *Nebraska symposium on motivation* (Vol. 17, pp. 237–307). Lincoln: University of Nebraska.

Zimmer, E. J., & Kallman, K. D. (1989). Genetic basis for alternative reproductive tactics in the pygmy swordtail, *Xiphophorus nigrensis. Evolution, 43,* 1298–1307.

Moods of Energy and Tension That Motivate

Robert E. Thayer

Abstract

Moods are perfect barometers of physiological and psychological functioning. Two biopsychological dimensions, Energetic and Tense Arousal, are keys to understanding moods. These dimensions interact under different activating conditions to form four complex moods that range from calm energy (pleasurable mood associated with full attentional focus, happiness, optimism, favorable athletic performance, and self-control) to tense tiredness (bad mood associated with depression, negative perception of problems, yielding to unwanted urges such as sugar snacking or smoking). Two other complex moods include tense energy (moderately positive state that combines vigor with moderate tension) and calm tiredness (ideal for restful sleep). Energetic and tense arousal are associated with many kinds of motivational processes, including various strategies of self-regulation (best strategy combines relaxation techniques, exercise, and cognitive control). Important to these moods are natural processes such as health, sleep, diet, diurnal energy cycles, movement (exercise), and stress. These moods are mediated by general bodily arousal states.

Key Words: mood, energy, tension, self-regulation, diet, exercise, arousal, sleep, stress, diurnal cycles

If we think of our moods as emphasizing meaning and enhancing or reducing the pleasure in our lives, we can understand how central they really are. In this respect they are more important than daily activities, money, status, and even personal relationships because these things are usually filtered through our moods. In many respects our moods are at the core of our being.

(*Thayer*, 1996, p. 4)

Contrary to a mistaken assumption that everyday moods are meaningless background feelings, these low-level emotional states appear to be barometers of both physiological and psychological functioning (Thayer, 2000). They have a physiological substrate. They are integrally tied to our thoughts and other cognitive precesses. They subtly influence our behavior, and they motivate us.

Unlike emotions that usually have an understandable cause, everyday moods are background feelings that seem to come and go with no apparent reason, although as we shall see they are integrally related to knowable bodily systems and processes. Moods can be regarded as dispositional variables that tend to amplify or inhibit existing causal relationships. I believe that the best moods involve high energy and lower tension, and the worst moods involve reduced energy or tiredness and increased tension.

Let me introduce an often overlooked motivational concept in this chapter with a personal anecdote. Being reminded of the approaching deadline for a draft of this work, I noticed that my motivation to finish it varied with the amount of requirements in my life and with time of day. The matter of other requirements being important to changing motivation levels is no surprise to any writer with many commitments, but often overlooked is time of day as a motivational variable. At times of day when I felt more energy, my motivation to complete this important task was unflagging because of its obvious significance, but when I was tired my motivation was reduced, often resulting in delay or procrastination.

An Endogenous Cycle of Energetic Arousal

This variation with time of day concerns a general biopsychological variable that I have named Energetic Arousal. Once established, this is an endogenous energy cycle (a kind of biological clock) that repeats itself with more or less the same pattern day after day unless there is significant change in such variables as physical activity, food intake, unusual emotional arousal, or crossing time zones with accordant behavioral changes. Energetic arousal directly affects level of motivation for everyday activities that require energy expenditure, and from this we can see one of the reasons for changes in motivation to finish this chapter. While experiencing more energy, my writing motivation increased, but with less energy (tiredness) motivation declined.

There are individual differences in this energy cycle such as the morningness/eveningness trait (moderately heritable), but in my experience feelings of energy and the physiological substrate that underlies it is highest in the first third of the waking day for most people, often reaching its peak at mid to late morning, dropping off in late afternoon, reaching a subpeak in the early evening and then declining to the lowest point just before sleep at night (see Fig. 23.1). Motivation for everyday activities varies directly with this diurnal (circadian)

rhythm. In the time of day when energy is high, motivation is strong, especially for physical activity. But as energy declines one is inclined to rest and to decrease energy expenditure. Although gross physical activity is most influenced by energy level in my view, cognitive activity also is influenced, and there is abundant evidence for this in the mood-cognition literature with the understanding that energy is a core component of mood.

Two Arousal Systems Mediate Mood

I regard mood as mediated by two bipolar biopsychological dimensions, Energetic Arousal and Tense Arousal, and the conjunction of these dimensions form four complex moods: calm energy, tense energy, calm tiredness, and tense tiredness (see Fig. 23.2).

Energetic Arousal

I think of energetic arousal as a kind of "go system." When it is high, we are motivated to move, to act, to do things. And when energetic arousal is low, our motivation predisposes rest and recuperation. There are a number of prominent associations of energetic arousal. Among the more important, this activation pattern is closely associated with health and illness (Thayer, 1989; cf. Ryan & Deci, 2008; Ryan & Frederick, 1997). This is immediately evident by the way in which a core element in the experience of sickness is fatigue and tiredness, while good health brings feelings of vitality and energy. Moreover, there are reliable correlations between mood (energy) and immune system functioning (Segerstrom, 2007). Subjective energy is an excellent indication of health and there are a variety of kinds of evidence for this. But this assertion was

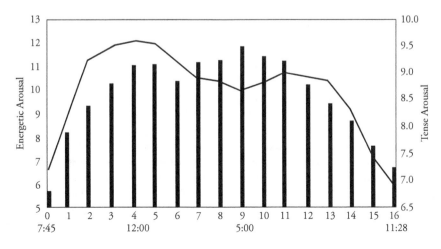

Fig. 23.1. Energy (line) and tension (bar) levels from waking to sleep. (Reproduced from Thayer, 2001, Oxford University Press.)

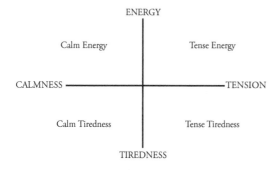

ENERGY

Calm Energy   Tense Energy

CALMNESS ——————————— TENSION

Calm Tiredness   Tense Tiredness

TIREDNESS

Fig. 23.2. Two biopsychological dimensions and four complex moods. (Reproduced from Thayer, 2001, Oxford University Press.)

nicely evidenced by a convincing study involving a panel of 310 masters-level nurses who systematically rated energy at present and in past decades (Dixon, Dixon, & Hickey, 1993). Their finding: Energy level was the best predictor of both physical and psychological health.

Another important association of energetic arousal is diet. Although there is no clear consensus about exactly what type of diet brings the greatest and most sustained energy feelings, we know from classic studies of starvation (e.g., Keys, Brozek, Henchel, Mickelsen, & Taylor, 1950) that reduced food intake has a primary effect of tiredness (low energy). As one example of my research in this area, an experiment involving sugar ingestion (Thayer, 1987a,) indicated that this resulted in increased energy followed an hour later by energy decreases and tension increases.

One of the most meaningful experimental demonstrations of the relationship between mood and a physiological substrate associated with food was carried out by Deary and his colleagues in their studies of hypoglycemia (e.g., Gold, MacLeod, Deary & Frier, 1995). Using random assignment and a placebo compared method of reducing blood glucose with an insulin drip, and at the same time periodically assessing mood over a 3-hour period, this group showed that as the blood glucose of the participants dropped from normal to near hypoglycemia tension increased and energy declined. The participants were left experiencing tense tiredness.

In my view, one important matter to bear in mind about the food-mood connection is that the moods which are experienced from typical food ingestion are subtle and require very reliable assessment for adequate understanding. Moreover, good understanding of the effects of food on mood is very complicated, and one must consider many variables

that are affected by food, including the immediate subjective reactions as well as changing reactions an hour or two later as the food is metabolized. And then there may be thoughts about what was eaten. For example, one may experience an immediate energy surge from a sugar snack (pleasant feeling) followed moments later by guilt about having broken one's diet (negative feeling), and as happened in my research, tense tiredness (negative feeling) some time later. These and other reasons are why I have used a short-term within-subjects approach such as those in which food-mood associations are repeatedly assessed and results are aggregated for maximal reliability (e.g., Thayer, 1987a, b; Thayer, Peters, Takahashi, & Birkhead-Flight, 1993).

Although there is no clear consensus about what type of food most affects energy and mood, there is much more unambiguous evidence about the way that mood affects diet. For example, in one review of over 50 scientific studies the causes of obesity and overeating could be traced to emotional eating (Ganley, 1989). Included here were such negative emotions as depression, anxiety, anger, boredom, and loneliness. A common pattern of these negative emotions was low energy and tension, or what I call tense tiredness (Thayer, 2001). And the scientific literature on overeating contains a number of studies showing that the mood conditions which are correlated with overeating are low energetic arousal and increased tense arousal. These negative moods exert powerful influences on behavior. When resources decline and feelings of low energy and increased tension prevail, people are often motivated to eat good tasting (energy-intensive) food as a way of feeling better. Eating such food can raise energy and reduce tension and from this we can see the locus of the motivation: It is to escape these negative feelings and enhance positive ones.

Another important association with energetic arousal is sleep. This is evident both from classic studies of sleep deprivation on feelings that are produced (Murrey, 1965; Thayer, 1989), as well as from correlational and quasi-experimental research in which energy level is manipulated and tracked with differing amounts of sleep. One very important reason why sleep and mood are related is the way that sleep or lack of sleep directly affects energy and tiredness and these feelings are core constituents of energetic arousal. As was true with diet mentioned earlier, time of day is likely to be important in assessment of sleep on mood, so for example, partial sleep deprivation one day may have its major mood effects the next day in the late afternoon or in the evening of the next day. But on the morning of the day following sleep deprivation there may be no apparent effect.

Physical activity also is an important component of energetic arousal. With regard to exercise, with which there are many scientific studies (e.g., Reed & Ones, 2006), certain conclusions seem apparent (also cf. Ryan, Williams, Patrick, & Deci, 2009). In my view (Thayer, 2001) the primary mood effect of moderate exercise (e.g., a short brisk walk) is increased energetic arousal and a secondary mood effect (less reliable) is reduced tense arousal. A tertiary effect is increased feelings of optimism. But with more intense exercise (e.g., an hour of intense aerobics) the primary mood effect is both reduced tense and energetic arousal, although there is some evidence that after recovery from intense exercise, there may be a resurgence of energetic arousal.

My work in recent years has involved self-regulation of mood, and this will be discussed more fully later. However, here let me say that exercise is a remarkably effective regulator of mood. Moreover, the amount of exercise necessary to impact mood is relatively little. We have focused on short exercise interventions that could be introduced into typical daily lifestyle—in particular, short brisk walks (Thayer, 1987a, b, 1989; Thayer et al., 1993). As indicated earlier, the primary mood effect of this form of exercise is increased energy.

One effective use of short brisk walks that indicates well the importance of exercise as a mood regulator occurred with a set of studies in which we assumed that unwanted behaviors such as smoking and sugar snacking often occur as a way of self-regulating mood, a kind of self-medication. Our idea was that if alternative ways of self-regulating mood were available the unhealthy behavior would diminish. In one experiment that focused on cigarette smoking and a second on sugar snacking, participants were randomly assigned to 5 minutes of a short brisk walk or to an alternative sedentary activity (Thayer et al., 1993) at times when they desired to smoke or snack. Before and after that 5 minutes, participants rated their urge to smoke (or snack) and their mood. After those post ratings they were free to smoke a cigarette or eat the sugar snack, but the time before smoking or snacking was recorded.

The brisk walk significantly reduced the urge to smoke (or snack) and significantly lengthened the time before the cigarette was smoked or the snack was eaten. Moreover, the walk significantly increased self-rated energy in both experiments. Finally, participants waited almost twice as long to smoke (or snack) if they walked than if they had engaged in some sedentary activity. It appeared that our hypothesis was correct and that the positive mood-regulating effect of exercise was verified.

Cognition and mood are quite interrelated, and this can be illustrated by the extensive research on mood-thought congruency (e.g., Blaney, 1986). And as I have indicated, energy and mood are closely related. But there is another often overlooked way that cognition and energy are likely to be closely associated. This has to do with the fact that motivation to act (particularly physical activity) is related to self-perception of the energy that would be necessary to act. This involves a kind of cybernetics analysis (cf., Carver & Scheier, 1982) incorporating feedback loops. Energy and motivation usually are integrated so that thoughts about a perspective action are associated with the perception of how much or little energy will be necessary. Usually the sensing of energy levels and the subsequent integration is so rapid and of such low awareness that it isn't noticed, but when one is tired it is easy to be unrealistic about the amount of energy that will be necessary for some future act and to believe it will not be possible (Thayer, 1987b).

Still another way that cognition and mood are interrelated was the subject of a series of our studies in which perception of personal problems and also optimistic thoughts was studied. The impetus for this research was my perception that seemingly unchanging personal problems did in fact vary substantially depending on the mood that preceded their consideration.

A group of volunteer participants who were experiencing a chronic personal problem were enlisted to rate the apparent seriousness of the agreed-upon problem as well as how optimistic they were that the problem would be solved. This was done five times during the day over several days in a 3-week period: beginning of day, late morning, late afternoon, and just before sleep. Additionally, they rated the problem after taking a 10-minute brisk walk as various times during the day.

The same problem was rated as significantly more serious (also less optimistic of being solved) at late afternoon than late morning. Moreover, regardless of time of day, the changing degree of apparent seriousness was rated as more serious when self-ratings of energy were low relative to higher tension (tense tired) compared to times when energy was high and tension low (calm energy). Lastly, the problem was rated as significantly less serious when consideration occurred after a 10-minute brisk walk. These findings were replicated in several quasi-experiments (Thayer, 1987b; Thayer, Takahashi, & Pauli, 1988).

One last prominent association with energetic arousal that should be mentioned is stress. Stress is evidenced by the subjective tension that it creates in interaction with energetic arousal. I believe that stress is related to a balance between resources and requirements (Thayer, 1996). When resources, which are indicated by one's energy level, are exceeded by requirements the result is tension and stress. One of the interesting implications of this is that the same experience may be sought out as pleasurable when resources are adequate but be stressful when ones resources are not equal to the requirements of the situation. More about this relationship will be discussed in the next section in relation to the interaction of energetic and tense arousal.

Tense Arousal

In addition to energetic arousal, I named the second of the two main mood systems Tense Arousal. This is a system that mediates danger, real or imagined (Thayer, 1989, 2009). While energetic arousal is a go system, tense arousal is a kind of stop system. Energy predisposes us to move and to act, but tension predisposes caution, waiting, or stopping. A primary marker that differentiates tense and energetic arousal is subjective experience, including tension/calmness denoting one dimension and energy/tiredness denoting the second. Other differences, which will be briefly described next, include some physiological patterns (primarily muscle tension) and also differences at the level of the brain (e.g., limbic system, cerebral cortical asymmetry).

Cognitive differences also exist between energetic and tense arousal. A major difference in my view is that cognition often is scattered with tension but is directed with energy. A tentative evolutionary explanation for this distinction may be that in a cautious (tense) mood it is adaptive to continuously scan the environment for danger. This primarily applies during circumstances in which the source of the danger is not fully known (e.g., generalized anxiety), but if the source of the danger were known it is likely that attention would be directed to that source even under high tension. On the other hand, the go system of energetic arousal facilitates fully directed attention (Thayer, 1989).

Alternate Models of Mood (Affect): Similarities and Differences

In the 1970s it became increasingly clear from factor analytic studies that affective space forms two bipolar dimensions rather than several independent factors as I had previously hypothesized. I then proposed a two-dimensional model (Thayer, 1978), and based in part on that empirical and theoretical work, four prominent models of affect and several less prominent ones exist today as the likely mappings of affect (Yik, Russell, & Barrett, 1999). My two-dimensional model involving energetic and tense arousal, plus combinations of the two kinds of arousal forming complex moods, currently stands as one of at least four competing models of mood. This model is the one I believe is the most valid representation of mood.

There is a substantial similarity between my two-dimensional model and other proposed models of affect. As alternatives to my two bipolar dimensions, two other prominent mappings of affect comprise similar but slightly different two-dimensional models. These include a model involving two dimensions named pleasure/displeasure and arousal, proposed by Russell (1980), and a second model involving two dimensions named positive and negative affect by Watson and Tellegen (1985). A third multidimensional circumplex model, including pleasantness and activation, also has been proposed by Larsen and Diener (1992).

The similarity between my two-dimensional model and Watson's model of positive and negative activation is quite apparent. In fact, the two models are substantially the same although the dimensions were given different names. The similarity between my model and Russell's model is also apparent with reference to combinations of energetic and tense arousal, which yield complex mood states. These complex mood states in my model match Russell's basic dimensions, especially the dimension of pleasure/displeasure (Yik et al., 1999).

That these multidimensional models are valid indicators of the most basic underlying dimensions of affect is suggested by various kinds of evidence. However, considering the four models of affect that are most prominent, which one is most valid?

I believe that energetic and tense arousal best capture the most elemental biopsychological processes that underlie affect. However,, there is substantial precedent for a basic psychological dimension of pleasure/displeasure (e.g., Russell). Affective states of energy and tiredness are more central from a biological perspective in my view. This energy-tiredness dimension underlies all health and general behavior. Wakefulness (closely correlated with energy) as well as sleep (tiredness) is a primary dimension of all life forms; thus, energetic arousal is a fundamental dimension of life. Also essential for survival is the ability to react to danger, and these reactions are mediated by tense arousal. Without the capacity to react to hostile environments, survival would be limited. Based on this very general biological perspective, energetic and tense arousal appear to be the most fundamental dimensions of affect.

This being said, I believe that all four models are basically compatible. Exploring this point further, cross-sectional studies have shown energetic and tense arousal to be orthogonal as the other competing models similarly exhibit orthogonality. But I believe that this apparent independence does not reflect the way that energy and tension interact under different activating conditions.

To illustrate this point, as we change from tiredness to high energy, tension states change and complex moods occur. At high levels of energy together with low tension, pleasurable moods are experienced. I call this complex mood "calm energy." On the other hand, for the moderately energized individual, as tension increases to the highest level, very negative moods occur and I call this complex negative mood "tense tiredness." Just as calm energy is very pleasurable, tense tiredness is experienced as displeasure. It is apparent then that my bipolar complex mood dimension represented by calm energy on one end and tense tiredness on the other end is the same as Russell's (2003) core mood that extends from pleasure to displeasure. Other combinations of the energy and tension dimensions yield the complex mood states that I call "tense energy" and "calm tiredness." Tense energy and calm tiredness represent different levels of arousal and from this we can see a similarity to all four models of affect. Thus, the four most prominent models of mood are compatible.

How Complex Moods Are Formed by Energetic and Tense Arousal Interactions

As indicated earlier, the four most prominent two-dimensional models of affect or mood are usually derived by cross-sectional studies in which all levels of both dimensions are represented (e.g., Yik et al., 1999). But in everyday experience changing activating conditions influence the two dimensions differentially. Thus, in my model, as activating conditions increase tense arousal, energetic arousal increases as well, yielding the complex mood of tense energy. But this only occurs up to a moderate level of activating conditions. Beyond that as tense arousal increases further, energetic arousal begins to decline, eventually resulting in the complex mood

of tense tiredness. In a similar way, as activating conditions increase energetic arousal from low to moderate levels, tense arousal also increases. But as tense arousal is increased further energetic arousal is decreased, thus yielding the complex mood that I call "tense tiredness."

In statistical terms, energetic and tense arousal bear a positive correlation from low to moderate levels of activating conditions and a negative correlation from moderate to high levels. Thus, it follows that these two types of correlation together result in orthogonal dimensions in cross-sectional studies. It is notable that these positive and negative correlations are the same regardless of whether activating conditions that drive energy result at high levels of energy and low tension (calm energy) or if activating conditions that drive tension result in high tension and low energy (tense tiredness). These relationships are portrayed in Figure 23.3.

This moderate level at which a positive correlation becomes negative has not been independently established from psychophysiological criteria other than affective response, but rather it must be observed on the basis of the shifting correlations. Speculating somewhat loosely, the moderate point at which increasing tense arousal results in decreasing energetic arousal probably is related to current physiological resources that can be assessed on the basis of subjective levels of energy. The moderate point at which increasing energy results in decreasing tense arousal is likely to be based on temperament (e.g., neuroticism).

Finally, as energy declines and tension increases there is a point at which energy is at such low ebb that exhaustion occurs. In my experience, this state of exhaustion may be quite pleasant, but in this condition an individual operates almost like an automaton in which behavior is directed cognitively without the usual subjective feedback that comes from sensing energy resources to sustain ongoing behavior. Although this may be experienced as a pleasant waking state, rest or sleep is the primary motivational directive. There is also some indication that this exhaustion state leaves one particularly vulnerable to serious physical breakdown (e.g., Prescott et al., 2003).

These interactions between the two arousal dimensions carry a number of motivational implications. For example, at different times of day different activities are likely to be more or less attractive. In the first part of the day as subjective energy increases in its natural circadian cycle physical activity is likely to be more attractive. But in the last part

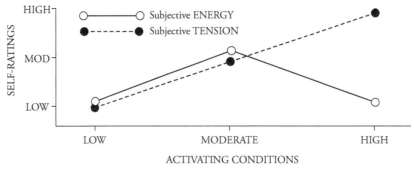

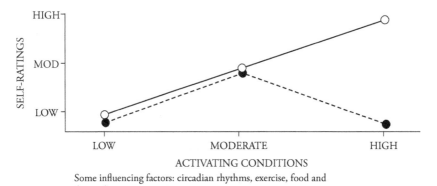

Fig. 23.3. Interactions of energy and tension under different activating conditions. (Reproduced from Thayer, 1996, Oxford University Press.)

of the day as energy declines and tiredness increases physical activity is likely to be less attractive. Likewise, cognitive demands probably vary in degree of attractiveness.

Calm Energy

It is useful to describe further the combination of energetic and tense arousal because this complex state relates to common emotions and thus leads to greater understanding of mood. One primary component is calm energy, the mixed mood state that I regard as most pleasurable and in many respects optimal for cognitive and physical functioning in waking hours when activity is appropriate. This mood is often not fully recognized. For example, in one talk I gave, a rather intense young man challenged the concept by saying that he does not understand calm energy because whenever he feels energetic he always feels slightly wired. (The feeling he was describing was a state I would call tense energy, a common mood in today's stress-filled society.)

Calm energy does exist during waking hours (primarily higher activity hours of day) when people experiencing it feel energetic and yet are very calm. In this state they experience little general muscular

tension. I regard this as a Zen-like state in which there are little or no tension-related stress reactions, a state in which natural cycles of greater and lesser energy occur, but tension is absent or at a low level.

Calm energy also bears a similarity, in my view, to Csikszentmihalyi's flow (1990), particularly on the basis of pleasurable attentional focus with full involvement. I also think of calm energy as enhancing athletic performance. In this regard, Morgan's (e.g., Morgan & Pollock, 1978) concept of the iceberg profile (high vigor coupled with low negative mood), which characterizes world-class athletes, is relevant. Probably related to this are anecdotal descriptions by athletes when their performance is so outstanding that they are in the zone. Calm energy also is an optimal predisposition in the martial arts such as karate and judo and is a valued state during the meditation in movement of Tai Chi Chuan. Calm energy is such an attractive state that people may seek it through self-medicating drugs such as caffeine, nicotine, and amphetamines.

Tense Tiredness

The bipolar opposite to calm energy in psychometric space is tense tiredness, a complex mood that is as negative as calm energy is positive. As resources decline and feelings of energy change to tiredness, vulnerability to stressful circumstances develops and tension arises. This state often develops late in the afternoon or later in the evening when stress is present. But tense tiredness may occur at any time when personal resources are depleted and stressful circumstances are present.

Although optimism and happiness are calm energetic states, feelings of depression and pessimism about the future are fostered by tense tiredness. As we shall see later when I discuss self-regulation, tense tiredness is a state that people self-regulate to feel better, often with food or drugs. For example, there is good evidence tense tiredness motivates breaking diets (also succumbing for other proscribed substances such as cigarettes) (Thayer, 2001). And in general, food urges are motivated by tense tiredness and overeating can be traced to this mood state.

Tense Energy

Two other complex mood states should be described to complete the picture of the interactions of energetic and tense arousal. One very common complex mood will be familiar to many people engaged in high-energy productive activity, but where stress-related tension is present. This is tense energy. Like calm energy, tense energy is also positively evaluated by many people. It is a state that combines energy and tension together. This is a common condition of a modern stress-filled society in which people may be quite productive and feel energetic but are never fully relaxed.

Calm Tired

The fourth complex mood to be described is calm tiredness. This state is optimal for sleep and is often sought through drugs by tired people who need sleep but suffer from the common condition of insomnia, which usually is due to low-level tense tiredness. In my view these sleep aids are not nearly as effective for restful sleep as naturally occurring tiredness together with the absence of tension because they involve side effects and they interfere with natural bodily processes.

Other commonly experienced emotions may be understood in relation to these interactions of energetic and tense arousal. Mentioned earlier is the observation that depression is a condition of low energy and increased tension (especially agitated depression). Other common emotions that can be understood in this context are happiness, optimism, anger, and boredom. Feelings of happiness are not to be confused with the trait of happiness, which we know is often correlated with the trait of extraversion (Pavot, Diener, & Fujita, 1990). Instead, it has to do with the state or the actual experience when one is feeling happiness (Yik et al., 1999). This calm energetic state is also related to feelings of optimism, a time when problems are perceived as most easily solvable (Thayer, 1987b).

In my view, anger is likely to represent a combination of energy and tension (tense energy). I base this idea on the observation that anger is diminished by extreme fatigue (moderate fatigue may increase tension and disinhibit angry thoughts). Additionally, one can observe that when angry and beginning to exercise—a common way of increasing energy—anger may increase at least until the exercise leads to exhaustion. Finally, boredom is often misunderstood as a low arousal state, but it is better interpreted as a state of tense tiredness (cf Berlyne, 1960). Boredom has been found to be an antecedent to overeating, and I have interpreted this as an example of self-regulation (Thayer, 2001).

General Bodily Arousal

General bodily arousal which underlies the mood dimensions that I have proposed represents interrelated multiple systems within the body on an arousal continuum that is associated with energy expenditure. When a resting individual becomes physically active, a wide variety of bodily systems are mobilized as energy expenditure increases. A similar pattern of mobilization occurs as a sleeping individual becomes maximally alert or as a calm person becomes intensely emotional. This mobilization occurs in a more or less integrated fashion, although the pattern of activation across bodily systems is not perfectly correlated. Reduced intraindividual correlation is likely due to differing latencies and strength of system responses. Plus there are unique responsibilities of each system for bodily homeostasis.

That a broad pattern of integration generally is the rule as the individual changes from low to high arousal with increasing amounts of energy expenditure is evident by comparing system levels from states of baseline or low arousal and reduced energy expenditure to states of high arousal and high-energy expenditure. As energy expenditure increases, each system evidences its own activation pattern. These patterns are not perfectly correlated, but the general interrelationship is apparent with reference to the low and high end points of energy expenditure.

To pursue this matter a bit further, consider an example of a resting individual who stands and begins to physically exercise (e.g., walks with increasing rapidity). Bodily arousal is reflected in a very general way throughout the body with increased cell metabolism, respiration, heart rate, blood pressure, adrenaline, cortisol, and other physiological systems associated with energy expenditure. At the brain level, infusions of neurotransmitters such as norepinephrine, dopamine, and serotonin mediate bodily arousal.

In my view, growing subjective energy and tension are part of this integrated pattern that constitutes general bodily arousal as increased feelings of energy and tension occur (Thayer, 1970, 1989). To summarize, in the bigger picture the subjective experience of energy and tension can be traced throughout the body from a basic level of the cellular mitochondria, up through neurotransmitter effects on relevant brain mechanisms (Brown, 1999; Duffy, 1962; Malmo, 1975; Thayer, 1989). Subjective energy and tension are the conscious representations of this general bodily arousal pattern.

Muscular Tension: The Activated Freeze Response

The similar activation pattern for both energetic and tense arousal follows from a biological perspective since both arousal systems predispose mobilization for action—ongoing actions with energetic arousal and preparation for (emergency) action with tense arousal. The most definitive difference between the two arousal patterns is in affect. However, there are other differences as well, although the full extent of the psychophysiological differences, including brain patterns, is not fully known. But several differences should be noted.

One physiological difference may be that tense arousal is associated more with anaerobic metabolism, whereas energetic arousal reflects aerobic metabolism (Thayer, 1989). For example, preparatory emergency arousal in the case of tension differs from energetic arousal at least in respect to skeletal-muscular activation. Thus, subjective states of tension, stress, and anxiety are characterized by preparatory muscle tension with an absence of directed motor activity. As one good indication, muscles around the thoracic cavity are tight, reflecting a pattern of restraint. Exemplifying this, breathing occurs at the top of the lungs in a short panting pattern. But with energetic arousal that is associated with ongoing activity, diaphramatic breathing is more the rule.

The skeletal-muscular inhibition associated with tension reflects what I have called the activated freeze

response. The fight-or-flight pattern made famous by Walter Cannon 100 years ago is preceded in danger situations by freezing, which optimizes avoidance of detection (Thayer, 1989). Although the fight-or-flight response is much better known than the kind of freeze response to which I refer, Cannon himself did note this initial reaction to danger (Cannon, 1929/1963). In my view, this activated freeze response plays an important role in the everyday experience of such states as nervousness, jitteriness, agitation, anxiety, and fear. This tension state (with the subjective opposite of calmness) experienced on a chronic level can produce headaches, as well as pain in the jaw, back, and shoulders.

Besides the degree and type of skeletal-muscular tension that differentiates energetic and tense arousal, other physiological differences probably exist such as the particular physiological patterns that differentiate adrenaline and cortisol (Dienstbier, 1989). Moreover, at the level of brain processes there undoubtedly are differences leading to the two kinds of subjective experience associated with the two dimensions of energy-tiredness and tension-calmness. Relevant here would be brain structures such as the reticular activating system, the limbic system, and cerebral cortical lateralized activation.

Self-Regulation of Mood

People seek pleasure and avoid pain. This hedonic principle has governed my work in relation to the self-regulation of mood (Thayer, 1989). When behavior is not required by schedules and previously made plans, when there is choice about what to do next, the preferred chosen behavior follows this hedonic principle. Sometimes this involves awareness of a negative mood followed by a conscious decision to take some action to feel better. But often there is only a low-level awareness of this process. In general, this probably is initiated by a thought about a pleasant activity that is sufficiently attractive to motivate action.

I maintain that people prefer moods of increased energy and reduced tension (calm energy), and they behave in various ways to achieve this state. They also act in various ways to reduce moods of tension and tiredness (tense tiredness). The direction of the preferred motivational process is from tense tiredness (mood to be avoided) and toward calm energy (optimal mood). For some types of people (e.g., Type As), however, tense energy may be preferred. Furthermore, when sleep is desired, the motivational direction would involve change from tense tiredness to calm tiredness.

To test this theory, my colleagues and I conducted a series of correlational studies in which a representative sample of adults from high school age through mid-eighties were first questioned about what they do when they are in a bad mood (also need increased energy and reduced tension) and what works (Thayer, Newman, & McClain, 1994). Hundreds of ways to self-regulate their mood were indicated and these were content analyzed yielding 29 categories of behaviors people regularly employ to try to change a bad mood. The categories that are used were then placed in an anonymous questionnaire that was administered to a representative sample of 308 respondents from 16 to 89 years who indicated methods they usually use to change a bad mood as well as the most common method they use. This most common method was then rated for success. Finally, people were given the opportunity to indicate things they do to change a bad mood but were not included in the 29 categories. Since none of these alternatives appeared to be sufficiently different from the list of 29, we assumed that the list was fairly all inclusive.

Of the 29 categories the most common response involved seeking social interaction (i.e., call, talk to, or be with someone) and this was endorsed by 54% of the respondents. Since we collected demographic information it was possible to determine that females were significantly more likely to endorse this activity, but many males chose this activity as well. Males, on the other hand, were significantly more likely to endorse the second more common response (51%), control thoughts (i.e., think positively, concentrate on something else, don't let things bother, give self pep talk), but many females chose this way as well.

The third most common response and judged second in effectiveness (listen to music, 47%) was a surprise to me at the time of the research, but since that time it has become more evident that our finding of a median split indicting that younger people were significantly more likely to chose this response than older people was valid. With audiences to whom I have spoken involving many young people, music listening to regulate mood is endorsed by the vast majority by a show of hands. Why listening to music would be so prevalent in regulating mood is not clear, but this mood regulation method currently is a vigorous research area, some focusing on the mood variables that I have proposed (e.g., Hirokawa, 2004; Lim, 2008).

Although seeking social interaction was the most commonly endorsed item, three of the first seven choices involved cognitive responses, thus indicating the importance that cognition has in mood regulation. This is a point that I have made in many ways, including the idea that the differences between emotions must involve the interactions of energetic and tense arousal and cognitive interpretations (Thayer, 1989, 1996).

We also looked at the 29 categories of mood regulation chosen by our research participants using factor analyses. Six factors were readily interpretable, and I have come to look at these factors as mood regulation strategies that have varying degrees of effectiveness. These degrees of effectiveness were judged both by our participants and also by a panel of 26 doctoral-level psychotherapists who graciously volunteered to make these kinds of assessments.

Of the six interpretable factors, the first one which we named Active Mood Management was judged the most effective both by our research participants and the panel of psychotherapists. This strategy nicely supported the mood theory that was one of the bases of our research. The five most highly loaded items of this strategy included, first and second, two ways for reducing tense arousal: relaxation techniques (e.g., deep breathing, stretching, muscle relaxation), and stress management activities (e.g., get organized, plan ahead). And the fifth item on this most effective strategy included the way that was judged the most effective way of changing a bad mood: exercise. The third and fourth items on this most effective strategy were cognitive items: put feelings in perspective and evaluate or analyze the situation. Thus, the best strategy for changing a bad mood involves simultaneously reducing tension, raising energy, and employing cognitive control.

Conclusion

The moods that influence our lives in all major aspects are affected in one biopsychological dimension by natural processes such as health, sleep, diet, and exercise (a go system) and in the second dimension by stress and perceived danger (a stop system). Complex moods arising from interactions of these dimensions account for many elements of motivation. These are not insignificant feelings, but rather they are excellent barometers of the overall psychology and physiology of the individual. One of the most important implications for motivation is the way that people both consciously and unconsciously self-regulate these moods in a wide variety of ways, and this generally follows the hedonic principle of motivation to optimize positive moods such as calm energy and reduce negative moods such as tense tiredness.

Future Directions

Further empirical and theoretical research could productively focus on the way that complex moods occur from the interactions of the two major biopsychological dimensions. This suggests potential solutions for previous points of confusion such as those concerning "paradoxical" effects of nicotine—that cigarettes both activate and deactivate simultaneously (Gilbert, 1979). Other seemingly paradoxical effects of drugs such as caffeine and cocaine may be important in this same respect. Likewise, these seemingly paradoxical effects occur with hyperactivity, a condition in which activating drugs such as caffeine and behaviors such as exercise appear to improve the condition. And in the exercise science literature, one finds similar dual arousal effects such as the fact that vigorous exercise produces calmness and tiredness simultaneously (Hall, Ekkekakis, Petruzello, 2007). These seemingly paradoxical effects may be understood, of course, by the orthogonality of energetic and tense arousal in cross-sectional studies but the complex interaction of these dimensions at different activation levels. Finally, what is not known well is how best to designate the moderate point at which increasing tension leads first to increased energy but at some point to reduced energy. Similarly, what is not known well is how to designate the moderate point at which increasing energy can lead first to increasing tension (in a stressful context) but at some moderate point to reduced tension.

Acknowledgment

Thanks to Martin Fiebert and Ralph Hupka for comments on a draft of this chapter.

References

Berlyne, D. E. (1960). *Conflict, arousal and curiosity*. New York: McGraw-Hill

Blaney, P. H. (1986). Affect and memory: A review. *Psychological Bulletin*, 99, 229–246.

Brown, G. (1999). *The energy of life*. New York: The Free Press

Cannon, W. B. (1929/1963). *Bodily changes in pain, hunger, fear and rage*. New York: Harper & Row.

Carver, C. S., & Scheier, M. F. (1982). Control theory: A useful conceptual framework for personality-social, clinical, and health psychology. *Psychological Bulletin*, 92, 111–135.

Csíkszentmihályi, M. (1990). *Flow: The psychology of optimal experience*. New York: Harper and Row

Dixon, J. K., Dixon, J. P., & Hickey, M. (1993). Energy as a central factor in the self-assessment of health. *Advances in Nursing Science*, 15, 1–12.

Dienstbier, R. A. (1989). Arousal and physiological toughness: Implications for mental and physical health. *Psychological Review*, 96, 84–100.

Duffy, E. (1962). *Activation and behavior*. New York: Wiley.

Ganley, R. M. (1989). Emotion and eating in obesity: A review of the literature. *International Journal of Eating Disorders*, 8, 342–361

Gilbert, D. G. (1979). Paradoxical tranquilizing and emotion-reducing effects of nicotine. *Psychological Bulletin*, 86, 643–661.

Gold, A. E., MacLeod, K. M., Deary, I. J., & Frier, B. M. (1995). Changes in mood during acute hypoglycemia in healthy participants. *Journal of Personality and Social Psychology*, 68, 498–504.

Hall, E. C., Ekkekakis, P., & Petruzello, S. J. (2007). Regional brain activity and strenuous exercise: Predicting affective responses using EEG asymmetry. *Biological Psychology*, 75, 194–200.

Hirokawa, E. (2004). Effects of music listening and relaxation instructions on arousal changes and the working memory task in older adults. *Journal of Music Therapy*, 41, 107–127.

Keys, A., Brozek, J., Henchel, A., Mickelsen, O., & Taylor, H. L. (1950). *The biology of human starvation*. Minneapolis: University of Minnesota Press.

Larsen, R. J., & Diener, E. (1992). Promises and problems with the circumplex model of emotion. *Review of Personality and Social Psychology*, 13, 25–59.

Lim, H. A. (2008). The effect of personality type and musical task on self-perceived arousal. *Journal of Music Therapy*, 45, 147–164.

Malmo, R. B. (1975). *On emotions, needs, and our archaic brain*. New York: Holt

Morgan, W. P., & Pollock, M. L. (1978). Psychological characterization of the elite distance runner. *Annals of the New York Academy of Science*, 301, 382–403.

Murrey, E. J. (1965). *Sleep, dreams and arousal*. New York: Appleton-Century-Crofts.

Pavot, W., Diener, E., & Fujita, F. (1990). Extraversion and happiness. *Personality and Individual Differences*, 11, 1299–1306.

Prescott, E., Holst, C., Gronbaek, M., Schnohr, P., Jensen, G., & Barefoot, J. (2003). Vital exhaustion as a risk factor for ischaemic heart disease and all-cause mortality in a community sample. *International Journal of Epidemiology*, 32, 990–997

Reed, J., & Ones, D. S. (2006). The effect of acute aerobic exercise on positive activated affect: A meta-analysis. *Psychology of Sport and Exercise*, 75, 477–514.

Russell, J. A. (1980). A circumplex model of affect. *Journal of Personality and Social Psychology*, 39, 1161–1178.

Russell, J. A. (2003). Core affect and the psychological construction of emotion. *Psychological Review*, 110, 145–172.

Ryan, R. M., & Deci, E. L. (2008). From ego depletion to vitality: Theory and findings concerning the facilitation of energy available to the self. *Social and Personality Psychology Compass*, 2, 702–717.

Ryan, R. M., & Frederick, C. (1997). On energy, personality and health: Subjective vitality as a dynamic reflection of well-being. *Journal of Personality*, 65, 529–565.

Ryan, R. M., Williams, G. C., Patrick, H., & Deci, E. L. (2009). Self-determination theory and physical activity: The dynamics of motivation in development and wellness. *Hellenic Journal of Psychology*, 6, 107–124.

Segerstrom, S. C. (2007). Stress, energy, and immunity: An ecological view. *Current Directions in Psychological Science*, 16, 326–330.

Thayer, R. E. (1970). Activation states as assessed by verbal report and four psychophysiological variables. *Psychophysiology, 7*, 86–94.

Thayer, R. E. (1978). Toward a psychological theory of multidimensional activation (Arousal). *Motivation and Emotion, 2*, 1–33.

Thayer, R. E. (1987a). Energy, tiredness, and tension effects of a sugar snack versus moderate exercise. *Journal of Personality and Social Psychology, 52*, 119–125.

Thayer, R. E. (1987b). Problem perception, optimism, and related states as a function of time of day (diurnal rhythm) and moderate exercise: Two arousal systems in interaction. *Motivation and Emotion, 11*, 19–36.

Thayer, R. E. (1989). *The biopsychology of mood and arousal.* New York: Oxford University Press.

Thayer, R. E., Newman, J., & McClain, T. M. (1994). Self-regulation of mood: Strategies for changing a bad mood, raising energy and reducing tension. *Journal of Personality and Social Psychology, 67*, 910–925.

Thayer, R. E. (1996). *The origin of everyday moods.* New York: Oxford University Press.

Thayer, R.E. (2000). Mood. In A. E. Kazdin (Ed.), *Encyclopedia of psychology* (pp. 394–395). Washington, DC: Oxford University Press and American Psychological Association.

Thayer, R. E. (2001). *Calm energy: How people regulate mood with food and exercise.* New York: Oxford University Press

Thayer, R. E. (2009). Tension. In D. Sander & K. R. Scherer (Eds.), *Emotion and the affective sciences* (pp. 390–391). New York: Oxford University Press.

Thayer, R. E., Peters, D. P., Takahashi, P. J., & Birkhead-Flight, A. M. (1993). Mood and behavior (smoking and sugar snacking) following moderate exercise: A partial test of self-regulation theory. *Personality and Individual Differences, 14*, 97–104.

Thayer, R. E., Takahashi, P. J., & Pauli, J. S. (1988). Multidimensional arousal states, diurnal rhythms, cognitive and social processes, and extraversion. *Personality and Individual Differences, 9*, 15–24.

Watson, D., & Tellegen, A. (1985). Toward a consensual structure of mood. *Psychological Bulletin, 98*, 219–235.

Yik, M. S. M., Russell, J. A., & Barrett, L. F. (1999). Structure of self-reported current affect: Integration and beyond. *Journal of Personality and Social Psychology, 77*, 600–619.

Effort Intensity: Some Insights From the Cardiovascular System

Guido H. E. Gendolla, Rex A. Wright, *and* Michael Richter

Abstract

This chapter deals with the psychological process that determines effort intensity in instrumental behavior. According to motivation intensity theory, effort should be proportional to experienced task difficulty as long as success is possible and justified and low when success is impossible or excessively difficult, given the available benefit. When task difficulty is unspecified or unknown, effort should be proportional to the importance of success. We report a program of experimental studies that have operationalized effort intensity as cardiovascular reactivity during task performance and used multiple manipulations of variables influencing subjective task difficulty (e.g., performance standards, ability, mood) and the amount of justified effort (e.g., material incentive, instrumentality, evaluation). The empirical evidence is in clear support of the principles of motivation intensity theory and challenges a number of other theoretical accounts. Directions for future research are discussed.

Key Words: effort, motivation intensity, cardiovascular response

Introduction

Motivation can be briefly defined as the process that determines the direction and energization of behavior (Elliot, 2006). Traditionally, the first aspect—what people do—has received more attention in motivation research than the second aspect—how much effort people mobilize to execute instrumental behavior. However, over the last 25 years a number of variables have been identified that influence effort intensity—that is, resource mobilization for instrumental behavior at a point in time (Gendolla & Wright, 2009). Drawing on the idea that effort has the function to deal with obstacles in the goal pursuit process, it was postulated at the beginning of the last century that effort mobilization follows the "difficulty law of motivation" (e.g., Ach, 1935; Hillgruber, 1912). Accordingly, effort is mobilized in proportion to the experienced difficulty of instrumental behavior—the higher the obstacles encountered during goal pursuit, the more

effort is mobilized. Over the years, this basic principle has been elaborated and modified, but it still has a major impact on current research. Its most influential elaboration has been formulated in Brehm's motivation intensity theory (Brehm & Self, 1989; Brehm, Wright, Solomon, Silka, & Greenberg, 1983). In the first part of this chapter we will discuss this theory and studies that have been inspired by it. In the second part we will discuss the relation of this approach to other theoretical accounts as well as future directions for research.

Motivation Intensity Theory

Motivation intensity theory (Brehm et al., 1983; Brehm & Self, 1989) draws on the basic idea that individuals try to avoid wasting resources. Following this resource conservation principle, performers are expected to expend effort *(1)* only to the degree that is needed, and *(2)* only when expenditure yields a return (i.e., a benefit) justifying the effort expended.

The need for effort is determined by the difficulty of instrumental behavior, which is the difficulty of activity that must be carried out to attain desired outcomes and avoid aversive ones. Thus, a central proposition of motivation intensity theory is that effort investment should vary nonmonotonically with the perceived difficulty of imminent or ongoing behavior (see Ach, 1935; Hillgruber, 1912). As long as success is viewed as both possible and worth the investment that it will require, effort should correspond to difficulty. That is, performers should invest greater effort the more difficult they perceive their task to be. On the other hand, if success is viewed as impossible or excessively difficult, given the benefit that it will accrue, then effort should be low (Fig. 24.1). Effort should also be low in the impossible case because it would yield no return, and it should be low in the excessively difficult case because it would yield a return lower than the value of the effort expended.

The Role of Benefit

An important point about the central proposition mentioned earlier is that it suggests that considerations of benefit in performance circumstances do not determine effort directly. Rather, they determine effort *indirectly* by setting the upper limit of what is justified and what performers are willing to do. Brehm referred to this upper limit as the performer's level of *potential* motivation. In theory, factors related to benefit (e.g., the value of and need for an available incentive) should have no impact on effort as long as success is possible and benefit is great enough to justify the required effort.

To illustrate, first consider a person offered at different points in time $10, $20, and $30 to lift a weight that he or she could lift and was willing to lift for $10. The present view suggests that the person's effort should correspond to the difficulty of the lift, and not the value of the incentive, at the different points. Next, consider what would happen under conditions where this person was unwilling to lift the weight even for $30. The present view suggests that his or her effort should be consistently low at the different points. Finally, consider what would happen if the person were offered the different incentives for lifting a weight that he or she knew exceeded his or her strength. Once again, effort should be low at all points.

Where Difficulty Is Unknown

A further point to note about the central proposition discussed earlier is that it assumes that performers know what will be required to succeed, which will not always be the case. Consider here, for example, *(1)* a student confronted with an exam from a new teacher, *(2)* a woman woken up in the middle of the night by a noise in her bedroom closet, or *(3)* a soldier confronted with random sniper fire over the course of a morning. People sometimes know that action is called for but are unsure what exactly needs to be done and how much effort needs to be mobilized for it. Motivation intensity theory asserts that effort in such circumstances will be proportional to potential motivation.

At first glance, the preceding assertion might seem contrary to the guiding principle of resource conservation. However, it arguably is not when one

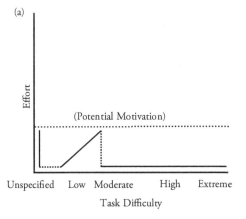
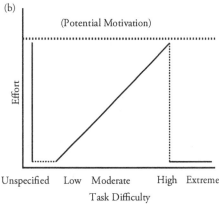

Fig. 24.1. Theoretical predictions of the joint impact of task difficulty and potential motivation on effort intensity. *A* shows predictions for effort mobilization when low effort is justified (i.e., low potential motivation). *B* shows predictions for the condition that high effort is justified (i.e., high potential motivation). (Adapted from Gendolla & Wright, 2009, p. 134. Copyright: Oxford University Press.)

considers that using potential motivation to guide effort investment allows performers to avoid investing more resources than is justified. Given that performers do not know what will be required to succeed when task difficulty is unknown, they are at risk of investing more than necessary. However, by investing effort proportional to potential motivation they can assure that they will never exceed the amount of justified effort.

Where Difficulty Is Not Fixed

A third point to note about the central proposition discussed earlier is that it recognizes that performance contingencies (i.e., benefits) do not always have an all-or-none character. The contingencies sometimes do, as would be the case if a person learned that he or she could earn an amount of money by lifting a given amount of weight. However, they sometimes do not. Consider, for example, a person told that he or she can earn $1 for every lift he or she makes or, alternatively, a child told he or she can earn a bite of dessert for every bite of broccoli that he or she takes. In circumstances like these, benefit rises in constant proportion to performance quality. Brehm referred to such circumstances as ones in which difficulty is not fixed (e.g., Brehm & Self, 1989). Additionally, persons can be asked to do their best (or what they want) without being confronted with a clear performance standard (see Locke & Latham, 1990). Also under this condition task difficulty is not fixed.

Once again, motivation intensity theory assumes that effort will be proportional to potential motivation (total benefit that can be accrued) up to the point that people can try no harder. Thus, the person in the previous example would be expected to exert more effort the more money he or she could make until attaining the effort peak. Similarly, the child would be expected to exert more effort the more delectable the available dessert until he or she attained his or her effort peak and persons who are asked to do their best should invest more effort the higher the benefits of success. Arguably, underlying processes are similar to those operating in unknown difficulty circumstances. Specifically, performers *(1)* aim to perform at the highest level that is both possible and justified, and *(2)* expend effort in proportion to the difficulty of that behavior (Wright & Kirby, 2001).

Summary

To summarize, motivation intensity theory maintains that effort intensity does not vary with potential benefit directly, but rather with the difficulty of behavior necessary to attain goals. So long as success is possible and worthwhile, effort should correspond to difficulty. Where success is deemed impossible or excessively difficult, given the available benefit, effort should be low. In theory, the role of benefit should be to determine the upper limit of what performers will be willing to do, thus determining the drop point of effort along possible levels of a difficulty continuum. Motivation intensity theory recognizes that people sometimes believe that action is—or might be—needed, but they are unsure what exactly needs to be done and that people sometimes can decide on their own how much effort they want to invest. In such circumstances, people are expected to expend effort in proportion to their potential motivation—that is, their willingness to act.

Measuring Effort

Motivation intensity theory provides an elegant picture of effort investment. However, its validity is by no means self-evident. Like any other theory worth serious consideration, it requires empirical testing and thus a measure of effort intensity. One idea to quantify effort intensity, applied for decades, has been to obtain self-reports of effort mobilization under different task conditions (e.g., Efklides, Kourkoulou, Mitsiou, & Ziliaskopoulou, 2006; Meyer & Hallermann, 1977; Roets, Van Hiel, Cornelis, & Soetens, 2008). However, self-report measures of effort are problematic for several reasons. For one thing, effort self-reports have been shown to be highly vulnerable to self-presentational influences (Pyszczynski & Greenberg, 1983; Rhodewalt & Fairfield, 1991). In addition, there is concern that people might not always apprehend how hard they are (or are not) trying, because introspection abilities are (very) limited (Wilson, 2002). A second idea has been to measure performance—an outcome that multiple motivation researchers have directly linked to the intensity aspect of motivation (e.g., Aarts, Custers, & Marien, 2008; Atkinson & Raynor, 1974; Bandura & Cervone, 1983; Eisenberger, 1992; Kukla, 1972; Locke & Latham, 1990). However, this is problematic as well because of obvious disconnections between effort and different performance outcomes, including the speed and quality of responses (see Harkins, 2006). Consider, for example, two people, one asked to memorize two nonsense trigrams and the other asked to memorize four. Within a period of 2 minutes, they both would be likely to succeed and therefore perform perfectly. But they would have to expend different degrees of effort to achieve their success. Moreover, performance is determined by more factors than effort alone—at least ability and strategy use also have (and sometimes even stronger) influences on it (see Locke & Latham, 1990).

A third idea is, in our view, more promising. It is to assess effort *physiologically*, that is, by examining adjustments in bodily systems that should—in theory—be involved in mobilizing people for action. This approach *(1)* takes as a given that effort either leads to energization or is simply part and parcel of the energy mobilization process, and *(2)* draws attention to the cardiovascular system.

Effort-Related Cardiovascular Reactivity

Effort investigators have looked to the cardiovascular system for two reasons. One reason is because there is growing agreement that the cardiovascular system functions chiefly to sustain behavior (Papillo & Shapiro, 1990). The second is because research in psychophysiology—particularly that by Elliott (1969) and Obrist (1976)—has indicated that effort not only affects cardiovascular responses but does so by way of certain sympathetic nervous system mechanisms, that is, mechanisms associated with the branch of the autonomic nervous system involved in activation. It is beyond the scope of this chapter to delve into all details of sympathetic cardiovascular influence or to examine carefully the evidence linking effort to it. For present purposes, it is sufficient to make two observations. First, in theory (Wright, 1996), the best indicators of the sympathetic mechanisms mentioned earlier should be heart contraction force (i.e., cardiac contractility—typically measured as pre-ejection period [PEP]) and outcomes affected by it, most notably systolic blood pressure (SBP—pressure at the peak of a pulse). Heart rate (HR—the pace of heart contraction) should tend to be indicative as well. However, it is affected not only by sympathetic activity but also by *para*sympathetic activity that can sometimes mask or even reverse the relevant sympathetic effects. Thus, HR must be interpreted cautiously in performance contexts. Other common cardiovascular parameters may have also some potential for reflecting effort, but less for reasons that we will not go into here. Interested readers are thus referred to relevant discussions by Berntson, Cacioppo, and Quigley (1993), Brownley, Hurwitz, and Schneiderman, (2000), Kelsey (2011), Obrist (1981), Papillo and Shapiro (1990), and Wright and Kirby (2001).

With the preceding background in place, we can now turn to relevant studies. The studies can be organized into two groups: *(1)* ones that addressed basic implications of the motivation intensity analysis and focused on psychological variables influencing subjective task difficulty, and *(2)* studies that focused on manipulations of variables that should impact potential motivation—the level of maximally justified effort—and its interaction with task difficulty.

Empirical Evidence

We will now present a series of studies that have systematically investigated the principles of motivation intensity theory and operationalized effort intensity as cardiovascular response—that is, performance-related changes in cardiovascular activity with reference to baseline values. The experimental protocol of a typical study consists of two phases. Participants are first habituated to the laboratory for a period of about 10 minutes. During that time, participants are inactive and cardiovascular baseline activity is assessed. Then participants work on a task, typically for about 5 minutes, and cardiovascular activity is again assessed during task performance. In some studies, cardiovascular activity was additionally assessed immediately before task performance. Participants' cardiovascular *re*activity—the dependent variable referring to effort intensity—is expressed in the mean performance-related changes in cardiovascular activity with reference to the individual baseline values.

The Role of Variables Affecting Difficulty

Numerous studies have investigated simple task difficulty effects on effort-related cardiovascular response. Examples are experiments conducted by Wright (1984) and Smith, Baldwin, and Christensen (1990). Wright (1984) told some participants that they could avoid an electric shock by performing an easy or difficult motor activity (a toggle switch grip or dynamometer grip, respectively) and other participants that they were in a control condition in which no (shock) avoidant behavior would be made available. HR data collected in the 30 seconds prior to a point at which participants were to either *(1)* perform their task (avoidance conditions) or *(2)* pause for further instructions (no avoidance) indicated greater responsiveness in the difficult avoidance condition. A measure of finger pulse volume (reflecting digital blood flow) indicated a similar response pattern. Smith et al. (1990) provided participants the chance to earn a monetary incentive by making a speech that was mildly, moderately, or extremely convincing to an audience. As expected, SBP, diastolic blood pressure (DBP—pressure between pulses) and HR responses measured just before and during the speech were greater when the performance standard was moderate than when it was low or extreme.

The most recent study to provide documentation for simple difficulty effects is an experiment by Richter, Friedrich, and Gendolla (2008) that included a measure of cardiac contractility (PEP) as well as measures of blood pressure and HR. Note that PEP is assessed in milliseconds and increased contractility is expressed by negative PEP reactivity values. The study presented participants a recognition memory task that required them to indicate repeatedly whether a probe character was in a preceding character string (Sternberg, 1966). Difficulty was manipulated by displaying the initial string for 1,000 milliseconds (difficulty low), 550 milliseconds (difficulty moderate), 100 milliseconds (difficulty high), or 15 milliseconds (difficulty extreme). As expected, contractility and SBP responses assessed during performance rose progressively from the low- to the moderate- to the high-difficulty condition, and then dropped (Fig. 24.2).

ABILITY AND DIFFICULTY

An ability elaboration from the motivation intensity analysis, which has been discussed in detail elsewhere (e.g., Wright, 1998), builds on two ideas. The first is that the proximal determinant of effort should be performers' personal appraisals of how difficult it will be to attain a goal. The second is that personal difficulty appraisals should be influenced by the performer's ability (i.e., capacity with respect

to the features of the task), with less capable performers viewing success at any given objective difficulty level as harder than more capable performers (Heider, 1958; Hockey, 1997; Kukla, 1972; cf. Bandura, 1982, 1986). It follows that (1) effort should be stronger for low- than high-ability performers as long as the low-ability performers perceive success as both possible and worthwhile; (2) low-ability performers should withhold effort and display reduced cardiovascular responses at a lower difficulty level than should high-ability performers, creating a window of difficulty levels within which effort is weaker for low- than high-ability performers; and (3) effort should be low for both ability groups under conditions where success calls for more than high-ability performers can or will do (Fig. 24.3).

One of the earliest ability studies (Wright, Wadley, Pharr, & Butler, 1994) examined ability as a measured, rather than a manipulated, factor. Investigators first administered in a mass testing session an ability questionnaire that allowed them to identify students who viewed themselves as highly incapable or highly capable with respect to math. They then invited the targeted students to participate in a study that gave them the chance to avoid noise by meeting a particular performance standard on a set of math problems. For some students, the problems were described as easy; for others, they were described as difficult; for still others, they were described as extremely difficult. Analysis of cardiovascular responses measured just before the performance period showed a difficulty x ability interaction for SBP. Among high-ability participants, anticipatory responses rose across the three difficulty levels. Among low-ability participants, they were higher at the easy- and high-difficulty levels, but low at the highest difficulty level.

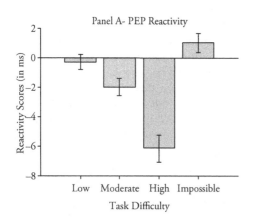
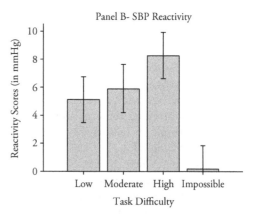

Fig. 24.2. PEP (*A*) and SBP (*B*) reactivity in dependence on task difficulty in the Study by Richter, Friedrich, and Gendolla (2008). (Reprinted with permission of John Wiley and Sons.)

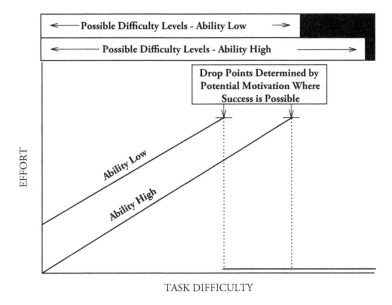

Fig. 24.3. Relation between effort and difficulty for people with low and high ability. (Adapted from Wright and Franklin, 2004, p. 190, with permission of Erlbaum Press.)

Other studies experimentally manipulated ability appraisals. One by Wright and Dill (1993) first used a performance feedback procedure to lead half of its participants to believe that they had low ability with respect to a scanning task and half to believe that they had high ability with respect to the task. Later, it presented a related scanning task and told the participants that they could earn a prize by meeting a high (85th percentile) or low (15th percentile) performance standard. As expected, SBP responses measured immediately before and during the work period were in an interactional pattern, reflecting relatively greater responsiveness for low-ability participants when the standard was low, but greater responsiveness for high-ability participants when the standard was high. Whereas ability tended to be negatively associated with SBP responsiveness when difficulty was low, it was positively associated with cardiovascular responsiveness when difficulty was high. Analysis of DBP data revealed an interactional response pattern corresponding closely with the SBP means.

A later study by Wright and Dismukes (1995) involved a similar procedure, but it utilized an aversive rather than an attractive incentive. As before, investigators first led participants to believe that they had low or high ability with respect to a scanning task. They then told participants that they could avoid noise by attaining a low (20th percentile) or high (95th percentile) performance standard on a version of the task. Results indicated a crossover response pattern for HR and, to a lesser degree,

SBP and DBP. Among high-ability participants, responses were or tended to be stronger under difficult conditions. Among low-ability participants, the reverse was true. Once again, whereas ability tended to be negatively associated with cardiovascular responsiveness when difficulty was low, it was positively associated with cardiovascular responsiveness when difficulty was high.

FATIGUE AND DIFFICULTY

Following from the ability reasoning and studies discussed in the previous section has been a series of studies concerned with fatigue influence on effort-related cardiovascular responses. Studies in the series have assumed that ability falls as fatigue rises. Accordingly, they have predicted that fatigue should interact with difficulty to determine effort-related cardiovascular responses in the same way that ability should do so, with high fatigue corresponding to low ability and low fatigue corresponding to high ability (Fig. 24.3).

The earliest of the fatigue studies was an experiment that involved a muscular challenge (Wright & Penacerrada, 2002). Its central purpose was to evaluate the implication that effort-related cardiovascular response should be proportional to fatigue where a performance challenge can and will be met. A secondary purpose was to evaluate the idea that muscular fatigue effects should tend to be challenge specific, that is, confined to challenges that involve the fatigued system. Participants first performed left- or right-handedly a set of 12 easy (low fatigue) or difficult (high fatigue) hand dynamometer grips. Following the initial grip period, the participants made and held with their right hand a modest grip while cardiovascular measures were taken. As expected, SBP responses were stronger under high fatigue conditions among participants who gripped first with their right hand, but not among participants who gripped first with their left hand.

Findings have been conceptually replicated and extended in multiple subsequent investigations, some involving muscular tasks and some involving mental tasks (for a review, see Wright & Stewart, 2011). One mental fatigue study (Wright, Martin, & Bland, 2003) examined the ideas that fatigue should *(1)* augment effort-related cardiovascular responses when it leaves unaltered a belief that success is possible and worthwhile, but *(2)* retard those responses when it causes success to appear impossible or excessively difficult. Investigators created low and high levels of mental fatigue by requiring participants initially to perform for 5 minutes an easy or difficult counting task. After the counting period, the investigators presented participants mental arithmetic problems with instructions that they could earn a prize if they attained a low (30th percentile) or high (80th percentile) performance standard. As expected, analysis of cardiovascular data collected during the arithmetic work period indicated a fatigue x difficulty interaction for SBP. High fatigue participants tended to have stronger responses than low fatigue participants when the standard was low; by contrast, they had weaker responses than low fatigue participants when the standard was high (Fig. 24.4). Analysis of the DBP and mean arterial pressure (MAP) data revealed the same interactions with means in similar crossover patterns.

Several mental fatigue studies aimed not only to reproduce cardiovascular effects like those mentioned previously but also to evaluate the extent to which mental fatigue effects are challenge specific, that is, limited to challenges highly relevant to the mental activity that induced the fatigue. An example is an experiment that *(1)* first required participants to perform an easy (fatigue low) or difficult (fatigue high) counting task, and then *(2)* presented the participants with either an arithmetic challenge (fatigue relevance high) or a letter scanning challenge (fatigue relevance low) with instructions that they would avoid a noise if they attained a modest (50th percentile) performance standard (Wright et al., 2007, Experiment 1). Analysis of the cardiovascular data collected during the second work period indicated stronger DBP and MAP responses for high fatigue participants regardless of the character of the task. SBP responses corresponded with DBP and MAP responses, although the fatigue effect in that case fell short of reliability. The other studies of this type also yielded no evidence that mental fatigue effects are challenge specific.

MOOD

Moods are defined as relatively long-lasting affective states that are experienced without concurrent awareness of their origins (Frijda, 1993). Typical examples are feeling elated or depressed. A series of experiments tested the idea of the mood-behavior-model (Gendolla, 2000) that moods have a systematic *informational* impact on effort intensity during task performance because they function as task-relevant information and have mood congruency effects on task appraisals. If effort mobilization is basically guided by a resource conservation principle, it follows that the default appraisal in face of a task should be that of the level of task demand. In those studies elated and depressed moods were first manipulated with exposure to funny or depressing video excerpts, elating or depressing music, or autobiographical recollection of positive or negative personal events. Subsequently, participants worked on a cognitive task (memory, attention, or verbal creativity). After an initial habituation period, cardiovascular measures were taken during mood inductions and task performance (see Gendolla & Brinkmann, 2005; Gendolla, Brinkmann, & Silvestrini, 2011 for more detailed reviews).

In support of the idea that moods systematically influence effort-related cardiovascular response

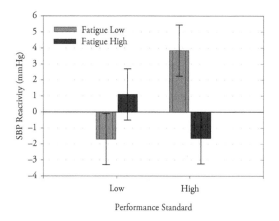

Fig. 24.4. SBP reactivity as a function of difficulty for low- and high fatigued participants. (Based on data presented by Wright et al., 2003.)

through their informational impact, it was found that *(1)* demand appraisals before and SBP reactivity during task performance were higher in a negative mood than in a positive mood for tasks with "do your best" instructions (e.g., Gendolla, Abele, & Krüsken, 2001; Gendolla & Krüsken, 2001a, 2002b); *(2)* these mood congruency effects on experienced demand and SBP response during task performance disappeared when moods' value as task-relevant information was called into question by providing a hint for the mood manipulations (Gendolla & Krüsken, 2002a); *(3)* when participants performed tasks with fixed performance standards, they used both their mood and the performance standard to appraise demand, resulting in the anticipated crossover pattern of mood and objective task difficulty (Gendolla & Krüsken, 2001b, 2002b) that resembles the interactive effect of ability beliefs and task difficulty discussed earlier: For easy tasks, SBP reactivity was stronger in a negative mood than in a positive mood, because subjective demand for participants in a negative mood was higher than for those in a positive mood. However, for difficult tasks, SBP reactivity was stronger in a positive mood than in a negative mood, because here subjective difficulty was high but still feasible in a positive mood, whereas it was too high in a negative mood, resulting in disengagement. Corresponding effects on effort-related cardiovascular response were found for individual differences in dysphoria/depression (Brinkmann & Gendolla, 2007, 2008) and extraversion (Kemper et al., 2008).

A recent study by de Burgo and Gendolla (2009) tested the mood-behavior-model postulate that that moods themselves are not motivational states and that they thus do not have an impact on effort-related cardiovascular response until they can be used as task-relevant information for demand appraisals. After being induced in positive versus negative moods with video excerpts, participants were exposed to a list of letter series. In an intentional learning condition, participants were explicitly instructed to correctly memorize the series within 5 minutes; in an incidental learning condition, the list was merely presented without framing it as achievement task. As in the mood studies discussed earlier, SBP did not differ between the mood conditions during the mood inductions, although the verbal mood manipulation checks indicated successfully manipulated positive and negative mood states. Most relevant, during task performance SBP reactivity in the intentional learning task was stronger in a negative mood than in a positive mood.

Mood had no effect on cardiovascular reactivity in the incidental learning task. The results support the idea that moods influence effort when they can be used as task-relevant information for task appraisals. However, when resources do not have to be mobilized, mood loses this informational impact. This influence of moods is clearly different from that of specific, object-related, and short-lived emotions, which directly mobilize resources for adaptive actions (see Kreibig, 2010).

In summary, the studies on mood effects on effort intensity discussed in this section show that moods function as task-relevant information. When tasks have an achievement character and judgments of task demand are possible, mood influences effort by informing about subjective task difficulty and has similar effects on effort intensity as ability beliefs, as discussed earlier.

The Role of Variables Affecting the Importance of Success

A number of studies have investigated the impact of variables influencing the level of potential motivation as determinant of the level of maximally justified effort for goal attainment. Most of these studies have focused on tasks with manipulated fixed difficulty levels. Others have focused on tasks where difficulty was unspecified. As outlined in the first section of this chapter, motivation intensity theory predicts that effort intensity should be proportional to task difficulty as long as success is justified. Consequently, high potential motivation justifies the high effort that is necessary to cope with highly difficult demands, while low potential motivation does not, resulting in earlier disengagement on lower difficulty levels. Moreover, effort intensity should be proportional to potential motivation when task difficulty is unspecified or unknown. These ideas were tested in experiments using various manipulations of potential motivation ranging from a material incentive to affective and self-esteem-related consequences of success.

MATERIAL INCENTIVE

Participants in a study by Eubanks, Wright, and Williams (2002) worked on a computerized recognition memory task. Depending on the difficulty condition, participants were presented with letter series that contained between three (very easy) and thirteen (very difficult) letters, followed by a target letter that was presented after a short delay. Participants learned before task onset that they could gain either $10 (low incentive) versus $100 (high incentive) if they responded correctly in at least 90% of the trials. The results were most pronounced for changes in HR, which increased over the whole range of difficulty conditions in the high-incentive condition. In the low-incentive condition, HR reactivity first increased with difficulty but dropped on the difficult and very difficult levels. This supports the idea that high monetary incentive leads to high effort for difficult tasks by justifying the necessary high effort. When task difficulty is rather low, incentive has no increasing effect on effort, because low effort is sufficient for succeeding.

Evidence for the incentive effects on effort-related cardiovascular response when task difficulty is unknown has come primarily from studies by Richter and Gendolla. The first study from these investigators (Richter & Gendolla, 2006, Experiment 1) used a computer to present participants over a 5-minute period in sequence a series of four nonsense quadrams, that is, character strings made up of four letters that convey no meaning (e.g., AEGD). Preliminary instructions informed participants that they could earn an attractive poster (incentive value high) or an unattractive poster (incentive value low) if they memorized their quadrams successfully, providing quadram and procedural details for some participants (difficulty low), but not for other participants (difficulty unknown). As expected, SBP reactivity during task performance was jointly determined by difficulty and incentive (potential motivation). Whereas reactivity was stronger under high- than low-incentive value conditions when difficulty was unknown, it was relatively low and constant across incentive value levels when difficulty was low.

Later studies conceptually replicated and extended the preceding cardiovascular effects. For example, Richter and Gendolla (2006, Experiment 2) used highly similar known and unknown difficulty protocols and manipulated incentive value by offering participants either 10 Swiss Francs or nothing for a good performance. As expected, SBP responses were greater in the payment condition than in the no-payment condition if difficulty was unknown, but not if difficulty was known and low. Another follow-up (Richter & Gendolla, 2007) ran a highly similar unknown difficulty protocol and manipulated incentive value across four levels, offering participants 10, 20, or 30 Swiss Francs, or nothing for success. Results showed that SBP responses measured during the performance period were directly proportional to the value of the incentive offered (i.e., to potential motivation).

The most recent experiment of this type (Richter & Gendolla, 2009a) examined PEP as well as blood pressure and HR. The experimental task required participants to match patterns displayed on a computer monitor to a target pattern, with success earning 1, 15, or 30 Swiss Francs. Instructions left details ambiguous and, furthermore, indicated that at the end of the work period, the computer would assign randomly the performance standard that would define success. As expected, PEP responsiveness increased steadily across the incentive value (potential motivation) conditions. SBP responses tended to rise with incentive value as well, although the comparison of the 15- and 30-Swiss Francs conditions did not approach significance.

In summary, studies that manipulated potential motivation by means of material incentive have well supported the predictions of motivation intensity theory. It has been shown that high incentive justifies the high necessary effort for coping with difficult tasks, while incentive itself does not boost effort when task difficulty is low and success only necessitates the mobilization of low resources. Moreover, there is replicated evidence that effort rises with the value of a material incentive when task difficulty is not specified.

OUTCOME EXPECTANCY (INSTRUMENTALITY)

A series of studies by Wright and colleagues operationalized potential motivation in terms of outcome expectancy, that is, the perceived likelihood that success on a task will lead to a desired outcome (Maddux, 1995). Outcome expectancy also is referred to as the instrumentality of behavior. In theory, importance should be greater where it is high than where it is low. Thus, outcome expectancy should determine performers' upper effort limit—the level of potential motivation.

An early experiment by Wright and Gregorich (1989) provided participants a low (1/15) or high (14/15) chance of winning a modest prize (a paper notebook) by succeeding on an easy (two-trigram) or moderately difficult (five-trigram) memorization task. Analysis of cardiovascular responses assessed just prior to work revealed difficulty x instrumentality (i.e., potential motivation) interaction patterns for SBP and HR. Among the high-chance participants, responses were proportional to difficulty; among the low-chance participants, the responses were low irrespective of difficulty.

A later experiment by Wright, Williams, and Dill (1992) manipulated the expectancy in an avoidance context rather than in an appetitive one and measured cardiovascular responses during, rather than immediately prior to, the work (see also Manuck, Harvey, Lechleiter, & Neal, 1978). Participants were presented trials of a recognition memory task similar to the one used by Richter et al. (2008). Specifically, they were presented a series of character strings, each followed by a question asking whether a probe was in the string. For half, each string had three characters, rendering success relatively easy. For the rest, each string had seven characters, rendering success relatively difficult. Instructions indicated that a good performance (90% success rate) would ensure a strong (19/20) or weak (1/20) chance of avoiding an aversive noise, thus yielding the same basic experimental design seen in the study mentioned earlier. Once again, there was a joint effect of chance and difficulty on cardiovascular response. Whereas responses were greater in the moderately difficult condition when outcome expectancy was high, they were low in both difficulty conditions when outcome expectancy (potential motivation) was low.

A recent study by Richter and Gendolla (2009b) extended the evidence on informational mood impact on effort mobilization discussed earlier. This experiment tested the idea that mood can influence effort mobilization through its informational impact on outcome expectancies when difficulty is unknown. Participants were induced into positive, neutral, or negative moods by an autobiographical recollection task and then worked on a memory task of *unknown* task difficulty—a setting in which participants orient effort mobilization on potential motivation, as discussed earlier. Before task onset, participants learned that they could earn the chance of winning a monetary reward if they succeeded and were asked to rate the probability of winning. Those subjective probability ratings were higher in a positive mood than in a negative mood—suggesting that potential motivation was higher in a positive mood (high probability to get the reward) than in a negative mood (low probability to get the reward). Corresponding to this, SBP reactivity during task performance increased from the negative via the neutral to the positive mood condition. The SBP effect was statistically mediated by participants' subjective probability ratings of winning the monetary reward for successful performance.

Another study—by Stewart, Wright, Hui, and Simmons (2009)—investigated combined effects of fatigue and outcome expectancy on effort-related cardiovascular response. Participants first performed an easy (fatigue low) or difficult (fatigue high) ver-

sion of a letter-cancellation task (see e.g., Gendolla & Krüsken, 2001b). They then were presented a set of single-digit multiplication problems with instructions that they would earn a strong (51/52—success importance high) or weak (1/52—success importance low) chance of winning a prize if they attained a moderate (50th percentile) performance standard. The central prediction was that fatigue would potentiate effort-related cardiovascular responses during the second period when the chance of winning (and, thus, importance) was high, but not when the chance of winning (and, thus, importance) was low. Potentiation was not expected under low chance (importance) conditions because available benefit under those conditions was not expected to be great enough to justify the added effort requirement associated with fatigue. SBP responses assessed during the period were supportive. Specifically, they were proportional to fatigue for high-chance participants, but low regardless of fatigue for low-chance participants. Analyses revealed the same interactional response pattern for DBP and MAP.

In summary, outcome expectancy studies have yielded effects highly compatible with the effects from the material incentive studies. In accordance with the principles of motivation intensity theory, they suggest that outcome expectancy moderates the relation between difficulty and effort when task difficulty is fixed and predicts effort directly when task difficulty is unknown.

SOCIAL EVALUATION

Some studies have tested the idea that social evaluation of one's performance augments the importance of success and thus increases the amount of justified effort (potential motivation). Wright, Tunstall, Williams, Goodwin, and Harmon-Jones (1995, Study 2) confronted participants with a recognition memory task that was either easy or had an unfixed performance standard. In the easy condition, participants tried to correctly identify in 90% of the trials if a target letter was part of a string of three letters that was presented for 5 seconds. In the unfixed difficulty condition, participants were also presented with strings of three letters but tried to attain 90% correct responses as fast as they could. Social evaluation was manipulated by telling participants explicitly that their responses could, versus could not, be monitored by the experimenter. The pattern of performance-related SBP reactivity occurred as expected: In the unfixed difficulty condition, social evaluation increased reactivity. But in the easy condition reactivity was low regardless of whether participants' responses could be monitored. A study by Wright, Killebrew, and Pimpalapure (2002) revealed corresponding results for social evaluation by high-, but not low-, status observers.

An experiment by Wright, Dill, Geen, and Anderson (1998) involved five difficulty levels, ranging from very easy to extremely difficult. Specifically, participants performed a recognition memory task and tried to correctly identify at least 90% of 40 trials in which two, four, six, eight, or ten letters were presented. Social evaluation was manipulated as in the previous experiment by Wright et al. (1995). In the social-evaluation condition, SBP reactivity increased from the two-letter condition to the six-letter condition and then sharply decreased, describing the anticipated saw-tooth shaped curve. In the no-evaluation condition, task difficulty had no significant impact on SBP reactivity, which was relatively low in all conditions. A study by Gendolla and Richter (2006a) found corresponding effects for implicit social evaluation manipulated by the mere presence of an observer.

It is of note that the preceding social evaluation studies challenge other approaches that have posited that social observation should lead to a general increase in autonomic nervous system activity (e.g., Baron, 1986; Cottrell, 1968; Zajonc, 1965) or a general increase in effort (Harkins, 2006). As outlined earlier and supporting the principles of motivational intensity theory, social evaluation resulted in relatively strong response of one specific autonomic arousal measure—cardiovascular activity—when a task was difficult and thus necessitated high resources, but not when it was easy, and required only relatively low resources.

EGO INVOLVEMENT

Ego involvement refers to an increased sense of success importance that occurs when people are in a performance setting and believe that a valuable ability is being evaluated (Klein & Schoenfeld, 1941). Studies by Gendolla and Richter tested the idea that ego involvement thus increases the level of potential motivation. In an experiment by Gendolla and Richter (2006b, Study 1), high-ego-involvement participants were told that a memory task would be diagnostic of an important ability—learning under time pressure—whereas low-ego-involvement participants were told that the task was only a filler without any diagnostic meaning. Task difficulty was low, moderate, or high. Additionally, there was a condition in which participants were instructed to "do their best" (unfixed difficulty). Figure 24.5 shows for the high-ego-involvement condition that SBP reactivity was, as expected, high in the unfixed difficulty condition where participants were instructed to correctly memorize as many items as they could. Moreover, SBP reactivity increased from the easy to the difficult condition. The unfixed and difficult conditions did not differ, suggesting that participants in these conditions mobilized effort up to the level of potential motivation, which was defined by the ego involvement manipulation. No significant differences emerged among the four difficulty cells in the low-ego—involvement condition.

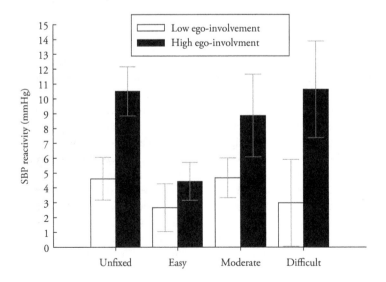

Fig. 24.5. SBP reactivity in dependence on ego involvement and task difficulty in Study 1 by Gendolla and Richter (2006b). (Reproduced with permission from Sage Publications.)

The effects for unfixed and fixed easy difficulty levels replicate the findings of a previous study using a mental concentration task that found identical effects on SBP, DBP, HR, and electrodermal reactivity (Gendolla & Richter, 2005).

A second experiment by Gendolla and Richter (2006b) involved a "do your best" condition and an excessively difficult, actually impossible, condition. Under "do your best" instructions high ego involvement led again to higher SBP reactivity than low ego involvement. More important, when task difficulty was so high that success was obviously impossible, participants disengaged even when ego involvement was high, resulting in low SBP reactivity.

The present studies on ego involvement challenge earlier views of Nicholls (1984) and Dweck (1986) who had formulated reservations against the assumption that the difficulty law of motivation applies to evaluations of important abilities. Those authors have suggested that the difficulty-effort relationship is only proportional when people *do not* try to demonstrate valuable abilities—that is, *not* under ego involvement. The findings of the Gendolla and Richter studies suggest, however, that the principle of resource conservation applies well under ego involvement and that effort intensity also follows the principles of motivation intensity theory when valuable abilities are evaluated.

SELF-EVALUATION

Self-awareness theory (Duval & Wicklund, 1972) posits that focusing individuals' attention to their self induces a state of self-evaluation: Persons compare their actual behavior with the momentarily relevant standards. In the context of achievement behavior, self-focused attention should, thus, justify relatively high resources, because self-evaluation makes success relatively important. Drawing on this logic, Gendolla, Richter, and Silvia (2008) tested the idea that self-focused attention determines the level of potential motivation. In their second study, participants performed a computer-based attention task. In a high-self-focus condition participants' face was filmed from the left-hand-side perspective during task performance. The picture was transmitted to a video monitor that was placed next to participants' computer screen, exposing them to a picture of their own face during task performance. In a contrasting low-self-focus condition, participants were not filmed because the camera was ostensibly out of order. The study involved a difficult and an extremely difficult (actually impossible) version of the attention task. It also included a condition in

which participants received "do your best" instructions. For the high-self-focus condition, where relatively much effort should have been justified, SBP reactivity was anticipated to be high in both the unfixed and the difficult conditions. By contrast, reactivity should have been low in the extremely difficult condition where participants were expected to disengage. In the low-self-focus condition, where only low effort should have been justified, reactivity was anticipated to be low in general. The results confirmed these predictions. A recent follow-up experiment by Silvia, McCord, and Gendolla (2010) conceptually replicated the joint effect of self-focus and task difficulty on effort-related cardiovascular response and clarified that self-focused attention also leads to high effort when success expectancies are low due to high task difficulty.

HEDONIC INCENTIVE: MODERATING EFFECTS OF MOOD AND DEPRESSIVE SYMPTOMS

A number of studies have also investigated the combined effects of mood, task difficulty, and the hedonic incentive of success on effort-related cardiovascular response. These studies tested the idea of the mood-behavior-model (Gendolla, 2000) that actions that are instrumental for mood regulation (maintaining a positive mood, repairing a negative mood) justify relatively high resources. One consequence of this suggestion is that positive hedonic incentive should eliminate the previously discussed effort withdrawal of people who face a difficult task in a negative mood (e.g., Brinkmann & Gendolla, 2008; Gendolla & Krüsken, 2001b). Building on initial evidence for this hypothesis (Gendolla & Krüsken, 2002c), Silvestrini and Gendolla (2009a) first induced participants into a positive or negative mood with film clips and then presented them a memory task that was either easy or difficult. Before performance, participants were informed about the hedonic consequences of success. In a positive incentive condition they were promised the presentation of a comedy video after success; in a negative incentive condition, participants expected the presentation of a distressing video after success. As depicted in Figure 24.6 SBP reactivity during task performance described the predicted pattern: When success incentive was negative, and thus did not justify high effort, SBP reactivity conformed to the crossover interaction pattern anticipated and shown for the joint effect of mood and objective task difficulty on experienced demand and corresponding effort intensity (e.g., Brinkmann & Gendolla, 2008; Gendolla & Krüsken, 2001b). However,

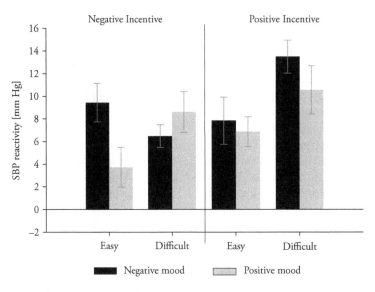

Fig. 24.6. Cell means and standard errors of systolic blood pressure reactivity during memory task performance in the experiment by Slivestrini and Gendolla (2009a). (Reproduced with permission from Elsevier.)

when success incentive was positive, SBP reactivity of participants who worked on the difficult task in a negative mood increased significantly. The anticipated pleasant consequences of success justified here the very high effort that was perceived as necessary when participants faced a difficult task in a negative mood. These results highlight the hedonic aspects of achievement motivation. Accordingly, it is not success per se that justifies the mobilization of high effort—success did not justify high resources when it led to unpleasant consequences. Rather, success has to be bound up with positive hedonic aspects to justify high effort. Another study that manipulated the hedonic aspects of task performance itself brought compatible results (Silvestrini & Gendolla, 2009b): A pleasant version of a sentence completion task justified higher effort than an unpleasant version.

Other research investigated the impact of incentive in individuals suffering from depressive symptoms. As discussed earlier, the effects of depressive symptoms on effort-related cardiovascular response resemble those of a negative mood when incentive is not manipulated (Brinkmann & Gendolla, 2007, 2008). But it is questionable whether promised performance-contingent reward has the same influences on effort mobilization in depressed/dysphoric individuals as in nondepressed/nondysphoric people. The reason is evidence that depressed individuals do not behaviorally respond to monetary reward and punishment (e.g., Henriques & Davidson, 2000). Brinkmann, Ancel Joye, Schüppach, and

Gendolla (2009, Study 2) therefore directly tested the hypothesis of a reduced reward responsiveness in dysphoric individuals in terms of effort mobilization. The studies used a task with unclear difficulty, because this type of task permits a direct test of reward effects on effort mobilization, as discussed earlier. In the reward condition participants learned that they could win money (10 Swiss Francs) for correctly solving an arithmetic problem. Participants received instructions to perform arithmetic operations over a 5-minute period, leading to a final correct or incorrect result in the end. No incentive was mentioned in the no-reward condition. Results showed strong increases in SBP, DBP, HR, and PEP for nondysphoric participants in the reward condition, reflecting the typical incentive effect in tasks with unclear difficulty (Richter & Gendolla, 2006, 2009a). In contrast, dysphorics' reactivity was significantly lower and did not differ from the no-reward condition. Taken together, these studies show that depressives' reduced responsiveness to reward is also evident in effort mobilization.

Conclusions

The present analysis has highlighted the question of what determines effort intensity in instrumental behavior. We have discussed empirical evidence from studies that have operationalized effort intensity as cardiovascular response in the context of task performance. The analysis was guided by the predictions of motivation intensity theory (Brehm et al., 1983; Brehm & Self, 1989), which state in brief that effort intensity corresponds to subjective difficulty as long as success is seen as possible and justified and that success importance (i.e., potential motivation) only influences effort directly when task difficulty is unspecified. As outlined in this chapter, many studies have investigated several psychological variables that have a systematic impact on subjective difficulty and potential motivation. Those studies have brought highly concordant evidence for the predictions. Additionally to supporting the principles of motivation intensity theory, this evidence challenges a number of other ideas about the determination of effort intensity.

Some of these challenges were already mentioned earlier in the context of the presentation of our empirical work. In addition to that, our findings also limit approaches suggesting that reward directly determines effort mobilization (e.g., Eisenberger, 1992; Fowles, 1983). The studies discussed here have revealed that a direct effect of incentive on the intensity of motivation only occurs when difficulty is unspecified or unknown rather than in general. Our findings are also not compatible with the idea that motivation is less intense if people perform tasks without a clear performance standard ("do your best") than if they perform tasks with fixed high standards (Locke & Latham, 1990). According to the findings presented here, these conditions produce the same effects on effort-related cardiovascular response. Moreover, our findings contradict the (historically popular) idea that the intensity of motivation is maximal on intermediate task difficulty levels, as, for example, expressed in Atkinson's (1957) influential risk taking model. The studies presented here have found that effort intensity is maximal on the highest possible and justified rather than an intermediate difficulty level. Compatible with this, and further challenging the risk taking model, recent experiments by Capa, Audiffen, and Ragot (2008a, 2008b) have found that a strong achievement orientation justifies high effort, resulting in stronger cardiovascular reactivity when task difficulty is high.

Future Directions

One interesting issue for future research might be the question of whether people are (always) cognizant of the effort they expend and if the factors influencing effort have their impact because they are deliberatively taken into account. Related to this issue is a point of critique that was occasionally raised in the earlier phases of the research presented here. The critique was that the principles of motivation

intensity theory may draw a picture of effort mobilization that is "too rational." The point was that the theory would not really capture the dynamics of human action, because it implies that people always consciously calculate how much effort they want and need to mobilize and decide to do so or to disengage—for example, in a deliberate process like this: "I'm highly able, thus this task must be easy for me, so I'll only invest little effort." This interpretation may have been caused in part by the fact that the function of effort has been regarded for long as allowing coping with obstacles and temptations during volitional goal pursuit. Some authors have thus seen effort as a proxy of *willpower* (e.g., Ach, 1910; Dewey, 1897) and the typical characteristic of an *action phase* in models of volition and action control (Heckhausen & Gollwitzer, 1987; Kuhl, 1983).

We agree that motivation intensity theory is well applicable to deliberate effort investment. However, according to our understanding the theory has not been conceptualized as being limited to this—although effort is surely necessary for self-control, because resisting temptations, changing habits, and coping with obstacles are difficult endeavors. However, according to our view, the principles of effort mobilization can be so well learned, or even internalized, that they also work implicitly. Some empirical support for this idea comes from recent studies that manipulated effort intensity with implicitly processed stimuli.

Implicit Determination of Effort

Participants in recent experiments by Gendolla and Silvestrini (2011) performed an attention or recognition memory task under "do your best" instructions. During the task, participants were exposed to briefly flashed and backward-masked happy, sad, or angry low-resolution pictures of facial expressions. The results revealed stronger reactivity of cardiac PEP and SBP in the masked sadness condition than in both the masked happiness and masked anger cells. Moreover, self-report measures found that, corresponding to this, task difficulty was experienced as higher in the masked sadness condition than in both the masked happiness and anger cells. The effects of masked sadness and happiness expressions resemble those of conscious moods discussed earlier—sadness was associated with difficulty and happiness was associated with ease (see Gendolla & Brinkmann, 2005)—although the masked emotional expressions did not have any effects on conscious feelings here. The effect of masked anger stimuli is explicable by the accumulating evidence that anger is associated with behavioral facilitation and experiences of control (Carver & Harmon-Jones, 2009), making a task subjectively easier. However, the important point is that effort intensity can be systematically manipulated with masked affective cues that are processed "on line"—that is, during performance—and have an effect on experienced task difficult.

Beside the effects of implicit affective stimuli on effort-related cardiovascular response, there is also evidence for the impact of masked incentive cues on performance-related sympathetic arousal. Stimulated by a study by Pessiglione et al. (2007) on implicit monetary incentive cues on the exertion of physical force, Bijleveld, Custers, and Aarts (2009) briefly flashed backward-masked pictures of low (1 cent coin) or high (50 cent coin) monetary incentive during a digit-retention task that was either easy or difficult. Measures of pupil dilation during task performance (which is related to sympathetic arousal and has been suggested to mirror mental effort; Kahneman, 1973) found higher arousal when the task was difficult and participants were flashed with pictures of valuable coins. This suggests that implicitly processed information about monetary incentive can augment potential motivation and justify the necessary effort for a difficult task—a finding that fully fits the principles of motivation intensity theory. Moreover, a recent study by Capa, Cleeremans, Bustin, Bouquet, and Hansenne (2011) primed university students with the goal of studying and combined the goal primes either with positive (i.e., rewarding) words or not. During the subsequent performance of a learning task of unspecified difficulty, participants in the goal priming-positive group showed larger decreases of mid-frequency band heart rate variability and pulse transit time, reflecting higher effort, according to the authors.

Another recent experiment by Gendolla and Silvestrini (2010) even went further and tested the possibility to manipulate effort intensity directly with masked stimuli that were processed "online" during task performance. Inspired by studies by Abarracín, et al. (2008) on the priming of general behavioral activation, participants were exposed to masked action versus inaction words during the trials of a recognition memory task. Additionally, there was a control condition in which participants were exposed to nonwords. Compared with the control group, the results showed stronger changes in cardiac contractility (PEP) in the action prime condition and weaker reactivity in the inaction prime condition. These results suggest that it is possible to influence effort intensity directly—that is, without taking effect on difficulty or potential motivation—with implicit cues that are processed online during task performance. This effect merits further attention because it suggests that effort intensity may not only be determined by experienced difficulty and potential motivation.

Personality and Individual Differences

Another issue that merits more attention in future research is the role of personality and individual differences in effort mobilization. Some data are already available and show that personality variables can moderate the effects of task difficulty and incentive on effort intensity. The studies on dysphoria/depression by Brinkmann and colleagues, discussed earlier, provide an example, the studies by Wright and colleagues on ability differences and fatigue provide another (see also Schmidt, Richter, Gendolla, & van der Linden, 2010). Other studies have investigated the moderating effects of individual differences in achievement motivation (Capa, 2011), agentic extraversion (Kemper, Leue, Chavanon, Henninghausen, & Stemmler, 2008), or self-focused attention (Silvia, Jones, Kelly, & Zibaie, 2011) on effort-related cardiovascular response. However, personality factors in effort mobilization are still far from being fully understood.

Task Context

Finally, another important issue that merits more attention in future research is the role of task context or task framing. Recent work by Richter (2010) shows that relationships among task difficulty, potential motivation, and cardiovascular reactivity are very flexible. Richter could show that the variables that take effect on effort-related cardiovascular reactivity largely depend on the task context. If participants had rated some "manipulation check" referring to task difficulty before performing a task, cardiovascular reactivity was a function of task difficulty. However, if participants had rated questions related to the reward that they could earn, cardiovascular reactivity was determined by reward value. This indicates that more variables than those referring to task difficulty and potential motivation have to be considered to fully understand the determination of effort intensity. Apparently, task context can determine which information individuals use for effort mobilization.

Link to Other Physiological Correlates of Effort Intensity

Taken together, there is solid evidence for the idea that effort-related cardiovascular response is systematically influenced by experienced task difficulty and potential motivation (the level of maximally justified effort), supporting the principles of motivation intensity theory. Moreover, there are new lines for future research addressing issues like the moderating role of individual differences, the impact of implicit cues on effort intensity, and the important role of context variables influencing effort mobilization.

Still another research field is the link between other physiological correlates and indicators of effort intensity. Earlier we have already mentioned pupil dilatation as another measure of sympathetic nervous system activity that has been related to effort (see also Granholm, Verney, Perivoliotis, & Miura, 2007). Other researchers have linked the investment of mental effort to glucose consumption (e.g., Fairclough & Houston, 2004) and have provided evidence that glucose administration can restore or even foster effortful cognitive performance (Kennedy & Scholey, 2000; see also Gailliot & Baumeister, 2007). Referring to the interplay between difficulty and reward on motivational central nervous system responses, Harmon-Jones et al. (2007) found greater left frontal cortical activation in manic individuals who were expecting to start working on a difficult anagram task where they could win money for correct answers. Moreover, research on brain activity and cardiovascular arousal during effortful cognitive processing has demonstrated that activity of the anterior cingulate cortex—which responds to the difficulty of mental challenges (Paus, Koski, Zografos, Caramanos, & Westbury, 1998)—is related to cardiovascular reactivity (Critchley, Corfield, Chandler, Mathias, & Dolan, 2000; Gianaros et al., 2005; Gray & Critchley, 2011). Further investigations in the interplay between central and autonomic nervous system responses during the performance of cognitive tasks could still enlarge the knowledge about physiological correlates and objective measures of the long disregarded but important intensity aspect of motivation. Although past research has revealed solid evidence for factors that systematically influence the mobilization of resources for instrumental behavior, the process of effort mobilization is certainly not yet fully understood.

Acknowledgments

The research reported in this chapter was facilitated by research grants from the Deutsche Forschungsgemeinschaft (Ge 987/1-1, Ge 987/3–1, Ge 987/7–1) and the Fonds National Suisse (100011–108144, 100014–122604) awarded to Guido Gendolla, from the National Science Foundation (BCS-0450941) awarded to Rex Wright, and from the Fonds National Suisse (100014–118220) awarded to Michael Richter.

References

Aarts, H., Custers, R., & Marien, H. (2008). Preparing and motivating behavior outside awareness. *Science, 319,* 1639.

Ach, N. (1910). *Über den Willensakt und das Temperament* [On the will and temperament]. Leipzig, Germany: Quelle und Meyer.

Ach, N. (1935). *Analyse des Willens* [Analysis of the will]. Berlin, Germany: Urban Schwarzenberg.

Abarracín, D., Handley, I. M., Noguchi, K., McCulloch, K. C., Li, H., Leeper, J.,…Hart, W. P. (2008). Increasing and decreasing motor and cognitive output: A model of general action and inaction goals. *Journal of Personality and Social Psychology, 95,* 510–523.

Atkinson, J. W. (1957). Motivational determinants of risk-taking behavior. *Psychological Review, 64,* 359–372.

Atkinson, J. W., & Raynor, J. O. (1974). *Motivation and achievement.* Washington, DC: Winston & Sons.

Bandura, A. (1982). Self-efficacy mechanism in human agency. *American Psychologist, 37,* 122–147.

Bandura, A. (1986). *Social foundations of thought and action.* Englewood Cliffs, NJ: Prentice Hall.

Bandura, A., & Cervone, D. (1983). Self-reactive mechanisms in goal motivators. *Journal of Personality and Social Psychology, 45,* 1017–1028.

Bijleveld, E., Custers, R., & Aarts, H. (2009). The unconscious eye opener: Pupil dilation reveals strategic recruitment of resources upon presentation of subliminal reward cues. *Psychological Science, 20,* 1313–1315.

Baron, R. S. (1986). Distraction-conflict theory: Progress and problems. *Advances in Experimental Social Psychology, 19,* 1–40.

Berntson, G. G., Cacioppo, J. T., & Quigley, K. S. (1993). Cardiac psychophysiology and autonomic space in humans: Empirical perspectives and conceptual implications. *Psychological Bulletin, 114,* 296–322.

Brehm, J. W., & Self, E. A. (1989). The intensity of motivation. *Annual Review of Psychology, 40,* 109–131.

Brehm, J. W., Wright, R. A., Solomon, S., Silka, L., & Greenberg, J. (1983). Perceived difficulty, energization, and the magnitude of goal valence. *Journal of Experimental Social Psychology, 19,* 21–48.

Brinkmann, K., & Gendolla, G. H. E. (2007). Dysphoria and mobilization of mental effort: Effects on cardiovascular reactivity. *Motivation and Emotion, 31,* 71–82.

Brinkmann, K., & Gendolla, G. H. E. (2008). Does depression interfere with effort mobilization? Effects of dysphoria and task difficulty on cardiovascular response. *Journal of Personality and Social Psychology, 94,* 146–157.

Brinkmann, K., Ancel Joye, I., Schüppach, L., & Gendolla, G. H. E. (2009). Anhedonia and effort mobilization in dysphoria: Reduced cardiovascular response to reward and punishment. *International Journal of Psychophysiology, 74,* 250–258.

Brownley, K. A., Hurwitz, B. E., & Schneiderman, N. (2000). Cardiovascular sychophysiology. In J. T. Cacioppo, L. G. Tassinary, & G. G. Berntson (Eds.), *Handbook of psychophysiology* (pp. 224–264). New York: Cambridge University Press.

Capa, R. L. (2011). Clarifying achievement motives and effort: Studies of cardiovascular response. In R. A. Wright & G. H. E. Gendolla (Eds.), *How motivation affects cardiovascular response: Mechanisms and applications* (pp. 383–398). Washington, DC: APA.

Capa, R. L., Audiffen, M., & Ragot, S. (2008a). The interactive effect of achievement motivation and task difficulty on mental effort. *International Journal of Psychophysiology, 70*, 144–150.

Capa, R. L., Audiffen, M., & Ragot, S. (2008b). The effects of achievement motivation, task difficulty, and goal difficulty on physiological, behavioral, and subjective effort. *Psychophysiology, 45*, 859–868.

Capa, R. L., Cleeremans, A., Bustin, G. M., Bouquet, C. A., & Hansenne, M. (2011). Effects of subliminal priming on nonconscious goal pursuit and effort-related cardiovascular response. *Social Cognition, 29*, 430–444.

Carver, C. S., & Harmon-Jones, E. (2009). Anger is approach-related affect: Evidence and implications. *Psychological Bulletin, 135*, 183–204.

Cottrell, N. B. (1968). Performance in the presence of other human beings: Mere presence, audience, and affiliation effects. In E. C. Simmel, R. A. Hoppe, & G. A. Milton (Eds), *Social facilitation and imitative behavior* (pp. 91–110). Boston, MA: Allyn & Bacon.

Critchley, H. D., Corfield, D. R., Chandler, M. P., Mathias, C. J., & Dolan, R. J. (2000). Cerebral correlates of autonomic cardiovascular arousal: a functional neuroimaging investigation in humans. *Journal of Physiology, 523*, 259–270.

De Burgo, J., & Gendolla, G. H. E. (2009). Are moods motivational states? A study on effort-related cardiovascular response. *Emotion, 9*, 892–697.

Dewey, J. (1897). The psychology of effort. *Psychological Review, 6*, 43–56.

Duval, S., & Wicklund, R. A. (1972). *A theory of objective self-awareness.* New York: Academic Press.

Dweck, C. S. (1986). Motivational processes affecting learning. *American Psychologist, 41*, 1040–1048.

Efklides, A., Kourkoulou, A., Mitsiou, F., & Ziliaskopoulou, D. (2006). Metacognitive knowledge of effort, personality factors, and mood state: Their relationships with effort-related metacognitive experiences. *Metacognition and Learning, 1*, 33–49.

Eisenberger, R. (1992). Learned industriousness. *Psychological Review, 99*, 248–267.

Elliot, A. J. (2006). The hierarchical model of approach-avoidance motivation. *Motivation and Emotion, 30*, 111–116.

Elliott, R. (1969). Tonic heart rate: Experiments on the effects of collative variables lead to a hypothesis about its motivational significance. *Journal of Personality and Social Psychology, 12*, 211–228.

Eubanks, L., Wright, R. A., & Williams, B. J. (2002). Reward influence on the heart: Cardiovascular response as a function of incentive value at five levels of task demand. *Motivation and Emotion, 26*, 139–152.

Fairclough, S. H., & Houston, K. (2004). A metabolic measure of mental effort. *Biological Psychology, 66*, 177–190.

Fowles, D. C. (1983). Motivational effects on heart rate and electrodermal activity: Implications for research on personality and psychopathology. *Journal of Research in Personality, 17*, 48–71.

Frijda, N. H. (1993). Moods, emotion episodes, and emotions. In M. Lewis & J. M. Haviland (Eds.), *Handbook of emotions* (pp. 381–404). New York: Guilford.

Gailliot, M. T., & Baumeister, R. F. (2007). The physiology of willpower: Linking blood glucose to self-control. *Personality and Social Psychology Review, 11*, 303–327.

Gendolla, G. H. E. (2000). On the impact of mood on behavior: An integrative theory and a review. *Review of General Psychology, 4*, 378–408.

Gendolla, G. H. E., Abele, A. E., & Krüsken, J. (2001). The informational impact of mood on effort mobilization: A study of cardiovascular and electrodermal responses. *Emotion, 1*, 12–24.

Gendolla, G. H. E., & Brinkmann, K. (2005). The role of mood states in self-regulation: Effects on action preferences and resource mobilization. *European Psychologist, 10*, 187–198.

Gendolla, G. H. E., Brinkmann, K., & Silvestrini, N. (2011). Gloomy and lazy? On the impact of mood and depressive symptoms on effort-related cardiovascular response. In R. A. Wright & G. H. E. Gendolla (Eds.), *How motivation affects cardiovascular response: Mechanisms and applications* (pp. 139–155). Washington, DC: APA.

Gendolla, G. H. E., & Krüsken, J. (2001a). Mood state and cardiovascular response in active coping with an affect-regulative challenge. *International Journal of Psychophysiology, 41*, 169–180.

Gendolla, G. H. E., & Krüsken, J. (2001b). The joint impact of mood state and task difficulty on cardiovascular and electrodermal reactivity in active coping. *Psychophysiology, 38*, 539–548.

Gendolla, G. H. E., & Krüsken, J. (2002a). Informational mood impact on effort-related ardiovascular response: The diagnostic value of moods counts. *Emotion, 2*, 251–262.

Gendolla, G. H. E, & Krüsken, J. (2002b). Mood, task demand, and effort-related cardiovascular response. *Cognition and Emotion, 16*, 577–603.

Gendolla, G. H. E, & Krüsken, J. (2002c). The joint effect of informational mood impact and performance-contingent incentive on effort-related cardiovascular response. *Journal of Personality and Social Psychology, 83*, 271–285.

Gendolla, G. H. E., & Richter, M. (2005). Ego involvement and effort: Cardiovascular, electrodermal, and performance effects. *Psychophysiology, 42*, 595–603.

Gendolla, G. H. E., & Richter, M. (2006a). Cardiovascular reactivity during performance under social observation: The moderating role of task difficulty. *International Journal of Psychophysiology, 62*, 185–192.

Gendolla, G. H. E., & Richter, M. (2006b). Ego involvement and the difficulty law of motivation: Effects on performance-related cardiovascular response. *Personality and Social Psychology Bulletin, 32*, 1188–1203.

Gendolla, G. H. E., Richter, M., & Silvia, P. (2008). Self-focus and task difficulty effects on effort-related cardiovascular reactivity. *Psychophysiology, 45*, 653–662.

Gendolla, G. H. E., & Silvestrini, N. (2010). The implicit "go": Masked action cues directly mobilize mental effort. *Psychological Science, 21*, 1389–1393.

Gendolla, G. H. E., & Silvestrini, N. (2011). Smiles make it easier and so do frowns: Masked affective stimuli influence mental effort. *Emotion, 11*, 320–328.

Gendolla, G. H. E., & Wright, R. A. (2009). Effort. In D. Sander & K. R. Scherer (Eds.), *Oxford companion to the affective sciences* (pp. 134–135). New York: Oxford University Press.

Gianaros, P. J., Derbyshire, S. W. G., May, C., Siegle, G., Gamalo, M. A., & Jennings, R. (2005). Anterior cingulate activity correlates with blood pressure during stress. *Psychophysiology, 42*, 627–635.

Gray, M. A., & Critchley, H. D. (2011). Integration of cardiac function with cognitive, motivational, and emotional processing: Evidence from neuroimaging. In R. A. Wright & G. H. E. Gendolla (Eds.), *How motivation affects cardiovascular response: Mechanisms and applications* (pp. 21–42). Washington, DC: APA Press.

Granholm, E., Verney, S. P., Perivoliotis, D., & Miura, T. (2007). Effortful cognitive resource allocation and negative symptom severity in chronic schizophrenia. *Schizophrenia Bulletin, 33*, 831–842.

Harkins, S. G. (2006). Mere effort as the mediator of the evaluation-performance relationship. *Journal of Personality and Social Psychology, 91*, 436–455.

Harmon-Jones, E., Abramson, L. Y., Nusslock, R., Sigelman, J. D., Urosevic, S., Turonie, L. D., … Fearn, M. (2007). Effect of bipolar disorder on left frontal cortical responses to goals differing in valence and task difficulty. *Biological Psychiatry, 63*, 693–698.

Heckhausen, H. & Gollwitzer, P. M. (1987). Thought contents and cognitive functioning in motivational versus volitional states. *Motivation and Emotion, 11*, 101–120.

Heider, F. (1958). *The psychology of interpersonal relations.* New York: Wiley.

Henriques, J. B., & Davidson, R. J. (2000). Decreased rsponsiveness to reward in depression. *Cognition and Emotion, 14*, 711–724.

Hillgruber, A. (1912). *Fortlaufende Arbeit und Willensbetätigung.* [Continuous work and the will]. Leipzig, Germany: Quelle und Meyer.

Hockey, G. R. (1997). Compensatory control in the regulation of human performance under stress and high workload: A cognitive-energetical framework. *Biological Psychology, 45*, 73–93.

Kahneman, D. (1973). *Attention and effort.* Englewood Cliffs, NJ: Prentice-Hall.

Kelsey, R. M. (2011). Beta-adrenergic cardiovascular reactivity and adaptation to stress: The cardiac pre-ejection period as an index of effort. In R. A. Wright, & G. H. E. Gendolla (Eds.), *How motivation affects cardiovascular response: Mechanisms and applications* (pp. 43–60). Washington, DC: APA Press.

Kemper, C. J., Leue, A., Wacker, J., Chavanon, M-L., Henninghausen, E., & Stemmler, G. (2008). Agentic extraversion as a predictor of effort-related cardiovascular response. *Biological Psychology, 76*, 191–199.

Kennedy, D. O., & Scholey, A. B. (2000). Glucose administration, heart rate and cognitve performance: Effects of increasing mental effort. *Psychopharmacology, 149*, 63–71.

Klein, G. S., & Schoenfeld, N. (1941). The influence of ego involvement on confidence. *Journal of Abnormal and Social Psychology, 36*, 249–258.

Kreibig, S. D. (2010). Autonomic nervous system activity in emotion: A review. *Biological Psychology, 84*, 394–421.

Kuhl, J. (1983). *Motivation, Konflikt und Handlungskontrolle* [Motivation, conflict, and action control]. Berlin, Germany: Springer.

Kukla, A. (1972). Foundations of an attributional theory of performance. *Psychological Review, 79*, 454–470.

Locke, E. A., & Latham, G. P. (1990). *A theory of goal setting task performance.* Upper Saddle River, NJ: Prentice Hall, Inc.

Maddux, J. E. (1995). Self-efficacy theory: An introduction. In J. E. Maddux (Ed.), *Self-efficacy, adaptation, and adjustment: Theory, research, and application* (pp. 3–27). New York: Plenum.

Manuck, S. B., Harvey, S. H., Lechleiter, S. L., & Neal, K. S. (1978). Effects of coping on blood pressure responses to threat and avoidance stimulation. *Psychophysiology, 15*, 544–549.

Meyer, W. U., & Hallermann, B. (1977). Intended effort and informational value of task outcome. *Archiv für Psychologie, 129*, 131–140.

Nicholls, J. G. (1984). Achievement motivation: Conceptions of ability, subjective experience, task choice, and performance. *Psychological Review, 91*, 328–346.

Obrist, P. A. (1976). The cardiovascular-behavioral interaction as it appears today. *Psychophysiology, 13*, 95–107.

Obrist, P. A. (1981). *Cardiovascular psychophysiology: A perspective.* New York: Plenum Press.

Papillo, J. F., & Shapiro, D. (1990). The cardiovascular system. In J. T. Cacioppo, & L. G. Tassinary (Eds), *Principles of psychophysiology* (pp. 465–512). New York: Cambridge University Press.

Paus, T., Koski, L., Caramanos, Z., & Westbury, C. (1998). Regional differences in the effect of task difficulty and motor output on blood flow response in the human cingulated cortex: A review of 107 PET activation studies. *NeuroReport, 9*, R37-R47.

Pessiglione, M., Schmidt, L., Draganski, B., Kalisch, R., Lau, H., Dolan, R. J., & Frith, C. D. (2007). How the brain translates money into force: A neuroimaging study of subliminal motivation. *Science, 316*, 904–906.

Pyszczynski, T., & Greenberg, T. (1983). Determinants of reduction in intended effort as a strategy for coping with anticipated failure. *Journal of Research in Personality, 17*, 412–422.

Rhodewalt, F., & Fairfield, M. (1991). Claimed self-handicaps and the self-handicapper: The relation of reduction in intended effort to performance. *Journal of Research in Personality, 25*, 402–417.

Richter, M. (2010). Pay attention to your manipulation checks! Reward impact on cardiac reactivity is moderated by task context. *Biological Psychology, 84*, 279–289.

Richter, M., Friedrich, A., & Gendolla, G. H. E. (2008). Task difficulty effects on cardiac activity. *Psychophysiology, 45*, 869–875.

Richter, M., & Gendolla, G. H. E. (2006). Incentive effects on cardiovascular reactivity in active coping with unclear task difficulty. *International Journal of Psychophysiology, 61*, 216–225.

Richter, M., & Gendolla, G. H. E. (2007). Incentive value, unclear task difficulty, and cardiovascular reactivity in active coping. *International Journal of Psychophysiology, 63*, 294–301.

Richter, M., & Gendolla, G. H. E. (2009a). The heart contracts to reward: Monetary incentives and preejection period. *Psychophysiology, 46*, 451–457.

Richter, M., & Gendolla, G. H. E. (2009b). Mood impact on cardiovascular reactivity when task difficulty is unclear. *Motivation and Emotion, 33*, 239–248.

Roets, A., Van Hiel, A., Cornelis, I., & Soetens, B. (2008). Determinants of task performance and invested effort: A need for closure by relative cognitive capacity interaction analysis. *Personality and Social Psychology Bulletin, 34*, 779–795.

Schmidt, R. E., Richter, M., Gendolla, G. H. E., & van der Linden, M. (2010). Young poor sleepers mobilize extra effort in an easy memory task: Evidence from cardiovascular measures. *Journal of Sleep Research, 19*, 487–495.

Silvestrini, N., & Gendolla, G. H. E. (2009a). Mood-regulative hedonic incentive interacts with mood and task difficulty to determine effort-related cardiovascular response and facial EMG. *Biological Psychology, 82*, 54–63.

Silvestrini, N., & Gendolla, G. H. E. (2009b). The joint effect of mood, task valence, and task difficulty on effort-related cardiovascular response and facial EMG. *International Journal of Psychophysiology, 73*, 226–234.

Silvia, P. J., Jones, H. C., Kelly, C. S., & Zibaie, A. (2011). Trait self-focused attention, task difficulty, and effort-related cardiovascular reactivitgy. *International Journal of Psychophysiology, 79*, 335–340.

Silvia, P. J., McCord, D. M., & Gendolla, G. H. E. (2010). Self-focused attention, performance expectancies, and the intensity of effort: Do people try harder for harder goals? *Motivation and Emotion, 34*, 363–370.

Smith, T. W., Baldwin, M., & Christensen, A. J. (1990). Interpersonal influence as active coping: Effects of task difficulty on cardiovascular reactivity. *Psychophysiology, 27*, 429–437.

Sternberg, S. (1966). High-speed scanning in human memory. *Science, 153*, 652–654.

Stewart, C. C., Wright, R. A., Hui, S. A., & Simmons, A. (2009). Outcome expectancy as a moderator of mental fatigue influence on cardiovascular response. *Psychophysiology, 46*, 1141–1149

Wilson, T. D. (2002). *Strangers to ourselves: Discovering the adaptive unconscious.* Cambridge, MA: Harvard University Press.

Wright, R. A. (1984). Motivation, anxiety, and the difficulty of control. *Journal of Personality and Social Psychology, 46*, 1376–1388.

Wright, R. A. (1996). Brehm's theory of motivation as a model of effort and cardiovascular response. In P. M. Gollwitzer & J. A. Bargh (Eds.), *The psychology of action: Linking cognition and motivation to behavior* (pp. 424–453). New York: Guilford.

Wright, R. A. (1998). Ability perception and cardiovascular response to behavioral challenge. In M. Kofta, G. Weary, & G. Sedek (Eds.), *Personal control in action: Cognitive and motivational mechanisms* (pp. 197–232). New York: Plenum.

Wright, R. A., & Dill, J. C. (1993). Blood pressure responses and incentive appraisals as a function of perceived ability and objective task demand. *Psychophysiology, 30*, 152–160.

Wright, R. A., Dill, J. C., Geen, R. G., & Anderson, C. A. (1998). Social evaluation influence on cardiovascular response to a fixed behavioral challenge: Effects across a range of difficulty levels. *Annals of Behavioral Medicine, 20*, 277–285.

Wright, R. A., & Dismukes, A. (1995). Cardiovascular effects of experimentally induced efficacy (ability) appraisals at low and high levels of avoidant task demand. *Psychophysiology, 32*, 172–176.

Wright, R. A., & Franklin, J. (2004). Ability perception determinants of effort-related cardiovascular response: Mood, optimism, and performance resources. In R. A. Wright, J. Greenberg, & S. S. Brehm (Eds), *Motivational analyses of social behavior: Building on Jack Brehm's contributions to psychology* (pp. 187–204). Hillsdale, NJ: Erlbaum.

Wright, R. A., & Gregorich, S. (1989). Difficulty and instrumentality of imminent behavior as determinants of cardiovascular response and self-reported energy. *Psychophysiology, 26*, 586–592.

Wright, R. A., Junious, T. R., Neal, C., Avello, A., Graham, C., Herrmann, L., Junious, S., & Walton, N. (2007). Mental fatigue influence on effort-related cardiovascular response: Difficulty effects and extension across cognitive performance domains. *Motivation and Emotion, 31*, 219–231.

Wright, R. A., Killebrew, K., & Pimpalapure, D. (2002). Cardiovascular incentive effects where a challenge is unfixed: Demonstrations involving social evaluation, evaluator status, and monetary reward. *Psychophysiology, 39*, 188–197.

Wright, R. A., & Kirby, L. D. (2001). Effort determination of cardiovascular response: An integrative analysis with applications in social psychology. *Advances in Experimental Social Psychology, 33*, 255–307.

Wright, R. A., Martin, R. E., & Bland, J. L. (2003). Energy resource depletion, task difficulty, and cardiovascular response to a mental arithmetic challenge. *Psychophysiology, 40*, 98–105.

Wright, R. A., & Penacerrada, D. (2002). Energy resource depletion, ability perception, and cardiovascular response to behavioral challenge. *Psychophysiology, 39*, 182–187.

Wright, R. A., & Stewart, C. C. (2011). Multifaceted effects of fatigue on effort and associated cardiovascular responses. In R. A. Wright & G. H. E. Gendolla (Eds.) *How motivation affects cardiovascular response: Mechanisms and applications* (pp. 199–218). Washington, DC: APA Press.

Wright, R. A., Tunstall, A. M., Williams, B. J., Goodwin, J. S., & Harmon-Jones, E. (1995). Social evaluation and cardiovascular response: An active coping approach. *Journal of Personality and Social Psychology, 69*, 530–543.

Wright, R. A., Wadley, V. G., Pharr, R. P., & Butler, M. (1994). Interactive influence of self-reported ability and avoidant task demand on anticipatory cardiovascular responsivity. *Journal of Research in Personality, 28*, 68–86.

Wright, R. A., Williams, B. J., & Dill, J. C. (1992). Interactive effects of difficulty and instrumentality of avoidant behavior on cardiovascular reactivity. *Psychophysiology, 29*, 677–686.

Zajonc, R. B. (1965). Social facilitation. *Science, 149*, 269–274.

PART 7

Motivation in Application

Motivation in Psychotherapy

Martin Grosse Holtforth *and* Johannes Michalak

Abstract

Motivational issues are central to human life. Correspondingly, they are also central to the challenging endeavor of psychotherapy. Assisting patients to change involves motivational issues at various levels and at various stages of therapy. Patients might be more or less motivated to begin and to participate in the different stages of psychotherapy (therapy motivation). Besides these differences in therapy motivation, an understanding of the broader concepts of motivation in psychotherapy should mandate that motivational issues be considered in the treatment of *all patients* and not only in those with obvious deficits in therapy motivation: Motivational issues influence the therapeutic relationship, they should be considered in tailoring specific interventions, and they might be important factors for the onset and maintenance of psychological disorders. This chapter presents theoretical and empirical background information and illustrates therapeutic approaches for dealing with patients' motivation. Moreover, it summarizes the implications of basic and clinical research for a motivationally informed psychotherapy.

Key Words: motivation, goals, psychotherapy, treatment, psychopathology

Motivation in Psychotherapy

Motivation is central in life and governs most psychological processes. According to Heckhausen and Heckhausen (2008):

> the psychology of motivation is specifically concerned with activities that reflect the pursuit of a particular goal and, in this function, form a meaningful unit of behavior. Motivational research seeks to explain these units of behavior in terms of their whys and hows.
> (p. 1)

Consequently, motivational processes also have a central importance for the change of experience and behavior, which is the main purpose of psychotherapy. Psychotherapy patients seek help for the parts of their lives that they failed to cope with themselves. Therapists strive to optimally assist their patients to

change behavior and experiences in order to enable them to live independently after therapy.

Because motivational issues are central to human life, they are also central to the challenging endeavor of psychotherapy. Assisting patients to change involves motivational issues at various levels and at various stages of therapy. First of all, patients might be more or less motivated to begin psychotherapy and to participate in the different stages of the psychotherapy process. Often, patients are willing to work very hard during the therapeutic process and to invest a lot to change their lives and their way of behavior. However, there are also patients who are ambivalent during different stages of the therapeutic process. They may be ambivalent about whether they should start therapy, whether they should frame a certain kind of behavior as a problematic behavior, or whether they should take steps to change a problematic behavior. All psychotherapists are confronted with these variations of *therapy motivation* in their patients, and they know that it is useful to skillfully deal with the patients who show reduced therapy motivation.

However, a broader perspective on motivation in psychotherapy would indicate that it might be useful to consider motivational issues in the treatment of *all patients* and not only in those with obvious deficits in therapy motivation: Motivational forces influence the therapeutic relationship, and it may be wise to consider them when trying to build a helpful therapeutic alliance. Moreover, specific interventions might be tailored to the motivational background of the patients. For example, the specific situation patients are confronted with in exposure therapy might not only be chosen because of the nature of their avoidance behavior but also because of the important personal goals the patient strives for. On the most fundamental level, some authors have identified insufficient satisfaction of basic psychological needs as an important factor in the etiology of various psychological problems and psychological disorders (Grawe, 2004; Ryan, 2005; Ryan, Deci, Grolnick, & La Guardia, 2006). Accordingly, from this perspective, the overall goal of psychotherapy should be to increase the degree of satisfaction of motivational needs in order to reduce psychopathological conditions.

Therapists dealing with motivational issues in psychotherapy could profit from a deeper understanding of basic motivational principles in human life. Therefore, the first part of our chapter presents theoretical and empirical background information as well as selected methods of assessing motivational constructs that might be relevant for psychotherapy research and practice. The second part of the chapter reviews important theoretical and empirical literature from *clinical research* pointing to the relevance of motivational variables in psychotherapy and illustrating therapeutic approaches for dealing with patients' motivation. In the final part of this chapter, we will summarize the implications of basic and clinical research for a motivationally informed psychotherapy.

Clinically Relevant Motivational Constructs

We will briefly introduce the following motivational constructs: psychological needs, motives, personal goals, values, therapy motivation, and treatment goals. The concept of psychological *needs* implies that everybody has the same needs, everybody must satisfy them, and, if the individual fails to satisfy these needs,

aversive outcomes such as diminished well-being or psychopathology might be consequences (Flanagan, 2010). Various lists of needs have been proposed, for example, self-enhancement, attachment, pleasure, and orientation/control by Epstein (1990), or relatedness, competence, and autonomy by Deci and Ryan (1985, 1995). Overarching metaneeds have also been suggested, such as a need for meaning (Heine, Proulx, & Vohs, 2006) or consistency as the most basic component of psychological functioning (Grawe, 2004).

Within the concept of *motives*, a general distinction can be made between *implicit* and *explicit* motives. Implicit motives are seen as enduring individual motive dispositions, whereas explicit motives refer to goals that are conscious or consciously accessible (Heckhausen & Heckhausen, 2008). The implicit motivational system consists of a relatively small number of motives (i.e., achievement, power, and affiliation motives) that are unconscious, holistically represented, and are more directly linked to emotional processes. It becomes apparent that the concept of implicit motives as used by Heckhausen and Heckhausen (2008) is very similar to the concept of needs described earlier, and the concept of explicit motives is very similar to the concept of high-level goals. Another general motivational construct is the construct of *values*. According to Rokeach (1973), "Values generally are defined as preferences for certain outcomes or modes of conduct" (as cited in Locke, 2000, p. 250). Such preferences can be shared by a whole community (cultural values) or be individual (personal values). The concept of personal values is also very similar to high-level goals.

A central and well-documented assumption of goal-oriented approaches is that, to a considerable extent, people's daily behaviors, thoughts, and emotions are linked to the pursuit of *personal goals* and are regulated by feedback regarding goal attainment (Austin & Vancouver, 1996; Carver & Scheier, 1996; Klinger, 1977). Personal goals can be defined as elaborate cognitive representations of what a person wants to achieve or avoid in his or her current life circumstances and are conscious, symbolically represented, and stored in a language-related manner (Brunstein, Schultheiss, & Graessmann, 1998). It is assumed that approach goals are developed to satisfy psychological needs, whereas avoidance goals are developed to prevent these needs from being hurt (Grawe, 2004; see also Elliot, 2008, for a review). People may pursue personal goals as diverse in content as, for example, making new friends, improving my professional situation, learning how to be more spontaneous, trying to be a better parent, or overcoming fear of rejection

(Chulef, Read, & Walsh, 2001). Grosse Holtforth and Grawe (2000) empirically identified the contents of personal goals that therapists considered to be especially relevant for their patients. Examples are to perform well, to be in a committed relationship, to avoid being humiliated, or to avoid showing weaknesses. The totality of all goals a person strives for (the person's goal structure) can be viewed as his or her individual future-oriented side giving purpose, structure, and meaning to life (Cantor, 1990; Emmons, 1986; Klinger, 1977; Michalak & Grosse Holtforth, 2006).

A patient usually seeks psychotherapy when he or she experiences an unbearable level of suffering being caused by unpleasant changes, experiences, and/or behaviors. Examples for such changes are psychopathological symptoms, unpleasant social interactions, inadequate performance at work, reduced enjoyment of leisure activities, or a general dissatisfaction with life. The person evaluates these experiences as problems because they are discrepant with his or her personal goals. When the person evaluates these changes as abnormal, believes that he or she is incapable of dealing with them alone, and has at least minimal hope that he or she will receive some relief from suffering through psychotherapy, the person may seek professional help (Schulte & Eifert, 2002). Apart from unbearable levels of suffering, other factors may also contribute to the person's decision to seek help, such as expectations or pressures by significant others or the wish to receive an absolution from guilt feelings by receiving a medical diagnosis, which may have been caused by a sense of burdensomeness to one's loved-ones (Schneider, 1990).

Therapy motivation is influenced by various experiences, including *(a)* suffering, *(b)* positive experiences (hope of relief), *(c)* fear of change, and *(d)* the therapeutic bond (wish to maintain the therapeutic relationship). Patient suffering may also be influenced by a multitude of factors, that is, *impairment* (psychopathological symptoms and negative affect), the experience of *being abnormal*, or the feeling of *helplessness* (Schulte & Eifert, 2002). Other factors may also be *gains from illness*, be they material (e.g., wish for a pension) or psychological (e.g., attention, support, protection; Schulte & Eifert, 2002).

Probably the most favorable approach that patients can bring to therapy would be one that is characterized by interest, curiosity, and commitment. The term *autonomous motivation* (Ryan & Deci, 2000) closely resembles this ideal kind of therapy motivation. For the purposes of psychotherapy, autonomous motivation can be defined as "the extent to which patients experience participation in treatment as a freely made choice emanating from themselves" (Zuroff et al., 2007, p. 137). If the patient has a favorable therapy motivation, he or she will cooperate with the therapist and the protocol, will disclose private experiences, will test out new patterns of behavior, will show low resistance to the therapist's intervention, and will unlikely drop out of treatment (*basic behavior*). The patient's *therapy expectations* may also influence the therapy process and outcome. Examples for therapy expectations are hope for improvement of well-being, hope for improvement of relationships, fear of adverse side effects, or fear of being ridiculed (Schulte & Eifert, 2002). The patient's motivation as well as his or her expectations may also be influenced by the patient's concepts of psychological illness and change (Calnan, 1987).

Treatment goals can be defined as "intended changes in behavior and experience to be attained by therapy, which patient and therapist agree upon at the beginning of treatment and on which successful psychotherapy should be instrumental" (Grosse Holtforth & Grawe, 2002, p. 79). Treatment goals have various functions in psychotherapy (Driessen et al., 2001). On an individual level, treatment goals focus patients' and therapists' attention, guide treatment planning, and provide criteria for outcome assessment (e.g., goal-attainment scaling, see earlier). In addition, treatment goals fulfill an ethical function by providing transparency for the patient, by balancing the power between the therapist and the patient, and by supporting the patient in giving his or her informed consent. Treatment goals also help to define similarities and differences between different therapeutic approaches. Finally, information on patients' treatment goals may support the optimization of treatment programs by providing feedback on the needs of specific patient groups (Uebelacker et al., 2008). Table 25.1 shows an empirically constructed list of patients' goals in psychotherapy (Grosse Holtforth & Grawe, 2002).

Assessing Motivational Constructs in Psychotherapy

As implicit motives are unconscious by definition, they cannot be assessed directly by self-report. Implicit motives have traditionally been assessed using projective techniques like the Thematic Apperception Test (TAT; Smith, 1992). During the TAT, respondents are asked to write fantasy stories in response to several pictures depicting motive-arousing scenarios. Several systems for deriving motive scores (achievement, power, and affiliation) from TAT stories have

Table 25.1. Bern Inventory of Treatment Goals (BIT-T)

Problem-/ Symptom- Oriented	Interpersonal	Well-Being/ Functioning	Existential	Personal Growth	Residual category (R)
Depression	Intimate	Exercise, activity	Self-	Attitude	Regeneration
Suicidality	relationships	Relaxation/	reflection	toward self	Psychosocial
Fears/anxiety	Current family	composure	and future	Desires and	rehabilitation
Obsessions/comp.	Family of origin	Well-being	Finding	wishes	Somatic
Traumatic experiences	Other specific		meaning	Self-control	rehabilitation
Substance use	relationships			Emotion	
Eating behavior	Loneliness, grief			regulation	
Sleep	Assertiveness				
Sexuality	Contact/closeness				
Somatic problems					
Stress					
Medication					

been developed (Smith, 1992). Although suitable for clinical research, these systems are not yet suited for routine clinical use due to missing norms, questionable or unknown test-retest reliability, and so on (Lilienfeld, Wood & Garb, 2000). Recently, several alternatives for assessing implicit motives (especially the achievement motive) have been introduced. For example, Brunstein and Schmitt (2004) developed an Implicit Association Test (IAT; Greenwald, McGhee, & Schwartz, 1998) to assess achievement motivation by evaluating the strength of association between achievement-related adjectives and the self-concept. However, such newer techniques are too time consuming for routine clinical use.

Explicit motivational constructs can be assessed efficiently using questionnaire methods. A sample questionnaire to assess various dimensions of therapy motivation is the Patient Motivation for Therapy Scale (CMTS; Pelletier, Tuson, & Haddad, 1997). Based on the self-determination theory proposed by Deci and Ryan (1985), the CMTS measures patients' intrinsic motivation, four forms of regulation for extrinsic motivation (integrated, identified, introjected, and external regulation), and motivation for therapy. An example for the assessment of values in the interpersonal realm is the Circumplex Scales of Interpersonal Values (CSIV; Locke, 2000). The principle of a circumplex structure implies that variables that measure interpersonal relations are arranged around a circle in a two-dimensional space, with the dimensions being agency and communion.

Personal goals are most often assessed in basic research using a combined idiographic-nomothetic approach. The first step (the idiographic part) is to ask the participants to generate a list of personal goals. In the second step (the nomothetic part), patients

rate these individual goals on various dimensions to allow for inter-individual comparisons. Goals can be rated by the participants themselves or by independent raters (e.g., categorization of goals by content or according to the approach and avoidance quality of the goals). Examples of this idiographic-nomothetic approach are the Personal Projects Matrix (Little, 1983), the Personal Concerns Inventory (Cox & Klinger, 2002), and its immediate antecedents, such as the Concern Dimensions Questionnaires (Klinger, Barta, & Maxeiner, 1980) and the Interview Questionnaire (Klinger, 1987). These instruments preceded and/or gave rise to other methods such as the Striving Assessment Scale (Emmons, 1986) and the Goal Assessment Battery (Karoly & Ruehlman, 1995). All of these approaches make it possible to assess theory-derived indices that seek to achieve a multilevel understanding of goals (e.g., goal importance, goal achievement, goal conflict, etc.).

Furthermore, various interviews to assess personal goals have been developed (e.g., AIMS; Wadsworth & Ford, 1983), allowing for an extensive description of the various goals and their mutual relationships. When standardized goal questionnaires (e.g., Ford & Nichols, 1991; Grosse Holtforth & Grawe, 2000; Grosse Holtforth & Grawe, 2003; Grosse Holtforth, Grawe, & Tamcan, 2004; Reiss & Havercamp, 1998; Ryff, 1989) are utilized, the participants are presented with goals that have to be evaluated with respect to dimensions such as importance, strain, progress, or realization. Compared to other methods, standardized questionnaires offer the advantage that the goal contents are comparable. Furthermore, goal assessment is less dependent on recall processes. However, the personal salience and ecological sensitivity of the idiographic-nomothetic approach associated with the individual formulation of goals is diminished by the standardized goal presentation. Conflict matrixes are used to examine the interrelationship and possible conflicts among goals (e.g., Cox, Klinger, & Blount, 1999; Emmons & King, 1988). To measure the amount of conflict that exists between pairs of goals, participants compare each goal with every other goal and ask themselves, "Does being successful in this goal have a helpful, a harmful, or no effect on the other goal?"

A strategy to assess the person's clinically relevant personal goals is Plan Analysis (Caspar, 2007). According to Caspar, Grossmann, Unmüssig, and Schramm (2005), a "person's Plan structure is the total of conscious and unconscious strategies this person has developed to satisfy his or her needs" (p. 92). The patient's Plan structure can be derived from various sources of information (e.g., biographical information, behavioral observations, and the patient's impact on others). The main question guiding the assessment process is: What is the explicit or implicit purpose of this patient's behavior? In a simplified form, Plan Analysis can be done and used in collaboration with the patient to enhance his or her understanding of certain parts of his or her functioning (Caspar, 2007). The result of a Plan Analysis is a graphic display of the structure of the patient's most important approach and avoidance goals as well as his or her individual means (Plans and behaviors) toward pursuing these goals (see Fig. 25.1).

Treatment goals can also be formulated and assessed in a more or less standardized form. Various questionnaires and checklists for a standardized assessment of treatment goals have been developed (e.g., Driessen et al., 2001; Grosse Holtforth, 2001;

Kunkel & Newsom, 1996; Miller & Thompson, 1973). The attainment of individually formulated therapy goals can be measured using, for example, the Goal Attainment Scaling (GAS) procedure (Kiresuk, Smith, & Cardillo, 1994). In the first step, GAS procedures define possible areas of change. Then, the patient and therapist join forces to explore and formulate as concretely as possible for each area what would constitute an improvement to, stagnation in, or a deterioration of the current state. The degree of goal attainment can be assessed in the course of treatment or after termination by patients, therapists, or independent raters. The goal-attainment scaling may then be viewed as individualized measures of treatment success (for a discussion of methodological limitations of GAS, see Hill & Lambert, 2004).

Personal Goals, Well-Being, and Psychological Problems

After considering methodological issues in assessing motivational constructs, we will now present research findings that underscore the importance of personal goals for well-being and psychological problems. We will focus on personal goals because most of the empirical research has used personal goals as a unit of analysis. In everyday life, humans pursue multiple goals in various areas, such as family, work, career, recreation, or spirituality using various individual strategies (Karoly, 2006). As there is a multitude of ways to pursue one's goals successfully, there are also many ways to fail in reaching one's goals. How effectively a person strives for his or her goals can be seen as key criterion for effective adjustment (Karoly, 2006). Succeeding or failing to reach one's goals not only has important consequences for the individual's happiness and well-being (for reviews see Brunstein, Schultheiss,

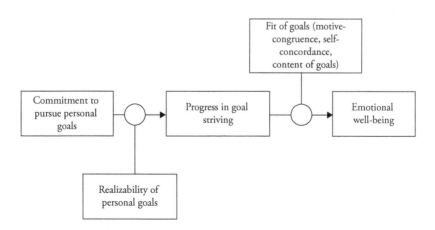

Fig. 25.1. Teleonomic model of subjective well-being (Brunstein & Maier, 2002, p. 163, modified).

& Maier, 1999; Emmons & Kaiser, 1996; Schmuck & Sheldon, 2001) but can also contribute to the development and maintenance of serious psychological problems and disorders.

In the following, we will highlight selected findings as pertaining to the associations of goal functioning to well-being and psychopathology. According to Pervin (1990), Karoly (1999), and Grawe (2004), psychopathology can develop when a person is unable to attain his or her goals over an extended period of time, when goal attainment is threatened by personal or external circumstances, or when dysfunctional processes occur in goal-oriented self-regulation. Concurrently, psychopathology can be seen as "disturbances to the normal processes and structures by which humans consciously and nonconsciously guide their actions, emotions, and thoughts in the service of achieving meaningful life goals" (Karoly, 2006, p. 367).

Brunstein and Maier (2002) summarized findings from basic research on personal goals in a *teleonomic model* of subjective well-being (see Fig. 25.1). In the teleonomic model, goal commitment, as well as goal realizability is assumed to causally influence well-being. If someone pursues his or her goals with commitment (i.e., he or she identifies with the goals and feels motivated to realize them), and if his or her life situation facilitates the attainment of these goals, progress in goal striving is more likely. Goal progress, in turn, is assumed to contribute to the person's emotional well-being.

The basic assumptions of the teleonomic model of emotional well-being have been supported by a multitude of research findings (Brunstein et al., 1999). For example, through longitudinal studies on various groups of participants (Brunstein, 1999; Maier & Brunstein, 2001, Wiese & Freund, 2005), it has been demonstrated that people who *(a)* are strongly committed to strive for their goals, and *(b)* who view their life circumstances as favorable for goal striving, achieved a greater degree of progress in goal attainment and greater increase in emotional well-being than people who were less committed to goals for which conditions were more unfavorable. In addition, people whose goals are in conflict with each other or are poorly integrated (Michalak, Heidenreich, & Hoyer, 2011) or who have goals that are abstract and not clearly formulated (Emmons, 1996) show lower subjective well-being and satisfaction with life. Furthermore, dysregulated goal/action identification seems to relate to various psychological symptoms and disorders such as depression or social anxiety in the sense that patients with these disorders identify negative events at a more abstract level

than healthy subjects (Watkins, 2011). In addition, more goal progress can be also expected if the social network supports a person's goals (Brunstein, 1993; Brunstein, Dangelmayer, & Schultheiss, 1996; Ruehlman & Wolchik, 1988). However, which goals the social network supports and what the consequences for the individual's well-being are may also depend on the cultural context. For example, whereas independent goal pursuit (fun and enjoyment) increased well-being among European Americans but less among Asian Americans, interdependent goal pursuit (pleasing parents and friends) increased the well-being of Asian Americans but not of European Americans (Oishi & Diener, 2001).

A central assumption in the teleonomic model is that successful goal striving does not inevitably lead to happiness and well-being, but rather if the goals *fit* the person. Goals may be pursued for extrinsic or intrinsic reasons, and the various content of goals also seems to make a difference. Many studies have shown that the pursuit of goals is especially associated with a sense of well-being if the goals are well integrated into the person's self-system (*self-concordance*; Sheldon, 2001), that is, if goals are pursued because one has consciously accepted the values underlying such behavior as personally important and meaningful (*identified regulation*) or because the pursuit of these goals is in itself satisfying and rewarding (*intrinsic regulation*). In contrast, goals are not integrated into the self-system if they are mainly pursued because of external reward ("extrinsic regulation") or internal pressure (e.g., feelings of guilt or embarrassment, "introjected regulation"; for reviews see Deci & Ryan, 2002; Ryan & Deci, 2000; Ryan, Sheldon, Kasser, & Deci, 1996; Sheldon, 2001). Whenever goals correspond with a person's personal values and interests, or the pursuit of the goals is itself satisfying, he or she will—even in times when the pursuit of goals is fraught with difficulties or exertion—be more able to activate emotional resources and thus persist in the pursuit. Concurrently, in a meta-analytical review by Koestner, Lekes, Powers, and Chicoine (2002), the positive effects of self-concordant goals on goal attainment were consistently shown even after controlling for other relevant variables such as neuroticism, goal efficiency, and commitment.

A closely related, but not quite the same aspect as self-concordance (Kasser & Ryan, 2001) refers to the content dimension of goals. Kasser and Ryan (1993, 1996) have coined the term *external goals* for goals the focus of which is to increase one's status in the eyes of others, as compared to *internal goals*, which are geared toward the fulfillment of inherently personal needs, such as competence, autonomy, and relatedness, and therefore fit people's deeper, psychologically fundamental needs. A series of studies (e.g., Kasser & Ryan, 1993, 1996; Schmuck, Kasser, & Ryan, 2000; Sheldon & Kasser, 1998) showed that people who mainly strove for external goals displayed a lower level of well-being than people who devoted their lives to the attainment of internal goals. Püschel, Schulte, and Michalak (2011) investigated associations between goal fit and psychopathology in a sample of 61 psychotherapy outpatients with heterogeneous diagnoses. In accordance with the teleonomic model, results showed that only motive-congruent goal progress was related to depressivity. Patients who made more progress at goals that matched their implicit motives experienced fewer depressive symptoms, whereas patients who failed to make progress at motive matching goals experienced more depressive symptoms. Motive-incongruent progress did not have any effect on depressive symptoms.

Several studies with student samples demonstrated associations between goal functioning and psychopathology. For example, in a study by Lecci, Karoly, Briggs, and Kuhn (1994) "negative" goal characteristics such as high stress and difficulty, low goal structure, low expectations regarding control, perceived insufficiency of own capabilities, and low expectations of success were associated with increased depression and anxiety. Correspondingly, Cohen and Cohen (1996, 2001) found in an extensive prospective longitudinal study that children and adolescents who set high priority on materialistic and hedonistic goals (i.e., external goals) showed a higher incidence of almost all Axis-I and Axis-II *DSM-III* diagnoses later in life. Furthermore, a number of studies found associations between goal conflicts, impaired well-being, and psychopathology (for a review, see Michalak, Heidenreich, & Hoyer, 2011).

Pursuing a high proportion of *avoidance goals* relative to approach goals is associated with less perceived goal progress and seems to be particularly detrimental to one's well-being and functioning (see Elliot & Friedman, 2007; Tamir & Diener, 2008, for reviews). Avoidance goals may exert this negative influence because the monitoring and management of goal process is harder for avoidance goals than for approach goals, because avoidance goals elicit more negative cognitions and emotions (Tamir & Diener, 2008), and avoidance goals hinder the satisfaction of important personal goals as well as associated psychological needs (Grawe, 2004). Particularly, an avoidance of aversive experiences may contribute to the development and perpetuation of mental problems (Grosse Holtforth, 2008; Hayes, Strosahl, &

Wilson, 1999). Such negative experiences can relate to various types of events, such as abandonment, criticism, or failure (Grosse Holtforth, Grawe, Egger, & Berking, 2005).

Empirical research showed that psychotherapy patients pursue more avoidance goals than normal controls, and that the intensity of avoidance goals correlates with the decreased levels of goal satisfaction, poor well-being, severity of psychopathology, and other psychological problems in psychotherapy patients as well as in normal controls (Grosse Holtforth & Grawe, 2000; Grosse Holtforth & Grawe, 2003). However, avoidance goals do not have to be uniformly maladaptive but might protect individuals from being deeply frustrated and hurt in harmful environments (Grosse Holtforth, Bents, Mauler, & Grawe, 2006). Michalak, Püschel, Joormann, and Schulte (2006) examined *avoidance tendencies* in the explicit and the implicit modes. In a sample of students and psychotherapy patients, avoidance tendencies within the explicit system of personal goals as well as in implicit motives were associated with symptoms, even when controlling for the other mode.

Several studies examined goal functioning in specific mental disorders (Michalak, Klappheck, & Kosfelder, 2004; Pöhlmann, 1999; Stangier, Ukrow, Schermelleh-Engel, Grabe, & Lauterbach, 2007). Pöhlmann (1999) compared the personal goals of psychosomatic patients with the goals of a psychologically healthy sample. Psychosomatic patients generally pursued more goals than psychologically healthy subjects. However, the goals were formulated as avoidance goals rather than approach goals, and the scope of the goals was narrower. Compared to psychologically healthy subjects, goals expressing the desire to change oneself were mentioned more often, as well as health-related goals. Michalak et al. (2004) investigated the aspect of goal attainment as well as goal fit in a study with psychotherapy outpatients with anxiety and mood disorders. Both probability of goal attainment as well as the self-concordance of goals (intrinsically vs. extrinsically motivated goal striving) correlated highly with symptom distress. In addition, Stangier and colleagues (2007) found that depressed inpatients showed higher scores for inconsistencies among different goals/values as well as between goals/values and their perceived realization as compared with controls. Strauman (2002) proposed in his self-regulation model of depression that individuals who are unable to pursue promotion goals effectively are at risk for mood disorder because of their chronic inability to satisfy these goals. In this model, depression results from and maintains disruption of the mechanisms of incentive motivation (Dickson & MacLeod, 2004; Strauman et al., 2006). Empirical studies indeed indicate that an inability to attain promotion goals is predictive of dysphoric mood and depressive symptoms (e.g., Scott & O'Hara, 1993).

In the motivational model of alcoholism by Cox and Klinger (1988, 1990), dysfunctional goal characteristics possess a central role as pathogenic factors in the development and maintenance of substance abuse and addictions. The model assumes that the balance between the expectation of positive and negative affective consequences of substance use determines the course and outcome of an episode of alcohol consumption. The satisfaction a person is able to draw from other areas of his or her life strongly contributes to the decision for or against the consumption of alcohol. When a person is unable to get satisfaction from other sources of reinforcement, the risk increases that he or she will use alcohol or other substances to find pleasure and emotional relief. In various studies with students with more pronounced alcohol-related problems, Cox et al. (2002) showed that unfavorable goal structures were associated with the amount of alcohol consumed. Compared with students, alcoholic patients reported fewer goals and reported less average commitment to them but also reported less average commitment relative to the return they expected from their goal striving (Man, Stuchlik-ova, & Klinger, 1998). It might be that alcoholics need more expected rewards to become committed to goals. A recent study by Sevincer and Oettingen (2009) demonstrated that the relationship between goal striving and psychopathology is not unidirectional but a "double-edged causal sword" (Karoly, 2006, p. 369). Sevincer and Oettingen (2009) found in an experimental study that alcohol consumption creates strong commitments even in light of low expectations. However, in a longitudinal study, once sober again, formerly intoxicated participants with low expectations did not follow up on their strong commitments over a 3-week period. The authors interpreted the findings as showing that alcohol seems to produce "empty goal commitments," as commitments are not based on individuals' expectations.

Motivational Factors in Psychotherapy Research and Practice

In the following, we will examine various ways in which motivational factors are relevant in the practice of psychotherapy—either as *facilitators* of treatment process and outcome or as *targets* of psychological change. First, we will examine the role of motivational factors in psychotherapy as they occur *naturally* in the process of treatment, then we will outline therapeutic interventions that explicitly aim at changing motivational factors.

GOALS, THERAPY MOTIVATION, AND MOTIVE CHANGE

Zuroff and colleagues (2007) examined the role of autonomous motivation in a randomized controlled trial comparing interpersonal therapy, cognitive behavior therapy, or pharmacotherapy with clinical management for depressed outpatients. They found that autonomous motivation assessed at session 3 was a stronger predictor of outcome than therapeutic alliance across all three treatments. In addition, patients who perceived their therapists as more autonomy supportive reported higher autonomous motivation. Thus, it seems that fostering autonomous motivation in psychotherapy is a general facilitator of favorable treatment outcomes.

Certain goal characteristics might influence the therapeutic process by enhancing or decreasing the motivation to actively engage in treatment and to attain treatment goals. Ryan, Plant, and O'Malley (1995) found that alcoholic patients who were pressured to participate in a treatment program showed higher dropout rates compared to patients who experienced their participation as more intrinsically motivated. In addition, Michalak, Klappheck, and Kosfelder (2004) investigated the correlation of optimism about goal attainment and the intrinsic orientation of patients' general goals with session outcome. Optimism as well as goal fit (i.e., self-concordance of goals) correlated strongly with session success. This correlation was not mediated by the patients' psychopathological state, so it can be assumed that motivational aspects are responsible for the correlation. Klappheck and Michalak (2009), analyzing the same sample, found that only optimism to reach the goal of symptom relief was related to treatment outcome. However, self-concordance of goals failed to predict treatment outcome.

Various studies have investigated the question of whether conflicts between a patient's general goals and poor integration of the goal structure (i.e., the extent of mutual support or hindrance of goals) is associated with the motivation to become actively involved in therapy (for a review, see Michalak et al., 2011). For example, in a study conducted by Michalak and Schulte (2002), goal conflicts in patients with anxiety disorders were negatively correlated with patients' basic behavior during therapy as well as treatment success. Conflict was measured using the Striving Instrumentality Matrix (SIM; Emmons & King, 1988). Moreover, basic behavior also correlated with some measures of treatment success (Michalak, Kosfelder, Meyer, & Schulte, 2003). However, Michalak et al. (2004) were unable to replicate correlations between goal conflicts and basic behavior in another sample of psychotherapy outpatients. In two studies with alcoholic inpatients and inpatients receiving treatment for drug addiction, Heidenreich (2000) showed negative correlations between the degree of conflict concerning the goal "personal change" and attitudes toward change-relevant topics. These attitudes were operationalized according to the transtheoretical model developed by Prochaska, DiClemente, and Norcross (1992): Willingness to contemplate changing problematic abuse ("Contemplation") and to actively cope with the abuse ("Action"; see also see Cox & Klinger, 2002).

MOTIVATIONAL INTERVENTIONS AS FACILITATORS OF CHANGE

Therapists can use motivational factors to facilitate change in at least two ways. Therapists can foster a good therapeutic relationship by tailoring the therapy to the patient's motives and they can try to formulate maximally helpful treatment goals.

Fostering the Therapeutic Relationship

One of the most important tasks of a therapist at the beginning of psychotherapy is to establish a good therapeutic relationship and productive working alliance (Horvath, 1995). From a motivational perspective, how well a behavior is received by another person depends on how effectively a behavior helps to satisfy the other person's needs and goals. According to Ryan and Deci (2000), a therapeutic relationship promoting the fundamental needs for competence, autonomy, and relatedness constitutes a prerequisite for a successful integration of goals into the self-system. However, a therapist can go beyond supporting generic psychological needs that are assumed to be shared by all human beings. For this, the therapist may individualize his or her behavior to accommodate the patient's individual goals. In their motivational attunement approach, Grosse Holtforth and Castonguay (2005) described ways to tailor therapeutic interventions to the patient's goals and motives in order to foster the therapeutic relationship and therapeutic outcome. By showing motivationally attuned behavior, the therapist attempts to satisfy important approach goals of the patient while activating avoidance goals no more than necessary. A motivationally attuned therapist

behavior is assumed to foster each of the essential parts of the therapeutic alliance: therapeutic bond, agreement on therapeutic tasks, and agreement on therapeutic goals (Bordin, 1979). The Motivational Attunement approach is similar to Alliance Fostering Therapy proposed by Crits-Christoph et al. (2006), which is conceptualized as a supplement to existing empirically supported therapies. Among others, maximally informing patients about the indicated therapeutic procedures and discussing them with the patients until reaching an agreement will foster task agreement (Crits-Christoph et al., 2006). The therapist may also bolster motivationally unattractive techniques by putting the task into the service of other approach goals and by activating other resources. For example, the therapist might say, "This exposure exercise will finally enable you to spend relaxed afternoons downtown shopping with your daughter and enjoying life a little more." Motivational attunement may also help to prevent alliance ruptures (Safran & Muran, 2000). Empirical results show that potential precipitants of alliance ruptures occur as either "therapist does something that the patient does not want or need" or as "the therapist fails to do something that the patient wants or needs" (Ackerman & Hilsenroth, 2001, p. 183). Therefore, a therapist will be well advised to be aware of the patient's salient approach and avoidance goals in order (a) not to miss important expectations or needs or (b) commit interactional blunders that fit the patient's individual vulnerabilities.

Formulating Treatment Goals

Treatment goals may first come to mind when thinking about goals in psychotherapy. As patients and therapists may have different goals for therapy, it is important to distinguish treatment goals from (a) naïve treatment concerns presented by the patients and (b) from treatment goals defined exclusively by the therapist. An agreement on therapy goals is considered a central ingredient of the working alliance. Naïve treatment concerns are what a patient hopes to accomplish in the course of therapy and are usually closely connected to the problem the person suffers from. These naïve treatment concerns can be seen as a subset of the patient's general personal goals (Pöhlmann, 1999). Naïve treatment concerns may or may not parallel the goals for therapy that the therapist holds. On the other hand, what the therapist sees as the goals of treatment may be strongly influenced by various factors, including therapeutic orientation (Arnow & Castonguay, 1996; Dirmaier, Harfst, Koch, & Schulz, 2006;

Philips, 2009). Empirically, agreement between the patients' and the therapists' treatment goals seems to have positive effects on the process and outcome of psychotherapy (Tryon & Winograd, 2001; see also Orlinsky, Ronnestad, & Willutzki, 2004). However, the rather low correspondence between patients' goals and therapists' goals found in earlier studies indicates that it is necessary for the therapist to explicitly strive for this agreement (Dimsdale, 1975; Dimsdale, Klerman, & Shershow, 1979; Polak, 1970; Thompson & Zimmerman, 1969).

In the process of goal definition, the therapist helps the patient to translate the often vaguely worded treatment objectives and wishes into well-formed therapeutic goals, so that they optimally fulfill the aforementioned functions. Several characteristics of a well-formed therapeutic goal can be formulated (Michalak & Grosse Holtforth, 2006; Willutzki & Koban, 2004). Optimally, treatment goals are negotiated and agreed upon with the patient. In the goal selection process, those goals should be preferred that correspond with a patient's intrinsic (approach) goals so that they hold a maximum positive valence, urgency, and importance for the patient. The goals should describe a change, an increase in skills, or the preservation of facilitative conditions. Therapists should ensure that the goals a patient chooses or formulates are attainable. Complex and long-term goals should be divided into sufficiently concrete and feasible low-level goals, and they should be divided into steps small enough for the patient to be able to translate them into action. Goal attainment should be initiated and maintained by the patient. Goals should not be in conflict with one another, and goal formulation should entail simple, concrete, specific, observable, and detailed descriptions of the current problematic state as well as the aspired goal state. In addition, therapeutic goals should be formulated positively as approach goals ("to be able to go shopping by myself") as opposed to avoidance goals ("no longer scared when alone outside"). The goal-striving process should be supported by implementation intentions (i.e., specifications as to when and where the goal will be pursued and how obstacles will be dealt with; see Gollwitzer & Brandstätter, 1997) and the patient's social environment should be motivated to support the patient's goals. Finally, goals should be clearly measurable so the patient can see the progress and feel motivated to further engage in therapy.

Empirical studies show that patients' treatment goals differ depending on patients' diagnoses. For example, psychotherapy patients with eating or anxiety disorder show a higher proportion of explicitly symptom-oriented goals (e.g., "having fewer episodes of binge-eating," "being able to go shopping by myself again"; Faller & Goßler, 1998) than do patients with mood disorders. The latter show—in addition to disorder-typical goals (e.g., "being able to find pleasure in everyday activities")—many goals that focus on interpersonal or existential issues (e.g., "resolving my marital conflicts"). Similar diagnostic differences could be found in other samples of inpatients and outpatients (Berking, Grosse Holtforth, Jacobi, & Kröner-Herwig, 2005; Dirmaier et al., 2006; Grosse Holtforth & Grawe, 2002; Grosse Holtforth, Reubi, Ruckstuhl, Berking, & Grawe, 2004; Grosse Holtforth, Wyss, Schulte, Trachsel, & Michalak, 2009; Uebelacker et al., 2008).

So far, only a few studies have examined the association between the content of therapeutic goals and therapy outcome. In a study analyzing the treatment goals of 2,770 inpatients in psychosomatic rehabilitation, Berking et al. (2005) found that the level of goal attainment differed between goal categories. For example, goals such as "reducing my panic attacks" or "learning to accept myself better" had much better prospects of success than the goal "coping with my sleep problems" or "experiencing less pain." Such findings help to adjust therapist expectations and may serve as references for evaluating treatment progress in various disorders.

For patients experiencing difficulties formulating clear and self-concordant therapy goals, Willutzki and Koban (2004) introduced the *EPOS* intervention (Development of Positive Perspectives in Psychotherapy). In the imagination phase, the therapist guides the patient in activating positive perspectives beyond presenting problems (e.g., "When your life progresses fine within the next years, what will a day in 5 years look like?"). In the analysis phase, the therapist supports the patient in specifying the personally relevant goals and relates these more concrete goals to the patient's imaginary activation of positive perspectives. These interventions usually take two to three sessions.

CHANGING MOTIVATIONAL FACTORS BY PSYCHOTHERAPY

First, we will describe general models of psychological change that ascribe a central role to motivational factors for change in psychotherapy. Then we will demonstrate examples of interventions that have an explicit motivational focus. A fundamental assumption of attempts to change motivational factors in psychotherapy is that motivational change will contribute to symptom change and improvement of well-being.

General Models of Change

We will describe three general models of behavior change that are particularly relevant to psychotherapy. These models are the Rubicon Model of Action Phases (Heckhausen, Gollwitzer & Weinert, 1987), the change model of General Psychotherapy (GPT; Grawe, 1997), as well as the Transtheoretical Model (TTM; Prochaska et al., 1992).

The Rubicon Model of Action Phases (Heckhausen et al., 1987) is a well-established psychological model for goal-oriented action that can be profitably applied to psychotherapy. Figure 25.2 shows the different phases of the model. In the *motivation phase*, a person contemplates on his or her goals, which is completed by the formulation of an intention, constituting the shift from choosing to wanting. From here on, all processes are directed toward the implementation of the decision, that is, toward the attainment of a particular goal. Subsequently, the person plans for how to reach the goal, screens out competing intentions, and ultimately executes adequate action. After realizing the action, the person evaluates the action consequences with reference to the pursued goal.

In General Psychotherapy (GPT; Grawe, 1997) the term generally denotes that rather than defining one's interventions by therapy *schools*, therapists conceptualize their interventions in terms of general *change factors*. The assumed general change factors are resource activation, problem actuation, motivational clarifications, and problem mastery. Whereas resource activation and problem actuation are considered catalysts for change, motivational clarification and problem mastery refer to specific types of corrective experiences (Alexander & French, 1946;

Goldfried, 1980). Motivational clarification, which is of particular relevance for this chapter, involves becoming aware of the motivational background of unpleasant emotions and reevaluating negative primary appraisals of situations and events (Grosse Holtforth, Grawe, & Castonguay, 2006). The psychotherapist for each patient individually combines empirically supported interventions that correspond to these mechanisms of change based on a case formulation and treatment plan (Caspar & Grosse Holtforth, 2010). In an experimental study with heterogeneous outpatients, Grosse Holtforth, Grawe, Fries, and Znoj (2008) demonstrated differential effects for general psychotherapy depending on motivational factors. General psychotherapy, which combines motivationally clarifying interventions with mastery-oriented interventions, yielded stronger reductions of interpersonal problems for patients with high levels of avoidance motivation, as compared to a cognitive-behavioral condition that focuses on mastery-oriented interventions only.

Grawe (2004) adapted the Rubicon Model described earlier for the systematization of change processes in psychotherapy. In the Rubicon Model, the therapist's goal is to help the patient to move through the phases of action to enable the patient to realize an action that fulfils his or her psychological needs. As the Rubicon constitutes the difference between choosing and wanting, the therapist may help the patient on both sides of the Rubicon. The therapist may help the patient to form clear intentions (motivational clarification) or to realize his or her intentions (problem mastery), or both. By motivationally clarifying interventions, the therapist guides the patient's attention to the process of choice, raises awareness for the involved motivational *forces* (wishes, fears, expectations, standards, etc.),

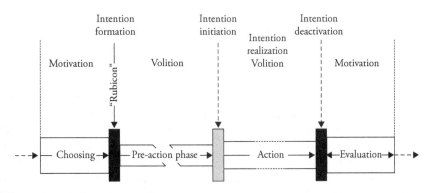

Fig. 25.2. The action phase model (Rubicon Model) by Heckhausen. (Adapted from Grawe, 2004, p. 50; reproduced by permission from Psychological Therapy by Klaus Grawe, ISBN 0-88937-217-9 ©2004 by Hogrefe& Huber Publishers www.hogrefe.com.)

and attempts to strengthen the patient's volition by changing the patient's intentions in clarity, direction, or strength. For example, psychodynamic therapies predominantly use interventions aiming at motivational clarification. To the *right of the Rubicon*, that is, when a patient has clear and strong intentions, the therapist's activities are geared toward supporting the patient in implementing his or her intentions. Behaviorally oriented therapies work predominantly on the right side of the Rubicon.

Perhaps the most testable of the general models is the Transtheoretical Model (TTM; Prochaska et al., 1992). The TTM describes the process of psychological change as going through six subsequent stages: *precontemplation, contemplation, preparation, action, maintenance,* and *termination.* Individuals may also return from action or maintenance to an earlier stage (relapse). Heckhausen et al.'s (1987) decisional Rubicon could be located between the contemplation and preparation phase. The authors also advise therapists to adjust their relational stance toward the patient to each individual's stage of change. Prochaska and Norcross (2001) proposed that in the precontemplation stage, the therapist should behave like an understanding parent, later morphing into a Socratic teacher in the contemplation phase. In the preparation phase, the therapist should assume the position of an experienced trainer, stepping behind again as a counselor in the action and maintenance phases. Research indicates that tailoring the therapy relationship and treatment intervention to the stage of change can enhance outcome, specifically in the percentage of patients completing therapy and in the ultimate success of treatment (Prochaska & Norcross, 2001).

Although the TTM has been criticized, for example, for inconclusive empirical foundation as well as unresolved assessment problems, the TTM, like the Rubicon Model and the change model of General Psychotherapy, possesses great heuristic value for practicing clinicians to conceptualize and structure their interventions.

Motivational Change as a Central Mechanism

Motivational factors may change in psychotherapy, even if motivational change is not explicitly part of the therapy rationale, or motivational factors may be the central mechanism of change that therapists explicitly try to implement. As an example of *naturalistic* motivational change, several authors found that unfavorable goal characteristics changed, even without an underlying explicit rationale for working on these goal characteristics. For example, motivational factors that

were found to change in psychotherapy were strong avoidance motivation (Grosse Holtforth et al., 2005), goal conflicts (Heidenreich, 2000; Hoyer, Fecht, Lauterbach, & Schneider, 2001; Michalak, 2000), or goal satisfaction (Berking, Grosse Holtforth, & Jacobi, 2003; Grosse Holtforth & Grawe, 2002).

Even though motivation can change even in therapies that do not explicitly target motivational variables, several approaches have been developed directly targeting motivational change. Some interventions have been tested in studies with nonclinical populations that might be used as a heuristic for clinical interventions. For example, Schultheiss and Brunstein (1999) used guided *goal imagery* to foster motive-congruent goal commitment (goal fit). They found that those subjects who had used guided goal imagery were more committed to goals that corresponded with their implicit motive dispositions. In an extension of this research, Job and Brandstätter (2009) showed in a series of experiments that goal fantasies focusing on affective incentives that are specific to a given motive promoted motive-congruent goal setting. Sheldon, Kasser, Smith, and Share (2002) designed an intervention to improve self-concordance and integration of goals. In the intervention, participants are asked to reflect upon their goals and are taught four specific strategies for the regulation of goal-related experience, such as Own the goal, Make it fun, Remember the big picture, and Keep a balance (Sheldon et al., 2002). Empirical results indicate that participants already high on personality integration benefited the most from the program in terms of goal attainment, whereas participants with low levels of self-concordance did not profit from the program. Also the formation of *implementation intentions* specifying the where, when, and how of goal pursuit may further goal attainment (Gollwitzer, 1993; Koestner et al., 2002).

In the following we will highlight sample therapeutic approaches that attempt to influence goal processes at various levels. Whereas motivational change is at the core of psychodynamic approaches and these therapeutic approaches are rather well known (e.g., Luborsky & Crits-Christoph, 1998), we will focus here on more recent approaches for the treatment of emotional problems that explicitly target motivational change. First, we will describe Motivational Interviewing (MI; Miller & Rollnick, 2002), an approach that combines various motivational strategies to further treatment motivation and therapy outcome, as well as other approaches that aim at the resolution of patient ambivalence. Two approaches for the treatment of emotional disorders that explicitly work on motivational factors are Self-System Therapy (SST; Strauman et al., 2006) and Well-Being Therapy (WBT; Fava & Tomba, 2009). Another approach that focuses on motivational change as a main change mechanism and has been explicated for several psychological disorders is the Acceptance and Commitment Therapy (ACT; Hayes et al., 1999). Finally, in the field of personality disorders, Clarification Oriented Therapy targets motivational change for changing patients' dysfunctional interactional behaviors (Sachse, 2004).

Motivational Interviewing (MI; Miller & Rollnick, 2002) is both a treatment philosophy and a set of methods employed to help people increase intrinsic motivation by exploring and resolving ambivalence about behavioral change. MI is highly compatible with the therapeutic goal of fostering autonomous motivation for therapy (Ryan & Deci, 2008). In MI, the therapist neither persuades nor coerces patients to change, but instead attempts to explore and resolve the patients' ambivalence, allowing them to decide for themselves about whether wanting to change or not (Ryan & Deci, 2008). When working with ambivalence and resulting resistance against change, the therapist supports the patient by confronting, exploring, and challenging introjected past experiences of conditional regard (Assor, Roth, & Deci, 2004). Such introjects may, for example, hinder a patient from disclosing his or her feelings to the therapist out of fear of disapproval. By providing an autonomy-supportive atmosphere, the MI therapist helps his or her patient find an internal source of motivation that guides and fuels his or her future change efforts (Markland, Ryan, Tobin, & Rollnick, 2005). The therapist tries to improve intrinsic motivation by helping the patient become the primary agent of change (Arkowitz & Westra, 2009). Initially, MI was established in the area of alcohol and other substance abuse (Miller & Rollnick, 2002), and more recently it has been used in the context of a wider range of clinical problems (see Buckner, 2009, for a review).

Patients may experience ambivalence not only regarding therapeutic change but also in other parts of their lives (e.g., the continuation of a marriage, finding a new job, etc.). Several methods are available to psychotherapists to help their patients deal with or resolve their ambivalences. A very pragmatic approach to this purpose is the work with the Decision Cube. More general interventions to change patient ambivalence are the Two-Chair-Exercise and the Decision-Fostering Intervention. The basis for the application of the Decision Cube is to assist the patient in making a deliberate decision for or against beginning psychotherapy. For this purpose, the intervention helps the patient to clarify the respective advantages and disadvantages of beginning psychotherapy (or not) using a 2 x 2 matrix. The therapist tries to activate the goals involved but takes an absolutely neutral stance toward the options. It is assumed that an autonomous decision to begin psychotherapy will lead to a greater commitment and endurance. The aim of the *two-chair-exercise* is to create awareness of both sides of an ambivalent experience and to prepare the two "split" sides for a later integration. As mentioned, this ambivalence may concern other ambivalences than starting a treatment. For this purpose, each of the two chairs used reflects one side of the ambivalence. The therapist actively guides the patient to activate and express the thoughts, feelings, and action tendencies of the different sides of the self by requesting the patient to switch chairs, whenever the patient assumes one respective side of the ambivalence. After some dialogue between the two sides, usually conflict/ambivalence weakens and the patient comes closer to a decision that integrates the two competing sides of himself or herself.

The Decision-Fostering Intervention (DFI) is a structured short group intervention aimed at motivating patients to actively participate in personal change. Central to the intervention is to frame the motivational problem as a decisional problem. DFI consists of the following successive parts: *Evaluation and Prioritization, Justification,* and *Planning*. In the *Evaluation and Prioritization* phases, patients imagine the change process, the range of possible outcomes, along with their own emotional reactions, the reactions of their significant others, and then subsequently prioritize their behavioral options. In the *Justification* phase, patients are asked to choose a decision and justify their decision in front of the group, while the therapist assumes the position of a (friendly) devil's advocate that the patient needs to convince. This dispute will lead to a *Decisional Statement* that the patient and therapist fixate in writing with the general structure: "I want to do X, because the consequence Y is more important to me than the consequence Z." To foster the *Presence* of the decision, the patients find a symbol for the decision (picture, posture, movement, etc.) and place it in a highly visible or noticeable position in their daily lives. In the *Planning* phase, patients plan the implementation of their decision by defining the where, when, and how of the associated actions, anticipate likely obstacles, and generate adequate responses. In addition, patients plan the specifics of *coming out* with their decision to significant others, and write these plans down. The therapist in DFI closely monitors and guides the patient through the process of decision formation, up to the implementation of the formulated decision.

Self-System Therapy (SST) has been developed by Strauman and colleagues (Strauman et al., 2006; Vieth et al., 2003) based on a model of depression as a disorder of motivation and goal pursuit resulting from chronic failure to attain certain kinds of personal goals. In an earlier study, Strauman et al. (2001) had found that various empirically supported treatments (cognitive therapy, CT; Beck, Rush, Shaw, & Emery, 1979; Beck, 1995), interpersonal psychotherapy (Klerman, Weissman, Rounsaville, & Chevron, 1984), and pharmacotherapy with selective serotonin reuptake inhibitors were less effective for depressed patients with chronic self-perceived failure in promotion goal pursuit than for other patients. According to Regulatory Focus Theory (RFT; Higgins, 1989), promotion goals are aimed at making good things happen, whereas prevention goals are aimed at preventing bad things from happening. If this subgroup of depressed patients was vulnerable to depression because of inadequate socialization toward pursuing promotion goals, then SST interventions to enhance promotion goal pursuit might help them recover from depression more completely. Strauman et al. (2006) summarized SST in four questions directed to the patient: "What are your promotion and prevention goals? What are you doing to try to attain them? What is keeping you from making progress? What can you do differently?" (Strauman et al., 2006, p. 368). To improve the patient's pursuit of promotion goals, SST flexibly combines techniques from other empirically supported psychotherapies, including cognitive therapy, interpersonal psychotherapy, and behavioral activation therapy in the service of improved goal pursuit. In a randomized trial comparing SST with cognitive therapy (CT) in a sample of 45 patients with depression, SST and CBT on average showed equal efficacy between treatments, but patients whose socialization history lacked an emphasis on promotion goals showed significantly greater improvement with SST (Strauman et al., 2006).

Well-Being Therapy (WBT; Fava & Tomba, 2009) is based on Ryff's cognitive model of psychological well-being (Ryff, 1989), which proposes six dimensions of psychological well-being: environmental mastery, personal growth, purpose in life, autonomy, self-acceptance, and positive relations with others. Although labeled as *dimensions of well-being*, these dimensions are very similar to other motivational constructs, for example, the dimensions of goal satisfaction (Grosse Holtforth & Grawe, 2003). A WBT therapist strives to help the patient achieve better well-being on all six dimensions to increase resilience (Fava, 1999; Fava & Ruini, 2003). To reach this goal, WBT integrates psychological techniques from various sources within a short-term format (8–12 sessions), that is, cognitive restructuring, scheduling of activities, and assertiveness training, and problem solving in addition to self-observation of positive experiences.

In early therapy the therapist helps the patient to develop skills to continuously attend to positive aspects of daily experience or positive emotions using structured diaries. Subsequently the therapist helps the patient to identify thoughts and beliefs leading to premature interruption of well-being by self-observation, and the therapist challenges these thoughts (Beck et al., 1979). In parallel, the therapist reinforces and encourages activities that are likely to elicit well-being by graded task assignments. In the final sessions, the therapist instructs the patient to self-monitor the course of episodes of well-being and optimize behaviors aiming at the attainment and preservation of well-being. WBT can be applied as a stand-alone therapy or as an addition to other forms of psychotherapy or pharmacotherapy. However, WBT is considered most appropriate for treating nonacute depression to address aspects that have been omitted by other approaches (Fava & Tomba, 2009). In an empirical test of WBT, 20 patients with depressive and/or anxiety disorders (major depression, panic disorder with agoraphobia, social phobia, generalized anxiety disorder, obsessive compulsive disorder) who had been successfully treated by behavioral (anxiety disorders) or pharmacological (mood disorders) methods were randomly assigned to either WBT or cognitive-behavioral therapy (CBT). Whereas both therapies showed a significant reduction of residual symptoms as well as increase in psychological well-being, WBT showed a significantly greater reduction of residual symptoms immediately after treatment (Fava & Tomba, 2009).

Acceptance and Commitment Therapy (ACT; Bach & Hayes, 2002; Hayes et al., 1999) focuses on reducing experiential avoidance, which is considered a pathological factor. Avoiding private experiences (i.e., certain thoughts, feelings, or body sensations) is assumed to result in failure to behave in a way that is in accord with one's values. As the acronym ACT indicates, patients learn to Accept their reactions and be present, Choose a valued direction, and Take action in order to develop more psychological flexibility (Hayes et al., 1999). Patients are guided to face and overcome experiential avoidance by learning to perceive their inner experiences (thoughts, images, emotions, memories etc.) without any evaluation, by allowing and accepting them to come and go without resisting them, by experiencing the here and now with openness and interest, and by observing the processes within the self. The therapist focuses on values by helping the patient to discover what he or she considers most important in life, to set goals according to these values, and to carry them out. A characteristic of ACT that distinguishes it from, for example, CBT is that ACT focuses less on symptom reduction than on empowering patients to pursue their goals in accordance with their important values. ACT has shown significant effects with a variety of clinical disorders and problems; however, the body of well-controlled studies does not suffice yet to conclude that ACT is generally more effective than other active treatments (Hayes, Luoma, Bond, Masuda, & Lillis, 2006). For example, Forman, Herbert, Moitra, Yeomans, and Geller (2007) found in a randomized controlled effectiveness trial of ACT and CT for anxiety and depression that patients in CT and ACT showed large and equivalent improvements in depression, anxiety, and other outcomes. However, the mechanisms of action differed between the therapies; in CT observing and describing one's experiences mediated outcomes for patients in the CT, whereas experiential avoidance, acting with awareness and acceptance, mediated outcomes for those in the ACT group.

Personality disorders can be characterized by the interpersonal problems the patients experience. According to the interpersonal theory of personality disorders, salient frustrated motives are the potential reasons underlying interpersonal problems (Horowitz, 2004). Accordingly in Horowitz's (2004; Horowitz et al., 2006) *model of interpersonal motives*, a person with a certain personality disorder is assumed to feel frustrated with respect to some salient motive. For example, for patients with a narcissistic personality disorder, the assumed organizing motive is the unrestricted admiration by other people. Consequently, narcissistic people may show behaviors like bragging about their exceptional achievements. As a result, they often appear rather arrogant and repel other people, so that the person reports characteristic recurring cognitions, fears, and interpersonal problems, which are described as the diagnostic criteria in the *DSM-IV-TR*. In response to failures to satisfy the predominant interpersonal motive, a person with a personality disorder may experience negative emotions, show maladaptive behavioral strategies (e.g., oversensitive counterattacks), or retreat to maladaptive coping strategies (e.g., abusing drugs or alcohol). Consequently, the goal of motivation-focused interventions for personality disorders according to Horowitz's model is to change problematic interpersonal behavior by changing the assumedly underlying motivational structure. This should lead to more adaptive interpersonal strategies and behaviors that, in turn, should lead to a better satisfaction of the full range of the person's goals.

Sachse (2010) proposed a conceptualization and treatment of personality disorders (Clarification-Oriented Psychotherapy, COP-PD) that is compatible with these assumptions. Like Horowitz (2004), Sachse (2010) assumed that over their lives, people with personality disorders have developed a preponderance of certain motives as well as dysfunctional interactional goals, strategies, behaviors, and cognitions for the satisfaction of these motives, which he calls *game structures*. These game structures (i.e., often manipulating and intransparent styles of interaction to force a partner to satisfy motives) constitute the characteristics of people with personality disorders. Thus, the actions of a patient with a personality disorder are governed by predominant motives as well as the developed game structures. In COP-PD, the therapist tries to help the patient explicate his or her interpersonal motives, change the associated dysfunctional interpersonal schemas (goals, strategies, and behaviors), and establish new need-satisfying motivational-behavioral patterns in real-life interactions. For example, with narcissistic patients, therapists attune their behavior to the assumed narcissistic motives by normalizing the patient's problems, maximally validating the patient's resources (but not the dysfunctional strategies), and cautiously directing attention to the discrepancy between the patient's self-doubts and his or her resources. This discrepancy in conjunction with awareness of the costs of the maladaptive behavior is assumed to fuel the patient's motivation for change. Subsequently, the therapist moves to reconstructing the schemas and to practicing new, more adaptive strategies and behaviors for motive satisfaction in real-life interactions with less adverse side effects. Clarification-Oriented Psychotherapy has been explicated also as a general strategy for other clinical disorders (Sachse, 2003).

Conclusion: A Motivationally Informed Psychotherapy

In the concluding section, we will try to summarize the implications of basic and clinical research for a motivationally informed psychotherapy. In a motivationally informed psychotherapy, psychotherapists are faced with at least two tasks: to help the patient change the factors maintaining his or her psychological disorder(s), and to foster conditions that support the patient's treatment motivation (see Schulte & Eifert, 2002).

A primary goal of psychotherapy is to decrease psychopathology and associated suffering. From a motivational perspective, the overall goal of psychotherapy can be defined more broadly as helping the patient to better satisfy his or her psychological needs, which should go along with better well-being and life satisfaction. Under this perspective, psychopathology is considered the principal source of psychological suffering that psychotherapy is supposed to change. However, part of the therapeutic enterprise may also be to assist the patient in accepting and coping with problems that are unchangeable, such as losses of significant others or one's own limitations as, for example, caused by physical disabilities.

To optimally be aware of, use, and change motivational factors in psychotherapy, a therapist has various options for assessing motivational constructs. For reasons of practicality, the therapist will use observational, interview, or questionnaire methods of assessment most likely in conjunction with anamnestic information, rather than more stringent yet time-consuming methods of assessing implicit motives. Motivational constructs that the therapist may assess at intake are therapy motivation, values, personal goals, motivational conflicts, and treatment goals. If the therapist wants to use motive-related measures for quality assurance purposes, the improvement of goal satisfaction may be the central construct to assess (Grosse Holtforth & Grawe, 2004).

For a motivation-focused case formulation, it will be central to get a clear picture of which approach goals the patient deems important, which avoidance goals he or she dreads most strongly, how strong the suffering from goal dissatisfaction is, which goals the patient cannot satisfy enough, and what the sources of the dissatisfaction are. The sources of lacking goal satisfaction may be heterogeneous, such as marital problems, academic failure, and discrimination at work. Motivational sources of goal dissatisfaction may be approach goals that are too strong (e.g., very high standards for personal achievement) or too strong avoidance goals (e.g., being very easily hurt by critical remarks of others). Additionally, goal conflicts or ambivalences may be powerful sources of goal dissatisfaction (e.g., being ambivalent about ending the relationship to an alcoholic spouse may

seriously hamper the patient's wishes to be in control of one's life). Goal satisfaction may also be hindered if the person has not developed adequate strategies for goal satisfaction (e.g., bragging behavior of narcissists). A motive-oriented treatment plan will then outline motive-related ways to improve the conditions for change as well as ways to change motivational factors that contribute to lacking goal satisfaction.

The therapist can create favorable conditions for change by fostering a good therapy relationship via motivational attunement and by formulating adequate therapy goals. As shown earlier, motivational attunement aims at strengthening the working alliance by attuning to the patient's most important approach goals, by avoiding to inadvertently activate avoidance goals, as well as using the motivational information to understand and resolve occurring alliance ruptures. The treatment goals that the patient and therapist agree on at the outset of treatment should concretize the directions the therapy should take for satisfying the patient's personal goals. If a patient experiences difficulties in formulating clear treatment goals, strategies of goal imagery and goal concretization (e.g., EPOS) may help the patient to get a clearer picture of what he or she wants to achieve with the help of the therapist. The therapist will focus goal formulation on positive outcomes associated with the planned changes and define goals that correspond well with the patient's values and motives and are compatible with each other.

Treatment goals should be formulated as approach goals ("I will be able to confront my boss assertively when I disagree") instead of avoidance goals ("I no longer avoid confronting my boss when I disagree"), should be controllable and attainable, should be formulated as concretely as possible, and the criteria for goal attainment should be explicitly stated. Well-chosen and well-formulated therapy goals will strengthen the patient's commitment and endurance in goal striving and participation in therapy. Goal attainment promises to be most likely if the patient develops clear intentions for goal attainment, as well as implementation intentions. Strategies like "Own the goal," "Make it fun," "Remember the big picture," or "Keep a balance" may help the patient in the process of goal striving (Sheldon et al., 2002, pp. 14–15).

To facilitate change, therapists may also question potential defensive justifications for preserving old goals and behaviors (Karoly, 2006). Another powerful force working against new goal striving may be the influence of *automaticity*. Patients may make the experience that "old" maladaptive behaviors or feelings are automatically triggered by situational cues. Such reactions may especially arise in situations that the patient previously dreaded and avoided. The therapist will need to make these automatized associations consciously accessible to the patient and work with the patient on accepting (not avoiding) his or her own aversive experiences. The sequence of awareness, acceptance, and new reactions/new behaviors will have to be repeatedly run through with the patient to result in more sustainable change. Such a training of deautomatizing previously automatic dysfunctional reactions and behaviors will help the patient to recognize and override the effects of automaticity in service of pursuing more need-satisfying goals (Karoly, 2006). An important factor to consider is the context of goal striving. The more the patient's social network supports the patient's goals, the more likely the patient will reach them. Depending on how changeable patient and therapist perceive the level of support for his or her goals, either couple, family, or systemic interventions will be indicated for trying to change the level of support.

We have highlighted several therapeutic approaches that attempt to influence goal processes at various levels. Motivational Interviewing as well as other techniques (Decision Cube, Two-Chair exercise, Decision-Fostering Interventions) are suited to change patient ambivalence toward treatment as well other forms of ambivalence. Both Self-System Therapy and Well-Being Therapy are designed to improve goal and need satisfaction in acutely or chronically depressed patients, respectively, with varying emphases. Acceptance and Commitment Therapy emphasizes overcoming experiential avoidance by accepting unpleasant experiences, developing clear values guiding one's actions, and trying to efficiently pursue one's goals. Clarification-Oriented Therapy for personality disorders intends to improve the patient's need and goal satisfaction by raising awareness for dysfunctional interactional strategies and behaviors and attempting to change these strategies and behaviors.

We hope to have demonstrated the centrality of motivational factors in psychotherapy, either as facilitators of change or as targets of change. Motivational considerations and interventions may be used in all kinds of psychotherapy and have a great potential for helping patients in overcoming their problems and living a happier and more satisfying life.

Future Research/Open Questions

As we have seen in this chapter, previous research on motivational factors in psychotherapy has already yielded findings that have great potential for advancing psychotherapy. However, as we have also seen, a multitude of questions remains to be investigated by future research. A few examples of such questions are as follows:

1. By which psychological mechanisms do motivational factors (treatment goals, motive satisfaction, conflicts, etc.) contribute to the development and maintenance of psychological disorders and problems? For example, how do the goals of patients with personality disorders influence their interpersonal behavior, and how does this behavior relate to the satisfaction of specific needs and goals?

2. Which motivation-focused interventions can foster motivational change, and how does this relate to therapy effectiveness? For example, is a treatment that fosters the formulation of well-formed therapy goals more effective than a treatment that does not?

3. Can therapists foster the quality of the therapeutic relationship by motivational attunement and does this improve therapy outcome? For example, do cognitive-behavioral therapists who try to tailor their interventions to the patient's motives attain better outcomes than therapists who do not?

4. What are the motivational mechanisms of change in psychotherapeutic treatments of various orientations? For example, how does the intensity of avoidance motivation change in cognitive-behavioral as compared to psychodynamic therapies?

5. Which motivational factors predict the process and outcome of psychotherapy, and how is this prediction mediated? For example, do high levels of ambivalence over the expression of emotion predict collaboration in treatment, and worse outcomes?

6. Do various psychotherapeutic approaches change explicit and implicit motivation differentially? What are the consequences for outcome? For example, do motivation-focused treatments change implicit motivational conflicts more effectively, and is this associated with longer-lasting improvements?

7. Do ethnically and culturally diverse groups of patients differ in motivational factors (values, treatment goals, response to motivational

interventions), how does this affect treatment, and how should practicing psychotherapists tailor their interventions to the ethnical backgrounds of their patients? For example, can clarification-focused interventions be applied similarly with Swiss patients with Asian background as with Moroccan patients with sub-Saharan African background, and which adaptations are necessary?

8. Which brain areas are associated with motivational characteristics of psychotherapy patients and how do they change over treatment? For example, can intense avoidance motivation be localized in the brain, and is change in avoidance motivation over therapy associated with changes in these brain areas?

Generally, future research on motivational factors would profit from a more frequent use of experimental methods, as well as causal hypotheses using longitudinal designs.

References

Ackerman, S. J., & Hilsenroth, M. J. (2001). A review of therapist characteristics and techniques negatively impacting the therapeutic alliance. *Psychotherapy: Theory, Research, Practice, Training, 38*, 171–185.

Alexander, F., & French, T. M. (1946). *Psychoanalytic therapy. Principles and applications*. New York: Wiley.

Arkowitz, H., & Westra, H. A. (2009). Introduction to the special series on motivational interviewing and psychotherapy. *Journal of Clinical Psychology, 65*, 1149–1155.

Arnow, B. A., & Castonguay, L. G. (1996). Treatment goals and strategies of cognitive-behavioral and psychodynamic therapists: A naturalistic investigation. *Journal of Psychotherapy Integration, 6*, 333–347.

Assor, A., Roth, G., & Deci, E. L. (2004). The emotional costs of parents' conditional regard: A self-determination theory analysis. *Journal of Personality, 72*, 47–88.

Austin, J. T., & Vancouver, J. B. (1996). Goal constructs in psychology: Structure, process, and content. *Psychological Bulletin, 120*, 338–375.

Bach, P., & Hayes, S. C. (2002). The use of acceptance and commitment therapy to prevent rehospitalization of psychotic patients. A randomized controlled trail. *Journal of Consulting and Clinical Psychology, 70*, 1129–1139.

Beck, A. T., Rush, A. J., Shaw, B. F., & Emery, G. (1979). *Cognitive therapy of depression*. New York: Guilford Press.

Beck, J. S. (1995). *Cognitive therapy: Basics and beyond*. New York: Guilford Press.

Berking, M., Grosse Holtforth, M., & Jacobi, C. (2003). Reduction of incongruence in inpatient psychotherapy. *Clinical Psychology and Psychotherapy, 10*, 86–92.

Berking, M., Grosse Holtforth, M., Jacobi, C., & Kröner-Herwig, B. (2005). Empirically based guidelines for goal-finding procedures in psychotherapy. *Psychotherapy Research, 15*, 316–324.

Bordin, E. S. (1979). The generalizability of the psycho-analytic concept of the working alliance. *Psychotherapy: Theory, Research, and Practice, 16*, 252–260.

Brunstein, J. C. (1993). Personal goals and subjective well-being: A longitudinal study. *Journal of Personality and Social Psychology, 65*, 1061–1070.

Brunstein, J. C. (1999). Persönliche Ziele und subjektives Wohlbefinden bei älteren Menschen [Personal goals and subjective well-being in elderly persons]. *Zeitschrift für Differentielle und Diagnostische Psychologie, 20*, 58–71.

Brunstein, J., Dangelmayer, G., & Schultheiss, O. (1996). Personal goals and social support in close relationships: Effects on relationship mood and marital satisfaction. *Journal of Personality and Social Psychology, 71*, 1006–1019.

Brunstein, J., & Maier, G. W. (2002). Das Streben nach persönlichen Zielen: Emotionales Wohlbefinden und proaktive Entwicklung über die Lebensspanne [Striving for personal goals: Emotional well-being and proactive development during the lifespan]. In H. Thomae (Ed.), *Persönlichkeit und Entwicklung* [Personality and development] (pp. 157–189). Weinheim, Germany: Beltz Verlag.

Brunstein, J. C., & Schmitt, C. H. (2004). Assessing individual differences in achievement motivation with the Implicit Association Test. *Journal of Research in Personality, 38*, 536–555.

Brunstein, J. C., Schultheiss, O. C., & Graessmann, R. (1998). Personal goals and emotional well-being: The moderating role of motive dispositions. *Journal of Personality and Social Psychology, 75*, 494–508.

Brunstein, J., Schultheiss, O., & Maier, G. W. (1999). The pursuit of personal goals: A motivational approach to well-being and life adjustment. In J. Brandstädter (Ed.), *Action self-development: Theory and research through the life span* (pp. 169–196). Thousand Oaks, CA: Sage.

Buckner, J. D. (2009). Motivation enhancement therapy can increase utilization of cognitive-behavioral therapy: The case of social anxiety disorder. *Journal of Clinical Psychology, 65*, 1195–1206.

Calnan, M. (1987). *Health and illness. The lay perspective*. London: Tavistock.

Cantor, N. (1990). From thought to behavior: "Having" and "doing" in the study of personality and cognition. *American Psychologist, 45*, 735–750.

Carver, C. S., & Scheier, M. F. (1996). *Perspectives on personality* (3rd. ed.). Needham Heights, MA: Allyn & Bacon.

Caspar, F. (2007). *Beziehungen und Probleme verstehen. Eine Einführung in die psychotherapeutische Plananalyse* [Understanding relationships and problems: Introduction into Plan Analysis] (3rd. ed.). Bern, Switzerland: Huber.

Caspar, F., & Grosse Holtforth, M. (2010). Klaus Grawe: On a constant quest for a truly integrative and research-based psychotherapy. In L. G. Castonguay, J. C. Muran, L. Angus, J. A. Hayes, N. Ladany, & T. Anderson (Eds.), *Bringing psychotherapy research to life* (pp. 113–123). Washington, DC: American Psychological Association.

Caspar, F., Grossmann, C., Unmüssig, C., & Schramm, E. (2005). Complementary therapeutic relationship: Therapist behavior, interpersonal patterns, and therapeutic effects. *Psychotherapy Research, 15*, 91–102.

Chulef, A. S., Read, S. J., & Walsh, D. A. (2001). A hierarchical taxonomy of human goals. *Motivation and Emotion, 25*, 191–232.

Cohen, P., & Cohen, J. (1996). *Life values and adolescent mental health*. Mahwah, NJ: Erlbaum.

Cohen, P., & Cohen, J. (2001). Life values and mental health in adolescence. In P. Schmuck & K. M. Sheldon (Eds.), *Life goals and well-being: Towards a positive psychology of human striving* (pp. 167–181). Seattle, WA: Hogrefe.

Cox, W. M., & Klinger, E. (1988). A motivational model of alcohol use. *Journal of Abnormal Psychology, 97,* 168–180.

Cox, W. M., & Klinger, E. (1990). Incentive motivation, affective change, and alcohol use: A model. In W. M. Cox (Ed.), *Why people drink: Parameters of alcohol as a reinforcer* (pp. 291–314). New York: Amereon Press.

Cox, W. M., & Klinger, E. (2002). Motivational structure relationships with substance use and processes of change. *Addictive Behaviors, 27,* 925–940.

Cox, W. M., Klinger, E., & Blount, J. P. (1999). *Systematic motivational counseling: A treatment manual.* Manual available from W. M. Cox, Professor of The Psychology of Addictive Behaviours, School of Psychology, Bangor University, UK.

Cox, W. M., Schippers, G. M., Klinger, E., Skutle, A., Stuchlikova, I., Man, F., King, A. L., & Inderhaug, R. (2002). Motivational structure and alcohol use in university students with consistency across nations. *Journal of Studies on Alcohol, 63,* 280–285.

Crits-Christoph, P., Connolly Gibbons, M. B., Crits-Christoph, K., Narducci, J., Schamberger, M., & Gallop, R. (2006). Can therapists be trained to improve their alliances? A pilot study of Alliance-Fostering Therapy. *Psychotherapy Research, 13,* 268–281.

Deci, E. L., & Ryan, R. M. (1985). *Intrinsic motivation and self-determination in human behavior.* New York: Plenum Press.

Deci, E. L., & Ryan, R. M. (1995). Human autonomy: The basis for true self-esteem. In M. Kernis (Ed.), *Efficacy, agency, and self-esteem* (pp. 31–49). New York: Plenum Press.

Deci, E. L., & Ryan, R. M. (2002). *Handbook of self-determination research.* Rochester, NY: University of Rochester Press.

Dickson, J. M., & MacLeod, A. K. (2004). Anxiety, depression, and approach and avoidance goals. *Cognition and Emotion, 18,* 423–430.

Dimsdale, J. E. (1975). Goals of therapy on psychiatric inpatient units. *Social Psychiatry, 10,* 1–7.

Dimsdale, J. E., Klerman, G., & Shershow, J. C. (1979). Conflict in treatment goals between patients and staff. *Social Psychiatry, 14,* 1–14.

Dirmaier, J., Harfst, T., Koch, U., & Schulz, H. (2006). Therapy goals in inpatient psychotherapy: Differences between diagnostic groups and psychotherapeutic orientations. *Clinical Psychology and Psychotherapy, 13,* 34–46.

Driessen, M., Sommer, B., Röstel, C., Malchow, C. P., Rumpf, H-J., & Adam, B. (2001). Therapieziele in der Psychologischen Medizin: Stand der Forschung und Entwicklung eines standardisierten Instruments. [Treatment goals in psychological medicine: State of research and development of standardized instruments]. *Zeitschrift für Psychotherapie, Psychosomatik und Medizinische Psychologie, 51,* 239–245.

Elliot, A. J. (2008). *Handbook of approach and avoidance motivation.* New York: Psychology Press.

Elliot, A. J. & Friedman R. (2007). Approach-avoidance: A central characteristic of personal goals. In B. R. Little, K. Salmela-Aro, & S. D. Philips (Eds.), *Personal project pursuit: Goals, action, and human flourishing* (pp. 97–118). Hillsdale, NJ: Erlbaum.

Emmons, R. A. (1986). Personal strivings: An approach to personality and subjective well-being. *Journal of Personality and Social Psychology, 51,* 1058–1068.

Emmons, R. A. (1996). Striving and feeling, personal goals and subjective well-being. In J. A. Bargh (Ed.), *The psychology of action: Linking cognition and motivation to behavior* (pp. 313–337). New York: Guilford Press.

Emmons, R. A., & Kaiser, H. A. (1996). Goal orientation and emotional well-being: Linking goals and affect through the self. In A. Tesser (Ed.), *Striving and feeling: Interactions among goals, affects, and self-regulation* (pp. 79–98). Hillsdale, NJ: Erlbaum.

Emmons, R. A., & King, L. A. (1988). Conflict among personal strivings: Immediate and long-term implications for psychological and physical well-being. *Journal of Personality and Social Psychology, 54,* 1040–1048.

Epstein, S. (1990). Cognitive-experiential self-theory. In L. A. Pervin (Ed.), *Handbook of personality: Theory and research* (pp. 165–192). New York: Guilford.

Faller, H., & Goßler, S. (1998). Probleme und Ziele von Psychotherapiepatienten [Problems and goals of psychotherapy patients]. *Psychotherapie, Psychosomatik, Medizinische Psychologie, 48,* 176–186.

Fava, G. A. (1999). Well-being therapy. *Psychotherapy and Psychosomatics, 68,* 171–178.

Fava, G. A., & Ruini, C. (2003). Development and characteristics of a well-being enhancing psychotherapeutic strategy: Well-being therapy. *Journal of Behavior Therapy and Experimental Psychiatry, 34,* 45–63.

Fava, G. A., & Tomba, E. (2009). Increasing psychological well-being and resilience by psychotherapeutic methods. *Journal of Personality, 77,* 1903–1934.

Flanagan, C. M. (2010). The case for needs in psychotherapy. *Journal of Psychotherapy Integration, 20,* 1–36.

Ford, M. E., & Nichols, C. W. (1991). Using goal assessments to identify motivational patterns and facilitate behavioral regulation and achievement. In M. L. Maehr & P. R. Pintrich (Eds.), *Advances in motivation and achievement.* (Vol. 7, pp. 51–84). Greenwich, CT: JAI.

Forman, E. M., Herbert, J. D., Moitra, E., Yeomans, P. D., & Geller, P. A. (2007). A randomized controlled therapy and cognitive therapy for anxiety and depression. *Behaviour Modification, 31,* 772–799.

Goldfried, M. R. (1980). Toward the delineation of therapeutic change principles. *American Psychologist, 35,* 991–999.

Gollwitzer, P. M. (1993). Goal achievement: The role of intentions. *European Review of Social Psychology, 4,* 141–185.

Gollwitzer, P. M., & Brandstätter, V. (1997). Implementation intentions and effective goal pursuit. *Journal of Personality and Social Psychology, 73,* 186–199.

Grawe, K. (1997). Research-informed psychotherapy. *Psychotherapy Research, 7,* 1–20.

Grawe, K. (2004). *Psychological therapy.* Cambridge, MA: Hogrefe.

Greenwald, A. G., McGhee, D. E., & Schwartz, J. L. K. (1998). Measuring individual differences in implicit cognition: The Implicit Association Test. *Journal of Personality and Social Psychology, 74,* 1464–1480.

Grosse Holtforth, M. (2001). Was möchten Patienten in ihrer Therapie erreichen?—Die Erfassung von Therapiezielen mit dem Berner Inventar für Therapieziele (BIT) [What do patients want to accomplish in psychotherapy?—Assessment and classification of treatment-goal themes with the Bern Inventory of Treatment Goals (BIT)]. *Verhaltenstherapie und psychosoziale Praxis, 33,* 241–258.

Grosse Holtforth, M. (2008). Avoidance motivation in psychological problems and psychotherapy. *Psychotherapy Research, 18,* 147–159.

Grosse Holtforth, M., Bents, H., Mauler, B., & Grawe, K. (2006). Interpersonal distress as a mediator between avoidance goals and goal satisfaction in psychotherapy inpatients. *Clinical Psychology and Psychotherapy*, 13, 172–182.

Grosse Holtforth, M., & Castonguay, L. G. (2005). Relationship and techniques in CBT—A motivational approach. *Psychotherapy: Theory, Research, Practice, Training*, 42, 443–455.

Grosse Holtforth, M., & Grawe, K. (2000). Fragebogen zur Analyse Motivationaler Schemata (FAMOS) [Questionnaire for the analysis of motivational schemata]. *Zeitschrift für Klinische Psychologie und Psychotherapie: Forschung und Praxis*, 29, 170–179.

Grosse Holtforth, M., & Grawe, K. (2002). Bern inventory or treatment goals: Part 1: Development and first application of a taxonomy of treatment goal themes. *Psychotherapy Research*, 12, 79–99.

Grosse Holtforth, M., & Grawe, K. (2003). Der Inkongruenzfragebogen (INK)—Ein Messinstrument zur Analyse motivationaler Inkongruenz [Questionnaire for assessing incongruence—an instrument for analysis of motivational incongruence]. *Zeitschrift für Klinische Psychologie und Psychotherapie*, 32, 315–323.

Grosse Holtforth, M., & Grawe, K. (2004). Inkongruenz und Fallkonzeption in der Psychologischen Therapie [Incongruence and case formulations in psychological therapy]. *Verhaltenstherapie und psychosoziale Praxis*, 36, 9–21.

Grosse Holtforth, M., Grawe, K., & Castonguay, L. G. (2006). Predicting a reduction of avoidance motivation in psychotherapy: Toward the delineation of differential processes of change operating at different phases of treatment. *Psychotherapy Research*, 16, 639–644.

Grosse Holtforth, M., Grawe, K., Egger, O., & Berking, M. (2005). Reducing the dreaded: Change of avoidance motivation in psychotherapy. *Psychotherapy Research*, 15, 262–271.

Grosse Holtforth, M., Grawe, K., Fries, A., & Znoj, H. (2008). Inconsistency as a criterion for differential indication in psychotherapy: A randomized controlled trial. *Zeitschrift für Klinische Psychologie und Psychotherapie*, 37, 103–111.

Grosse Holtforth, M., Grawe, K., & Tamcan, Ö. (2004). Der Inkongruenzfragebogen (INK)—Handanweisung [Questionnaire for assessing incongruence—manual]. Göttingen, Germany: Hogrefe.

Grosse Holtforth, M., Reubi, I., Ruckstuhl, L., Berking, M., & Grawe, K. (2004). The value of treatment goals in the outcome evaluation of psychiatric inpatients. *International Journal of Social Psychiatry*, 50, 80–91.

Grosse Holtforth, M., Wyss, T., Schulte, D., Trachsel, M., & Michalak, J. (2009). Some like it specific: The difference between treatment goals of anxious and depressed patients. *Psychology and Psychotherapy: Theory, Research and Practice*, 82, 279–290.

Hayes, S. C., Luoma, J., Bond, F., Masuda, A., & Lillis, J. (2006). Acceptance and commitment therapy. *Research and Therapy*, 44, 1–25.

Hayes, S. C., Strosahl, K. D., & Wilson, K. G. (1999). *Acceptance and commitment therapy: An experiential approach to behavior change.* New York: Guilford Press.

Heckhausen, H., Gollwitzer, P. M., & Weinert, F. E. (1987). *Jenseits des Rubikon: Der Wille in den Humanwissenschaften* [Beyond the Rubicon: The will in human sciences]. Berlin, Germany: Springer.

Heckhausen, J., & Heckhausen, H. (2008). *Motivation and action.* Cambridge University Press.

Heidenreich, T. (2000*). Intrapsychische Konflikte und Therapiemotivation in der Behandlung von Substanzabhängigkeit* [Intrapsychic conflict and therapy motivation in the treatment of substance abuse]. Regensburg, Germany: Roderer.

Heine, S. J., Proulx, T., & Vohs, K. D. (2006). The meaning maintenance model: On the coherence of social motivations. *Personality and Social Psychology Review*, 10, 88–110.

Higgins, E. T. (1989). Continuities and discontinuities in self-regulatory and self-evaluative processes: A developmental theory relating self and affect. *Journal of Personality*, 57, 407–444.

Hill, C. E., & Lambert, M. J. (2004). Methodological issues in studying psychotherapy process and outcomes. In M. J. Lambert (Ed.), *Handbook of psychotherapy and behavior change* (pp. 84–135). New York: Wiley.

Horowitz, L. M. (2004). *Interpersonal foundations of psychopathology.* Washington, DC: American Psychological Association.

Horowitz, L. M., Wilson, K. R., Turan, B., Zolotsev, P., Constantino, M. J., & Henderson, L. (2006). How interpersonal motives clarify the meaning of interpersonal behavior: A revised circumplex model. *Personality and Social Psychology Review*, 10, 67–86.

Horvath, A. O. (1995). The therapeutic relationship: From transference to alliance. *In Session: Psychotherapy in Practice*, 1, 7–18.

Hoyer, J., Fecht, J., Lauterbach, W., & Schneider, R. (2001). Changes in conflict, symptoms, and well-being during psychodynamic and cognitive-behavioral alcohol inpatient treatment. *Psychotherapy and Psychosomatics*, 70, 209–215.

Job, V., & Brandstätter, V. (2009). Get a taste of your goals: Promoting motive-goal congruence through affect-focus goal fantasy. *Journal of Personality*, 77, 1527–1560.

Karoly, P. (1999). A goal systems-self-regulatory perspective on personality, psychopathology, and change. *Review of General Psychology*, 3, 264–291.

Karoly, P. (2006). Tracking the leading edge of self-regulatory failure: Commentary on "Where do we go from here? The goal perspective in psychotherapy." *Clinical Psychology Science and Practice*, 13, 366–370.

Karoly, P., & Ruehlman, L. S. (1995). Goal cognition and its clinical implications: Development and preliminary validation of four motivational assessment instruments. *Assessment*, 2, 113–129.

Kasser, T., & Ryan, R. M. (1993). A dark side of the American dream: Correlates of financial success as a central life aspiration. *Journal of Personality and Social Psychology*, 65, 410–422.

Kasser, T., & Ryan, R. M. (1996). Further examining the American dream: Differential correlates of intrinsic and extrinsic goals. *Personality and Social Psychology Bulletin*, 22, 280–287.

Kasser, T., & Ryan, R. M. (2001). Be careful of what you wish for: Optimal functioning and the relative attainment of intrinsic and extrinsic goals. In P. Schmuck & K. M. Sheldon (Eds.), *Life goals and well-being: towards a positive psychology of human striving* (pp. 116–131). Seattle, WA: Hogrefe.

Kiresuk, T. J., Smith, A., & Cardillo, J. E. (1994). *Goal Attainment Scaling: Applications, theory, and measurement.* Hillsdale, NJ: Erlbaum.

Klappheck, M. A., & Michalak, J. (2009). Patientenziele und Therapieerfolg [Patients' goals and treatment outcome]. *Zeitschrift für Klinische Psychologie und Psychotherapie*, 38, 24–33.

Klerman, G. L., Weissman, M. M., Rounsaville, B. J., & Chevron, E. S. (1984). *Interpersonal psychotherapy of depression.* New York: Basic Books.

Klinger, E. (1977). *Meaning and void: Inner experience and the incentives in people's lives*. Minneapolis: University of Minnesota Press.

Klinger, E. (1987). The Interview Questionnaire technique: Reliability and validity of a mixed idiographic-nomothetic measure of motivation. In J. N. Butcher & C. D. Spielberger (Eds.), *Advances in personality assessment* (Vol. 6., pp. 31–48). Hillsdale, NJ: Lawrence Erlbaum Associates.

Klinger, E., Barta, S. G., & Maxeiner, M. E. (1980). Motivational correlates of thought content frequency and commitment. *Journal of Personality and Social Psychology, 39*, 1222–1237.

Koestner, R., Lekes, N., Powers, T. A., & Chicoine, E. (2002). Attaining personal goals: Self-concordance plus implementation equals success. *Journal of Personality and Social Psychology, 83*, 231–244.

Kunkel, M. A., & Newsom, S. (1996). Presenting problems for mental health services: A concept map. *Journal of Mental Health Counseling, 18*, 53–63.

Lecci, L., Karoly, P., Briggs, C., & Kuhn, K. (1994). Specificity and generality of motivational components in depression: A personal projects analysis. *Journal of Abnormal Psychology, 103*, 404–408.

Lilienfeld, S. O., Wood, J. M., & Garb, H. N. (2000). The scientific status of projective techniques. *Psychological Science in the Public Interest, 1*, 27–66.

Little, B. R. (1983). Personal projects: A rational and method for investigation. *Environment and Behavior, 15*, 273–309.

Locke, K. D. (2000). Circumplex Scales of Interpersonal Values: Reliability, validity, and applicability to interpersonal problems and personality disorders. *Journal of Personality Assessment, 75*, 249–267.

Luborsky, L., & Crits-Christoph, P. (1998). *Understanding transference: The core conflictual relationship theme method* (2nd ed.). Washington, DC: American Psychological Association.

Maier, G. W., & Brunstein, J. C. (2001). The role of personal work goals in newcomers' job satisfaction and organizational commitment: A longitudinal analysis. *Journal of Applied Psychology, 86*, 1034–1042.

Man, F., Stuchlikova, I., & Klinger, E. (1998). Motivational structure of alcoholic and nonalcoholic Czech men. *Psychological Reports, 82*, 1091–1106.

Markland, D., Ryan, R. M., Tobin, V., & Rollnick, S. (2005). Motivational interviewing and self-determination theory. *Journal of Social and Clinical Psychology, 24*, 811–831.

Michalak, J. (2000). *Zielkonflikte im therapeutischen Prozess* [Goal conflicts in the therapeutic process]. Wiesbaden, Germany: Deutscher Universitätsverlag.

Michalak, J., & Grosse Holtforth, M. (2006). Where do we go from here? The goal perspective in psychotherapy. *Clinical Psychology Science and Practice, 13*, 346–365.

Michalak, J., Heidenreich, T., & Hoyer, J. (2011). Goal conflicts and goal integration: Theory, assessment, and clinical implications. In W. M. Cox & E. Klinger (Eds.), *Handbook of motivational counseling: Motivating people for change* (2nd. ed., pp. 89–107). London: Wiley

Michalak, J., Klappheck, M., & Kosfelder, J. (2004). Personal goals of psychotherapy patients: The intensity and the "why" of goal-motivated behavior and their implications for the therapeutic process. *Psychotherapy Research, 14*, 193–209.

Michalak, J., Kosfelder, J., Meyer, F., & Schulte, D. (2003). Messung des Therapieerfolgs—Veränderungsmessung oder retrospektive Erfolgsbeurteilung [Assessing treatment success- change scores or retrospective measures of success].

Zeitschrift für Klinische Psychologie und Psychotherapie, 32, 94–103.

Michalak, J., Püschel, O., Joormann, J., & Schulte, D. (2006). Implicit motives and explicit goals: Two distinctive modes of motivational functioning and their relations to psychopathology. *Clinical Psychology and Psychotherapy, 13*, 81–96.

Michalak, J., & Schulte, D. (2002). Zielkonflikte und Therapiemotivation [Goal conflicts and treatment motivation]. *Zeitschrift für Klinische Psychologie und Psychotherapie, 31*, 213–219.

Miller, A., & Thompson, A. (1973). Factor structure of a goal checklist for patients. *Psychological Reports, 32*, 497–498.

Miller, W. R., & Rollnick, S. (2002). *Motivational interviewing: Preparing people for change* (2nd ed.). New York: Guilford Press.

Oishi, S., & Diener, E. (2001). Goals, culture, and subjective well-being. *Personality and Social Psychology Bulletin, 27*, 1674–1682.

Orlinsky, D. E., Ronnestad, M. H., & Willutzki, U. (2004). Fifty years of process-outcome research: Continuity and change. In M. J. Lambert (Ed.), *Handbook of psychotherapy and behavior change* (pp. 307–389). New York: Wiley.

Pelletier, L. G., Tuson, K. M., & Haddad, N. K. (1997). Client motivation for therapy scale: A measure of intrinsic motivation, extrinsic motivation, and amotivation for therapy. *Journal of Personality Assessment, 68*, 414–435.

Pervin, L. A. (1990). *Handbook of personality: Theory and research.* New York: Guilford Press.

Philips, B. (2009). Comparing apples and oranges: How do patient characteristics and treatment goals vary between different forms of psychotherapy? *Psychology and Psychotherapy: Theory, Research and Practice, 82*, 323–336.

Pöhlmann, K. (1999). Persönliche Ziele: Ein neuer Ansatz zur Erfassung von Therapiezielen [Personal goals: A new approach for assessing treatment goals]. *Praxis Klinische Verhaltensmedizin und Rehabilitation, 45*, 14–20.

Polak, P. (1970). Patterns of discord: Goals of patients, therapists and community members. *Archives of General Psychiatry, 23*, 277–283.

Prochaska, J. O., DiClemente, C. C., & Norcross, J. C. (1992). In search of how people change. Applications to addictive behavior. *American Psychologist, 47*, 1002–1014.

Prochaska, J. O., & Norcross, J. C. (2001). Stages of change. *Psychotherapy: Theory, Research, Practice, Training, 38*, 443–448.

Püschel, O., Schulte, D., & Michalak, J. (2011). Be careful what you strive for. The significance of motive-goal-congruence for depressivity. *Clinical Psychology and Psychotherapy, 18*, 23–33.

Reiss, S., & Havercamp, S. M. (1998). Toward a comprehensive assessment of fundamental motivation: Factor structure of the Reiss Profiles. *Psychological Assessment, 10*, 97–106.

Rokeach, M. (1973). *The nature of human values.* New York: Free Press.

Ruehlman, L. S., & Wolchik, S. A. (1988). Personal goals and interpersonal support and hindrance as factors in psychological distress and well-being. *Journal of Personality and Social Psychology, 55*, 293–301.

Ryan, R. M. (2005). The development line of autonomy in the etiology, dynamics, and treatment of borderline personality disorders. *Development and Psychopathology, 17*, 987–1006.

Ryan, R. M., & Deci, E. L. (2000). Self-determination theory and the facilitation of intrinsic motivation, social development, and well-being. *American Psychologist, 55*, 68–78.

Ryan, R. M., & Deci, E. L. (2008). A self-determination theory approach to psychotherapy: The motivational basis for effective change. *Canadian Psychology, 49*, 186–193.

Ryan, R. M., Deci, E. L., Grolnick, W. S., & La Guardia, J. G. (2006). The significance of autonomy and autonomy support in psychological development and psychopathology. In D. Cicchetti & D. Cohen (Eds.), *Developmental psychopathology. Vol. 1: Theory and methods* (2nd ed., pp. 295–849). New York: Wiley.

Ryan, R. M., Plant, R. W., & O'Malley, S. (1995). Initial motivations for alcohol treatment: Relations with treatment involvement and dropout. *Addictive Behaviors, 20*, 279–297.

Ryan, R. M., Sheldon, K. M., Kasser, T., & Deci, E. L. (1996). All goals are not created equal: An organismic perspective on the nature of goals and their regulation. In P. M. Gollwitzer & J. A. Bargh (Eds.), *The psychology of action: Linking cognition and motivation to behavior* (pp. 7–26). New York: Guilford Press.

Ryff, C. D. (1989). Happiness is everything, or is it? Explorations on the meaning of psychological well-being. *Journal of Personality and Social Psychology, 6*, 1069–1081.

Sachse, R. (2003). *Klärungsorientierte Psychotherapie* [Clarification-Oriented Psychotherapy]. Göttingen, Germany: Hogrefe.

Sachse, R. (2004). *Persönlichkeitsstörungen* [Personality disorders]. Göttingen, Germany: Hogrefe.

Sachse, R. (2010). *Persönlichkeitsstörungen verstehen: Zum Umgang mit schwierigen Klienten* [Understanding personality disorders: Treating difficult patients]. Bonn, Germany: Psychiatrie-Verlag.

Safran, J. D., & Muran, J. C. (2000). *Negotiating the therapeutic alliance: A relational treatment guide.* New York: Guilford Press.

Schmuck, P., Kasser, T., & Ryan, R. M. (2000). Intrinsic and extrinsic goals: Their structure and relationship to well-being in German and U.S. college students. *Social Indicators Research, 50*, 225–241.

Schmuck, P., & Sheldon, K. M. (Eds.). (2001). *Life goals and well-being: towards a positive psychology of human striving.* Seattle, WA: Hogrefe.

Schneider, W. (1990). *Indikationen zur Psychotherapie. Anwendungsbereiche und Forschungsprobleme* [Indication for psychotherapy]. Weinheim, Germany: Beltz.

Schulte, D., & Eifert, G. H. (2002). What to do when manuals fail? The dual model of psychotherapy. *Clinical Psychology: Science and Practice, 9*, 312–328.

Schultheiss, O. C., & Brunstein, J. C. (1999). Goal imagery: Bridging the gap between implicit motives and explicit goals. *Journal of Personality, 67*, 1–38.

Scott, L., & O'Hara, M. W. (1993). Self-discrepancies in clinically anxious and depressed university students. *Journal of Abnormal Psychology, 102*, 282–287.

Sevincer, A. T., & Oettingen, G. (2009). Alcohol breeds empty goal commitments. *Journal of Abnormal Psychology, 118*, 623–633.

Sheldon, K. (2001). The self-concordance model of healthy goal striving: When personal goals correctly represent the person. In P. Schmuck & K. Sheldon (Eds.), *Life goals and well-being: Towards a positive psychology of human striving* (pp. 18–36). Seattle, WA: Hogrefe.

Sheldon, K., & Kasser, T. (1998). Pursuing personal goals: Skills enable progress but not all progress is beneficial. *Personality and Social Psychology Bulletin, 24*, 1319–1331.

Sheldon, K. M., Kasser, T., Smith, K., & Share, T. (2002). Personal goals and psychological growth: Testing an intervention to enhance goal attainment and personality integration. *Journal of Personality, 70*, 5–31.

Smith, C. P. (1992). *Motivation and personality: Handbook of thematic content analysis.* Cambridge, England: Cambridge University Press.

Stangier, U., Ukrow, U., Schermelleh-Engel, K., Grabe, M., & Lauterbach, W.(2007). Intrapersonal conflict in goals and values of patients with unipolar depression. *Psychotherapy and Psychosomatics, 76*, 162–170.

Strauman, T. J. (2002). Self-regulation and depression. *Self and Identity, 1*, 151–157.

Strauman, T. J., Koldon, G. G., Stromquist, V., Davis, N., Kwapil, L., Heerey, E., & Schneider, K. (2001). The effects of treatments for depression on perceived failure in self-regulation. *Cognitive Therapy and Research, 25*, 693–712.

Strauman, T. J., Vieth, A. Z., Merrill, K. A., Kolden, G. G., Woods, T. E., Klein, M. H.,...Kwapil, L. (2006). Self-system therapy as an intervention for self-regulatory dysfunction in depression: A randomized comparison with cognitive therapy. *Journal of Consulting and Clinical Psychology, 74*, 367–376.

Tamir, M., & Diener, E. (2008). Approach-avoidance goals and well-being: One size does not fit all. In A. Elliot (Ed.), *Handbook of approach and avoidance motivation* (pp. 415–430). New York: Psychology Press.

Thompson, H., & Zimmerman, R. (1969). Goals of counseling: Whose? When? *Journal of Counceling Psychology, 16*, 121–125.

Tryon, G. S., & Winograd, G. (2001). Goal consensus and collaboration. *Psychotherapy: Theory, Research, Practice, Training, 38*, 385–389.

Uebelacker, L. A., Battle, C. L., Friedman, M. A., Cardemil, E. V., Beevers, C. G., & Miller, I. W. (2008). The importance of interpersonal treatment goals for depressed inpatients. *Journal of Nervous and Mental Disease, 196*, 217–222.

Vieth, A., Strauman, T. J., Kolden, G., Woods, T., Michels, J., & Klein, M. H. (2003). Self-System Therapy: A theory-based psychotherapy for depression. *Clinical Psychology: Science and Practice, 10*, 245–268.

Wadsworth, M., & Ford, D. H. (1983). Assessment of personal goal hierachies. *Journal of Counseling Psychology, 39*, 514–526.

Watkins, E. (2011). Dysregulation in level of goal and action identification across psychological disorders. *Clinical Psychology Review, 31*, 260–278.

Wiese, B. S., & Freund, A. M. (2005). Goal progress makes one happy, or does it? Longitudinal findings from the work domain. *Journal of Occupational and Organizational Psychology, 78*, 287–304.

Willutzki, U., & Koban, C. (2004). Enhancing motivation for psychotherapy: The eloboration of positive perspectives (EPOS) to develop patients' goal structure. In W. M. Cox & E. Klinger (Eds.), *Motivating people to change: A handbook of motivational counseling* (pp. 337–256). London: Wiley.

Zuroff, D. C., Koestner, R., Moskowitz, D. S., McBride, C., Marshall, M., & Bagby, R. M. (2007). Autonomous motivation for therapy: A new common factor in brief treatments for depression. *Psychotherapy Research, 17*, 137–147.

Motivation in Education

Allan Wigfield, Jenna Cambria, *and* Jacquelynne S. Eccles

Abstract

In this chapter we discuss the nature of children's achievement motivation and how it develops over the school years. We focus on the competence-related belief, value, goal, interest, and intrinsic aspects of motivation that have been emphasized in much of the research on motivation. We then discuss how different aspects of classroom and school practices influence motivation, and how teacher–student relationships and peer relationships impact students' motivation. We next consider how school transitions influence students' motivation, describing important differences in the structure and organization of schools at different levels of schooling. In the final section we describe some recent intervention work to boost children's motivation in different ways. Suggestions for future research include how students' motivation varies in different classroom contexts, the need to study motivation in diverse groups of children, methodological issues with respect to studying motivation, what other kinds of further motivation intervention studies are needed, and how work on motivation can inform educational policy.

Key Words: achievement motivation, development of motivation, motivation and instruction, teacher–student relationships and motivation, peers and motivation

Overview

Motivation theorists are interested in the "whys" of human behavior: what moves people to act (Weiner, 1992). In terms of motivation and education, researchers studying school motivation look at things like the engagement and interest students have in different academic activities, the choices students make about which academic activities to do, their persistence at continuing the activities, and the degree of effort they expend. But what determines individuals' choices, effort, and persistence at different academic activities? Many motivation researchers have focused on students' self-beliefs, values, and goals and how these relate to their achievement behaviors, such as choice, persistence, and performance (Maehr & Zusho, 2009; Ryan & Deci, 2009; Schiefele, 2009; Schunk & Pajares, 2009; Wigfield &

Eccles, 2002; Wigfield, Tonks, & Klauda, 2009). Because of this emphasis on *self* variables, much research on motivation has focused on motivation as a characteristic of the individual.

Motivation researchers also recognize the importance of social influences on learning and motivation (Ladd, Herald-Brown, & Kochel, 2009; Wentzel, 2009). Indeed, many researchers and theorists now posit that learning is an inherently social activity (Hickey & Granade, 2004; Vygotsky, 1978). Learning in classrooms is not done in isolation, but instead occurs in the context of relationships with teachers and peers (O'Donnell, 2006; Webb & Palincsar, 1996; Wentzel, 2009). These relationships, and the different roles that emerge for students and teachers in various classrooms, strongly influence how students learn. Furthermore, opportunities for social interactions around learning have been shown to improve children's achievement in reading and other areas (e.g., Guthrie, McRae, & Klauda, 2007; Johnson & Johnson, 2009). Along with social relationships, it is increasingly clear that the social contexts and organization of classrooms and schools also have major influences on students' motivation and achievement (Nolen & Ward, 2008; Perry, Turner, & Meyer, 2006; Wigfield, Eccles, & Rodriguez, 1998).

In this chapter we discuss children's motivation in school. We begin with a brief discussion of the belief, value, and goal constructs prevalent in current motivation research and how they develop. We then discuss the influence of different aspects of classrooms and schools on the development of students' motivation. We also discuss how school structures change as children move from elementary into secondary school, and how such changes affect students' motivation. We close with discussion of some recent intervention efforts to improve children's motivation.

The Nature of Student Motivation

Researchers have assessed many different constructs that are crucial to students' motivation. To organize our discussion of these constructs, we separate them into two broad groups. One group includes individuals' sense of their competence and agency to achieve different outcomes. Another group concerns intrinsic and extrinsic motivation, interest, values, and goals. Many of these constructs are discussed in greater detail in other chapters in this book.

Individuals' Sense of Competence and Control

Many researchers interested in motivation focus on students' beliefs about their ability and efficacy to perform achievement tasks as crucial motivational mediators of achievement behavior (e.g., Bandura, 1997; Eccles et al., 1983; Wigfield, Tonks, & Klauda, 2009). Ability beliefs are children's evaluations of their competence in different areas. Researchers have documented that children's and adolescents' ability beliefs relate to and predict their achievement performance in different achievement domains like math and reading, even when previous performance is controlled (see Wigfield et al., 2009, for review).

Bandura's (1997) construct of self-efficacy also deals with individuals' sense of competence; however, Bandura defined self-efficacy as a generative capacity where different subskills are organized into courses of action. Bandura (1997) reviewed research showing that individuals' efficacy for different achievement tasks is a major determinant of activity choice, willingness to expend effort, and persistence in and out of school (see also Schunk & Pajares, 2009).

Researchers interested in individuals' control beliefs initially made a major distinction between internal and external locus of control (e.g., Crandall, Katkovsky, & Crandall, 1965; Rotter, 1966. Internal control means the individual believes that he or she controls the outcome; external control means the outcome is determined by other things. Researchers have confirmed the positive association between internal locus of control and academic achievement (see Skinner, 1995). Connell and Wellborn (1991) integrated control beliefs into a broader theoretical framework based on psychological needs for competence, autonomy, and relatedness from self-determination theory (Ryan & Deci, 2009). They linked control beliefs to competence needs: Children who believe they control their achievement outcomes should feel more competent. When the family, peer, and school contexts support children's autonomy, develop their competence, and provide positive relations with others, then children's motivation (which Connell and Wellborn conceptualized as *engagement*) will be positive, and they will become fully engaged in different activities, such as their school work. When one or more of the needs is not fulfilled, children will become disaffected (see Connell, Spencer, & Aber, 1994; Skinner, Kindermann, Connell, & Wellborn, 2009).

Individuals' Intrinsic Motivation, Interests, Values, and Goals

Although theories dealing with competence, expectancy, and control beliefs provide powerful explanations of individuals' performance on different kinds of achievement activities, these theories do not systematically address another important motivational question: Does the individual *want* to do the task? Even if people are certain they can do a task and think they can control the outcome, they may not want to engage in it. Once the decision is made to engage in a task or activity, there are different reasons for doing so. The constructs discussed next focus on these aspects of motivation.

A basic distinction in the motivation literature is between intrinsic motivation and extrinsic motivation (Deci & Ryan, 1985; Harter, 1981). When individuals are intrinsically motivated, they do activities for their own sake and out of interest in the activity. Deci, Ryan, and their colleagues (e. g., Deci & Ryan, 1985; Ryan & Deci, 2009) went beyond the extrinsic-intrinsic motivation dichotomy in their discussion of *internalization*, the process of transferring the regulation of behavior from outside to inside the individual. They defined several levels in the process of going from external to more internalized regulation: *external*—regulation coming from outside the individual; *introjected*—internal regulation based on feelings that he or she should or has to do the behavior; *identified*—internal regulation of behavior that is based on the utility of that behavior (e.g., studying hard to get grades to get into college); and finally, *integrated*—regulation based on what the individual thinks is valuable and important to the self. Even though the integrated level is self-determined, it still does not reflect intrinsically motivated behavior. Intrinsic motivation only occurs when the individual autonomously controls the behavior, which may not be the case even at the integrated level of regulation.

A construct closely related to intrinsic motivation is interest (Hidi & Renninger, 2006; Schiefele, 2009), and researchers studying interest distinguish between individual and situational interest. As the name implies, individual or personal interest is a characteristic of the individual, and it is conceptualized either as a relatively stable disposition or an active state. Hidi and Renninger (2006) suggested that individual interest includes both knowledge and value about a topic or object and represents an enduring involvement with an activity. By contrast, situational interest stems from conditions in the environment. Hidi and Renninger (2006) described how situational interest generates curiosity, which can lead individuals to explore an activity further and develop individual interest in it. This point is a crucial one for this chapter; features of activities that individuals do in school can increase their personal interest in the activities. Furthermore, there are significant but moderate relations between interest and learning of different kinds (Schiefele, 2009).

Eccles and her colleagues have defined different ways in which individuals can value activities such as schoolwork (see Eccles et al., 1983; Wigfield et al., 2009). Eccles et al. (1983) outlined four motivational components of task value: attainment value, intrinsic value, utility value, and cost. Attainment value refers to the importance of the activity to the individual. Intrinsic value is the enjoyment the individual gets from performing the activity, and so it is conceptually linked to intrinsic motivation and

interest (Wigfield & Cambria, 2010). Utility value is determined by how well a task relates to current and future goals, such as career goals. A task can have positive value to a person because it facilitates important future goals, even if he or she is not interested in a task for its own sake. For instance, students often take classes that they do not particularly enjoy but that they need in order to pursue other interests, to please their parents, or to be with their friends. In one sense then this component captures the more "extrinsic" reasons for engaging in a task. But it also relates directly to individuals' internalized short- and long-term goals. Finally, cost refers to what one has to give up to do something else; spending time on homework means less time for socializing with friends.

Eccles and her colleagues have found that individuals' task values predict course plans and enrollment decisions in mathematics, physics, and English and involvement in sport activities even after controlling for prior performance levels (Durik, Vida, & Eccles, 2006; Eccles et al., 1983; Meece, Wigfield, & Eccles, 1990; Simpkins, Davis-Kean, & Eccles, 2006). They have also shown that both competence beliefs and values predict career choices (see Eccles, 2005).

The construct perhaps most directly related to the purposes for doing an activity is achievement goals. Researchers (e.g., Ames, 1992; Dweck & Leggett, 1988; Nicholls, 1984) initially distinguished three broad goal orientations that students can have toward their learning (see Maehr & Zusho, 2009; Elliot, 2005, for review). One orientation, called learning, task involved, or mastery goal orientation, means that the child is focused on improving his or her skills, mastering material, and learning new things. The second goal orientation, called performance or ego orientation, means that the child focuses on maximizing favorable evaluations of his or her competence and minimizing negative evaluations of competence. The different terms used to label the first two goal orientations occurred because different researchers were working on them simultaneously, with each having a somewhat distinctive view of each orientation (see Pintrich, 2000a, and Thorkildsen & Nicholls, 1998). Nicholls and his colleagues (e.g., Nicholls, Cobb, Wood, Yackel, & Patashnick, 1990; Nicholls, Cobb, Yackel, Wood, & Wheatley, 1990) and Meece (1991, 1994) also described a work-avoidant goal orientation, which means that the child does not wish to engage in academic activities. This orientation has received less research attention compared to the others.

In the 1990s, researchers differentiated performance and mastery goal orientations into approach and avoidance components. Elliot and Harackiewicz (1996) and Skaalvik (1997), among others, defined performance-approach goals as students' desire to demonstrate competence and outperform others. Performance-avoidance goals involve the desire to avoid looking incompetent. Elliot (1999; Elliot & McGregor, 2001) and Pintrich (2000b) proposed that the mastery goal orientation also may be divided into approach and avoid components, rather than being solely conceived as reflecting an approach tendency.

One issue with the approach-avoidance distinction that continues among goal orientation theorists is debate about their relative merits of the different kinds of goal orientation. Most goal orientation theorists believe in the benefits of mastery goals for both students and teachers (because they focus students on meaningful learning and improvement) and many of these theorists state that such goal orientations should be focused on more strongly in school. Theorists also agree that performance-avoid goals are debilitating. There is debate, however, about the relative merits of performance-approach goals. Because these goals relate positively to some important achievement outcomes such as grades, some theorists believe that performance-approach goals can be beneficial to students; other theorists continue to think that mastery goals are the most favorable goals students can have. A complete discussion of this debate is beyond the scope of this chapter; interested readers should see Linnenbrink (2005) and Maehr and Zusho (2009).

To conclude this section, researchers have identified a number of important beliefs, value, and goal constructs that impact students' motivation. These variables relate to achievement and choice in many different academic areas. We discussed these constructs individually and many researchers indeed have studied each separately. There is increasing interest currently in how they interrelate and relate to various achievement outcomes (e.g., Harackiewicz, Durik, Barron, Linnenbrink-Garcia, & Tauer, 2008; Wigfield & Cambria, 2010). For instance, having positive competence beliefs, intrinsic motivation, and mastery goals for activities may be the most adaptive pattern for positive motivation.

Researchers also have studied how students' beliefs, values, and goals change across the school years; that is, how they change across the school years; that is the topic of the next section.

Development of Children's Motivation

A substantial body of research shows that children's academic motivation declines across the elementary and secondary school years (see Wigfield, Eccles, Schiefele, Roeser, & Davis-Kean, 2006, for review). Many young children are quite optimistic about their competencies in different areas, and this optimism changes to greater realism and (sometimes) pessimism for many children as they go through school (Fredricks & Eccles, 2002; Jacobs, Lanza, Osgood, Eccles, & Wigfield, 2002; Watt, 2004). Children's intrinsic motivation for different academic subjects also declines (Gottfried, Fleming, & Gottfried., 2001), as does their valuing of achievement (Jacobs et al., 2002). Children also appear to focus more on performance goals as they get older (Maehr & Zusho, 2009). Although the pattern of these findings is clear, most of the research just mentioned is normative, describing mean-level change across all children. Researchers have shown that these patterns do vary for children achieving at different levels (Harter, Whitesell, & Kowalski, 1992; Wigfield, Eccles, Mac Iver, Reuman, & Midgley, 1991); more work of this kind is needed.

These changes have been explained with respect to children's understanding of their performance and changes in the school environments children experience. First, children both receive more information about their performance and learn to interpret it more clearly. Because they are with same-aged peers in school they also learn to compare themselves more systematically with others, which can lead to decreases in motivation for some children (see Wigfield et al., 2009). Second, schools focus more on evaluation and performance outcomes as children go through school, which can negatively impact some children's motivation. We turn next to a more detailed consideration of schooling's influences on students' motivation.

School's Influences on Students' Motivation

How do different kinds of tasks, activities, and structures in school impact children's motivation? How do the relationships children have with their teachers and peers influence their motivation? We focus on these issues in this section.

Tasks and Classroom Practices and Student Motivation

Stipek (1996) reviewed the effects of tasks and classroom practices on student outcomes. She argued that although students do have certain motivational characteristics that they bring with them to the classroom, teachers and the kinds of environment they provide are primary influences on students' motivation and achievement. Stipek (1996) discussed how teachers can foster motivation by specific classroom practices that enhance achievement-related beliefs, intrinsic motivation, and learning goals.

From her review of the research, Stipek (1996) posited that the classroom practices that are associated with changes in achievement-related beliefs are task-level practices, criteria for success, evaluation, rewards, and teacher behaviors toward students. Task-level practices that are motivating are those with appropriate level of challenge. In addition, tasks should be differentiated over time so that tasks do not become redundant or uninteresting. Next, teachers can foster more positive achievement-related beliefs by creating clear achievable criterion for success and offer rewards for achieving this criterion. Stipek suggested that improvement on previous work be the primary mark of success and students should receive clear and positive feedback about how to attain this goal. Rewards should be given on the basis of improvement, effort, and performance. The final classroom practice that Stipek (1996) discussed as a primary influence on achievement-related beliefs is how teachers treat their students. Teachers' behaviors reflect their beliefs about student competence; therefore, they should avoid treating students of varying abilities differently and express that all students can achieve if they put effort into the task. These classroom practices are associated with student competence beliefs, having an internal locus of control, and holding the perception that achievement is due to effort and not attributable solely to ability. These beliefs are associated with more positive achievement-related beliefs, which are related to positive student outcomes such as help seeking, persistence, effort, and pride in success.

Stipek (1996) also discussed how classroom practices influence intrinsic motivation in students. In this case there is significant overlap with her discussion of fostering achievement-related beliefs. The classroom practices that are associated with intrinsic motivation are use of rewards, evaluation, and task-level practices. When rewards are used as indicators of performance and to provide information as opposed to trying to gain control over students, they can enhance intrinsic motivation (see also Ryan & Deci, 2009). Next, overly emphasizing evaluation has negative effects on intrinsic motivation. Evaluation is best used to inform students about their best or less effective practices as opposed to threatening or controlling evaluation techniques. Similar

to the use of rewards, intrinsic motivation is most enhanced when evaluation provides information about progress. Teachers also can foster intrinsic motivation by varying the format of tasks, offering appropriate levels of challenges for students, and allowing choice. Each of these classroom practices is associated with students' perceptions of control over their academic outcomes, mastery goals, and competence beliefs. Increasing these positive beliefs and feelings are associated with task engagement, enjoyment, understanding, and ultimately increased intrinsic motivation.

Stipek (1996) also described the importance of classroom practices on fostering learning or mastery goals. This is important because learning goals (also called mastery or task goals) are associated with developing skills and a desire to master the material. This builds on her discussion of fostering intrinsic motivation in students because it includes each of those practices and is supplemented by several other practices such as adapting instruction to students existing background knowledge, providing opportunities for exploration of the topic, and treating mistakes as an expected part of the learning process. Engaging in these practices is associated with increase in students' goals. Students are more likely to understand, gain skills, and learn and master tasks. These goals are associated with attentiveness, conceptual learning, and feeling satisfaction from gaining knowledge.

Stipek's (1996) discussion of the merit of these instructional practices on achievement-related beliefs, intrinsic motivation, and learning goals was based on observational, correlational, and experimental research; however, these task-level and instructional practices likely interact, and it remains unclear how practices may interact, what the best combination of practices is, and at what magnitude these practices are most helpful for students' motivation and learning.

TARGET

Ames (1992) used the acronym TARGET to describe a set of instructional practices designed to increase the levels of student motivation, especially their mastery goals. She focused on mastery goals because these goals are associated with more time spent on tasks (Butler, 1987) and the amount of effort put into learning (Elliot & Dweck, 1988) than performance goals. TARGET is an evidence-based set of classroom practices that includes task design, authority, recognition, grouping arrangements, evaluation practices, and time allocation.

Strategic design of tasks is the first element of TARGET. Each task should be designed with useful learning goals in mind and use a variety of tasks. The focus of these tasks should be gaining skills and learning. Such thoughtful planning of classroom tasks is associated with increased interest and skills. Distributing authority in the classroom is essential to increasing student autonomy and allows them ownership over their learning by allowing them to make decisions and schedules for their tasks. By shifting autonomy in the classroom from teacher to student, students gain ownership over their learning activities by increasing their participation in classroom choices. This increases mastery goals and interest. Recognizing students' success and improvement is similar to Stipek's (1996) discussion of rewards and evaluation. Students' effort and successes should be recognized and rewarded.

The next element of TARGET is grouping arrangements, which should be organized to promote discussion that leads to a deeper understanding of points and support in the face of challenging tasks. These classroom groups should be heterogeneous and should not reflect ability differences (see Wigfield et al., 1998, for a review of how ability grouping impacts students' motivation). Students generally are aware of ability-based groups, and this is undermining for mastery goals. Evaluation techniques that encourage learning and not normative comparison are essential to TARGET. They should be based on progress and achieving attainable goals. The final piece of a TARGET classroom is time allocation. Allowing students to make decisions about how to pace and schedule their assignments and understanding that students work successfully at difference paces is essential for fostering mastery goals. With respect to enhancing the probability that students adopt a mastery goal orientation, a TARGET classroom structure uses motivational principles that could contribute or contribute multiplicatively toward an orientation to develop new skills.

Teacher–Student Relationships and Student Motivation

There is a growing body of literature that shows how the affective relationships teachers have with students impact students' motivation and achievement in school (see Juvonen, 2006, and Wentzel, 2009, for review). When teachers support students emotionally, they have higher school-related perceptions of competence, clearer positive social and academic goals, and willingness to engage in school activities. These relations emerge even when children's relations with peers and parents are taken into account; research measuring support from all three kinds of socialization agents shows that teacher support is particularly important for academic motivation and adjustment.

Teachers' relations with students are crucial to students' early adjustment in school (Birch & Ladd, 1996), and the emotional quality of student–teacher relations during the early school years predicts growth in their reading and math achievement (Pianta, Belsky, Vandegrift, Houts, & Morrison, 2008). The importance of such relations continues into middle school and beyond. Goodenow (1993) found that students' perceptions of support from teachers and their sense of belongingness in their classrooms related strongly to their perceived valuing of the schoolwork they were doing. Similarly, Wentzel (2002) found that students' academic goals and performance were strongly related to their sense that their middle school teachers were "caring."

Wentzel (2009) noted that much of the work showing how teacher–student relations impact student achievement is correlational and discussed a variety of design and measurement issues that need to be considered in the next generation of this research. These include the complexity of these relations and the need to examine students' impact on teachers along with teachers' impact on students. Additionally, researchers need to take the "nested" nature of these relationships into account; teacher–student relations occur in complex classroom settings and the kinds of relations teachers have with individual students likely is influenced by the relations they have with others in their classes. Wentzel argued that we need a clearer understanding of the mechanisms underlying the observed relations of teacher emotional support and student motivation and achievement.

Peers and Motivation

Peers are another important social influence on motivation. When children are socially supported and accepted by their peers, they have stronger motivation, better achievement outcomes, and are more engaged in school (see Ladd, Herald-Brown, & Kochel., 2009 for review). Furthermore, social competence and social support can help ease school transitions, including the transition from home to school (Ladd et al., 2009. In contrast, socially rejected and highly aggressive children, and also those who are victimized by others, are at risk for poorer achievement and motivation (Birch & Ladd, 1996; Ladd et al., 2009). Moreover, it appears that both the quantity of children's friendships with peers and the quality of the friendships are related to positive outcomes; in fact, the quality of children's friendships may be especially key, particularly as children move into adolescence (Berndt & Keefe, 1995).

Peer groups in school can have either a positive or negative effect on motivation across various activity settings. Children who come together in peer groups often share similar motivational orientations and activity preferences, and such groupings reinforce and strengthen their existing motivational orientation and activity preferences over time (e.g., Berndt & Keefe, 1995; Kindermann, 1993, 2007). Whether such effects are positive or negative depends on the nature of the peer groups' motivational orientation. High-achieving children who seek out other high achievers as friends develop even more positive academic motivation over time. The role of peer group influences is likely to vary across age. Peers may play an especially important role vis-à-vis motivation and achievement during adolescence, for two reasons: Adolescents are more aware of, and concerned about, peer group acceptance and they spend much more unsupervised time with peers groups than younger children (Rubin, Bukowski, & Parker, 2006). Consequently, adolescents should be especially susceptible to peer group influences on motivation and achievement.

Learning in Groups and Motivation

There is an extensive body of research on how students learn in groups and the impact of students on each others' learning and motivation; much of this work has focused on cooperative learning (see O'Donnell, 2006; Webb & Palincsar, 1996, for systematic reviews of the research on group processes in the classroom, and Johnson & Johnson, 2009, for a review of the effects of cooperative learning). One issue motivation researchers have focused on is how cooperative and competitive reward structures in classrooms influence students' motivation. Ames (1984) discussed how competitive reward structures heighten social comparison and a focus on one's ability relative to others. Cooperative reward structures help children focus on shared effort and interdependence. More broadly, the research on cooperative learning shows that children's achievement often improves, social relations are more positive, and students' motivation is enhanced (Johnson & Johnson, 2009). Peers can also help each other understand and learn the material through group discussion, sharing of resources, modeling academic skills, and interpreting and clarifying the tasks for each other

(Cohen, 1994; O'Donnell, 2006). By working together students can create communities of learners and learn to co-regulate each others' motivation and achievement (McCaslin & Good, 1996).

School Transitions and Changes in Student Motivation.

Entrance into kindergarten and then the transition from kindergarten to first grade introduces several systematic changes in children's social worlds (Pianta, Rimm-Kaufman, & Cox, 1999). First, classes are age stratified, making within-age ability social comparison much easier. Second, formal evaluations of competence by "experts" begin. Third, formal ability grouping begins usually with reading group assignment. Fourth, peers have the opportunity to play a much more constant and salient role in children' lives. Each of these changes can impact children's motivational development (Pianta et al., 1999). Unfortunately, very little longitudinal research has focused on this transition and how it influences children's motivation and achievement (one important exception is Pianta and colleagues' work; see Pianta et al., 2008).

Instead, most of the research on the early elementary school years has focused on individual differences in the link between children's early school experiences and their subsequent development. This research suggests significant long-term consequences of children's experiences in the early school years, particularly experiences associated with ability grouping and within-class differential teacher treatment. For example, teachers use a variety of information to assign first graders to reading groups, including temperamental characteristics like interest and persistence, race, gender, and social class (e.g., Alexander, Dauber & Entwisle, 1993; Brophy & Good, 1974). Alexander et al. (1993) demonstrated that differences in first grade reading group placement and teacher–student interactions predict subsequent motivation and achievement even after controlling for initial differences in reading competence. Furthermore, these effects are mediated by both differential instruction and the amplifying impact of ability group placement on parents' and teachers' views of the children's abilities, talents, and motivation (Pallas et al., 1994).

As noted earlier, there are substantial changes in academic motivation and achievement across the upper elementary and secondary school years, including changes in grades, interest in school, perceptions of competence in different areas, and increases in performance goals at the expense of mastery goals. These changes are particularly large for students who are doing poorly (either emotionally or academically) in school (Lord, Eccles, & McCarthy, 1994). The transition from elementary to middle school can accelerate these negative changes. In explaining them, Eccles et al. (1998) discussed how the multiple changes that occur during this time period (puberty, school transitions, changing relations with parents, increasing cognitive maturity, increasing concern with identity, increasing sexuality and heterosociality, and increasing focus on peer relationships) likely have an impact on students' motivation and achievement. They also discussed how differences in school environments between elementary and secondary schools could contribute to these changes (see also NRC, 2004). Traditional secondary schools differ structurally in important ways from elementary schools. Most secondary schools are substantially larger than elementary schools. As a result, students' friendship networks often are disrupted as they attend classes with students from several different schools. In addition, students are likely to feel more anonymous and alienated because of the large size of many secondary schools. Finally, the opportunity to participate in and play leadership roles in school activities often declines over these school transitions due to the limited number of slots in such niches and the increasing size of the student body. These kinds of changes should affect the students' sense of belonging as well as their sense of social competence.

The nature of instruction also changes: Secondary school instruction is organized and taught departmentally—making it likely that secondary school teachers teach several different groups of students each day and are unlikely to teach any particular students for more than one year. This departmental structure can create a number of difficulties for students. First, the curriculum often is not integrated across different subjects. Second, students typically have several teachers each day with little opportunity to interact with any one teacher on any deeper dimension beyond the academic content of what is being taught and disciplinary issues. As a result, the likelihood of students and teachers forming close, supportive bonds is much less in secondary than in elementary schools.

Finally, grading systems are more likely to be based on social comparative performance, ability level tracking via curricular tracking is common, and teachers are more likely to hold entity, rather than incremental, views of ability differences (Eccles & Midgley, 1989; Wigfield Eccles, & Pintrich, 1996). These characteristics, in turn, are likely to lead to an increase in performance rather than mastery goal focus in the classroom and the school building. As noted earlier, these changes are likely to undermine low-performing students' sense of competence.

Research on the transition to high school suggests that similar changes occur at this transition (Lee & Smith, 2001; Mac Iver et al., 1995; NRC, 2004). For example, high schools are typically even larger and more bureaucratic than middle and junior high schools. Lee and Smith (2001) provide numerous examples of how the sense of community among teachers and students is undermined by the size and bureaucratic structure of most high schools. There is less opportunity for students and teachers to get to know each other and, likely as a consequence, there is distrust between them and little agreement on a common set of goals and values. There is also less opportunity for the students to form mentor-like relationships with the teachers, and there is little effort to make instruction meaningful to the students.

Such environments are likely to undermine the motivation and involvement of many students, especially those not doing particularly well academically, and those who are alienated from the values of the adults in the high school. Furthermore, research based upon both teacher and student reports shows that schools become more socially comparative and competitive in orientation as students progression from elementary to middle to high school (Wigfield et al., 1996). The coincidence of declining social support and increased social comparison and competition at both the middle and high school levels likely contributes to some adolescents' decisions, especially those who are already on the margins of the school community, to withdraw from school prior to graduation (Finn, 1989).

Middle School Reform Efforts and Student Motivation

Based in part on the research just reviewed, during the 1990s different middle school reform efforts were undertaken; many of the recommendations were included in a report by the Carnegie Foundation (1989). There are a number of important ways in which these recommendations have been implemented in different middle schools. One is replacing departmentalized curriculum structures with teams of teachers working with the same group of students. This practice allows groups of teachers to spend more time with the same group of adolescents, thus getting to know them better. It also allows for greater integration across the curriculum. Teachers serving as advisors and counselors has become more prevalent, so that adolescents can develop closer relationships with their teachers. To create smaller learning communities in often-large middle schools, "schools within schools" have been created, in part through the teaming approach just discussed. This is particularly likely to occur for the youngest group in a middle school, be they fifth graders, sixth graders, or seventh graders. Cooperative learning practices are used more frequently, in part to reduce the use of ability grouping or tracking. Juvonen (2007) discussed middle school reform efforts designed specifically to promote student engagement in school by facilitating social relationships among students and between students and teachers.

Relatively few of the middle school reform efforts focused specifically on students' motivation. An important exception is the work of Maehr and Midgley (1996), who worked with teachers and administrators to change the culture organization and climate of a middle school and an elementary school in a city in Michigan from performance goal based to mastery goal based (similar to Ames, 1992). The school-university team worked extensively to restructure the school toward a focus on mastery goal; they spent 3 years in each school. At the middle school they focused on creating teams of teachers, "schools within the school," lessening the use of ability grouping practices, and changing the student recognition patterns so that not just the "honor roll" students were recognized. They also worked to loosen the rigid bell schedule so that longer class periods were sometimes possible. Changing the school culture in the middle school was very difficulty due to some teachers' (especially the math teachers) resistance to change. Despite these difficulties, the changes had positive effects on students' motivation (E. Anderman, Maehr, & Midgley, 1999).

Even less work has been done on high school reform effort with respect to motivation and the results of this work are less consistent (NRC, 2004). Reform efforts have followed similar principles aimed at creating schools that better meet the competence, belonging, autonomy, and mattering needs of the adolescent students. As is true for the middle school reform efforts, when these principles are well implemented, improvements in students' motivation, school engagement, and academic performance are obtained (NRC, 2004). But successfully implementing these kinds of changes has proven to be very difficult at the high school level.

One of the challenges for motivation researchers is that many of the reform efforts they espouse do not fit well with the current focus on performance, testing, and accountability that are hallmarks of the No Child Left Behind era. The severe pressure that many teachers and principals face to produce higher test scores and other indicators of student performance can lead to a strong focus on performance on the tests used to gauge student growth, at the expense of focusing on how efforts to enhance students' interest and mastery can enhance their performance (Deci & Ryan, 2002). We understand the importance of students showing continual progress in their learning and believe teachers and principals need to be accountable for this progress. However, we also believe that a focus on enhancing students' sense of competence, interest and enjoyment of learning, and mastery also can lead to gains in students' performance, and it is more likely to foster students' healthy development in other areas as well. We turn next to a discussion of some successful interventions that have enhanced students' motivation and achievement

Motivation Interventions

Many researchers studying students' motivation have used correlational methods measuring aspects of students' motivation and relating them to different achievement outcomes, experimental studies done in controlled laboratory settings, or classroom-based observation studies. From this work we now have a substantial body of information about the nature of students' motivation and how different teaching practices and classroom environments impact motivation and achievement. There is a growing body of work examining the effectiveness of different kinds of interventions designed to improve students' motivation; we discuss examples of this kind of work in this section (see also Wentzel & Wigfield, 2007). This work can be done at different levels, including working with individual students to improve aspects of their motivation such as their self-efficacy or changing their failure attributions to focus on lack of effort rather than lack of ability (e.g., Dweck, 1975; Schunk, 1983) or working at the classroom or school levels; we focus here on the latter kind of work.

Blackwell, Trzesniewski, and Dweck (2007) provided seventh grade students with an eight-session intervention designed to help them develop an incremental rather than entity view of their ability. Dweck and her colleagues have shown that students who believe that their intelligence is incremental or modifiable are more positively motivated than those who believe it is fixed (see Dweck & Master, 2009, for review). The intervention involved teaching children that they can grow their intelligence through their efforts and students were assigned randomly by classroom to the intervention or control group. The intervention produced significant changes in the intervention group's theories of intelligence; these children became more incremental in their views about their intelligence. Overall, students' math grades declined over the course of the year; this decline was reversed for the students in the intervention group. Interestingly, there was an (marginally significant) interaction of student's initial theory of intelligence and condition showing that students who initially endorsed the entity view of intelligence were most impacted by the intervention with respect to their grades. The decline in grades for such students in the intervention group reversed, whereas for control group students holding this view the decline continued. Blackwell et al. concluded that altering students' views of their intelligence impacted both their motivation and mathematics achievement.

Felner, Seitsinger, Brand, Burns, and Bolton (2007) reviewed their work on reforming middle schools to create effective small learning communities in middle school. They call their approach the High Performance Learning Communities Project (Project HiPlace). Project HiPlace is being conducted in middle schools across the country, including many middle schools serving minority students living in poverty. Felner and his colleagues have conducted a number of large-scale studies on the effectiveness of Project HiPlace, and they have documented that creating smaller learning communities in middle school has positive effects on students' motivation and achievement.

Balfanz, Herzog, and Mac Iver (2007) and other colleagues developed a system for identifying middle school students who are most at risk for academic disengagement and later dropping out of school. They focus on student grades, attendance, and behavior in school (as rated by the teacher) as possible indicators of disengagement, and they examine how each of these factors individually and together affect student engagement and school attendance over the middle and high school years. These researchers also developed and evaluated a middle school reform effort called the Talent Development Middle School Project, a broad-scale instructional program implemented in urban middle schools in Philadelphia and other cities. Talent Development

includes instruction in math, English, and science. The program focuses on developing strong learning communities and providing an engaging curriculum in each subject area. Analyses of the effects of the program on student outcomes indicate that the program has been effective in improving student achievement and engagement because the specific kinds of instruction are important for motivation and achievement.

Guthrie, McRae, and Klauda (2007) review the research on how different kinds of reading instruction programs influence motivation and achievement, focusing specifically on Concept-Oriented Reading Instruction (CORI), a reading comprehension instruction program that integrates science and reading. CORI focuses on instructional practices to enhance students' motivation for reading and ability to use cognitive reading strategies. The classroom practices that are designed to enhance reading motivation include increasing personal relevance of the material being learned, providing choices with respect to learning activities, ensuring enough success that students' self-efficacy is fostered, giving many opportunities for student collaboration, and teaching in thematic units so that students have clear content goals for learning. Guthrie et al.'s meta-analysis of the work to date on CORI's effectiveness in boosting students' reading motivation, reading comprehension, and strategy use showed that CORI is indeed effective in increasing these outcomes for students in grades 3–5.

Hudley, Graham, and Taylor (2007) focused on a somewhat different issue that has implications for students' school engagement and achievement, helping students interact more positively with their peers. Their interventions focus on reducing elementary school aged children's aggression toward peers. Many of their interventions have been conducted with African American boys. The theoretical grounding of their work is attribution theory, a theory that characterizes individuals' understanding of their own and others' actions. Hudley et al. discuss how aggressive children often interpret the acts of others as hostile, even when the intention behind the act is benign. Their interventions focus on changing these children's interpretations of others' actions, and reducing their aggressive responses to other children. Results of studies evaluating the effectiveness of the interventions show that they have had positive effects both on students' social behavior and attitudes, and academic motivation. Hudley et al. discuss how this work shows that children's social behaviors indeed can be altered in positive ways during the elementary school years, leading to increased achievement or improved motivation. They also discuss the importance of tailoring the interventions to the cultural and ethnic backgrounds of the participants, in order for the interventions to be optimally effective.

In sum, research on the nature of motivation has informed important interventions that aim to increase motivation in various domains, increase achievement, and improve students' social behaviors and perceptions. Work is needed to take these successful interventions to scale and to examine them for different groups of children and children of different ages.

Conclusion and Future Directions

We have learned much about the nature of students' motivation and how it changes across the school years. We also have learned much about how different kinds of tasks, activities, and other characteristics of school and classroom environments impact students' motivation, as well as how teacher–student and peer relations influence motivation. Although the frequently observed declines in student motivation continue to be cause for concern, various motivation-based intervention studies have shown that the declines can be reversed. We have a growing body of knowledge about how students' motivation can be enhanced in classrooms, which is a reason for optimism. We close our chapter with some issues that need research attention over the next few years.

How Do Different Classroom Contexts Influence Students' Motivation?

Perry et al. (2006) reviewed research on how the interactions among students, teachers, and the contextual features of different classrooms impact students' motivation. They take a sociocultural approach to student motivation and learning, arguing that students' participation in different classroom environments and interactions with others co-create motivation. They discuss research on some of the same topics that Stipek (1996) reviewed such as how different kinds of academic tasks influence students, how different kinds of instructional practices influence students, and how teacher–student relations and student–student relations influence motivation. They agree with many of Stipek's points about instructional practices and tasks, but they note that the dynamic and complex nature of classrooms means that the practices may have different meanings in different classrooms.

A number of motivation researchers taking sociocultural approaches to motivation have made similar points about the dynamic, situation-based nature of motivation (Hickey, 1997, 2008; Hickey & Granade, 2004; Nolen, 2007; Nolen & Ward, 2008; Urdan, 1999). These researchers argue that motivation is not a stable individual characteristic that operates similarly in different settings. Additionally, classrooms themselves are fluid structures that change depending upon who is in them and the mutual influences teachers, students, and activities all have on one another. Motivation theorists taking a sociocultural perspective challenge some of the premises of the social cognitive models of motivation that focus on the individual, and they also challenge the notion that practices thought to optimize motivation will operate similar in different classrooms (see in particular Hickey, 2008, and Hickey & Granade, 2004). An important research implication of these points is that we need to look carefully at how practices shown to facilitate motivation operate in different classroom settings, to understand the breadth of their impact as well as their limits.

How Does Motivation Vary in Different Groups of Children?

Researchers studying children's motivation have long been interested in group differences, with a particular focus on gender and ethnic differences in motivation (see Graham & Hudley, 2005; Meece, Glienke, & Askew, 2009; Murdock, 2009; and Wigfield et al., 2006 for review). This work shows that boys' and girls' competence-related beliefs and values tend to follow gender stereotypic patterns, with boys having more positive beliefs and values in domains such as math and sports, and girls in reading/English and music (Eccles, 1984; Eccles et al., 1993). More recent studies that these patterns may be changing; for instance, Jacobs et al. (2002) did not find significant gender differences in value of math, though gender differences in competence beliefs in math (favoring boys) and English (favoring girls) were found, along with gender differences in English value (favoring girls) and sport value and competence beliefs favoring boys.

Furthermore, researchers working in other countries find somewhat different patterns in gender differences in children's competence and values (Watt, 2004). The changing patterns in gender differences as well as the different findings from studies done in different cultural context demonstrate the importance of continuing to assess gender differences in achievement motivation.

With respect to ethnic differences in motivation, some research shows that African American children have more positive competence beliefs than do European American children, but that these beliefs do not relate as strongly to achievement for the African American children (see Graham, 1994). Graham, Taylor, and Hudley have found interesting interactions of ethnicity and gender, using a peer nomination measure asking who students admire in their school that they describe as a way to measure task value (Graham, Taylor, & Hudley, 1998; Taylor & Graham, 2007). They found that during elementary school African American, European American, and Hispanic American children chose students who were fashionable, athletic, and high achievers as ones they admired; females in all groups and European American boys continued to do so in middle school. However, in middle school African American and Hispanic American males nominated classmates who were fashionable and athletic but who were not high achievers. This work shows why it is important to consider gender and ethnicity together, as there are different patterns for boys and girls in different ethnic groups with respect to motivation-related beliefs.

Researchers interested in ethnic differences in motivation point to broader cultural and societal issues such as the perceived opportunity structure for different groups (e.g., if I work hard in school, will it lead to more economic opportunities for me and members of my group), discrimination, and stereotypes about the capabilities of individuals from different groups as impacting motivation and achievement (Aronson, 2002; Graham & Hudley, 2005; Murdock, 2009). The complex influences of these factors on students' motivation need further research attention.

How Should Motivation Be Studied?

Much of the research on children's beliefs, values, interests, and goals has relied on self-report questionnaires. There are numerous reasons why student self-report is a good way to measure motivation; if one is interested in measuring individuals' beliefs, then self-report needs to be used. However, such measures are subject to social desirability effects, and it is challenging to use them in studies of young children, despite the efforts of researchers to develop good measures for use with younger children.

We urge researchers to include other kinds of measures along with participant self-report measures, to get a more complete picture of students' motivation-related beliefs, values, and goals, their interrelations, and relations to outcomes. Classroom observations and interviews can provide a richer depiction of situated motivation. Measures of actual choices, persistence, and effort can provide information about outcomes tied to motivation. Teacher and parent ratings of children's motivation have been used successfully, and they have been shown to relate to various achievement outcomes (e.g., see Wigfield et al., 2008 for a teacher rating measure of student engagement). Having multiple informants and multiple kinds of measures adds complexity to a study, but it has many benefits as well.

What Are the Next Steps in Motivation Interventions?

We are encouraged by the results from the different motivation intervention studies discussed earlier. There are several important next steps for research of this kind. We continue to need both quasi-experimental and randomized trial design intervention studies done in classrooms, to build a strong experimental support for effective interventions. Second, we need to do these kinds of studies at different grade levels, to see how effective programs are with different aged students, and how they need to be modified for use with students of different ages. We predict that it may be easier to change students' motivation when they are younger, before long-term patterns of failure and avoidance set in for children performing poorly in school. However, because some motivation problems emerge later we need effective interventions for middle and high school students as well.

What Are the Implications of Motivation Research for School Reform?

As noted earlier, many of the principles derived from research on motivation about how to enhance students' motivation in school do not mesh well with the current press for more assessments and evaluation of student performance, and teacher and principal accountability for student performance on these tests. These pressures can lead to a strong focus on teaching to the tests being used and the (sometimes) surface learning needed to do well on such tests, rather than a deep engagement in meaningful and interesting learning activities. We do not believe that the motivational principles we have discussed are antithetical to student achievement in school; indeed, we think that when students believe they are competent, see that what they are learning is relevant and interesting, and have the goals of mastering material and increasing their skills they will perform very well in school. Motivation researchers, particularly those doing intervention work, should work with policy makers to be sure that motivation is included in the debates about effective education policy and how best to assess children's learning and promote both achievement and motivation. One good example of this type of work is the National Research Council's (2004) book on engaging schools. More of this kind of work is needed.

References

Alexander, K. L., Dauber, S. L., Entwisle, D. R. (1993). First-grade classroom behavior: Its short- and long-term consequences for school performance. *Child Development, 64*, 801–803

Ames, C. (1984). Competitive, cooperative, and individualistic goal structures: A cognitive-motivational analysis. In R. E. Ames & C. Ames (Eds.), *Research on motivation in education* (Vol. 1). San Diego, CA: Academic Press.

Ames, C. (1992). Classrooms: Goals, structures, and student motivation. *Journal of Educational Psychology, 84*, 261–271.

Anderman, E. M., Maehr, M. L., & Midgley, C. (1999). Declining motivation after the transition to middle school: Schools can make a difference. *Journal of Research and Development in Education, 32*, 131–147.

Aronson, J. (2002). Stereotype threat: Contending and coping with unnerving expectations. In J. Aronson (Ed.), *Improving academic achievement: Impact of psychological factors on education* (pp. 279–300). San Diego, CA: Academic Press.

Balfanz, R., Herzog, L., & Mac Iver, D. J. (2007). Preventing student disengagement and keeping students on the graduation path in urban middle-grades schools: Early identification and effective intervention. *Educational Psychologist, 42*, 223–236.

Bandura, A. (1997). *Self-efficacy: The exercise of control.* New York: W. H. Freeman.

Berndt, T. J., & Keefe, K. (1995). Friends' influence on adolescents' adjustment to school. *Child Development, 66*, 1312–1219.

Birch, S. H., & Ladd, G. W. (1996). Interpersonal relationships in the school environment and children's early school adjustment: The role of teachers and peers. In J. Juvonen & K. R. Wentzel (Eds.), *Social motivation: Understanding children's school adjustment* (pp. 199–225). New York: Cambridge University Press.

Blackwell, L. S., Trzesniewski, K. H., & Dweck, C. S. (2007). Implicit theories of intelligence predict achievement across an adolescent transition: A longitudinal study and an intervention. *Child Development, 78*, 246–263.

Butler, R. (1987). Task-involving and ego-involving properties of evaluation: Effects of different feedback conditions on motivational perceptions, interest, and performance. *Journal of Educational Psychology, 79*, 474–482.

Carnegie Council on Adolescent Development. (1989). *Turning points: Preparing American youth for the 21st century.* Washington, DC: Author.

Connell, J. P., Spencer, M. B., & Aber, J. L. (1994). Educational risk and resilience in African American Youth: Context, self, and action outcomes in school. *Child Development, 65*, 493–506.

Connell, J. P., & Wellborn, J. G. (1991). Competence, autonomy, and relatedness: A motivational analysis of self-system

processes. In R. Gunnar & L. A. Sroufe (Eds.), *Minnesota symposia on child psychology* (Vol. 23, pp. 43–77). Hillsale, NJ: Lawrence Erlbaum Associates.

Crandall, V. C., Katkovsky, W., & Crandall, V. J. (1965). Children's beliefs in their own control of reinforcements in intellectual-academic achievement situations. *Child Development, 36*, 91–109.

Deci, E. L., & Ryan, R. M. (1985). *Intrinsic motivation and self-determination in human behavior.* New York: Plenum Press.

Deci, E. L., & Ryan, R. M. (2002). The paradox of achievement: The harder you push, the worse it gets. In J. Aronson (Ed.), *Improving academic achievement: Impact of psychological factors on education* (pp. 61–87). San Diego, CA: Academic Press.

Durik, A. M., Vida, M., & Eccles, J. S. (2006). Task values and ability beliefs as predictors of high school literacy choices: A developmental analysis. *Journal of Educational Psychology, 98*, 382–393.

Dweck, C. S. (1975). The role of expectations and attributions in the alleviation of learned helplessness. *Journal of Personality and Social Psychology, 31*, 674–685.

Dweck, C. S., & Leggett, E. (1988). A social-cognitive approach to motivation and personality. *Psychological Review, 95*, 256–273.

Dweck, C. S., & Master, A. (2009). Self-theories and motivation: Students' beliefs about intelligence. In K. R. Wentzel & A. Wigfield (Eds.), *Handbook of motivation at school* (pp. 123–140). New York: Routledge.

Eccles, J. S. (1984). Sex differences in achievement patterns. In T. Sonderegger (Ed.), *Nebraska Symposium on Motivation* (Vol. 32, pp. 97–132). Lincoln: University of Nebraska Press.

Eccles, J. S. (2005). Subjective task values and the Eccles et al. model of achievement related choices. In A. J. Elliott & C. S. Dweck (Eds.), *Handbook of competence and motivation* (pp. 105–121). New York: Guilford.

Eccles, J. S., & Midgley, C. (1989). Stage/environment fit: Developmentally appropriate classrooms for early adolescents. In R. Ames & C. Ames (Eds.), *Research on motivation in education* (Vol. 3, pp. 139–181). New York: Academic Press.

Eccles, J. S., & Wigfield, A. (1995). In the mind of the achiever: The structure of adolescents' academic achievement related-beliefs and self-perceptions. *Personality and Social Psychology Bulletin, 21*, 215–225.

Eccles, J. S., Wigfield, A., Harold, R., & Blumenfeld, P. B. (1993). Age and gender differences in children's self- and task perceptions during elementary school. *Child Development, 64*, 830–847.

Eccles, J. S., Adler, T. F., Futterman, R., Goff, S. B., Kaczala, C. M., Meece, J. L., & Midgley, C. (1983). Expectancies, values, and academic behaviors. In J. T. Spence (Ed.), *Achievement and achievement motivation* (pp. 75–146). San Francisco, CA: W. H. Freeman.

Elliot, A. J. (1999). Approach and avoidance motivation and achievement goals. *Educational Psychologist, 34*, 169–189.

Elliot, A. J. (2005). A conceptual history of the achievement goal construct. In A. J. Elliot & C. S. Dweck (Eds.), *Handbook of competence and motivation* (pp. 52–72). New York: Guilford Publications.

Elliot, A. J., & Harackiewicz, J. M. (1996). Approach and avoidance goals and intrinsic motivation: A mediational analysis. *Journal of Personality and Social Psychology, 70*, 461–475.

Elliot, A. J., & McGregor, H. (2001). A 2 x 2 achievement goal framework. *Journal of Personality and Social Psychology, 80*, 501–509.

Elliott, E. S., & Dweck, C. S. (1988). Goals: An approach to motivation and achievement. *Journal of Personality and Social Psychology,54*, 5–12.

Felner, R. D., Seitsinger, A. M., Brand, S., Burns, A., & Bolton, N. (2007). Creating small learning communities: Lessons from the project on high-performing learning communities about "what works" in creating productive, developmentally enhancing, learning contexts. *Educational Psychologist, 42*, 209–221.

Finn, J. D. (1989). Withdrawing from school. *Review of Educational Research, 59*, 117–142.

Fredricks, J., & Eccles, J. S. (2002). Children's competence and value beliefs from childhood through adolescence: Growth trajectories in two male sex-typed domains. *Developmental Psychology, 38*, 519–533.

Goodenow, C. (1993). Classroom belonging among early adolescent students: Relationships to motivation and achievement. *Journal of Early Adolescence, 13*(1), 21–43.

Gottfried, A. E., Fleming, J. S., & Gottfried, A. W. (2001). Continuity of academic intrinsic motivation from childhood through late adolescence: A longitudinal study. *Journal of Educational Psychology, 93*, 3–13.

Graham, S. (1994). Motivation in African Americans. *Review of Educational Research, 64*, 55–117.

Graham, S., & Hudley, C. (2005). Race and ethnicity in the study of motivation and competence. In A. Elliot & C. S. Dweck (Eds.), *Handbook of competence and motivation* (pp. 392–413). New York: Guilford Press.

Graham, S., Taylor, A. Z., & Hudley, C. (1998).Exploring achievement values among ethnic minority early adolescents. *Journal of Educational Psychology, 90*, 606–620.

Guthrie, J. T., McRae, A., & Klauda, S. L. (2007). Contributions of concept-oriented reading instruction to knowledge about interventions for motivation in reading. *Educational Psychologist, 42*, 237–250.

Harackiewicz, J. M., Durik, A. M., Barron, K. E., Linnenbrink-Garcia, L., & Tauer, J. M. (2008). The role of achievement goals in the development of interest: Reciprocal relations between achievement goals, interest, and performance. *Journal of Educational Psychology, 100*, 105–122.

Harter, S. (1981). A new self-report scale of intrinsic versus extrinsic orientation in the classroom: Motivational and informational components. *Developmental Psychology, 17*, 300–312.

Harter, S., Whitesell, N. R., & Kowalski, P. (1992). Individual differences in the effects of educational transitions on young adolescents' perceptions of competence and motivational orientation. *American Educational Research Journal, 29*, 809–835.

Hickey, D. T., (1997). Motivation and contemporary socio-constructivist instructional perspectives. *Educational Psychologist, 32*, 175–193.

Hickey, D. T. (2008). Sociocultural theories of motivation. In E. M. Anderman & L. Anderman (Eds.), *Psychology of classroom learning*. Farmington Hills, MI: Thomson Gale Publishers.

Hickey, D. T., & Granade, J. B. (2004). The influence of sociocultural theory on our theories of engagement and motivation. In D. M. McInerney & S. Van Etten (Eds.), *Big theories revisited. Vol. 4: Research on sociocultural influences on motivation and learning* (pp. 223–247). Greenwich, CT: Information Age Publishing.

Hidi, S., & Renninger, K. A. (2006). The four phase model of interest development. *Educational Psychologist, 41*, 111–127.

Hudley, C., Graham, S., & Taylor, A. (2007). Reducing aggressive behavior and increasing motivation in school: The evolution of an intervention to strengthen school adjustment. *Educational Psychologist, 42*, 251–260.

Jacobs, J., Lanza, S., Osgood, D. W., Eccles, J. S., & Wigfield, A. (2002). Ontogeny of children's self-beliefs: Gender and domain differences across grades one through 12. *Child Development, 73*, 509–527.

Johnson, D. W., & Johnson, R. T. (2009). An educational psychology success story: Social interdependence theory and cooperative learning. *Educational Researcher, 38*, 365–379.

Juvonen, J. (2006). Sense of belonging, social bonds, and school functioning. In P. A. Alexander & P. H. Winne (Eds.), *Handbook of educational psychology* (2nd ed., pp. 655–674). Mahwah, NJ: Erlbaum.

Juvonen, J. (2007). Reforming middle schools: Focus on continuity, social connectedness, and engagement. *Educational Psychologist, 42*, 197–208.

Kindermann, T. A. (1993). Natural peer groups as contexts for individual development: The case of children's motivation in school. *Developmental Psychology, 29*, 970–977.

Kindermann, T. A. (2007). Effects of naturally existing peer groups on changes in academic engagement in a cohort of sixth graders. *Child Development, 78, 1186–1203*.

Ladd, G.W., Herald-Brown, S. L., & Kochel, K. (2009). Peers and motivation. In K. R. Wentzel & A. Wigfield (Eds.), *Handbook of motivation at school* (pp. 323–348). New York: Routledge.

Lee, V. E., & Smith, J. (2001). *Restructuring high schools for equity and excellence: What works*. New York: Teachers College Press.

Linnenbrink, E. A. (2005). The dilemma of performance-approach goals: The use of multiple goal contexts to promote students' motivation and learning. *Journal of Educational Psychology, 97*, 197–213.

Lord, S., Eccles, J. S., & McCarthy, K. (1994). Risk and protective factors in the transition to junior high school. *Journal of Early Adolescence, 14*, 162–199.

Maehr, M. L., & Midgley, C. (1996). *Transforming school cultures*. Boulder, CO: Westview Press.

Maehr, M. L., & Zusho, A. (2009). Achievement goal theory: Past, present, and future. In K. R. Wentzel & A. Wigfield (Eds.), *Handbook of motivation at school* (pp. 77–104). New York: Routledge.

McCaslin, M., & Good, T. L. (1996). The informal curriculum. In D. C. Berliner & R. C. Calfee (Eds.), *Handbook of educational psychology* (pp 622–670). New York: Macmillan.

Meece, J. L. (1991). The classroom context and students' motivational goals. In M. Maehr & P. Pintrich (Eds.), *Advances in motivation and achievement* (Vol. 7, pp. 261–286). Greenwich, CT: JAI Press,

Meece, J. L. (1994). The role of motivation in self-regulated learning. In D. H. Schunk & B. J. Zimmerman (Eds.), *Self-regulation of learning and performance* (pp. 25–44). Hillsdale, NJ: Lawrence Erlbaum Associates.

Meece, J. Glienke, B. B., & Askew, K. (2009). Gender and motivation. In K. R. Wentzel & A. Wigfield (Eds.), *Handbook of motivation at school* (pp. 411–431). New York: Routledge.

Meece, J. L., Wigfield, A., & Eccles, J. S. (1990). Predictors of math anxiety and its consequences for young adolescents' course enrollment intentions and performances in mathematics. *Journal of Educational Psychology, 82*, 60–70.

Murdock, T. (2009). Achievement motivation in racial and ethnic context. In K. R. Wentzel & A. Wigfield (Eds.), *Handbook of motivation at school* (pp. 433–461). New York: Routledge.

National Research Council. (2004). *Engaging schools: Fostering high school students' motivation to learn.* Washington, DC: National Academies Press.

Nicholls, J. G. (1984). Achievement motivation: Conceptions of ability, subjective experience, task choice, and performance. *Psychological Review, 91*, 328–346.

Nicholls, J. G., Cobb, P., Wood, T., Yackel, E., & Patashnick, M. (1990). Dimensions of success in mathematics: Individual and classroom differences. *Journal for Research in Mathematics Education, 21*, 109–122.

Nicholls, J. G., Cobb, P., Yackel, E., Wood, T., & Wheatley, G. (1990). Students' theories of mathematics and their mathematical knowledge: Multiple dimensions of assessment. In G. Kulm (Ed.), *Assessing higher order thinking in mathematics* (pp. 137–154). Washington, DC: American Association for the Advancement of Science.

Nolen, S. B. (2007). Young children's motivation to read and write: Development in social contexts. *Cognition and Instruction, 25*, 219–270.

Nolen, S. B., & Ward, C. J. (2008). Sociocultural and situative approaches to studying motivation. In M. L. Maehr, S. Karabenick & T. Urdan (Eds.), *Advances in motivation and achievement. Vol. 15: Social psychological perspectives* (pp. 425–461). Bingley, England: Emerald Publishing Group.

O'Donnell, A. M. (2006). The role of peers and group learning. In P. A. Alexander & P. H. Winne (Eds.), *Handbook of educational psychology* (2nd ed., pp. 781–802). Mahwah, NJ: Erlbaum.

Pallas, A. M., Entwisle, D. R., Alexander, K. L. & Stluka. M. F. (1994). Ability-group effects: Instructional, social, or institutional? *Sociology of Education, 67*, 27–46.

Perry, N. E., Turner, J. C., & Meyer, D. K. (2006). Classrooms as contexts for motivating learning. In P. A. Alexander & P. H. Winne (Eds.), *Handbook of educational psychology* (2nd ed., pp. 327–348). Mahwah, NJ: Erlbaum.

Pianta, R. C., Belsky, J., Vandegrift, N., Houts, R., & Morrison, F. J. (2008). Classroom effects on children's achievement trajectories in elementary school. *American Educational Reserach Journal, 45*, 365–397.

Pianta, R. C., Rimm-Kaufman, S. E., & Cox, M. J. (1999). Introduction: An ecological approach to kindergarten transition. In R. C. Pianta & M. J. Cox (Eds.), *The transition to kindergarten* (pp. 3–12). Baltimore, MD: P. H. Brookes Publishing.

Pintrich, P. R. (2000a). An achievement goal theory perspective on issues in motivation terminology, theory, and research. *Contemporary Educational Psychology, 25*, 92–104.

Pintrich, P. R. (200b). Multiple goals, multiple pathways: The role of goal orientation in learning and achievement. *Journal of Educational Psychology, 92*, 544–555.

Rotter, J. B. (1966). Generalized expectancies for internal versus external control of reinforcement. *Psychological Monographs, 80*, 1–28.

Rubin, K. H., Bukowski, W. M., & Parker, J. G. (2006). Peer interactions, relationships, and groups. In W. Damon (Series Ed.) & N. Eisenberg (Vol. Ed.), *Handbook of child psychology* (6th ed., Vol. 3, pp. 571–645). New York: Wiley.

Ryan, R. M., & Deci, E. L. (2009). Promoting self-determined school engagement: Motivation, learning, and well-being. In K. R. Wentzel & A. Wigfield (Eds.), *Handbook of motivation in school* (pp. 171–196). New York: Routledge.

Schiefele, U. (2009). Situational and individual interest. In K. R. Wentzel & A. Wigfield (Eds.), *Handbook of motivation in school* (pp. 197–222). New York: Routledge.

Schunk, D. H. (1983). Developing children's self-efficacy and skills: The roles of social comparative information and goal setting. *Contemporary Educational Psychology, 8*, 76–86.

Schunk, D. H., & Pajares, F. (2009). Self-efficacy theory. In K. R. Wentzel & A. Wigfield (Eds.), *Handbook of motivation in school* (pp. 35–54). New York: Routledge.

Simpkins, S. D., Davis-Kean, P. E., & Eccles, J. S. (2006). Math and science motivation: A longitudinal examination of the links between choice and beliefs. *Developmental Psychology, 42*, 70–83.

Skaalvik, E. (1997). Self-enhancing and self-defeating ego orientation: Relations with task and task avoidance orientation, achievement, self-perceptions, and anxiety. *Journal of Educational Psychology, 89*, 71–81.

Skinner, E. A. (1995). *Perceived control, motivation, and coping.* Thousand Oaks, CA: Sage Publications.

Skinner, E. A., Kindermann, T. A., Connell, J. P., & Wellborn, J. G. (2009). Engagement and disaffection as organizational constructs in the dynamics of motivational development. In K. R. Wentzel & A. Wigfield (Eds.), *Handbool of motivation at school* (pp. 223–245). New York: Routledge.

Stipek, D. J. (1996). Motivation and instruction. In R. C. Calfee & D. C. Berliner (Eds.), *Handbook of educational psychology* (pp. 85–113). New York: Macmillan.

Taylor, A. Z., & Graham, S. (2007). An examination of the relationship between achievement values and perceptions of barriers among low-SES African American and Latino students. *Journal of Educational Psychology, 99*, 52–64.

Thorkildsen, T., & Nicholls, J. G. (1998). Fifth graders' achievement orientations and beliefs: Individual and classroom differences. *Journal of Educational Psychology, 90*, 179–201.

Urdan, T. C. (Ed.). (1999). *The role of context: Advances in motivation and achievement* (Vol. 11). Greenwich, CT: JAI Press.

Vygotsky, L. S. (1978). *Mind and society: The development of higher mental processes.* Cambridge, MA: Harvard University Press.

Watt, H. (2004). Development of adolescents' self-perceptions, values, and task perceptions. *Child Development, 75*, 1556–1574.

Webb, N. M., & Palincsar, A. M. (1996). Group processes in the classroom. In D. C. Berliner & R. C. Calfee (Eds.), *Handbook of educational psychology* (pp 841–873). New York: Macmillan.

Weiner, B. (1992). *Human motivation: Metaphors, theories, and research.* Newbury Park, CA: Sage Publications.

Wentzel, K. (2002). Are effective teachers like good parents? Teaching styles and student adjustment in early adolescence. *Child Development, 73*, 287–301.

Wentzel, K. R. (2009). Students' relationships with teachers as motivational constructs. In K. R. Wentzel & A. Wigfield (Eds.), *Handbook of motivation at school* (pp. 301–322). New York: Routledge.

Wentzel, K. R., & Wigfield, A. (2007). *Motivational interventions that work.* Special Issue,, Educational Psychologist, 42, No. 4.

Wigfield, A., & Cambria, J. M. (2010). Children's achievement values, goal orientations, and interest: Definitions, development, and relations to achievement outcomes. *Developmental Review, 35*, 1–30.

Wigfield, A., & Eccles, J. S. (2002). The development of competence beliefs, expectancies for success, and achievement values from childhood through adolescence. In A. Wigfield & J. S. Eccles (Eds.), *Development of achievement motivation* (pp. 91–120). San Diego, CA: Academic Press.

Wigfield, A., Eccles, J. S., MacIver, D., Reuman, D., & Midgley, C. (1991). Transitions at early adolescence: Changes in children's domain-specific self-perceptions and general self-esteem across the transition to junior high school. *Developmental Psychology, 27,* 552–565.

Wigfield, A., Eccles, J. S., & Pintrich, P. R. (1996). Development between the ages of eleven and twenty-five. In D.C. Berliner and R.C. Calfee (Eds.), *The handbook of educational psychology,* New York: Macmillan Publishing.

Wigfield, A., Eccles, J. S., & Rodriguez, D. (1998). The development of children's motivation in school contexts. In A. Iran-Nejad & P. D. Pearson (Eds.), *Review of research in education* (Vol. 23, pp. 73–118). Washington, DC: American Educational Research Association.

Wigfield, A., Eccles, J. S., Schiefele, U., Roeser, R. W., & Davis-Kean, P. (2006). Development of achievement motivation. In N. Eisenberg (Ed.), *Handbook of child psychology* (Vol. 3, pp. 933–1002). New York: John Wiley.

Wigfield, A., Guthrie, J. T., Perencevich, K., Taboada, A., Klauda, S. L., McRae, S., & Barbosa, P. (2008). The role of reading engagement in mediating the effects of instruction on reading outcomes. *Psychology in the Schools, 45,* 432–445.

Wigfield, A., Tonks, S., & Klauda, S. L. (2009). Expectancy—value theory. In K. R. Wentzel & A. Wigfield (Eds.), *Handbook of motivation in school* (pp. 55–76). New York: Routledge.

Advances in Motivation in Exercise and Physical Activity

Martin S. Hagger

Abstract

Given the considerable epidemiological evidence linking regular physical activity with good health and reduced risk of chronic disease, exercise psychologists have adopted theories and models of motivation to understand the antecedents and processes that give rise to health-related physical activity. These theories are important because they provide the basis for the development and evaluation of interventions aimed at promoting increased physical activity in a largely sedentary population. This chapter reviews three of the leading theories that have been applied in physical activity contexts: the theory of planned behavior, self-determination theory, and achievement goal theory. Advances in research that have aimed to promote better understanding of the factors that underpin motivation in physical activity and the relevant processes are also reviewed, including implementation intentions, the increasing importance of psychological needs, and theoretical integration. In addition, the role of methodological improvements such as the measurement of implicit motivational processes and the need for "gold standard" designs when evaluating physical activity interventions based on these theories are highlighted. It is concluded that future research needs to develop hybrid interventions adopting both motivational and implemental strategies to change physical activity behavior, research should extend knowledge of the relative contribution of implicit and explicit motivational processes on physical activity behavior, and investigations to evaluate physical activity interventions should pay careful attention to design and evaluation.

Key Words: exercise, planned behavior, intention, autonomous motivation, achievement goals, implicit processes, intervention design

Introduction

There is strong epidemiological evidence linking low levels of physical activity with chronic health conditions such as cardiovascular disease (Williams, 2001), obesity (Ross, Freeman, & Janssen, 2000), diabetes (Jeon, Lokken, Hu, & van Dam, 2007), and cancer (Byers et al., 2002). International reports have highlighted the importance of regular physical activity as an important preventive behavior in managing these health risks (U.S. Department of Health and Human Services, 1996; World Health Organization, 2004). However, it is clear that people

in industrialized nations do not engage in sufficient physical activity to minimize risks from these chronic conditions (Bauman et al., 2009; Martinez-Gonzalez et al., 2001). Such reports have catalyzed considerable investigation into the motivational variables that are associated with individual leisure-time physical activity in order to develop population-based interventions to change behavior (Marteau, Dieppe, Foy, Kinmonth, & Schneiderman, 2006).

Many behavioral approaches adopted to understand people's motivation to engage in physical activity have been based on social psychological theories and models. The purpose of these theories is three-fold: *(1)* to identify the motivational correlates and antecedents of physical activity behavior; *(2)* to identify the mechanisms and processes by which these correlates affect physical activity (e.g., mediation and moderation effects); and *(3)* to use knowledge of the antecedents and mechanisms to inform and design interventions aimed at changing behavior to promote desirable health outcomes (Baum & Posluszny, 1999; Hagger, 2009; Taylor, 2008). In this chapter I will review three dominant social psychological approaches to understanding motivation in physical activity and review recent advances in the field that have aimed to enhance understanding and advance knowledge of how to increase motivation and behavior in physical activity. I will first review the research on the motivational theories and the contribution such research has made in identifying the key constructs that influence physical activity behavior and which have been most effective in explaining variance in physical activity behavior. The theories are Ajzen's (1985, 1991) theory of planned behavior, Deci and Ryan's (1985b, 2000) self-determination theory, and Nicholls' (1989) achievement goal theory. I will very briefly review the research adopting these approaches and evaluate their importance and level of contribution to the literature on motivation and physical activity. Most important, I will identify the advances, theoretically, that researchers in the physical activity domain have made to each of these theories such as the use of implementation intention strategies, the adoption of new perspectives on psychological needs (e.g., "need thwarting"), and the introduction of a 2 x 2 achievement goal framework. I will also outline how theoretical integration may benefit theoretical research in physical activity contexts. Finally, I will review recent methodological advances in the psychology of physical activity such as the use of implicit measures of motivation and the importance of randomized controlled trials, intervention mapping, and intervention fidelity to ensure that the effective components of motivational interventions to change physical activity can be identified and replicated precisely.

Three Key Motivational Theories in Physical Activity

The psychology of physical activity is a theory-rich discipline with many motivational theories and models proposed to provide comprehensive and definitive explanations of health behavior (Hagger, 2010a). It is, however, important to note that many of these theories have similar components and hypotheses, such that there is considerable overlap in the definitions of constructs and the proposed mechanisms by which these constructs affect physical activity behavior (Hagger, 2009). For example, self-efficacy, a very important construct in the field of social psychology and derived from Bandura's (1977, 1995) influential social cognitive theory, is a key component in numerous theories of motivated social behavior such as protection motivation theory (Rogers, 1975) and the theory of planned behavior (Ajzen, 1985) and both have been applied to physical activity (Hagger, Chatzisarantis, & Biddle, 2002b; Rhodes, Plotnikoff, & Courneya, 2008). Similarly, the construct of intention, which is a motivational construct reflecting the degree of effort and planning an individual is prepared to invest in pursuing a behavior, is also a key component of numerous theories such as the theory of planned behavior, protection motivation theory, the theories of self-regulation and trying (Bagozzi & Kimmel, 1995), and the theory of goal-directed behavior (Perugini & Conner, 2000). Again these theories have been adopted to explain behavior in a physical activity context (Bagozzi & Kimmel, 1995; Perugini & Conner, 2000). Similarly, these theories have different assumptions and perspectives. For example, attitudinal theories like the theory of planned behavior are belief based and focus on behavioral predictions based on estimates of the future outcomes of a given behavior and individuals' evaluation of those outcomes. In contrast, theories such as self-determination theory (Deci & Ryan, 1985b, 2000) adopt an organismic approach, steeped in the humanist tradition, focusing on the contextual influences on motivated behavior and motivational orientations derived from the satisfaction of innate psychological needs. In this chapter I will focus on three dominant motivational theories applied in physical activity contexts: the theory of planned behavior, self-determination theory, and achievement goal theory. I will outline how the adoption of these theories has contributed to the understanding of physical activity behavior. I will also review how these theories might help move the field forward in terms of developing a more comprehensive theory of the antecedents and mechanisms of physical activity behavior and informing interventions and practical solutions to increase motivation to participate in physical activity and promote engagement in physical activity behavior.

The Theory of Planned Behavior

The theory of planned behavior (Ajzen, 1985, 1991; Fishbein & Ajzen, 2009) is a widely adopted social cognitive theory aimed at explaining intentional behavior. It has been applied to many health-related behaviors, including physical activity (Hagger et al., 2002b; Symons Downs & Hausenblas, 2005). In the theory, intention is considered a motivational construct and represents the degree of planning and effort people are willing to invest in performing any future planned action or behavior. Intention is conceptualized within the theory as the most proximal influence on behavior and is a function of a set of personal, normative, and control-related belief-based social-cognitive constructs regarding the performance of the future behavior, termed *attitudes, subjective norms*, and *perceived behavioral control*, respectively.

Attitudes refer to an individual's overall evaluation of the behavior and are usually tapped using *direct* measures and psychometric scales (Ajzen, 2003). However, the sets of personal beliefs that the target behavior will result in outcomes (behavioral beliefs) and whether such outcomes are salient (outcome expectations) are hypothesized to underpin the direct attitude measure (Ajzen, 2003). These can also be measured individually for each belief and outcome and are considered *indirect* measures of attitude. Similarly, subjective norms are typically measured directly as a person's overall evaluation that significant others would want them to engage in the target behavior. As with attitudes, subjective norms are sourced indirectly from sets of beliefs that reflect expectations that significant others will exert pressure or cajole the individual to engage in the behavior (normative beliefs) and the individual's propensity to comply with those significant others (motivation to comply). The construct of perceived behavioral control encompasses control-related perceptions with respect to the target behavior, including actual barriers and personal evaluations of limitation or capacity with respect to the behavior. This led Ajzen to indicate that perceived behavioral control contained elements of Bandura's (1977) self-efficacy construct in that it captures judgments of how well one can execute required actions to produce important outcomes. The construct is also underpinned by a set of beliefs (Ajzen, 1985). *Control beliefs* refer to the perceived presence of factors that may facilitate or impede performance of behavior, and *perceived power* refers to the perceived impact that facilitative or inhibiting factors may have on performance of behavior (Ajzen & Driver, 1991). An indirect measure of perceived behavioral control is formed from the composite of the control beliefs multiplied by its perceived power (Ajzen & Driver, 1991).

In terms of process and the operationalization of the model, intentions are hypothesized to lead directly to behavior and mediate the effects of attitudes, subjective norms, and perceived behavioral control on behavior. This means that intentions *explain* the effects of attitudes, subjective norms, and perceived behavioral control on behavior. Intentions are therefore necessary to convert these constructs into behavior. Ajzen (1985) also predicted direct and indirect effects for the perceived behavioral control construct on behavior. The effects of perceived behavioral control that are mediated by intention reflect the level of perceived volitional control an individual has over the performance of the behavior in the future, similar to self-efficacy. However, if perceived behavioral control closely reflected the degree to which participation in the behavior was impaired by real environmental barriers or impedances, the construct would serve as a "proxy" measure of actual control and directly affect behavior unmediated by intention.

The most frequently cited or "modal" beliefs that underpin the attitude, subjective norms, and perceived behavioral control constructs in physical activity contexts have been identified. The beliefs are typically elicited from pilot research using open-ended measures that are content analyzed to provide sufficient information to develop the salient outcomes for the behavioral belief and outcome evaluation measures, the salient referents for the normative belief and motivation to comply measures, and the salient barriers and control-related issues for the control beliefs and perceived power measures (Ajzen & Fishbein, 1980). Research in physical activity has typically identified the following most frequently cited (modal) outcomes: "good companionship," "weight control," "benefit my overall health," "take too much time," "fun," "get fit," "stay in shape," "improve skills," "get an injury," and "makes you hot and sweaty" (Hagger, Chatzisarantis, & Biddle, 2001). Similarly, important referents identified include friends, colleagues, and family members like parents, grandparents, and siblings (Hagger et al., 2001). The modal control beliefs identified include barriers and facilitators that underpin the direct measure of perceived behavioral control: "bad weather," "age," "heart pain," "costs," "fatigue," and "no time" (Godin, Valois, Jobin, & Ross, 1991). As with behavioral and normative beliefs, research shows that control beliefs demonstrate considerable variance across different populations and behaviors. For example, studies in the physical activity domain have identified "age" and "fear of having a heart attack" among the control beliefs for older and clinical populations (Godin et al., 1991), but these beliefs do not feature among the control beliefs of younger populations who focus more on inclement weather and lack of time (Hagger et al., 2001). Interestingly, the comparatively limited research examining relations between the indirect belief-based measures and the direct measures suggests that multiplicative composites of the belief and value systems do not account for a high degree of variance in the direct measures of attitudes, subjective norms, and perceived behavioral control (Hagger et al., 2001). Few definitive solutions have been put forward for this problem, and the role of beliefs and expectancy-value models within the theory of planned behavior is an area of surprisingly sparse attention in the literature (Ajzen & Fishbein, 2008; Bagozzi, 1984; French & Hankins, 2003).

Formative research adopting the theory of planned behavior in physical activity contexts has demonstrated that attitudes and perceived behavioral control consistently and significantly predict intentions and explain approximately equal proportions of the variance in physical activity behavior with a substantially lesser role for subjective norms (Hagger & Chatzisarantis, 2005; Hagger et al., 2002b). In addition to individual empirical studies, a meta-analysis of 72 studies applying the theory of planned behavior in physical activity contexts supported the trends in the physical activity data across the literature (Hagger et al., 2002b). Using a meta-analytic path analysis, intention was found to be the sole proximal predictor of physical activity and that the effects of attitudes and perceived behavioral control on intentions were medium in magnitude and stronger than the effects of subjective norms. In addition, studies that separated measures of self-efficacy (reflecting personal capacity and confidence estimates) and perceived controllability (reflecting perceived barriers) indicated that self-efficacy explained additional variance in the prediction of both intentions and behavior. Past behavior also predicted all of the theory constructs and attenuated their effects on intention and behavior. Nevertheless, the influences of the social cognitive constructs on intentions and behavior remained significant even after controlling for previous experience. This indicated that previous decision-making processes were accounted for by the variables in the model, but the

most recent decision-making variables remained salient as explanations of variance in physical activity intentions and behavior. It was concluded that "...while past behavior had a significant and direct influence on intention, attitude, perceived behavioral control, and self-efficacy, these cognitions are also necessary for translating past decisions about behavioral involvement into action. This is consistent with the notion that involvement in volitional behaviors such as regular physical activity involves both conscious and automatic influences" (p. 23).

This evidence indicates the general recognition of theory of planned behavior as an important theoretical approach to the understanding of the motivational influences on physical activity behavior. The considerable attention paid to the theory in the literature is attributable to its effectiveness in accounting for variance in physical activity intention and behavior as well as its relative parsimony and role as a flexible framework for the study of psychosocial influences and processes that underpin physical activity behavior. For example, its role as a "flexible framework" has been supported by research that has shown the attitude, subjective norm, and perceived behavioral control constructs mediate the effect of other distal constructs on intentions and behavior such as personality (Bozionelos & Bennett, 1999; Chatzisarantis & Hagger, 2008; Conner & Abraham, 2001; Conner, Rodgers, & Murray, 2007; Hoyt, Rhodes, Hausenblas, & Giacobbi, 2009; Rhodes & Courneya, 2003; Rhodes, Courneya, & Jones, 2002, 2003) and other individual difference variables (Chatzisarantis & Hagger, 2007; Fitch & Ravlin, 2005; Hagger, Anderson, Kyriakaki, & Darkings, 2007). However, researchers have also indicated that the theory does not account for all of the variance in intention and behavior, nor does it mediate the effects of certain "external variables" on intentions and behavior (e.g., Bagozzi & Kimmel, 1995; Conner & Abraham, 2001; Conner & Armitage, 1998; Rhodes & Courneya, 2003; Rhodes et al., 2002). Paradoxically, this "weakness" has become the theory's greatest strength. Ajzen (1991) states that the theory should be viewed as a *flexible framework* into which other variables can be incorporated provided they make a meaningful and unique contribution to the prediction of intentions and there is a theoretical precedence for the inclusion of such variables.

As a consequence, the theory has been adopted by researchers in physical activity as a general framework to investigate the effect of a number of additional social cognitive constructs on intention and behavior (Conner & Armitage, 1998). To the extent that such constructs have a unique effect on intention or behavior and are not mediated by the core theory variables of attitude, subjective norm, and perceived behavioral control, the researcher has evidence to support the inclusion of that construct within the theory. A number of constructs have been found to have a unique effect on intentions and/or behavior, including anticipated affect and attitude ambivalence (Armitage & Conner, 2000), anticipated regret (Sheeran & Orbell, 1999a), cultural norms and ethnicity (Blanchard et al., 2008; Blanchard et al., 2009; Blanchard et al., 2003; Van Hooft & De Jong, 2009; Walker, Courneya, & Deng, 2006), descriptive norms (Sheeran & Orbell, 1999a), group norms and membership (Terry, Hogg, & White, 2000; White, Hogg, & Terry, 2002), health locus of control (Armitage, 2003; Hagger & Armitage, 2004), moral norms (Godin, Conner, & Sheeran, 2005; Lam, 1999), past behavior (Aarts, Verplanken, & van Knippenberg, 1998; Albarracín & Wyer, 2000; Conner, Warren, Close, & Sparks, 1999; Hagger et al., 2001), prototypes (Norman, Armitage, & Quigley, 2007), self-identity (Hagger & Chatzisarantis, 2006), and self-schemas (Sheeran & Orbell, 2000a).

In addition to the effects of other constructs, the influence of variations in the characteristics and nature of the core theory of planned behavior constructs on intentions, and of intention itself, on behavior have been investigated (Sheeran, 2002). Examples include the stability of intentions (Sheeran, Orbell, & Trafimow, 1999), the accessibility of attitudes (Doll & Ajzen, 1992; Verplanken, Hofstee, & Janssen, 1998), and hypothetical bias (Ajzen, Brown, & Carvahal, 2004). In addition, researchers have sought to differentiate between the independent and fundamental concepts within each of the psychosocial components that predict intentions. For example, attitudes have been differentiated into cognitive or instrumental attitudes and affective attitudes (Lowe, Eves, & Carroll, 2002; Trafimow & Sheeran, 1998), subjective norms have been differentiated into injunctive norms and descriptive norms (Rivis & Sheeran, 2003), and, as mentioned previously, perceived behavioral control has been differentiated into self-efficacy and perceived controllability (Armitage & Conner, 1999a, 1999b; Hagger et al., 2001; Povey, Conner, Sparks, James, & Shepherd, 2000; Sniehotta, Scholz, & Schwarzer, 2005; Terry & O'Leary, 1995). Even intentions have been distinguished from desires, the latter being "emotional" forms of intention (Perugini &

Bagozzi, 2001, 2004). In the same vein, researchers have also investigated the extent to which individuals are orientated toward or base their intentions on each of the core theory constructs (Sheeran, Trafimow, Finlay, & Norman, 2002; Trafimow & Finlay, 1996). These modifications suggest that the antecedents of volitional behaviors, like physical activity, may be more complex than originally conceived by the theory (Conner & Armitage, 1998). However, it is important to note that many of these modifications make relatively modest increases in the predictions within the model and the separation of the theory components into more specific, differentiated constructs does not appear to affect the prediction of intentions and behavior at the global level (Hagger & Chatzisarantis, 2005). Notwithstanding these modifications, the theory still performs relatively well in terms of explaining physical activity behavior and in its most parsimonious form can inform successful interventions to promote physical activity (e.g., Chatzisarantis & Hagger, 2005; Darker, French, Eves, & Sniehotta, 2010).

Although the theory of planned behavior has demonstrated considerable success in terms of predicting physical activity in numerous contexts and groups, the theory and the research that has adopted it does have considerable documented limitations. First, the relationship between intentions and behavior is far from perfect. In fact, it frequently falls considerably short of a large effect size and meta-analytic studies have typically indicated that the relationship between intentions and behavior is relatively modest (Hagger et al., 2002b), perhaps medium in size, according to Cohen's (1987) taxonomy of effect sizes. Numerous reasons have been cited for this problem such as a lack of correspondence between the measures of intention and behavior, the relative instability of intentions, and the moderating effect of numerous individual difference factors such as self-schema. These have been frequently investigated and research has shown that the intention-behavior "gap" is strengthened under conditions of high intention stability and among self-schematics (Sheeran & Orbell, 2000a). However, the relationship remains relatively modest in effect size, which means that people frequently do not convert their "good" intentions to engage in physical activity into actual behavior. Researchers have therefore sought to develop strategies that might assist in moderating the intention–behavior relationship, particularly strategies that enable individuals to convert their "good" intentions to engage in physical activity behavior into actual action.

These strategies and advances will be reviewed in the "Theoretical Advances" section of this chapter.

Self-Determination Theory

Self-determination theory (Deci & Ryan, 1985b, 2000) is a prominent motivational theory adopted to identify the contextual and interpersonal influences on human behavior and has received much attention in the physical activity literature (Hagger & Chatzisarantis, 2007a, 2008, 2007d; Ryan & Deci, 2007). Self-determination theory is actually a meta-theory comprising a number of subtheories that seek to explain human motivation and behavior on the basis of individual differences in motivational orientations, contextual influences on motivation, and interpersonal perceptions. Central to self-determination theory is the distinction between self-determined or *autonomous* forms of motivation relative to non-self-determined or *controlling* forms of motivation. The extent to which people experience motivation to engage in activities and behaviors as autonomous or controlling will determine their persistence with the behavior in the future and whether they gain certain adaptive outcomes such as satisfaction, enjoyment, and psychological well-being. Organismic integration theory (OIT), a subtheory of self-determination theory, seeks to provide an explanation for the processes by which people assimilate behaviors that are externally regulated and incorporate them into their repertoire of behaviors that are self-determined and integrated into their personal system. Central to OIT is the perceived locus of causality, which represents a graduated continuum of motivational styles or *regulations*. The continuum, known as the perceived locus of causality, is characterized by two relatively autonomous forms of motivation: *intrinsic motivation* and *identified regulation*, and two relatively controlling forms of motivation: *external regulation* and *introjected regulation* (Ryan & Connell, 1989). Important for researchers and practitioners in the field of physical activity, individuals who act for autonomous reasons are more likely to persist in the absence of discernable external rewards or contingencies. Therefore, if interventions can promote autonomous motives for engaging in physical activity among individuals, it is likely to lead to persistence over time and cede the health benefits of physical activity to those individuals. The major theoretical tenets of self-determination theory have been outlined in detail elsewhere in this volume (see Chapter 6), so the present review will focus on the specific application of self-determination in the domain of health-related physical activity.

Research adopting the perceived locus of causality from OIT has shown that autonomous forms of regulation are positively related to adaptive behavioral and psychological outcomes in the domain of physical activity. Autonomous motivation is associated with physical activity participation and adherence over time (Barbeau, Sweet, & Fortier, 2009; Chatzisarantis, Biddle, & Meek, 1997; Chatzisarantis, Hagger, Biddle, & Karageorghis, 2002; Chatzisarantis, Hagger, Biddle, Smith, & Wang, 2003; Fortier & Kowal, 2007; Pelletier, Dion, Slovinec-D'Angelo, & Reid, 2004; Vansteenkiste, Simons, Soenens, & Lens, 2004), perceived competence (Goudas, Biddle, & Fox, 1994), physical activity intentions (Hagger & Chatzisarantis, 2007b; Hagger, Chatzisarantis, Culverhouse, & Biddle, 2003; Phillips, Abraham, & Bond, 2003; Standage, Duda, & Ntoumanis, 2005; Wilson & Rodgers, 2004), Csikzentmihalyi's (1990) flow state (Fortier & Kowal, 2007), and psychological well-being (Wilson & Rodgers, 2007). Furthermore, environmental antecedents such as autonomy support (Edmunds, Ntoumanis, & Duda, 2007) and people's perceptions that the motivational context is supportive of their autonomous motivation (Hagger, Chatzisarantis, Barkoukis, Wang, & Baranowski, 2005; Hagger et al., 2003; Hein & Koka, 2007; Koka & Hein, 2003; Standage et al., 2005) have also been linked with autonomous motivational regulations from OIT. Findings from previous research have been supported by a recent meta-analysis of the effects of perceived locus of causality on behavior and outcomes in physical activity settings (Chatzisarantis et al., 2003). The analysis supported the proposed effects of the motivational regulations on physical activity behavior and outcomes such as perceived competence and physical activity intentions across a set of 21 studies (Chatzisarantis et al., 2003). Interestingly, autonomous forms of motivation mediated the effect of perceived competence on physical activity intentions, suggesting that competence perceptions affect behavior because competence perceptions tend to be self-determined in nature.

Another fundamental subtheory of self-determination theory is Basic needs theory. Deci and Ryan (2000) suggest that the origins of self-determined motivation stem from individuals' innate propensity to satisfy three basic psychological needs: *autonomy, competence,* and *relatedness*. These needs are perceived to be *fundamental* to all humans, and people approach behaviors in an intrinsically motivated fashion because they perceive it as being efficacious in satisfying psychological needs. The existence of these needs has been justified empirically and research has illustrated that these needs are pervasive across different cultures (Sheldon, Elliot, Kim, & Kasser, 2001). Basic needs theory is linked with OIT because it charts the origins of autonomous or self-determined motivational regulations. The perceived locus of causality is proposed to reflect the degree to which behaviors have become internalized or "taken in." Behaviors that have the propensity to fulfill personally relevant goals that are valued by individuals (e.g., participating in physical activity to gain more energy for other activities in life or to increase fitness) are perceived as efficacious in satisfying psychological needs. Increased participation in such behaviors will likely lead to the behavior being internalized and finally integrated into the person's repertoire of behaviors that satisfy these needs. As a result, people may not perform physical activity for the activity itself as in the "classic" definition of intrinsic motivation. Rather, they perform it to achieve an intrinsic "outcome" that is highly valued and perceived as part of the person's "true self."

It is also important to note that the three basic needs are complementary—that is, optimal functioning and truly integrated behavior can only result if all three psychological needs are supported. For example, competence alone, that is, mastering a technique or skilled action alone is not sufficient for a behavior to be perceived to be need satisfying. Competence along with a perception that the behavior is performed out of a true sense of self, without external contingency, perceived or real, and out of choice and volition (i.e., autonomously motivated) and that behavioral engagement is supported by others in an autonomous fashion (i.e., relatedness) is necessary for an action to be fully integrated and to support psychological needs. Research in the physical activity domain has suggested that the basic needs tend to be strongly correlated and can be subsumed by a single global factor (Hagger, Chatzisarantis, & Harris, 2006; Ntoumanis, 2005; Standage et al., 2005) and interventions that provide synergistic support for the needs of autonomy, competence, and relatedness tend to result in greater behavioral engagement than support for each individual need alone (Deci, Eghrari, Patrick, & Leone, 1994). Overall, the satisfaction of basic psychological needs has been shown to be related to autonomous forms of motivation in physical activity contexts from the perceived locus of causality consistent with self-determination theory (Edmunds et al., 2007; Hagger et al., 2006; Standage, Gillison, & Treasure, 2007) and interventions supporting autonomous motivation were found to increase psychological

need satisfaction as well as motivational regulations (Edmunds et al., 2007). While research examining the role of psychological need satisfaction as the origin of autonomous motivation in physical activity, this research is relatively new and there is considerable scope for further investigation to answer questions relating to the role of needs in determining physical activity behavior. For example, what happens to physical activity when needs are not fulfilled or thwarted? Such questions will be addressed in the "Theoretical Advances" section of this chapter.

Achievement Goal Theory and the 2 x 2 Framework

Achievement goal theory was developed to examine the effects of perceptions of success and failure on motivation in education contexts (Nicholls, 1989). Central to the theory is the manner in which people tend to view or interpret success or failure when engaged in competence-relevant behaviors. The original conceptualization of the theory identified two pervading dispositional and enduring motivational orientations: mastery oriented and performance oriented. Individuals with a mastery-oriented or *self-referenced* goal orientation tend to view success and failure in terms of personal improvement, effort, self-referenced goals, and learning. Analogously, people with a performance-oriented or *other-referenced* goal perspective tend to view their success and failure in terms of their performance compared to others, fulfilling normative standards, other-referenced goals, competition, and normative comparison. This classic dichotomous conceptualization of achievement motivation has formed the basis of numerous theoretical traditions that have viewed achievement goals as generalized orientations that affect individuals' interpretation of competence across a wide variety of contexts (Ames, 1992; Dweck, 1986; Nicholls, 1984), including physical activity (e.g., Cury et al., 1996; Treasure & Roberts, 2001; Vlachopoulos & Biddle, 1997).

A relatively recent framework proposed by Elliot and others (Elliot, 1999; Pintrich, 2000) views achievement goals as more dynamic, flexible, and changeable interpersonal constructs that not only vary in terms of the definition of competence in achievement settings but also in their valence as either approach or avoidant. The integration of an approach-avoidance valence concurrent with the mastery-performance dichotomy has led to the development of a 2 x 2 conceptualization of achievement goals (Elliot & Church, 1997; Elliot & Conroy, 2005; Elliot & McGregor, 2001). The theory proposes that not only can people define their competence with respect to future actions as self-referenced, either according to a personal or absolute standard, or other referenced, but also in terms of whether it will lead to adaptive, desirable outcomes or maladaptive, undesirable outcomes. Such evaluations are automatically paired with an approach or avoidance response such that courses of action that are expected to lead to desirable outcomes are approach valenced and actions leading to undesired outcomes are avoidance valenced (Bargh, 1997; Elliot & McGregor, 2001). As a consequence, people will tend to perceive their competence with respect to future actions in terms of both the definition and valence dimensions.

The 2 x 2 framework integrates the definition and competence dimensions to produce four distinct achievement goal constructs: mastery-approach goals in which competence is defined in terms of mastering skills, improving technique, and enhancing self-referenced outcomes and is positively valenced; performance-approach goals in which competence is defined in normative terms and relative to the performance of others and is positively valenced; mastery-avoidance goals in which competence is defined as personally referenced and is negatively valenced; and performance-avoidance goals in which competence is defined normatively and is negatively valenced. These goal orientations should be viewed as "situation-specific regulators of achievement behavior that are energized and impelled by underlying motive dispositions" (Elliot & Church, 1997, p. 228). Therefore, global goal orientations and motivational dispositions may influence or give rise to these goals and the goals are also affected by environmental and situational factors that define the behavioral response.

Research with the 2 x 2 model has illustrated that mastery-approach goals are most strongly related to adaptive outcomes such as need for achievement (Elliot & Murayama, 2008), self-concept (Hein & Hagger, 2007), perceived competence (Cury, Elliot, Da Fonseca, & Moller, 2006), self-determined forms of motivation (Barkoukis, Ntoumanis, & Nikitaras, 2007; Hein & Hagger, 2007; Wang, Biddle, & Elliot, 2007), enjoyment (Pekrun, Elliot, & Maier, 2006; Wang et al., 2007), and behavioral persistence (Elliot, Cury, Fryer, & Huguet, 2006; Elliot & Murayama, 2008). Research has also investigated relations between achievement goals using the 2 x 2 framework in physical activity contexts, but investigations have largely focused on competitive sport behavior (e.g., Adie, Duda, &

Ntoumanis, 2008; Barkoukis et al., 2007; Conroy, Elliot, & Hofer, 2003; Conroy, Kaye, & Coatsworth, 2006). Elliot and Conroy (2005) point out that relations between the 2 x 2 achievement goal constructs and health-related physical activity have not been fully investigated: "Although the value of the expanded 2 x 2 conceptual framework [of achievement goals] in sport and physical activity domains is a relatively open empirical question, we are optimistic of its potential for enhancing our understanding of achievement motivation in these contexts and eagerly await further investigation" (p. 21).

Recent research has provided evidence to support to Elliot and Conroy's suggestion that the 2 x 2 model may offer a useful framework for the understanding of motivation in health-related physical activity contexts. Variables such as intrinsic motivation (Barkoukis et al., 2007), perceived competence (Wang et al., 2007), and self-efficacy (Cumming & Hall, 2004) have been shown to be related to approach goals, whereas fear of failure and extrinsic motivation have been shown to be related to avoidance goals (Barkoukis et al., 2007; Conroy & Elliot, 2004). This provides an indication of the utility and content of achievement goals in this context. For example, people may perceive engaging in physical activity as an opportunity to achieve personally relevant or self-determined outcomes such as mastering an exercise technique or losing the most weight in an aerobics class. They are therefore more likely to develop approach-valenced mastery or performance goals toward their behavioral regulation. However, they may also be motivated to avoid physical activity contexts if they perceive that they are unlikely to demonstrate competence and have a high likelihood of failure. For example, people may perceive that doing physical activities may reveal their lack of skills or that they are not as competent as others when it comes to lifting weights or running at speed on a treadmill. Such undesirable outcomes are likely to result in the development of avoidance-valenced mastery or performance goals. Just as high perceived competence and fear of failure may lead to the development of approach and avoidance goals, respectively, other variables related to competence may also be linked to achievement goals (Hein & Hagger, 2007).

While research in the field of achievement goals has been somewhat rejuvenated with the introduction of the 2 x 2 conceptual framework, questions still remain, particularly for the field of health-related physical activity. At the forefront of this future research should be the development of specific inventories for the physical activity context. Conroy et al.'s (2003) achievement goal questionnaire for sport (AGQ-S) has been shown to be a useful and valid instrument in measuring constructs from the 2 x 2 framework in sport contexts, but it is not likely to be applicable to noncompetitive, health-related physical activity contexts. In addition, future research in the physical activity domain should be directed toward establishing the links between the achievement goals from the 2 x 2 framework and the degree of internalization of physical activity behavior using the perceived locus of causality. It may be that the graded conceptualization of motivational regulations in the exercise domain may discriminate the different goal perspectives. There is also the need to examine achievement goals in relation to constructs from other theories. For example, there are recognized congruences between achievement goal and self-determination theories, and these have been well documented, generally (Ryan & Deci, 1989) and in the domain of physical activity (Standage, Duda, & Ntoumanis, 2003a). However, there is increased need to look at the overlap and distinctions in the context of the 2 x 2 framework. This will be investigated in more detail in the "Integration of Theories" section of this chapter.

Theoretical Advances

While the three motivational theories have informed exercise psychologists' understanding of the factors that influence physical activity behavior and also provided a useful basis for interventions aimed at changing physical activity behavior and health-related outcomes, questions remain with respect to some of the limitations of the theories and the lack of information or research in particular areas in the physical activity context. I outlined some of these limitations and needs for research in the previous sections. For example, the theory of planned behavior is limited in that the link between intentions and behavior was relatively modest; there is relatively limited information on self-determination theory in the role that psychological need satisfaction plays on physical activity behavior; and there is little research on the conceptual and empirical links between theories like achievement goal theory, the theory of planned behavior, and self-determination theory in the physical activity domain. In the next two sections, I will outline recent developments in the field of motivation in physical activity that attempt to address these outstanding questions with a view to advancing knowledge and understanding of physical activity behavior.

Implementation Intention Approaches

One of the problems with motivational interventions based on theories like the theory of planned behavior is that their effects on actual behavior have been relatively modest (Hardeman et al., 2002). The limited success of such interventions has been attributed to the comparatively weak relationship between intentions and behavior observed in formative research on the theory. For example, meta-analyses have demonstrated that the average effect size of the intention–behavior relationship for many health behaviors, including physical activity, although significant, is comparatively weak and is further compromised by the inclusion of past behavior (Armitage & Conner, 2001; Hagger et al., 2002b). Furthermore, meta-analyses of interventions and experimental manipulations based on the theory of planned behavior aimed at changing intentions have corroborated these findings, demonstrating substantially larger effects of interventions on intentions than behavior (Webb & Sheeran, 2006). These data present a problem for interventions based on this theory as it seems that even though people may report that they have "good intentions" to engage in physical activity, people do not always behave in accordance with their intentions.

Solutions to this problem have been presented in the form of implemental approaches to behavioral engagement. Heckhausen and Gollwitzer (1987) presented an action-phase model that identifies two complementary processes that lead to action: an intentional (motivational) phase and an implemental (volitional) phase. The intentional phase encompasses the processes that lead to the formation of intentions to engage in a behavior captured aptly in the theory of planned behavior by the antecedents of intention. However, while intentions to engage in health-related behaviors may be a prerequisite for behavioral engagement, they are not always sufficient. The implemental phase outlines the process of how the identification of critical cues in the environment leads to the enactment of intentions and promotes strong links between the cue and the planned action. Proponents of the action-phase model have proposed that engaging in strategies that highlight a critical situation or contingency in which the behavior will be initiated will be effective in promoting behavioral engagement. Such strategies, known as *implementation intentions*, require people to propose and write down when and where they will enact their planned behavior (e.g., "*if* situation *Y* occurs, *then* I will perform response *Z*!"). Such exercises promote behavioral engagement by promoting increased accessibility of the critical cue in the environment (Aarts, Dijksterhuis, & Midden, 1999) and developing a link in memory between the critical situation (Y) and the planned action (Z) (Brandstätter, Lengfelder, & Gollwitzer, 2001). When intentions are furnished with implementation intentions, behavioral initiation is therefore more efficient, guided by automatic processes, and less vulnerable to lapses in memory or reliant on conscious processing.

Augmenting intentions with implementation intentions has shown to be effective in promoting behavioral engagement in numerous health-related contexts, including cancer screening (Orbell, Hodgkins, & Sheeran, 1997; Prestwich et al., 2005; Sheeran & Orbell, 2000b), dietary behaviors (Chapman, Armitage, & Norman, 2009; Prestwich, Ayres, & Lawton, 2008; Prestwich, Perugini, & Hurling, 2009; Scholz, Schuz, Ziegelmann, Lippke, & Schwarzer, 2008; van Osch et al., 2009; Verplanken & Faes, 1999), alcohol consumption (Murgraff, Abraham, & McDermott, 2007), and physical activity (Arbour & Martin Ginis, 2009; Chatzisarantis, Hagger, & Thøgersen-Ntoumani, 2008; De Vet, Oenema, Sheeran, & Brug, 2009; Luszczynska, 2006; Milne, Orbell, & Sheeran, 2002; Prestwich, Lawton, & Conner, 2003; Sniehotta, Scholz, Schwarzer et al., 2005). A meta-analysis has also demonstrated that implementation exercises have a strong effect on behavioral enactment (Gollwitzer & Sheeran, 2006). In addition, investigations have demonstrated that changes in behavior as a result of forming implementation intentions are not due to changes in intentions or other constructs from the theory of planned behavior (Orbell et al., 1997; Sheeran & Orbell, 1999b). Instead, there is evidence that the effect of implementation intention manipulations is mediated by the extent to which participants engage in the implementation intention exercises and form plans to enact their intentions (Scholz et al., 2008). Such mediators are important because they demonstrate the mechanisms for the effects and also highlight the dependence of the effect on compliance with the implementation intention manipulations (Michie, 2008).

In the context of physical activity behavior, implementation intentions have been shown to be effective in producing increased physical activity participation and, therefore, reducing the intention-behavior "gap." The body of research adopting these kinds of intervention is increasing has been applied to numerous types of physical activity such as walking (Arbour & Martin Ginis, 2009) and regular moderate-to-vigorous physical activity (Luszczynska & Haynes, 2009; Prestwich et al., 2008; Prestwich et al., 2009; Stadler, Oettingen, & Gollwitzer, 2009) and in different populations such as those with chronic diseases like obesity (De Vet et al., 2009) and cardiovascular disease (Luszczynska, 2006; Sniehotta, Scholz, Schwarzer et al., 2005). A recent meta-analysis of interventions and experimental trials adopting implementation intentions in the context of physical activity demonstrated a small-to-medium effect size of implementation intentions on physical activity behavior (Bélanger-Gravel, Godin, & Amireault, 2011). Suffice to say that the trends in this research generally support the significant and positive effects for implementation intention interventions on physical activity behavior found in studies adopting this intervention approach in other behavioral contexts.

A relatively recent advance in this field is the adoption of hybrid intervention approaches that target both intention promotion using traditional intervention approaches targeting the antecedents of intention from the theory of planned behavior and implementation using implementation intention strategies. This research has demonstrated that motivational interventions combined with implementation intentions have a synergistic effect on physical activity behavior (Milne et al., 2002; Prestwich et al., 2003). Such interventions have demonstrated considerable promise and indicate the importance of both motivation and implementation when it comes to intervening to enhance physical activity behavior. Hybrid interventions should therefore be advocated in the development of physical activity interventions based on motivational theories in the future.

Psychological Needs and Need Thwarting

Self-determination theory is a relatively unique approach in the melee of psychological theories applied to physical activity because it is an organismic approach that is based on three innate psychological needs: autonomy, competence, and relatedness (Deci & Ryan, 2000). According to the theory, it is the environmental support for these needs as well as the extent to which an individual perceives these needs to be satisfied that gives rise to autonomously motivated behavior. The latter "state" of motivation is clearly desirable for exercise psychologists, practitioners, and interventionists when it comes to behaviors like physical activity because it means that individuals are more likely to engage and persist with the behavior (i.e., be more effective at self-regulating their physical activity) in the absence of any external contingency (e.g., the presence of a social agent to "prod" and "coerce") or tangible reward (e.g., money). In the theory, it is assumed that all individuals require these needs to be satisfied to function effectively in their environment, and research has suggested that people recognize the value of these needs and that they are universal (Sheldon et al., 2001). As a consequence, there has been considerable recent interest in the role of psychological need satisfaction, motivational orientations toward physical activity, and actual physical activity engagement and behavior.

For example, several studies have shown global psychological need satisfaction to be associated with actual physical activity behavior (Edmunds et al., 2007; Hagger et al., 2003; Hagger et al., 2006; Wilson, Rodgers, Blanchard, & Gessell, 2003). However, this association was, unsurprisingly, mediated by contextual-level motivational orientations, indicating a process model. Psychological need satisfaction therefore acts as a distal factor influencing physical activity behavior by promoting autonomous forms of motivation toward that specific behavior. Support for this process model has been relatively consistent in the literature for both physical activity and other health-related behaviors. In fact, a recent meta-analysis has demonstrated a significant indirect effect of satisfaction of the three psychological needs on health-related behavior, many of which were conducted in a physical activity context (McLachlan, 2011). This demonstrates the relatively consistent effects of psychological needs and the process model proposed by Deci and Ryan (1985b, 2000) in their exposition of the theory.

So what does the future hold for research into psychological needs? I propose two new steps. First, there has been comparatively little attention paid to occasions where psychological needs remain unsatisfied or are thwarted (Bartholomew, Ntoumanis, & Thogersen-Ntoumani, 2009). It could be argued that is equally important to examine the effects of occasions when individuals in physical activity contexts fail to have their psychological needs satisfied and whether that impacts on their physical activity participation. If a person perceives the physical activity domain not to be a context in which his or her needs are likely to be satisfied, this will probably have two effects on the person's behavior in that domain. First, it would likely lead to an avoidance response and desistance from physical activity participation and, second, the individual may likely seek the satisfaction of those needs elsewhere, in other behavioral domains. These effects are most

likely to occur when the context fails to support needs. Recent evidence for this comes from some research conducted on adolescent girls' unhealthy weight-control behaviors (such as skipping meals, taking laxatives, and vomiting). The research demonstrated that low psychological need satisfaction was associated with high levels of these behaviors and this was mediated by body image concerns (Thøgersen-Ntoumani, Ntoumanis, & Nikitaras, 2010). However, perceptions that significant social agents such a parents supported autonomy was positively related to psychological need satisfaction. This indicates that interventions that target autonomy-supportive behaviors of social agents may be a useful means to promote psychological need satisfaction and, as a consequence, autonomous motivation to engage in physical activity. Indeed, our meta-analysis has demonstrated a significant relationship between both perceived and actual autonomy support and psychological need satisfaction (McLachlan, 2011). It may be that thwarted psychological needs in certain contexts are not irreparable, and the provision of autonomy support may be most effective in bringing about changes in motivation for people with low need satisfaction. However, there is relatively little research adopting this approach in a physical activity context, and there is a clear need for further inquiry in this direction to confirm these hypotheses.

Integration of Theories
THE THEORY OF PLANNED BEHAVIOR AND SELF-DETERMINATION THEORY

Recently, researchers have sought to integrate psychosocial models such as the theory of planned behavior with other motivational theories like self-determination theory. This is because these approaches are deemed to provide complementary explanations of the processes that underlie motivated behavior (Hagger, 2009). This is important with regard to the theory of planned behavior because it provides information as to the origins of the attitudes, subjective norm, and perceived behavioral control constructs. Several researchers have integrated these approaches in mediational models to illustrate the processes that lead to decisions to engage in social behavior. For example, self-determined or autonomous motives from self-determination theory have been shown to directly predict behavioral intentions (Chatzisarantis et al., 2002; Hagger, Chatzisarantis, & Biddle, 2002a; Standage et al., 2003a; Wilson & Rodgers, 2004). However, some researchers have tested a more complete model in which different regulatory styles of autonomous and controlled motivation from self-determination theory predict intentions via the mediation of attitudes and perceived behavioral control. This motivational sequence has been supported in a number of studies (Chatzisarantis et al., 2002; Hagger et al., 2005; Hagger et al., 2002a; Hagger et al., 2003; Hagger et al., 2006).

The proposition that self-determination theory (Deci & Ryan, 1985b, 2000) can augment social cognitive theories such as the theory of planned behavior has been suggested previously, but it has only recently received empirical support. Numerous authors have proposed that motivational, organismic theories such as self-determination theory could potentially offer explanations for the origins of constructs in social cognitive theories. As Andersen, Chen, and Carter (2000) state, "most information processing [social cognitive] models are silent on matters central to self-determination theory" (p. 272). Deci and Ryan (1985b) have suggested that social cognitive theories identify the immediate antecedents of behavior but neglect the origins of the antecedents: "Cognitive theories begin their analysis with what Kagan (1972) called a motive, which is a cognitive representation of some future desired state. What is missing, of course, is the consideration of the conditions of the organism that makes these future states desired" (p. 228). Constructs such as attitudes, perceived behavioral control, and intentions from social cognitive theories like the theory of planned behavior are measured as explicitly stated expectancies regarding future behavioral engagement. Therefore, the integration of these theories may offer more information as to the mechanisms that underlie intentional behavior such as physical activity.

The integration of the theory of planned behavior and self-determination theory is based on two key premises. The first premise is based on the hypothesis that the relationship between autonomous motives from self-determination theory and the constructs from the theory of planned behavior is a *formative* one. People who have high levels of autonomous motivation in a given domain are likely to experience their behavior in that domain as personally relevant and valued in that it is concordant with their psychological need for self-determination (Sheldon, 2002). As a consequence, autonomously motivated people will have a greater tendency to critically examine the importance and value of the outcomes of engaging in any future target behavior. In the case of physical activity, autonomous people will be likely to find information that points to the importance of activity and thus form a positive attitude toward future participation in that physical activity. In contrast, people who report high levels of controlled forms of motivation will tend to focus on external contingencies of the future engagement in physical activity, which are likely to have little to do with the valued consequences of participating in physical activity. Individuals with high levels of autonomous motivation are likely to feel more confident in reaching their goals and engaging in subsequent behavior to satisfy these goals because they quench their need for competence. Links between autonomous motivation and perceived competence have been found in previous research (e.g., Williams, Gagne, Ryan, & Deci, 2002; Williams, McGregor, Zeldman, & Freedman, 2004).

The second premise relates to the relative degree of generality reflected by the constructs from the two theories. The autonomous motives from self-determination theory reflect dispositional motivational orientations in a particular context and are therefore expected to predict behavioral engagement across a variety of behaviors in that context. In the case of physical activity this can mean formal kinds of exercise (e.g., going to the gym, participating in an aerobics class), sport (e.g., training for a particular sport and competition), and informal or incidental physical activity (e.g., walking to work, using stairs instead of the elevator). Vallerand (2000) labels this form of motivation *contextual-level motivation* because it reflects motivational orientations that affect all forms of behavior in a given context. However, the constructs from the theory of planned behavior are *expectations* for engaging in the behavior in the future, and measures of these constructs therefore specify explicitly the behavior and time frame of that bout of behavior. Vallerand suggested that contextual-level motivation affects motivational orientations at the situational level in a top-down fashion (see also Guay, Mageau, & Vallerand, 2003). Intentions in the theory of planned behavior are hypothesized to be located at this level because they reflect expectations for engaging in a specific target behavior at a specific future point in time. They are therefore conceptualized as orientations to engage in a behavior at the situational level. In addition, Vallerand also hypothesized that contextual-level motivation would also influence cognitions at the situational level. It is therefore expected that motivation at the contextual level would influence the beliefs that underlie engagement in specific bouts of a behavior in the future, which, according to the theory of planned behavior, are constructs like attitudes and perceived behavioral control. In accordance with this theory, it would be expected that contextual-level motives would predict the performance of behavior at the situational level and its antecedents.

There is a growing body of research that has supported the integration of the theory of planned behavior and self-determination theory. The development of research in this area began with Chatzisarantis, Biddle, and Meek (1997) who found that intentions based on self-determination theory (autonomous intentions) were a better predictor of behavior than "traditional" forms of intentions. Similarly, Sheeran, Norman, and Orbell (1999) found that intentions based on attitudes were more likely to predict behavior than intentions based on subjective norms, and they suggested that intentions based on attitudes reflected pursuing behaviors for personally valued outcomes (akin to an identified regulation) and, therefore, for more autonomous reasons than intentions based on subjective norms, which reflected more controlling aspects of motivation such as external or introjected regulations. Together these results paved the way for more comprehensive studies in which the effects of self-determined forms of motivation influenced behavior.

Following these pioneering studies, researchers have been committed to comprehensive tests integrating the theories adopting hypotheses from both component theories to address hypotheses relating to behavior in numerous contexts. Prominent among these studies are those that outline a clear motivational sequence in which the generalized motivational orientations from self-determination theory influence constructs from the theory of planned behavior in a physical activity context (e.g., Chatzisarantis et al., 2002; Hagger et al., 2002a). In such studies, the theory of planned behavior acts as a conduit for the effects of autonomous forms of motivation on physical activity behavior. The decision-making constructs from the theory of planned behavior reflect the formation of plans to engage in physical activity in the future and represent situational motivational orientations toward physical activity behavior. The self-determination theory motives serve to indicate a source of information that influences the decision-making process. For example, autonomous forms of motivation from self-determination theory are hypothesized to influence attitudes from the theory of planned behavior; an autonomous motivational disposition in a particular domain is likely to be

an impetus to the formation of attitudes oriented toward servicing personally valued goals and mediate the effects of autonomous motivation on physical activity intentions.

Hagger, Chatzisarantis, and Biddle (2002a) found that self-determined forms of motivation affected intentions to engage in physical activity behavior, but only via the mediation of attitudes and perceived behavioral control. This provided support for the hypothesis that autonomous forms of motivation bias individuals' decision making in favor of forming attitudes congruent with their personal goals (attitudes) and perceptions that the behavior will lead to competence-related outcomes (perceived behavioral control). This was corroborated in a subsequent study that furthered these findings to actual behavior. Autonomous motives affected behavior via a motivational sequence beginning with autonomous forms of motivation and ending with behavioral engagement mediated by attitudes, perceived behavioral control, intentions, and effort (Chatzisarantis et al., 2002). Since this initial research, the indirect effect of autonomous motives from self-determination theory on intentions and behavior as stipulated by the proposed motivational sequence has been corroborated in several studies in the domain of physical activity (e.g., Hagger et al., 2005; Hagger et al., 2003; Hagger, Chatzisarantis et al., 2009; Shen, McCaughtry, & Martin, 2007, 2008). A recent meta-analysis of all studies adopting these theories and testing some of the components of the integrated motivational sequence has provided support for the sequence (Hagger & Chatzisarantis, 2009b). The meta-analysis demonstrated across 36 studies, the majority of which were in a physical activity context, that the effect of self-determined motivation on behavior was mediated by the theory of planned behavior variables. This provides useful information for the process by which social contexts influence behavior and provides recommendations for intervention. For example, we have shown that interventions can be designed in such a way to change perceptions at any stage of the motivational sequence, targeting either autonomous motives as a distal influence on intentions or attitudes and perceived control as a proximal influence. This may lead to hybrid interventions that adopt techniques from both self-determination theory (Chatzisarantis & Hagger, 2009) and the theory of planned behavior (Chatzisarantis & Hagger, 2005) to promote increased physical activity participation.

2 X 2 ACHIEVEMENT GOAL PERSPECTIVES AND SELF-DETERMINATION THEORY

Achievement goal theory was developed by researchers interested in examining the effects of young people's perceptions of success and failure on motivation in education contexts (Ames, 1992; Nicholls, 1989). An important tenet of the theory is that cues from the social context, known as the *motivational climate*, have pervasive effects on motivation and behavior. Two dimensions have emerged from research examining the effects of motivational climate on motivation in educational settings: a task or *mastery*-oriented climate and an ego- or *performance*-oriented climate. A mastery-oriented motivational climate tends to promote hard work, effort, cooperation, and personal development among individuals acting in that climate, whereas a performance-oriented climate tends to engender comparisons with others, competition, success based on ability, and reward and punishment schedules for success and failure. Research in education has suggested that a mastery-oriented climate tends to engender adaptive motivational patterns and is linked to increased psychological well-being and persistence in behavior (Ames, 1995; Ntoumanis & Biddle, 1999).

The concepts of motivational climate and intrinsic motivation from self-determination theory have been viewed as providing complementary explanations of motivation. A mastery-oriented motivational climate, in supporting effort, personal improvement, and self-references improvement is directly compatible with autonomous motivation because such contexts have been shown to enhance intrinsic motivation (Butler, 1987). In contrast, performance-oriented climates have not been associated with autonomous forms of motivation, and they may even undermine autonomous motivation given its focus on external contingencies for success. Recently, Deci and Ryan (2000) have explicitly linked a mastery-oriented motivational climate with the development of intrinsic motivation, stating that "both [theories] suggest that the use of salient performance-based rewards, social comparisons, and normatively based goal standards as motivational strategies yield manifold hidden costs [and] that environments that are less evaluative and more supportive of the intrinsic desire to learn provide the basis for enhanced achievement and well-being" (p. 260). These theoretical links have been supported empirically across many achievement-related behaviors (Rawsthorne & Elliot, 1999). A burgeoning body of literature in the physical activity domain has also supported these theoretical links, and it seems a mastery motivational climate promotes exercise adherence and is attributable to the context enhancing intrinsic motivation and competence (Cury et al., 1996; Cury, Da Fonséca, Rufo, Peres, & Sarrazin, 2003; Cury, Elliot, Sarrazin, Da Fonseca, & Rufo, 2002; Escarti & Gutierrez, 2001; Goudas & Biddle, 1994; Hein & Hagger, 2007; Kavussanu & Roberts, 1996; Papaioannou, 2004; Treasure & Roberts, 2001).

Recent research has sought to examine the role of motivational climate in physical activity contexts in promoting or thwarting autonomous forms of motivation (Ntoumanis, 2001; Standage, Duda, & Ntoumanis, 2003b). Such studies adopt a longitudinal approach, similar to those examining the effect of perceived autonomy support on motivation and intention (Hagger & Chatzisarantis, 2007b, 2007c), and there is considerable congruence in the motivational sequences put forward in these models. However, these models have tended to focus on participation within physical education rather than physical activity outside of school. Importantly, these authors make explicit the links between a mastery-oriented motivational climate and contexts that support psychological needs and recognize the congruences between the features of the social context that support autonomous forms of motivation from both theoretical perspectives (Ntoumanis, 2005; Standage et al., 2005; Standage et al., 2007).

The achievement goal perspective has also been adopted alongside constructs from self-determination theory in terms of dispositional orientations that reflect perceptions about success and failure (Ntoumanis, 2005; Standage et al., 2003b). Until recently, research in achievement goal perspectives had identified two pervading achievement goal orientations: task oriented and ego oriented. A task-oriented motivational orientation means an individual will tend to view success and failure in physical activity contexts relative to personal improvement, effort, self-referenced goals, learning, and improvement. Analogously, ego-oriented persons will tend to view their success and failure relative to their performance compared to others, fulfilling normative standards, other-referenced goals, and competition and normative comparison. Research in physical activity contexts has suggested that individuals who attach high value to task-oriented goals tend to have more adaptive motivational patterns and, in particular, report high levels of intrinsic motivation in tasks (Boyd, Weinmann, & Yin, 2002;

Brunel, 1996; Hein & Hagger, 2007; Newton & Duda, 1999; Standage et al., 2003b; Wang & Biddle, 2003). This is irrespective to whether they also endorse an ego-oriented goal perspective, and it is only when task orientation is comparatively low that maladaptive motivational patterns such as avoiding evaluative situations and low intrinsic motivation arise (Goudas et al., 1994; Goudas, Biddle, & Underwood, 1995). It must, however, be stressed that there is a relative dearth of research examining the effects of motivational climate on autonomous forms of motivation in physical activity contexts, and, most important, even fewer studies that have examined the role of interventions to manipulate or change motivational climate and its effects on self-determination theory variables and physical activity behavior (Hagger, Hein, & Chatzisarantis, 2011). These should be prioritized in future research.

Measurement and Methodological Advances

In this final section I outline two important methodological advances that offer much promise in contributing to the understanding of the motivational influences on physical activity behavior. The first focuses on the development of new measures of implicit, nonconscious constructs in the field of social psychology and applying them alongside the explicit measures of motivation traditionally operationalized in theories and models of motivation in physical activity contexts. Such an approach acknowledges that motivated behaviors like physical activity are not simply a function of explicit, conscious decision-making processes but are also subject to more spontaneous, impulsive psychological variables (Hagger, 2010c; Hagger, Wood, Stiff, & Chatzisarantis, 2009, 2010; Hofmann, Friese, & Wiers, 2008). The second focuses on the importance of using cutting-edge methodological features when designing interventions based on motivational theories in physical activity research. I will argue for the consideration of intervention mapping and reporting of intervention protocols such that there is clear congruence between the target theoretical constructs and the intervention components as well as the need for state-of-the-art techniques to establish the effectiveness of the intervention, including treatment fidelity checks.

Implicit Motivation

Research in social psychology over the past 10 years has begun to shift away from models that focus solely on deliberative, intentional, and explicit influences on behavior and sought to develop theories that account for the nonconscious, impulsive, and implicit influences on human behavior (Bargh & Chartrand, 1999; Greenwald et al., 2002; Hofmann, Friese, & Strack, 2009; Kehr, 2004; Nosek, Greenwald, & Banaji, 2007; Strack & Deutsch, 2004). Such approaches have given rise to so-called *dual route* models of motivation that recognize that behavior is a function of reflective, deliberative, volitional, and planned inferences as well as those that are impulsive, automatic, nonconscious, and unplanned (Hofmann et al., 2009; Strack & Deutsch, 2004). Interest in these automatic and implicit processes has been mirrored by concomitant advances in methods to measure implicit processes. Research adopting implicit processes alongside more traditional self-report measures of cognition has illustrated that behavior is influenced by both explicit and implicit social cognitive variables and these effects are relatively independent (Perugini, 2005; Spence & Townsend, 2007).

Given the increasing attention being paid to implicit processes, recent research has endeavored to examine the role of implicit processes in self-determined motivation and behavior. This is based on theoretical premises that suggest that people have an implicit bias or propensity to approach behaviors in an autonomous or controlling manner. For example, Deci and Ryan (1985a) proposed causality orientations theory, which introduced the notion that people have a generalized capacity to be oriented toward and interpret situations as supportive of their self-determination. Therefore, people exhibit interindividual differences in their generalized causality orientations, which are global and relatively enduring, developed through experience, and affect motivation and behavior in a variety of contexts. Such orientations may moderate the effects of situational factors that support or thwart intrinsic motivation on behavior (Hagger & Chatzisarantis, 2011). In addition, it has been supposed that these causality orientations may affect behavior independent of conscious decision making (Elliot, McGregor, & Thrash, 2002), in much the same way as individual difference and personality constructs tend to influence behaviors independent of intentional processes (Conner & Abraham, 2001; Rhodes et al., 2002). Indeed, recent evidence examining mediational models of motivation adopting OIT and basic needs theory have indicated that generalized constructs such as basic need satisfaction predict exercise behavior directly independent of contextual motivational orientations and intentions (Hagger et al., 2006). These processes therefore transcend the deliberative route by which these psychological constructs lead to behavior and suggests that people's global causality orientations may affect behavior directly, and the process is likely to be one with which the person is unaware and therefore implicit in nature.

Recent research has included implicit motivational constructs in the prediction of behavior adopting a self-determination theory approach. Levesque and Pelletier (2003) adopted priming techniques used in previous studies examining implicit processes to activate either autonomous or nonautonomous (termed *heteronomous*) motivational orientations. Using this method, they found that priming autonomous and heteronomous motivation influenced participants' perceptions of intrinsic motivation, choice, and competence as well as persistence with subsequent problem-solving tasks consistent with explicit, consciously regulated motivational orientations. Similarly, Burton, Lydon, D'Alessandro, and Koestner (2006) used a lexical decision task to measure implicit autonomous motivation and found that this measure predicted psychological well-being and academic performance independent of explicit measures of autonomous motivation. Together these studies suggest that the motivational influences from self-determination theory can influence behavior and other outcomes implicitly and these effects are independent of explicit motivational orientations.

Recently we have conducted a series of studies to extend this research to a physical activity context and adopt recently developed measures of implicit motivational orientations from self-determination theory (Harris, 2008; Keatley, Clarke, & Hagger, 2011). The studies required the development of an implicit measure of motivational orientations based on self-determination theory using the Implicit Association Test (IAT) and then evaluate the extent to which the implicit motives tapped by the new measure predicted variance in physical activity behavior. The IAT is essentially a sorting task that requires individuals to sort items from two pairs of contrasted categories into logical sets and in doing so measures the strength of association between mental constructs that are bipolar in nature. The IAT was developed with the distinction between "intrinsic" and "extrinsic" as categories of motivation and "pleasant" or "unpleasant" as the associated attributes. The words that represented the category were derived from a pilot study in which participants were required to write down words associated with intrinsic and extrinsic categories.

In our studies, we used the newly developed implicit measure of motivation to predict self-reported physical activity behavior alongside more explicit measures of motivational orientations from the perceived locus of causality. Scores on the IAT were such that higher scores represented a strong link between the positive attribute and self-determined motivation. Although there were relations between the implicit and explicit measures of motivation, there was no direct effect of the implicit motivational orientations on physical activity behavior. Rather, the explicit measures of autonomous and controlling motivation both significantly predicted physical activity intentions and behavior. In one sample, there was a mediated effect from the implicit motivational orientation to intentions via the mediation of explicit controlling forms motivation. This preliminary evidence suggests that the implicit measure of self-determined motivation may have a role in influencing physical activity intentions, but the route is subsumed by explicit forms of motivation. Nevertheless, this is an important finding because it suggests that physical activity is largely an intentional behavior under the volitional control of the individual and requires conscious and deliberative motivational factors to be enacted. However, research using implicit measures is in its infancy and requires further validation work and research examining the independent prediction of implicit autonomous motives on motivation and physical activity. Furthermore, the present studies focused on self-reported physical activity and, therefore, likely a more considered, intentional form. It may be that implicit motivational orientations are more important in predicting forms of activity which are less to do with explicit, deliberate motivational processes. This is clearly an important avenue for future research, and it will provide new and important information on the relative contribution of the implicit and explicit motivational systems on physical activity behavior.

Randomized Controlled Trials and Intervention Mapping

The randomized controlled trial (RCT) has often been cited as the gold standard for the evaluation of clinical trials of any intervention, and a considerable body of evidence has been recently established examining the efficacy of theory-based psychological intervention on physical activity behavior (Michie & Abraham, 2008). Indeed, meta-analyses have extolled the effectiveness of RCT evaluations of theory-based interventions on physical activity behavior and health-related outcomes such as fitness and weight loss in numerous contexts (e.g., Conn, Hafdahl, Cooper, Brown, & Lusk, 2009; Harris, Kuramoto, Schulzer, & Retallack, 2009; Jenkins, Christensen, Walker, & Dear, 2009; Wu, Gao, Chen, & van Dam, 2009). There have also been meta-analyses focusing on intervention based on specific theories like the theory of planned behavior (Hardeman et al., 2002) and self-determination theory (McLachlan, 2011) or theory-based intervention protocols like motivational interviewing (Lundahl, Kunz, Brownell, Tollefson, & Burke, 2010). However, many of these systematic reviews and meta-analyses have been hampered and limited by the low quality of many of the constituent studies. A key quality component that has often be cited a lacking is the sufficient detail in the reporting of the intervention and a lack of provision of clear protocols to permit the replication of the intervention and the identification of the components of the intervention that are effective in changing behavior (Michie & Abraham, 2008; Michie et al., 2005; Michie, Johnston, Francis, Hardeman, & Eccles, 2008). These limitations have made it difficult to draw definitive conclusions as to the effectiveness of particular interventions based on particular theories. For example, without sufficient detail it is difficult to establish whether the intervention satisfactorily targeted the theoretical variable proposed by the researchers running the intervention and resulted in changes in the dependent variable (Michie & Abraham, 2008). Recent solutions to this have arisen in the need to clearly map the intervention components onto the theoretical constructs the components are purported to change (Michie, 2008; Michie et al., 2008). A further problem is whether there is sufficient detail and checks regarding whether the intervention has been carried out by those administering the intervention as it is outlined in the intervention protocol. This would require checks to ensure that those administering the intervention were keeping to task and whether the participants reported carrying out the intervention correctly and accurately. This is known as *treatment fidelity* (Bellg et al., 2004) and has only very recently been applied to behavioral interventions in physical activity contexts (Hardeman et al., 2007).

The aforementioned intervention components have been termed the "active ingredients" of interventions, and this has received much recent attention in the literature. Abraham and Michie (2008) have published a taxonomy of health-related behavior change intervention components. The aim of the taxonomy is to provide a more systematic description of the components of interventions that target specific constructs from motivational theories of behavior change. This is an important step forward in terms of assisting researchers and intervention designers in being more explicit in identifying the specific components of interventions that are proposed to be making the change in behavior (Michie, 2008). This is clearly important when it comes to translational research aiming to capitalize on the research identifying antecedents and mechanisms from motivational theories applied to physical activity contexts (Hagger, 2010a; Moss-Morris & Yardley, 2008). Furthermore, there is now a specific protocol for the coding of intervention components which provides a blueprint for mapping the intervention components that are the likely "active ingredients" of interventions (Michie & Prestwich, 2010). This is not only a tool for those conducting systematic reviews and meta-analyses but also for those designing interventions to consider when it comes to pinpointing the components from formative research examining psychological correlates likely to be the most viable target for intervention. Interventions aimed at changing physical activity behavior should therefore pay careful attention to providing clear details of the constructs that are the targets of interventions (based on formative research), the intervention components that will be adopted to give rise to the intervention, and a clear protocol, similar to an instruction manual, giving the precise details of the intervention so that it can be replicated.

Two other important methodological issues must be considered when it comes to the design, implementation, and evaluation of theory-based physical activity interventions. First, it is important that intervention designers include means to evaluate the treatment fidelity of the intervention (Bellg et al., 2004). This must come in two forms. First, it is important to evaluate whether the intervention has actually caused change in the specific theoretical variable or variables targeted by the intervention, similar to manipulation checks in experimental research. It is therefore essential that the intervention not only includes the primary outcome variables whether that be physical activity behavior, or any target outcome variables related to physical activity, but also measures of the psychological variables related to the intervention, both before and after the implementation of the intervention. Second, it is important that interventionists include means to identify whether the intervention has been carried out according to the proscribed protocol. If the intervention is delivered by a clinician or a social agent, an example of a fidelity check might include some sort of observation of a subgroup of the agents delivering the intervention and coded independently for the specific behaviors expected of those carrying out the intervention. Of course, it is important that this is compared to similar observations for the social agents executing the control condition components of the intervention. This will ensure that the intervention is carried out precisely and effectively in the manner outlined in the protocol.

Finally, I mentioned previously the importance of including measures relating to the target theory-related variables that the intervention components are purported to target as a means to establish the effectiveness of the intervention (Hagger, 2010b; Hagger & Chatzisarantis, 2009a). However, these components are also likely to be the salient mediators of intervention components and will provide an important test of the mechanisms by which the intervention affects behavioral outcomes. As an illustration, two of our recent interventions adopting theory-based interventions have demonstrated the importance of examining the psychological mediators of intervention components on behavior and motivational outcomes in physical activity (Chatzisarantis & Hagger, 2005, 2009). For example, in a school-based intervention aimed at increasing physical activity behavior among school pupils, we trained teachers to present their lessons in an autonomy-supportive manner versus an information-only intervention (Chatzisarantis & Hagger, 2009). As predicted, physical activity behavior increased among the children randomly allocated to the intervention group, but this was mediated perceived autonomy support, which also served as the manipulation check, and autonomous motivation and behavioral intentions. Similarly, we found that the effects of a school-based intervention adopting the theory of planned behavior on physical activity intentions was mediated by attitudes and perceived behavioral control (Chatzisarantis & Hagger, 2005). These data were analyses using path analyses, and the mediation analyses were conducted according to the criteria proposed by Baron and Kenny (1986). These analyses should be considered essential for the identification the process by which the intervention exerts its effects on physical activity behavior and is recommended practice.

Conclusion

In this chapter I have reviewed three important motivational theories that have provided exercise psychologists and those interested in promoting physical activity behavior in a largely sedentary population with important knowledge of the factors that influence physical activity and the processes by which these factors affect physical activity: the theory of planned behavior, self-determination theory, and achievement goal theory. Although these theories have had success in explaining variance in physical activity behavior and serving as the basis for interventions to change physical activity, there are limitations and shortcoming in the theories and in current knowledge of the application of these theories to physical activity. These limitations include the link between intentions and behavior and the relations between constructs in the theories. I have therefore reviewed recent advances that have aimed to address these limitations and gaps in the research such as the adoption of implementation intentions and theoretical integration. In addition, I have also highlighted the importance of recent methodological advances in implicit motivational research and the design of interventions in developing future research in physical activity behavior and advancing knowledge and understanding of physical activity behavior. I think the overall message of this chapter, distilling the research on motivation in physical activity, is that there is some high-quality and innovative research that is not only moving motivational theory forward but has genuine application and practical relevance to interventionists and policy makers to adopt in order to promote physical activity in populations and produce healthier lifestyles.

Future Directions

(1) Can an intervention designed to increase motivational climate as outlined by achievement goal theory result in changes in self-determined motivation, achievement goal orientations, and actual physical activity behavior?

(2) How do hybrid interventions that use motivational and implemental intervention components to promote physical activity affect the behavior people who are resistant to change and have low motivation versus those with high motivation?

(3) What are the differential effects of implicit and explicit motivational constructs on different types of physical activity such as formal exercise (e.g., going to the gym, attending an aerobics class) and more "habitual" forms of physical activity (e.g., walking to work)?

References

Aarts, H., Dijksterhuis, A., & Midden, C. (1999). To plan or not to plan? Goal achievement or interrupting the performance of mundane behaviors. *European Journal of Social Psychology, 29*, 971–979.

Aarts, H., Verplanken, B., & van Knippenberg, A. (1998). Predicting behavior from actions in the past: Repeated decision-making or a matter of habit? *Journal of Applied Social Psychology, 28*, 1355–1374.

Abraham, C., & Michie, S. (2008). A taxonomy of behavior change techniques used in interventions. *Health Psychology, 27*, 379–387.

Adie, J. W., Duda, J. L., & Ntoumanis, N. (2008). Achievement goals, competition appraisals, and the psychological and emotional welfare of sport participants. *Journal of Sport and Exercise Psychology, 30*, 302–322.

Ajzen, I. (1985). From intentions to actions: A theory of planned behavior. In J. Kuhl & J. Beckmann (Eds.), *Action-control: From cognition to behavior* (pp. 11–39). Heidelberg, Germany: Springer.

Ajzen, I. (1991). The theory of planned behavior. *Organizational Behavior and Human Decision Processes, 50*, 179–211.

Ajzen, I. (2003, April 14). Constructing a TPB questionnaire: Conceptual and methodological considerations. Retrieved September 1, 2009, from http://www-unix.oit.umass.edu/~aizen

Ajzen, I., Brown, T. C., & Carvahal, F. (2004). Explaining the discrepancy between intentions and actions: The case of hypothetical bias in contingent valuation. *Personality and Social Psychology Bulletin, 30*, 1108–1121.

Ajzen, I., & Driver, B. E. (1991). Prediction of leisure participation from behavioral, normative, and control beliefs: An application of the theory of planned behavior. *Leisure Sciences, 13*, 185–204.

Ajzen, I., & Fishbein, M. (1980). *Understanding attitudes and predicting social behavior*. Englewood Cliffs, NJ: Prentice Hall.

Ajzen, I., & Fishbein, F. (2008). Scaling and testing multiplicative combinations in the expectancy-value model of attitudes. *Journal of Applied Social Psychology, 38*, 2222–2247.

Albarracín, D., & Wyer, R. S. (2000). The cognitive impact of past behavior: Influences on beliefs, intentions, and future behavioral decisions. *Journal of Personality and Social Psychology, 79*, 5–22.

Ames, C. (1992). Classrooms: Goals, structures, and student motivation. *Journal of Educational Psychology, 84*, 261–271.

Ames, C. (1995). Achievement goals, motivational climate, and motivational processes. In G. C. Roberts (Ed.), *Motivation in sport and exercise* (pp. 161–176). Champaign, IL: Human Kinetics.

Andersen, S. M., Chen, S., & Carter, C. (2000). Fundamental human needs: Making social cognition relevant. *Psychological Inquiry, 4*, 269–275.

Arbour, K. P., & Martin Ginis, K. A. (2009). A randomised controlled trial of the effects of implementation intentions on women's walking behaviour. *Psychology and Health, 24*, 49–65.

Armitage, C. J. (2003). The relationship between multidimensional health locus of control and perceived behavioural control: How are distal perceptions of control related to proximal perceptions of control? *Psychology and Health, 18*, 723–738.

Armitage, C. J., & Conner, M. (1999a). Distinguishing perceptions of control from self-efficacy: Predicting consumption of a low fat diet using the theory of planned behavior. *Journal of Applied Social Psychology, 29*, 72–90.

Armitage, C. J., & Conner, M. (1999b). The theory of planned behavior: Assessment of predictive validity and "perceived control." *British Journal of Social Psychology, 38*, 35–54.

Armitage, C. J., & Conner, M. (2000). Attitudinal ambivalence: A test of three key hypotheses. *Personality and Social Psychology Bulletin, 26*, 1421–1432.

Armitage, C. J., & Conner, M. (2001). Efficacy of the theory of planned behaviour: A meta-analytic review. *British Journal of Social Psychology, 40*, 471–499.

Bagozzi, R. P. (1984). Expectancy-value attitude models: An analysis of critical measurement issues. *International Journal of Research in Marketing, 1*, 295–310.

Bagozzi, R. P., & Kimmel, S. K. (1995). A comparison of leading theories for the prediction of goal directed behaviours. *British Journal of Social Psychology, 34*, 437–461.

Bandura, A. (1977). Self-efficacy: Toward a unifying theory of behavioral change. *Psychological Review, 84*, 191–215.

Bandura, A. (1995). Health promotion from the perspective of social cognitive theory. *Psychology and Health, 13*, 623–649.

Barbeau, A., Sweet, S. N., & Fortier, M. (2009). A path-analytic model of self-determination theory in a physical activity context. *Journal of Applied Biobehavioral Research, 14*, 103–118.

Bargh, J. A. (1997). The automaticity of everyday life. In R. Wyer (Ed.), *Advances in social cognition* (Vol. 10, pp. 1–61). Mahwah, NJ: Erlbaum.

Bargh, J. A., & Chartrand, T. L. (1999). The unbearable automaticity of being. *American Psychologist, 54*, 462–479.

Barkoukis, V., Ntoumanis, N., & Nikitaras, N. (2007). Comparing dichotomous and trichotomous approaches to achievement goal theory: An example using motivational regulations as outcome variables. *British Journal of Educational Psychology, 77*, 683–702.

Baron, R. M., & Kenny, D. A. (1986). The moderator-mediator variable distinction in social psychological research: Conceptual, strategic and statistical considerations. *Journal of Personality and Social Psychology, 51*, 1173–1182.

Bartholomew, K., Ntoumanis, N., & Thogersen-Ntoumani, C. (2009). A review of controlling motivational strategies from a self-determination theory perspective: Implications for sports coaches. *International Review of Sport and Exercise Psychology, 2*, 215–233.

Baum, A., & Posluszny, D. M. (1999). Health psychology: Mapping biobehavioral contributions to health and illness. *Annual Review of Psychology, 50*, 137–163.

Bauman, A., Bull, F., Chey, T., Craig, C. L., Ainsworth, B. E., Sallis, J. F.,...The IPS Group. (2009). The International Prevalence Study on Physical Activity: Results from 20 countries. *International Journal of Behavioral Nutrition and Physical Activity, 6*, 21.

Bélanger-Gravel, A., Godin, G., & Amireault, S. (2011). A meta-analytic review of the effect of implementation intentions on physical activity. *Health Psychology Review*, Advance online publication. doi: 10.1080/17437199.2011.560095

Bellg, A. J., Borrelli, B., Resnick, B., Hecht, J., Minicucci, D. S., Ory, M.,...Treatment Fidelity Workgroup of the NIH Behavior Change Consortium. (2004). Special NIH committee report—Enhancing treatment fidelity in health behavior change studies: Best practices and recommendations from the NIH behavior change consortium. *Health Psychology, 23*, 443–451.

Blanchard, C. M., Kupperman, J., Sparling, P., Nehld, E., Rhodes, R. E., Courneya, K. S.,...Rupph, J. C. (2008).

Ethnicity and the theory of planned behavior in an exercise context: A mediation and moderation perspective. *Psychology of Sport and Exercise, 9,* 527–545.

Blanchard, C. M., Kupperman, J., Sparling, P. B., Nehl, E., Rhodes, R. E., Courneya, K. S., & Baker, F. (2009). Do ethnicity and gender matter when using the theory of planned behavior to understand fruit and vegetable consumption? *Appetite, 52,* 15–20.

Blanchard, C. M., Rhodes, R. E., Nehl, E., Fisher, J., Sparling, P., & Courneya, K. S. (2003). Ethnicity and the theory of planned behavior in the exercise domain. *American Journal of Health Behavior, 27,* 579–591.

Boyd, M. P., Weinmann, C., & Yin, Z. (2002). The relationship of physical self-perceptions and goal orientations to intrinsic motivation for exercise. *Journal of Sport Behavior, 25,* 1–18.

Bozionelos, G., & Bennett, P. (1999). The theory of planned behaviour as predictor of exercise: The moderating influence of beliefs and personality variables. *Journal of Health Psychology, 4,* 517–529.

Brandstätter, V., Lengfelder, A., & Gollwitzer, P. M. (2001). Implementation intentions and efficient action initiation. *Personality and Social Psychology Bulletin, 81,* 946–960.

Brunel, P. C. (1996). The relationship of task and ego orientation and intrinsic and extrinsic motivation. *Journal of Sport and Exercise Psychology, 17 (Suppl.),* S18.

Burton, K. D., Lydon, J. E., D'Alessandro, D., & Koestner, R. (2006). The differential effects of intrinsic and identified motivation on well-being and performance: Prospective, experimental, and implicit approaches to self-determination theory. *Journal of Personality and Social Psychology, 91,* 750–762.

Butler, R. (1987). Task-involving and ego-involving properties of evaluation: Effects of different feedback conditions on motivational perceptions, interest, and performance. *Journal of Educational Psychology, 79,* 474–482.

Byers, T., Nestle, M., McTiernan, A., Doyle, C., Currie-Williams, A., Gansler, T., & Thun, M. (2002). American Cancer Society guidelines on nutrition and physical activity for cancer prevention: Reducing the risk of cancer with healthy food choices and physical activity. *CA—Cancer Journal of Clinicians, 52,* 92–119.

Chapman, J., Armitage, C. J., & Norman, P. (2009). Comparing implementation intention interventions in relation to young adults' intake of fruit and vegetables. *Psychology and Health, 24,* 317–332.

Chatzisarantis, N. L. D., Biddle, S. J. H., & Meek, G. A. (1997). A self-determination theory approach to the study of intentions and the intention-behaviour relationship in children's physical activity. *British Journal of Health Psychology, 2,* 343–360.

Chatzisarantis, N. L. D., & Hagger, M. S. (2005). Effects of a brief intervention based on the theory of planned behavior on leisure time physical activity participation. *Journal of Sport and Exercise Psychology, 27,* 470–487.

Chatzisarantis, N. L. D., & Hagger, M. S. (2007). Mindfulness and the intention-behavior relationship within the theory of planned behavior. *Personality and Social Psychology Bulletin, 33,* 663–676.

Chatzisarantis, N. L. D., & Hagger, M. S. (2008). Influences of personality traits and continuation intentions on physical activity participation within the theory of planned behaviour. *Psychology and Health, 23,* 347–367.

Chatzisarantis, N. L. D., & Hagger, M. S. (2009). Effects of an intervention based on self-determination theory on self-reported leisure-time physical activity participation. *Psychology and Health, 24,* 29–48.

Chatzisarantis, N. L. D., Hagger, M. S., Biddle, S. J. H., & Karageorghis, C. (2002). The cognitive processes by which perceived locus of causality predicts participation in physical activity. *Journal of Health Psychology, 7,* 685–699.

Chatzisarantis, N. L. D., Hagger, M. S., Biddle, S. J. H., Smith, B., & Wang, C. K. J. (2003). A meta-analysis of perceived locus of causality in exercise, sport, and physical education contexts. *Journal of Sport and Exercise Psychology, 25,* 284–306.

Chatzisarantis, N. L. D., Hagger, M. S., & Thøgersen-Ntoumani, C. (2008). Effects of implementation intentions and self concordance on health behavior. *Journal of Applied Biobehavioral Research, 13,* 198–214.

Cohen, J. (1987). *Statistical power analysis for the behavioral sciences* (2nd ed.). Hillsdale, NJ: Erlbaum.

Conn, V. S., Hafdahl, A. R., Cooper, P. S., Brown, L. M., & Lusk, S. L. (2009). Meta-analysis of workplace physical activity interventions. *American Journal of Preventive Medicine, 37,* 330–339.

Conner, M., & Abraham, C. (2001). Conscientiousness and the theory of planned behavior: Toward a more complete model of the antecedents of intentions and behavior. *Personality and Social Psychology Bulletin, 27,* 1547–1561.

Conner, M., & Armitage, C. J. (1998). Extending the theory of planned behavior: A review and avenues for further research. *Journal of Applied Social Psychology, 28,* 1429–1464.

Conner, M., Rodgers, W., & Murray, T. (2007). Conscientiousness and the intention-behavior relationship: Predicting exercise behavior. *Journal of Sport and Exercise Psychology, 29,* 518–533.

Conner, M., Warren, R., Close, S., & Sparks, P. (1999). Alcohol consumption and the theory of planned behavior: An examination of the cognitive mediation of past behavior. *Journal of Applied Social Psychology, 29,* 1676–1704.

Conroy, D. E., & Elliot, A. J. (2004). Fear of failure and achievement goals in sport: Addressing the issue of the chicken and the egg. *Anxiety, Stress and Coping, 17,* 271–285.

Conroy, D. E., Elliot, A. J., & Hofer, S. M. (2003). A 2 x 2 achievement goals questionnaire for sport: Evidence for factorial invariance, temporal stability, and external validity. *Journal of Sport and Exercise Psychology, 25,* 456–476.

Conroy, D. E., Kaye, M. P., & Coatsworth, J. D. (2006). Coaching climates and the destructive effects of mastery-avoidance achievement goals on situational motivation. *Journal of Sport and Exercise Psychology, 28,* 69–92.

Csikzentmihalyi, M. (1990). *Flow: The psychology of optimal experience.* New York.: Harper & Rowe.

Cumming, J., & Hall, C. (2004). The relationship between goal orientation and self-efficacy for exercise. *Journal of Applied Social Psychology, 34,* 747–763.

Cury, F., Biddle, S. J. H., Famose, J. P., Goudas, M., Sarrazin, P., & Durand, M. (1996). Personal and situational factors influencing intrinsic interest of adolescent girls in school physical education: A structural equation modeling analysis. *Educational Psychologist, 16,* 305–315.

Cury, F., Da Fonséca, D., Rufo, M., Peres, C., & Sarrazin, P. (2003). The trichotomous model and investment in learning to prepare for a sport test: A mediational analysis. *British Journal of Educational Psychology, 73,* 529–543.

Cury, F., Elliot, A. J., Da Fonseca, D., & Moller, A. C. (2006). The social-cognitive model of achievement motivation and the 2x2 achievement goal framework. *Journal of Personality and Social Psychology, 90,* 666–679.

Cury, F., Elliot, A. J., Sarrazin, P., Da Fonseca, D., & Rufo, M. (2002). The trichotomous achievement goal model and intrinsic motivation: A sequential mediational analysis. *Journal of Experimental Social Psychology, 38*, 473–481.

Darker, C. D., French, D. P., Eves, F. F., & Sniehotta, F. F. (2010). An intervention to promote walking amongst the general population based on an 'extended' theory of planned behaviour: A waiting list randomised controlled trial. *Psychology and Health, 25*, 71–88.

Deci, E. L., Eghrari, H., Patrick, B. C., & Leone, D. R. (1994). Facilitating internalization: The self-determination theory perspective. *Journal of Personality, 62*, 119–142.

Deci, E. L., & Ryan, R. M. (1985a). The general causality orientations scale: Self-determination in personality. *Journal of Research in Personality, 19*, 109–134.

Deci, E. L., & Ryan, R. M. (1985b). *Intrinsic motivation and self-determination in human behavior.* New York: Plenum Press.

Deci, E. L., & Ryan, R. M. (2000). The "what" and "why" of goal pursuits: Human needs and the self-determination of behavior. *Psychological Inquiry, 11*, 227–268.

De Vet, E., Oenema, A., Sheeran, P., & Brug, J. (2009). Should implementation intentions interventions be implemented in obesity prevention: The impact of if-then plans on daily physical activity in Dutch adults. *International Journal of Behavioral Nutrition and Physical Activity, 6*, 11.

Doll, J., & Ajzen, I. (1992). Accessibility and stability of predictors in the theory of planned behavior. *Journal of Personality and Social Psychology, 63*, 754–765.

Dweck, C. S. (1986). Motivational processes affecting learning. *American Psychologist, 41*, 1040–1048.

Edmunds, J. K., Ntoumanis, N., & Duda, J. L. (2007). Perceived autonomy support and psychological need satisfaction in exercise. In M. S. Hagger & N. L. D. Chatzisarantis (Eds.), *Intrinsic motivation and self-determination in exercise and sport* (pp. 35–51). Champaign, IL: Human Kinetics.

Elliot, A. J. (1999). Approach and avoidance motivation and achievement goals. *Educational Psychologist, 34*, 169–189.

Elliot, A. J., & Church, M. (1997). A hierarchical model of approach and avoidance achievement motivation. *Journal of Personality and Social Psychology, 72*, 218–232.

Elliot, A. J., & Conroy, D. E. (2005). Beyond the dichotomous model of achievement goals in sport and exercise psychology. *Sport and Exercise Psychology Review, 1*, 17–25.

Elliot, A. J., Cury, F., Fryer, J. W., & Huguet, P. (2006). Achievement goals, self-handicapping, and performance attainment: A mediational analysis. *Journal of Sport and Exercise Psychology, 28*, 344–361.

Elliot, A. J., & McGregor, H. A. (2001). A 2 x 2 achievement goal framework. *Journal of Personality and Social Psychology, 80*, 501–519.

Elliot, A. J., McGregor, H. A., & Thrash, T. M. (2002). The need for competence. In E. L. Deci & R. M. Ryan (Eds.), *Handbook of self-determination research* (pp. 361–387). Rochester, NY: University of Rochester Press.

Elliot, A. J., & Murayama, K. (2008). On the measurement of achievement goals: Critique, illustration, and application. *Journal of Educational Psychology, 100*, 613–628.

Escarti, A., & Gutierrez, M. (2001). Influence of motivational climate in physical education on the intention to practice physical activity or sport. *European Journal of Sport Science, 1*, 1–12.

Fishbein, M., & Ajzen, I. (2009). *Predicting and changing behavior: The reasoned action approach.* New York: Psychology Press.

Fitch, J. L., & Ravlin, E. C. (2005). Willpower and perceived behavioral control: Influences on the intention-behavior relationship and postbehavior attributions. *Social Behavior and Personality, 33*, 105–123.

Fortier, M., & Kowal, J. (2007). The flow state and physical activity behaviour change as motivational outcomes: A self-determination theory perspective. In M. S. Hagger & N. L. D. Chatzisarantis (Eds.), *Intrinsic motivation and self-determination theory in exercise and sport* (pp. 113–125). Champaign, IL: Human Kinetics.

French, D. P., & Hankins, M. (2003). The expectancy-value muddle in the theory of planned behaviour—and some proposed solutions. *British Journal of Health Psychology, 8*, 37–55.

Godin, G., Conner, M., & Sheeran, P. (2005). Bridging the intention-behaviour 'gap': The role of moral norm. *British Journal of Social Psychology, 44*, 497–512.

Godin, G., Valois, R., Jobin, J., & Ross, A. (1991). Prediction of intention to exercise of individuals who have suffered from coronary heart disease. *Journal of Clinical Psychology, 47*, 762–772.

Gollwitzer, P. M., & Sheeran, P. (2006). Implementation intentions and goal achievement: A meta-analysis of effects and processes. *Advances in Experimental Social Psychology, 38*, 69–119.

Goudas, M., & Biddle, S. J. H. (1994). Perceived motivational climate and intrinsic motivation in school physical education classes. *European Journal of Psychology of Education, 9*, 241–250.

Goudas, M., Biddle, S. J. H., & Fox, K. R. (1994). Perceived locus of causality, goal orientations, and perceived competence in school physical education classes. *British Journal of Educational Psychology, 64*, 453–563.

Goudas, M., Biddle, S. J. H., & Underwood, M. (1995). A prospective study of the relationships between motivational orientations and perceived competence with intrinsic motivation and achievement in a teacher education course. *Educational Psychology Review, 5*, 89–96.

Greenwald, A. G., Banaji, M. R., Rudman, L. A., Farnham, S. D., Nosek, B. A., & Mellott, D. S. (2002). A unified theory of implicit attitudes, stereotypes, self-esteem, and self-concept. *Psychological Review, 109*, 3–25.

Guay, F., Mageau, G. A., & Vallerand, R. J. (2003). On the hierarchical structure of self-determined motivation: A test of top-down, bottom-up, reciprocal, and horizontal effects. *Personality and Social Psychology Bulletin, 29*, 992–1004.

Hagger, M. S. (2009). Theoretical integration in health psychology: Unifying ideas and complementary explanations. *British Journal of Health Psychology, 14*, 189–194.

Hagger, M. S. (2010a). Current issues and new directions in psychology and health: Physical activity research showcasing theory into practice. *Psychology and Health, 25*, 1–5.

Hagger, M. S. (2010b). Health Psychology Review: Advancing theory and research in health psychology and behavioural medicine. *Health Psychology Review, 4*, 1–5.

Hagger, M. S. (2010c). Self-regulation: An important construct in health psychology research and practice. *Health Psychology Review, 4*, 57–65.

Hagger, M. S., Anderson, M., Kyriakaki, M., & Darkings, S. (2007). Aspects of identity and their influence on intentional behaviour: Comparing effects for three health behaviours. *Personality and Individual Differences, 42*, 355–367.

Hagger, M. S., & Armitage, C. (2004). The influence of perceived loci of control and causality in the theory of planned behavior in a leisure-time exercise context. *Journal of Applied Biobehavioral Research, 9*, 45–64.

Hagger, M. S., Chatzisarantis, N., & Biddle, S. J. H. (2001). The influence of self-efficacy and past behaviour on the physical activity intentions of young people. *Journal of Sports Sciences, 19*, 711–725.

Hagger, M. S., & Chatzisarantis, N. L. D. (2005). First- and higher-order models of attitudes, normative influence, and perceived behavioural control in the theory of planned behaviour. *British Journal of Social Psychology, 44*, 513–535.

Hagger, M. S., & Chatzisarantis, N. L. D. (2006). Self-identity and the theory of planned behaviour: Between-and within-participants analyses. *British Journal of Social Psychology, 45*, 731–757.

Hagger, M. S., & Chatzisarantis, N. L. D. (2007a). Advances in self-determination theory research in sport and exercise. *Psychology of Sport and Exercise, 8*, 597–599.

Hagger, M. S., & Chatzisarantis, N. L. D. (2007b). Self-determination theory and the theory of planned behavior: An integrative approach toward a more complete model of motivation. In L. V. Brown (Ed.), *Psychology of motivation* (pp. 83–98). Hauppauge, NY: Nova Science.

Hagger, M. S., & Chatzisarantis, N. L. D. (2007c). The trans-contextual model of motivation. In M. S. Hagger & N. L. D. Chatzisarantis (Eds.), *Intrinsic motivation and self-determination in exercise and sport* (pp. 53–70). Champaign, IL: Human Kinetics.

Hagger, M. S., & Chatzisarantis, N. L. D. (Eds.). (2007d). *Intrinsic motivation and self-determination in exercise and sport*. Champaign, IL: Human Kinetics.

Hagger, M. S., & Chatzisarantis, N. L. D. (2008). Self-determination theory and the psychology of exercise. *International Review of Sport and Exercise Psychology, 1*, 79–103.

Hagger, M. S., & Chatzisarantis, N. L. D. (2009a). Assumptions in research in sport and exercise psychology. *Psychology of Sport and Exercise, 10*, 511–519.

Hagger, M. S., & Chatzisarantis, N. L. D. (2009b). Integrating the theory of planned behaviour and self-determination theory in health behaviour: A meta-analysis. *British Journal of Health Psychology, 14*, 275–302.

Hagger, M. S., & Chatzisarantis, N. L. D. (2011). Causality orientations moderate the undermining effect of rewards on intrinsic motivation. *Journal of Experimental Social Psychology, 47*, 485–489

Hagger, M. S., Chatzisarantis, N. L. D., Barkoukis, V., Wang, C. K. J., & Baranowski, J. (2005). Perceived autonomy support in physical education and leisure-time physical activity: A cross-cultural evaluation of the trans-contextual model. *Journal of Educational Psychology, 97*, 376–390.

Hagger, M. S., Chatzisarantis, N. L. D., & Biddle, S. J. H. (2002a). The influence of autonomous and controlling motives on physical activity intentions within the theory of planned behaviour. *British Journal of Health Psychology, 7*, 283–297.

Hagger, M. S., Chatzisarantis, N. L. D., & Biddle, S. J. H. (2002b). A meta-analytic review of the theories of reasoned action and planned behavior in physical activity: Predictive validity and the contribution of additional variables. *Journal of Sport and Exercise Psychology, 24*, 3–32.

Hagger, M. S., Chatzisarantis, N. L. D., Culverhouse, T., & Biddle, S. J. H. (2003). The processes by which perceived autonomy support in physical education promotes leisure-time physical activity intentions and behavior:

A trans-contextual model. *Journal of Educational Psychology, 95*, 784–795.

Hagger, M. S., Chatzisarantis, N. L. D., & Harris, J. (2006). From psychological need satisfaction to intentional behavior: Testing a motivational sequence in two behavioral contexts. *Personality and Social Psychology Bulletin, 32*, 131–138.

Hagger, M. S., Chatzisarantis, N. L. D., Hein, V., Pihu, M., Soós, I., Karsai, I., . . . Leemans, S. (2009). Teacher, peer, and parent autonomy support in physical education and leisure-time physical activity: A trans-contextual model of motivation in four cultures. *Psychology and Health, 24*, 689–711.

Hagger, M. S., Hein, V., & Chatzisarantis, N. L. D. (2011). Achievement goals, physical self-concept and social physique anxiety in a physical activity context. *Journal of Applied Social Psychology, 41*, 1299–1339.

Hagger, M. S., Wood, C., Stiff, C., & Chatzisarantis, N. L. D. (2009). The strength model of self-regulation failure and health-related behavior. *Health Psychology Review, 3*, 208–238.

Hagger, M. S., Wood, C., Stiff, C., & Chatzisarantis, N. L. D. (2010). Ego depletion and the strength model of self-control: A meta-analysis. *Psychological Bulletin, 136*, 495–525.

Hardeman, W., Johnston, M., Johnston, D. W., Bonetti, D., Wareham, N. J., & Kinmonth, A. L. (2002). Application of the theory of planned behaviour change interventions: A systematic review. *Psychology and Health, 17*, 123–158.

Hardeman, W., Michie, S., Fanshawe, T., Prevost, T., Mcloughlin, K., & Kinmonth, A. L. (2007). Fidelity of delivery of a physical activity intervention: Predictors and consequences *Psychology and Health, 23*, 11–24.

Harris, J. (2008). *Psychological need satisfaction and the prediction of behaviour*. PhD thesis, University of Essex, Colchester, UK.

Harris, K. C., Kuramoto, L. K., Schulzer, M., & Retallack, J. E. (2009). Effect of school-based physical activity interventions on body mass index in children: A meta-analysis. *Canadian Medical Association Journal, 180*, 719–726.

Heckhausen, H., & Gollwitzer, P. M. (1987). Thought contents and cognitive functioning in motivational and volitional states of mind. *Motivation and Emotion, 11*, 101–120.

Hein, V., & Hagger, M. S. (2007). Global self-esteem, goal achievement orientations and self-determined behavioural regulations in physical education setting. *Journal of Sports Sciences, 25*, 149–259.

Hein, V., & Koka, A. (2007). Perceived feedback and motivation in physical education and physical activity. In M. S. Hagger & N. L. D. Chatzisarantis (Eds.), *Intrinsic motivation and self-determination in exercise and sport* (pp. 127–140). Champaign, IL: Human Kinetics.

Hofmann, W., Friese, M., & Strack, F. (2009). Impulse and self-control from a dual-systems perspective. *Perspectives on Psychological Science, 4*, 162–176.

Hofmann, W., Friese, M., & Wiers, R. W. (2008). Impulsive versus reflective influences on health behavior: A theoretical framework and empirical review. *Health Psychology Review, 2*, 111–137.

Hoyt, A. L., Rhodes, R. E., Hausenblas, H. A., & Giacobbi, P. R., Jr. (2009). Integrating five-factor model facet-level traits with the theory of planned behavior and exercise. *Psychology of Sport and Exercise, 10*, 565–572.

Jenkins, A., Christensen, H., Walker, J. G., & Dear, K. (2009). The effectiveness of distance interventions for increasing physical activity: A review. *American Journal of Health Promotion, 24*, 102–117.

Jeon, C. Y., Lokken, R. P., Hu, F. B., & van Dam, R. M. (2007). Physical activity of moderate intensity and risk of type 2 diabetes. *Diabetes Care, 30*, 744–752.

Kagan, J. (1972). Motives and development. *Journal of Personality and Social Psychology, 22*, 51–66.

Kavussanu, M., & Roberts, G. C. (1996). Motivation in physical activity contexts: The relationship of perceived motivational climate to intrinsic motivation and self-efficacy. *Journal of Sport and Exercise Psychology, 18*, 264–280.

Keatley, D., Clarke, D., & Hagger, M. S. (2011). Assessing the predictive validity of implicit and explicit measures of motivation on condom use, physical activity, and healthy eating. *Psychology and Health*. Advance online publication. doi: 10.1080/08870446.2011.605451.

Kehr, H. M. (2004). Implicit/explicit motive discrepancies and volitional depletion among managers. *Personality and Social Psychology Bulletin, 30*, 315–327.

Koka, A., & Hein, V. (2003). Perceptions of teacher's feedback and learning environment as components of motivation in physical education. *Psychology of Sport and Exercise, 4*, 333–346.

Lam, S. (1999). Predicting intentions to conserve water from the theory of planned behavior, perceived moral obligation, and perceived water right. *Journal of Applied Social Psychology, 29*, 1058–1071.

Levesque, C., & Pelletier, L. G. (2003). On the investigation of primed and chronic autonomous and heteronomous motivational orientations. *Personality and Social Psychology Bulletin, 29*, 1570–1584.

Lowe, R., Eves, F., & Carroll, D. (2002). The influence of affective and instrumental beliefs on exercise intentions and behavior: A longitudinal analysis. *Journal of Applied Social Psychology, 32*, 1241–1252.

Lundahl, B. W., Kunz, C., Brownell, C., Tollefson, D., & Burke, B. L. (2010). A meta-analysis of motivational interviewing: Twenty-five years of empirical studies. *Research on Social Work Practice, 20*, 137–160.

Luszczynska, A. (2006). An implementation intentions intervention, the use of a planning strategy, and physical activity after myocardial infarction. *Social Science and Medicine, 62*, 900–908.

Luszczynska, A., & Haynes, C. (2009). Changing nutrition, physical activity and body weight among student nurses and midwives: Effects of a planning intervention and self-efficacy beliefs. *Journal of Health Psychology, 14*, 1075–1084.

Marteau, T. M., Dieppe, P., Foy, R., Kinmonth, A-L., & Schneiderman, N. (2006). Behavioural medicine: Changing our behaviour. *British Medical Journal, 332*, 437–438.

Martinez-Gonzalez, M. A., Varo, J. J., Santos, J. L., De Irala, J., Gibney, M., Kearney, J., & Martinez, J. A. (2001). Prevalence of physical activity during leisure time in the European Union. *Medicine and Science in Sports and Exercise, 33*, 1142–1146.

McLachlan, S. (2011). *The role of autonomy support and integration in predicting and changing behaviour: theoretical and practical perspectives on self-determination theory*. PhD thesis, School of Psychology, University of Nottingham, Nottingham, UK.

Michie, S. (2008). What works and how? Designing more effective interventions needs answers to both questions. *Addiction, 103*, 886–887.

Michie, S., & Abraham, C. (2008). Advancing the science of behaviour change: A plea for scientific reporting. *Addiction, 103*, 1409–1410.

Michie, S., Johnston, M., Abraham, C., Lawton, R., Parker, D., & Walker, A. (2005). Making psychological theory useful for implementing evidence based practice: A consensus approach. *Quality and Safety in Health Care, 14*, 26–33.

Michie, S., Johnston, M., Francis, J., Hardeman, W., & Eccles, M. (2008). From theory to intervention: Mapping theoretically derived behavioural determinants to behaviour change techniques. *Applied Psychology-an International Review-Psychologie Appliquee-Revue Internationale, 57*, 660–680.

Michie, S., & Prestwich, A. (2010). Are interventions theory-based? Development of a theory coding scheme. *Health Psychology, 29*, 1–8.

Milne, S. E., Orbell, S., & Sheeran, P. (2002). Combining motivational and volitional interventions to promote exercise participation: Protection motivation theory and implementation intentions. *British Journal of Health Psychology, 7*, 163–184.

Moss-Morris, R., & Yardley, L. (2008). Current issues and new directions in Psychology and Health: Contributions to translational research. *Psychology and Health, 23*, 1–4.

Murgraff, V., Abraham, C., & McDermott, M. (2007). Reducing Friday alcohol consumption among moderate, women drinkers: Evaluation of a brief evidence-based intervention. *Alcohol and Alcoholism, 42*, 37–41.

Newton, M. L., & Duda, J. L. (1999). The interaction of motivational climate, dispositional goal orientations, and perceived ability in predicting indices of motivation. *International Journal of Sport Psychology, 30*, 63–82.

Nicholls, J. G. (1984). Achievement motivation: Conceptions of ability, subjective experience, task choice, and performance. *Psychological Review, 91*, 328–346.

Nicholls, J. G. (1989). *The competitive ethos and democratic education*. Cambridge, MA: Harvard University Press.

Norman, P., Armitage, C. J., & Quigley, C. (2007). The theory of planned behavior and binge drinking: Assessing the impact of binge drinker prototypes. *Addictive Behaviors, 32*, 1753–1768.

Nosek, B. A., Greenwald, A. G., & Banaji, M. R. (2007). The implicit association test at age 7: A methodological and conceptual review. In J. A. Bargh (Ed.), *Automatic processes in social thinking and behavior* (pp. 265–292). New York: Psychology Press.

Ntoumanis, N. (2001). A self-determination approach to the understanding of motivation in physical education. *British Journal of Educational Psychology, 71*, 225–242.

Ntoumanis, N. (2005). A prospective study of participation in optional school physical education based on self-determination theory. *Journal of Educational Psychology, 97*, 444–453.

Ntoumanis, N., & Biddle, S. J. H. (1999). A review of motivational climate in physical activity. *Journal of Sports Sciences, 17*, 543–665.

Orbell, S., Hodgkins, S., & Sheeran, P. (1997). Implementation intentions and the theory of planned behavior. *Personality and Social Psychology Bulletin, 23*, 945–954.

Papaioannou, A. (2004). A multi-level approach to motivational climate in physical education and sport settings: An individual or group level construct? *Journal of Sport and Exercise Psychology, 26*, 90–118.

Pekrun, R., Elliot, A. J., & Maier, M. A. (2006). Achievement goals and discrete achievement emotions: A theoretical model and prospective test. *Journal of Educational Psychology, 98*, 583–597.

Pelletier, L. G., Dion, S. C., Slovinec-D'Angelo, M., & Reid, R. (2004). Why do you regulate what you eat? Relationships between forms of regulation, eating behaviors, sustained dietary behavior change, and psychological adjustment. *Motivation and Emotion, 28,* 245–277.

Perugini, M. (2005). Predictive models of implicit and explicit attitudes. *British Journal of Social Psychology, 44,* 29–45

Perugini, M., & Bagozzi, R. P. (2001). The role of desires and anticipated emotions in goal-directed behaviours: Broadening and deepening the theory of planned behavior. *British Journal of Social Psychology, 40,* 79–98.

Perugini, M., & Bagozzi, R. P. (2004). The distinction between desires and intentions. *European Journal of Social Psychology, 34,* 69–84.

Perugini, M., & Conner, M. (2000). Predicting and understanding behavioral volitions: The interplay between goals and behaviors. *European Journal of Social Psychology, 30,* 705–731.

Phillips, P., Abraham, C., & Bond, R. (2003). Personality, cognition, and university students' examination performance. *European Journal of Personality, 17,* 435–448.

Pintrich, P. (2000). An achievement goal theory perspective on issues in motivation terminology, theory, and research. *Contemporary Educational Psychology, 25,* 92–104.

Povey, R., Conner, M., Sparks, P., James, R., & Shepherd, R. (2000). Application of the theory of planned behaviour to two dietary behaviours: Roles of perceived control and self-efficacy. *British Journal of Health Psychology, 5,* 121–139.

Prestwich, A., Ayres, K., & Lawton, R. (2008). Crossing two types of implementation intentions with a protection motivation intervention for the reduction of saturated fat intake: A randomized trial. *Social Science and Medicine, 67,* 1550–1558.

Prestwich, A., Conner, M., Lawton, R., Bailey, W., Litman, J., & Molyneaux, V. (2005). Individual and collaborative implementation intentions and the promotion of breast self-examination. *Psychology and Health, 20,* 743–760.

Prestwich, A., Lawton, R., & Conner, M. (2003). The use of implementation intentions and the decision balance sheet in promoting exercise behaviour. *Psychology and Health, 10,* 707–721.

Prestwich, A., Perugini, M., & Hurling, R. (2009). Can the effects of implementation intentions on exercise be enhanced using text messages? *Psychology and Health, 24,* 677–687.

Rawsthorne, L. J., & Elliot, A. J. (1999). Achievement goals and intrinsic motivation: A meta-analytic review. *Personality and Social Psychology Review, 3,* 326–344.

Rhodes, R. E., & Courneya, K. S. (2003). Relationships between personality, an extended theory of planned behaviour model and exercise behaviour. *British Journal of Health Psychology, 8,* 19–36.

Rhodes, R. E., Courneya, K. S., & Jones, L. W. (2002). Personality, the theory of planned behavior, and exercise: A unique role for extroversion's activity facet. *Journal of Applied Social Psychology, 32,* 1721–1736.

Rhodes, R. E., Courneya, K. S., & Jones, L. W. (2003). Translating exercise intentions into behavior: Personality and social cognitive correlates. *Journal of Health Psychology, 8,* 449–460.

Rhodes, R. E., Plotnikoff, R., & Courneya, K. (2008). Predicting the physical activity intention-behavior profiles of adopters and maintainers using three social cognition models. *Annals of Behavioral Medicine, 36,* 244–252.

Rivis, A., & Sheeran, P. (2003). Descriptive norms as an additional predictor in the theory of planned behaviour: A meta-analysis. *Current Psychology, 22,* 218–233.

Rogers, R. W. (1975). A protection motivation theory of fear appeals and attitude change. *Journal of Psychology, 91,* 93–114.

Ross, R., Freeman, J. A., & Janssen, I. (2000). Exercise alone is an effective strategy for reducing obesity and related comorbidities. *Exercise and Sport Science Review, 28,* 165–170.

Ryan, R. M., & Connell, J. P. (1989). Perceived locus of causality and internalization: Examining reasons for acting in two domains. *Journal of Personality and Social Psychology, 57,* 749–761.

Ryan, R. M., & Deci, E. L. (1989). Bridging the research traditions of task/ego involvement and intrinsic/extrinsic motivation: Comment on Butler (1987). *Journal of Educational Psychology, 81,* 265–268.

Ryan, R. M., & Deci, E. L. (2007). Active human nature: Self-determination theory and the promotion and maintenance of sport, exercise, and health. In M. S. Hagger & N. L. D. Chatzisarantis (Eds.), *Intrinsic motivation and self-determination in exercise and sport* (pp. 1–20). Champaign, IL: Human Kinetics.

Scholz, U., Schuz, B., Ziegelmann, J. R., Lippke, S., & Schwarzer, R. (2008). Beyond behavioural intentions: Planning mediates between intentions and physical activity. *British Journal of Health Psychology, 13,* 479–494.

Sheeran, P. (2002). Intention-behavior relations: A conceptual and empirical review. In W. Stroebe & M. Hewstone (Eds.), *European review of social psychology* (pp. 1–36). London: Wiley.

Sheeran, P., Norman, P., & Orbell, S. (1999). Evidence that intentions based on attitudes better predict behaviour than intentions based on subjective norms. *European Journal of Social Psychology, 29,* 403–406.

Sheeran, P., & Orbell, S. (1999a). Augmenting the theory of planned behavior: Roles for anticipated regret and descriptive norms. *Journal of Applied Social Psychology, 29,* 2107–2142.

Sheeran, P., & Orbell, S. (1999b). Implementation intentions and repeated behaviour: Augmenting the predictive validity of the theory of planned behaviour. *European Journal of Social Psychology, 29,* 349–369.

Sheeran, P., & Orbell, S. (2000a). Self schemas and the theory of planned behaviour. *European Journal of Social Psychology, 30,* 533–550.

Sheeran, P., & Orbell, S. (2000b). Using implementation intentions to increase attendance for cervical cancer screening. *Health Psychology, 19,* 283–289.

Sheeran, P., Orbell, S., & Trafimow, D. (1999). Does the temporal stability of behavioral intentions moderate intention-behavior and past behavior-future behavior relations? *Personality and Social Psychology Bulletin, 25,* 721–730.

Sheeran, P., Trafimow, D., Finlay, K. A., & Norman, P. (2002). Evidence that the type of person affects the strength of the perceived behavioural control-intention relationship. *British Journal of Social Psychology, 41,* 253–270.

Sheldon, K. M. (2002). The self-concordance model of health goal striving: When personal goals correctly represent the person. In E. L. Deci & R. M. Ryan (Eds.), *Handbook of self-determination research* (pp. 65–86). Rochester, NY: University of Rochester Press.

Sheldon, K. M., Elliot, A. J., Kim, Y., & Kasser, T. (2001). What is satisfying about satisfying events? Testing 10 candidate psychological needs. *Journal of Personality and Social Psychology, 80,* 325–339.

Shen, B., McCaughtry, N., & Martin, J. (2007). The influence of self-determination in physical education on leisure-time physical activity behavior *Research Quarterly for Exercise and Sport, 78,* 328–338.

Shen, B., McCaughtry, N., & Martin, J. (2008). Urban adolescents' exercise intentions and behaviors: An exploratory study of a trans-contextual model. *Contemporary Educational Psychology, 33,* 841–858.

Sniehotta, F. F., Scholz, U., & Schwarzer, R. (2005). Bridging the intention—behaviour gap: Planning, self-efficacy, and action control in the adoption and maintenance of physical exercise. *Psychology and Health, 20,* 143–160.

Sniehotta, F. F., Scholz, U., Schwarzer, R., Fuhrmann, B., Kiwus, U., & Voller, H. (2005). Long-term effects of two psychological interventions on physical exercise and self-regulation following coronary rehabilitation. *International Journal of Behavioral Medicine, 12,* 244–255.

Spence, A., & Townsend, E. (2007). Predicting behaviour towards genetically modified (GM) food using implicit and explicit attitudes. *British Journal of Social Psychology, 46,* 437–457.

Stadler, G., Oettingen, G., & Gollwitzer, P. M. (2009). Physical activity in women effects of a self-regulation intervention. *American Journal of Preventive Medicine, 36,* 29–34.

Standage, M., Duda, J. L., & Ntoumanis, N. (2003a). A model of contextual motivation in physical education: Using constructs from self-determination and achievement goal theories to predict physical activity intentions. *Journal of Educational Psychology, 95,* 97–110.

Standage, M., Duda, J. L., & Ntoumanis, N. (2003b). Predicting motivational regulations in physical education: The interplay between dispositional goal orientations, motivational climate and perceived competence. *Journal of Sports Sciences, 21,* 631–647.

Standage, M., Duda, J. L., & Ntoumanis, N. (2005). A test of self-determination theory in school physical education. *British Journal of Educational Psychology, 75,* 411–433.

Standage, M., Gillison, F. B., & Treasure, D. C. (2007). Self-determination and motivation in physical education. In M. S. Hagger & N. L. D. Chatzisarantis (Eds.), *Intrinsic motivation and self-determination in exercise and sport* (pp. 71–85). Champaign, IL: Human Kinetics.

Strack, F., & Deutsch, R. (2004). Reflective and impulsive determinants of social behavior. *Personality and Social Psychology Review, 8,* 220–247.

Symons Downs, D., & Hausenblas, H. A. (2005). The theories of reasoned action and planned behavior applied to exercise: A meta-analytic update. *Journal of Physical Activity and Health, 2,* 76–97.

Taylor, S. E. (2008). Current issues and new directions in psychology and health: Bringing basic and applied research together to address underlying mechanisms. *Psychology and Health, 23,* 131–134.

Terry, D. J., Hogg, M. A., & White, K. M. (2000). Attitude-behavior relations: Social identity and group membership. In D. J. Terry & M. A. Hogg (Eds.), *Attitudes, behavior, and social context: The role of norms and group membership* (pp. 67–93). Mahwah, NJ: Erlbaum.

Terry, D. J., & O'Leary, J. E. (1995). The theory of planned behaviour: The effects of perceived behavioural control and self-efficacy. *British Journal of Social Psychology, 34,* 199–220.

Thøgersen-Ntoumani, C., Ntoumanis, N., & Nikitaras, N. (2010). Unhealthy weight control behaviours in adolescent girls: A process model based on self-determination theory. *Psychology and Health, 25,* 535–550.

Trafimow, D., & Finlay, K. A. (1996). The importance of subjective norms for a minority of people: Between-subjects and within-subjects effects. *Personality and Social Psychology Bulletin, 22,* 820–828.

Trafimow, D., & Sheeran, P. (1998). Some tests of the distinction between cognitive and affective beliefs. *Journal of Experimental Social Psychology, 34,* 378–397.

Treasure, D. C., & Roberts, G. C. (2001). Students' perceptions of the motivational climate, achievement beliefs and satisfaction in physical education. *Research Quarterly for Exercise and Sport, 72,* 165–175.

U.S. Department of Health and Human Services. (1996). *Physical activity and health: A report of the surgeon general.* Atlanta, GA: Centers for Disease Control and Prevention, National Center for Chronic Disease Prevention and Health Promotion.

Vallerand, R. J. (2000). Deci and Ryan's self-determination theory: A view from the hierarchical model of intrinsic and extrinsic motivation. *Psychological Inquiry, 11,* 312–318.

Van Hooft, E. A. J., & De Jong, M. (2009). Predicting job seeking for temporary employment using the theory of planned behaviour: The moderating role of individualism and collectivism. *Journal of Occupational and Organizational Psychology, 82,* 295–316.

van Osch, L., Beenackers, M., Reubsaet, A., Lechner, L., Candel, M., & de Vries, H. (2009). Action planning as predictor of health protective and health risk behavior: An investigation of fruit and snack consumption. *International Journal of Behavioral Nutrition and Physical Activity, 6,* 69.

Vansteenkiste, M., Simons, J., Soenens, B., & Lens, W. (2004). How to become a persevering exerciser? Providing a clear, future intrinsic goal in an autonomy-supportive way. *Journal of Sport and Exercise Psychology, 26,* 232–249.

Verplanken, B., & Faes, S. (1999). Good intentions, bad habits, and effects of forming implementation intentions on healthy eating. *European Journal of Social Psychology, 29,* 591–604.

Verplanken, B., Hofstee, G., & Janssen, H. (1998). Accessibility of affective versus cognitive components of attitudes. *European Journal of Social Psychology, 28,* 23–35.

Vlachopoulos, S., & Biddle, S. J. H. (1997). Modeling the relation of goal orientations to achievement-related affect in physical activity: Does perceived ability matter? *Journal of Sport and Exercise Psychology, 19,* 169–187.

Walker, G. J., Courneya, K. S., & Deng, J. (2006). Ethnicity, gender, and the theory of planned behavior: The case of playing the lottery. *Journal of Leisure Research, 38,* 224–248.

Wang, C. K. J., & Biddle, S. J. H. (2003). Intrinsic motivation towards sports in Singaporean students: The role of sport ability beliefs. *Journal of Health Psychology, 8,* 515–523.

Wang, C. K. J., Biddle, S. J. H., & Elliot, A. J. (2007). The 2×2 achievement goal framework in a physical education context. *Psychology of Sport and Exercise, 8,* 147–168.

Webb, T. L., & Sheeran, P. (2006). Does changing behavioral intentions engender behavior change? A meta-analysis of the experimental evidence. *Psychological Bulletin, 132,* 249–268.

White, K. M., Hogg, M. A., & Terry, D. J. (2002). Improving attitude-behavior correspondence through exposure to normative support from a salient ingroup. *Basic and Applied Social Psychology, 24,* 91–103.

Williams, G. C., Gagne, M., Ryan, R. M., & Deci, E. L. (2002). Facilitating autonomous motivation for smoking cessation. *Health Psychology, 21,* 40–50.

Williams, G. C., McGregor, H. A., Zeldman, A., & Freedman, Z. R. (2004). Testing a self-determination theory process model for promoting glycemic control through diabetes self-management. *Health Psychology, 23,* 58–66.

Williams, P. T. (2001). Physical fitness and activity as separate heart disease risk factors: A meta-analysis. *Medicine and Science in Sports and Exercise, 33,* 754–761.

Wilson, P. M., & Rodgers, W. M. (2004). The relationship between perceived autonomy support, exercise regulations and behavioral intentions in women. *Psychology of Sport and Exercise, 5,* 229–242.

Wilson, P. M., & Rodgers, W. M. (2007). Self-determination theory, exercise and well-being. In M. S. Hagger & N. L. D. Chatzisarantis (Eds.), *Intrinsic motivation and self-determination in exercise and sport* (pp. 101–112). Champiagn, IL: Human Kinetics.

Wilson, P. M., Rodgers, W. M., Blanchard, C. M., & Gessell, J. (2003). The relationship between psychological needs, self-determined motivation, exercise attitudes, and physical fitness. *Journal of Applied Social Psychology, 33,* 2373–2392.

World Health Organization (WHO). (2004). *Global strategy on diet, physical activity and health.* Geneva: Author.

Wu, T., Gao, X., Chen, M., & van Dam, R. M. (2009). Long-term effectiveness of diet-plus-exercise interventions vs. diet-only interventions for weight loss: A meta-analysis. *Obesity Reviews, 10,* 313–323.

Work Motivation: Directing, Energizing, and Maintaining Effort (and Research)

Adam M. Grant *and* Jihae Shin

Abstract

This chapter provides an overview of contemporary research on work motivation. We start by identifying the central premises, controversies, and unanswered questions related to five core theoretical perspectives on work motivation: expectancy theory, equity theory, goal-setting theory, job design, and self-determination theory. We then discuss four current topics and new directions: collective motivation and organizing, temporal dynamics, creativity, and the effects of rewards.

Key Words: work motivation, expectancy theory, equity theory, goal setting, job design, self-determination theory, organizing, creativity, rewards

Introduction

Work motivation is an important phenomenon for both scholars and practitioners to understand. It helps to explain what drove Thomas Edison to invent the first light bulb, Florence Nightingale to improve nursing practices, Nelson Mandela to become the president of South Africa, Benjamin Franklin to create fire and police departments, Maya Angelou to write poetry, and Michelangelo to paint the Sistine Chapel. Knowledge of work motivation also has the potential to shed light on major collective accomplishments such as discovering flight, landing on the moon, curing river blindness, and inventing the telephone and the computer. Underlying all of these accomplishments is a desire to take action.

Work motivation is described as the psychological processes that direct, energize, and maintain action toward a job, task, role, or project (Campbell & Pritchard, 1976; Kanfer, 1990). Our chapter is not designed to be exhaustive; comprehensive reviews of work motivation theory and research are available in other outlets (e.g., Ambrose & Kulik, 1999; Diefendorff & Chandler, 2010; Kanfer, Chen, & Pritchard, 2008; Latham & Pinder, 2005; Mitchell & Daniels, 2003). Rather, our goal is to provide an

overview of core theoretical perspectives, key studies, important controversies and unanswered questions, as well as call attention to hot topics and new directions for work motivation theory and research. We start by discussing five core theoretical perspectives on work motivation: expectancy theory, equity theory, goal-setting theory, job design, and self-determination theory. We then turn our attention to four new directions and underexplored topics for work motivation research: group motivation and organizing, motivation over time, motivation and creativity, and the effects of rewards.

Core Theoretical Perspectives on Work Motivation

Scholars have distinguished between two principal types of work motivation theories: endogenous process theories and exogenous cause theories (Katzell & Thompson, 1990). Endogenous process theories focus primarily on the psychological mechanisms that explain motivation inside employees' heads, while exogenous cause theories focus primarily on contextual influences on work motivation that can be changed and altered. We begin with a consideration of two key endogenous process theories: expectancy theory and equity theory. Next, we cover two central exogenous cause theories: goal setting and job design. Finally, we examine self-determination theory as a hybrid perspective that places equivalent emphasis on endogenous processes and exogenous causes.

Expectancy Theory

According to expectancy theory, employees choose to invest effort in courses of action by weighing their relative utilities—that is, their probabilities of achieving desired outcomes (Vroom, 1964). Effort is a function of three beliefs: expectancy (effort will lead to performance), instrumentality (performance will lead to outcomes), and valence (these outcomes are important or valued). These beliefs are thought to interactively influence effort, such that if any one of the beliefs is missing, the course of action will not be selected (Porter & Lawler, 1968). Without expectancy beliefs, employees feel that effort is futile; without instrumentality and valence beliefs, employees question whether performance is worth the effort. Critically, expectancy theory is designed to account for the within-person decisions that employees make about whether, where, and how to invest their time and energy, rather than for differences in effort between employees.

Expectancy theory has been tested in many studies, but it is more often used as an organizing framework for generating and testing context-specific hypotheses. For example, researchers have applied expectancy theory to guide the development of models to explain variations in DUI arrests among police officers (Mastrofski, Ritti, & Snipes, 1994), efforts by middle managers to champion issues for senior executives to pursue (Ashford, Rothbard, Piderit, & Dutton, 1998), home runs hit by major league baseball players (Harder, 1991), and strategic decisions in competitive markets (Chen & Miller, 1994). In a meta-analysis of 77 studies, Van Eerde and Thierry (1996) found that expectancy, instrumentality, and valence beliefs were better predictors of psychological indicators of motivation (intentions and preferences) than of behavioral indicators (performance, effort, and choices), which may be an artifact of common method and source biases. Supporting one fundamental tenet of the theory, they found that expectancy, instrumentality, and valence beliefs were more accurate predictors of within-person than between-person differences in criteria. However, they found that the multiplicative model explained little variance over and above the additive model. This may be an artifact of the low reliabil-ity of multiplicative measures. Moreover, the meta-analysis provided little information about causality, as most studies have been correlational rather than experimental. Nevertheless, the overall results suggest that expectancy, instrumentality, and valence beliefs do take a valuable step toward explaining variance in work motivation.

Research on expectancy theory has generated several controversies and unanswered questions. In light of evidence that expectancy, instrumentality, and valence beliefs leave considerable variance in motivation unexplained (Van Eerde & Thierry, 1996), it is critical to understand other forces that influence motivation. The theory of planned behavior (Ajzen, 1991) takes a productive step in this direction. According to this theory, planned actions are directly caused by intentions as micromediators of the belief–behavior relationship. Intentions are in turn a function of perceived behavioral control over the behavior, attitudes toward the behavior, and subjective norms about the behavior.[1]

Comparing the planned behavior and expectancy theories reveals both similarities and useful distinctions. Perceived behavioral control, which is akin to self-efficacy (Bandura, 1977)[2], corresponds to expectancy beliefs, as both describe employees' judgments about whether they are capable of performing if they expend effort. Attitudes, which capture the extent to which an employee evaluates the behavior favorably, appear to overlap with both instrumentality and valence beliefs, which—in tandem—connote that the behavior will lead to favorable outcomes. Moving beyond expectancy theory, the theory of planned behavior adds subjective norms, or social expectations and pressure to engage in the behavior. The underlying premise is that employees derive utility not only from personal outcomes but also from social rewards that convey approval, respect, and community and social punishments that convey disapproval, disrespect, and alienation. In a meta-analysis of 185 studies, Armitage and Conner (2001) found that perceived behavioral control, attitudes, subjective norms, and intentions combined to explain 27% of the variance in behaviors (31% when self-reported and 21% when objectively measured or observer-rated) and 39% of the variance in intentions. Both subjective norms and intentions explained unique variance in behaviors after accounting for perceived behavioral control and attitudes, which highlights the potential value of including these two psychological constructs to expand the predictive validity of expectancy theory.

A second limitation of expectancy theory is that it is often viewed as overly calculative (Ashford et al., 1998; Mitchell & Daniels, 2003; Staw, 1984). Although the theory is reasonably effective in predicting motivation and behavior, it creates a caricature of how employees actually make decisions and experience motivation. With the possible exceptions of mathematicians, engineers, financial analysts, and economists, rarely have we seen an employee sit down and calculate the probabilities of effort leading to performance and performance leading to outcomes, and the utility of these outcomes. It would be even more uncommon for an employee to perform these calculations for multiple possible courses of action. With this limitation in mind, scholars have begun to incorporate "hot" affective components into expectancy theory (Seo, Barrett, & Bartunek, 2004). For example, Erez and Isen (2002) demonstrated that positive affect can increase expectancy, instrumentality, and valence beliefs, but only under task conditions that are supportive of these beliefs (e.g., working on a task in which performance is based on effort rather than chance). This research takes a step toward capturing the real-time, affect-laden processes through which expectancy, instrumentality, and valence judgments are made (see also Seo et al., 2004).

Expectancy theory has also been criticized for failing to specify the nature and sources of variations in employees' beliefs and judgments. Employees can attach valence not only to outcomes of performance but also to effort and performance as ends in and of themselves. For example, Eisenberger's (1992) theory of learned industriousness explains how, when employees are rewarded for effort over time, hard work can take on secondary reward properties, such that employees naturally enjoy the very experience of expending effort. In addition, employees tend to view performance as a reward in and of itself when they are growth oriented (Hackman & Oldham, 1976), conscientious (Grant, 2008b), and achievement motivated (McClelland, 1961), suggesting that they will place valence on performance even when there are no external outcomes attached to it.

Finally, expectancy theory falls short of explaining how employees update and change their beliefs over time (Mitchell & Biglan, 1971). For example, valence beliefs can change as employees realize that their actual satisfaction with an outcome is different (e.g., lower or higher) than the satisfaction that they anticipated (e.g., Wilson & Gilbert, 2005). As an endogenous process theory (Katzell & Thompson, 1990), the focus of expectancy theory has been on identifying the key psychological forces that guide decisions about effort and understanding their consequences, rather than specifying their causes or fluctuations. Despite these limitations, expectancy theory is appealing in its theoretical parsimony and its applications to diagnosing and resolving motivational problems in organizations, and thus it remains a popular and widely used theory.

Equity Theory

Equity theory (Adams, 1963, 1965) takes a step toward placing motivation more squarely in a social context. The central assumption of equity theory is that employees are motivated when their inputs (e.g., effort, knowledge, skill, loyalty) are matched by outcomes (e.g., pay, bonuses, benefits, recognition), which creates a sense of equity or fairness. When outcomes do not match inputs, the resulting perceptions of inequity lead to distress, which motivates employees to take action to reduce it. When employees feel underrewarded, they may restore perceived equity by reducing their inputs (slacking off), attempting to reduce others' inputs (convincing coworkers to do less work or sabotaging their efforts to be productive), seeking to increase their outcomes (asking for a raise or vacation time), or aiming to decrease coworkers' outcomes (asking them to take a pay cut or lobbying a boss to standardize salaries). When employees feel overrewarded, they may restore perceived equity by increasing their inputs (working harder) or reducing their outcomes (requesting a pay cut or redistributing their salaries to coworkers).

How do employees make judgments of equity? To evaluate input-outcome ratios, employees can make a range of comparisons (Adams, 1963, 1965). One set of comparisons is between outcomes and inputs such as effort (the time and energy that I invested), ability (my knowledge, skills, and talents), and seniority (my tenure and loyalty). Another set of comparisons is of the input-outcome ratios to other input-outcome ratios, including my own past input-outcome ratios (what I have received elsewhere or before, relative to my contributions) and others' input-outcome ratios (are mine appropriate in light of the ratios of similar others?). This last comparison, the social comparison, is often viewed as the central theoretical insight offered by equity theory (Weick, 1966): Even when employees receive outcomes that match their inputs, their motivation can suffer when they perceive others as maintaining more favorable input-outcome ratios. For example, studies have shown that higher pay dispersion—the disparity in compensation between the highest-paid and lowest-paid employees in an organization—predicts greater manager and employee turnover (Bloom & Michel, 2002), lower job satisfaction, productivity, and collaboration (Pfeffer & Langton, 1993), and in major league baseball teams, fewer runs scored, more runs given up by pitchers, and more losses (Bloom, 1999).

Equity theory assumes that both underrewarding employees and overrewarding employees can be detrimental to motivation. Although research has consistently shown negative motivational and behavioral effects of underreward inequity, evidence reveals mixed results about the consequences of overreward inequity: Some employees appear to decrease their motivation, others increase it, and still others show no significant changes (Ambrose & Kulik, 1999). One approach to resolving these conflicting findings has involved understanding individual differences in equity sensitivity. Huseman, Hatfield, and Miles (1987) proposed that employees can be classified into one of three categories of equity preferences: benevolent (preferring a lower outcome/input ratio than comparison others), equity sensitive (preferring an equal outcome/input ratio to comparison others), and entitled (preferring a higher outcome/input ratio than comparison others). Accordingly, overreward inequity leads to higher motivation among benevolent and equity-sensitive employees than entitled employees (Miles, Hatfield, & Huseman, 1989). Benevolent and equity-sensitive employees are willing to work to restore fairness, whereas entitled employees may be quite content with receiving more than they contribute.

A key controversy in work motivation research concerns competing predictions between equity and expectancy theories in situations characterized by the combination of perceived underreward inequity and high instrumentality beliefs (Harder, 1991). According to equity theory, when instrumentality is high, employees who feel underrewarded will be distressed by perceived inequity and may reduce their effort to create a more appropriate balance between their inputs and outcomes. On the other hand, expectancy theory predicts that when instrumentality is high, employees who feel underrewarded will be motivated to achieve higher performance, as they are confident that this will result in the rewards they feel they deserve. Harder (1991) provided a theoretical and empirical resolution of this controversy in a study of major league baseball free agents. He found that under low instrumentality, negative performance effects of inequity were

visible, but under high instrumentality, individuals maintained their performance: "individuals faced with inequitable underreward will choose the avenue of decreased performance to the extent that it does not affect future rewards. If decreasing performance will adversely affect future rewards, then alternative avenues for restoring equity will be undertaken" (Harder, 1991, pp. 463–464).

Another issue facing equity theory concerns how organizations and employees handle inconsistencies in equity that emerge between different types of comparisons. For example, when pay dispersion is high, star performers making self-comparisons perceive high equity, but average and low performers making social comparisons may perceive low equity. In general, research suggests that in some circumstances, the costs of perceived inequity among the latter group can outweigh the benefits of perceived equity among the former group (Bloom, 1999; Messersmith, Guthrie, Ji, & Lee, 2011; Siegel & Hambrick, 2005). However, this research has yet to identify conditions under which organizations can create favorable perceptions of equity for different groups of employees. One practical solution, pay secrecy, appears to be a mixed bag, as employees often view it as a signal of inequity and resist by going out of their way to publicize their salaries (Colella, Paetzold, Zardkoohi, & Wesson, 2007).

Goal-Setting Theory

One criticism of both expectancy and equity theories is that they focus primarily on psychological processes involved in work motivation, providing little explicit theory and guidance for explaining the role of contextual forces (Katzell & Thompson, 1990). Goal-setting theory overcomes these limitations by focusing on the motivational effects of goals, or targets for action. Extensive research has shown that difficult, specific goals motivate high performance by focusing attention, increasing effort and persistence, and encouraging the development of novel task strategies (Locke & Latham, 1990). For instance, classic studies showed that setting specific, difficult goals—relative to "do your best," easy, or no goals—for 36 truck drivers transporting logs led them to increase from 60% to 90% of legal allowable weight, saving the company approximately $250,000 in less than a year (for a review, see Locke & Latham, 2002). In another study, Latham and Saari (1982) gave 39 truck drivers the goal of enhancing the number of daily trips that they took to the mill, which yielded 15% average daily increases in trips and saved the company approximately $2.7 million in less than 4 months.

Difficult, specific goals are most likely to produce these effects when employees are committed to them, when they receive feedback, and when tasks are simple rather than complex. Without commitment, employees question whether it is worthwhile to work toward difficult goals. Without feedback, employees cannot gauge their progress and adjust effort, persistence, and task strategies accordingly. When tasks are simple, effort is a key determinant of performance, but when tasks are complex, ability and task strategies become more influential, reducing the performance effects of goal setting as a motivational technique (Locke & Latham, 2002).

At first glance, the principle of difficult goals motivating higher performance than easy goals appears to conflict with expectancy theory. From an expectancy theory standpoint, easy goals yield greater effort-to-performance expectancy beliefs, and thus greater motivation and performance, than difficult goals. Researchers have resolved this tension by showing that when goal difficulty is held constant, higher expectancy beliefs are associated with higher performance, but when goal difficulty varies, more difficult goals are linked with higher performance, as the attention, effort, persistence, and task strategy benefits of difficult goals appear to outweigh the costs of lower expectancy beliefs (Locke, Motowidlo, & Bobko, 1986). Furthermore, expectancy beliefs moderate the effects of goal difficulty on performance, such that setting difficult goals only motivates employees to take action if they believe such action has the potential to achieve the goals (Locke & Latham, 2002).

As goal-setting theory gained prominence, scholars began to raise concerns about managers using goals as manipulative tools, and they expressed growing interest in understanding the motivational effects of goals that were self-set by employees. This yielded a major controversy about whether participation in goal setting increases motivation and performance. Holding goal difficulty constant, studies by Latham and colleagues showed null effects of participation, whereas studies by Erez and colleagues identified significant benefits. The authors collaborated, with Locke as a mediator (not a moderator), to jointly design experiments to resolve the dispute. They discovered that the effects of participation in goal setting depend on goal commitment. When the purpose of the goals is clear, participation offers little benefit, but when the purpose is unclear, allowing employees to participate serves the function of increasing goal commitment and thereby

motivates higher performance (Latham, Erez, & Locke, 1988). Subsequent studies suggested that participation may achieve these benefits not only through motivational mechanisms but also through cognitive mechanisms of enabling employees to share information about task strategies and building self-efficacy (Locke & Latham, 2002). Moreover, employees who have high self-efficacy with respect to assigned goals tend to set higher goals, experience greater goal commitment, choose better task strategies, and maintain goal pursuit in the face of negative feedback (Locke & Latham, 2002).

Of course, if employees' goals are not aligned with organizational goals, goal setting can reduce rather than increase performance (Locke & Latham, 2002). This raises important ethical issues, as employees can take unethical or illegal shortcuts to achieve goals. For example, Schweitzer, Ordoñez, and Douma (2004) conducted a laboratory experiment showing that participants were more likely to cheat by overstating their productivity when they had unmet goals than when they were simply asked to do their best. These effects were observed for goals with and without monetary incentives, and they were particularly pronounced when participants narrowly missed goal accomplishment (Schweitzer et al., 2004). A heated debate has ensued about whether goal-setting theory adequately addresses and accounts for these and other risks of goal setting, such as tunnel vision, stress, reduced learning and intrinsic motivation, and excessive risk taking and competition (Latham & Locke, 2009; Locke & Latham, 2009; Ordoñez, Schweitzer, Galinsky, & Bazerman, 2009a, 2009b). We are sympathetic to the arguments of both sides. On one hand, goal-setting theorists have acknowledged many of these risks, and demonstrating that goals can increase unethical behavior is consistent with a premise of goal-setting theory that when employees are committed to goals, they will be motivated to discover and create task strategies for achieving them (Locke & Latham, 2002). After all, unethical behavior is a task strategy. On the other hand, although much is known about the motivation and performance effects of goal setting, substantially less theory and research has addressed the conditions under which goals are more versus less likely to encourage unethical behavior and other unintended consequences (e.g., Barsky, 2008). This represents an important direction for future research: Scholars should systematically build and test theories about the factors that amplify and mitigate the negative effects of goal setting.

Job Design

Goals are one important contextual influence on motivation, but how employees' jobs are structured also has a substantial impact on their motivation (for reviews, see Fried, Levi, & Laurence, 2008; Grant & Parker, 2009; Morgeson & Humphrey, 2008; Oldham & Hackman, 2010; Parker & Ohly, 2008). Classic research on job design focused on the principle of job enrichment, which refers to altering the structural characteristics of employees' tasks to increase their motivating potential (Herzberg, 1959). The dominant approach to job enrichment is based on the Job Characteristics Model (Hackman & Oldham, 1976, 1980), which proposes that motivation, satisfaction, performance quality, and withdrawal behaviors such as absenteeism and turnover are a function of three critical psychological states: experienced meaningfulness, responsibility for outcomes, and knowledge of results. Experienced meaningfulness is thought to be determined by three core job characteristics: skill variety (being challenged to use a variety of one's capabilities), task identity (completing a whole, identifiable piece of work from start to finish), and task significance (having an impact on other people inside or outside the organization). Experienced responsibility is thought to be shaped by the job characteristic of autonomy (freedom and discretion about when and how to complete the work) and experienced knowledge of results by the job characteristic of feedback (information from completing the work itself about one's progress and effectiveness). Thus, from a motivational standpoint, well-designed jobs are high in at least one of the dimensions of skill variety, task identity, and task significance, as well as in autonomy and feedback. These effects are moderated by individual differences in growth need strength, such that employees who value learning and development should be more responsive to both the enriched job characteristics and the critical psychological states, as well as by knowledge, skill, and satisfaction with the work context.

Field experiments and meta-analytic reviews have shown that as a whole, these job characteristics have good explanatory power for work motivation (Fried & Ferris, 1987; Griffin, 1983). At the same time, the model has been critiqued and expanded on a number of grounds to include curvilinear effects of jobs that are "too" enriched (Xie & Johns, 1995), consider how job perceptions are shaped by social information as well as objective task structures (Salancik & Pfeffer, 1978; Zalesny & Ford, 1990), account for variations between the different tasks that employees perform (Wong & Campion,

1991) and workday schedules (Elsbach & Hargadon, 2006), include knowledge and learning as well as motivational mechanisms for explaining job design effects (Parker, Wall, & Jackson, 1997; Parker, Wall, & Cordery, 2001), and examine how motivational approaches to job design from organizational psychology may involve tradeoffs with respect to mechanistic approaches from industrial engineering, perceptual-motor approaches from human factors and cognitive psychology, and biological approaches from medicine (Campion & McClelland, 1993; Morgeson & Campion, 2002).

From a motivational standpoint, one critique of the Job Characteristics Model is that it focused on the enrichment of assigned tasks, overlooking the important role that interpersonal relationships play in motivation (for a review, see Grant & Parker, 2009). Although early research included relational characteristics of jobs such as interactions with others and friendship opportunities (Hackman & Lawler, 1971; Trist & Bamforth, 1951; Turner & Lawrence, 1965), they fell out of favor as Hackman and Oldham (1976) sought to focus squarely on the task characteristics that composed jobs. Recent research has examined the motivational effects of redesigning jobs to connect employees to their impact on the beneficiaries of their work—the clients, customers, patients, and other who are affected by their efforts (Grant, 2007). Studies have shown, for example, that when employees even have a short interaction with an end user of their work, they come to perceive their actions as having a greater impact and as more socially valued, and feel more committed to their end users in general, which motivates them to work harder and achieve higher performance and productivity (Grant, 2008b; Grant et al., 2007). As will be discussed in more detail later, this opens up the opportunity to understand how jobs can be designed not only to enhance intrinsic motivation but also to foster prosocial motivation—the desire to protect and promote the well-being of others (Grant, 2007).

Similar to the growing attention to self-set as opposed to manager-set goals, scholars have observed that managers are not the only architects of jobs; employees also take initiative to proactively alter the characteristics of their own jobs (for a review, see Grant & Parker, 2009). Scholars have developed conceptual frameworks to explain the factors that motivate employees to adjust their roles (Nicholson, 1984) and craft or modify their jobs (Wrzesniewski & Dutton, 2001). Recent research has revealed how employees take initiative to craft their jobs in pursuit of "unanswered callings" (Berg, Grant, & Johnson, 2010), craft their jobs not only in isolation but also in collaboration (Leana, Appelbaum, & Shevchuk, 2009), and experience and respond to challenges encountered in job crafting (Berg, Wrzesniewski, & Dutton, 2010). Research has also explored how managers and employees work together to negotiate "idiosyncratic deals" about the motivational characteristics of jobs (Hornung, Rousseau, Glaser, Angerer, & Weigl, 2010; Rousseau, Ho, & Greenberg, 2006).

Self-Determination Theory

Scholars have long viewed intrinsic motivation—a desire to act based on interest and enjoyment of the work itself—as a key influence on work motivation, especially in the literatures on job design (Hackman & Oldham, 1980) and creativity (Amabile & Mueller, 2007; George, 2007; Shalley, Zhou, & Oldham, 2004). Self-determination theory has begun to play a central role in expanding our understanding of intrinsic motivation and informing work motivation research more generally (for a review, see Gagné & Deci, 2005). In work motivation research, self-determination theory has been particularly useful in resolving controversies about the conditions under which rewards and incentives have positive versus negative effects. According to self-determination theory, employees have three basic psychological needs: autonomy, competence, and relatedness (Ryan & Deci, 2000). Autonomy refers to the feeling of choice and discretion, competence refers to feeling capable and efficacious, and relatedness refers to feelings of connectedness and belongingness with others.

Self-determination theorists propose that when these three psychological needs are fulfilled, employees are more likely to be intrinsically motivated and internalize external goals and objectives. Thus, when rewards and incentives are delivered in a manner that threatens feelings of autonomy, competence, and/or relatedness, employees will tend to react negatively. For example, explaining a reward system in a controlling rather than supportive manner can compromise employees' feelings of autonomy and relatedness (e.g., Deci, Connell, & Ryan, 1989; Deci, Koestner, & Ryan, 1999; see also Kramer, 1999). On the other hand, as long as rewards and incentives are delivered in a manner that supports autonomy, competence, and relatedness, intrinsic motivation and internalization are more likely (e.g., Amabile, 1993). Other research suggests that additional features of compensation systems, such as variable versus fixed pay ratios and the number of people whose performance determines the reward (Gagné & Forest, 2008), as well as the symbolic features of rewards—who distributes them, why, how, and to whom (Mickel & Barron, 2008)—may affect self-determination and intrinsic motivation.

Self-determination theory also makes a valuable contribution to our understanding of work motivation by elaborating our understanding of extrinsic motivation. Rather than viewing extrinsic motivation as a unitary construct, Ryan and Deci (2000) proposed that extrinsic motivation is a matter of degree, varying along a continuum of autonomous regulation. They identified four different types of extrinsic motivation that employees experience as successively less controlled and more autonomous: external (based on outside reward and punishment contingencies), introjected (based on internal reward and punishment contingencies, such as guilt and self-esteem), identified (based on consistency with a personal value), and integrated (assimilated into one's system of values).

In the work domain, researchers have proposed that since external reward and incentive contingencies are virtually omnipresent, extrinsic and intrinsic motivations often coexist (Adler & Chen, 2009; Staw, 1984). If this is true, employees might be expected to invest more time and energy in their work when they find it both intrinsically motivating and are able to identify or integrate it with their values (e.g., with prosocial values related to helping others). Consistent with this prediction, research has shown that intrinsic and prosocial motivations interact synergistically to predict higher levels of persistence, performance, and productivity among firefighters and fundraisers (Grant, 2008a), as well as higher levels of creativity achieved by military security officers, water treatment employees, and participants in an experiment helping a local band make money (Grant & Berry, 2011). Thus, intrinsic and identified-integrated motivations appear to be particularly potent in combination. Other research has shown that autonomous motivations (intrinsic, integrated, identified) are more important for performance on complex rather than simple tasks, where autonomous motivations encourage exploration and persistence (for a review, see Gagné & Deci, 2005).

Organizational scholars have also used self-determination theory to explain the motivational effects of transformational leadership—acting to inspire employees, model important values, and provide individualized consideration and intellectual stimulation. Bono and Judge (2003) conducted a field study and a laboratory experiment showing that transformational leaders encouraged employees to set autonomous rather than controlled goals, resulting in more positive attitudes and higher performance. Interestingly, their field study suggested that transformational leadership was associated positively with autonomous motivation but had no relationship with controlled motivation, while their lab experiment indicated that transformational leadership reduced controlled motivation more strongly than it increased autonomous motivation. Further research is still needed to explain this discrepancy, but the difference in the strength and content of rewards and incentives between the field and lab may be one key factor (Bono & Judge, 2003).

Integrating job design and self-determination theories, we know much more about how intrinsic motivation is influenced by the structure than the content of employees' tasks. According to self-determination theory, feelings of autonomy, competence, and relatedness are important for intrinsic motivation. However, intrinsic motivation depends on enjoying the work itself, and some tasks are experienced by employees as "not in themselves interesting" (Gagné & Deci, 2005, p. 347). Thus, even when employees feel autonomous, competent, and connected to others, they may not experience intrinsic motivation in tasks that they do not find interesting or enjoyable. Currently, we lack a theoretical framework for specifying how particular task contents are more intrinsically interesting than others, and how different employees find different types of tasks interesting. It may be the case that one of the benefits of providing employees with autonomy is that it gives them the freedom and discretion to craft their jobs in ways that they find intrinsically motivating, but this has yet to be studied.

Finally, little research has explored the costs of intrinsic motivation in organizational settings. Research suggests that intrinsic motivation is less effective for performance in tasks that are simple or require considerable self-control and discipline (Gagné & Deci, 2005; Koestner & Losier, 2002). Scholars have begun to speculate that intrinsic motivation can distract attention away from organizational goals, or at the very least, is not necessarily aligned with them (Grant & Berry, 2011; Osterloh & Frey, 2000). In addition, scholars have raised concerns that employees can be intrinsically motivated toward activities that are directly destructive or harmful, such as theft and sabotage (Osterloh & Frey, 2000). As we noted for goal setting, more research is needed on the contingencies that affect whether and when intrinsic motivation

is conducive to effective task performance and organizational citizenship behaviors (Gagné & Deci, 2005).

Motivating New Directions

Beyond these core theoretical perspectives, we see a range of contemporary issues and unanswered questions for work motivation research to address. In the following sections, we discuss four key current and new directions for motivation research: group motivation and organizing, motivation over time, motivation and creativity, and the effects of rewards.

Group Motivation and Organizing

Moving beyond the dominant emphasis on individual-level motivation, scholars have paid increasing attention to the role of motivation in work groups and teams. The most comprehensive perspective on this phenomenon is Chen and Kanfer's (2006) theoretical model integrating individual-level, group-level, and cross-level processes. They adopt a systems perspective to explain how, at both individual and team levels, motivational states affect goal generation and goal striving, and thus influence performance. They propose that individual motivational states are a function of employees' traits, work experience, the quality of relationships with their leaders, and individual feedback, while team motivational states are a function of leadership climate, group norms, work design, and team feedback. They further discuss how team and individual motivational processes reciprocally influence each other, as do individual and team performance. Recent research provides support for the general premises of the model. For example, Chen, Kanfer, DeShon, Mathieu, and Kozlowski (2009) demonstrated the cross-level influence of prior team performance on subsequent individual performance in two samples. They found that prior team performance influences self-efficacy by shaping prior individual performance and team efficacy, that team efficacy affects goal striving through self-efficacy and team action processes (e.g., helping and cooperation), and that these team action processes influence individual performance by shaping individual goal striving.

One exciting pathway for extending the Chen and Kanfer model involves examining the influence of motivation on organizing. Organizing refers to the processes through which individual members coordinate their actions to achieve collective goals (Weick, 1979), and it is among the most important yet neglected topics in all of organizational research

(Heath & Sitkin, 2001). Surprisingly little research has examined the impact of motivation on organizing. For example, there is a large literature on "high-reliability organizing" that examines how groups coordinate actions to achieve consistent, safe performance in uncertain, complex, consequential, high-risk contexts such as nuclear power plants, wildland firefighting, hospital emergency departments, and aircraft carriers (e.g., Hofmann & Stetzer, 1998; Waller & Roberts, 2003; Weick & Roberts, 1993). Traditional approaches to increasing reliability have focused on building collective capabilities for systems to manage unexpected events through the structuring of roles, routines, and norms (e.g., Bierly & Spender, 1995; Bigley & Roberts, 2001; Vogus & Welbourne, 2003; Weick, Sutcliffe, & Obstfeld, 1999, 2005; Zohar & Luria, 2003). However, these collective capabilities are nearly useless if employees are not motivated to put them into action. Researchers have yet to explore how individual and team motivational processes affect the effective implementation of collective capabilities for high reliability. Moreover, individual and team motivational processes may be important catalysts of the decision to create and develop collective capabilities in the first place.

More generally, the impact of motivation on organizing has been neglected. One notable exception to this trend is the fascinating work by Adler and Chen (2009) on large-scale collaborative creativity. These authors focus on how social collectives are able to organize or coordinate efforts to develop and implement novel, useful solutions to problems, such as when hundreds or thousands of software developers collaborate to introduce a new computer program, aircraft engineers collaborate to develop a new design, and scientists create new pharmaceutical drugs. Building on self-determination theory, Adler and Chen (2009) present propositions to explain how large-scale collaborative creativity can be organized effectively through simultaneously activating intrinsic and identified motivations. We hope to see more research follow suit by examining how individual-level and team-level motivations influence the propensity and capacity to organize. Research on social motivations that are directed toward others, such as collectivistic work motivation (Shamir, 1990, 1991), motivation to innovate (Amabile, 1988), and prosocial motivation (Grant, 2007, 2008a; Grant & Berry, 2011), may prove especially useful in drawing sharper theoretical and empirical links between motivation and the organizing of individual efforts into collective outcomes. In addition, recent developments in knowledge about proactive motivation—the desire to take anticipatory action to create change (for reviews, see Grant & Parker, 2009; Parker, Bindl, & Strauss, 2010)—may help to explain the disproportionate influence of particular individual efforts on organizing.

Motivation Over Time

In response to critiques that most motivation theory and research is overly static, scholars have begun to examine dynamic and temporal perspectives on motivation. One dynamic view adopts an adult development perspective to explain how motivations change across the life span (Kanfer & Ackerman, 2004). These authors review research suggesting that aging is associated with declines in fluid intelligence (working memory, abstract reasoning, attention, and processing of novel information), but increases in crystallized intelligence (educational and experiential knowledge). They propose that as employees age, these changes increase the likelihood of enhancing effort to cope with jobs that place heavy demands on fluid intelligence, but this may compromise motivation and performance, as declining performance in the face of increased effort can reduce self-efficacy. In contrast, aging may be associated with more effective maintenance of motivation and performance in jobs that primarily require crystallized intelligence, as employees are able to sustain high performance in the absence of greater effort. As a result, from an instrumentality and valence standpoint, stronger rewards and incentives may be necessary to increase the performance of midlife employees (above current levels) in jobs requiring crystallized intelligence, compared to younger workers. Kanfer and Ackerman (2004) further propose that aging reduces the valence that employees place on effort and on increasing job performance, although the latter effect can be attenuated by performance standards that fit age-graded values, such as rising emphasis on social rather than technical competence.

Aging also has important implications for how employees grapple with death awareness and respond to mortality cues, and Grant and Wade-Benzoni (2009) proposed that these changes can have substantial effects on work motivation. These authors distinguished between two states of death awareness—the "hot" death anxiety typically studied by terror management theorists and the "cool" death reflection typically studied by generativity and posttraumatic growth theorists. They proposed that death anxiety is likely to motivate withdrawal behaviors from work, such as absenteeism, tardiness, and turnover, except when work serves as an escape from mortality cues. They argued that in contrast, death reflection has the potential to motivate generative work behaviors, such as helping, mentoring, and transitions to more prosocially focused or service-oriented occupations, especially for employees who view work as a calling. However, since empirical research has yet to test, challenge, complicate, and expand the propositions developed by Kanfer and Ackerman (2004) and Grant and Wade-Benzoni (2009), we encourage future studies on the impact of aging and death awareness on work motivation.

A different perspective on temporal changes in motivation appears in research on generational differences in work values. Twenge, Campbell, Hoffman, and Lance (2010) used a nationally representative sample of U.S. high school seniors in 1976, 1991, and 2006 to compare mean work values between the Baby Boomer, Generation X, and Millennial generations. A key feature of their analytic approach is that while cross-sectional studies confound generational cohorts with age and life experience, longitudinal studies comparing participants at the same ages can isolate these factors. They discovered that on average, leisure values have increased with each new generation, corresponding with declines in work centrality. Extrinsic values, although highest among Generation X, remain higher among Millennials than Baby Boomers. Millennials appear to place less importance on social and intrinsic work values than Baby Boomers, and there were no significant differences in emphasis placed on altruistic work values.

There is a heavy debate about the practical significance of the effect sizes in this program of research (e.g., Trzesniewski & Donnellan, 2010), and how they may be small in comparison to those of developmental and age effects (e.g., Roberts, Edmonds, & Grijalva, 2010). However, because of its ability to isolate generational differences from age differences, this is the most rigorous study to date of generational differences in work values. The Twenge et al. (2010) findings raise interesting questions about whether, on average, employees from the Millennial generation will display stronger responses to motivational interventions focusing on leisure rewards (e.g., time off, paid vacations) and weaker responses to social rewards (e.g., making contacts and friendship opportunities) and intrinsic rewards (e.g., learning, interesting work, creative challenges).

These perspectives on life-span development and generational differences emphasize relatively macroscopic changes in motivation, but it is also important to understand more microscopic changes in motivation. Compared to research on the direction and intensity of effort, few theoretical models and empirical studies have focused on the maintenance or persistence of effort (e.g., Grant et al., 2007; Penner, Dovidio, Piliavin, & Schroeder, 2005). Are the factors that sustain motivation different from those that initiate it—and if so, how, why, and when? Furthermore, little research has examined the factors that influence changes in the valence that employees place on different outcomes over time. For example, outside of changes in job designs and incentives, what leads employees to develop more intrinsic motivation toward a specific occupation, job, project, or task? As another example, researchers have established that employees vary in their orientations toward work as a job, a career, or a calling (Wrzesniewski, McCauley, Rozin, & Schwartz, 1997; see also Bunderson & Thompson, 2009). However, we know little about what leads employees to shift from viewing work as a job to a career or a career to a calling. We need a deeper understanding of the factors that shift employees' motivational orientations toward work over time.

Motivation and Creativity

Motivation is known to play a central role in creativity, or the production of novel and useful ideas, which is a topic of increasing interest and importance to organizations as the pace and uncertainty of work continue to accelerate. Amabile and colleagues have developed a componential theory of creativity that features intrinsic motivation prominently as an important influence on the creative process (Amabile, 1996; Amabile & Mueller, 2007). Intrinsic motivation is thought to enhance creativity by encouraging exploration and risk taking (Amabile, Hennessey, & Grossman, 1986; Hennessey, Amabile, & Martinage, 1989), psychological engagement in work and in learning (Amabile, Hill, Hennessey, & Tighe, 1994), and active processing of information and selection of novel, challenging tasks (Conti, Amabile, & Pollack, 1995), as well as persistence (Shalley, Zhou, & Oldham, 2004). Interestingly, research has shown mixed effects of intrinsic motivation on creativity, with some laboratory and field studies indicating a positive relationship, and others suggesting a null relationship (e.g., George, 2007; Shalley et al., 2004).

Grant and Berry (2011) sought to resolve this discrepancy by examining whether the effect of intrinsic motivation on creativity is contingent on prosocial motivation. They proposed that while intrinsic motivation fosters a focus on novel ideas, prosocial motivation is important for encouraging perspective taking about what others find useful (Grant & Berry, 2011). They found support for these hypotheses across field studies of military officers and water treatment employees, as well as in a laboratory experiment. We hope to see further research build on this evidence to examine other motivational processes that foster a focus on usefulness, complementing the attention to novelty cultivated by intrinsic motivation. Such investigations will further enhance our understanding of the effects of motivation on creativity.

More broadly, we hope to see scholars investigate the impact of motivation on a wider range of dependent variables. Our discussion of creativity aligns with increasing attention of organizational researchers to employee behaviors that go beyond core task requirements: organizational citizenship behaviors such as helping and sportsmanship (e.g., Organ, 1988; Podsakoff, MacKenzie, Paine, & Bachrach, 2000), proactive behaviors such as voicing suggestions and taking charge to introduce new work methods (Grant & Parker, 2009; Parker et al., 2010), and counterproductive behaviors such as aggression, theft, and sabotage (Griffin & Lopez, 2005; Spector & Fox, 2010). Different motivations may play a key role in shaping which of these behavioral directions employees pursue.

Rewards and Motivation

Another key direction involves identifying the conditions under which rewards increase motivation. A debate currently exists about whether managers underestimate the power of intrinsic relative to extrinsic rewards for motivating employees (Heath, 1999), or whether there is a discrepancy between what employees say and what they do, such that employees report that extrinsic rewards are relatively unimportant, but the preferences revealed by their behaviors suggest otherwise (Rynes, Gerhart, & Minette, 2004). Scholars may take steps to resolve this debate by attending not only to the instrumental features of rewards but also to their symbolic features. For example, Mickel and Barron (2008) propose that rewards will be more likely to increase motivation when they are distributed by high-status authority figures, for high performance and accomplishments, and in public ceremonies.

This raises a more general issue with respect to rewards: We believe that lumping all rewards into a common category has obscured the importance of understanding the effects of different types of rewards on motivation. In particular, researchers have focused primarily on pay and financial incentives, giving far less emphasis to more symbolic rewards such as recognition and appreciation, even though these rewards are frequently intended to motivate and can be effective (Stajkovic & Luthans, 2001; see also Frey, 2007, and Grant & Gino, 2010). We hope to see scholars build and test theories about the motivational effects of different types of recognition systems.

Conclusion

Scholars have explored many other issues related to work motivation that fall outside the scope of this chapter. For example, important developments have examined how motivation is shaped by needs and motives (for reviews, see Ambrose & Kulik, 1999; Steers, Mowday, & Shapiro, 2004), personality traits (e.g., Barrick, Stewart, & Piotrowski, 2002; Judge & Ilies, 2002), culture (Erez, 2010), and nonwork factors (George & Brief, 1996; Kossek & Misra, 2008; Rothbard, 2001). Furthermore, extensive treatments of the role of self-regulation processes are available elsewhere (Diefendorff & Chandler, 2010). In addition, some scholars have developed integrative perspectives and models that bring together multiple motivation theories (Locke & Latham, 2004; Mitchell & Daniels, 2003; Steel & König, 2006). It remains to be seen whether an integrative model of motivation is desirable, or even possible. Our own view is that given the complexity of psychological, social, and situational influences on motivation, researchers are best advised to develop, test, and elaborate middle-range theories (Weick, 1974) that are problem driven—designed to explain particular phenomena and outcomes, rather than seeking to generalize to all outcomes (Lawrence, 1992). Nevertheless, we hope this chapter is useful in summarizing key trends in the study of work motivation and directing, energizing, and maintaining future research.

Notes

1. More recent work suggests that the psychological processes underlying the model can be further illuminated by including desires as micromediators of the effects of beliefs on intentions (Perugini & Bagozzi, 2001).

2. Some scholars have challenged the theoretical and empirical appropriateness of lumping self-efficacy and perceived behavioral control together. The central distinction lies in that

self-efficacy describes judgments of one's internal capability to perform a behavior, whereas perceived behavioral control also incorporates judgments of whether external forces may limit the controllability of the behavior (see Armitage & Conner, 2001, p. 476), which suggests that perceived behavioral control and expectancy beliefs share greater similarity with each other than they do with self-efficacy.

References

Adams, J. S. (1963). Toward an understanding of inequity. *Journal of Abnormal and Social Psychology*, *67*, 422–436.

Adams, J. S. (1965). Inequity in social exchange. In L. Berkowitz (Ed.), *Advances in experimental social psychology* (Vol. 2, pp. 267–299). New York: Academic Press.

Adler, P. S., & Chen, C. X. (2009). Beyond intrinsic motivation: On the nature of individual motivation in large-scale collaborative creativity. *Social Science Research Network*. Retrieved August 2, 2011, from https://msbfile03.usc.edu/digitalmeasures/padler/intellcont/BEYOND%20INTRINSIC%20MOTIVATION-1.pdf

Ajzen, I. (1991). The theory of planned behavior. *Organizational Behavior and Human Decision Processes*, *50*, 179–211.

Amabile, T. M. (1988). A model of creativity and innovation in organizations. *Research in Organizational Behavior*, *10*, 123–167.

Amabile, T. M. (1993). Motivational synergy: Toward new conceptualizations of intrinsic and extrinsic motivation in the workplace. *Human Resource Management Review*, *3*, 185–201.

Amabile, T.M. (1996). *Creativity in context*. Boulder, CO: Westview Press.

Amabile, T. M., Hennessey, B. A., & Grossman, B. S. (1986). Social influences on creativity: The effects of contracted-for reward. *Journal of Personality and Social Psychology*, *50*, 14–23.

Amabile, T. M., Hill, K. G., Hennessey, B. A., & Tighe, E. M. (1994). The Work Preference Inventory: Assessing intrinsic and extrinsic motivational orientations. *Journal of Personality and Social Psychology*, *66*, 950–967.

Amabile, T. M., & Mueller, J. S. (2007). Studying creativity, its processes, and its antecedents: An exploration of the componential theory of creativity. In J. Zhou & C. Shalley (Eds.), *Handbook of organizational creativity* (pp. 31–62). Mahwah, NJ: Erlbaum.

Ambrose, M. L., & Kulik, C. T. (1999). Old friends, new faces: Motivation in the 1990s. *Journal of Management*, *25*, 231–292.

Armitage, C. J., & Conner, M. (2001). Efficacy of the theory of planned behaviour: A meta-analytic review. *British Journal of Social Psychology*, *40*, 471–499.

Ashford, S. J., Rothbard, N. P., Piderit, S. K., & Dutton, J. E. (1998). Out on a limb: The role of context and impression management in selling gender-equity issues. *Administrative Science Quarterly*, *43*, 23–57.

Bandura, A. (1977). Self-efficacy: Toward a unifying theory of behavioral change. *Psychological Review*, *84*, 191–215.

Barrick, M. R., Stewart, G. L., & Piotrowski, M. (2002). Personality and job performance: Test of the mediating effects of motivation among sales representatives. *Journal of Applied Psychology*, *87*, 43–51.

Barsky, A. (2008). Understanding the ethical cost of organizational goal-setting: A review and theory development. *Journal of Business Ethics*, *81*, 63–81.

Berg, J. M., Grant, A. M., & Johnson, V. (2010). When callings are calling: Crafting work and leisure in pursuit of unanswered occupational callings. *Organization Science*, *21*, 973–994.

Berg, J. M., Wrzesniewski, A., & Dutton, J. E. (2010). Perceiving and responding to challenges in job crafting at different ranks: When proactivity requires adaptivity. *Journal of Organizational Behavior*, *31*, 158–186.

Bierly, P. E., & Spender, J-C. (1995). Culture and high reliability organizations: The case of the nuclear submarine. *Journal of Management*, *21*, 639–656.

Bigley, G. A., & Roberts K. H. (2001). The incident command system: High-reliability organizing for complex and volatile task environments. *Academy of Management Journal*, *44*, 1281–1299.

Bloom, M. (1999). The performance effects of pay dispersion on individuals and organizations. *Academy of Management Journal*, *42*, 25–40.

Bloom, M., & Michel, J. G. (2002). The relationships among organizational context, pay dispersion, and managerial turnover. *Academy of Management Journal*, *45*, 33–42.

Bono, J. E., & Judge, T. A. (2003). Self-concordance at work: Toward understanding the motivational effects of transformational leaders. *Academy of Management Journal*, *46*, 554–571.

Bunderson, J. S., & Thompson, J. A. (2009). The call of the wild: Zookeepers, callings, and the double-edged sword of deeply meaningful work. *Administrative Science Quarterly*, *54*, 32–57.

Campbell, D. J., & Pritchard, R. (1976). Motivation theory in industrial and organizational psychology. In M. D. Dunnette (Ed.), *Handbook of industrial and organizational psychology* (pp. 63–130). Chicago, IL: Rand McNally.

Campion, M. A., & McClelland, C. L. (1993). Follow-up and extension of the interdisciplinary costs and benefits of enlarged jobs. *Journal of Applied Psychology*, *78*, 339–351.

Chen, G., & Kanfer, R. (2006). Toward a systems theory of motivated behavior in work teams. *Research in Organizational Behavior*, *27*, 223–267.

Chen, G., Kanfer, R., DeShon, R. P., Mathieu, J. E., & Kozlowski, S. W. J. (2009). The motivating potential of teams: Test and extension of Chen & Kanfer's (2006) cross-level model of motivation in teams. *Organizational Behavior and Human Decision Processes*, *110*, 45–55.

Chen, M. J., & Miller, D. (1994). Competitive attack, retaliation and performance: An expectancy-valence framework. *Strategic Management Journal*, *15*, 85–102.

Colella, A., Paetzold, R. L., Zardkoohi, A., & Wesson, M. J. (2007). Exposing pay secrecy. *Academy of Management Review*, *32*, 55–71.

Conti, R., Amabile, T. M., & Pollack, S. (1995). Enhancing intrinsic motivation, learning, and creativity. *Personality and Social Psychology Bulletin*, *21*, 1107–1116.

Deci, E. L., Connell, J. P., & Ryan, R. M. (1989). Self-determination in a work organization. *Journal of Applied Psychology*, *74*, 580–590.

Deci, E. L., Koestner, R., & Ryan, R. M. (1999). A meta-analytic review of experiments examining the effects of extrinsic rewards on intrinsic motivation. *Psychological Bulletin*, *125*, 627–668.

Diefendorff, J. M., & Chandler, M. M. (2010). Motivating employees. In S. Zedeck (Ed.), *Handbook of industrial and organizational psychology* (pp. 65–135). Washington, DC: American Psychological Association.

Eisenberger, R. (1992). Learned industriousness. *Psychological Review, 99*, 248–267.

Elsbach, K. D., & Hargadon, A. B. (2006). Enhancing creativity through "mindless" work: A framework of workday design. *Organization Science, 17*, 470–483.

Erez, M. (2010). Culture and job design. *Journal of Organizational Behavior, 31*, 389–400.

Erez, A., & Isen, A. M. (2002). The influence of positive affect on the components of expectancy motivation. *Journal of Applied Psychology, 87*, 1055–1067.

Frey, B. S. (2007). Awards as compensation. *European Management Review, 4*, 6–14.

Fried, Y., & Ferris, G. R. (1987). The validity of the job characteristics model: A review and meta-analysis. *Personnel Psychology, 40*, 287–322.

Fried, Y., Levi, A. S., & Laurence, G. (2008). Motivation and job design in the new world of work. In S. Cartwright and C. L. Cooper (Eds.), *The Oxford handbook of personnel psychology* (Vol. 24, pp. 586–611). Oxford, England: Oxford University Press.

Gagné, M., & Deci, E. L. (2005). Self-determination theory and work motivation. *Journal of Organizational Behavior, 26*, 331–362.

Gagné, M., & Forest, J. (2008). The study of compensation systems through the lens of self-determination theory: Reconciling 35 years of debate. *Canadian Psychology, 49*, 225–232.

George, J. M. (2007). Creativity in organizations. *Academy of Management Annals, 1*, 439–477.

George, J. M., & Brief, A. P. (1996). Motivational agendas in the workplace: The effects of feelings on focus of attention and work motivation. *Research in Organizational Behavior, 18*, 75–109.

Grant, A. M. (2007). Relational job design and the motivation to make a prosocial difference. *Academy of Management Review, 32*, 393–417.

Grant, A. M. (2008a). Does intrinsic motivation fuel the prosocial fire? Motivational synergy in predicting persistence, performance, and productivity. *Journal of Applied Psychology, 93*, 48–58.

Grant, A. M. (2008b). The significance of task significance: Job performance effects, relational mechanisms, and boundary conditions. *Journal of Applied Psychology, 93*, 108–124.

Grant, A. M., & Berry, J. (2011). The necessity of others is the mother of invention: Intrinsic and prosocial motivations, perspective-taking, and creativity. *Academy of Management Journal, 54*, 73–96.

Grant, A. M., Campbell, E. M., Chen, G., Cottone, K., Lapedis, D., & Lee, K. (2007). Impact and the art of motivation maintenance: The effects of contact with beneficiaries on persistence behavior. *Organizational Behavior and Human Decision Processes, 103*, 53–67.

Grant, A. M., & Gino, F. (2010). A little thanks goes a long way: Explaining why gratitude expressions motivate prosocial behavior. *Journal of Personality and Social Psychology, 98*.

Grant, A. M., & Parker, S. K. (2009). Redesigning work design theories: The rise of relational and proactive perspectives. *Academy of Management Annals, 3*, 317–375.

Grant, A. M., & Wade-Benzoni, K. (2009). The hot and cool of death awareness at work: Mortality cues, aging, and self-protective and prosocial motivations. *Academy of Management Review, 34*, 600–622.

Griffin, R. W. (1983). Objective and social sources of information in task redesign: A field experiment. *Administrative Science Quarterly, 28*, 184–200.

Griffin, R. W., & Lopez, Y. P. (2005). 'Bad behavior' in organizations: A review and typology for future research. *Journal of Management, 31*, 988–1005.

Hackman, J. R., & Lawler, E. E. (1971). Employee reactions to job characteristics. *Journal of Applied Psychology, 55*, 259–286.

Hackman, J. R., & Oldham, G. R. (1976). Motivation through the design of work: Test of a theory. *Organizational Behavior and Human Performance, 16*, 250–279.

Hackman, J. R., & Oldham, G. R. (1980). *Work redesign*. Reading, MA: Addison-Wesley.

Harder, J. W. (1991). Equity theory versus expectancy theory: The case of major league baseball free agents. *Journal of Applied Psychology, 76*, 458–464.

Heath, C. (1999). On the social psychology of agency relationships: Lay theories of motivation overemphasize extrinsic incentives. *Organizational Behavior and Human Decision Processes, 78*, 25–62.

Heath, C., & Sitkin, S. (2001). Big-B versus Big-O: What is organizational about organizational behavior? *Journal of Organizational Behavior, 22*, 43–58.

Hennessey, B. A., Amabile, T. M., & Martinage, M. (1989). Immunizing children against the negative effects of reward. *Contemporary Educational Psychology, 14*, 212–227.

Herzberg, F. (1959). *The motivation to work*. New York: Wiley.

Hofmann, D. A., & Stetzer, A. (1998). The role of safety climate and communication in accident interpretation: Implications for learning from negative events. *Academy of Management Journal, 41*, 644-657.

Hornung, S., Rousseau, D. M., Glaser, J., Angerer, P., & Weigl, M. (2010). Beyond top-down and bottom-up work redesign: Customizing job content through idiosyncratic deals. *Journal of Organizational Behavior, 31*, 187–215.

Huseman, R. C., Hatfield, J. D., & Miles, E. W. (1987). A new perspective on *equity* theory: The *equity sensitivity* construct. *Academy of Management Review, 12*, 222–234.

Judge, T. A., & Ilies, R. (2002). Relationship of *personality* to performance motivation: A meta-analytic review. *Journal of Applied Psychology, 87*, 797–807.

Kanfer, R. (1990). Motivation theory and industrial and organizational psychology. In M. D. Dunnette (Ed.), *Handbook of industrial and organizational psychology* (Vol. 1, 2nd ed., pp. 75–130). Palo Alto, CA: Consulting Psychologists Press.

Kanfer, R., & Ackerman, P. L. (2004). Aging, adult development, and work motivation. *Academy of Management Review, 29*, 440–458.

Kanfer, R., Chen, G., & Pritchard, R. D. (Eds.). (2008). *Work motivation: Past, present, and future*. New York: Taylor and Francis Group.

Katzell, R. A., & Thompson, D. E. (1990). Work motivation: Theory and practice. *American Psychologist, 45*, 144–153.

Koestner, R., & Losier, G. F. (2002). Distinguishing three ways of being highly motivated: A closer look at introjection, identification, and intrinsic motivation. In R. Koestner, G. F. Losier, E. L. Deci, & R. M. Ryan (Eds.), *Handbook of self-determination research* (pp. 101–121). Rochester, NY: University of Rochester Press.

Kossek, E., & Misra, K. (2008). Non-work influences on work motivation. In R. Kanfer, G. Chen, & R. Pritchard (Eds.),

Work motivation: Past, present, and future (pp. 471–500). New York: Taylor and Francis Group.

Kramer, R. (1999). Trust and distrust in organizations: Emerging perspectives, enduring questions. *Annual Review of Psychology, 50*, 569–598.

Latham, G. P., Erez, M., & Locke, E. A. (1988). Resolving scientific disputes by the joint design of crucial experiments by the antagonists: Application to the Erez-Latham dispute regarding participation in goal setting. *Journal of Applied Psychology, 73*, 753–772.

Latham, G. P., & Locke, E. A. (2009). Science and ethics: What should count as evidence against the use of goal setting? *Academy of Management Perspectives, 23*, 88–91.

Latham, G. P., & Pinder, C. C. (2005). Work motivation theory and research at the dawn of the twenty-first century. *Annual Review of Psychology, 56*, 495–516.

Latham, G. P., & Saari, L. M. (1982). The importance of union acceptance for productivity improvement through goal setting. *Personnel Psychology, 35*, 781–787.

Lawrence, P. R. (1992). The challenge of problem-oriented research. *Journal of Management Inquiry, 1*, 139–142.

Leana, C., Appelbaum, E., & Shevchuk, I. (2009). Work process and quality of care in early childhood education: The role of job crafting. *Academy of Management Journal, 52*, 1169–1192.

Locke, E. A., & Latham, G. P. (1990). *A theory of goal-setting and task performance.* Englewood Cliffs, NJ: Prentice-Hall.

Locke, E. A., & Latham, G. P. (2002). Building a practically useful theory of goal setting and task motivation: A 35-year odyssey. *American Psychologist, 57*, 705–717.

Locke, E. A., & Latham, G. P. (2004). What should we do about motivation theory? Six recommendations for the twenty-first century. *Academy of Management Review, 29*, 388–403.

Locke, E. A., & Latham, G. P. (2009). Has goal setting gone wild, or have its attackers abandoned good scholarship? *Academy of Management Perspectives, 23*, 17–23.

Locke, E. A., Motowidlo, S. J., & Bobko, P. (1986). Using self-efficacy theory to resolve the conflict between goal-setting theory and expectancy theory in organizational behavior and industrial/organizational psychology. *Journal of Social and Clinical Psychology, 4*, 328–338.

Mastrofski, S. D., Ritti, R. R., & Snipes, J. B. (1994). Expectancy theory and police productivity in DUI enforcement. *Law and Society Review, 28*, 113–148.

McClelland, D. C. (1961). *The achieving society.* New York: Van Nostrom Reinhold.

Messersmith, J. G., Guthrie, J. P., Ji, Y.-Y., & Lee, J.-Y. (2011). Executive turnover: The influence of dispersion and other pay system characteristics. *Journal of Applied Psychology, 96*, 457–469.

Mickel, A. E., & Barron, L. A. (2008). Getting "more bang for the buck": Symbolic value of monetary rewards in organizations. *Journal of Management Inquiry, 17*, 329–338.

Miles, E. W., Hatfield, J. D., & Huseman, R. C. (1989). The equity sensitivity construct: Potential implications for worker performance. *Journal of Management, 15*, 581–588.

Mitchell, T. R., & Biglan, A. (1971). Instrumentality theories: Current uses in psychology. *Psychological Bulletin, 76*, 432–454.

Mitchell, T. R., & Daniels, D. (2003). Motivation. In W. Borman, D. Ilgen, & R. Klimoski (Eds.), *Handbook of psychology. Vol. 12: Industrial/organizational psychology* (pp. 225–254). New York: Wiley.

Morgeson, F. P., & Campion, M. A. (2002). Avoiding tradeoffs when redesigning work: Evidence from a longitudinal quasi-experiment. *Personnel Psychology, 55*, 589–612.

Morgeson, F. P., & Humphrey, S. E. (2008). Job and team design: Toward a more integrative conceptualization of work design. In J. Martocchio (Ed.), *Research in personnel and human resource management* (Vol. 27, pp. 39–92). Bingley, England: Emerald Group Publishing Limited.

Nicholson, N. (1984). A theory of work role transitions. *Administrative Science Quarterly, 29*, 172–191.

Oldham, G. R., & Hackman, J. R. (2010). Not what it was and not what it will be: The future of job design research. *Journal of Organizational Behavior, 31*, 463–479.

Ordoñez, L. D., Schweitzer, M. E., Galinsky, A. D. & Bazerman, M. H. (2009a). Goals gone wild: The systematic side effects of overprescribing goal setting. *Academy of Management Perspectives, 23*, 6–22.

Ordoñez, L. D., Schweitzer, M. E., Galinsky, A. D., & Bazerman, M. H. (2009b). On good scholarship, goal setting, and scholars gone wild. *Academy of Management Perspectives, 23*, 82–87.

Organ, D. W. (1988). *Organizational citizenship behavior: The good soldier syndrome.* Lexington, MA: Lexington Books.

Osterloh, M., & Frey, B. (2000). Motivation, knowledge transfer and organizational form. *Organization Science, 11*, 538–550.

Parker, S. K., Bindl, U. K., & Strauss, K. (2010). Making things happen: A model of proactive motivation. *Journal of Management, 36*, 827–856.

Parker, S. K., & Ohly, S. (2008). Designing motivating jobs. In R. Kanfer, G. Chen, & R. Pritchard (Eds.), *Work motivation: Past, present, and future* (pp. 233–284). New York: LEA/Psychology Press.

Parker, S. K., Wall, T. D., & Cordery, J. L. (2001). Future work design research and practice: Towards an elaborated model of work design. *Journal of Occupational and Organizational Psychology, 74*, 413–440.

Parker, S. K., Wall, T. D., & Jackson, P. R. (1997). 'That's not my job': Developing flexible employee work orientations. *Academy of Management Journal, 40*, 899–929.

Penner, L. A., Dovidio, J. F., Piliavin, J. A., & Schroeder, D. A. (2005). Prosocial behavior: Multilevel perspectives. *Annual Review of Psychology, 56*, 365–392.

Perugini, M., & Bagozzi, R. P. (2001). The role of desires and anticipated emotions in goal-directed behaviours: Broadening and deepening the theory of planned behavior. *British Journal of Social Psychology, 40*, 79–98.

Pfeffer, J., & Langton, N. (1993). The effect of wage dispersion on satisfaction, productivity, and working collaboratively: Evidence from college and university faculty. *Administrative Science Quarterly, 38*, 382–407.

Podsakoff, P. M., MacKenzie, S. B., Paine, J. B., & Bachrach, D. G. (2000). Organizational citizenship behaviors: A critical review of the theoretical and empirical literature and suggestions for future research. *Journal of Management, 26*, 513–563.

Porter, L. W., & Lawler, E. E., III. (1968). *Managerial attitudes and performance.* Homewood, IL: Dorsey Press.

Roberts, B. W., Edmonds, G., & Grijalva, E. (2010). It is developmental me, not generation me: Developmental changes are more important than generational changes in narcissism—comment on Trzesniewski & Donnellan (2010). *Perspectives on Psychological Science, 5*, 97–102.

Rothbard, N. P. (2001). Enriching or depleting? The dynamics of engagement in work and family roles. *Administrative Science Quarterly, 46*, 655–684.

Rousseau, D. M., Ho, V. T., & Greenberg, J. (2006). I-deals: Idiosyncratic terms in employment relationships. *Academy of Management Review, 31*, 977–994.

Ryan, R. M., & Deci, E. L. (2000). Self-determination theory and the facilitation of intrinsic motivation, social development, and well-being. *American Psychologist, 55*, 68–78.

Rynes, S. L., Gerhart, B., & Minette, K. A. (2004). The importance of pay in employee motivation: Discrepancies between what people say and what they do. *Human Resource Management, 43*, 381–394.

Salancik, G. R., & Pfeffer, J. (1978). A social information processing approach to job attitudes and task design. *Administrative Science Quarterly, 23*, 224–253.

Schweitzer, M. E., Ordóñez, L., & Douma, B. (2004). Goal setting as a motivator of unethical behavior. *Academy of Management Journal, 47*, 422–432.

Seo, M., Barrett, L. F., & Bartunek, J. M. (2004). The role of affective experience in work motivation. *Academy of Management Review, 29*, 423–439.

Shalley, C. E., Zhou, J., & Oldham, G. R. (2004). The effects of personal and contextual characteristics on creativity: Where should we go from here? *Journal of Management, 30*, 933–958.

Shamir, B. (1990). Calculations, values, and identities: The sources of collectivistic work motivation. *Human Relations, 43*, 313–332.

Shamir, B. (1991). Meaning, self and motivation in organizations. *Organization Studies, 12*, 405–424.

Siegel, P. A., & Hambrick, D. C. (2005). Pay disparities within top management groups: Evidence of harmful effects on performance of high-technology firms. *Organization Science, 16*, 259-274.

Spector, P. E., & Fox, S. (2010). Theorizing about the deviant citizen: An attributional explanation of the interplay of organizational citizenship and counterproductive work behavior. *Human Resource Management Review, 20*, 132–143.

Stajkovic, A. D., & Luthans, F. (2001). Differential effects of incentive motivators on work performance. *Academy of Management Journal, 44*, 580–590.

Staw, B. M. (1984). Organizational behavior: A review and reformulation of the field's outcome variables. *Annual review of Psychology, 35*, 627–666.

Steel, P., & König, C. J. (2006). Integrating theories of motivation. *Academy of Management Review, 31*, 889–913.

Steers, R., Mowday, R., & Shapiro, D. (2004). The future of work motivation theory. *Academy of Management Review, 29*, 379–387.

Trist, E. L., & Bamforth, K. M. (1951). Some social and psychological consequences of the longwall method of coal-getting. *Human Relations, 4*, 3–38.

Trzesniewski, K. H., & Donnellan, M. B. (2010). Rethinking "Generation Me": A study of cohort effects from 1976–2006. *Perspectives on Psychological Science, 5*, 58–75.

Turner, A. N., & Lawrence, P. R. (1965). *Industrial jobs and the worker*. Boston, MA: Harvard University Press.

Twenge, J. M., Campbell, S. M., Hoffman, B. J., & Lance, C. E. (2010). Generational differences in work values: Leisure and extrinsic values increasing, social and intrinsic values decreasing. *Journal of Management, 36*, 1117–1142.

Van Eerde, W., & Thierry, H. (1996). Vroom's expectancy models and work-related criteria: A meta-analysis. *Journal of Applied Psychology, 81*, 575–586.

Vogus, T. J., & Welbourne, T. M. (2003). Structuring for high reliability: HR practices and mindful processes in reliability-seeking organizations. *Journal of Organizational Behavior, 24*, 877–903.

Vroom, V. H. (1964). *Work and motivation*. New York: Wiley.

Waller, M. J., & Roberts, K. H. 2003. High reliability and organizational behavior: Finally the twain must meet. *Journal of Organizational Behavior, 24*, 813–814.

Weick, K. E. (1966). The concept of equity in the perception of pay. *Administrative Science Quarterly, 11*, 414–439.

Weick, K. E. (1974). Middle range theories of social systems. *Behavioral Science, 19*, 357–367.

Weick, K. E. (1979). *The social psychology of organizing* (2nd ed.). Reading, MA: Addison-Wesley.

Weick, K. E., & Roberts, K. (1993). Collective mind in organizations: Heedful interrelating on flight decks. *Administrative Science Quarterly, 38*, 357–381.

Weick, K. E., Sutcliffe, K. M., & Obstfeld, D. (1999). Organizing for high reliability: Processes of collective mindfulness. *Research in Organizational Behavior, 21*, 81–123.

Weick, K. E., Sutcliffe, K. M., & Obstfeld, D. (2005). Organizing and the process of sensemaking. *Organization Science, 16*, 409–421.

Wilson, T. D., & Gilbert, D. T. (2005). Affective forecasting: Knowing what to want. *Current Directions in Psychological Science, 14*, 131–134.

Wong, C., & Campion, M. A. (1991). Development and test of a task level model of motivational job design. *Journal of Applied Psychology, 76*, 825–837.

Wrzesniewski, A., & Dutton, J. E. (2001). Crafting a job: Revisioning employees as active crafters of their work. *Academy of Management Review, 26*, 179–201.

Wrzesniewski, A., McCauley, C. R., Rozin, P., & Schwartz, B. (1997). Jobs, careers, and callings: People's relations to their work. *Journal of Research in Personality, 31*, 21–33.

Xie, J. L., & Johns, G. (1995). Job scope and stress: Can job scope be too high? *Academy of Management Journal, 38*, 1288–1309.

Zalesny, M. D., & Ford, J. K. (1990). Extending the social information processing perspective: New links to attitudes, behaviors, and perceptions. *Organizational Behavior and Human Decision Processes, 47*, 205–246.

Zohar, D., & Luria, G. (2003). Organizational meta-scripts as a source of high reliability: The case of an army armored brigade. *Journal of Organizational Behavior, 24*, 837–859.

Youth Motivation and Participation in Sport and Physical Activity

Maureen R. Weiss, Anthony J. Amorose, *and* Lindsay E. Kipp

Abstract

Sports and physical activities are ubiquitous achievement contexts for children and adolescents worldwide. Motivation to initiate, continue, and sustain physical activity involvement is important for ensuring positive developmental and healthy outcomes. In this chapter we synthesize and consolidate theory-driven knowledge about determinants and outcomes of youth motivation and participation in sport and physical activity. First, we discuss relevant theoretical frameworks for understanding youth motivation in the physical activity domain. Second, we review empirical research on social-contextual factors and individual differences related to youths' desire to continue physical activity and opportunities for accruing the many benefits from such participation. Finally, based on our review of literature, we offer several avenues for future research that address gaps in the knowledge base about mechanisms of influence on youths' motivation and participation in physical activity.

Key Words: parental influence, coaching behaviors, teacher influence, peer acceptance, friendship, self-esteem, perceived competence, enjoyment, anxiety, physical activity interventions

"Get up and play an hour a day!" The television ad featuring LPGA (Ladies Professional Golf Association) players made it clear that children and adolescents can glean physical, social, and psychological benefits from engaging in at least 1 hour of physical activity per day (U.S. Department of Health and Human Services [USDHHS], 2008). Other sport organizations have followed suit with catchy phrases delivered by sport role models. The onslaught of media attention has been fueled by efforts to stem the obesity epidemic among youth, with a focus on sufficient types and levels of physical activity coupled with healthy eating patterns. Because of the frequent news reports, doesn't everyone *know* youth should be physically active to accrue health benefits? But if everybody *knows* that regular physical activity is important, why isn't this knowledge translated to actual *behavior*? One reason is that youth vary in their motivation to initiate, continue, and sustain

sufficient physical activity to attain positive developmental outcomes.

We define motivation in terms of *because* answers to *why* questions (Weiss & Amorose, 2008; Weiss & Williams, 2004). In physical activity, such *why* questions include the following: *(a)* Why do some individuals regularly play sports or engage in physical activity, whereas others are not sufficiently active? *(b)* Why do some individuals participate for the inherent pleasure they get out of activity, whereas others participate primarily to obtain some external goal? *(c)* Why do some youth exert maximal effort and persevere in physical activities, whereas others give up easily or even discontinue altogether? Answers to these questions begin with the word *because* and depend, in part, on the theoretical framework adopted for understanding youth physical activity motivation and participation. In this chapter we review several theories and empirical studies that sharpen our lens for answering these *why* questions. But first we define the scope of our chapter in terms of physical activity contexts and populations of interest.

The term *physical activity* applies to a range of structured and unstructured contexts (Weiss & Wiese-Bjornstal, 2009). Structured activities include school and community sport programs, school physical education, after-school youth programs, and community classes (e.g., dance, martial arts). Unstructured activities include recess, free play, recreational activities, and active transport (e.g., riding a bike to school). We focus our review on structured activities for youth, namely organized sport and physical education, but we also consider correlates of physical activity behavior in general. Sport is a ubiquitous phenomenon among children and youth worldwide (De Knop, Engstrom, Skirstad, & Weiss, 1996), and physical education is inclusive of all children, regardless of skill level or external resources (Payne & Morrow, 2009). These settings consist of social and contextual factors (e.g., adults and peers, psychological climate) that are conducive to modifying motivation and participation behavior. We review research on elementary-age children through emerging adults (i.e., college students) because most studies in structured contexts have been conducted with these age groups.

We begin the chapter with an overview of theoretical frameworks that are applicable to understanding youth motivation in physical activity. Next we discuss research on determinants and consequences of physical activity motivation, with an eye toward robust findings on social-environmental (parent, coach, peer influence) and individual difference factors (self-perceptions, emotions). We conclude with suggesting several research directions based on our extensive review. In sum, physical activity is a very important context for understanding youth motivation in our efforts to maximize participation levels and achieve positive benefits of an active lifestyle.

Theoretical Frameworks for Understanding Physical Activity Motivation[1]

We purposefully selected competence motivation (Harter, 1978), self-determination (Deci & Ryan, 1985), achievement goal (Nicholls, 1989), and expectancy-value (Eccles et al., 1983) theories for our comprehensive review. First, each theory highlights major reasons *why* youth are motivated to engage in physical activity: *(a)* to develop or demonstrate physical competence, *(b)* to attain social acceptance or approval, and *(c)* to experience fun and enjoyment (Reeve & Weiss, 2006; Weiss & Williams, 2004). Second, empirical research provides strong evidence that these theories, which were originally developed for the academic domain, are applicable to youth motivation and participation in physical activity. Finally, they are deemed "practical theories" of motivation (Gill & Williams, 2008); that is, theoretical constructs and their relationships are easily translated to behavioral interventions, which is essential for considering links among physical activity motivation, participation behavior, and health-related outcomes (Reeve & Weiss, 2006; Stuntz & Weiss, 2010).

Competence Motivation Theory

Susan Harter's (1978) classic paper revitalized Robert White's (1959) concept of *effectance motivation* and set in motion her line of research that expanded and operationally defined theoretical constructs. White argued that individuals are motivated to have an *effect* on their environment, and they subsequently engage in mastery attempts to develop or demonstrate competence. Such mastery attempts are influenced by the desire for challenge, curiosity, and independence. If challenge-seeking behavior is successful, then feelings of efficacy and inherent pleasure are experienced that serve to maintain or enhance effectance or competence motivation.

Harter (1978, 1981a) revised White's (1959) original model in several ways (see Fig. 29.1). First, she specified that *competence motivation is domain specific*. Children will differ in desire, curiosity, and interest to demonstrate competence depending on academic, physical, or social skills. In fact, Harter (1981b) explicitly identified sports and physical activities as a salient achievement domain. Second, Harter contended that competence or success at *optimal challenges*—difficult but realistic skills—is most likely to contribute to positive emotions and intrinsic motivation. Third, Harter highlighted *significant adults and peers* as central to developing children's mastery motivation. She clarified that socializers, especially parents, must reinforce *independent mastery attempts* and not just praise successful outcomes. Fourth, Harter added *perceptions of competence and control* as individual factors that influence affective responses and competence motivation. Fifth, Harter situated intrinsic pleasure or *positive affect* in response to successful task mastery in the center of her model. Harter's call to "restore affect and emotion to its rightful place, as central to

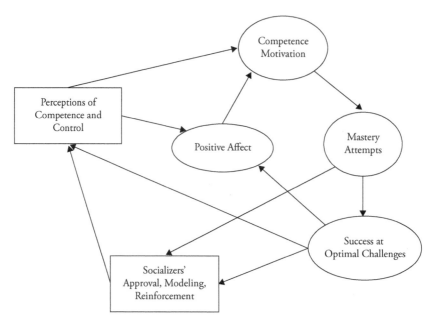

Fig. 29.1. Model of competence motivation theory. Reprinted, with permission, from Weiss, M. R., & Amorose, A. J. (2008). Motivational orientation and sport behavior. In T. S. Horn (Ed.), *Advances in sport psychology* (3rd ed., p. 119). Champaign, IL: Human Kinetics.

an understanding of behavior" (Harter, 1981b, p. 4) resonates with enjoyment being consistently named as a primary reason for youth physical activity motivation (Weiss & Williams, 2004).

Within physical activity contexts, parents and coaches have been frequently studied as important sources of competence motivation among children and adolescents (see Weiss & Amorose, 2008; Weiss & Williams, 2004). Mechanisms of parental influence, such as providing positive feedback for effort and improvement, showing confidence in their child's potential, and modeling positive attitudes and behaviors, are associated with youth reporting higher perceived competence, enjoyment, and intrinsic motivation for physical activity (e.g., Babkes & Weiss, 1999; Bois, Sarrazin, Brustad, Trouilloud, & Cury, 2002; Brustad, 1993). Similarly, youth report more favorable self-perceptions, affective responses, and motivational orientations when they indicate coaches provide more frequent informational feedback, respond positively to performance attempts, and place greater emphasis on a mastery climate (e.g., Black & Weiss, 1992; R.E. Smith, Smoll, & Cumming, 2007; Weiss, Amorose, & Wilko, 2009).

In youth physical activity motivation research, perceived competence is the most frequently studied individual difference factor (see Weiss & Amorose, 2008; Weiss & Williams, 2004). Perceived physical competence (or sport-specific competence)

is a strong predictor of cognitive (e.g., self-esteem), affective (e.g., enjoyment, anxiety), and behavioral (e.g., effort, persistence) outcomes (e.g., Amorose, 2001; Ebbeck & Weiss, 1998; Ferrer Caja & Weiss, 2000, 2002; Weiss, Bredemeier, & Shewchuk, 1986). Because perceived competence is strongly related to physical activity motivation, many studies have also focused on identifying the information sources children and adolescents use to form judgments about how physically competent they are (e.g., Horn & Weiss, 1991; Weiss & Amorose, 2005; see Horn, 2004; Horn & Amorose, 1998).

Competence motivation is a multidimensional construct that is influenced by cognitive (perceived competence), affective (joy), and social (parents, coaches) factors. Starting with the box labeled competence motivation in Figure 29.1, we see that a child's desire to demonstrate competence will lead her to attempt mastering physical skills. If she is successful, and if *significant adults and peers* respond to her efforts with approval, she will experience heightened *perceived competence and control* and positive *affect* such as joy, pride, and pleasure. Positive self-perceptions and affective reactions will maintain or enhance competence motivation, or the child's desire to continue seeking challenge and mastery in physical activities. Maintaining physical activity motivation, in turn, will optimize acquiring the physical, social, and psychological benefits that are afforded from such participation.

Self-Determination Theory

Self-determination theory, developed and refined by Deci and Ryan (1985, Ryan & Deci, 2000, 2002), is a popular framework for understanding youth motivation in sport and physical activity. Self-determination theory is really a meta-theory comprised of four related mini-theories (i.e., cognitive evaluation theory, organismic integration theory, causality orientation theory, and basic needs theory), which together identify and explain principles and processes for understanding motivation, personality and social development, and overall psychological functioning (see Ryan & Deci, 2000, 2002). Given the extensiveness of the theory, a comprehensive description is beyond the scope of this chapter (see Ryan & Deci, 2002, Weiss & Amorose, 2008, for reviews). Rather, our focus will be on elements of the overall theory that have been used to understand youth motivation in sport and physical activity.

One of the main contributions of self-determination theory to understanding physical activity motivation is distinguishing between various forms of behavioral regulation. As mentioned, youth engage in sport and physical activity to develop or demonstrate physical competence, gain social acceptance or approval, and enjoy one's experiences (see Weiss & Amorose, 2008). Self-determination theory categorizes each specific reason into one of three global types of motivation—intrinsic, extrinsic, and amotivation. Each form of motivation is situated along a continuum of self-determination (see Fig. 29.2) insomuch as the motives vary in terms of locus of causality (i.e., whether behavior

is initiated and controlled by internal versus external sources) and the degree to which the behavior is regulated autonomously (i.e., the extent to which action emanates from the self).

Intrinsic motivation represents the most self-determined form of behavioral regulation and is defined as engaging in an activity for the pleasure and satisfaction derived from the activity itself (Ryan & Deci, 2000, 2007). When intrinsically motivated, individuals will freely engage in physical activity and experience a sense of enjoyment while doing so as opposed to performing to obtain some separable outcome (e.g., to please others). The most non-self-determined form of motivation is *amotivation*, which refers to lack of intention to act and absence of motivated behavior, resulting from devaluing an activity, feeling incompetent, or not perceiving contingency between actions and desired outcomes (Ryan & Deci, 2007).

Extrinsic motivation, situated between amotivation and intrinsic motivation on the self-determination continuum, involves engaging in an activity for some instrumental reason (Vallerand, 1997). Ryan and colleagues (Ryan & Connell, 1989; Ryan & Deci, 2000, 2002) identified four specific types of extrinsic motivation that range on a continuum from lower to higher levels of self-determined behavior. The two forms of extrinsic motivation falling on the non-self-determined side include external and introjected regulation. *External regulation* involves behavior that is controlled by external means such as rewards or punishments, whereas *introjected regulation* refers to behavior regulated by internalized

Type of Motivation	Amotivation	Extrinsic Motivation				Intrinsic Motivation
Type of Regulation	non-regulation	external	introjected	identified	integrated	intrinsic
Example Motive "I participate in sport because…"	"I have nothing better to do with myself."	"because my parents are making me."	"I don't want to let others down by quitting."	"it will help open doors for my future career as a coach."	"it helps to confirm my identity as an athlete"	"I love the rush I feel when running down the field."
Locus of Causality	impersonal	external	somewhat external	somewhat internal	internal	internal
		←				→
Degree of Autonomy	non-self-determined					self-determined

Fig. 29.2. Continuum of motivation according to self-determination theory. Reprinted, with permission, from Weiss, M. R., & Amorose, A. J. (2008). Motivational orientation and sport behavior. In T. S. Horn (Ed.), *Advances in sport psychology* (3rd ed., p. 133). Champaign, IL: Human Kinetics.

pressure such as worry or shame and/or a desire to enhance one's ego. Identified and integrated regulations represent self-determined or autonomous forms of extrinsic motivation. *Identified regulation* involves behavior performed out of choice because an individual values the activity or perceives benefits from involvement. *Integrated regulation* reflects behavior that has been fully integrated into the self and assimilated with one's values, goals, and needs (e.g., identity as a physically active person).

Youth will likely have multiple reasons, both intrinsic and extrinsic, for their participation in sport and physical activity (Weiss & Amorose, 2008). What is most critical is the extent to which the pattern of motives tends to be more or less self-determined in nature. In other words, a central aspect of understanding motivation from a self-determination perspective centers on whether one has a self-determined or non-self-determined motivational orientation for an activity. Numerous behavioral, cognitive, and affective benefits are associated with engaging in physical activities for self-determined reasons (e.g., Blanchard, Amiot, Perreault, Vallerand, & Provencher, 2009; Ferrer Caja & Weiss, 2000, 2002; Gagné, Ryan, & Bargmann, 2003; Ntoumanis, 2001, 2005; Pelletier, Fortier, Vallerand, & Briére, 2001; Standage, Duda, & Ntoumanis, 2006). As such, an important goal of self-determination theory is to understand the processes by which youth develop self-determined motivation, particularly when the initial motive for an activity is not inherently enjoyable but rather instrumental in nature (Ryan & Deci, 2002). While a number of interpersonal and social-contextual factors contribute to variations in motivational regulations (e.g., coaching behaviors, motivational climate), the theory highlights the central role of psychological needs for competence, autonomy, and relatedness. Satisfaction of these needs is essential to maintaining and enhancing self-determined motivation.

The *need for competence* reflects a desire to perceive our behavior and interaction with the social environment as effective (Deci, 1975; Harter, 1978, White, 1959). The *need for autonomy* refers to perceiving behaviors as freely chosen and that we are the origins of our actions (deCharms, 1968; Deci & Ryan, 1987; Ryan & Connell, 1989). The *need for relatedness* reflects our desire to feel connected to others and experience a sense of belonging (Baumeister & Leary, 1995; Ryan, 1995). According to self-determination theory, the degree to which youths' needs for competence, autonomy, and relatedness are supported will facilitate or obstruct their tendencies toward autonomous regulation of

behavior (Ryan & Deci, 2002). A central tenet of the theory is that functionally significant events—intrapersonal or social-contextual—that impact a person's sense of competence, autonomy, and relatedness will affect the type of motivation she or he develops for an activity (i.e., self-determined or non-self-determined). The extent to which these needs are fulfilled provides a mechanism by which intrapersonal events and social-contextual factors affect motivated behavior and personal well-being (Ryan & Deci, 2002, 2007). Situational events (e.g., coach/teacher styles, motivational climate) that satisfy psychological needs will promote optimal functioning, such as self-determined motivation, while those that inhibit need satisfaction will lead to nonoptimal outcomes in physical activity contexts (e.g., Blanchard et al., 2009; Cox & Williams, 2008; Hollembeak & Amorose, 2005; Ntoumanis, 2005; Standage et al., 2006).

In summary, self-determination theory makes distinctions among the motives that underlie youths' actions and specifies that behavioral regulation varies along a continuum of self-determination. The theory also describes how social-contextual and intrapersonal events can facilitate or thwart people's natural tendency toward psychological growth and self-regulated behavior. Specifically, the extent to which events impact one's needs for competence, autonomy, and relatedness will ultimately influence motivational orientation, behavior, and psychological functioning. A model summarizing theoretical relationships is seen in Figure 29.3.

Achievement Goal Theory

The achievement goal perspective has been one of the more popular approaches to understanding youth motivation and participation in physical activity over the past 25 years (Harwood, Spray, & Keegan, 2008; Roberts, Treasure, & Conroy, 2007). This perspective is actually a cluster of related yet distinct theories proffered by a number of scholars, notably Nicholls (1989), Dweck (1999), Ames (1992), and Elliot (1999). As with other theories (e.g., competence motivation, self-determination, expectancy-value), perceptions of competence are considered a critical determinant of motivated behavior. In fact, a goal of developing or demonstrating competence or avoiding the demonstration of low competence is considered the primary energizing force guiding engagement in achievement-related activities (Harwood et al., 2008; Roberts et al., 2007). This approach also highlights the means by which youth construe

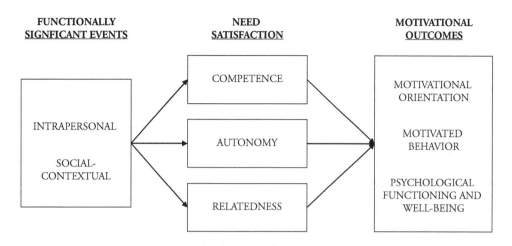

| FUNCTIONALLY SIGNFICANT EVENTS | NEED SATISFACTION | MOTIVATIONAL OUTCOMES |

Fig. 29.3. Summary model of key relationships in self-determination theory. Reprinted, with permission, from Weiss, M. R., & Amorose, A. J. (2008). Motivational orientation and sport behavior. In T. S. Horn (Ed.), *Advances in sport psychology* (3rd ed., p. 137). Champaign, IL: Human Kinetics.

competence-related beliefs. That is, understanding motivational orientations and behaviors requires knowledge of the criteria used to judge whether performance attempts are successful or unsuccessful—otherwise known as *achievement goals*.

The labels used to distinguish between different subjective definitions of success and failure varies across the specific theories; however, task and ego goals are predominantly adopted in physical activity settings (Nicholls, 1989). People who adopt task-oriented goals—also referred to as mastery or learning goals—construe competence in self-referenced terms. Experiencing success is rooted in exerting high levels of effort and learning and improving skills. Ego-oriented goals—also referred to as performance or outcome goals—are based in social comparison. Successful demonstration of competence is derived from outperforming others at a task, especially if accomplished with relatively less effort. Achievement goals are presumed to function at both a dispositional and state level. We can distinguish achievement goal *orientations*, which reflect people's dispositional proneness to define success and failure in specific ways, from people's goal *involvement*, which reflect the achievement goal adopted in a particular situation (Harwood et al., 2008; Roberts et al., 2007).

In early writings, *social* goals were also considered as a means of defining success, such as attaining acceptance and approval from significant adults or peers (Maehr & Nicholls, 1980). This goal faded away in the literature for awhile, but heeding the call of Urdan and Maehr (1995) to revive social goals, researchers have included social along with task and ego goals in studies of youth participants' psychosocial and behavioral outcomes in physical activity (e.g., Allen, 2003; Stuntz & Weiss,

2003, 2009). Nevertheless, the majority of scholarship in physical activity from an achievement goal perspective has focused exclusively on task and ego goals.

These subjective definitions of success and failure govern achievement-related beliefs and are the central influence guiding motivational processes in achievement settings (Roberts et al., 2007). For instance, achievement goals combined with perceived competence are predicted to influence motivated behavior (Dweck, 1999; Nicholls, 1989). Specifically, youth seek optimal challenges, exert high levels of effort, and persist even in the face of difficulty when their achievement goal is task oriented regardless of their perceived competence at the activity. This same adaptive motivational pattern would be expected for those who adopt an ego-oriented goal as long as they possess high expectations of success. Highly ego-oriented individuals who doubt their ability, however, are expected to demonstrate a helpless motivational pattern such as avoiding challenge and demonstrating low effort and persistence. A number of studies conducted in physical activity settings provide support for these predictions (e.g., Cury, Biddle, Sarrazin, & Famose, 1997; Sarrazin, Roberts, Cury, Biddle, & Famose, 2002).

Achievement goal orientations have been linked to a variety of motivational outcomes among youth (e.g., level of perceived competence, motivational orientation, enjoyment and interest, burnout, effort, and performance) (see Harwood et al., 2008; Roberts et al., 2007; Weiss & Ferrer Caja, 2002). Positive outcomes are associated with adopting higher task-oriented goals, either alone or in combination with a higher ego orientation. Conversely, negative motivational outcomes are associated with a higher ego orientation, especially when paired with a lower task orientation. Recent work also shows that positive motivational outcomes are associated with the adoption of social goals (e.g., Stuntz & Weiss, 2009).

Given the critical motivational implications of achievement goals, a host of intrapersonal and social-contextual factors impact adoption of achievement goals, such as cognitive development, implicit theories of ability, and motivational climate (see Elliot, 1999; Roberts et al., 2007). Because motivational climate is especially relevant for the physical activity context, we focus our remaining discussion on this construct. According to Ames (1992), *motivational climate* refers to how success is defined in a social environment such as a physical education class or athletic team. Two primary climates, which parallel the two main achievement goals, are presumed to function in achievement settings. A *mastery* (also called *task-involving*) *motivational climate* describes an environment that defines success in terms of learning, improvement, and effort. In contrast, a *performance* (also called *ego-involving*) *motivational climate* emphasizes competition, winning, and outperforming others as the basis for defining success (see Duda & Balaguer, 2007; Harwood et al., 2008; Roberts et al., 2007).

The prevailing motivational climate will be a function of various factors. For instance, dimensions distinguishing mastery and performance climates include the following: *(a)* the nature and design of tasks, *(b)* who is given authority for making decisions, *(c)* how participants are evaluated and recognized, *(d)* how much time is allotted for learning skills, and *(e)* how people are grouped (see Ames, 1992; Duda & Balaguer, 2007; Harwood et al., 2008; Ntoumanis & Biddle, 1999). Ames asserts that individuals' *perceptions* of the motivational climate is the key factor driving motivation; that is, the subjective meaning attached to significant others' behaviors within the environment will ultimately affect achievement goals and patterns of motivated behavior.

In summary, situational (e.g., motivational climate) and intrapersonal variations (e.g., goal orientation, perceived competence) in how success and failure are defined are central to understanding motivational processes and outcomes according to achievement goal theory. A summary model identifying some of the key motivational constructs and their relationships is presented in Figure 29.4.

Expectancy-Value Theory

Eccles et al.'s (1983) expectancy-value theory describes and explains variations in achievement choices and behaviors across multiple domains. Achievement motivation is predicted directly by an individual's

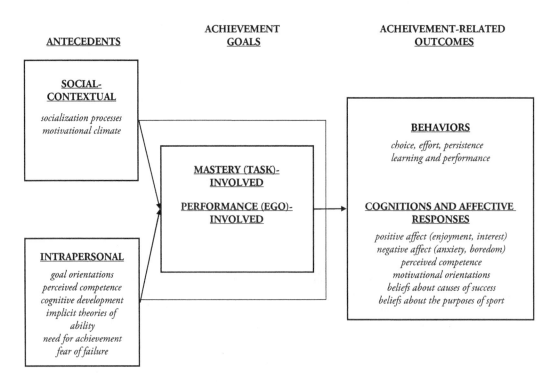

Fig. 29.4. Summary model of the achievement goal perspective.

expectations of success and subjective task values, and it is indirectly influenced by socializers' beliefs and behaviors; gender and activity stereotypes; children's schema, goals, and interests; and past achievement experiences, among other influences (see Fig. 29.5). Expectancy-value theory has been an especially productive approach for investigating parental influence on youths' physical activity beliefs and behaviors (see Fredricks & Eccles, 2004; Weiss & Amorose, 2008).

Expectation of success is defined as the individual's belief in successfully completing a task or mastering an activity, and thus it is synonymous with the construct of perceived competence (Eccles et al., 1983). Subjective task value generally refers to the importance placed on being successful in an achievement domain. Eccles and colleagues (1983) identified four components of subjective task value: attainment value, interest value, utility value, and cost. *Attainment value* refers to personal importance of doing well in a certain achievement domain that confirms one's self-identity, such as opportunities for demonstrating or developing competence. *Interest value* refers to how much youth enjoy participating in the activity (i.e., how intrinsically rewarding is the activity?). *Utility value* describes one's perception of how useful the activity is relative to short- or long-term goals (i.e., extrinsic value of the activity). Finally, *cost* refers to one's appraisal of the time, effort, and other resources that would be lost by engaging in a particular achievement activity. Most research by Eccles and colleagues has emphasized the three positive task values (attainment, interest, utility), but cost of participating in especially high-level sport is a salient factor explaining variations in motivated behavior (e.g., W.M. Weiss & Weiss, 2003, 2006, 2007; W.M. Weiss, Weiss, & Amorose, 2010). Consistent with theoretical predictions, expectancies and values are strongly related to youths' achievement behaviors in physical activity (e.g., Cox & Whaley, 2004; Fredricks & Eccles, 2005).

Expectancy-value theory originated as a means of explaining gender differences in achievement choices and behaviors (Eccles et al., 1983). Eccles and colleagues conducted several studies that revealed variations in physical activity motivation among males and females that were linked to expectations of success and subjective task values (e.g., Eccles et al., 1983; Eccles & Harold, 1991; Fredricks & Eccles, 2002, 2005). Girls reported lower expectancies, value, and participation in physical activities and sports than boys. In addition to differential expectancies and task values, gender differences in expectancy-value constructs are also linked to parents' beliefs and behaviors about the value of various achievement domains.

Fredricks and Eccles (2004) classified three mechanisms of parental influence: *(a)* providers of experience (e.g., tangible support, encouragement), *(b)* interpreters of experience (e.g., conveying beliefs about child's domain-specific competence, goal orientation, or how success is defined), and *(c)* role models (e.g., expressing

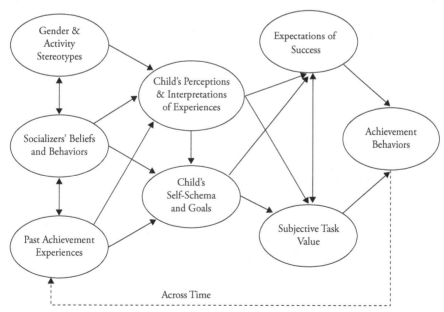

Fig. 29.5. Relationships in expectancy-value theory. Reprinted, with permission, from Weiss, M. R., & Amorose, A. J. (2008). Motivational orientation and sport behavior. In T. S. Horn (Ed.), Advances in sport psychology (3rd ed., p. 139). Champaign, IL: Human Kinetics. [Previously adapted, with permission of Taylor & Francis, Inc., from Eccles, J. S., & Harold, R.D. (1991). Gender differences in sport involvement: Applying Eccles' expectancy-value model, *Journal of Applied Sport Psychology, 32,* 7–35.]

attitudes and demonstrating behaviors that endorse value of a domain). In several studies, youths' perceptions of their parents' beliefs about participating and performing well in sport, and parents' importance ratings for boys and girls being good in sports, were related to youths' self-judgments of sport competence (e.g., Babkes & Weiss, 1999; Bois et al., 2002; Fredricks & Eccles, 2002; Sabiston & Crocker, 2008).

Because of strong linkages between parental beliefs and behaviors with youths' expectations of success, task values, and achievement behaviors, Eccles situated expectancy-value constructs within a comprehensive model of parental influence (Eccles, Wigfield, & Schiefele, 1998; Fredricks & Eccles, 2004). Compatible with the original theory, this model (see Fig. 29.6) accentuates the role of family characteristics (e.g., culture, siblings), general parental beliefs and behaviors (e.g., gender stereotypes, parenting styles), and parents' child-specific beliefs and behaviors on children's achievement outcomes (perceived competence, task values, participation behavior). Parent–child relationships among competence beliefs, task values, and achievement behavior as specified by Eccles' theory have been a focus of research in physical activity contexts (see Horn & Horn, 2007; Weiss & Amorose, 2008).

In sum, expectancy-value theory identifies social and contextual factors that influence youths' expectancies of success and subjective task values that, in turn, relate to domain-specific achievement behaviors. It should be noted that the developmental emphasis of this theory suggests that children's achievement behaviors (e.g., participation, performance) can, in turn, modify socializers' beliefs and behaviors. That is, the parent–child relationship for expectancies, task values, and motivation is bidirectional and reciprocal. This latter aspect has not been studied as frequently as the parent-to-child pathway but denotes a particularly relevant area to pursue in the physical activity domain.

Research on Youth Motivation and Participation in Physical Activity

The four theoretical frameworks highlighted for explaining youth physical activity motivation possess two common threads of similarity. First, they identify *social and contextual* factors that influence motivational orientations and behaviors, including parents' beliefs and behaviors, peer influence, and coach–athlete relationships. Second they recognize key *individual differences* that directly or indirectly impact participation motivation—notably perceived competence and affective responses. In this section we review research on social-contextual factors and individual differences as they relate to youths' physical activity motivation and behavior. We report findings that cut across theoretical frameworks in an effort to be parsimonious and systematic.

Social-Contextual Factors

This section is divided into parental influence, coach–athlete relationships, and peer relationships. We identify robust findings on these topics, thereby revealing consistent mechanisms of influence on youth motivation and participation in physical activity.

PARENTAL INFLUENCE ON YOUTH PHYSICAL ACTIVITY MOTIVATION

In 1992, Brustad published an influential paper in which he advocated using appropriate theory-driven

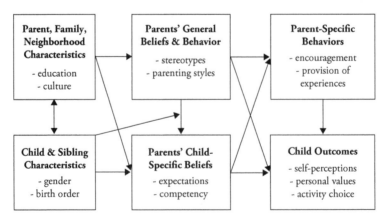

Figure 29.6. Model of parental influence (Eccles et al., 1998). Reprinted, with permission, from Weiss, M. R., & Amorose, A. J. 2008. Motivational orientation and sport behavior. In T. S. Horn (Ed.), *Advances in sport psychology* (3rd ed., p. 144). Champaign, IL: Human Kinetics. [Previously adapted, with permission of John Wiley & Sons, from Eccles, J. S., Wigfield, A., & Schiefele, U. (1998). Motivation to succeed. In W. Damon (Series Ed.) & N. Eisenberg (Vol. Ed.), *Handbook of child psychology. Vol. 3: Social, emotional, and personality development* (5th ed., pp. 1017–1095).]

approaches to integrate socialization and motivational factors into the study of youth in sport. He lamented that few studies delved into parents as sources of motivation, and that existing descriptive studies were limited compared to explanatory theories that would reveal points of intervention. Now 20 years later, the literature abounds with theory-driven studies investigating mechanisms of parental influence on children's motivational orientations. We organized empirical research on parental influence and children's psychosocial and behavioral outcomes along Eccles et al.'s (1983, 1998) notion of parents as *providers of experience*, as *role models*, and as *interpreters of experience*.

Within these categories, we discuss specific parental behaviors that relate to children's physical activity motivation. These include *(a)* providing social support, *(b)* modeling attitudes and behaviors, *(c)* expressing beliefs about the child's competence, *(d)* expressing beliefs about the value of physical activity, and *(e)* conveying pressure to perform or be successful (see Garcia Bengoechea & Strean, 2007). Other reviews provide additional perspectives on the role of the family in youth physical activity (Brustad, 2010; Fredricks & Eccles, 2004; Horn & Horn, 2007).

Providing Social Support

Forms of social support include logistical, emotional, intimacy, affection, companionship, and instrumental support (Furman & Buhrmester, 1985; Garcia Bengoechea & Strean, 2007). Logistical support includes signing children up for sports teams and transporting them to practices and games. Emotional support refers to encouragement for playing a sport and giving one's best effort and responding positively to mastery attempts. Instrumental support includes teaching children sport skills and being actively involved in their experiences, while intimacy and affection support refer to unconditional warmth, admiration, and respect between parent and child. Companionship support might include parents and children doing physical activities and attending sporting events together.

In line with parents as providers of experience, mothers and fathers who show greater social support for their child's activity involvement are associated with youth reporting favorable ability perceptions, value toward physical activity, and emotional experiences, and greater intrinsic motivation and physical activity behavior (e.g., Bhalla & Weiss, 2010; Brustad, 1993; Davison, Cutting, & Birch, 2003; Sabiston & Crocker, 2008; Ullrich-French &

Smith, 2006, 2009; M.R. Weiss & Hayashi, 1995; W.M. Weiss & Weiss, 2003, 2006). For example, Ullrich-French and Smith (2006, 2009) investigated parent–child relationship quality and motivational constructs among youth soccer players. In the first study they found that stronger mother–child and father–child relationship quality, defined as emotional, loyalty, intimacy, and companionship support, was positively related to children's perceived competence, enjoyment, and self-determined motivation. One year later, mother–child relationship quality (along with perceived competence and close friendships) distinguished participants who continued versus discontinued their soccer involvement. W.M. Weiss and Weiss (2003) investigated sources of attraction- and entrapment-based commitment to participate among adolescent gymnasts. In the first study, gymnasts who showed attraction-based commitment (high enjoyment and perceived benefits, low perceived costs) reported higher emotional support from parents than entrapped gymnasts (low enjoyment and perceived benefits, high perceived costs) as well as higher intrinsic motivation and greater effort and persistence in the gym.

Modeling Attitudes and Behaviors

Modeling or observational learning is a powerful mechanism of transmitting attitudes and behaviors in the physical activity domain (see McCullagh & Weiss, 2002). As role models, parents communicate through words and actions how valuable they believe it is for their child to be successful in the physical domain. Some authors have assessed modeling effects as a correlation between parents' and child's level of physical activity (e.g., Dempsey, Kimiecik, & Horn, 1993; Fredricks & Eccles, 2002; Freedson & Evenson, 1991), but observational learning effects go beyond simple correspondence of activity levels to parents' specific expressions of attitudes and behaviors. Parents' enjoyment of doing physical activities, comments made about the importance and utility of physical activity as a healthy behavior, and past or present involvement as an athlete or coach exemplify ways in which parents serve as physical activity models for their children (e.g., Babkes & Weiss, 1999; Bois, Sarrazin, Brustad, Trouilliard, & Cury, 2005; Brustad, 1993; Davison et al., 2003; Davison & Jago, 2009; Weiss & Fretwell, 2005). The diverse ways in which modeling has been defined and assessed may explain why some authors conclude that equivocal support exists for parents as role models of children's physical activity behavior (Fredricks & Eccles, 2004).

In reality, it is difficult to separate parent behaviors neatly into categories of providers, interpreters, or models of physical activity experiences. When parents facilitate participation opportunities and encourage children to continue involvement (i.e., provide experiences), or express confidence about their child's ability to be successful and discuss the importance of being physically active to stay fit (i.e., interpret experiences), we would argue that parents are modeling attitudes and behaviors they want their child to emulate. That is, parents are communicating beliefs and exhibiting behaviors that provide children with information and motivation to embrace physical activity as an integral part of their lifestyle. In line with this theorizing, some researchers have included social support, role modeling, and competence/value beliefs as indices of a broader parental influence construct (Davison, Symons Downs, & Birch, 2006; Fredricks & Eccles, 2005; Sabiston & Crocker, 2008). For example, Sabiston and Crocker tested a model of relationships among social influence (parents, best friend), expectancy-value constructs, and physical activity behavior. They situated emotional support, value beliefs, and role modeling as observed indicators of a latent construct of parental influence, and they examined associations with adolescent girls' and boys' perceived competence, subjective task values, and physical activity. Strong support emerged for an indirect effect of parents' beliefs and behaviors on youths' physical activity as mediated by perceived competence and task values.

Studies that operationally defined parent modeling in more inclusive terms (e.g., show enjoyment of physical activity, participate in activities with children, be a parent-coach, have athletic experience) provide substantive support for parents as influential role models. For example, Davison and Jago (2009) assessed modeling effects in terms of parent-reported enjoyment of physical activity, frequency of physical activity, family using sport as recreation, and use of own behavior to encourage activity. In a longitudinal investigation, they found that girls who maintained physical activity levels from ages 9 to 15 had parents who reported higher scores on these facets of modeling than girls who did not maintain physical activity levels. Thus, even though parent modeling has been assessed using varied definitions (level of physical activity vs. other behaviors and attitudes) and methods (objective, parent report, child report), ample evidence exists to support modeling as a salient mechanism of parental influence.

Expressing Beliefs About Child's Competence in Physical Activity

As interpreters of experience, parents communicate directly or indirectly how confident they are in their child's potential to be successful in sport and how physically talented they believe their child to be. Parents' appraisals of their child's ability influence children's *perceptions* of their parents' ability beliefs, which ultimately affect their self-appraisals of ability (e.g., Amorose, 2002; Bois, Sarrazin, Brustad, Chanal, & Trouilloud, 2005). By far, parents' expression of beliefs about their child's competence is one of the most robust findings related to children's self-competence beliefs and participation motivation (e.g., Babkes & Weiss, 1999; Bois et al., 2002; Fredricks & Eccles, 2002, 2005; Kimiecik & Horn, 1998; Kimiecik, Horn, & Shurin, 1996). In these studies, youths' perceptions of parents' beliefs about their sport or fitness competence were strongly related to their own self-reported ability ratings and physical activity behavior.

Some studies show that parents hold gender-stereotyped beliefs about children's competence. Jacobs and Eccles (1992) found that mothers who held stronger gender-stereotyped beliefs assigned boys higher ability ratings for math and sports and girls higher ratings in social activities. Mothers' appraisals, in turn, predicted children's self-perceptions of ability in these domains. Fredricks and Eccles (2005) examined parent-child beliefs and behaviors in sport among children in grades 2, 4, and 5. A total support score was based on parents' beliefs (e.g., child's sport ability, value of sport) and behaviors (e.g., encouragement, time involved in sports). Boys recorded a greater number of family supports, which were positively associated with children's perceptions of ability, value toward sport, and time spent in sports. It should be noted that other studies did not find differential parent beliefs and behaviors for sons and daughters (Babkes & Weiss, 1999; Bois, Sarrazin, Brustad, Trouilloud, & Cury, 2005; Kimiecik & Horn, 1998; Sabiston & Crocker, 2008). Factors that distinguish when and why gender differences in physical activity motivation occur are important directions for future research.

The finding that parents' and children's competence beliefs are interrelated is typically interpreted as a parent-to-child pathway. An alternative explanation is that the pathway is bidirectional or reciprocal (e.g., Davison et al., 2006; Dorsch, Smith, & McDonough, 2009; Eccles et al., 1998; M.R. Weiss & Hayashi, 1995). Children showing interest, talent, and confidence in sport may spark parents' interest in their child's participation, influence competence beliefs, and inspire them to invest time facilitating their child's experiences. Davison et al. tested two models linking parental support, child's perceived athletic competence, and child's physical activity. The "traditional" pathway specified that parental support at age 9 predicts perceived competence at age 11, which predicts physical activity at age 11. The "child elicitation" pathway specified that perceived competence at age 9 predicts parental support at age 11, which predicts physical activity at age 11. Path analyses and tests of mediation provided support for the model in which child characteristics elicit a response from parents (i.e., social support for sport participation) that, in turn, impacts the child's physical activity behavior. Dorsch et al. also found support for bidirectional socialization influences in sport. Focus group responses by youth sport parents revealed changes in cognitions (knowledge about sport), behaviors (physical activity), and emotions (pride, anxiety) as a result of being socialized through their child's participation.

In sum, evidence exists for multiple pathways in the parent–child socialization process. Children's perceptions of parents' competence beliefs influence their own self-beliefs and motivated behavior, *and* children's perceptions of physical competence and skill-related behavior influence parents' perceptions of the child's competence and their behaviors toward their child.

Expressing Beliefs About the Value of Physical Activity

Parallel with parents as interpreters of experience by conveying beliefs about their child's sport competence, parents also express thoughts and feelings about the value they place on being successful in physical activity domains. Similar to the parent–child linkages in beliefs about sport competence, so too is the connection between parents' importance and utility value of physical activity with children's self-reported task values and participation behavior (e.g., Bhalla & Weiss, 2010; Fredricks & Eccles, 2002, 2005; Kimiecik & Horn, 1998; Kimiecik et al., 1996; Stuart, 2003). In the Fredricks and Eccles (2002, 2005) studies, children's perceptions of the value their parents place on being successful in sport were related to their own ratings of importance and utility value as well as time spent in sports activities.

Using an innovative design, Stuart (2003) divided adolescent boys and girls into low and high sport value groups, then interviewed them about why they thought sport was interesting, important,

and useful (or not). Among the sources that emerged were parents' positive or negative influences—participants with high sport value said they were sparked by their parents' interest in sport ("grew up around sports"), whereas the low-value group spoke about unsupportive parents, parents' lack of sport experiences, and parents not providing choices. Bhalla and Weiss (2010) interviewed adolescent girls of Anglo and East Indian ethnicity about parents' value toward sport. Although Anglo parents were seen as placing greater value on sports than East Indian parents, themes such as "bring honor to the family" (i.e., family is recognized when child achieves in sport), "proud of accomplishments" (i.e., telling others that sport achievement is special), and "change routine" (i.e., makes adjustment to schedule to pick up daughter from practice) suggest that East Indian parents modify their value beliefs as part of the acculturation process, and these beliefs made a positive impact on their daughters' sport participation.

Conveying Pressure to Perform or Be Successful

Social sources of stress and burnout have long been topics of interest in youth sport (see Crocker, Hoar, McDonough, Kowalski, & Niefer, 2004). Several studies have shown that young athletes worry about fear of failure and negative evaluations from parents (e.g., Gould, Horn, & Spreeman, 1983; Scanlan & Lewthwaite, 1984; Weiss, Wiese, & Klint, 1989). For example, Weiss et al. found that youth gymnasts identified parents' expectations about performance as a frequent source of worry prior to competition, such as "what my parents will say" and "letting my parents down."

Parents can unknowingly place pressure or unrealistic expectations on youth to perform and be successful in sport. This is a fine line—parents might think and say they are being "supportive" while children interpret the same behaviors as "pressure" (Babkes & Weiss, 1999; Fredricks & Eccles, 2004; Gould, Udry, Tuffey, & Loehr, 1996). Because youths' interpretations of parents' behaviors are the important factor explaining behavioral outcomes, parents' verbal and nonverbal actions that are translated by youth as pressuring should have negative psychosocial and behavioral consequences.

Indeed, many studies show a negative relationship between perceived parental pressure and youths' enjoyment, motivation, and participation behavior (e.g., Babkes & Weiss, 1999; Bois, Lalanne, & Delforge, 2009; Brustad, 1988; Sagar & Lavallee, 2010; Scanlan & Lewthwaite, 1984; W.M. Weiss &

Weiss, 2007). For example, Bois et al. found that parents' presence at competitive events was perceived as pressure by adolescent tennis and basketball players, resulting in elevated precompetitive anxiety levels. If such anxiety levels persist, we would expect lower motivation to continue sport. Sagar and Lavallee interviewed adolescent athletes and their parents about contributors to fear of failure. Themes included parents' use of punitive behavior (e.g., criticism), controlling behavior (e.g., attending trainings and competitions), and high expectations (e.g., reaching top national ranking). Chronic exposure to such negative parent behaviors is likely to result in heightened stress and dropping out of sport.

COACH/TEACHER INFLUENCE ON YOUTH MOTIVATION AND PARTICIPATION IN PHYSICAL ACTIVITY

At all competitive levels—from youth to collegiate sport—coaches can significantly impact the behaviors, cognitions, and affective responses of their athletes (see Amorose, 2007; Chelladurai, 2007; Horn, 2008; Mageau & Vallerand, 2003; Smoll & Smith, 2002). The way in which coaches structure practices and games, make decisions, provide quality and quantity of feedback in response to performances, establish relationships with athletes, and use techniques to motivate players have important implications for psychological development and motivational orientations. While the physical education context is different than sport (e.g., students are more variable in ability; focus is on skill development, not outcomes), teachers function in a similar role as coaches—they structure the setting, use teaching styles, give informational and motivational feedback, and form teacher–student relationships. Thus, teachers' instructional behaviors and interpersonal interactions also contribute important motivational consequences for their students (see Biddle, 2001; Hein & Koka, 2007; Standage, Gillison, & Treasure, 2007).

We overview key findings from research exploring the motivational influences of coaches and teachers. The review is broken down by mechanisms of coaching/teaching influence: (a) feedback patterns, (b) general leadership styles, (c) motivational climate, and (d) autonomy-supportive versus controlling behaviors. Other important aspects of teaching and coaching behavior are motivationally relevant (e.g., see Jowett & Poczwardowski, 2007); however, the behavioral mechanisms we review are the ones most systematically examined in youth sport and physical activity (Amorose, 2007; Horn, 2008).

Feedback Patterns

All the theories we highlighted either implicitly or explicitly suggest that performance-related feedback from significant others will influence performers' motivation. Studies in sport and physical activity settings have explored various dimensions of feedback—mostly focusing on the motivational implications of the *content* and *frequency* of feedback (Horn, 2008). In general, coaches/teachers who provide frequent performance-contingent praise and technical information should be associated with positive motivational outcomes among youth participants (e.g., higher perceived competence, self-esteem, and self-determined motivation), whereas criticizing athletes/students or ignoring their performance altogether should have the opposite effect (see Amorose, 2007; Hein & Koka, 2007; Horn, 2008).

An illustrative example of this type of work comes from the systematic line of research by R.E. Smith, Smoll, and colleagues (see Smith & Smoll, 2007; Smoll & Smith, 2002). Based on extensive observations of youth sport coaches, Smith and Smoll noted the common types of feedback coaches use in practices and games and examined the degree to which different types of feedback were related to participants' psychosocial and behavioral outcomes. Using this information, they developed what they termed the "positive approach" to coaching—meaning high frequencies of reinforcement for effort and good performances, encouragement following errors, and mistake-contingent instruction, while at the same time minimizing punitive behaviors and nonresponses. In a number of field-based experiments, Smith, Smoll, and colleagues found that coaches who were trained to and actually engaged in these behaviors had players who reported higher self-esteem, enjoyment, and intentions of returning the following season, and lower anxiety and attrition rates (e.g., Barnett, Smoll, & Smith, 1992; Smith, Smoll, & Barnett, 1995; Smoll, Smith, Barnett, & Everett, 1993).

Smith and Smoll's scholarship stimulated considerable research on coaching behaviors and youth motivation (e.g., Allen & Howe, 1998; Amorose & Horn, 2000; Black & Weiss, 1992; Coatsworth & Conroy, 2006) and to a lesser extent teacher behaviors in physical education (e.g., Nicaise, Bois, Fairclough, Amorose, & Cogérino, 2007; Nicaise, Cogérino, Bois, & Amorose, 2006). In general, results of these studies support the motivational benefits of adopting a positive approach to providing feedback. Despite the intuitive implications of these findings (e.g., coaches and teachers should provide lots of praise and encouragement and avoid criticism), it is important to acknowledge that providing effective feedback is considerably more complex. For instance, providing seemingly effective feedback, such as praise and technical instruction, may actually lead to negative motivational outcomes if the feedback is not given contingent or appropriate to performance attempts, is given in a controlling or demeaning manner, and is insincere or condescending. Similarly, negative motivational effects are likely when feedback provided to athletes suggests unrealistic performance expectations and promotes ego involvement (see Henderlong & Lepper, 2002; Horn, 2008; Mageau & Vallerand, 2003).

General Leadership Styles

Studies also provide support for the motivational influence of general leadership styles exhibited by coaches and teachers (see Amorose, 2007; Chelladurai, 2007, Horn, 2008). This research, conducted mainly with coaches, has focused primarily on leadership styles assessed with the Leadership Scale for Sport (Chelladurai & Saleh, 1980). With this measure, participants indicate their perceptions of the coach's general decision-making style (democratic and autocratic), motivational tendencies (social support and positive feedback), and instructional tendencies (training and instruction). In general, positive athlete outcomes are associated with each of these dimensions, with the exception of autocratic behavior (see Amorose, 2007; Chelladurai, 2007; Horn, 2008). For example, Price and Weiss (2000) found that adolescent female soccer players who rated their coaches higher in training and instruction, social support, positive feedback, and democratic decisions, and lower in autocratic behavior, reported more positive (i.e., perceived competence, enjoyment) and fewer negative (i.e., anxiety, burnout) motivational outcomes.

A series of studies by Amorose and colleagues (Amorose & Horn, 2000, 2001; Hollembeak & Amorose, 2005) linked these leadership styles with college athletes' intrinsic motivation. For instance, Hollembeak and Amorose found that the various dimensions, with the exception of social support, were predictive of athletes' perceptions of competence, autonomy, and relatedness, which in turn predicted athletes' level of intrinsic motivation. The motivational effect was particularly strong for coaches' decision-making style—athletes perceiving their coaches as more democratic in decision-making style reported higher levels of autonomy and intrinsic motivation, while athletes who perceived coaches higher in autocratic behavior reported lower levels of autonomy, relatedness, and intrinsic motivation.

A recent study in the physical education setting by Koka and Hagger (2010) shows that general leadership behaviors of secondary school teachers are related to students' motivation. Specifically, these researchers found that teachers' positive feedback predicted satisfaction of competence, autonomy, and relatedness needs and indirectly predicted students' self-determined motivation. Higher autocratic behavior and negative nonverbal feedback predicted lower self-determined motivation, whereas frequency of instruction and a teaching style that provided for situational considerations (e.g., accounting for students' abilities when setting goals) showed positive relationships with self-determination constructs. Finally, higher autonomy need satisfaction was predicted by greater use of a democratic teaching style, whereas higher competence need satisfaction was related to less negative nonverbal feedback.

Overall, research shows that perceived leadership styles exhibited by coaches and teachers have important motivational implications (see Amorose, 2007; Chelladurai, 2007; Horn, 2008). From a practical standpoint, getting teachers and coaches to provide social support and positive feedback, engage in high levels of training and instruction, and adopt a democratic decision-making style should facilitate self-determined forms of motivation. It should be noted, however, that these recommendations may be too simplistic. For instance, researchers contend that the most effective leadership styles will depend on other factors such as characteristics and preferences of athletes/students and the situation or context in which coaches/teachers and athletes/students are interacting (e.g., level of competition, type of sport, practice versus game context) (Amorose, 2007; Chelladurai, 2007; Horn, 2008).

Motivational Climate

The way coaches and teachers structure learning experiences, how they provide feedback and give recognition, and strategies they adopt for grouping athletes or students help to establish what has been referred to as the *motivational climate* (Ames, 1992). The climate refers to how success and failure are defined and emphasized in the social environment (Duda & Balaguer, 2007). A mastery (task-involved) motivational climate focuses on learning, improvement, and effort as ways of conceptualizing success. Behaviors exhibited by coaches and teachers who create this type of climate will provide optimally challenging and meaningful learning activities, reward and encourage progress toward individualized goals, evaluate performance based on effort and skill improvement, and promote cooperation among group members. Conversely, a performance (ego-involved) motivational climate describes an environment where the focus is on defining success and failure in terms of favorable comparison to others and other norm-referenced criteria. In this climate, coaches and teachers reinforce players/students for demonstrating superior performance relative to others, use punishment for making mistakes, and encourage intrateam rivalry as a means to achieve norm-referenced goals (Newton, Duda, & Yin, 2000).

Considerable research has demonstrated that the climate created by teachers and coaches carries motivational significance for youth participants (Biddle, 2001; Duda & Balaguer, 2007; Harwood et al., 2008; Horn, 2008; Roberts et al., 2007). For instance, youth who report a higher mastery climate within their sport/physical activity setting also report positive achievement-related outcomes such as higher perceptions of competence and enjoyment, lower anxiety, more adaptive coping strategies, and higher self-determined motivation, whereas participating under a higher performance climate generally is associated with less positive achievement-related outcomes.

We present a few studies demonstrating the diversity of achievement-related outcomes associated with coaches' and teachers' structuring of the motivational climate. A longitudinal study of adolescent female handball players (ages 13–15 years) provides a nice illustration of the effects of perceived motivational climate (Sarrazin, Vallerand, Guillet, Pelletier, & Cury, 2002). Findings revealed that higher perceived mastery climate predicted higher levels of the three psychological needs (i.e., perceived competence, autonomy, and relatedness), whereas a higher performance climate negatively predicted perceived autonomy. In turn, need satisfaction predicted level of self-determined motivation, which was directly and negatively related to intention to drop out and indirectly related to actual dropout behavior 21 months later.

Studies in the physical education context also highlight the relevance of the motivational climate. For instance, Barkoukis, Ntoumanis, and Thøgersen-Ntoumanis (2010) explored changes in junior high school students' achievement motivation over the course of 3 years. A mastery motivational climate was positively associated with a task goal orientation

and enjoyment of physical education and negatively related to boredom. A performance climate, on the other hand, was positively associated with an ego goal orientation and boredom. The positive effect of a mastery compared to a performance climate was also supported by Papaioannou, Marsh, and Theodorakis (2004), who found that motivational climate at the beginning of a school year was predictive of goal orientations, enjoyment, effort, perceived control, physical self-concept, and exercise intentions at the end of the year.

Because motivational climate contributes significantly to variations in affective, cognitive, and behavioral outcomes in sport and physical activity, coaches and teachers should engage in instructional practices and interpersonal behaviors that emphasize a mastery relative to a performance climate (Duda & Treasure, 2010; Standage et al., 2007). This is more easily accomplished in physical education compared to competitive sport settings, and thus more research is merited on how to balance mastery and performance climates in contexts where favorable outcomes and being the best are considered benchmarks of successful achievement.

Autonomy-Supportive Versus Controlling Behaviors

One of the more frequently studied aspects of coach and teacher behavior is the degree to which autonomy-supportive versus controlling behaviors are used in their interactions with athletes and students. An autonomy-supportive coach/teacher engages in behaviors that acknowledge athletes'/students' thoughts and feelings; encourages choice, self-initiation, and self-regulation; and minimizes the use of pressure and demands to control others (Deci & Ryan, 1985, 1987). A controlling interpersonal style, on the other hand, is characterized by pressuring another to think, feel, and act in a way consistent with the coach's/teacher's needs and wants (Deci & Ryan, 1985, 1987).

In the sport setting, Mageau and Vallerand (2003) contend that autonomy-supportive coaches engage in a number of specific behaviors to optimize motivation in athletes. These include *(a)* providing choice to athletes within specific limits and rules, *(b)* providing athletes with a meaningful rationale for activities, limits, and rules, *(c)* asking about and acknowledging athletes' feelings, *(d)* providing opportunity for athletes to take initiative and act independently, *(e)* providing noncontrolling performance feedback, *(f)* avoiding overt control, guilt-induced criticism and controlling statements, and *(g)* minimizing behaviors that promote ego involvement. A controlling interpersonal coaching style, according to Bartholomew, Ntoumanis, and Thøgersen-Ntoumani (2009), includes the following behavioral dimensions: *(a)* using rewards to manipulate athletes' behavior, *(b)* using overly critical feedback in an attempt to motivate athletes to perform better, *(c)* attempting to influence athletes' behaviors and lives outside the sport setting, *(d)* using power assertive techniques to force athlete compliance, *(e)* using social comparison as the reference for evaluating athletes, and *(f)* recognizing athletes when they are performing well and withdrawing attention when athletes are struggling.

Considerable research has shown that teachers and coaches who exhibit more autonomy-supportive and less controlling behaviors facilitate positive motivational outcomes in students/athletes (see Amorose, 2007; Bartholomew et al., 2009; Mageau & Vallerand, 2003; Standage et al., 2007). Studies in sport contexts have consistently shown that autonomy-supportive behaviors are effective in promoting a wide range of positive psychological and behavioral outcomes (e.g., Adie, Duda, & Ntoumanis, 2008; Amorose & Anderson-Butcher, 2007; Coatsworth & Conroy, 2009; Gagné, Ryan, & Bargmann, 2003; Gillet, Vallerand, Amoura, & Baldes, 2010; Smith, Ntoumanis, & Duda, 2007). Similar findings occur in physical education settings (e.g., Hagger, Chatzisarantis, Barkoukis, Wang, & Baranowski, 2005; Ntoumanis, 2005; Standage et al., 2006; Standage & Gillison, 2007; Vierling, Standage, & Treasure, 2007). For instance, Standage and colleagues (2006) showed that students' (ages 11–14) perceptions of greater autonomy-supportive behaviors by their physical education teacher predicted higher perceived competence, autonomy, and relatedness in students, which in turn positively related to students' motivational orientation for physical education. Furthermore, higher levels of self-determined motivation related to greater effort and persistence in physical education. A similar pattern of results was reported by Amorose and Anderson-Butcher (2007), who found that the degree to which high school and college athletes perceived their coaches to be autonomy-supportive positively related to athletes' perceived competence, autonomy, and relatedness, which in turn predicted self-determined motivation.

The effects of controlling behaviors on motivational outcomes have also been examined (e.g., Blanchard et al., 2009; Conroy & Coatsworth, 2007; Pelletier, Fortier, Vallerand, & Brière, 2001; Smith, Ntoumanis, & Duda, 2010). In many cases, these studies looked at both controlling and autonomy-supportive behaviors given these dimensions are relatively independent (see Bartholomew et al., 2009, 2010; Tessier, Sarrazin, & Ntoumanis, 2008). For example, Pelletier and colleagues found positive associations between perceived autonomy support and self-determined forms of motivation in a sample of 13–22-year-old swimmers, whereas controlling coaching behaviors related to less self-determined forms of motivation. They also reported that swimmers who dropped out over the course of the 2-year study reported lower autonomy support and greater controlling behaviors from their coaches relative to swimmers who maintained their participation.

It is clear that an autonomy-supportive interpersonal style is an effective motivational technique for coaches and physical educators. Unfortunately, many teachers and coaches tend to rely on a more controlling interpersonal style and may actually be seen as effective leaders (see Mageau & Vallerand, 2003). The data-based evidence, however, implies numerous benefits if coaches and teachers are more autonomy supportive in their instructional style (see Amorose, 2007; Mageau & Vallerand, 2003; Standage et al., 2007).

PEER INFLUENCE ON YOUTH PHYSICAL ACTIVITY MOTIVATION

One's peers, such as classmates, teammates, and friends, are just as important as significant adults when it comes to physical activity motivation, especially as youth seek to demonstrate autonomy from adult figures (A.L. Smith, 2003; Weiss & Stuntz, 2004). The two main peer constructs in the developmental literature are *peer group acceptance* and *friendship* (Bukowski & Hoza, 1989; Rubin, Bukowski, & Parker, 1998). Peer group acceptance, or popularity, refers to how much a child is liked or accepted by members of the peer group (e.g., teammates). It is a general, unilateral view that entails how well the peer group regards one of its members. Friendship refers to a close, dyadic relationship (e.g., best friends) and represents a specific, reciprocated view of experiences between two persons (e.g., intimacy, loyalty). These constructs are conceptually distinct and thus examined separately as determinants of youth physical activity motivation (Weiss & Stuntz, 2004).

Over the last decade, more attention has been given to the role of peer groups and close friendships in physical activity motivation. This is essential because peer interactions and relationships are best understood within the *social context* in which they occur (e.g., Zarbatany, Ghesquiere, & Mohr,

1992). Sport and physical activity is a unique social context in that behavior and performance are highly visible. It is not surprising, then, that peer comparison and evaluation are salient sources of information whereby youth participants judge how physically competent they are (Horn, 2004; Horn & Amorose, 1998). In turn, self-judgments about ability are strongly related to motivation to continue participation. Consistent with our discussion of adult influence, we organize our review around mechanisms of peer influence: *(a)* social acceptance and approval, *(b)* social support/friendship quality, *(c)* observational learning, *(d)* leadership behaviors, and *(e)* negative evaluative behaviors.

Social Acceptance and Approval

One of the most robust findings is that children and adolescents are motivated to participate in physical activity for social reasons—to be with and make friends, attain acceptance and approval from peers, and feel part of a group or team (Weiss & Petlichkoff, 1989; Weiss & Williams, 2004). These findings generalize across age, gender, race/ethnicity, socioeconomic status, culture, and sport type (e.g., Brodkin & Weiss, 1990; Gill, Gross, & Huddleston, 1983; Hayashi & Weiss, 1994; Sirard, Pfeiffer, & Pate, 2006; Wilson, Williams, Evans, Mixon, & Rheaume, 2005). For example, Brodkin and Weiss assessed participation motives among age-group swimmers ranging from 6 to 60+ years old. Participating to attain social status was highest for 15–22-year-olds, to obtain friends' approval was highest for 6–9 and 10–14-year-olds, and affiliation reasons were important for all age groups. Klint and Weiss (1987) found that higher peer acceptance was associated with higher affiliation motives among 8–16-year-old gymnasts, suggesting that youth who feel socially accepted are motivated to demonstrate ability in getting along with teammates.

Theory-driven studies show that peer group acceptance is positively related to perceived competence, affective responses, motivational orientations, and physical activity behavior (e.g., Cox, Duncheon, & McDavid, 2009; A.L. Smith, 1999; A.L. Smith, Ullrich-French, Walker, & Hurley, 2006; Ullrich-French & Smith, 2006; Weiss & Duncan, 1992). For example, A.L. Smith (1999) tested a model of relationships between peer and motivational variables and found that adolescents higher in peer acceptance reported higher physical self-worth, positive affect, and intrinsic motivation. In turn, higher physical self-worth was indirectly related to intrinsic motivation and physical activity level through the

mediation of positive affect. By contrast, Cox et al. found that perceived peer acceptance was predictive of enjoyment and self-determined motivation for adolescent physical education students through perceived relatedness (feeling supported and valued in the classroom).

Social acceptance and approval by peers has also been studied within the concept of social goal orientations (e.g., Allen, 2003; Petlichkoff, 1993; Lewthwaite & Piparo, 1993; Schilling & Hayashi, 2001; Stuntz & Weiss, 2003, 2009). Social goal orientations, like task and ego orientations, refer to how one defines success in an achievement domain; individuals who are high in social goal orientations define success as having positive relationships with others. Stuntz and Weiss (2009) examined three social goal orientations among adolescent sport participants. Group acceptance orientation refers to defining success as being liked and regarded highly by peers; friendship orientation refers to defining success in terms of developing a close, mutual relationship; and coach praise orientation refers to defining success as gaining approval from a coach. They assessed social, task, and ego orientations in relation to motivational outcomes and found that youth scoring higher in group acceptance and friendship orientations reported more adaptive outcomes (perceived competence, enjoyment, and intrinsic motivation).

Social cohesion is a complementary construct for understanding peer group acceptance and approval in youth physical activity. Carron and Brawley (2008) define cohesion as a tendency for a group (e.g., team) to remain unified in its efforts to achieve instrumental (task cohesion) and social goals (i.e., social cohesion). Social cohesion refers to developing and maintaining relationships within the group and is assessed by individuals' perceptions of how well the group gets along and members like each other. Thus, the construct of social cohesion is conceptually consistent with peer group acceptance and approval. Adolescents' ratings of greater team harmony, satisfaction, and mutual liking are associated with effective coach and peer leadership behaviors (e.g., Price & Weiss, 2011b; Westre & Weiss, 1991; Zacharatos, Barling, & Kelloway, 2000).

Social Support/Friendship Quality

Considerable evidence exists that peers serve as sources of companionship, instrumental, affection, admiration, and emotional support, which relate to physical activity motivation (see Weiss & Stuntz, 2004). For example, British adolescents were interviewed to uncover reasons influencing their decisions to maintain or discontinue physical activity (Coakley & White, 1992). Social support from same-sex friends (i.e., companionship and emotional support) and social constraints from opposite-sex friends (i.e., peer pressure) emerged as common themes, with girls indicating these factors as more influential than boys for determining activity choices. Duncan (1993) found that perceptions of greater companionship and esteem support in physical education predicted adolescent students' enjoyment within the classroom and choices to be active outside of class.

To understand the nature and significance of friendships on youths' psychosocial and behavioral outcomes, Hartup (1995) identified three perspectives: *(a)* whether one has a close friendship, *(b) who* one's friends are, and *(c)* the quality of one's friendships. Friendship quality is essentially synonymous with friendship support and refers to positive and negative dimensions that characterize one's relationship. Weiss and colleagues conducted interrelated studies to provide conceptual clarity to the construct of "sport friendship quality" (Weiss & Smith, 1999, 2002; Weiss, Smith, & Theeboom, 1996). In the first study, Weiss et al. interviewed 8–16-year-old sport participants about their friendships in physical activities. Twelve positive dimensions (e.g., companionship, intimacy, loyalty, self-esteem enhancement) and four negative dimensions (e.g., conflict, betrayal) emerged that were similar to social support types in the developmental literature, whereas context-specific higher-order themes showed unique qualities (e.g., "we help each other in sport," "he motivates me in sports," "negative competitiveness"). Dimensions and themes were used to develop a pool of items and provide factorial and construct validity for a measure of sport friendship quality (Weiss & Smith, 1999, 2002).

Subsequent studies investigated friendship quality or peer social support in relation to psychosocial and motivational variables in the physical domain (e.g., Cox et al., 2009; Moran & Weiss, 2006; A.L. Smith, Ullrich-French, et al., 2006; Ullrich-French & Smith, 2006, 2009; W.M. Weiss & Weiss, 2003, 2006, 2007). For example, A.L. Smith, Ullrich-French, et al. assessed 10–14-year-old sport participants on positive friendship quality, conflict, and peer acceptance, and they compared relationship profiles to motivational outcomes. Youth with a positive relationship profile (higher peer acceptance, higher friendship quality, and lower conflict) showed more adaptive outcomes—higher perceived competence, enjoyment, and self-determined motivation, and less anxiety and self-presentational concerns—than youth with negative profiles (lower peer acceptance, lower friendship quality, higher or lower conflict).

Taking a different approach, Stuntz and Spearance (2010) explored cross-domain relationships by determining whether teammate–athlete interactions extend outside the sport context (e.g., school, family, goals). Path analyses revealed that positive cross-domain teammate relationships were predictive of high sport enjoyment for collegiate athletes and high sport commitment for youth and collegiate athletes. The concept of cross-domain relationships resonates with a positive youth development approach, whereby caring and supportive peers (and adults) contribute to psychosocial growth experiences in one domain (e.g., physical activity) that transcend to other domains (Weiss & Wiese-Bjornstal, 2009).

Observational Learning

According to Bandura (1986), modeling or observational learning is acknowledged "to be one of the most powerful means of transmitting values, attitudes, and patterns of thought and behavior" (p. 47). Peer models are similar in age, gender, competence level, and other characteristics (Schunk, 1998), and they connote effective sources of physical activity information and motivation (McCullagh & Weiss, 2002). A similar model is thought to elicit selective attention in observers and change in their competence beliefs, emotions, and motivated behavior through an attitude of "if he or she can do it, so can I!"

Schunk (1998) contends that peer models convey information and motivation to observers about learning strategies, self-regulation skills, outcome expectations, and self-efficacy. These psychological processes translate to motivated behavior and improved performance. Peer models may be effective because observers identify better with skills and learning strategies conveyed by similar others, and they may be especially helpful when observers are uncertain about their abilities to do a task, are unfamiliar with skills, or have experienced difficulty or anxiety in past performance attempts. Weiss, McCullagh, Smith, and Berlant (1998) conducted an experimental study to determine effects of peer modeling on motivation and skill development of children who were fearful of and lacked confidence in swimming. Children (ages 5–8 years) viewed a peer mastery, peer coping, or no model (control) in combination with swim instruction for 3 days. Peer modeling groups showed stronger pre- to postintervention improvements than controls in swim skills, self-efficacy, and fear of swimming, and differences held up in a retention test. Results highlight the utility of an intervention that combines peer modeling and swim lessons to enhance motivation and skill learning.

Other researchers have examined modeling effects through correlating physical activity levels of youth and their peers or identifying whether youth had friends who participated in sport or physical activity (e.g., Denault & Poulin, 2009; King, Tergerson, & Wilson, 2008; Salvy et al., 2008, 2009; Schofield, Mummery, Schofield, & Hopkins, 2007). For example, adolescents who indicated they had friends who exercise or participate in sports reported being more physically active and spending more hours doing sports than their counterparts (Denault & Poulin, 2009; King et al., 2008). Schofield et al. used an objective measure (pedometry) to assess adolescent girls' physical activity with that of three closest friends, including reciprocated (mutually nominated) and nonreciprocated friends. Girls with a larger number of active friends were more likely to reach the criterion of 10,000 steps than those with no active friends; and a moderate relationship emerged for a girl's physical activity level with that of a reciprocated friend, whereas a trivial correlation was found for nonreciprocated friendships.

Davison (2004) investigated sources and types of support for physical activity among middle school girls and boys. Interestingly, items for her "peer support" variable included the following items: "friends' level of activity," "importance friends assign to being physically active," "frequency of being active with friends," "friends' admiration of people who are active," and "friends' admiration of people who are athletic." The content of these items refers to friends' attitudes and behaviors for endorsing physical activity, thereby consistent with definition and characteristics of peer modeling discussed earlier. She found that high-active girls reported greater peer support/modeling than low active girls (along with other sources of social support). Salvy et al. (2008, 2009) found that doing physical activity with a friend was particularly effective for overweight youth, who showed increased motivation to be active and a higher intensity level in physical activity. Concomitant effects were not significant for lean youth; that is, doing physical activity alone or with a friend was equally effective.

Leadership Behaviors

An exciting area of research that has gained momentum is peer leadership. Coaches occupy a formal leadership role on sport teams, but team members also represent sources of leadership that can motivate others to achieve instrumental and social goals (e.g., team harmony) (Glenn & Horn, 1993; Moran & Weiss, 2006; Price & Weiss, 2011b). Peer leaders can fulfill roles such as team captain or they can emerge from within the group by demonstrating ability to inspire group members' effort and performance (i.e., lead by example). Thus, peer leadership represents an important mechanism of peer influence on teammates' individual (e.g., self-determined) and group motivation (e.g., task and social cohesion).

Early research focused on correlates of peer leadership, with those higher in interpersonal attraction and sociability being rated higher in leadership attributes (e.g., Tropp & Landers, 1979; Yukelson, Weinberg, Richardson, & Jackson, 1983). Interpersonal attraction is akin to peer group acceptance and shows a linkage with peer variables of leadership and sociability. Recent research has adopted theory-driven approaches to understand qualities of effective peer leaders and relationships between leadership behaviors and team outcomes (e.g., Glenn & Horn, 1993; Moran & Weiss, 2006; Price and Weiss, 2011a, b; Zacharatos et al., 2000).

Several studies show that effective peer leaders are characterized by both instrumental (task-oriented) and expressive (social-oriented) behaviors, such as facilitating teammates in attaining group goals and promoting a positive and accepting environment (e.g., Eys, Loughead, & Hardy, 2007; Glenn & Horn, 1993; Price & Weiss, 2011a; Rees, 1983). Extending the social-oriented behaviors of peer leaders, studies show that peer attributes of group acceptance, positive friendship quality, and leadership are intertwined (Moran & Weiss, 2006; Price & Weiss, 2011a; Yukelson et al., 1983; Zacharatos et al., 2000). Team members who were rated higher in leadership qualities and behaviors were also liked by their teammates, scored higher on social support (e.g., loyalty, intimacy, self-esteem enhancement), and maintained sport friendships "off the field." Based on these links among peer constructs, Moran and Weiss suggested that social competence is the glue that binds these characteristics and behaviors together. Individuals who are outgoing, get along with others, and enjoy and respect the "company they keep" (Bukowski, Newcomb, & Hartup, 1996) are favorably appraised by their peers, are chosen as friends, engage in high-quality friendships, and are seen as team leaders.

Transformational leadership theory (Bass, 1998) has been embraced as an appropriate and useful framework for understanding peer and coach leadership in sport (e.g., Price & Weiss, 2011a, b; Rowold, 2006). According to this theory, leaders motivate followers to adopt attitudes and behaviors that maximize achieving group goals. This occurs through engaging in four behaviors: (a) inspirational motivation (setting high achievement standards and exhibiting confidence in attaining them), (b) idealized influence (modeling desirable attitudes and behaviors), (c) intellectual stimulation (facilitating problem solving among teammates), and (d) individualized consideration (recognizing the needs and interests of each teammate). Price examined the unique and combined influence of peer and coach leadership on individual and team outcomes for adolescent female soccer players. For the unique influence of peer leadership, transformational behaviors were positively related to athletes' enjoyment, intrinsic motivation, task and social cohesion, and collective efficacy. When peer and coach leadership were simultaneously modeled, coach transformational behaviors were positively related to individual and team outcomes while peer transformational behaviors were positively related only to task and social cohesion. These findings demonstrate the utility of considering the interaction of peer and coach leadership, because inspirational, idealized, intellectual, and individualized behaviors were related to team members' psychosocial attributes and team dynamics differently depending on the source of leadership influence.

Negative Evaluative Behaviors

Unfortunately interactions and relationships among peers are not always positive. Peer group relationships can be characterized as low in social acceptance (e.g., rejected, neglected), high in negative friendship quality (e.g., conflict, betrayal), and low in positive friendship quality (e.g., loyalty, intimacy) (Bukowski et al., 1996; Rubin et al., 1998). Such can also be the case in sport and physical activity (e.g., Evans & Roberts, 1987; Jensen & Steele, 2009; Kunesh, Hasbrook, & Lewthwaite, 1992; A.L. Smith, Ullrich-French, et al., 2006; Storch et al., 2007). For example, Evans and Roberts observed elementary-age boys (grades 3–6) while they interacted with their peers on the school playground and interviewed them about their experiences. Low-skilled boys were chosen last for teams, were relegated to noncentral positions (e.g., right field), and were often denied playing time. Interview responses from these boys were vivid with examples of negative affect and low motivation for sport activities. These disparate opportunities and behaviors denied low-skilled boys from developing physically (i.e., improve sport skills) and socially (i.e., attain acceptance, strengthen friendships), and are examples of factors that squelch motivation for continuing in sport activities.

Kunesh et al. (1992) conducted a naturalistic study of 11–12-year-old girls and their peer groups using multiple methods (observations, sociometric ratings, interviews), contexts (school, neighborhood), and activities (sport, games, unstructured physical activity). Male classmates rated the girls low in peer acceptance (i.e., rejected, neglected) and treated them negatively, such as teasing, criticizing, name-calling, taunting, and excluding. Girls disclosed feelings of anxiety and embarrassment as a result of the boys' behaviors at school, which resulted in girls' attempts to avoid physical activity (e.g., PE, games at recess). By contrast, girls reported having fun doing unstructured physical activity in their neighborhood with close friends and viewed the few negative peer interactions in this setting as natural because they were with reciprocated friends. Importantly, the girls continued to be motivated to play games and be physically active in their home environments. The girls' age group (11–12 years) was an important feature of the study as evidence shows that girls starting at this age show a decline in physical activity that continues over the adolescent years (USDHHS, 2008). Negative peer interactions that promote high anxiety and embarrassment and low motivation for physical activity are counter to our efforts to maintain and enhance a physically active lifestyle and associated health benefits.

The study by Kunesh et al. (1992) is reminiscent of peer victimization, a subject of concern in school contexts. Peer victimization refers to verbal, physical, and relational aggressive behaviors toward others (e.g., Crick, Bigbee, & Howes, 1996; Ladd & Price, 1993). Youth who are victims of peer aggression report anxiety, loneliness, and depression, which is related to lower self-evaluations and decreased motivation in achievement situations. The literature on moral development in sport indicates that organized sport is a context where physical and verbal aggression occurs frequently and is even encouraged in some sports (Weiss, Smith, & Stuntz, 2008). However, such behaviors have been studied in relation to sources of social influence and individual differences (e.g., moral reasoning) and not motivation per se. However, youth who are fearful and anxious about the physical nature of sports are likely to be prone to dropping out, but little empirical evidence exists to verify a link between aggressive behaviors in sport and motivation to participate.

A few studies have investigated links between peer victimization, psychosocial variables, and physical activity among overweight youth (e.g., Jensen & Steele, 2009; Storch et al., 2007). Children who are overweight or at risk of overweight have much to benefit from regular physical activity, not only the obvious physical health benefits but social (e.g., making friends, attaining high friendship quality) and psychological (e.g., self-esteem, positive affect, motivation) benefits as well. Storch et al. found that, among 8–18-year-old youth, higher ratings of peer victimization were related to lower physical activity levels, and depressive symptoms and loneliness mediated this relationship. Similarly, Jensen and Steele found that fifth- and sixth-grade girls who reported high levels of weight criticism combined with body dissatisfaction were much less physically active than girls who experienced criticism in the absence of body dissatisfaction. These same results were not applicable to boys. Given a major focus of physical activity researchers on strategies for reducing or preventing overweight and obesity, it seems reasonable to suggest that peer interventions are essential for helping to stem the tide.

SUMMARY

Parents, coaches/teachers, and peers connote salient sources of social influence on young people's motivational orientations and behaviors in physical activity contexts. Through expressing beliefs about competence and task value, as well as exhibiting behaviors that convey information, inspiration, and evaluation, significant adults and peers influence participants' psychological needs, behavioral regulations, and physical activity levels. In the next section we highlight individual difference factors that are associated with motivational orientations and participation behavior.

Individual Difference Factors

In sport and physical activity, self-perceptions, notably global self-esteem and domain-specific self-evaluations, are consistently strong predictors of motivational orientations and behaviors. Emotional responses, such as enjoyment and anxiety, are also prevalent in the physical domain and frequently mediate the relationship between social influence and motivational outcomes. In the following sections, we discuss self-perceptions and emotions as antecedents and as consequences of physical activity

motivation. A major focus is on physical activity as a context for promoting positive cognitive, affective, and behavioral outcomes as shown through intervention and longitudinal studies.

SELF-PERCEPTIONS AND YOUTH PHYSICAL ACTIVITY MOTIVATION

In the physical activity domain, self-perceptions have been examined as antecedents of participation motivation and as consequences of physical activity participation (see Fox & Wilson, 2008; Horn, 2004; Weiss, Bhalla, & Price, 2008). We discuss the constructs of perceived competence and self-esteem as predictors of physical activity motivation and as outcomes derived from one's experiences in physical activity. Perceived competence is a belief about one's ability in a particular achievement domain (e.g., academic, physical, social) or subdomain (e.g., math, soccer, peer acceptance). Individuals appraise their abilities in domains that they value, and these domain-specific appraisals make up one's global sense of self, or self-esteem. Self-esteem is multidimensional meaning that individuals can have domain-specific self-evaluations as well as more global self-evaluations that are not tied to specific abilities. In all four theories we highlighted, self-evaluations of ability and one's overall self-concept are important individual differences explaining motivational orientations and behaviors.

Perceived Competence and Self-Esteem as Determinants of Physical Activity Motivation

Perceived physical competence is strongly related to self-determined forms of motivation for both physical education students (e.g., Cox & Williams, 2008; Ferrer Caja & Weiss, 2000, 2002; Ntoumanis, 2001; Standage, Duda, & Ntoumanis, 2003, 2006; Standage & Gillison, 2007; Taylor, Ntoumanis, Standage, & Spray, 2010) and sport participants (e.g., Amorose, 2001; Amorose & Anderson-Butcher, 2007; Hollembeak & Amorose, 2005; Kipp & Amorose, 2008; Sarrazin, Vallerand, Guillet, Pelletier, & Cury, 2002). In these studies, self-determined forms of motivation include both intrinsic motivation and self-determined forms of extrinsic motivation (i.e., identified and integrated regulations).

Physical education contexts have provided strong support for the link between perceived physical competence and self-determined motivation, whereas the sport context has received less attention. In the physical education domain, Ferrer Caja and Weiss (2000, 2002) surveyed high school students who took physical education as either a requirement

(2000 study) or as an elective (2002 study). Model testing showed that perceived physical competence (along with task orientation and mastery motivational climate) was a significant predictor of intrinsic motivation for both groups of students. Cox and Williams (2008) administered surveys to fifth- and sixth-grade physical education students and found that perceived physical competence (along with perceived autonomy and relatedness) was a significant predictor of self-determined motivation. The relationship was the strongest when perceived physical competence mediated the relationship between mastery climate and self-determined motivation. In the sport domain, Amorose and Anderson-Butcher (2007) assessed high school and college athletes on self-determination constructs and found that perceived competence (as well as perceived autonomy and relatedness) mediated the relationship between perceived autonomy support by the coach and self-determined motivation.

Perceived competence has also been examined as a determinant of motivational behaviors in physical activity, such as effort, intention to participate in future activity, persistence, and dropout (Davison, Symons Downs, & Birch, 2006; Ferrer Caja & Weiss, 2000, 2002; Ntoumanis, 2001; Sarrazin et al., 2002; Standage et al., 2003, 2006; Taylor et al., 2010; Ullrich-French & Smith, 2009). For example, Ferrer Caja and Weiss also included teacher ratings of students' effort and persistence in physical education. In both studies (2000, 2002), intrinsic motivation mediated the relationship between perceived physical competence and effort and persistence in physical education. In another study, Taylor and colleagues assessed adolescent physical education students' perceived physical competence, motivational orientations, effort in physical education, intention to exercise outside of physical education class, and leisure-time physical activity at three times over a school trimester. Results revealed that perceived physical competence and self-determined motivation were the strongest predictors of effort, intentions, and physical activity levels.

Global self-evaluations like self-esteem and physical self-worth have also been examined in relation to self-determined motivation (Amorose, 2001; Hein & Hagger, 2007; Standage & Gillison, 2007). For example, Amorose surveyed middle school physical education students, most who indicated they participated in organized sports. Both global self-evaluations (self-worth) and domain-specific self-evaluations (physical self-worth, perceived physical competence) were related to intrinsic motivation.

Students with positive and stable self-evaluations over time reported higher levels of intrinsic motivation compared to students with less positive and less stable self-evaluations. Standage and Gillison took a different approach by examining self-determined motivation as a predictor of self-esteem. They assessed adolescent physical education students on self-determination constructs—perceptions of competence, autonomy, and relatedness; teacher's use of autonomy-supportive behavior; self-determined motivation; self-esteem; and health-related quality of life. In all model testing, perceived competence predicted self-determined motivation. Furthermore, three models supported differing relationships between self-determined motivation and self-esteem. In model 1, self-determined motivation directly predicted self-esteem, which in turn predicted quality of life. In model 2, self-determined motivation indirectly predicted self-esteem through quality of life. In model 3, self-determined motivation directly predicted both self-esteem and quality of life. These results mean that self-esteem, quality of life, and self-determined motivation are intricately related.

To improve levels of self-determined motivation and motivated behavior in physical activity contexts, research clearly shows that maintaining and enhancing perceived competence and self-esteem are important points of intervention. The next question is: How do we improve physical activity participants' self-perceptions? Sport and physical activity program intervention studies have been helpful in answering this question.

Perceived Competence and Self-Esteem as Outcome of Physical Activity Experiences

Several studies have shown that self-evaluations can be improved as a result of theory-driven physical activity interventions (e.g., Ebbeck & Gibbons, 1998; Marsh & Peart, 1988; Schneider, Fridlund Dunton, & Cooper, 2008; Smoll, Smith, Barnett, & Everett, 1993; Taymoori & Lubans, 2008; Theeboom, De Knop, & Weiss, 1995). In line with research on coaches' feedback patterns and motivational climate, several studies have focused on coach-training interventions to bring about positive self-evaluations in young sport participants (e.g., Smoll et al., 1993; Theeboom et al., 1995). Smoll and colleagues trained 10–12-year-old boys' baseball coaches through a coach effectiveness workshop designed to emphasize reinforcement for good performance and effort, mistake-contingent encouragement, and corrective and technical instruction.

Coaches were also asked to avoid or minimize using punishment and punitive instruction. At the end of the season, boys who played for the trained coaches viewed their coaches as more supportive compared to boys in the control group. Importantly for the present discussion, boys who played for the trained coaches and started the season with low self-esteem showed significant increases in self-esteem over the season, whereas those in the control group did not. No differences in trained versus control groups occurred for youth who scored moderate or high in self-esteem at the beginning of the season. These results suggest that children who have the most to gain from a positive sport experience (i.e., those who are low in self-esteem) benefited greatly from having a coach who used positive forms of instruction and evaluative feedback.

Other intervention studies have emphasized cooperation among peers in physical education classes to bring about positive self-evaluations (Ebbeck & Gibbons, 1998; Marsh & Peart, 1988). For example, Ebbeck and Gibbons conducted an intervention where middle school physical education teachers were trained in using team-building challenges with their students throughout the school year. At the end of the intervention, boys and girls in the intervention group were significantly higher on perceptions of global self-worth, athletic competence, physical appearance, and social acceptance than the control group (regular physical education activities). In addition, female students in the intervention group were significantly higher on perceived academic competence and behavioral conduct than those in the control group. Effect sizes for group differences were large and meaningful. Thus, a physical activity intervention that required group interdependence and positive peer interactions was successful in modifying a range of global and domain-specific self-evaluations.

Some recent studies have incorporated health promotion interventions to increase physical activity and improve self-perceptions (Schneider et al., 2008; Taymoori & Lubans, 2008). Schneider and colleagues conducted a 9-month, school-based physical activity intervention for sedentary adolescent girls. Physical education classes designed exclusively for study participants included supervised activity four times per week (e.g., aerobic dance, yoga, basketball, swimming, Tae Bo) and educational instruction one day per week to promote physical activity outside of school. Self-concept, physical activity level, and cardiovascular fitness were assessed before, during, and after

the 9-month school-based intervention. Changes in study variables were analyzed in relation to a comparison group, which included physical education students at another school. Results showed that intervention group participants who improved their fitness levels showed significant increases in global physical self-concept over the school year, and they suggest that organized physical activity that improves fitness levels can promote positive self-evaluations.

Collectively the intervention studies discussed in this section suggest causal links between physical activity participation and improvement in self-evaluations. It is clear that quality physical activity programs can positively impact participants' perceived physical competence and self-esteem. In addition, studies have supported links between higher perceived competence and self-esteem with greater self-determined motivation and physical activity participation. Coaches, teachers, and physical activity instructors are in an important position to structure the environment to positively shape the self-perceptions of their participants. Parents can also help shape their children's perceptions of physical competence. As shown in earlier sections, significant adults who model physical activity, emphasize a mastery climate, and exhibit autonomy-supportive behavior can positively impact participants' self-perceptions. In sum, theory-driven physical activity programs can effect positive changes in participants' sense of self. In turn, higher levels of perceived competence and self-esteem can ultimately promote more self-determined reasons for participation, greater effort and persistence in physical activity, and higher physical activity levels.

EMOTIONS AND YOUTH PHYSICAL ACTIVITY MOTIVATION

The physical domain provides a unique context for experiencing emotions, both positive and negative. People often experience joy and pride after successful physical performances and frustration, anxiety, and anger following poor performances. Emotions have been examined as antecedents of participation motivation and as consequences of participation in physical activity (see Crocker, Hoar, McDonough, Kowalski, & Niefer, 2004; Crocker, Kowalski, Hoar, & McDonough, 2004). In this section, we discuss consistent findings about the relationship between emotions and motivation. Participants' feeling states are important individual difference factors that help explain motivation and participation in physical activity.

Research on emotional responses and physical activity motivation has focused mainly on enjoyment, anxiety, stress, and burnout. However, definitions of emotion have not always been conceptually clear, with terms such as feeling states, affect, moods, and emotions used interchangeably. Crocker, Kowalski, et al. (2004) provide a guide for defining emotions: quick onset, cognitive appraisal, distinct physiological patterns, subjective feeling states, and facial or bodily expression (e.g., happy, angry, anxious, and excited). Affect is described as a global feeling state that can vary in tone (pleasant to unpleasant) and intensity (low to high).

To understand emotions in the physical domain, early research identified sources of enjoyment such as perceived competence, positive peer interactions, perceived coach support, effort, and skill mastery (e.g., Scanlan, Carpenter, Lobel, & Simons, 1993; Scanlan, Ravizza, & Stein, 1989; Scanlan & Simons, 1992; Wankel & Kreisel, 1985). Sources of anxiety, competitive stress, and burnout have also been frequently studied, such as negative performance expectancies, negative social evaluation, performance evaluation potential, and negative coach relationships (e.g., Gould, Horn, & Spreeman, 1983; Passer, 1988; Raedeke, 1997; Scanlan & Passer, 1979; Scanlan, Stein, & Ravizza, 1991; see Gould, 1993). Research describing the nature of positive and negative emotions in the physical domain led to theory-driven studies on the emotion–motivation relationship (see Crocker, Hoar, et al., 2004; Crocker, Kowalski, et al., 2004).

Emotions and Affect as Determinants of Participation Motivation and Motivated Behaviors

Enjoyment and positive affect strongly predict self-determined motivation, psychological commitment to physical activity, and motivated behaviors like effort and persistence (Raedeke, 1997; Schneider, Dunn, & Cooper, 2009; A.L. Smith, 1999; Weiss, Kimmel, & Smith, 2001; W.M. Weiss & Weiss, 2003, 2006, 2007; W.M. Weiss, Weiss, & Amorose, 2010). For example, W.M. Weiss and Weiss (2003, 2006) used cluster analysis to group 10–18-year-old gymnasts into commitment profiles. Gymnasts with an adaptive profile (committed to sport for attraction reasons) reported higher enjoyment, intrinsic motivation, and effort and persistence in their training behaviors, compared to gymnasts with a maladaptive profile (committed to sport because they feel entrapped). In another study, A.L. Smith (1999) surveyed adolescents involved in organized sport and physical activity on

competence motivation constructs (peer influence, self-perceptions, affect, motivation). Among the findings, model testing showed that greater positive affect toward physical activity was related to higher intrinsic motivation and physical activity behavior.

Negative emotions in sport, notably performance anxiety, competitive stress, and burnout, have been linked to a range of social and motivational outcomes among athletes (e.g., Gould, Tuffey, Udry, & Loehr, 1996; Gould, Udry, Tuffey, & Loehr, 1996; Price & Weiss, 2000; Raedeke, 1997; Raedeke & Smith, 2001, 2004; Vealey, Armstrong, Comar, & Greenleaf, 1998). For example, Price and Weiss found that adolescent female athletes who reported higher anxiety and burnout rated their coaches as exhibiting lower frequency of instruction, social support, positive feedback, and democratic decision-making behaviors, and greater autocratic behaviors. Athlete burnout has been a topic of great concern among scholars and practitioners due to the demands and pressures often present in competitive sport (see Reeve & Weiss, 2006; Schmidt & Stein, 1991). Athlete burnout is defined as *(a)* emotional and physical exhaustion, *(b)* reduced sense of accomplishment, and *(c)* sport devaluation (e.g., Raedeke, 1997; Raedeke & Smith, 2001). For example, Raedeke and Smith (2004) found that adolescent swimmers who reported higher levels of stress in their sport scored higher on burnout. In addition, results provided support for stress as a mediator of the relationship between coping behaviors and social support satisfaction with burnout. These contextual factors (coping behaviors and social support) may help reduce stress levels and in turn promote more adaptive forms of motivation for physical activity participants.

Emotions and Affect as Consequences of Motivational Orientations and Physical Activity Participation

Recently, researchers have examined physical activity in relation to aspects of well-being such as positive affect, subjective vitality, satisfaction, self-esteem, depressive symptoms, and physical symptoms of illness. Emotional aspects of well-being (e.g., positive affect, depressive symptoms, anxiety, enjoyment) have been studied as outcomes of motivational orientations and physical activity levels (e.g., Blanchard, Amiot, Perriault, Vallerand, & Provencher, 2009; Boone & Leadbeater, 2006; Cox, Duncheon, & McDavid, 2009; Gore, Farrell, & Gordon, 2001; Sanders, Field, Diego, & Kaplan, 2000; Vierling, Standage, & Treasure, 2007). For example, Cox and colleagues found that self-determined motivation predicted greater enjoyment and less worry among sixth- through eighth-grade physical education students. Blanchard et al. tested a model of relationships among team cohesion; coach behaviors; perceived competence, autonomy, and relatedness; self-determined motivation; and emotional outcomes among 16–22-year-old basketball players. Among other findings, self-determined motivation predicted greater levels of positive emotions while playing basketball and satisfaction with their sport participation. Boone and Leadbeater found that greater positive team sport involvement among adolescents predicted fewer depressive symptoms, and that perceived social acceptance and body dissatisfaction predicted depressive symptoms through positive team sport involvement. These studies provide evidence of interrelationships among emotions, motivational orientations, and physical activity involvement.

Several intervention studies provide further evidence for the role of sport and physical activity in fostering emotional well-being. Theory-based physical activity programs have positively changed participants' emotional experiences (MacPhail, Gorely, Kirk, & Kinchin, 2008; R.E. Smith, Smoll, & Barnett, 1995; R.E. Smith, Smoll, & Cumming, 2007; Theeboom, De Knop, & Weiss, 1995). R.E. Smith and colleagues (1995) trained youth baseball coaches using their coach effectiveness program at the beginning of a season. The training program emphasized providing social support, encouraging and reinforcing effort, and deemphasizing the importance of winning. Thus, the intervention was hypothesized to reduce athletes' competitive anxiety levels. At the end of the season, players in the experimental group evaluated their coaches more positively, reported having more fun, and experienced reduced trait anxiety compared to players in the control group. R.E. Smith et al. (2007) conducted a similar intervention and added a mastery climate component in the coach training (emphasis on effort and improvement and positive control rather than aversive control). Over the course of a basketball season, boys and girls in the experimental group showed decreases in cognitive, somatic, and overall anxiety, while control group players reported increases in anxiety.

Other intervention studies were conducted in physical education-type settings. Theeboom and colleagues (1995) examined the effect of mastery (experimental group) and performance (control group) motivational climates with youth ages 8–12 years in a summer sports program. After a 3-week program in martial arts, youth in the intervention group reported greater enjoyment, perceived competence, and intrinsic motivation, and they were rated higher in physical skills, compared to the control group. MacPhail and colleagues (2008) incorporated a 16-week sport education unit in elementary school physical education classes. The program consisted of activities that encouraged autonomy, such as choosing a team name, choosing a role on the team, and taking part in determining winners in the tournament. Students were interviewed about their experiences throughout the program and several themes emerged: fun and enjoyment, team affiliation, autonomy, perceived sport competence, and formal competition. Survey responses for motivational variables reinforced past research on sources of enjoyment: affiliation, autonomy, competition, and learning skills. These intervention studies show that participation in theory-driven physical activity programs can foster positive emotional outcomes, including increased enjoyment and reduced anxiety.

In sum, emotions have been examined in the sport domain as both antecedents and consequences of motivational orientations and physical activity participation. It is clear that the more youth enjoy their sport experiences, the more they will be motivated for self-determined reasons and exert greater effort and persistence. In turn, greater self-determined motivation and skill mastery should result in greater positive emotions. Intervention studies contribute to our understanding of how physical activity can impact emotional well-being. Programs that emphasize improvement rather than winning, provide opportunities to be autonomous, and provide social support bring about greater levels of enjoyment and lower levels of anxiety in physical activity participants. These contextual factors can be fostered by coaches and parents and can lead to overall well-being (e.g., improved self-esteem, greater perceived competence, higher intrinsic motivation, and successful skill learning).

Future Research Directions

In this chapter we extensively reviewed the knowledge base on antecedents, correlates, and outcomes of physical activity motivation. Still there is much yet to be known about factors that influence individuals to initiate and maintain their involvement in sport and physical activities. It is not possible within the scope of this chapter to provide a comprehensive set of recommendations for future research. Thus, we limit our suggestions to a few that we consider to be major areas necessitating attention in the literature. Readers are directed to other sources for more detailed discussion of future research ideas (Amorose, 2007; Horn, 2008; Horn & Horn, 2007; Weiss & Amorose, 2008; Weiss & Stuntz, 2004; Weiss & Williams, 2004).

Since Brustad's (1992) plea for conducting research blending socialization and motivation influences, an explosion of studies occurred in the past decade on mechanisms of parental influence and youths' physical activity experiences. Still much is unknown about the role of the family on participants' physical activity- and achievement-related outcomes (Fredricks & Eccles, 2004; Horn & Horn, 2007). Based on Eccles et al.'s (1998) model of parental influence, family characteristics (e.g., education, number of children, culture, employment status) and child characteristics (e.g., gender, birth order, sibling characteristics) should influence parents' beliefs and behaviors and subsequently the child's beliefs and behaviors. Additionally, children can socialize and motivate parents through their active involvement in sports. Yet most studies have been conducted with intact two-parent families (mother and father), of mostly European American ethnicity, and with little attention to sibling influence (Horn & Horn, 2007). Clearly more empirical study is needed on variations in family structure (e.g., single-parent, step-parents, same-sex parents), bidirectional and reciprocal parent-child influences, and family characteristics (e.g., socioeconomic status, culture, number and birth order of siblings) on youth participants' physical activity motivation. A few studies have initiated momentum on these issues (e.g., Bhalla & Weiss, 2010; Davison et al., 2006; Dorsch et al., 2009), but clearly more complete testing is needed of Eccles et al.'s model of parental influence in the context of physical activity.

Coaches and teachers clearly have an important influence on the athletes and students with whom they work, yet many questions remain to be answered in the study of these social-contextual determinants of motivation (see Amorose, 2007; Horn, 2008; Mageau & Vallerand, 2003). For instance, we know relatively little about *why* coaches and physical education teachers act the way they do. A number of scholars have identified potentially important determinants such as characteristics of the coach/teacher, the situation, and characteristics of the athletes/students (see Chelladurai, 2007; Horn, 2008; Horn, Lox, & Labrador, 2010; Mageau & Vallerand, 2003; Smoll & Smith, 2002). However, with the exception of a few studies (e.g., Price & Weiss, 2000; Taylor, Ntoumanis, & Smith, 2009; Taylor, Ntoumanis, & Standage, 2008), these relationships remain understudied.

The value in expanding our understanding of antecedents of coaching and teaching behaviors is that it will be useful in designing effective intervention programs (Horn, 2008). While examples of interventions exist that have manipulated key coaching and teaching behaviors (e.g., Barnett et al., 1992; Coatsworth & Conroy, 2006; Chatzisarantis & Hagger, 2009; Jaakkola & Liukkonen, 2006; Tessier, Sarrazin, & Ntoumanis, 2008; Theeboom et al., 1995), scholars need to expand this type of research. Such research will help us *(a)* understand aspects of intervention that are more or less effective for modifying motivational outcomes, *(b)* determine the optimal length of time required to acquire meaningful changes in motivation, and *(c)* examine the most effective ways to train coaches and teachers to adopt these behaviors.

Peers such as teammates, classmates, and close friends represent a salient source of competence and motivational information for physical activity participants. In our review, we teased out potential behavioral mechanisms based on a limited amount of empirical research in the physical domain. Thus, considerably more theory-driven research is needed to determine *how* and *why* peer groups and friendships make an impact on youths' self-perceptions, emotions, and physical activity motivation (see A.L. Smith, 2003; Weiss & Stuntz, 2004). All the theories we highlighted explicitly acknowledge the powerful contribution of significant others on motivational processes; thus, questions couched within competence motivation, self-determination, achievement goal, and expectancy-value theories present attractive opportunities to investigate peer interactions and relationships as sources of physical activity motivation.

Given that children and adolescents possess an entire social network of significant adults and peers, an important direction is to simultaneously examine children's relationships with all relevant socializers and their physical activity motivation (see Weiss & Amorose, 2008; Weiss & Stuntz, 2004). Recent studies have begun to assess the contribution of two sources of social influence on youth participants' motivation-related constructs using statistical modeling techniques (e.g., Cox et al., 2009; Price & Weiss, 2011b; Sabiston & Crocker, 2008; Ullrich-French & Smith, 2006, 2009). However, investigating the influence of children's social networks on psychosocial and behavioral outcomes will no doubt necessitate a variety of methodologies, including ethnographic, interview, observational, and survey techniques, to obtain a complete picture of this process (see Garcia Bengoechea & Strean, 2007).

Concluding Remarks

Physical activity is a unique context for promoting positive youth development, including self-perceptions, emotional responses, motivational orientations, and participation behaviors (Weiss & Wiese-Bjornstal, 2009). We cannot assume findings from other domains such as school, neighborhood, and community clubs translate to youths' experiences in sport and physical activity. It is necessary to consider the nuances and complexities of this context that is so ubiquitous among boys' and girls' involvement today. Practical theories for the physical activity domain include competence motivation, self-determination, achievement goal, and expectancy-value theories. All have been supported through model testing that reveals theoretically consistent relationships among social, psychological, and motivational constructs. However, experimental, intervention, longitudinal, and qualitative designs and methodologies can contribute substantially to filling the gaps in our understanding of temporal, short- versus long-lasting, and strength and meaningfulness of effects on youths' physical activity motivation. Such work can notably elevate our knowledge about determinants of physical activity motivation and, in turn, health and well-being.

Note

1. Other theoretical frameworks have been used to study youth sport and physical activity motivation, such as the sport commitment model and causal attribution theory (see Crocker, Hoar, et al., 2004; Weiss & Amorose, 2008). It is beyond the scope of this chapter to review all theories, so we selected ones that have been most productive for understanding physical activity motivation among youth.

References

Adie, J. W., Duda, J. L., & Ntoumanis, N. (2008). Autonomy support, basic need satisfaction and the optimal functioning of adult male and female sport participants: A test of basic needs theory. *Motivation and Emotion, 32,* 189–199.

Allen, J. B. (2003). Social motivation in youth sport. *Journal of Sport and Exercise Psychology, 25,* 551–567.

Ames, C. (1992). Achievement goals, motivational climate, and motivational processes. In G. C. Roberts (Ed.), *Motivation in sport and exercise* (pp. 161–176). Champaign, IL: Human Kinetics.

Amorose, A. J. (2001). Intraindividual variability of self-evaluations in the physical domain: Prevalence, consequences, and antecedents. *Journal of Sport and Exercise Psychology, 23,* 222–244.

Amorose, A. J. (2002). The influence of reflected appraisals on middle school and high school athletes' self-perceptions of sport competence. *Pediatric Exercise Science, 14,* 377–390.

Amorose, A. J. (2007). Coaching effectiveness: Exploring the relationship between coaching behavior and motivation from a self-determination theory perspective. In M. S. Hagger &

N. L. D. Chatzisarantis (Eds.), *Intrinsic motivation and self-determination in exercise and sport* (pp. 209–227). Champaign, IL: Human Kinetics.

Amorose, A. J., & Anderson-Butcher, D. (2007). Autonomy-supportive coaching and self-determined motivation in high school and college athletes: A test of self-determination theory. *Psychology of Sport and Exercise, 8,* 654–670.

Amorose, A. J., & Horn, T. S. (2000). Intrinsic motivation: Relationships with collegiate athletes' gender, scholarship status, and perceptions of their coaches' behavior. *Journal of Sport and Exercise Psychology, 22,* 63–84.

Amorose, A. J., & Horn, T. S. (2001). Pre- to post-season changes in the intrinsic motivation of first year college athletes: Relationships with coaching behavior and scholarship status. *Journal of Applied Sport Psychology, 13,* 355–373.

Babkes, M. L., & Weiss, M. R. (1999). Parental influence on cognitive and affective responses in children's competitive soccer participation. *Pediatric Exercise Science, 11,* 44–62.

Bandura, A. (1986). *Social foundations of thought and action: A social cognitive theory.* Englewood Cliffs, NJ: Prentice-Hall.

Barkoukis, V., Ntoumanis, N., & Thøgersen-Ntoumani, C. (2010). Developmental changes in achievement motivation and affect in physical education: Growth trajectories and demographic differences. *Psychology of Sport and Exercise, 11,* 83–90.

Barnett, N. P., Smoll, F. L., & Smith, R. E. (1992). Effects of enhancing coach-athlete relationships on youth sport attrition. *The Sport Psychologist, 6,* 111–127.

Bartholomew, K. J., Ntoumanis, N., & Thøgersen-Ntoumani, C. (2009). A review of controlling motivation strategies from a self-determination theory perspective: Implications for coaches. *International Review of Sport and Exercise Psychology, 2,* 215–233.

Bartholomew, K. J., Ntoumanis, N., & Thøgersen-Ntoumani, C. (2010). The controlling interpersonal style in a coaching context: Development and initial validation of a psychometric scale. *Journal of Sport and Exercise Psychology, 32,* 193–216.

Bass, B. M. (1998). *Transformational leadership: Industry, military, and educational impact.* Mahwah, NJ: Erlbaum.

Baumeister, R., & Leary, M. R. (1995). The need to belong: Desire for interpersonal attachments as a fundamental human motive. *Psychological Bulletin, 117,* 497–529.

Bhalla, J. A., & Weiss, M. R. (2010). A cross-cultural perspective of parental influence on achievement beliefs and behaviors in sport and school domains. *Research Quarterly for Exercise and Sport, 81,* 494–505.

Biddle, S. J. H. (2001). Enhancing motivation in physical education. In G. C. Roberts (Ed.), *Advances in motivation in sport and exercise* (pp. 101–128). Champaign, IL: Human Kinetics.

Black, S. J., & Weiss, M. R. (1992). The relationship among perceived coaching behaviors, perceptions of ability, and motivation in competitive age-group swimmers. *Journal of Sport and Exercise Psychology, 14,* 309–325.

Blanchard, C. M., Amiot, C. E., Perreault, S., Vallerand, R. J., & Provencher, P. (2009). Cohesiveness, coach's interpersonal style and psychological needs: Their effects on self-determination and athletes' subjective well-being. *Psychology of Sport and Exercise, 10,* 545–551.

Bois, J. E., Lalanne, J., & Delforge, C. (2009). The influence of parenting practices and parental presence on children's and adolescents' pre-competitive anxiety. *Journal of Sports Sciences, 27,* 995–1005.

Bois, J. E., Sarrazin, P. G., Brustad, R. J., Trouilloud, D. O., & Cury, F. (2002). Mothers' expectancies and young adolescents' perceived physical competence: A yearlong study. *Journal of Early Adolescence, 22*, 384–406.

Bois, J. E., Sarrazin, P. G., Brustad, R. J., Chanal, J. P., & Trouilloud, D. O. (2005). Parents' appraisals, reflected appraisals, and children's self-appraisals of sport competence: A yearlong study. *Journal of Applied Sport Psychology, 17*, 273–289.

Bois, J. E., Sarrazin, P. G., Brustad, R. J., Trouilloud, D. O., & Cury, F. (2005). Elementary schoolchildren's perceived competence and physical activity involvement: The influence of parents' role modeling behaviours and perceptions of their child's competence. *Psychology of Sport and Exercise, 6*, 381–397.

Boone, E. M., & Leadbeater, B. J. (2006). Game on: Diminishing risks for depressive symptoms in early adolescence through positive involvement in team sports. *Journal of Research on Adolescence, 16*, 79–90.

Brodkin, P., & Weiss, M. R. (1990). Developmental differences in motivation for participating in competitive swimming. *Journal of Sport and Exercise Psychology, 12*, 248–263.

Brustad, R. J. (1992). Integrating socialization influences into the study of children's motivation in sport. *Journal of Sport and Exercise Psychology, 14*, 59–77.

Brustad, R. J. (1993). Who will go out and play? Parental and psychological influences on children's attraction to physical activity. *Pediatric Exercise Science, 5*, 210–223.

Brustad, R. J. (2010). The role of family in promoting physical activity. *President's Council on Physical Fitness and Sports Research Digest, Series 10* (3), 1–8.

Bukowski, W. M., & Hoza, B. (1989). Popularity and friendship: Issues in theory, measurement, and outcome. In T. J. Berndt & G. W. Ladd (Eds.), *Peer relationships in child development* (pp. 15–45). New York: Wiley.

Bukowski, W. M., Newcomb, A. F., & Hartup, W. W. (1996). Friendship and its significance in childhood and adolescence: Introduction and comment. In W. M. Bukowski, A. F. Newcomb, & W. W. Hartup (Eds.), *The company they keep: Friendship in childhood and adolescence* (pp. 1–15). New York: Cambridge University Press.

Carron, A. V., & Brawley, L. R. (2008). Group dynamics in sport and physical activity. In T. S. Horn (Ed.), *Advances in sport psychology* (3rd ed., pp. 213–237). Champaign, IL: Human Kinetics.

Chatzisarantis, N. L. D., & Hagger, M. S. (2009). Effects of an intervention based on self-determination theory on self-reported leisure-time physical activity participation. *Psychology and Health, 24*, 29–48.

Chelladurai, P. (2007). Leadership in sports. In G. Tenenbaum & R. C. Eklund (Eds.), *Handbook of sport psychology* (3rd ed., pp. 113–135). Hoboken, NJ: Wiley.

Chelladurai, P., & Saleh, S. D. (1980). Dimensions of leader behavior in sports: Development of a leadership scale. *Journal of Sport Psychology, 2*, 34–45.

Coakley, J. J., & White, A. (1992). Making decisions: Gender and sport participation among British adolescents. *Sociology of Sport Journal, 9*, 20–35.

Coatsworth, J. D., & Conroy, D. E. (2006). Enhancing self-esteem of youth swimmers through coach training: Gender and age effects. *Psychology of Sport and Exercise, 7*, 173–192.

Coatsworth, J. D., & Conroy, D. E. (2009). The effect of autonomy-supportive coaching, need satisfaction, and self-perceptions on initiative and identity in youth swimmers. *Developmental Psychology, 45*, 320–328.

Conroy, D. E., & Coatsworth, J. D. (2007). Coaching behaviors associated with changes in fear of failure: Changes in self-talk and need satisfaction as potential mechanisms. *Journal of Personality, 75*, 383–419.

Cox, A., Duncheon, N., & McDavid, L. (2009). Teachers as sources of relatedness perceptions, motivation, and affective responses in physical education. *Research Quarterly for Exercise and Sport, 80*, 765–773.

Cox, A. E., & Whaley, D. E. (2004). The influence of task value, expectancies for success, and identity on athletes' achievement behaviors. *Journal of Applied Sport Psychology, 16*, 103–117.

Cox, A., & Williams, L. (2008). The roles of perceived teacher support, motivational climate, and psychological need satisfaction in students' physical education motivation. *Journal of Sport and Exercise Psychology, 30*, 222–239.

Crick, N. R., Bigbee, M. A., & Howes, C. (1996). Gender differences in children's normative beliefs about aggression: How do I hurt thee? Let me count the ways. *Child Development, 67*, 1003–1014.

Crocker, P.R.E., Hoar, S.D., McDonough, M.H., Kowalski, K.C., & Niefer, C. B. (2004). Emotional experience in youth sport. In M. R. Weiss (Ed.), *Developmental sport and exercise psychology: A lifespan perspective* (pp. 197–221). Morgantown, WV: Fitness Information Technology.

Crocker, P. R. E., Kowalski, K. C., Hoar, S. D., & McDonough, M. H. (2004). Emotion in sport across adulthood. In M. R. Weiss (Ed.), *Developmental sport and exercise psychology: A lifespan perspective* (pp. 197–221). Morgantown, WV: Fitness Information Technology.

Cury, F., Biddle, S. J. H., Sarrazin, P., & Famose, J. P. (1997). Achievement goals and perceived ability predict investment in learning a sport task. *British Journal of Educational Psychology, 67*, 293–309.

Davison, K. K. (2004). Activity-related support from parents, peers, and siblings and adolescents' physical activity: Are there gender differences? *Journal of Physical Activity and Health, 1*, 363–376.

Davison, K. K., Cutting, T. M., & Birch, L. L. (2003). Parents' activity-related parenting practices predict girls' physical activity. *Medicine and Science in Sports and Exercise, 35*, 1589–1595.

Davison, K. K., & Jago, R. (2009). Change in parent and peer support across ages 9 to 15 yr and adolescent girls' physical activity. *Medicine and Science in Sports and Exercise, 41*, 1816–1825.

Davison, K. K., Symons Downs, D., & Birch, L. L. (2006). Pathways linking perceived athletic competence and parental support at age 9 years to girls' physical activity at age 11 years. *Research Quarterly for Exercise and Sport, 77*, 23–31.

deCharms, R. (1968). *Personal causation: The internal affective determinants of behavior.* New York: Academic Press.

De Knop, P., Engstrom, L. M., Skirstad, B., & Weiss, M. R. (Eds.). (1996). *Worldwide trends in youth sport.* Champaign, IL: Human Kinetics.

Deci, E. L. (1975). *Intrinsic motivation.* New York: Plenum.

Deci, E. L., & Ryan, R. M. (1985). *Intrinsic motivation and self-determination in human behavior.* New York: Plenum Publishing Corporation.

Deci, E. L., & Ryan, R. M. (1987). The support of autonomy and the control of behavior. *Journal of Personality and Social Psychology, 53*, 1024–1037.

Dempsey, J. M., Kimiecik, J. C., & Horn, T. S. (1993). Parental influence on children's moderate to vigorous physical activity participation: An expectancy-value approach. *Pediatric Exercise Science, 5,* 151–167.

Denault, A-S., & Poulin, F. (2009). Predictors of adolescent participation in organized activities: A five-year longitudinal study. *Journal of Research on Adolescence, 19,* 287–311.

Dorsch, T. E., Smith, A. L., & McDonough, M. H. (2009). Parents' perceptions of child-to-parent socialization in organized youth sport. *Journal of Sport and Exercise Psychology, 31,* 444–468.

Duda, J. L., & Balaguer, I. (2007). Coach-created motivational climate. In S. Jowett & D. Lavallee (Eds.), *Social psychology in sport* (pp. 117–130). Champaign, IL: Human Kinetics.

Duda, J. L, & Treasure, D. C. (2010). Motivational processes and the facilitation of quality engagement in sport. In J. Williams (Ed.), *Applied sport psychology: Personal growth to peak performance* (6th ed., pp. 59–80). Boston, MA: McGraw Hill.

Duncan, S. C. (1993). The role of cognitive appraisal and friendship provisions in adolescents' affect and motivation toward activity in physical education. *Research Quarterly for Exercise and Sport, 64,* 314–323.

Dweck, C. S. (1999). *Self theories: Their role in motivation, personality, and development.* Philadelphia, PA: Psychology Press.

Ebbeck, V., & Gibbons, S. L. (1998). The effect of a team building program on the self-conceptions of grade 6 and 7 physical education students. *Journal of Sport and Exercise Psychology, 20,* 300–310.

Ebbeck, V., & Weiss, M. R. (1998). Determinants of children's self-esteem: An examination of perceived competence and affect in sport. *Pediatric Exercise Science, 10,* 285–298.

Eccles, J. S., Adler, T. E., Futterman, R., Goff, S. B., Kaczala, C. M., Meece, J. L., & Midgley, C. (1983). Expectancies, values, and academic behaviors. In J. T. Spence (Ed.), *Achievement and achievement motivation* (pp. 75–146). San Francisco, CA: W.H. Freeman.

Eccles, J. S., & Harold, R. D. (1991). Gender differences in sport involvement: Applying the Eccles' expectancy-value model. *Journal of Applied Sport Psychology, 3,* 7–35.

Eccles, J. S., Wigfield, A. W., & Schiefele, U. (1998). Motivation to succeed. In W. Damon (Series Ed.) & N. Eisenberg (Vol. Ed.), *Handbook of child psychology. Vol. 3: Social, emotional, and personality development* (5th ed., pp. 1017–1095). New York: Wiley.

Elliot, A. J. (1999). Approach and avoidance motivation and achievement goals. *Educational Psychologist, 34,* 169–189.

Evans, J., & Roberts, G. C. (1987). Physical competence and the development of children's peer relations. *Quest, 39,* 23–35.

Eys, M. A., Loughead, T. M., & Hardy, J. (2007). Athlete leadership dispersion and satisfaction in interactive sport teams. *Psychology of Sport and Exercise, 8,* 281–296.

Ferrer Caja, E., & Weiss, M. R. (2000). Predictors of intrinsic motivation among adolescent students in physical education. *Research Quarterly for Exercise and Sport, 71,* 267–279.

Ferrer Caja, E., & Weiss, M. R. (2002). Cross-validation of a model of intrinsic motivation with students enrolled in high school elective courses. *The Journal of Experimental Education, 71,* 41–65.

Fox, K. R., & Wilson, P. M. (2008). Self-perceptual systems and physical activity. In T. S. Horn (Ed.), *Advances in sport psychology* (3rd. ed., pp. 49–64). Champaign, IL: Human Kinetics.

Fredricks, J. A., & Eccles, J. S. (2002). Children's competence and value beliefs from childhood through adolescence:

Growth trajectories in two male-sex-typed domains. *Developmental Psychology, 38,* 519–533.

Fredricks, J. A., & Eccles, J. S. (2004). Parental influences on youth involvement in sports. In M. R. Weiss (Ed.), *Developmental sport and exercise psychology: A lifespan perspective* (pp. 145–164). Morgantown, WV: Fitness Information Technology.

Fredricks, J. A., & Eccles, J. S. (2005). Family socialization, gender, and sport motivation and involvement. *Journal of Sport and Exercise Psychology, 27,* 3–31.

Freedson, P. S., & Evenson, S. (1991). Familial aggregation in physical activity. *Research Quarterly for Exercise and Sport, 62,* 384–389.

Furman, W., & Buhrmester, D. (1985). Children's perceptions of the personal relationships in their social networks. *Developmental Psychology, 21,* 1016–1024.

Gagné, M., Ryan, R. M., & Bargmann, K. (2003). Autonomy support and need satisfaction in the motivation and well-being of gymnasts. *Journal of Applied Sport Psychology, 15,* 372–389.

Garcia Bengoechea, E., & Strean, W. B. (2007). On the interpersonal context of adolescents' sport motivation. *Psychology of Sport and Exercise, 8,* 195–217.

Gill, D. L., Gross, J. B., & Huddleston, S. (1983). Participation motivation in youth sports. *International Journal of Sport Psychology, 14,* 1–14.

Gill, D. L., & Williams, L. (2008). *Psychological dynamics of sport and exercise* (3rd ed.). Champaign, IL: Human Kinetics.

Gillet, N., Vallerand, R. J., Amoura, S., & Baldes, B. (2010). Influence of coaches' autonomy support on athletes' motivation and sport performance: A test of the hierarchical model of intrinsic and extrinsic motivation. *Psychology of Sport and Exercise, 11,* 155–161.

Glenn, S. D., & Horn, T. S. (1993). Psychological and personal predictors of leadership behavior in female soccer athletes. *Journal of Applied Sport Psychology, 5,* 17–34.

Gore, S., Farrell, F., & Gordon, J. (2001). Sports involvement as protection against depressed mood. *Journal of Research on Adolescence, 11,* 119–130.

Gould, D. (1993). Intensive sport participation and the prepubescent athlete: Competitive stress and burnout. In B. R. Cahill & A. J. Pearl (Eds.), *Intensive participation in children's sports* (pp. 19–38). Champaign, IL: Human Kinetics.

Gould, D., Horn, T., & Spreeman, J. (1983). Sources of stress in junior elite wrestlers. *Journal of Sport Psychology, 5,* 159–171.

Gould, D., Tuffey, S., Udry, E., & Loehr, J. (1996). Burnout in competitive junior tennis players: II. Qualitative analysis. *The Sport Psychologist, 10,* 341–366.

Gould, D., Udry, E., Tuffey, S., & Loehr, J. (1996). Burnout in competitive junior tennis players: I. A quantitative psychological assessment. *The Sport Psychologist, 10,* 322–340.

Hagger, M. S., Chatzisarantis, N. L. D., Barkoukis, V., Wang, C. K. J., & Baranowski, J. (2005). Perceived autonomy support in physical education and leisure-time physical activity: A cross-cultural evaluation of the trans-contextual model. *Journal of Educational Psychology, 97,* 376–390.

Harter, S. (1978). Effectance motivation reconsidered. *Human Development, 21,* 34–64.

Harter, S. (1981a). A model of intrinsic mastery motivation in children: Individual differences and developmental change. In W. A. Collins (Ed.), *Minnesota Symposium on Child Psychology* (Vol. 14, pp. 215–255). Hillsdale, NJ: Erlbaum.

Harter, S. (1981b). The development of competence motivation in the mastery of cognitive and physical skills: Is there still a place for joy? In G. C. Roberts & D. M. Landers (Eds.), *Psychology of motor behavior and sport—1980* (pp. 3–29). Champaign, IL: Human Kinetics.

Hartup, W. W. (1995). The three faces of friendship. *Journal of Social and Personal Relationships, 12*, 569–574.

Harwood, C., Spray, C. M., & Keegan, R. (2008). Achievement goal theories in sport. In T. S. Horn (Ed.), Advances in sport psychology (3rd. ed., pp. 157–186). Champaign, IL: Human Kinetics.

Hayashi, C. T., & Weiss, M. R. (1994). A cross-cultural analysis of achievement motivation in Anglo and Japanese marathon runners. *International Journal of Sport Psychology, 25*, 187–202.

Hein, V., & Hagger, M. S. (2007). Global self-esteem, goal achievement orientations, and self-determined behavioral regulations in a physical education setting. *Journal of Sport Sciences, 25*, 149–159.

Hein, V., & Koka, A. (2007), Perceived feedback and motivation in physical education and physical activity. In M. S. Hagger & N. L. D. Chatzisarantis (Eds.), *Intrinsic motivation and self-determination in exercise and sport* (pp. 127–140). Champaign, IL: Human Kinetics.

Henderlong, J., & Lepper, M. R. (2002). The effects of praise on children's intrinsic motivation: A review and synthesis. *Psychological Bulletin, 128*, 774–795.

Hollembeak, J., & Amorose, A. J. (2005). Perceived coaching behaviors and college athletes' intrinsic motivation: A test of self-determination theory. *Journal of Applied Sport Psychology.17*, 20–36.

Horn, T. S. (2004). Developmental perspectives on self-perceptions in children and adolescents. In M. R. Weiss (Ed.), *Developmental sport and exercise psychology: A lifespan perspective* (pp. 101–143). Morgantown, WV: Fitness Information Technology.

Horn, T. S. (2008). Coaching effectiveness in the sport domain. In T. S. Horn (Ed.), *Advances in sport psychology* (3rd ed., pp. 240–267). Champaign, IL: Human Kinetics.

Horn, T. S., & Amorose, A. J. (1998). Sources of competence information. In J. L. Duda (Ed.), *Advances in sport and exercise psychology measurement* (pp. 49–64). Morgantown, WV: Fitness Information Technology.

Horn, T. S., & Horn, J. L. (2007). Family influences on children's sport and physical activity participation, behavior, and psychosocial responses. In G. Tenenbaum & R. C. Eklund (Eds.), *Handbook of sport psychology* (pp. 685–711). Hoboken, NJ: Wiley.

Horn, T. S., Lox, C. L. & Labrador, F. (2010). The self-fulfilling prophecy theory: When coaches' expectations become reality. In J. M. Williams (Ed.), *Applied sport psychology: Personal growth to peak performance* (6th ed., pp. 81–105). Palo Alto, CA: Mayfield.

Horn, T. S., & Weiss, M. R. (1991). A developmental analysis of children's self-ability judgments. *Pediatric Exercise Science, 3*, 312–328.

Jaakkola, T., & Liukkonen, J. (2006). Changes in students' self-determined motivation and goal orientation as a result of motivational climate intervention within high school physical education classes. *International Journal of Sport and Exercise Psychology, 4*, 302–324.

Jacobs, J. E., & Eccles, J. S. (1992). The impact of mothers' gender-role stereotypic beliefs on mothers' and children's ability perceptions. *Journal of Personality and Social Psychology, 63*, 932–944.

Jensen, C. D., & Steele, R. G. (2009). Body dissatisfaction, weight criticism, and self-reported physical activity in pre-adolescent children. *Journal of Pediatric Psychology, 34*, 822–826.

Jowett, S., & Poczwardowski, A. (2007), Understanding the coach-athlete relationship. In S. Jowett & D. Lavallee (Eds.), *Social psychology in sport* (pp. 3–14). Champaign, IL: Human Kinetics.

Kimiecik, J. C., & Horn, T. S. (1998). Parental beliefs and children's moderate-to-vigorous physical activity. *Research Quarterly for Exercise and Sport, 69*, 163–175.

Kimiecik, J. C., Horn, T. S., & Shurin, C. S. (1996). Relationships among children's beliefs, perceptions of their parents' beliefs, and their moderate-to-vigorous physical activity. *Research Quarterly for Exercise and Sport, 67*, 324–336.

King, K. A., Tergerson, J. L., & Wilson, B. R. (2008). Effect of social support on adolescents' perceptions of and engagement in physical activity. *Journal of Physical Activity and Health, 5*, 374–384.

Kipp, L. E., & Amorose, A. J. (2008). Perceived motivational climate and self-determined motivation in female high-school athletes. *Journal of Sport Behavior, 31*, 108–129.

Klint, K. A., & Weiss, M. R. (1987). Perceived competence and motives for participating in youth sports: A test of Harter's competence motivation theory. *Journal of Sport Psychology, 9*, 55–65.

Koka, A., & Hagger, M. (2010). Perceived teaching behaviors and self-determined motivation in physical education: A test of self-determination theory. *Research Quarterly for Exercise and Sport, 81*, 74–86.

Kunesh, M. A., Hasbrook, C. A., & Lewthwaite, R. (1992). Physical activity socialization: Peer interactions and affective responses among a sample of sixth grade girls. *Sociology of Sport Journal, 9*, 385–396.

Ladd, G. W., & Price, J. M. (1993). Playstyles of peer-accepted and peer-rejected children on the playground. In C. H. Hart (Ed.), *Children on playgrounds: Research perspectives and applications* (pp. 130–161). Albany: State University of New York Press.

Lewthwaite, R., & Piparo, A. J. (1993). Goal orientations in young competitive athletes: Physical achievement, social-relational, and experiential concerns. *Journal of Research in Personality, 27*, 103–117.

MacPhail, A., Gorely, T., Kirk, D., & Kinchin, G. (2008). Children's experiences of fun and enjoyment during a season of sport education. *Research Quarterly for Exercise and Sport, 79*, 344–355.

Mageau, G. A., & Vallerand, R. J. (2003). The coach-athlete relationship: A motivational model. *Journal of Sports Sciences, 21*, 883–904.

Maehr, M. L., & Nicholls, J. G. (1980). Culture and achievement motivation: A second look. In N. Warren (Ed.), *Studies in cross-cultural psychology* (Vol. 3, pp. 221–267). New York: Academic Press.

Marsh, H. W., & Peart, N. D. (1988). Competitive and cooperative physical fitness training programs for girls: Effects on physical fitness and multidimensional self-concepts. *Journal of Sport and Exercise Psychology, 10*, 390–407.

McCullagh, P., & Weiss, M. R. (2002). Observational learning: The forgotten psychological method in sport psychology. In J. Van Raalte & B. W. Brewer (Eds.), *Exploring sport and exercise psychology* (2nd ed., pp. 131–149). Washington, DC: American Psychological Association.

Moran, M. M., & Weiss, M. R. (2006). Peer leadership in sport: Links with friendship, peer acceptance, psychological characteristics, and athletic ability. *Journal of Applied Sport Psychology, 2*, 97–113.

Newton, M., Duda, J. L., & Yin, Z. N. (2000). Examination of the psychometric properties of the Perceived Motivational Climate in Sport Questionnaire-2 in a sample of female athletes. *Journal of Sport Sciences, 18*, 275–290.

Nicaise, V, Bois, J., Fairclough, S. J., Amorose, A. J., & Cogérino, G. (2007). Girls' and boys' perceptions of physical education teachers' feedback: Effects on performance and psychological responses. *Journal of Sports Sciences, 25*, 915–926.

Nicaise, V, Cogérino, G., Bois, J., & Amorose, A. J. (2006). Students' perceptions of teacher's feedback and physical competence in physical education classes: Gender effects. *Journal of Teaching in Physical Education, 25*, 36–57.

Nicholls, J. G. (1989). *The competitive ethos and democratic education*. Cambridge, MA: Harvard University Press.

Ntoumanis, N. (2001). A self-determination approach to the understanding of motivation in physical education. *British Journal of Educational Psychology, 71*, 225–242.

Ntoumanis, N. (2005). A prospective study of participation in optional school physical education using a self-determination theory framework. *Journal of Educational Psychology, 97*, 444–453.

Ntoumanis, N., & Biddle, S. (1999). A review of motivational climate in physical activity. *Journal of Sports Sciences, 17*, 643–665.

Papaioannou, A., Marsh, H., & Theodorakis, Y. (2004). A multi-level approach to motivational climate in physical education and sport settings: An individual or group level construct? *Journal of Sport and Exercise Psychology, 26*, 90–118.

Passer, M. W. (1988). Determinants and consequences of children's competitive stress. In F. L. Smoll (Ed.), *Children in sport* (3rd ed., pp. 203–227). Champaign, IL: Human Kinetics.

Payne, V. G., & Morrow, J. R., Jr. (2009). School physical education as a viable change agent to increase youth physical activity. *President's Council on Physical Fitness and Sports Research Digest, 10* (2), 1–8.

Pelletier, L. G., Fortier, M. S., Vallerand, R. J., & Briére, N. M. (2001). Associations among perceived autonomy support, forms of self-regulation, and persistence: A prospective study. *Motivation and Emotion, 25*, 279–306.

Petlichkoff, L. M. (1993). Relationship of player status and time of season to achievement goals and perceived ability in inter-scholastic athletes. *Pediatric Exercise Science, 5*, 242–252.

Price, M. S., & Weiss, M. R. (2000). Relationships among coach burnout, coach behaviors, and athletes' psychological responses. *The Sport Psychologist, 14*, 391–409.

Price, M. S., & Weiss, M. R. (2011a). Peer leadership in sport: Relationships among personal characteristics, leader behaviors, and team outcomes. *Journal of Applied Sport Psychology, 23*, 49–64.

Price, M. S., & Weiss, M. R. (2011b). Relationships among coach leadership, peer leadership, and adolescent athletes' psychosocial and team outcomes: A test of transformational leadership theory. Manuscript submitted for publication.

Raedeke, T. D. (1997). Is athlete burnout more than just stress? A sport commitment perspective. *Journal of Sport and Exercise Psychology, 19*, 396–417.

Raedeke, T. D., & Smith, A. L. (2001). Development and preliminary validation of an athlete burnout measure. *Journal of Sport and Exercise Psychology, 23*, 281–306.

Raedeke, T. D., & Smith, A. L. (2004). Coping resources and athlete burnout: An examination of stress mediated and moderation hypothesis. *Journal of Sport and Exercise Psychology, 26*, 525–541.

Rees, C. R. (1983). Instrumental and expressive leadership in team sports: A test of leadership role differentiation theory. *Journal of Sport Behavior, 6*, 17–27.

Reeve, R. E., & Weiss, M. R. (2006). Sports and physical activities. In G. G. Bear & K. M. Minke (Eds.), *Children's needs III: Development, prevention, and intervention* (pp. 485–498). Bethesda, MD: National Association of School Psychologists.

Roberts, G. C., Treasure, D. C., & Conroy, D. E. (2007). Understanding the dynamics of motivation in sport and physical activity: An achievement goal interpretation. In G. Tenenbaum & R. C. Eklund (Eds.), *Handbook of sport psychology* (3rd ed., pp. 3–30). Hoboken, NJ: Wiley.

Rowold, J. (2006). Transformational and transactional leadership in martial arts. *Journal of Applied Sport Psychology, 18*, 312–325.

Rubin, K. H., Bukowski, W. M., & Parker, J. G. (1998). Peer interactions, relationships, and groups. In W. Damon (Series Ed.) & N. Eisenberg (Vol. Ed.), *Handbook of child psychology. Vol. 3: Social, emotional, and personality development* (pp. 619–700). New York: Wiley.

Ryan, R. M. (1995). Psychological need and the facilitation of integrative processes. *Journal of Personality, 63*, 397–427.

Ryan, R. M., & Connell, J. P. (1989). Perceived locus of causality and internalization: Examining reasons for acting in two domains. *Journal of Personality and Social Psychology, 57*, 749–761.

Ryan, R. M., & Deci, E. L. (2000). Self determination theory and the facilitation of intrinsic motivation, social development, and well being. *American Psychologist, 55*, 68–78.

Ryan, R. M., & Deci, E. L. (2002). An overview of self-determination theory: An organismic-dialectical perspective. In E. L. Deci & R. M. Ryan (Eds.), *Handbook of self-determination research* (pp. 3–33). Rochester, NY: The University of Rochester Press.

Ryan, R. M., & Deci, E. L. (2007). Active human nature: Self-determination theory and the promotion and maintenance of sport, exercise, and health. In M. S. Hagger & N. L. D. Chatzisarantis (Eds.), *Intrinsic motivation and self-determination in exercise and sport* (pp. 1–20). Champaign, IL: Human Kinetics.

Sabiston, C. M., & Crocker, P. R. E. (2008). Exploring self-perceptions and social influences as correlates of adolescent leisure-time physical activity. *Journal of Sport and Exercise Psychology, 30*, 3–22.

Sagar, S. S., & Lavallee, D. (2010). The developmental origins of fear of failure in adolescent athletes: Examining parental practices. *Psychology of Sport and Exercise, 11*, 177–187.

Salvy, S-J., Bowker, J. W., Roemmich, J. N., Romero, N., Kieffer, E., Paluch, R., & Epstein, L. H. (2008). Peer influence on children's physical activity: An experience sampling study. *Journal of Pediatric Psychology, 33*, 29–49.

Salvy, S-J., Roemmich, J. N., Bowker, J. C., Romero, N. D., Stadler, P. J., & Epstein, L. H. (2009). Effect of peers and friends on youth physical activity and motivation to be physically active. *Journal of Pediatric Psychology, 34*, 217–225.

Sanders, C. E., Field, T. M., Diego, M., & Kaplan, M. (2000). Moderate involvement in sports is related to lower depression levels among adolescents. *Adolescence*, 35, 793–797.

Sarrazin, P., Roberts, G. C., Cury, F., Biddle, S. J. H., & Famose, J. P. (2002). Exerted effort and performance in climbing among boys: The influence of achievement goals, perceived ability, and task difficulty. *Research Quarterly for Exercise and Sport*, 73, 425–436.

Sarrazin, P., Vallerand, R., Guillet, E., Pelletier, L., & Cury, F. (2002). Motivation and dropout in female handballers: A 21-month prospective study. *European Journal of Social Psychology*, 32, 395–418.

Scanlan, T. K., Carpenter, P. J., Lobel, M., & Simons, J. P. (1993). Sources of enjoyment for youth sport athletes. *Pediatric Exercise Science*, 5, 275–285.

Scanlan, T. K., & Lewthwaite, R. (1984). Social psychological aspects of competition for male youth sport participants: I: Predictors of competitive stress. *Journal of Sport Psychology*, 6, 208–226.

Scanlan, T. K., & Passer, M. W. (1979). Sources of competitive stress in young female athletes. *Journal of Sport Psychology*, 1, 151–159.

Scanlan, T. K., Ravizza, K. & Stein, G. L. (1989). An in-depth study of former elite figure skaters: I. Introduction to the project. *Journal of Sport and Exercise Psychology*, 11, 54–64.

Scanlan, T. K., & Simons, J. P. (1992). The construct of sport enjoyment. In G. C. Roberts (Ed.), *Motivation in sport and exercise* (pp. 199–216). Champaign, IL: Human Kinetics.

Scanlan, T. K., Stein, G. L., & Ravizza, K. (1991). An in-depth study of former elite figure skaters: II. Sources of stress. *Journal of Sport and Exercise Psychology*, 13, 102–120.

Schilling, T. A., & Hayashi, C. T. (2001). Achievement motivation among high school basketball and cross-country athletes: A personal investment perspective. *Journal of Applied Sport Psychology*, 13, 103–128.

Schmidt, G. W., & Stein, G. L. (1991). Sport Commitment: A model integrating enjoyment, dropout, and burnout. *Journal of Sport and Exercise Psychology*, 8, 254–265.

Schneider, M., Dunn, A., & Cooper, D. (2009). Affect, exercise, and physical activity among healthy adolescents. *Journal of Sport and Exercise Psychology*, 31, 706–723.

Schneider, M., Fridlund Dunton, G., & Cooper, D. M. (2008). Physical activity and physical self-concept among sedentary adolescent females: An intervention study. *Psychology of Sport and Exercise*, 9, 1–14.

Schofield, L., Mummery, W. K., Schofield, G., & Hopkins, W. (2007). The association of objectively determined physical activity behavior among adolescent female friends. *Research Quarterly for Exercise and Sport*, 78, 9–15.

Schunk, D. H. (1998). Peer modeling. In K. Topping & S. Ehly (Eds.), *Peer-assisted learning* (pp. 185–202). Mahwah, NJ: Erlbaum.

Sirard, J. R., Pfeiffer, K. A., & Pate, R. R. (2006). Motivational factors associated with sports program participation in middle school students. *Journal of Adolescent Health*, 38, 696–703.

Smith, A., Ntoumanis, N., & Duda, J. (2007). Goal striving, goal attainment, and well-being: Adapting and testing the self-concordance model in sport. *Journal of Sport and Exercise Psychology*, 29, 763–782.

Smith, A., Ntoumanis, N., & Duda, J. (2010). An investigation of coaching behavior, goal motives, and implementation intentions as predictors of well-being in sport. *Journal of Applied Sport Psychology*, 22, 17–33.

Smith, A. L. (1999). Perceptions of peer relationships and physical activity participation in early adolescence. *Journal of Sport and Exercise Psychology*, 21, 329–350.

Smith, A. L. (2003). Peer relationships in physical activity contexts: A road less traveled in youth sport and exercise psychology research. *Psychology of Sport and Exercise*, 4, 25–39.

Smith, A. L., Ullrich-French, S., Walker, E., II, & Hurley, K. S. (2006). Peer relationship profiles and motivation in youth sport. *Journal of Sport and Exercise Psychology*, 28, 362–382.

Smith, R. E., & Smoll, F. L. (2007). Social-cognitive approach to coaching behaviors. In S. Jowett & D. Lavallee (Eds.), *Social psychology in sport* (pp. 3–14). Champaign, IL: Human Kinetics.

Smith, R. E., Smoll, F. L, & Barnett, N. P. (1995). Reduction of children's sport performance anxiety through social support and stress-reduction training for coaches. *Journal of Applied Developmental Psychology*, 16, 125–142.

Smith, R. E., Smoll, F. L., & Cumming, S. P. (2007). Effects of a motivational climate intervention for coaches on young athletes' sport performance anxiety. *Journal of Sport and Exercise Psychology*, 29, 39–59.

Smoll, F. L., & Smith, R. E. (2002). Coaching behavior research and intervention in youth sport. In F. L. Smoll & R. E. Smith (Eds.), *Children and youth in sport* (pp. 211–231). Dubuque, IA: Kendall/Hunt.

Smoll, F. L., Smith, R. E., Barnett, N. P., & Everett, J. J. (1993). Enhancement of children's self-esteem through social support training for youth sport coaches. *Journal of Applied Psychology*, 78, 602–610.

Standage, M., Duda, J. L., & Ntoumanis, N. (2003). A model of contextual motivation in physical education: Using constructs from self-determination and achievement goal theories to predict physical activity intentions. *Journal of Educational Psychology*, 95, 97–110.

Standage, M., Duda, J. L., & Ntoumanis, N. (2006). Students' motivational processes and their relationship to teacher ratings in school physical education: A self-determination theory approach. *Research Quarterly for Exercise and Sport*, 77, 100–110.

Standage, M., & Gillison, F. (2007). Students' motivational responses toward school physical education and their relationship to general self-esteem and health-related quality of life. *Psychology of Sport and Exercise*, 8, 704–721.

Standage, M., Gillison, F., & Treasure, D. C. (2007), Self-determination theory and motivation in physical education. In M. S. Hagger & N. L. D. Chatzisarantis (Eds.), *Intrinsic motivation and self-determination in exercise and sport* (pp. 71–86). Champaign, IL: Human Kinetics.

Storch, E. A., Milsom, V. A., DeBraganza, N., Lewin, A. B., Geffken, G. R., & Silverstein, J. H. (2007). Peer victimization, psychological adjustment, and physical activity in overweight and at-risk-for-overweight youth. *Journal of Pediatric Psychology*, 32, 80–89.

Stuart, M. E. (2003). Sources of subjective task value in sport: An examination of adolescents with high or low value for sport. *Journal of Applied Sport Psychology*, 15, 239–255.

Stuntz, C. P., & Spearance, A. L. (2010). Cross-domain relationships in two sport populations: Measurement validation including prediction of motivation-related variables. *Psychology of Sport and Exercise*, 11, 267–274.

Stuntz, C. P., & Weiss, M. R. (2003). Influence of social goal orientations and peers on unsportsmanlike play. *Research Quarterly for Exercise and Sport, 74*, 421–435.

Stuntz, C. P., & Weiss, M. R. (2009). Achievement goal orientations and motivational outcomes in youth sport: The role of social orientations. *Psychology of Sport and Exercise, 10*, 255–262.

Stuntz, C. P., & Weiss, M. R. (2010). Motivating children and adolescents to sustain a physically active lifestyle. *American Journal of Lifestyle Medicine, 4*, 433–444.

Taylor, I. M., Ntoumanis, N., & Smith, B. (2009). The social context as a determinant of teacher motivational strategies in physical education. *Psychology of Sport and Exercise, 10*, 235–243.

Taylor, I. M., Ntoumanis, N., & Standage, M. (2008). A self-determination theory approach to understanding the antecedents of teachers' motivational strategies in physical education. *Journal of Sport and Exercise Psychology, 30*, 75–94.

Taylor, I. M., Ntoumanis, N., Standage, M., & Spray, C. M. (2010). Motivational predictors of physical education students' effort, exercise intentions, and leisure-time physical activity: A multilevel linear growth analysis. *Journal of Sport and Exercise Psychology, 32*, 99–120.

Taymoori, P., & Lubans, D. R. (2008). Mediators of behavior change in two tailored physical activity interventions for adolescent girls. *Psychology of Sport and Exercise, 9*, 605–619.

Tessier, D., Sarrazin, P., & Ntoumanis, N. (2008). The effects of an experimental programme to support students' autonomy on the overt behaviors of physical education teachers. *European Journal of Psychology of Education, 23*, 239–253.

Theeboom, M., De Knop, P., & Weiss, M. R. (1995). Motivational climate, psychosocial responses, and motor skill development in children's sport: A field-based intervention study. *Journal of Sport and Exercise Psychology, 17*, 294–311.

Tropp, K. J., & Landers, D. M. (1979). Team interaction and the emergence of leadership and interpersonal attraction in field hockey. *Journal of Sport Psychology, 1*, 228–240.

U.S. Department of Health and Human Services (2008). *2008 Physical Activity Guidelines for Americans.* Washington, DC.

Ullrich-French, S., & Smith, A. L. (2006). Perceptions of relationships with parents and peers in youth sport: Independent and combined prediction of motivational outcomes. *Psychology of Sport and Exercise, 7*, 193–214.

Ullrich-French, S., & Smith, A. L. (2009). Social and motivational predictors of continued youth sport participation. *Psychology of Sport and Exercise, 10*, 87–95.

Urdan, T. C., & Maehr, M. L. (1995). Beyond a two-goal theory of motivation and achievement: A case for social goals. *Review of Educational Research, 65*, 213–243.

Vallerand, R. J. (1997). Toward a hierarchical model of intrinsic and extrinsic motivation. In M. P. Zanna (Ed.), *Advances in experimental social psychology* (pp. 271–360). San Diego, CA: Academic Press.

Vealey, R. S., Armstrong, L., Comar, W., & Greenleaf, C. A. (1998). Influence of perceived coaching behaviors on burnout and competitive anxiety in female college athletes. *Journal of Applied Sport Psychology, 10*, 297–318.

Vierling, K. K., Standage, M., & Treasure, D. C. (2007). Predicting attitudes and physical activity in an "at-risk" minority youth sample: A test of self-determination theory. *Psychology of Sport and Exercise, 8*, 795–817.

Wankel, L. M., & Kreisel, P. S. J. (1985). Factors underlying enjoyment of youth sports: Sport and age group comparisons. *Journal of Sport Psychology, 7*, 51–64.

Weiss, M. R., & Amorose, A. J. (2005). Children's self-perceptions in the physical domain: Between- and within-age variability in level, accuracy, and sources of perceived competence. *Journal of Sport and Exercise Psychology, 27*, 226–244.

Weiss, M. R., & Amorose, A. J. (2008). Motivational orientations and sport behavior. In T. S. Horn (Ed.), *Advances in sport psychology* (3rd ed., pp. 115–155). Champaign, IL: Human Kinetics.

Weiss, M. R., Amorose, A. J., & Wilko, A. M. (2009). Coaching behaviors, motivational climate, and psychosocial outcomes among female adolescent athletes. *Pediatric Exercise Science, 21*, 475–492.

Weiss, M. R., Bhalla, J. A., & Price, M. S. (2007). Developing positive self-perceptions through youth sport participation. In H. Hebestreit & O. Bar-Or (Eds.), *The encyclopaedia of sports medicine. Vol. 10: The young athlete* (pp. 302–318). Oxford, England: Blackwell.

Weiss, M. R., Bredemeier, B. J., & Shewchuk, R. M. (1986). The dynamics of perceived competence, perceived control, and motivational orientation in youth sports. In M. R. Weiss & D. Gould (Eds.), *Sport for children and youths* (pp. 89–101). Champaign, IL: Human Kinetics.

Weiss, M. R., & Duncan, S. C. (1992). The relation between physical competence and peer acceptance in the context of children's sport participation. *Journal of Sport and Exercise Psychology, 14*, 177–191.

Weiss, M. R., & Ferrer Caja, E. (2002). Motivational orientations and sport behavior. In T. S. Horn (Ed.), *Advances in sport psychology* (2nd ed., pp. 101–184). Champaign, IL: Human Kinetics.

Weiss, M. R., & Fretwell, S. D. (2005). The parent-coach/child-athlete relationship in youth sport: Cordial, contentious, or conundrum? *Research Quarterly for Exercise and Sport, 76*, 286–305.

Weiss, M. R., & Hayashi, C. T. (1995). All in the family: Parent-child socialization influences in competitive youth gymnastics. *Pediatric Exercise Science, 7*, 36–48.

Weiss, M. R., Kimmel, L. A., & Smith, A. L. (2001). Determinants of sport commitment among junior tennis players: Enjoyment as a mediating variable. *Pediatric Exercise Science, 13*, 131–144.

Weiss, M. R., McCullagh, P., Smith, A. L., & Berlant, A. R. (1998). Observational learning and the fearful child: Influence of peer models on swimming skill performance and psychological responses. *Research Quarterly for Exercise and Sport, 69*, 380–394.

Weiss, M. R., & Petlichkoff, L. M. (1989). Children's motivation for participation in and withdrawal from sport: Identifying the missing links. *Pediatric Exercise Science, 1*, 195–211.

Weiss, M. R., & Smith, A. L. (1999). Quality of youth sport friendships: Measurement development and validation. *Journal of Sport and Exercise Psychology, 21*, 145–166.

Weiss, M. R., & Smith, A. L. (2002). Friendship quality in youth sport: Relationship to age, gender, and motivation variables. *Journal of Sport and Exercise Psychology, 24*, 420–437.

Weiss, M. R., Smith, A. L., & Stuntz, C. P. (2008). Moral development in sport and physical activity: Theory, research, and intervention. In T. S. Horn (Ed.), *Advances in sport psychology* (3rd ed. pp. 187–210). Champaign, IL: Human Kinetics.

Weiss, M. R., Smith, A. L., & Theeboom, M. (1996). "That's what friends are for": Children's and teenagers' perceptions of peer relationships in the sport domain. *Journal of Sport and Exercise Psychology, 18,* 347–379.

Weiss, M. R., & Stuntz, C. P. (2004). A little friendly competition: Peer relationships and psychosocial development in youth sport and physical activity contexts. In M. R. Weiss (Ed.), *Developmental sport and exercise psychology: A lifespan perspective* (pp. 165–196). Morgantown, WV: Fitness Information Technology.

Weiss, M. R., & Wiese-Bjornstal, D. M. (2009). Promoting positive youth development through physical activity. *President's Council on Physical Fitness and Sports Research Digest, 10*(3), 1–8.

Weiss, M. R., Wiese, D. M., & Klint, K. A. (1989). Head over heels with success: The relationship between self-efficacy and performance in competitive youth gymnastics. *Journal of Sport and Exercise Psychology, 11,* 444–451.

Weiss, M. R., & Williams, L. (2004). The *why* of youth sport involvement: A developmental perspective on motivational processes. In M. R. Weiss (Ed.), *Developmental sport and exercise psychology: A lifespan perspective* (pp. 223–268). Morgantown, WV: Fitness Information Technology.

Weiss, W. M., & Weiss, M. R. (2003). Attraction- and entrapment-based commitment among competitive female gymnasts. *Journal of Sport and Exercise Psychology, 25,* 229–247.

Weiss, W. M., & Weiss, M. R. (2006). A longitudinal analysis of sport commitment among competitive female gymnasts. *Psychology of Sport and Exercise, 7,* 309–323.

Weiss, W. M., & Weiss, M. R. (2007). Sport commitment among competitive female gymnasts: A developmental perspective. *Research Quarterly for Exercise and Sport, 78,* 90–102.

Weiss, W. M., Weiss, M. R., & Amorose, A. J. (2010). Sport commitment among competitive female athletes: Test of an expanded model. *Journal of Sports Sciences, 28,* 423–434.

Westre, K. R., & Weiss, M. R. (1991). The relationship between perceived coaching behaviors and group cohesion in high school football teams. *The Sport Psychologist, 5,* 41–54.

White, R. W. (1959). Motivation reconsidered: The concept of competence. *Psychological Review, 66,* 297–330.

Wilson, D. K., Williams, J., Evans, A., Mixon, G., & Rheaume, C. (2005). A qualitative study of gender preferences and motivational factors for physical activity in underserved adolescents. *Journal of Pediatric Psychology, 30,* 293–297.

Yukelson, D., Weinberg, R., Richardson, P., & Jackson, A. (1983). Interpersonal attraction and leadership within collegiate sport teams. *Journal of Sport Behavior, 6,* 28–36.

Zacharatos, A., Barling, J., & Kelloway, E. K. (2000). Development and effects of transformational leadership in adolescents. *The Leadership Quarterly, 11,* 211–226.

Zarbatany, L., Ghesquiere, K., & Mohr, K. (1992). A context perspective on early adolescents' friendship expectations. *Journal of Early Adolescence, 12,* 111–126.

Through a Fly's Eye: Multiple Yet Overlapping Perspectives on Future Directions for Human Motivation Research

Richard M. Ryan *and* Nicole Legate

Abstract

In this final chapter we examine future directions in motivation research by looking through the individual lenses of our volume authors. We review each chapter for viewpoints on new directions for research. Each chapter offers some unique ideas relevant to the particular area of inquiry, but there is also overlapping emphasis on several issues facing the field as a whole. The most widely cited future direction was for more research into dual-process models of motivation. There were also frequent calls for more intervention research, especially interventions in which process variables and active ingredients can be carefully assessed. A desire for more developmental and neuropsychological studies of motivation was also common among this selected group. The centrality of motivation for human adaptation and wellness makes the pursuit of these topics a central task for psychology.

Key Words: human motivation, dual processes, interventions, development, well-being

The centrality of motivation in human functioning and wellness is clear, and it supplies the rationale for this volume. As the papers included here highlight, motivation plays an essential role in adaptation and in both individual and collective well-being. In addition, many of the common assumptions about human motivation are wrong or overly simplistic, and contemporary research is yielding new insights into what moves us into action, for better or for worse.

Collectively these papers also underscore another fact: The factors that both underlie and influence motivation are complex and multilayered. In this volume, motivation is variously described as being molded through evolution; engendered by culture; facilitated or undermined by parents; impacted by social contexts such as work, school, and leisure settings; and dependent upon underlying neurological mechanisms. In other words, the science of

human motivation involves the fluid interplay of biological, psychological and sociocultural determinants of what moves us to action.

Given the importance and the level of complexity inherent in the study of human motivation, there is clearly only going to be increasing research activity on this topic in the years ahead. Where is the field headed? What gaps do motivation studies need to address? What are the proximal and distal problems in line for exploration and discovery?

Each Oxford volume in this series finishes with a "future directions" chapter, typically expressing the views of the editor(s). Although we could finish this volume with a chapter centering on our own views on the future of motivation research, our sensibilities suggest that we provide readers with a more democratic offering. So in this chapter, rather than letting the editor's singular (and rather myopic) views predominate, we will look through the multiple and independent lenses of our chapter authors to provide a "compound eye" view of the field's future directions.

To really see the benefits of presenting a "compound eye" view on future directions in motivation, it is important to understand a bit more about this system. A compound eye has some advantages, especially when looking ahead. For example, flies see through such a system, equipped with a convex surface carpeted by multiple "eyes" called *ommatidia*. Each ommatidium has its own lens, and it is pointed in a slightly different direction, much like the current perspectives represented in these handbook chapters. Yet in the fly, what each of the separate "eyes" senses significantly overlaps with those next to it (see, e.g., Riley, Harmann, Barrett, & Wright, 2008). These sensory inputs come together so that the fly perceives one image. Such a complex system of vision has both scope and redundancy built into it, contributing to the fly's highly skilled capacity to navigate and "find the sugar."

Within the present volume are 29 chapters from articulate leaders in the field of motivation, each peering into the future of our field. They are pursuing separate but interrelated theoretical questions, and in doing so harnessing and refining the scientific tools available. Each takes a unique perspective, but there is also overlap in visions of where the field should go. Why not let each of these ommatidium contribute its own uniquely weighted input to our perception? No doubt each will be distinct, but they may also overlap and offer redundancies that highlight the most pressing issues for future work in human motivation research. What compound vision might result?

Accordingly, in what follows we have reviewed each of the chapters in this volume to distill some of the salient directions for future research in the field of human motivation the chapter authors believe should be pursued. It is important to recognize that the authors, when invited to write for this volume, were not specifically asked to reflect on future directions in their chapters. Though some said little in this regard, many devoted significant attention to raising issues that they believe merit future pursuit. Some explicitly commented on the important questions needing to be further explored in their specific areas of research, and many reflected on the methodological and substantive directions the field of human motivation more generally ought to follow. Once presenting these "nutshell" summaries of the authors' reflections on future directions, we will see whether we can benefit from their compound vision.

Future Directions in Motivation: Assembling a Compound View

Each of the authors of this volume highlights important new directions for the study of motivation as he or she sees it. We present these in the order they appear in the volume. Some of these recommendations for future research are specific to the theoretical framework reviewed in the chapter, but just as often authors also pointed to common gaps in motivation research that currently leave important questions less than fully answered.

General Theories of Human Motivation
SOCIAL COGNITIVE THEORY AND MOTIVATION
Dale H. Schunk and Ellen L. Usher

• Schunk and Usher raised questions about the applicability of social cognitive theory across all age groups. Because some learning and experiences of self-efficacy may often require complex cognitive capacities, the authors believe that understanding developmental constraints on these motivational processes represents an important area of further research. Longitudinal methods may help elucidate these questions about developmental changes in self-efficacy and learning.

• Moreover, because most social cognitive research in motivation has been conducted in Western societies, Shunck and Usher called for a broader examination of the cross-cultural relevancy of the theory.

• Specific to social cognitive theory, Schunk and Usher believe that future research should focus on how modeled observations can combine with learner practice to "optimize motivational effects." They pointed to the importance of technology in carrying out this objective. Making modeling more accessible to learners through computers and hand-held devices could make new and diverse modeling opportunities possible. Moreover, having learners watch their own performance on video could improve their ability to self-model.

CYBERNETIC CONTROL AND SELF-REGULATION OF BEHAVIOR
Charles S. Carver and Michael F. Scheier

• In their discussion of the self-regulation of behavior and emotion, Carver and Scheier reexamined some previous assumptions about the hierarchy of behavioral controls. New insights about the dual modes of functioning, and dimensionality within emotions, have prompted this reconsideration. They suggested that a model of hierarchical organization of the self and its goals likely involves "pressures toward compatibility" among values and attitudes. At the same time, lower levels of self-regulation may operate independently of higher levels of self-regulation and may sometimes be in conflict with them. Testing this idea of compatibility (which in our work in self-determination theory we might think of in terms of integration) is seen by Carver and Scheier as an important area for investigation.

• The authors also raised questions concerning other compatibility-related conflicts in self-control. For example, does self-control pit longer and shorter term goals against each other, as usually thought, or does self-control pit the two mental modes against each other (automatic tendencies vs. planful effort to restrain behavior)?

• They also wondered whether future research might apply their feedback theory to more fully address the core motivational processes involved in growth and optimal functioning. For example, perhaps enjoyment signals that engaging in the experience is moving the person toward another goal that is already part of the self. More generally understanding ties between affective feedback and growth functions is an agenda for future research.

TERROR MANAGEMENT THEORY
Pelin Kasebir and Tom Pyszczynski

• In line with terror management theory's (TMT) tradition of employing innovative methods, Kasebir and Pyszczynski called for more new and creative methods, beyond death-thought accessibility methodology, to explore new territory in terror management processes.

• The authors saw TMT's applications to psychopathology and fostering peace as other important future directions of research.

• They also saw further investigation into meaning and certainty, both epistemic and existential forms, as helping to reconcile TMT with other theories about meaning (Heine, Proulx, & Vohs, 2006; Lind & van den Bos, 2002).

• Recognizing that death reminders can have a positive impact on some individuals, the authors suggest that TMT move beyond only looking at the "darker side" of human motivation and begin

to explore in more depth how death can be a "constructive, empowering force" for people.

TOO MUCH OF A GOOD THING? TRADE-OFFS IN PROMOTION AND PREVENTION FOCUS
Abigail A. Scholer and E. Tory Higgins

• Scholer and Higgins hoped to see future research move beyond analysis at the individual level to explore how groups of individuals with different levels of promotion and prevention orientations work together. This line of research could help elucidate what work environments look like when they are maximizing the benefits of these two motivational systems.

• Understanding how promotion and prevention motivations work together with other motivations (namely locomotion and assessment motivations) was another area identified for future investigation. The authors reasoned that understanding the bigger picture of how these different regulatory systems interact could help to maximize the benefits and minimize the costs of each particular motivational system. This is in line with their main argument throughout the chapter that more motivation isn't necessarily better—there are trade-offs involved with each motivational system.

MOTIVATION, PERSONALITY, AND DEVELOPMENT WITHIN EMBEDDED SOCIAL CONTEXTS: AN OVERVIEW OF SELF-DETERMINATION THEORY
Edward L. Deci and Richard M. Ryan

• A theme of this chapter was how people exist within embedded social contexts that affect their psychological need satisfactions and wellness both directly and indirectly. Deci and Ryan were thus especially interested in developing a better understanding of how different levels of social influence (e.g., interpersonal, institutional, cultural, politico-economic) interact to impact motivational outcomes and well-being.

• There was special interest in both new historical and technological trends that are changing the traditional avenues of socialization and modes of influence on goals and values. Particularly noted was the extending reach of corporate capitalism, and increasing exposure to media and interactive technologies, and their role in facilitating or undermining basic need satisfactions.

• Their comments also focused on the study of forces that thwart or facilitate peoples' basic needs within and across diverse settings as potentially informing policy and interventions aimed at fostering individual and community wellness.

Motivational Processes

EGO DEPLETION: THEORY AND EVIDENCE
Mark Muraven

• Muraven sees a better understanding of how practicing self-control helps to build self-control as a critical next step in ego-depletion research. Understanding this pathway will be valuable for the theory and for designing interventions. Knowing more about practice effects can specifically inform interventions by identifying tasks that are most effective to practice, and by specifying the optimum practice time and frequency that leads to improvements in self-control. Interventions that aim to build self-control could have value for the individual for society, as self-control is involved in many important behaviors like controlling aggression, getting along with others, and resisting temptation.

• Another direction for future research that Muraven identified involves the finding that depletion leads to greater passivity. Exploring this finding further and connecting it to changes in the brain may help create a more comprehensive and unified theory of depletion.

FLOW
Susan A. Jackson

• Jackson pointed to the importance of investigating neurological and psychophysiological correlates of flow for the theory's advancement. Utilizing such methods, she argues, is crucial to a deeper understanding about what systems are in play when an individual is in a state of flow.

• She also recommended that future research continue to examine both individual differences and situational factors (e.g., competition) that facilitate and hinder the flow experience. Furthermore, Jackson also raised questions as to how person and situational variables interact to affect the different dimensions of flow. Additionally, how do these dimensions of flow shift across contexts and within individuals? She identified this interplay of context and person as one of the most important directions for the future of flow research.

IMPLICIT-EXPLICIT MOTIVATION CONGRUENCE
Todd M. Thrash, Laura A. Maruskin, and Chris C. Martin

• In their chapter, Thrash, Maruskin and Martin pointed out a lot of variation in how congruence in implicit and explicit motivation is operationalized and modeled across studies. Because these differences lead to different conceptualizations and different robustness of findings, the authors called for a more careful and explicit rationale when operationalizing the construct and presenting one's analytic approach in future studies on congruence.

• They also raised an interesting question that we have sometimes wondered ourselves: Why not cite Freud? Many of Freud's writings can speak to congruence in implicit and explicit motives, and the authors argue that ignoring these insights "undermines rather than serves scientific credibility and progress." Thrash et al. suggested that when possible, researchers should better understand and utilize historical insights.

• Practicing what they preach, the authors highlight insights from Freud about integrating incongruence as a direction for future research. Though acceptance is typically thought to be the only way to integrate incongruence, there are two other "healthy" ways to integrate incongruent motives posited by Freud that merit exploration: rejection and sublimation. The authors encouraged researchers to consider these other options as a means of integration, as both rejection and sublimation of motives (especially implicit ones) can be accomplished in self-determined and mindful ways.

• Another future direction of research in congruence that the authors identified is to move beyond a between-persons level of analysis. Exploring how an individual varies across time and across "content domains" in the congruence of their implicit and explicit motives represents an important and unexplored area of investigation.

CURIOSITY AND MOTIVATION
Paul J. Silvia

• Silvia wondered whether the different lines of thought on curiosity couldn't be connected in future pursuits on curiosity and motivation. He suggested some connections between self-determination theory and emotion psychology, for example. He encouraged researchers to be open to bridging theories in an effort to better understand the motive of curiosity, with the risk that doing so might result in changes to the concept of curiosity.

- Silvia also pointed to exploring the interplay of traits and states as a direction of future research in curiosity. Looking at how "curious traits influence curious states" using a variety of new methods could advance the field of curiosity in motivation. He also suggested examining the "midrange" level of curiosity (the level of idiosyncratic interests), especially how it develops, as a future direction.

INTEREST AND ITS DEVELOPMENT
K. Ann Renninger and Stephanie Su

- Renninger and Su suggest that future interest research focus more on developmental transformations. For example, can the meaning of factors like novelty vary across phases of interest and across age groups?
- The authors also wondered about the role of contextual supports in facilitating interest at different phases of interest development, and they suggested this too as an important future area of research.
- They also encouraged interest researchers to draw upon the existing body of work in interest to better understand differences in studies using different measures and methods. This could help provide a more unified and comprehensive understanding of interest.

Goals and Motivation
ACHIEVEMENT GOALS: EXAMINING THE THOUGHTS, ATTITUDES, AND BEHAVIORS THAT CHARACTERIZE PEOPLE'S COMPETENCE-BASED PURSUITS
Kou Murayama, Andrew J. Elliot, and Ron Friedman

- Murayama, Elliot, and Friedman identified the processes underlying goal pursuit as an important priority for future investigation in achievement goals. Understanding this process could help inform interventions.
- They also detailed ways to advance achievement goal work, including extending the framework by using a "3x2 framework" to understand different types of achievement goals, and better understanding the consequences of mastery-avoidance goals.

- The authors also called for broader methodologies such as priming, diary methodologies, and continued work on developing interventions.
- Other areas of needed investigation identified by the authors involved a more fine-tuned understanding of the interdependent relations between achievement goals.
- They also suggested that understanding how situational factors may affect achievement goals and understanding potential cultural differences in these effects would be an important area for future research.

GOAL REGULATION AND IMPLEMENTATION: GOAL SETTING AND GOAL STRIVING
Peter M. Gollwitzer and Gabriele Oettingen

- Gollwitzer and Oettingen saw future directions in goal regulation and implementation as better understanding how mental contrasting and implementation intentions can best help people create goals that help them fulfill their wishes.
- The authors discussed an intervention that taught people how to effectively set and implement goals by themselves, and carrying out more of these interventions would be a worthy pursuit for future goal research.
- They also called for more focus on potential mediators of the effects of goal regulation and implementation, such as increased efficacy or control beliefs.

UNCONSCIOUS GOAL PURSUIT: NONCONSCIOUS GOAL REGULATION AND MOTIVATION
Henk Aarts and Ruud Custers

- Aarts and Custers encouraged more investigation of the role of awareness of goals in producing behavior. Many questions remained unanswered, such as whether consciousness mediates goal-priming effects. To answer such questions, they recommend that manipulation checks always be used, and eventually researchers should develop more refined methods to examine just how conscious people are of goal primes directing their behavior (e.g., Seth, Dienes, Cleeremans, Overgaard, & Pessoa, 2008).
- The authors highlighted another challenging question for future research: How do unconscious goals "flexibly control" behavior?

• The authors also raised many questions about when consciousness can play a role in goal pursuit. They wondered whether consciousness may facilitate performance in some contexts more than others, and whether consciousness may be especially important in stopping, or overriding behavior.

• Moreover, the authors suggested that an important avenue of future research is determining whether consciously and unconsciously activated goals stimulate cognitions and the brain in similar or distinct ways. Diverse methods and levels of analysis, especially at the neurological level, are likely needed to answer these questions and yield additional insights on goal-related processes and efficacy.

THE MOTIVATIONAL COMPLEXITY OF CHOOSING: A REVIEW OF THEORY AND RESEARCH
Erika A. Patall

• Patall believes that future research in choice should explore whether the effects of choice go beyond the effect of having one's preferences.

• She also thought it was important that researchers focus on factors that enhance or inhibit choice effects. She raised the important issue of systematically testing, through experimental design, certain assumptions that are made in the literature about choice, such as about the effort required for making different types of choices.

• Future research in choice should also test how factors like interest, perceived competence, and developmental age interact to affect different motivational outcomes.

• Patall also saw research on the mechanisms and pathways through which choice leads to different motivational outcomes as another important direction.

ON GAINS AND LOSSES, MEANS AND ENDS: GOAL ORIENTATION AND GOAL FOCUS ACROSS ADULTHOOD
Alexandra M. Freund, Marie Hennecke, and Maida Mustafić

• Freund, Hennecke, and Mustafić discussed the potential benefits and mechanisms of a process focus as opposed to an outcome focus in people's goal orientation. They found that a process focus helps with adaptation after failure, and they encouraged future research on goal focus to test this relatively new idea. Yet because age-related shifts in goal orientation research are relatively new, future research should continue to examine the trajectories of people's orientation of goal focus across the life span using longer term longitudinal designs.

• The authors also state that future research will have to show the incremental validity of goal focus above and beyond well-established motivational constructs such as intrinsic and extrinsic motivation.

Motivation in Relationships
SELF-ENHANCEMENT AND SELF-PROTECTION MOTIVES
Constantine Sedikides and Mark D. Alicke

• Sedikides and Alicke believe that exploring the dynamic between self-enhancement and self-protection motives is an important pursuit for new research. As these motives can operate independently, and may also interact in unknown ways, they recommended that researchers treat these motives as separate dimensions rather than as two ends of a continuum. Treating these motives as separate dimensions can help answer questions about how they may facilitate or impede one another in different contexts and also help to examine their interplay with other self-evaluation motives.

• The authors wondered about the relations between implicit and explicit self-enhancement and self-protection motives. They advocated using new methodologies to help elucidate these relations and their functional effects.

• They also called for future research exploring the situational factors and individual differences that constrain self-enhancement and self-protection.

THE GENDERED BODY PROJECT: MOTIVATIONAL COMPONENTS OF OBJECTIFICATION THEORY
Tomi-Ann Roberts and Patricia L. Waters

• In discussing self-objectification and its many adverse consequences to health and psychological well-being, Roberts and Waters wondered why some individuals are motivated to engage in self-objectification behaviors and others aren't.

• Given the current cultural climate, understanding the factors that promote resilience in the face of societal pressures to conform is critical for developing interventions that could start to bolster resilience to self-objectification in girls and women. Designing interventions to reduce objectification of girls and women at the community and societal level, and interventions to promote resilience to societal pressures at the individual level, represent important next steps to reduce adverse outcomes like disordered eating, body shame, and depressive symptoms.

• The authors suggested that self-objectification can be thought of as motivated behavior but also as a type of amotivation, or external locus of control with respect to norms of physical attractiveness. Testing these ideas in relation to other theories of motivation will be important in advancing self-objectification theory.

PARENTS AND MOTIVATION: THE ROLE OF RELATEDNESS
Eva M. Pomerantz, Cecilia Sin-Sze Cheung, and Lili Qin

• Many themes emerged in Pomerantz, Cheung, and Qin's chapter about parenting and motivation that they identified as important empirical questions to test. For example, understanding how different phases of the parent–child relationship impact children's academic functioning, and understanding the limits of relatedness to children's academic functioning represent two closely related lines of future research discussed by the authors.

• The authors also believe that further understanding of developmental pathways, such as how children's sense of responsibility to parents may have an increased effect on their motivation over time, is needed in future research. They also called for examination of this issue cross-culturally.

AVOIDING THE PITFALLS AND APPROACHING THE PROMISES OF CLOSE RELATIONSHIPS
Shelly L. Gable and Thery Prok

• Gable and Prok called for the field of approach and avoidance social motivation to move beyond examining individual differences to look at the situational factors, such as environmental cues for incentive or threat, that influence an individual to pursue interpersonal goals. Understanding cues in the environment and other situational influences represents a fruitful area of future research.

• They considered it important for future research to examine implicit incentives and threats and their impacts on motivation.

• They also wondered whether it is possible for people to learn to focus on different relationship

goals, especially those low in approach or high in avoidance goals. Interventions on people's relationship goal tendencies, such as by cueing incentives, could be important for improving relationship functioning and wellness.

• The authors called for more careful study of how motives and goals operate in long-term relationships over time.

Evolutionary and Biological Perspectives
NEUROPSYCHOLOGY AND HUMAN MOTIVATION
Johnmarshall Reeve and Woogul Lee

• A goal of Revee and Lee's chapter was to show the relevance of neuroscience to motivation research in an effort to expand the field through introducing new methodology and theoretical conceptualizations. They wondered about the future of motivation and neuroscience, and how much the two fields will come to influence one another. They put this future in the hands of motivation researchers, who will need to be open and willing to learn more about neuroscience and its methods for this advancement to occur.

• The authors raised many questions that will require a good deal of empirical support to eventually answer. For example, they asked whether neuroscience is relevant to only some parts of motivation or whether it is relevant to more general and complex types of motivation. Another question they posed as meriting inquiry: Can the brain generate motivation of its own? Or is the motivation at the neurological level always a response to environmental events?

• They also encouraged more research on the compatibility of dependent measures in neuroscience, such as reaction times and cortical activations, with typical outcomes in motivation research. Research in motivational neuroscience has begun to identify neural bases of different motivational states, but completing such an endeavor might arguably be the biggest challenge facing this field.

EVOLVED INDIVIDUAL DIFFERENCES IN HUMAN EMOTION
Larry C. Bernard

• Bernard advocates for more support from other areas of investigation, including comparative psychology and behavioral genetics, to further the study of evolved individual differences in personality and motivation.

He believes that future research should test multiple and conflicting motives to understand how they may interact to shape behavior. Moreover, it is important to test how different strengths in motive dimensions shape social cognition.

• Bernard highlighted experimental personality research as a direction of future research.

• He also saw potential utility of evolved individual differences in applied areas such as education, industrial/organizational, health, and clinical psychology.

MOODS OF ENERGY AND TENSION THAT MOTIVATE
Robert E. Thayer

• Thayer hoped that future investigations could help clarify how complex moods arise. He discussed "seemingly paradoxical effects" resulting from biopsychological states that simultaneously activate and deactivate the body, and thus suggested investigating these biopsychological states further as an important avenue in future research. He implied that moving beyond cross-sectional designs could help clarify the interplay of energetic and tense arousal producing complex moods. Experience or event sampling methodologies could be useful to future work.

• Another unanswered issue that Thayer raised as a direction for future research concerns determining the "moderate point at which increasing tension leads first to increased energy but at some point to reduced energy."

EFFORT INTENSITY: INSIGHTS FROM THE CARDIOVASCULAR SYSTEM
Guido H. E. Gendolla, Rex A. Wright, and Michael Richter

• Gendolla, Wright, and Richter identified more investigation into the roles that consciousness and automaticity play in expending effort as an important future direction. Do people always consciously determine how much effort to mobilize for a behavior? The authors asserted that effort could become learned to the point of automaticity. Although the authors reviewed some evidence supporting this, they suggested that more research needs to be conducted before clear claims can be made about implicit effort mobilization.

• They wondered whether awareness might also explain some of the mechanisms through which certain effort mobilization effects occur.

• The authors suggested that future research examine the roles of personality and individual differences, and situational variables like task context and task framing on effort intensity and mobilization.

• They also encouraged future researchers to conduct studies using other physiological correlates, such as brain activity, in tandem with cardiovascular measurements to better understand how the central and autonomic nervous systems interact to mobilize effort.

Motivation in Application
MOTIVATION IN PSYCHOTHERAPY
Martin Grosse Holtforth and Johannes Michalak

• Grosse Holtforth and Michalak asserted that motivation is critical for psychotherapy in all patients, and as such it should inform many aspects of therapy. A great deal of research is needed to answer the questions that they raise about motivational factors in psychotherapy. For example, insofar as motivational factors are linked to the onset and maintenance of psychopathology, what are the mechanisms underlying these links? Also on the issue of mechanism, the authors wonder about the mechanisms that underlie change in different therapeutic approaches.

• Are there changes in both implicit and explicit motivation during psychotherapy interventions? Do different types of therapies change these two motivations in different ways?

• To the extent that cultural factors impact motivation, how do they impact treatment?

• Addressing the authors' question about brain changes corresponding to changes in motivation during the course of therapy necessitates incorporating neuroscience methods into treatment outcome studies.

• Clearly, diverse methodologies are needed to answer these complex questions. The authors proposed that experimental and longitudinal designs can help clarify these questions and advance future research in this field.

MOTIVATION IN EDUCATION
Allan Wigfield, Jenna Cambria, and Jacquelynne S. Eccles

• Wigfield, Cambria, and Eccles believe that the issue of how individual differences in children, namely gender and ethnic differences, and different classroom contexts impact student's motivation merits attention for future research.

• They encouraged future research to move beyond self-report measures of motivations and outcomes. They noted that conducting interviews and having multiple informants could help create a more complete picture of children's motivation in the classroom.

• They urged researchers to continue to do intervention work, especially quasi-experimental designs and randomized trials, in classrooms at all education levels (from early elementary grades to high school).

• The authors also identified collaboration with policy makers as an important next step to make sure that findings from motivation research, especially interventions, can better inform school reform in an effort to optimize children's motivation in school.

ADVANCES IN MOTIVATION IN EXERCISE AND PHYSICAL ACTIVITY
Martin S. Hagger

• Hagger identified interventions to change physical activity behavior as a main avenue for future research. He believes that careful evaluation of physical activity interventions is critical for understanding the "active ingredients" of change and of basic mechanisms of motivation.

• He prioritized replicating and manualizing interventions as a direction for future studies, and as such called upon researchers to detail all aspects of their interventions, including how they evaluate treatment fidelity.

• Hagger also pointed to research about implicit and explicit motivational processes on physical activity behavior as another valuable future area.

WORK MOTIVATION: DIRECTING, ENERGIZING, AND MAINTAINING RESEARCH
Adam M. Grant and Jihae Shin

• Grant and Shin hope to see researchers extend the scope of outcomes of work motivation into more specific topics such as creativity and task persistence.

• They also would like to see more work on the effects of a broader range of rewards, such as recognition and appreciation, on motivation. Understanding these other reward structures

may also help elucidate other conditions that can facilitate motivation.

• Grant and Shin suggest that moving beyond the individual level of analysis is an important area for advancement of work motivation. Examining how motivation operates in work groups and teams, for example, merits more research attention.

• They also encouraged future research focusing on the issue of worker motivation over time. Research that employs longitudinal methods could address this issue.

MOTIVATION IN SPORT AND PHYSICAL ACTIVITY
Maureen R. Weiss, Anthony J. Amorose, and Lindsay E. Kipp

• Weiss, Amorose, and Kipp identified the issue of how family dynamics affect physical activity motivation in youth as a needed direction for future research. For example, family structure differences (e.g., single- vs. two-parent households) and family characteristics such as socioeconomic status may differentially impact sports and physical activity motivation. Understanding how these factors interact to facilitate or hinder motivation may serve to elucidate risk and protective factors, and help inform interventions and populations to be targeted.

• Furthermore, these authors would like to understand in a fine-tuned way the parts of interventions that are more or less effective, such as the optimum length of time for a coaching intervention. They encouraged further investigation into the "active ingredients" producing change in coaching and teaching behaviors that lead to enhanced motivation in children.

• They also thought that it is important for future research to determine *how* and *why* peer groups and friendships affect physical activity motivation.

• They proposed that a variety of methodologies are necessary to accomplish these objectives, including ethnographic, interview, observational, and survey methods.

Motivation's Future: What's the Buzz?
Remembering that our *Oxford Handbook of Human Motivation* authors were not explicitly asked to write about future directions, most nonetheless did make some forward-looking comments. In our review of articles we tried to cull these visions

into a cohesive picture of the future of motivation work. Of course, each of our "ommatidium" provided some unique ideas, typically connected with the specific area of research. But some overlap, or redundancy occurred, and we focus on that.

Perhaps the most widely cited future direction that emerged was, at least for us, a somewhat surprising one. Mentioned more than any other area for future research was investigations of *dual-process models* or more study of the distinctions and relations between automatic, or implicit, and deliberative, or explicit, goals. The fact that this interest emerged in so many papers reflects motivation researchers' renewed interest in nonconscious processes and the motivated behavior they can organize. We would add to this the strong interest in the dynamic nature of motivation, as implicit and explicit processes can operate congruently or be in conflict. So despite our surprise it should have been of little wonder that this was the most saliently expressed future direction in the field, since it has both basic research and broad applied implications.

Alongside more examination of implicit and explicit processes, perhaps the next most frequently mentioned future direction was a call for more intervention research, including controlled or randomized clinical trials. The ideas expressed in this vein were not simply calls to "do good" with our knowledge. Instead, oft echoed was the idea that through intervention research we can significantly advance the basic science of human motivation. In attempting to test the efficacy and "stickiness" of interventions we gain greater understanding of mechanisms and basic processes at work, especially if we are careful to both appropriately randomize and measure potential mediators and moderators of obtained effects. Insofar as many theoretical traditions in the field of motivation are experimentally based, intervention research can also help establish the generalizability and relevance of theory to representative populations and everyday contexts.

A third frequently cited direction for future research was the call for more developmental and longitudinal research. Reflecting again the fact that so much theory in this volume is primarily founded upon experimental methods, and therefore focuses on short timeframes and proximal outcomes, the call for longitudinal research has at least two implications. First, longitudinal research advances our causal models because it can allow for some quasi-causal modeling and hypothesis testing. More important perhaps, developmental research would take seriously the idea that motivation transforms over time—changing in its qualities and complexity. Understanding these transformations and the systematic influences of maturation, context, and culture on motivational changes and manifestations over time clearly concerns our volume authors.

Following these "big three" themes of dual process, intervention and developmental research, emerging as important future directions were calls for greater integration between biological and psychological methods and theorizing. As Reeve and Lee point out in their chapter on the neuroscience of human motivation, more of a two-way street needs to develop between neuropsychology and behavioral scientists, one that navigates between the dual hazards of reductionism on the one hand and "floating" unanchored psychological constructs on the other. The excitement here is that mapping of psychological processes onto real-time biological correspondents offers opportunities to test hypothetical processes with a level of detail and resolution not previously accessible in our science. We might add here that this call for more integration was not limited to neuroscience. It is clear that we more broadly need to attach our motivation theories to biological functioning, including physiological measures of effort, exertion, arousal, and fatigue, as exemplified in the work reviewed by Gendolla, Wright, and Richter in this volume.

The only final big category that spanned across the majority of chapters was a desire for more understanding of how individual differences influence motivation. Here we include both calls for more studies of behavioral genetics, as well as more measurement of traits and stable characteristics that emerge in development from interactions of the genome with cultural and environmental factors. Individual differences are indeed understudied in a field that tends to focus on experimental methodologies and situational manipulations and effects. But clearly our experimental effects are frequently moderated by individual differences, many of which are still to be identified in their importance and mechanisms of influence. Put differently, individual differences qualify even the most common effects we study in this field, from the effects of mortality salience on defenses, to the impact of interpersonal controls on intrinsic motivation. Our authors identify our lack of focus on these moderating differences (other than as control variables) as a major gap in our knowledge.

Among the other topics for future direction that were mentioned frequently were the following: more studies of within-person changes over time, more studies of cultural and economic system influences on motivation, more studies of group (as opposed to individual) motivational processes, and more attention to motivation at the interface between humans and technology. And of course most every author called for more refined and sharper tools for digging into their particular plots within this field of study.

When all of these authors' perspectives coalesce into one compound eye, it is clear that there is plenty of territory yet to explore within the field of human motivation. To get there, the fly's eye view suggests that we will especially need to intensify research efforts with regard to nonconscious motivational processes, accomplish more integrative work with biologists and comparative psychologists, and engage in more informative, research-intensive interventions, among other important future directions. Our hope is that the contributions within this volume help researchers envision new ways forward, so that we can satisfy not only our curiosity about human nature but also optimize our derived knowledge to help enhance human well-being, adaptation, and our collective quality of life. So let's get buzzing.

Reference

Riley, D. T., Harmann, W. M., Barrett, S. F., & Wright, C. H. (2008). *Musca domestica* inspired machine vision sensor with hyperacuity. *Bioinspiration and Biomimetics*, 3, 026003.

INDEX

A

ability, effort intensity and, 424–425
academic function. *See also* student
    motivation
    achievement goals for, 200
    autonomy climates, 95
    choice as benefit for, 254–255, 255
    high-stakes rewards for, 99–100
    lack of willpower for, 222
    responsibility of children to parents
        and, 341–342, 344–345
Acceptance and Commitment Therapy
    (ACT), 453, 454–455, 457
achievement goals, 558
    approach-avoidance distinctions in,
        194–195
    in classroom setting, 200
    competence and, 195–196
    contextual effects of, 199–201
    definition of, 195–196
    dichotomous model of, 191–193
    extrinsic, 196
    future research on, methodological
        expansion in, 201–202
    goal pursuit and, 234
    historical development of, 191–195
    integrated model for, 193
    learning-performance model of,
        192
    measurement of, 197–198
    in multiple goals model, 198
    as omnibus construct, 195
    performance-approach, 198–199
    performance-avoidance, 198–199
    social, 196–197
    as specific aim, 195–196
    task-ego model of, 192–193
    as theory, physical activity and,
        485–487, 492–493, 524–526
    trichotomous model of, 194
    2 x 2 model of, 194–195
    work-avoidance, 196
achievement goal theory, youth motivation
    and, 524–526

achievement motivation theory,
    choice in, 250
The Achievement Motive (McClelland/
    Atkinson/Clark/Lowell), 142–143
ACT. *See* Acceptance and Commitment
    Therapy
action, affect and, 34
actional phase, for motivations, 291,
    292–293
action awareness, in flow, 128–129
activated freeze response, 416
activation, of motives, 8
activity. *See* physical activity
adaptation
    for adult development goals, 283
    of goal focus, 289–290
    in objectification theory, 324–325
addictive behaviors. *See also* alcohol
    consumption; tobacco use
    self-control and, 112
ADHD. *See* attention-deficit hyperactivity
    disorder
adult development, goals for, 281
    adaptation in, 283
    age as influence on, 283
    compensation in, 282–283
    goal focus and, 285–288
    goal selection and, 282
    multidirectionality of, 281–283
    multiple goal management and, 282
    optimization for, 282–283
    resource conservation in, 282–283
affect. *See also* complex moods; moods;
        negative affect; positive affect
    action and, 34
    approach-related, 34
    associative learning and, 369
    avoidance-related, 34
    biological mechanisms for, 32–33
    bipolar dimensions, 34–35
    dimensions of, 33–34
    emotion and, 32
    feedback control and, 32–36
    interest development and, 176

lack of willpower and, 223
    motive congruence and, 151
    negative, priority management and, 30
    parental, in SDT, 339–340
    positive, as counterintuitive, 35–36
    priority management and, 36
    reference criterion for, 33
affiliation, need for, 353
affiliation motives, 353
    approach, 353
    avoidance, 353
age
    adult goal development by, 283
    change goals and, 289–290
    gender development for girls by,
        328–329
    goal focus and, 285–288
    outcome focus for goals and, 290
    process focus for goals and, 290
    responsibility of children to parents
        by, 344
    stability goals and, 290
    work motivation influenced by,
        513–514
agency
    collective, 15
    neural foundation for, 372–373
    reciprocal interactions and, 14–15
aggressive behavior
    ego depletion and, 116
    evolved individual motives for,
        392–393
AIM-Q. *See* Assessment of Individual
    Motives-Questionnaire
akrasia, 221. *See also* willpower, lack of
alcohol consumption
    dysfunctional goals and, 448
    ego depletion and, 114–115
    self-awareness and, 57
Alliance Fostering Therapy, 449
Allport, Gordon, 304
altruism, 395
Ames, C., 193
analytical processing, prevention-focused

individuals and, 77
anxiety-buffer hypothesis, 47
   PTSD and, 51
anxiety disorders, in prevention-focused
      individuals, 70
appearance motive, 393
approach affiliation motives, 353
approach-related affect, 34
approach *versus* avoidance processes
   in achievement goal models, 194–195
   affect and, 34, 34
   for close relationship formation,
      352–353, 355–356
   eagerness-related approach strategies,
      215
   in feedback control, 32
   in goal focus, 288
   in goal striving, 215
Aristotle, 221
Arnold, Felix, 159
aspirations. *See also* extrinsic life goals;
      goals; intrinsic life goals
   cultural contexts for, 97
   in goal striving, 215
Assessment of Individual Motives-
      Questionnaire (AIM-Q), 398
assimilation, in BTAE, 310–311
associative learning, as motivational state,
      369–370
   affect and, 369
   environmental incentives in, 369
   liking in, 369–370
Atkinson, J.W., 142–143
attachment, personal relationships and,
      53–54
   existential threats and, response to, 54
attachment theory, 336–339
   parental relationships in, 337–338
   parental sensitivity in, 338
   peer relationships in, 338
   security perceptions in, 343
   teacher relationships in, 338
attention-deficit hyperactivity disorder
      (ADHD), 219
attitudes, in planned behavior theory, 481
attribution theory, choice in, 252
autonomous motivation. *See also* extrinsic
      motivation; intrinsic motivation
   benefits of, 90
   causality orientations for, 87, 90–91
   within corporate capitalism, 99
   cultural influences on, 89–90, 96–97
   feedback for, 94
   identified regulation in, 89
   integrated regulation in, 89
   introjection in, 89
   outcomes from, 89–90
   in psychotherapy, 443, 448–449
   social-contextual effects of, 93–96
   wellness and, 96–97
autonomy. *See also* choice
   as basic psychological need, 87
   causality orientations for, 87, 90–91

for children, in SDT, 340
controlling climates for, 94–95
ego depletion and, 121
intrinsic motivation and, 87–88
in personal relationships, 95–96
purpose of, 85
in SDT, 85–86
self-awareness and, 102
self-control and, 121
supportive climates for, 94–95
autonomy-controlling climates, 94–95
   in health care settings, 95
   in school settings, 95
   social contexts for, 95
   in workplace settings, 95
autonomy orientation, 90–91
autonomy-supportive climates, 94–95
   in health care settings, 95
   relational supports in, 94
   in school settings, 95
   social contexts for, 95
   in workplace settings, 95
autotelic experience, 129–130
avoidance affiliation motives, 353
avoidance goals, well-being and, 447
avoidance processes. *See* approach
      versus avoidance processes; illness
      avoidance; performance-avoidance
      goals; threat avoidance, in close
      relationships; work-avoidance goals
avoidance-related affect, 34

B

balanced selection for phenotypes,
      in FFM, 384
BAS. *See* Behavioral Activity System
basic psychological needs, in SDT, 87,
      101–102
   autonomy as, 87
   for children, 339
   extrinsic life goals and, as antagonistic
      to, 92
   intrinsic life goals for, 92
   physical activity and, 484–485,
      488–489, 524
   weekend effect and, 101
Becker, Ernest, 45
Behavioral Activity System (BAS), 356
behavioral control, self-efficacy and,
      515–516
Behavioral Inhibition System (BIS), 356
behavioral syndrome theory, 382
   in evolved individual difference theory,
      389–390
   extraversion in, 386
   FFM and, 385–386
behavior theory, curiosity in, 160
better-than-average-effect (BTAE),
      307–311
   aggregate comparisons in, 310
   assimilation in, 310–311
   attribute valence in, 308
   contrast in, 310–311

controllability of traits in, 308
egocentrism and, 309–310
focalism and, 310
individuated entities in, 310
nonmotivational explanations for,
      309–311
as pancultural, 308
prevalence of, among populations,
      307–308
psychological health and, 314
psychological interests and, 315
self-affirmation and, 309
self-threat and, 309
verifiability of attributes in, 308–309
Beyond Boredom and Anxiety
      (Csikszentmihalyi), 130
bias. *See* encoding biases; self-serving bias
Billings, Josh, 311
binge eating, self-awareness and, 57
Binswanger, Ludwig, 48
BIS. *See* Behavioral Inhibition System
breasts, sexual objectification of, 326–327
Brumberg, Joan, 323
BTAE. *See* better-than-average-effect

C

calm energy, 414
   flow and, 414
calm tiredness, 415
capitalism. *See* corporate capitalism
cardiovascular reactivity, to effort intensity,
      423
career choice, self-efficacy and, 23
causality orientations, 87, 90–91
   autonomy orientation, 90–91
challenge in flow, skills in balance with,
      128, 130
change goals, 289–290
children. *See also* relatedness, for children;
      youth motivation, for physical activity
   adoption of parental values, 342
   attachment theory perspective on,
      336–339
   autonomy for, in SDT, 340
   basic psychological needs of, in SDT,
      339
   investment and engagement in, 336
   parental affect and, in SDT, 339–340
   parental relationships for, in
      attachment theory, 337–338
   parental sensitivity towards, in
      attachment theory, 338
   peer relationships for, in attachment
      theory, 338
   responsibility to parents, 341–342
   SDT perspective on, 339–341
   self-efficacy in, 25
   socialization of, in SDT, 339
   teacher relationships for, in attachment
      theory, 338
choices, 559
   in academic achievement motivation,
      254–255, 255

in achievement motivation theory, 250
in attribution theory, 252
autonomy and, 258–260, 264
characteristics of, 257–263
cognitive dissonance and, 252
competence from, perceptions of, 261,
   263–264
control and, 258
correspondence with target and,
   269–270
cultural differences as influence on,
   265–267
as demotivator, 255–257
by developmental level, 267
disadvantages of, 256
in dissonance theory, 252
in drive theories, 249
effort level for, 260–262
ego depletion from, 256
in expectancy-value theories, 249–
   250, 250
as experience, 251–257
frame of reference for, 262
future research on, 271–272, 272
individual orientations for, 250–251,
   263–268
interest level and, 263
intrinsic motivation and, 253
maladaptive, 249
maximization strategies for, 264–265
motivations for, 249–251
as motivator, 251–255
multiplicity of, influence of, 261–262
through nonconscious processes, 251
outcome desirability and, 269
perceived versus actual, 257
perceptions of, 257–260
in planned behavior theory, 250
power of, 248
preferences as influence on, 270–271
in psychological theory, 248
realism of setting and, 268–269
in regulatory focus theory, 265
as reward-based, 249
satisficing strategies for, 264–265
in SDT, 253
self-efficacy from, 254, 264
in self-perception theory, 252–253
in self-presentational enhancement
   situations, 268
self-regulation and, 250, 256
situational characteristics and,
   268–270
in social learning theory, 250
socioeconomic differences influenced
   by, 265–267
task type and, 269
Clarification Oriented Therapy, 453, 457
Clark, R.A., 142–143
classical conditioning, unconscious goal
   pursuit and, 233
close relationships, 560
advantages of, 351–352

approach versus avoidance processes in,
   352–353, 355–356
BAS for, 356
BIS for, 356
disadvantages of, 351–352
emotion in, 357–358
evolutionary development of, 351
functional development of, 351
goal type and, 355
incentives for, 354
interpersonal outcomes, in approach
   versus avoidance motivation,
   355–356
intimacy motivation in, 353–354
outcome-goal link processes for,
   356–358
social bonds as, 350–351
social information in, 356–357, 357
social motivation and, 353–354
threat avoidance for, 354
coasting, positive affect and, 35
cognition
ego depletion and, 116
energetic arousal and, 411–412
environmental inquisitiveness and, 392
cognitive modeling, for vicarious
   learning, 17
collective agency, in reciprocal
   interactions, 15
collective efficacy, 24
sources of, 24
for teachers, 24
commitment, as tradeoff
benefits of, 74–75
evolved individual motives for,
   394–395
in mental contrasting, 212
in prevention-focused individuals,
   72–75
signal detection paradigms, 74
in women, 395
comparative psychology, in FFM,
   384–385
compensation, in adult development
   goals, 282–283
competence
achievement goals and, 195–196
from choice, 261, 263–264
in physical activity motivation,
   parental expression of, 530–531
student motivation and, 464
youth physical activity motivation
   and, 540–542
competence motivation theory
as domain specific, 521
effectance motivation in, 521
peer influence in, 521
for physical activity, 521–522
positive effect in, 521–522
self-perception of competence in, 521
skill mastery in, 521
youths and, for physical activity,
   521–522

competitions, lack of willpower, 222
complex moods, 413–415
calm energy, 414
calm tiredness, 415
tense energy, 415
tense tiredness, 414–415
computer-mediated environments, flow
   in, 132
concentration, in flow, 129
Concept-Oriented Reading Instruction
   (CORI), 472
conditioning. See classical conditioning
conscientiousness, willpower and,
   224–225
consciousness. See private body
   consciousness
consilience, in motivation studies, 6
consistency, in motives, 150–151
context learning, stimulus-response rules
   and, 236
control. See also control theory; feedback
   control; self-control
choice and, 258
in flow, 129
in planned behavior theory, 481–482
self-efficacy and, 515–516
student motivation and, 464
controlled motivations. See extrinsic
   motivation
control theory, 6
individual differences in motivation,
   400
cooperative learning, 471
Core flow scales, 135
CORI. See Concept-Oriented Reading
   Instruction
corporate capitalism, 98
autonomous motivation within, 99
extrinsic life goals and, 99
materialism from, 99
reward contingencies in, 98–99,
   99–100
correspondence of content, for motives,
   147–148
creativity
flow and, 132
in promotion-focused individuals,
   76–77
within work motivation, 514–515
Csikszentmihalyi, M., 130
cultural values
evaluation of, 97
female self-objectification and, 330
need satisfaction and, 97
culture
aspirations and, contexts for, 97
autonomous motivation influenced by,
   89–90, 96–97
BTAE and, as pancultural, 308
choice influenced by, 265–267
female self-objectification and, 330
group belonging and, 52–53
need satisfaction and, 97

responsibility of children to parents
and, 345
SDT and, 86–87, 96–97
social cognitive theory and, relevance
of, 25–26
student motivation influenced by,
473–474
values in, 97, 97
worldview validation through, 52
curiosity, 557–558
in behavior theory, 160
diversive, 159
drive-reduction model for, 158
emotional theory for, 160–161
as "for its own sake" motivation,
159–161
future research applications for,
163–164
global, 162
I-D model of, 162
individual differences in, 161–163
information gaps model for, 159
interest as influence on, 161
novelty reduction and, 157–159
openness to experience and, 162–163
reward-aversion model for, 160
specific, 159
uncertainty reduction and, 157–159
cybernetic processes, for self-regulation,
28–29, 555–556
feedback control, 29–31
hierarchy for, 29
for motivations, 38–40
theory development for, 28–29
Cyrenaics, 304

D

death, awareness of. See also existential
anxiety; existential psychology
DTA hypothesis and, 47
escaping from, 56–58
flight fantasies and, 49
from frailty of human body, 48–49
health-promoting behaviors from,
48–49
religious belief and, 55
self-esteem and, 49–51
in TMT, 46
in wilderness settings, 49
death-thought accessibility (DTA)
hypothesis, 47
Decision-Fostering Intervention (DFI),
453–454
decision making
dopamine hypothesis of positive
affect and, 370
ego depletion and, 116
implicit motivational states for, neural
bases of, 370–371
rational motivational states for, neural
bases of, 371–372
somatic marker hypothesis for, 371
delay of gratification tasks, 221–222

delegation hypothesis, 219
democratic systems, 100–101
Demosthenes, 304
depression
failure and, 69–70
hedonic incentive and, 431–432
personal goals and, 447–448
priority management and, 36
promotion-focused individuals
and, 70
self-system theory and, 70
desirability, motivation and, 209
developmental psychology
children's responsibility to parents
in, 344
choice in, 267
effortful control in, 37
Dewey, John, 159–160, 160
DFI. See Decision-Fostering Intervention
DFS-2. See dispositional flow scale-2
diet and nutrition, energetic arousal
and, 410
Dinnerstein, Dorothy, 326
discrepancy-enlarging feedback loop,
29–30
for overt behavior, 30
in personality psychology, 30
in social psychology, 30
discrepancy-reducing feedback loop, 29
for overt behavior, 30
in personality psychology, 30
in social psychology, 30
disinhibition effects, in vicarious
learning, 16
dispositional flow scale-2 (DFS-2), 134
dissonance theory, choice in, 252
cognitive dissonance, 252
diversive curiosity, 159
diversive exploration, 158
dopamine system, in reward-based
motivated action, 367–368
dopamine hypothesis of positive
affect, 370
expectancy and, 376
drive-reduction model, 158
diversive exploration as revision
of, 158
optimal arousal approach to, 158–159
drive theories, choice in, 249
DTA hypothesis. See death-thought
accessibility hypothesis
Dweck, C.S., 192
dysfunctional goals, alcohol
consumption and, 448

E

eagerness-related approach strategies, 215
early grade school, student motivation
during, 469–471
economic systems, in SDT, 97–99
corporate capitalism, 98
human capital in, 98
The Economist, 50–51

education, 561–562. See also academic
function; learning; student
motivation
grading systems and, 470
transition to schools and, 469–471
as value, in student motivation, 465
EEG. See electroencephalography
effectance motivation, 521
efficacy. See collective efficacy; self-efficacy
effortful control, in feedback control, 37
effort intensity, 561
ability and, 424–425
cardiovascular reactivity to, 423
difficulty in, variability of status for,
421–422, 423–427
ego involvement in, 430–431
empirical evidence for, 423–432
fatigue and, 425–426
future research implications for,
433–435
hedonic incentive for, 431–432
implicit determination of, 433–434
individual differences in, 434
measurement for, 422–423
mood and, 426–427, 431–432
in motivation intensity theory,
420–422
outcome expectancy for, 428–429
personality and, 434
physiological correlates of, 435
self-evaluation of, 431
social evaluation of, 429–430
success in, variables for, 427–432
task context and, 434
theory development for, 418
egocentrism, BTAE and, 309–310
ego depletion, 7, 557
aggressive behavior and, 116
alcohol consumption and, 114–115
autonomy and, 121
as biologically mediated, 118
causes of, 113–114
from choice, 256
cognitive effects of, 116
consequences of, 114–117
conservation of resources and,
119–120
decision making with, 116
EEG methodology for, 117
ego strength and, 112–113
EMG activation and, 116–117
expectancy accounts in, 117–118
future research models for, 123
glucose levels and, 118
implementation intentions in, 120
inhibitions of urges with, 115
interpersonal behaviors and, 113–114
interpersonal effects from, 115–116
moderators of, 120–121
motivation and, 119
operations for, 117–118
physiological markers of, 116–117
positive affect and, 120–121

after rest, 120–121
risk taking and, 116
self-affirmation and, 121
self-control and, 111
as self-fulfilling, 117–118
self-perception with, 116
from suppression of self, 114
susceptibility to persuasion with, 115
ego involvement
in achievement goal model, 192–193
success and, 430–431
ego strength
development of, 121–122
from self-control, 112–113, 122
electroencephalography (EEG), 117
electromyographic (EMG) activation,
116–117
embedded contexts, motivations in, 86–87
EMG activation. *See* electromyographic
activation
emotions, 560–561
affect and, 32
in close relationships, 357–358
curiosity and, 160–161
interest and, 172
mood compared to, 408
priority management and, influenced
by, 36
self-efficacy and, 22
in social interaction, 357–358
youth physical activity motivation
and, 542–544
employees, in expectancy theory, 507
enactive learning, 15
encoding biases, 311–312
End Poem (Rilke), 59
energetic arousal, 409–412
calm energy mood, 414
cognition and, 411–412
complex moods from, 413–415
diet and, 410
endogenous cycle of, 409
physical activity and, 411
sleep and, 410–411
stress and, 412
subjective, 409–410
well-being and, 409–410
environmental incentives, 369
environmental inquisitiveness, 392
cognitive function and, 392
Epicureans, 304
episodic memory, self-efficacy and, 376
equity theory, work motivation and,
507–508
critical assessment of, 508
ESM. *See* Experience Sampling Method
evolutionary psychology, sexual
objectification in, 324–325
evolutionary theory, individual differences
in motivation in, 382
evolved individual differences, in
motivation, 386–397
with aggression, 392–393

for altruism, 395
for appearance, 393
background for, 386–387
behavioral syndromes and, 389–390
for commitment, 394–395
components of, 388
in dyadic domains, 392–394
for environmental inquisitiveness, 392
for illness avoidance, 391–392
in individual domains, 391–392
for interpersonal inquisitiveness, 392
in large group domains, 395–396
MAT for, 387
for meaning, 397
for mental efforts, 393–394
motives in, 389–390
in multilevel selection theory, 395
operational definitions for, 389–390
physical stature and status, 394
PRF for, 387
sexuality and, 393
for social exchange, 395–396
theory development for, 387–391
for threat avoidance, 391
tradeoffs in, 391–397
in very large group domains, 396–397
for wealth accumulation, 394
existential anxiety, 48–58
flight fantasies and, 49
future research on, 58–59
group belonging and, 52–53
health-promoting behaviors from,
48–49
hero worship and, 56
from human sexuality, 49
materialism and, 49
after 9/11 attacks, 57
personal dimensions of, 49–51
personal relationships and, 53–54
physical dimensions of, 48–49
from problems of body, 48–49
psychopathology of, 51
religious belief and, 55
self-esteem and, 49–51
social dimension of, 52–54
spiritual dimension of, 54–56
SSB and, 50
symbolic immortality and, 50–51
worldview validation in, 52–53
existential psychology, 45
objectification theory and, 326–327
TMT and, 45–48
existential self-awareness, 45
anxiety from, motivational role of,
48–58
expectancy
dopamine systems and, influence on,
376
ego depletion and, 117–118
neural foundation for, 375–376
reward prediction error and, 375
in self-enhancement, 313
in self-protection, 313

in SSB, 306
success and, from effort intensity,
428–429
expectancy theory, work motivation and,
506–507
critical assessment of, 506–507
employee belief changes under, 507
planned behavior theory and, 506
expectancy-value theories
attainment values in, 527
choice in, 249–250, 250
gender in, 527
interest values in, 527
in neuroscience, 373–374
parental influence in, 527–528
utility values in, 527
for youth motivation, for physical
activity, 526–528
Experience Sampling Method (ESM),
130, 133–134
experiential system, in feedback control,
37
explicit motives, 557
consistency in, 150–151
correspondence of content for,
147–148
disattenuation approaches in,
148–149
incongruence in, 154
independence of, 154
integrative general model for, 145–146
measure methodology for, 142–146,
148–149
MTMM analysis of, 149
omnibus effect of multiple
methodological factors, 146–147,
154
private body consciousness in,
150–151
in psychotherapeutic motivation, 442
self-monitoring of, 150–151
statistical independence in, 144
exploration, as tradeoff
through materialism, 75
maximization desires and, 75
for promotion-focused individuals,
75–76
unintended losses from, 76
external regulation, in OIT, 484
extraversion
in behavioral syndrome theory, 386
in fluctuating phenotype selection,
for FFM, 384
in personality psychology, 381
extrinsic achievement goals, 196
process focus for goals and, 284
extrinsic life goals, 91–93
attainment of, 92–93
basic psychological needs and, as
antagonistic to, 92
corporate capitalism and, 99
manipulation of, 93
psychological health influenced by, 92

pursuit of, 92
research on, 93
extrinsic motivation, 88–89
as external regulation, 88
identified regulation in, 89
integrated regulation in, 89
introjection in, 89
neural foundation for, 374–375
outcome focus for goals and, 284
for physical activity, 523–524
social context effects on, 96
work motivation and, 511

F

failure, as tradeoff, 67, 67–71
affective consequences of, 295–296
behavioral consequences of, 294–295
depression and, 69–70
emotional intensity for, 68
emotional quality of, 68–69
goal focus after, consequences of, 294–296
happiness and, 69
as means-related, 294
as outcome-related, 294
strategic preferences and, 71–72
fantasy realization, theory of, 211
fatigue, effort intensity and, 425–426
mental, 426
feedback
autonomous motivation and, 94
in flow, 129
self-enhancement and, 313–314
self-protection and, 313–314
in unconscious goal pursuit, 239
for youth motivation, 532–533
feedback control, 29–31. See also negative feedback; positive feedback
affect and, 32–36
approach and avoidance processes in, 32
effortful control in, 37
experiential system in, 37
goal sequences in, 31, 38
hierarchical organization of, 31–32, 37–38
impulsive systems in, 37
levels of abstraction in, 31
loops in, 29–30
in overt behavior, 30–31
planfulness in, 38
principles in, 31
processes in, 29–30, 30–31
programs in, 31
rational system in, 37
reflecting systems in, 37
self-control and, 38
two-mode models for, 37–38
feedback loops, 29–30
concurrent function for, 34
discrepancy-enlarging, 29–30
discrepancy-reducing, 29
elements of, 29
homeostasis in, 30–31

females. See women
feminism, sexual objectification and, 324
Five-Factor model of personality (FFM), 382–386
background of, 382
balanced selection in, for phenotypes, 384
behavioral syndromes and, 385–386
comparative psychology in, 384–385
criticisms of, 386
evolution mechanisms for, 382–386
fluctuating selection in, for phenotypes, 383–384
life history theory and, 385
stabilizing selection in, for phenotypes, 382–383
tradeoffs in, 383–384
flight fantasies, 49
flow, as concept, 57, 557
action awareness in, 128–129
autotelic experience and, 129–130
calm energy mood and, 414
challenge-skills balance in, 128, 130
in computer-mediated environments, 132
control in, 129
creativity and, 132
definition of, 127–128
dimensions of, 128–130
ESM for, 130, 133–134
facilitation of, 136–137
feedback in, 129
Flow Scales for, 132, 134–136, 137–138
FSS for, 132
future research applications for, 137–138
goal clarity in, 129
hypnotic susceptibility and, 137
identification of, 127
influential factors for, 136
macro experiences, 128
measurement of, 133–136
model for, 128
motive congruence and, 152
neural foundation for, 375
perfectionism and, 132
qualitative methodology for, 133
quantitative methodology for, 133–136
research examples of, 130–132
self-consciousness in, loss of, 129
self-reporting measures for, 138
in sports settings, 131
task concentration with, 129
time perception and, 129
Flow Scales, 132, 134–136, 137–138
Core, 135
Long, 134, 134–135
potential uses of, 135–136
Short, 135
Flow State Scale (FSS), 132
FSS-2, 134

fluctuating selection for phenotypes, in FFM, 383–384
extraversion in, 384
focalism, BTAE and, 310
forethought, 376
"for its own sake" motivation, 159–161
Four-Phase model, of interest, 167, 169–171
developmental factors in, 170–171
individual interest in, 169
learner characteristics in, 175
situational interest in, 169
Frenzel, A.C., 178–179
Freud, Anna, 304
Freud, Sigmund, 153–154, 304
friendships, youth motivation influenced by, 536–537
FSS. See Flow State Scale

G

game structures, 455
game theory, 400
gender. See also objectification theory
in expectancy-value theories, 527
vicarious learning and, 17
gender development, for girls
by age level, 328–329
cognitive developmental theories for, 328–330
media influences on, 331
sexual objectification and, 328–330
socialization theories for, 328
gendered body project, 323, 331
self-esteem and, 331
general bodily arousal, 415–416
General Psychotherapy (GPT) model, 451
generational differences, in work motivation, 514
global curiosity, 162
glucose levels, ego depletion and, 118
goals. See also achievement goals; goal orientation; goal pursuit; goal setting; goal striving; learning goals; performance goals
abstractness of, 210–211
for adult development, 281
avoidance, 447
change, 289–290
close relationships and, 355
definition of, 4, 18, 191
difficulty of, 18
dysfunctional, 448
extrinsic, in life, 91–93
extrinsic achievement, 196
feedback control and, as sequences, 31, 38
in flow, 129
habits and, as automatic, 237
inequality of, 281
inhibition of, in prevention orientation, 69
inhibition of, in promotion orientation, 69

interference of, 239
intervention studies for, 225–226
intrinsic, in life, 91–93
learning, 18–19
of motivational psychotherapy, 456
motivation compared to, 208–210
new, sources of, 39–40
performance-approach, 198–199
performance-avoidance, 198–199
shielding of, 217
social, for physical activity, 525
social achievement, 196–197
in social cognitive theory, 18–19
stability, 290
work-avoidance, 196
goal focus, 283–296, 559. *See also* goal
    orientation; outcome focus, for
    goals; process focus, for goals
adaptation of, 289–290
affective consequences after failure,
    295–296
age and, 285–288
approach *versus* avoidance processes
    in, 288
behavioral consequences after failure,
    294–295
for change goals, 289–290
change in, 288–290
after failure, consequences of,
    294–296
maintenance in, 286
means usage frequency in, 289
motivational phase and, 291–293
resources for, 287, 289
in self-system theory, 287–288
for stability goals, 290
stability of, 288–290
time perspectives and, 287–288
goal-interference, 239
goal orientation, 281, 559
adaptation of, 283
age as influence on, 283
compensation in, 282–283
goal selection and, 282
multidirectionality of, 281–283
multiple goal management and, 282
optimization for, 282–283
outcome focus for goals and, 284–285
process focus for goals and, 284–285
resource conservation in, 282–283
student motivation and, 466
goal pursuit, 558–559
achievement goals and, 234
performance and, 281
research on, 233, 234–235
triggers for, 234
goal setting, 558
determinants of, for content and
    structure, 210–211
future research applications for,
    225–226
intervention studies for, 225–226
for learning goals, 210

by life domain, 212
mental contrasting in, 212, 212–213
for performance goals, 210
psychopathology and, 447
self-regulation of, 211–214
as theory, for work motivation,
    508–509
theory of fantasy realization and, 211
goal striving, 214–225, 558
approach *versus* avoidance processes
    in, 215
aspirational standards and, 215
content as influence on, 214
delegation hypothesis for, 219
determinants of, 214–218
eagerness-related approach strategies
    in, 215
functions of, 214
future research applications for,
    225–226
identity-relatedness in, 216
implementation intentions in, 218–
    219, 219–221
intervention studies for, 225–226
lack of willpower and, 221–225
learning-performance model for, 215
orientation framing in, 215
positive affect and, 217
power status and, 217–218
in self-completion theory, 216
self-regulation of, 218–225
shielding in, 217
structural features of goals in,
    214–215
Goetz, T., 178–179
GPT. *See* General Psychotherapy model
grading systems, student motivation and,
    470
groups, work motivation for, 512–513
group belonging, 52–53
culture and, 52–53
group learning, student motivation
    and, 469

H
habits
    as automatic goal-directed behavior, 237
    stimulus-response rules and, 235–236
    in unconscious goal pursuit, 235–238
happiness, 69
Harter, Susan, 521
health care, autonomy climates in, 95
health-promoting behaviors, 48–49
Heckhausen, Heinz, 291, 292, 373
Heckhausen, J., 283, 291
hedonic incentive, for success, 431–432
hedonism, 304
hegemonic masculinity
    definition of, 325
    power and, 325
    sexual objectification of women and,
        325–326
hero worship, 56

High Performance Learning Communities
    Project (Project HiPlace), 472
high school, student motivation during,
    470
high-stakes rewards, 99–100
    economic malfeasance from, 100
    in SDT, 99–100
homeostasis, in feedback loops, 30–31
human capital, 98
human sexuality. *See* sexuality
hypnotic susceptibility, flow and, 137

I
IAT. *See* Implicit Association Test
identified regulation, 89
    in OIT, 484
    for physical activity, 524
identity-relatedness, in goal striving, 216
identity status, 152
I-D model, of curiosity, 162
illness avoidance, 391–392
immortality
    through religious belief, 55
    symbolic, 50–51
implementation approach, to physical
    activity, 487–488
implementation intentions, in goal
    striving, 218–219, 219–221
    ADHD and, 219
    lack of willpower, 224
Implicit Association Test (IAT), 494
implicit motives, 8, 557
    consistency in, 150–151
    correspondence of content for,
        147–148
    disattenuation approaches in, 148–149
    IAT for, 494
    incongruence in, 154
    independence of, 154
    integrative general model for, 145–146
    measure methodology for, 142–146,
        148–149
    MTMM analysis of, 149
    omnibus effect of multiple
        methodological factors, 146–147,
        154
    for physical activity, 493–494
    private body consciousness in,
        150–151
    in psychotherapeutic motivation, 442
    self-monitoring of, 150–151
    statistical independence in, 144
impression management, in SSB, 307
impulsive systems, in feedback control, 37
incentives, motivation and, 209
    for close relationships, 354
    current, 354
    environmental, 369
    hedonic, for success, 431–432
    material, for success, 427–428
incongruence, of motives, 154
individual differences, in motivation,
    560–561, 563–564

AIM-Q for, 398
assessment strategy development for,
   398–399
in behavioral syndrome theory, 382
in control theory, 400
for effort intensity, 434
in evolutionary theory, 382
evolved, 386–397
in FFM, 382–386
future research applications for,
   399–400
in game theory, 400
for legacies, 396–397
in life history theory, 382
in personality psychology, 381–382
reliability of, 398
theory development for, 381–382
validity of, 398–399
for youth physical activity, 540–544
in Zurich Model of Social Motivation,
   400
individual interest, 169
information gaps model, for curiosity, 159
inhibition effects, in vicarious learning, 16
inquisitiveness
  environmental, 392
  interpersonal, 392
integrated regulation, 89
  in physical activity, 524
intention, physical activity and, 480
  in planned behavior theory, 483
interest. *See also* interest development
  awareness of, 168–169
  choice influenced by, 263
  conceptualizations of, 171–172
  curiosity influenced by, 161
  definition of, 169
  development of, 170–171, 175–181
  emotions and, 172
  Four-Phase model of, 167, 169–171
  future research applications for,
     183–184
  individual, 169
  knowledge and, 169
  measurement considerations for,
     172–175
  Punnett square for, 182–183
  research on, 168–169
  situational, 169
  student motivation and, 465
  study methodology for, 173, 175–181
  survey methodology for, 173
  task competence and, 172
  vocational, 172
Interest and Effort in Education (Dewey), 160
interest development, 169, 170–171,
   558
  affect and, 176
  case studies for, 178–179, 179–180,
    180–181
  fluctuations in, 176, 177–178
  future research applications for,
    183–184

knowledge in, 181
learning and, 177
Punnett square for, 182–183
research on, 175–181
shifts in, 176, 177–178
study methodology for, 173, 175–181
survey methodology for, 173
sustainment factors, 176, 177–178
triggers for, 175–176, 176–177
International Association for Positive
  Psychology (IPPA), 127
interpersonal inquisitiveness, 392
interpersonal motives, model for, 455
interventions
  DFI, 453–454
  for physical activity, mapping of,
    495–496
  in psychotherapeutic motivation,
    449–450
  for student motivation, 471–473, 474
intervention studies, for goals, 225–226
interviews. *See* motivational interviewing
intimacy motivation, 353–354
intrinsic life goals, 91–93
  attainment of, 92–93
  for basic psychological needs, 92
  manipulation of, 93
  pursuit of, 92
  research on, 93
intrinsic motivation, 87–88
  choice and, 253
  external pressure and, 94
  information internalization in, 88
  neural foundation for, 374–375
  in OIT, 484
  organizational goal-setting and, 512
  outcome focus for goals and, 284
  outcomes from, 89–90
  for physical activity, 523
  as pleasurable, 88
  process focus for goals and, 284
  social context effects on, 96
  for students, 464–466, 467
  work motivation and, 511
introjection, 89
  in OIT, 484
IPPA. *See* International Association for
  Positive Psychology

J
James, William, 48, 304
Job Characteristics Model, 510
job design, work motivation and,
  510–511
  from Job Characteristics Model, 510

K
Keillor, Garrison, 307
Keller, Helen, 167–168, 167–168
knowledge
  interest and, 169
  in interest development, 181
Koskey, K.L., 179–180

L
lack of willpower. *See* willpower, lack of
leadership
  Leadership Scale for Sport, 533
  transformational, 511–512
  for youth motivation, 533, 538–539
Leadership Scale for Sport, 533
learners, in Four-Phase model of interest,
  175
learning. *See also* vicarious learning
  in achievement goal models, 192
  associative, as motivational state,
    369–370
  context, stimulus-response rules and,
    236
  cooperative, 471
  enactive, 15
  goals, 18, 18–19
  in goal striving, 215
  in groups, student motivation and,
    469
  interest development and, 177
  observational, 16, 16, 537–538
  performance compared to, 15
  social influences on, 463–464
learning goals, 18, 18–19
  goal setting for, 210
learning-performance model
  of achievement goals, 192
  for goal striving, 215
learning theory, motivation in, 209
legacy motive, 396–397
Lewin, Kurt, 251
life history theory, 382
  FFM and, 385
liking, in associative learning, 369–370
Linnenbrink-Garcia, L., 179–180
Long flow Scales, 134, 134–135
  DFS-2, 134
  psychometric characteristics
    of, 134–135
Lowell, E.L., 142–143

M
MacKinnon, Catherine, 325
macro flow experiences, 128
maladaptive choices, 249
Manzy, C., 179–180
mastery experiences
  outcome focus for goals and, 284–285
  process focus for goals and, 284–285
  self-efficacy and, 23–24
  in student motivation, 467
MAT. *See* Motivation Analysis Test
material incentives, for success, 427–428
materialism. *See also* wealth accumulation,
  evolved individual motives for
  from corporate capitalism, 99
  existential anxiety and, 49
  exploration through, in promotion-
    focused individuals, 75
maximization desires, exploration and, 75
Mayer, Richard, 365

McClelland, David, 141–142, 142–143
  independence interpretation of,
    143–145
McDougall, William, 161–162
meaning schemas
  evolved individual motives for, 397
  through religious belief, 55
media, sexual objectification of women
    and, 331
memory. *See* episodic memory, self-efficacy
    and; selective self-memory
menstruation, sexual objectification and,
    327
mental contrasting, in goal setting, 212,
    212–213
  commitment in, 212
  mediating processes for, 213
  motivation and, 213
  for negative futures, 212–213
  for present reality associations, 213
  as problem-solving strategy, 213
mental fatigue, 426
middle school, student motivation during,
    470–471
Mill, John Stuart, 304
Mischel, Walter, 222
mnemic neglect, 312
moods, 561. *See also* depression
  alternative models for, 412–413
  arousal systems, 113, 409–412
  cognition and, 411–412
  complex, formation of, 413–415
  diet and nutrition and, 410
  effort intensity and, 426–427, 431–432
  emotion compared to, 408
  energetic arousal, 409–412
  function of, 408
  future research applications, 418
  general bodily arousal, 415–416
  in motivation intensity theory, 426–427
  muscular tension and, 416
  pleasantness and activation model
    for, 412
  pleasure/displeasure model for, 412
  positive and negative activation model
    for, 412
  positive and negative affect model
    for, 412
  self-regulation of, 416–417
  task difficulty and, 426–427
  tense arousal, 412
  two-dimensional models for, 412
mortality salience (MS) hypothesis, 46–47
motivations. *See also* curiosity; evolved
    individual differences, in
    motivation; extrinsic motivation;
    goals; intrinsic motivation;
    motivational theory; neuroscience,
    motivation and; psychotherapy,
    motivation in; relatedness, for
    children; rewards, motivation and;
    individual differences, in motivation
  actional phase for, 291, 292–293

activation of, 8
appearance, 393
biological purpose of, 4–5
for choice, 249–251
cybernetic approach to, 38–40
definition of, 13, 367
desirability and, 209
drive-reduction model for, 158
ego depletion and, 119
within embedded contexts, 86–87
"for its own sake," 159–161
goal focus and, 291–293
goals compared to, 208–210
as implicit, 8
incentives and, 209
individual differences for, 563–564
intimacy, 353–354
in learning theory, 209
mental contrasting and, 213
nonconscious, 8, 8, 251
in observational learning, 16
for physical activity, theoretical
    frameworks for, 521–528
postactional phase for, 291
preactional phase for, 291, 292
predecisional phase for, 291, 291–292
priming methods for, 8
psychological models for, 5–7
social, 353–354
in social cognitive theory, processes
    for, 18, 17–24, 209
for student, 464–466
tradeoffs for, 67–78
in unconscious goal pursuit, 239–242
motivation, studies on
  academic resurgence for, 7–9
  causal explanations in, 5
  consilience in, 6
  coordinated analyses for, 9
  experimental methods in, 8–9
  interdisciplinary nature of, 4–7
  practical applications for, 9–10
  psychological models in, 5–7
  statistical methodology changes for, 8
Motivational Attunement approach, 449
motivational climate
  for physical activity, 492, 533–534
  for SDT, 492
  for youths, for physical activity, 526,
    533–534
motivational interviewing, 453
motivational theory, 4. *See also* control
    theory; regulatory focus theory;
    self-determination theory;
    social cognitive theory; terror
    management theory
  cognitive approaches to, 3
  coordinated analyses for, 9
  psychological models in, 5–7
Motivation Analysis Test (MAT), 387
motivation intensity theory, 420–422
  ability in, 424–425
  benefit in, 421

difficulty in, variability of status for,
    421–422, 423–427
fatigue in, 425–426
mood in, 426–427
motives. *See also* explicit motives;
    implicit motives
  activation of, 8
  affiliation, 353
  appearance, 393
  congruence, 142
  consistency in, 150–151
  correspondence of content for, 147–148
  definition of, 141
  disattenuation approaches in,
    148–149
  in evolved individual difference theory,
    389–390
  game structures as, in personality
    disorders, 455
  incongruence and, 154
  integrative general model for, 145–146
  interpersonal model, 455
  legacy, 396–397
  measure methodology for, 142–146,
    148–149
  MTMM analysis of, 149
  omnibus effect of multiple
    methodological factors, 146–147,
    154
  private body consciousness in, 150–151
  PSEs for, 141–142
  questionnaires for, 141–142
  self-determination in, 150
  self-monitoring of, 150–151
  social exchange, 395–396
  statistical independence in
    measurement for, 143
  TAT for, 141
motive congruence, 142
  affect regulation and, 151
  analysis of, 154
  antecedents of, 151
  consequences of, 151–153
  flow and, 152
  Freud and, 153–154
  identity status and, 152
  incongruence and, 154
  need satisfaction in, 151
  research models for, 153
  stress and, 151
  unintegration of, 154
  volitional strength and, 152
  well-being and, 152–153
MS hypothesis. *See* mortality salience
    hypothesis
MTMM analysis. *See* multitrait-method
    analysis framework
multilevel selection theory, 395
multiple goals model, 198
multitrait-method (MTMM) analysis
    framework, 149
Murray, J. Clark, 159
muscular tension, 416

N

need for affiliation. *See* affiliation, need for
need satisfaction, 151. *See also* basic
  psychological needs, in SDT
  cultural values and, 97
need thwarting, 488–489
negative affect
  goal striving and, 216–217
  priority management and, 30
  unconscious goal pursuit and, 243
negative feedback, for overt behavior, 30
neuroscience, motivation and, 560. *See also* decision making
  for agency, 372–373
  associative learning states for,
    369–370
  automatic states for, 368–369
  dopamine hypothesis of positive affect,
    370
  dopamine system in, 367–368
  for expectancy, 375–376
  in expectancy-value theory, 373–374
  for extrinsic motivation, 374–375
  for flow, 375
  future research applications in,
    377–378
  implicit states for, 370–371
  for intrinsic motivation, 374–375
  key constructs in, 372–377
  neural core for, 367–372
  neurotransmitters in, 378
  priming in, 370–371
  rational motivational states, 371–372
  for self-efficacy, 376
  for self-regulation, 376–377
  somatic marker hypothesis, 371
  taxonomy for, 366–367
  for value, 373–374
  for volition, 373
Nicholls, J.G., 192–193
9/11 attacks, existential anxiety after, 57
nonconscious motivations, 8, 8
  choice and, 251
Nussbaum, Martha, 324

O

objectification theory, 559–560
  evolutionary adaptation in, 324–325
  existential motivations in, 326–327
  framework of, 324–327
  gendered body project and, 323, 331
  girls' gender development and,
    328–330
  hegemonic masculinity maintenance
    in, 325–326
  media influences in, 331
  power in, role of, 325
  self-objectification in, 327–331
objective self-awareness theory, 44
observational learning, 16
  motivation in, 16
  for youth motivation, 537–538
OIT. *See* organismic integration theory

openness to experience, curiosity and,
  162–163
optimal arousal approach, to drive-
  reduction model, 158–159
optimal experience, 127. *See also* flow, as
  concept
organismic integration theory (OIT),
  484
  external regulation in, 484
  identified regulation in, 484
  intrinsic motivation in, 484
  introjection regulation in, 484
organization
  intrinsic motivation and, 512
  purpose of, 3
  work motivation and, 513
outcome expectations
  choice and, 269
  self-efficacy and, 19, 19, 23
  in social cognitive theory, 19
outcome focus, for goals
  age and, 290
  definition of, 284
  extrinsic motivation and, 284
  goal orientation and, 284–285
  intrinsic motivation and, 284
  performance and, 284–285
  process focus compared to, 285, 285
An Outline of Intellectual Rubbish
  (Russell), 315–316
overt behavior, 30–31
  discrepancy-enlarging feedback loop
    for, 30
  for discrepancy-reducing feedback
    loop, 30
  negative feedback processes for, 30
  positive feedback processes for, 30

P

parents. *See also* attachment, personal
  relationships and; attachment
  theory; relatedness, for children
  in attachment theory, 337–338
  parental affect, in SDT, 339–340
  physical activity motivation, influence
    on, 528–532
  pressure by, for physical activity,
    531–532
  responsibility of children to, 341–342,
    344–345
  sensitivity of, in attachment theory,
    338
parental relationships, in attachment
  theory, 337–338
  sensitivity towards child in, 338
PDP. *See* Process Dissociation Procedure
peer relationships
  in attachment theory, 338
  in competence motivation theory, 521
  mutual autonomy support in, 95–96
  student motivation and, 468–469
  youth motivation influenced by,
    535–540

perceived *versus* actual choice, 257
perfectionism, flow and, 132
performance
  in achievement goal models, 192
  goal pursuit and, 281
  in goal striving, 215
  learning compared to, 15
  outcome focus for goals and, 284–285
  process focus for goals and, 284–285
  self-efficacy and, 21
  tradeoffs in, 76–78
performance-approach goals, 198–199
performance-avoidance goals, 198–199
performance goals, 18–19
  goal setting for, 210
Perkun, R., 178–179
persistence, self-efficacy and, 23
personal goals
  alcohol consumption and, dysfunction
    in, 448
  content dimension of, 446–447
  depression and, 447–448
  in psychotherapeutic motivation,
    442–443, 444–445
  in teleonomic model, 446
  well-being as, 445–448
personality
  effort intensity and, 434
  lack of willpower and, 224
  structure, 143
personality disorders, 455
  game structures in, 455
  model of interpersonal motives, 455
personality psychology
  comparative psychology for, 384–385
  discrepancy-enlarging feedback loop
    in, 30
  discrepancy-reducing feedback loop
    in, 30
  extraversion in, 381
  feedback control hierarchy in, 32
  FFM in, 382–386
  focus of, 386
  individual differences in motivation,
    381–382
Personality Research Form (PRF), 387
personal relationships. *See also* attachment
  theory; parental relationships,
  in attachment theory; peer
  relationships; teacher relationships
  attachment and, 53–54
  existential anxiety and, 53–54
  mutual autonomy support in, 95–96
  teacher-student, student motivation
    and, 468, 466–469
persuasive messages
  ego depletion and, 115
  from self-efficacy, 21–22, 24
physical activity, 562
  achievement goal theory and,
    485–487, 492–493, 524–526
  basic psychological needs and,
    484–485, 488–489, 524

competence motivation theory for, 521–522
energetic arousal and, 411
expectancy-value theories for, 526–528
extrinsic motivation for, 523–524
identified regulation of, 524
implementation intention approach to, 487–488
implicit motivation for, 493–494
integrated regulation of, 524
intention and, 480
intervention mapping for, 495–496
intrinsic motivation for, 523
measurement methodology for, 493–496
motivational climate for, 492, 533–534
need thwarting and, 488–489
in planned behavior theory, 481–484, 489–491
psychology of, 480
range of, 521
RCTs for, 494–495
in SDT, 484–485, 488–489, 489–491, 492–493, 523–524
self-efficacy and, 480
social goals for, 525
theoretical advances for, 487–493
theoretical motivation frameworks for, 521–528
theory integration for, 489–493
2 x 2 model for, 486–487, 492–493
as value, 531
well-being and, 479
youth motivation for, 528–540
physical stature and status, evolved individual motives for, 394
Picture-Story Exercises (PSEs), 141–142
statistical independence in, 143
Plan Analysis, 445
planfulness, 38
planned behavior theory, 481–484
attitudes in, 481
choice in, 250
control beliefs in, 481–482
critical assessment of, 482, 483–484
expectancy theory and, 506
intention in, 483
SDT and, integration of, 489–491
subjective norms in, 481
pleasantness and activation model, for mood, 412
pleasure centers, of brain, 235–236
pleasure/displeasure model, for mood, 412
political systems, 100–101
democratic, 100–101
totalitarianism, 100
positive affect
coasting and, 35
in competence motivation theory, 521–522
as counterintuitive, 35–36

dopamine hypothesis, 370
ego depletion and, 120–121
goal striving and, 217
with multiple concerns, 36
unconscious goal pursuit and, 240, 241–242
positive and negative activation model, for mood, 412
positive and negative affect model, for mood, 412
positive feedback, for overt behavior, 30
postactional phase, for motivations, 291
posttraumatic stress disorder (PTSD), 51
power. See also willpower, lack of
of choices, 248
goal striving and, through status, 217–218
in objectification theory, 325
rape and, 325–326
Powers, William, 29
preactional phase, for motivations, 291, 292
implementational mindset for, 292
predecisional phase, for motivations, 291, 291–292
preferences, choice influenced by, 270–271
prevention orientation, in regulatory focus theory, 6, 66. See also failure, as tradeoff; success, as tradeoff
analytical processing and, 77
anxiety disorders and, 70
commitment and, 72–75
desired end states for, 66–67
for failure, 67
happiness and, 69
intergoal inhibition in, 69
life experiences and, 71–72
performance and, 76–78
safety as focus in, 78
satisfactory state as motivational necessity for, 70
strategic preferences for, 71–72
for success, 67
system constraints for, 78–80
tradeoffs, for motivations, 67–78
PRF. See Personality Research Form
priming methods, for motives, 8
neural basis for, 370–371
principles, in feedback control, 31
priority management
affect and, 36
depression and, 36
emotions and, influence on, 36
private body consciousness, 150–151
problem-solving strategies, mental contrasting as, 213
Process Dissociation Procedure (PDP), 223
process focus, for goals
age and, 290
definition of, 284
extrinsic motivation and, 284
goal orientation and, 284–285

intrinsic motivation and, 284
outcome focus compared to, 285, 285
performance and, 284–285
programs, in feedback control, 31
Project HiPlace. See High Performance Learning Communities Project
promotion orientation, in regulatory focus theory, 6, 66. See also failure, as tradeoff; success, as tradeoff
creativity and, 76–77
depression and, 70
desired end states for, 66–67
exploration and, 75–76
for failure, 67, 67–71
happiness and, 69
intergoal inhibition in, 69
life experiences and, 71–72
performance and, 76–78
strategic preferences for, 71–72
for success, 67, 67–71
system constraints for, 78–80
tradeoffs, for motivations, 67–78
PSEs. See Picture-Story Exercises
psychological distance, in goal striving, 216
psychopathology, development of, 446
goal setting and, 447
psychotherapy, motivation in, 561
ACT, 453, 454–455, 457
Alliance Fostering Therapy, 449
autonomous motivation approach to, 443, 448–449
Clarification Oriented Therapy, 453, 457
clinically relevant constructs in, 442–443
DFI in, 453–454
experience as influence on, 443
explicit motives in, 442
factors in, 448–455
future research applications for, 457–458
general models of change in, 451–452
goals of, 456
GPT, 451
implicit motives in, 442
intervention facilitation in, 449–450
Motivational Attunement approach, 449
motivational construct assessment in, 443–445
motivational interviewing in, 453
patient ambivalence over, 453
patient relationship in, 449
personal goals in, 442–443, 444–445
Plan Analysis in, 445
Rubicon Model of Action Phases in, 451
SDT in, 444
SIM in, 448–449
SST, 452–453, 454, 457
theory development for, 441–442
treatment goals in, 444, 443, 445, 449–450

TTM, 452
values in, 442
WBT, 454
well-being as goal in, 445–448
PTSD. *See* posttraumatic stress disorder
Pugh, K.J., 179–180
Punnett square, for interest, 182–183

R

randomized controlled trials (RCTs),
    494–495
    treatment fidelity in, 495–496
rape, feelings of power from, 325–326
rational system, in feedback control, 37
RCTs. *See* randomized controlled trials
reciprocal interactions, 14–15
    agency and, 14–15
    collective agency in, 15
    self-efficacy and, 14
    triadic reciprocality, 14
reflecting systems, in feedback control, 37
reflection, in self-regulation, 376
reform, of student motivation practices,
    470–471
    research implications for, 474–475
regulation. *See* external regulation, in
    OIT; identified regulation;
    integrated regulation;
    self-regulation
regulatory fit, 6
regulatory focus theory, 6, 66–67
    choice in, 265
    prevention orientation in, 6, 66
    promotion orientation in, 6, 66
    regulatory fit in, 6
    tradeoffs in, for motivations, 67–78
relatedness, for children, 560. *See also*
    attachment, personal relationships
    and
    alternative factors to, 345–346
    attachment theory and, 336–339
    contextual variations, 344–345
    early, 342–344
    function of, 335
    responsibility to parents and, 341–342
    SDT and, 339–341
    theory integration for, 342–346
relationships. *See* attachment theory; close
    relationships; peer relationships;
    personal relationships
religious beliefs. *See also* spirituality
    existential anxiety and, 55
    immortality and, 55
    intrinsic, 55
    meaning schemas through, 55
    psychological consequences of, 55
    worldview validation through, 55
resources
    in adult goal development, 282–283
    ego depletion and, 119–120
    for goal focus, 287
    self-control and, 119–120
response facilitation, 16

responsibility, of children to parents,
    341–342
    academic functioning and, 341–342,
    344–345
    cultural variations of, 345
    by developmental stage, 344
    parental values and, adoption of, 342
resting
    ego depletion after, 120–121
    energetic arousal after, 410–411
retention, for vicarious learning, 16
rewards, motivation and
    automatic states for, 368–369
    choice based on, 249
    dopamine system-influenced,
    367–368
    neural foundations for, in motivated
    actions, 367–372
    neurotransmitters for, 378
    reward prediction error, 375
    sources of, 368–372
    in work settings, 515
reward-aversion model, for curiosity, 160
reward contingencies, in corporate
    capitalism, 98–99
    as high-stakes, 99–100
reward prediction error, 375
reward processing, in unconscious goal
    pursuit, 240–241
Rilke, Rainer Maria, 59
risk taking, ego depletion and, 116
Rubicon Model of Action Phases, 451
Russell, Bertrand, 315–316
safety, as focus, 78

S

SDT. *See* self-determination theory
selective self-memory
    from encoding bias, 311–312
    prevalence of, 311
    psychological health and, 314–315
    psychological interests and, 315
the self
    ego depletion and, from suppression,
    114
    four constituents of, 48
self-affirmation
    BTAE and, 309
    ego depletion and, 121
    self-enhancement and, 306, 312
    self-protection and, 312
    SSB and, 306
self-awareness, 44–45. *See also* existential
    anxiety; existential psychology
    autonomy and, 102
    avoidance behaviors, 57
    behavioral flexibility and, 44–45
    escaping from, 56–58
    existential issues with, 45
    in flow, 128–129
    flow concept and, 57
    functions of, 44
    in objective self-awareness theory, 44

purpose of, 43
    in SDT, 102
    self-regulation and, 44, 58
    TMT and, 57
    well-being and, 102
self-awareness theory, success in, 431
self-completion theory, 216
self-consciousness, in flow, 129
self-control
    addictive behaviors and, 112
    autonomy and, 121
    conservation of resources and,
    119–120
    ego depletion and, 111
    ego strength from, 112–113, 122
    feedback control and, 38
    mood arousal and, 113
    as process, 111
    self-regulation compared to, 111–112
self-determination, in motives, 150
self-determination theory (SDT), 4, 7,
    556–557. *See also* autonomous
    motivation; extrinsic motivation;
    intrinsic motivation
    autonomy in, 85–86, 340
    basic psychological needs in, 87,
    101–102, 484–485
    causality orientations in, 87, 90–91
    for children, 339–341
    choice in, 253
    cultural contexts for, 86–87, 96–97
    economic systems under, 97–99
    embedded contexts and, motivations
    in, 86–87
    extrinsic life goals in, 91–93
    high-stakes rewards in, 99–100
    intrinsic life goals in, 91–93
    motivational climate for, 492
    OIT as subtheory of, 484
    overview of, 85
    parental affect in, 339–340
    physical activity in, 484–485, 488–
    489, 489–491, 492–493, 523–524
    planned behavior theory and,
    integration of, 489–491
    political systems under, 100–101
    in psychotherapeutic motivation, 444
    self-awareness in, 102
    social contexts in, 87
    socialization of children, 339
    transformational leadership and,
    511–512
    2 x 2 model and, integration of,
    492–493
    work motivation and, 511–512
    youth motivation and, 523–524
self-efficacy. *See also* collective efficacy
    behavioral control and, 515–516
    career choice and, 23
    in children, 25
    from choice, 254, 264
    effects of, 22–23, 23
    emotional reactions and, 22

environmental factors for, 14
episodic memory and, 376
informational sources for, 21, 20–22
mastery experiences and, 23–24
multiplicative influences on, 22
neural foundation for, 376
outcome expectations and, 19, 19, 23
performance behavior and, 21
persistence and, 23
personal factors for, 14
from persuasive messages, 21–22, 24
physical activity and, 480
reciprocal interactions and, 14
research evidence for, 23–24
self-modeling for, 21
self-regulation and, 23
in social cognitive theory, 20–24
social comparisons and, 20, 21
student motivation and, 464
task choice and, 23
self-enhancement, 559
    BTAE in, 307–311
    definition of, 303
    expectancy differentials in, 313
    feedback inconsistency and, 313–314
    future research development for, 316
    in hedonism, 304
    information valences in, 313–314
    instantiations of, 304–314
    nonmotivational explanations for,
        312–314
    psychological health and, 314–315
    psychological interests and, 315
    selective self-memory and, 311–312
    self-affirmation and, 306, 312
    self-threat and, 312
    self-view valences in, 313–314
    SSB in, 305–307
    theory development for, 304
self-esteem
    existential anxiety and, 49–51
    gendered body project and, 331
    youth physical activity motivation
        and, 540–542
self-evaluation. See also self-enhancement;
        self-protection
    of effort intensity, 431
    in social cognitive theory, 19
    social comparisons and, 20
    of success, 431
self-modeling, for vicarious learning, 17
self-monitoring, of motives, 150–151
self-objectification, by women, 327–331
    cognitive developmental theories for,
        328–330
    cultural messages and, 330
    factors for, 327–328
    gendered body project and, 323, 331
    girls' gender development and,
        328–330
    through media, 331
    situational motivators for, 330
    socialization theories for, 328

self-perception. See also self-awareness
    in competence motivation theory, 521
    ego depletion and, 116
    for youth physical activity motivation,
        540–542
self-perception theory, choice in, 252–253
self-presentation, choice and, 268
self-protection, 559
    BTAE in, 307–311
    definition of, 303
    expectancy differentials in, 313
    feedback inconsistency and, 313–314
    future research development for, 316
    in hedonism, 304
    information valences in, 313–314
    instantiations of, 304–314
    nonmotivational explanations for,
        312–314
    psychological health and, 314–315
    psychological interests and, 315
    selective self-memory and, 311–312
    self-affirmation and, 312
    self-threat and, 312
    self-view valences in, 313–314
    SSB in, 305–307
    theory development for, 304
self-regulation. See also commitment, as
        tradeoff; feedback control; self-
        control; self-determination
    choice and, 250, 256
    cybernetic processes for, 28–29,
        555–556
    forethought in, 376
    of goal setting, 211–214
    of goal striving, 218–225
    happiness and, 69
    of mood, 416–417
    neural foundation for, 376–377
    reflection in, 376
    self-awareness and, 44
    self-control compared to, 111–112
    self-efficacy and, 23
    in social cognitive theory, 17
    unconscious goal pursuit and, 243
self-serving bias (SSB), 50
    expectancies in, 306
    impression management in, 307
    nonmotivational explanations for,
        306–307
    prevalence of, among populations, 305
    psychological health and, 314
    psychological interests and, 315
    self-affirmation and, 306
    in self-enhancement, 305–307
    in self-protection, 305–307
    self-threat and, 305–306
self-system theory
    depression and, 70
    goal focus in, 287–288
Self-System Therapy (SST), 452–453,
        454, 457
self-threat, 312
    BTAE and, 309

mnemic neglect and, 312
    SSB and, 305–306
sexuality
    evolved individual motives for, 393
    existential anxiety and, 49
sexual masochism, self-awareness and, 57
sexual objectification, of women. See also
        objectification theory
    breasts and, 326–327
    components of, 324
    definition of, 324
    as evolutionary adaptation, 324–325
    existential motivations for, 326–327
    feminism and, 324
    gendered body project and, 323, 331
    hegemonic masculinity maintenance
        from, 325–326
    media influences in, 331
    menstruation and, 327
    power from, 325
    theoretical frameworks for, 324–327
    by women, 327–331
shielding, of goals, 217
Short flow scales, 135
SIM. See Striving Instrumentality Matrix
situational interest, 169
skills
    in competence motivation theory, 521
    in flow, challenges in balance with,
        128, 130
    in unconscious goal pursuit, 236–238
sleep, energetic arousal and, 410–411. See
        also resting
Smith R.E., 532
social achievement goals, 196–197
social bonds, 350–351
    social isolation and, 350–351
social cognitive theory, 6, 555
    collective efficacy and, 24
    conceptual framework for, 14–15
    cross-cultural relevance of, 25–26
    developmental appropriateness of, 25
    enactive learning in, 15
    future research applications for, 24–26
    goals in, 18–19
    modeled observations in, benefits
        of, 25
    motivational processes in, 18, 17–24,
        209
    outcome expectations in, 19
    performance in, learning compared
        to, 15
    reciprocal interactions in, 14–15
    self-efficacy in, 20–24
    self-evaluation in, 19
    self-regulatory processes in, 17
    social comparisons in, 20
    symbolic processes in, 17
    values in, 19–20
    vicarious learning in, 15, 15–17
social comparisons
    development of, 20
    self-efficacy and, 20, 21

self-evaluation and, 20
in social cognitive theory, 20
social competence, student motivation
  and, 468–469
social contexts, in SDT, 87
social exchange motive, 395–396
social goals, for youth physical activity,
  525
social information, in close relationships
  interpretation of, 356–357
  weight of, 357
social interaction, emotion in, 357–358
social isolation, negative effects of,
  350–351
socialization, of children, 339
social learning theory, choice in, 250
social motivation
  affiliation motives in, 353
  Zurich Model, 400
social psychology
  discrepancy-enlarging feedback loop
    in, 30
  discrepancy-reducing feedback loop
    in, 30
  feedback control hierarchy in, 32
socioeconomics, choice influenced
  by, 265–267
somatic marker hypothesis, 371
specific curiosity, 159
spirituality, 56
  existential anxiety and, 54–56
sports, flow in, 131. See also youth
  motivation, for physical activity
SSB. See self-serving bias
SST. See Self-System Therapy
stability goals, 290
stabilizing selection for phenotypes,
  in FFM, 382–383
statistical independence, in motive
  measurement, 143
  in explicit motives, 144
  in implicit motives, 144
  McClelland's interpretation of, 143–145
  in personality structure, 143
  problems in, 143
Steinbeck, John, 50
Stewart, V.C., 179–180
stimulus-response rules, 235–236
  context learning and, 236
  in pleasure centers, of brain, 235–236
stress
  energetic arousal and, 412
  motive congruence and, 151
Striving Instrumentality Matrix (SIM),
  448–449
student motivation, 464–466
  classroom practices, 466–467, 473
  competence and, 464
  control and, 464
  cooperative learning approach to, 471
  with CORI, 472
  cultural influences on, 473–474
  development of, 466

in early grade school, 469–471
education as value in, 465
goal orientation and, 466
by grade level, 469–470
grading systems and, 470
group learning and, 469
in high school, 470
interest and, 465
interventions for, 471–473, 474
intrinsic motivation and, 464–466, 467
mastery experiences as part of, 467
in middle school, 470–471
peer influence on, 468–469
through Project HiPlace, 472
reform efforts for, 470–471, 474–475
in research study, 474
school influence on, 466–469
self-efficacy and, 464
social competence and, 468–469
TARGET approach to, 467–468
task assignment and, 466–467
teachers' influence on, 468, 466–469
transition to school and, 470,
  469–471
subjective energy, 409–410
subjective norms, in planned behavior
  theory, 481
success, as tradeoff, 67, 67–71
  ego involvement in, 430–431
  emotional intensity for, 68
  emotional quality of, 68–69
  happiness and, 69
  material incentives for, 427–428
  outcome expectancy for, 428–429
  in self-awareness theory, 431
  self-evaluation of, 431
  social evaluation of, 429–430
  strategic preferences and, 71–72
success, effort intensity and, 427–432
  material incentives for, 427–428
Sullivan, Anne, 167
symbolic immortality, 50–51
  hero worship and, 56

T

TARGET approach, to student
  motivation, 467–468
  evaluation techniques in, 468
  grouping arrangements in, 468
  task design in, 468
  time allocation in, 468
tasks
  in achievement goal model, 192–193
  choice and, by type, 269
  delay of gratification, 221–222
  effort intensity by, 434
  flow and, 129
  interest in, competence and, 172
  mood and, 426–427
  self-control, with tobacco use, 122
  self-efficacy from, 23
  student motivation from, 466–467
  in TARGET approach, 468

task-ego model, of achievement goals,
  192–193
TAT. See Thematic Apperception Test
teacher relationships
  children and, in attachment theory, 338
  collective efficacy for, 24
  student motivation and, 468,
    466–469
  for youth motivation, for physical
    activity, 532–535
teleonomic model, of well-being, 446
  personal goals in, 446
television consumption, self-awareness
  and, 57
tense arousal, 412
  calm energy mood, 414
  complex moods from, 413–415
  muscular tension and, 416
tense energy, 415
tense tiredness, 414–415
terror management theory (TMT), 4,
  6–7, 45–48, 556
  anxiety-buffer hypothesis in, 47
  criticism of, 58–59
  death as inevitability in, 46
  development of, 45–46
  DTA hypothesis in, 47
  existential anxiety in, 48–58
  future research on, 58–59
  group belonging and, 52–53
  MS hypothesis in, 46–47
  psychopathology of, 51
  PTSD and, 51
  purpose of, 43
  research strategy for, 46–48
  self-awareness and, 57
  worldview validation in, 52–53
Thematic Apperception Test (TAT), 141
theory of fantasy realization. See fantasy
  realization, theory of
theory of planned behavior. See planned
  behavior theory
The Story of My Life (Keller), 167–168
thirst, as motivational state, 368–369
threat avoidance
  in close relationships, 354
  evolved individual motives for, 391
time
  goal focus and, 287–288
  perception of, flow and, 129
  in TARGET approach, 468
  work motivation influenced by,
    513–514
TMT. See terror management theory
tobacco use, self-control tasks and, 122
Tomkins, Silvan, 160–161
totalitarianism, 100
tradeoffs, for motivations, 67–78, 556.
  See also prevention orientation, in
  regulatory focus theory; promotion
  orientation, in regulatory focus theory
  commitment as, 72–75
  in emotional life, 67–72

within evolved individual differences, 391–397
exploration as, 75–76
for failure, 67, 67–71
in FFM, 383–384
in performance, 76–78
for success, 67, 67–71
transformational leadership, 511–512
transition to schools, student motivation and
in grade school, 469–471
in high school, 470
Transtheoretical Model (TTM), 452
triadic reciprocality, 14
trichotomous model, of achievement goals, 194
TTM. *See* Transtheoretical Model
2 x 2 model, of achievement goals, 194–195
for physical activity, 486–487
SDT and, integration of, 492–493

U

unconscious goal pursuit. *See also* goal setting; goal striving
academic development of, theories for, 232–233
active maintenance of representations in, 238–239
classical conditioning and, 233
conceptual parameters of, 233–235
control of, 235–239
feedback processing in, 239
flexibility of, 238–239, 243
goal-interference and, inhibition of, 239
habits in, 235–238
monitoring in, 239
motivation in, 239–242
negative affect and, 243
positive affect and, 240, 241–242
research on, 233–234
reward processing in, 240–241
self-regulation and, 243
skills adjustment in, 236–238
stimulus-response rules and, 235–236
will and, 240
urges, with ego depletion, 115

V

values
education as, 465
as internalized process, 374
neural foundations for, 373–374
physical activity as, 531
in psychotherapeutic motivation, 442
in social cognitive theory, 19–20
vicarious learning, 15, 15–17
cognitive modeling for, 17
disinhibition effects in, 16
gender and, 17
inhibition effects in, 16
modeling for, 16–17

through observation, 16
production processes of, 16
response facilitation in, 16
retention of, 16
self-modeling for, 17
types of, 16, 16
violence, from threats to worldview validation, 53
vocational interest, 172
volition
neural foundation for, 373
strength of, 152

W

Watt, H.M.G., 178–179
WBT. *See* Well-Being Therapy
wealth accumulation, evolved individual motives for, 394
weekend effect, 101
well-being
avoidance goals and, 447
energetic arousal and, 409–410
motive congruence and, 152–153
as personal goal, 445–448
physical activity and, 479
self-awareness and, 102
social isolation and, 350–351
teleonomic model of, 446
Well-Being Therapy (WBT), 454
wellness, autonomous motivation and, 96–97
White, Robert, 521
will, unconscious goal pursuit and, 240
willpower, lack of, 221–225
in academic settings, 222
affective responses and, 223
behavioral responses and, 223–224
cognitive responses and, 223
competition and, 222
conscientiousness and, 224–225
delay of gratification tasks and, 221–222
habitual responses and, 222–223
implementation intention and, 224
PDP for, 223
personality attributes and, 224
women. *See also* gender; gender development, for girls; objectification theory; sexual objectification, of women
commitment motivations in, 395
in media, sexual objectification of, 331
self-objectification by, 327–331
work-avoidance goals, 196
work motivation, 562
aging of employees and, 513–514
autonomy climates in, 95
creativity within, 514–515
equity theory and, 507–508
expectancy theory and, 506–507
extrinsic motivation and, 511
generational differences in, 514
goal setting theory and, 508–509

for groups, 512–513
intrinsic motivation and, 511
job design and, 510–511
organization through, 513
parameters of, 505
rewards in, 515
SDT and, 511–512
temporal perspectives on, 513–514
theoretical perspectives on, 505–512
transformational leadership and, 511–512
worldview validation, 52–53
through culture, 52
through religious belief, 55
threats to, violence from, 53

Y

Yalom, Irvin, 45, 49, 51. *See also* existential anxiety
Young, Iris Marion, 326–327
youth motivation, for physical activity, 528–540, 562
achievement goal theory and, 524–526
attitude and behavioral modeling for, 529–530
autonomy-supportive behaviors for, 534–535
coach/teacher influence on, 532–535
competence for, 540–542
competence motivation theory and, 521–522
controlling behaviors in, 534–535
emotional influences on, 542–544
expectancy-value theories for, 526–528
expressions of competence for, 530–531
feedback patterns for, 532–533
friendship quality as influence on, 536–537
future research applications for, 544–545
individual differences in, 540–544
leadership styles for, 533, 538–539
motivational climate for, 526, 533–534
negative evaluative behaviors, 539–540
observational learning for, 537–538
parental influence on, 528–532
peer influence on, 535–540
perceived competence and, 540–542
pressure by parents for, 531–532
SDT and, 523–524
self-esteem and, 540–542
self-perceptions and, 540–542
social-contextual factors for, 528–540
social goals for, 525
social support for, 529, 536
as value, 531

Z

Zurich Model of Social Motivation, 400